5-Year Cost Index is a composite of each fund's individual cost factors that may affect a fund, including sales loads, redemption fees, tax loads, a[...] [...]. Each factor is weighted by its relative importance to an investor that i[...] for five years before redeeming. Cost Index ratings are Ver[...] cost of ownership), High, Medium, Low, and Very Low.

Benefits

The trade-off to investment costs are investment benefits, principally return, safety, and current yield:

Investment Objectives are Growth, Income, Growth & Income (growth primarily and income secondarily), and Income & Growth (income primarily and growth secondarily).

5-Year Projected Returns use econometric model forecasts of the general market plus an econometric model based on each fund's historical volatility, performance, and correlation with the Standard & Poor's 500 Index. Projections are made for all equity funds with at least 52 weeks of price history. Projected returns are not computed for gold, international, sector, bond, or tax-free funds because their performances are not closely related to the U.S. stock market.

Safety Ratings range from 0% safe (extremely volatile funds) to 100% safe (funds whose prices are absolutely stable from week to week). They are based on the volatility of weekly total returns of each fund (with at least one year of price history) over the past five years, and on any demonstrated inferior performance. The Safety Ratings permit direct comparisons of the safety of dissimilar types of funds.

Yield is the current 30-day standardized yield as defined by the Securities and Exchange Commission for income funds, and the *estimated* yield for equity funds based on actual income distributions paid over the last twelve months, adjusted for subsequent changes in portfolio value.

Performance

Performance returns include reinvestment of all dividends and distributions. They do not reflect sales or redemption charges.

Worst-Ever Loss is the largest "drawdown" on a total-return basis since 1980. The period during which that loss occurred is also shown. Funds not in existence in 1987 tend to have smaller losses than funds that experienced that year's decline.

Correlations show the relationships between each fund and the S&P 500 Index and the Lehman Bros. Long Treasury Bond Index. A fund whose weekly total returns are perfectly correlated with an index has a correlation of 100%. If its weekly fluctuations are completely independent of the index, its correlation is 0%. If a fund tends to move in the opposite direction of the index, its correlation is negative. Blue-chip stock funds are most highly correlated with the S&P 500 Index, while sector funds specializing in the securities of a single industry and international funds tend to be least correlated with the S&P 500. Long-term Treasury bond funds are most highly correlated with the Bond Index, while shorter-maturity and lower-quality bond funds are normally less correlated with the Bond Index.

Up-Market and Down-Market Rankings range from "A" (best performance), to "E" (worst). Stock funds are graded according to their performance during all swings of 10% or more by the Standard & Poor's 500 Index since 1980. Bond funds are graded on their performance in all up and down swings of 5% or more in the Lehman Bros. Treasury Long Bond Index. Every fund is graded relative to the performance of all other funds in its category that have been in existence as long or longer. A fund must experience at least two up-market swings to receive an Up-Market Ranking and at least two Down-Market swings to receive a Down-Market Ranking.

Investment Information

Minimum Initial Investments are often waived or reduced for IRA, Keogh, and pension accounts.

Telephone Switching frequency limits and charges indicate the usefulness of a fund for frequent trading. Switching privileges may be subject to minimum share or dollar amounts, and in some cases may also incur sales and redemption fees shown under "Maximum Charges."

Total Assets is the size of a fund's portfolio at the end of the third quarter of 1993.

1994 MUTUAL FUND BUYER'S GUIDE

The author is Editor of

Mutual Fund Forecaster
Mutual Fund Plus
Market Logic
Fund Watch
New Issues
The Insiders
Investor's Digest
Stock Market Weekly
Mutual Fund Weekly
Income Fund Outlook
The Professional Investor
Mutual Fund Buyer's Guide

These advisory services are published by:

The Institute for Econometric Research
3471 N. Federal, Fort Lauderdale, FL 33306
800-442-9000

The author is also Managing Editor of
Mutual Funds Magazine

MUTUAL FUND BUYER'S GUIDE

1994

Five-Year Profit Projections · Safety Ratings
Winning Investment Strategies · Tax Guide
All-Star Ratings · 1,700 Charts · and more

Stock Funds · Bond Funds
Tax-Free Funds

Norman G. Fosback

1994 MUTUAL FUND BUYER'S GUIDE

International Standard Book Number: 1-55738-586-6

TABLE OF CONTENTS

Introduction

Financial historians may eventually look back on the 1990s as "The Decade of the Mutual Fund" . . . were it not for the fact that the 1970s and 1980s were also "decades of the mutual fund." In truth, the mutual fund expansion of the last 20 years has been the single greatest financial boom ever. In 1974, the entire mutual fund industry managed $34 billion. Today, the industry is more than fifty *times* $34 billion – approximately two trillion dollars of Americans' monies under pooled, professional, investment management.

This growth is without parallel in financial history. But it is easy to explain. Once a business characterized by a handful of relatively homogeneous funds, the mutual fund business has evolved into a vast heterogeneous industry offering an extraordinary breadth, and depth, of choices for investors.

Beginning with the invention of money market funds in the early 1970s, the mutual fund industry has grown to encompass funds that invest in virtually every publicly-traded financial instrument invented by man – stocks, bonds, options, futures, derivatives; both domestic and foreign securities. And within these groups, there are numerous subclassifications such as growth stocks, income stocks, and specialized industry stocks. On the income side, investors can choose from funds specializing in every type of bond, from Treasuries to high and low-grade corporates, municipals of all quality ratings, exotic collateralized mortgage obligations, zero-coupon issues, and issues of foreign governments, to name just a few. In the money market arena, not only T-bills and CDs are represented, but also commercial paper, Eurodollars, repos, put bonds . . . you name it and a mutual fund owns it.

The only financial instruments not now owned by mutual funds are those that have yet to be invented, and you may rest assured that this dynamic industry will own those, too, as soon as they are created. Indeed, many of the most innovative financial instrument derivatives are being developed to cater to the investment needs of mutual funds.

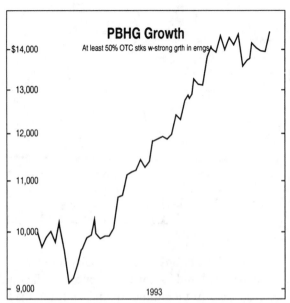

PBHG Growth
At least 50% OTC stks w-strong grth in erngs

The top diversified domestic equity fund in 1993 was PBHG Growth, up +47%.

The proliferation of mutual funds, and the securities in which they invest, has been an extraordinary service to the American public. The better-than-50-fold growth of money under management in just two decades is the proof. More choices means that more Americans own funds, in the process obtaining instant diversification, while avoiding the plagues of market complexity and manipulation that so often ensnare investors attempting a "do-it-yourself" approach to stocks and bonds. Furthermore, the investments are protected by a rich tradition of success and a regulatory apparatus that, while not perfect, effectively deters most abuses.

But with proliferation of choice comes complication and risk. As more investors transfer their savings and investments to mutual funds, the average level of investor sophistication is bound to fall . . . in inverse relation to the need for more sophistication in an increasingly complex marketplace. The mutual fund public, in other words, must be better informed of their choices, not less. And they must have information that will enable them to exercise these choices intelligently. That is the role of this book, our first annual edition of the *Mutual Fund Buyer's Guide*.

It was relatively easy to select a fund forty years ago when only 150 were on the market. Today, with thousands of funds from which to choose, and with mutual funds promoting themselves in every available medium, buy-and-sell decision-making is vastly more difficult. The chance of making a bad decision is greater simply because the breadth of choice is wider. To illustrate the complexity of the choices facing investors, consider that there are now more mutual funds than there are NYSE and Amex-listed common stocks.

Furthermore, as with all industries in a capitalistic society, the mutual fund industry is entirely self-serving. It offers investors a broader choice of funds not because it is necessarily better for investors, but because it is *profitable*. The industry also understands that in a financial bull market, such as that which has prevailed the last two decades, it can increase its profitability by other means, as well. The most disturbing of these is the rapid escalation of loads and fees.

Even though fund sponsors realize enormous economies of scale with larger funds, and even though funds have, indeed, become much larger, fees are spiraling upward. Today, the average fund keeps for itself approximately $1 of every $6 of portfolio profits – mainly to compensate portfolio managers and to support far-flung marketing efforts, little of which benefits fund shareholders.

Plus, sponsors charge investors an average of 3% in direct sales and redemption commissions. That so little price competition exists in an otherwise competitive industry, can be attributed only to the ignorance of investors. Fund investors must become better informed, and recognize that choosing the most *cost-effective* fund alternative is almost as important as choosing the fund whose portfolio will perform the best. The *Buyer's Guide* is dedicated to helping you here, too.

This is the first-ever book that brings to investors the entire panoply of critical mutual fund investing information in a single low-priced volume. High-precision charts, concise summaries of costs and benefits, historical performances, and how-to invest information, all capped off with a unique Star Rating System for each of more than 1,700 of the leading funds in America – funds that, in aggregate, account for more than 98% of all the assets in equity and bond funds.

The investment choices are yours. And now, the information and evaluation you need is, literally, in your hands. Happy reading, and good investing!

Chapter One

Guide to Mutual Funds

Mutual funds are among the most flexible and potentially advantageous investments in the financial universe. They are equally suited to beginning, intermediate, and advanced investors.

What is a Mutual Fund?

A mutual fund is simply a corporation (or business trust) that sells shares of its stock to the public, and invests the proceeds in securities, such as stocks and bonds, of other companies. Mutual fund stockholders share in the income, profits, and losses of their funds' investments. At the end of every business day, the typical fund calculates the total market value of all of its investments and other assets and deducts its liabilities to determine the precise value of each outstanding share. That value is called its "net asset value per share."

Mutual funds originated in Europe in the early 1800s, attaining great popularity in Scotland and England in the middle part of that century. The first mutual fund in the United States was formed in 1924. The industry has grown rapidly since, and today consists of over 3,000 funds investing approximately $2 trillion on behalf of stockholders.

Funds, also known as "investment companies," are broadly classified into two categories, open-end and closed-end.

Open-end funds are nearly always *open* to investors, who at any time can buy new shares from the funds at net asset value, or sell (redeem) the shares they own back to the funds, also at the net asset value. Some open-end funds charge a sales commission (also called a "load") to investors when they buy or sell shares, and are therefore known as "load" funds. Funds that do not charge a load are called "no-load" funds.

In contrast to open-end funds, closed-end funds make a single public sale of shares to the public, and then *close* their doors to new investors. Such funds will not sell new shares to the public nor will they repurchase shares from existing investors. To enable stockholders of closed-end funds to sell shares from time to time, and to allow other investors to buy shares, closed-end funds trade on stock exchanges or in the over-the-counter market just like thousands of other stocks. Investors buy and sell them through a stockbroker (who will charge his usual commission) at whatever price the market determines. Depending on market conditions, that price may be above, below, or the same as the fund's net asset value.

For beginning investors, open-end funds are usually more attractive, for they can always be bought and sold at their net asset value. Closed-end funds may be particularly advantageous investments when they sell at a discount below their net asset value.

Advantages

The key advantages of mutual funds are diversification, liquidity, and professional management. Many funds also provide cost advantages and offer a plethora of useful features.

Diversification: Without question, the single greatest advantage of a mutual fund is that it is a *portfolio* of many securities. There is, indeed, safety in numbers. Portfolios consisting of many securities are safer than portfolios with few securities. Most investors, especially those with limited assets, are unable to purchase a large number of different securities. Mutual funds enable individuals to obtain partial ownership of portfolios consisting of dozens, or even hundreds, of different stocks, bonds, money market instruments, and other securities, all for an investment of just a few hundred or a few thousand dollars.

Liquidity: The ability to sell an investment at a moment's notice is an important attribute. Investors can sell some or all of their shares back to mutual funds on a single day's notice, usually without any of the costs entailed in liquidating a portfolio of individual stocks or bonds. Closed-end funds can be sold in the open market at any time at the cost of a small commission.

Professional Management: Mutual funds provide professional portfolio supervision for investors that are unable or unwilling to manage their own portfolios. Nevertheless, professional management is probably the most over-stated advantage of mutual funds. In truth, management is "professional" only if it generates a reasonable return on an investment portfolio relative to the risks assumed. Some fund managers do, indeed, consistently beat the market in which they are investing by exercising superior security selection, market timing, or portfolio strategies. Others, however, have inferior track records.

These "professional" managers are little better than "amateurs." Overall, the average mutual fund portfolio slightly underperforms the market. Somewhat less than half of all professional portfolio manages actually "earn their keep." One purpose of the *Buyer's Guide* is to help you separate the wheat from the chaff.

Low Trading Costs: Small investors usually have to pay commission rates equal to several percent of the amount of their investment when they buy and sell securities. Mutual funds buy and sell securities in large blocks and obtain much lower trading costs, passing the resulting savings on to shareholders.

Retirement Plans: Most funds offer several types of accounts, including tax-deferred retirement plans, such as Keoghs and Individual Retirement Accounts (IRAs). Fees, if any, for these special services are modest.

Dollar Cost Averaging: Because mutual funds can be purchased in small-dol-

Reward and risk possiblities are abundant with mutual funds. In the last decade, Fidelity Magellan soared eight fold, while 44 Wall Street Equity contracted sharply.

lar amounts at periodic intervals, even in fractional shares, they are ideal vehicles for "dollar cost averaging." This intriguing method of accumulating fund shares is analyzed in detail in Chapter 4. Briefly, dollar cost averaging *guarantees* that an investor's average cost of fund shares will be *less* than the average of the prices at the times the shares were purchased. Some funds will even arrange to have amounts regularly transferred from your bank account to automate your DCA program.

Automatic Withdrawal Plans: Many funds also allow investors to gradually sell their shares in an amount and frequency of their own choosing, and will mail a check for the proceeds monthly or quarterly. This enables investors to receive a periodic cash flow from their investment irrespective of a fund's yield or the normal frequency of its distributions.

Distribution Reinvestment: At shareholder request, mutual funds will automatically reinvest all income and capital-gains distributions in additional shares at no charge. In other words, you can have your profits in cash or in

Fidelity offers investors a choice of three dozen "sector" funds specializing in individual industries.

more stock, an option most stock investors do not have.

Dividend Direction Plans: These programs allow you to reinvest dividend and capital-gain distributions received from one fund into another fund in the same family.

Ease of Investment: Buying a fund is "as easy as pie" – certainly much easier than opening a bank account. Later in this chapter, we shall show precisely how easy it is to open a mutual fund account.

Special Purpose Funds: The mutual fund industry has expanded and become extremely diverse during the last two decades. Funds are now available that invest in almost every type of security imaginable. Here is a representative, but by no means exhaustive, list: blue chips, growth stocks, small-company stocks, over-the-counter stocks, preferred stocks, high-grade corporate bonds, junk bonds, Government agency bonds, Ginnie Maes, U.S. Treasuries, zero coupons, gold stocks, health-care stocks, computer stocks, utility stocks (and stocks of many other specialized industries), gold bullion, convertible securities, Treasury bills, bank CDs, commercial paper, and foreign stocks. Regardless of the type of investment you seek, there is likely to be a mutual fund to serve you with a diversified portfolio.

Telephone Switching: Many mutual fund organizations allow investors to switch from one fund to another via telephone instruction, or even to allocate their investments among multiple funds. This service, usually available at no charge, enables investors to switch objectives with a minimum of bother. One extremely popular application of this feature is to switch back and forth between a growth-oriented mutual fund and a conservative income or money fund on the basis of an investor's expectations about the direction of the stock market.

Less Paperwork: One nice thing about funds is that they do most of the paperwork for their stockholders. Capital gains and losses on the purchase and sale of securities, as well as dividend and interest earnings, are neatly totaled for each stockholder at the end of the year for his or her tax purposes. Funds also do all of the day-to-day paperwork chores, including handling of stock certificates, brokerage tickets, statements, transfer agents, stock offerings, etc. All investors have to do is send their money to a fund and it does the rest.

Costs of Mutual Fund Investing

Mutual funds are not a one-way road to riches. For every reward on Wall Street, there is usually an offsetting cost or risk; for every advantage, a disadvantage. In addition to the risk of poor performance, an investor owning a mutual fund subjects himself to a variety of costs and charges.

Sales Charge: Many mutual funds impose a "sales charge" or "load" on investors that buy new shares. Sales charges can range up to 9.3%, although the maximum charge ever published by a fund is 8.5%. This means that $85 of a $1,000 investment is kept by the salesperson or sales organization, and only $915 worth of fund shares are actually purchased. Note that the sales fee equals 9.3% of the amount actually invested. Sadly, most funds quote their sales charges as a percentage of the cost of shares purchased *plus* the commission. This somewhat deceptive practice makes commission rates appear to be

Match the Market

Solid Line: Vanguard Index 500
Dotted Line: Standard & Poor's 500 Index

An index fund like Vanguard Index 500 lets you virtually "buy the market."

slightly lower than they really are. The fees shown in the *Buyer's Guide* are calculated to correctly show the actual percentage commission rate. Sales charges are usually reduced for larger transactions. Many mutual funds, including virtually all money market mutual funds, are "no-load" and do not charge any sales loads at all. (See Chapter Three for more details on maximum load charges.)

Redemption Fee: When an investor sells – i.e., redeems – shares back to a fund, he may incur another charge, a redemption fee. Most funds do not levy any redemption fee at all, but some charge up to 5.3% of the amount of money initially invested. These "back-end loads," also known as contingent deferred sales charges, are sales charges deducted at the end of the transaction rather than the beginning. However, the charges usually scale down with the passage of time. For example, a fund might charge a 5% redemption fee on the sale of shares sold within one year of purchase, while shares sold in their second year of holding would incur a 4% fee, and so on down to a 1% fee in the fifth year, and nothing thereafter.

Other funds levy a small redemption fee on the full sale value of shares sold within a specified period – say, within the first six months or one year after purchase. Such redemption fees are usually imposed to discourage investors from frequent trading.

Redemption fees and sales charges assessed on a particular value of an investment have the same effect on profits and losses. Whether a fund charges a 5% load at the time shares are bought, or charges a 5% fee to redeem, the effect is *exactly* the same on an investor's final value. However, when a redemption fee is levied only on the value of the shares purchased, and if the fund appreciates in value between the times of purchase and sale, a redemption fee costs less than an initial sales charge.

Reloading Charge: Nearly all funds permit investors to automatically reinvest all capital-gain and income distributions in new shares with no sales charge. However, a few funds levy what might be called a "reloading" charge on reinvestments of income distributions.

Hidden Load: A growing, and particularly obnoxious, practice in the mutual fund industry is the imposition of hidden-load charges on investors. Hidden loads are enacted pursuant to so-called "12b-1 plans," also called "distribution plans." Most new funds now levy these charges, and more are adding them. They typically range as high as ¾ of 1% per year.

The money that fund sponsors receive from hidden-load charges supposedly benefits existing fund stockholders by funding promotional efforts that hopefully increase the size of the fund and lead to reduced management fees and operating expenses as a percentage of assets. In practice, however, it is impossible for such cost reductions to offset the hidden loads themselves. Furthermore, large funds lack the operating flexibility of small funds, so if promotions financed by hidden-load charges significantly increase the size of a fund, they may ultimately actually harm existing fund shareholders.

Service (or Administrative) Fees: Beginning in 1990, some mutual funds began levying this fee to compensate brokers for "servicing" the accounts of investors that bought fund shares through their firms. These charges typically range up to 0.25% per year. They are nothing more than a different type of hidden load. Whether such charges are said to be pursuant to a distribution plan or an administration services agreement, they end up enriching salesmen and fund sponsors, not investors.

Additional Costs

All of the charges discussed above should be avoided by mutual fund investors, other considerations being equal. For example, sales charges, redemption fees, hidden loads, and service fees are not necessary to the operation and management of a mutual fund portfolio; they merely pay, directly or indirectly, for sales efforts. The fact that many of the best funds impose *none* of these charge is the ultimate proof they are completely unnecessary.

In addition, mutual funds require their shareholders to bear the burden of several other types of expenses. Though necessary, these costs are usually (though not always) quite modest. Most investors would incur far greater costs themselves if they bypassed mutual funds and purchased stocks and bonds directly. Nevertheless, informed investors should be aware of these additional costs of fund ownership.

Transaction Costs: As a fund buys and sells securities, it incurs brokerage commissions. Transaction costs are normally much lower for mutual funds than for individual investors because funds buy and sell in large quantities. Nevertheless, all trading costs are ultimately borne by shareholders. The more actively a fund turns over (trades) its portfolio, naturally, the more transaction costs it will incur.

Portfolio Management Fees: Every mutual fund contracts with an investment advisor to make investment decisions. Shareholders must bear the cost of the fee paid to the manager, which usually ranges from 0.25% to 1¼% of fund assets per annum. Generally, the larger the fund, the lower the percentage fee. Annual management fees in excess of 0.75% should generally be considered excessive.

Operating Expenses: Mutual funds incur various day-to-day operating costs, including rent, telephone expense, employee salaries, prospectus and annual report printing, and so forth. As these expenses are incurred, they are paid from fund assets, and therefore reduce stockholders' returns. Typical fund operating expenses range from 0.10% to 1¼% per year. Added to management fees, total operating expenses exceed 2% per annum for some funds. Total annual expenses average 1.45% for all equity funds, 1.05% for all taxable bond funds, and 0.85% for all tax-free bond funds.

Balancing the Pluses and Minuses

The nice thing about free markets is that they give investors extraordinarily wide choices. Not all funds, for example, offer all the attractive plans and features enumerated in the list of advantages above. And many funds levy obnoxious layers of expenses and fees on their shareholders. However, with thousands of mutual funds from which to choose, investors can find the features they need without assuming costs they don't need.

The Prospectus

Mutual funds are required to send a "prospectus" to all new and prospective investors. The prospectus is supposed to give an investor all the information he needs to decide whether a fund's shares are a suitable investment. Unfortunately, many are needlessly complex, only slightly more enlightening than an insurance policy. Nevertheless, here are the four basic factors that should be considered when reading a prospectus:

Lexington Strategic Invstmnts

South African gold stocks

1993

The top specialized equity fund in 1993 was Lexington Strategic Investments, up +270%.

First, the front page of a prospectus concisely states the fund's investment objective (growth or income, for example).

Second, a "fee table," usually appearing on the second or third page, summarizes all of the loads, fees, and other costs associated with an investment in the fund.

Third, the next few pages usually discuss the fund's portfolio strategy and list any restricted investments.

Fourth, the availability of various plans such as IRAs, Keoghs, automatic withdrawal, switching with other funds, and so forth are discussed in the remaining prospectus pages.

Do-it-yourselfers should also ask a fund to enclose its latest annual, or interim, stockholder report along with its prospectus. These reports include an itemization of the fund's investment holdings. Viewed in conjunction with the investment objective and portfolio strategy stated in the prospectus, the portfolio listing will show whether a fund owns stocks, bonds, or other types of securities, reveal whether it is purchasing securities of household-name companies or little-known firms, and show the extent to which the fund concentrates investments in particular industries.

How to Buy a Fund

Open-end funds that charge sales commissions of 4% or more (i.e., high-load funds) can be purchased through stockbrokers or independent fund sales-men, who will retain a good chunk of the sales fee as a commission. Most high-load funds can also be purchased directly from the funds themselves, but the sales commission must still be paid.

To buy shares of low-load funds, those with sales commissions of less than 4%, as well as no-load funds, which levy no sales charge at all, investors must usually deal directly with the funds themselves. Alternatively, several dis-count brokerage firms – see Chapter Five – will buy and sell shares of many low-load and no-load funds for their clients . . . and usually (though not always) charge an extra commission for the service.

To buy shares directly from a fund, simply write to it or call it by telephone. (Most funds have toll-free "800" telephone numbers.) Phone numbers are provided for all funds in the *Buyer's Guide*. When calling a fund, ask if it is available for sale in your state (not all funds are available in all states), and if it is, ask it to send you a new account application form. The fund will automati-cally send a current prospectus along with the application form. If you wish, you can also request any or all of the following items: (1) special forms that may be necessary to open an IRA, Keogh, or retirement account; (2) a "Statement of Additional Information," which provides much more detailed information than the prospectus (this report is only for really serious fund students); (3) the current annual report; and (4) any report to stockholders that has been issued since the latest annual report.

After these documents have been received, and studied if desired, the next step is to fill out the account application form. If the application leaves any ambiguities or unanswered questions, simply call the fund once again and ask for assistance. Most funds are extremely responsive and want to help investors open new accounts. (It is invariably easier to open a new account with a mutual fund than with a bank.) Be sure to consider and check the alternatives offered for future redemption of your shares. Most funds give you a choice of telephone, mail, and wire redemption. Finally, simply mail or overnight-express the form back to the fund, along with a check or money order. To speed new investments, most funds will alternatively accept wire transfers from a bank.

Closed-end funds are traded in the marketplace just like the stocks of thousands of companies. They may be bought and sold directly through a broker who will charge his standard commission. (When a closed-end fund goes public by selling shares for the first time, brokers frequently market them as "commission-free." Buyer beware! Brokerage firms never sell anything without a commission, and this no exception; a commission ranging from 5%

to 9% is invariably embedded in the initial offering prices of closed-end funds.)

How to Sell a Fund

All open-end mutual funds, load and no-load, can be sold directly back to the fund itself. Methods of sale vary from fund to fund but generally include the options of notifying a fund by mail, telephone, or wire. Account application forms generally provide a space for new shareholders to designate the sale options they wish to use. However, the actual procedures to use to liquidate some funds can be a bit tricky, so to avoid an unwelcome surprise later, we suggest that you cover this base directly with a fund representative *before* you invest. Funds originally bought through a stockbroker can be sold through a broker, as well.

Most fund groups also permit free, or very low-cost, transfers of investments to another fund (such as a money fund) in the same group, by either mail or telephone instruction.

Dividends

Mutual funds are required to distribute to their shareholders at least 90% of all investment profits. In practice, most funds pay out virtually 100% of their investment income after expenses. In fund parlance, a dividend is call a "distribution."

Funds make two kinds of distributions: (1) *capital gains*, which consist only of long-term capital gains; and (2) *ordinary dividends*, which may consist of interest and dividends earned on investments, as well as short-term capital gains. The nature of a distribution is always specified by the fund in an accompanying statement. Ordinary dividends, except those from tax-free funds, are currently taxable at ordinary income tax rates. Long-term capital gains distributions are currently capped at 28%. (Caution: Tax rates are extremely fluid these days, as Washington copes with budgetary deficits. Check with your tax advisor for up-to-the minute tax-rate details.)

At the end of the calendar year, funds also send to shareholders a summary, for income tax purposes, of all distributions made during the year. That summary is known as a Form 1099. A copy of the Form 1099 is also sent to the Internal Revenue Service, which then attempts to match taxpayers' reported income with what the funds have reported paying.

Nearly all funds give investors a choice of taking distributions in cash or reinvesting them in new fund shares. (The option you choose has no effect on the taxability of the distribution.) Investors should indicate their preference for cash payment or reinvestment of distributions on the account application filled out at the time of initial investment. The choice may, of course, be changed at any time.

Tracking Your Investment

Price quotations for all mutual funds with at least 1,000 stockholders or $25 million of assets are published daily in *The Wall Street Journal* and in most newspapers. All of these publications receive their price quotations from a trade group, the National Association of Securities Dealers (NASD). To obtain current prices on a fund with less than 1,000 shareholders or under $25 million of assets, it is usually necessary to call the fund directly.

Most funds are listed in newspapers' mutual fund tables under the name of their sponsor. For example, all of the several dozen funds in the Vanguard organization are listed under the Vanguard heading, even though some of the funds do not have "Vanguard" as part of their names. The *Buyer's Guide* has adapted this standard, grouping funds in the same fashion as in their newspaper listings.

In the newspaper listings, a fund is quoted with either one or two prices. The first price (or the only price if just one is shown) is usually presented under the heading "NAV," which stands for "Net Asset Value," although some papers use the heading "Bid." This is the actual value of the fund's shares and the price at which redeeming fund shareholders were permitted to *sell* their shares at the end of the previous day.

The best-performing international equity fund in 1993 was Turkish Investment, up +171%.

The second price, called "Offer Price" or "Asked," represents the price paid by new investors at the end of the previous day. For no-load funds, the price new investors pay for shares is the net asset value. The Offer Price can be higher than the Net Asset Value because it includes the maximum sales charge paid by new investors. However, that does not necessarily mean the fund has no back-end load (redemption charge) or hid-

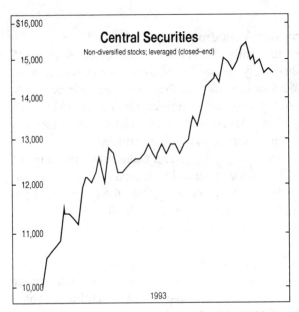

Central Securities

Non-diversified stocks; leveraged (closed–end)

$16,000

15,000

14,000

13,000

12,000

11,000

10,000

1993

The #1 closed-end domestic equity fund in 1993 was Central Securities, up +46%.

den load (12b-1 plan). Some newspapers identify funds that levy redemption fees with an "r" and funds that levy 12b-1 hidden loads with a "p." In neither case, however, is the amount of the charge indicated. If, instead of a second price, the initials "NL" appear, the fund does not levy a front-end sales charge.

When measuring the performance of an investment in a mutual fund, it is vital to consider the fund's distributions. Whenever a fund makes a distribution, its net asset value is reduced by precisely the amount of the distribution. Because the fund also fluctuates in value due to market changes on the day the distribution is deducted, the actual price change is usually different than the amount of the distribution. Ultimately, funds distribute to investors nearly all of their profits and losses, so a fund's net asset value could be unchanged over a period of time in which its investors nevertheless made a considerable amount of money from the distributions.

For example, an investor may have initially purchased shares of a fund at $10 per share, and some years later, each share may still be priced at $10. The investor may nevertheless have fared well because of income and capital gains distributions paid over the years. What counts, then, is not the price performance of a fund's shares, but the fund's total investment performance; that is, the total return to shareholders. All fund performance statistics in the *Buyer's Guide* assume reinvestment in additional fund shares of all income and capital-gains distributions, and therefore present total returns to fund shareholders.

Regulation

Mutual funds are among the most tightly-regulated businesses in America. They must be registered with the U.S. Securities and Exchange Commission under a law, the Investment Company Act of 1940, that was passed in the aftermath of the Great Depression. Pursuant to this law, funds are required to print a prospectus for new investors at least once a year and disseminate reports to stockholders, including a portfolio, at least twice a year. The SEC regularly examines the books of fund groups managing more than $1 billion.

Predicting Performance

What are the best predictors of a mutual fund's future performance? The tools that can be used to forecast performance

G.T. Global Strategic Incm "A"
Foreign & U.S. – govts & corps; emerg mkts

The top taxable bond fund in 1993 was G.T. Global Strategic Income "A," which returned +44%.

range from general guidelines, such as fund size, to precise scientific measurements based on individual econometric models of each fund. Here is an overview of the factors that do and do not matter in selecting a fund.

Fund Size: Many academic studies have examined the correlation between the size of a fund and its performance. The universal conclusion has been that big is not necessarily beautiful.

The largest mutual funds are rarely among the top performers in a rising market, but neither are they likely to be among the worst performers in a falling market. Some very large funds have excellent long-term records, although most were *not* large funds at the beginning when they were recording the bulk of their cumulative gains. (An exception is Fidelity Magellan, which continued to be a star performer long after it became the largest stock fund in America.)

Large funds are constrained by their sheer size to invest in highly-capitalized stocks that are generally among the least volatile in the marketplace. Smaller funds can be more flexible. With only a few million, or few tens of millions, of dollars to invest, they can take positions in relatively small-capitalization equities. While such stocks tend to be among the worst performers in bear markets, they are usually the best in bull markets.

But smallness is not beneficial *per se*. A badly managed small fund will still be a bad investment. Further, management fees and expenses are relatively higher for small funds, penalizing their performance before the game even starts. A billion-dollar fund typically incurs annual costs of about three-quarters of one percent, while a $10 million fund normally incurs expenses equal to two to three times that.

The advantage of smallness, then, is that it gives a fund a greater *opportunity* to realize the benefits of superior portfolio management.

Load v. No-Load: There is absolutely no evidence that sales loads enhance performance. Loads don't buy performance; they only buy a salesman. Indeed, as will be shown in Chapter 2, no-load stock funds appear to be better performers than their load-fund counterparts, even before deducting the loads from performance. There is also direct evidence that a fund's performance is penalized by the amount of its annual management fees and 12b-1 "hidden loads."

What this means, of course, is that net returns to investors will, all other things equal, be relatively inferior for funds that charge loads or levy high fees. That is because all of the loads and fees come, directly or indirectly, out of the pockets of fund shareholders. Therefore, in the absence of rare over-riding performance considerations, no-load funds are a better buy than load funds, and funds with low expense ratios are better buys than funds with high expense ratios.

Short-term traders in particular should use no-load, or very low load, funds exclusively. However, investors that contemplate holding a fund for many years should recognize that an apparently heavy initial sales charge may ultimately be proved inconsequential. (Investors that paid Templeton Growth Fund's 9.3% sales

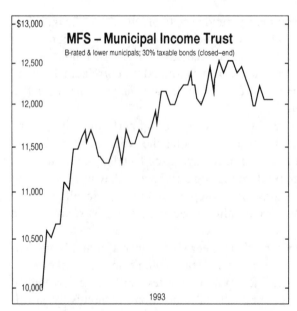

MFS – Municipal Income Trust
B-rated & lower municipals; 30% taxable bonds (closed–end)

$13,000

12,500

12,000

11,500

11,000

10,500

10,000

1993

The top tax-free bond fund in 1993 was MFS – Municipal Income Trust, with a total return of +21%.

load in the 1950s obviously didn't mind a whit after their fund subsequently soared more than a hundred-fold.) This is especially true if the planned investment is large enough, typically $25,000 or more, to entitle you to a discount on the sales charge. In these instances, the prospective reward and risk associated with owning a fund's shares is what really counts.

Fund Price: The price of a stock can provide an excellent indication of its prospective performance. Low-priced stocks, although more risky, persistently outperform higher priced stocks. A mutual fund's price, however, is completely arbitrary, usually established by the fund's management merely to maximize its sales potential to new investors. Hence, the price of a fund is inconsequential. Most funds try to keep the price below $20 a share and will split the shares if necessary to do so. There is no reason why a fund whose net asset value is, say, $100 per share, should not be just as good, or bad, a performer as a fund whose share price is $10 or $1.

Type of Fund: Mutual funds are commonly classified by their investment objective; e.g., growth, aggressive growth, income, etc. Such classifications can provide a useful guide to what an investor is buying, but only preliminarily. Some funds classified in relatively conservative categories are actually managed more aggressively than funds in more speculative categories. What counts is performance. Regardless of claimed objectives, funds are much better categorized on the basis of purely statistical analyses of how they actually perform relative to one another in the marketplace.

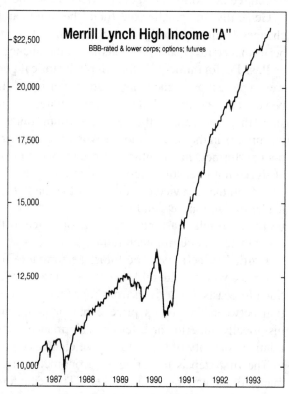

Junk bonds have a bad name, but many junk bond mutual funds have made their shareholders rich.

Management Changes: What usually happens when a fund switches managers? This question is of more than just academic interest, because a new Securities and Exchange Commission rule requires fund to identify their portfolio managers and inform investors when changes occur.

The surprising answer, according to a recent study by CDA/Weisenberger, a Maryland research organization, is that it all depends on how well the fund was doing *before* the switch in managers. A study of portfolio manager changes in growth funds over a ten-year period found that when good-performing funds switched managers, performance tended to slump . . . to about 10% worse than average. But when lagging funds switched managers, performances perked up . . . to 27% better than average.

Finally, bear in mind that many of the larger fund groups have sufficient depth of management expertise that the departure of one individual makes little difference; witness Fidelity Magellan's continuing superior performance with three portfolio managers between 1990 and 1993.

Generally, the smaller the fund, the more carefully one should watch for changes at the top levels of management. And on average, expect a relative performance reversal when an equity fund changes managers.

Past Performance: If the simple historical performance of a mutual fund were a perfect prologue to its future performance, the selection question would be very easily solved. Indeed, recent studies at Harvard and Yale Universities show that, on average, the best-performing funds in the past tend to be good performers in the future, and the worst-performing funds in the past tend to be poor performers in the future. However, a mutual fund's performance is *better* analyzed not in absolute terms, but in relation to the market.

A fund that is twice as volatile as the market is likely to be a performance leader in bull markets and among the worst performers in bear markets. The best way to relate a fund's past performance to the market is to develop an econometric model for each fund.

Profit Projections: The future performance of most mutual funds can be estimated with considerable accuracy using econometric modeling techniques. Such forecasts are derived from four factors: A market forecast; the correlation between the fund's price behavior and that of the market; the fund's historically superior or inferior performance relative to the market; and the relative volatility of the fund's price changes compared with the market.

The first step is to derive an econometric model of the expected performance of the general stock market. (This technique, discussed at length in the author's book, *Stock Market Logic*, was pioneered in the early 1970s by The Institute for Econometric Research.) In terms of forecasting future mutual

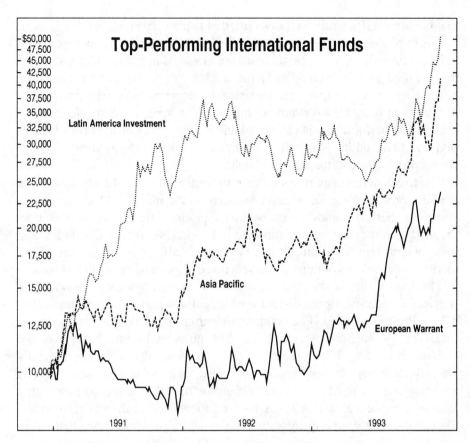

Top-Performing International Funds

Latin America Investment

Asia Pacific

European Warrant

1991   1992   1993

Around the world with mutual funds

fund performance, it is worth keeping in mind that the market is more easily and accurately predicted over long periods of time, such as one, two, or five years, than over shorter periods of, say, three months or less. The *Buyer's Guide* makes an econometric model forecast of the performance of Standard & Poor's 500 Index, the best benchmark of mutual fund performance, for the next five years. This forecast is the primary component of each mutual fund 5-Year Profit Projection in this *Guide*.

The second step in forecasting fund performance is to measure the correlation between each fund's price behavior and that of the market in general. The movements of most funds are fairly well correlated with the market because their diversification reduces portfolio fluctuations unrelated to the market. Although only so-called "index funds" are completely diversified, most mutual funds are sufficiently well diversified as to act very much like the market.

The third element to be measured is the fund's propensity to underper-form or outperform the market. Some funds are managed in a consistently superior manner, and even in a completely flat market can be expected to provide a positive return. Other funds are consistently inferior to the market and tend to decline even in a sideways-moving market. The superiority or inferiority of each fund's performance is calculated and becomes part of the Profit Projection for that fund. We call this statistic a fund's Superiority Rating. (Econometricians call the statistic "alpha.")

The fourth component of each Profit Projection is the Volatility Rating – a measure of a fund's price volatility relative to the market. (This statistic is known as "beta.") Funds whose price changes have been more volatile than the market in the past tend to continue to be more volatile in the future, and funds whose relative volatility has been, say, half, or equal to, that of the market, will usually continue to possess those degrees of volatility, as well.

The final result of this statistical analysis is an econometric model that provides a scientific estimate of how each fund will perform in the future – its 5-Year Profit Projection. For example, we currently project that the market, as measured by the S&P 500, will rise 26% on a total-return basis over the coming five years. If our statistical analysis shows that a particular fund's price fluctuations are very highly correlated with the market and that it is normally about a third more volatile than the market, we should expect that fund to advance about 26% times 1.33, or about 35% in the next five years. Then, if the fund's Superiority Rating is, say +5% a year (indicating that, on an annual basis, it tends to consistently beat the market by that amount, regardless of what the market does), the final 5-Year Profit Projection is 35% plus five times 5%, which equals +60%.

Conclusion

You now know all the rudiments of mutual fund investing – the opportunities and the pitfalls. In fact, you probably know more now than 99% of all fund investors. You are ready to begin, so charge right ahead.

Chapter Two

Loads versus No-Loads

For years, the argument has raged: Which are better, no-load funds or load funds? Several studies, limited in scope, have provided tentative evidence that paying sales commissions (loads) does not produce superior performance. Until now, comprehensive evidence has not been available.

However, a 23-year performance study by the *Buyer's Guide* of no-load funds provides definitive proof that no-loads reward their shareholders with superior returns. And that superiority exists *before* adjusting for the sales charges. In other words, the performance gap widens further in favor of no-load funds when the sales loads are charged against the performance of the load funds. Put another way, sales charges do not buy superior performance, they just buy a salesman.

Growth Funds
Annual Rates of Return: 1971-1993

	No-Load Funds Only	All Funds
1971-1975	− 0.4%	− 1.0%
1976-1980	+24.0%	+16.9%
1981-1985	+11.2%	+11.2%
1986-1990	+10.5%	+10.2%
1991-1993	+23.1%	+21.1%
All 23 Years	+12.5%	+10.6%

Our first table shows the performance of all U.S. growth funds over five separate intervals from 1971 through 1993. In each of the periods, no-load growth funds performed as well, or better, than all growth funds combined, including both load and no-load. Over the entire 23 years, the no-loads provided an average annual return of 12.5%, the equivalent of a 23-year growth of $10,000 to $150,100. Meanwhile, all growth funds together returned only 10.6% per annum, the equivalent of an initial $10,000 investment increasing to $101,500.

To verify these results on an independent group of funds, we also compared the returns of so-called "growth and income" funds, which strive to achieve both capital appreciation and yield for their shareholders. In two periods, no-

Growth & Income Funds
Annual Rates of Return: 1971-1993

	No-Load Funds Only	All Funds
1971-1975	+ 3.2%	+ 3.8%
1976-1980	+16.5%	+15.9%
1981-1985	+15.1%	+13.8%
1986-1990	+ 8.9%	+ 9.5%
1991-1993	+16.5%	+16.2%
All 23 Years	+11.5%	+11.4%

load funds slightly underperformed all funds in aggregate. However, in the entire 23-year period, no-loads produced very slightly higher returns. Again, sales commissions did not buy superior performance. All other factors being equal, then, no-load funds should be preferred to load funds.

Chapter Three

Beware Hidden Loads

Without question, the worst abuses imposed on mutual fund shareholders during the last decade have been "12b-1 hidden load" charges. In a nutshell, these are continuing sales charges imposed on existing fund shareholders year after year to finance current and future marketing efforts. Nearly half of all funds now impose these egregious charges. The total cost to all fund shareholders now exceeds $2 *billion* a year.

The Securities and Exchange Commission – ostensibly the public's protector – first encouraged hidden loads in the early 1980s, but the funds were slow to grab for the new-found treasure. Then, as the market soared, many fund managers apparently decided their shareholders were profiting so handsomely they wouldn't miss a few percentage points of profit one way or another.

The result has been a proliferation of schemes known variously as "Rule 12b-1 Plans" (after the SEC rule that permits such fees) or "distribution plans." For the first few years, most funds buried the disclosure of these fees deep in their prospectuses, and we coined the still-popular descriptive term "hidden load." Now, 12b-1 fees are disclosed in the table of fund fees and expenses near the front of their prospectus.

We recognized the dangers of SEC Rule 12b-1 – and vehemently opposed it – from the sad day it was first proposed. The Rule's trip through the SEC to ultimate approval is said to have involved the most expensive industry lobbying campaign in the history of U.S. securities regulation. It paid off.

The Keystone Caper

To see how a 12b-1 Plan works, let's take a look at one of the earliest – and still most abusive – examples: the plan used by the Keystone Custodian Fund Series S-4, offered by a subsidiary of Travelers Insurance. Keystone S-4 was a full-load fund until it implemented a pacesetting 12b-1 Plan and eliminated the front-end load to ostensibly become a "no-load" fund. But under its 12b-1 Plan, up to 1% of *all* shareholders' investments can be taken *every* year to pay for the costs of selling new shares. (Initially, the 12b-1 charge was 1¼% annually.)

The fee is used to pay a commission to Keystone's sales distributor on all future sales of fund shares – whether made to new or existing shareholders. Shareholders' assets are also used to pay royalty-like commissions to selling brokers for as long as each new investment remains in the fund, possibly forever. Finally, new shareholders that redeem their investments within four years now pay a redemption fee of up to 4.2% back to the fund.

One of the worst aspects of most new 12b-1 Plans is that, when enacted, existing shareholders, who may well have previously paid sales charges on their own investments, are now, by virtue of the annual 12b-1 assessments, forced to pay more sales commissions on purchases of the fund by new investors. In the case of Keystone, investors paid a 9.3% sales charge in the old pre no-load days, but still have their investments reduced by a further sales charge of up to 1% every year for as long as they remain in the fund, even if they make no further transactions. This incredibly unfair situation is tantamount to paying your broker a commission to buy a stock and then, months or years later, paying *extra commissions* every month to compensate him for selling stocks to *new* clients.

No Justification

The economic "rationale" for allowing a fund to have a 12b-1 Plan to pay sales costs is that it helps a fund grow, and that shareholders benefit, either because bigger funds are more efficient, or because management fees and other costs decline somewhat as a percentage of total assets for larger funds. As for equity funds, the first hypothesis is simply false. There is no evidence that large funds consistently perform better than small funds.

As for the cost savings of larger funds, Keystone S-4 again provides an excellent case study. If the 12b-1 program succeeds in doubling assets over a period of years, the annual management fee will decline a mere 0.05% (based on the fee schedule in Keystone's own prospectus). Compare that with the 12b-1 load of 1% a year, and you readily see that investors can lose 20 times as much paying for hoped-for growth as they will benefit *if* the growth occurs.

Who really profits from larger fund size? The managers of the fund itself! Their incomes from management fees soar as fund size increases, regardless of whether that increase ensues from good portfolio management or from sales efforts paid out of shareholders' assets. It costs little more to manage the portfolio of a large fund than a small one, but management fees are levied as a percentage of total assets and every additional dollar of assets increases the management fee.

Fortunately, most hidden-load plans are not as expensive as Keystone's. Some 12b-1 Plans cost shareholders only ¼ of 1% a year, and amount to little more than a slightly higher management fee. In fact, the total of the annual management fee and hidden-load fee of some funds is *less* than the management fee alone of some funds with no 12b-1 Plan.

The annual fees levied under various 12b-1 Plans range from 0.06% to 0.75%. A rule implemented in 1993 effectively capped 12b-1 fees at 0.75% but also permitted "adminstrative service fees" of an additional 0.25% per annum, so total hidden loads are often 1% a year – a clearly abusive level. Charges of less than 0.10% are so insignificant they can be ignored when selecting a fund. Fees of up to 0.30% per annum are no greater than the existing range of variance of management fees among different funds, so up to that level, 12b-1 costs are a minor consideration in choosing a fund.

The 12b-1 charges to watch out for are those that are greater than 0.30%. Since annual stock returns average about 10% (bond and money market returns are much less than that), high 12b-1 charges are clearly abusive. A 1% annual hidden load confiscates a tenth or more of investors' expected total return for no purpose other than to enable the fund to sell shares to other investors.

For short-term traders contemplating only a brief holding period, even an unusually high 12b-1 charge is preferable to any size sales or redemption load. That is because a charge at a rate of, say, 1.00% per annum is trivial over one or two months.

The potential for catastrophic abuse in Rule 12b-1 was apparent from the start, but the SEC's lame-brained excuse was that it was only an experimental program with built-in "safeguards." In fact, Rule 12b-1 only requires (1) initial shareholder approval, and (2) annual reapproval by a fund's directors.

Shareholder approval has proven to be a sham. Mutual fund shareholder approval of almost anything is virtually a *fait accompli*. (Most stockholders would vote away half their profits if the proposal were obfuscated in sufficiently misleading legalese.) In practice, 99.8% of funds seeking shareholder approval of 12b-1 Plans have received it.

The other "safeguard," annual director reapproval, has proven equally meaningless. Every year, the directors of every mutual fund with a Rule 12b-1 Plan make a "finding" that the continuance of the hidden load is reasonably likely to benefit shareholders. Although such a conclusion certainly deserves a ranking high on the list of "Great American Lies," no fund has ever acknowledged that its Board has voted against management and recommended discontinuing a hidden load.

At least 40% of a mutual fund's directors must be "disinterested." These are directors that, in theory, are not beholden to fund management, and are sufficiently independent to speak up for shareholders' rights. Unfortunately, many disinterested directors are individuals that make a profession of serving as outside directors to mutual funds or other public companies. It is a lucrative profession, one that can provide thousands of dollars a year in fees for a few hours of work.

Who selects "disinterested" directors? Why, a fund's management, naturally. Not surprisingly, disinterested directors that prove to be *too disinterested* sometimes don't get invited back. As a result, most disinterested directors get along by going along . . . and vote to continue 12b-1 Plans.

Contrary Evidence

An exhaustive study by two professors at State University of New York in Buffalo provides proof that if anyone benefits from hidden loads, it certainly is not the shareholders. Their research is the most comprehensive examination of 12b-1 charges ever conducted, and is enhanced by the fact that it was commissioned by the SEC's own Office of Economic Analysis.

Charles Tszcinka's and Robert Zweig's meticulously-documented report concludes in part, "Rule 12b-1 has increased expenses, lowered net [shareholder] returns, and [has] had no effect on [fund] growth." It goes on to say that "many of the benefits claimed for Rule 12b-1 do not exist." For example, the professors found "no evidence" that hidden loads lower expense ratios through economies of scale or promote growth of assets.

12b-1 Abuses

According to the SEC, fund officials have used the proceeds of 12b-1 Plans for such diverse purposes as buying cases of whiskey, paying off their accounts at Bloomingdale's, expensing away dinner at New York's posh 21 Club, and even buying boxes of chocolate bonbons. Exotic vacations for fund salesmen, financed with 12b-1 fees, are common practice in the fund industry. All of this despite a strict requirement that all 12b-1 fees be spent to benefit fund *shareholders*.

In 1988, the SEC finally decided to put a stop to the worst abuses of hidden loads. It drafted a 137-page proposal requiring full disclosure of hidden loads and drastic changes to the way the 12b-1 scam works. If ever adopted, the new rules could mark the end of the hidden-load heyday. Unfortunately, the proposals were lobbied to a standstill by the fund industry and ultimately dropped.

The proposed rules, literally years in preparation, were voluminous and provide a glimpse into other 12b-1 malpractices. The key feature was a requirement for annual *shareholder* approval of all hidden-load schemes. We still hope the SEC will mandate such clear disclosure regarding 12b-1 Plans that shareholder approval will become more difficult to obtain.

The proposed rules would have barred the popular practice of funds with hidden loads misleading investors by characterizing themselves as "no-loads." They would also have forbidden fund distributors from levying hidden loads for "distribution services" and then keeping the money while providing absolutely no distribution services whatsoever – a scam that amazingly is legal under current rules. Another proposed rule would have required disclosure of the obnoxious practice of combining full front-end loads plus hidden loads to produce total fees that exceed the maximum front-end load now permitted by law – a ploy that is also legal, although now requiring disclosure in the prospectus.

Yet another proposed rule would have forbidden accruing distribution costs under Rule 12b-1 as an undisclosed fund liability to be repaid many years in the future. Some funds have undisclosed liabilities of more than $100 million that will eventually have to be repaid, with interest, from future hidden loads, or simply as a levy directly on shareholders' assets if the hidden load ends. Funds now avoid disclosing such liabilities by claiming that accounting rules do not require disclosure of obligations that "cannot be reasonably estimated." The funds argue that since hidden-load fees are tied to the unknown future level of fund assets, they can't be reasonably estimated, and hence don't have to be disclosed.

Load Caps Imposed in 1993

In 1993, the National Association of Securities Dealers (NASD), under the sanction of the SEC, imposed a 12b-1 industry cap of 0.75% per annum plus an additional 0.25% maximum annual account-service (or administrative) fee, which is really just another hidden load. The most constructive aspect of the NASD approach is its concurrent imposition of partial limits on maximum aggregate sales charges (front-end and back-end loads), depending on whether a fund has a service fee. If a fund has an annual service fee, its maximum combined front-end and back-end load is 7.25% of the total amount paid including the sales charge (or 7.82% of the dollar value of shares purchased). If a fund does *not* have a service fee, its maximum combined front-end and back-end load is 6.25% (or 6.67% of the value of shares bought).

However, there is a loophole in the new regulation: The load caps are imposed upon the fund as a whole, not on individual shareholders. This means that a fund can continue to levy combined front-end and back-end loads on individual shareholders up to the old maximum of 8.5% (an actual load of 9.3% of the dollar value of shares bought or sold) provided the *average* charges to all shareholders do not exceed the new caps. Since most funds reduce their percentage sales charges on large-dollar purchases, this loophole effectively allows them to keep levying the larger charge on small investors.

The rules also unfortunately allow funds that impose 12b-1 and service fees totaling as much as 0.25% per annum to legally call themselves "*no*-load." Such a gross distortion of the English language is but the latest deceit in the long-running 12b-1 fiasco.

Chapter Four

Dollar Cost Averaging

Ah, to be able to "beat the market." Investors that beat the market consistently can look forward to a secure future. But, of course, not everyone cannot beat the market, simply because everyone *is* the market. In fact, over any given period, about half of all investors must do worse than average. Is it possible, then, to develop a long-term investment strategy that can absolutely *guarantee* you will come out ahead of the market?

The answer is, Yes, and the strategy is "dollar cost averaging." The name may sound complicated, but the concept has been around since the 1920s and it is simplicity itself. It is a long-term investment technique that beats the market . . . by ignoring the market.

What is Dollar Cost Averaging?

To set up a dollar cost averaging system, you merely invest a fixed amount of money at regular time intervals. For example, you could invest $1,000 every three months. Or $100 every month. Or $500 every week. The amount and frequency of investments are dependent solely upon your financial means.

Once you initiate the system, it is essential to the success of your dollar cost averaging program that you stick with it – at least to the extent of *ignoring all market fluctuations*. Therefore, be careful to establish an investment schedule that is consistent with your financial means. You will find, then, a secondary value in dollar cost averaging: It is, in effect, a "forced" savings plan.

By now, you are probably asking yourself, How can such a simple system beat the market? Isn't there some catch? The answers are, Yes, it really is just that simple; and, No, there isn't any catch.

Why Does Averaging Work?

The wonders of dollar cost averaging can be best illustrated with a simple example: Let's assume you have decided to invest $1,000 in a mutual fund every six months. At the outset, the fund shares sell for $10. You therefore open an account and buy 100 shares with your first $1,000.

Six months later, the market has soared and the fund is selling for $20. You buy 50 shares for another investment of $1,000.

A few months later, the market has corrected some of its advance and the fund's price has fallen back to $15, the midpoint of your $10 and $20 purchases. That puts you even, right?

Wrong! You really have a nice profit! Your $2,000 total investment first bought you 100 shares and then another 50 shares. Your total holding of 150 shares times their $15 price is worth $2,250. That's about a 12% gain over your $2,000 cost.

In case you're scratching your head over this result, let's go directly to the explanation. Your superior return occurred because your two fixed-dollar investment bought relatively more shares when the price was low and fewer shares when the price was high. As a result, your *average cost per share* is $13.33 (your $2,000 total investment divided by the 150 shares purchased). So now that the fund is selling at $15, you obviously have a profit.

Looked at another way, it is interesting to observe that the average of the two transaction prices, $15, is above the real average cost per share, only $13.33. This amazing phenomenon always holds true with dollar cost averaging.

Dollar cost averaging operates on this principle: Because you invest a fixed-dollar amount at each interval, you always buy a larger number of shares when the price is low and a smaller number of shares when the price is high. In effect, you are buying a lot at bargain prices and relatively little at what might be considered exorbitantly high prices.

Of course, only looking back years from now will we know for a fact what prices really were bargains and what prices truly were exorbitant. The beauty of dollar cost averaging is that we don't need to know the answer when we are making our investments; it's handled automatically.

Time Diversification

Time diversification is one of the newest ideas in modern portfolio theory. To reduce risk and maximize expected total return, the theory holds that you should own securities across all time periods. Some recent academic evidence suggests that when it comes to reducing total risk, time diversification is more important than the traditional diversification of buying many different securities. As we can see, dollar cost averaging, now more than a half-century old, is really pure time diversification. Thus, not only does dollar cost averaging help to improve your returns, it also works to reduce your total portfolio risk.

Discipline

It is critically important to ignore all market fluctuations when employing dollar cost averaging. Most investors that obtain poor returns in the market are victims of their own emotions. Only after security prices have been rising sharply do they work up enough courage to buy stocks or mutual fund shares. And about the only time they ever sell shares is when they become especially fearful *after* prices have already been plunging. The consequence of their naiveté, of course, is that they buy high and sell low – a ticket to disaster.

Dollar cost averaging enables you to ignore market fluctuations because you automatically buy more shares low and buy fewer shares high – a ticket to success.

It is important, then, not to let your emotions get the best of you. You must exercise the discipline of maintaining your systematic investment program. Unless you have a well-established expertise in timing the market, don't try it. Let dollar cost averaging do your market timing for you.

Investment Frequency

As we have noted, you can make your dollar cost average investments as frequently as you wish – weekly, monthly, even annually. However, to optimize the program, it is better to make more frequent investments.

The stock and bond markets can swing violently up and down, and it is desirable, from a dollar cost averaging standpoint, to buy a large number of shares with your fixed dollar investment when the market is at a low. But market lows may not occur at the precise time you are scheduled to make an investment. The more frequently your program calls for reinvestment, then, the closer it will come to enabling you to buy a lot of shares near the precise low of an intermediate or major market downtrend.

In fact, dollar cost averaging almost makes you *hope* that prices will go *down* so you can buy more shares and build up your portfolio.

Starting at the Top – A Worst Case

It is *never* too late in a market cycle to start a dollar cost averaging program, as the following example attests: In his 1967 book, *Handbook of Formula Plans in the Stock Market*, Dr. Robert H. Persons created a hypothetical dollar cost averaging portfolio with the Dow Jones Industrial Average. The Dow, of course, is a motley group of 30 supposedly "blue-chip" stocks. Its performance nearly always lags the rest of the market.

The program began right at the market high in 1929, just before the Great Crash. Persons made a hypothetical equal-dollar investment in the Dow Jones Industrial Average in each year from 1929 to 1966. However, instead of buying the Dow at the same time each year, he assumed purchase at the *high* price each year – a worst-case scenario, if you will.

Obviously, the program showed a loss in the first couple of years as the market plunged. But amidst the gloom and despair of the depression low in 1932 and 1933, the program was purchasing large numbers of shares at very low prices. (Even the years' high prices were low in the early '30s.) The result was that by 1935, the portfolio already showed a profit. Nineteen years later, 1954 to be exact, the Dow Jones Industrial Average itself finally struggled back to its 1929 peak, but by then the program had doubled in value.

At the conclusion of the illustration, the Dow had appreciated 161% above its 1929 high. By that time, the dollar cost averaging program had appreciated 336% over its cost, despite the fact that some of the shares purchased were acquired just one, two, or three years previously.

A New Concept

Although dollar cost averaging has been around for more than a half-century, it has traditionally been used and illustrated in extremely simple portfolios, usually with just a single stock or a single mutual fund. A refined approach is to use dollar cost averaging with many different stocks, bonds, or mutual funds.

It is fairly obvious that the prices of most securities move roughly together, rising and falling with the market. Of course, some are more or less volatile than others, and not *every one* moves in the same direction as the market *all* of the time. But over the course of months and years, you will find that individual security returns are correlated with the market itself more than with any other factor. (A possible exception to this pattern is gold stocks, which seem to have a mind of their own.)

It follows that investors using a dollar cost averaging program can buy shares of *different* stocks, bonds, or mutual funds at each regular purchase date. Because most securities will move up and down with the market, you will purchase relatively more shares of any security when the market is low, and buy fewer shares of virtually any security when the market is high. The diversification into multiple issues provides added protection against the prospect of a complete collapse in any one issue.

In other words, there is no need to tie your hands to the point of buying shares of only a single security or one mutual fund. You can pick and choose whatever ones you think are best at the scheduled time of investment.

To carry this concept to its natural, most profitable, conclusion, we propose the following strategy: At the time of a scheduled dollar cost averaging investment, buy shares of the mutual fund that carries our "Best Buy" in our investment advisory letters. The benefit of this strategy will be two-fold: First, you will build added protection into your portfolio by eventually diversifying into many different mutual funds. Second, the fund you buy at any moment is the one that is likely to provide the best return in the year immediately ahead.

Even if our forecasts for all funds is down – which could occur if the market outlook is particularly gloomy – you should buy the "Best Buy" fund. That might mean, of course, buying a fund that we nevertheless project will appreciate only slightly in the period just ahead. But again, it is important to the ultimate success of dollar cost averaging to discipline yourself to making the investments at the allotted times. The payoff will be when your portfolio decisively beats the market. Not only will you profit from dollar cost averaging's built-in market-timing program, but you will benefit from superior investment selection – the best of both worlds!

TECHNICAL NOTE

Dollar cost averaging works on the principle of the harmonic mean, the least known of the three most common averaging methods. The most popular averaging technique, of course, is the simple arithmetic average (or arithmetic mean) in which several values are added together and then divided by the number of values. A second averaging system is the geometric mean, computed by multiplying several values together and taking a root (equal to the number of values being averaged) of their product.

The harmonic mean is a little more complicated to compute, but is nevertheless straightforward: Instead of averaging the values, one averages the *reciprocals* of the values. (The reciprocal of 10, for example, is .10; the reciprocal of .10 is 10; the reciprocal of 2 is .5; the reciprocal of 25 is .04.) Once the average reciprocal is determined, simply find the reciprocal of that average. The harmonic mean of a series consisting of different values will *always* be below the arithmetic and geometric means of those same values.

The example used in the article above to illustrate dollar cost averaging assumed a $1,000 purchase of a fund when the price was $10 and again when the price was $20. The average cost of the acquired shares, $13.33, is actually the harmonic mean of those two prices: First, find the reciprocals of $10 and $20, which are .10 and .05, respectively. The average of these two reciprocals is .075. Finally, determine the reciprocal of .075 (which is 1.0 divided by .075). The answer is $13.33. Note that $13.33 is below the simple arithmetic average of $15, and below the geometric mean price of $14.14.

Of course, in this particular example, we could also have computed the average cost by dividing the 150 shares bought into the $2,000 total investment, which also yields the $13.33 answer. The harmonic mean becomes a more straightforward way of computing average cost when there are many values involved, and the answer is independent of the dollar amount of the periodic investments, assuming each such investment is the same total amount.

Chapter Five

Specialized Investing Techniques

There are more mutual funds today than common stocks on the New York and American Stock Exchanges combined. And with individual investors committing an ever-growing proportion of their money to funds, discount brokers are taking an increasingly active role in this dynamic market. In addition to transaction services, many discount brokers offer ways to buy funds on margin or sell short, two highly-speculative trading techniques.

Overview

You can buy no-load mutual funds for no commission at all directly from the funds themselves. Likewise, most no-loads levy no redemption fee to sell your shares. So why ever use a discount broker, who will normally charge a separate commission, albeit a small one, for each fund purchase or sale?

The answer, in a word, is *convenience*. If you hold funds in an account with a discount broker, you can easily switch from fund to fund using only that broker as a middleman. Gone forever are the days of dealing with each fund individually; working your way through redemption procedures with a fund you own and want to sell, awaiting receipt of the liquidation proceeds, and finally sending your money on to a new fund you wish to buy (along with another load of paperwork).

Plus, with a discount broker, you will receive just a single monthly account statement, rather than individual statements from all of the different funds you own. At the end of the year, your tax information will be conveniently summarized for all funds on a single Form 1099, rather than individual Form 1099s from many different funds.

No Free Lunch

The cost of this convenience is the broker's commission. There aren't many free lunches in the financial markets, and discount brokers levy commission fees even on no-load funds. This has the effect of transforming no-load funds into low-load funds. (If a discount broker buys a *load* fund for you, it will normally take its commission out of the load itself rather than charging you extra.)

The good news for investors is that the fees discount brokers charge to handle mutual fund transactions have been systematically declining in recent years. As we shall see below, in some cases the fees have completely disappeared.

We have surveyed the entire discount brokerage field, an industry that now has more than a hundred participants. Only a handful of discount brokers are set up to buy and sell mutual funds for clients. Five are "major players," with at least several hundred funds in their repertoire:

Broker	Telephone	Commission Free Trading?	Margin?	Shorting?
Jack White	800-323-3263	Yes	Yes	Yes
Fidelity	800-544-9697	Yes	Yes	Yes
Muriel Siebert	800-872-0711	Yes	No	No
Charles Schwab	800-435-4000	Yes	Yes	No
Waterhouse Secs.	800-930-4410	Yes	Yes	No

The accompanying tables also show the mutual fund commission schedules for each firm, and compare the commission rates for different-sized transactions. In general, Jack White currently offers the widest range of services and the lowest commission rates. [Note: Commission schedules change frequently, so check with the broker for current rates.]

Commission-Free Trading

Each of these discount brokers now offer commission-free trading of some funds. Typically, this option is available for select funds whose sponsors have special compensation arrangements with the broker. These commission-free trades generally require a minimum holding period to avoid the transaction fee, with shares sold in a shorter period of time reverting to the broker's standard commission schedule. Each broker's list of commission-free funds constantly changes, so call the broker of your choice for an up-to-date list.

Account Insurance

Fund shares held in accounts with discount brokers are insured up to $500,000 with the Securities Investors Protection Corp. (SIPC), a government-sponsored agency. Some brokerages buy hundreds of thousands or millions of dollars of additional account insurance from independent insurers. Insurance

Discount Broker Commission Schedules

Charles Schwab

Transaction Size	Commission to Buy or Sell
0 – $ 15,000	0.60% of transaction amount*
$15,001 – $100,000	$90.00 + 0.20% of amount over $15,000
$100,001 – and up	$260.00 + 0.08% of amount over $100,000

(*subject to $29 minimum commission)

Fidelity

Transaction Size	Commission to Buy or Sell
0 – $ 5,000	$17.50 + 0.80% of transaction amount*
$5,001 – $10,000	$29.50 + 0.40% of transaction amount
$10,001 – $25,000	$39.50 + 0.20% of transaction amount
$25,001 – $95,000	$67.50 + 0.10% of transaction amount
$95,001 – and up	$157.50 + 0.08% of transaction amount

(*subject to $28 minimum commission)

Muriel Siebert

Transaction Size	Commission to Buy or Sell
0 – $ 5,000	$17.50 + 0.80% of transaction amount*
$5,001 – $10,000	$29.50 + 0.40% of transaction amount*
$10,001 – $25,000	$39.50 + 0.20% of transaction amount
$25,001 – $95,000	$67.50 + 0.10% of transaction amount
$95,001 – and up	$157.50 + 0.08% of transaction amount

(*subject to $39.50 minimum commission)

Waterhouse

Transaction Size	Commission to Buy or Sell
0 – $ 15,000	0.60% of transaction amount*
$15,001 – $100,000	$90.00 + 0.20% of amount over $15,000
$100,001 – and up	$260.00 + 0.08% of amount over $100,000

(*subject to $29 minimum commission)

Jack White

Transaction Size	Commission to Buy or Sell
0 – $ 5,000	$27.00
$5,001 – $25,000	$35.00
$25,001 – and up	$50.00

protects brokerage clients in the event the brokerage firm fails. Note that this is *not* an extra level of investor protection, but rather one that is necessitated when investors leave fund shares in a brokerage account. If you simply deal directly with funds themselves, you won't have the insurance . . . because you won't need it.

Margin Trading

Margin is a term used in the securities industry to denote the financing of securities transactions with borrowed money. Since 1974, the minimum initial margin requirement, as set by the Federal Reserve Board, has been 50%. This means investors buying securities on margin must pay at least 50 cents in cash for every dollar's worth of securities purchased. The remaining 50 cents can be borrowed, usually from the brokerage firm executing the transaction.

Naturally, brokers do not provide loans for nothing. Investors must pay interest on margin loans, typically a percent or two above the prime lending rate of commercial banks (the rate banks charge their best customers for short-term loans). Margin-loan interest is generally tax-deductible except when money is borrowed to buy tax-exempt securities, such as tax-free bond funds.

Margin borrowing significantly increases both profit and loss potential of fund investments. For example, suppose an investor buys $10,000 of a fund on 50% margin, paying $5,000 in cash and borrowing the other $5,000 from his brokerage firm. If the fund doubles in value to $20,000, the investor's own capital grows to $15,000. The remaining $5,000 is still owed to the broker. Note that a 100% increase in the value of the fund (from $10,000 to $20,000) provides a 200% increase in the investor's net equity (from $5,000 to $15,000). A 50% margin rate, in other words, is the equivalent of two-to-one leverage.

The reverse side of the coin is that losses are also magnified. Assume, in the above example, that the initial $10,000 fund position falls in value to just $5,000. In this case, the investor's entire initial $5,000 cash investment is wiped out because all of the remaining $5,000 is owed to the lending broker. Thus, a 50% price decline causes a 100% loss to the investor; again two-to-one leverage. Of course, long before the fund's value falls 50%, the investor will receive a "margin call" from his brokerage firm, demanding more cash.

Remember that any profit on a margined holding is reduced by the amount of interest paid on the loan, and any loss is increased by the interest. If an investor is to come out ahead, the fund must provide a rate of return – from capital gains, dividends, or interest – greater than the interest rate being charged on the borrowed capital. It does not pay, for example, to buy a Government bond fund yielding 5% on margin if the annual interest rate on the loan is 9%, unless you expect the price of that bond to increase. But it might

Comparative Commissions

Dollar Commissions (One-Way Trade)

Broker	$1,000 Trade	$5,000 Trade	$10,000 Trade	$25,000 Trade	$100,000 Trade	$500,000 Trade
Jack White	$27.00	$27.00	$35.00	$35.00	$ 50.00	$ 50.00
Fidelity	28.00	57.50	49.50	89.50	237.50	557.50
Muriel Siebert	39.50	57.50	49.50	89.50	237.50	557.50
Charles Schwab	29.00	30.00	60.00	110.00	260.00	580.00
Waterhouse	29.00	30.00	60.00	110.00	260.00	580.00

Percentage Commissions (One-Way Trade)

Broker	$1,000 Trade	$5,000 Trade	$10,000 Trade	$25,000 Trade	$100,000 Trade	$500,000 Trade
Jack White	2.70%	0.54%	0.35%	0.14%	0.01%	0.01%
Fidelity	2.80	1.15	0.50	0.36	0.24	0.11
Muriel Siebert	3.95	1.15	0.50	0.36	0.24	0.11
Charles Schwab	2.90	0.60	0.60	0.44	0.26	0.12
Waterhouse	2.90	0.60	0.60	0.44	0.26	0.12

prove profitable to buy on margin a "junk bond" fund yielding 10% if the interest rate on the loan is 8%. Most mutual fund investors consider using margin only to buy capital-gains-oriented funds for an expected market rally. In truth, any investment whose expected total return exceeds the margin lending rate is a margin-purchase candidate.

Four of the five leading discount brokers – Jack White, Fidelity, Charles Schwab, and Waterhouse – offer margin services for their customers. Most full-service brokerage firms also allow investors to buy load funds on margin, but only after they have received the stock certificates from the fund. This delay can be up to one to two months. During that time, investors must advance the entire purchase price in cash. Alternatively, investors with borrowing power in existing full-service brokerage house margin accounts (based on other security holdings) can borrow against the value of those other securities at the time of mutual fund share purchases, and thereby indirectly buy funds on margin.

Another source for borrowing to buy funds on margin, potentially the cheapest, is from your bank. Lending policies vary from bank to bank, and not all will lend money for the purchase of mutual funds. Nevertheless, it is definitely worth a try, especially for investors that have a well-established relationship with their banker. Obviously, the lowest-cost way to buy a no-load fund is to invest directly with the fund, eliminating additional commissions levied by discount brokers. Investors that borrow from a bank to help finance purchase of no-load fund shares avoid these extra transaction fees on both the buying and selling side. Lending rates from banks fluctuate widely. The rate any individual investor is likely to obtain will depend upon his personal credit standing with his bank. Finally, borrowing money from a bank may result in considerable paperwork and inconvenience. For some investors, it may not be worth all the trouble; for others it will be.

One frequently overlooked vehicle for buying funds on margin is closed-end funds. Most trade along with other common stocks on the New York Stock Exchange (others on the American Stock Exchange or over-the-counter) and can be bought or sold short on margin through any brokerage firm. The commission and interest rate charges on these transactions are usually the same as for any common stocks.

A Leveraging Alternative

Investors seeking to gain extra leverage, but without borrowing, should consider this alternative: Simply purchase funds with above-average volatility. Buying a fund whose price fluctuations are more volatile than the market is equivalent to buying on margin a fund with average volatility . . . without loan interest and margin calls.

Investors can obtain the greatest leverage by purchasing especially volatile funds on margin. The compounding effect of the two leveraging sources can result in price fluctuations (up and down) several times as great as the market – equivalent to owning an average-volatility fund on less than 50% margin.

Short Selling

Short selling is an extremely speculative trading technique, one that is utilized by traders betting that prices will go down rather than up. Of the major discount brokers, Jack White allows investors to sell short selected mutual funds and maintain the positions in their brokerage accounts, and Fidelity permits shorting its own group of 36 industry "Select" funds. The risk of selling short any type of securities, except in risk-reducing hedge positions, normally far outweighs the potential rewards, and we do not generally recommend the technique for mutual fund traders or investors.

Short selling involves the sale of shares first and the purchase of those shares second – exactly the reverse of the normal purchase-and-sale sequence. How do you sell shares before you buy them? Simply borrow someone else's shares and sell them. Later, you buy back equivalent shares and return them to the lender. Brokerage firms hold many shares for their customers, and gladly act as conduits between lender and borrower for that purpose. (The typical lender doesn't even know the transaction has occurred.)

As for profits and losses, you score short selling the same way you score normal long transactions: If your selling price is more than your purchase (or repurchase) price, you pocket a profit; if it's less, you take a loss. The difference, of course, is that in short selling, because you sell first and buy back later, you want the shares to go down to a lower buy price, rather than up to a higher sell price.

The biggest difference between buying a fund and selling one short is the risk/reward relationship. If you buy a fund (or a stock), your profit potential is infinite, but your risk is limited to the loss of your entire investment. If you sell short, your maximum profit is 100% (in the unlikely event the shares become totally worthless), but your potential loss can be infinite, for there is no limit to how high a price can rise by the time you cover your short sale.

Finally, it is useful to keep in mind that while investors earn dividends (in fact, dividends provide a third to half of the long-run return of common stocks and stock funds), short sellers have to pay them. That's because the person that buys the shares from the short seller is entitled to his dividends just as is the owner of the original shares that were borrowed by the short seller. In other words, two investors get dividends, and since the fund itself pays only one, the short seller is obligated to pay the second.

Assuming you are bold enough to chance the short side, shorting a mutual fund rather than a stock at least has the benefit of "diversification." As noted above, a major risk of short selling is unlimited loss. But funds are less risky than stocks here because their diversified portfolios do not move as fast.

You can also put yourself on the short side of the market by shorting closed-end funds. Since closed-ends trade on the leading exchanges and in the over-the-counter market, they can be sold short through *any* brokerage firm, just like all other common stocks.

Chapter Six

Technical Trading Systems

Moving-average systems are a popular and easy way to trade mutual funds. They represent a purely "technical" approach to timing, because all trading decisions are the automatic result of price action, with no consideration given to any fundamental factor.

The goal of a moving-average system is to keep investors in the market during most price uptrends, while offering some prospect that they will be out of the market during downtrends. All such systems are based upon, and dependent on, the tendency of the market, and the prices of individual funds, to move in trends.

What is a Moving Average?

The heart of these systems, of course, is the moving average itself. This is simply a statistical tool for smoothing a series of price values to eliminate minor fluctuations. For example, a ten-week arithmetic moving average – the dotted line in our chart of Fidelity Magellan – consists of successive averages of that fund's ten most recent week-ending prices. Just add up the ten latest Friday prices and divide the total by ten. With each subsequent week, the newest value is incorporated into the average, and the value of eleven weeks previous is dropped, so that the ten most recent weekly prices are always used to calculate the moving average.

Also pictured in Fidelity Magellan's chart is a 40-week moving average, denoted by a dashed line. It is useful to compare the 10-week and 40-week moving averages because they reveal how moving averages perform and how timing systems that are based on moving averages work in practice.

Note that the 10-week moving average is nearly always closer to the price series than is the 40-week average. This is because the former consists only of

Fidelity Magellan

Net Asset Value Adjusted for all Distributions
(Ratio Scale)
Dashed line represents 40-week Moving Average
Dotted line represents 10-week Moving Average

$80	
70	
60	
50	
40	
30	
20	
10	
5	1981 1982 1983 1984 1985 1986 1987 1988 1989 1990 1991 1992 1993

the ten most recent fund prices whereas the 40-week moving average is also a function of much older prices that may be far removed from the current fund price.

Because they are more sensitive to price, shorter-term moving averages, such as a 10-week, have more twists and turns than longer-term averages. For example, assume an investor uses this timing system: Buy a fund when its current price moves up through a moving average, and sell when the price falls below the moving average. He will obtain many more buy and sell signals with a short-term moving average simply because that moving average is closer to the price series. Longer-term moving averages would produce fewer buy and sell signals.

Simple arithmetic moving average are, however, subject to criticism on two counts: First, they assign equal weight to each of the base observations. In a ten-week average, for example, each of the ten values is counted once and has a one-tenth importance (or weight) in the average. But, it would seem logical that more recent observations may, by their very nature, be more relevant and should receive more weight.

Second, as a simple arithmetic average moves through time, its point-to-point fluctuations are strictly dependent upon two numbers, the new one being added and the old one being dropped. If the new number is greater than the old one, the average of the values will increase and so, too, will the moving average. If the new number is less than the old one, the average will decrease. Therefore, even though the *level* of an arithmetic moving average is dependent upon all of the prices being averaged, *fluctuations* in the moving average are dependent solely upon two numbers, the one being added and the one being dropped, and the last of these is older and of questionable relevance.

An alternative type of moving average, one that overcomes both of these objections, is an *exponential* moving average. An exponential system is based upon the assignment of a fixed weight (say, 10%) to the current price, and all of the remaining weight (in this case, 90%) to the previous value of the moving average itself. The proportional weight assigned to the most recent observation is frequently called a "smoothing constant."

To determine the exponential smoothing constant roughly proportionate to a simple arithmetic moving average of a given length, use the following easy formula: Divide "2"

Calculating an Exponential Moving Average			
Week	Price	Method of Calculation	Exponential Moving Average
1	$ 10	(to start)	$10.00
2	11	(0.18 x 11.00 + 0.82 x 10.00)	10.18
3	10	(0.18 x 10.00 + 0.82 x 10.18)	10.15
4	11	(0.18 x 11.00 + 0.82 x 10.15)	10.30
5	13	(0.18 x 13.00 + 0.82 x 10.30)	10.79
6	14	(0.18 x 14.00 + 0.82 x 10.79)	11.38
7	13	(0.18 x 13.00 + 0.82 x 11.38)	11.67
8	12	(0.18 x 12.00 + 0.82 x 11.67)	11.73
9	13	(0.18 x 13.00 + 0.82 x 11.73)	11.96
10	15	(0.18 x 15.00 + 0.82 x 11.96)	12.51

by one more than the number of terms in the simple moving average you wish to duplicate. For example, to find a smoothing constant to construct an exponential moving average equivalent to a ten-week arithmetic moving average, divide 2 by 11. The result, 0.18, is the smoothing constant. The following table illustrates how this smoothing constant is used to construct an exponential average of a price series.

After initially establishing the moving average as equal to the beginning price, the moving average is updated by multiplying the newest price by 0.18 (the smoothing constant) and adding that to the product derived from multiplying the previous exponential moving average value by 0.82 (1.00 minus the

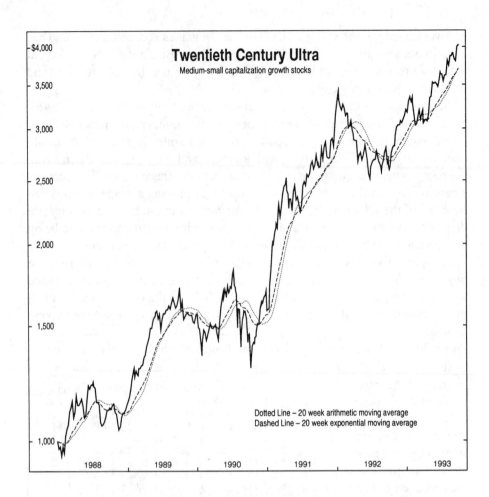

Twentieth Century Ultra
Medium-small capitalization growth stocks

Dotted Line – 20 week arithmetic moving average
Dashed Line – 20 week exponential moving average

smoothing constant). After ten weeks, the exponential moving average value is \$12.51. That value is greater than the simple ten-week arithmetic average of \$12.20 because proportionately greater weight has been assigned to the more recent, and in this case higher, prices. In this example, the most recent price in the 10-week exponential average has 18% of the weight; the most recent price in a 10-week arithmetic average has only 10% of the weight.

In an exponential moving average, the weight effectively assigned to any given historical value declines as it becomes older, but it is worth noting that *every* historical price always has *some* weight in an exponential moving average. That weight never declines completely to zero but merely trends closer and closer to zero and never quite reaches it.

The chart of 20th Century Ultra Fund displays its price over a recent six-year period along with two 20-week moving averages – a 20-week arithmetic moving average and a 20-week exponential moving average.

We can quickly see that the two different types of moving averages seldom have the same value. A close inspection reveals that the exponential moving average is usually somewhat more sensitive to price; that is, it tends to move more quickly toward the price series itself. That is because the exponential moving average gives more weight to recent prices while the arithmetic moving average gives an equal amount of weight to all of the different prices (in this case, 20 weeks of prices) contained within it. As a result, an investor using price penetrations of an exponential moving average for buy and sell signals will usually get those signals earlier than an investor using the same length arithmetic moving average. Whether this actually proves to be more or less profitable, of course, depends upon the prices at which the buy and sell signals are derived. In all of our studies, we have found that the profitability of the arithmetic and exponential moving averages is similar, with a *slight* edge going to the exponential system.

Although exponential moving averages are typically not as well known to investors, they are easier to update in real time. Given a marginal superiority in the profitability of trading strategies, they are therefore generally to be preferred.

How Profitable
Are Moving Average Systems?

The basic theory underlying virtually all moving-average systems is that when the price of a fund is above the moving average, the fund is in an uptrend and should be owned. When the price is below the moving average, the fund is downtrending and should be avoided.

We have created an elaborate computer-based simulation model to test moving-average trading systems. Our initial findings will no doubt be surprising to technicians, and to the Wall Street establishment. In general, we have discovered that over the last decade, moving-average trading systems have a decidedly mixed track record in terms of producing profit relative to a simple no trading "buy-and-hold" strategy. However, they are invariably excellent at reducing risk.

Our study is based on the total-return performances of all 263 open-end (both load and no-load) and closed-end funds that were continuously available during the ten-year period June 30, 1981, to June 30, 1991. Obviously, high-frequency trading strategies cannot be used profitably on funds that levy substantial sales loads. We include such funds in our simulations merely to broaden the statistical base. Once defined, of course, any trading system involving even moderately high turnover must be applied exclusively to no-load funds.

The first year of the ten-year study period is used to accumulate the values of the moving averages, so the simulation results are based on actual returns for the nine-year period June 30, 1982, through June 30, 1991.

Our initial investigation tests this simple trading rule:

> If the price of a fund at the end of a week is above its moving average, own the fund during the following week.
> If the price of a fund at the end of a week is below its moving average, own Treasury bills in the following week.

This system is designed to capitalize on trend persistency in the market; to own funds when they are relatively strong (above their moving averages), and to avoid them when they are weak (below their moving averages). We test two types of moving averages – arithmetic, which gives equal weight to each price, and exponential, which assigns more weight to recent prices and less weight to older values. We test every moving average strategy from a 2-week moving average to 52 weeks. The table presents the average nine-year trading results across all 263 funds for the trading strategies using arithmetic moving averages of 5, 10, 15, 20, 25, 30, 35, 40, 45, and 50 weeks. (The results using exponential averaging are only slightly superior.)

The profits of the various arithmetic moving-average strategies range from a low of $25,490 (the 50-week strategy) to a high of $31,600 (the 15-week), based on initial $10,000 investments. Half the strategies produce a lower return than the $28,170 an investor could have earned simply by buying the average fund at the beginning of the nine-year period and holding throughout. The 10, 15, and 20-week strategies most clearly beat buy-and-hold, producing

Arithmetic Moving-Average Trading Strategies				
Moving-Average Strategy	Profit on $10,000 Initial Investment	Profit Compared to $28,170 Profit of Buy & Hold	% of Time Out of Funds and in T-bills	Number of Round-Trip Trades
5 Week MA Strategy	$27,040	4% less profit	37% less risk	58
10 Week MA Strategy	30,400	8% more profit	33% less risk	36
15 Week MA Strategy	31,600	12% more profit	31% less risk	26
20 Week MA Strategy	30,770	9% more profit	29% less risk	21
25 Week MA Strategy	29,420	4% more profit	28% less risk	17
30 Week MA Strategy	28,300	1% more profit	27% less risk	15
35 Week MA Strategy	27,880	1% less profit	26% less risk	14
40 Week MA Strategy	27,190	3% less profit	26% less risk	13
45 Week MA Strategy	26,210	7% less profit	25% less risk	12
50 Week MA Strategy	25,490	10% less profit	24% less risk	11

extra profits of 8%, 12%, and 9%, respectively, while the longest-term strategies produce significantly less profit.

Strategies based on moving-average lengths between those shown in the table generally produce proportionate returns. For example, the profits achieved with 21, 22, 23, and 24-week moving-averages are between the amounts earned, and shown in the table, for the 20 and 25-week systems.

Among those moving-average systems now in popular use, the widely-publicized 39-week average approximately matches the 40-week strategy result, producing 3% less profit than a naive buy-and-hold strategy.

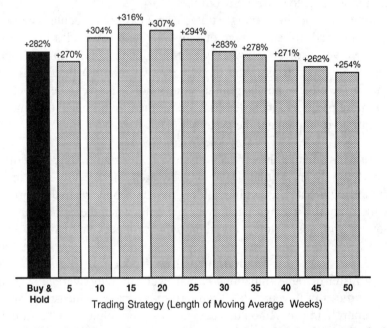

Moving-Average Trading Systems
Versus Buy & Hold Return

Buy when fund price moves above the moving average
Sell when fund price moves below the moving average

Trading Strategy (Length of Moving Average Weeks)

In defense of the longer-term moving averages, which show poorly in this study, it should be noted that the market was unusually strong in the 1980s. The $28,170 buy-and-hold profit is equal to a compounded annual return of 16%, substantially more than the 10% total return realized in the typical year in this century. Such an environment is not amenable to trading systems. The only hope of a moving-average system is to take a trader out of the market during price downtrends. But when the market is in a broad uptrend, it pays to own mutual funds most of the time; in other words, forget trading, and just buy and hold. In the 1980s, market corrections were few and brief.

Short-term moving averages, such as 5, 10, 15, and 20-week, stay closer to their price series and therefore generate more buy and sell signals. This enables a trader to get in and out of funds faster when prices turn. The downside is that a trader can be whipsawed back and forth when the market is fluctuating in an essentially sideways direction. In contrast, long-term moving-average systems produce fewer buy and sell signals, but those signals tend to occur well after an actual price turn. If price declines are relatively short, long-term moving-averages simply get a trader out of equities at about the time that it would be better to get back in. Long-term moving-average strategies perform much better in a market environment, such as that in the 1960s and 1970s, that is characterized by occasional long bear markets, which the moving-average systems help avoid.

The long-term moving-average strategies *are* easier to execute because they require fewer trades – an average of only 11 round-trip trades in nine years (about one a year) for the 50-week system in this test, as contrasted with an average of 58 round-trips (about one every two months) for the five-week system. On the other hand, the primary concern of an active trader should be to achieve more profit and incur less risk rather than to minimize the amount of work required to implement the system.

Reverse Strategies

We further validated the efficacy of moving average trading systems, and the underlying theory of trend-following, by applying the strategies to every fund *in reverse* – that is, assuming holding the funds only when their prices are below their moving averages, and owning T-bills when their prices are above the moving averages. Almost invariably, this produces dramatically inferior profits.

Traders Incur Less Risk

A key result of our simulations is that every moving-average system we tested significantly lowers risk. There are many ways to measure risk. The one we report here is based on this easy-to-grasp principle: To the extent that a trader is out of the market and safely ensconced in T-bills, all risk of a price decline has been avoided. For example, the average result for all 263 funds (see table, previous page) for the five-week strategy is that a trader is out of funds, and in T-bills, 37% of the time. Such a strategy is therefore 37% less risky than a buy-and-hold strategy that is continuously invested in funds and always exposed to the risk of price decline.

Since every one of the trading strategies is, from time to time, out of funds and in Treasury bills, *all* of them are less risky than buy-and-hold. In the cases of the 10, 15, 20, 25, and 30-week strategies, traders earn more profit than buy-and-hold *and* incur less risk. Even the strategies that earn *slightly less profit* than buy-and-hold are *much less risky* than buy-and-hold. Thus, on a risk-adjusted basis they, too, are superior.

Results Vary

Naturally, the results vary dramatically among different funds. Some strategies produce enormous profits for some funds and relatively minuscule profits for other funds. For example, the 5, 10, 15, 20, and 25-week arithmetic and exponential moving-average strategies applied to *Wood Struthers Neuwirth* (a no-load fund with unlimited telephone switching) all produce profits from a $10,000 initial investment of between $45,000 and $73,000. That's two to three times more than the $22,000 profit that buy-and-hold investors earned in that fund during the same period.

The extent to which moving-average systems can reduce risk is wonderfully illustrated in the case of 44 Wall Street, the worst-performing fund in our 263-fund population over the ten-year period. 44 Wall Street investors that put $10,000 in the fund and never sold, lost $6,814, more than two-thirds of their capital. However, *every* moving-average system applied to 44 Wall Street makes money: The worst makes $8,000, the best $20,000, and the average gain is about $15,000.

Of course, several of these returns are less than those achieved by the average trading strategy applied to all 263 funds. This is simply because 44 Wall Street was such a terrible performer during the period that it was usually better to own some other fund *under any circumstances*. The moving-average systems, however, placed the 44 Wall Street trader in Treasury bills as often, or more often, than in the fund itself. During the periods of time that the moving-average systems are invested in the fund, the fund generally made money.

For example, the 15-week arithmetic moving-average system produces a $20,010 total profit. With this system, a trader owns 44 Wall Street less than half the time, during which he achieves a 105% compounded total return. During the balance of the time, the trader is invested in Treasury bills, which earn another 47% compounded profit. During the latter times, the fund incurred an incredible 85% cumulative loss. That loss is suffered by buy-and-hold investors that own the fund continuously, but is neatly escaped by a moving-average investor. This illustrates how the risk-reduction capability of moving-average systems can actually transform a loser like 44 Wall Street into a winner.

Moving Average Interactions

The next step in our exploration of moving average timing systems is to determine the profitability of buying and selling when a short-term moving average of a fund's price moves above or below other moving averages.

Basing trading strategies on the crossing of two moving-average series is a common technique among technicians. For example, they might buy a stock or a mutual fund when the 10-week moving average rises above the 30-week moving average, and sell when the 10-week average falls below the 30-week average. Or, they might buy when the 5-week moving average rises above the

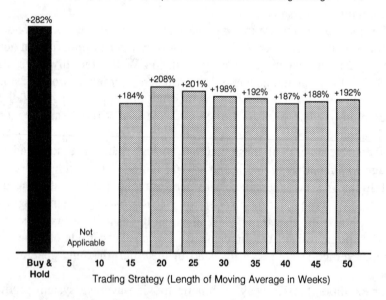

Moving-Average Trading Systems Versus Buy & Hold Return

Buy when 10-week fund price moves above the moving average
Sell when 10-week fund price moves below the moving average

40-week average, and sell when the 5-week average falls below the 40-week. The guiding principle in all cases is to buy when the short-term moving average rises above a longer-term moving average and to sell when the short-term average falls below the longer-term average.

We tested *every combination* of moving averages – more than 1,300 different strategies – from 2-week to 52-week – across the same nine-year period tested earlier, for our 263-fund population. The average profit-loss results from buying and selling funds when the *10-week arithmetic moving average* crosses various longer-term averages is representative. We report these results in the accompanying chart.

We discovered that nearly every timing strategy using one moving average versus another is *inferior* to the strategies based on current price versus a moving average tested earlier, and inferior as well to a naive buy and hold strategy. In fact, the typical nine-year total return of this variant of the system (see charts) is about 100 percentage points less than the original system. Both techniques reduce risk by about the same amount versus buy and hold (approximately one-fourth), but with their lower returns, the moving average versus moving average systems are clearly inferior to the price versus moving average approaches.

Chapter Seven

Tax Tactics

Mutual funds are among the most flexible of all investments from a tax standpoint. However, their unique status in the financial world carries with it special risks for the poorly informed. Investors need to know all of the tax angles to mutual funds if they are to profit from their tax *advantages* and avoid their tax *risks*.

This chapter examines the factors investors should consider to correctly foresee the tax impact of their mutual fund transactions and holdings. It also analyzes several strategies investors can utilize to legally reduce the tax impact of their mutual fund transactions.

Overview

Mutual funds are simply conduits through which individuals make indirect investments in securities. The funds realize capital gains and losses and receive dividend and interest income on investments, all in behalf of their shareholders.

For tax purposes, funds are considered "regulated investment companies." This means they can avoid paying any taxes on the portion of their investment income and capital gains distributed to their shareholders, who are then taxed on those distributions. As a result, the vast majority of funds distribute virtually all of their profits to shareholders. Funds make distributions at different frequencies, some monthly, and others quarterly, semi-annually, or annually.

Taxability of Fund Distributions

Taxable mutual fund distributions fall into two classifications, *capital gains distributions* and *ordinary dividends*.

Capital gains are the amount by which long-term gains realized by a fund exceed its realized long-term losses. To qualify as long-term, a security must have been owned by the fund for longer than one year before sale. Shareholders report such distributions as long-term gains regardless of how long they have owned the fund.

Ordinary dividends from a fund consist of its dividend and interest earnings, less management fees and other operating expenses, plus the amount by which a fund's short-term gains exceed its short-term losses. (Short-term refers to securities owned one year or less.) Shareholders report ordinary dividend distributions as "dividend income" regardless of the fact that they may include short-term gains.

Ordinary dividends received by fund shareholders is taxed at ordinary income tax rates, which range from 15% to 39.6% depending on the taxpayer's total taxable income. Capital gains distributions are subject to a maximum tax rate of 28%. However, phase-out revisions relating to personal exemptions and itemized deductions can boost the *effective* tax rate on capital gains above 28% for certain high-income individuals.

To facilitate investor reporting of distributions to the IRS, mutual funds send all shareholders a year-end summary on Form 1099-DIV, listing gross dividends broken down into capital gains distributions and ordinary dividends. Alternatively, some funds merely send you their usual form of statement, marking it as a "Substitute Form 1099." Either way, the funds send an indentical copy, usually computerized, to the IRS, which uses it to match against taxpayer returns.

Reinvested distributions are taxed as of the distribution date, although in some cases, dividends paid in January may be considered paid as of December of the preceding year.

Note: Investors need not declare distributions by funds held in IRA and Keogh plans.

Profits and Losses

When an investor redeems (sells) or exchanges fund shares for any reason, including via check writing, automatic withdrawal plans, and automatic exchange plans, the capital gain or loss from the purchase of the shares sold must be reported on Schedule D of the Form 1040 tax return (except, again, for IRAs, Keoghs, and other retirement plans.)

Traditionally, the Internal Revenue Service has done a very poor job holding investors liable for taxes owed on gains (other than from distributions) from their fund investments. Billions of dollars of income have gone unreported, or have been reported erroneously, to the IRS. When the Government will tighten its hold on taxpayers remains to be seen. As the IRS brings on-line more sophisticated and streamlined data-processing systems to match taxpayers' returns with reports filed by the funds and brokers, its oversight will become more rigorous. But today, its ability to track the tax basis of investors' holdings is far from perfect.

Avoiding Double Taxation

To avoid double taxation, investors must add the amount of reinvested distributions to their original cost when determining a capital gain or loss. For example, take an investor who buys $10,000 of mutual fund shares, receives and reinvests $2,000 of distributions on which taxes are incurred at the time of the distribution, and later redeems the shares for $15,000. The total cost for capital gains purposes is the initial $10,000 *plus* the $2,000 of distributions that were taxed independently. Thus, the taxable gain from the $15,000 sale is only $3,000 instead of $5,000.

Many investors fail to make this critical adjustment and double-pay their income tax. We suggest accumulating your Form 1099-DIVs in a file with your records of your fund shareholdings.

Which Shares Were Sold?

If an investor purchases shares of a particular fund on more than one occasion and at differing prices, and later sells only part of the shares, the tax laws allow great flexibility in choosing which shares are assumed to be the ones sold.

Imagine an investor who bought 400 shares of a mutual fund according to this schedule:

$$
\begin{array}{lll}
100 \text{ shares at} & \$\ 8 & = \$\ \ \ 800 \\
200 \text{ shares at} & \$12 & = \ \ 2,400 \\
\underline{100} \text{ shares at} & \$\ 9 & = \ \ \ \underline{900} \\
400 & & \$\ 4,100
\end{array}
$$

Average cost = $10.25 a share

Now, assume the investor sells 100 shares of his cumulative 400-share holding for $10 a share. What is the capital gain or loss?

Don't guess too fast, for . . . sorry about this . . . there are at least *four* possible answers. The method chosen for a particular fund holding must be indicated on the investor's tax return, and that method must continue to be utilized for all subsequent sales of the position in that fund until the position is completely liquidated. The method you choose should generally be the one that minimizes any taxable gain or maximizes a tax loss. (The losses can be used to offset other gains up to $3,000 a year of ordinary income.)

The most common technique, and the one automatically used by the IRS if an investor declines to choose one of the other methods, is "first in – first out." This means that the first shares bought are the first ones to be sold. In our example, the first shares were purchased for $8, so the investor realizes a $2-per-share capital gain from the $10 sale, on which a tax is naturally due.

The second alternative is the so-called "single category" or perhaps, better termed, "single average cost" method: The average cost of all shares owned *in a single account* is the cost basis for any of those shares when sold. To determine whether a gain is long or short-term, the shares sold are considered to be those owned for the longest period of time. In the example, the average cost of the 400 shares is $10.25, so the investor selling 100 shares at $10 can report a $.25-per-share capital loss.

The third alternative, the "double category average cost" method, permits an investor first to divide all the shares owned prior to a sale into two groups: (1) those owned long enough to qualify for long-term capital gain or loss treatment – currently more than one year, and (2) all the rest, which are called short-term shares. The average per-share cost for both groups is calculated, and the investor may elect the group from which he chooses to assign the shares to be sold. When lower tax rates are applicable to long-term gains than to short term gains, most investors will elect to sell shares from the long-term group in the case of a capital gain. In the case of a capital loss, investors would usually sell shares from the short-term group for the most advantageous tax treatment.

Finally, the fourth alternative enables an investor to specifically identify *any shares* in his portfolio as the ones being sold. This is obviously the most flexible and most advantageous method in the vast majority of cases. Generally, investors will simply select the shares with the highest cost, for they will provide the largest loss for tax purposes (and hence, the largest tax savings), or the smallest gain (and hence the smallest tax due). In our example above, 100 of the shares bought at $12 would be selected for sale, yielding a $2-per-share capital loss and a nice tax saving.

Identification of which securities are sold is usually based on which stock certificate is delivered to the buyer. In the case of mutual fund shares held in an account, there are no certificates so you must obtain a written acknowledgement from the custodian confirming your instructions regarding which shares are to be sold. It is best to check with the custodian in advance.

Wash Sale Rule

When a taxpayer sells a security at a loss, that loss is valid for tax purposes only if "substantially identical" securities were not purchased within 31 days before or after the date of sale. Any time securities are sold at a loss, the investor should be sure to not violate this rule, or loss or deferral of the tax benefit will result.

The wash-sale problem usually arises when an investor has a loss on an investment that he or she wishes to realize for tax purposes, but also desires to retain ownership of the shares. This is an especially important consideration near the end of the year when investors consider selling securities on which they have losses in order to reduce their tax burden. The ways to avoid triggering the wash-sale rule are either to (1) double up – i.e., 31 days before the sale, purchase an identical number of shares as the original investment; or (2) repurchase the shares sold 31 days after the sale.

Mutual funds are just like any other security, when it comes to wash sales. Fortunately, it is often possible for mutual fund investors to avoid the wash-sale pitfall. The ploy is very simple: At the same time a mutual fund is sold to realize a loss, simply purchase an identical dollar amount of a *similar* fund. This strategy is used by many common stock investors – e.g., sell General Motors and buy Ford, sell K-mart and buy Wal-Mart, etc. The problem with individual common stocks is that they frequently move in different directions over short periods of time. Most mutual funds, on the other hand, generally move in the same direction as the market. It is usually rather straightforward to find two funds with similar volatility and portfolio objectives. Some fund organizations even offer multiple mutual funds with similar investment philosophies. A simple telephone call can frequently switch an investment from one fund to another, and, if desired, back to the original fund 31 days later.

If the frequency of your mutual fund trades triggers the wash-sale rule, the disallowed loss increases the basis of your subsequent purchase, postponing but never eliminating your tax saving.

The Distribution Tax Problem

Mutual fund distributions can cause a thorny problem for fund investors.

If an investor buys a fund today, and the fund pays a distribution tomorrow, the investor owes tax on the amount of the distribution. This seems rather unfair, inasmuch as the capital gains and ordinary income may have been earned by the fund long before the new investor's purchase. Nevertheless, *somebody* has to pay the tax on those profits, and the current owners of fund shares are the unlucky victims.

One partial saving grace is that when a fund makes a distribution, the price of its shares falls by the amount of the distribution, in effect reducing the investor's future capital gains tax liability. Still, having to cope with the immediate tax liability of a distribution is not mouth-watering, especially if a fund investment is earmarked for a several-year holding.

Fortunately, most funds make distributions at roughly the same time each year, and announce them in advance. Herein lie opportunities for significant savings.

First, just before purchasing shares of any mutual fund, call the fund and ask if a distribution will be made soon. If a distribution is scheduled, defer purchase until the day after the record date of the distribution to avoid its tax impact.

Second, when contemplating the sale of a fund's shares, first contact the fund to determine if a distribution is scheduled shortly. If so, sell the shares before the distribution to avoid its tax liability. (Your capital gain will be higher, or your loss smaller, but you won't risk receiving a distribution that includes ordinary income, which can be taxed at higher rates than capital gains.)

Deducting Mutual Fund Fees

Custodial fees incurred in connection with mutual fund investments, including maintenance fees paid on tax-deferred IRA and Keogh plans, are deductible from ordinary income by taxpayers who itemize. The deduction is limited to the portion of total miscellaneous deductions that exceed 2% of a taxpayer's adjusted gross income. These deductions are itemized on Schedule A of Form 1040.

Sales charges (loads) paid to a broker or to a fund's sponsor at the time of share purchases must be added to the cost of the shares, so they ultimately reduce the amount of the taxable capital gain (or increase the capital loss) when the shares are sold. Similarly, redemption fees paid to a fund at the time shares are sold back to a fund must be deducted from the sale proceeds and similarly reduce the net taxable capital gain (or increase the loss) of an investment. Sales and redemption fees are therefore *not* deductible as investment expenses against ordinary income.

Extra IRA Deductions

Every wage earner under the retirement age should have an Individual Retirement Account. Unless you already participate in another pension plan *and* have an adjusted gross income of $25,000 or more ($40,000 for a joint return), your annual IRA contribution is tax-deductible – up to a maximum of $2,000 a year. Interest, dividends, and capital gains compound tax-free in the account until you retire.

In addition, you may deduct all fees and expenses incurred in conjunction with maintaining an IRA. This means that in addition to the annual $2,000 deduction, you can write off trustee, custodial, and management costs related

Early Start IRA: How $6,750 Grows to Over $1 Million

This table show four ways to accumulate approximately $1,000,000 in an IRA by age 65 assuming a 10%-per-annum return. **Investor A** contributes $2,000 at the beginning of each year for forty years (ages 26-65); **Investor B**, $2,000 a year for only seven years (ages 19-25); **Investor C**, $2,000 a year for only five years (ages 14-18); and **Investor D** smaller sums still from ages 8 through 13. Finally **Investor E** shows the IRA growth achieved by making all of these contributions at every age from 8 to 65.

| | Investor A | | Investor B | | Investor C | | Investor D | | Investor E | |
| | Contri- | Year-End | Contri- | Year-End | Contri- | Year-End | Contri- | Year-End | Contri- | Year-End |
Age	bution	Value	bution	Value	bution	Value	bution	Value	bution	Value
8	-0-	-0-	-0-	-0-	-0-	-0-	500	550	500	550
9	-0-	-0-	-0-	-0-	-0-	-0-	750	1,430	750	1,430
10	-0-	-0-	-0-	-0-	-0-	-0-	1,000	2,673	1,000	2,673
11	-0-	-0-	-0-	-0-	-0-	-0-	1,250	4,315	1,250	4,315
12	-0-	-0-	-0-	-0-	-0-	-0-	1,500	6,397	1,500	6,397
13	-0-	-0-	-0-	-0-	-0-	-0-	1,750	8,962	1,750	8,962
14	-0-	-0-	-0-	-0-	2,000	2,200	-0-	9,858	2,000	12,058
15	-0-	-0-	-0-	-0-	2,000	4,620	-0-	10,843	2,000	15,463
16	-0-	-0-	-0-	-0-	2,000	7,282	-0-	11,928	2,000	19,210
17	-0-	-0-	-0-	-0-	2,000	10,210	-0-	13,121	2,000	23,331
18	-0-	-0-	-0-	-0-	2,000	13,431	-0-	14,433	2,000	27,864
19	-0-	-0-	2,000	2,200	-0-	14,774	-0-	15,876	2,000	32,850
20	-0-	-0-	2,000	4,620	-0-	16,252	-0-	17,463	2,000	38,335
21	-0-	-0-	2,000	7,282	-0-	17,877	-0-	19,210	2,000	44,369
22	-0-	-0-	2,000	10,210	-0-	19,665	-0-	21,131	2,000	51,006
23	-0-	-0-	2,000	13,431	-0-	21,631	-0-	23,244	2,000	58,306
24	-0-	-0-	2,000	16,974	-0-	23,794	-0-	25,568	2,000	66,337
25	-0-	-0-	2,000	20,872	-0-	26,174	-0-	28,125	2,000	75,170
26	2,000	2,200	-0-	22,959	-0-	28,791	-0-	30,938	2,000	84,888
27	2,000	4,620	-0-	25,255	-0-	31,670	-0-	34,031	2,000	95,576
28	2,000	7,282	-0-	27,780	-0-	34,837	-0-	37,434	2,000	107,334
29	2,000	10,210	-0-	30,558	-0-	38,321	-0-	41,178	2,000	120,267
30	2,000	13,431	-0-	33,614	-0-	42,153	-0-	45,296	2,000	134,494
31	2,000	16,974	-0-	36,976	-0-	46,368	-0-	49,825	2,000	150,143
32	2,000	20,872	-0-	40,673	-0-	51,005	-0-	54,808	2,000	167,358
33	2,000	25,159	-0-	44,741	-0-	56,106	-0-	60,289	2,000	186,294
34	2,000	29,875	-0-	49,215	-0-	61,716	-0-	66,317	2,000	207,123
35	2,000	35,062	-0-	54,136	-0-	67,888	-0-	72,949	2,000	230,035
36	2,000	40,769	-0-	59,550	-0-	74,676	-0-	80,244	2,000	255,239
37	2,000	47,045	-0-	65,505	-0-	82,144	-0-	88,269	2,000	282,963
38	2,000	53,950	-0-	72,055	-0-	90,359	-0-	97,095	2,000	313,459
39	2,000	61,545	-0-	79,261	-0-	99,394	-0-	106,805	2,000	347,005
40	2,000	69,899	-0-	87,187	-0-	109,334	-0-	117,485	2,000	383,905
41	2,000	79,089	-0-	95,905	-0-	120,267	-0-	129,234	2,000	424,496
42	2,000	89,198	-0-	105,496	-0-	132,294	-0-	142,157	2,000	469,145
43	2,000	100,318	-0-	116,045	-0-	145,523	-0-	156,373	2,000	518,269
44	2,000	112,550	-0-	127,650	-0-	160,076	-0-	172,010	2,000	572,286
45	2,000	126,005	-0-	140,415	-0-	176,083	-0-	189,211	2,000	631,714
46	2,000	140,805	-0-	154,456	-0-	193,692	-0-	208,133	2,000	697,086
47	2,000	157,086	-0-	169,902	-0-	213,061	-0-	228,946	2,000	768,995
48	2,000	174,995	-0-	186,892	-0-	234,367	-0-	251,840	2,000	848,094
49	2,000	194,694	-0-	205,581	-0-	257,803	-0-	277,024	2,000	935,103
50	2,000	216,364	-0-	226,140	-0-	283,358	-0-	304,727	2,000	1,030,814
51	2,000	240,200	-0-	248,754	-0-	311,942	-0-	335,209	2,000	1,136,095
52	2,000	266,420	-0-	273,629	-0-	343,136	-0-	368,719	2,000	1,251,905
53	2,000	295,262	-0-	300,992	-0-	377,450	-0-	405,591	2,000	1,379,295
54	2,000	326,988	-0-	331,091	-0-	415,195	-0-	446,150	2,000	1,519,425
55	2,000	361,887	-0-	364,200	-0-	456,715	-0-	490,766	2,000	1,673,567
56	2,000	400,276	-0-	400,620	-0-	502,386	-0-	539,842	2,000	1,843,124
57	2,000	442,503	-0-	440,682	-0-	552,625	-0-	593,826	2,000	2,029,636
58	2,000	488,953	-0-	484,750	-0-	607,887	-0-	653,209	2,000	2,234,800
59	2,000	540,049	-0-	533,225	-0-	668,676	-0-	718,530	2,000	2,460,480
60	2,000	596,254	-0-	586,548	-0-	735,543	-0-	790,383	2,000	2,708,728
61	2,000	658,079	-0-	645,203	-0-	809,098	-0-	869,421	2,000	2,981,800
62	2,000	726,087	-0-	709,723	-0-	890,007	-0-	956,363	2,000	3,282,180
63	2,000	800,896	-0-	780,695	-0-	979,008	-0-	1,052,000	2,000	3,612,598
64	2,000	883,185	-0-	858,765	-0-	1,076,909	-0-	1,157,200	2,000	3,976,058
65	2,000	973,704	-0-	944,641	-0-	1,184,600	-0-	1,272,930	2,000	4,375,864
Less Total Invested:		(80,000)		(14,000)		(10,000)		(6,750)		(110,750)
Equals Net Earnings:		893,704		930,641		1,174,600		1,266,170		4,265,114
Money Grew:		11-fold		66-fold		117-fold		188-fold		38-fold

to your IRA. These expenses are, however, deductible only to the extent that all of your investment-related expenses exceed, in aggregate, 2% of your adjusted gross income.

We recommend deducting every possible cost related to maintaining your IRA. Take these deductions on the "Miscellaneous Deductions" line of Schedule A of Form 1040.

A Final Tax Word

Regardless of your investment and tax strategy, remember that the most important consideration is *not* minimizing your tax bill, but *maximizing your aftertax profits*.

Chapter Eight

The Buyer's Guide to Equity Funds

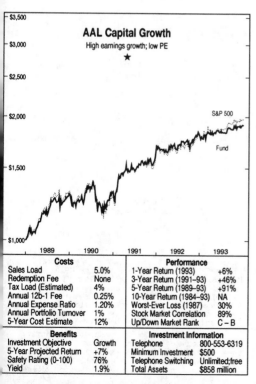

AAL Capital Growth
High earnings growth; low PE
★

S&P 500

Fund

Costs		Performance	
Sales Load	5.0%	1-Year Return (1993)	+6%
Redemption Fee	None	3-Year Return (1991–93)	+46%
Tax Load (Estimated)	4%	5-Year Return (1989–93)	+91%
Annual 12b-1 Fee	0.25%	10-Year Return (1984–93)	NA
Annual Expense Ratio	1.20%	Worst-Ever Loss (1987)	30%
Annual Portfolio Turnover	1%	Stock Market Correlation	89%
5-Year Cost Estimate	12%	Up/Down Market Rank	C – B

Benefits		Investment Information	
Investment Objective	Growth	Telephone	800-553-6319
5-Year Projected Return	+7%	Minimum Investment	$500
Safety Rating (0-100)	76%	Telephone Switching	Unlimited;free
Yield	1.9%	Total Assets	$858 million

AARP Capital Growth
Diversified growth stocks

Costs		Performance	
Sales Load	None	1-Year Return (1993)	+16%
Redemption Fee	None	3-Year Return (1991–93)	+71%
Tax Load (Estimated)	4%	5-Year Return (1989–93)	+92%
Annual 12b-1 Fee	None	10-Year Return (1984–93)	NA
Annual Expense Ratio	1.13%	Worst-Ever Loss (1987)	38%
Annual Portfolio Turnover	101%	Stock Market Correlation	68%
5-Year Cost Estimate	10%	Up/Down Market Rank	B – E

Benefits		Investment Information	
Investment Objective	Growth	Telephone	800-253-2277
5-Year Projected Return	+7%	Minimum Investment	$500
Safety Rating (0-100)	67%	Telephone Switching	See prospectus
Yield	0.1%	Total Assets	$585 million

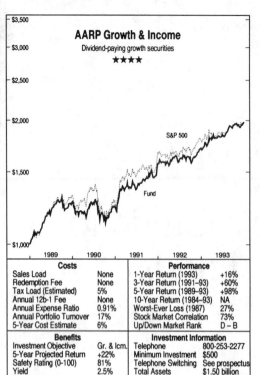

AARP Growth & Income
Dividend-paying growth securities
★★★★

S&P 500

Fund

Costs		Performance	
Sales Load	None	1-Year Return (1993)	+16%
Redemption Fee	None	3-Year Return (1991–93)	+60%
Tax Load (Estimated)	5%	5-Year Return (1989–93)	+98%
Annual 12b-1 Fee	None	10-Year Return (1984–93)	NA
Annual Expense Ratio	0.91%	Worst-Ever Loss (1987)	27%
Annual Portfolio Turnover	17%	Stock Market Correlation	73%
5-Year Cost Estimate	6%	Up/Down Market Rank	D – B

Benefits		Investment Information	
Investment Objective	Gr. & Icm.	Telephone	800-253-2277
5-Year Projected Return	+22%	Minimum Investment	$500
Safety Rating (0-100)	81%	Telephone Switching	See prospectus
Yield	2.5%	Total Assets	$1.50 billion

ABT - Emerging Growth
Common stocks of emerging growth companies
★

Costs		Performance	
Sales Load	5.0%	1-Year Return (1993)	+18%
Redemption Fee	None	3-Year Return (1991–93)	+138%
Tax Load (Estimated)	7%	5-Year Return (1989–93)	+204%
Annual 12b-1 Fee	0.25%	10-Year Return (1984–93)	NA
Annual Expense Ratio	1.44%	Worst-Ever Loss (1987)	49%
Annual Portfolio Turnover	40%	Stock Market Correlation	49%
5-Year Cost Estimate	19%	Up/Down Market Rank	A – E

Benefits		Investment Information	
Investment Objective	Growth	Telephone	800-553-7838
5-Year Projected Return	+54%	Minimum Investment	$1,000
Safety Rating (0-100)	58%	Telephone Switching	Unlimited;free
Yield	0.0%	Total Assets	$55 million

ABT - Growth & Income
Dividend-paying securities

Costs		Performance	
Sales Load	5.0%	1-Year Return (1993)	+3%
Redemption Fee	None	3-Year Return (1991–93)	+38%
Tax Load (Estimated)	6%	5-Year Return (1989–93)	+45%
Annual 12b-1 Fee	0.25%	10-Year Return (1984–93)	+179%
Annual Expense Ratio	1.23%	Worst-Ever Loss (1987)	30%
Annual Portfolio Turnover	50%	Stock Market Correlation	79%
5-Year Cost Estimate	17%	Up/Down Market Rank	D – C

Benefits		Investment Information	
Investment Objective	Icm. & Gr.	Telephone	800-553-7838
5-Year Projected Return	–11%	Minimum Investment	$1,000
Safety Rating (0-100)	75%	Telephone Switching	Unlimited;free
Yield	1.7%	Total Assets	$81 million

ABT - Utility Income
Utility securities
★

Costs		Performance	
Sales Load	5.0%	1-Year Return (1993)	+8%
Redemption Fee	None	3-Year Return (1991–93)	+40%
Tax Load (Estimated)	4%	5-Year Return (1989–93)	+76%
Annual 12b-1 Fee	0.25%	10-Year Return (1984–93)	+222%
Annual Expense Ratio	1.17%	Worst-Ever Loss (1986-87)	19%
Annual Portfolio Turnover	24%	Stock Market Correlation	46%
5-Year Cost Estimate	13%	Up/Down Market Rank	E – A

Benefits		Investment Information	
Investment Objective	Gr. & Icm.	Telephone	800-553-7838
5-Year Projected Return	NA	Minimum Investment	$1,000
Safety Rating (0-100)	81%	Telephone Switching	Unlimited;free
Yield	3.7%	Total Assets	$159 million

Acorn Fund
Small firms in growth industries
★★★★

Costs		Performance	
Sales Load	None	1-Year Return (1993)	+32%
Redemption Fee	2.0%	3-Year Return (1991–93)	+142%
Tax Load (Estimated)	7%	5-Year Return (1989–93)	+148%
Annual 12b-1 Fee	None	10-Year Return (1984–93)	+418%
Annual Expense Ratio	0.64%	Worst-Ever Loss (1987)	29%
Annual Portfolio Turnover	19%	Stock Market Correlation	49%
5-Year Cost Estimate	6%	Up/Down Market Rank	D – B

Benefits		Investment Information	
Investment Objective	Growth	Telephone	800-922-6769
5-Year Projected Return	+53%	Minimum Investment	$4,000
Safety Rating (0-100)	76%	Telephone Switching	Unlimited;free
Yield	0.5%	Total Assets	$1.89 billion

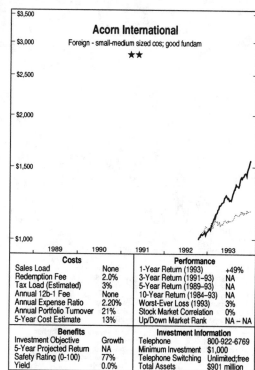

Acorn International
Foreign - small-medium sized cos; good fundam
★★

Costs		Performance	
Sales Load	None	1-Year Return (1993)	+49%
Redemption Fee	2.0%	3-Year Return (1991–93)	NA
Tax Load (Estimated)	3%	5-Year Return (1989–93)	NA
Annual 12b-1 Fee	None	10-Year Return (1984–93)	NA
Annual Expense Ratio	2.20%	Worst-Ever Loss (1993)	3%
Annual Portfolio Turnover	21%	Stock Market Correlation	0%
5-Year Cost Estimate	13%	Up/Down Market Rank	NA – NA

Benefits		Investment Information	
Investment Objective	Growth	Telephone	800-922-6769
5-Year Projected Return	NA	Minimum Investment	$1,000
Safety Rating (0-100)	77%	Telephone Switching	Unlimited;free
Yield	0.0%	Total Assets	$901 million

Adams Express
Diversified stocks

Costs		Performance	
Sales Load	None	1-Year Return (1993)	–3%
Redemption Fee	None	3-Year Return (1991–93)	+54%
Tax Load (Estimated)	8%	5-Year Return (1989–93)	+94%
Annual 12b-1 Fee	None	10-Year Return (1984–93)	+238%
Annual Expense Ratio	0.52%	Worst-Ever Loss (1987)	29%
Annual Portfolio Turnover	18%	Stock Market Correlation	21%
5-Year Cost Estimate	7%	Up/Down Market Rank	E – A

Benefits		Investment Information	
Investment Objective	Icm. & Gr.	Telephone	800-638-2479
5-Year Projected Return	+12%	Minimum Investment	None
Safety Rating (0-100)	69%	Telephone Switching	Via broker
Yield	2.5%	Total Assets	$696 million

Addison Capital
Undervalued; low PE securities

Costs		Performance	
Sales Load	3.1%	1-Year Return (1993)	+13%
Redemption Fee	None	3-Year Return (1991–93)	+57%
Tax Load (Estimated)	6%	5-Year Return (1989–93)	+88%
Annual 12b-1 Fee	0.65%	10-Year Return (1984–93)	NA
Annual Expense Ratio	2.13%	Worst-Ever Loss (1987)	34%
Annual Portfolio Turnover	30%	Stock Market Correlation	76%
5-Year Cost Estimate	19%	Up/Down Market Rank	B – D

Benefits		Investment Information	
Investment Objective	Growth	Telephone	800-526-6397
5-Year Projected Return	+8%	Minimum Investment	$1,000
Safety Rating (0-100)	73%	Telephone Switching	Not available
Yield	1.0%	Total Assets	$39 million

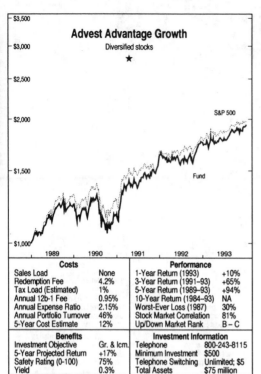

Advest Advantage Growth
Diversified stocks
★

S&P 500

Fund

Costs		Performance	
Sales Load	None	1-Year Return (1993)	+10%
Redemption Fee	4.2%	3-Year Return (1991–93)	+65%
Tax Load (Estimated)	1%	5-Year Return (1989–93)	+94%
Annual 12b-1 Fee	0.95%	10-Year Return (1984–93)	NA
Annual Expense Ratio	2.15%	Worst-Ever Loss (1987)	30%
Annual Portfolio Turnover	46%	Stock Market Correlation	81%
5-Year Cost Estimate	12%	Up/Down Market Rank	B – C

Benefits		Investment Information	
Investment Objective	Gr. & Icm.	Telephone	800-243-8115
5-Year Projected Return	+17%	Minimum Investment	$500
Safety Rating (0-100)	75%	Telephone Switching	Unlimited; $5
Yield	0.3%	Total Assets	$75 million

Advest Advantage Income
Diversified stocks and bonds
★★★★

Costs		Performance	
Sales Load	None	1-Year Return (1993)	+14%
Redemption Fee	4.2%	3-Year Return (1991–93)	+49%
Tax Load (Estimated)	3%	5-Year Return (1989–93)	+77%
Annual 12b-1 Fee	0.75%	10-Year Return (1984–93)	NA
Annual Expense Ratio	1.82%	Worst-Ever Loss (1987)	17%
Annual Portfolio Turnover	59%	Stock Market Correlation	62%
5-Year Cost Estimate	13%	Up/Down Market Rank	D – A

Benefits		Investment Information	
Investment Objective	Icm. & Gr.	Telephone	800-243-8115
5-Year Projected Return	+26%	Minimum Investment	$500
Safety Rating (0-100)	87%	Telephone Switching	Unlimited; $5
Yield	3.8%	Total Assets	$74 million

Advest Advantage Special
Diversified growth securities
★

Costs		Performance	
Sales Load	None	1-Year Return (1993)	+20%
Redemption Fee	4.2%	3-Year Return (1991–93)	+116%
Tax Load (Estimated)	1%	5-Year Return (1989–93)	+141%
Annual 12b-1 Fee	0.95%	10-Year Return (1984–93)	NA
Annual Expense Ratio	2.84%	Worst-Ever Loss (1986-87)	34%
Annual Portfolio Turnover	40%	Stock Market Correlation	48%
5-Year Cost Estimate	16%	Up/Down Market Rank	C – C

Benefits		Investment Information	
Investment Objective	Growth	Telephone	800-243-8115
5-Year Projected Return	+47%	Minimum Investment	$500
Safety Rating (0-100)	68%	Telephone Switching	Unlimited; $5
Yield	0.0%	Total Assets	$22 million

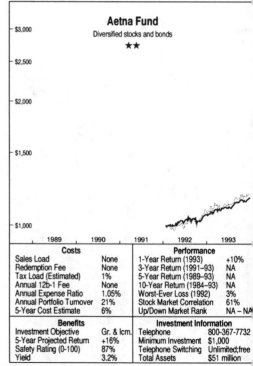

Aetna Fund
Diversified stocks and bonds
★★

Costs		Performance	
Sales Load	None	1-Year Return (1993)	+10%
Redemption Fee	None	3-Year Return (1991–93)	NA
Tax Load (Estimated)	1%	5-Year Return (1989–93)	NA
Annual 12b-1 Fee	None	10-Year Return (1984–93)	NA
Annual Expense Ratio	1.05%	Worst-Ever Loss (1992)	3%
Annual Portfolio Turnover	21%	Stock Market Correlation	61%
5-Year Cost Estimate	6%	Up/Down Market Rank	NA – NA

Benefits		Investment Information	
Investment Objective	Gr. & Icm.	Telephone	800-367-7732
5-Year Projected Return	+16%	Minimum Investment	$1,000
Safety Rating (0-100)	87%	Telephone Switching	Unlimited;free
Yield	3.2%	Total Assets	$51 million

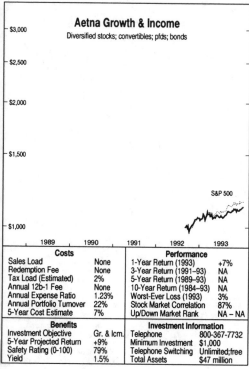

Aetna Growth & Income
Diversified stocks; convertibles; pfds; bonds

(chart with S&P 500 line; years 1989–1993; $1,000–$3,000 scale)

Costs		Performance	
Sales Load	None	1-Year Return (1993)	+7%
Redemption Fee	None	3-Year Return (1991–93)	NA
Tax Load (Estimated)	2%	5-Year Return (1989–93)	NA
Annual 12b-1 Fee	None	10-Year Return (1984–93)	NA
Annual Expense Ratio	1.23%	Worst-Ever Loss (1993)	3%
Annual Portfolio Turnover	22%	Stock Market Correlation	87%
5-Year Cost Estimate	7%	Up/Down Market Rank	NA – NA

Benefits		Investment Information	
Investment Objective	Gr. & Icm.	Telephone	800-367-7732
5-Year Projected Return	+9%	Minimum Investment	$1,000
Safety Rating (0-100)	79%	Telephone Switching	Unlimited;free
Yield	1.5%	Total Assets	$47 million

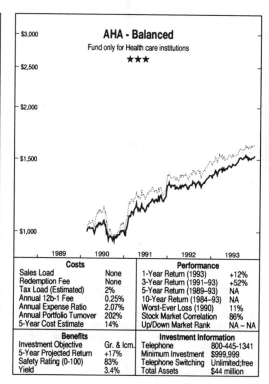

AHA - Balanced
Fund only for Health care institutions
★★★

(chart; years 1989–1993; $1,000–$3,000 scale)

Costs		Performance	
Sales Load	None	1-Year Return (1993)	+12%
Redemption Fee	None	3-Year Return (1991–93)	+52%
Tax Load (Estimated)	2%	5-Year Return (1989–93)	NA
Annual 12b-1 Fee	0.25%	10-Year Return (1984–93)	NA
Annual Expense Ratio	2.07%	Worst-Ever Loss (1990)	11%
Annual Portfolio Turnover	202%	Stock Market Correlation	86%
5-Year Cost Estimate	14%	Up/Down Market Rank	NA – NA

Benefits		Investment Information	
Investment Objective	Gr. & Icm.	Telephone	800-445-1341
5-Year Projected Return	+17%	Minimum Investment	$999,999
Safety Rating (0-100)	83%	Telephone Switching	Unlimited;free
Yield	3.4%	Total Assets	$44 million

Aim - Aggressive Growth
Stocks with expected EPS growth over 15%
★

(chart; years 1989–1993; $1,000–$3,000 scale)

Costs		Performance	
Sales Load	5.8%	1-Year Return (1993)	+32%
Redemption Fee	None	3-Year Return (1991–93)	+163%
Tax Load (Estimated)	2%	5-Year Return (1989–93)	+197%
Annual 12b-1 Fee	0.25%	10-Year Return (1984–93)	NA
Annual Expense Ratio	1.00%	Worst-Ever Loss (1987)	48%
Annual Portfolio Turnover	98%	Stock Market Correlation	53%
5-Year Cost Estimate	13%	Up/Down Market Rank	A – E

Benefits		Investment Information	
Investment Objective	Growth	Telephone	800-959-4246
5-Year Projected Return	+55%	Minimum Investment	$500
Safety Rating (0-100)	63%	Telephone Switching	Unlimited;free
Yield	0.0%	Total Assets	$273 million

Aim - Balanced "A"
60% stocks; 40% bonds
★★

(chart; years 1989–1993; $1,000–$3,500 scale)

Costs		Performance	
Sales Load	5.0%	1-Year Return (1993)	+16%
Redemption Fee	None	3-Year Return (1991–93)	+82%
Tax Load (Estimated)	4%	5-Year Return (1989–93)	+101%
Annual 12b-1 Fee	0.25%	10-Year Return (1984–93)	+145%
Annual Expense Ratio	2.07%	Worst-Ever Loss (1987)	30%
Annual Portfolio Turnover	166%	Stock Market Correlation	64%
5-Year Cost Estimate	21%	Up/Down Market Rank	E – B

Benefits		Investment Information	
Investment Objective	Icm. & Gr.	Telephone	800-959-4246
5-Year Projected Return	+28%	Minimum Investment	$500
Safety Rating (0-100)	76%	Telephone Switching	Unlimited;free
Yield	2.4%	Total Assets	$31 million

Aim - Charter
Dividend-paying growth stocks
★★★

Fund

S&P 500

| 1989 | 1990 | 1991 | 1992 | 1993 |

Costs		Performance	
Sales Load	5.8%	1-Year Return (1993)	+9%
Redemption Fee	None	3-Year Return (1991–93)	+52%
Tax Load (Estimated)	2%	5-Year Return (1989–93)	+128%
Annual 12b-1 Fee	0.30%	10-Year Return (1984–93)	+260%
Annual Expense Ratio	1.17%	Worst-Ever Loss (1987)	32%
Annual Portfolio Turnover	146%	Stock Market Correlation	82%
5-Year Cost Estimate	15%	Up/Down Market Rank	C – C

Benefits		Investment Information	
Investment Objective	Gr. & Icm.	Telephone	800-959-4246
5-Year Projected Return	+22%	Minimum Investment	$500
Safety Rating (0-100)	77%	Telephone Switching	Unlimited;free
Yield	1.8%	Total Assets	$1.65 billion

Aim - Constellation Growth
Small-medium emerging growth stocks
★

| 1989 | 1990 | 1991 | 1992 | 1993 |

Costs		Performance	
Sales Load	5.8%	1-Year Return (1993)	+17%
Redemption Fee	None	3-Year Return (1991–93)	+130%
Tax Load (Estimated)	3%	5-Year Return (1989–93)	+204%
Annual 12b-1 Fee	0.30%	10-Year Return (1984–93)	+410%
Annual Expense Ratio	1.21%	Worst-Ever Loss (1981-82)	51%
Annual Portfolio Turnover	68%	Stock Market Correlation	57%
5-Year Cost Estimate	16%	Up/Down Market Rank	A – E

Benefits		Investment Information	
Investment Objective	Gr. & Icm.	Telephone	800-959-4246
5-Year Projected Return	+45%	Minimum Investment	$500
Safety Rating (0-100)	62%	Telephone Switching	Unlimited;free
Yield	0.0%	Total Assets	$2.92 billion

Aim - Growth "A"
Established growth companies

| 1989 | 1990 | 1991 | 1992 | 1993 |

Costs		Performance	
Sales Load	5.8%	1-Year Return (1993)	+4%
Redemption Fee	None	3-Year Return (1991–93)	+42%
Tax Load (Estimated)	2%	5-Year Return (1989–93)	+74%
Annual 12b-1 Fee	0.25%	10-Year Return (1984–93)	+180%
Annual Expense Ratio	1.17%	Worst-Ever Loss (1987)	34%
Annual Portfolio Turnover	188%	Stock Market Correlation	75%
5-Year Cost Estimate	14%	Up/Down Market Rank	B – E

Benefits		Investment Information	
Investment Objective	Growth	Telephone	800-959-4246
5-Year Projected Return	–5%	Minimum Investment	$500
Safety Rating (0-100)	63%	Telephone Switching	Unlimited;free
Yield	0.0%	Total Assets	$157 million

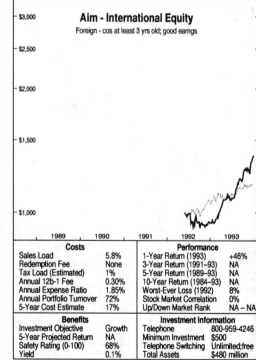

Aim - International Equity
Foreign - cos at least 3 yrs old; good earngs

| 1989 | 1990 | 1991 | 1992 | 1993 |

Costs		Performance	
Sales Load	5.8%	1-Year Return (1993)	+46%
Redemption Fee	None	3-Year Return (1991–93)	NA
Tax Load (Estimated)	1%	5-Year Return (1989–93)	NA
Annual 12b-1 Fee	0.30%	10-Year Return (1984–93)	NA
Annual Expense Ratio	1.85%	Worst-Ever Loss (1992)	8%
Annual Portfolio Turnover	72%	Stock Market Correlation	0%
5-Year Cost Estimate	17%	Up/Down Market Rank	NA – NA

Benefits		Investment Information	
Investment Objective	Growth	Telephone	800-959-4246
5-Year Projected Return	NA	Minimum Investment	$500
Safety Rating (0-100)	68%	Telephone Switching	Unlimited;free
Yield	0.1%	Total Assets	$480 million

Aim - Summit
Contractual plan
★

Costs		Performance	
Sales Load	9.3%	1-Year Return (1993)	+8%
Redemption Fee	None	3-Year Return (1991–93)	+63%
Tax Load (Estimated)	3%	5-Year Return (1989–93)	+115%
Annual 12b-1 Fee	None	10-Year Return (1984–93)	NA
Annual Expense Ratio	0.76%	Worst-Ever Loss (1987)	39%
Annual Portfolio Turnover	139%	Stock Market Correlation	84%
5-Year Cost Estimate	17%	Up/Down Market Rank	A – E

Benefits		Investment Information	
Investment Objective	Growth	Telephone	800-959-4246
5-Year Projected Return	+12%	Minimum Investment	$50
Safety Rating (0-100)	71%	Telephone Switching	Not available
Yield	1.0%	Total Assets	$712 million

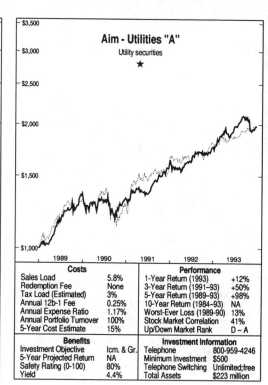

Aim - Utilities "A"
Utility securities
★

Costs		Performance	
Sales Load	5.8%	1-Year Return (1993)	+12%
Redemption Fee	None	3-Year Return (1991–93)	+50%
Tax Load (Estimated)	3%	5-Year Return (1989–93)	+98%
Annual 12b-1 Fee	0.25%	10-Year Return (1984–93)	NA
Annual Expense Ratio	1.17%	Worst-Ever Loss (1989-90)	13%
Annual Portfolio Turnover	100%	Stock Market Correlation	41%
5-Year Cost Estimate	15%	Up/Down Market Rank	D – A

Benefits		Investment Information	
Investment Objective	Icm. & Gr.	Telephone	800-959-4246
5-Year Projected Return	NA	Minimum Investment	$500
Safety Rating (0-100)	80%	Telephone Switching	Unlimited;free
Yield	4.4%	Total Assets	$223 million

Aim - Value "A"
Undervalued stocks
★★★

Costs		Performance	
Sales Load	5.8%	1-Year Return (1993)	+19%
Redemption Fee	None	3-Year Return (1991–93)	+98%
Tax Load (Estimated)	1%	5-Year Return (1989–93)	+166%
Annual 12b-1 Fee	0.25%	10-Year Return (1984–93)	NA
Annual Expense Ratio	1.16%	Worst-Ever Loss (1987)	32%
Annual Portfolio Turnover	152%	Stock Market Correlation	71%
5-Year Cost Estimate	14%	Up/Down Market Rank	A – C

Benefits		Investment Information	
Investment Objective	Gr. & Icm.	Telephone	800-959-4246
5-Year Projected Return	+41%	Minimum Investment	$500
Safety Rating (0-100)	72%	Telephone Switching	Unlimited;free
Yield	0.2%	Total Assets	$826 million

Aim - Weingarten Equity
Seasoned cos; above-avg grth & earnings accel

Costs		Performance	
Sales Load	5.8%	1-Year Return (1993)	+2%
Redemption Fee	None	3-Year Return (1991–93)	+47%
Tax Load (Estimated)	2%	5-Year Return (1989–93)	+111%
Annual 12b-1 Fee	0.30%	10-Year Return (1984–93)	+312%
Annual Expense Ratio	1.13%	Worst-Ever Loss (1987)	36%
Annual Portfolio Turnover	108%	Stock Market Correlation	76%
5-Year Cost Estimate	15%	Up/Down Market Rank	A – E

Benefits		Investment Information	
Investment Objective	Growth	Telephone	800-959-4246
5-Year Projected Return	+7%	Minimum Investment	$500
Safety Rating (0-100)	68%	Telephone Switching	Unlimited;free
Yield	0.6%	Total Assets	$4.71 billion

Alger Growth
Large; diversified stocks
★

Fund

S&P 500

Costs		Performance	
Sales Load	None	1-Year Return (1993)	+20%
Redemption Fee	5.3%	3-Year Return (1991–93)	+93%
Tax Load (Estimated)	2%	5-Year Return (1989–93)	+166%
Annual 12b-1 Fee	0.75%	10-Year Return (1984–93)	NA
Annual Expense Ratio	2.32%	Worst-Ever Loss (1987)	37%
Annual Portfolio Turnover	79%	Stock Market Correlation	62%
5-Year Cost Estimate	15%	Up/Down Market Rank	A – E
Benefits		**Investment Information**	
Investment Objective	Growth	Telephone	800-992-3863
5-Year Projected Return	+46%	Minimum Investment	None
Safety Rating (0-100)	68%	Telephone Switching	6 per yr; free
Yield	0.0%	Total Assets	$35 million

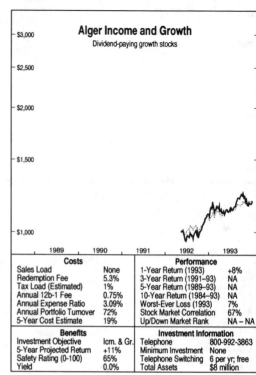

Alger Income and Growth
Dividend-paying growth stocks

Costs		Performance	
Sales Load	None	1-Year Return (1993)	+8%
Redemption Fee	5.3%	3-Year Return (1991–93)	NA
Tax Load (Estimated)	1%	5-Year Return (1989–93)	NA
Annual 12b-1 Fee	0.75%	10-Year Return (1984–93)	NA
Annual Expense Ratio	3.09%	Worst-Ever Loss (1993)	7%
Annual Portfolio Turnover	72%	Stock Market Correlation	67%
5-Year Cost Estimate	19%	Up/Down Market Rank	NA – NA
Benefits		**Investment Information**	
Investment Objective	Icm. & Gr.	Telephone	800-992-3863
5-Year Projected Return	+11%	Minimum Investment	None
Safety Rating (0-100)	65%	Telephone Switching	6 per yr; free
Yield	0.0%	Total Assets	$8 million

Alger Small Capitalization
Stocks with under $1-billion market value
★

Costs		Performance	
Sales Load	None	1-Year Return (1993)	+13%
Redemption Fee	5.3%	3-Year Return (1991–93)	+82%
Tax Load (Estimated)	0%	5-Year Return (1989–93)	+220%
Annual 12b-1 Fee	0.75%	10-Year Return (1984–93)	NA
Annual Expense Ratio	2.17%	Worst-Ever Loss (1992)	29%
Annual Portfolio Turnover	75%	Stock Market Correlation	42%
5-Year Cost Estimate	12%	Up/Down Market Rank	A – E
Benefits		**Investment Information**	
Investment Objective	Growth	Telephone	800-992-3863
5-Year Projected Return	+41%	Minimum Investment	None
Safety Rating (0-100)	60%	Telephone Switching	6 per yr; free
Yield	0.0%	Total Assets	$283 million

Alliance "A"
Diversified stocks

Costs		Performance	
Sales Load	4.4%	1-Year Return (1993)	+14%
Redemption Fee	None	3-Year Return (1991–93)	+76%
Tax Load (Estimated)	7%	5-Year Return (1989–93)	+107%
Annual 12b-1 Fee	0.30%	10-Year Return (1984–93)	+255%
Annual Expense Ratio	1.05%	Worst-Ever Loss (1987)	40%
Annual Portfolio Turnover	60%	Stock Market Correlation	78%
5-Year Cost Estimate	18%	Up/Down Market Rank	A – E
Benefits		**Investment Information**	
Investment Objective	Gr. & Icm.	Telephone	800-221-5672
5-Year Projected Return	+19%	Minimum Investment	$250
Safety Rating (0-100)	68%	Telephone Switching	Unlimited; free
Yield	0.3%	Total Assets	$857 million

Alliance Balanced Shares "A"
Diversified stocks and bonds

S&P 500

Fund

Costs		Performance	
Sales Load	4.4%	1-Year Return (1993)	+10%
Redemption Fee	None	3-Year Return (1991–93)	+40%
Tax Load (Estimated)	3%	5-Year Return (1989–93)	+57%
Annual 12b-1 Fee	0.30%	10-Year Return (1984–93)	NA
Annual Expense Ratio	1.40%	Worst-Ever Loss (1987)	22%
Annual Portfolio Turnover	206%	Stock Market Correlation	84%
5-Year Cost Estimate	15%	Up/Down Market Rank	D – B

Benefits		Investment Information	
Investment Objective	Icm. & Gr.	Telephone	800-221-5672
5-Year Projected Return	+4%	Minimum Investment	$250
Safety Rating (0-100)	80%	Telephone Switching	Unlimited;free
Yield	2.9%	Total Assets	$185 million

Alliance Canadian
Foreign - Canadian stocks

Costs		Performance	
Sales Load	4.4%	1-Year Return (1993)	+17%
Redemption Fee	None	3-Year Return (1991–93)	+7%
Tax Load (Estimated)	0%	5-Year Return (1989–93)	+4%
Annual 12b-1 Fee	0.30%	10-Year Return (1984–93)	+75%
Annual Expense Ratio	2.69%	Worst-Ever Loss (1987)	33%
Annual Portfolio Turnover	46%	Stock Market Correlation	19%
5-Year Cost Estimate	20%	Up/Down Market Rank	E – C

Benefits		Investment Information	
Investment Objective	Growth	Telephone	800-221-5672
5-Year Projected Return	NA	Minimum Investment	$250
Safety Rating (0-100)	64%	Telephone Switching	Unlimited;free
Yield	0.0%	Total Assets	$14 million

Alliance Counterpoint
Low PE depressed securities

Costs		Performance	
Sales Load	4.4%	1-Year Return (1993)	+7%
Redemption Fee	None	3-Year Return (1991–93)	+50%
Tax Load (Estimated)	6%	5-Year Return (1989–93)	+91%
Annual 12b-1 Fee	0.30%	10-Year Return (1984–93)	NA
Annual Expense Ratio	1.62%	Worst-Ever Loss (1987)	33%
Annual Portfolio Turnover	66%	Stock Market Correlation	78%
5-Year Cost Estimate	20%	Up/Down Market Rank	B – D

Benefits		Investment Information	
Investment Objective	Gr. & Icm.	Telephone	800-221-5672
5-Year Projected Return	+3%	Minimum Investment	$250
Safety Rating (0-100)	70%	Telephone Switching	Unlimited;free
Yield	0.0%	Total Assets	$66 million

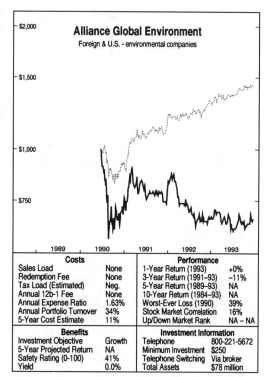

Alliance Global Environment
Foreign & U.S. - environmental companies

Costs		Performance	
Sales Load	None	1-Year Return (1993)	+0%
Redemption Fee	None	3-Year Return (1991–93)	–11%
Tax Load (Estimated)	Neg.	5-Year Return (1989–93)	NA
Annual 12b-1 Fee	None	10-Year Return (1984–93)	NA
Annual Expense Ratio	1.63%	Worst-Ever Loss (1990)	39%
Annual Portfolio Turnover	34%	Stock Market Correlation	16%
5-Year Cost Estimate	11%	Up/Down Market Rank	NA – NA

Benefits		Investment Information	
Investment Objective	Growth	Telephone	800-221-5672
5-Year Projected Return	NA	Minimum Investment	$250
Safety Rating (0-100)	41%	Telephone Switching	Via broker
Yield	0.0%	Total Assets	$78 million

Alliance Global Small Cap "A"
Foreign & U.S. - small capitalization cos

S&P 500

Fund

Costs		Performance	
Sales Load	4.4%	1-Year Return (1993)	+20%
Redemption Fee	None	3-Year Return (1991–93)	+43%
Tax Load (Estimated)	Neg.	5-Year Return (1989–93)	+34%
Annual 12b-1 Fee	0.30%	10-Year Return (1984–93)	+114%
Annual Expense Ratio	2.34%	Worst-Ever Loss (1987)	43%
Annual Portfolio Turnover	104%	Stock Market Correlation	47%
5-Year Cost Estimate	18%	Up/Down Market Rank	B – E

Benefits		Investment Information	
Investment Objective	Growth	Telephone	800-221-5672
5-Year Projected Return	NA	Minimum Investment	$250
Safety Rating (0-100)	59%	Telephone Switching	Unlimited;free
Yield	0.0%	Total Assets	$70 million

Alliance Growth "B"
Stocks with favorable earnings; good growth
★★

Costs		Performance	
Sales Load	None	1-Year Return (1993)	+28%
Redemption Fee	4.2%	3-Year Return (1991–93)	+129%
Tax Load (Estimated)	Neg.	5-Year Return (1989–93)	NA
Annual 12b-1 Fee	1.00%	10-Year Return (1984–93)	NA
Annual Expense Ratio	2.10%	Worst-Ever Loss (1990)	30%
Annual Portfolio Turnover	137%	Stock Market Correlation	63%
5-Year Cost Estimate	11%	Up/Down Market Rank	A – NA

Benefits		Investment Information	
Investment Objective	Gr. & Icm.	Telephone	800-221-5672
5-Year Projected Return	+51%	Minimum Investment	$250
Safety Rating (0-100)	69%	Telephone Switching	Unlimited;free
Yield	0.0%	Total Assets	$238 million

Alliance Growth & Income "A"
Good quality, dividend-paying securities

Costs		Performance	
Sales Load	4.4%	1-Year Return (1993)	+10%
Redemption Fee	None	3-Year Return (1991–93)	+46%
Tax Load (Estimated)	1%	5-Year Return (1989–93)	+80%
Annual 12b-1 Fee	0.30%	10-Year Return (1984–93)	+262%
Annual Expense Ratio	1.09%	Worst-Ever Loss (1987)	30%
Annual Portfolio Turnover	94%	Stock Market Correlation	87%
5-Year Cost Estimate	12%	Up/Down Market Rank	C – C

Benefits		Investment Information	
Investment Objective	Icm. & Gr.	Telephone	800-221-5672
5-Year Projected Return	+3%	Minimum Investment	$250
Safety Rating (0-100)	73%	Telephone Switching	Unlimited;free
Yield	2.5%	Total Assets	$534 million

Alliance International "A"
Foreign - diversified

Costs		Performance	
Sales Load	4.4%	1-Year Return (1993)	+28%
Redemption Fee	None	3-Year Return (1991–93)	+30%
Tax Load (Estimated)	4%	5-Year Return (1989–93)	+33%
Annual 12b-1 Fee	0.30%	10-Year Return (1984–93)	NA
Annual Expense Ratio	1.88%	Worst-Ever Loss (1987)	34%
Annual Portfolio Turnover	76%	Stock Market Correlation	10%
5-Year Cost Estimate	20%	Up/Down Market Rank	D – B

Benefits		Investment Information	
Investment Objective	Growth	Telephone	800-221-5672
5-Year Projected Return	NA	Minimum Investment	$250
Safety Rating (0-100)	66%	Telephone Switching	Unlimited;free
Yield	0.7%	Total Assets	$186 million

Alliance New Europe "A"
Foreign - European stocks; non-diversified

Costs		Performance	
Sales Load	4.4%	1-Year Return (1993)	+35%
Redemption Fee	None	3-Year Return (1991–93)	NA
Tax Load (Estimated)	Neg.	5-Year Return (1989–93)	NA
Annual 12b-1 Fee	0.30%	10-Year Return (1984–93)	NA
Annual Expense Ratio	2.25%	Worst-Ever Loss (1991)	16%
Annual Portfolio Turnover	94%	Stock Market Correlation	2%
5-Year Cost Estimate	17%	Up/Down Market Rank	NA – NA

Benefits		Investment Information	
Investment Objective	Growth	Telephone	800-221-5672
5-Year Projected Return	NA	Minimum Investment	$250
Safety Rating (0-100)	66%	Telephone Switching	Unlimited;free
Yield	0.0%	Total Assets	$91 million

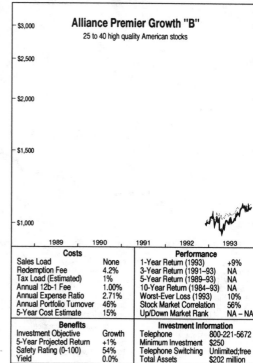

Alliance Premier Growth "B"
25 to 40 high quality American stocks

Costs		Performance	
Sales Load	None	1-Year Return (1993)	+9%
Redemption Fee	4.2%	3-Year Return (1991–93)	NA
Tax Load (Estimated)	1%	5-Year Return (1989–93)	NA
Annual 12b-1 Fee	1.00%	10-Year Return (1984–93)	NA
Annual Expense Ratio	2.71%	Worst-Ever Loss (1993)	10%
Annual Portfolio Turnover	46%	Stock Market Correlation	56%
5-Year Cost Estimate	15%	Up/Down Market Rank	NA – NA

Benefits		Investment Information	
Investment Objective	Growth	Telephone	800-221-5672
5-Year Projected Return	+1%	Minimum Investment	$250
Safety Rating (0-100)	54%	Telephone Switching	Unlimited;free
Yield	0.0%	Total Assets	$202 million

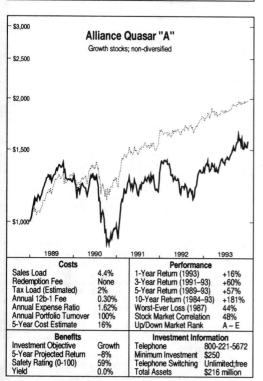

Alliance Quasar "A"
Growth stocks; non-diversified

Costs		Performance	
Sales Load	4.4%	1-Year Return (1993)	+16%
Redemption Fee	None	3-Year Return (1991–93)	+60%
Tax Load (Estimated)	2%	5-Year Return (1989–93)	+57%
Annual 12b-1 Fee	0.30%	10-Year Return (1984–93)	+181%
Annual Expense Ratio	1.62%	Worst-Ever Loss (1987)	44%
Annual Portfolio Turnover	100%	Stock Market Correlation	48%
5-Year Cost Estimate	16%	Up/Down Market Rank	A – E

Benefits		Investment Information	
Investment Objective	Growth	Telephone	800-221-5672
5-Year Projected Return	–8%	Minimum Investment	$250
Safety Rating (0-100)	59%	Telephone Switching	Unlimited;free
Yield	0.0%	Total Assets	$216 million

Alliance Technology "A"
Technology stocks

Costs		Performance	
Sales Load	4.4%	1-Year Return (1993)	+22%
Redemption Fee	None	3-Year Return (1991–93)	+117%
Tax Load (Estimated)	6%	5-Year Return (1989–93)	+123%
Annual 12b-1 Fee	0.30%	10-Year Return (1984–93)	+215%
Annual Expense Ratio	1.61%	Worst-Ever Loss (1987)	48%
Annual Portfolio Turnover	52%	Stock Market Correlation	41%
5-Year Cost Estimate	19%	Up/Down Market Rank	B – E

Benefits		Investment Information	
Investment Objective	Growth	Telephone	800-221-5672
5-Year Projected Return	NA	Minimum Investment	$250
Safety Rating (0-100)	57%	Telephone Switching	Unlimited;free
Yield	0.0%	Total Assets	$176 million

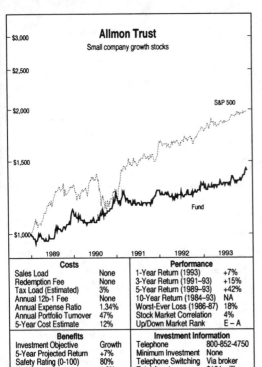

Allmon Trust
Small company growth stocks

S&P 500

Fund

Costs		Performance	
Sales Load	None	1-Year Return (1993)	+7%
Redemption Fee	None	3-Year Return (1991–93)	+15%
Tax Load (Estimated)	3%	5-Year Return (1989–93)	+42%
Annual 12b-1 Fee	None	10-Year Return (1984–93)	NA
Annual Expense Ratio	1.34%	Worst-Ever Loss (1986–87)	18%
Annual Portfolio Turnover	47%	Stock Market Correlation	4%
5-Year Cost Estimate	12%	Up/Down Market Rank	E – A

Benefits		Investment Information	
Investment Objective	Growth	Telephone	800-852-4750
5-Year Projected Return	+7%	Minimum Investment	None
Safety Rating (0-100)	80%	Telephone Switching	Via broker
Yield	1.8%	Total Assets	$124 million

Ambassador Growth Stock Fiduc
65% stks & converts; good financials & erngs

Costs		Performance	
Sales Load	None	1-Year Return (1993)	+17%
Redemption Fee	None	3-Year Return (1991–93)	NA
Tax Load (Estimated)	8%	5-Year Return (1989–93)	NA
Annual 12b-1 Fee	None	10-Year Return (1984–93)	NA
Annual Expense Ratio	0.95%	Worst-Ever Loss (1992)	13%
Annual Portfolio Turnover	56%	Stock Market Correlation	59%
5-Year Cost Estimate	14%	Up/Down Market Rank	NA – NA

Benefits		Investment Information	
Investment Objective	Gr. & Icm.	Telephone	800-892-4366
5-Year Projected Return	+30%	Minimum Investment	$500
Safety Rating (0-100)	63%	Telephone Switching	Unlimited;free
Yield	0.1%	Total Assets	$197 million

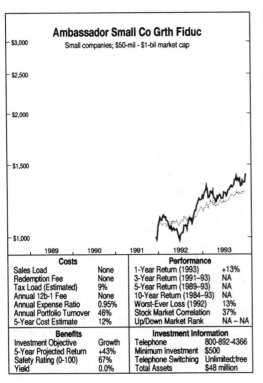

Ambassador Small Co Grth Fiduc
Small companies; $50-mil - $1-bil market cap

Costs		Performance	
Sales Load	None	1-Year Return (1993)	+13%
Redemption Fee	None	3-Year Return (1991–93)	NA
Tax Load (Estimated)	9%	5-Year Return (1989–93)	NA
Annual 12b-1 Fee	None	10-Year Return (1984–93)	NA
Annual Expense Ratio	0.95%	Worst-Ever Loss (1992)	13%
Annual Portfolio Turnover	46%	Stock Market Correlation	37%
5-Year Cost Estimate	12%	Up/Down Market Rank	NA – NA

Benefits		Investment Information	
Investment Objective	Growth	Telephone	800-892-4366
5-Year Projected Return	+43%	Minimum Investment	$500
Safety Rating (0-100)	67%	Telephone Switching	Unlimited;free
Yield	0.0%	Total Assets	$48 million

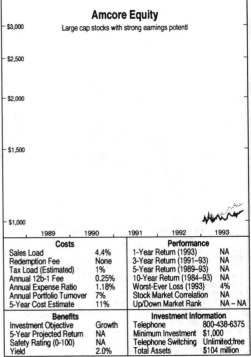

Amcore Equity
Large cap stocks with strong earnings potentl

Costs		Performance	
Sales Load	4.4%	1-Year Return (1993)	NA
Redemption Fee	None	3-Year Return (1991–93)	NA
Tax Load (Estimated)	1%	5-Year Return (1989–93)	NA
Annual 12b-1 Fee	0.25%	10-Year Return (1984–93)	NA
Annual Expense Ratio	1.18%	Worst-Ever Loss (1993)	4%
Annual Portfolio Turnover	7%	Stock Market Correlation	NA
5-Year Cost Estimate	11%	Up/Down Market Rank	NA – NA

Benefits		Investment Information	
Investment Objective	Growth	Telephone	800-438-6375
5-Year Projected Return	NA	Minimum Investment	$1,000
Safety Rating (0-100)	NA	Telephone Switching	Unlimited;free
Yield	2.0%	Total Assets	$104 million

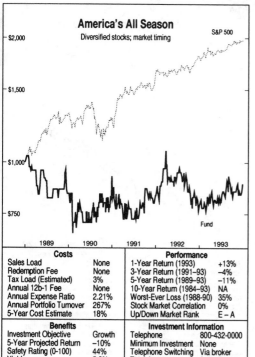

America's All Season

Diversified stocks; market timing

S&P 500

Fund

Costs		Performance	
Sales Load	None	1-Year Return (1993)	+13%
Redemption Fee	None	3-Year Return (1991–93)	–4%
Tax Load (Estimated)	3%	5-Year Return (1989–93)	–11%
Annual 12b-1 Fee	None	10-Year Return (1984–93)	NA
Annual Expense Ratio	2.21%	Worst-Ever Loss (1988-90)	35%
Annual Portfolio Turnover	267%	Stock Market Correlation	0%
5-Year Cost Estimate	18%	Up/Down Market Rank	E – A

Benefits		Investment Information	
Investment Objective	Growth	Telephone	800-432-0000
5-Year Projected Return	–10%	Minimum Investment	None
Safety Rating (0-100)	44%	Telephone Switching	Via broker
Yield	5.8%	Total Assets	$43 million

America's Utility

Minimum 65% electric utility & telephone cos

Costs		Performance	
Sales Load	None	1-Year Return (1993)	+13%
Redemption Fee	None	3-Year Return (1991–93)	NA
Tax Load (Estimated)	2%	5-Year Return (1989–93)	NA
Annual 12b-1 Fee	None	10-Year Return (1984–93)	NA
Annual Expense Ratio	1.21%	Worst-Ever Loss (1993)	9%
Annual Portfolio Turnover	24%	Stock Market Correlation	31%
5-Year Cost Estimate	7%	Up/Down Market Rank	NA – NA

Benefits		Investment Information	
Investment Objective	Icm. & Gr.	Telephone	800-487-3863
5-Year Projected Return	NA	Minimum Investment	$1,000
Safety Rating (0-100)	73%	Telephone Switching	Not available
Yield	4.0%	Total Assets	$130 million

American - Amcap

Fast growing companies

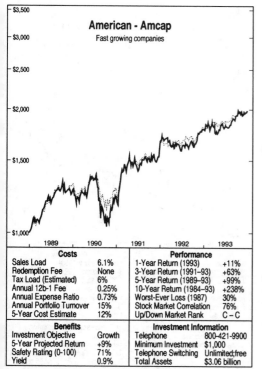

Costs		Performance	
Sales Load	6.1%	1-Year Return (1993)	+11%
Redemption Fee	None	3-Year Return (1991–93)	+63%
Tax Load (Estimated)	6%	5-Year Return (1989–93)	+99%
Annual 12b-1 Fee	0.25%	10-Year Return (1984–93)	+238%
Annual Expense Ratio	0.73%	Worst-Ever Loss (1987)	30%
Annual Portfolio Turnover	15%	Stock Market Correlation	76%
5-Year Cost Estimate	12%	Up/Down Market Rank	C – C

Benefits		Investment Information	
Investment Objective	Growth	Telephone	800-421-9900
5-Year Projected Return	+9%	Minimum Investment	$1,000
Safety Rating (0-100)	71%	Telephone Switching	Unlimited;free
Yield	0.9%	Total Assets	$3.06 billion

American - American Mutual

Conservative stocks

★★★

Costs		Performance	
Sales Load	6.1%	1-Year Return (1993)	+14%
Redemption Fee	None	3-Year Return (1991–93)	+50%
Tax Load (Estimated)	6%	5-Year Return (1989–93)	+85%
Annual 12b-1 Fee	0.25%	10-Year Return (1984–93)	+259%
Annual Expense Ratio	0.60%	Worst-Ever Loss (1987)	22%
Annual Portfolio Turnover	15%	Stock Market Correlation	86%
5-Year Cost Estimate	11%	Up/Down Market Rank	D – A

Benefits		Investment Information	
Investment Objective	Gr. & Icm.	Telephone	800-421-9900
5-Year Projected Return	+10%	Minimum Investment	$250
Safety Rating (0-100)	83%	Telephone Switching	Unlimited;free
Yield	3.9%	Total Assets	$5.19 billion

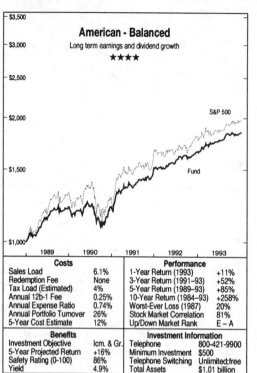

American - Balanced
Long term earnings and dividend growth
★★★★

Costs		Performance	
Sales Load	6.1%	1-Year Return (1993)	+11%
Redemption Fee	None	3-Year Return (1991–93)	+52%
Tax Load (Estimated)	4%	5-Year Return (1989–93)	+85%
Annual 12b-1 Fee	0.25%	10-Year Return (1984–93)	+258%
Annual Expense Ratio	0.74%	Worst-Ever Loss (1987)	20%
Annual Portfolio Turnover	26%	Stock Market Correlation	81%
5-Year Cost Estimate	12%	Up/Down Market Rank	E – A

Benefits		Investment Information	
Investment Objective	Icm. & Gr.	Telephone	800-421-9900
5-Year Projected Return	+16%	Minimum Investment	$500
Safety Rating (0-100)	86%	Telephone Switching	Unlimited;free
Yield	4.9%	Total Assets	$1.01 billion

American - Capital Incm Buildr
Stocks with above-average yield
★★★★

Costs		Performance	
Sales Load	6.1%	1-Year Return (1993)	+15%
Redemption Fee	None	3-Year Return (1991–93)	+60%
Tax Load (Estimated)	4%	5-Year Return (1989–93)	+100%
Annual 12b-1 Fee	0.30%	10-Year Return (1984–93)	NA
Annual Expense Ratio	0.98%	Worst-Ever Loss (1987)	9%
Annual Portfolio Turnover	17%	Stock Market Correlation	48%
5-Year Cost Estimate	13%	Up/Down Market Rank	D – A

Benefits		Investment Information	
Investment Objective	Icm. & Gr.	Telephone	800-421-9900
5-Year Projected Return	+30%	Minimum Investment	$1,000
Safety Rating (0-100)	87%	Telephone Switching	Unlimited;free
Yield	4.7%	Total Assets	$1.57 billion

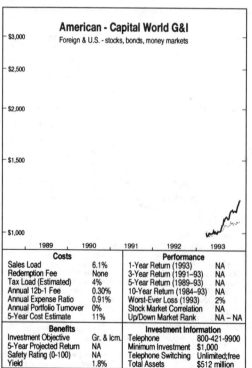

American - Capital World G&I
Foreign & U.S. - stocks, bonds, money markets

Costs		Performance	
Sales Load	6.1%	1-Year Return (1993)	NA
Redemption Fee	None	3-Year Return (1991–93)	NA
Tax Load (Estimated)	4%	5-Year Return (1989–93)	NA
Annual 12b-1 Fee	0.30%	10-Year Return (1984–93)	NA
Annual Expense Ratio	0.91%	Worst-Ever Loss (1993)	2%
Annual Portfolio Turnover	0%	Stock Market Correlation	NA
5-Year Cost Estimate	11%	Up/Down Market Rank	NA – NA

Benefits		Investment Information	
Investment Objective	Gr. & Icm.	Telephone	800-421-9900
5-Year Projected Return	NA	Minimum Investment	$1,000
Safety Rating (0-100)	NA	Telephone Switching	Unlimited;free
Yield	1.8%	Total Assets	$512 million

American - Europacific Growth
Foreign - diversified stocks
★

Costs		Performance	
Sales Load	6.1%	1-Year Return (1993)	+36%
Redemption Fee	None	3-Year Return (1991–93)	+65%
Tax Load (Estimated)	4%	5-Year Return (1989–93)	+105%
Annual 12b-1 Fee	0.25%	10-Year Return (1984–93)	NA
Annual Expense Ratio	1.10%	Worst-Ever Loss (1987)	29%
Annual Portfolio Turnover	10%	Stock Market Correlation	15%
5-Year Cost Estimate	13%	Up/Down Market Rank	D – A

Benefits		Investment Information	
Investment Objective	Growth	Telephone	800-421-9900
5-Year Projected Return	NA	Minimum Investment	$250
Safety Rating (0-100)	79%	Telephone Switching	Unlimited;free
Yield	1.2%	Total Assets	$2.65 billion

1994 Mutual Fund Buyer's Guide

American - Fundamental Invstrs

High quality stocks
★★

S&P 500

Fund

| | 1989 | 1990 | 1991 | 1992 | 1993 |

Costs		Performance	
Sales Load	6.1%	1-Year Return (1993)	+18%
Redemption Fee	None	3-Year Return (1991–93)	+70%
Tax Load (Estimated)	6%	5-Year Return (1989–93)	+105%
Annual 12b-1 Fee	0.25%	10-Year Return (1984–93)	+304%
Annual Expense Ratio	0.65%	Worst-Ever Loss (1987)	33%
Annual Portfolio Turnover	38%	Stock Market Correlation	84%
5-Year Cost Estimate	14%	Up/Down Market Rank	B – D

Benefits		Investment Information	
Investment Objective	Gr. & Icm.	Telephone	800-421-9900
5-Year Projected Return	+13%	Minimum Investment	$250
Safety Rating (0-100)	76%	Telephone Switching	Unlimited;free
Yield	2.4%	Total Assets	$1.48 billion

American - Growth Fund of Amer

High earnings growth stocks
★

| | 1989 | 1990 | 1991 | 1992 | 1993 |

Costs		Performance	
Sales Load	6.1%	1-Year Return (1993)	+14%
Redemption Fee	None	3-Year Return (1991–93)	+67%
Tax Load (Estimated)	9%	5-Year Return (1989–93)	+108%
Annual 12b-1 Fee	0.25%	10-Year Return (1984–93)	+269%
Annual Expense Ratio	0.77%	Worst-Ever Loss (1987)	32%
Annual Portfolio Turnover	25%	Stock Market Correlation	68%
5-Year Cost Estimate	15%	Up/Down Market Rank	B – D

Benefits		Investment Information	
Investment Objective	Growth	Telephone	800-421-9900
5-Year Projected Return	+13%	Minimum Investment	$1,000
Safety Rating (0-100)	72%	Telephone Switching	Unlimited;free
Yield	0.4%	Total Assets	$4.46 billion

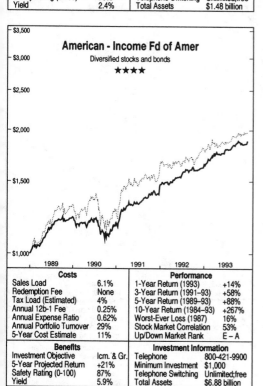

American - Income Fd of Amer

Diversified stocks and bonds
★★★★

| | 1989 | 1990 | 1991 | 1992 | 1993 |

Costs		Performance	
Sales Load	6.1%	1-Year Return (1993)	+14%
Redemption Fee	None	3-Year Return (1991–93)	+58%
Tax Load (Estimated)	4%	5-Year Return (1989–93)	+88%
Annual 12b-1 Fee	0.25%	10-Year Return (1984–93)	+267%
Annual Expense Ratio	0.62%	Worst-Ever Loss (1987)	16%
Annual Portfolio Turnover	29%	Stock Market Correlation	53%
5-Year Cost Estimate	11%	Up/Down Market Rank	E – A

Benefits		Investment Information	
Investment Objective	Icm. & Gr.	Telephone	800-421-9900
5-Year Projected Return	+21%	Minimum Investment	$1,000
Safety Rating (0-100)	87%	Telephone Switching	Unlimited;free
Yield	5.9%	Total Assets	$6.88 billion

American - Inv Co of America

Diversified stocks
★★

| | 1989 | 1990 | 1991 | 1992 | 1993 |

Costs		Performance	
Sales Load	6.1%	1-Year Return (1993)	+12%
Redemption Fee	None	3-Year Return (1991–93)	+51%
Tax Load (Estimated)	7%	5-Year Return (1989–93)	+97%
Annual 12b-1 Fee	0.25%	10-Year Return (1984–93)	+307%
Annual Expense Ratio	0.58%	Worst-Ever Loss (1987)	28%
Annual Portfolio Turnover	21%	Stock Market Correlation	90%
5-Year Cost Estimate	12%	Up/Down Market Rank	C – B

Benefits		Investment Information	
Investment Objective	Gr. & Icm.	Telephone	800-421-9900
5-Year Projected Return	+11%	Minimum Investment	$250
Safety Rating (0-100)	80%	Telephone Switching	Unlimited;free
Yield	2.5%	Total Assets	$15.95 billion

American - New Economy
Service and information companies
★★

Costs		Performance	
Sales Load	6.1%	1-Year Return (1993)	+31%
Redemption Fee	None	3-Year Return (1991–93)	+98%
Tax Load (Estimated)	9%	5-Year Return (1989–93)	+134%
Annual 12b-1 Fee	0.25%	10-Year Return (1984–93)	+370%
Annual Expense Ratio	0.89%	Worst-Ever Loss (1987)	31%
Annual Portfolio Turnover	28%	Stock Market Correlation	65%
5-Year Cost Estimate	16%	Up/Down Market Rank	A – D

Benefits		Investment Information	
Investment Objective	Growth	Telephone	800-421-9900
5-Year Projected Return	+27%	Minimum Investment	$1,000
Safety Rating (0-100)	73%	Telephone Switching	Unlimited;free
Yield	0.7%	Total Assets	$1.27 billion

American - New Perspective
Foreign & U.S. - 50% each
★

Costs		Performance	
Sales Load	6.1%	1-Year Return (1993)	+27%
Redemption Fee	None	3-Year Return (1991–93)	+62%
Tax Load (Estimated)	9%	5-Year Return (1989–93)	+100%
Annual 12b-1 Fee	0.25%	10-Year Return (1984–93)	+327%
Annual Expense Ratio	0.87%	Worst-Ever Loss (1987)	27%
Annual Portfolio Turnover	15%	Stock Market Correlation	45%
5-Year Cost Estimate	14%	Up/Down Market Rank	D – B

Benefits		Investment Information	
Investment Objective	Growth	Telephone	800-421-9900
5-Year Projected Return	NA	Minimum Investment	$250
Safety Rating (0-100)	80%	Telephone Switching	Unlimited;free
Yield	1.4%	Total Assets	$3.38 billion

American - SmallCap World
Foreign & U.S. - small cap stocks
★★

Costs		Performance	
Sales Load	6.1%	1-Year Return (1993)	+30%
Redemption Fee	None	3-Year Return (1991–93)	+84%
Tax Load (Estimated)	7%	5-Year Return (1989–93)	NA
Annual 12b-1 Fee	0.25%	10-Year Return (1984–93)	NA
Annual Expense Ratio	1.15%	Worst-Ever Loss (1990)	17%
Annual Portfolio Turnover	25%	Stock Market Correlation	50%
5-Year Cost Estimate	16%	Up/Down Market Rank	NA – NA

Benefits		Investment Information	
Investment Objective	Growth	Telephone	800-421-9900
5-Year Projected Return	NA	Minimum Investment	$1,000
Safety Rating (0-100)	78%	Telephone Switching	Unlimited;free
Yield	0.3%	Total Assets	$1.57 billion

American - Washington Mutual
Prudent man rule
★

Costs		Performance	
Sales Load	6.1%	1-Year Return (1993)	+13%
Redemption Fee	None	3-Year Return (1991–93)	+53%
Tax Load (Estimated)	6%	5-Year Return (1989–93)	+89%
Annual 12b-1 Fee	0.25%	10-Year Return (1984–93)	+297%
Annual Expense Ratio	0.70%	Worst-Ever Loss (1987)	29%
Annual Portfolio Turnover	18%	Stock Market Correlation	87%
5-Year Cost Estimate	12%	Up/Down Market Rank	B – B

Benefits		Investment Information	
Investment Objective	Gr. & Icm.	Telephone	800-421-9900
5-Year Projected Return	+5%	Minimum Investment	$250
Safety Rating (0-100)	75%	Telephone Switching	Unlimited;free
Yield	3.2%	Total Assets	$10.30 billion

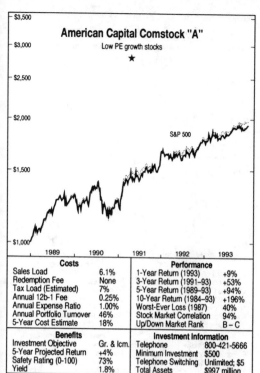

American Capital Comstock "A"
Low PE growth stocks
★

S&P 500

Costs		Performance	
Sales Load	6.1%	1-Year Return (1993)	+9%
Redemption Fee	None	3-Year Return (1991–93)	+53%
Tax Load (Estimated)	7%	5-Year Return (1989–93)	+94%
Annual 12b-1 Fee	0.25%	10-Year Return (1984–93)	+196%
Annual Expense Ratio	1.00%	Worst-Ever Loss (1987)	40%
Annual Portfolio Turnover	46%	Stock Market Correlation	94%
5-Year Cost Estimate	18%	Up/Down Market Rank	B – C

Benefits		Investment Information	
Investment Objective	Gr. & Icm.	Telephone	800-421-5666
5-Year Projected Return	+4%	Minimum Investment	$500
Safety Rating (0-100)	73%	Telephone Switching	Unlimited; $5
Yield	1.8%	Total Assets	$997 million

American Capital Conv Secs
Convertible securities

Costs		Performance	
Sales Load	None	1-Year Return (1993)	+19%
Redemption Fee	None	3-Year Return (1991–93)	+66%
Tax Load (Estimated)	3%	5-Year Return (1989–93)	+63%
Annual 12b-1 Fee	None	10-Year Return (1984–93)	+145%
Annual Expense Ratio	0.88%	Worst-Ever Loss (1987)	27%
Annual Portfolio Turnover	134%	Stock Market Correlation	3%
5-Year Cost Estimate	10%	Up/Down Market Rank	E – A

Benefits		Investment Information	
Investment Objective	Gr. & Icm.	Telephone	800-421-5666
5-Year Projected Return	+17%	Minimum Investment	None
Safety Rating (0-100)	74%	Telephone Switching	Via broker
Yield	5.1%	Total Assets	$79 million

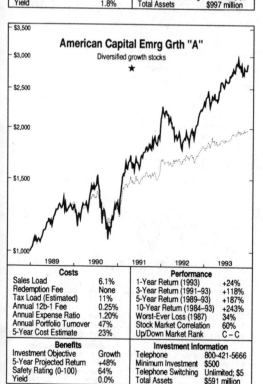

American Capital Emrg Grth "A"
Diversified growth stocks
★

Costs		Performance	
Sales Load	6.1%	1-Year Return (1993)	+24%
Redemption Fee	None	3-Year Return (1991–93)	+118%
Tax Load (Estimated)	11%	5-Year Return (1989–93)	+187%
Annual 12b-1 Fee	0.25%	10-Year Return (1984–93)	+243%
Annual Expense Ratio	1.20%	Worst-Ever Loss (1987)	34%
Annual Portfolio Turnover	47%	Stock Market Correlation	60%
5-Year Cost Estimate	23%	Up/Down Market Rank	C – C

Benefits		Investment Information	
Investment Objective	Growth	Telephone	800-421-5666
5-Year Projected Return	+48%	Minimum Investment	$500
Safety Rating (0-100)	64%	Telephone Switching	Unlimited; $5
Yield	0.0%	Total Assets	$591 million

American Capital Enterprs "A"
Growth stocks

Costs		Performance	
Sales Load	6.1%	1-Year Return (1993)	+11%
Redemption Fee	None	3-Year Return (1991–93)	+67%
Tax Load (Estimated)	2%	5-Year Return (1989–93)	+114%
Annual 12b-1 Fee	0.25%	10-Year Return (1984–93)	+224%
Annual Expense Ratio	0.99%	Worst-Ever Loss (1987)	39%
Annual Portfolio Turnover	198%	Stock Market Correlation	79%
5-Year Cost Estimate	14%	Up/Down Market Rank	A – E

Benefits		Investment Information	
Investment Objective	Growth	Telephone	800-421-5666
5-Year Projected Return	+14%	Minimum Investment	$500
Safety Rating (0-100)	70%	Telephone Switching	Unlimited; $5
Yield	0.5%	Total Assets	$847 million

American Capital Eqty Icm "A"
High-yield stocks and bonds
★★★

S&P 500 / Fund

Costs		Performance	
Sales Load	6.1%	1-Year Return (1993)	+16%
Redemption Fee	None	3-Year Return (1991–93)	+63%
Tax Load (Estimated)	2%	5-Year Return (1989–93)	+89%
Annual 12b-1 Fee	0.25%	10-Year Return (1984–93)	+195%
Annual Expense Ratio	1.01%	Worst-Ever Loss (1987)	29%
Annual Portfolio Turnover	134%	Stock Market Correlation	87%
5-Year Cost Estimate	14%	Up/Down Market Rank	D – A

Benefits		Investment Information	
Investment Objective	Icm. & Gr.	Telephone	800-421-5666
5-Year Projected Return	+17%	Minimum Investment	$500
Safety Rating (0-100)	82%	Telephone Switching	Unlimited; $5
Yield	3.1%	Total Assets	$312 million

American Capital Eqty Incm "B"
Income producing stocks; inv-grade bonds

Costs		Performance	
Sales Load	None	1-Year Return (1993)	NA
Redemption Fee	5.3%	3-Year Return (1991–93)	NA
Tax Load (Estimated)	2%	5-Year Return (1989–93)	NA
Annual 12b-1 Fee	1.00%	10-Year Return (1984–93)	NA
Annual Expense Ratio	1.87%	Worst-Ever Loss (1993)	3%
Annual Portfolio Turnover	134%	Stock Market Correlation	NA
5-Year Cost Estimate	12%	Up/Down Market Rank	NA – NA

Benefits		Investment Information	
Investment Objective	Icm. & Gr.	Telephone	800-421-5666
5-Year Projected Return	NA	Minimum Investment	$500
Safety Rating (0-100)	NA	Telephone Switching	Unlimited; $5
Yield	2.3%	Total Assets	$312 million

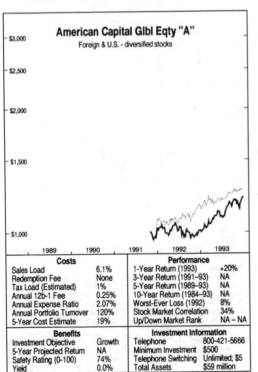

American Capital Glbl Eqty "A"
Foreign & U.S. - diversified stocks

Costs		Performance	
Sales Load	6.1%	1-Year Return (1993)	+20%
Redemption Fee	None	3-Year Return (1991–93)	NA
Tax Load (Estimated)	1%	5-Year Return (1989–93)	NA
Annual 12b-1 Fee	0.25%	10-Year Return (1984–93)	NA
Annual Expense Ratio	2.07%	Worst-Ever Loss (1992)	8%
Annual Portfolio Turnover	120%	Stock Market Correlation	34%
5-Year Cost Estimate	19%	Up/Down Market Rank	NA – NA

Benefits		Investment Information	
Investment Objective	Growth	Telephone	800-421-5666
5-Year Projected Return	NA	Minimum Investment	$500
Safety Rating (0-100)	74%	Telephone Switching	Unlimited; $5
Yield	0.0%	Total Assets	$59 million

American Capital Gr & Icm "A"
Diversified securities

Costs		Performance	
Sales Load	6.1%	1-Year Return (1993)	+16%
Redemption Fee	None	3-Year Return (1991–93)	+66%
Tax Load (Estimated)	2%	5-Year Return (1989–93)	+82%
Annual 12b-1 Fee	0.25%	10-Year Return (1984–93)	+191%
Annual Expense Ratio	1.15%	Worst-Ever Loss (1987)	38%
Annual Portfolio Turnover	120%	Stock Market Correlation	90%
5-Year Cost Estimate	15%	Up/Down Market Rank	C – C

Benefits		Investment Information	
Investment Objective	Gr. & Icm.	Telephone	800-421-5666
5-Year Projected Return	+12%	Minimum Investment	$500
Safety Rating (0-100)	75%	Telephone Switching	Unlimited; $5
Yield	2.0%	Total Assets	$210 million

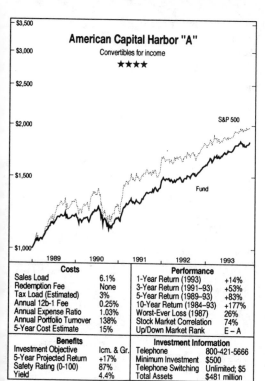

American Capital Harbor "A"

Convertibles for income

★★★★

S&P 500

Fund

$3,500			
$3,000			
$2,500			
$2,000			
$1,500			
$1,000			
1989	1990	1991	1992	1993

Costs		Performance	
Sales Load	6.1%	1-Year Return (1993)	+14%
Redemption Fee	None	3-Year Return (1991–93)	+53%
Tax Load (Estimated)	3%	5-Year Return (1989–93)	+83%
Annual 12b-1 Fee	0.25%	10-Year Return (1984–93)	+177%
Annual Expense Ratio	1.03%	Worst-Ever Loss (1987)	26%
Annual Portfolio Turnover	138%	Stock Market Correlation	74%
5-Year Cost Estimate	15%	Up/Down Market Rank	E – A

Benefits		Investment Information	
Investment Objective	Icm. & Gr.	Telephone	800-421-5666
5-Year Projected Return	+17%	Minimum Investment	$500
Safety Rating (0-100)	87%	Telephone Switching	Unlimited; $5
Yield	4.4%	Total Assets	$481 million

American Capital Pace "A"

Growth company stocks

$3,500			
$3,000			
$2,500			
$2,000			
$1,500			
$1,000			
1989	1990	1991	1992	1993

Costs		Performance	
Sales Load	6.1%	1-Year Return (1993)	+11%
Redemption Fee	None	3-Year Return (1991–93)	+52%
Tax Load (Estimated)	2%	5-Year Return (1989–93)	+84%
Annual 12b-1 Fee	0.25%	10-Year Return (1984–93)	+183%
Annual Expense Ratio	1.06%	Worst-Ever Loss (1987)	37%
Annual Portfolio Turnover	113%	Stock Market Correlation	90%
5-Year Cost Estimate	14%	Up/Down Market Rank	C – C

Benefits		Investment Information	
Investment Objective	Growth	Telephone	800-421-5666
5-Year Projected Return	–1%	Minimum Investment	$500
Safety Rating (0-100)	70%	Telephone Switching	Unlimited; $5
Yield	1.2%	Total Assets	$2.51 billion

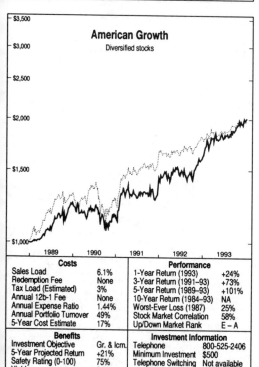

American Growth

Diversified stocks

$3,500			
$3,000			
$2,500			
$2,000			
$1,500			
$1,000			
1989	1990	1991	1992	1993

Costs		Performance	
Sales Load	6.1%	1-Year Return (1993)	+24%
Redemption Fee	None	3-Year Return (1991–93)	+73%
Tax Load (Estimated)	3%	5-Year Return (1989–93)	+101%
Annual 12b-1 Fee	None	10-Year Return (1984–93)	NA
Annual Expense Ratio	1.44%	Worst-Ever Loss (1987)	25%
Annual Portfolio Turnover	49%	Stock Market Correlation	58%
5-Year Cost Estimate	17%	Up/Down Market Rank	E – A

Benefits		Investment Information	
Investment Objective	Gr. & Icm.	Telephone	800-525-2406
5-Year Projected Return	+21%	Minimum Investment	$500
Safety Rating (0-100)	75%	Telephone Switching	Not available
Yield	0.5%	Total Assets	$64 million

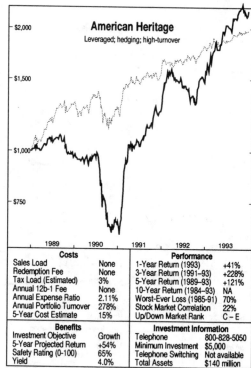

American Heritage

Leveraged; hedging; high-turnover

$2,000			
$1,500			
$1,000			
$750			
1989	1990	1991	1992	1993

Costs		Performance	
Sales Load	None	1-Year Return (1993)	+41%
Redemption Fee	None	3-Year Return (1991–93)	+228%
Tax Load (Estimated)	3%	5-Year Return (1989–93)	+121%
Annual 12b-1 Fee	None	10-Year Return (1984–93)	NA
Annual Expense Ratio	2.11%	Worst-Ever Loss (1985-91)	70%
Annual Portfolio Turnover	278%	Stock Market Correlation	22%
5-Year Cost Estimate	15%	Up/Down Market Rank	C – E

Benefits		Investment Information	
Investment Objective	Growth	Telephone	800-828-5050
5-Year Projected Return	+54%	Minimum Investment	$5,000
Safety Rating (0-100)	65%	Telephone Switching	Not available
Yield	4.0%	Total Assets	$140 million

EQUITY

American National Growth
Diversified stocks

S&P 500

Fund

1989 1990 1991 1992 1993

Costs		Performance	
Sales Load	6.1%	1-Year Return (1993)	+7%
Redemption Fee	None	3-Year Return (1991–93)	+44%
Tax Load (Estimated)	0%	5-Year Return (1989–93)	+74%
Annual 12b-1 Fee	0.25%	10-Year Return (1984–93)	+156%
Annual Expense Ratio	1.07%	Worst-Ever Loss (1983-84)	33%
Annual Portfolio Turnover	36%	Stock Market Correlation	71%
5-Year Cost Estimate	12%	Up/Down Market Rank	B – D

Benefits		Investment Information	
Investment Objective	Growth	Telephone	800-231-4639
5-Year Projected Return	–3%	Minimum Investment	$100
Safety Rating (0-100)	71%	Telephone Switching	1 per mo; free
Yield	0.6%	Total Assets	$112 million

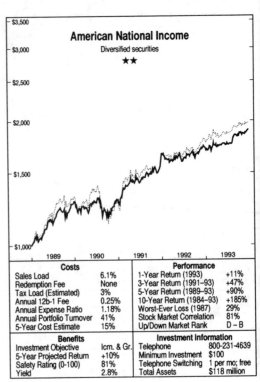

American National Income
Diversified securities
★★

1989 1990 1991 1992 1993

Costs		Performance	
Sales Load	6.1%	1-Year Return (1993)	+11%
Redemption Fee	None	3-Year Return (1991–93)	+47%
Tax Load (Estimated)	3%	5-Year Return (1989–93)	+90%
Annual 12b-1 Fee	0.25%	10-Year Return (1984–93)	+185%
Annual Expense Ratio	1.18%	Worst-Ever Loss (1987)	29%
Annual Portfolio Turnover	41%	Stock Market Correlation	81%
5-Year Cost Estimate	15%	Up/Down Market Rank	D – B

Benefits		Investment Information	
Investment Objective	Icm. & Gr.	Telephone	800-231-4639
5-Year Projected Return	+10%	Minimum Investment	$100
Safety Rating (0-100)	81%	Telephone Switching	1 per mo; free
Yield	2.8%	Total Assets	$118 million

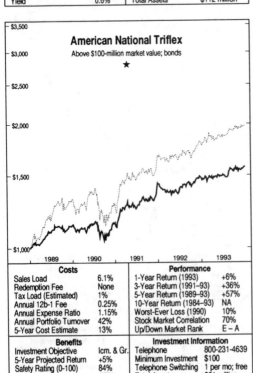

American National Triflex
Above $100-million market value; bonds
★

1989 1990 1991 1992 1993

Costs		Performance	
Sales Load	6.1%	1-Year Return (1993)	+6%
Redemption Fee	None	3-Year Return (1991–93)	+36%
Tax Load (Estimated)	1%	5-Year Return (1989–93)	+57%
Annual 12b-1 Fee	0.25%	10-Year Return (1984–93)	NA
Annual Expense Ratio	1.15%	Worst-Ever Loss (1990)	10%
Annual Portfolio Turnover	42%	Stock Market Correlation	70%
5-Year Cost Estimate	13%	Up/Down Market Rank	E – A

Benefits		Investment Information	
Investment Objective	Icm. & Gr.	Telephone	800-231-4639
5-Year Projected Return	+5%	Minimum Investment	$100
Safety Rating (0-100)	84%	Telephone Switching	1 per mo; free
Yield	2.7%	Total Assets	$21 million

American Performance Equity
Diversif; 70% stocks & conv; 30% corp bonds

1989 1990 1991 1992 1993

Costs		Performance	
Sales Load	4.2%	1-Year Return (1993)	+10%
Redemption Fee	None	3-Year Return (1991–93)	+35%
Tax Load (Estimated)	5%	5-Year Return (1989–93)	NA
Annual 12b-1 Fee	0.25%	10-Year Return (1984–93)	NA
Annual Expense Ratio	1.16%	Worst-Ever Loss (1992)	14%
Annual Portfolio Turnover	133%	Stock Market Correlation	70%
5-Year Cost Estimate	16%	Up/Down Market Rank	NA – NA

Benefits		Investment Information	
Investment Objective	Gr. & Icm.	Telephone	800-762-7085
5-Year Projected Return	–12%	Minimum Investment	$1,000
Safety Rating (0-100)	69%	Telephone Switching	Unlimited;free
Yield	0.9%	Total Assets	$58 million

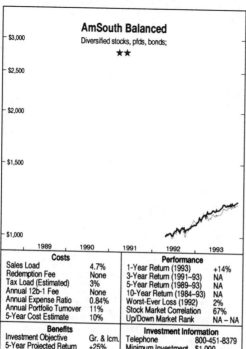

AmSouth Balanced
Diversified stocks, pfds, bonds;
★★

Costs		Performance	
Sales Load	4.7%	1-Year Return (1993)	+14%
Redemption Fee	None	3-Year Return (1991–93)	NA
Tax Load (Estimated)	3%	5-Year Return (1989–93)	NA
Annual 12b-1 Fee	None	10-Year Return (1984–93)	NA
Annual Expense Ratio	0.84%	Worst-Ever Loss (1992)	2%
Annual Portfolio Turnover	11%	Stock Market Correlation	67%
5-Year Cost Estimate	10%	Up/Down Market Rank	NA – NA

Benefits		Investment Information	
Investment Objective	Gr. & Icm.	Telephone	800-451-8379
5-Year Projected Return	+25%	Minimum Investment	$1,000
Safety Rating (0-100)	85%	Telephone Switching	Unlimited;free
Yield	3.4%	Total Assets	$174 million

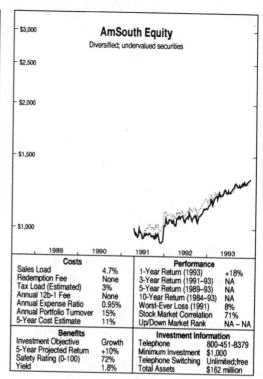

AmSouth Equity
Diversified; undervalued securities

Costs		Performance	
Sales Load	4.7%	1-Year Return (1993)	+18%
Redemption Fee	None	3-Year Return (1991–93)	NA
Tax Load (Estimated)	3%	5-Year Return (1989–93)	NA
Annual 12b-1 Fee	None	10-Year Return (1984–93)	NA
Annual Expense Ratio	0.95%	Worst-Ever Loss (1991)	8%
Annual Portfolio Turnover	15%	Stock Market Correlation	71%
5-Year Cost Estimate	11%	Up/Down Market Rank	NA – NA

Benefits		Investment Information	
Investment Objective	Growth	Telephone	800-451-8379
5-Year Projected Return	+10%	Minimum Investment	$1,000
Safety Rating (0-100)	72%	Telephone Switching	Unlimited;free
Yield	1.8%	Total Assets	$162 million

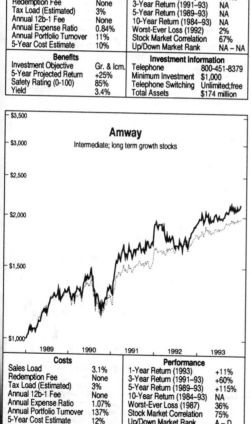

Amway
Intermediate; long term growth stocks

Costs		Performance	
Sales Load	3.1%	1-Year Return (1993)	+11%
Redemption Fee	None	3-Year Return (1991–93)	+60%
Tax Load (Estimated)	3%	5-Year Return (1989–93)	+115%
Annual 12b-1 Fee	None	10-Year Return (1984–93)	NA
Annual Expense Ratio	1.07%	Worst-Ever Loss (1987)	36%
Annual Portfolio Turnover	137%	Stock Market Correlation	75%
5-Year Cost Estimate	12%	Up/Down Market Rank	A – D

Benefits		Investment Information	
Investment Objective	Gr. & Icm.	Telephone	800-346-2670
5-Year Projected Return	+13%	Minimum Investment	$500
Safety Rating (0-100)	66%	Telephone Switching	Unlimited;free
Yield	0.3%	Total Assets	$62 million

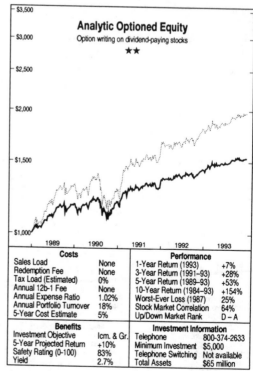

Analytic Optioned Equity
Option writing on dividend-paying stocks
★★

Costs		Performance	
Sales Load	None	1-Year Return (1993)	+7%
Redemption Fee	None	3-Year Return (1991–93)	+28%
Tax Load (Estimated)	0%	5-Year Return (1989–93)	+53%
Annual 12b-1 Fee	None	10-Year Return (1984–93)	+154%
Annual Expense Ratio	1.02%	Worst-Ever Loss (1987)	25%
Annual Portfolio Turnover	18%	Stock Market Correlation	64%
5-Year Cost Estimate	5%	Up/Down Market Rank	D – A

Benefits		Investment Information	
Investment Objective	Icm. & Gr.	Telephone	800-374-2633
5-Year Projected Return	+10%	Minimum Investment	$5,000
Safety Rating (0-100)	83%	Telephone Switching	Not available
Yield	2.7%	Total Assets	$65 million

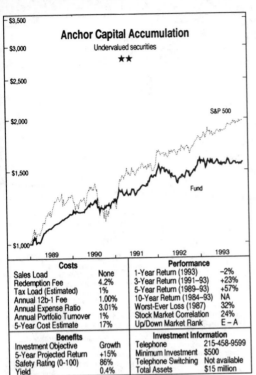

Anchor Capital Accumulation
Undervalued securities
★★

Costs		Performance	
Sales Load	None	1-Year Return (1993)	–2%
Redemption Fee	4.2%	3-Year Return (1991–93)	+23%
Tax Load (Estimated)	1%	5-Year Return (1989–93)	+57%
Annual 12b-1 Fee	1.00%	10-Year Return (1984–93)	NA
Annual Expense Ratio	3.01%	Worst-Ever Loss (1987)	32%
Annual Portfolio Turnover	1%	Stock Market Correlation	24%
5-Year Cost Estimate	17%	Up/Down Market Rank	E – A

Benefits		Investment Information	
Investment Objective	Growth	Telephone	215-458-9599
5-Year Projected Return	+15%	Minimum Investment	$500
Safety Rating (0-100)	86%	Telephone Switching	Not available
Yield	0.4%	Total Assets	$15 million

API Trust Growth
Owns other mutual funds

Costs		Performance	
Sales Load	None	1-Year Return (1993)	+19%
Redemption Fee	None	3-Year Return (1991–93)	+76%
Tax Load (Estimated)	2%	5-Year Return (1989–93)	+93%
Annual 12b-1 Fee	1.00%	10-Year Return (1984–93)	NA
Annual Expense Ratio	2.05%	Worst-Ever Loss (1987)	36%
Annual Portfolio Turnover	157%	Stock Market Correlation	42%
5-Year Cost Estimate	13%	Up/Down Market Rank	B – E

Benefits		Investment Information	
Investment Objective	Growth	Telephone	800-544-6060
5-Year Projected Return	+14%	Minimum Investment	$500
Safety Rating (0-100)	66%	Telephone Switching	Unlimited;free
Yield	0.0%	Total Assets	$45 million

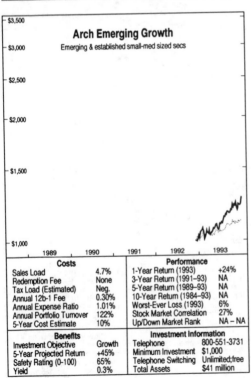

Arch Emerging Growth
Emerging & established small-med sized secs

Costs		Performance	
Sales Load	4.7%	1-Year Return (1993)	+24%
Redemption Fee	None	3-Year Return (1991–93)	NA
Tax Load (Estimated)	Neg.	5-Year Return (1989–93)	NA
Annual 12b-1 Fee	0.30%	10-Year Return (1984–93)	NA
Annual Expense Ratio	1.01%	Worst-Ever Loss (1993)	6%
Annual Portfolio Turnover	122%	Stock Market Correlation	27%
5-Year Cost Estimate	10%	Up/Down Market Rank	NA – NA

Benefits		Investment Information	
Investment Objective	Growth	Telephone	800-551-3731
5-Year Projected Return	+45%	Minimum Investment	$1,000
Safety Rating (0-100)	65%	Telephone Switching	Unlimited;free
Yield	0.3%	Total Assets	$41 million

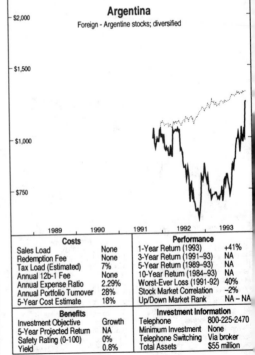

Argentina
Foreign - Argentine stocks; diversified

Costs		Performance	
Sales Load	None	1-Year Return (1993)	+41%
Redemption Fee	None	3-Year Return (1991–93)	NA
Tax Load (Estimated)	7%	5-Year Return (1989–93)	NA
Annual 12b-1 Fee	None	10-Year Return (1984–93)	NA
Annual Expense Ratio	2.29%	Worst-Ever Loss (1991-92)	40%
Annual Portfolio Turnover	28%	Stock Market Correlation	–2%
5-Year Cost Estimate	18%	Up/Down Market Rank	NA – NA

Benefits		Investment Information	
Investment Objective	Growth	Telephone	800-225-2470
5-Year Projected Return	NA	Minimum Investment	None
Safety Rating (0-100)	0%	Telephone Switching	Via broker
Yield	0.8%	Total Assets	$55 million

Armstrong Associates
Growth stocks; 1-3 year outlook

S&P 500

$1,500

$1,000

1989 1990 1991 1992 1993

Costs		Performance	
Sales Load	None	1-Year Return (1993)	+15%
Redemption Fee	None	3-Year Return (1991–93)	+46%
Tax Load (Estimated)	5%	5-Year Return (1989–93)	+56%
Annual 12b-1 Fee	None	10-Year Return (1984–93)	+114%
Annual Expense Ratio	1.87%	Worst-Ever Loss (1987)	33%
Annual Portfolio Turnover	35%	Stock Market Correlation	70%
5-Year Cost Estimate	13%	Up/Down Market Rank	D – D

Benefits		Investment Information	
Investment Objective	Growth	Telephone	214-720-9101
5-Year Projected Return	+8%	Minimum Investment	$250
Safety Rating (0-100)	79%	Telephone Switching	Not available
Yield	0.0%	Total Assets	$10 million

ASA
South African gold stocks

$3,500
$3,000
$2,500
$2,000
$1,500
$1,000

1989 1990 1991 1992 1993

Costs		Performance	
Sales Load	None	1-Year Return (1993)	+62%
Redemption Fee	None	3-Year Return (1991–93)	+24%
Tax Load (Estimated)	27%	5-Year Return (1989–93)	+76%
Annual 12b-1 Fee	None	10-Year Return (1984–93)	+68%
Annual Expense Ratio	0.70%	Worst-Ever Loss (1983-86)	53%
Annual Portfolio Turnover	2%	Stock Market Correlation	1%
5-Year Cost Estimate	7%	Up/Down Market Rank	E – B

Benefits		Investment Information	
Investment Objective	Gr. & Icm.	Telephone	201-377-3535
5-Year Projected Return	NA	Minimum Investment	None
Safety Rating (0-100)	44%	Telephone Switching	Via broker
Yield	4.1%	Total Assets	$279 million

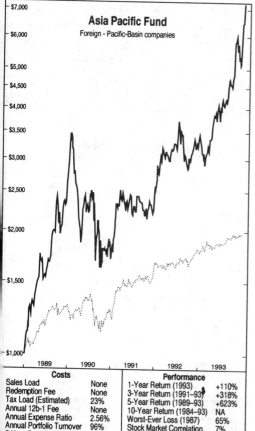

Asia Pacific Fund
Foreign - Pacific-Basin companies

$7,000
$6,000
$5,000
$4,500
$4,000
$3,500
$3,000
$2,500
$2,000
$1,500
$1,000

1989 1990 1991 1992 1993

Costs		Performance	
Sales Load	None	1-Year Return (1993)	+110%
Redemption Fee	None	3-Year Return (1991–93)	+318%
Tax Load (Estimated)	23%	5-Year Return (1989–93)	+623%
Annual 12b-1 Fee	None	10-Year Return (1984–93)	NA
Annual Expense Ratio	2.56%	Worst-Ever Loss (1987)	65%
Annual Portfolio Turnover	96%	Stock Market Correlation	7%
5-Year Cost Estimate	51%	Up/Down Market Rank	B – E

Benefits		Investment Information	
Investment Objective	Growth	Telephone	800-451-6788
5-Year Projected Return	NA	Minimum Investment	None
Safety Rating (0-100)	26%	Telephone Switching	Via broker
Yield	0.2%	Total Assets	$144 million

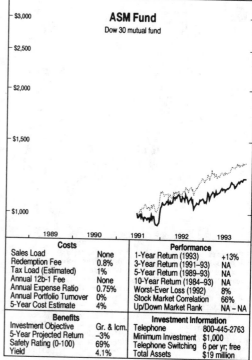

ASM Fund
Dow 30 mutual fund

$3,000
$2,500
$2,000
$1,500
$1,000

1989 1990 1991 1992 1993

Costs		Performance	
Sales Load	None	1-Year Return (1993)	+13%
Redemption Fee	0.8%	3-Year Return (1991–93)	NA
Tax Load (Estimated)	1%	5-Year Return (1989–93)	NA
Annual 12b-1 Fee	None	10-Year Return (1984–93)	NA
Annual Expense Ratio	0.75%	Worst-Ever Loss (1992)	8%
Annual Portfolio Turnover	0%	Stock Market Correlation	66%
5-Year Cost Estimate	4%	Up/Down Market Rank	NA – NA

Benefits		Investment Information	
Investment Objective	Gr. & Icm.	Telephone	800-445-2763
5-Year Projected Return	–3%	Minimum Investment	$1,000
Safety Rating (0-100)	69%	Telephone Switching	6 per yr; free
Yield	4.1%	Total Assets	$19 million

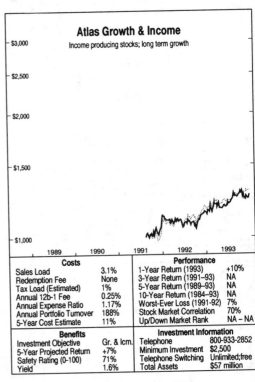

Atlanta Growth

50 large cap companies in Atlanta area

Costs		Performance	
Sales Load	3.9%	1-Year Return (1993)	+6%
Redemption Fee	None	3-Year Return (1991–93)	NA
Tax Load (Estimated)	5%	5-Year Return (1989–93)	NA
Annual 12b-1 Fee	0.25%	10-Year Return (1984–93)	NA
Annual Expense Ratio	3.30%	Worst-Ever Loss (1993)	4%
Annual Portfolio Turnover	9%	Stock Market Correlation	54%
5-Year Cost Estimate	24%	Up/Down Market Rank	NA – NA

Benefits		Investment Information	
Investment Objective	Growth	Telephone	800-762-0227
5-Year Projected Return	+18%	Minimum Investment	$500
Safety Rating (0-100)	76%	Telephone Switching	Not available
Yield	0.0%	Total Assets	$9 million

Atlas Growth & Income

Income producing stocks; long term growth

Costs		Performance	
Sales Load	3.1%	1-Year Return (1993)	+10%
Redemption Fee	None	3-Year Return (1991–93)	NA
Tax Load (Estimated)	1%	5-Year Return (1989–93)	NA
Annual 12b-1 Fee	0.25%	10-Year Return (1984–93)	NA
Annual Expense Ratio	1.17%	Worst-Ever Loss (1991-92)	7%
Annual Portfolio Turnover	188%	Stock Market Correlation	70%
5-Year Cost Estimate	11%	Up/Down Market Rank	NA – NA

Benefits		Investment Information	
Investment Objective	Gr. & Icm.	Telephone	800-933-2852
5-Year Projected Return	+7%	Minimum Investment	$2,500
Safety Rating (0-100)	71%	Telephone Switching	Unlimited;free
Yield	1.6%	Total Assets	$57 million

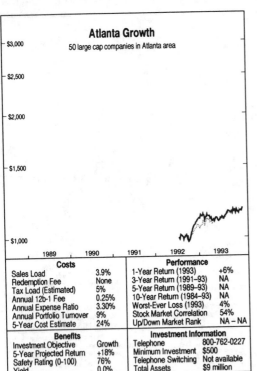

Austria

Foreign - Austrian stocks

Costs		Performance	
Sales Load	None	1-Year Return (1993)	+47%
Redemption Fee	None	3-Year Return (1991–93)	+3%
Tax Load (Estimated)	6%	5-Year Return (1989–93)	NA
Annual 12b-1 Fee	None	10-Year Return (1984–93)	NA
Annual Expense Ratio	2.13%	Worst-Ever Loss (1990-92)	72%
Annual Portfolio Turnover	32%	Stock Market Correlation	4%
5-Year Cost Estimate	18%	Up/Down Market Rank	E – C

Benefits		Investment Information	
Investment Objective	Growth	Telephone	800-247-4154
5-Year Projected Return	NA	Minimum Investment	None
Safety Rating (0-100)	0%	Telephone Switching	Via broker
Yield	1.0%	Total Assets	$80 million

Babson Enterprise

Small; undervalued growth stocks
★★★★

Costs		Performance	
Sales Load	None	1-Year Return (1993)	+16%
Redemption Fee	None	3-Year Return (1991–93)	+107%
Tax Load (Estimated)	Neg.	5-Year Return (1989–93)	+114%
Annual 12b-1 Fee	None	10-Year Return (1984–93)	NA
Annual Expense Ratio	1.11%	Worst-Ever Loss (1987)	35%
Annual Portfolio Turnover	15%	Stock Market Correlation	37%
5-Year Cost Estimate	6%	Up/Down Market Rank	C – C

Benefits		Investment Information	
Investment Objective	Growth	Telephone	800-422-2766
5-Year Projected Return	+36%	Minimum Investment	$1,000
Safety Rating (0-100)	78%	Telephone Switching	1 per mo; free
Yield	0.3%	Total Assets	$209 million

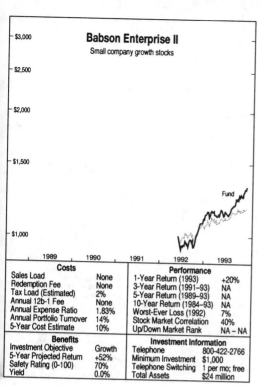

Babson Enterprise II
Small company growth stocks

| 1989 | 1990 | 1991 | 1992 | 1993 |

Costs		Performance	
Sales Load	None	1-Year Return (1993)	+20%
Redemption Fee	None	3-Year Return (1991–93)	NA
Tax Load (Estimated)	2%	5-Year Return (1989–93)	NA
Annual 12b-1 Fee	None	10-Year Return (1984–93)	NA
Annual Expense Ratio	1.83%	Worst-Ever Loss (1992)	7%
Annual Portfolio Turnover	14%	Stock Market Correlation	40%
5-Year Cost Estimate	10%	Up/Down Market Rank	NA – NA

Benefits		Investment Information	
Investment Objective	Growth	Telephone	800-422-2766
5-Year Projected Return	+52%	Minimum Investment	$1,000
Safety Rating (0-100)	70%	Telephone Switching	1 per mo; free
Yield	0.0%	Total Assets	$24 million

Babson Growth
Growth companies; long term

| 1989 | 1990 | 1991 | 1992 | 1993 |

Costs		Performance	
Sales Load	None	1-Year Return (1993)	+10%
Redemption Fee	None	3-Year Return (1991–93)	+52%
Tax Load (Estimated)	11%	5-Year Return (1989–93)	+68%
Annual 12b-1 Fee	None	10-Year Return (1984–93)	+212%
Annual Expense Ratio	0.86%	Worst-Ever Loss (1987)	34%
Annual Portfolio Turnover	13%	Stock Market Correlation	89%
5-Year Cost Estimate	7%	Up/Down Market Rank	B – E

Benefits		Investment Information	
Investment Objective	Gr. & Icm.	Telephone	800-422-2766
5-Year Projected Return	+2%	Minimum Investment	$500
Safety Rating (0-100)	72%	Telephone Switching	2 per mo; free
Yield	1.5%	Total Assets	$249 million

Babson Shadow Stock
20% smallest stocks; neglected
★★

| 1989 | 1990 | 1991 | 1992 | 1993 |

Costs		Performance	
Sales Load	None	1-Year Return (1993)	+15%
Redemption Fee	None	3-Year Return (1991–93)	+90%
Tax Load (Estimated)	6%	5-Year Return (1989–93)	+70%
Annual 12b-1 Fee	None	10-Year Return (1984–93)	NA
Annual Expense Ratio	1.25%	Worst-Ever Loss (1989-90)	31%
Annual Portfolio Turnover	15%	Stock Market Correlation	37%
5-Year Cost Estimate	8%	Up/Down Market Rank	D – C

Benefits		Investment Information	
Investment Objective	Growth	Telephone	800-422-2766
5-Year Projected Return	+22%	Minimum Investment	$2,500
Safety Rating (0-100)	81%	Telephone Switching	1 per mo; free
Yield	0.8%	Total Assets	$34 million

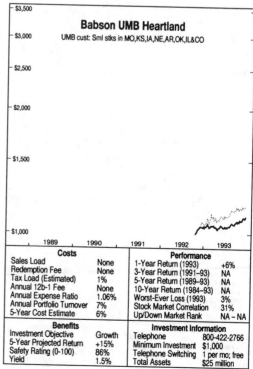

Babson UMB Heartland
UMB cust: Sml stks in MO,KS,IA,NE,AR,OK,IL&CO

| 1989 | 1990 | 1991 | 1992 | 1993 |

Costs		Performance	
Sales Load	None	1-Year Return (1993)	+6%
Redemption Fee	None	3-Year Return (1991–93)	NA
Tax Load (Estimated)	1%	5-Year Return (1989–93)	NA
Annual 12b-1 Fee	None	10-Year Return (1984–93)	NA
Annual Expense Ratio	1.06%	Worst-Ever Loss (1993)	3%
Annual Portfolio Turnover	7%	Stock Market Correlation	31%
5-Year Cost Estimate	6%	Up/Down Market Rank	NA – NA

Benefits		Investment Information	
Investment Objective	Growth	Telephone	800-422-2766
5-Year Projected Return	+15%	Minimum Investment	$1,000
Safety Rating (0-100)	86%	Telephone Switching	1 per mo; free
Yield	1.5%	Total Assets	$25 million

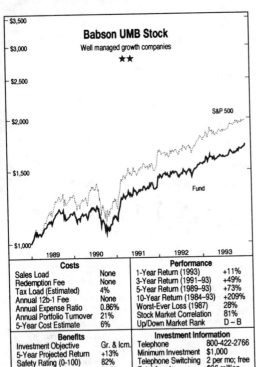

Babson UMB Stock
Well managed growth companies
★★

S&P 500

Fund

Costs		Performance	
Sales Load	None	1-Year Return (1993)	+11%
Redemption Fee	None	3-Year Return (1991–93)	+49%
Tax Load (Estimated)	4%	5-Year Return (1989–93)	+73%
Annual 12b-1 Fee	None	10-Year Return (1984–93)	+209%
Annual Expense Ratio	0.86%	Worst-Ever Loss (1987)	28%
Annual Portfolio Turnover	21%	Stock Market Correlation	81%
5-Year Cost Estimate	6%	Up/Down Market Rank	D – B

Benefits		Investment Information	
Investment Objective	Gr. & Icm.	Telephone	800-422-2766
5-Year Projected Return	+13%	Minimum Investment	$1,000
Safety Rating (0-100)	82%	Telephone Switching	2 per mo; free
Yield	2.1%	Total Assets	$96 million

Babson Value
High-quality, undervalued stocks
★★

Costs		Performance	
Sales Load	None	1-Year Return (1993)	+23%
Redemption Fee	None	3-Year Return (1991–93)	+83%
Tax Load (Estimated)	2%	5-Year Return (1989–93)	+92%
Annual 12b-1 Fee	None	10-Year Return (1984–93)	NA
Annual Expense Ratio	1.01%	Worst-Ever Loss (1987)	33%
Annual Portfolio Turnover	17%	Stock Market Correlation	73%
5-Year Cost Estimate	6%	Up/Down Market Rank	C – C

Benefits		Investment Information	
Investment Objective	Growth	Telephone	800-422-2766
5-Year Projected Return	+22%	Minimum Investment	$1,000
Safety Rating (0-100)	77%	Telephone Switching	1 per mo; free
Yield	2.2%	Total Assets	$39 million

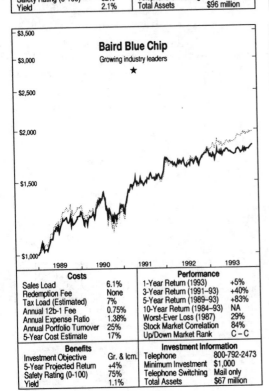

Baird Blue Chip
Growing industry leaders
★

Costs		Performance	
Sales Load	6.1%	1-Year Return (1993)	+5%
Redemption Fee	None	3-Year Return (1991–93)	+40%
Tax Load (Estimated)	7%	5-Year Return (1989–93)	+83%
Annual 12b-1 Fee	0.75%	10-Year Return (1984–93)	NA
Annual Expense Ratio	1.38%	Worst-Ever Loss (1987)	29%
Annual Portfolio Turnover	25%	Stock Market Correlation	84%
5-Year Cost Estimate	17%	Up/Down Market Rank	C – C

Benefits		Investment Information	
Investment Objective	Gr. & Icm.	Telephone	800-792-2473
5-Year Projected Return	+4%	Minimum Investment	$1,000
Safety Rating (0-100)	75%	Telephone Switching	Mail only
Yield	1.1%	Total Assets	$67 million

Baird Capital Development
Undervalued stocks
★

Costs		Performance	
Sales Load	6.1%	1-Year Return (1993)	+12%
Redemption Fee	None	3-Year Return (1991–93)	+86%
Tax Load (Estimated)	5%	5-Year Return (1989–93)	+114%
Annual 12b-1 Fee	0.75%	10-Year Return (1984–93)	NA
Annual Expense Ratio	1.56%	Worst-Ever Loss (1987)	37%
Annual Portfolio Turnover	25%	Stock Market Correlation	53%
5-Year Cost Estimate	17%	Up/Down Market Rank	A – E

Benefits		Investment Information	
Investment Objective	Gr. & Icm.	Telephone	800-792-2473
5-Year Projected Return	+25%	Minimum Investment	$1,000
Safety Rating (0-100)	75%	Telephone Switching	Mail only
Yield	0.2%	Total Assets	$52 million

Baker Fentress
Non-diversified stocks

S&P 500

Fund

Costs		Performance	
Sales Load	None	1-Year Return (1993)	+10%
Redemption Fee	None	3-Year Return (1991–93)	+52%
Tax Load (Estimated)	9%	5-Year Return (1989–93)	+45%
Annual 12b-1 Fee	None	10-Year Return (1984–93)	+156%
Annual Expense Ratio	0.79%	Worst-Ever Loss (1987)	39%
Annual Portfolio Turnover	74%	Stock Market Correlation	23%
5-Year Cost Estimate	17%	Up/Down Market Rank	D – B
Benefits		**Investment Information**	
Investment Objective	Gr. & Icm.	Telephone	312-236-9190
5-Year Projected Return	–10%	Minimum Investment	None
Safety Rating (0-100)	62%	Telephone Switching	Via broker
Yield	2.9%	Total Assets	$433 million

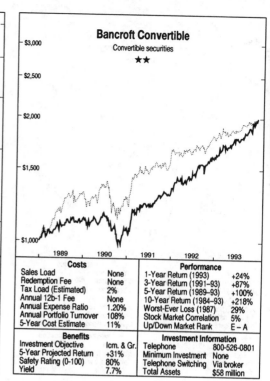

Bancroft Convertible
Convertible securities
★★

Costs		Performance	
Sales Load	None	1-Year Return (1993)	+24%
Redemption Fee	None	3-Year Return (1991–93)	+87%
Tax Load (Estimated)	2%	5-Year Return (1989–93)	+100%
Annual 12b-1 Fee	None	10-Year Return (1984–93)	+218%
Annual Expense Ratio	1.20%	Worst-Ever Loss (1987)	29%
Annual Portfolio Turnover	108%	Stock Market Correlation	5%
5-Year Cost Estimate	11%	Up/Down Market Rank	E – A
Benefits		**Investment Information**	
Investment Objective	Icm. & Gr.	Telephone	800-526-0801
5-Year Projected Return	+31%	Minimum Investment	None
Safety Rating (0-100)	80%	Telephone Switching	Via broker
Yield	7.7%	Total Assets	$58 million

Baron Asset
$100-$500 mil mkt value; underv grth stocks

Costs		Performance	
Sales Load	None	1-Year Return (1993)	+23%
Redemption Fee	None	3-Year Return (1991–93)	+89%
Tax Load (Estimated)	9%	5-Year Return (1989–93)	NA
Annual 12b-1 Fee	0.25%	10-Year Return (1984–93)	NA
Annual Expense Ratio	1.70%	Worst-Ever Loss (1989-90)	35%
Annual Portfolio Turnover	108%	Stock Market Correlation	48%
5-Year Cost Estimate	19%	Up/Down Market Rank	B – E
Benefits		**Investment Information**	
Investment Objective	Growth	Telephone	800-992-2766
5-Year Projected Return	+18%	Minimum Investment	$2,000
Safety Rating (0-100)	69%	Telephone Switching	Mail only
Yield	1.5%	Total Assets	$57 million

Bartlett Basic Value
Undervalued stocks

Costs		Performance	
Sales Load	None	1-Year Return (1993)	+12%
Redemption Fee	None	3-Year Return (1991–93)	+55%
Tax Load (Estimated)	5%	5-Year Return (1989–93)	+56%
Annual 12b-1 Fee	None	10-Year Return (1984–93)	+198%
Annual Expense Ratio	1.21%	Worst-Ever Loss (1987)	23%
Annual Portfolio Turnover	39%	Stock Market Correlation	71%
5-Year Cost Estimate	10%	Up/Down Market Rank	E – B
Benefits		**Investment Information**	
Investment Objective	Growth	Telephone	800-800-4612
5-Year Projected Return	+7%	Minimum Investment	$5,000
Safety Rating (0-100)	78%	Telephone Switching	Unlimited;free
Yield	1.4%	Total Assets	$102 million

Bartlett Value International
Foreign & U.S. - undervalued securities

S&P 500

Fund

Costs		Performance	
Sales Load	None	1-Year Return (1993)	+31%
Redemption Fee	None	3-Year Return (1991–93)	+57%
Tax Load (Estimated)	5%	5-Year Return (1989–93)	NA
Annual 12b-1 Fee	None	10-Year Return (1984–93)	NA
Annual Expense Ratio	1.91%	Worst-Ever Loss (1990-91)	20%
Annual Portfolio Turnover	16%	Stock Market Correlation	14%
5-Year Cost Estimate	11%	Up/Down Market Rank	NA – NA

Benefits		Investment Information	
Investment Objective	Growth	Telephone	800-800-4612
5-Year Projected Return	NA	Minimum Investment	$5,000
Safety Rating (0-100)	74%	Telephone Switching	Unlimited;free
Yield	0.6%	Total Assets	$35 million

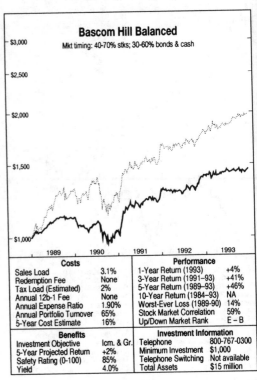

Bascom Hill Balanced
Mkt timing: 40-70% stks; 30-60% bonds & cash

Costs		Performance	
Sales Load	3.1%	1-Year Return (1993)	+4%
Redemption Fee	None	3-Year Return (1991–93)	+41%
Tax Load (Estimated)	2%	5-Year Return (1989–93)	+46%
Annual 12b-1 Fee	None	10-Year Return (1984–93)	NA
Annual Expense Ratio	1.90%	Worst-Ever Loss (1989-90)	14%
Annual Portfolio Turnover	65%	Stock Market Correlation	59%
5-Year Cost Estimate	16%	Up/Down Market Rank	E – B

Benefits		Investment Information	
Investment Objective	Icm. & Gr.	Telephone	800-767-0300
5-Year Projected Return	+2%	Minimum Investment	$1,000
Safety Rating (0-100)	85%	Telephone Switching	Not available
Yield	4.0%	Total Assets	$15 million

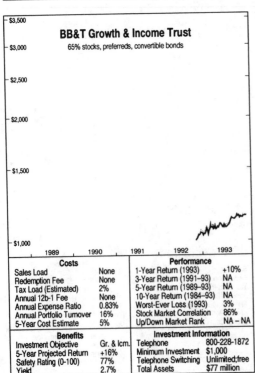

BB&T Growth & Income Trust
65% stocks, preferreds, convertible bonds

Costs		Performance	
Sales Load	None	1-Year Return (1993)	+10%
Redemption Fee	None	3-Year Return (1991–93)	NA
Tax Load (Estimated)	2%	5-Year Return (1989–93)	NA
Annual 12b-1 Fee	None	10-Year Return (1984–93)	NA
Annual Expense Ratio	0.83%	Worst-Ever Loss (1993)	3%
Annual Portfolio Turnover	16%	Stock Market Correlation	86%
5-Year Cost Estimate	5%	Up/Down Market Rank	NA – NA

Benefits		Investment Information	
Investment Objective	Gr. & Icm.	Telephone	800-228-1872
5-Year Projected Return	+16%	Minimum Investment	$1,000
Safety Rating (0-100)	77%	Telephone Switching	Unlimited;free
Yield	2.7%	Total Assets	$77 million

Beacon Hill Mutual
Diversified secs; well established companies

Costs		Performance	
Sales Load	None	1-Year Return (1993)	–5%
Redemption Fee	None	3-Year Return (1991–93)	+18%
Tax Load (Estimated)	17%	5-Year Return (1989–93)	+51%
Annual 12b-1 Fee	None	10-Year Return (1984–93)	+143%
Annual Expense Ratio	2.60%	Worst-Ever Loss (1987)	32%
Annual Portfolio Turnover	3%	Stock Market Correlation	57%
5-Year Cost Estimate	15%	Up/Down Market Rank	D – C

Benefits		Investment Information	
Investment Objective	Gr. & Icm.	Telephone	800-343-0529
5-Year Projected Return	–8%	Minimum Investment	None
Safety Rating (0-100)	68%	Telephone Switching	Not available
Yield	0.0%	Total Assets	$5 million

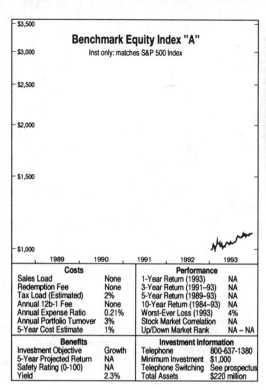

Benchmark Diversified Grth "A"
Inst only: Stocks, pfds & converts; grwth cos

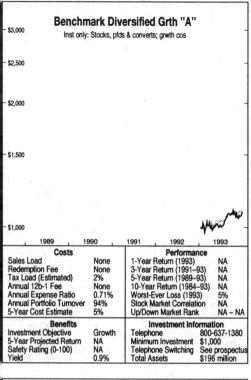

Costs		Performance	
Sales Load	None	1-Year Return (1993)	NA
Redemption Fee	None	3-Year Return (1991–93)	NA
Tax Load (Estimated)	2%	5-Year Return (1989–93)	NA
Annual 12b-1 Fee	None	10-Year Return (1984–93)	NA
Annual Expense Ratio	0.71%	Worst-Ever Loss (1993)	5%
Annual Portfolio Turnover	94%	Stock Market Correlation	NA
5-Year Cost Estimate	5%	Up/Down Market Rank	NA – NA

Benefits		Investment Information	
Investment Objective	Growth	Telephone	800-637-1380
5-Year Projected Return	NA	Minimum Investment	$1,000
Safety Rating (0-100)	NA	Telephone Switching	See prospectus
Yield	0.9%	Total Assets	$196 million

Benchmark Equity Index "A"
Inst only: matches S&P 500 Index

Costs		Performance	
Sales Load	None	1-Year Return (1993)	NA
Redemption Fee	None	3-Year Return (1991–93)	NA
Tax Load (Estimated)	2%	5-Year Return (1989–93)	NA
Annual 12b-1 Fee	None	10-Year Return (1984–93)	NA
Annual Expense Ratio	0.21%	Worst-Ever Loss (1993)	4%
Annual Portfolio Turnover	3%	Stock Market Correlation	NA
5-Year Cost Estimate	1%	Up/Down Market Rank	NA – NA

Benefits		Investment Information	
Investment Objective	Growth	Telephone	800-637-1380
5-Year Projected Return	NA	Minimum Investment	$1,000
Safety Rating (0-100)	NA	Telephone Switching	See prospectus
Yield	2.3%	Total Assets	$220 million

Benchmark Small Co Index "A"
Inst only: matches Russell 2000 Small Stk Idx

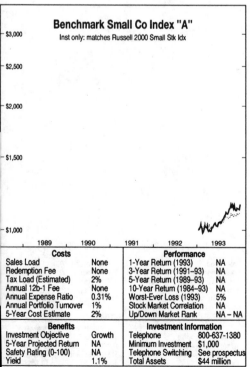

Costs		Performance	
Sales Load	None	1-Year Return (1993)	NA
Redemption Fee	None	3-Year Return (1991–93)	NA
Tax Load (Estimated)	2%	5-Year Return (1989–93)	NA
Annual 12b-1 Fee	None	10-Year Return (1984–93)	NA
Annual Expense Ratio	0.31%	Worst-Ever Loss (1993)	5%
Annual Portfolio Turnover	1%	Stock Market Correlation	NA
5-Year Cost Estimate	2%	Up/Down Market Rank	NA – NA

Benefits		Investment Information	
Investment Objective	Growth	Telephone	800-637-1380
5-Year Projected Return	NA	Minimum Investment	$1,000
Safety Rating (0-100)	NA	Telephone Switching	See prospectus
Yield	1.1%	Total Assets	$44 million

Benham Equity Growth
Select from 2000 largest stks to beat S&P 500

Costs		Performance	
Sales Load	None	1-Year Return (1993)	+11%
Redemption Fee	None	3-Year Return (1991–93)	NA
Tax Load (Estimated)	2%	5-Year Return (1989–93)	NA
Annual 12b-1 Fee	None	10-Year Return (1984–93)	NA
Annual Expense Ratio	0.75%	Worst-Ever Loss (1992)	10%
Annual Portfolio Turnover	111%	Stock Market Correlation	84%
5-Year Cost Estimate	6%	Up/Down Market Rank	NA – NA

Benefits		Investment Information	
Investment Objective	Growth	Telephone	800-321-8321
5-Year Projected Return	+21%	Minimum Investment	$1,000
Safety Rating (0-100)	74%	Telephone Switching	6 per yr; free
Yield	1.9%	Total Assets	$85 million

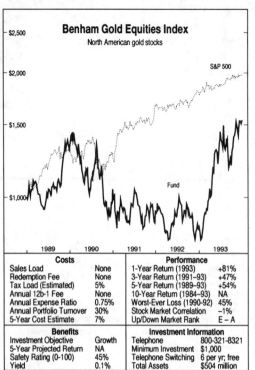

Benham Gold Equities Index
North American gold stocks

Costs		Performance	
Sales Load	None	1-Year Return (1993)	+81%
Redemption Fee	None	3-Year Return (1991–93)	+47%
Tax Load (Estimated)	5%	5-Year Return (1989–93)	+54%
Annual 12b-1 Fee	None	10-Year Return (1984–93)	NA
Annual Expense Ratio	0.75%	Worst-Ever Loss (1990-92)	45%
Annual Portfolio Turnover	30%	Stock Market Correlation	–1%
5-Year Cost Estimate	7%	Up/Down Market Rank	E – A

Benefits		Investment Information	
Investment Objective	Growth	Telephone	800-321-8321
5-Year Projected Return	NA	Minimum Investment	$1,000
Safety Rating (0-100)	45%	Telephone Switching	6 per yr; free
Yield	0.1%	Total Assets	$504 million

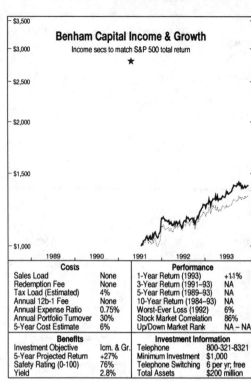

Benham Capital Income & Growth
Income secs to match S&P 500 total return
★

Costs		Performance	
Sales Load	None	1-Year Return (1993)	+11%
Redemption Fee	None	3-Year Return (1991–93)	NA
Tax Load (Estimated)	4%	5-Year Return (1989–93)	NA
Annual 12b-1 Fee	None	10-Year Return (1984–93)	NA
Annual Expense Ratio	0.75%	Worst-Ever Loss (1992)	6%
Annual Portfolio Turnover	30%	Stock Market Correlation	86%
5-Year Cost Estimate	6%	Up/Down Market Rank	NA – NA

Benefits		Investment Information	
Investment Objective	Icm. & Gr.	Telephone	800-321-8321
5-Year Projected Return	+27%	Minimum Investment	$1,000
Safety Rating (0-100)	76%	Telephone Switching	6 per yr; free
Yield	2.8%	Total Assets	$200 million

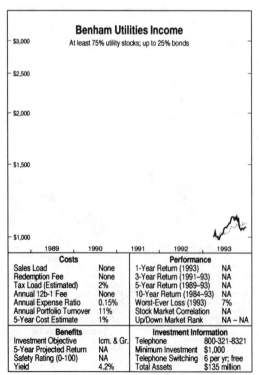

Benham Utilities Income
At least 75% utility stocks; up to 25% bonds

Costs		Performance	
Sales Load	None	1-Year Return (1993)	NA
Redemption Fee	None	3-Year Return (1991–93)	NA
Tax Load (Estimated)	2%	5-Year Return (1989–93)	NA
Annual 12b-1 Fee	None	10-Year Return (1984–93)	NA
Annual Expense Ratio	0.15%	Worst-Ever Loss (1993)	7%
Annual Portfolio Turnover	11%	Stock Market Correlation	NA
5-Year Cost Estimate	1%	Up/Down Market Rank	NA – NA

Benefits		Investment Information	
Investment Objective	Icm. & Gr.	Telephone	800-321-8321
5-Year Projected Return	NA	Minimum Investment	$1,000
Safety Rating (0-100)	NA	Telephone Switching	6 per yr; free
Yield	4.2%	Total Assets	$135 million

Berger - One Hundred
Established growth stocks
★★★★

Costs		Performance	
Sales Load	None	1-Year Return (1993)	+21%
Redemption Fee	None	3-Year Return (1991–93)	+148%
Tax Load (Estimated)	5%	5-Year Return (1989–93)	+247%
Annual 12b-1 Fee	0.75%	10-Year Return (1984–93)	+393%
Annual Expense Ratio	1.64%	Worst-Ever Loss (1983-84)	42%
Annual Portfolio Turnover	74%	Stock Market Correlation	52%
5-Year Cost Estimate	15%	Up/Down Market Rank	B – D

Benefits		Investment Information	
Investment Objective	Growth	Telephone	800-333-1001
5-Year Projected Return	+63%	Minimum Investment	$250
Safety Rating (0-100)	63%	Telephone Switching	4 per yr; free
Yield	0.0%	Total Assets	$1.65 billion

Berger - One Hundred and One

Highly predictable firms
★★★

Costs		Performance	
Sales Load	None	1-Year Return (1993)	+23%
Redemption Fee	None	3-Year Return (1991–93)	+107%
Tax Load (Estimated)	2%	5-Year Return (1989–93)	+130%
Annual 12b-1 Fee	0.75%	10-Year Return (1984–93)	+251%
Annual Expense Ratio	2.31%	Worst-Ever Loss (1987)	27%
Annual Portfolio Turnover	62%	Stock Market Correlation	53%
5-Year Cost Estimate	15%	Up/Down Market Rank	D – B
Benefits		**Investment Information**	
Investment Objective	Gr. & Icm.	Telephone	800-333-1001
5-Year Projected Return	+46%	Minimum Investment	$250
Safety Rating (0-100)	76%	Telephone Switching	4 per yr; free
Yield	0.2%	Total Assets	$189 million

Bergstrom Capital

Long term growth stocks

Costs		Performance	
Sales Load	None	1-Year Return (1993)	–27%
Redemption Fee	None	3-Year Return (1991–93)	+69%
Tax Load (Estimated)	12%	5-Year Return (1989–93)	+150%
Annual 12b-1 Fee	None	10-Year Return (1984–93)	+440%
Annual Expense Ratio	0.79%	Worst-Ever Loss (1987)	36%
Annual Portfolio Turnover	22%	Stock Market Correlation	2%
5-Year Cost Estimate	11%	Up/Down Market Rank	E – A
Benefits		**Investment Information**	
Investment Objective	Growth	Telephone	800-426-5523
5-Year Projected Return	+35%	Minimum Investment	None
Safety Rating (0-100)	62%	Telephone Switching	Via broker
Yield	1.2%	Total Assets	$128 million

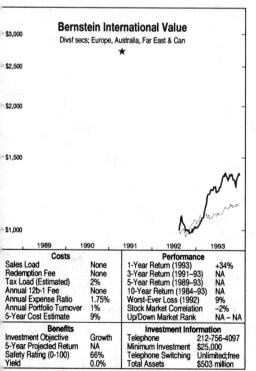

Bernstein International Value

Divsf secs; Europe, Australia, Far East & Can
★

Costs		Performance	
Sales Load	None	1-Year Return (1993)	+34%
Redemption Fee	None	3-Year Return (1991–93)	NA
Tax Load (Estimated)	2%	5-Year Return (1989–93)	NA
Annual 12b-1 Fee	None	10-Year Return (1984–93)	NA
Annual Expense Ratio	1.75%	Worst-Ever Loss (1992)	9%
Annual Portfolio Turnover	1%	Stock Market Correlation	-2%
5-Year Cost Estimate	9%	Up/Down Market Rank	NA – NA
Benefits		**Investment Information**	
Investment Objective	Growth	Telephone	212-756-4097
5-Year Projected Return	NA	Minimum Investment	$25,000
Safety Rating (0-100)	66%	Telephone Switching	Unlimited;free
Yield	0.0%	Total Assets	$503 million

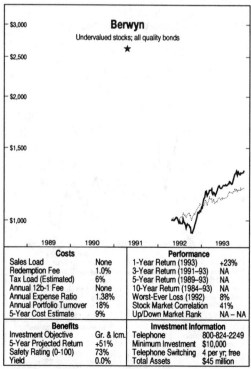

Berwyn

Undervalued stocks; all quality bonds
★

Costs		Performance	
Sales Load	None	1-Year Return (1993)	+23%
Redemption Fee	1.0%	3-Year Return (1991–93)	NA
Tax Load (Estimated)	6%	5-Year Return (1989–93)	NA
Annual 12b-1 Fee	None	10-Year Return (1984–93)	NA
Annual Expense Ratio	1.38%	Worst-Ever Loss (1992)	8%
Annual Portfolio Turnover	18%	Stock Market Correlation	41%
5-Year Cost Estimate	9%	Up/Down Market Rank	NA – NA
Benefits		**Investment Information**	
Investment Objective	Gr. & Icm.	Telephone	800-824-2249
5-Year Projected Return	+51%	Minimum Investment	$10,000
Safety Rating (0-100)	73%	Telephone Switching	4 per yr; free
Yield	0.0%	Total Assets	$45 million

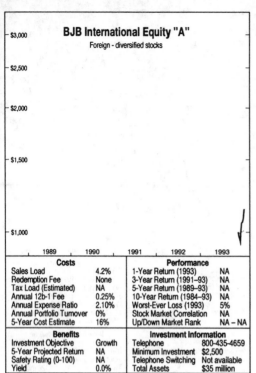

BJB International Equity "A"
Foreign - diversified stocks

Costs		Performance	
Sales Load	4.2%	1-Year Return (1993)	NA
Redemption Fee	None	3-Year Return (1991–93)	NA
Tax Load (Estimated)	NA	5-Year Return (1989–93)	NA
Annual 12b-1 Fee	0.25%	10-Year Return (1984–93)	NA
Annual Expense Ratio	2.10%	Worst-Ever Loss (1993)	5%
Annual Portfolio Turnover	0%	Stock Market Correlation	NA
5-Year Cost Estimate	16%	Up/Down Market Rank	NA – NA

Benefits		Investment Information	
Investment Objective	Growth	Telephone	800-435-4659
5-Year Projected Return	NA	Minimum Investment	$2,500
Safety Rating (0-100)	NA	Telephone Switching	Not available
Yield	0.0%	Total Assets	$35 million

Blanchard Global Growth
Foreign & U.S. - diversified sector allocatn

Costs		Performance	
Sales Load	None	1-Year Return (1993)	+24%
Redemption Fee	None	3-Year Return (1991–93)	+39%
Tax Load (Estimated)	Neg.	5-Year Return (1989–93)	+51%
Annual 12b-1 Fee	0.75%	10-Year Return (1984–93)	NA
Annual Expense Ratio	2.40%	Worst-Ever Loss (1987)	18%
Annual Portfolio Turnover	138%	Stock Market Correlation	42%
5-Year Cost Estimate	13%	Up/Down Market Rank	E – A

Benefits		Investment Information	
Investment Objective	Growth	Telephone	800-922-7771
5-Year Projected Return	NA	Minimum Investment	$3,000
Safety Rating (0-100)	85%	Telephone Switching	Unlimited;free
Yield	0.0%	Total Assets	$89 million

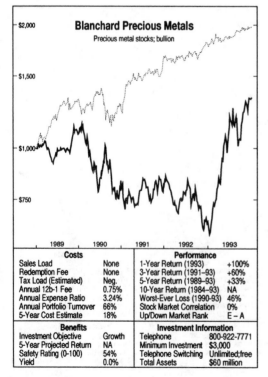

Blanchard Precious Metals
Precious metal stocks; bullion

Costs		Performance	
Sales Load	None	1-Year Return (1993)	+100%
Redemption Fee	None	3-Year Return (1991–93)	+60%
Tax Load (Estimated)	Neg.	5-Year Return (1989–93)	+33%
Annual 12b-1 Fee	0.75%	10-Year Return (1984–93)	NA
Annual Expense Ratio	3.24%	Worst-Ever Loss (1990-93)	46%
Annual Portfolio Turnover	66%	Stock Market Correlation	0%
5-Year Cost Estimate	18%	Up/Down Market Rank	E – A

Benefits		Investment Information	
Investment Objective	Growth	Telephone	800-922-7771
5-Year Projected Return	NA	Minimum Investment	$3,000
Safety Rating (0-100)	54%	Telephone Switching	Unlimited;free
Yield	0.0%	Total Assets	$60 million

Blue Chip Value
Undervalued; dividend-paying stocks

Costs		Performance	
Sales Load	None	1-Year Return (1993)	+12%
Redemption Fee	None	3-Year Return (1991–93)	+81%
Tax Load (Estimated)	7%	5-Year Return (1989–93)	+124%
Annual 12b-1 Fee	None	10-Year Return (1984–93)	NA
Annual Expense Ratio	1.42%	Worst-Ever Loss (1987)	52%
Annual Portfolio Turnover	118%	Stock Market Correlation	8%
5-Year Cost Estimate	18%	Up/Down Market Rank	B – E

Benefits		Investment Information	
Investment Objective	Growth	Telephone	800-624-4190
5-Year Projected Return	+7%	Minimum Investment	None
Safety Rating (0-100)	57%	Telephone Switching	Via broker
Yield	10.5%	Total Assets	$77 million

Boston Co Retail Cap App "A"
Growth stocks; long term

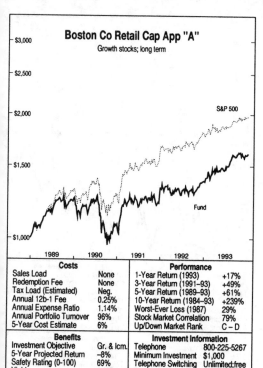

Costs		Performance	
Sales Load	None	1-Year Return (1993)	+17%
Redemption Fee	None	3-Year Return (1991–93)	+49%
Tax Load (Estimated)	Neg.	5-Year Return (1989–93)	+61%
Annual 12b-1 Fee	0.25%	10-Year Return (1984–93)	+239%
Annual Expense Ratio	1.14%	Worst-Ever Loss (1987)	29%
Annual Portfolio Turnover	96%	Stock Market Correlation	79%
5-Year Cost Estimate	6%	Up/Down Market Rank	C – D

Benefits		Investment Information	
Investment Objective	Gr. & Icm.	Telephone	800-225-5267
5-Year Projected Return	–8%	Minimum Investment	$1,000
Safety Rating (0-100)	69%	Telephone Switching	Unlimited;free
Yield	1.1%	Total Assets	$461 million

Boston Co Retail Spcl Grth "A"
Small company growth stocks
★

Costs		Performance	
Sales Load	None	1-Year Return (1993)	+20%
Redemption Fee	None	3-Year Return (1991–93)	+96%
Tax Load (Estimated)	Neg.	5-Year Return (1989–93)	+122%
Annual 12b-1 Fee	0.25%	10-Year Return (1984–93)	+233%
Annual Expense Ratio	1.79%	Worst-Ever Loss (1987)	34%
Annual Portfolio Turnover	134%	Stock Market Correlation	56%
5-Year Cost Estimate	9%	Up/Down Market Rank	B – E

Benefits		Investment Information	
Investment Objective	Growth	Telephone	800-225-5267
5-Year Projected Return	+39%	Minimum Investment	$1,000
Safety Rating (0-100)	66%	Telephone Switching	Unlimited;free
Yield	0.0%	Total Assets	$87 million

Brandywine
Financial strength; EPS growth
★★

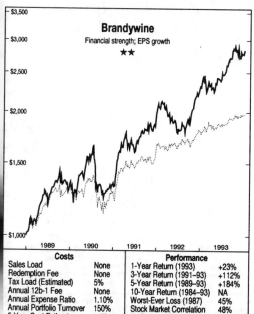

Costs		Performance	
Sales Load	None	1-Year Return (1993)	+23%
Redemption Fee	None	3-Year Return (1991–93)	+112%
Tax Load (Estimated)	5%	5-Year Return (1989–93)	+184%
Annual 12b-1 Fee	None	10-Year Return (1984–93)	NA
Annual Expense Ratio	1.10%	Worst-Ever Loss (1987)	45%
Annual Portfolio Turnover	150%	Stock Market Correlation	48%
5-Year Cost Estimate	11%	Up/Down Market Rank	A – E

Benefits		Investment Information	
Investment Objective	Gr. & Icm.	Telephone	800-338-1579
5-Year Projected Return	+59%	Minimum Investment	$25,000
Safety Rating (0-100)	67%	Telephone Switching	Not available
Yield	0.0%	Total Assets	$1.51 billion

Brazil Fund
Foreign - Brazilian stocks

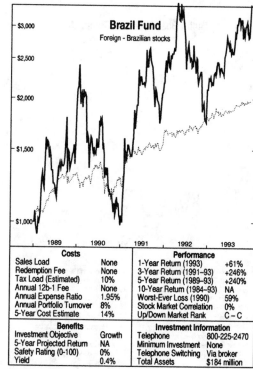

Costs		Performance	
Sales Load	None	1-Year Return (1993)	+61%
Redemption Fee	None	3-Year Return (1991–93)	+246%
Tax Load (Estimated)	10%	5-Year Return (1989–93)	+240%
Annual 12b-1 Fee	None	10-Year Return (1984–93)	NA
Annual Expense Ratio	1.95%	Worst-Ever Loss (1990)	59%
Annual Portfolio Turnover	8%	Stock Market Correlation	0%
5-Year Cost Estimate	14%	Up/Down Market Rank	C – C

Benefits		Investment Information	
Investment Objective	Growth	Telephone	800-225-2470
5-Year Projected Return	NA	Minimum Investment	None
Safety Rating (0-100)	0%	Telephone Switching	Via broker
Yield	0.4%	Total Assets	$184 million

Brazilian Equity
Foreign - Brazilian stocks

Costs		Performance	
Sales Load	None	1-Year Return (1993)	+75%
Redemption Fee	None	3-Year Return (1991–93)	NA
Tax Load (Estimated)	2%	5-Year Return (1989–93)	NA
Annual 12b-1 Fee	None	10-Year Return (1984–93)	NA
Annual Expense Ratio	2.48%	Worst-Ever Loss (1992)	59%
Annual Portfolio Turnover	50%	Stock Market Correlation	–2%
5-Year Cost Estimate	17%	Up/Down Market Rank	NA – NA

Benefits		Investment Information	
Investment Objective	Growth	Telephone	212-832-2626
5-Year Projected Return	NA	Minimum Investment	None
Safety Rating (0-100)	0%	Telephone Switching	Via broker
Yield	0.5%	Total Assets	$44 million

Bruce
Diversified securities

Costs		Performance	
Sales Load	None	1-Year Return (1993)	+19%
Redemption Fee	None	3-Year Return (1991–93)	+34%
Tax Load (Estimated)	2%	5-Year Return (1989–93)	+53%
Annual 12b-1 Fee	None	10-Year Return (1984–93)	+171%
Annual Expense Ratio	2.12%	Worst-Ever Loss (1987)	34%
Annual Portfolio Turnover	14%	Stock Market Correlation	21%
5-Year Cost Estimate	12%	Up/Down Market Rank	D – C

Benefits		Investment Information	
Investment Objective	Growth	Telephone	800-872-7823
5-Year Projected Return	+6%	Minimum Investment	$1,000
Safety Rating (0-100)	67%	Telephone Switching	Not available
Yield	6.2%	Total Assets	$3 million

Bull & Bear Fin News Composite
Financial News Composite Index

Costs		Performance	
Sales Load	None	1-Year Return (1993)	+13%
Redemption Fee	None	3-Year Return (1991–93)	+45%
Tax Load (Estimated)	2%	5-Year Return (1989–93)	NA
Annual 12b-1 Fee	0.25%	10-Year Return (1984–93)	NA
Annual Expense Ratio	1.79%	Worst-Ever Loss (1990)	22%
Annual Portfolio Turnover	0%	Stock Market Correlation	76%
5-Year Cost Estimate	9%	Up/Down Market Rank	C – D

Benefits		Investment Information	
Investment Objective	Growth	Telephone	800-847-4200
5-Year Projected Return	NA	Minimum Investment	$1,000
Safety Rating (0-100)	64%	Telephone Switching	Unlimited;free
Yield	1.0%	Total Assets	$6 million

Bull & Bear Gold Investors
International & U.S. gold stocks

Costs		Performance	
Sales Load	None	1-Year Return (1993)	+88%
Redemption Fee	None	3-Year Return (1991–93)	+54%
Tax Load (Estimated)	5%	5-Year Return (1989–93)	+43%
Annual 12b-1 Fee	1.00%	10-Year Return (1984–93)	+67%
Annual Expense Ratio	3.01%	Worst-Ever Loss (1987-92)	53%
Annual Portfolio Turnover	156%	Stock Market Correlation	0%
5-Year Cost Estimate	23%	Up/Down Market Rank	E – B

Benefits		Investment Information	
Investment Objective	Gr. & Icm.	Telephone	800-847-4200
5-Year Projected Return	NA	Minimum Investment	$1,000
Safety Rating (0-100)	60%	Telephone Switching	Unlimited;free
Yield	0.0%	Total Assets	$57 million

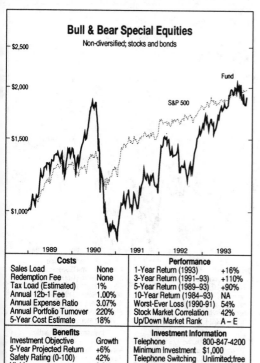

Bull & Bear Special Equities
Non-diversified; stocks and bonds

Costs		Performance	
Sales Load	None	1-Year Return (1993)	+16%
Redemption Fee	None	3-Year Return (1991–93)	+110%
Tax Load (Estimated)	1%	5-Year Return (1989–93)	+90%
Annual 12b-1 Fee	1.00%	10-Year Return (1984–93)	NA
Annual Expense Ratio	3.07%	Worst-Ever Loss (1990-91)	54%
Annual Portfolio Turnover	220%	Stock Market Correlation	42%
5-Year Cost Estimate	18%	Up/Down Market Rank	A – E

Benefits		Investment Information	
Investment Objective	Growth	Telephone	800-847-4200
5-Year Projected Return	+6%	Minimum Investment	$1,000
Safety Rating (0-100)	42%	Telephone Switching	Unlimited;free
Yield	0.0%	Total Assets	$84 million

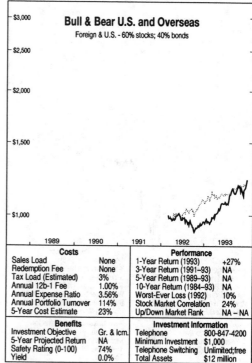

Bull & Bear U.S. and Overseas
Foreign & U.S. - 60% stocks; 40% bonds

Costs		Performance	
Sales Load	None	1-Year Return (1993)	+27%
Redemption Fee	None	3-Year Return (1991–93)	NA
Tax Load (Estimated)	3%	5-Year Return (1989–93)	NA
Annual 12b-1 Fee	1.00%	10-Year Return (1984–93)	NA
Annual Expense Ratio	3.56%	Worst-Ever Loss (1992)	10%
Annual Portfolio Turnover	114%	Stock Market Correlation	24%
5-Year Cost Estimate	23%	Up/Down Market Rank	NA – NA

Benefits		Investment Information	
Investment Objective	Gr. & Icm.	Telephone	800-847-4200
5-Year Projected Return	NA	Minimum Investment	$1,000
Safety Rating (0-100)	74%	Telephone Switching	Unlimited;free
Yield	0.0%	Total Assets	$12 million

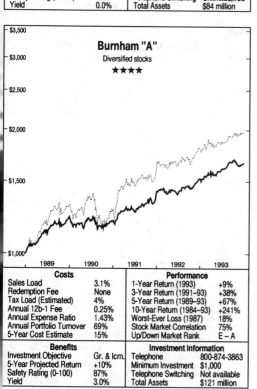

Burnham "A"
Diversified stocks
★★★★

Costs		Performance	
Sales Load	3.1%	1-Year Return (1993)	+9%
Redemption Fee	None	3-Year Return (1991–93)	+38%
Tax Load (Estimated)	4%	5-Year Return (1989–93)	+67%
Annual 12b-1 Fee	0.25%	10-Year Return (1984–93)	+241%
Annual Expense Ratio	1.43%	Worst-Ever Loss (1987)	18%
Annual Portfolio Turnover	69%	Stock Market Correlation	75%
5-Year Cost Estimate	15%	Up/Down Market Rank	E – A

Benefits		Investment Information	
Investment Objective	Gr. & Icm.	Telephone	800-874-3863
5-Year Projected Return	+10%	Minimum Investment	$1,000
Safety Rating (0-100)	87%	Telephone Switching	Not available
Yield	3.0%	Total Assets	$121 million

Calamos Convertible
Convertible securities
★★★

Costs		Performance	
Sales Load	4.7%	1-Year Return (1993)	+18%
Redemption Fee	None	3-Year Return (1991–93)	+74%
Tax Load (Estimated)	5%	5-Year Return (1989–93)	+94%
Annual 12b-1 Fee	0.50%	10-Year Return (1984–93)	NA
Annual Expense Ratio	1.70%	Worst-Ever Loss (1987)	22%
Annual Portfolio Turnover	85%	Stock Market Correlation	64%
5-Year Cost Estimate	20%	Up/Down Market Rank	E – B

Benefits		Investment Information	
Investment Objective	Icm. & Gr.	Telephone	800-323-9943
5-Year Projected Return	+26%	Minimum Investment	$2,500
Safety Rating (0-100)	81%	Telephone Switching	Mail only
Yield	4.3%	Total Assets	$18 million

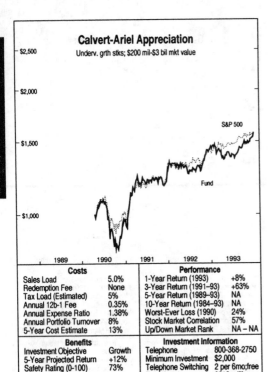

Calvert-Ariel Appreciation
Underv. grth stks; $200 mil-$3 bil mkt value

S&P 500

Fund

Costs		Performance	
Sales Load	5.0%	1-Year Return (1993)	+8%
Redemption Fee	None	3-Year Return (1991–93)	+63%
Tax Load (Estimated)	5%	5-Year Return (1989–93)	NA
Annual 12b-1 Fee	0.35%	10-Year Return (1984–93)	NA
Annual Expense Ratio	1.38%	Worst-Ever Loss (1990)	24%
Annual Portfolio Turnover	8%	Stock Market Correlation	57%
5-Year Cost Estimate	13%	Up/Down Market Rank	NA – NA

Benefits		Investment Information	
Investment Objective	Growth	Telephone	800-368-2750
5-Year Projected Return	+12%	Minimum Investment	$2,000
Safety Rating (0-100)	73%	Telephone Switching	2 per 6mo;free
Yield	0.2%	Total Assets	$210 million

Calvert-Ariel Growth
Undervalued stocks

Costs		Performance	
Sales Load	5.0%	1-Year Return (1993)	+9%
Redemption Fee	None	3-Year Return (1991–93)	+61%
Tax Load (Estimated)	4%	5-Year Return (1989–93)	+69%
Annual 12b-1 Fee	0.25%	10-Year Return (1984–93)	NA
Annual Expense Ratio	1.17%	Worst-Ever Loss (1987)	31%
Annual Portfolio Turnover	14%	Stock Market Correlation	48%
5-Year Cost Estimate	12%	Up/Down Market Rank	C – C

Benefits		Investment Information	
Investment Objective	Growth	Telephone	800-368-2750
5-Year Projected Return	–2%	Minimum Investment	$2,000
Safety Rating (0-100)	73%	Telephone Switching	2 per 6mo;free
Yield	1.0%	Total Assets	$235 million

Calvert Social Equity
Socially responsible stocks

Costs		Performance	
Sales Load	5.0%	1-Year Return (1993)	+2%
Redemption Fee	None	3-Year Return (1991–93)	+35%
Tax Load (Estimated)	5%	5-Year Return (1989–93)	+64%
Annual 12b-1 Fee	0.35%	10-Year Return (1984–93)	NA
Annual Expense Ratio	1.17%	Worst-Ever Loss (1990)	16%
Annual Portfolio Turnover	43%	Stock Market Correlation	72%
5-Year Cost Estimate	16%	Up/Down Market Rank	D – C

Benefits		Investment Information	
Investment Objective	Growth	Telephone	800-368-2750
5-Year Projected Return	–8%	Minimum Investment	$1,000
Safety Rating (0-100)	75%	Telephone Switching	2 per 6mo;free
Yield	1.3%	Total Assets	$86 million

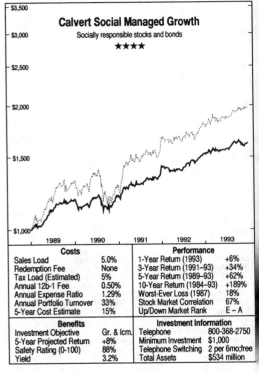

Calvert Social Managed Growth
Socially responsible stocks and bonds
★★★★

Costs		Performance	
Sales Load	5.0%	1-Year Return (1993)	+6%
Redemption Fee	None	3-Year Return (1991–93)	+34%
Tax Load (Estimated)	5%	5-Year Return (1989–93)	+62%
Annual 12b-1 Fee	0.50%	10-Year Return (1984–93)	+189%
Annual Expense Ratio	1.29%	Worst-Ever Loss (1987)	18%
Annual Portfolio Turnover	33%	Stock Market Correlation	67%
5-Year Cost Estimate	15%	Up/Down Market Rank	E – A

Benefits		Investment Information	
Investment Objective	Gr. & Icm.	Telephone	800-368-2750
5-Year Projected Return	+8%	Minimum Investment	$1,000
Safety Rating (0-100)	88%	Telephone Switching	2 per 6mo;free
Yield	3.2%	Total Assets	$534 million

1994 Mutual Fund Buyer's Guide

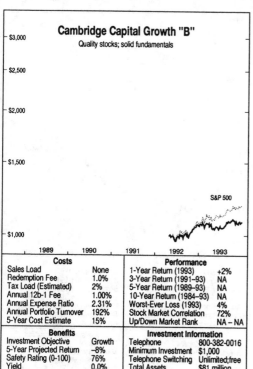

Cambridge Capital Growth "B"
Quality stocks; solid fundamentals

S&P 500

Costs		Performance	
Sales Load	None	1-Year Return (1993)	+2%
Redemption Fee	1.0%	3-Year Return (1991–93)	NA
Tax Load (Estimated)	2%	5-Year Return (1989–93)	NA
Annual 12b-1 Fee	1.00%	10-Year Return (1984–93)	NA
Annual Expense Ratio	2.31%	Worst-Ever Loss (1993)	4%
Annual Portfolio Turnover	192%	Stock Market Correlation	72%
5-Year Cost Estimate	15%	Up/Down Market Rank	NA – NA

Benefits		Investment Information	
Investment Objective	Growth	Telephone	800-382-0016
5-Year Projected Return	–8%	Minimum Investment	$1,000
Safety Rating (0-100)	76%	Telephone Switching	Unlimited;free
Yield	0.0%	Total Assets	$81 million

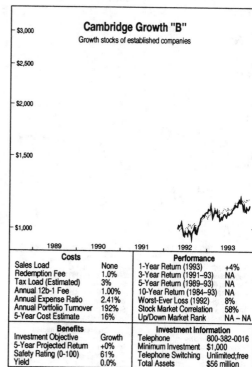

Cambridge Growth "B"
Growth stocks of established companies

Costs		Performance	
Sales Load	None	1-Year Return (1993)	+4%
Redemption Fee	1.0%	3-Year Return (1991–93)	NA
Tax Load (Estimated)	3%	5-Year Return (1989–93)	NA
Annual 12b-1 Fee	1.00%	10-Year Return (1984–93)	NA
Annual Expense Ratio	2.41%	Worst-Ever Loss (1992)	8%
Annual Portfolio Turnover	192%	Stock Market Correlation	58%
5-Year Cost Estimate	16%	Up/Down Market Rank	NA – NA

Benefits		Investment Information	
Investment Objective	Growth	Telephone	800-382-0016
5-Year Projected Return	+0%	Minimum Investment	$1,000
Safety Rating (0-100)	61%	Telephone Switching	Unlimited;free
Yield	0.0%	Total Assets	$56 million

Capstone - Fund of the S.W.
Firms in TX, OK, AR, LA, NM and AZ

Costs		Performance	
Sales Load	5.0%	1-Year Return (1993)	+8%
Redemption Fee	None	3-Year Return (1991–93)	+74%
Tax Load (Estimated)	15%	5-Year Return (1989–93)	+111%
Annual 12b-1 Fee	0.35%	10-Year Return (1984–93)	NA
Annual Expense Ratio	1.96%	Worst-Ever Loss (1987)	33%
Annual Portfolio Turnover	2%	Stock Market Correlation	65%
5-Year Cost Estimate	17%	Up/Down Market Rank	A – D

Benefits		Investment Information	
Investment Objective	Growth	Telephone	800-262-6631
5-Year Projected Return	+13%	Minimum Investment	$200
Safety Rating (0-100)	68%	Telephone Switching	2 per mo; free
Yield	0.0%	Total Assets	$16 million

Capstone - Medical Research
Medical research and health-care securities

Costs		Performance	
Sales Load	5.0%	1-Year Return (1993)	+26%
Redemption Fee	None	3-Year Return (1991–93)	+84%
Tax Load (Estimated)	0%	5-Year Return (1989–93)	NA
Annual 12b-1 Fee	0.25%	10-Year Return (1984–93)	NA
Annual Expense Ratio	2.48%	Worst-Ever Loss (1990)	21%
Annual Portfolio Turnover	84%	Stock Market Correlation	17%
5-Year Cost Estimate	19%	Up/Down Market Rank	NA – NA

Benefits		Investment Information	
Investment Objective	Growth	Telephone	800-262-6631
5-Year Projected Return	NA	Minimum Investment	$200
Safety Rating (0-100)	62%	Telephone Switching	2 per mo; free
Yield	0.7%	Total Assets	$10 million

Capstone - U.S. Trend
Conservative stocks

Costs		Performance	
Sales Load	5.0%	1-Year Return (1993)	+6%
Redemption Fee	None	3-Year Return (1991–93)	+44%
Tax Load (Estimated)	8%	5-Year Return (1989–93)	+82%
Annual 12b-1 Fee	0.35%	10-Year Return (1984–93)	+181%
Annual Expense Ratio	1.10%	Worst-Ever Loss (1987)	30%
Annual Portfolio Turnover	17%	Stock Market Correlation	89%
5-Year Cost Estimate	13%	Up/Down Market Rank	B – D

Benefits		Investment Information	
Investment Objective	Growth	Telephone	800-262-6631
5-Year Projected Return	–2%	Minimum Investment	$200
Safety Rating (0-100)	70%	Telephone Switching	2 per mo; free
Yield	1.3%	Total Assets	$99 million

Cardinal
Diversified stocks
★

Costs		Performance	
Sales Load	6.4%	1-Year Return (1993)	+6%
Redemption Fee	None	3-Year Return (1991–93)	+54%
Tax Load (Estimated)	8%	5-Year Return (1989–93)	+76%
Annual 12b-1 Fee	None	10-Year Return (1984–93)	NA
Annual Expense Ratio	0.67%	Worst-Ever Loss (1987)	27%
Annual Portfolio Turnover	33%	Stock Market Correlation	80%
5-Year Cost Estimate	15%	Up/Down Market Rank	D – B

Benefits		Investment Information	
Investment Objective	Gr. & Icm.	Telephone	800-848-7734
5-Year Projected Return	+3%	Minimum Investment	$1,000
Safety Rating (0-100)	78%	Telephone Switching	1 per mo; $5
Yield	2.1%	Total Assets	$285 million

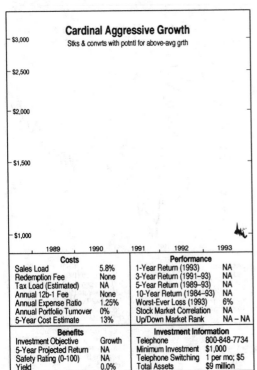

Cardinal Aggressive Growth
Stks & convrts with potntl for above-avg grth

Costs		Performance	
Sales Load	5.8%	1-Year Return (1993)	NA
Redemption Fee	None	3-Year Return (1991–93)	NA
Tax Load (Estimated)	NA	5-Year Return (1989–93)	NA
Annual 12b-1 Fee	None	10-Year Return (1984–93)	NA
Annual Expense Ratio	1.25%	Worst-Ever Loss (1993)	6%
Annual Portfolio Turnover	0%	Stock Market Correlation	NA
5-Year Cost Estimate	13%	Up/Down Market Rank	NA – NA

Benefits		Investment Information	
Investment Objective	Growth	Telephone	800-848-7734
5-Year Projected Return	NA	Minimum Investment	$1,000
Safety Rating (0-100)	NA	Telephone Switching	1 per mo; $5
Yield	0.0%	Total Assets	$9 million

Castle Convertible
Convertible securities
★

Costs		Performance	
Sales Load	None	1-Year Return (1993)	+23%
Redemption Fee	None	3-Year Return (1991–93)	+101%
Tax Load (Estimated)	0%	5-Year Return (1989–93)	+111%
Annual 12b-1 Fee	None	10-Year Return (1984–93)	+140%
Annual Expense Ratio	1.10%	Worst-Ever Loss (1987)	26%
Annual Portfolio Turnover	53%	Stock Market Correlation	8%
5-Year Cost Estimate	8%	Up/Down Market Rank	E – A

Benefits		Investment Information	
Investment Objective	Gr. & Icm.	Telephone	800-992-3863
5-Year Projected Return	+35%	Minimum Investment	None
Safety Rating (0-100)	73%	Telephone Switching	Via broker
Yield	6.4%	Total Assets	$58 million

Central Fund of Canada
Gold and silver bullion

S&P 500 / Fund

Costs		Performance	
Sales Load	None	1-Year Return (1993)	+44%
Redemption Fee	None	3-Year Return (1991–93)	+21%
Tax Load (Estimated)	Neg.	5-Year Return (1989–93)	+10%
Annual 12b-1 Fee	None	10-Year Return (1984–93)	NA
Annual Expense Ratio	1.04%	Worst-Ever Loss (1987-92)	52%
Annual Portfolio Turnover	0%	Stock Market Correlation	1%
5-Year Cost Estimate	7%	Up/Down Market Rank	E – A

Benefits		Investment Information	
Investment Objective	Growth	Telephone	416-648-7878
5-Year Projected Return	NA	Minimum Investment	None
Safety Rating (0-100)	47%	Telephone Switching	Via broker
Yield	0.0%	Total Assets	$86 million

Central Securities
Non-diversified stocks; leveraged
★

Costs		Performance	
Sales Load	None	1-Year Return (1993)	+46%
Redemption Fee	None	3-Year Return (1991–93)	+152%
Tax Load (Estimated)	10%	5-Year Return (1989–93)	+138%
Annual 12b-1 Fee	None	10-Year Return (1984–93)	+251%
Annual Expense Ratio	0.88%	Worst-Ever Loss (1987)	31%
Annual Portfolio Turnover	16%	Stock Market Correlation	10%
5-Year Cost Estimate	10%	Up/Down Market Rank	D – C

Benefits		Investment Information	
Investment Objective	Gr. & Icm.	Telephone	212-688-3011
5-Year Projected Return	+49%	Minimum Investment	None
Safety Rating (0-100)	67%	Telephone Switching	Via broker
Yield	0.6%	Total Assets	$166 million

Centurion Growth
Diversified common stocks & convertibles

Costs		Performance	
Sales Load	5.0%	1-Year Return (1993)	+0%
Redemption Fee	None	3-Year Return (1991–93)	+1%
Tax Load (Estimated)	Neg.	5-Year Return (1989–93)	+1%
Annual 12b-1 Fee	0.25%	10-Year Return (1984–93)	–15%
Annual Expense Ratio	3.33%	Worst-Ever Loss (1983-87)	40%
Annual Portfolio Turnover	210%	Stock Market Correlation	19%
5-Year Cost Estimate	24%	Up/Down Market Rank	E – B

Benefits		Investment Information	
Investment Objective	Growth	Telephone	800-448-6984
5-Year Projected Return	–24%	Minimum Investment	$500
Safety Rating (0-100)	64%	Telephone Switching	Not available
Yield	0.1%	Total Assets	$5 million

Century Shares Trust
Insurance and bank stocks
★

Costs		Performance	
Sales Load	None	1-Year Return (1993)	+0%
Redemption Fee	None	3-Year Return (1991–93)	+66%
Tax Load (Estimated)	15%	5-Year Return (1989–93)	+117%
Annual 12b-1 Fee	None	10-Year Return (1984–93)	+319%
Annual Expense Ratio	0.84%	Worst-Ever Loss (1989-90)	28%
Annual Portfolio Turnover	1%	Stock Market Correlation	49%
5-Year Cost Estimate	5%	Up/Down Market Rank	C – C

Benefits		Investment Information	
Investment Objective	Gr. & Icm.	Telephone	800-321-1928
5-Year Projected Return	NA	Minimum Investment	$500
Safety Rating (0-100)	74%	Telephone Switching	Not available
Yield	1.9%	Total Assets	$292 million

CGM - Capital Development
Diversified stocks
★★

Fund

Costs		Performance	
Sales Load	None	1-Year Return (1993)	+29%
Redemption Fee	None	3-Year Return (1991–93)	+201%
Tax Load (Estimated)	1%	5-Year Return (1989–93)	+260%
Annual 12b-1 Fee	None	10-Year Return (1984–93)	+618%
Annual Expense Ratio	0.86%	Worst-Ever Loss (1987)	47%
Annual Portfolio Turnover	163%	Stock Market Correlation	58%
5-Year Cost Estimate	6%	Up/Down Market Rank	A – D

Benefits		Investment Information	
Investment Objective	Growth	Telephone	800-345-4048
5-Year Projected Return	+66%	Minimum Investment	$2,500
Safety Rating (0-100)	59%	Telephone Switching	4 per yr; free
Yield	0.3%	Total Assets	$462 million

CGM - Mutual
Diversified securities
★★★

Costs		Performance	
Sales Load	None	1-Year Return (1993)	+22%
Redemption Fee	None	3-Year Return (1991–93)	+82%
Tax Load (Estimated)	4%	5-Year Return (1989–93)	+125%
Annual 12b-1 Fee	None	10-Year Return (1984–93)	+371%
Annual Expense Ratio	0.93%	Worst-Ever Loss (1987)	34%
Annual Portfolio Turnover	86%	Stock Market Correlation	58%
5-Year Cost Estimate	9%	Up/Down Market Rank	C – B

Benefits		Investment Information	
Investment Objective	Gr. & Icm.	Telephone	800-345-4048
5-Year Projected Return	+43%	Minimum Investment	$2,500
Safety Rating (0-100)	75%	Telephone Switching	4 per yr; free
Yield	3.1%	Total Assets	$799 million

Charter Blue Chip
Stocks; market timing

Costs		Performance	
Sales Load	None	1-Year Return (1993)	+2%
Redemption Fee	None	3-Year Return (1991–93)	+40%
Tax Load (Estimated)	2%	5-Year Return (1989–93)	+50%
Annual 12b-1 Fee	None	10-Year Return (1984–93)	NA
Annual Expense Ratio	2.28%	Worst-Ever Loss (1987-90)	30%
Annual Portfolio Turnover	202%	Stock Market Correlation	69%
5-Year Cost Estimate	15%	Up/Down Market Rank	D – B

Benefits		Investment Information	
Investment Objective	Growth	Telephone	414-257-1842
5-Year Projected Return	+1%	Minimum Investment	$50
Safety Rating (0-100)	70%	Telephone Switching	Unlimited; free
Yield	0.0%	Total Assets	$11 million

Chile
Foreign - Chilean stocks

Costs		Performance	
Sales Load	None	1-Year Return (1993)	+39%
Redemption Fee	None	3-Year Return (1991–93)	+257%
Tax Load (Estimated)	23%	5-Year Return (1989–93)	NA
Annual 12b-1 Fee	None	10-Year Return (1984–93)	NA
Annual Expense Ratio	1.68%	Worst-Ever Loss (1990)	47%
Annual Portfolio Turnover	19%	Stock Market Correlation	5%
5-Year Cost Estimate	20%	Up/Down Market Rank	C – NA

Benefits		Investment Information	
Investment Objective	Growth	Telephone	212-832-2626
5-Year Projected Return	NA	Minimum Investment	None
Safety Rating (0-100)	19%	Telephone Switching	Via broker
Yield	1.6%	Total Assets	$181 million

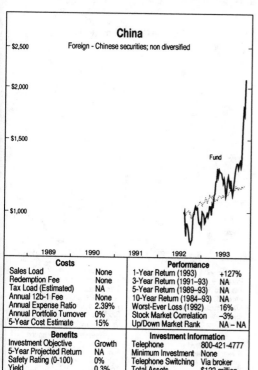

China

Foreign - Chinese securities; non diversified

Fund

| | | 1989 | 1990 | 1991 | 1992 | 1993 |

Costs		Performance	
Sales Load	None	1-Year Return (1993)	+127%
Redemption Fee	None	3-Year Return (1991–93)	NA
Tax Load (Estimated)	NA	5-Year Return (1989–93)	NA
Annual 12b-1 Fee	None	10-Year Return (1984–93)	NA
Annual Expense Ratio	2.39%	Worst-Ever Loss (1992)	16%
Annual Portfolio Turnover	0%	Stock Market Correlation	–3%
5-Year Cost Estimate	15%	Up/Down Market Rank	NA – NA

Benefits		Investment Information	
Investment Objective	Growth	Telephone	800-421-4777
5-Year Projected Return	NA	Minimum Investment	None
Safety Rating (0-100)	0%	Telephone Switching	Via broker
Yield	0.3%	Total Assets	$122 million

Clemente Global Growth

Foreign - small-medium stocks

| | | 1989 | 1990 | 1991 | 1992 | 1993 |

Costs		Performance	
Sales Load	None	1-Year Return (1993)	+53%
Redemption Fee	None	3-Year Return (1991–93)	+63%
Tax Load (Estimated)	5%	5-Year Return (1989–93)	+91%
Annual 12b-1 Fee	None	10-Year Return (1984–93)	NA
Annual Expense Ratio	2.23%	Worst-Ever Loss (1987)	54%
Annual Portfolio Turnover	73%	Stock Market Correlation	10%
5-Year Cost Estimate	20%	Up/Down Market Rank	D – C

Benefits		Investment Information	
Investment Objective	Growth	Telephone	212-765-0700
5-Year Projected Return	NA	Minimum Investment	None
Safety Rating (0-100)	63%	Telephone Switching	Via broker
Yield	5.1%	Total Assets	$63 million

Clipper

Undervalued securities
★

| | | 1989 | 1990 | 1991 | 1992 | 1993 |

Costs		Performance	
Sales Load	None	1-Year Return (1993)	+11%
Redemption Fee	None	3-Year Return (1991–93)	+71%
Tax Load (Estimated)	2%	5-Year Return (1989–93)	+93%
Annual 12b-1 Fee	None	10-Year Return (1984–93)	NA
Annual Expense Ratio	1.12%	Worst-Ever Loss (1989-90)	25%
Annual Portfolio Turnover	85%	Stock Market Correlation	65%
5-Year Cost Estimate	8%	Up/Down Market Rank	B – C

Benefits		Investment Information	
Investment Objective	Growth	Telephone	800-776-5033
5-Year Projected Return	+24%	Minimum Investment	$5,000
Safety Rating (0-100)	75%	Telephone Switching	Not available
Yield	1.5%	Total Assets	$282 million

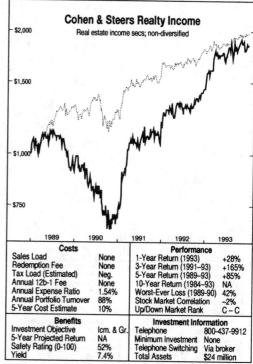

Cohen & Steers Realty Income

Real estate income secs; non-diversified

| | | 1989 | 1990 | 1991 | 1992 | 1993 |

Costs		Performance	
Sales Load	None	1-Year Return (1993)	+28%
Redemption Fee	None	3-Year Return (1991–93)	+165%
Tax Load (Estimated)	Neg.	5-Year Return (1989–93)	+85%
Annual 12b-1 Fee	None	10-Year Return (1984–93)	NA
Annual Expense Ratio	1.54%	Worst-Ever Loss (1989-90)	42%
Annual Portfolio Turnover	88%	Stock Market Correlation	–2%
5-Year Cost Estimate	10%	Up/Down Market Rank	C – C

Benefits		Investment Information	
Investment Objective	Icm. & Gr.	Telephone	800-437-9912
5-Year Projected Return	NA	Minimum Investment	None
Safety Rating (0-100)	52%	Telephone Switching	Via broker
Yield	7.4%	Total Assets	$24 million

Colonial Fund "A"
Financially sound companies
★

Costs		Performance	
Sales Load	6.1%	1-Year Return (1993)	+12%
Redemption Fee	None	3-Year Return (1991–93)	+58%
Tax Load (Estimated)	3%	5-Year Return (1989–93)	+76%
Annual 12b-1 Fee	0.25%	10-Year Return (1984–93)	+249%
Annual Expense Ratio	1.13%	Worst-Ever Loss (1987)	24%
Annual Portfolio Turnover	37%	Stock Market Correlation	72%
5-Year Cost Estimate	14%	Up/Down Market Rank	D – A
Benefits		Investment Information	
Investment Objective	Icm. & Gr.	Telephone	800-322-2847
5-Year Projected Return	+7%	Minimum Investment	$1,000
Safety Rating (0-100)	79%	Telephone Switching	Unlimited; $5
Yield	1.9%	Total Assets	$623 million

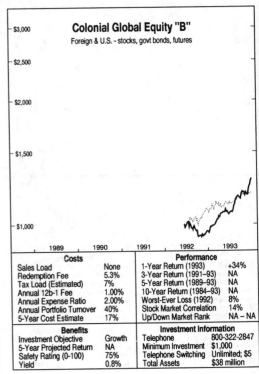

Colonial Global Equity "B"
Foreign & U.S. - stocks, govt bonds, futures

Costs		Performance	
Sales Load	None	1-Year Return (1993)	+34%
Redemption Fee	5.3%	3-Year Return (1991–93)	NA
Tax Load (Estimated)	7%	5-Year Return (1989–93)	NA
Annual 12b-1 Fee	1.00%	10-Year Return (1984–93)	NA
Annual Expense Ratio	2.00%	Worst-Ever Loss (1992)	8%
Annual Portfolio Turnover	40%	Stock Market Correlation	14%
5-Year Cost Estimate	17%	Up/Down Market Rank	NA – NA
Benefits		Investment Information	
Investment Objective	Growth	Telephone	800-322-2847
5-Year Projected Return	NA	Minimum Investment	$1,000
Safety Rating (0-100)	75%	Telephone Switching	Unlimited; $5
Yield	0.8%	Total Assets	$38 million

Colonial Growth Shares "A"
Growth stocks and convertibles

Costs		Performance	
Sales Load	6.1%	1-Year Return (1993)	+10%
Redemption Fee	None	3-Year Return (1991–93)	+64%
Tax Load (Estimated)	0%	5-Year Return (1989–93)	+91%
Annual 12b-1 Fee	0.35%	10-Year Return (1984–93)	+258%
Annual Expense Ratio	1.19%	Worst-Ever Loss (1987)	34%
Annual Portfolio Turnover	47%	Stock Market Correlation	75%
5-Year Cost Estimate	13%	Up/Down Market Rank	A – D
Benefits		Investment Information	
Investment Objective	Gr. & Icm.	Telephone	800-322-2847
5-Year Projected Return	+2%	Minimum Investment	$1,000
Safety Rating (0-100)	71%	Telephone Switching	Unlimited; $5
Yield	0.6%	Total Assets	$209 million

Colonial International Equity
Foreign - diversified

Costs		Performance	
Sales Load	6.1%	1-Year Return (1993)	+31%
Redemption Fee	None	3-Year Return (1991–93)	+24%
Tax Load (Estimated)	3%	5-Year Return (1989–93)	+13%
Annual 12b-1 Fee	0.25%	10-Year Return (1984–93)	NA
Annual Expense Ratio	1.79%	Worst-Ever Loss (1990-92)	25%
Annual Portfolio Turnover	25%	Stock Market Correlation	10%
5-Year Cost Estimate	17%	Up/Down Market Rank	E – A
Benefits		Investment Information	
Investment Objective	Gr. & Icm.	Telephone	800-225-2365
5-Year Projected Return	NA	Minimum Investment	$1,000
Safety Rating (0-100)	61%	Telephone Switching	Unlimited; $5
Yield	0.6%	Total Assets	$10 million

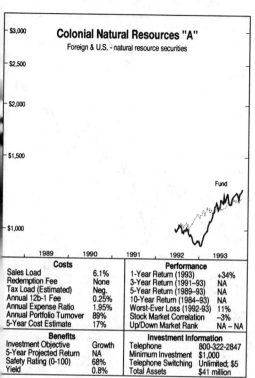

Colonial Natural Resources "A"

Foreign & U.S. - natural resource securities

Costs		Performance	
Sales Load	6.1%	1-Year Return (1993)	+34%
Redemption Fee	None	3-Year Return (1991–93)	NA
Tax Load (Estimated)	Neg.	5-Year Return (1989–93)	NA
Annual 12b-1 Fee	0.25%	10-Year Return (1984–93)	NA
Annual Expense Ratio	1.95%	Worst-Ever Loss (1992-93)	11%
Annual Portfolio Turnover	89%	Stock Market Correlation	–3%
5-Year Cost Estimate	17%	Up/Down Market Rank	NA – NA

Benefits		Investment Information	
Investment Objective	Growth	Telephone	800-322-2847
5-Year Projected Return	NA	Minimum Investment	$1,000
Safety Rating (0-100)	68%	Telephone Switching	Unlimited; $5
Yield	0.8%	Total Assets	$41 million

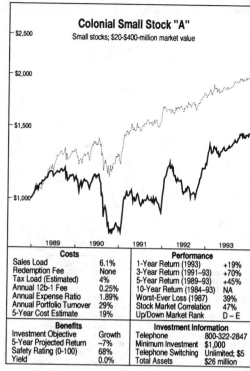

Colonial Small Stock "A"

Small stocks; $20-$400-million market value

Costs		Performance	
Sales Load	6.1%	1-Year Return (1993)	+19%
Redemption Fee	None	3-Year Return (1991–93)	+70%
Tax Load (Estimated)	4%	5-Year Return (1989–93)	+45%
Annual 12b-1 Fee	0.25%	10-Year Return (1984–93)	NA
Annual Expense Ratio	1.89%	Worst-Ever Loss (1987)	39%
Annual Portfolio Turnover	29%	Stock Market Correlation	47%
5-Year Cost Estimate	19%	Up/Down Market Rank	D – E

Benefits		Investment Information	
Investment Objective	Growth	Telephone	800-322-2847
5-Year Projected Return	–7%	Minimum Investment	$1,000
Safety Rating (0-100)	68%	Telephone Switching	Unlimited; $5
Yield	0.0%	Total Assets	$26 million

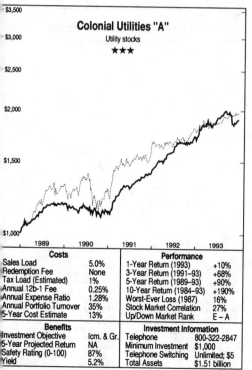

Colonial Utilities "A"

Utility stocks

★★★

Costs		Performance	
Sales Load	5.0%	1-Year Return (1993)	+10%
Redemption Fee	None	3-Year Return (1991–93)	+68%
Tax Load (Estimated)	1%	5-Year Return (1989–93)	+90%
Annual 12b-1 Fee	0.25%	10-Year Return (1984–93)	+190%
Annual Expense Ratio	1.28%	Worst-Ever Loss (1987)	16%
Annual Portfolio Turnover	35%	Stock Market Correlation	27%
5-Year Cost Estimate	13%	Up/Down Market Rank	E – A

Benefits		Investment Information	
Investment Objective	Icm. & Gr.	Telephone	800-322-2847
5-Year Projected Return	NA	Minimum Investment	$1,000
Safety Rating (0-100)	87%	Telephone Switching	Unlimited; $5
Yield	5.2%	Total Assets	$1.51 billion

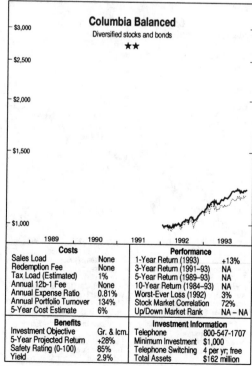

Columbia Balanced

Diversified stocks and bonds

★★

Costs		Performance	
Sales Load	None	1-Year Return (1993)	+13%
Redemption Fee	None	3-Year Return (1991–93)	NA
Tax Load (Estimated)	1%	5-Year Return (1989–93)	NA
Annual 12b-1 Fee	None	10-Year Return (1984–93)	NA
Annual Expense Ratio	0.81%	Worst-Ever Loss (1992)	3%
Annual Portfolio Turnover	134%	Stock Market Correlation	72%
5-Year Cost Estimate	6%	Up/Down Market Rank	NA – NA

Benefits		Investment Information	
Investment Objective	Gr. & Icm.	Telephone	800-547-1707
5-Year Projected Return	+28%	Minimum Investment	$1,000
Safety Rating (0-100)	85%	Telephone Switching	4 per yr; free
Yield	2.9%	Total Assets	$162 million

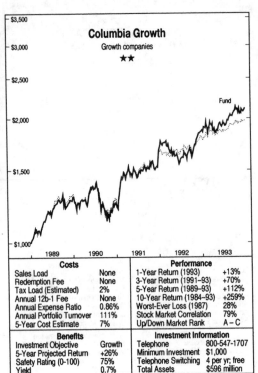

Columbia Growth
Growth companies
★★

Costs		Performance	
Sales Load	None	1-Year Return (1993)	+13%
Redemption Fee	None	3-Year Return (1991–93)	+70%
Tax Load (Estimated)	2%	5-Year Return (1989–93)	+112%
Annual 12b-1 Fee	None	10-Year Return (1984–93)	+259%
Annual Expense Ratio	0.86%	Worst-Ever Loss (1987)	28%
Annual Portfolio Turnover	111%	Stock Market Correlation	79%
5-Year Cost Estimate	7%	Up/Down Market Rank	A – C

Benefits		Investment Information	
Investment Objective	Growth	Telephone	800-547-1707
5-Year Projected Return	+26%	Minimum Investment	$1,000
Safety Rating (0-100)	75%	Telephone Switching	4 per yr; free
Yield	0.7%	Total Assets	$596 million

Columbia Special
Smaller stocks; more aggressive than S&P 500
★

Costs		Performance	
Sales Load	None	1-Year Return (1993)	+22%
Redemption Fee	None	3-Year Return (1991–93)	+108%
Tax Load (Estimated)	2%	5-Year Return (1989–93)	+142%
Annual 12b-1 Fee	None	10-Year Return (1984–93)	NA
Annual Expense Ratio	1.19%	Worst-Ever Loss (1987)	43%
Annual Portfolio Turnover	184%	Stock Market Correlation	58%
5-Year Cost Estimate	8%	Up/Down Market Rank	A – E

Benefits		Investment Information	
Investment Objective	Growth	Telephone	800-547-1707
5-Year Projected Return	+31%	Minimum Investment	$2,000
Safety Rating (0-100)	66%	Telephone Switching	4 per yr; free
Yield	0.1%	Total Assets	$708 million

Common Sense Growth
Diversified stocks; no alcohol, tobacco

Costs		Performance	
Sales Load	9.3%	1-Year Return (1993)	+9%
Redemption Fee	None	3-Year Return (1991–93)	+63%
Tax Load (Estimated)	1%	5-Year Return (1989–93)	+101%
Annual 12b-1 Fee	None	10-Year Return (1984–93)	NA
Annual Expense Ratio	1.18%	Worst-Ever Loss (1987)	38%
Annual Portfolio Turnover	134%	Stock Market Correlation	86%
5-Year Cost Estimate	17%	Up/Down Market Rank	B – D

Benefits		Investment Information	
Investment Objective	Growth	Telephone	800-544-5445
5-Year Projected Return	+6%	Minimum Investment	$250
Safety Rating (0-100)	71%	Telephone Switching	Mail only
Yield	0.8%	Total Assets	$2.04 billion

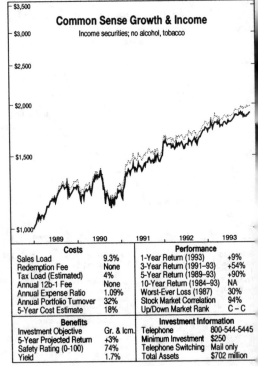

Common Sense Growth & Income
Income securities; no alcohol, tobacco

Costs		Performance	
Sales Load	9.3%	1-Year Return (1993)	+9%
Redemption Fee	None	3-Year Return (1991–93)	+54%
Tax Load (Estimated)	4%	5-Year Return (1989–93)	+90%
Annual 12b-1 Fee	None	10-Year Return (1984–93)	NA
Annual Expense Ratio	1.09%	Worst-Ever Loss (1987)	30%
Annual Portfolio Turnover	32%	Stock Market Correlation	94%
5-Year Cost Estimate	18%	Up/Down Market Rank	C – C

Benefits		Investment Information	
Investment Objective	Gr. & Icm.	Telephone	800-544-5445
5-Year Projected Return	+3%	Minimum Investment	$250
Safety Rating (0-100)	74%	Telephone Switching	Mail only
Yield	1.7%	Total Assets	$702 million

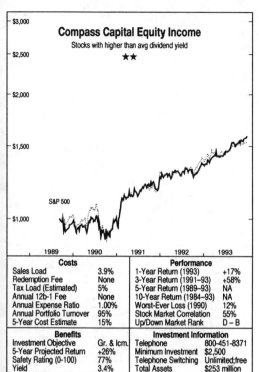

Compass Capital Equity Income

Stocks with higher than avg dividend yield

★★

Costs		Performance	
Sales Load	3.9%	1-Year Return (1993)	+17%
Redemption Fee	None	3-Year Return (1991–93)	+58%
Tax Load (Estimated)	5%	5-Year Return (1989–93)	NA
Annual 12b-1 Fee	None	10-Year Return (1984–93)	NA
Annual Expense Ratio	1.00%	Worst-Ever Loss (1990)	12%
Annual Portfolio Turnover	95%	Stock Market Correlation	55%
5-Year Cost Estimate	15%	Up/Down Market Rank	D – B

Benefits		Investment Information	
Investment Objective	Gr. & Icm.	Telephone	800-451-8371
5-Year Projected Return	+26%	Minimum Investment	$2,500
Safety Rating (0-100)	77%	Telephone Switching	Unlimited;free
Yield	3.4%	Total Assets	$253 million

Compass Capital Growth

Favorable debt-equity; mid-cap; earnings grth

Costs		Performance	
Sales Load	3.9%	1-Year Return (1993)	+4%
Redemption Fee	None	3-Year Return (1991–93)	+43%
Tax Load (Estimated)	2%	5-Year Return (1989–93)	NA
Annual 12b-1 Fee	None	10-Year Return (1984–93)	NA
Annual Expense Ratio	0.98%	Worst-Ever Loss (1990)	21%
Annual Portfolio Turnover	126%	Stock Market Correlation	75%
5-Year Cost Estimate	12%	Up/Down Market Rank	C – D

Benefits		Investment Information	
Investment Objective	Gr. & Icm.	Telephone	800-451-8371
5-Year Projected Return	−1%	Minimum Investment	$2,500
Safety Rating (0-100)	68%	Telephone Switching	Unlimited;free
Yield	0.6%	Total Assets	$153 million

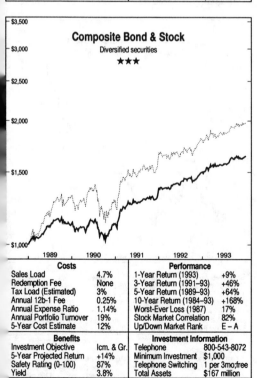

Composite Bond & Stock

Diversified securities

★★★

Costs		Performance	
Sales Load	4.7%	1-Year Return (1993)	+9%
Redemption Fee	None	3-Year Return (1991–93)	+46%
Tax Load (Estimated)	3%	5-Year Return (1989–93)	+64%
Annual 12b-1 Fee	0.25%	10-Year Return (1984–93)	+168%
Annual Expense Ratio	1.14%	Worst-Ever Loss (1987)	17%
Annual Portfolio Turnover	19%	Stock Market Correlation	82%
5-Year Cost Estimate	12%	Up/Down Market Rank	E – A

Benefits		Investment Information	
Investment Objective	Icm. & Gr.	Telephone	800-543-8072
5-Year Projected Return	+14%	Minimum Investment	$1,000
Safety Rating (0-100)	87%	Telephone Switching	1 per 3mo;free
Yield	3.8%	Total Assets	$167 million

Composite Growth

Undervalued stocks

Costs		Performance	
Sales Load	4.7%	1-Year Return (1993)	+7%
Redemption Fee	None	3-Year Return (1991–93)	+51%
Tax Load (Estimated)	4%	5-Year Return (1989–93)	+59%
Annual 12b-1 Fee	0.25%	10-Year Return (1984–93)	+190%
Annual Expense Ratio	1.12%	Worst-Ever Loss (1987)	25%
Annual Portfolio Turnover	54%	Stock Market Correlation	81%
5-Year Cost Estimate	15%	Up/Down Market Rank	D – B

Benefits		Investment Information	
Investment Objective	Gr. & Icm.	Telephone	800-543-8072
5-Year Projected Return	+3%	Minimum Investment	$1,000
Safety Rating (0-100)	76%	Telephone Switching	1 per 3mo;free
Yield	1.6%	Total Assets	$96 million

Composite Northwest 50
Matches N.W. 50 Index; pacific northwest cos

Costs		Performance	
Sales Load	4.7%	1-Year Return (1993)	+2%
Redemption Fee	None	3-Year Return (1991–93)	+53%
Tax Load (Estimated)	6%	5-Year Return (1989–93)	+108%
Annual 12b-1 Fee	0.25%	10-Year Return (1984–93)	NA
Annual Expense Ratio	1.11%	Worst-Ever Loss (1987)	41%
Annual Portfolio Turnover	8%	Stock Market Correlation	68%
5-Year Cost Estimate	12%	Up/Down Market Rank	B – D

Benefits		Investment Information	
Investment Objective	Growth	Telephone	800-543-8072
5-Year Projected Return	+2%	Minimum Investment	$1,000
Safety Rating (0-100)	64%	Telephone Switching	1 per 3mo;free
Yield	0.5%	Total Assets	$172 million

Connecticut Mutual - Growth
Diversified stocks
★★

Costs		Performance	
Sales Load	5.3%	1-Year Return (1993)	+21%
Redemption Fee	None	3-Year Return (1991–93)	+85%
Tax Load (Estimated)	2%	5-Year Return (1989–93)	+130%
Annual 12b-1 Fee	0.10%	10-Year Return (1984–93)	NA
Annual Expense Ratio	1.12%	Worst-Ever Loss (1987)	34%
Annual Portfolio Turnover	142%	Stock Market Correlation	75%
5-Year Cost Estimate	14%	Up/Down Market Rank	A – D

Benefits		Investment Information	
Investment Objective	Growth	Telephone	800-322-2642
5-Year Projected Return	+20%	Minimum Investment	$1,000
Safety Rating (0-100)	75%	Telephone Switching	Unlimited; $5
Yield	2.0%	Total Assets	$59 million

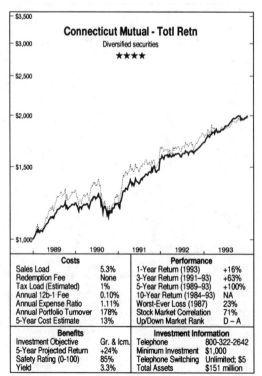

Connecticut Mutual - Totl Retn
Diversified securities
★★★★

Costs		Performance	
Sales Load	5.3%	1-Year Return (1993)	+16%
Redemption Fee	None	3-Year Return (1991–93)	+63%
Tax Load (Estimated)	1%	5-Year Return (1989–93)	+100%
Annual 12b-1 Fee	0.10%	10-Year Return (1984–93)	NA
Annual Expense Ratio	1.11%	Worst-Ever Loss (1987)	23%
Annual Portfolio Turnover	178%	Stock Market Correlation	71%
5-Year Cost Estimate	13%	Up/Down Market Rank	D – A

Benefits		Investment Information	
Investment Objective	Gr. & Icm.	Telephone	800-322-2642
5-Year Projected Return	+24%	Minimum Investment	$1,000
Safety Rating (0-100)	85%	Telephone Switching	Unlimited; $5
Yield	3.3%	Total Assets	$151 million

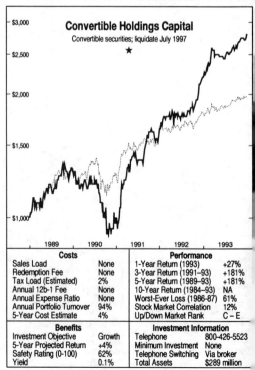

Convertible Holdings Capital
Convertible securities; liquidate July 1997
★

Costs		Performance	
Sales Load	None	1-Year Return (1993)	+27%
Redemption Fee	None	3-Year Return (1991–93)	+181%
Tax Load (Estimated)	2%	5-Year Return (1989–93)	+181%
Annual 12b-1 Fee	None	10-Year Return (1984–93)	NA
Annual Expense Ratio	None	Worst-Ever Loss (1986-87)	61%
Annual Portfolio Turnover	94%	Stock Market Correlation	12%
5-Year Cost Estimate	4%	Up/Down Market Rank	C – E

Benefits		Investment Information	
Investment Objective	Growth	Telephone	800-426-5523
5-Year Projected Return	+4%	Minimum Investment	None
Safety Rating (0-100)	62%	Telephone Switching	Via broker
Yield	0.1%	Total Assets	$289 million

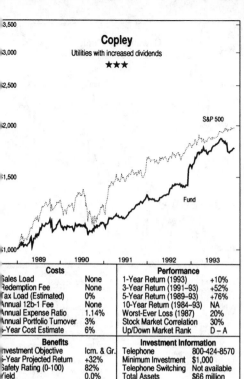

Copley
Utilities with increased dividends
★★★

(chart showing S&P 500 and Fund, 1989–1993)

Costs		Performance	
Sales Load	None	1-Year Return (1993)	+10%
Redemption Fee	None	3-Year Return (1991–93)	+52%
Tax Load (Estimated)	0%	5-Year Return (1989–93)	+76%
Annual 12b-1 Fee	None	10-Year Return (1984–93)	NA
Annual Expense Ratio	1.14%	Worst-Ever Loss (1987)	20%
Annual Portfolio Turnover	3%	Stock Market Correlation	30%
5-Year Cost Estimate	6%	Up/Down Market Rank	D – A

Benefits		Investment Information	
Investment Objective	Icm. & Gr.	Telephone	800-424-8570
5-Year Projected Return	+32%	Minimum Investment	$1,000
Safety Rating (0-100)	82%	Telephone Switching	Not available
Yield	0.0%	Total Assets	$66 million

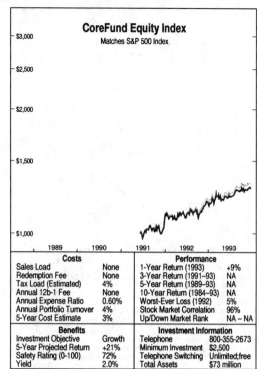

CoreFund Equity Index
Matches S&P 500 Index

(chart, 1989–1993)

Costs		Performance	
Sales Load	None	1-Year Return (1993)	+9%
Redemption Fee	None	3-Year Return (1991–93)	NA
Tax Load (Estimated)	4%	5-Year Return (1989–93)	NA
Annual 12b-1 Fee	None	10-Year Return (1984–93)	NA
Annual Expense Ratio	0.60%	Worst-Ever Loss (1992)	5%
Annual Portfolio Turnover	4%	Stock Market Correlation	96%
5-Year Cost Estimate	3%	Up/Down Market Rank	NA – NA

Benefits		Investment Information	
Investment Objective	Growth	Telephone	800-355-2673
5-Year Projected Return	+21%	Minimum Investment	$2,500
Safety Rating (0-100)	72%	Telephone Switching	Unlimited;free
Yield	2.0%	Total Assets	$73 million

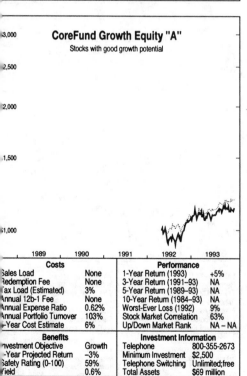

CoreFund Growth Equity "A"
Stocks with good growth potential

(chart, 1989–1993)

Costs		Performance	
Sales Load	None	1-Year Return (1993)	+5%
Redemption Fee	None	3-Year Return (1991–93)	NA
Tax Load (Estimated)	3%	5-Year Return (1989–93)	NA
Annual 12b-1 Fee	None	10-Year Return (1984–93)	NA
Annual Expense Ratio	0.62%	Worst-Ever Loss (1992)	9%
Annual Portfolio Turnover	103%	Stock Market Correlation	63%
5-Year Cost Estimate	6%	Up/Down Market Rank	NA – NA

Benefits		Investment Information	
Investment Objective	Growth	Telephone	800-355-2673
5-Year Projected Return	–3%	Minimum Investment	$2,500
Safety Rating (0-100)	59%	Telephone Switching	Unlimited;free
Yield	0.6%	Total Assets	$69 million

Counsellors Tandem Capitl Shrs
Utility securities
★

(chart, 1989–1993)

Costs		Performance	
Sales Load	None	1-Year Return (1993)	+6%
Redemption Fee	None	3-Year Return (1991–93)	+46%
Tax Load (Estimated)	6%	5-Year Return (1989–93)	+152%
Annual 12b-1 Fee	None	10-Year Return (1984–93)	NA
Annual Expense Ratio	1.30%	Worst-Ever Loss (1987)	58%
Annual Portfolio Turnover	40%	Stock Market Correlation	14%
5-Year Cost Estimate	14%	Up/Down Market Rank	C – D

Benefits		Investment Information	
Investment Objective	Gr. & Icm.	Telephone	800-888-6878
5-Year Projected Return	+3%	Minimum Investment	None
Safety Rating (0-100)	61%	Telephone Switching	Via broker
Yield	0.0%	Total Assets	$79 million

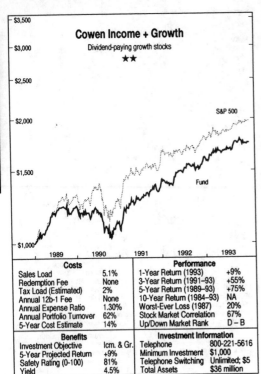

Cowen Income + Growth
Dividend-paying growth stocks
★★

Costs		Performance	
Sales Load	5.1%	1-Year Return (1993)	+9%
Redemption Fee	None	3-Year Return (1991–93)	+55%
Tax Load (Estimated)	2%	5-Year Return (1989–93)	+75%
Annual 12b-1 Fee	None	10-Year Return (1984–93)	NA
Annual Expense Ratio	1.30%	Worst-Ever Loss (1987)	20%
Annual Portfolio Turnover	62%	Stock Market Correlation	67%
5-Year Cost Estimate	14%	Up/Down Market Rank	D – B

Benefits		Investment Information	
Investment Objective	Icm. & Gr.	Telephone	800-221-5616
5-Year Projected Return	+9%	Minimum Investment	$1,000
Safety Rating (0-100)	81%	Telephone Switching	Unlimited; $5
Yield	4.5%	Total Assets	$36 million

Cowen Opportunity
Science and technology stocks

Costs		Performance	
Sales Load	5.1%	1-Year Return (1993)	+32%
Redemption Fee	None	3-Year Return (1991–93)	+101%
Tax Load (Estimated)	Neg.	5-Year Return (1989–93)	+149%
Annual 12b-1 Fee	None	10-Year Return (1984–93)	NA
Annual Expense Ratio	1.83%	Worst-Ever Loss (1990)	33%
Annual Portfolio Turnover	160%	Stock Market Correlation	45%
5-Year Cost Estimate	15%	Up/Down Market Rank	A – E

Benefits		Investment Information	
Investment Objective	Growth	Telephone	800-221-5616
5-Year Projected Return	NA	Minimum Investment	$1,000
Safety Rating (0-100)	63%	Telephone Switching	Unlimited; $5
Yield	0.0%	Total Assets	$16 million

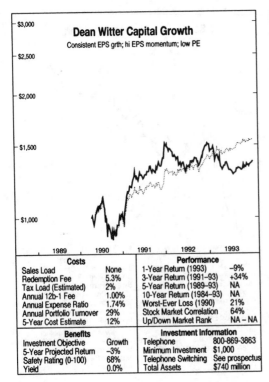

Dean Witter Capital Growth
Consistent EPS grth; hi EPS momentum; low PE

Costs		Performance	
Sales Load	None	1-Year Return (1993)	–9%
Redemption Fee	5.3%	3-Year Return (1991–93)	+34%
Tax Load (Estimated)	2%	5-Year Return (1989–93)	NA
Annual 12b-1 Fee	1.00%	10-Year Return (1984–93)	NA
Annual Expense Ratio	1.74%	Worst-Ever Loss (1990)	21%
Annual Portfolio Turnover	29%	Stock Market Correlation	64%
5-Year Cost Estimate	12%	Up/Down Market Rank	NA – NA

Benefits		Investment Information	
Investment Objective	Growth	Telephone	800-869-3863
5-Year Projected Return	–3%	Minimum Investment	$1,000
Safety Rating (0-100)	68%	Telephone Switching	See prospectus
Yield	0.0%	Total Assets	$740 million

Dean Witter Convertible
Convertible securities

Costs		Performance	
Sales Load	None	1-Year Return (1993)	+16%
Redemption Fee	5.3%	3-Year Return (1991–93)	+57%
Tax Load (Estimated)	Neg.	5-Year Return (1989–93)	+56%
Annual 12b-1 Fee	1.00%	10-Year Return (1984–93)	NA
Annual Expense Ratio	1.92%	Worst-Ever Loss (1987)	32%
Annual Portfolio Turnover	194%	Stock Market Correlation	64%
5-Year Cost Estimate	11%	Up/Down Market Rank	E – C

Benefits		Investment Information	
Investment Objective	Gr. & Icm.	Telephone	800-869-3863
5-Year Projected Return	+6%	Minimum Investment	$1,000
Safety Rating (0-100)	79%	Telephone Switching	See prospectu
Yield	3.5%	Total Assets	$208 million

Dean Witter Developing Growth
High earnings growth stocks

Costs		Performance	
Sales Load	None	1-Year Return (1993)	+31%
Redemption Fee	5.3%	3-Year Return (1991–93)	+89%
Tax Load (Estimated)	0%	5-Year Return (1989–93)	+109%
Annual 12b-1 Fee	1.00%	10-Year Return (1984–93)	+122%
Annual Expense Ratio	1.86%	Worst-Ever Loss (1990)	38%
Annual Portfolio Turnover	153%	Stock Market Correlation	50%
5-Year Cost Estimate	11%	Up/Down Market Rank	C – E
Benefits		**Investment Information**	
Investment Objective	Growth	Telephone	800-869-3863
5-Year Projected Return	+32%	Minimum Investment	$1,000
Safety Rating (0-100)	58%	Telephone Switching	See prospectus
Yield	0.0%	Total Assets	$214 million

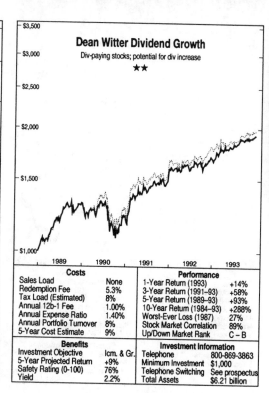

Dean Witter Dividend Growth
Div-paying stocks; potential for div increase
★★

Costs		Performance	
Sales Load	None	1-Year Return (1993)	+14%
Redemption Fee	5.3%	3-Year Return (1991–93)	+58%
Tax Load (Estimated)	8%	5-Year Return (1989–93)	+93%
Annual 12b-1 Fee	1.00%	10-Year Return (1984–93)	+288%
Annual Expense Ratio	1.40%	Worst-Ever Loss (1987)	27%
Annual Portfolio Turnover	8%	Stock Market Correlation	89%
5-Year Cost Estimate	9%	Up/Down Market Rank	C – B
Benefits		**Investment Information**	
Investment Objective	Icm. & Gr.	Telephone	800-869-3863
5-Year Projected Return	+9%	Minimum Investment	$1,000
Safety Rating (0-100)	76%	Telephone Switching	See prospectus
Yield	2.2%	Total Assets	$6.21 billion

Dean Witter Equity Income
Diversified; div-paying stocks; option stratg

Costs		Performance	
Sales Load	None	1-Year Return (1993)	+0%
Redemption Fee	5.3%	3-Year Return (1991–93)	+29%
Tax Load (Estimated)	Neg.	5-Year Return (1989–93)	+56%
Annual 12b-1 Fee	1.00%	10-Year Return (1984–93)	NA
Annual Expense Ratio	2.04%	Worst-Ever Loss (1987)	30%
Annual Portfolio Turnover	120%	Stock Market Correlation	68%
5-Year Cost Estimate	12%	Up/Down Market Rank	C – C
Benefits		**Investment Information**	
Investment Objective	Icm. & Gr.	Telephone	800-869-3863
5-Year Projected Return	+0%	Minimum Investment	$1,000
Safety Rating (0-100)	76%	Telephone Switching	See prospectus
Yield	5.1%	Total Assets	$159 million

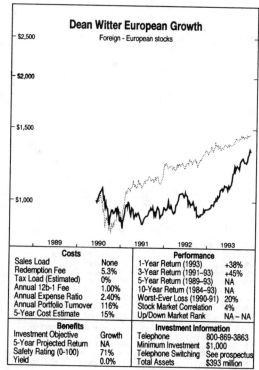

Dean Witter European Growth
Foreign - European stocks

Costs		Performance	
Sales Load	None	1-Year Return (1993)	+38%
Redemption Fee	5.3%	3-Year Return (1991–93)	+45%
Tax Load (Estimated)	0%	5-Year Return (1989–93)	NA
Annual 12b-1 Fee	1.00%	10-Year Return (1984–93)	NA
Annual Expense Ratio	2.40%	Worst-Ever Loss (1990-91)	20%
Annual Portfolio Turnover	116%	Stock Market Correlation	4%
5-Year Cost Estimate	15%	Up/Down Market Rank	NA – NA
Benefits		**Investment Information**	
Investment Objective	Growth	Telephone	800-869-3863
5-Year Projected Return	NA	Minimum Investment	$1,000
Safety Rating (0-100)	71%	Telephone Switching	See prospectus
Yield	0.0%	Total Assets	$393 million

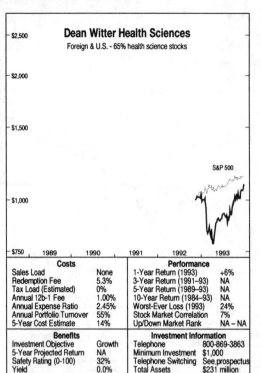

Dean Witter Health Sciences
Foreign & U.S. - 65% health science stocks

Costs		Performance	
Sales Load	None	1-Year Return (1993)	+6%
Redemption Fee	5.3%	3-Year Return (1991–93)	NA
Tax Load (Estimated)	0%	5-Year Return (1989–93)	NA
Annual 12b-1 Fee	1.00%	10-Year Return (1984–93)	NA
Annual Expense Ratio	2.45%	Worst-Ever Loss (1993)	24%
Annual Portfolio Turnover	55%	Stock Market Correlation	7%
5-Year Cost Estimate	14%	Up/Down Market Rank	NA – NA

Benefits		Investment Information	
Investment Objective	Growth	Telephone	800-869-3863
5-Year Projected Return	NA	Minimum Investment	$1,000
Safety Rating (0-100)	32%	Telephone Switching	See prospectus
Yield	0.0%	Total Assets	$231 million

Dean Witter Managed Assets
Equities, fixed-income, money market
★

Costs		Performance	
Sales Load	None	1-Year Return (1993)	+9%
Redemption Fee	5.3%	3-Year Return (1991–93)	+46%
Tax Load (Estimated)	Neg.	5-Year Return (1989–93)	+58%
Annual 12b-1 Fee	1.00%	10-Year Return (1984–93)	NA
Annual Expense Ratio	1.79%	Worst-Ever Loss (1990)	12%
Annual Portfolio Turnover	76%	Stock Market Correlation	78%
5-Year Cost Estimate	11%	Up/Down Market Rank	E – A

Benefits		Investment Information	
Investment Objective	Gr. & Icm.	Telephone	800-869-3863
5-Year Projected Return	+12%	Minimum Investment	$1,000
Safety Rating (0-100)	84%	Telephone Switching	See prospectus
Yield	2.1%	Total Assets	$247 million

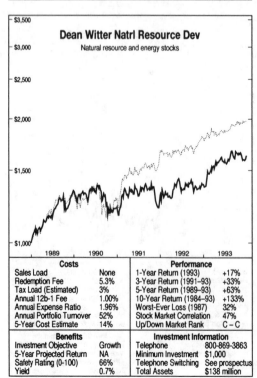

Dean Witter Natrl Resource Dev
Natural resource and energy stocks

Costs		Performance	
Sales Load	None	1-Year Return (1993)	+17%
Redemption Fee	5.3%	3-Year Return (1991–93)	+33%
Tax Load (Estimated)	3%	5-Year Return (1989–93)	+63%
Annual 12b-1 Fee	1.00%	10-Year Return (1984–93)	+133%
Annual Expense Ratio	1.96%	Worst-Ever Loss (1987)	32%
Annual Portfolio Turnover	52%	Stock Market Correlation	47%
5-Year Cost Estimate	14%	Up/Down Market Rank	C – C

Benefits		Investment Information	
Investment Objective	Growth	Telephone	800-869-3863
5-Year Projected Return	NA	Minimum Investment	$1,000
Safety Rating (0-100)	66%	Telephone Switching	See prospectus
Yield	0.7%	Total Assets	$138 million

Dean Witter Pacific Growth
Foreign - Pac-Basin; high EPS growth; low PE
★

Costs		Performance	
Sales Load	None	1-Year Return (1993)	+95%
Redemption Fee	5.3%	3-Year Return (1991–93)	+145%
Tax Load (Estimated)	2%	5-Year Return (1989–93)	NA
Annual 12b-1 Fee	1.00%	10-Year Return (1984–93)	NA
Annual Expense Ratio	2.97%	Worst-Ever Loss (1992)	12%
Annual Portfolio Turnover	50%	Stock Market Correlation	2%
5-Year Cost Estimate	19%	Up/Down Market Rank	NA – NA

Benefits		Investment Information	
Investment Objective	Growth	Telephone	800-869-3863
5-Year Projected Return	NA	Minimum Investment	$1,000
Safety Rating (0-100)	70%	Telephone Switching	See prospectus
Yield	0.0%	Total Assets	$1.10 billion

Dean Witter Precious Metals
International & U.S. gold stocks & bullion

S&P 500

Costs		Performance	
Sales Load	None	1-Year Return (1993)	+56%
Redemption Fee	5.3%	3-Year Return (1991–93)	NA
Tax Load (Estimated)	2%	5-Year Return (1989–93)	NA
Annual 12b-1 Fee	1.00%	10-Year Return (1984–93)	NA
Annual Expense Ratio	3.30%	Worst-Ever Loss (1991-93)	22%
Annual Portfolio Turnover	36%	Stock Market Correlation	–1%
5-Year Cost Estimate	22%	Up/Down Market Rank	NA – NA

Benefits		Investment Information	
Investment Objective	Growth	Telephone	800-869-3863
5-Year Projected Return	NA	Minimum Investment	$1,000
Safety Rating (0-100)	49%	Telephone Switching	See prospectus
Yield	0.0%	Total Assets	$43 million

Dean Witter Strategist
Asset alloc; equities; bonds & money markets
★

Costs		Performance	
Sales Load	None	1-Year Return (1993)	+8%
Redemption Fee	5.3%	3-Year Return (1991–93)	+53%
Tax Load (Estimated)	2%	5-Year Return (1989–93)	+93%
Annual 12b-1 Fee	1.00%	10-Year Return (1984–93)	NA
Annual Expense Ratio	1.62%	Worst-Ever Loss (1990)	18%
Annual Portfolio Turnover	98%	Stock Market Correlation	83%
5-Year Cost Estimate	12%	Up/Down Market Rank	B – B

Benefits		Investment Information	
Investment Objective	Gr. & Icm.	Telephone	800-869-3863
5-Year Projected Return	+19%	Minimum Investment	$1,000
Safety Rating (0-100)	77%	Telephone Switching	See prospectus
Yield	1.8%	Total Assets	$809 million

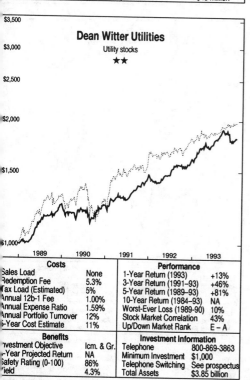

Dean Witter Utilities
Utility stocks
★★

Costs		Performance	
Sales Load	None	1-Year Return (1993)	+13%
Redemption Fee	5.3%	3-Year Return (1991–93)	+46%
Tax Load (Estimated)	5%	5-Year Return (1989–93)	+81%
Annual 12b-1 Fee	1.00%	10-Year Return (1984–93)	NA
Annual Expense Ratio	1.59%	Worst-Ever Loss (1989-90)	10%
Annual Portfolio Turnover	12%	Stock Market Correlation	43%
5-Year Cost Estimate	11%	Up/Down Market Rank	E – A

Benefits		Investment Information	
Investment Objective	Icm. & Gr.	Telephone	800-869-3863
5-Year Projected Return	NA	Minimum Investment	$1,000
Safety Rating (0-100)	86%	Telephone Switching	See prospectus
Yield	4.3%	Total Assets	$3.85 billion

Dean Witter Value-Added Mkt Eq
S&P 500; equal dollar investments

Costs		Performance	
Sales Load	None	1-Year Return (1993)	+13%
Redemption Fee	5.3%	3-Year Return (1991–93)	+68%
Tax Load (Estimated)	6%	5-Year Return (1989–93)	+83%
Annual 12b-1 Fee	1.00%	10-Year Return (1984–93)	NA
Annual Expense Ratio	1.71%	Worst-Ever Loss (1989-90)	26%
Annual Portfolio Turnover	6%	Stock Market Correlation	88%
5-Year Cost Estimate	11%	Up/Down Market Rank	B – E

Benefits		Investment Information	
Investment Objective	Gr. & Icm.	Telephone	800-869-3863
5-Year Projected Return	+6%	Minimum Investment	$1,000
Safety Rating (0-100)	71%	Telephone Switching	See prospectus
Yield	0.8%	Total Assets	$330 million

Dean Witter Worldwide Invstmnt
Foreign & U.S. - diversified securities

Costs		Performance	
Sales Load	None	1-Year Return (1993)	+41%
Redemption Fee	5.3%	3-Year Return (1991–93)	+55%
Tax Load (Estimated)	0%	5-Year Return (1989–93)	+63%
Annual 12b-1 Fee	1.00%	10-Year Return (1984–93)	+237%
Annual Expense Ratio	2.40%	Worst-Ever Loss (1987)	25%
Annual Portfolio Turnover	72%	Stock Market Correlation	27%
5-Year Cost Estimate	14%	Up/Down Market Rank	E – A

Benefits		Investment Information	
Investment Objective	Gr. & Icm.	Telephone	800-869-3863
5-Year Projected Return	NA	Minimum Investment	$1,000
Safety Rating (0-100)	77%	Telephone Switching	See prospectus
Yield	0.0%	Total Assets	$264 million

Delaware Decatur I
Quality stocks, high yield

Costs		Performance	
Sales Load	9.3%	1-Year Return (1993)	+15%
Redemption Fee	None	3-Year Return (1991–93)	+53%
Tax Load (Estimated)	0%	5-Year Return (1989–93)	+62%
Annual 12b-1 Fee	None	10-Year Return (1984–93)	+243%
Annual Expense Ratio	0.72%	Worst-Ever Loss (1987)	27%
Annual Portfolio Turnover	132%	Stock Market Correlation	78%
5-Year Cost Estimate	13%	Up/Down Market Rank	D – B

Benefits		Investment Information	
Investment Objective	Icm. & Gr.	Telephone	800-523-1918
5-Year Projected Return	–10%	Minimum Investment	$250
Safety Rating (0-100)	73%	Telephone Switching	Unlimited;free
Yield	4.6%	Total Assets	$1.56 billion

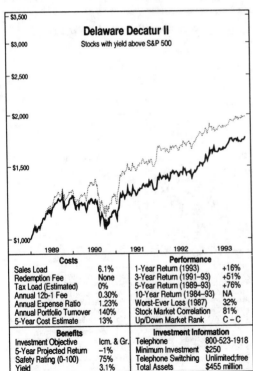

Delaware Decatur II
Stocks with yield above S&P 500

Costs		Performance	
Sales Load	6.1%	1-Year Return (1993)	+16%
Redemption Fee	None	3-Year Return (1991–93)	+51%
Tax Load (Estimated)	0%	5-Year Return (1989–93)	+76%
Annual 12b-1 Fee	0.30%	10-Year Return (1984–93)	NA
Annual Expense Ratio	1.23%	Worst-Ever Loss (1987)	32%
Annual Portfolio Turnover	140%	Stock Market Correlation	81%
5-Year Cost Estimate	13%	Up/Down Market Rank	C – C

Benefits		Investment Information	
Investment Objective	Icm. & Gr.	Telephone	800-523-1918
5-Year Projected Return	–1%	Minimum Investment	$250
Safety Rating (0-100)	75%	Telephone Switching	Unlimited;free
Yield	3.1%	Total Assets	$455 million

Delaware DelCap
Growth companies

Costs		Performance	
Sales Load	6.1%	1-Year Return (1993)	+12%
Redemption Fee	None	3-Year Return (1991–93)	+62%
Tax Load (Estimated)	4%	5-Year Return (1989–93)	+110%
Annual 12b-1 Fee	0.30%	10-Year Return (1984–93)	NA
Annual Expense Ratio	1.39%	Worst-Ever Loss (1987)	36%
Annual Portfolio Turnover	50%	Stock Market Correlation	53%
5-Year Cost Estimate	18%	Up/Down Market Rank	A – E

Benefits		Investment Information	
Investment Objective	Growth	Telephone	800-523-1918
5-Year Projected Return	+11%	Minimum Investment	$250
Safety Rating (0-100)	69%	Telephone Switching	Unlimited;free
Yield	0.0%	Total Assets	$1.04 billion

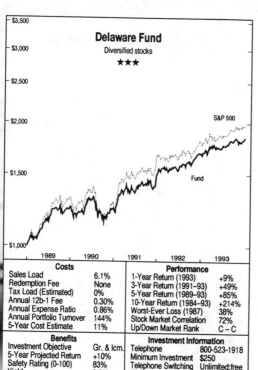

Delaware Fund
Diversified stocks
★★★

Costs		Performance	
Sales Load	6.1%	1-Year Return (1993)	+9%
Redemption Fee	None	3-Year Return (1991–93)	+49%
Tax Load (Estimated)	0%	5-Year Return (1989–93)	+85%
Annual 12b-1 Fee	0.30%	10-Year Return (1984–93)	+214%
Annual Expense Ratio	0.86%	Worst-Ever Loss (1987)	38%
Annual Portfolio Turnover	144%	Stock Market Correlation	72%
5-Year Cost Estimate	11%	Up/Down Market Rank	C – C

Benefits		Investment Information	
Investment Objective	Gr. & Icm.	Telephone	800-523-1918
5-Year Projected Return	+10%	Minimum Investment	$250
Safety Rating (0-100)	83%	Telephone Switching	Unlimited;free
Yield	3.3%	Total Assets	$507 million

Delaware Trend
Stocks; fundamental investment analysis
★

Costs		Performance	
Sales Load	6.1%	1-Year Return (1993)	+22%
Redemption Fee	None	3-Year Return (1991–93)	+161%
Tax Load (Estimated)	Neg.	5-Year Return (1989–93)	+194%
Annual 12b-1 Fee	0.30%	10-Year Return (1984–93)	NA
Annual Expense Ratio	1.33%	Worst-Ever Loss (1987)	46%
Annual Portfolio Turnover	67%	Stock Market Correlation	48%
5-Year Cost Estimate	13%	Up/Down Market Rank	A – E

Benefits		Investment Information	
Investment Objective	Growth	Telephone	800-523-1918
5-Year Projected Return	+36%	Minimum Investment	$250
Safety Rating (0-100)	65%	Telephone Switching	Unlimited;free
Yield	0.0%	Total Assets	$245 million

Delaware Value
Undervalued; out-of-favor stocks
★★

Costs		Performance	
Sales Load	6.1%	1-Year Return (1993)	+19%
Redemption Fee	None	3-Year Return (1991–93)	+106%
Tax Load (Estimated)	3%	5-Year Return (1989–93)	NA
Annual 12b-1 Fee	0.30%	10-Year Return (1984–93)	NA
Annual Expense Ratio	1.93%	Worst-Ever Loss (1989-90)	25%
Annual Portfolio Turnover	46%	Stock Market Correlation	63%
5-Year Cost Estimate	19%	Up/Down Market Rank	B – E

Benefits		Investment Information	
Investment Objective	Growth	Telephone	800-523-1918
5-Year Projected Return	+28%	Minimum Investment	$250
Safety Rating (0-100)	75%	Telephone Switching	Unlimited;free
Yield	0.2%	Total Assets	$127 million

Dimensional - Continental
Foreign - 20% smallest European stocks

Costs		Performance	
Sales Load	1.5%	1-Year Return (1993)	+24%
Redemption Fee	None	3-Year Return (1991–93)	-5%
Tax Load (Estimated)	4%	5-Year Return (1989–93)	+33%
Annual 12b-1 Fee	None	10-Year Return (1984–93)	NA
Annual Expense Ratio	0.90%	Worst-Ever Loss (1990-93)	38%
Annual Portfolio Turnover	6%	Stock Market Correlation	3%
5-Year Cost Estimate	7%	Up/Down Market Rank	D – A

Benefits		Investment Information	
Investment Objective	Growth	Telephone	310-395-8005
5-Year Projected Return	NA	Minimum Investment	$50,000
Safety Rating (0-100)	65%	Telephone Switching	See prospectus
Yield	0.1%	Total Assets	$258 million

Dimensional - Japan
Foreign - Japanese small companies

S&P 500

Costs		Performance	
Sales Load	1.0%	1-Year Return (1993)	+13%
Redemption Fee	None	3-Year Return (1991–93)	–11%
Tax Load (Estimated)	Neg.	5-Year Return (1989–93)	–17%
Annual 12b-1 Fee	None	10-Year Return (1984–93)	NA
Annual Expense Ratio	0.78%	Worst-Ever Loss (1990-92)	58%
Annual Portfolio Turnover	10%	Stock Market Correlation	4%
5-Year Cost Estimate	5%	Up/Down Market Rank	E – B

Benefits		Investment Information	
Investment Objective	Growth	Telephone	310-395-8005
5-Year Projected Return	NA	Minimum Investment	$50,000
Safety Rating (0-100)	23%	Telephone Switching	Not available
Yield	0.0%	Total Assets	$289 million

Dimensional - US Small Company
20% smallest NYSE, AMEX and OTC stocks
★

Costs		Performance	
Sales Load	None	1-Year Return (1993)	+20%
Redemption Fee	None	3-Year Return (1991–93)	+115%
Tax Load (Estimated)	Neg.	5-Year Return (1989–93)	+85%
Annual 12b-1 Fee	None	10-Year Return (1984–93)	NA
Annual Expense Ratio	0.70%	Worst-Ever Loss (1987)	36%
Annual Portfolio Turnover	4%	Stock Market Correlation	40%
5-Year Cost Estimate	4%	Up/Down Market Rank	D – D

Benefits		Investment Information	
Investment Objective	Growth	Telephone	310-395-8005
5-Year Projected Return	+32%	Minimum Investment	$50,000
Safety Rating (0-100)	76%	Telephone Switching	See prospectus
Yield	0.2%	Total Assets	$614 million

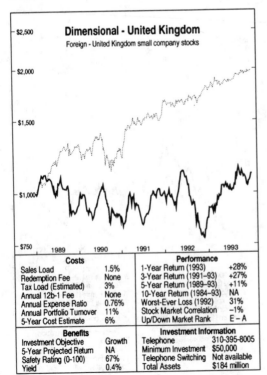

Dimensional - United Kingdom
Foreign - United Kingdom small company stocks

Costs		Performance	
Sales Load	1.5%	1-Year Return (1993)	+28%
Redemption Fee	None	3-Year Return (1991–93)	+27%
Tax Load (Estimated)	3%	5-Year Return (1989–93)	+11%
Annual 12b-1 Fee	None	10-Year Return (1984–93)	NA
Annual Expense Ratio	0.76%	Worst-Ever Loss (1992)	31%
Annual Portfolio Turnover	11%	Stock Market Correlation	–1%
5-Year Cost Estimate	6%	Up/Down Market Rank	E – A

Benefits		Investment Information	
Investment Objective	Growth	Telephone	310-395-8005
5-Year Projected Return	NA	Minimum Investment	$50,000
Safety Rating (0-100)	67%	Telephone Switching	Not available
Yield	0.4%	Total Assets	$184 million

Dodge & Cox Balanced
Diversified securities
★★★★★

Costs		Performance	
Sales Load	None	1-Year Return (1993)	+16%
Redemption Fee	None	3-Year Return (1991–93)	+55%
Tax Load (Estimated)	5%	5-Year Return (1989–93)	+92%
Annual 12b-1 Fee	None	10-Year Return (1984–93)	+275%
Annual Expense Ratio	0.63%	Worst-Ever Loss (1987)	22%
Annual Portfolio Turnover	6%	Stock Market Correlation	81%
5-Year Cost Estimate	4%	Up/Down Market Rank	D – A

Benefits		Investment Information	
Investment Objective	Icm. & Gr.	Telephone	415-434-0311
5-Year Projected Return	+24%	Minimum Investment	$2,500
Safety Rating (0-100)	83%	Telephone Switching	Mail only
Yield	2.7%	Total Assets	$424 million

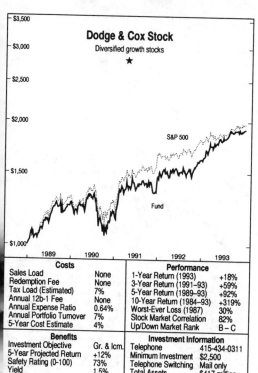

Dodge & Cox Stock
Diversified growth stocks
★

S&P 500

Fund

Costs			Performance	
Sales Load	None	1-Year Return (1993)	+18%
Redemption Fee	None	3-Year Return (1991–93)	+59%
Tax Load (Estimated)	7%	5-Year Return (1989–93)	+92%
Annual 12b-1 Fee	None	10-Year Return (1984–93)	+319%
Annual Expense Ratio	0.64%	Worst-Ever Loss (1987)	30%
Annual Portfolio Turnover	7%	Stock Market Correlation	82%
5-Year Cost Estimate	4%	Up/Down Market Rank	B – C
Benefits		**Investment Information**	
Investment Objective	Gr. & Icm.	Telephone	415-434-0311
5-Year Projected Return	+12%	Minimum Investment	$2,500
Safety Rating (0-100)	73%	Telephone Switching	Mail only
Yield	1.5%	Total Assets	$417 million

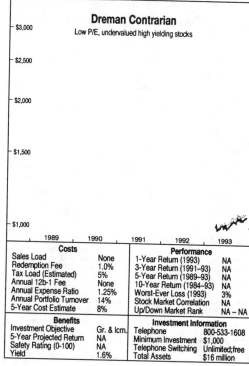

Dreman Contrarian
Low P/E, undervalued high yielding stocks

Costs			Performance	
Sales Load	None	1-Year Return (1993)	NA
Redemption Fee	1.0%	3-Year Return (1991–93)	NA
Tax Load (Estimated)	5%	5-Year Return (1989–93)	NA
Annual 12b-1 Fee	None	10-Year Return (1984–93)	NA
Annual Expense Ratio	1.25%	Worst-Ever Loss (1993)	3%
Annual Portfolio Turnover	14%	Stock Market Correlation	NA
5-Year Cost Estimate	8%	Up/Down Market Rank	NA – NA
Benefits		**Investment Information**	
Investment Objective	Gr. & Icm.	Telephone	800-533-1608
5-Year Projected Return	NA	Minimum Investment	$1,000
Safety Rating (0-100)	NA	Telephone Switching	Unlimited;free
Yield	1.6%	Total Assets	$16 million

Dreyfus Appreciation
Undervalued stocks; market timing
★

Costs			Performance	
Sales Load	None	1-Year Return (1993)	+1%
Redemption Fee	None	3-Year Return (1991–93)	+45%
Tax Load (Estimated)	4%	5-Year Return (1989–93)	+80%
Annual 12b-1 Fee	0.23%	10-Year Return (1984–93)	NA
Annual Expense Ratio	1.14%	Worst-Ever Loss (1987)	35%
Annual Portfolio Turnover	3%	Stock Market Correlation	75%
5-Year Cost Estimate	6%	Up/Down Market Rank	C – C
Benefits		**Investment Information**	
Investment Objective	Gr. & Icm.	Telephone	800-645-6561
5-Year Projected Return	+7%	Minimum Investment	$2,500
Safety Rating (0-100)	73%	Telephone Switching	Unlimited;free
Yield	1.8%	Total Assets	$244 million

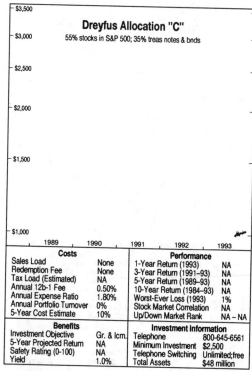

Dreyfus Allocation "C"
55% stocks in S&P 500; 35% treas notes & bnds

Costs			Performance	
Sales Load	None	1-Year Return (1993)	NA
Redemption Fee	None	3-Year Return (1991–93)	NA
Tax Load (Estimated)	NA	5-Year Return (1989–93)	NA
Annual 12b-1 Fee	0.50%	10-Year Return (1984–93)	NA
Annual Expense Ratio	1.80%	Worst-Ever Loss (1993)	1%
Annual Portfolio Turnover	0%	Stock Market Correlation	NA
5-Year Cost Estimate	10%	Up/Down Market Rank	NA – NA
Benefits		**Investment Information**	
Investment Objective	Gr. & Icm.	Telephone	800-645-6561
5-Year Projected Return	NA	Minimum Investment	$2,500
Safety Rating (0-100)	NA	Telephone Switching	Unlimited;free
Yield	1.0%	Total Assets	$48 million

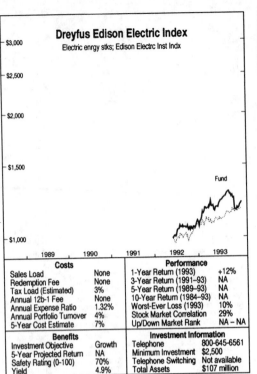

Dreyfus Edison Electric Index
Electric enrgy stks; Edison Electrc Inst Indx

Fund

Costs		Performance	
Sales Load	None	1-Year Return (1993)	+12%
Redemption Fee	None	3-Year Return (1991–93)	NA
Tax Load (Estimated)	3%	5-Year Return (1989–93)	NA
Annual 12b-1 Fee	None	10-Year Return (1984–93)	NA
Annual Expense Ratio	1.32%	Worst-Ever Loss (1993)	10%
Annual Portfolio Turnover	4%	Stock Market Correlation	29%
5-Year Cost Estimate	7%	Up/Down Market Rank	NA – NA

Benefits		Investment Information	
Investment Objective	Growth	Telephone	800-645-6561
5-Year Projected Return	NA	Minimum Investment	$2,500
Safety Rating (0-100)	70%	Telephone Switching	Not available
Yield	4.9%	Total Assets	$107 million

Dreyfus Fund
Diversified stocks
★

Costs		Performance	
Sales Load	None	1-Year Return (1993)	+6%
Redemption Fee	None	3-Year Return (1991–93)	+44%
Tax Load (Estimated)	4%	5-Year Return (1989–93)	+72%
Annual 12b-1 Fee	None	10-Year Return (1984–93)	+202%
Annual Expense Ratio	0.74%	Worst-Ever Loss (1987)	26%
Annual Portfolio Turnover	42%	Stock Market Correlation	85%
5-Year Cost Estimate	7%	Up/Down Market Rank	D – B

Benefits		Investment Information	
Investment Objective	Gr. & Icm.	Telephone	800-645-6561
5-Year Projected Return	+8%	Minimum Investment	$2,500
Safety Rating (0-100)	77%	Telephone Switching	Unlimited;free
Yield	2.5%	Total Assets	$2.84 billion

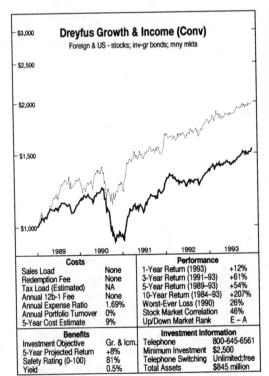

Dreyfus Growth & Income (Conv)
Foreign & US - stocks; inv-gr bonds; mny mkts

Costs		Performance	
Sales Load	None	1-Year Return (1993)	+12%
Redemption Fee	None	3-Year Return (1991–93)	+61%
Tax Load (Estimated)	NA	5-Year Return (1989–93)	+54%
Annual 12b-1 Fee	None	10-Year Return (1984–93)	+207%
Annual Expense Ratio	1.69%	Worst-Ever Loss (1990)	26%
Annual Portfolio Turnover	0%	Stock Market Correlation	46%
5-Year Cost Estimate	9%	Up/Down Market Rank	E – A

Benefits		Investment Information	
Investment Objective	Gr. & Icm.	Telephone	800-645-6561
5-Year Projected Return	+8%	Minimum Investment	$2,500
Safety Rating (0-100)	81%	Telephone Switching	Unlimited;free
Yield	0.5%	Total Assets	$845 million

Dreyfus Growth Opportunity
Small; undervalued stocks

Costs		Performance	
Sales Load	None	1-Year Return (1993)	+2%
Redemption Fee	None	3-Year Return (1991–93)	+48%
Tax Load (Estimated)	1%	5-Year Return (1989–93)	+59%
Annual 12b-1 Fee	None	10-Year Return (1984–93)	+165%
Annual Expense Ratio	1.00%	Worst-Ever Loss (1981-82)	39%
Annual Portfolio Turnover	44%	Stock Market Correlation	53%
5-Year Cost Estimate	6%	Up/Down Market Rank	D – D

Benefits		Investment Information	
Investment Objective	Gr. & Icm.	Telephone	800-645-6561
5-Year Projected Return	+7%	Minimum Investment	$2,500
Safety Rating (0-100)	66%	Telephone Switching	Unlimited;free
Yield	0.0%	Total Assets	$521 million

Dreyfus International Equity

Frgn & U.S - 65% non US stks, conv, pfd, bnds

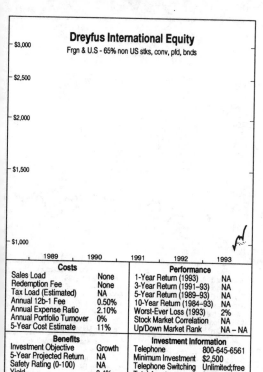

Costs		Performance	
Sales Load	None	1-Year Return (1993)	NA
Redemption Fee	None	3-Year Return (1991–93)	NA
Tax Load (Estimated)	NA	5-Year Return (1989–93)	NA
Annual 12b-1 Fee	0.50%	10-Year Return (1984–93)	NA
Annual Expense Ratio	2.10%	Worst-Ever Loss (1993)	2%
Annual Portfolio Turnover	0%	Stock Market Correlation	NA
5-Year Cost Estimate	11%	Up/Down Market Rank	NA – NA
Benefits		**Investment Information**	
Investment Objective	Growth	Telephone	800-645-6561
5-Year Projected Return	NA	Minimum Investment	$2,500
Safety Rating (0-100)	NA	Telephone Switching	Unlimited;free
Yield	0.4%	Total Assets	$127 million

Dreyfus New Leaders

Emerging growth stocks; market timing
★★★

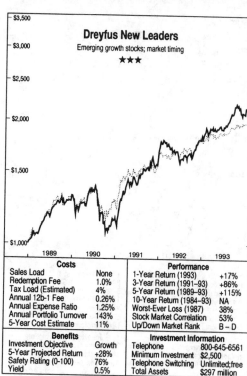

Costs		Performance	
Sales Load	None	1-Year Return (1993)	+17%
Redemption Fee	1.0%	3-Year Return (1991–93)	+86%
Tax Load (Estimated)	4%	5-Year Return (1989–93)	+115%
Annual 12b-1 Fee	0.26%	10-Year Return (1984–93)	NA
Annual Expense Ratio	1.25%	Worst-Ever Loss (1987)	38%
Annual Portfolio Turnover	143%	Stock Market Correlation	53%
5-Year Cost Estimate	11%	Up/Down Market Rank	B – D
Benefits		**Investment Information**	
Investment Objective	Growth	Telephone	800-645-6561
5-Year Projected Return	+28%	Minimum Investment	$2,500
Safety Rating (0-100)	76%	Telephone Switching	Unlimited;free
Yield	0.5%	Total Assets	$297 million

Dreyfus Peoples Index

Matches S&P 500 Index
★

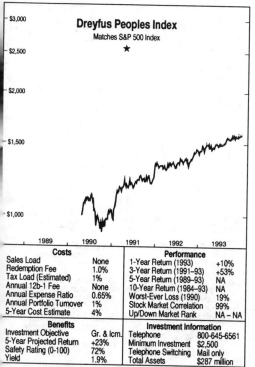

Costs		Performance	
Sales Load	None	1-Year Return (1993)	+10%
Redemption Fee	1.0%	3-Year Return (1991–93)	+53%
Tax Load (Estimated)	1%	5-Year Return (1989–93)	NA
Annual 12b-1 Fee	None	10-Year Return (1984–93)	NA
Annual Expense Ratio	0.65%	Worst-Ever Loss (1990)	19%
Annual Portfolio Turnover	1%	Stock Market Correlation	99%
5-Year Cost Estimate	4%	Up/Down Market Rank	NA – NA
Benefits		**Investment Information**	
Investment Objective	Gr. & Icm.	Telephone	800-645-6561
5-Year Projected Return	+23%	Minimum Investment	$2,500
Safety Rating (0-100)	72%	Telephone Switching	Mail only
Yield	1.9%	Total Assets	$287 million

Dreyfus Peoples S&P MidCap Idx

Matches S&P MidCap 400 Index
★

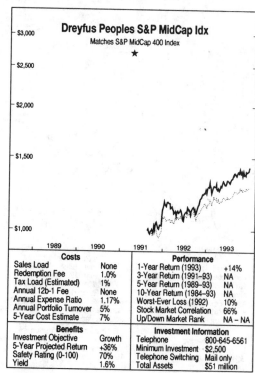

Costs		Performance	
Sales Load	None	1-Year Return (1993)	+14%
Redemption Fee	1.0%	3-Year Return (1991–93)	NA
Tax Load (Estimated)	1%	5-Year Return (1989–93)	NA
Annual 12b-1 Fee	None	10-Year Return (1984–93)	NA
Annual Expense Ratio	1.17%	Worst-Ever Loss (1992)	10%
Annual Portfolio Turnover	5%	Stock Market Correlation	66%
5-Year Cost Estimate	7%	Up/Down Market Rank	NA – NA
Benefits		**Investment Information**	
Investment Objective	Growth	Telephone	800-645-6561
5-Year Projected Return	+36%	Minimum Investment	$2,500
Safety Rating (0-100)	70%	Telephone Switching	Mail only
Yield	1.6%	Total Assets	$51 million

Dreyfus Third Century
Socially responsible companies
★

Costs		Performance	
Sales Load	None	1-Year Return (1993)	+5%
Redemption Fee	None	3-Year Return (1991–93)	+48%
Tax Load (Estimated)	2%	5-Year Return (1989–93)	+80%
Annual 12b-1 Fee	0.25%	10-Year Return (1984–93)	+212%
Annual Expense Ratio	1.11%	Worst-Ever Loss (1981-82)	30%
Annual Portfolio Turnover	48%	Stock Market Correlation	57%
5-Year Cost Estimate	8%	Up/Down Market Rank	D – C

Benefits		Investment Information	
Investment Objective	Gr. & Icm.	Telephone	800-645-6561
5-Year Projected Return	+19%	Minimum Investment	$2,500
Safety Rating (0-100)	77%	Telephone Switching	Unlimited;free
Yield	0.5%	Total Assets	$527 million

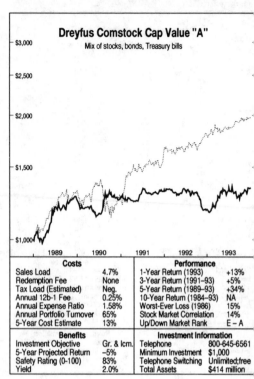

Dreyfus Comstock Cap Value "A"
Mix of stocks, bonds, Treasury bills

Costs		Performance	
Sales Load	4.7%	1-Year Return (1993)	+13%
Redemption Fee	None	3-Year Return (1991–93)	+5%
Tax Load (Estimated)	Neg.	5-Year Return (1989–93)	+34%
Annual 12b-1 Fee	0.25%	10-Year Return (1984–93)	NA
Annual Expense Ratio	1.58%	Worst-Ever Loss (1986)	15%
Annual Portfolio Turnover	65%	Stock Market Correlation	14%
5-Year Cost Estimate	13%	Up/Down Market Rank	E – A

Benefits		Investment Information	
Investment Objective	Gr. & Icm.	Telephone	800-645-6561
5-Year Projected Return	–5%	Minimum Investment	$1,000
Safety Rating (0-100)	83%	Telephone Switching	Unlimited;free
Yield	2.0%	Total Assets	$414 million

Dreyfus Prem Capital Growth
Short selling; leveraged
★

Costs		Performance	
Sales Load	3.1%	1-Year Return (1993)	+15%
Redemption Fee	None	3-Year Return (1991–93)	+62%
Tax Load (Estimated)	0%	5-Year Return (1989–93)	+92%
Annual 12b-1 Fee	None	10-Year Return (1984–93)	+267%
Annual Expense Ratio	1.07%	Worst-Ever Loss (1987)	32%
Annual Portfolio Turnover	142%	Stock Market Correlation	65%
5-Year Cost Estimate	9%	Up/Down Market Rank	C – B

Benefits		Investment Information	
Investment Objective	Growth	Telephone	800-645-6561
5-Year Projected Return	+17%	Minimum Investment	$1,000
Safety Rating (0-100)	78%	Telephone Switching	2 per yr; free
Yield	4.9%	Total Assets	$607 million

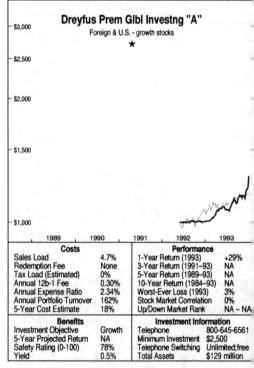

Dreyfus Prem Glbl Investng "A"
Foreign & U.S. - growth stocks
★

Costs		Performance	
Sales Load	4.7%	1-Year Return (1993)	+29%
Redemption Fee	None	3-Year Return (1991–93)	NA
Tax Load (Estimated)	0%	5-Year Return (1989–93)	NA
Annual 12b-1 Fee	0.30%	10-Year Return (1984–93)	NA
Annual Expense Ratio	2.34%	Worst-Ever Loss (1993)	3%
Annual Portfolio Turnover	162%	Stock Market Correlation	0%
5-Year Cost Estimate	18%	Up/Down Market Rank	NA – NA

Benefits		Investment Information	
Investment Objective	Growth	Telephone	800-645-6561
5-Year Projected Return	NA	Minimum Investment	$2,500
Safety Rating (0-100)	78%	Telephone Switching	Unlimited;free
Yield	0.5%	Total Assets	$129 million

E
Q
U
I
T
Y

Dreyfus Strategic Growth LP
Leveraged; short selling; futures

Costs		Performance	
Sales Load	3.1%	1-Year Return (1993)	+25%
Redemption Fee	None	3-Year Return (1991–93)	+40%
Tax Load (Estimated)	6%	5-Year Return (1989–93)	+49%
Annual 12b-1 Fee	0.32%	10-Year Return (1984–93)	NA
Annual Expense Ratio	1.79%	Worst-Ever Loss (1987)	23%
Annual Portfolio Turnover	199%	Stock Market Correlation	38%
5-Year Cost Estimate	20%	Up/Down Market Rank	D – B

Benefits		Investment Information	
Investment Objective	Growth	Telephone	800-645-6561
5-Year Projected Return	–6%	Minimum Investment	$1,000
Safety Rating (0-100)	71%	Telephone Switching	2 per yr; free
Yield	0.0%	Total Assets	$43 million

Dreyfus Strategic Invstmnt "A"
Diversified securities; hedging

Costs		Performance	
Sales Load	4.7%	1-Year Return (1993)	+17%
Redemption Fee	None	3-Year Return (1991–93)	+56%
Tax Load (Estimated)	4%	5-Year Return (1989–93)	+108%
Annual 12b-1 Fee	0.25%	10-Year Return (1984–93)	NA
Annual Expense Ratio	1.68%	Worst-Ever Loss (1987)	23%
Annual Portfolio Turnover	264%	Stock Market Correlation	42%
5-Year Cost Estimate	19%	Up/Down Market Rank	C – B

Benefits		Investment Information	
Investment Objective	Growth	Telephone	800-645-6561
5-Year Projected Return	+23%	Minimum Investment	$1,000
Safety Rating (0-100)	73%	Telephone Switching	2 per yr; free
Yield	0.6%	Total Assets	$289 million

Dreyfus Strategic World Inv LP
Foreign & U.S. - diversified
★★

Costs		Performance	
Sales Load	3.1%	1-Year Return (1993)	+22%
Redemption Fee	None	3-Year Return (1991–93)	+39%
Tax Load (Estimated)	1%	5-Year Return (1989–93)	+78%
Annual 12b-1 Fee	0.31%	10-Year Return (1984–93)	NA
Annual Expense Ratio	1.62%	Worst-Ever Loss (1989)	8%
Annual Portfolio Turnover	452%	Stock Market Correlation	6%
5-Year Cost Estimate	13%	Up/Down Market Rank	E – A

Benefits		Investment Information	
Investment Objective	Growth	Telephone	800-645-6561
5-Year Projected Return	NA	Minimum Investment	$1,000
Safety Rating (0-100)	86%	Telephone Switching	2 per yr; free
Yield	0.0%	Total Assets	$150 million

Duff & Phelps Utilities
Utility securities
★

Costs		Performance	
Sales Load	None	1-Year Return (1993)	+8%
Redemption Fee	None	3-Year Return (1991–93)	+54%
Tax Load (Estimated)	1%	5-Year Return (1989–93)	+104%
Annual 12b-1 Fee	None	10-Year Return (1984–93)	NA
Annual Expense Ratio	0.98%	Worst-Ever Loss (1987)	23%
Annual Portfolio Turnover	73%	Stock Market Correlation	4%
5-Year Cost Estimate	8%	Up/Down Market Rank	E – A

Benefits		Investment Information	
Investment Objective	Icm. & Gr.	Telephone	800-426-5523
5-Year Projected Return	NA	Minimum Investment	None
Safety Rating (0-100)	76%	Telephone Switching	Via broker
Yield	7.3%	Total Assets	$2.08 billion

Eagle Growth Shares
Diversified stocks

S&P 500

Fund

Costs		Performance	
Sales Load	9.3%	1-Year Return (1993)	+1%
Redemption Fee	None	3-Year Return (1991–93)	+47%
Tax Load (Estimated)	9%	5-Year Return (1989–93)	+77%
Annual 12b-1 Fee	None	10-Year Return (1984–93)	NA
Annual Expense Ratio	2.50%	Worst-Ever Loss (1987)	38%
Annual Portfolio Turnover	94%	Stock Market Correlation	51%
5-Year Cost Estimate	36%	Up/Down Market Rank	C – D

Benefits		Investment Information	
Investment Objective	Growth	Telephone	800-749-9933
5-Year Projected Return	–18%	Minimum Investment	None
Safety Rating (0-100)	67%	Telephone Switching	Not available
Yield	0.0%	Total Assets	$3 million

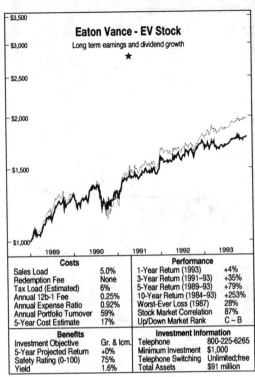

Eaton Vance - EV Stock
Long term earnings and dividend growth
★

Costs		Performance	
Sales Load	5.0%	1-Year Return (1993)	+4%
Redemption Fee	None	3-Year Return (1991–93)	+35%
Tax Load (Estimated)	6%	5-Year Return (1989–93)	+79%
Annual 12b-1 Fee	0.25%	10-Year Return (1984–93)	+253%
Annual Expense Ratio	0.92%	Worst-Ever Loss (1987)	28%
Annual Portfolio Turnover	59%	Stock Market Correlation	87%
5-Year Cost Estimate	17%	Up/Down Market Rank	C – B

Benefits		Investment Information	
Investment Objective	Gr. & Icm.	Telephone	800-225-6265
5-Year Projected Return	+0%	Minimum Investment	$1,000
Safety Rating (0-100)	75%	Telephone Switching	Unlimited;free
Yield	1.6%	Total Assets	$91 million

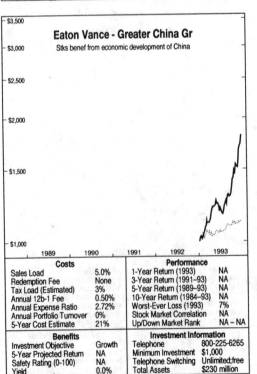

Eaton Vance - Greater China Gr
Stks benef from economic development of China

Costs		Performance	
Sales Load	5.0%	1-Year Return (1993)	NA
Redemption Fee	None	3-Year Return (1991–93)	NA
Tax Load (Estimated)	3%	5-Year Return (1989–93)	NA
Annual 12b-1 Fee	0.50%	10-Year Return (1984–93)	NA
Annual Expense Ratio	2.72%	Worst-Ever Loss (1993)	7%
Annual Portfolio Turnover	0%	Stock Market Correlation	NA
5-Year Cost Estimate	21%	Up/Down Market Rank	NA – NA

Benefits		Investment Information	
Investment Objective	Growth	Telephone	800-225-6265
5-Year Projected Return	NA	Minimum Investment	$1,000
Safety Rating (0-100)	NA	Telephone Switching	Unlimited;free
Yield	0.0%	Total Assets	$230 million

Eaton Vance - Growth
Diversified stocks

Costs		Performance	
Sales Load	5.0%	1-Year Return (1993)	–3%
Redemption Fee	None	3-Year Return (1991–93)	+43%
Tax Load (Estimated)	2%	5-Year Return (1989–93)	+77%
Annual 12b-1 Fee	0.25%	10-Year Return (1984–93)	+209%
Annual Expense Ratio	0.87%	Worst-Ever Loss (1987)	33%
Annual Portfolio Turnover	74%	Stock Market Correlation	73%
5-Year Cost Estimate	12%	Up/Down Market Rank	A – D

Benefits		Investment Information	
Investment Objective	Gr. & Icm.	Telephone	800-225-6265
5-Year Projected Return	–5%	Minimum Investment	$1,000
Safety Rating (0-100)	68%	Telephone Switching	Unlimited;free
Yield	0.4%	Total Assets	$143 million

Eaton Vance - Special Equities
Established growth stocks

Costs		Performance	
Sales Load	5.0%	1-Year Return (1993)	+1%
Redemption Fee	None	3-Year Return (1991–93)	+63%
Tax Load (Estimated)	7%	5-Year Return (1989–93)	+107%
Annual 12b-1 Fee	0.25%	10-Year Return (1984–93)	NA
Annual Expense Ratio	0.96%	Worst-Ever Loss (1987)	34%
Annual Portfolio Turnover	68%	Stock Market Correlation	60%
5-Year Cost Estimate	18%	Up/Down Market Rank	A – D

Benefits		Investment Information	
Investment Objective	Growth	Telephone	800-225-6265
5-Year Projected Return	+15%	Minimum Investment	$1,000
Safety Rating (0-100)	66%	Telephone Switching	Unlimited;free
Yield	0.0%	Total Assets	$84 million

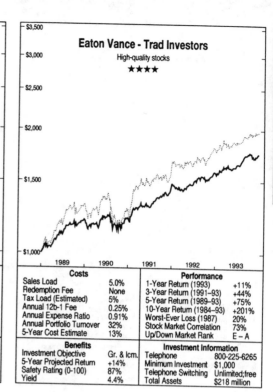

Eaton Vance - Trad Investors
High-quality stocks
★★★★

Costs		Performance	
Sales Load	5.0%	1-Year Return (1993)	+11%
Redemption Fee	None	3-Year Return (1991–93)	+44%
Tax Load (Estimated)	5%	5-Year Return (1989–93)	+75%
Annual 12b-1 Fee	0.25%	10-Year Return (1984–93)	+201%
Annual Expense Ratio	0.91%	Worst-Ever Loss (1987)	20%
Annual Portfolio Turnover	32%	Stock Market Correlation	73%
5-Year Cost Estimate	13%	Up/Down Market Rank	E – A

Benefits		Investment Information	
Investment Objective	Gr. & Icm.	Telephone	800-225-6265
5-Year Projected Return	+14%	Minimum Investment	$1,000
Safety Rating (0-100)	87%	Telephone Switching	Unlimited;free
Yield	4.4%	Total Assets	$218 million

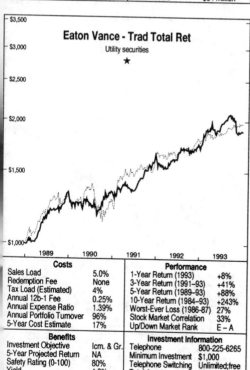

Eaton Vance - Trad Total Ret
Utility securities
★

Costs		Performance	
Sales Load	5.0%	1-Year Return (1993)	+8%
Redemption Fee	None	3-Year Return (1991–93)	+41%
Tax Load (Estimated)	4%	5-Year Return (1989–93)	+88%
Annual 12b-1 Fee	0.25%	10-Year Return (1984–93)	+243%
Annual Expense Ratio	1.39%	Worst-Ever Loss (1986-87)	27%
Annual Portfolio Turnover	96%	Stock Market Correlation	33%
5-Year Cost Estimate	17%	Up/Down Market Rank	E – A

Benefits		Investment Information	
Investment Objective	Icm. & Gr.	Telephone	800-225-6265
5-Year Projected Return	NA	Minimum Investment	$1,000
Safety Rating (0-100)	80%	Telephone Switching	Unlimited;free
Yield	4.0%	Total Assets	$687 million

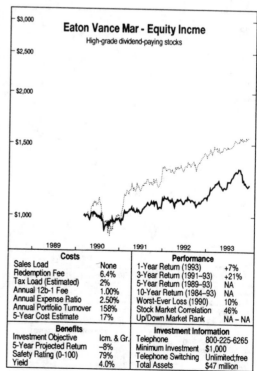

Eaton Vance Mar - Equity Incme
High-grade dividend-paying stocks

Costs		Performance	
Sales Load	None	1-Year Return (1993)	+7%
Redemption Fee	6.4%	3-Year Return (1991–93)	+21%
Tax Load (Estimated)	2%	5-Year Return (1989–93)	NA
Annual 12b-1 Fee	1.00%	10-Year Return (1984–93)	NA
Annual Expense Ratio	2.50%	Worst-Ever Loss (1990)	10%
Annual Portfolio Turnover	158%	Stock Market Correlation	46%
5-Year Cost Estimate	17%	Up/Down Market Rank	NA – NA

Benefits		Investment Information	
Investment Objective	Icm. & Gr.	Telephone	800-225-6265
5-Year Projected Return	–8%	Minimum Investment	$1,000
Safety Rating (0-100)	79%	Telephone Switching	Unlimited;free
Yield	4.0%	Total Assets	$47 million

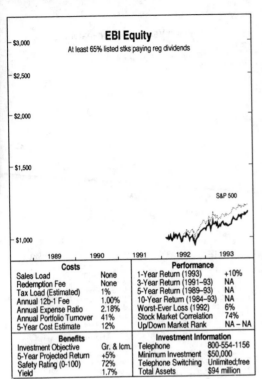

EBI Equity
At least 65% listed stks paying reg dividends

S&P 500

Costs		Performance	
Sales Load	None	1-Year Return (1993)	+10%
Redemption Fee	None	3-Year Return (1991–93)	NA
Tax Load (Estimated)	1%	5-Year Return (1989–93)	NA
Annual 12b-1 Fee	1.00%	10-Year Return (1984–93)	NA
Annual Expense Ratio	2.18%	Worst-Ever Loss (1992)	6%
Annual Portfolio Turnover	41%	Stock Market Correlation	74%
5-Year Cost Estimate	12%	Up/Down Market Rank	NA – NA

Benefits		Investment Information	
Investment Objective	Gr. & Icm.	Telephone	800-554-1156
5-Year Projected Return	+5%	Minimum Investment	$50,000
Safety Rating (0-100)	72%	Telephone Switching	Unlimited;free
Yield	1.7%	Total Assets	$94 million

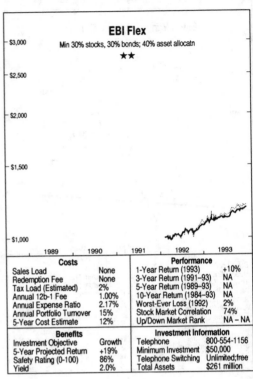

EBI Flex
Min 30% stocks, 30% bonds; 40% asset allocatn
★★

Costs		Performance	
Sales Load	None	1-Year Return (1993)	+10%
Redemption Fee	None	3-Year Return (1991–93)	NA
Tax Load (Estimated)	2%	5-Year Return (1989–93)	NA
Annual 12b-1 Fee	1.00%	10-Year Return (1984–93)	NA
Annual Expense Ratio	2.17%	Worst-Ever Loss (1992)	2%
Annual Portfolio Turnover	15%	Stock Market Correlation	74%
5-Year Cost Estimate	12%	Up/Down Market Rank	NA – NA

Benefits		Investment Information	
Investment Objective	Growth	Telephone	800-554-1156
5-Year Projected Return	+19%	Minimum Investment	$50,000
Safety Rating (0-100)	86%	Telephone Switching	Unlimited;free
Yield	2.0%	Total Assets	$261 million

Eclipse Equity
Smaller; undervalued stocks
★

Costs		Performance	
Sales Load	None	1-Year Return (1993)	+17%
Redemption Fee	None	3-Year Return (1991–93)	+82%
Tax Load (Estimated)	2%	5-Year Return (1989–93)	+83%
Annual 12b-1 Fee	None	10-Year Return (1984–93)	NA
Annual Expense Ratio	1.15%	Worst-Ever Loss (1989-90)	25%
Annual Portfolio Turnover	106%	Stock Market Correlation	64%
5-Year Cost Estimate	9%	Up/Down Market Rank	D – B

Benefits		Investment Information	
Investment Objective	Gr. & Icm.	Telephone	800-872-2710
5-Year Projected Return	+23%	Minimum Investment	$1,000
Safety Rating (0-100)	78%	Telephone Switching	Unlimited;free
Yield	0.6%	Total Assets	$182 million

Ellsworth Conv Growth & Income
Convertible securities

Costs		Performance	
Sales Load	None	1-Year Return (1993)	+17%
Redemption Fee	None	3-Year Return (1991–93)	+75%
Tax Load (Estimated)	3%	5-Year Return (1989–93)	+93%
Annual 12b-1 Fee	None	10-Year Return (1984–93)	NA
Annual Expense Ratio	1.30%	Worst-Ever Loss (1986-87)	32%
Annual Portfolio Turnover	99%	Stock Market Correlation	6%
5-Year Cost Estimate	12%	Up/Down Market Rank	D – A

Benefits		Investment Information	
Investment Objective	Gr. & Icm.	Telephone	212-269-9236
5-Year Projected Return	+24%	Minimum Investment	None
Safety Rating (0-100)	71%	Telephone Switching	Via broker
Yield	2.6%	Total Assets	$61 million

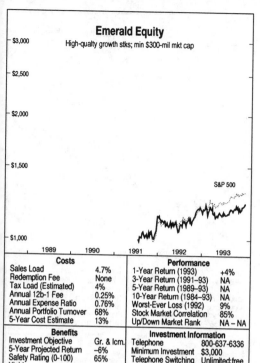

Emerald Equity
High-qualty growth stks; min $300-mil mkt cap

S&P 500

Costs		Performance	
Sales Load	4.7%	1-Year Return (1993)	+4%
Redemption Fee	None	3-Year Return (1991–93)	NA
Tax Load (Estimated)	4%	5-Year Return (1989–93)	NA
Annual 12b-1 Fee	0.25%	10-Year Return (1984–93)	NA
Annual Expense Ratio	0.76%	Worst-Ever Loss (1992)	9%
Annual Portfolio Turnover	68%	Stock Market Correlation	85%
5-Year Cost Estimate	13%	Up/Down Market Rank	NA – NA
Benefits		**Investment Information**	
Investment Objective	Gr. & lcm.	Telephone	800-637-6336
5-Year Projected Return	–6%	Minimum Investment	$3,000
Safety Rating (0-100)	65%	Telephone Switching	Unlimited;free
Yield	1.2%	Total Assets	$154 million

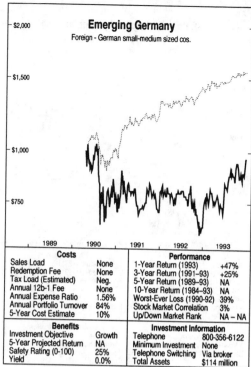

Emerging Germany
Foreign - German small-medium sized cos.

Costs		Performance	
Sales Load	None	1-Year Return (1993)	+47%
Redemption Fee	None	3-Year Return (1991–93)	+25%
Tax Load (Estimated)	Neg.	5-Year Return (1989–93)	NA
Annual 12b-1 Fee	None	10-Year Return (1984–93)	NA
Annual Expense Ratio	1.56%	Worst-Ever Loss (1990-92)	39%
Annual Portfolio Turnover	84%	Stock Market Correlation	3%
5-Year Cost Estimate	10%	Up/Down Market Rank	NA – NA
Benefits		**Investment Information**	
Investment Objective	Growth	Telephone	800-356-6122
5-Year Projected Return	NA	Minimum Investment	None
Safety Rating (0-100)	25%	Telephone Switching	Via broker
Yield	0.0%	Total Assets	$114 million

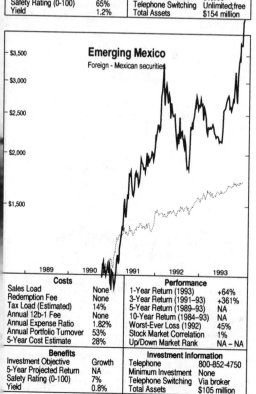

Emerging Mexico
Foreign - Mexican securities

Costs		Performance	
Sales Load	None	1-Year Return (1993)	+64%
Redemption Fee	None	3-Year Return (1991–93)	+361%
Tax Load (Estimated)	14%	5-Year Return (1989–93)	NA
Annual 12b-1 Fee	None	10-Year Return (1984–93)	NA
Annual Expense Ratio	1.82%	Worst-Ever Loss (1992)	45%
Annual Portfolio Turnover	53%	Stock Market Correlation	1%
5-Year Cost Estimate	28%	Up/Down Market Rank	NA – NA
Benefits		**Investment Information**	
Investment Objective	Growth	Telephone	800-852-4750
5-Year Projected Return	NA	Minimum Investment	None
Safety Rating (0-100)	7%	Telephone Switching	Via broker
Yield	0.8%	Total Assets	$105 million

Engex
Non-diversified growth stocks

Costs		Performance	
Sales Load	None	1-Year Return (1993)	+16%
Redemption Fee	None	3-Year Return (1991–93)	+85%
Tax Load (Estimated)	0%	5-Year Return (1989–93)	+45%
Annual 12b-1 Fee	None	10-Year Return (1984–93)	+19%
Annual Expense Ratio	2.11%	Worst-Ever Loss (1987)	73%
Annual Portfolio Turnover	65%	Stock Market Correlation	6%
5-Year Cost Estimate	14%	Up/Down Market Rank	E – B
Benefits		**Investment Information**	
Investment Objective	Growth	Telephone	212-495-4000
5-Year Projected Return	–6%	Minimum Investment	None
Safety Rating (0-100)	31%	Telephone Switching	Via broker
Yield	0.0%	Total Assets	$12 million

Enterprise Capital Appreciatn
Stocks with increasing earnings; strong finls
★

Fund

S&P 500

Costs		Performance	
Sales Load	5.0%	1-Year Return (1993)	+6%
Redemption Fee	None	3-Year Return (1991–93)	+78%
Tax Load (Estimated)	5%	5-Year Return (1989–93)	NA
Annual 12b-1 Fee	0.45%	10-Year Return (1984–93)	NA
Annual Expense Ratio	1.75%	Worst-Ever Loss (1990)	26%
Annual Portfolio Turnover	68%	Stock Market Correlation	62%
5-Year Cost Estimate	21%	Up/Down Market Rank	A – NA

Benefits		Investment Information	
Investment Objective	Growth	Telephone	800-432-4320
5-Year Projected Return	+31%	Minimum Investment	$1,000
Safety Rating (0-100)	68%	Telephone Switching	Unlimited;free
Yield	0.0%	Total Assets	$101 million

Enterprise Growth
Growth stocks

Costs		Performance	
Sales Load	5.0%	1-Year Return (1993)	+11%
Redemption Fee	None	3-Year Return (1991–93)	+67%
Tax Load (Estimated)	4%	5-Year Return (1989–93)	+101%
Annual 12b-1 Fee	0.45%	10-Year Return (1984–93)	NA
Annual Expense Ratio	1.60%	Worst-Ever Loss (1987)	31%
Annual Portfolio Turnover	110%	Stock Market Correlation	69%
5-Year Cost Estimate	19%	Up/Down Market Rank	C – C

Benefits		Investment Information	
Investment Objective	Growth	Telephone	800-432-4320
5-Year Projected Return	+16%	Minimum Investment	$1,000
Safety Rating (0-100)	72%	Telephone Switching	Unlimited;free
Yield	0.1%	Total Assets	$88 million

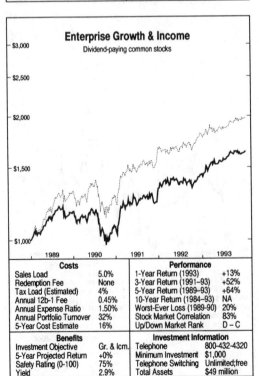

Enterprise Growth & Income
Dividend-paying common stocks

Costs		Performance	
Sales Load	5.0%	1-Year Return (1993)	+13%
Redemption Fee	None	3-Year Return (1991–93)	+52%
Tax Load (Estimated)	4%	5-Year Return (1989–93)	+64%
Annual 12b-1 Fee	0.45%	10-Year Return (1984–93)	NA
Annual Expense Ratio	1.50%	Worst-Ever Loss (1989-90)	20%
Annual Portfolio Turnover	32%	Stock Market Correlation	83%
5-Year Cost Estimate	16%	Up/Down Market Rank	D – C

Benefits		Investment Information	
Investment Objective	Gr. & Icm.	Telephone	800-432-4320
5-Year Projected Return	+0%	Minimum Investment	$1,000
Safety Rating (0-100)	75%	Telephone Switching	Unlimited;free
Yield	2.9%	Total Assets	$49 million

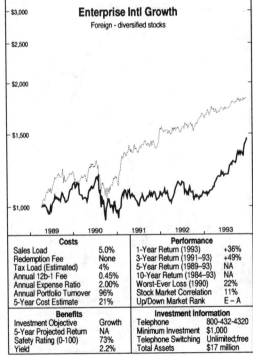

Enterprise Intl Growth
Foreign - diversified stocks

Costs		Performance	
Sales Load	5.0%	1-Year Return (1993)	+36%
Redemption Fee	None	3-Year Return (1991–93)	+49%
Tax Load (Estimated)	4%	5-Year Return (1989–93)	NA
Annual 12b-1 Fee	0.45%	10-Year Return (1984–93)	NA
Annual Expense Ratio	2.00%	Worst-Ever Loss (1990)	22%
Annual Portfolio Turnover	96%	Stock Market Correlation	11%
5-Year Cost Estimate	21%	Up/Down Market Rank	E – A

Benefits		Investment Information	
Investment Objective	Growth	Telephone	800-432-4320
5-Year Projected Return	NA	Minimum Investment	$1,000
Safety Rating (0-100)	73%	Telephone Switching	Unlimited;free
Yield	2.2%	Total Assets	$17 million

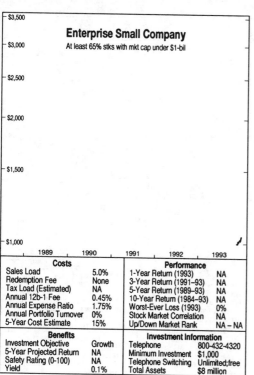

Enterprise Small Company

At least 65% stks with mkt cap under $1-bil

Costs		Performance	
Sales Load	5.0%	1-Year Return (1993)	NA
Redemption Fee	None	3-Year Return (1991–93)	NA
Tax Load (Estimated)	NA	5-Year Return (1989–93)	NA
Annual 12b-1 Fee	0.45%	10-Year Return (1984–93)	NA
Annual Expense Ratio	1.75%	Worst-Ever Loss (1993)	0%
Annual Portfolio Turnover	0%	Stock Market Correlation	NA
5-Year Cost Estimate	15%	Up/Down Market Rank	NA – NA
Benefits		**Investment Information**	
Investment Objective	Growth	Telephone	800-432-4320
5-Year Projected Return	NA	Minimum Investment	$1,000
Safety Rating (0-100)	NA	Telephone Switching	Unlimited;free
Yield	0.1%	Total Assets	$8 million

Equity Strategies

Non diversified; value oriented securities

Costs		Performance	
Sales Load	None	1-Year Return (1993)	+18%
Redemption Fee	None	3-Year Return (1991–93)	+36%
Tax Load (Estimated)	4%	5-Year Return (1989–93)	+94%
Annual 12b-1 Fee	0.75%	10-Year Return (1984–93)	+202%
Annual Expense Ratio	1.17%	Worst-Ever Loss (1987-88)	36%
Annual Portfolio Turnover	0%	Stock Market Correlation	4%
5-Year Cost Estimate	6%	Up/Down Market Rank	E – B
Benefits		**Investment Information**	
Investment Objective	Gr. & Icm.	Telephone	800-443-1021
5-Year Projected Return	+46%	Minimum Investment	$1,000
Safety Rating (0-100)	32%	Telephone Switching	Not available
Yield	0.0%	Total Assets	$99 million

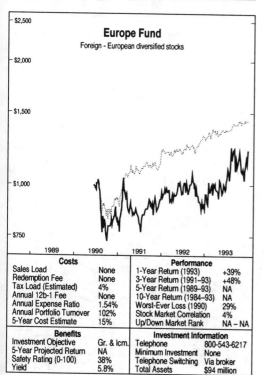

Europe Fund

Foreign - European diversified stocks

Costs		Performance	
Sales Load	None	1-Year Return (1993)	+39%
Redemption Fee	None	3-Year Return (1991–93)	+48%
Tax Load (Estimated)	4%	5-Year Return (1989–93)	NA
Annual 12b-1 Fee	None	10-Year Return (1984–93)	NA
Annual Expense Ratio	1.54%	Worst-Ever Loss (1990)	29%
Annual Portfolio Turnover	102%	Stock Market Correlation	4%
5-Year Cost Estimate	15%	Up/Down Market Rank	NA – NA
Benefits		**Investment Information**	
Investment Objective	Gr. & Icm.	Telephone	800-543-6217
5-Year Projected Return	NA	Minimum Investment	None
Safety Rating (0-100)	38%	Telephone Switching	Via broker
Yield	5.8%	Total Assets	$94 million

European Warrant

Foreign - Western European equity warrants

Costs		Performance	
Sales Load	None	1-Year Return (1993)	+108%
Redemption Fee	None	3-Year Return (1991–93)	+130%
Tax Load (Estimated)	2%	5-Year Return (1989–93)	NA
Annual 12b-1 Fee	None	10-Year Return (1984–93)	NA
Annual Expense Ratio	2.13%	Worst-Ever Loss (1990-91)	47%
Annual Portfolio Turnover	100%	Stock Market Correlation	9%
5-Year Cost Estimate	16%	Up/Down Market Rank	NA – NA
Benefits		**Investment Information**	
Investment Objective	Growth	Telephone	800-331-1710
5-Year Projected Return	NA	Minimum Investment	None
Safety Rating (0-100)	23%	Telephone Switching	Via broker
Yield	0.0%	Total Assets	$58 million

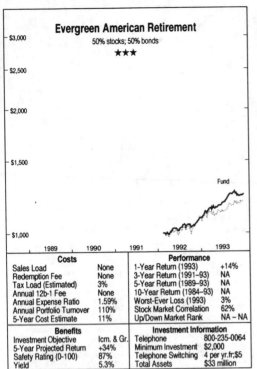

Evergreen American Retirement
50% stocks; 50% bonds
★★★

Fund

Costs		Performance	
Sales Load	None	1-Year Return (1993)	+14%
Redemption Fee	None	3-Year Return (1991–93)	NA
Tax Load (Estimated)	3%	5-Year Return (1989–93)	NA
Annual 12b-1 Fee	None	10-Year Return (1984–93)	NA
Annual Expense Ratio	1.59%	Worst-Ever Loss (1993)	3%
Annual Portfolio Turnover	110%	Stock Market Correlation	62%
5-Year Cost Estimate	11%	Up/Down Market Rank	NA – NA

Benefits		Investment Information	
Investment Objective	Icm. & Gr.	Telephone	800-235-0064
5-Year Projected Return	+34%	Minimum Investment	$2,000
Safety Rating (0-100)	87%	Telephone Switching	4 per yr.fr;$5
Yield	5.3%	Total Assets	$33 million

Evergreen Fund
Small; little known stocks

Costs		Performance	
Sales Load	None	1-Year Return (1993)	+6%
Redemption Fee	None	3-Year Return (1991–93)	+62%
Tax Load (Estimated)	9%	5-Year Return (1989–93)	+64%
Annual 12b-1 Fee	None	10-Year Return (1984–93)	+200%
Annual Expense Ratio	1.13%	Worst-Ever Loss (1987)	32%
Annual Portfolio Turnover	21%	Stock Market Correlation	75%
5-Year Cost Estimate	9%	Up/Down Market Rank	B – D

Benefits		Investment Information	
Investment Objective	Growth	Telephone	800-235-0064
5-Year Projected Return	+5%	Minimum Investment	$2,000
Safety Rating (0-100)	70%	Telephone Switching	4 per yr.fr;$5
Yield	0.6%	Total Assets	$678 million

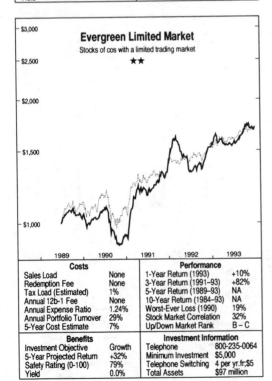

Evergreen Limited Market
Stocks of cos with a limited trading market
★★

Costs		Performance	
Sales Load	None	1-Year Return (1993)	+10%
Redemption Fee	None	3-Year Return (1991–93)	+82%
Tax Load (Estimated)	1%	5-Year Return (1989–93)	NA
Annual 12b-1 Fee	None	10-Year Return (1984–93)	NA
Annual Expense Ratio	1.24%	Worst-Ever Loss (1990)	19%
Annual Portfolio Turnover	29%	Stock Market Correlation	32%
5-Year Cost Estimate	7%	Up/Down Market Rank	B – C

Benefits		Investment Information	
Investment Objective	Growth	Telephone	800-235-0064
5-Year Projected Return	+32%	Minimum Investment	$5,000
Safety Rating (0-100)	79%	Telephone Switching	4 per yr.fr;$5
Yield	0.0%	Total Assets	$97 million

Evergreen Total Return
Diversified securities
★★★★

Costs		Performance	
Sales Load	None	1-Year Return (1993)	+15%
Redemption Fee	None	3-Year Return (1991–93)	+56%
Tax Load (Estimated)	1%	5-Year Return (1989–93)	+71%
Annual 12b-1 Fee	None	10-Year Return (1984–93)	+224%
Annual Expense Ratio	1.18%	Worst-Ever Loss (1987)	22%
Annual Portfolio Turnover	54%	Stock Market Correlation	71%
5-Year Cost Estimate	7%	Up/Down Market Rank	E – A

Benefits		Investment Information	
Investment Objective	Gr. & Icm.	Telephone	800-235-0064
5-Year Projected Return	+17%	Minimum Investment	$2,000
Safety Rating (0-100)	84%	Telephone Switching	4 per yr.fr;$5
Yield	5.6%	Total Assets	$1.20 billion

Evergreen Value Timing
Undervalued securities
★★★

Costs		Performance	
Sales Load	None	1-Year Return (1993)	+14%
Redemption Fee	None	3-Year Return (1991–93)	+64%
Tax Load (Estimated)	7%	5-Year Return (1989–93)	+96%
Annual 12b-1 Fee	None	10-Year Return (1984–93)	NA
Annual Expense Ratio	1.33%	Worst-Ever Loss (1987)	30%
Annual Portfolio Turnover	24%	Stock Market Correlation	80%
5-Year Cost Estimate	10%	Up/Down Market Rank	B – C
Benefits		**Investment Information**	
Investment Objective	Gr. & Icm.	Telephone	800-235-0064
5-Year Projected Return	+22%	Minimum Investment	$2,000
Safety Rating (0-100)	78%	Telephone Switching	4 per yr.fr;$5
Yield	0.9%	Total Assets	$76 million

Excel Midas Gold Shares
North American gold stocks

Costs		Performance	
Sales Load	4.7%	1-Year Return (1993)	+99%
Redemption Fee	None	3-Year Return (1991–93)	+85%
Tax Load (Estimated)	1%	5-Year Return (1989–93)	+87%
Annual 12b-1 Fee	0.25%	10-Year Return (1984–93)	NA
Annual Expense Ratio	2.25%	Worst-Ever Loss (1987-92)	47%
Annual Portfolio Turnover	72%	Stock Market Correlation	–2%
5-Year Cost Estimate	18%	Up/Down Market Rank	E – A
Benefits		**Investment Information**	
Investment Objective	Gr. & Icm.	Telephone	800-783-3444
5-Year Projected Return	NA	Minimum Investment	$100
Safety Rating (0-100)	61%	Telephone Switching	Unlm;$7.50
Yield	0.0%	Total Assets	$9 million

Excel Value
Seasoned stocks

Costs		Performance	
Sales Load	4.7%	1-Year Return (1993)	–8%
Redemption Fee	None	3-Year Return (1991–93)	+2%
Tax Load (Estimated)	4%	5-Year Return (1989–93)	–8%
Annual 12b-1 Fee	0.25%	10-Year Return (1984–93)	NA
Annual Expense Ratio	3.51%	Worst-Ever Loss (1989-90)	29%
Annual Portfolio Turnover	151%	Stock Market Correlation	33%
5-Year Cost Estimate	30%	Up/Down Market Rank	E – C
Benefits		**Investment Information**	
Investment Objective	Gr. & Icm.	Telephone	800-783-3444
5-Year Projected Return	–21%	Minimum Investment	$100
Safety Rating (0-100)	61%	Telephone Switching	Unlm;$7.50
Yield	0.0%	Total Assets	$1 million

Fairmont
Undervalued securities

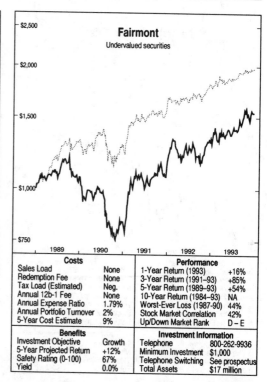

Costs		Performance	
Sales Load	None	1-Year Return (1993)	+16%
Redemption Fee	None	3-Year Return (1991–93)	+85%
Tax Load (Estimated)	Neg.	5-Year Return (1989–93)	+54%
Annual 12b-1 Fee	None	10-Year Return (1984–93)	NA
Annual Expense Ratio	1.79%	Worst-Ever Loss (1987-90)	44%
Annual Portfolio Turnover	2%	Stock Market Correlation	42%
5-Year Cost Estimate	9%	Up/Down Market Rank	D – E
Benefits		**Investment Information**	
Investment Objective	Growth	Telephone	800-262-9936
5-Year Projected Return	+12%	Minimum Investment	$1,000
Safety Rating (0-100)	67%	Telephone Switching	See prospectus
Yield	0.0%	Total Assets	$17 million

FBL Growth

Growth stocks; above-average earnings growth
★★★★

Costs		Performance	
Sales Load	None	1-Year Return (1993)	+27%
Redemption Fee	5.3%	3-Year Return (1991–93)	+60%
Tax Load (Estimated)	8%	5-Year Return (1989–93)	+91%
Annual 12b-1 Fee	0.50%	10-Year Return (1984–93)	NA
Annual Expense Ratio	1.69%	Worst-Ever Loss (1987)	29%
Annual Portfolio Turnover	92%	Stock Market Correlation	13%
5-Year Cost Estimate	20%	Up/Down Market Rank	E – B

Benefits		Investment Information	
Investment Objective	Gr. & Icm.	Telephone	800-247-4170
5-Year Projected Return	+35%	Minimum Investment	$250
Safety Rating (0-100)	90%	Telephone Switching	Unlimited; $5
Yield	16.2%	Total Assets	$53 million

Federated Exchange Fund

Diversified securities

Costs		Performance	
Sales Load	None	1-Year Return (1993)	+11%
Redemption Fee	None	3-Year Return (1991–93)	+58%
Tax Load (Estimated)	8%	5-Year Return (1989–93)	+77%
Annual 12b-1 Fee	None	10-Year Return (1984–93)	+253%
Annual Expense Ratio	1.07%	Worst-Ever Loss (1987)	31%
Annual Portfolio Turnover	66%	Stock Market Correlation	82%
5-Year Cost Estimate	14%	Up/Down Market Rank	B – D

Benefits		Investment Information	
Investment Objective	Gr. & Icm.	Telephone	800-245-2423
5-Year Projected Return	+11%	Minimum Investment	$25,000
Safety Rating (0-100)	73%	Telephone Switching	Unlimited;free
Yield	1.6%	Total Assets	$94 million

Federated Growth Trust

Earnings and dividend growth stocks

Costs		Performance	
Sales Load	None	1-Year Return (1993)	+8%
Redemption Fee	None	3-Year Return (1991–93)	+59%
Tax Load (Estimated)	2%	5-Year Return (1989–93)	+95%
Annual 12b-1 Fee	None	10-Year Return (1984–93)	NA
Annual Expense Ratio	0.96%	Worst-Ever Loss (1987)	38%
Annual Portfolio Turnover	46%	Stock Market Correlation	52%
5-Year Cost Estimate	7%	Up/Down Market Rank	A – E

Benefits		Investment Information	
Investment Objective	Growth	Telephone	800-245-2423
5-Year Projected Return	+16%	Minimum Investment	$25,000
Safety Rating (0-100)	73%	Telephone Switching	Unlimited;free
Yield	0.8%	Total Assets	$454 million

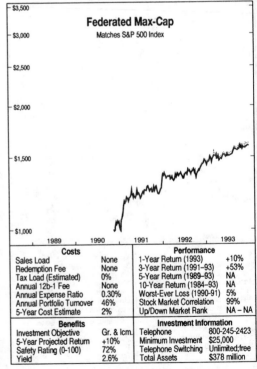

Federated Max-Cap

Matches S&P 500 Index

Costs		Performance	
Sales Load	None	1-Year Return (1993)	+10%
Redemption Fee	None	3-Year Return (1991–93)	+53%
Tax Load (Estimated)	0%	5-Year Return (1989–93)	NA
Annual 12b-1 Fee	None	10-Year Return (1984–93)	NA
Annual Expense Ratio	0.30%	Worst-Ever Loss (1990-91)	5%
Annual Portfolio Turnover	46%	Stock Market Correlation	99%
5-Year Cost Estimate	2%	Up/Down Market Rank	NA – NA

Benefits		Investment Information	
Investment Objective	Gr. & Icm.	Telephone	800-245-2423
5-Year Projected Return	+10%	Minimum Investment	$25,000
Safety Rating (0-100)	72%	Telephone Switching	Unlimited;free
Yield	2.6%	Total Assets	$378 million

EQUITY

Federated Stock & Bond
Diversified securities
★★★★★

S&P 500

Fund

Costs		Performance	
Sales Load	None	1-Year Return (1993)	+11%
Redemption Fee	None	3-Year Return (1991–93)	+41%
Tax Load (Estimated)	3%	5-Year Return (1989–93)	+58%
Annual 12b-1 Fee	None	10-Year Return (1984–93)	+169%
Annual Expense Ratio	1.04%	Worst-Ever Loss (1987)	14%
Annual Portfolio Turnover	72%	Stock Market Correlation	78%
5-Year Cost Estimate	9%	Up/Down Market Rank	E – A

Benefits		Investment Information	
Investment Objective	Icm. & Gr.	Telephone	800-245-2423
5-Year Projected Return	+15%	Minimum Investment	$25,000
Safety Rating (0-100)	88%	Telephone Switching	Mail only
Yield	3.3%	Total Assets	$116 million

Federated Stock Trust
Large, high-quality stocks

Costs		Performance	
Sales Load	None	1-Year Return (1993)	+12%
Redemption Fee	None	3-Year Return (1991–93)	+63%
Tax Load (Estimated)	2%	5-Year Return (1989–93)	+75%
Annual 12b-1 Fee	None	10-Year Return (1984–93)	+265%
Annual Expense Ratio	0.99%	Worst-Ever Loss (1987)	30%
Annual Portfolio Turnover	54%	Stock Market Correlation	82%
5-Year Cost Estimate	7%	Up/Down Market Rank	B – D

Benefits		Investment Information	
Investment Objective	Gr. & Icm.	Telephone	800-245-2423
5-Year Projected Return	+13%	Minimum Investment	$25,000
Safety Rating (0-100)	73%	Telephone Switching	Mail only
Yield	1.8%	Total Assets	$545 million

Fidel Adv - Global Resources
Foreign - natural resource securities
★

Costs		Performance	
Sales Load	5.0%	1-Year Return (1993)	+38%
Redemption Fee	None	3-Year Return (1991–93)	+79%
Tax Load (Estimated)	Neg.	5-Year Return (1989–93)	+126%
Annual 12b-1 Fee	0.65%	10-Year Return (1984–93)	NA
Annual Expense Ratio	2.65%	Worst-Ever Loss (1990-91)	19%
Annual Portfolio Turnover	274%	Stock Market Correlation	34%
5-Year Cost Estimate	20%	Up/Down Market Rank	B – A

Benefits		Investment Information	
Investment Objective	Growth	Telephone	800-522-7297
5-Year Projected Return	NA	Minimum Investment	$2,500
Safety Rating (0-100)	71%	Telephone Switching	Unlimited;free
Yield	0.0%	Total Assets	$57 million

Fidel Adv - Growth Opportunity
Diversified stocks
★

Costs		Performance	
Sales Load	5.0%	1-Year Return (1993)	+22%
Redemption Fee	None	3-Year Return (1991–93)	+101%
Tax Load (Estimated)	Neg.	5-Year Return (1989–93)	+145%
Annual 12b-1 Fee	0.65%	10-Year Return (1984–93)	NA
Annual Expense Ratio	1.70%	Worst-Ever Loss (1990)	27%
Annual Portfolio Turnover	94%	Stock Market Correlation	74%
5-Year Cost Estimate	14%	Up/Down Market Rank	A – E

Benefits		Investment Information	
Investment Objective	Growth	Telephone	800-522-7297
5-Year Projected Return	+33%	Minimum Investment	$2,500
Safety Rating (0-100)	71%	Telephone Switching	Unlimited;free
Yield	0.3%	Total Assets	$2.34 billion

EQUITY

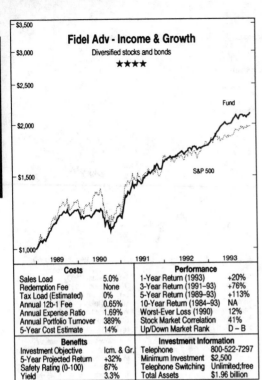

Fidel Adv - Income & Growth
Diversified stocks and bonds
★★★★

(chart shows Fund and S&P 500, $1,000–$3,500 scale, 1989–1993)

Costs		Performance	
Sales Load	5.0%	1-Year Return (1993)	+20%
Redemption Fee	None	3-Year Return (1991–93)	+76%
Tax Load (Estimated)	0%	5-Year Return (1989–93)	+113%
Annual 12b-1 Fee	0.65%	10-Year Return (1984–93)	NA
Annual Expense Ratio	1.69%	Worst-Ever Loss (1990)	12%
Annual Portfolio Turnover	389%	Stock Market Correlation	41%
5-Year Cost Estimate	14%	Up/Down Market Rank	D – B

Benefits		Investment Information	
Investment Objective	Icm. & Gr.	Telephone	800-522-7297
5-Year Projected Return	+32%	Minimum Investment	$2,500
Safety Rating (0-100)	87%	Telephone Switching	Unlimited;free
Yield	3.3%	Total Assets	$1.96 billion

Fidel Adv - Overseas
Foreign - diversified securities

(chart shows Fund, $750–$2,500 scale, 1989–1993)

Costs		Performance	
Sales Load	5.0%	1-Year Return (1993)	+42%
Redemption Fee	None	3-Year Return (1991–93)	+44%
Tax Load (Estimated)	0%	5-Year Return (1989–93)	NA
Annual 12b-1 Fee	0.65%	10-Year Return (1984–93)	NA
Annual Expense Ratio	2.65%	Worst-Ever Loss (1990-91)	23%
Annual Portfolio Turnover	120%	Stock Market Correlation	6%
5-Year Cost Estimate	21%	Up/Down Market Rank	NA – NA

Benefits		Investment Information	
Investment Objective	Growth	Telephone	800-522-7297
5-Year Projected Return	NA	Minimum Investment	$2,500
Safety Rating (0-100)	69%	Telephone Switching	Unlimited;free
Yield	0.2%	Total Assets	$268 million

Fidel Adv - Strtgc Opportuntys
Unusual developments
★★★★

(chart, $1,000–$3,500 scale, 1989–1993)

Costs		Performance	
Sales Load	5.0%	1-Year Return (1993)	+20%
Redemption Fee	None	3-Year Return (1991–93)	+67%
Tax Load (Estimated)	Neg.	5-Year Return (1989–93)	+106%
Annual 12b-1 Fee	0.65%	10-Year Return (1984–93)	NA
Annual Expense Ratio	1.55%	Worst-Ever Loss (1989-90)	14%
Annual Portfolio Turnover	275%	Stock Market Correlation	59%
5-Year Cost Estimate	14%	Up/Down Market Rank	D – A

Benefits		Investment Information	
Investment Objective	Growth	Telephone	800-522-7297
5-Year Projected Return	+23%	Minimum Investment	$2,500
Safety Rating (0-100)	83%	Telephone Switching	Unlimited;free
Yield	2.1%	Total Assets	$310 million

Fidelity Asset Manager
10-50% stocks; 20-60% bonds; 0-70% money mkt
★★★★★

(chart, $1,000–$3,000 scale, 1989–1993)

Costs		Performance	
Sales Load	None	1-Year Return (1993)	+23%
Redemption Fee	None	3-Year Return (1991–93)	+72%
Tax Load (Estimated)	1%	5-Year Return (1989–93)	NA
Annual 12b-1 Fee	None	10-Year Return (1984–93)	NA
Annual Expense Ratio	1.17%	Worst-Ever Loss (1990)	9%
Annual Portfolio Turnover	79%	Stock Market Correlation	69%
5-Year Cost Estimate	7%	Up/Down Market Rank	C – A

Benefits		Investment Information	
Investment Objective	Gr. & Icm.	Telephone	800-544-8888
5-Year Projected Return	+43%	Minimum Investment	$2,500
Safety Rating (0-100)	89%	Telephone Switching	4 per yr; free
Yield	3.9%	Total Assets	$9.07 billion

EQUITY

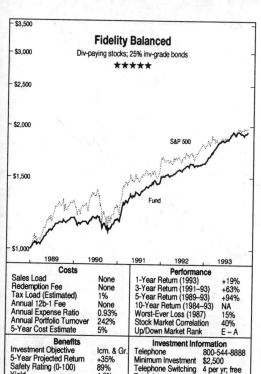

Fidelity Balanced
Div-paying stocks; 25% inv-grade bonds
★★★★★

S&P 500

Fund

1989 1990 1991 1992 1993

Costs		Performance	
Sales Load	None	1-Year Return (1993)	+19%
Redemption Fee	None	3-Year Return (1991–93)	+63%
Tax Load (Estimated)	1%	5-Year Return (1989–93)	+94%
Annual 12b-1 Fee	None	10-Year Return (1984–93)	NA
Annual Expense Ratio	0.93%	Worst-Ever Loss (1987)	15%
Annual Portfolio Turnover	242%	Stock Market Correlation	40%
5-Year Cost Estimate	5%	Up/Down Market Rank	E – A

Benefits		Investment Information	
Investment Objective	Icm. & Gr.	Telephone	800-544-8888
5-Year Projected Return	+35%	Minimum Investment	$2,500
Safety Rating (0-100)	89%	Telephone Switching	4 per yr; free
Yield	4.6%	Total Assets	$4.67 billion

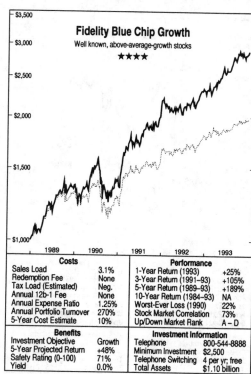

Fidelity Blue Chip Growth
Well known, above-average-growth stocks
★★★★

1989 1990 1991 1992 1993

Costs		Performance	
Sales Load	3.1%	1-Year Return (1993)	+25%
Redemption Fee	None	3-Year Return (1991–93)	+105%
Tax Load (Estimated)	Neg.	5-Year Return (1989–93)	+189%
Annual 12b-1 Fee	None	10-Year Return (1984–93)	NA
Annual Expense Ratio	1.25%	Worst-Ever Loss (1990)	22%
Annual Portfolio Turnover	270%	Stock Market Correlation	73%
5-Year Cost Estimate	10%	Up/Down Market Rank	A – D

Benefits		Investment Information	
Investment Objective	Growth	Telephone	800-544-8888
5-Year Projected Return	+48%	Minimum Investment	$2,500
Safety Rating (0-100)	71%	Telephone Switching	4 per yr; free
Yield	0.0%	Total Assets	$1.10 billion

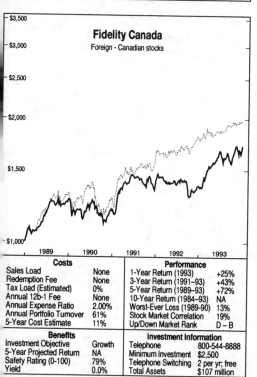

Fidelity Canada
Foreign - Canadian stocks

1989 1990 1991 1992 1993

Costs		Performance	
Sales Load	None	1-Year Return (1993)	+25%
Redemption Fee	None	3-Year Return (1991–93)	+43%
Tax Load (Estimated)	0%	5-Year Return (1989–93)	+72%
Annual 12b-1 Fee	None	10-Year Return (1984–93)	NA
Annual Expense Ratio	2.00%	Worst-Ever Loss (1989–90)	13%
Annual Portfolio Turnover	61%	Stock Market Correlation	19%
5-Year Cost Estimate	11%	Up/Down Market Rank	D – B

Benefits		Investment Information	
Investment Objective	Growth	Telephone	800-544-8888
5-Year Projected Return	NA	Minimum Investment	$2,500
Safety Rating (0-100)	79%	Telephone Switching	2 per yr; free
Yield	0.0%	Total Assets	$107 million

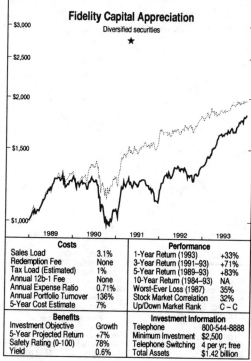

Fidelity Capital Appreciation
Diversified securities
★

1989 1990 1991 1992 1993

Costs		Performance	
Sales Load	3.1%	1-Year Return (1993)	+33%
Redemption Fee	None	3-Year Return (1991–93)	+71%
Tax Load (Estimated)	1%	5-Year Return (1989–93)	+83%
Annual 12b-1 Fee	None	10-Year Return (1984–93)	NA
Annual Expense Ratio	0.71%	Worst-Ever Loss (1987)	35%
Annual Portfolio Turnover	136%	Stock Market Correlation	32%
5-Year Cost Estimate	7%	Up/Down Market Rank	C – C

Benefits		Investment Information	
Investment Objective	Growth	Telephone	800-544-8888
5-Year Projected Return	+7%	Minimum Investment	$2,500
Safety Rating (0-100)	78%	Telephone Switching	4 per yr; free
Yield	0.6%	Total Assets	$1.42 billion

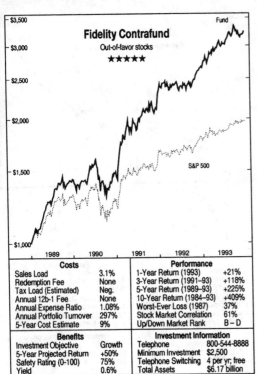

Fidelity Contrafund

Out-of-favor stocks

★★★★★

Fund

S&P 500

Costs		Performance	
Sales Load	3.1%	1-Year Return (1993)	+21%
Redemption Fee	None	3-Year Return (1991–93)	+118%
Tax Load (Estimated)	Neg.	5-Year Return (1989–93)	+225%
Annual 12b-1 Fee	None	10-Year Return (1984–93)	+409%
Annual Expense Ratio	1.08%	Worst-Ever Loss (1987)	37%
Annual Portfolio Turnover	297%	Stock Market Correlation	61%
5-Year Cost Estimate	9%	Up/Down Market Rank	B – D

Benefits		Investment Information	
Investment Objective	Growth	Telephone	800-544-8888
5-Year Projected Return	+50%	Minimum Investment	$2,500
Safety Rating (0-100)	75%	Telephone Switching	4 per yr; free
Yield	0.6%	Total Assets	$6.17 billion

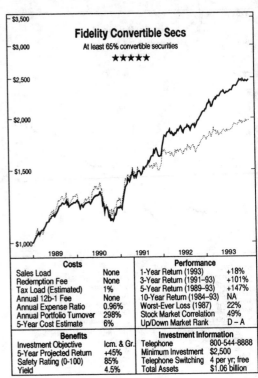

Fidelity Convertible Secs

At least 65% convertible securities

★★★★★

Costs		Performance	
Sales Load	None	1-Year Return (1993)	+18%
Redemption Fee	None	3-Year Return (1991–93)	+101%
Tax Load (Estimated)	1%	5-Year Return (1989–93)	+147%
Annual 12b-1 Fee	None	10-Year Return (1984–93)	NA
Annual Expense Ratio	0.96%	Worst-Ever Loss (1987)	22%
Annual Portfolio Turnover	298%	Stock Market Correlation	49%
5-Year Cost Estimate	6%	Up/Down Market Rank	D – A

Benefits		Investment Information	
Investment Objective	Icm. & Gr.	Telephone	800-544-8888
5-Year Projected Return	+45%	Minimum Investment	$2,500
Safety Rating (0-100)	85%	Telephone Switching	4 per yr; free
Yield	4.5%	Total Assets	$1.06 billion

Fidelity Destiny I (cont plan)

Diversified securities; contractual plan

★

Costs		Performance	
Sales Load	13.6%	1-Year Return (1993)	+26%
Redemption Fee	None	3-Year Return (1991–93)	+102%
Tax Load (Estimated)	1%	5-Year Return (1989–93)	+146%
Annual 12b-1 Fee	None	10-Year Return (1984–93)	+396%
Annual Expense Ratio	0.50%	Worst-Ever Loss (1987)	37%
Annual Portfolio Turnover	75%	Stock Market Correlation	79%
5-Year Cost Estimate	17%	Up/Down Market Rank	A – E

Benefits		Investment Information	
Investment Objective	Growth	Telephone	800-522-7297
5-Year Projected Return	+26%	Minimum Investment	$50
Safety Rating (0-100)	73%	Telephone Switching	Not available
Yield	1.5%	Total Assets	$2.98 billion

Fidelity Destiny II (cont plan)

Diversified securities; contractual plan

★

Costs		Performance	
Sales Load	13.6%	1-Year Return (1993)	+27%
Redemption Fee	None	3-Year Return (1991–93)	+107%
Tax Load (Estimated)	Neg.	5-Year Return (1989–93)	+155%
Annual 12b-1 Fee	None	10-Year Return (1984–93)	NA
Annual Expense Ratio	0.84%	Worst-Ever Loss (1987)	39%
Annual Portfolio Turnover	75%	Stock Market Correlation	76%
5-Year Cost Estimate	18%	Up/Down Market Rank	A – E

Benefits		Investment Information	
Investment Objective	Growth	Telephone	800-522-7297
5-Year Projected Return	+43%	Minimum Investment	$50
Safety Rating (0-100)	72%	Telephone Switching	Not available
Yield	1.0%	Total Assets	$1.13 billion

Fidelity Disciplined Equity
At least 65% undervalued stocks; good fundam
★★★★

Fund
S&P 500

Costs		Performance	
Sales Load	None	1-Year Return (1993)	+14%
Redemption Fee	None	3-Year Return (1991–93)	+75%
Tax Load (Estimated)	Neg.	5-Year Return (1989–93)	NA
Annual 12b-1 Fee	None	10-Year Return (1984–93)	NA
Annual Expense Ratio	1.16%	Worst-Ever Loss (1990)	20%
Annual Portfolio Turnover	304%	Stock Market Correlation	82%
5-Year Cost Estimate	6%	Up/Down Market Rank	A – D

Benefits		Investment Information	
Investment Objective	Growth	Telephone	800-544-8888
5-Year Projected Return	+32%	Minimum Investment	$2,500
Safety Rating (0-100)	76%	Telephone Switching	4 per yr; free
Yield	1.2%	Total Assets	$795 million

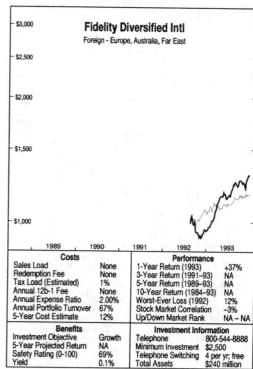

Fidelity Diversified Intl
Foreign - Europe, Australia, Far East

Costs		Performance	
Sales Load	None	1-Year Return (1993)	+37%
Redemption Fee	None	3-Year Return (1991–93)	NA
Tax Load (Estimated)	1%	5-Year Return (1989–93)	NA
Annual 12b-1 Fee	None	10-Year Return (1984–93)	NA
Annual Expense Ratio	2.00%	Worst-Ever Loss (1992)	12%
Annual Portfolio Turnover	67%	Stock Market Correlation	–3%
5-Year Cost Estimate	12%	Up/Down Market Rank	NA – NA

Benefits		Investment Information	
Investment Objective	Growth	Telephone	800-544-8888
5-Year Projected Return	NA	Minimum Investment	$2,500
Safety Rating (0-100)	69%	Telephone Switching	4 per yr; free
Yield	0.1%	Total Assets	$240 million

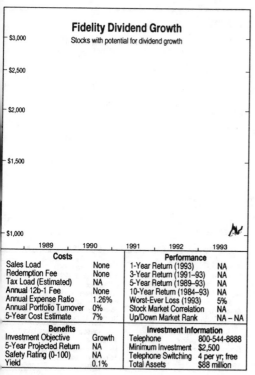

Fidelity Dividend Growth
Stocks with potential for dividend growth

Costs		Performance	
Sales Load	None	1-Year Return (1993)	NA
Redemption Fee	None	3-Year Return (1991–93)	NA
Tax Load (Estimated)	NA	5-Year Return (1989–93)	NA
Annual 12b-1 Fee	None	10-Year Return (1984–93)	NA
Annual Expense Ratio	1.26%	Worst-Ever Loss (1993)	5%
Annual Portfolio Turnover	0%	Stock Market Correlation	NA
5-Year Cost Estimate	7%	Up/Down Market Rank	NA – NA

Benefits		Investment Information	
Investment Objective	Growth	Telephone	800-544-8888
5-Year Projected Return	NA	Minimum Investment	$2,500
Safety Rating (0-100)	NA	Telephone Switching	4 per yr; free
Yield	0.1%	Total Assets	$88 million

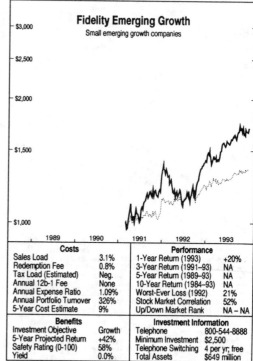

Fidelity Emerging Growth
Small emerging growth companies

Costs		Performance	
Sales Load	3.1%	1-Year Return (1993)	+20%
Redemption Fee	0.8%	3-Year Return (1991–93)	NA
Tax Load (Estimated)	Neg.	5-Year Return (1989–93)	NA
Annual 12b-1 Fee	None	10-Year Return (1984–93)	NA
Annual Expense Ratio	1.09%	Worst-Ever Loss (1992)	21%
Annual Portfolio Turnover	326%	Stock Market Correlation	52%
5-Year Cost Estimate	9%	Up/Down Market Rank	NA – NA

Benefits		Investment Information	
Investment Objective	Growth	Telephone	800-544-8888
5-Year Projected Return	+42%	Minimum Investment	$2,500
Safety Rating (0-100)	58%	Telephone Switching	4 per yr; free
Yield	0.0%	Total Assets	$649 million

EQUITY

Fidelity Equity-Income
High-yield conservative stocks
★★

Costs		Performance	
Sales Load	2.0%	1-Year Return (1993)	+21%
Redemption Fee	None	3-Year Return (1991–93)	+80%
Tax Load (Estimated)	3%	5-Year Return (1989–93)	+84%
Annual 12b-1 Fee	None	10-Year Return (1984–93)	+258%
Annual Expense Ratio	0.67%	Worst-Ever Loss (1987)	25%
Annual Portfolio Turnover	97%	Stock Market Correlation	76%
5-Year Cost Estimate	9%	Up/Down Market Rank	D – A

Benefits		Investment Information	
Investment Objective	Icm. & Gr.	Telephone	800-544-8888
5-Year Projected Return	+18%	Minimum Investment	$2,500
Safety Rating (0-100)	80%	Telephone Switching	4 per yr; free
Yield	3.4%	Total Assets	$6.65 billion

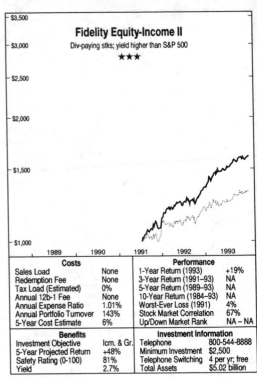

Fidelity Equity-Income II
Div-paying stks; yield higher than S&P 500
★★★

Costs		Performance	
Sales Load	None	1-Year Return (1993)	+19%
Redemption Fee	None	3-Year Return (1991–93)	NA
Tax Load (Estimated)	0%	5-Year Return (1989–93)	NA
Annual 12b-1 Fee	None	10-Year Return (1984–93)	NA
Annual Expense Ratio	1.01%	Worst-Ever Loss (1991)	4%
Annual Portfolio Turnover	143%	Stock Market Correlation	67%
5-Year Cost Estimate	6%	Up/Down Market Rank	NA – NA

Benefits		Investment Information	
Investment Objective	Icm. & Gr.	Telephone	800-544-8888
5-Year Projected Return	+48%	Minimum Investment	$2,500
Safety Rating (0-100)	81%	Telephone Switching	4 per yr; free
Yield	2.7%	Total Assets	$5.02 billion

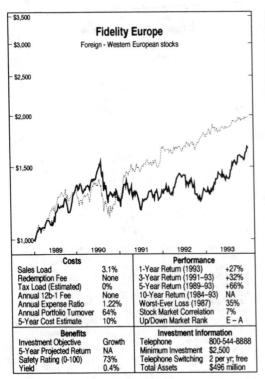

Fidelity Europe
Foreign - Western European stocks

Costs		Performance	
Sales Load	3.1%	1-Year Return (1993)	+27%
Redemption Fee	None	3-Year Return (1991–93)	+32%
Tax Load (Estimated)	0%	5-Year Return (1989–93)	+66%
Annual 12b-1 Fee	None	10-Year Return (1984–93)	NA
Annual Expense Ratio	1.22%	Worst-Ever Loss (1987)	35%
Annual Portfolio Turnover	64%	Stock Market Correlation	7%
5-Year Cost Estimate	10%	Up/Down Market Rank	E – A

Benefits		Investment Information	
Investment Objective	Growth	Telephone	800-544-8888
5-Year Projected Return	NA	Minimum Investment	$2,500
Safety Rating (0-100)	73%	Telephone Switching	2 per yr; free
Yield	0.4%	Total Assets	$496 million

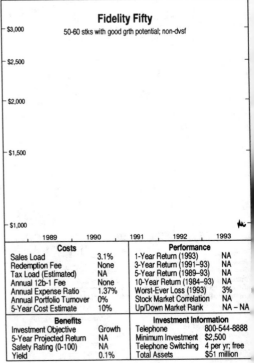

Fidelity Fifty
50-60 stks with good grth potential; non-dvsf

Costs		Performance	
Sales Load	3.1%	1-Year Return (1993)	NA
Redemption Fee	None	3-Year Return (1991–93)	NA
Tax Load (Estimated)	NA	5-Year Return (1989–93)	NA
Annual 12b-1 Fee	None	10-Year Return (1984–93)	NA
Annual Expense Ratio	1.37%	Worst-Ever Loss (1993)	3%
Annual Portfolio Turnover	0%	Stock Market Correlation	NA
5-Year Cost Estimate	10%	Up/Down Market Rank	NA – NA

Benefits		Investment Information	
Investment Objective	Growth	Telephone	800-544-8888
5-Year Projected Return	NA	Minimum Investment	$2,500
Safety Rating (0-100)	NA	Telephone Switching	4 per yr; free
Yield	0.1%	Total Assets	$51 million

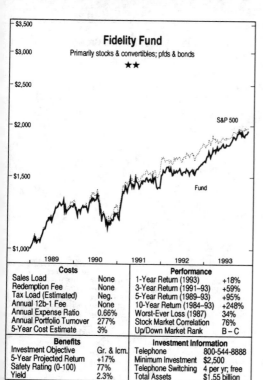

Fidelity Fund
Primarily stocks & convertibles; pfds & bonds
★★

S&P 500

Fund

| 1989 | 1990 | 1991 | 1992 | 1993 |

Costs		Performance	
Sales Load	None	1-Year Return (1993)	+18%
Redemption Fee	None	3-Year Return (1991–93)	+59%
Tax Load (Estimated)	Neg.	5-Year Return (1989–93)	+95%
Annual 12b-1 Fee	None	10-Year Return (1984–93)	+248%
Annual Expense Ratio	0.66%	Worst-Ever Loss (1987)	34%
Annual Portfolio Turnover	277%	Stock Market Correlation	76%
5-Year Cost Estimate	3%	Up/Down Market Rank	B – C

Benefits		Investment Information	
Investment Objective	Gr. & Icm.	Telephone	800-544-8888
5-Year Projected Return	+17%	Minimum Investment	$2,500
Safety Rating (0-100)	77%	Telephone Switching	4 per yr; free
Yield	2.3%	Total Assets	$1.55 billion

Fidelity Growth & Income
Dividend-paying growth stocks
★★★★

| 1989 | 1990 | 1991 | 1992 | 1993 |

Costs		Performance	
Sales Load	3.1%	1-Year Return (1993)	+20%
Redemption Fee	None	3-Year Return (1991–93)	+89%
Tax Load (Estimated)	0%	5-Year Return (1989–93)	+128%
Annual 12b-1 Fee	None	10-Year Return (1984–93)	NA
Annual Expense Ratio	0.83%	Worst-Ever Loss (1987)	29%
Annual Portfolio Turnover	108%	Stock Market Correlation	78%
5-Year Cost Estimate	8%	Up/Down Market Rank	B – C

Benefits		Investment Information	
Investment Objective	Gr. & Icm.	Telephone	800-544-8888
5-Year Projected Return	+30%	Minimum Investment	$2,500
Safety Rating (0-100)	78%	Telephone Switching	4 per yr; free
Yield	2.4%	Total Assets	$7.68 billion

Fidelity Growth Company
Stocks with high earnings or sales growth
★★

| 1989 | 1990 | 1991 | 1992 | 1993 |

Costs		Performance	
Sales Load	3.1%	1-Year Return (1993)	+16%
Redemption Fee	None	3-Year Return (1991–93)	+86%
Tax Load (Estimated)	Neg.	5-Year Return (1989–93)	+173%
Annual 12b-1 Fee	None	10-Year Return (1984–93)	+365%
Annual Expense Ratio	1.09%	Worst-Ever Loss (1987)	41%
Annual Portfolio Turnover	240%	Stock Market Correlation	67%
5-Year Cost Estimate	9%	Up/Down Market Rank	A – E

Benefits		Investment Information	
Investment Objective	Growth	Telephone	800-544-8888
5-Year Projected Return	+36%	Minimum Investment	$2,500
Safety Rating (0-100)	69%	Telephone Switching	4 per yr; free
Yield	0.2%	Total Assets	$2.55 billion

Fidel Instl - Eqty Portf Grwth
Diversified common and preferred stocks
★★★

| 1989 | 1990 | 1991 | 1992 | 1993 |

Costs		Performance	
Sales Load	None	1-Year Return (1993)	+15%
Redemption Fee	None	3-Year Return (1991–93)	+109%
Tax Load (Estimated)	Neg.	5-Year Return (1989–93)	+224%
Annual 12b-1 Fee	None	10-Year Return (1984–93)	NA
Annual Expense Ratio	1.28%	Worst-Ever Loss (1987)	40%
Annual Portfolio Turnover	281%	Stock Market Correlation	64%
5-Year Cost Estimate	7%	Up/Down Market Rank	A – E

Benefits		Investment Information	
Investment Objective	Growth	Telephone	800-843-3001
5-Year Projected Return	+56%	Minimum Investment	$100,000
Safety Rating (0-100)	67%	Telephone Switching	4 per yr; free
Yield	0.0%	Total Assets	$425 million

Fidel Instl - Equity Portf Icm
Yield exceeding S&P 500; up to 20% junk bonds
★

Costs		Performance	
Sales Load	None	1-Year Return (1993)	+19%
Redemption Fee	None	3-Year Return (1991–93)	+77%
Tax Load (Estimated)	Neg.	5-Year Return (1989–93)	+74%
Annual 12b-1 Fee	None	10-Year Return (1984–93)	NA
Annual Expense Ratio	0.96%	Worst-Ever Loss (1989-90)	27%
Annual Portfolio Turnover	109%	Stock Market Correlation	76%
5-Year Cost Estimate	5%	Up/Down Market Rank	D – C
Benefits		**Investment Information**	
Investment Objective	Icm. & Gr.	Telephone	800-843-3001
5-Year Projected Return	+16%	Minimum Investment	$100,000
Safety Rating (0-100)	78%	Telephone Switching	4 per yr; free
Yield	2.0%	Total Assets	$184 million

Fidelity International Growth
Foreign - EPS, dividend growth stocks

Costs		Performance	
Sales Load	None	1-Year Return (1993)	+35%
Redemption Fee	None	3-Year Return (1991–93)	+41%
Tax Load (Estimated)	0%	5-Year Return (1989–93)	+63%
Annual 12b-1 Fee	None	10-Year Return (1984–93)	NA
Annual Expense Ratio	1.62%	Worst-Ever Loss (1987)	26%
Annual Portfolio Turnover	60%	Stock Market Correlation	9%
5-Year Cost Estimate	9%	Up/Down Market Rank	E – A
Benefits		**Investment Information**	
Investment Objective	Gr. & Icm.	Telephone	800-544-8888
5-Year Projected Return	NA	Minimum Investment	$2,500
Safety Rating (0-100)	78%	Telephone Switching	2 per yr; free
Yield	0.3%	Total Assets	$1.07 billion

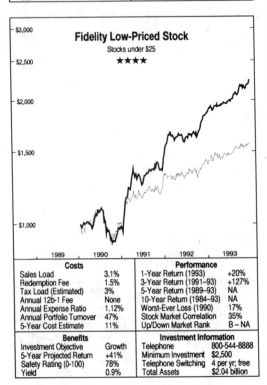

Fidelity Low-Priced Stock
Stocks under $25
★★★★

Costs		Performance	
Sales Load	3.1%	1-Year Return (1993)	+20%
Redemption Fee	1.5%	3-Year Return (1991–93)	+127%
Tax Load (Estimated)	3%	5-Year Return (1989–93)	NA
Annual 12b-1 Fee	None	10-Year Return (1984–93)	NA
Annual Expense Ratio	1.12%	Worst-Ever Loss (1990)	17%
Annual Portfolio Turnover	47%	Stock Market Correlation	35%
5-Year Cost Estimate	11%	Up/Down Market Rank	B – NA
Benefits		**Investment Information**	
Investment Objective	Growth	Telephone	800-544-8888
5-Year Projected Return	+41%	Minimum Investment	$2,500
Safety Rating (0-100)	78%	Telephone Switching	4 per yr; free
Yield	0.9%	Total Assets	$2.04 billion

Fidelity Magellan
Diversified stocks
★★★★

Costs		Performance	
Sales Load	3.1%	1-Year Return (1993)	+25%
Redemption Fee	None	3-Year Return (1991–93)	+88%
Tax Load (Estimated)	4%	5-Year Return (1989–93)	+142%
Annual 12b-1 Fee	None	10-Year Return (1984–93)	+440%
Annual Expense Ratio	1.00%	Worst-Ever Loss (1987)	36%
Annual Portfolio Turnover	125%	Stock Market Correlation	73%
5-Year Cost Estimate	13%	Up/Down Market Rank	A – D
Benefits		**Investment Information**	
Investment Objective	Growth	Telephone	800-544-8888
5-Year Projected Return	+29%	Minimum Investment	$2,500
Safety Rating (0-100)	75%	Telephone Switching	4 per yr; free
Yield	1.1%	Total Assets	$31.67 billion

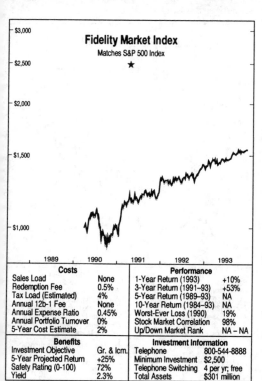

Fidelity Market Index
Matches S&P 500 Index
★

Costs		Performance	
Sales Load	None	1-Year Return (1993)	+10%
Redemption Fee	0.5%	3-Year Return (1991–93)	+53%
Tax Load (Estimated)	4%	5-Year Return (1989–93)	NA
Annual 12b-1 Fee	None	10-Year Return (1984–93)	NA
Annual Expense Ratio	0.45%	Worst-Ever Loss (1990)	19%
Annual Portfolio Turnover	0%	Stock Market Correlation	98%
5-Year Cost Estimate	2%	Up/Down Market Rank	NA – NA

Benefits		Investment Information	
Investment Objective	Gr. & Icm.	Telephone	800-544-8888
5-Year Projected Return	+25%	Minimum Investment	$2,500
Safety Rating (0-100)	72%	Telephone Switching	4 per yr; free
Yield	2.3%	Total Assets	$301 million

Fidelity OTC
Over-the-counter securities
★★★

Costs		Performance	
Sales Load	3.1%	1-Year Return (1993)	+8%
Redemption Fee	None	3-Year Return (1991–93)	+86%
Tax Load (Estimated)	Neg.	5-Year Return (1989–93)	+131%
Annual 12b-1 Fee	None	10-Year Return (1984–93)	NA
Annual Expense Ratio	1.08%	Worst-Ever Loss (1987)	39%
Annual Portfolio Turnover	213%	Stock Market Correlation	54%
5-Year Cost Estimate	9%	Up/Down Market Rank	B – D

Benefits		Investment Information	
Investment Objective	Growth	Telephone	800-544-8888
5-Year Projected Return	+30%	Minimum Investment	$2,500
Safety Rating (0-100)	76%	Telephone Switching	4 per yr; free
Yield	0.4%	Total Assets	$1.33 billion

Fidelity Overseas
Foreign - diversified stocks

Costs		Performance	
Sales Load	3.1%	1-Year Return (1993)	+40%
Redemption Fee	None	3-Year Return (1991–93)	+35%
Tax Load (Estimated)	0%	5-Year Return (1989–93)	+47%
Annual 12b-1 Fee	None	10-Year Return (1984–93)	NA
Annual Expense Ratio	1.52%	Worst-Ever Loss (1987)	29%
Annual Portfolio Turnover	84%	Stock Market Correlation	10%
5-Year Cost Estimate	11%	Up/Down Market Rank	E – A

Benefits		Investment Information	
Investment Objective	Growth	Telephone	800-544-8888
5-Year Projected Return	NA	Minimum Investment	$2,500
Safety Rating (0-100)	71%	Telephone Switching	2 per yr; free
Yield	1.6%	Total Assets	$1.52 billion

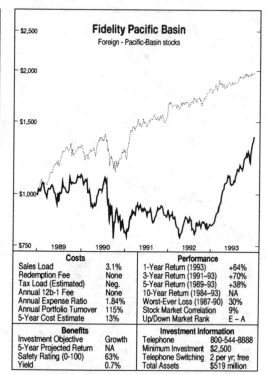

Fidelity Pacific Basin
Foreign - Pacific-Basin stocks

Costs		Performance	
Sales Load	3.1%	1-Year Return (1993)	+64%
Redemption Fee	None	3-Year Return (1991–93)	+70%
Tax Load (Estimated)	Neg.	5-Year Return (1989–93)	+38%
Annual 12b-1 Fee	None	10-Year Return (1984–93)	NA
Annual Expense Ratio	1.84%	Worst-Ever Loss (1987-90)	30%
Annual Portfolio Turnover	115%	Stock Market Correlation	9%
5-Year Cost Estimate	13%	Up/Down Market Rank	E – A

Benefits		Investment Information	
Investment Objective	Growth	Telephone	800-544-8888
5-Year Projected Return	NA	Minimum Investment	$2,500
Safety Rating (0-100)	63%	Telephone Switching	2 per yr; free
Yield	0.7%	Total Assets	$519 million

Fidelity Puritan
High-yield stocks and bonds
★★★★★

S&P 500

Fund

Costs		Performance	
Sales Load	None	1-Year Return (1993)	+21%
Redemption Fee	None	3-Year Return (1991–93)	+74%
Tax Load (Estimated)	2%	5-Year Return (1989–93)	+95%
Annual 12b-1 Fee	None	10-Year Return (1984–93)	+292%
Annual Expense Ratio	0.74%	Worst-Ever Loss (1987)	21%
Annual Portfolio Turnover	76%	Stock Market Correlation	63%
5-Year Cost Estimate	6%	Up/Down Market Rank	D – A

Benefits		Investment Information	
Investment Objective	Icm. & Gr.	Telephone	800-544-8888
5-Year Projected Return	+30%	Minimum Investment	$2,500
Safety Rating (0-100)	84%	Telephone Switching	4 per yr; free
Yield	4.7%	Total Assets	$8.98 billion

Fidelity Real Estate Invstmnt
Real estate stocks
★★★

Costs		Performance	
Sales Load	None	1-Year Return (1993)	+13%
Redemption Fee	None	3-Year Return (1991–93)	+87%
Tax Load (Estimated)	2%	5-Year Return (1989–93)	+94%
Annual 12b-1 Fee	None	10-Year Return (1984–93)	NA
Annual Expense Ratio	1.16%	Worst-Ever Loss (1987)	23%
Annual Portfolio Turnover	102%	Stock Market Correlation	24%
5-Year Cost Estimate	8%	Up/Down Market Rank	D – A

Benefits		Investment Information	
Investment Objective	Gr. & Icm.	Telephone	800-544-8888
5-Year Projected Return	NA	Minimum Investment	$2,500
Safety Rating (0-100)	83%	Telephone Switching	4 per yr; free
Yield	4.5%	Total Assets	$422 million

Fidelity Retirement Growth
For retirement plans only
★★★

Costs		Performance	
Sales Load	None	1-Year Return (1993)	+22%
Redemption Fee	None	3-Year Return (1991–93)	+97%
Tax Load (Estimated)	Neg.	5-Year Return (1989–93)	+130%
Annual 12b-1 Fee	None	10-Year Return (1984–93)	+342%
Annual Expense Ratio	1.02%	Worst-Ever Loss (1987)	37%
Annual Portfolio Turnover	93%	Stock Market Correlation	65%
5-Year Cost Estimate	5%	Up/Down Market Rank	A – D

Benefits		Investment Information	
Investment Objective	Growth	Telephone	800-544-8888
5-Year Projected Return	+31%	Minimum Investment	$500
Safety Rating (0-100)	75%	Telephone Switching	4 per yr; free
Yield	0.8%	Total Assets	$2.84 billion

Fidelity Select Air Transport
Airline and freight stocks

Costs		Performance	
Sales Load	3.1%	1-Year Return (1993)	+31%
Redemption Fee	0.8%	3-Year Return (1991–93)	+91%
Tax Load (Estimated)	Neg.	5-Year Return (1989–93)	+98%
Annual 12b-1 Fee	None	10-Year Return (1984–93)	NA
Annual Expense Ratio	2.64%	Worst-Ever Loss (1987)	40%
Annual Portfolio Turnover	96%	Stock Market Correlation	38%
5-Year Cost Estimate	18%	Up/Down Market Rank	B – E

Benefits		Investment Information	
Investment Objective	Growth	Telephone	800-544-8888
5-Year Projected Return	NA	Minimum Investment	$2,500
Safety Rating (0-100)	66%	Telephone Switching	See prospectus
Yield	0.0%	Total Assets	$15 million

Fidelity Select American Gold
Western Hemisphere gold stocks

Costs		Performance	
Sales Load	3.1%	1-Year Return (1993)	+79%
Redemption Fee	0.8%	3-Year Return (1991–93)	+63%
Tax Load (Estimated)	Neg.	5-Year Return (1989–93)	+64%
Annual 12b-1 Fee	None	10-Year Return (1984–93)	NA
Annual Expense Ratio	1.59%	Worst-Ever Loss (1987-92)	42%
Annual Portfolio Turnover	30%	Stock Market Correlation	–1%
5-Year Cost Estimate	12%	Up/Down Market Rank	E – A

Benefits		Investment Information	
Investment Objective	Growth	Telephone	800-544-8888
5-Year Projected Return	NA	Minimum Investment	$2,500
Safety Rating (0-100)	55%	Telephone Switching	See prospectus
Yield	0.0%	Total Assets	$365 million

Fidelity Select Automotive
Automotive stocks
★★

Costs		Performance	
Sales Load	3.1%	1-Year Return (1993)	+35%
Redemption Fee	0.8%	3-Year Return (1991–93)	+163%
Tax Load (Estimated)	1%	5-Year Return (1989–93)	+156%
Annual 12b-1 Fee	None	10-Year Return (1984–93)	NA
Annual Expense Ratio	1.57%	Worst-Ever Loss (1987)	36%
Annual Portfolio Turnover	140%	Stock Market Correlation	52%
5-Year Cost Estimate	13%	Up/Down Market Rank	C – D

Benefits		Investment Information	
Investment Objective	Growth	Telephone	800-544-8888
5-Year Projected Return	NA	Minimum Investment	$2,500
Safety Rating (0-100)	71%	Telephone Switching	See prospectus
Yield	0.2%	Total Assets	$197 million

Fidelity Select Biotechnology
Biotechnology stocks
★★

Costs		Performance	
Sales Load	3.1%	1-Year Return (1993)	+1%
Redemption Fee	0.8%	3-Year Return (1991–93)	+79%
Tax Load (Estimated)	Neg.	5-Year Return (1989–93)	+273%
Annual 12b-1 Fee	None	10-Year Return (1984–93)	NA
Annual Expense Ratio	1.50%	Worst-Ever Loss (1987)	43%
Annual Portfolio Turnover	79%	Stock Market Correlation	25%
5-Year Cost Estimate	11%	Up/Down Market Rank	A – D

Benefits		Investment Information	
Investment Objective	Growth	Telephone	800-544-8888
5-Year Projected Return	NA	Minimum Investment	$2,500
Safety Rating (0-100)	58%	Telephone Switching	See prospectus
Yield	0.0%	Total Assets	$551 million

Fidelity Select Brdcst & Media
Broadcast and media stocks

Costs		Performance	
Sales Load	3.1%	1-Year Return (1993)	+38%
Redemption Fee	0.8%	3-Year Return (1991–93)	+131%
Tax Load (Estimated)	1%	5-Year Return (1989–93)	+126%
Annual 12b-1 Fee	None	10-Year Return (1984–93)	NA
Annual Expense Ratio	2.54%	Worst-Ever Loss (1989-90)	43%
Annual Portfolio Turnover	70%	Stock Market Correlation	55%
5-Year Cost Estimate	18%	Up/Down Market Rank	B – E

Benefits		Investment Information	
Investment Objective	Growth	Telephone	800-544-8888
5-Year Projected Return	NA	Minimum Investment	$2,500
Safety Rating (0-100)	69%	Telephone Switching	See prospectus
Yield	0.0%	Total Assets	$65 million

Fidelity Select Brokerage

Brokerage house stocks

★

Fund

S&P 500

Costs		Performance	
Sales Load	3.1%	1-Year Return (1993)	+49%
Redemption Fee	0.8%	3-Year Return (1991–93)	+186%
Tax Load (Estimated)	Neg.	5-Year Return (1989–93)	+174%
Annual 12b-1 Fee	None	10-Year Return (1984–93)	NA
Annual Expense Ratio	2.21%	Worst-Ever Loss (1987)	54%
Annual Portfolio Turnover	111%	Stock Market Correlation	53%
5-Year Cost Estimate	15%	Up/Down Market Rank	C – D

Benefits		Investment Information	
Investment Objective	Growth	Telephone	800-544-8888
5-Year Projected Return	NA	Minimum Investment	$2,500
Safety Rating (0-100)	65%	Telephone Switching	See prospectus
Yield	0.1%	Total Assets	$94 million

Fidelity Select Chemicals

Chemical company stocks

Costs		Performance	
Sales Load	3.1%	1-Year Return (1993)	+13%
Redemption Fee	0.8%	3-Year Return (1991–93)	+70%
Tax Load (Estimated)	Neg.	5-Year Return (1989–93)	+91%
Annual 12b-1 Fee	None	10-Year Return (1984–93)	NA
Annual Expense Ratio	1.89%	Worst-Ever Loss (1987)	38%
Annual Portfolio Turnover	214%	Stock Market Correlation	61%
5-Year Cost Estimate	13%	Up/Down Market Rank	C – C

Benefits		Investment Information	
Investment Objective	Growth	Telephone	800-544-8888
5-Year Projected Return	NA	Minimum Investment	$2,500
Safety Rating (0-100)	76%	Telephone Switching	See prospectus
Yield	0.8%	Total Assets	$26 million

Fidelity Select Computers

Computer stocks

Costs		Performance	
Sales Load	3.1%	1-Year Return (1993)	+29%
Redemption Fee	0.8%	3-Year Return (1991–93)	+106%
Tax Load (Estimated)	1%	5-Year Return (1989–93)	+160%
Annual 12b-1 Fee	None	10-Year Return (1984–93)	NA
Annual Expense Ratio	1.81%	Worst-Ever Loss (1987)	48%
Annual Portfolio Turnover	254%	Stock Market Correlation	40%
5-Year Cost Estimate	14%	Up/Down Market Rank	B – E

Benefits		Investment Information	
Investment Objective	Growth	Telephone	800-544-8888
5-Year Projected Return	NA	Minimum Investment	$2,500
Safety Rating (0-100)	54%	Telephone Switching	See prospectus
Yield	0.0%	Total Assets	$61 million

Fidelity Select Construction

Construction and housing stocks

★

Costs		Performance	
Sales Load	3.1%	1-Year Return (1993)	+34%
Redemption Fee	0.8%	3-Year Return (1991–93)	+124%
Tax Load (Estimated)	1%	5-Year Return (1989–93)	+136%
Annual 12b-1 Fee	None	10-Year Return (1984–93)	NA
Annual Expense Ratio	2.02%	Worst-Ever Loss (1987)	46%
Annual Portfolio Turnover	60%	Stock Market Correlation	55%
5-Year Cost Estimate	16%	Up/Down Market Rank	B – E

Benefits		Investment Information	
Investment Objective	Growth	Telephone	800-544-8888
5-Year Projected Return	NA	Minimum Investment	$2,500
Safety Rating (0-100)	71%	Telephone Switching	See prospectus
Yield	0.0%	Total Assets	$64 million

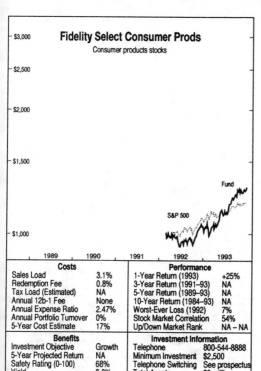

Fidelity Select Consumer Prods
Consumer products stocks

Costs		Performance	
Sales Load	3.1%	1-Year Return (1993)	+25%
Redemption Fee	0.8%	3-Year Return (1991–93)	NA
Tax Load (Estimated)	NA	5-Year Return (1989–93)	NA
Annual 12b-1 Fee	None	10-Year Return (1984–93)	NA
Annual Expense Ratio	2.47%	Worst-Ever Loss (1992)	7%
Annual Portfolio Turnover	0%	Stock Market Correlation	54%
5-Year Cost Estimate	17%	Up/Down Market Rank	NA – NA

Benefits		Investment Information	
Investment Objective	Growth	Telephone	800-544-8888
5-Year Projected Return	NA	Minimum Investment	$2,500
Safety Rating (0-100)	68%	Telephone Switching	See prospectus
Yield	0.0%	Total Assets	$9 million

Fidelity Select Defense & Aero
Defense and aerospace stocks

Costs		Performance	
Sales Load	3.1%	1-Year Return (1993)	+29%
Redemption Fee	0.8%	3-Year Return (1991–93)	+64%
Tax Load (Estimated)	Neg.	5-Year Return (1989–93)	+70%
Annual 12b-1 Fee	None	10-Year Return (1984–93)	NA
Annual Expense Ratio	2.48%	Worst-Ever Loss (1987)	40%
Annual Portfolio Turnover	87%	Stock Market Correlation	53%
5-Year Cost Estimate	17%	Up/Down Market Rank	D – C

Benefits		Investment Information	
Investment Objective	Growth	Telephone	800-544-8888
5-Year Projected Return	NA	Minimum Investment	$2,500
Safety Rating (0-100)	74%	Telephone Switching	See prospectus
Yield	0.5%	Total Assets	$3 million

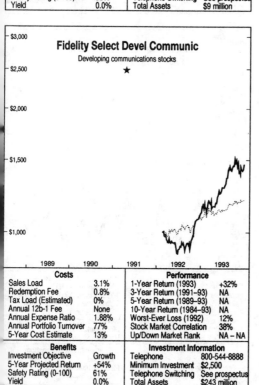

Fidelity Select Devel Communic
Developing communications stocks
★

Costs		Performance	
Sales Load	3.1%	1-Year Return (1993)	+32%
Redemption Fee	0.8%	3-Year Return (1991–93)	NA
Tax Load (Estimated)	0%	5-Year Return (1989–93)	NA
Annual 12b-1 Fee	None	10-Year Return (1984–93)	NA
Annual Expense Ratio	1.88%	Worst-Ever Loss (1992)	12%
Annual Portfolio Turnover	77%	Stock Market Correlation	38%
5-Year Cost Estimate	13%	Up/Down Market Rank	NA – NA

Benefits		Investment Information	
Investment Objective	Growth	Telephone	800-544-8888
5-Year Projected Return	+54%	Minimum Investment	$2,500
Safety Rating (0-100)	61%	Telephone Switching	See prospectus
Yield	0.0%	Total Assets	$243 million

Fidelity Select Electric Util
Electric utility stocks
★★

Costs		Performance	
Sales Load	3.1%	1-Year Return (1993)	+13%
Redemption Fee	0.8%	3-Year Return (1991–93)	+56%
Tax Load (Estimated)	5%	5-Year Return (1989–93)	+97%
Annual 12b-1 Fee	None	10-Year Return (1984–93)	NA
Annual Expense Ratio	1.70%	Worst-Ever Loss (1986-87)	30%
Annual Portfolio Turnover	55%	Stock Market Correlation	37%
5-Year Cost Estimate	17%	Up/Down Market Rank	D – A

Benefits		Investment Information	
Investment Objective	Growth	Telephone	800-544-8888
5-Year Projected Return	NA	Minimum Investment	$2,500
Safety Rating (0-100)	83%	Telephone Switching	See prospectus
Yield	2.8%	Total Assets	$23 million

Fidelity Select Electronics
Electronics stocks

Fund

S&P 500

Costs		Performance	
Sales Load	3.1%	1-Year Return (1993)	+32%
Redemption Fee	0.8%	3-Year Return (1991–93)	+128%
Tax Load (Estimated)	Neg.	5-Year Return (1989–93)	+179%
Annual 12b-1 Fee	None	10-Year Return (1984–93)	NA
Annual Expense Ratio	1.71%	Worst-Ever Loss (1986-88)	50%
Annual Portfolio Turnover	293%	Stock Market Correlation	41%
5-Year Cost Estimate	12%	Up/Down Market Rank	B – D

Benefits		Investment Information	
Investment Objective	Growth	Telephone	800-544-8888
5-Year Projected Return	NA	Minimum Investment	$2,500
Safety Rating (0-100)	59%	Telephone Switching	See prospectus
Yield	0.0%	Total Assets	$45 million

Fidelity Select Energy
Energy stocks

Costs		Performance	
Sales Load	3.1%	1-Year Return (1993)	+19%
Redemption Fee	0.8%	3-Year Return (1991–93)	+16%
Tax Load (Estimated)	1%	5-Year Return (1989–93)	+59%
Annual 12b-1 Fee	None	10-Year Return (1984–93)	+130%
Annual Expense Ratio	1.71%	Worst-Ever Loss (1981-82)	43%
Annual Portfolio Turnover	72%	Stock Market Correlation	17%
5-Year Cost Estimate	14%	Up/Down Market Rank	D – B

Benefits		Investment Information	
Investment Objective	Growth	Telephone	800-544-8888
5-Year Projected Return	NA	Minimum Investment	$2,500
Safety Rating (0-100)	68%	Telephone Switching	See prospectu
Yield	0.2%	Total Assets	$81 million

Fidelity Select Enrgy Services
Energy service stocks

Costs		Performance	
Sales Load	3.1%	1-Year Return (1993)	+21%
Redemption Fee	0.8%	3-Year Return (1991–93)	–4%
Tax Load (Estimated)	Neg.	5-Year Return (1989–93)	+55%
Annual 12b-1 Fee	None	10-Year Return (1984–93)	NA
Annual Expense Ratio	1.76%	Worst-Ever Loss (1987)	52%
Annual Portfolio Turnover	236%	Stock Market Correlation	13%
5-Year Cost Estimate	13%	Up/Down Market Rank	D – C

Benefits		Investment Information	
Investment Objective	Growth	Telephone	800-544-8888
5-Year Projected Return	NA	Minimum Investment	$2,500
Safety Rating (0-100)	47%	Telephone Switching	See prospectus
Yield	0.4%	Total Assets	$39 million

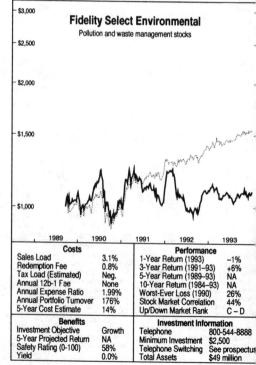

Fidelity Select Environmental
Pollution and waste management stocks

Costs		Performance	
Sales Load	3.1%	1-Year Return (1993)	–1%
Redemption Fee	0.8%	3-Year Return (1991–93)	+6%
Tax Load (Estimated)	Neg.	5-Year Return (1989–93)	NA
Annual 12b-1 Fee	None	10-Year Return (1984–93)	NA
Annual Expense Ratio	1.99%	Worst-Ever Loss (1990)	26%
Annual Portfolio Turnover	176%	Stock Market Correlation	44%
5-Year Cost Estimate	14%	Up/Down Market Rank	C – D

Benefits		Investment Information	
Investment Objective	Growth	Telephone	800-544-8888
5-Year Projected Return	NA	Minimum Investment	$2,500
Safety Rating (0-100)	58%	Telephone Switching	See prospectu
Yield	0.0%	Total Assets	$49 million

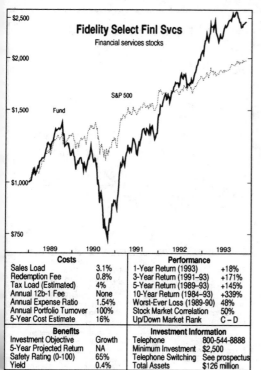

Fidelity Select Finl Svcs
Financial services stocks

Costs		Performance	
Sales Load	3.1%	1-Year Return (1993)	+18%
Redemption Fee	0.8%	3-Year Return (1991–93)	+171%
Tax Load (Estimated)	4%	5-Year Return (1989–93)	+145%
Annual 12b-1 Fee	None	10-Year Return (1984–93)	+339%
Annual Expense Ratio	1.54%	Worst-Ever Loss (1989-90)	48%
Annual Portfolio Turnover	100%	Stock Market Correlation	50%
5-Year Cost Estimate	16%	Up/Down Market Rank	C – D

Benefits		Investment Information	
Investment Objective	Growth	Telephone	800-544-8888
5-Year Projected Return	NA	Minimum Investment	$2,500
Safety Rating (0-100)	65%	Telephone Switching	See prospectus
Yield	0.4%	Total Assets	$126 million

Fidelity Select Food & Agric
Food and agricultural stocks
★ ★

Costs		Performance	
Sales Load	3.1%	1-Year Return (1993)	+9%
Redemption Fee	0.8%	3-Year Return (1991–93)	+55%
Tax Load (Estimated)	Neg.	5-Year Return (1989–93)	+135%
Annual 12b-1 Fee	None	10-Year Return (1984–93)	NA
Annual Expense Ratio	1.67%	Worst-Ever Loss (1987)	29%
Annual Portfolio Turnover	515%	Stock Market Correlation	64%
5-Year Cost Estimate	12%	Up/Down Market Rank	B – B

Benefits		Investment Information	
Investment Objective	Growth	Telephone	800-544-8888
5-Year Projected Return	NA	Minimum Investment	$2,500
Safety Rating (0-100)	78%	Telephone Switching	See prospectus
Yield	0.3%	Total Assets	$173 million

Fidelity Select Health
Health-care products and services stocks

Costs		Performance	
Sales Load	3.1%	1-Year Return (1993)	+2%
Redemption Fee	0.8%	3-Year Return (1991–93)	+55%
Tax Load (Estimated)	Neg.	5-Year Return (1989–93)	+175%
Annual 12b-1 Fee	None	10-Year Return (1984–93)	+472%
Annual Expense Ratio	1.46%	Worst-Ever Loss (1987)	38%
Annual Portfolio Turnover	112%	Stock Market Correlation	35%
5-Year Cost Estimate	11%	Up/Down Market Rank	A – D

Benefits		Investment Information	
Investment Objective	Growth	Telephone	800-544-8888
5-Year Projected Return	NA	Minimum Investment	$2,500
Safety Rating (0-100)	62%	Telephone Switching	See prospectus
Yield	0.1%	Total Assets	$576 million

Fidelity Select Home Finance
Companies engaged in real estate investing
★ ★

Costs		Performance	
Sales Load	3.1%	1-Year Return (1993)	+27%
Redemption Fee	0.8%	3-Year Return (1991–93)	+231%
Tax Load (Estimated)	8%	5-Year Return (1989–93)	+209%
Annual 12b-1 Fee	None	10-Year Return (1984–93)	NA
Annual Expense Ratio	1.55%	Worst-Ever Loss (1989-90)	47%
Annual Portfolio Turnover	61%	Stock Market Correlation	44%
5-Year Cost Estimate	21%	Up/Down Market Rank	B – D

Benefits		Investment Information	
Investment Objective	Growth	Telephone	800-544-8888
5-Year Projected Return	NA	Minimum Investment	$2,500
Safety Rating (0-100)	67%	Telephone Switching	See prospectus
Yield	0.0%	Total Assets	$160 million

Fidelity Select Industrl Equip
Industrial equipment stocks

Costs		Performance	
Sales Load	3.1%	1-Year Return (1993)	+43%
Redemption Fee	0.8%	3-Year Return (1991–93)	+102%
Tax Load (Estimated)	Neg.	5-Year Return (1989–93)	+102%
Annual 12b-1 Fee	None	10-Year Return (1984–93)	NA
Annual Expense Ratio	2.49%	Worst-Ever Loss (1987)	46%
Annual Portfolio Turnover	407%	Stock Market Correlation	47%
5-Year Cost Estimate	17%	Up/Down Market Rank	B – D

Benefits		Investment Information	
Investment Objective	Growth	Telephone	800-544-8888
5-Year Projected Return	NA	Minimum Investment	$2,500
Safety Rating (0-100)	69%	Telephone Switching	See prospectus
Yield	0.1%	Total Assets	$84 million

Fidelity Select Industrial Mat
Industrial material stocks

Costs		Performance	
Sales Load	3.1%	1-Year Return (1993)	+21%
Redemption Fee	0.8%	3-Year Return (1991–93)	+85%
Tax Load (Estimated)	Neg.	5-Year Return (1989–93)	+60%
Annual 12b-1 Fee	None	10-Year Return (1984–93)	NA
Annual Expense Ratio	2.02%	Worst-Ever Loss (1987)	49%
Annual Portfolio Turnover	273%	Stock Market Correlation	46%
5-Year Cost Estimate	14%	Up/Down Market Rank	D – E

Benefits		Investment Information	
Investment Objective	Growth	Telephone	800-544-8888
5-Year Projected Return	NA	Minimum Investment	$2,500
Safety Rating (0-100)	69%	Telephone Switching	See prospectus
Yield	0.3%	Total Assets	$36 million

Fidelity Select Insurance
Insurance stocks
★★

Costs		Performance	
Sales Load	3.1%	1-Year Return (1993)	+8%
Redemption Fee	0.8%	3-Year Return (1991–93)	+81%
Tax Load (Estimated)	1%	5-Year Return (1989–93)	+125%
Annual 12b-1 Fee	None	10-Year Return (1984–93)	NA
Annual Expense Ratio	2.49%	Worst-Ever Loss (1986-87)	32%
Annual Portfolio Turnover	81%	Stock Market Correlation	49%
5-Year Cost Estimate	18%	Up/Down Market Rank	B – C

Benefits		Investment Information	
Investment Objective	Growth	Telephone	800-544-8888
5-Year Projected Return	NA	Minimum Investment	$2,500
Safety Rating (0-100)	75%	Telephone Switching	See prospectus
Yield	0.0%	Total Assets	$18 million

Fidelity Select Leisre & Enter
Leisure and entertainment stocks
★

Costs		Performance	
Sales Load	3.1%	1-Year Return (1993)	+40%
Redemption Fee	0.8%	3-Year Return (1991–93)	+116%
Tax Load (Estimated)	1%	5-Year Return (1989–93)	+120%
Annual 12b-1 Fee	None	10-Year Return (1984–93)	NA
Annual Expense Ratio	1.90%	Worst-Ever Loss (1987)	38%
Annual Portfolio Turnover	109%	Stock Market Correlation	57%
5-Year Cost Estimate	15%	Up/Down Market Rank	C – E

Benefits		Investment Information	
Investment Objective	Growth	Telephone	800-544-8888
5-Year Projected Return	NA	Minimum Investment	$2,500
Safety Rating (0-100)	72%	Telephone Switching	See prospectus
Yield	0.0%	Total Assets	$117 million

Fidelity Select Med Delivery Fund
Health-care delivery stocks

S&P 500

Costs		Performance	
Sales Load	3.1%	1-Year Return (1993)	+6%
Redemption Fee	0.8%	3-Year Return (1991–93)	+63%
Tax Load (Estimated)	Neg.	5-Year Return (1989–93)	+199%
Annual 12b-1 Fee	None	10-Year Return (1984–93)	NA
Annual Expense Ratio	1.77%	Worst-Ever Loss (1987)	39%
Annual Portfolio Turnover	155%	Stock Market Correlation	27%
5-Year Cost Estimate	13%	Up/Down Market Rank	A – D

Benefits		Investment Information	
Investment Objective	Growth	Telephone	800-544-8888
5-Year Projected Return	NA	Minimum Investment	$2,500
Safety Rating (0-100)	56%	Telephone Switching	See prospectus
Yield	0.0%	Total Assets	$148 million

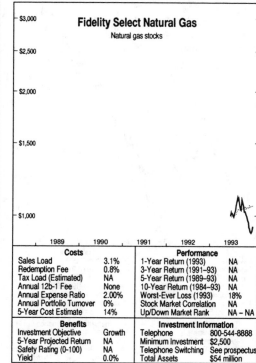

Fidelity Select Natural Gas
Natural gas stocks

Costs		Performance	
Sales Load	3.1%	1-Year Return (1993)	NA
Redemption Fee	0.8%	3-Year Return (1991–93)	NA
Tax Load (Estimated)	NA	5-Year Return (1989–93)	NA
Annual 12b-1 Fee	None	10-Year Return (1984–93)	NA
Annual Expense Ratio	2.00%	Worst-Ever Loss (1993)	18%
Annual Portfolio Turnover	0%	Stock Market Correlation	NA
5-Year Cost Estimate	14%	Up/Down Market Rank	NA – NA

Benefits		Investment Information	
Investment Objective	Growth	Telephone	800-544-8888
5-Year Projected Return	NA	Minimum Investment	$2,500
Safety Rating (0-100)	NA	Telephone Switching	See prospectus
Yield	0.0%	Total Assets	$54 million

Fidelity Select Paper & Forest
Paper and forest products stocks

Costs		Performance	
Sales Load	3.1%	1-Year Return (1993)	+19%
Redemption Fee	0.8%	3-Year Return (1991–93)	+79%
Tax Load (Estimated)	Neg.	5-Year Return (1989–93)	+58%
Annual 12b-1 Fee	None	10-Year Return (1984–93)	NA
Annual Expense Ratio	2.21%	Worst-Ever Loss (1987-90)	43%
Annual Portfolio Turnover	222%	Stock Market Correlation	38%
5-Year Cost Estimate	15%	Up/Down Market Rank	D – D

Benefits		Investment Information	
Investment Objective	Growth	Telephone	800-544-8888
5-Year Projected Return	NA	Minimum Investment	$2,500
Safety Rating (0-100)	66%	Telephone Switching	See prospectus
Yield	0.1%	Total Assets	$48 million

Fidelity Select Precious Metal
International gold stocks

Costs		Performance	
Sales Load	3.1%	1-Year Return (1993)	+112%
Redemption Fee	0.8%	3-Year Return (1991–93)	+68%
Tax Load (Estimated)	Neg.	5-Year Return (1989–93)	+75%
Annual 12b-1 Fee	None	10-Year Return (1984–93)	+61%
Annual Expense Ratio	1.73%	Worst-Ever Loss (1987-92)	56%
Annual Portfolio Turnover	36%	Stock Market Correlation	1%
5-Year Cost Estimate	13%	Up/Down Market Rank	E – B

Benefits		Investment Information	
Investment Objective	Growth	Telephone	800-544-8888
5-Year Projected Return	NA	Minimum Investment	$2,500
Safety Rating (0-100)	52%	Telephone Switching	See prospectus
Yield	1.2%	Total Assets	$497 million

Fidelity Select Regional Banks
Regional bank stocks
★

Costs		Performance	
Sales Load	3.1%	1-Year Return (1993)	+11%
Redemption Fee	0.8%	3-Year Return (1991–93)	+173%
Tax Load (Estimated)	6%	5-Year Return (1989–93)	+175%
Annual 12b-1 Fee	None	10-Year Return (1984–93)	NA
Annual Expense Ratio	1.49%	Worst-Ever Loss (1989-90)	43%
Annual Portfolio Turnover	63%	Stock Market Correlation	43%
5-Year Cost Estimate	18%	Up/Down Market Rank	C – C

Benefits		Investment Information	
Investment Objective	Growth	Telephone	800-544-8888
5-Year Projected Return	NA	Minimum Investment	$2,500
Safety Rating (0-100)	66%	Telephone Switching	See prospectus
Yield	0.9%	Total Assets	$115 million

Fidelity Select Retailing
Retailing stocks
★

Costs		Performance	
Sales Load	3.1%	1-Year Return (1993)	+13%
Redemption Fee	0.8%	3-Year Return (1991–93)	+132%
Tax Load (Estimated)	0%	5-Year Return (1989–93)	+185%
Annual 12b-1 Fee	None	10-Year Return (1984–93)	NA
Annual Expense Ratio	1.77%	Worst-Ever Loss (1987)	43%
Annual Portfolio Turnover	171%	Stock Market Correlation	50%
5-Year Cost Estimate	13%	Up/Down Market Rank	A – E

Benefits		Investment Information	
Investment Objective	Growth	Telephone	800-544-8888
5-Year Projected Return	NA	Minimum Investment	$2,500
Safety Rating (0-100)	67%	Telephone Switching	See prospectus
Yield	0.0%	Total Assets	$61 million

Fidelity Select Software
Software and computer services stocks

Costs		Performance	
Sales Load	3.1%	1-Year Return (1993)	+32%
Redemption Fee	0.8%	3-Year Return (1991–93)	+162%
Tax Load (Estimated)	Neg.	5-Year Return (1989–93)	+196%
Annual 12b-1 Fee	None	10-Year Return (1984–93)	NA
Annual Expense Ratio	1.64%	Worst-Ever Loss (1987)	39%
Annual Portfolio Turnover	402%	Stock Market Correlation	38%
5-Year Cost Estimate	12%	Up/Down Market Rank	B – D

Benefits		Investment Information	
Investment Objective	Growth	Telephone	800-544-8888
5-Year Projected Return	NA	Minimum Investment	$2,500
Safety Rating (0-100)	58%	Telephone Switching	See prospectus
Yield	0.0%	Total Assets	$162 million

Fidelity Select Technology
Technology stocks

Costs		Performance	
Sales Load	3.1%	1-Year Return (1993)	+29%
Redemption Fee	0.8%	3-Year Return (1991–93)	+122%
Tax Load (Estimated)	Neg.	5-Year Return (1989–93)	+188%
Annual 12b-1 Fee	None	10-Year Return (1984–93)	+104%
Annual Expense Ratio	1.64%	Worst-Ever Loss (1987)	48%
Annual Portfolio Turnover	259%	Stock Market Correlation	40%
5-Year Cost Estimate	12%	Up/Down Market Rank	A – E

Benefits		Investment Information	
Investment Objective	Growth	Telephone	800-544-8888
5-Year Projected Return	NA	Minimum Investment	$2,500
Safety Rating (0-100)	58%	Telephone Switching	See prospectus
Yield	0.3%	Total Assets	$229 million

Fidelity Select Telecommun

Telecommunications stocks

★★

Fund

S&P 500

| 1989 | 1990 | 1991 | 1992 | 1993 |

Costs		Performance	
Sales Load	3.1%	1-Year Return (1993)	+30%
Redemption Fee	0.8%	3-Year Return (1991–93)	+96%
Tax Load (Estimated)	Neg.	5-Year Return (1989–93)	+147%
Annual 12b-1 Fee	None	10-Year Return (1984–93)	NA
Annual Expense Ratio	1.74%	Worst-Ever Loss (1989-90)	27%
Annual Portfolio Turnover	115%	Stock Market Correlation	53%
5-Year Cost Estimate	13%	Up/Down Market Rank	B – C
Benefits		**Investment Information**	
Investment Objective	Growth	Telephone	800-544-8888
5-Year Projected Return	NA	Minimum Investment	$2,500
Safety Rating (0-100)	72%	Telephone Switching	See prospectus
Yield	0.5%	Total Assets	$413 million

Fidelity Select Transportation

Transportation stocks

★

| 1989 | 1990 | 1991 | 1992 | 1993 |

Costs		Performance	
Sales Load	3.1%	1-Year Return (1993)	+29%
Redemption Fee	0.8%	3-Year Return (1991–93)	+147%
Tax Load (Estimated)	1%	5-Year Return (1989–93)	+149%
Annual 12b-1 Fee	None	10-Year Return (1984–93)	NA
Annual Expense Ratio	2.48%	Worst-Ever Loss (1987)	43%
Annual Portfolio Turnover	116%	Stock Market Correlation	50%
5-Year Cost Estimate	18%	Up/Down Market Rank	B – E
Benefits		**Investment Information**	
Investment Objective	Growth	Telephone	800-544-8888
5-Year Projected Return	NA	Minimum Investment	$2,500
Safety Rating (0-100)	70%	Telephone Switching	See prospectus
Yield	0.0%	Total Assets	$10 million

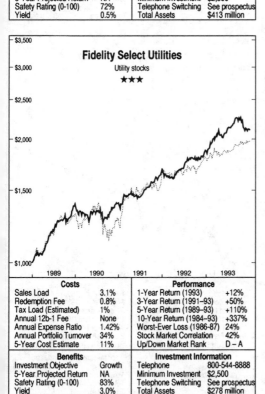

Fidelity Select Utilities

Utility stocks

★★★

| 1989 | 1990 | 1991 | 1992 | 1993 |

Costs		Performance	
Sales Load	3.1%	1-Year Return (1993)	+12%
Redemption Fee	0.8%	3-Year Return (1991–93)	+50%
Tax Load (Estimated)	1%	5-Year Return (1989–93)	+110%
Annual 12b-1 Fee	None	10-Year Return (1984–93)	+337%
Annual Expense Ratio	1.42%	Worst-Ever Loss (1986-87)	24%
Annual Portfolio Turnover	34%	Stock Market Correlation	42%
5-Year Cost Estimate	11%	Up/Down Market Rank	D – A
Benefits		**Investment Information**	
Investment Objective	Growth	Telephone	800-544-8888
5-Year Projected Return	NA	Minimum Investment	$2,500
Safety Rating (0-100)	83%	Telephone Switching	See prospectus
Yield	3.0%	Total Assets	$278 million

Fidelity Small Cap Stock

65% stocks & pfds; $750-mil or less mkt cap

| 1989 | 1990 | 1991 | 1992 | 1993 |

Costs		Performance	
Sales Load	3.1%	1-Year Return (1993)	NA
Redemption Fee	None	3-Year Return (1991–93)	NA
Tax Load (Estimated)	NA	5-Year Return (1989–93)	NA
Annual 12b-1 Fee	None	10-Year Return (1984–93)	NA
Annual Expense Ratio	1.31%	Worst-Ever Loss (1993)	4%
Annual Portfolio Turnover	0%	Stock Market Correlation	NA
5-Year Cost Estimate	10%	Up/Down Market Rank	NA – NA
Benefits		**Investment Information**	
Investment Objective	Growth	Telephone	800-544-8888
5-Year Projected Return	NA	Minimum Investment	$2,500
Safety Rating (0-100)	NA	Telephone Switching	4 per yr; free
Yield	0.2%	Total Assets	$659 million

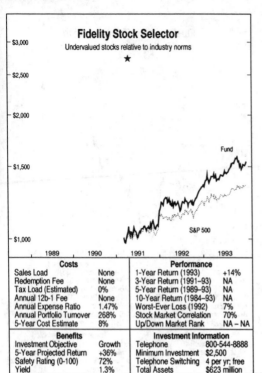

Fidelity Stock Selector
Undervalued stocks relative to industry norms
★

Costs		Performance	
Sales Load	None	1-Year Return (1993)	+14%
Redemption Fee	None	3-Year Return (1991–93)	NA
Tax Load (Estimated)	0%	5-Year Return (1989–93)	NA
Annual 12b-1 Fee	None	10-Year Return (1984–93)	NA
Annual Expense Ratio	1.47%	Worst-Ever Loss (1992)	7%
Annual Portfolio Turnover	268%	Stock Market Correlation	70%
5-Year Cost Estimate	8%	Up/Down Market Rank	NA – NA

Benefits		Investment Information	
Investment Objective	Growth	Telephone	800-544-8888
5-Year Projected Return	+36%	Minimum Investment	$2,500
Safety Rating (0-100)	72%	Telephone Switching	4 per yr; free
Yield	1.3%	Total Assets	$623 million

Fidelity Strategic Oppor
Unusual development stocks
★★★★

Costs		Performance	
Sales Load	5.0%	1-Year Return (1993)	+21%
Redemption Fee	None	3-Year Return (1991–93)	+70%
Tax Load (Estimated)	4%	5-Year Return (1989–93)	+111%
Annual 12b-1 Fee	None	10-Year Return (1984–93)	NA
Annual Expense Ratio	0.90%	Worst-Ever Loss (1987)	27%
Annual Portfolio Turnover	275%	Stock Market Correlation	59%
5-Year Cost Estimate	14%	Up/Down Market Rank	C – B

Benefits		Investment Information	
Investment Objective	Growth	Telephone	800-544-8888
5-Year Projected Return	+25%	Minimum Investment	$1,000
Safety Rating (0-100)	83%	Telephone Switching	4 per yr; free
Yield	2.4%	Total Assets	$20 million

Fidelity Trend
Diversified stocks
★

Costs		Performance	
Sales Load	None	1-Year Return (1993)	+19%
Redemption Fee	None	3-Year Return (1991–93)	+90%
Tax Load (Estimated)	1%	5-Year Return (1989–93)	+118%
Annual 12b-1 Fee	None	10-Year Return (1984–93)	+269%
Annual Expense Ratio	0.74%	Worst-Ever Loss (1987)	39%
Annual Portfolio Turnover	65%	Stock Market Correlation	73%
5-Year Cost Estimate	5%	Up/Down Market Rank	A – E

Benefits		Investment Information	
Investment Objective	Growth	Telephone	800-544-8888
5-Year Projected Return	+23%	Minimum Investment	$2,500
Safety Rating (0-100)	70%	Telephone Switching	4 per yr; free
Yield	0.5%	Total Assets	$1.39 billion

Fidelity U.S. Equity Index
Matches S&P 500; $100,000 minimum investment
★

Costs		Performance	
Sales Load	None	1-Year Return (1993)	+10%
Redemption Fee	None	3-Year Return (1991–93)	+53%
Tax Load (Estimated)	4%	5-Year Return (1989–93)	NA
Annual 12b-1 Fee	None	10-Year Return (1984–93)	NA
Annual Expense Ratio	0.28%	Worst-Ever Loss (1990)	19%
Annual Portfolio Turnover	4%	Stock Market Correlation	99%
5-Year Cost Estimate	2%	Up/Down Market Rank	B – C

Benefits		Investment Information	
Investment Objective	Growth	Telephone	800-624-0133
5-Year Projected Return	+24%	Minimum Investment	$100,000
Safety Rating (0-100)	72%	Telephone Switching	4 per yr; free
Yield	3.2%	Total Assets	$1.67 billion

Fidelity Utilities Income

Utility securities
★★★★

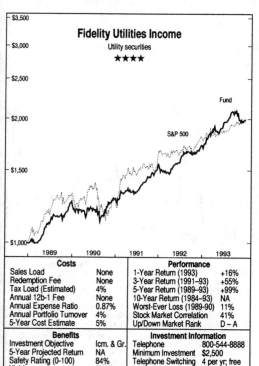

Costs		Performance	
Sales Load	None	1-Year Return (1993)	+16%
Redemption Fee	None	3-Year Return (1991–93)	+55%
Tax Load (Estimated)	4%	5-Year Return (1989–93)	+99%
Annual 12b-1 Fee	None	10-Year Return (1984–93)	NA
Annual Expense Ratio	0.87%	Worst-Ever Loss (1989–90)	11%
Annual Portfolio Turnover	4%	Stock Market Correlation	41%
5-Year Cost Estimate	5%	Up/Down Market Rank	D – A

Benefits		Investment Information	
Investment Objective	Icm. & Gr.	Telephone	800-544-8888
5-Year Projected Return	NA	Minimum Investment	$2,500
Safety Rating (0-100)	84%	Telephone Switching	4 per yr; free
Yield	3.5%	Total Assets	$1.47 billion

Fidelity Value

Undervalued stocks
★

Costs		Performance	
Sales Load	None	1-Year Return (1993)	+23%
Redemption Fee	None	3-Year Return (1991–93)	+88%
Tax Load (Estimated)	Neg.	5-Year Return (1989–93)	+101%
Annual 12b-1 Fee	None	10-Year Return (1984–93)	NA
Annual Expense Ratio	1.00%	Worst-Ever Loss (1987)	34%
Annual Portfolio Turnover	81%	Stock Market Correlation	65%
5-Year Cost Estimate	5%	Up/Down Market Rank	C – D

Benefits		Investment Information	
Investment Objective	Growth	Telephone	800-544-8888
5-Year Projected Return	+23%	Minimum Investment	$2,500
Safety Rating (0-100)	74%	Telephone Switching	4 per yr; free
Yield	0.8%	Total Assets	$1.71 billion

Fidelity Worldwide

Foreign - No. America; Europe; Pacific-Basin

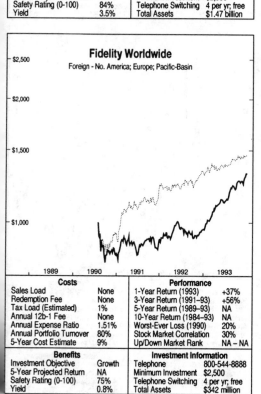

Costs		Performance	
Sales Load	None	1-Year Return (1993)	+37%
Redemption Fee	None	3-Year Return (1991–93)	+56%
Tax Load (Estimated)	1%	5-Year Return (1989–93)	NA
Annual 12b-1 Fee	None	10-Year Return (1984–93)	NA
Annual Expense Ratio	1.51%	Worst-Ever Loss (1990)	20%
Annual Portfolio Turnover	80%	Stock Market Correlation	30%
5-Year Cost Estimate	9%	Up/Down Market Rank	NA – NA

Benefits		Investment Information	
Investment Objective	Growth	Telephone	800-544-8888
5-Year Projected Return	NA	Minimum Investment	$2,500
Safety Rating (0-100)	75%	Telephone Switching	4 per yr; free
Yield	0.8%	Total Assets	$342 million

Fiduciary Capital Growth

Undervalued growth stocks
★

Costs		Performance	
Sales Load	None	1-Year Return (1993)	+15%
Redemption Fee	None	3-Year Return (1991–93)	+79%
Tax Load (Estimated)	0%	5-Year Return (1989–93)	+86%
Annual 12b-1 Fee	None	10-Year Return (1984–93)	+163%
Annual Expense Ratio	1.33%	Worst-Ever Loss (1987)	33%
Annual Portfolio Turnover	33%	Stock Market Correlation	56%
5-Year Cost Estimate	7%	Up/Down Market Rank	C – E

Benefits		Investment Information	
Investment Objective	Gr. & Icm.	Telephone	800-338-1579
5-Year Projected Return	+21%	Minimum Investment	$1,000
Safety Rating (0-100)	75%	Telephone Switching	Mail only
Yield	0.3%	Total Assets	$47 million

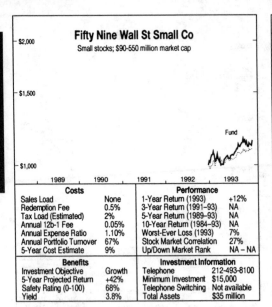

Fifty Nine Wall St Small Co
Small stocks; $90-550 million market cap

Costs		Performance	
Sales Load	None	1-Year Return (1993)	+12%
Redemption Fee	0.5%	3-Year Return (1991–93)	NA
Tax Load (Estimated)	2%	5-Year Return (1989–93)	NA
Annual 12b-1 Fee	0.05%	10-Year Return (1984–93)	NA
Annual Expense Ratio	1.10%	Worst-Ever Loss (1993)	7%
Annual Portfolio Turnover	67%	Stock Market Correlation	27%
5-Year Cost Estimate	9%	Up/Down Market Rank	NA – NA

Benefits		Investment Information	
Investment Objective	Growth	Telephone	212-493-8100
5-Year Projected Return	+42%	Minimum Investment	$15,000
Safety Rating (0-100)	68%	Telephone Switching	Not available
Yield	3.8%	Total Assets	$35 million

First Australia
Foreign - Australian stocks

Costs		Performance	
Sales Load	None	1-Year Return (1993)	+56%
Redemption Fee	None	3-Year Return (1991–93)	+75%
Tax Load (Estimated)	2%	5-Year Return (1989–93)	+75%
Annual 12b-1 Fee	None	10-Year Return (1984–93)	NA
Annual Expense Ratio	1.90%	Worst-Ever Loss (1987)	54%
Annual Portfolio Turnover	102%	Stock Market Correlation	0%
5-Year Cost Estimate	14%	Up/Down Market Rank	D – C

Benefits		Investment Information	
Investment Objective	Growth	Telephone	800-451-6788
5-Year Projected Return	NA	Minimum Investment	None
Safety Rating (0-100)	41%	Telephone Switching	Via broker
Yield	1.1%	Total Assets	$120 million

First Financial
Savings & loan and bank stocks

Costs		Performance	
Sales Load	None	1-Year Return (1993)	+55%
Redemption Fee	None	3-Year Return (1991–93)	+391%
Tax Load (Estimated)	10%	5-Year Return (1989–93)	+283%
Annual 12b-1 Fee	None	10-Year Return (1984–93)	NA
Annual Expense Ratio	1.21%	Worst-Ever Loss (1989-90)	56%
Annual Portfolio Turnover	120%	Stock Market Correlation	14%
5-Year Cost Estimate	20%	Up/Down Market Rank	B – E

Benefits		Investment Information	
Investment Objective	Growth	Telephone	800-451-6788
5-Year Projected Return	NA	Minimum Investment	None
Safety Rating (0-100)	42%	Telephone Switching	Via broker
Yield	0.1%	Total Assets	$175 million

First Iberian
Foreign - Spanish; Portuguese stocks

Costs		Performance	
Sales Load	None	1-Year Return (1993)	+46%
Redemption Fee	None	3-Year Return (1991–93)	+18%
Tax Load (Estimated)	1%	5-Year Return (1989–93)	+33%
Annual 12b-1 Fee	None	10-Year Return (1984–93)	NA
Annual Expense Ratio	2.33%	Worst-Ever Loss (1990-92)	67%
Annual Portfolio Turnover	20%	Stock Market Correlation	1%
5-Year Cost Estimate	15%	Up/Down Market Rank	E – C

Benefits		Investment Information	
Investment Objective	Growth	Telephone	800-451-6788
5-Year Projected Return	NA	Minimum Investment	None
Safety Rating (0-100)	11%	Telephone Switching	Via broker
Yield	0.7%	Total Assets	$49 million

First Investors Blue Chip
S&P 500 stocks with $300+ mil market value

Costs		Performance	
Sales Load	6.7%	1-Year Return (1993)	+8%
Redemption Fee	None	3-Year Return (1991–93)	+50%
Tax Load (Estimated)	6%	5-Year Return (1989–93)	NA
Annual 12b-1 Fee	0.30%	10-Year Return (1984–93)	NA
Annual Expense Ratio	1.60%	Worst-Ever Loss (1990)	22%
Annual Portfolio Turnover	52%	Stock Market Correlation	90%
5-Year Cost Estimate	22%	Up/Down Market Rank	B – C

Benefits		Investment Information	
Investment Objective	Gr. & Icm.	Telephone	800-423-4026
5-Year Projected Return	+0%	Minimum Investment	$1,000
Safety Rating (0-100)	72%	Telephone Switching	1 per mo; free
Yield	0.6%	Total Assets	$115 million

First Investors Global
Foreign & U.S. - diversified securities

Costs		Performance	
Sales Load	6.7%	1-Year Return (1993)	+23%
Redemption Fee	None	3-Year Return (1991–93)	+37%
Tax Load (Estimated)	3%	5-Year Return (1989–93)	+66%
Annual 12b-1 Fee	0.30%	10-Year Return (1984–93)	+241%
Annual Expense Ratio	1.92%	Worst-Ever Loss (1987)	28%
Annual Portfolio Turnover	40%	Stock Market Correlation	28%
5-Year Cost Estimate	20%	Up/Down Market Rank	D – A

Benefits		Investment Information	
Investment Objective	Gr. & Icm.	Telephone	800-423-4026
5-Year Projected Return	NA	Minimum Investment	$1,000
Safety Rating (0-100)	67%	Telephone Switching	1 per mo; free
Yield	0.2%	Total Assets	$187 million

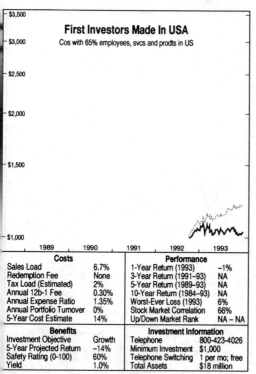

First Investors Made In USA
Cos with 65% employees, svcs and prodts in US

Costs		Performance	
Sales Load	6.7%	1-Year Return (1993)	–1%
Redemption Fee	None	3-Year Return (1991–93)	NA
Tax Load (Estimated)	2%	5-Year Return (1989–93)	NA
Annual 12b-1 Fee	0.30%	10-Year Return (1984–93)	NA
Annual Expense Ratio	1.35%	Worst-Ever Loss (1993)	6%
Annual Portfolio Turnover	0%	Stock Market Correlation	66%
5-Year Cost Estimate	14%	Up/Down Market Rank	NA – NA

Benefits		Investment Information	
Investment Objective	Growth	Telephone	800-423-4026
5-Year Projected Return	–14%	Minimum Investment	$1,000
Safety Rating (0-100)	60%	Telephone Switching	1 per mo; free
Yield	1.0%	Total Assets	$18 million

First Investors Total Return
Stocks, bonds and money market securities

Costs		Performance	
Sales Load	6.7%	1-Year Return (1993)	+7%
Redemption Fee	None	3-Year Return (1991–93)	+29%
Tax Load (Estimated)	2%	5-Year Return (1989–93)	NA
Annual 12b-1 Fee	0.30%	10-Year Return (1984–93)	NA
Annual Expense Ratio	1.64%	Worst-Ever Loss (1992)	10%
Annual Portfolio Turnover	134%	Stock Market Correlation	60%
5-Year Cost Estimate	18%	Up/Down Market Rank	NA – NA

Benefits		Investment Information	
Investment Objective	Gr. & Icm.	Telephone	800-423-4026
5-Year Projected Return	+3%	Minimum Investment	$1,000
Safety Rating (0-100)	81%	Telephone Switching	1 per mo; free
Yield	2.2%	Total Assets	$61 million

First Philippine
Foreign - Philippine stocks
S&P 500

Fund

Costs		Performance	
Sales Load	None	1-Year Return (1993)	+135%
Redemption Fee	None	3-Year Return (1991–93)	+299%
Tax Load (Estimated)	28%	5-Year Return (1989–93)	NA
Annual 12b-1 Fee	None	10-Year Return (1984–93)	NA
Annual Expense Ratio	1.79%	Worst-Ever Loss (1990)	59%
Annual Portfolio Turnover	37%	Stock Market Correlation	4%
5-Year Cost Estimate	35%	Up/Down Market Rank	C – NA

Benefits		Investment Information	
Investment Objective	Growth	Telephone	800-524-4458
5-Year Projected Return	NA	Minimum Investment	None
Safety Rating (0-100)	32%	Telephone Switching	Via broker
Yield	0.0%	Total Assets	$126 million

First Union Value "B"
Stocks with $100-million minimum equity
★

Costs		Performance	
Sales Load	4.2%	1-Year Return (1993)	+9%
Redemption Fee	None	3-Year Return (1991–93)	+47%
Tax Load (Estimated)	NA	5-Year Return (1989–93)	+80%
Annual 12b-1 Fee	0.75%	10-Year Return (1984–93)	NA
Annual Expense Ratio	1.01%	Worst-Ever Loss (1987)	29%
Annual Portfolio Turnover	24%	Stock Market Correlation	86%
5-Year Cost Estimate	10%	Up/Down Market Rank	C – C

Benefits		Investment Information	
Investment Objective	Gr. & Icm.	Telephone	800-326-3241
5-Year Projected Return	+4%	Minimum Investment	$1,000
Safety Rating (0-100)	77%	Telephone Switching	5 per yr; free
Yield	2.0%	Total Assets	$189 million

Flag Investors - Emerging Grth
Quality emerging growth stocks

Costs		Performance	
Sales Load	4.7%	1-Year Return (1993)	–1%
Redemption Fee	None	3-Year Return (1991–93)	+35%
Tax Load (Estimated)	2%	5-Year Return (1989–93)	+41%
Annual 12b-1 Fee	0.25%	10-Year Return (1984–93)	NA
Annual Expense Ratio	1.46%	Worst-Ever Loss (1989-90)	37%
Annual Portfolio Turnover	69%	Stock Market Correlation	44%
5-Year Cost Estimate	15%	Up/Down Market Rank	B – E

Benefits		Investment Information	
Investment Objective	Growth	Telephone	800-767-3524
5-Year Projected Return	–9%	Minimum Investment	$2,000
Safety Rating (0-100)	49%	Telephone Switching	Unlimited;free
Yield	0.0%	Total Assets	$31 million

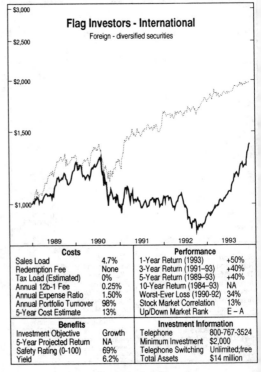

Flag Investors - International
Foreign - diversified securities

Costs		Performance	
Sales Load	4.7%	1-Year Return (1993)	+50%
Redemption Fee	None	3-Year Return (1991–93)	+40%
Tax Load (Estimated)	0%	5-Year Return (1989–93)	+40%
Annual 12b-1 Fee	0.25%	10-Year Return (1984–93)	NA
Annual Expense Ratio	1.50%	Worst-Ever Loss (1990-92)	34%
Annual Portfolio Turnover	98%	Stock Market Correlation	13%
5-Year Cost Estimate	13%	Up/Down Market Rank	E – A

Benefits		Investment Information	
Investment Objective	Growth	Telephone	800-767-3524
5-Year Projected Return	NA	Minimum Investment	$2,000
Safety Rating (0-100)	69%	Telephone Switching	Unlimited;free
Yield	6.2%	Total Assets	$14 million

Flag Investors - Quality Grwth
High-quality growth companies

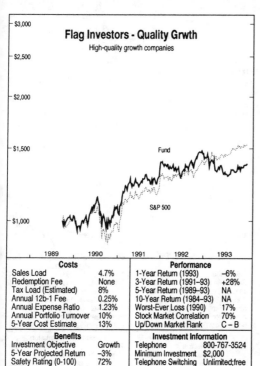

Costs

Sales Load	4.7%	1-Year Return (1993)	–6%
Redemption Fee	None	3-Year Return (1991–93)	+28%
Tax Load (Estimated)	8%	5-Year Return (1989–93)	NA
Annual 12b-1 Fee	0.25%	10-Year Return (1984–93)	NA
Annual Expense Ratio	1.23%	Worst-Ever Loss (1990)	17%
Annual Portfolio Turnover	10%	Stock Market Correlation	70%
5-Year Cost Estimate	13%	Up/Down Market Rank	C – B

Benefits / Investment Information

Investment Objective	Growth	Telephone	800-767-3524
5-Year Projected Return	–3%	Minimum Investment	$2,000
Safety Rating (0-100)	72%	Telephone Switching	Unlimited;free
Yield	0.6%	Total Assets	$56 million

Flag - Telephone Income "A"
Telephone securities
★★

Costs

Sales Load	4.7%	1-Year Return (1993)	+18%
Redemption Fee	None	3-Year Return (1991–93)	+63%
Tax Load (Estimated)	9%	5-Year Return (1989–93)	+124%
Annual 12b-1 Fee	0.25%	10-Year Return (1984–93)	NA
Annual Expense Ratio	0.92%	Worst-Ever Loss (1987)	22%
Annual Portfolio Turnover	25%	Stock Market Correlation	52%
5-Year Cost Estimate	14%	Up/Down Market Rank	C – B

Benefits / Investment Information

Investment Objective	Icm. & Gr.	Telephone	800-767-3524
5-Year Projected Return	NA	Minimum Investment	$2,000
Safety Rating (0-100)	77%	Telephone Switching	Unlimited;free
Yield	2.8%	Total Assets	$438 million

Flex-Funds Growth
Small stocks; market timing

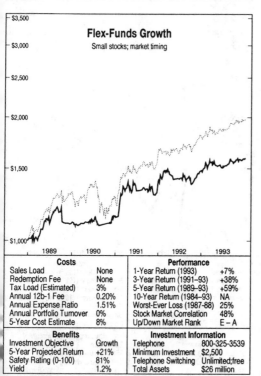

Costs

Sales Load	None	1-Year Return (1993)	+7%
Redemption Fee	None	3-Year Return (1991–93)	+38%
Tax Load (Estimated)	3%	5-Year Return (1989–93)	+59%
Annual 12b-1 Fee	0.20%	10-Year Return (1984–93)	NA
Annual Expense Ratio	1.51%	Worst-Ever Loss (1987-88)	25%
Annual Portfolio Turnover	0%	Stock Market Correlation	48%
5-Year Cost Estimate	8%	Up/Down Market Rank	E – A

Benefits / Investment Information

Investment Objective	Growth	Telephone	800-325-3539
5-Year Projected Return	+21%	Minimum Investment	$2,500
Safety Rating (0-100)	81%	Telephone Switching	Unlimited;free
Yield	1.2%	Total Assets	$26 million

Flex-Funds Muirfield
Owns other no-load and low-load funds
★★★

Costs

Sales Load	None	1-Year Return (1993)	+22%
Redemption Fee	None	3-Year Return (1991–93)	+70%
Tax Load (Estimated)	0%	5-Year Return (1989–93)	+98%
Annual 12b-1 Fee	0.20%	10-Year Return (1984–93)	NA
Annual Expense Ratio	1.40%	Worst-Ever Loss (1990)	9%
Annual Portfolio Turnover	0%	Stock Market Correlation	15%
5-Year Cost Estimate	7%	Up/Down Market Rank	D – A

Benefits / Investment Information

Investment Objective	Growth	Telephone	800-325-3539
5-Year Projected Return	+45%	Minimum Investment	$2,500
Safety Rating (0-100)	79%	Telephone Switching	Unlimited;free
Yield	1.1%	Total Assets	$77 million

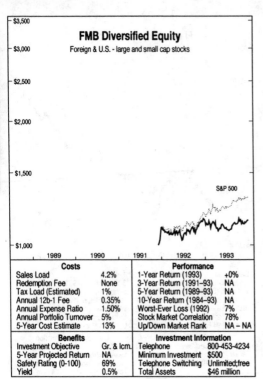

FMB Diversified Equity
Foreign & U.S. - large and small cap stocks

S&P 500

Costs		Performance	
Sales Load	4.2%	1-Year Return (1993)	+0%
Redemption Fee	None	3-Year Return (1991–93)	NA
Tax Load (Estimated)	1%	5-Year Return (1989–93)	NA
Annual 12b-1 Fee	0.35%	10-Year Return (1984–93)	NA
Annual Expense Ratio	1.50%	Worst-Ever Loss (1992)	7%
Annual Portfolio Turnover	5%	Stock Market Correlation	78%
5-Year Cost Estimate	13%	Up/Down Market Rank	NA – NA

Benefits		Investment Information	
Investment Objective	Gr. & Icm.	Telephone	800-453-4234
5-Year Projected Return	NA	Minimum Investment	$500
Safety Rating (0-100)	69%	Telephone Switching	Unlimited;free
Yield	0.5%	Total Assets	$46 million

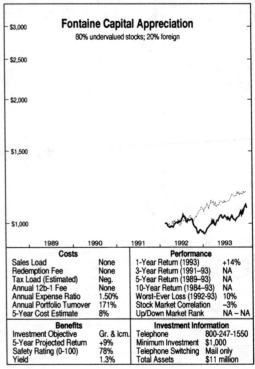

Fontaine Capital Appreciation
80% undervalued stocks; 20% foreign

Costs		Performance	
Sales Load	None	1-Year Return (1993)	+14%
Redemption Fee	None	3-Year Return (1991–93)	NA
Tax Load (Estimated)	Neg.	5-Year Return (1989–93)	NA
Annual 12b-1 Fee	None	10-Year Return (1984–93)	NA
Annual Expense Ratio	1.50%	Worst-Ever Loss (1992-93)	10%
Annual Portfolio Turnover	171%	Stock Market Correlation	–3%
5-Year Cost Estimate	8%	Up/Down Market Rank	NA – NA

Benefits		Investment Information	
Investment Objective	Gr. & Icm.	Telephone	800-247-1550
5-Year Projected Return	+9%	Minimum Investment	$1,000
Safety Rating (0-100)	78%	Telephone Switching	Mail only
Yield	1.3%	Total Assets	$11 million

Fortis Asset Allocation
Foreign & U.S. - common stocks
★★★

Costs		Performance	
Sales Load	4.7%	1-Year Return (1993)	+11%
Redemption Fee	None	3-Year Return (1991–93)	+53%
Tax Load (Estimated)	4%	5-Year Return (1989–93)	+86%
Annual 12b-1 Fee	0.45%	10-Year Return (1984–93)	NA
Annual Expense Ratio	1.58%	Worst-Ever Loss (1990)	13%
Annual Portfolio Turnover	45%	Stock Market Correlation	58%
5-Year Cost Estimate	17%	Up/Down Market Rank	C – B

Benefits		Investment Information	
Investment Objective	Gr. & Icm.	Telephone	800-800-2638
5-Year Projected Return	+19%	Minimum Investment	$500
Safety Rating (0-100)	84%	Telephone Switching	Unlimited;free
Yield	2.6%	Total Assets	$105 million

Fortis Capital
Blue chip stocks

Costs		Performance	
Sales Load	5.0%	1-Year Return (1993)	+3%
Redemption Fee	None	3-Year Return (1991–93)	+63%
Tax Load (Estimated)	6%	5-Year Return (1989–93)	+105%
Annual 12b-1 Fee	0.25%	10-Year Return (1984–93)	+245%
Annual Expense Ratio	1.23%	Worst-Ever Loss (1987)	33%
Annual Portfolio Turnover	68%	Stock Market Correlation	64%
5-Year Cost Estimate	18%	Up/Down Market Rank	A – D

Benefits		Investment Information	
Investment Objective	Gr. & Icm.	Telephone	800-800-2638
5-Year Projected Return	+8%	Minimum Investment	$500
Safety Rating (0-100)	69%	Telephone Switching	Unlimited;free
Yield	0.9%	Total Assets	$246 million

Fortis Fiduciary
Diversified securities

Costs		Performance	
Sales Load	5.0%	1-Year Return (1993)	+3%
Redemption Fee	None	3-Year Return (1991–93)	+68%
Tax Load (Estimated)	6%	5-Year Return (1989–93)	+105%
Annual 12b-1 Fee	0.25%	10-Year Return (1984–93)	NA
Annual Expense Ratio	1.49%	Worst-Ever Loss (1987)	37%
Annual Portfolio Turnover	53%	Stock Market Correlation	63%
5-Year Cost Estimate	20%	Up/Down Market Rank	A – E

Benefits		Investment Information	
Investment Objective	Growth	Telephone	800-800-2638
5-Year Projected Return	+4%	Minimum Investment	$500
Safety Rating (0-100)	65%	Telephone Switching	Unlimited;free
Yield	0.0%	Total Assets	$48 million

Fortis Growth
Diversified growth stocks
★

Costs		Performance	
Sales Load	5.0%	1-Year Return (1993)	+10%
Redemption Fee	None	3-Year Return (1991–93)	+87%
Tax Load (Estimated)	10%	5-Year Return (1989–93)	+149%
Annual 12b-1 Fee	0.25%	10-Year Return (1984–93)	+301%
Annual Expense Ratio	1.13%	Worst-Ever Loss (1987)	40%
Annual Portfolio Turnover	49%	Stock Market Correlation	51%
5-Year Cost Estimate	21%	Up/Down Market Rank	A – E

Benefits		Investment Information	
Investment Objective	Growth	Telephone	800-800-2638
5-Year Projected Return	+24%	Minimum Investment	$500
Safety Rating (0-100)	64%	Telephone Switching	Unlimited;free
Yield	0.0%	Total Assets	$585 million

Fortis Special Stock Portfolio
For Fortis Employees only
★

Costs		Performance	
Sales Load	None	1-Year Return (1993)	+10%
Redemption Fee	None	3-Year Return (1991–93)	+90%
Tax Load (Estimated)	6%	5-Year Return (1989–93)	+157%
Annual 12b-1 Fee	None	10-Year Return (1984–93)	NA
Annual Expense Ratio	1.21%	Worst-Ever Loss (1987)	41%
Annual Portfolio Turnover	50%	Stock Market Correlation	51%
5-Year Cost Estimate	12%	Up/Down Market Rank	A – E

Benefits		Investment Information	
Investment Objective	Growth	Telephone	800-800-2638
5-Year Projected Return	+36%	Minimum Investment	$500
Safety Rating (0-100)	65%	Telephone Switching	Unlimited;free
Yield	0.0%	Total Assets	$70 million

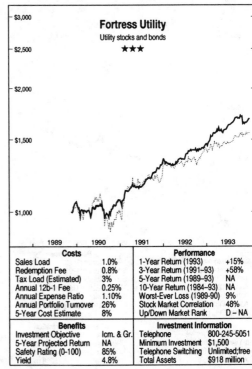

Fortress Utility
Utility stocks and bonds
★★★

Costs		Performance	
Sales Load	1.0%	1-Year Return (1993)	+15%
Redemption Fee	0.8%	3-Year Return (1991–93)	+58%
Tax Load (Estimated)	3%	5-Year Return (1989–93)	NA
Annual 12b-1 Fee	0.25%	10-Year Return (1984–93)	NA
Annual Expense Ratio	1.10%	Worst-Ever Loss (1989-90)	9%
Annual Portfolio Turnover	26%	Stock Market Correlation	48%
5-Year Cost Estimate	8%	Up/Down Market Rank	D – NA

Benefits		Investment Information	
Investment Objective	Icm. & Gr.	Telephone	800-245-5051
5-Year Projected Return	NA	Minimum Investment	$1,500
Safety Rating (0-100)	85%	Telephone Switching	Unlimited;free
Yield	4.8%	Total Assets	$918 million

Forty Four Wall Street Equity
Non-diversified stocks; leveraged

S&P 500

Fund

| | 1989 | 1990 | 1991 | 1992 | 1993 |

Costs		Performance	
Sales Load	None	1-Year Return (1993)	+43%
Redemption Fee	None	3-Year Return (1991–93)	+74%
Tax Load (Estimated)	1%	5-Year Return (1989–93)	+48%
Annual 12b-1 Fee	None	10-Year Return (1984–93)	−69%
Annual Expense Ratio	4.39%	Worst-Ever Loss (1983-87)	90%
Annual Portfolio Turnover	167%	Stock Market Correlation	45%
5-Year Cost Estimate	26%	Up/Down Market Rank	B – E

Benefits		Investment Information	
Investment Objective	Growth	Telephone	800-543-2620
5-Year Projected Return	−6%	Minimum Investment	$1,000
Safety Rating (0-100)	74%	Telephone Switching	Not available
Yield	0.0%	Total Assets	$8 million

Founders Balanced
Dividend-paying stocks, govt secs and bonds
★★★★★

| | 1989 | 1990 | 1991 | 1992 | 1993 |

Costs		Performance	
Sales Load	None	1-Year Return (1993)	+22%
Redemption Fee	None	3-Year Return (1991–93)	+59%
Tax Load (Estimated)	0%	5-Year Return (1989–93)	+89%
Annual 12b-1 Fee	0.25%	10-Year Return (1984–93)	+208%
Annual Expense Ratio	1.42%	Worst-Ever Loss (1987)	16%
Annual Portfolio Turnover	149%	Stock Market Correlation	65%
5-Year Cost Estimate	8%	Up/Down Market Rank	E – A

Benefits		Investment Information	
Investment Objective	Icm. & Gr.	Telephone	800-525-2440
5-Year Projected Return	+26%	Minimum Investment	$1,000
Safety Rating (0-100)	85%	Telephone Switching	4 per yr; free
Yield	1.9%	Total Assets	$51 million

Founders Blue Chip
Large; strong companies
★

| | 1989 | 1990 | 1991 | 1992 | 1993 |

Costs		Performance	
Sales Load	None	1-Year Return (1993)	+14%
Redemption Fee	None	3-Year Return (1991–93)	+47%
Tax Load (Estimated)	1%	5-Year Return (1989–93)	+100%
Annual 12b-1 Fee	0.25%	10-Year Return (1984–93)	+253%
Annual Expense Ratio	1.29%	Worst-Ever Loss (1987)	34%
Annual Portfolio Turnover	183%	Stock Market Correlation	83%
5-Year Cost Estimate	8%	Up/Down Market Rank	B – D

Benefits		Investment Information	
Investment Objective	Gr. & Icm.	Telephone	800-525-2440
5-Year Projected Return	+12%	Minimum Investment	$1,000
Safety Rating (0-100)	73%	Telephone Switching	4 per yr; free
Yield	0.5%	Total Assets	$298 million

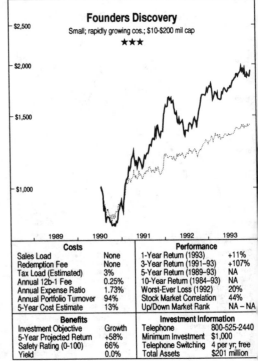

Founders Discovery
Small; rapidly growing cos.; $10-$200 mil cap
★★★

| | 1989 | 1990 | 1991 | 1992 | 1993 |

Costs		Performance	
Sales Load	None	1-Year Return (1993)	+11%
Redemption Fee	None	3-Year Return (1991–93)	+107%
Tax Load (Estimated)	3%	5-Year Return (1989–93)	NA
Annual 12b-1 Fee	0.25%	10-Year Return (1984–93)	NA
Annual Expense Ratio	1.73%	Worst-Ever Loss (1992)	20%
Annual Portfolio Turnover	94%	Stock Market Correlation	44%
5-Year Cost Estimate	13%	Up/Down Market Rank	NA – NA

Benefits		Investment Information	
Investment Objective	Growth	Telephone	800-525-2440
5-Year Projected Return	+58%	Minimum Investment	$1,000
Safety Rating (0-100)	66%	Telephone Switching	4 per yr; free
Yield	0.0%	Total Assets	$201 million

Founders Frontier

Small-medium sized cos; $150-$600 mil mkt cap

★★

Fund

S&P 500

Costs		Performance	
Sales Load	None	1-Year Return (1993)	+17%
Redemption Fee	None	3-Year Return (1991–93)	+90%
Tax Load (Estimated)	4%	5-Year Return (1989–93)	+153%
Annual 12b-1 Fee	0.25%	10-Year Return (1984–93)	NA
Annual Expense Ratio	1.73%	Worst-Ever Loss (1989-90)	25%
Annual Portfolio Turnover	116%	Stock Market Correlation	51%
5-Year Cost Estimate	13%	Up/Down Market Rank	B – B

Benefits		Investment Information	
Investment Objective	Growth	Telephone	800-525-2440
5-Year Projected Return	+35%	Minimum Investment	$1,000
Safety Rating (0-100)	67%	Telephone Switching	4 per yr; free
Yield	0.0%	Total Assets	$223 million

Founders Growth

Established companies

★★

Costs		Performance	
Sales Load	None	1-Year Return (1993)	+26%
Redemption Fee	None	3-Year Return (1991–93)	+93%
Tax Load (Estimated)	3%	5-Year Return (1989–93)	+145%
Annual 12b-1 Fee	0.25%	10-Year Return (1984–93)	+287%
Annual Expense Ratio	1.42%	Worst-Ever Loss (1987)	32%
Annual Portfolio Turnover	202%	Stock Market Correlation	58%
5-Year Cost Estimate	11%	Up/Down Market Rank	A – D

Benefits		Investment Information	
Investment Objective	Gr. & Icm.	Telephone	800-525-2440
5-Year Projected Return	+33%	Minimum Investment	$1,000
Safety Rating (0-100)	68%	Telephone Switching	4 per yr; free
Yield	0.0%	Total Assets	$334 million

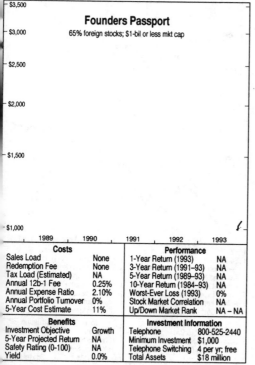

Founders Passport

65% foreign stocks; $1-bil or less mkt cap

Costs		Performance	
Sales Load	None	1-Year Return (1993)	NA
Redemption Fee	None	3-Year Return (1991–93)	NA
Tax Load (Estimated)	NA	5-Year Return (1989–93)	NA
Annual 12b-1 Fee	0.25%	10-Year Return (1984–93)	NA
Annual Expense Ratio	2.10%	Worst-Ever Loss (1993)	0%
Annual Portfolio Turnover	0%	Stock Market Correlation	NA
5-Year Cost Estimate	11%	Up/Down Market Rank	NA – NA

Benefits		Investment Information	
Investment Objective	Growth	Telephone	800-525-2440
5-Year Projected Return	NA	Minimum Investment	$1,000
Safety Rating (0-100)	NA	Telephone Switching	4 per yr; free
Yield	0.0%	Total Assets	$18 million

Founders Special

Medium sized U.S. companies

★★

Costs		Performance	
Sales Load	None	1-Year Return (1993)	+16%
Redemption Fee	None	3-Year Return (1991–93)	+106%
Tax Load (Estimated)	1%	5-Year Return (1989–93)	+156%
Annual 12b-1 Fee	0.25%	10-Year Return (1984–93)	+274%
Annual Expense Ratio	1.37%	Worst-Ever Loss (1987)	36%
Annual Portfolio Turnover	271%	Stock Market Correlation	55%
5-Year Cost Estimate	8%	Up/Down Market Rank	A – E

Benefits		Investment Information	
Investment Objective	Growth	Telephone	800-525-2440
5-Year Projected Return	+38%	Minimum Investment	$1,000
Safety Rating (0-100)	68%	Telephone Switching	4 per yr; free
Yield	0.0%	Total Assets	$447 million

EQUITY

Founders Worldwide Growth
Foreign - established growth companies
★★★

Fund

S&P 500

Costs		Performance	
Sales Load	None	1-Year Return (1993)	+30%
Redemption Fee	None	3-Year Return (1991–93)	+78%
Tax Load (Estimated)	4%	5-Year Return (1989–93)	NA
Annual 12b-1 Fee	0.25%	10-Year Return (1984–93)	NA
Annual Expense Ratio	2.01%	Worst-Ever Loss (1990)	11%
Annual Portfolio Turnover	119%	Stock Market Correlation	31%
5-Year Cost Estimate	15%	Up/Down Market Rank	NA – NA

Benefits		Investment Information	
Investment Objective	Growth	Telephone	800-525-2440
5-Year Projected Return	NA	Minimum Investment	$1,000
Safety Rating (0-100)	78%	Telephone Switching	4 per yr; free
Yield	0.0%	Total Assets	$49 million

FPA - Capital
Diversified growth stocks

Costs		Performance	
Sales Load	7.0%	1-Year Return (1993)	+17%
Redemption Fee	None	3-Year Return (1991–93)	+133%
Tax Load (Estimated)	7%	5-Year Return (1989–93)	+149%
Annual 12b-1 Fee	None	10-Year Return (1984–93)	NA
Annual Expense Ratio	1.06%	Worst-Ever Loss (1990)	39%
Annual Portfolio Turnover	13%	Stock Market Correlation	41%
5-Year Cost Estimate	15%	Up/Down Market Rank	B – D

Benefits		Investment Information	
Investment Objective	Gr. & Icm.	Telephone	800-982-4372
5-Year Projected Return	+33%	Minimum Investment	$1,500
Safety Rating (0-100)	61%	Telephone Switching	4 per yr; $5
Yield	0.1%	Total Assets	$145 million

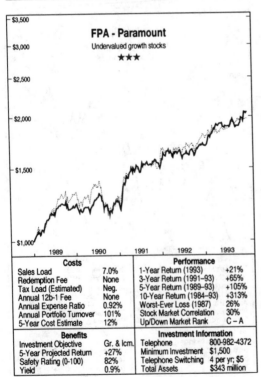

FPA - Paramount
Undervalued growth stocks
★★★

Costs		Performance	
Sales Load	7.0%	1-Year Return (1993)	+21%
Redemption Fee	None	3-Year Return (1991–93)	+65%
Tax Load (Estimated)	Neg.	5-Year Return (1989–93)	+105%
Annual 12b-1 Fee	None	10-Year Return (1984–93)	+313%
Annual Expense Ratio	0.92%	Worst-Ever Loss (1987)	26%
Annual Portfolio Turnover	101%	Stock Market Correlation	30%
5-Year Cost Estimate	12%	Up/Down Market Rank	C – A

Benefits		Investment Information	
Investment Objective	Gr. & Icm.	Telephone	800-982-4372
5-Year Projected Return	+27%	Minimum Investment	$1,500
Safety Rating (0-100)	82%	Telephone Switching	4 per yr; $5
Yield	0.9%	Total Assets	$343 million

FPA - Perennial
Growth and undervalued stocks
★★★

Costs		Performance	
Sales Load	7.0%	1-Year Return (1993)	+5%
Redemption Fee	None	3-Year Return (1991–93)	+44%
Tax Load (Estimated)	1%	5-Year Return (1989–93)	+83%
Annual 12b-1 Fee	None	10-Year Return (1984–93)	NA
Annual Expense Ratio	1.08%	Worst-Ever Loss (1987)	23%
Annual Portfolio Turnover	29%	Stock Market Correlation	67%
5-Year Cost Estimate	14%	Up/Down Market Rank	D – B

Benefits		Investment Information	
Investment Objective	Gr. & Icm.	Telephone	800-982-4372
5-Year Projected Return	+9%	Minimum Investment	$1,500
Safety Rating (0-100)	85%	Telephone Switching	4 per yr; $5
Yield	0.9%	Total Assets	$86 million

EQUITY

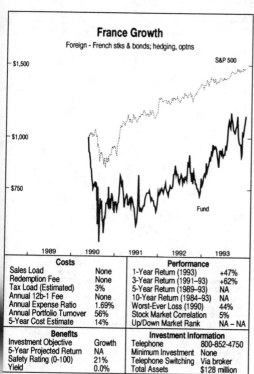

France Growth

Foreign - French stks & bonds; hedging, optns

S&P 500

$1,500

$1,000

$750

Fund

1989 1990 1991 1992 1993

Costs		Performance	
Sales Load	None	1-Year Return (1993)	+47%
Redemption Fee	None	3-Year Return (1991–93)	+62%
Tax Load (Estimated)	3%	5-Year Return (1989–93)	NA
Annual 12b-1 Fee	None	10-Year Return (1984–93)	NA
Annual Expense Ratio	1.69%	Worst-Ever Loss (1990)	44%
Annual Portfolio Turnover	56%	Stock Market Correlation	5%
5-Year Cost Estimate	14%	Up/Down Market Rank	NA – NA

Benefits		Investment Information	
Investment Objective	Growth	Telephone	800-852-4750
5-Year Projected Return	NA	Minimum Investment	None
Safety Rating (0-100)	21%	Telephone Switching	Via broker
Yield	0.0%	Total Assets	$128 million

Franklin California Growth

Non divsf; 65% sml-med Cal stks; $2.5 bil cap

$3,000

$2,500

$2,000

$1,500

$1,000

1989 1990 1991 1992 1993

Costs		Performance	
Sales Load	4.7%	1-Year Return (1993)	+18%
Redemption Fee	None	3-Year Return (1991–93)	NA
Tax Load (Estimated)	1%	5-Year Return (1989–93)	NA
Annual 12b-1 Fee	0.25%	10-Year Return (1984–93)	NA
Annual Expense Ratio	2.28%	Worst-Ever Loss (1992)	21%
Annual Portfolio Turnover	38%	Stock Market Correlation	41%
5-Year Cost Estimate	18%	Up/Down Market Rank	NA – NA

Benefits		Investment Information	
Investment Objective	Growth	Telephone	800-632-2180
5-Year Projected Return	+2%	Minimum Investment	$100
Safety Rating (0-100)	58%	Telephone Switching	Unlimited;free
Yield	1.2%	Total Assets	$4 million

Franklin Convertible Secs

Convertible securities

★★★★

$3,000

$2,500

$2,000

$1,500

$1,000

1989 1990 1991 1992 1993

Costs		Performance	
Sales Load	4.2%	1-Year Return (1993)	+20%
Redemption Fee	None	3-Year Return (1991–93)	+86%
Tax Load (Estimated)	4%	5-Year Return (1989–93)	+96%
Annual 12b-1 Fee	None	10-Year Return (1984–93)	NA
Annual Expense Ratio	0.81%	Worst-Ever Loss (1990)	18%
Annual Portfolio Turnover	23%	Stock Market Correlation	53%
5-Year Cost Estimate	10%	Up/Down Market Rank	D – A

Benefits		Investment Information	
Investment Objective	Gr. & Icm.	Telephone	800-632-2180
5-Year Projected Return	+37%	Minimum Investment	$100
Safety Rating (0-100)	85%	Telephone Switching	Unlimited;free
Yield	5.5%	Total Assets	$41 million

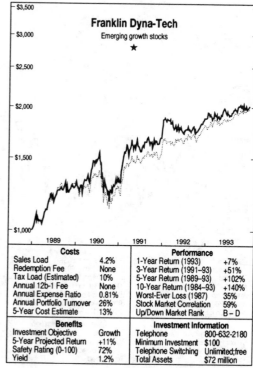

Franklin Dyna-Tech

Emerging growth stocks

★

$3,500

$3,000

$2,500

$2,000

$1,500

$1,000

1989 1990 1991 1992 1993

Costs		Performance	
Sales Load	4.2%	1-Year Return (1993)	+7%
Redemption Fee	None	3-Year Return (1991–93)	+51%
Tax Load (Estimated)	10%	5-Year Return (1989–93)	+102%
Annual 12b-1 Fee	None	10-Year Return (1984–93)	+140%
Annual Expense Ratio	0.81%	Worst-Ever Loss (1987)	35%
Annual Portfolio Turnover	26%	Stock Market Correlation	59%
5-Year Cost Estimate	13%	Up/Down Market Rank	B – D

Benefits		Investment Information	
Investment Objective	Growth	Telephone	800-632-2180
5-Year Projected Return	+11%	Minimum Investment	$100
Safety Rating (0-100)	72%	Telephone Switching	Unlimited;free
Yield	1.2%	Total Assets	$72 million

Franklin Equity
Low PE growth stocks

(Chart showing S&P 500 and Fund from 1989 to 1993, $1,000–$3,000 scale)

Costs		Performance	
Sales Load	4.2%	1-Year Return (1993)	+8%
Redemption Fee	None	3-Year Return (1991–93)	+41%
Tax Load (Estimated)	0%	5-Year Return (1989–93)	+50%
Annual 12b-1 Fee	None	10-Year Return (1984–93)	+222%
Annual Expense Ratio	0.69%	Worst-Ever Loss (1987)	38%
Annual Portfolio Turnover	51%	Stock Market Correlation	75%
5-Year Cost Estimate	8%	Up/Down Market Rank	A – E

Benefits		Investment Information	
Investment Objective	Gr. & Icm.	Telephone	800-632-2180
5-Year Projected Return	–12%	Minimum Investment	$100
Safety Rating (0-100)	67%	Telephone Switching	Unlimited;free
Yield	1.6%	Total Assets	$352 million

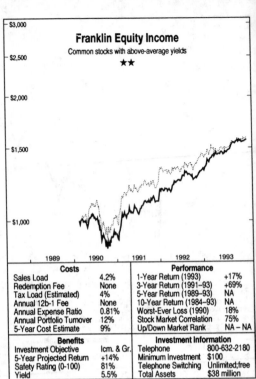

Franklin Equity Income
Common stocks with above-average yields
★★

(Chart from 1989 to 1993, $1,000–$3,000 scale)

Costs		Performance	
Sales Load	4.2%	1-Year Return (1993)	+17%
Redemption Fee	None	3-Year Return (1991–93)	+69%
Tax Load (Estimated)	4%	5-Year Return (1989–93)	NA
Annual 12b-1 Fee	None	10-Year Return (1984–93)	NA
Annual Expense Ratio	0.81%	Worst-Ever Loss (1990)	18%
Annual Portfolio Turnover	12%	Stock Market Correlation	75%
5-Year Cost Estimate	9%	Up/Down Market Rank	NA – NA

Benefits		Investment Information	
Investment Objective	Icm. & Gr.	Telephone	800-632-2180
5-Year Projected Return	+14%	Minimum Investment	$100
Safety Rating (0-100)	81%	Telephone Switching	Unlimited;free
Yield	5.5%	Total Assets	$38 million

Franklin Gold
International gold stocks

(Chart from 1989 to 1993, $1,000–$3,000 scale)

Costs		Performance	
Sales Load	4.2%	1-Year Return (1993)	+73%
Redemption Fee	None	3-Year Return (1991–93)	+46%
Tax Load (Estimated)	11%	5-Year Return (1989–93)	+65%
Annual 12b-1 Fee	None	10-Year Return (1984–93)	+93%
Annual Expense Ratio	0.75%	Worst-Ever Loss (1984-86)	48%
Annual Portfolio Turnover	2%	Stock Market Correlation	–1%
5-Year Cost Estimate	9%	Up/Down Market Rank	E – B

Benefits		Investment Information	
Investment Objective	Gr. & Icm.	Telephone	800-632-2180
5-Year Projected Return	NA	Minimum Investment	$100
Safety Rating (0-100)	56%	Telephone Switching	Unlimited;free
Yield	1.2%	Total Assets	$337 million

Franklin Growth
Diversified growth stocks
★

(Chart from 1989 to 1993, $1,000–$3,500 scale)

Costs		Performance	
Sales Load	4.2%	1-Year Return (1993)	+7%
Redemption Fee	None	3-Year Return (1991–93)	+39%
Tax Load (Estimated)	6%	5-Year Return (1989–93)	+75%
Annual 12b-1 Fee	None	10-Year Return (1984–93)	+233%
Annual Expense Ratio	0.66%	Worst-Ever Loss (1981)	24%
Annual Portfolio Turnover	3%	Stock Market Correlation	72%
5-Year Cost Estimate	8%	Up/Down Market Rank	B – C

Benefits		Investment Information	
Investment Objective	Growth	Telephone	800-632-2180
5-Year Projected Return	+3%	Minimum Investment	$100
Safety Rating (0-100)	76%	Telephone Switching	Unlimited;free
Yield	1.7%	Total Assets	$578 million

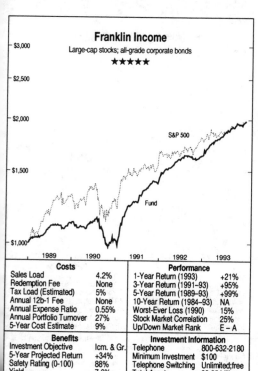

Franklin Income
Large-cap stocks; all-grade corporate bonds
★★★★★

S&P 500

Fund

Costs		Performance	
Sales Load	4.2%	1-Year Return (1993)	+21%
Redemption Fee	None	3-Year Return (1991–93)	+95%
Tax Load (Estimated)	5%	5-Year Return (1989–93)	+99%
Annual 12b-1 Fee	None	10-Year Return (1984–93)	NA
Annual Expense Ratio	0.55%	Worst-Ever Loss (1990)	15%
Annual Portfolio Turnover	27%	Stock Market Correlation	25%
5-Year Cost Estimate	9%	Up/Down Market Rank	E – A

Benefits		Investment Information	
Investment Objective	Icm. & Gr.	Telephone	800-632-2180
5-Year Projected Return	+34%	Minimum Investment	$100
Safety Rating (0-100)	88%	Telephone Switching	Unlimited;free
Yield	7.6%	Total Assets	$3.85 billion

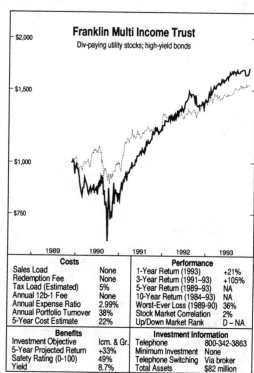

Franklin Multi Income Trust
Div-paying utility stocks; high-yield bonds

Costs		Performance	
Sales Load	None	1-Year Return (1993)	+21%
Redemption Fee	None	3-Year Return (1991–93)	+105%
Tax Load (Estimated)	5%	5-Year Return (1989–93)	NA
Annual 12b-1 Fee	None	10-Year Return (1984–93)	NA
Annual Expense Ratio	2.99%	Worst-Ever Loss (1989-90)	36%
Annual Portfolio Turnover	38%	Stock Market Correlation	2%
5-Year Cost Estimate	22%	Up/Down Market Rank	D – NA

Benefits		Investment Information	
Investment Objective	Icm. & Gr.	Telephone	800-342-3863
5-Year Projected Return	+33%	Minimum Investment	None
Safety Rating (0-100)	49%	Telephone Switching	Via broker
Yield	8.7%	Total Assets	$82 million

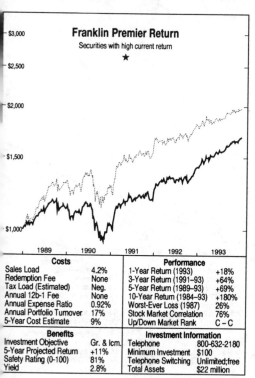

Franklin Premier Return
Securities with high current return
★

Costs		Performance	
Sales Load	4.2%	1-Year Return (1993)	+18%
Redemption Fee	None	3-Year Return (1991–93)	+64%
Tax Load (Estimated)	Neg.	5-Year Return (1989–93)	+69%
Annual 12b-1 Fee	None	10-Year Return (1984–93)	+180%
Annual Expense Ratio	0.92%	Worst-Ever Loss (1987)	26%
Annual Portfolio Turnover	17%	Stock Market Correlation	76%
5-Year Cost Estimate	9%	Up/Down Market Rank	C – C

Benefits		Investment Information	
Investment Objective	Gr. & Icm.	Telephone	800-632-2180
5-Year Projected Return	+11%	Minimum Investment	$100
Safety Rating (0-100)	81%	Telephone Switching	Unlimited;free
Yield	2.8%	Total Assets	$22 million

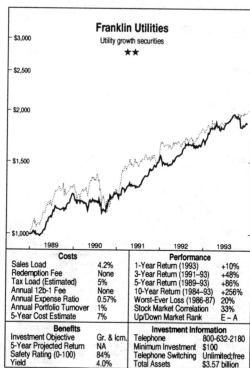

Franklin Utilities
Utility growth securities
★★

Costs		Performance	
Sales Load	4.2%	1-Year Return (1993)	+10%
Redemption Fee	None	3-Year Return (1991–93)	+48%
Tax Load (Estimated)	5%	5-Year Return (1989–93)	+86%
Annual 12b-1 Fee	None	10-Year Return (1984–93)	+256%
Annual Expense Ratio	0.57%	Worst-Ever Loss (1986-87)	20%
Annual Portfolio Turnover	1%	Stock Market Correlation	33%
5-Year Cost Estimate	7%	Up/Down Market Rank	E – A

Benefits		Investment Information	
Investment Objective	Gr. & Icm.	Telephone	800-632-2180
5-Year Projected Return	NA	Minimum Investment	$100
Safety Rating (0-100)	84%	Telephone Switching	Unlimited;free
Yield	4.0%	Total Assets	$3.57 billion

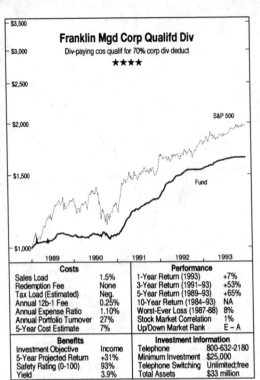

Franklin Mgd Corp Qualifd Div

Div-paying cos qualif for 70% corp div deduct

★★★★

Costs		Performance	
Sales Load	1.5%	1-Year Return (1993)	+7%
Redemption Fee	None	3-Year Return (1991–93)	+53%
Tax Load (Estimated)	Neg.	5-Year Return (1989–93)	+65%
Annual 12b-1 Fee	0.25%	10-Year Return (1984–93)	NA
Annual Expense Ratio	1.10%	Worst-Ever Loss (1987-88)	8%
Annual Portfolio Turnover	27%	Stock Market Correlation	1%
5-Year Cost Estimate	7%	Up/Down Market Rank	E – A

Benefits		Investment Information	
Investment Objective	Income	Telephone	800-632-2180
5-Year Projected Return	+31%	Minimum Investment	$25,000
Safety Rating (0-100)	93%	Telephone Switching	Unlimited;free
Yield	3.9%	Total Assets	$33 million

Franklin Mgd Rising Dividends

Cos with increased dividends in last 10 years

★★

Costs		Performance	
Sales Load	4.2%	1-Year Return (1993)	–3%
Redemption Fee	None	3-Year Return (1991–93)	+45%
Tax Load (Estimated)	2%	5-Year Return (1989–93)	+73%
Annual 12b-1 Fee	0.50%	10-Year Return (1984–93)	NA
Annual Expense Ratio	1.46%	Worst-Ever Loss (1987)	22%
Annual Portfolio Turnover	11%	Stock Market Correlation	63%
5-Year Cost Estimate	13%	Up/Down Market Rank	D – B

Benefits		Investment Information	
Investment Objective	Gr. & Icm.	Telephone	800-632-2180
5-Year Projected Return	+9%	Minimum Investment	$100
Safety Rating (0-100)	81%	Telephone Switching	Unlimited;free
Yield	1.7%	Total Assets	$358 million

Fundtrust Aggressive Growth

Diversified stocks

★

Costs		Performance	
Sales Load	1.5%	1-Year Return (1993)	+14%
Redemption Fee	None	3-Year Return (1991–93)	+67%
Tax Load (Estimated)	2%	5-Year Return (1989–93)	+81%
Annual 12b-1 Fee	0.50%	10-Year Return (1984–93)	NA
Annual Expense Ratio	1.61%	Worst-Ever Loss (1987)	30%
Annual Portfolio Turnover	34%	Stock Market Correlation	46%
5-Year Cost Estimate	11%	Up/Down Market Rank	D – B

Benefits		Investment Information	
Investment Objective	Growth	Telephone	800-344-9033
5-Year Projected Return	+18%	Minimum Investment	$1,000
Safety Rating (0-100)	77%	Telephone Switching	Unlimited;free
Yield	1.1%	Total Assets	$32 million

Fundtrust Growth

Diversified stocks

★

Costs		Performance	
Sales Load	1.5%	1-Year Return (1993)	+13%
Redemption Fee	None	3-Year Return (1991–93)	+58%
Tax Load (Estimated)	1%	5-Year Return (1989–93)	+73%
Annual 12b-1 Fee	0.50%	10-Year Return (1984–93)	NA
Annual Expense Ratio	1.60%	Worst-Ever Loss (1987)	26%
Annual Portfolio Turnover	40%	Stock Market Correlation	52%
5-Year Cost Estimate	10%	Up/Down Market Rank	E – B

Benefits		Investment Information	
Investment Objective	Gr. & Icm.	Telephone	800-344-9033
5-Year Projected Return	+15%	Minimum Investment	$1,000
Safety Rating (0-100)	80%	Telephone Switching	Unlimited;free
Yield	1.0%	Total Assets	$22 million

1994 Mutual Fund Buyer's Guide

Fundtrust Growth & Income
Diversified securities
★

S&P 500

Fund

Costs		Performance	
Sales Load	1.5%	1-Year Return (1993)	+13%
Redemption Fee	None	3-Year Return (1991–93)	+53%
Tax Load (Estimated)	4%	5-Year Return (1989–93)	+67%
Annual 12b-1 Fee	0.50%	10-Year Return (1984–93)	NA
Annual Expense Ratio	1.50%	Worst-Ever Loss (1987)	24%
Annual Portfolio Turnover	10%	Stock Market Correlation	52%
5-Year Cost Estimate	10%	Up/Down Market Rank	E – A

Benefits		Investment Information	
Investment Objective	Gr. & Icm.	Telephone	800-344-9033
5-Year Projected Return	+9%	Minimum Investment	$1,000
Safety Rating (0-100)	80%	Telephone Switching	Unlimited;free
Yield	2.6%	Total Assets	$41 million

Future Germany
Foreign - German stocks

Costs		Performance	
Sales Load	None	1-Year Return (1993)	+41%
Redemption Fee	None	3-Year Return (1991–93)	+46%
Tax Load (Estimated)	3%	5-Year Return (1989–93)	NA
Annual 12b-1 Fee	None	10-Year Return (1984–93)	NA
Annual Expense Ratio	1.47%	Worst-Ever Loss (1990)	42%
Annual Portfolio Turnover	43%	Stock Market Correlation	9%
5-Year Cost Estimate	12%	Up/Down Market Rank	NA – NA

Benefits		Investment Information	
Investment Objective	Growth	Telephone	800-437-6269
5-Year Projected Return	NA	Minimum Investment	None
Safety Rating (0-100)	32%	Telephone Switching	Via broker
Yield	0.5%	Total Assets	$164 million

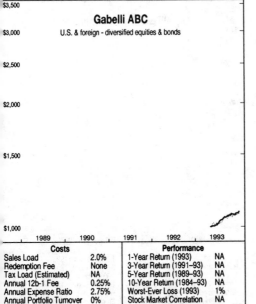

Gabelli ABC
U.S. & foreign - diversified equities & bonds

Costs		Performance	
Sales Load	2.0%	1-Year Return (1993)	NA
Redemption Fee	None	3-Year Return (1991–93)	NA
Tax Load (Estimated)	NA	5-Year Return (1989–93)	NA
Annual 12b-1 Fee	0.25%	10-Year Return (1984–93)	NA
Annual Expense Ratio	2.75%	Worst-Ever Loss (1993)	1%
Annual Portfolio Turnover	0%	Stock Market Correlation	NA
5-Year Cost Estimate	17%	Up/Down Market Rank	NA – NA

Benefits		Investment Information	
Investment Objective	Gr. & Icm.	Telephone	800-422-3554
5-Year Projected Return	NA	Minimum Investment	$2,000
Safety Rating (0-100)	NA	Telephone Switching	Unlimited;free
Yield	2.9%	Total Assets	$10 million

Gabelli Asset
Diversified stocks
★★★★★

Costs		Performance	
Sales Load	None	1-Year Return (1993)	+22%
Redemption Fee	None	3-Year Return (1991–93)	+66%
Tax Load (Estimated)	5%	5-Year Return (1989–93)	+99%
Annual 12b-1 Fee	0.25%	10-Year Return (1984–93)	NA
Annual Expense Ratio	1.31%	Worst-Ever Loss (1987)	26%
Annual Portfolio Turnover	14%	Stock Market Correlation	69%
5-Year Cost Estimate	8%	Up/Down Market Rank	C – B

Benefits		Investment Information	
Investment Objective	Growth	Telephone	800-422-3554
5-Year Projected Return	+27%	Minimum Investment	$1,000
Safety Rating (0-100)	83%	Telephone Switching	Unlimited;free
Yield	0.7%	Total Assets	$857 million

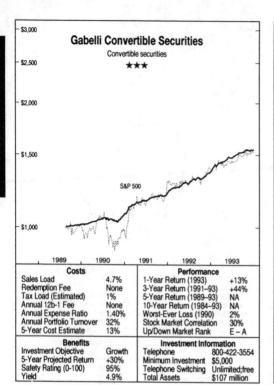

Gabelli Convertible Securities
Convertible securities
★★★

S&P 500

Costs		Performance	
Sales Load	4.7%	1-Year Return (1993)	+13%
Redemption Fee	None	3-Year Return (1991–93)	+44%
Tax Load (Estimated)	1%	5-Year Return (1989–93)	NA
Annual 12b-1 Fee	None	10-Year Return (1984–93)	NA
Annual Expense Ratio	1.40%	Worst-Ever Loss (1990)	2%
Annual Portfolio Turnover	32%	Stock Market Correlation	30%
5-Year Cost Estimate	13%	Up/Down Market Rank	E – A

Benefits		Investment Information	
Investment Objective	Growth	Telephone	800-422-3554
5-Year Projected Return	+30%	Minimum Investment	$5,000
Safety Rating (0-100)	95%	Telephone Switching	Unlimited;free
Yield	4.9%	Total Assets	$107 million

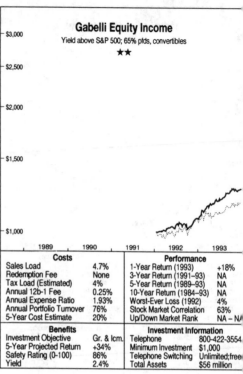

Gabelli Equity Income
Yield above S&P 500; 65% pfds, convertibles
★★

Costs		Performance	
Sales Load	4.7%	1-Year Return (1993)	+18%
Redemption Fee	None	3-Year Return (1991–93)	NA
Tax Load (Estimated)	4%	5-Year Return (1989–93)	NA
Annual 12b-1 Fee	0.25%	10-Year Return (1984–93)	NA
Annual Expense Ratio	1.93%	Worst-Ever Loss (1992)	4%
Annual Portfolio Turnover	76%	Stock Market Correlation	63%
5-Year Cost Estimate	20%	Up/Down Market Rank	NA – NA

Benefits		Investment Information	
Investment Objective	Gr. & Icm.	Telephone	800-422-3554
5-Year Projected Return	+34%	Minimum Investment	$1,000
Safety Rating (0-100)	86%	Telephone Switching	Unlimited;free
Yield	2.4%	Total Assets	$56 million

Gabelli Equity Trust
Undervalued stocks

Costs		Performance	
Sales Load	None	1-Year Return (1993)	+30%
Redemption Fee	None	3-Year Return (1991–93)	+57%
Tax Load (Estimated)	8%	5-Year Return (1989–93)	+106%
Annual 12b-1 Fee	None	10-Year Return (1984–93)	NA
Annual Expense Ratio	1.26%	Worst-Ever Loss (1989-90)	35%
Annual Portfolio Turnover	23%	Stock Market Correlation	33%
5-Year Cost Estimate	12%	Up/Down Market Rank	C – C

Benefits		Investment Information	
Investment Objective	Growth	Telephone	800-422-3554
5-Year Projected Return	–10%	Minimum Investment	None
Safety Rating (0-100)	55%	Telephone Switching	Via broker
Yield	9.5%	Total Assets	$750 million

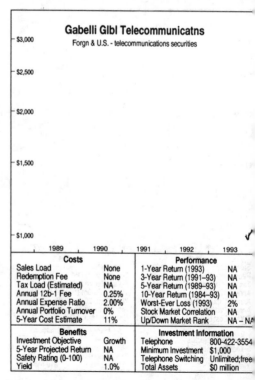

Gabelli Glbl Telecommunicatns
Forgn & U.S. - telecommunications securities

Costs		Performance	
Sales Load	None	1-Year Return (1993)	NA
Redemption Fee	None	3-Year Return (1991–93)	NA
Tax Load (Estimated)	NA	5-Year Return (1989–93)	NA
Annual 12b-1 Fee	0.25%	10-Year Return (1984–93)	NA
Annual Expense Ratio	2.00%	Worst-Ever Loss (1993)	2%
Annual Portfolio Turnover	0%	Stock Market Correlation	NA
5-Year Cost Estimate	11%	Up/Down Market Rank	NA – NA

Benefits		Investment Information	
Investment Objective	Growth	Telephone	800-422-3554
5-Year Projected Return	NA	Minimum Investment	$1,000
Safety Rating (0-100)	NA	Telephone Switching	Unlimited;free
Yield	1.0%	Total Assets	$0 million

Gabelli Growth
Growth stocks with favorable earnings
★★★★

Chart labels: Fund, S&P 500; Y-axis $1,000–$3,500; X-axis 1989–1993

Costs		Performance	
Sales Load	None	1-Year Return (1993)	+11%
Redemption Fee	None	3-Year Return (1991–93)	+56%
Tax Load (Estimated)	6%	5-Year Return (1989–93)	+114%
Annual 12b-1 Fee	0.25%	10-Year Return (1984–93)	NA
Annual Expense Ratio	1.41%	Worst-Ever Loss (1987)	27%
Annual Portfolio Turnover	78%	Stock Market Correlation	72%
5-Year Cost Estimate	14%	Up/Down Market Rank	B – B

Benefits		Investment Information	
Investment Objective	Growth	Telephone	800-422-3554
5-Year Projected Return	+18%	Minimum Investment	$1,000
Safety Rating (0-100)	76%	Telephone Switching	Unlimited;free
Yield	0.4%	Total Assets	$703 million

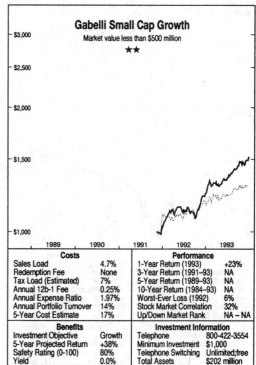

Gabelli Small Cap Growth
Market value less than $500 million
★★

Y-axis $1,000–$3,000; X-axis 1989–1993

Costs		Performance	
Sales Load	4.7%	1-Year Return (1993)	+23%
Redemption Fee	None	3-Year Return (1991–93)	NA
Tax Load (Estimated)	7%	5-Year Return (1989–93)	NA
Annual 12b-1 Fee	0.25%	10-Year Return (1984–93)	NA
Annual Expense Ratio	1.97%	Worst-Ever Loss (1992)	6%
Annual Portfolio Turnover	14%	Stock Market Correlation	32%
5-Year Cost Estimate	17%	Up/Down Market Rank	NA – NA

Benefits		Investment Information	
Investment Objective	Growth	Telephone	800-422-3554
5-Year Projected Return	+38%	Minimum Investment	$1,000
Safety Rating (0-100)	80%	Telephone Switching	Unlimited;free
Yield	0.0%	Total Assets	$202 million

Gabelli Value
Undervalued special situations
★★★

Y-axis $1,000–$3,000; X-axis 1989–1993

Costs		Performance	
Sales Load	5.8%	1-Year Return (1993)	+39%
Redemption Fee	None	3-Year Return (1991–93)	+81%
Tax Load (Estimated)	4%	5-Year Return (1989–93)	NA
Annual 12b-1 Fee	0.25%	10-Year Return (1984–93)	NA
Annual Expense Ratio	1.52%	Worst-Ever Loss (1990)	18%
Annual Portfolio Turnover	1%	Stock Market Correlation	44%
5-Year Cost Estimate	14%	Up/Down Market Rank	C – B

Benefits		Investment Information	
Investment Objective	Growth	Telephone	800-422-3554
5-Year Projected Return	+31%	Minimum Investment	$1,000
Safety Rating (0-100)	77%	Telephone Switching	Not available
Yield	0.4%	Total Assets	$470 million

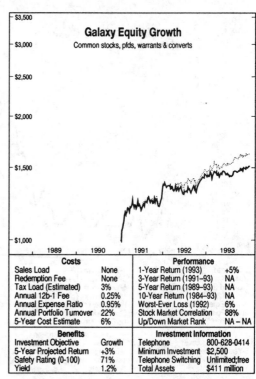

Galaxy Equity Growth
Common stocks, pfds, warrants & converts

Y-axis $1,000–$3,500; X-axis 1989–1993

Costs		Performance	
Sales Load	None	1-Year Return (1993)	+5%
Redemption Fee	None	3-Year Return (1991–93)	NA
Tax Load (Estimated)	3%	5-Year Return (1989–93)	NA
Annual 12b-1 Fee	0.25%	10-Year Return (1984–93)	NA
Annual Expense Ratio	0.95%	Worst-Ever Loss (1992)	6%
Annual Portfolio Turnover	22%	Stock Market Correlation	88%
5-Year Cost Estimate	6%	Up/Down Market Rank	NA – NA

Benefits		Investment Information	
Investment Objective	Growth	Telephone	800-628-0414
5-Year Projected Return	+3%	Minimum Investment	$2,500
Safety Rating (0-100)	71%	Telephone Switching	Unlimited;free
Yield	1.2%	Total Assets	$411 million

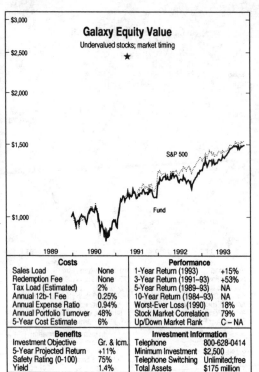

Galaxy Equity Value
Undervalued stocks; market timing
★

Costs		Performance	
Sales Load	None	1-Year Return (1993)	+15%
Redemption Fee	None	3-Year Return (1991–93)	+53%
Tax Load (Estimated)	2%	5-Year Return (1989–93)	NA
Annual 12b-1 Fee	0.25%	10-Year Return (1984–93)	NA
Annual Expense Ratio	0.94%	Worst-Ever Loss (1990)	18%
Annual Portfolio Turnover	48%	Stock Market Correlation	79%
5-Year Cost Estimate	6%	Up/Down Market Rank	C – NA

Benefits		Investment Information	
Investment Objective	Gr. & Icm.	Telephone	800-628-0414
5-Year Projected Return	+11%	Minimum Investment	$2,500
Safety Rating (0-100)	75%	Telephone Switching	Unlimited;free
Yield	1.4%	Total Assets	$175 million

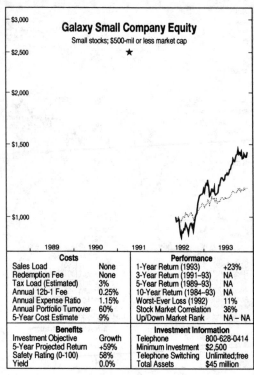

Galaxy Small Company Equity
Small stocks; $500-mil or less market cap
★

Costs		Performance	
Sales Load	None	1-Year Return (1993)	+23%
Redemption Fee	None	3-Year Return (1991–93)	NA
Tax Load (Estimated)	3%	5-Year Return (1989–93)	NA
Annual 12b-1 Fee	0.25%	10-Year Return (1984–93)	NA
Annual Expense Ratio	1.15%	Worst-Ever Loss (1992)	11%
Annual Portfolio Turnover	60%	Stock Market Correlation	36%
5-Year Cost Estimate	9%	Up/Down Market Rank	NA – NA

Benefits		Investment Information	
Investment Objective	Growth	Telephone	800-628-0414
5-Year Projected Return	+59%	Minimum Investment	$2,500
Safety Rating (0-100)	58%	Telephone Switching	Unlimited;free
Yield	0.0%	Total Assets	$45 million

GAM Global
Foreign & U.S. - diversified stocks

Costs		Performance	
Sales Load	5.3%	1-Year Return (1993)	+75%
Redemption Fee	None	3-Year Return (1991–93)	+85%
Tax Load (Estimated)	9%	5-Year Return (1989–93)	NA
Annual 12b-1 Fee	None	10-Year Return (1984–93)	NA
Annual Expense Ratio	2.33%	Worst-Ever Loss (1990-91)	24%
Annual Portfolio Turnover	140%	Stock Market Correlation	7%
5-Year Cost Estimate	31%	Up/Down Market Rank	NA – NA

Benefits		Investment Information	
Investment Objective	Growth	Telephone	212-888-4200
5-Year Projected Return	NA	Minimum Investment	$10,000
Safety Rating (0-100)	69%	Telephone Switching	See prospectus
Yield	0.4%	Total Assets	$22 million

GAM International
Foreign - Europe, Pacific-Basin and Canada
★

Costs		Performance	
Sales Load	5.3%	1-Year Return (1993)	+80%
Redemption Fee	None	3-Year Return (1991–93)	+114%
Tax Load (Estimated)	11%	5-Year Return (1989–93)	NA
Annual 12b-1 Fee	None	10-Year Return (1984–93)	NA
Annual Expense Ratio	2.11%	Worst-Ever Loss (1990-91)	19%
Annual Portfolio Turnover	116%	Stock Market Correlation	2%
5-Year Cost Estimate	31%	Up/Down Market Rank	NA – NA

Benefits		Investment Information	
Investment Objective	Growth	Telephone	212-888-4200
5-Year Projected Return	NA	Minimum Investment	$10,000
Safety Rating (0-100)	68%	Telephone Switching	See prospectus
Yield	0.4%	Total Assets	$47 million

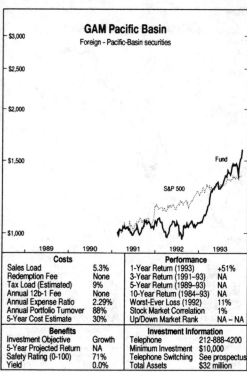

GAM Pacific Basin
Foreign - Pacific-Basin securities

Costs		Performance	
Sales Load	5.3%	1-Year Return (1993)	+51%
Redemption Fee	None	3-Year Return (1991–93)	NA
Tax Load (Estimated)	9%	5-Year Return (1989–93)	NA
Annual 12b-1 Fee	None	10-Year Return (1984–93)	NA
Annual Expense Ratio	2.29%	Worst-Ever Loss (1992)	11%
Annual Portfolio Turnover	88%	Stock Market Correlation	1%
5-Year Cost Estimate	30%	Up/Down Market Rank	NA – NA

Benefits		Investment Information	
Investment Objective	Growth	Telephone	212-888-4200
5-Year Projected Return	NA	Minimum Investment	$10,000
Safety Rating (0-100)	71%	Telephone Switching	See prospectus
Yield	0.0%	Total Assets	$32 million

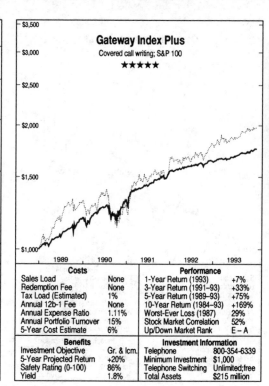

Gateway Index Plus
Covered call writing; S&P 100
★★★★★

Costs		Performance	
Sales Load	None	1-Year Return (1993)	+7%
Redemption Fee	None	3-Year Return (1991–93)	+33%
Tax Load (Estimated)	1%	5-Year Return (1989–93)	+75%
Annual 12b-1 Fee	None	10-Year Return (1984–93)	+169%
Annual Expense Ratio	1.11%	Worst-Ever Loss (1987)	29%
Annual Portfolio Turnover	15%	Stock Market Correlation	52%
5-Year Cost Estimate	6%	Up/Down Market Rank	E – A

Benefits		Investment Information	
Investment Objective	Gr. & Icm.	Telephone	800-354-6339
5-Year Projected Return	+20%	Minimum Investment	$1,000
Safety Rating (0-100)	86%	Telephone Switching	Unlimited;free
Yield	1.8%	Total Assets	$215 million

Gateway SWRW Growth Plus
Well established companies; buys puts
★★

Costs		Performance	
Sales Load	None	1-Year Return (1993)	+9%
Redemption Fee	None	3-Year Return (1991–93)	+54%
Tax Load (Estimated)	6%	5-Year Return (1989–93)	+100%
Annual 12b-1 Fee	None	10-Year Return (1984–93)	NA
Annual Expense Ratio	1.68%	Worst-Ever Loss (1987)	41%
Annual Portfolio Turnover	51%	Stock Market Correlation	81%
5-Year Cost Estimate	15%	Up/Down Market Rank	C – D

Benefits		Investment Information	
Investment Objective	Growth	Telephone	800-354-6339
5-Year Projected Return	+9%	Minimum Investment	$1,000
Safety Rating (0-100)	72%	Telephone Switching	Unlimited;free
Yield	0.4%	Total Assets	$20 million

Gemini II - Capital Shares
Dividend-paying stocks; liquidate Jan. 1997

Costs		Performance	
Sales Load	None	1-Year Return (1993)	+34%
Redemption Fee	None	3-Year Return (1991–93)	+113%
Tax Load (Estimated)	4%	5-Year Return (1989–93)	+61%
Annual 12b-1 Fee	None	10-Year Return (1984–93)	NA
Annual Expense Ratio	None	Worst-Ever Loss (1989-90)	54%
Annual Portfolio Turnover	36%	Stock Market Correlation	34%
5-Year Cost Estimate	4%	Up/Down Market Rank	B – E

Benefits		Investment Information	
Investment Objective	Growth	Telephone	800-662-7447
5-Year Projected Return	–3%	Minimum Investment	None
Safety Rating (0-100)	45%	Telephone Switching	Via broker
Yield	0.0%	Total Assets	$188 million

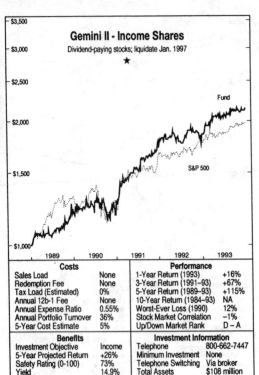

Gemini II - Income Shares
Dividend-paying stocks; liquidate Jan. 1997
★

Costs		Performance	
Sales Load	None	1-Year Return (1993)	+16%
Redemption Fee	None	3-Year Return (1991–93)	+67%
Tax Load (Estimated)	0%	5-Year Return (1989–93)	+115%
Annual 12b-1 Fee	None	10-Year Return (1984–93)	NA
Annual Expense Ratio	0.55%	Worst-Ever Loss (1990)	12%
Annual Portfolio Turnover	36%	Stock Market Correlation	–1%
5-Year Cost Estimate	5%	Up/Down Market Rank	D – A

Benefits		Investment Information	
Investment Objective	Income	Telephone	800-662-7447
5-Year Projected Return	+26%	Minimum Investment	None
Safety Rating (0-100)	73%	Telephone Switching	Via broker
Yield	14.9%	Total Assets	$108 million

General American Investors
Long term capital appreciation
★

Costs		Performance	
Sales Load	None	1-Year Return (1993)	–16%
Redemption Fee	None	3-Year Return (1991–93)	+75%
Tax Load (Estimated)	Neg.	5-Year Return (1989–93)	+168%
Annual 12b-1 Fee	None	10-Year Return (1984–93)	+238%
Annual Expense Ratio	1.16%	Worst-Ever Loss (1987)	40%
Annual Portfolio Turnover	16%	Stock Market Correlation	29%
5-Year Cost Estimate	8%	Up/Down Market Rank	C – C

Benefits		Investment Information	
Investment Objective	Gr. & Icm.	Telephone	800-436-8401
5-Year Projected Return	+18%	Minimum Investment	None
Safety Rating (0-100)	64%	Telephone Switching	Via broker
Yield	0.0%	Total Assets	$586 million

General Elec Svgs & Security
For General Electric employees only
★★

Costs		Performance	
Sales Load	None	1-Year Return (1993)	+11%
Redemption Fee	None	3-Year Return (1991–93)	+58%
Tax Load (Estimated)	1%	5-Year Return (1989–93)	+100%
Annual 12b-1 Fee	None	10-Year Return (1984–93)	+245%
Annual Expense Ratio	0.24%	Worst-Ever Loss (1987)	32%
Annual Portfolio Turnover	29%	Stock Market Correlation	94%
5-Year Cost Estimate	2%	Up/Down Market Rank	C – C

Benefits		Investment Information	
Investment Objective	Growth	Telephone	800-242-0134
5-Year Projected Return	+16%	Minimum Investment	None
Safety Rating (0-100)	75%	Telephone Switching	Not available
Yield	2.8%	Total Assets	$1.79 billion

General Securities
Long term holdings; call writing
★★★★

Costs		Performance	
Sales Load	None	1-Year Return (1993)	+6%
Redemption Fee	None	3-Year Return (1991–93)	+53%
Tax Load (Estimated)	3%	5-Year Return (1989–93)	+78%
Annual 12b-1 Fee	None	10-Year Return (1984–93)	+214%
Annual Expense Ratio	1.32%	Worst-Ever Loss (1981-82)	19%
Annual Portfolio Turnover	54%	Stock Market Correlation	59%
5-Year Cost Estimate	10%	Up/Down Market Rank	D – B

Benefits		Investment Information	
Investment Objective	Growth	Telephone	800-331-4923
5-Year Projected Return	+18%	Minimum Investment	$500
Safety Rating (0-100)	84%	Telephone Switching	Not available
Yield	2.2%	Total Assets	$27 million

EQUITY

Germany
Foreign - German stocks

Fund

S&P 500

Costs
Sales Load	None	
Redemption Fee	None	
Tax Load (Estimated)	4%	
Annual 12b-1 Fee	None	
Annual Expense Ratio	1.61%	
Annual Portfolio Turnover	37%	
5-Year Cost Estimate	14%	

Performance
1-Year Return (1993)	+26%
3-Year Return (1991–93)	+23%
5-Year Return (1989–93)	+91%
10-Year Return (1984–93)	NA
Worst-Ever Loss (1990-92)	58%
Stock Market Correlation	1%
Up/Down Market Rank	D – C

Benefits
Investment Objective	Growth
5-Year Projected Return	NA
Safety Rating (0-100)	0%
Yield	0.5%

Investment Information
Telephone	800-437-6269
Minimum Investment	None
Telephone Switching	Via broker
Total Assets	$129 million

Gintel Erisa
For retirement plans only

Costs
Sales Load	None	
Redemption Fee	None	
Tax Load (Estimated)	1%	
Annual 12b-1 Fee	0.40%	
Annual Expense Ratio	1.46%	
Annual Portfolio Turnover	138%	
5-Year Cost Estimate	9%	

Performance
1-Year Return (1993)	+5%
3-Year Return (1991–93)	+37%
5-Year Return (1989–93)	+50%
10-Year Return (1984–93)	+181%
Worst-Ever Loss (1987)	29%
Stock Market Correlation	42%
Up/Down Market Rank	C – B

Benefits
Investment Objective	Gr. & Icm.
5-Year Projected Return	–1%
Safety Rating (0-100)	71%
Yield	7.7%

Investment Information
Telephone	800-243-5808
Minimum Investment	$2,000
Telephone Switching	Unlimited;free
Total Assets	$52 million

Gintel Fund
Non-diversified; high-quality stocks

Costs
Sales Load	None	
Redemption Fee	None	
Tax Load (Estimated)	Neg.	
Annual 12b-1 Fee	None	
Annual Expense Ratio	1.72%	
Annual Portfolio Turnover	135%	
5-Year Cost Estimate	9%	

Performance
1-Year Return (1993)	+2%
3-Year Return (1991–93)	+47%
5-Year Return (1989–93)	+70%
10-Year Return (1984–93)	+166%
Worst-Ever Loss (1987)	34%
Stock Market Correlation	43%
Up/Down Market Rank	C – C

Benefits
Investment Objective	Growth
5-Year Projected Return	+4%
Safety Rating (0-100)	66%
Yield	3.4%

Investment Information
Telephone	800-243-5808
Minimum Investment	$5,000
Telephone Switching	Unlimited;free
Total Assets	$150 million

GIT Equity Special Growth
Small; growth companies

Costs
Sales Load	None	
Redemption Fee	None	
Tax Load (Estimated)	8%	
Annual 12b-1 Fee	None	
Annual Expense Ratio	1.35%	
Annual Portfolio Turnover	6%	
5-Year Cost Estimate	8%	

Performance
1-Year Return (1993)	+15%
3-Year Return (1991–93)	+54%
5-Year Return (1989–93)	+62%
10-Year Return (1984–93)	NA
Worst-Ever Loss (1987)	33%
Stock Market Correlation	38%
Up/Down Market Rank	D – B

Benefits
Investment Objective	Growth
5-Year Projected Return	+0%
Safety Rating (0-100)	74%
Yield	0.8%

Investment Information
Telephone	800-336-3063
Minimum Investment	$2,500
Telephone Switching	Unlimited;free
Total Assets	$40 million

EQUITY

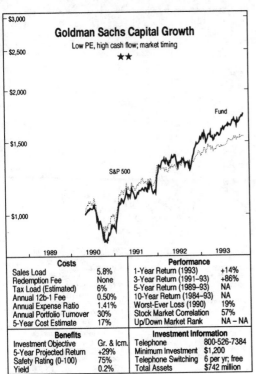

Goldman Sachs Capital Growth
Low PE, high cash flow; market timing
★★

Fund

S&P 500

Costs		Performance	
Sales Load	5.8%	1-Year Return (1993)	+14%
Redemption Fee	None	3-Year Return (1991–93)	+86%
Tax Load (Estimated)	6%	5-Year Return (1989–93)	NA
Annual 12b-1 Fee	0.50%	10-Year Return (1984–93)	NA
Annual Expense Ratio	1.41%	Worst-Ever Loss (1990)	19%
Annual Portfolio Turnover	30%	Stock Market Correlation	57%
5-Year Cost Estimate	17%	Up/Down Market Rank	NA – NA

Benefits		Investment Information	
Investment Objective	Gr. & Icm.	Telephone	800-526-7384
5-Year Projected Return	+29%	Minimum Investment	$1,200
Safety Rating (0-100)	75%	Telephone Switching	6 per yr; free
Yield	0.2%	Total Assets	$742 million

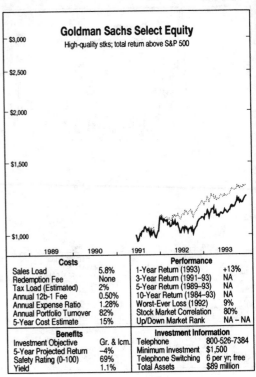

Goldman Sachs Select Equity
High-quality stks; total return above S&P 500

Costs		Performance	
Sales Load	5.8%	1-Year Return (1993)	+13%
Redemption Fee	None	3-Year Return (1991–93)	NA
Tax Load (Estimated)	2%	5-Year Return (1989–93)	NA
Annual 12b-1 Fee	0.50%	10-Year Return (1984–93)	NA
Annual Expense Ratio	1.28%	Worst-Ever Loss (1992)	9%
Annual Portfolio Turnover	82%	Stock Market Correlation	80%
5-Year Cost Estimate	15%	Up/Down Market Rank	NA – NA

Benefits		Investment Information	
Investment Objective	Gr. & Icm.	Telephone	800-526-7384
5-Year Projected Return	–4%	Minimum Investment	$1,500
Safety Rating (0-100)	69%	Telephone Switching	6 per yr; free
Yield	1.1%	Total Assets	$89 million

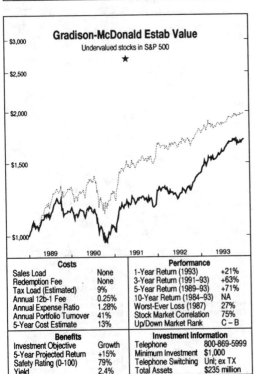

Gradison-McDonald Estab Value
Undervalued stocks in S&P 500
★

Costs		Performance	
Sales Load	None	1-Year Return (1993)	+21%
Redemption Fee	None	3-Year Return (1991–93)	+63%
Tax Load (Estimated)	9%	5-Year Return (1989–93)	+71%
Annual 12b-1 Fee	0.25%	10-Year Return (1984–93)	NA
Annual Expense Ratio	1.28%	Worst-Ever Loss (1987)	27%
Annual Portfolio Turnover	41%	Stock Market Correlation	75%
5-Year Cost Estimate	13%	Up/Down Market Rank	C – B

Benefits		Investment Information	
Investment Objective	Growth	Telephone	800-869-5999
5-Year Projected Return	+15%	Minimum Investment	$1,000
Safety Rating (0-100)	79%	Telephone Switching	Unl; ex TX
Yield	2.4%	Total Assets	$235 million

Gradison-McDonald Oppor Value
Smaller cos; hi earnings grth; not in S&P 500
★★

Costs		Performance	
Sales Load	None	1-Year Return (1993)	+11%
Redemption Fee	None	3-Year Return (1991–93)	+73%
Tax Load (Estimated)	8%	5-Year Return (1989–93)	+86%
Annual 12b-1 Fee	0.25%	10-Year Return (1984–93)	NA
Annual Expense Ratio	1.44%	Worst-Ever Loss (1987)	29%
Annual Portfolio Turnover	42%	Stock Market Correlation	47%
5-Year Cost Estimate	14%	Up/Down Market Rank	D – C

Benefits		Investment Information	
Investment Objective	Growth	Telephone	800-869-5999
5-Year Projected Return	+18%	Minimum Investment	$1,000
Safety Rating (0-100)	78%	Telephone Switching	Unl; ex TX
Yield	0.4%	Total Assets	$76 million

EQUITY

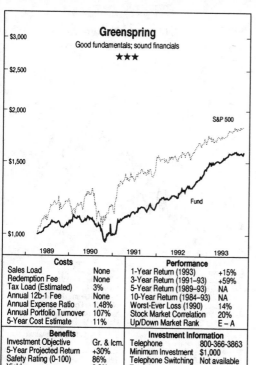

Greenspring
Good fundamentals; sound financials
★★★

S&P 500

Fund

Costs		Performance	
Sales Load	None	1-Year Return (1993)	+15%
Redemption Fee	None	3-Year Return (1991–93)	+59%
Tax Load (Estimated)	3%	5-Year Return (1989–93)	NA
Annual 12b-1 Fee	None	10-Year Return (1984–93)	NA
Annual Expense Ratio	1.48%	Worst-Ever Loss (1990)	14%
Annual Portfolio Turnover	107%	Stock Market Correlation	20%
5-Year Cost Estimate	11%	Up/Down Market Rank	E – A

Benefits		Investment Information	
Investment Objective	Gr. & Icm.	Telephone	800-366-3863
5-Year Projected Return	+30%	Minimum Investment	$1,000
Safety Rating (0-100)	86%	Telephone Switching	Not available
Yield	2.9%	Total Assets	$28 million

Growth Fund of Spain
Foreign - Spanish stocks

Costs		Performance	
Sales Load	None	1-Year Return (1993)	+34%
Redemption Fee	None	3-Year Return (1991–93)	+28%
Tax Load (Estimated)	2%	5-Year Return (1989–93)	NA
Annual 12b-1 Fee	None	10-Year Return (1984–93)	NA
Annual Expense Ratio	1.22%	Worst-Ever Loss (1990)	40%
Annual Portfolio Turnover	170%	Stock Market Correlation	17%
5-Year Cost Estimate	10%	Up/Down Market Rank	NA – NA

Benefits		Investment Information	
Investment Objective	Growth	Telephone	800-621-1148
5-Year Projected Return	NA	Minimum Investment	None
Safety Rating (0-100)	39%	Telephone Switching	Via broker
Yield	0.0%	Total Assets	$195 million

G.T. Global America Growth "A"
Small-med sized cos; undervalued; EPS accel

Costs		Performance	
Sales Load	5.0%	1-Year Return (1993)	+8%
Redemption Fee	None	3-Year Return (1991–93)	+70%
Tax Load (Estimated)	6%	5-Year Return (1989–93)	NA
Annual 12b-1 Fee	0.35%	10-Year Return (1984–93)	NA
Annual Expense Ratio	1.78%	Worst-Ever Loss (1990)	32%
Annual Portfolio Turnover	114%	Stock Market Correlation	39%
5-Year Cost Estimate	22%	Up/Down Market Rank	A – E

Benefits		Investment Information	
Investment Objective	Growth	Telephone	800-824-1580
5-Year Projected Return	+11%	Minimum Investment	$500
Safety Rating (0-100)	62%	Telephone Switching	See prospectus
Yield	0.0%	Total Assets	$138 million

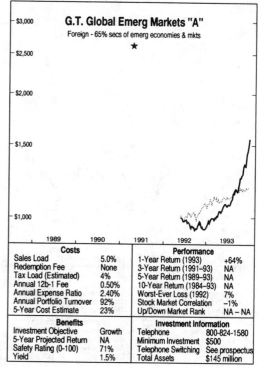

G.T. Global Emerg Markets "A"
Foreign - 65% secs of emerg economies & mkts
★

Costs		Performance	
Sales Load	5.0%	1-Year Return (1993)	+64%
Redemption Fee	None	3-Year Return (1991–93)	NA
Tax Load (Estimated)	4%	5-Year Return (1989–93)	NA
Annual 12b-1 Fee	0.50%	10-Year Return (1984–93)	NA
Annual Expense Ratio	2.40%	Worst-Ever Loss (1992)	7%
Annual Portfolio Turnover	92%	Stock Market Correlation	–1%
5-Year Cost Estimate	23%	Up/Down Market Rank	NA – NA

Benefits		Investment Information	
Investment Objective	Growth	Telephone	800-824-1580
5-Year Projected Return	NA	Minimum Investment	$500
Safety Rating (0-100)	71%	Telephone Switching	See prospectus
Yield	1.5%	Total Assets	$145 million

G.T. Global Europe "A"
Foreign - European stocks

(Chart: S&P 500 and Fund, years 1989–1993, $1,000–$3,500 scale)

Costs		Performance	
Sales Load	5.0%	1-Year Return (1993)	+28%
Redemption Fee	None	3-Year Return (1991–93)	+19%
Tax Load (Estimated)	Neg.	5-Year Return (1989–93)	+43%
Annual 12b-1 Fee	0.35%	10-Year Return (1984–93)	NA
Annual Expense Ratio	2.05%	Worst-Ever Loss (1987)	33%
Annual Portfolio Turnover	67%	Stock Market Correlation	10%
5-Year Cost Estimate	16%	Up/Down Market Rank	E – B

Benefits		Investment Information	
Investment Objective	Growth	Telephone	800-824-1580
5-Year Projected Return	NA	Minimum Investment	$500
Safety Rating (0-100)	66%	Telephone Switching	See prospectus
Yield	0.7%	Total Assets	$867 million

G.T. Global Health Care "A"
Foreign & US - health care;65% stks;35% bonds

(Chart: years 1989–1993, $1,000–$3,000 scale)

Costs		Performance	
Sales Load	5.0%	1-Year Return (1993)	+3%
Redemption Fee	None	3-Year Return (1991–93)	+40%
Tax Load (Estimated)	3%	5-Year Return (1989–93)	NA
Annual 12b-1 Fee	0.50%	10-Year Return (1984–93)	NA
Annual Expense Ratio	2.03%	Worst-Ever Loss (1992-93)	34%
Annual Portfolio Turnover	104%	Stock Market Correlation	32%
5-Year Cost Estimate	20%	Up/Down Market Rank	C – NA

Benefits		Investment Information	
Investment Objective	Growth	Telephone	800-824-1580
5-Year Projected Return	NA	Minimum Investment	$500
Safety Rating (0-100)	67%	Telephone Switching	See prospectus
Yield	0.3%	Total Assets	$451 million

G.T. Global International "A"
Foreign - diversified

(Chart: years 1989–1993, $1,000–$3,500 scale)

Costs		Performance	
Sales Load	5.0%	1-Year Return (1993)	+34%
Redemption Fee	None	3-Year Return (1991–93)	+43%
Tax Load (Estimated)	9%	5-Year Return (1989–93)	+70%
Annual 12b-1 Fee	0.35%	10-Year Return (1984–93)	NA
Annual Expense Ratio	1.93%	Worst-Ever Loss (1987)	34%
Annual Portfolio Turnover	91%	Stock Market Correlation	14%
5-Year Cost Estimate	27%	Up/Down Market Rank	E – A

Benefits		Investment Information	
Investment Objective	Growth	Telephone	800-824-1580
5-Year Projected Return	NA	Minimum Investment	$500
Safety Rating (0-100)	75%	Telephone Switching	See prospectus
Yield	0.0%	Total Assets	$497 million

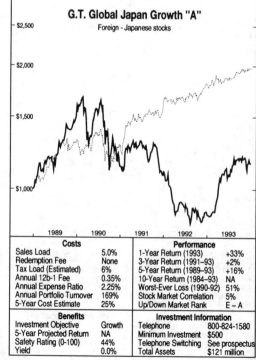

G.T. Global Japan Growth "A"
Foreign - Japanese stocks

(Chart: years 1989–1993, $1,000–$2,500 scale)

Costs		Performance	
Sales Load	5.0%	1-Year Return (1993)	+33%
Redemption Fee	None	3-Year Return (1991–93)	+2%
Tax Load (Estimated)	6%	5-Year Return (1989–93)	+16%
Annual 12b-1 Fee	0.35%	10-Year Return (1984–93)	NA
Annual Expense Ratio	2.25%	Worst-Ever Loss (1990-92)	51%
Annual Portfolio Turnover	169%	Stock Market Correlation	5%
5-Year Cost Estimate	25%	Up/Down Market Rank	E – A

Benefits		Investment Information	
Investment Objective	Growth	Telephone	800-824-1580
5-Year Projected Return	NA	Minimum Investment	$500
Safety Rating (0-100)	44%	Telephone Switching	See prospectus
Yield	0.0%	Total Assets	$121 million

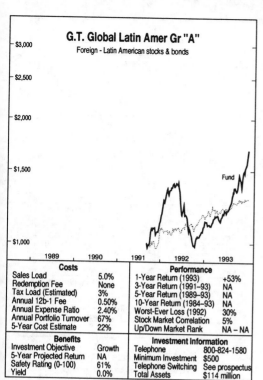

G.T. Global Latin Amer Gr "A"
Foreign - Latin American stocks & bonds

Costs		Performance	
Sales Load	5.0%	1-Year Return (1993)	+53%
Redemption Fee	None	3-Year Return (1991–93)	NA
Tax Load (Estimated)	3%	5-Year Return (1989–93)	NA
Annual 12b-1 Fee	0.50%	10-Year Return (1984–93)	NA
Annual Expense Ratio	2.40%	Worst-Ever Loss (1992)	30%
Annual Portfolio Turnover	67%	Stock Market Correlation	5%
5-Year Cost Estimate	22%	Up/Down Market Rank	NA – NA

Benefits		Investment Information	
Investment Objective	Growth	Telephone	800-824-1580
5-Year Projected Return	NA	Minimum Investment	$500
Safety Rating (0-100)	61%	Telephone Switching	See prospectus
Yield	0.0%	Total Assets	$114 million

G.T. Global Pacific Growth "A"
Foreign - Pacific-Basin stocks
★

Costs		Performance	
Sales Load	5.0%	1-Year Return (1993)	+61%
Redemption Fee	None	3-Year Return (1991–93)	+67%
Tax Load (Estimated)	5%	5-Year Return (1989–93)	+120%
Annual 12b-1 Fee	0.35%	10-Year Return (1984–93)	+417%
Annual Expense Ratio	2.03%	Worst-Ever Loss (1987)	34%
Annual Portfolio Turnover	102%	Stock Market Correlation	9%
5-Year Cost Estimate	22%	Up/Down Market Rank	E – A

Benefits		Investment Information	
Investment Objective	Growth	Telephone	800-824-1580
5-Year Projected Return	NA	Minimum Investment	$500
Safety Rating (0-100)	73%	Telephone Switching	See prospectus
Yield	0.0%	Total Assets	$401 million

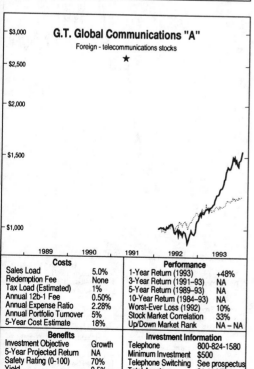

G.T. Global Communications "A"
Foreign - telecommunications stocks
★

Costs		Performance	
Sales Load	5.0%	1-Year Return (1993)	+48%
Redemption Fee	None	3-Year Return (1991–93)	NA
Tax Load (Estimated)	1%	5-Year Return (1989–93)	NA
Annual 12b-1 Fee	0.50%	10-Year Return (1984–93)	NA
Annual Expense Ratio	2.28%	Worst-Ever Loss (1992)	10%
Annual Portfolio Turnover	5%	Stock Market Correlation	33%
5-Year Cost Estimate	18%	Up/Down Market Rank	NA – NA

Benefits		Investment Information	
Investment Objective	Growth	Telephone	800-824-1580
5-Year Projected Return	NA	Minimum Investment	$500
Safety Rating (0-100)	70%	Telephone Switching	See prospectus
Yield	0.5%	Total Assets	$1.11 billion

G.T. Global Wldwde Growth "A"
Foreign & U.S. - diversified stocks
★

Costs		Performance	
Sales Load	5.0%	1-Year Return (1993)	+28%
Redemption Fee	None	3-Year Return (1991–93)	+58%
Tax Load (Estimated)	5%	5-Year Return (1989–93)	+91%
Annual 12b-1 Fee	0.35%	10-Year Return (1984–93)	NA
Annual Expense Ratio	2.07%	Worst-Ever Loss (1990-91)	22%
Annual Portfolio Turnover	116%	Stock Market Correlation	35%
5-Year Cost Estimate	23%	Up/Down Market Rank	D – B

Benefits		Investment Information	
Investment Objective	Growth	Telephone	800-824-1580
5-Year Projected Return	NA	Minimum Investment	$500
Safety Rating (0-100)	76%	Telephone Switching	See prospectus
Yield	0.0%	Total Assets	$182 million

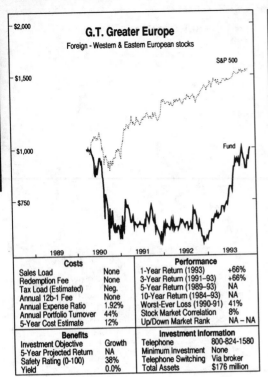

G.T. Greater Europe
Foreign - Western & Eastern European stocks

S&P 500

Fund

Costs		Performance	
Sales Load	None	1-Year Return (1993)	+66%
Redemption Fee	None	3-Year Return (1991–93)	+66%
Tax Load (Estimated)	Neg.	5-Year Return (1989–93)	NA
Annual 12b-1 Fee	62%	10-Year Return (1984–93)	NA
Annual Expense Ratio	1.92%	Worst-Ever Loss (1990-91)	41%
Annual Portfolio Turnover	44%	Stock Market Correlation	8%
5-Year Cost Estimate	12%	Up/Down Market Rank	NA – NA

Benefits		Investment Information	
Investment Objective	Growth	Telephone	800-824-1580
5-Year Projected Return	NA	Minimum Investment	None
Safety Rating (0-100)	38%	Telephone Switching	Via broker
Yield	0.0%	Total Assets	$176 million

Guardian Park Avenue
Diversified growth stocks
★★★

Costs		Performance	
Sales Load	4.7%	1-Year Return (1993)	+20%
Redemption Fee	None	3-Year Return (1991–93)	+95%
Tax Load (Estimated)	6%	5-Year Return (1989–93)	+111%
Annual 12b-1 Fee	0.15%	10-Year Return (1984–93)	+366%
Annual Expense Ratio	0.83%	Worst-Ever Loss (1987)	32%
Annual Portfolio Turnover	92%	Stock Market Correlation	65%
5-Year Cost Estimate	16%	Up/Down Market Rank	B – C

Benefits		Investment Information	
Investment Objective	Growth	Telephone	800-221-3253
5-Year Projected Return	+27%	Minimum Investment	$1,000
Safety Rating (0-100)	79%	Telephone Switching	Unlimited;free
Yield	1.8%	Total Assets	$516 million

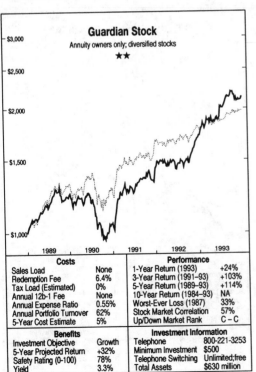

Guardian Stock
Annuity owners only; diversified stocks
★★

Costs		Performance	
Sales Load	None	1-Year Return (1993)	+24%
Redemption Fee	6.4%	3-Year Return (1991–93)	+103%
Tax Load (Estimated)	0%	5-Year Return (1989–93)	+114%
Annual 12b-1 Fee	None	10-Year Return (1984–93)	NA
Annual Expense Ratio	0.55%	Worst-Ever Loss (1987)	33%
Annual Portfolio Turnover	62%	Stock Market Correlation	57%
5-Year Cost Estimate	5%	Up/Down Market Rank	C – C

Benefits		Investment Information	
Investment Objective	Growth	Telephone	800-221-3253
5-Year Projected Return	+32%	Minimum Investment	$500
Safety Rating (0-100)	78%	Telephone Switching	Unlimited;free
Yield	3.3%	Total Assets	$630 million

H & Q Healthcare Investors
Health services and medical technology stocks

Costs		Performance	
Sales Load	None	1-Year Return (1993)	–8%
Redemption Fee	None	3-Year Return (1991–93)	+66%
Tax Load (Estimated)	11%	5-Year Return (1989–93)	+206%
Annual 12b-1 Fee	None	10-Year Return (1984–93)	NA
Annual Expense Ratio	1.74%	Worst-Ever Loss (1987)	51%
Annual Portfolio Turnover	28%	Stock Market Correlation	12%
5-Year Cost Estimate	17%	Up/Down Market Rank	A – D

Benefits		Investment Information	
Investment Objective	Growth	Telephone	800-327-6679
5-Year Projected Return	NA	Minimum Investment	None
Safety Rating (0-100)	41%	Telephone Switching	Via broker
Yield	0.0%	Total Assets	$114 million

Hampton Utilities Capital Shrs
Utility securities; liquidate March 1994

Costs		Performance	
Sales Load	None	1-Year Return (1993)	+16%
Redemption Fee	None	3-Year Return (1991–93)	+75%
Tax Load (Estimated)	4%	5-Year Return (1989–93)	+113%
Annual 12b-1 Fee	None	10-Year Return (1984–93)	NA
Annual Expense Ratio	0.58%	Worst-Ever Loss (1989-90)	24%
Annual Portfolio Turnover	19%	Stock Market Correlation	6%
5-Year Cost Estimate	6%	Up/Down Market Rank	C – A

Benefits		Investment Information	
Investment Objective	Growth	Telephone	800-221-0856
5-Year Projected Return	NA	Minimum Investment	None
Safety Rating (0-100)	70%	Telephone Switching	Via broker
Yield	1.2%	Total Assets	$18 million

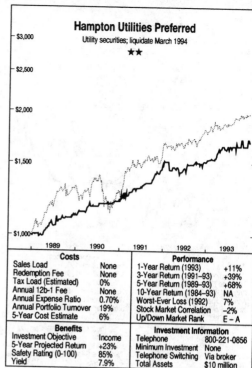

Hampton Utilities Preferred
Utility securities; liquidate March 1994
★★

Costs		Performance	
Sales Load	None	1-Year Return (1993)	+11%
Redemption Fee	None	3-Year Return (1991–93)	+39%
Tax Load (Estimated)	0%	5-Year Return (1989–93)	+68%
Annual 12b-1 Fee	None	10-Year Return (1984–93)	NA
Annual Expense Ratio	0.70%	Worst-Ever Loss (1992)	7%
Annual Portfolio Turnover	19%	Stock Market Correlation	–2%
5-Year Cost Estimate	6%	Up/Down Market Rank	E – A

Benefits		Investment Information	
Investment Objective	Income	Telephone	800-221-0856
5-Year Projected Return	+23%	Minimum Investment	None
Safety Rating (0-100)	85%	Telephone Switching	Via broker
Yield	7.9%	Total Assets	$10 million

Harbor - Capital Appreciation
Companies with market value over $700-million
★

Costs		Performance	
Sales Load	None	1-Year Return (1993)	+12%
Redemption Fee	None	3-Year Return (1991–93)	+91%
Tax Load (Estimated)	1%	5-Year Return (1989–93)	+133%
Annual 12b-1 Fee	None	10-Year Return (1984–93)	NA
Annual Expense Ratio	0.91%	Worst-Ever Loss (1990)	27%
Annual Portfolio Turnover	98%	Stock Market Correlation	66%
5-Year Cost Estimate	6%	Up/Down Market Rank	A – E

Benefits		Investment Information	
Investment Objective	Growth	Telephone	800-422-1050
5-Year Projected Return	+35%	Minimum Investment	$2,000
Safety Rating (0-100)	68%	Telephone Switching	See prospectus
Yield	0.2%	Total Assets	$135 million

Harbor - Growth
Earnings growth; undervalued stocks

Costs		Performance	
Sales Load	None	1-Year Return (1993)	+18%
Redemption Fee	None	3-Year Return (1991–93)	+68%
Tax Load (Estimated)	Neg.	5-Year Return (1989–93)	+93%
Annual 12b-1 Fee	None	10-Year Return (1984–93)	NA
Annual Expense Ratio	0.90%	Worst-Ever Loss (1987)	35%
Annual Portfolio Turnover	257%	Stock Market Correlation	59%
5-Year Cost Estimate	5%	Up/Down Market Rank	A – E

Benefits		Investment Information	
Investment Objective	Growth	Telephone	800-422-1050
5-Year Projected Return	+16%	Minimum Investment	$2,000
Safety Rating (0-100)	63%	Telephone Switching	See prospectus
Yield	0.1%	Total Assets	$216 million

Harbor - International

Foreign - Europe, Pacific emrg indust nations

★

Fund

| 1989 | 1990 | 1991 | 1992 | 1993 |

Costs		Performance	
Sales Load	None	1-Year Return (1993)	+45%
Redemption Fee	None	3-Year Return (1991–93)	+76%
Tax Load (Estimated)	3%	5-Year Return (1989–93)	NA
Annual 12b-1 Fee	None	10-Year Return (1984–93)	NA
Annual Expense Ratio	1.28%	Worst-Ever Loss (1990-91)	24%
Annual Portfolio Turnover	24%	Stock Market Correlation	13%
5-Year Cost Estimate	8%	Up/Down Market Rank	D – B

Benefits		Investment Information	
Investment Objective	Growth	Telephone	800-422-1050
5-Year Projected Return	NA	Minimum Investment	$2,000
Safety Rating (0-100)	74%	Telephone Switching	See prospectus
Yield	0.9%	Total Assets	$1.90 billion

Harbor - Value

Div-paying underv. stks; at least $300-ml cap

| 1989 | 1990 | 1991 | 1992 | 1993 |

Costs		Performance	
Sales Load	None	1-Year Return (1993)	+8%
Redemption Fee	None	3-Year Return (1991–93)	+41%
Tax Load (Estimated)	1%	5-Year Return (1989–93)	NA
Annual 12b-1 Fee	None	10-Year Return (1984–93)	NA
Annual Expense Ratio	0.94%	Worst-Ever Loss (1990)	21%
Annual Portfolio Turnover	25%	Stock Market Correlation	81%
5-Year Cost Estimate	5%	Up/Down Market Rank	D – NA

Benefits		Investment Information	
Investment Objective	Gr. & Icm.	Telephone	800-422-1050
5-Year Projected Return	–2%	Minimum Investment	$2,000
Safety Rating (0-100)	71%	Telephone Switching	See prospectus
Yield	2.4%	Total Assets	$60 million

Heartland Value

Undervalued stocks

★★

| 1989 | 1990 | 1991 | 1992 | 1993 |

Costs		Performance	
Sales Load	None	1-Year Return (1993)	+19%
Redemption Fee	3.1%	3-Year Return (1991–93)	+153%
Tax Load (Estimated)	1%	5-Year Return (1989–93)	+124%
Annual 12b-1 Fee	0.30%	10-Year Return (1984–93)	NA
Annual Expense Ratio	1.48%	Worst-Ever Loss (1987)	34%
Annual Portfolio Turnover	76%	Stock Market Correlation	29%
5-Year Cost Estimate	9%	Up/Down Market Rank	C – D

Benefits		Investment Information	
Investment Objective	Growth	Telephone	800-432-7856
5-Year Projected Return	+49%	Minimum Investment	$1,000
Safety Rating (0-100)	74%	Telephone Switching	Unlimited;free
Yield	0.0%	Total Assets	$151 million

Heritage Capital Appreciation

Undervalued stocks

★

| 1989 | 1990 | 1991 | 1992 | 1993 |

Costs		Performance	
Sales Load	4.2%	1-Year Return (1993)	+18%
Redemption Fee	None	3-Year Return (1991–93)	+76%
Tax Load (Estimated)	5%	5-Year Return (1989–93)	+85%
Annual 12b-1 Fee	0.50%	10-Year Return (1984–93)	NA
Annual Expense Ratio	1.66%	Worst-Ever Loss (1987)	29%
Annual Portfolio Turnover	55%	Stock Market Correlation	66%
5-Year Cost Estimate	19%	Up/Down Market Rank	B – D

Benefits		Investment Information	
Investment Objective	Growth	Telephone	800-421-4184
5-Year Projected Return	+16%	Minimum Investment	$1,000
Safety Rating (0-100)	77%	Telephone Switching	1 per mo; free
Yield	1.8%	Total Assets	$75 million

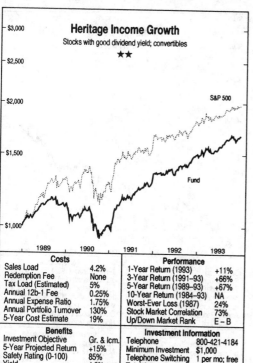

Heritage Income Growth
Stocks with good dividend yield; convertibles
★★

Costs		Performance	
Sales Load	4.2%	1-Year Return (1993)	+11%
Redemption Fee	None	3-Year Return (1991–93)	+66%
Tax Load (Estimated)	5%	5-Year Return (1989–93)	+67%
Annual 12b-1 Fee	0.25%	10-Year Return (1984–93)	NA
Annual Expense Ratio	1.75%	Worst-Ever Loss (1987)	24%
Annual Portfolio Turnover	130%	Stock Market Correlation	73%
5-Year Cost Estimate	19%	Up/Down Market Rank	E – B

Benefits		Investment Information	
Investment Objective	Gr. & Icm.	Telephone	800-421-4184
5-Year Projected Return	+15%	Minimum Investment	$1,000
Safety Rating (0–100)	85%	Telephone Switching	1 per mo; free
Yield	4.2%	Total Assets	$34 million

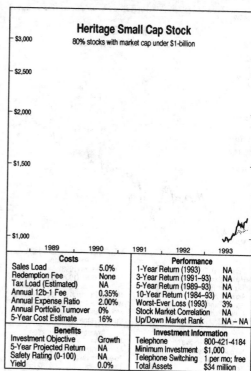

Heritage Small Cap Stock
80% stocks with market cap under $1-billion

Costs		Performance	
Sales Load	5.0%	1-Year Return (1993)	NA
Redemption Fee	None	3-Year Return (1991–93)	NA
Tax Load (Estimated)	NA	5-Year Return (1989–93)	NA
Annual 12b-1 Fee	0.35%	10-Year Return (1984–93)	NA
Annual Expense Ratio	2.00%	Worst-Ever Loss (1993)	3%
Annual Portfolio Turnover	0%	Stock Market Correlation	NA
5-Year Cost Estimate	16%	Up/Down Market Rank	NA – NA

Benefits		Investment Information	
Investment Objective	Growth	Telephone	800-421-4184
5-Year Projected Return	NA	Minimum Investment	$1,000
Safety Rating (0–100)	NA	Telephone Switching	1 per mo; free
Yield	0.0%	Total Assets	$34 million

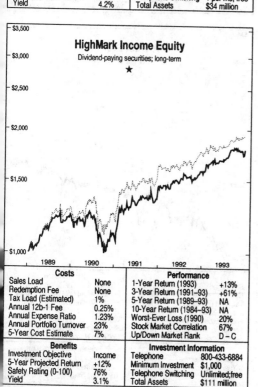

HighMark Income Equity
Dividend-paying securities; long-term
★

Costs		Performance	
Sales Load	None	1-Year Return (1993)	+13%
Redemption Fee	None	3-Year Return (1991–93)	+61%
Tax Load (Estimated)	1%	5-Year Return (1989–93)	NA
Annual 12b-1 Fee	0.25%	10-Year Return (1984–93)	NA
Annual Expense Ratio	1.23%	Worst-Ever Loss (1990)	20%
Annual Portfolio Turnover	23%	Stock Market Correlation	67%
5-Year Cost Estimate	7%	Up/Down Market Rank	D – C

Benefits		Investment Information	
Investment Objective	Income	Telephone	800-433-6884
5-Year Projected Return	+12%	Minimum Investment	$1,000
Safety Rating (0–100)	76%	Telephone Switching	Unlimited;free
Yield	3.1%	Total Assets	$111 million

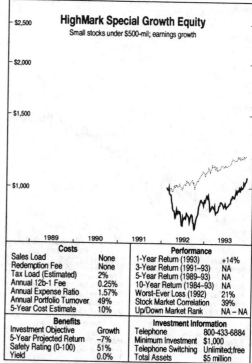

HighMark Special Growth Equity
Small stocks under $500-mil; earnings growth

Costs		Performance	
Sales Load	None	1-Year Return (1993)	+14%
Redemption Fee	None	3-Year Return (1991–93)	NA
Tax Load (Estimated)	2%	5-Year Return (1989–93)	NA
Annual 12b-1 Fee	0.25%	10-Year Return (1984–93)	NA
Annual Expense Ratio	1.57%	Worst-Ever Loss (1992)	21%
Annual Portfolio Turnover	49%	Stock Market Correlation	39%
5-Year Cost Estimate	10%	Up/Down Market Rank	NA – NA

Benefits		Investment Information	
Investment Objective	Growth	Telephone	800-433-6884
5-Year Projected Return	–7%	Minimum Investment	$1,000
Safety Rating (0–100)	51%	Telephone Switching	Unlimited;free
Yield	0.0%	Total Assets	$5 million

Horace Mann Growth
Annuity contracts; diversified growth stocks

Fund
S&P 500

Costs		Performance	
Sales Load	None	1-Year Return (1993)	+20%
Redemption Fee	8.7%	3-Year Return (1991–93)	+68%
Tax Load (Estimated)	0%	5-Year Return (1989–93)	+106%
Annual 12b-1 Fee	None	10-Year Return (1984–93)	+248%
Annual Expense Ratio	2.08%	Worst-Ever Loss (1987)	33%
Annual Portfolio Turnover	35%	Stock Market Correlation	67%
5-Year Cost Estimate	11%	Up/Down Market Rank	A – D

Benefits		Investment Information	
Investment Objective	Growth	Telephone	800-999-1030
5-Year Projected Return	+19%	Minimum Investment	$100
Safety Rating (0-100)	73%	Telephone Switching	Mail only
Yield	2.6%	Total Assets	$152 million

HT Insight Equity
Dividend-paying large stocks

Costs		Performance	
Sales Load	4.7%	1-Year Return (1993)	+18%
Redemption Fee	None	3-Year Return (1991–93)	+64%
Tax Load (Estimated)	1%	5-Year Return (1989–93)	+92%
Annual 12b-1 Fee	0.25%	10-Year Return (1984–93)	NA
Annual Expense Ratio	0.98%	Worst-Ever Loss (1989-90)	21%
Annual Portfolio Turnover	78%	Stock Market Correlation	84%
5-Year Cost Estimate	11%	Up/Down Market Rank	B – D

Benefits		Investment Information	
Investment Objective	Gr. & Icm.	Telephone	800-441-7379
5-Year Projected Return	+8%	Minimum Investment	$1,000
Safety Rating (0-100)	72%	Telephone Switching	Unlimited;free
Yield	1.6%	Total Assets	$33 million

Hummer Growth
Cyclical growth stocks
★★★

Costs		Performance	
Sales Load	None	1-Year Return (1993)	+4%
Redemption Fee	None	3-Year Return (1991–93)	+47%
Tax Load (Estimated)	6%	5-Year Return (1989–93)	+92%
Annual 12b-1 Fee	None	10-Year Return (1984–93)	NA
Annual Expense Ratio	1.23%	Worst-Ever Loss (1987)	30%
Annual Portfolio Turnover	3%	Stock Market Correlation	74%
5-Year Cost Estimate	7%	Up/Down Market Rank	C – B

Benefits		Investment Information	
Investment Objective	Gr. & Icm.	Telephone	800-621-4477
5-Year Projected Return	+20%	Minimum Investment	$1,000
Safety Rating (0-100)	80%	Telephone Switching	Unlimited;free
Yield	1.3%	Total Assets	$96 million

IAA Trust Growth
Diversified stocks

Costs		Performance	
Sales Load	3.1%	1-Year Return (1993)	+6%
Redemption Fee	None	3-Year Return (1991–93)	+39%
Tax Load (Estimated)	4%	5-Year Return (1989–93)	+68%
Annual 12b-1 Fee	None	10-Year Return (1984–93)	NA
Annual Expense Ratio	0.85%	Worst-Ever Loss (1987)	29%
Annual Portfolio Turnover	14%	Stock Market Correlation	85%
5-Year Cost Estimate	9%	Up/Down Market Rank	C – C

Benefits		Investment Information	
Investment Objective	Growth	Telephone	800-245-2100
5-Year Projected Return	–3%	Minimum Investment	$100
Safety Rating (0-100)	72%	Telephone Switching	Unlimited;free
Yield	1.4%	Total Assets	$72 million

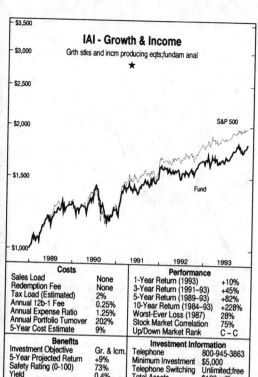

IAI - Growth & Income

Grth stks and incm producing eqts;fundam anal
★

Costs		Performance	
Sales Load	None	1-Year Return (1993)	+10%
Redemption Fee	None	3-Year Return (1991–93)	+45%
Tax Load (Estimated)	2%	5-Year Return (1989–93)	+82%
Annual 12b-1 Fee	0.25%	10-Year Return (1984–93)	+228%
Annual Expense Ratio	1.25%	Worst-Ever Loss (1987)	28%
Annual Portfolio Turnover	202%	Stock Market Correlation	75%
5-Year Cost Estimate	9%	Up/Down Market Rank	C – C
Benefits		**Investment Information**	
Investment Objective	Gr. & Icm.	Telephone	800-945-3863
5-Year Projected Return	+9%	Minimum Investment	$5,000
Safety Rating (0-100)	73%	Telephone Switching	Unlimited;free
Yield	0.4%	Total Assets	$186 million

IAI - International

Foreign - diversified stocks

Costs		Performance	
Sales Load	None	1-Year Return (1993)	+39%
Redemption Fee	None	3-Year Return (1991–93)	+53%
Tax Load (Estimated)	4%	5-Year Return (1989–93)	+57%
Annual 12b-1 Fee	0.25%	10-Year Return (1984–93)	NA
Annual Expense Ratio	1.91%	Worst-Ever Loss (1987)	22%
Annual Portfolio Turnover	36%	Stock Market Correlation	7%
5-Year Cost Estimate	13%	Up/Down Market Rank	E – A
Benefits		**Investment Information**	
Investment Objective	Gr. & Icm.	Telephone	800-945-3863
5-Year Projected Return	NA	Minimum Investment	$5,000
Safety Rating (0-100)	76%	Telephone Switching	Unlimited;free
Yield	2.5%	Total Assets	$82 million

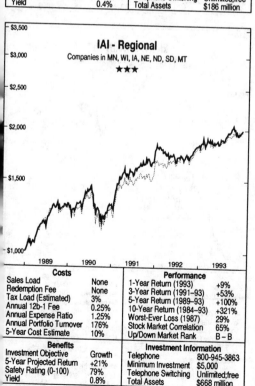

IAI - Regional

Companies in MN, WI, IA, NE, ND, SD, MT
★★★

Costs		Performance	
Sales Load	None	1-Year Return (1993)	+9%
Redemption Fee	None	3-Year Return (1991–93)	+53%
Tax Load (Estimated)	3%	5-Year Return (1989–93)	+100%
Annual 12b-1 Fee	0.25%	10-Year Return (1984–93)	+321%
Annual Expense Ratio	1.25%	Worst-Ever Loss (1987)	29%
Annual Portfolio Turnover	176%	Stock Market Correlation	65%
5-Year Cost Estimate	10%	Up/Down Market Rank	B – B
Benefits		**Investment Information**	
Investment Objective	Growth	Telephone	800-945-3863
5-Year Projected Return	+21%	Minimum Investment	$5,000
Safety Rating (0-100)	79%	Telephone Switching	Unlimited;free
Yield	0.8%	Total Assets	$668 million

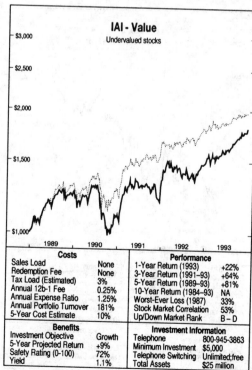

IAI - Value

Undervalued stocks

Costs		Performance	
Sales Load	None	1-Year Return (1993)	+22%
Redemption Fee	None	3-Year Return (1991–93)	+64%
Tax Load (Estimated)	3%	5-Year Return (1989–93)	+81%
Annual 12b-1 Fee	0.25%	10-Year Return (1984–93)	NA
Annual Expense Ratio	1.25%	Worst-Ever Loss (1987)	33%
Annual Portfolio Turnover	181%	Stock Market Correlation	53%
5-Year Cost Estimate	10%	Up/Down Market Rank	B – D
Benefits		**Investment Information**	
Investment Objective	Growth	Telephone	800-945-3863
5-Year Projected Return	+9%	Minimum Investment	$5,000
Safety Rating (0-100)	72%	Telephone Switching	Unlimited;free
Yield	1.1%	Total Assets	$25 million

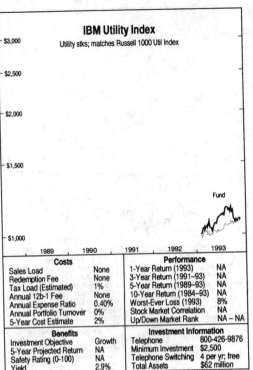

IBM Utility Index

Utility stks; matches Russell 1000 Util Index

Fund

Costs			Performance	
Sales Load	None		1-Year Return (1993)	NA
Redemption Fee	None		3-Year Return (1991–93)	NA
Tax Load (Estimated)	1%		5-Year Return (1989–93)	NA
Annual 12b-1 Fee	None		10-Year Return (1984–93)	NA
Annual Expense Ratio	0.40%		Worst-Ever Loss (1993)	8%
Annual Portfolio Turnover	0%		Stock Market Correlation	NA
5-Year Cost Estimate	2%		Up/Down Market Rank	NA – NA
Benefits			**Investment Information**	
Investment Objective	Growth		Telephone	800-426-9876
5-Year Projected Return	NA		Minimum Investment	$2,500
Safety Rating (0-100)	NA		Telephone Switching	4 per yr; free
Yield	2.9%		Total Assets	$62 million

Idex

Companies with good fundamentals
★

Costs			Performance	
Sales Load	9.3%		1-Year Return (1993)	+3%
Redemption Fee	None		3-Year Return (1991–93)	+67%
Tax Load (Estimated)	4%		5-Year Return (1989–93)	+137%
Annual 12b-1 Fee	None		10-Year Return (1984–93)	NA
Annual Expense Ratio	1.28%		Worst-Ever Loss (1987)	28%
Annual Portfolio Turnover	104%		Stock Market Correlation	64%
5-Year Cost Estimate	21%		Up/Down Market Rank	A – C
Benefits			**Investment Information**	
Investment Objective	Growth		Telephone	800-624-4339
5-Year Projected Return	+13%		Minimum Investment	$50
Safety Rating (0-100)	69%		Telephone Switching	See prospectus
Yield	0.4%		Total Assets	$353 million

Idex 3

Stocks with market value above $1-billion
★

Costs			Performance	
Sales Load	9.3%		1-Year Return (1993)	+5%
Redemption Fee	None		3-Year Return (1991–93)	+71%
Tax Load (Estimated)	2%		5-Year Return (1989–93)	+139%
Annual 12b-1 Fee	None		10-Year Return (1984–93)	NA
Annual Expense Ratio	1.21%		Worst-Ever Loss (1987)	27%
Annual Portfolio Turnover	124%		Stock Market Correlation	64%
5-Year Cost Estimate	18%		Up/Down Market Rank	A – C
Benefits			**Investment Information**	
Investment Objective	Growth		Telephone	800-624-4339
5-Year Projected Return	+15%		Minimum Investment	$50
Safety Rating (0-100)	69%		Telephone Switching	See prospectus
Yield	0.5%		Total Assets	$204 million

Idex II Growth "A"

Companies with good fundamentals
★

Costs			Performance	
Sales Load	5.8%		1-Year Return (1993)	+4%
Redemption Fee	None		3-Year Return (1991–93)	+66%
Tax Load (Estimated)	4%		5-Year Return (1989–93)	+139%
Annual 12b-1 Fee	0.35%		10-Year Return (1984–93)	NA
Annual Expense Ratio	1.70%		Worst-Ever Loss (1987)	30%
Annual Portfolio Turnover	97%		Stock Market Correlation	64%
5-Year Cost Estimate	20%		Up/Down Market Rank	A – D
Benefits			**Investment Information**	
Investment Objective	Growth		Telephone	800-624-4339
5-Year Projected Return	+17%		Minimum Investment	$50
Safety Rating (0-100)	69%		Telephone Switching	See prospectus
Yield	0.2%		Total Assets	$542 million

IDS Blue Chip Advantage
S&P stocks selected for superior performance
★

Costs		Performance	
Sales Load	5.3%	1-Year Return (1993)	+12%
Redemption Fee	None	3-Year Return (1991–93)	+55%
Tax Load (Estimated)	1%	5-Year Return (1989–93)	NA
Annual 12b-1 Fee	None	10-Year Return (1984–93)	NA
Annual Expense Ratio	1.10%	Worst-Ever Loss (1990)	20%
Annual Portfolio Turnover	202%	Stock Market Correlation	94%
5-Year Cost Estimate	13%	Up/Down Market Rank	NA – NA

Benefits		Investment Information	
Investment Objective	Gr. & Icm.	Telephone	800-437-4332
5-Year Projected Return	+6%	Minimum Investment	$2,000
Safety Rating (0-100)	72%	Telephone Switching	3 per mo; free
Yield	1.6%	Total Assets	$140 million

IDS Discovery
Small stocks and growth stocks

Costs		Performance	
Sales Load	5.3%	1-Year Return (1993)	+10%
Redemption Fee	None	3-Year Return (1991–93)	+82%
Tax Load (Estimated)	6%	5-Year Return (1989–93)	+138%
Annual 12b-1 Fee	None	10-Year Return (1984–93)	+173%
Annual Expense Ratio	1.03%	Worst-Ever Loss (1987)	39%
Annual Portfolio Turnover	76%	Stock Market Correlation	47%
5-Year Cost Estimate	18%	Up/Down Market Rank	B – D

Benefits		Investment Information	
Investment Objective	Growth	Telephone	800-437-4332
5-Year Projected Return	+28%	Minimum Investment	$2,000
Safety Rating (0-100)	66%	Telephone Switching	3 per mo; free
Yield	0.0%	Total Assets	$471 million

IDS Equity Plus
Diversified securities
★★

Costs		Performance	
Sales Load	5.3%	1-Year Return (1993)	+15%
Redemption Fee	None	3-Year Return (1991–93)	+68%
Tax Load (Estimated)	4%	5-Year Return (1989–93)	+110%
Annual 12b-1 Fee	None	10-Year Return (1984–93)	+262%
Annual Expense Ratio	0.74%	Worst-Ever Loss (1987)	31%
Annual Portfolio Turnover	42%	Stock Market Correlation	75%
5-Year Cost Estimate	13%	Up/Down Market Rank	B – D

Benefits		Investment Information	
Investment Objective	Gr. & Icm.	Telephone	800-437-4332
5-Year Projected Return	+18%	Minimum Investment	$2,000
Safety Rating (0-100)	75%	Telephone Switching	3 per mo; free
Yield	1.0%	Total Assets	$621 million

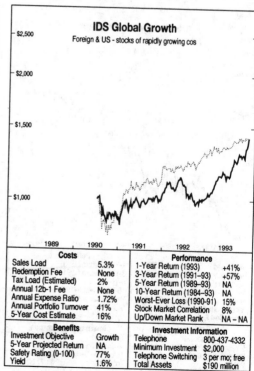

IDS Global Growth
Foreign & US - stocks of rapidly growing cos

Costs		Performance	
Sales Load	5.3%	1-Year Return (1993)	+41%
Redemption Fee	None	3-Year Return (1991–93)	+57%
Tax Load (Estimated)	2%	5-Year Return (1989–93)	NA
Annual 12b-1 Fee	None	10-Year Return (1984–93)	NA
Annual Expense Ratio	1.72%	Worst-Ever Loss (1990-91)	15%
Annual Portfolio Turnover	41%	Stock Market Correlation	8%
5-Year Cost Estimate	16%	Up/Down Market Rank	NA – NA

Benefits		Investment Information	
Investment Objective	Growth	Telephone	800-437-4332
5-Year Projected Return	NA	Minimum Investment	$2,000
Safety Rating (0-100)	77%	Telephone Switching	3 per mo; free
Yield	1.6%	Total Assets	$190 million

EQUITY

IDS Growth

Diversified growth stocks

★

Fund

S&P 500

Costs		Performance	
Sales Load	5.3%	1-Year Return (1993)	+9%
Redemption Fee	None	3-Year Return (1991–93)	+72%
Tax Load (Estimated)	4%	5-Year Return (1989–93)	+143%
Annual 12b-1 Fee	None	10-Year Return (1984–93)	+243%
Annual Expense Ratio	0.87%	Worst-Ever Loss (1987)	42%
Annual Portfolio Turnover	44%	Stock Market Correlation	68%
5-Year Cost Estimate	13%	Up/Down Market Rank	A – E

Benefits		Investment Information	
Investment Objective	Growth	Telephone	800-437-4332
5-Year Projected Return	+25%	Minimum Investment	$2,000
Safety Rating (0-100)	69%	Telephone Switching	3 per mo; free
Yield	0.0%	Total Assets	$970 million

IDS International

Foreign - diversified stocks

Costs		Performance	
Sales Load	5.3%	1-Year Return (1993)	+34%
Redemption Fee	None	3-Year Return (1991–93)	+41%
Tax Load (Estimated)	2%	5-Year Return (1989–93)	+51%
Annual 12b-1 Fee	None	10-Year Return (1984–93)	NA
Annual Expense Ratio	1.45%	Worst-Ever Loss (1987)	30%
Annual Portfolio Turnover	94%	Stock Market Correlation	14%
5-Year Cost Estimate	15%	Up/Down Market Rank	E – A

Benefits		Investment Information	
Investment Objective	Growth	Telephone	800-437-4332
5-Year Projected Return	NA	Minimum Investment	$2,000
Safety Rating (0-100)	72%	Telephone Switching	3 per mo; free
Yield	2.4%	Total Assets	$382 million

IDS Managed Retirement

Divsf; 65% U.S. stks; pfds, converts & bonds

★★★

Costs		Performance	
Sales Load	5.3%	1-Year Return (1993)	+15%
Redemption Fee	None	3-Year Return (1991–93)	+83%
Tax Load (Estimated)	2%	5-Year Return (1989–93)	+147%
Annual 12b-1 Fee	None	10-Year Return (1984–93)	NA
Annual Expense Ratio	0.85%	Worst-Ever Loss (1987)	32%
Annual Portfolio Turnover	46%	Stock Market Correlation	74%
5-Year Cost Estimate	12%	Up/Down Market Rank	A – D

Benefits		Investment Information	
Investment Objective	Gr. & Icm.	Telephone	800-437-4332
5-Year Projected Return	+31%	Minimum Investment	$2,000
Safety Rating (0-100)	74%	Telephone Switching	3 per mo; free
Yield	1.4%	Total Assets	$1.77 billion

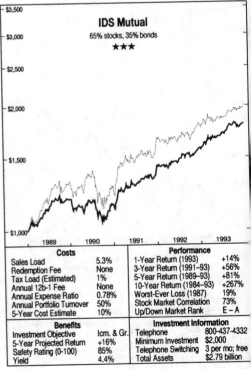

IDS Mutual

65% stocks, 35% bonds

★★★

Costs		Performance	
Sales Load	5.3%	1-Year Return (1993)	+14%
Redemption Fee	None	3-Year Return (1991–93)	+56%
Tax Load (Estimated)	1%	5-Year Return (1989–93)	+81%
Annual 12b-1 Fee	None	10-Year Return (1984–93)	+267%
Annual Expense Ratio	0.78%	Worst-Ever Loss (1987)	19%
Annual Portfolio Turnover	50%	Stock Market Correlation	73%
5-Year Cost Estimate	10%	Up/Down Market Rank	E – A

Benefits		Investment Information	
Investment Objective	Icm. & Gr.	Telephone	800-437-4332
5-Year Projected Return	+16%	Minimum Investment	$2,000
Safety Rating (0-100)	85%	Telephone Switching	3 per mo; free
Yield	4.4%	Total Assets	$2.79 billion

IDS New Dimensions
Dynamic growth stocks
★★★

Fund

S&P 500

Costs		Performance	
Sales Load	5.3%	1-Year Return (1993)	+14%
Redemption Fee	None	3-Year Return (1991–93)	+81%
Tax Load (Estimated)	2%	5-Year Return (1989–93)	+151%
Annual 12b-1 Fee	None	10-Year Return (1984–93)	+384%
Annual Expense Ratio	0.95%	Worst-Ever Loss (1987)	30%
Annual Portfolio Turnover	75%	Stock Market Correlation	71%
5-Year Cost Estimate	12%	Up/Down Market Rank	A – C

Benefits		Investment Information	
Investment Objective	Growth	Telephone	800-437-4332
5-Year Projected Return	+36%	Minimum Investment	$2,000
Safety Rating (0-100)	73%	Telephone Switching	3 per mo; free
Yield	0.5%	Total Assets	$3.45 billion

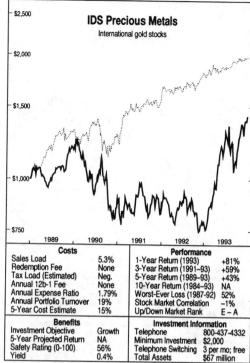

IDS Precious Metals
International gold stocks

Costs		Performance	
Sales Load	5.3%	1-Year Return (1993)	+81%
Redemption Fee	None	3-Year Return (1991–93)	+59%
Tax Load (Estimated)	Neg.	5-Year Return (1989–93)	+43%
Annual 12b-1 Fee	None	10-Year Return (1984–93)	NA
Annual Expense Ratio	1.79%	Worst-Ever Loss (1987-92)	52%
Annual Portfolio Turnover	19%	Stock Market Correlation	–1%
5-Year Cost Estimate	15%	Up/Down Market Rank	E – A

Benefits		Investment Information	
Investment Objective	Growth	Telephone	800-437-4332
5-Year Projected Return	NA	Minimum Investment	$2,000
Safety Rating (0-100)	56%	Telephone Switching	3 per mo; free
Yield	0.4%	Total Assets	$67 million

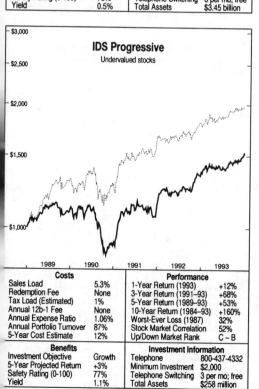

IDS Progressive
Undervalued stocks

Costs		Performance	
Sales Load	5.3%	1-Year Return (1993)	+12%
Redemption Fee	None	3-Year Return (1991–93)	+68%
Tax Load (Estimated)	1%	5-Year Return (1989–93)	+53%
Annual 12b-1 Fee	None	10-Year Return (1984–93)	+160%
Annual Expense Ratio	1.06%	Worst-Ever Loss (1987)	32%
Annual Portfolio Turnover	87%	Stock Market Correlation	52%
5-Year Cost Estimate	12%	Up/Down Market Rank	C – B

Benefits		Investment Information	
Investment Objective	Growth	Telephone	800-437-4332
5-Year Projected Return	+3%	Minimum Investment	$2,000
Safety Rating (0-100)	77%	Telephone Switching	3 per mo; free
Yield	1.1%	Total Assets	$258 million

IDS Stock
Diversified stocks
★★★

Costs		Performance	
Sales Load	5.3%	1-Year Return (1993)	+18%
Redemption Fee	None	3-Year Return (1991–93)	+60%
Tax Load (Estimated)	Neg.	5-Year Return (1989–93)	+112%
Annual 12b-1 Fee	None	10-Year Return (1984–93)	+277%
Annual Expense Ratio	0.72%	Worst-Ever Loss (1987)	28%
Annual Portfolio Turnover	77%	Stock Market Correlation	80%
5-Year Cost Estimate	9%	Up/Down Market Rank	C – B

Benefits		Investment Information	
Investment Objective	Gr. & Icm.	Telephone	800-437-4332
5-Year Projected Return	+21%	Minimum Investment	$2,000
Safety Rating (0-100)	79%	Telephone Switching	3 per mo; free
Yield	8.8%	Total Assets	$1.94 billion

IDS Strategy Aggressive
Stocks in growth industries

Fund

S&P 500

Costs		Performance	
Sales Load	None	1-Year Return (1993)	+8%
Redemption Fee	5.3%	3-Year Return (1991–93)	+62%
Tax Load (Estimated)	4%	5-Year Return (1989–93)	+125%
Annual 12b-1 Fee	1.00%	10-Year Return (1984–93)	NA
Annual Expense Ratio	1.75%	Worst-Ever Loss (1987)	41%
Annual Portfolio Turnover	49%	Stock Market Correlation	56%
5-Year Cost Estimate	14%	Up/Down Market Rank	A – E

Benefits		Investment Information	
Investment Objective	Growth	Telephone	800-437-4332
5-Year Projected Return	+24%	Minimum Investment	$2,000
Safety Rating (0-100)	68%	Telephone Switching	3 per mo; free
Yield	0.0%	Total Assets	$618 million

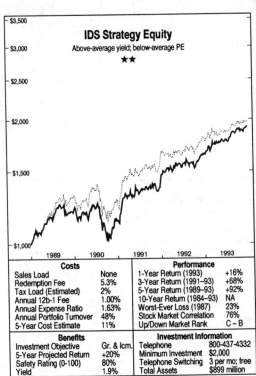

IDS Strategy Equity
Above-average yield; below-average PE
★★

Costs		Performance	
Sales Load	None	1-Year Return (1993)	+16%
Redemption Fee	5.3%	3-Year Return (1991–93)	+68%
Tax Load (Estimated)	2%	5-Year Return (1989–93)	+92%
Annual 12b-1 Fee	1.00%	10-Year Return (1984–93)	NA
Annual Expense Ratio	1.63%	Worst-Ever Loss (1987)	23%
Annual Portfolio Turnover	48%	Stock Market Correlation	76%
5-Year Cost Estimate	11%	Up/Down Market Rank	C – B

Benefits		Investment Information	
Investment Objective	Gr. & Icm.	Telephone	800-437-4332
5-Year Projected Return	+20%	Minimum Investment	$2,000
Safety Rating (0-100)	80%	Telephone Switching	3 per mo; free
Yield	1.9%	Total Assets	$899 million

IDS Strategy Worldwide Growth
Foreign & U.S. - Pac-Basin & No. American cos

Costs		Performance	
Sales Load	None	1-Year Return (1993)	+31%
Redemption Fee	5.3%	3-Year Return (1991–93)	+34%
Tax Load (Estimated)	2%	5-Year Return (1989–93)	+30%
Annual 12b-1 Fee	1.00%	10-Year Return (1984–93)	NA
Annual Expense Ratio	2.91%	Worst-Ever Loss (1987)	36%
Annual Portfolio Turnover	106%	Stock Market Correlation	17%
5-Year Cost Estimate	20%	Up/Down Market Rank	E – C

Benefits		Investment Information	
Investment Objective	Growth	Telephone	800-437-4332
5-Year Projected Return	NA	Minimum Investment	$2,000
Safety Rating (0-100)	68%	Telephone Switching	3 per mo; free
Yield	0.0%	Total Assets	$104 million

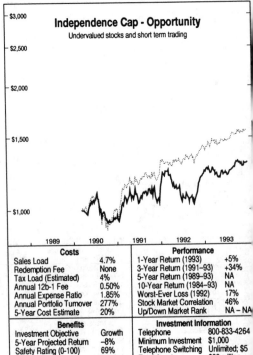

Independence Cap - Opportunity
Undervalued stocks and short term trading

Costs		Performance	
Sales Load	4.7%	1-Year Return (1993)	+5%
Redemption Fee	None	3-Year Return (1991–93)	+34%
Tax Load (Estimated)	4%	5-Year Return (1989–93)	NA
Annual 12b-1 Fee	0.50%	10-Year Return (1984–93)	NA
Annual Expense Ratio	1.85%	Worst-Ever Loss (1992)	17%
Annual Portfolio Turnover	277%	Stock Market Correlation	46%
5-Year Cost Estimate	20%	Up/Down Market Rank	NA – NA

Benefits		Investment Information	
Investment Objective	Growth	Telephone	800-833-4264
5-Year Projected Return	–8%	Minimum Investment	$1,000
Safety Rating (0-100)	69%	Telephone Switching	Unlimited; $5
Yield	2.2%	Total Assets	$33 million

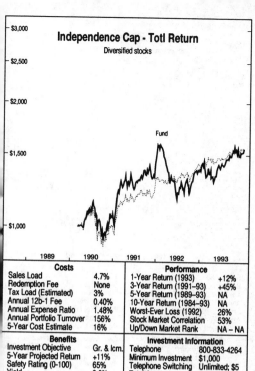

Independence Cap - Totl Return
Diversified stocks

Fund

Costs		Performance	
Sales Load	4.7%	1-Year Return (1993)	+12%
Redemption Fee	None	3-Year Return (1991–93)	+45%
Tax Load (Estimated)	3%	5-Year Return (1989–93)	NA
Annual 12b-1 Fee	0.40%	10-Year Return (1984–93)	NA
Annual Expense Ratio	1.48%	Worst-Ever Loss (1992)	26%
Annual Portfolio Turnover	156%	Stock Market Correlation	53%
5-Year Cost Estimate	16%	Up/Down Market Rank	NA – NA
Benefits		**Investment Information**	
Investment Objective	Gr. & Icm.	Telephone	800-833-4264
5-Year Projected Return	+11%	Minimum Investment	$1,000
Safety Rating (0-100)	65%	Telephone Switching	Unlimited; $5
Yield	0.0%	Total Assets	$35 million

India Growth
Foreign - Indian stocks

Costs		Performance	
Sales Load	None	1-Year Return (1993)	+112%
Redemption Fee	None	3-Year Return (1991–93)	+213%
Tax Load (Estimated)	18%	5-Year Return (1989–93)	+304%
Annual 12b-1 Fee	None	10-Year Return (1984–93)	NA
Annual Expense Ratio	2.79%	Worst-Ever Loss (1990-91)	45%
Annual Portfolio Turnover	19%	Stock Market Correlation	0%
5-Year Cost Estimate	25%	Up/Down Market Rank	E – A
Benefits		**Investment Information**	
Investment Objective	Growth	Telephone	800-553-8080
5-Year Projected Return	NA	Minimum Investment	None
Safety Rating (0-100)	23%	Telephone Switching	Via broker
Yield	0.0%	Total Assets	$73 million

Indonesia
Foreign - Indonesian stocks

Costs		Performance	
Sales Load	None	1-Year Return (1993)	+131%
Redemption Fee	None	3-Year Return (1991–93)	+111%
Tax Load (Estimated)	Neg.	5-Year Return (1989–93)	NA
Annual 12b-1 Fee	None	10-Year Return (1984–93)	NA
Annual Expense Ratio	2.04%	Worst-Ever Loss (1990-91)	50%
Annual Portfolio Turnover	32%	Stock Market Correlation	0%
5-Year Cost Estimate	13%	Up/Down Market Rank	NA – NA
Benefits		**Investment Information**	
Investment Objective	Growth	Telephone	212-832-2626
5-Year Projected Return	NA	Minimum Investment	None
Safety Rating (0-100)	12%	Telephone Switching	Via broker
Yield	0.0%	Total Assets	$39 million

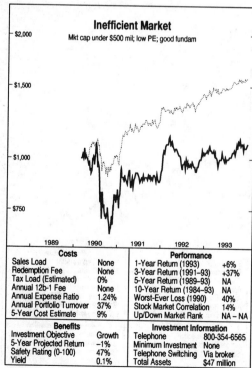

Inefficient Market
Mkt cap under $500 mil; low PE; good fundam

Costs		Performance	
Sales Load	None	1-Year Return (1993)	+6%
Redemption Fee	None	3-Year Return (1991–93)	+37%
Tax Load (Estimated)	0%	5-Year Return (1989–93)	NA
Annual 12b-1 Fee	None	10-Year Return (1984–93)	NA
Annual Expense Ratio	1.24%	Worst-Ever Loss (1990)	40%
Annual Portfolio Turnover	37%	Stock Market Correlation	14%
5-Year Cost Estimate	9%	Up/Down Market Rank	NA – NA
Benefits		**Investment Information**	
Investment Objective	Growth	Telephone	800-354-6565
5-Year Projected Return	–1%	Minimum Investment	None
Safety Rating (0-100)	47%	Telephone Switching	Via broker
Yield	0.1%	Total Assets	$47 million

Invesco - Dynamics
Fundamental and technical analysis
★★

Fund

S&P 500

Costs		Performance	
Sales Load	None	1-Year Return (1993)	+19%
Redemption Fee	None	3-Year Return (1991–93)	+125%
Tax Load (Estimated)	4%	5-Year Return (1989–93)	+159%
Annual 12b-1 Fee	0.25%	10-Year Return (1984–93)	+246%
Annual Expense Ratio	1.20%	Worst-Ever Loss (1987)	44%
Annual Portfolio Turnover	144%	Stock Market Correlation	54%
5-Year Cost Estimate	11%	Up/Down Market Rank	A – E

Benefits		Investment Information	
Investment Objective	Growth	Telephone	800-525-8085
5-Year Projected Return	+53%	Minimum Investment	$1,000
Safety Rating (0-100)	65%	Telephone Switching	4 per yr; free
Yield	0.0%	Total Assets	$274 million

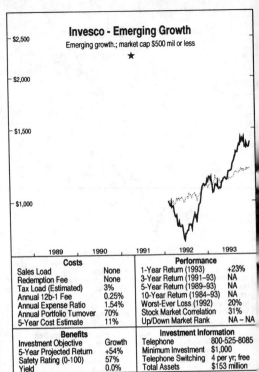

Invesco - Emerging Growth
Emerging growth.; market cap $500 mil or less
★

Costs		Performance	
Sales Load	None	1-Year Return (1993)	+23%
Redemption Fee	None	3-Year Return (1991–93)	NA
Tax Load (Estimated)	3%	5-Year Return (1989–93)	NA
Annual 12b-1 Fee	0.25%	10-Year Return (1984–93)	NA
Annual Expense Ratio	1.54%	Worst-Ever Loss (1992)	20%
Annual Portfolio Turnover	70%	Stock Market Correlation	31%
5-Year Cost Estimate	11%	Up/Down Market Rank	NA – NA

Benefits		Investment Information	
Investment Objective	Growth	Telephone	800-525-8085
5-Year Projected Return	+54%	Minimum Investment	$1,000
Safety Rating (0-100)	57%	Telephone Switching	4 per yr; free
Yield	0.0%	Total Assets	$153 million

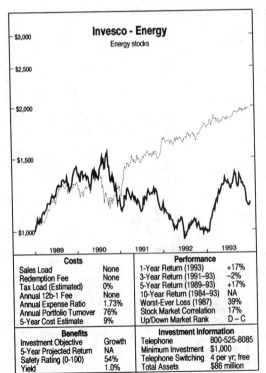

Invesco - Energy
Energy stocks

Costs		Performance	
Sales Load	None	1-Year Return (1993)	+17%
Redemption Fee	None	3-Year Return (1991–93)	–2%
Tax Load (Estimated)	0%	5-Year Return (1989–93)	+17%
Annual 12b-1 Fee	None	10-Year Return (1984–93)	NA
Annual Expense Ratio	1.73%	Worst-Ever Loss (1987)	39%
Annual Portfolio Turnover	76%	Stock Market Correlation	17%
5-Year Cost Estimate	9%	Up/Down Market Rank	D – C

Benefits		Investment Information	
Investment Objective	Growth	Telephone	800-525-8085
5-Year Projected Return	NA	Minimum Investment	$1,000
Safety Rating (0-100)	54%	Telephone Switching	4 per yr; free
Yield	1.0%	Total Assets	$86 million

Invesco - European
Foreign - Western European stocks

Costs		Performance	
Sales Load	None	1-Year Return (1993)	+25%
Redemption Fee	None	3-Year Return (1991–93)	+24%
Tax Load (Estimated)	1%	5-Year Return (1989–93)	+56%
Annual 12b-1 Fee	None	10-Year Return (1984–93)	NA
Annual Expense Ratio	1.29%	Worst-Ever Loss (1987)	30%
Annual Portfolio Turnover	46%	Stock Market Correlation	9%
5-Year Cost Estimate	7%	Up/Down Market Rank	E – A

Benefits		Investment Information	
Investment Objective	Growth	Telephone	800-525-808
5-Year Projected Return	NA	Minimum Investment	$1,000
Safety Rating (0-100)	73%	Telephone Switching	4 per yr; free
Yield	1.0%	Total Assets	$256 million

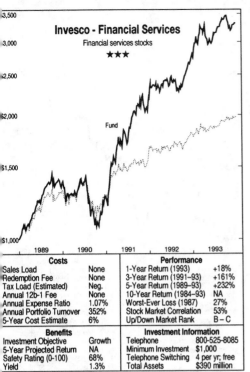

Invesco - Financial Services
Financial services stocks
★★★

Costs		Performance	
Sales Load	None	1-Year Return (1993)	+18%
Redemption Fee	None	3-Year Return (1991–93)	+161%
Tax Load (Estimated)	Neg.	5-Year Return (1989–93)	+232%
Annual 12b-1 Fee	None	10-Year Return (1984–93)	NA
Annual Expense Ratio	1.07%	Worst-Ever Loss (1987)	27%
Annual Portfolio Turnover	352%	Stock Market Correlation	53%
5-Year Cost Estimate	6%	Up/Down Market Rank	B – C

Benefits		Investment Information	
Investment Objective	Growth	Telephone	800-525-8085
5-Year Projected Return	NA	Minimum Investment	$1,000
Safety Rating (0-100)	68%	Telephone Switching	4 per yr; free
Yield	1.3%	Total Assets	$390 million

Invesco - Gold
International gold stocks

Costs		Performance	
Sales Load	None	1-Year Return (1993)	+73%
Redemption Fee	None	3-Year Return (1991–93)	+48%
Tax Load (Estimated)	0%	5-Year Return (1989–93)	+38%
Annual 12b-1 Fee	None	10-Year Return (1984–93)	NA
Annual Expense Ratio	1.41%	Worst-Ever Loss (1987-92)	62%
Annual Portfolio Turnover	128%	Stock Market Correlation	0%
5-Year Cost Estimate	8%	Up/Down Market Rank	E – A

Benefits		Investment Information	
Investment Objective	Growth	Telephone	800-525-8085
5-Year Projected Return	NA	Minimum Investment	$1,000
Safety Rating (0-100)	52%	Telephone Switching	4 per yr; free
Yield	0.0%	Total Assets	$290 million

Invesco - Growth
Earnings growth stocks
★

Costs		Performance	
Sales Load	None	1-Year Return (1993)	+17%
Redemption Fee	None	3-Year Return (1991–93)	+71%
Tax Load (Estimated)	5%	5-Year Return (1989–93)	+122%
Annual 12b-1 Fee	0.25%	10-Year Return (1984–93)	+222%
Annual Expense Ratio	1.04%	Worst-Ever Loss (1987)	36%
Annual Portfolio Turnover	77%	Stock Market Correlation	73%
5-Year Cost Estimate	10%	Up/Down Market Rank	C – D

Benefits		Investment Information	
Investment Objective	Gr. & Icm.	Telephone	800-525-8085
5-Year Projected Return	+25%	Minimum Investment	$1,000
Safety Rating (0-100)	70%	Telephone Switching	4 per yr; free
Yield	0.6%	Total Assets	$484 million

Invesco - Health Sciences
Health-care stocks
★

Costs		Performance	
Sales Load	None	1-Year Return (1993)	–8%
Redemption Fee	None	3-Year Return (1991–93)	+52%
Tax Load (Estimated)	Neg.	5-Year Return (1989–93)	+204%
Annual 12b-1 Fee	None	10-Year Return (1984–93)	NA
Annual Expense Ratio	1.00%	Worst-Ever Loss (1987)	42%
Annual Portfolio Turnover	76%	Stock Market Correlation	30%
5-Year Cost Estimate	5%	Up/Down Market Rank	A – E

Benefits		Investment Information	
Investment Objective	Growth	Telephone	800-525-8085
5-Year Projected Return	NA	Minimum Investment	$1,000
Safety Rating (0-100)	61%	Telephone Switching	4 per yr; free
Yield	0.0%	Total Assets	$525 million

Invesco - Industrial Income
High-yield stocks; stable return
★★★★★

Costs		Performance	
Sales Load	None	1-Year Return (1993)	+17%
Redemption Fee	None	3-Year Return (1991–93)	+72%
Tax Load (Estimated)	2%	5-Year Return (1989–93)	+129%
Annual 12b-1 Fee	0.25%	10-Year Return (1984–93)	+356%
Annual Expense Ratio	0.98%	Worst-Ever Loss (1987)	28%
Annual Portfolio Turnover	121%	Stock Market Correlation	74%
5-Year Cost Estimate	8%	Up/Down Market Rank	D – A

Benefits		Investment Information	
Investment Objective	Icm. & Gr.	Telephone	800-525-8085
5-Year Projected Return	+34%	Minimum Investment	$1,000
Safety Rating (0-100)	79%	Telephone Switching	4 per yr; free
Yield	3.7%	Total Assets	$3.57 billion

Invesco - Leisure
Leisure stocks
★★

Costs		Performance	
Sales Load	None	1-Year Return (1993)	+36%
Redemption Fee	None	3-Year Return (1991–93)	+156%
Tax Load (Estimated)	0%	5-Year Return (1989–93)	+215%
Annual 12b-1 Fee	None	10-Year Return (1984–93)	NA
Annual Expense Ratio	1.51%	Worst-Ever Loss (1987)	36%
Annual Portfolio Turnover	108%	Stock Market Correlation	59%
5-Year Cost Estimate	8%	Up/Down Market Rank	A – E

Benefits		Investment Information	
Investment Objective	Growth	Telephone	800-525-8085
5-Year Projected Return	NA	Minimum Investment	$1,000
Safety Rating (0-100)	69%	Telephone Switching	4 per yr; free
Yield	0.0%	Total Assets	$219 million

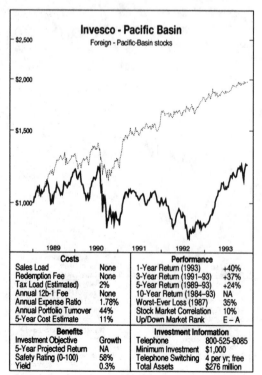

Invesco - Pacific Basin
Foreign - Pacific-Basin stocks

Costs		Performance	
Sales Load	None	1-Year Return (1993)	+40%
Redemption Fee	None	3-Year Return (1991–93)	+37%
Tax Load (Estimated)	2%	5-Year Return (1989–93)	+24%
Annual 12b-1 Fee	None	10-Year Return (1984–93)	NA
Annual Expense Ratio	1.78%	Worst-Ever Loss (1987)	35%
Annual Portfolio Turnover	44%	Stock Market Correlation	10%
5-Year Cost Estimate	11%	Up/Down Market Rank	E – A

Benefits		Investment Information	
Investment Objective	Growth	Telephone	800-525-8085
5-Year Projected Return	NA	Minimum Investment	$1,000
Safety Rating (0-100)	58%	Telephone Switching	4 per yr; free
Yield	0.3%	Total Assets	$276 million

Invesco - Technology
Technology stocks
★

Costs		Performance	
Sales Load	None	1-Year Return (1993)	+15%
Redemption Fee	None	3-Year Return (1991–93)	+142%
Tax Load (Estimated)	Neg.	5-Year Return (1989–93)	+219%
Annual 12b-1 Fee	None	10-Year Return (1984–93)	NA
Annual Expense Ratio	1.12%	Worst-Ever Loss (1987)	49%
Annual Portfolio Turnover	214%	Stock Market Correlation	43%
5-Year Cost Estimate	6%	Up/Down Market Rank	A – E

Benefits		Investment Information	
Investment Objective	Growth	Telephone	800-525-8085
5-Year Projected Return	NA	Minimum Investment	$1,000
Safety Rating (0-100)	58%	Telephone Switching	4 per yr; free
Yield	0.0%	Total Assets	$246 million

Invesco - Utilities
Utility securities
★★★

(Chart showing Fund and S&P 500, y-axis $1,000–$3,500, years 1989–1993)

Costs		Performance	
Sales Load	None	1-Year Return (1993)	+21%
Redemption Fee	None	3-Year Return (1991–93)	+72%
Tax Load (Estimated)	Neg.	5-Year Return (1989–93)	+103%
Annual 12b-1 Fee	None	10-Year Return (1984–93)	NA
Annual Expense Ratio	1.13%	Worst-Ever Loss (1987)	20%
Annual Portfolio Turnover	162%	Stock Market Correlation	47%
5-Year Cost Estimate	6%	Up/Down Market Rank	C – B

Benefits		Investment Information	
Investment Objective	Growth	Telephone	800-525-8085
5-Year Projected Return	NA	Minimum Investment	$1,000
Safety Rating (0-100)	80%	Telephone Switching	4 per yr; free
Yield	2.5%	Total Assets	$200 million

Investment Ser Cap Grwth Invst
Above-avg earnings & dividend grwth prospects
★

(Chart, y-axis $1,000–$3,000, years 1989–1993)

Costs		Performance	
Sales Load	6.1%	1-Year Return (1993)	+11%
Redemption Fee	None	3-Year Return (1991–93)	+63%
Tax Load (Estimated)	6%	5-Year Return (1989–93)	NA
Annual 12b-1 Fee	None	10-Year Return (1984–93)	NA
Annual Expense Ratio	1.00%	Worst-Ever Loss (1990)	25%
Annual Portfolio Turnover	23%	Stock Market Correlation	47%
5-Year Cost Estimate	14%	Up/Down Market Rank	NA – NA

Benefits		Investment Information	
Investment Objective	Growth	Telephone	800-245-4770
5-Year Projected Return	+17%	Minimum Investment	$500
Safety Rating (0-100)	73%	Telephone Switching	Unlimited;free
Yield	0.8%	Total Assets	$15 million

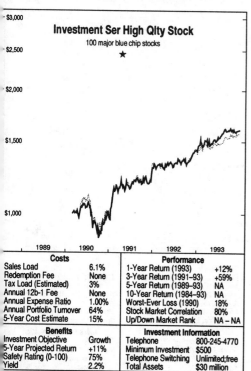

Investment Ser High Qlty Stock
100 major blue chip stocks
★

(Chart, y-axis $1,000–$3,000, years 1989–1993)

Costs		Performance	
Sales Load	6.1%	1-Year Return (1993)	+12%
Redemption Fee	None	3-Year Return (1991–93)	+59%
Tax Load (Estimated)	3%	5-Year Return (1989–93)	NA
Annual 12b-1 Fee	None	10-Year Return (1984–93)	NA
Annual Expense Ratio	1.00%	Worst-Ever Loss (1990)	18%
Annual Portfolio Turnover	64%	Stock Market Correlation	80%
5-Year Cost Estimate	15%	Up/Down Market Rank	NA – NA

Benefits		Investment Information	
Investment Objective	Growth	Telephone	800-245-4770
5-Year Projected Return	+11%	Minimum Investment	$500
Safety Rating (0-100)	75%	Telephone Switching	Unlimited;free
Yield	2.2%	Total Assets	$30 million

Investors Research
Market timing; leveraged

(Chart, y-axis $1,000–$3,500, years 1989–1993)

Costs		Performance	
Sales Load	6.0%	1-Year Return (1993)	+6%
Redemption Fee	None	3-Year Return (1991–93)	+36%
Tax Load (Estimated)	Neg.	5-Year Return (1989–93)	+62%
Annual 12b-1 Fee	None	10-Year Return (1984–93)	NA
Annual Expense Ratio	0.91%	Worst-Ever Loss (1987)	30%
Annual Portfolio Turnover	70%	Stock Market Correlation	61%
5-Year Cost Estimate	11%	Up/Down Market Rank	D – B

Benefits		Investment Information	
Investment Objective	Growth	Telephone	800-732-1733
5-Year Projected Return	+0%	Minimum Investment	None
Safety Rating (0-100)	72%	Telephone Switching	Not available
Yield	1.1%	Total Assets	$49 million

Irish Investment
Foreign - Irish stocks

S&P 500

Fund

Costs		Performance	
Sales Load	None	1-Year Return (1993)	+41%
Redemption Fee	None	3-Year Return (1991–93)	+38%
Tax Load (Estimated)	Neg.	5-Year Return (1989–93)	NA
Annual 12b-1 Fee	None	10-Year Return (1984–93)	NA
Annual Expense Ratio	1.80%	Worst-Ever Loss (1990)	33%
Annual Portfolio Turnover	10%	Stock Market Correlation	8%
5-Year Cost Estimate	12%	Up/Down Market Rank	NA – NA

Benefits		Investment Information	
Investment Objective	Growth	Telephone	800-468-6475
5-Year Projected Return	NA	Minimum Investment	None
Safety Rating (0-100)	45%	Telephone Switching	Via broker
Yield	0.8%	Total Assets	$40 million

Istel
Diversified securities
★

Costs		Performance	
Sales Load	None	1-Year Return (1993)	+14%
Redemption Fee	None	3-Year Return (1991–93)	+40%
Tax Load (Estimated)	3%	5-Year Return (1989–93)	+60%
Annual 12b-1 Fee	1.00%	10-Year Return (1984–93)	+116%
Annual Expense Ratio	1.54%	Worst-Ever Loss (1980-82)	26%
Annual Portfolio Turnover	22%	Stock Market Correlation	65%
5-Year Cost Estimate	9%	Up/Down Market Rank	E – C

Benefits		Investment Information	
Investment Objective	Gr. & Icm.	Telephone	800-338-157
5-Year Projected Return	+5%	Minimum Investment	$500
Safety Rating (0-100)	79%	Telephone Switching	Not available
Yield	2.2%	Total Assets	$17 million

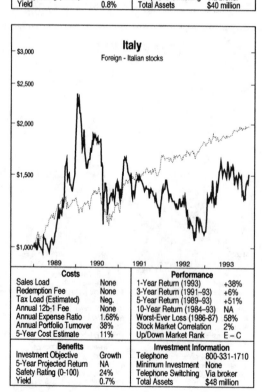

Italy
Foreign - Italian stocks

Costs		Performance	
Sales Load	None	1-Year Return (1993)	+38%
Redemption Fee	None	3-Year Return (1991–93)	+6%
Tax Load (Estimated)	Neg.	5-Year Return (1989–93)	+51%
Annual 12b-1 Fee	None	10-Year Return (1984–93)	NA
Annual Expense Ratio	1.68%	Worst-Ever Loss (1986-87)	58%
Annual Portfolio Turnover	38%	Stock Market Correlation	2%
5-Year Cost Estimate	11%	Up/Down Market Rank	E – C

Benefits		Investment Information	
Investment Objective	Growth	Telephone	800-331-1710
5-Year Projected Return	NA	Minimum Investment	None
Safety Rating (0-100)	24%	Telephone Switching	Via broker
Yield	0.7%	Total Assets	$48 million

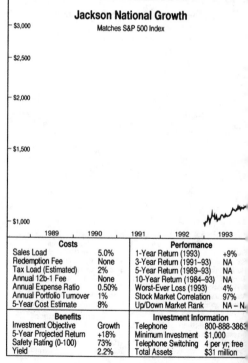

Jackson National Growth
Matches S&P 500 Index

Costs		Performance	
Sales Load	5.0%	1-Year Return (1993)	+9%
Redemption Fee	None	3-Year Return (1991–93)	NA
Tax Load (Estimated)	2%	5-Year Return (1989–93)	NA
Annual 12b-1 Fee	None	10-Year Return (1984–93)	NA
Annual Expense Ratio	0.50%	Worst-Ever Loss (1993)	4%
Annual Portfolio Turnover	1%	Stock Market Correlation	97%
5-Year Cost Estimate	8%	Up/Down Market Rank	NA – N.

Benefits		Investment Information	
Investment Objective	Growth	Telephone	800-888-3863
5-Year Projected Return	+18%	Minimum Investment	$1,000
Safety Rating (0-100)	73%	Telephone Switching	4 per yr; free
Yield	2.2%	Total Assets	$31 million

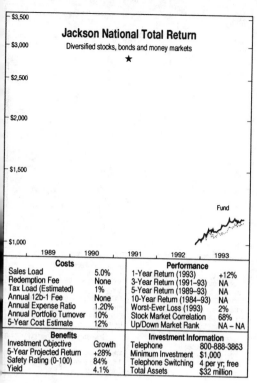

Jackson National Total Return
Diversified stocks, bonds and money markets
★

Fund

Costs		Performance	
Sales Load	5.0%	1-Year Return (1993)	+12%
Redemption Fee	None	3-Year Return (1991–93)	NA
Tax Load (Estimated)	1%	5-Year Return (1989–93)	NA
Annual 12b-1 Fee	None	10-Year Return (1984–93)	NA
Annual Expense Ratio	1.20%	Worst-Ever Loss (1993)	2%
Annual Portfolio Turnover	10%	Stock Market Correlation	68%
5-Year Cost Estimate	12%	Up/Down Market Rank	NA – NA

Benefits		Investment Information	
Investment Objective	Growth	Telephone	800-888-3863
5-Year Projected Return	+28%	Minimum Investment	$1,000
Safety Rating (0-100)	84%	Telephone Switching	4 per yr; free
Yield	4.1%	Total Assets	$32 million

Jakarta Growth
Foreign - Indonesian stocks

Costs		Performance	
Sales Load	None	1-Year Return (1993)	+94%
Redemption Fee	None	3-Year Return (1991–93)	+104%
Tax Load (Estimated)	Neg.	5-Year Return (1989–93)	NA
Annual 12b-1 Fee	None	10-Year Return (1984–93)	NA
Annual Expense Ratio	2.06%	Worst-Ever Loss (1990-91)	57%
Annual Portfolio Turnover	24%	Stock Market Correlation	2%
5-Year Cost Estimate	13%	Up/Down Market Rank	NA – NA

Benefits		Investment Information	
Investment Objective	Growth	Telephone	800-833-0018
5-Year Projected Return	NA	Minimum Investment	None
Safety Rating (0-100)	19%	Telephone Switching	Via broker
Yield	0.4%	Total Assets	$36 million

Janus
Diversified growth stocks
★★★★★

Costs		Performance	
Sales Load	None	1-Year Return (1993)	+11%
Redemption Fee	None	3-Year Return (1991–93)	+69%
Tax Load (Estimated)	0%	5-Year Return (1989–93)	+146%
Annual 12b-1 Fee	None	10-Year Return (1984–93)	+313%
Annual Expense Ratio	0.97%	Worst-Ever Loss (1981)	22%
Annual Portfolio Turnover	117%	Stock Market Correlation	73%
5-Year Cost Estimate	5%	Up/Down Market Rank	B – B

Benefits		Investment Information	
Investment Objective	Growth	Telephone	800-525-8983
5-Year Projected Return	+30%	Minimum Investment	$1,000
Safety Rating (0-100)	76%	Telephone Switching	4 per yr; free
Yield	2.0%	Total Assets	$8.68 billion

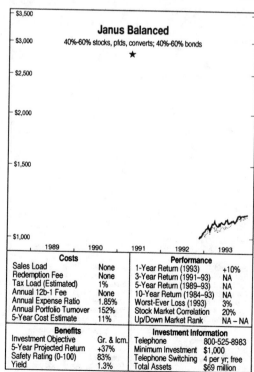

Janus Balanced
40%-60% stocks, pfds, converts; 40%-60% bonds
★

Costs		Performance	
Sales Load	None	1-Year Return (1993)	+10%
Redemption Fee	None	3-Year Return (1991–93)	NA
Tax Load (Estimated)	1%	5-Year Return (1989–93)	NA
Annual 12b-1 Fee	None	10-Year Return (1984–93)	NA
Annual Expense Ratio	1.85%	Worst-Ever Loss (1993)	3%
Annual Portfolio Turnover	152%	Stock Market Correlation	20%
5-Year Cost Estimate	11%	Up/Down Market Rank	NA – NA

Benefits		Investment Information	
Investment Objective	Gr. & Icm.	Telephone	800-525-8983
5-Year Projected Return	+37%	Minimum Investment	$1,000
Safety Rating (0-100)	83%	Telephone Switching	4 per yr; free
Yield	1.3%	Total Assets	$69 million

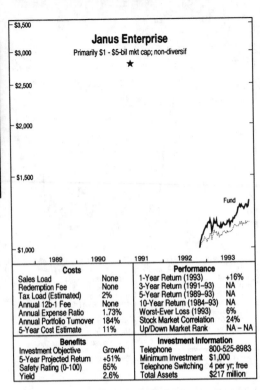

Janus Enterprise
Primarily $1 - $5-bil mkt cap; non-diversif
★

Fund

1989	1990	1991	1992	1993

Costs		Performance	
Sales Load	None	1-Year Return (1993)	+16%
Redemption Fee	None	3-Year Return (1991–93)	NA
Tax Load (Estimated)	2%	5-Year Return (1989–93)	NA
Annual 12b-1 Fee	None	10-Year Return (1984–93)	NA
Annual Expense Ratio	1.73%	Worst-Ever Loss (1993)	6%
Annual Portfolio Turnover	184%	Stock Market Correlation	24%
5-Year Cost Estimate	11%	Up/Down Market Rank	NA – NA

Benefits		Investment Information	
Investment Objective	Growth	Telephone	800-525-8983
5-Year Projected Return	+51%	Minimum Investment	$1,000
Safety Rating (0-100)	65%	Telephone Switching	4 per yr; free
Yield	2.6%	Total Assets	$217 million

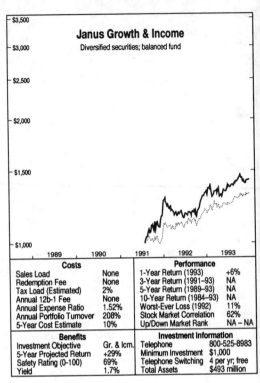

Janus Growth & Income
Diversified securities; balanced fund

1989	1990	1991	1992	1993

Costs		Performance	
Sales Load	None	1-Year Return (1993)	+6%
Redemption Fee	None	3-Year Return (1991–93)	NA
Tax Load (Estimated)	2%	5-Year Return (1989–93)	NA
Annual 12b-1 Fee	None	10-Year Return (1984–93)	NA
Annual Expense Ratio	1.52%	Worst-Ever Loss (1992)	11%
Annual Portfolio Turnover	208%	Stock Market Correlation	62%
5-Year Cost Estimate	10%	Up/Down Market Rank	NA – NA

Benefits		Investment Information	
Investment Objective	Gr. & Icm.	Telephone	800-525-8983
5-Year Projected Return	+29%	Minimum Investment	$1,000
Safety Rating (0-100)	69%	Telephone Switching	4 per yr; free
Yield	1.7%	Total Assets	$493 million

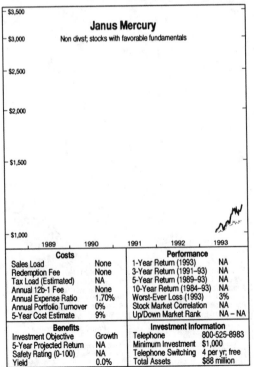

Janus Mercury
Non divsf; stocks with favorable fundamentals

1989	1990	1991	1992	1993

Costs		Performance	
Sales Load	None	1-Year Return (1993)	NA
Redemption Fee	None	3-Year Return (1991–93)	NA
Tax Load (Estimated)	NA	5-Year Return (1989–93)	NA
Annual 12b-1 Fee	None	10-Year Return (1984–93)	NA
Annual Expense Ratio	1.70%	Worst-Ever Loss (1993)	3%
Annual Portfolio Turnover	0%	Stock Market Correlation	NA
5-Year Cost Estimate	9%	Up/Down Market Rank	NA – NA

Benefits		Investment Information	
Investment Objective	Growth	Telephone	800-525-8983
5-Year Projected Return	NA	Minimum Investment	$1,000
Safety Rating (0-100)	NA	Telephone Switching	4 per yr; free
Yield	0.0%	Total Assets	$88 million

Janus Twenty
20 to 25 undervalued stocks
★★★

1989	1990	1991	1992	1993

Costs		Performance	
Sales Load	None	1-Year Return (1993)	+3%
Redemption Fee	None	3-Year Return (1991–93)	+78%
Tax Load (Estimated)	2%	5-Year Return (1989–93)	+171%
Annual 12b-1 Fee	None	10-Year Return (1984–93)	NA
Annual Expense Ratio	1.07%	Worst-Ever Loss (1987)	34%
Annual Portfolio Turnover	122%	Stock Market Correlation	63%
5-Year Cost Estimate	8%	Up/Down Market Rank	A – D

Benefits		Investment Information	
Investment Objective	Growth	Telephone	800-525-8983
5-Year Projected Return	+33%	Minimum Investment	$1,000
Safety Rating (0-100)	68%	Telephone Switching	4 per yr; free
Yield	1.0%	Total Assets	$3.78 billion

Janus Venture
Small company stocks
★★★★★

Costs		Performance	
Sales Load	None	1-Year Return (1993)	+9%
Redemption Fee	None	3-Year Return (1991–93)	+73%
Tax Load (Estimated)	3%	5-Year Return (1989–93)	+139%
Annual 12b-1 Fee	None	10-Year Return (1984–93)	NA
Annual Expense Ratio	1.02%	Worst-Ever Loss (1987)	23%
Annual Portfolio Turnover	125%	Stock Market Correlation	53%
5-Year Cost Estimate	9%	Up/Down Market Rank	C – B

Benefits		Investment Information	
Investment Objective	Growth	Telephone	800-525-8983
5-Year Projected Return	+37%	Minimum Investment	$1,000
Safety Rating (0-100)	78%	Telephone Switching	4 per yr; free
Yield	1.1%	Total Assets	$1.87 billion

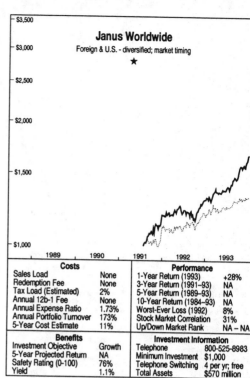

Janus Worldwide
Foreign & U.S. - diversified; market timing
★

Costs		Performance	
Sales Load	None	1-Year Return (1993)	+28%
Redemption Fee	None	3-Year Return (1991–93)	NA
Tax Load (Estimated)	2%	5-Year Return (1989–93)	NA
Annual 12b-1 Fee	None	10-Year Return (1984–93)	NA
Annual Expense Ratio	1.73%	Worst-Ever Loss (1992)	8%
Annual Portfolio Turnover	173%	Stock Market Correlation	31%
5-Year Cost Estimate	11%	Up/Down Market Rank	NA – NA

Benefits		Investment Information	
Investment Objective	Growth	Telephone	800-525-8983
5-Year Projected Return	NA	Minimum Investment	$1,000
Safety Rating (0-100)	76%	Telephone Switching	4 per yr; free
Yield	1.1%	Total Assets	$570 million

Japan
Foreign - Japanese stocks

Costs		Performance	
Sales Load	None	1-Year Return (1993)	+24%
Redemption Fee	None	3-Year Return (1991–93)	+6%
Tax Load (Estimated)	Neg.	5-Year Return (1989–93)	–2%
Annual 12b-1 Fee	None	10-Year Return (1984–93)	+276%
Annual Expense Ratio	1.42%	Worst-Ever Loss (1990-92)	40%
Annual Portfolio Turnover	64%	Stock Market Correlation	6%
5-Year Cost Estimate	7%	Up/Down Market Rank	E – A

Benefits		Investment Information	
Investment Objective	Growth	Telephone	800-535-2726
5-Year Projected Return	NA	Minimum Investment	$1,000
Safety Rating (0-100)	46%	Telephone Switching	4 per yr; free
Yield	2.7%	Total Assets	$630 million

Japan OTC Equity
Foreign - Japanese OTC stocks

Costs		Performance	
Sales Load	None	1-Year Return (1993)	+29%
Redemption Fee	None	3-Year Return (1991–93)	+20%
Tax Load (Estimated)	Neg.	5-Year Return (1989–93)	NA
Annual 12b-1 Fee	None	10-Year Return (1984–93)	NA
Annual Expense Ratio	1.59%	Worst-Ever Loss (1990)	53%
Annual Portfolio Turnover	36%	Stock Market Correlation	10%
5-Year Cost Estimate	11%	Up/Down Market Rank	NA – NA

Benefits		Investment Information	
Investment Objective	Growth	Telephone	800-933-3440
5-Year Projected Return	NA	Minimum Investment	None
Safety Rating (0-100)	10%	Telephone Switching	Via broker
Yield	0.0%	Total Assets	$65 million

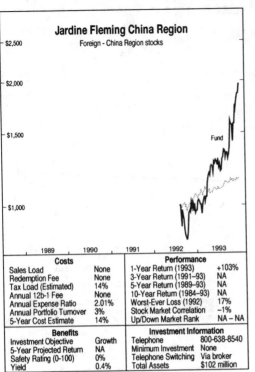

Jardine Fleming China Region
Foreign - China Region stocks

Fund

Costs		Performance	
Sales Load	None	1-Year Return (1993)	+103%
Redemption Fee	None	3-Year Return (1991–93)	NA
Tax Load (Estimated)	14%	5-Year Return (1989–93)	NA
Annual 12b-1 Fee	None	10-Year Return (1984–93)	NA
Annual Expense Ratio	2.01%	Worst-Ever Loss (1992)	17%
Annual Portfolio Turnover	3%	Stock Market Correlation	–1%
5-Year Cost Estimate	14%	Up/Down Market Rank	NA – NA

Benefits		Investment Information	
Investment Objective	Growth	Telephone	800-638-8540
5-Year Projected Return	NA	Minimum Investment	None
Safety Rating (0-100)	0%	Telephone Switching	Via broker
Yield	0.4%	Total Assets	$102 million

John Hanc Freedom Aviatn & Tch
Aviation and technology stocks

Costs		Performance	
Sales Load	5.3%	1-Year Return (1993)	+21%
Redemption Fee	None	3-Year Return (1991–93)	+63%
Tax Load (Estimated)	15%	5-Year Return (1989–93)	+83%
Annual 12b-1 Fee	None	10-Year Return (1984–93)	+170%
Annual Expense Ratio	1.53%	Worst-Ever Loss (1987)	40%
Annual Portfolio Turnover	31%	Stock Market Correlation	48%
5-Year Cost Estimate	23%	Up/Down Market Rank	C – E

Benefits		Investment Information	
Investment Objective	Growth	Telephone	800-225-5291
5-Year Projected Return	NA	Minimum Investment	$1,000
Safety Rating (0-100)	59%	Telephone Switching	Unlimited;free
Yield	0.0%	Total Assets	$84 million

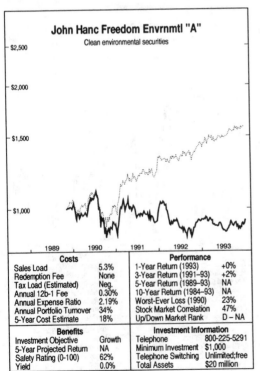

John Hanc Freedom Envrnmtl "A"
Clean environmental securities

Costs		Performance	
Sales Load	5.3%	1-Year Return (1993)	+0%
Redemption Fee	None	3-Year Return (1991–93)	+2%
Tax Load (Estimated)	Neg.	5-Year Return (1989–93)	NA
Annual 12b-1 Fee	0.30%	10-Year Return (1984–93)	NA
Annual Expense Ratio	2.19%	Worst-Ever Loss (1990)	23%
Annual Portfolio Turnover	34%	Stock Market Correlation	47%
5-Year Cost Estimate	18%	Up/Down Market Rank	D – NA

Benefits		Investment Information	
Investment Objective	Growth	Telephone	800-225-5291
5-Year Projected Return	NA	Minimum Investment	$1,000
Safety Rating (0-100)	62%	Telephone Switching	Unlimited;free
Yield	0.0%	Total Assets	$20 million

John Hanc Freedom Global "B"
Foreign & U.S. - diversified stocks

Costs		Performance	
Sales Load	None	1-Year Return (1993)	+34%
Redemption Fee	4.2%	3-Year Return (1991–93)	+92%
Tax Load (Estimated)	8%	5-Year Return (1989–93)	+106%
Annual 12b-1 Fee	1.00%	10-Year Return (1984–93)	NA
Annual Expense Ratio	2.99%	Worst-Ever Loss (1987)	38%
Annual Portfolio Turnover	104%	Stock Market Correlation	24%
5-Year Cost Estimate	29%	Up/Down Market Rank	E – B

Benefits		Investment Information	
Investment Objective	Growth	Telephone	800-225-5291
5-Year Projected Return	NA	Minimum Investment	$1,000
Safety Rating (0-100)	70%	Telephone Switching	Unlimited;free
Yield	0.0%	Total Assets	$98 million

John Hanc Freedom Global Tech
Foreign & U.S. - technology stocks

Costs		Performance	
Sales Load	5.3%	1-Year Return (1993)	+32%
Redemption Fee	None	3-Year Return (1991–93)	+86%
Tax Load (Estimated)	Neg.	5-Year Return (1989–93)	+77%
Annual 12b-1 Fee	None	10-Year Return (1984–93)	NA
Annual Expense Ratio	2.05%	Worst-Ever Loss (1987)	37%
Annual Portfolio Turnover	60%	Stock Market Correlation	42%
5-Year Cost Estimate	17%	Up/Down Market Rank	B – E

Benefits		Investment Information	
Investment Objective	Gr. & Icm.	Telephone	800-225-5291
5-Year Projected Return	NA	Minimum Investment	$1,000
Safety Rating (0-100)	58%	Telephone Switching	Unlimited;free
Yield	0.0%	Total Assets	$39 million

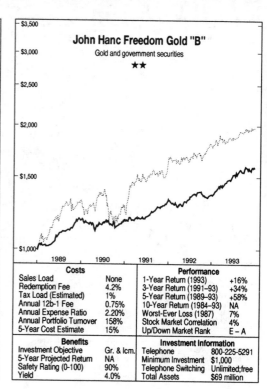

John Hanc Freedom Gold "B"
Gold and government securities
★★

Costs		Performance	
Sales Load	None	1-Year Return (1993)	+16%
Redemption Fee	4.2%	3-Year Return (1991–93)	+34%
Tax Load (Estimated)	1%	5-Year Return (1989–93)	+58%
Annual 12b-1 Fee	0.75%	10-Year Return (1984–93)	NA
Annual Expense Ratio	2.20%	Worst-Ever Loss (1987)	7%
Annual Portfolio Turnover	158%	Stock Market Correlation	4%
5-Year Cost Estimate	15%	Up/Down Market Rank	E – A

Benefits		Investment Information	
Investment Objective	Gr. & Icm.	Telephone	800-225-5291
5-Year Projected Return	NA	Minimum Investment	$1,000
Safety Rating (0-100)	90%	Telephone Switching	Unlimited;free
Yield	4.0%	Total Assets	$69 million

John Hanc Freedom Pac Basin
Foreign - Pacific-Basin except U.S. & Japan

Costs		Performance	
Sales Load	5.3%	1-Year Return (1993)	+70%
Redemption Fee	None	3-Year Return (1991–93)	+96%
Tax Load (Estimated)	1%	5-Year Return (1989–93)	+79%
Annual 12b-1 Fee	0.50%	10-Year Return (1984–93)	NA
Annual Expense Ratio	2.73%	Worst-Ever Loss (1990)	28%
Annual Portfolio Turnover	179%	Stock Market Correlation	10%
5-Year Cost Estimate	22%	Up/Down Market Rank	E – B

Benefits		Investment Information	
Investment Objective	Growth	Telephone	800-225-5291
5-Year Projected Return	NA	Minimum Investment	$1,000
Safety Rating (0-100)	68%	Telephone Switching	Unlimited;free
Yield	0.0%	Total Assets	$15 million

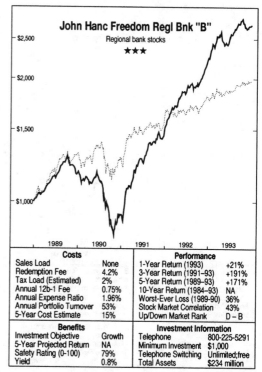

John Hanc Freedom Regl Bnk "B"
Regional bank stocks
★★★

Costs		Performance	
Sales Load	None	1-Year Return (1993)	+21%
Redemption Fee	4.2%	3-Year Return (1991–93)	+191%
Tax Load (Estimated)	2%	5-Year Return (1989–93)	+171%
Annual 12b-1 Fee	0.75%	10-Year Return (1984–93)	NA
Annual Expense Ratio	1.96%	Worst-Ever Loss (1989-90)	36%
Annual Portfolio Turnover	53%	Stock Market Correlation	43%
5-Year Cost Estimate	15%	Up/Down Market Rank	D – B

Benefits		Investment Information	
Investment Objective	Growth	Telephone	800-225-5291
5-Year Projected Return	NA	Minimum Investment	$1,000
Safety Rating (0-100)	79%	Telephone Switching	Unlimited;free
Yield	0.8%	Total Assets	$234 million

John Hancock Sovrgn Achvrs "B"
Undervalued stocks

S&P 500

Fund

Costs		Performance	
Sales Load	None	1-Year Return (1993)	+9%
Redemption Fee	4.2%	3-Year Return (1991–93)	+59%
Tax Load (Estimated)	1%	5-Year Return (1989–93)	+67%
Annual 12b-1 Fee	0.75%	10-Year Return (1984–93)	NA
Annual Expense Ratio	2.27%	Worst-Ever Loss (1987)	34%
Annual Portfolio Turnover	84%	Stock Market Correlation	80%
5-Year Cost Estimate	15%	Up/Down Market Rank	B – D
Benefits		**Investment Information**	
Investment Objective	Growth	Telephone	800-225-5291
5-Year Projected Return	+5%	Minimum Investment	$1,000
Safety Rating (0-100)	72%	Telephone Switching	Unlimited;free
Yield	0.2%	Total Assets	$111 million

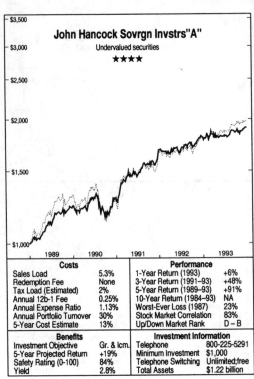

John Hancock Sovrgn Invstrs "A"
Undervalued securities
★★★★

Costs		Performance	
Sales Load	5.3%	1-Year Return (1993)	+6%
Redemption Fee	None	3-Year Return (1991–93)	+48%
Tax Load (Estimated)	2%	5-Year Return (1989–93)	+91%
Annual 12b-1 Fee	0.25%	10-Year Return (1984–93)	NA
Annual Expense Ratio	1.13%	Worst-Ever Loss (1987)	23%
Annual Portfolio Turnover	30%	Stock Market Correlation	83%
5-Year Cost Estimate	13%	Up/Down Market Rank	D – B
Benefits		**Investment Information**	
Investment Objective	Gr. & Icm.	Telephone	800-225-5291
5-Year Projected Return	+19%	Minimum Investment	$1,000
Safety Rating (0-100)	84%	Telephone Switching	Unlimited;free
Yield	2.8%	Total Assets	$1.22 billion

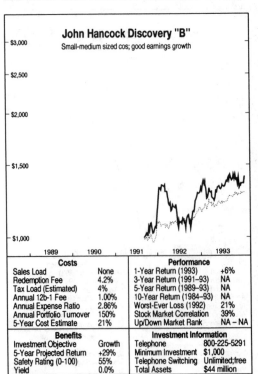

John Hancock Discovery "B"
Small-medium sized cos; good earnings growth

Costs		Performance	
Sales Load	None	1-Year Return (1993)	+6%
Redemption Fee	4.2%	3-Year Return (1991–93)	NA
Tax Load (Estimated)	4%	5-Year Return (1989–93)	NA
Annual 12b-1 Fee	1.00%	10-Year Return (1984–93)	NA
Annual Expense Ratio	2.86%	Worst-Ever Loss (1992)	21%
Annual Portfolio Turnover	150%	Stock Market Correlation	39%
5-Year Cost Estimate	21%	Up/Down Market Rank	NA – NA
Benefits		**Investment Information**	
Investment Objective	Growth	Telephone	800-225-5291
5-Year Projected Return	+29%	Minimum Investment	$1,000
Safety Rating (0-100)	55%	Telephone Switching	Unlimited;free
Yield	0.0%	Total Assets	$44 million

John Hancock Growth
Diversified stocks; long-intermediate term

Costs		Performance	
Sales Load	5.3%	1-Year Return (1993)	+13%
Redemption Fee	None	3-Year Return (1991–93)	+70%
Tax Load (Estimated)	7%	5-Year Return (1989–93)	+103%
Annual 12b-1 Fee	0.50%	10-Year Return (1984–93)	NA
Annual Expense Ratio	1.60%	Worst-Ever Loss (1987)	32%
Annual Portfolio Turnover	94%	Stock Market Correlation	66%
5-Year Cost Estimate	23%	Up/Down Market Rank	A – D
Benefits		**Investment Information**	
Investment Objective	Gr. & Icm.	Telephone	800-225-5291
5-Year Projected Return	+11%	Minimum Investment	$1,000
Safety Rating (0-100)	68%	Telephone Switching	Unlimited;free
Yield	0.0%	Total Assets	$165 million

John Hancock Special Eqtys "A"
Emerging growth; special situations
★

Costs		Performance	
Sales Load	5.3%	1-Year Return (1993)	+20%
Redemption Fee	None	3-Year Return (1991–93)	+188%
Tax Load (Estimated)	2%	5-Year Return (1989–93)	+236%
Annual 12b-1 Fee	0.30%	10-Year Return (1984–93)	NA
Annual Expense Ratio	0.94%	Worst-Ever Loss (1987)	44%
Annual Portfolio Turnover	125%	Stock Market Correlation	46%
5-Year Cost Estimate	13%	Up/Down Market Rank	A – E

Benefits		Investment Information	
Investment Objective	Growth	Telephone	800-225-5291
5-Year Projected Return	+56%	Minimum Investment	$1,000
Safety Rating (0-100)	61%	Telephone Switching	Unlimited;free
Yield	0.0%	Total Assets	$348 million

JP Growth
Industry leaders
★

Costs		Performance	
Sales Load	4.7%	1-Year Return (1993)	+8%
Redemption Fee	None	3-Year Return (1991–93)	+50%
Tax Load (Estimated)	4%	5-Year Return (1989–93)	+95%
Annual 12b-1 Fee	None	10-Year Return (1984–93)	NA
Annual Expense Ratio	0.87%	Worst-Ever Loss (1987)	32%
Annual Portfolio Turnover	37%	Stock Market Correlation	85%
5-Year Cost Estimate	12%	Up/Down Market Rank	B – D

Benefits		Investment Information	
Investment Objective	Gr. & Icm.	Telephone	800-458-4498
5-Year Projected Return	+7%	Minimum Investment	$300
Safety Rating (0-100)	73%	Telephone Switching	Unlimited;free
Yield	1.3%	Total Assets	$37 million

Kaufmann
Small stocks; diversified
★★★★

Costs		Performance	
Sales Load	None	1-Year Return (1993)	+18%
Redemption Fee	0.2%	3-Year Return (1991–93)	+136%
Tax Load (Estimated)	7%	5-Year Return (1989–93)	+225%
Annual 12b-1 Fee	0.75%	10-Year Return (1984–93)	NA
Annual Expense Ratio	2.60%	Worst-Ever Loss (1987)	50%
Annual Portfolio Turnover	80%	Stock Market Correlation	44%
5-Year Cost Estimate	23%	Up/Down Market Rank	B – D

Benefits		Investment Information	
Investment Objective	Growth	Telephone	800-237-0132
5-Year Projected Return	+57%	Minimum Investment	$1,500
Safety Rating (0-100)	65%	Telephone Switching	See prospectus
Yield	1.0%	Total Assets	$790 million

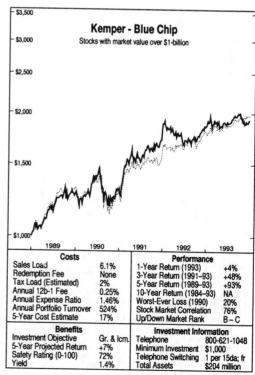

Kemper - Blue Chip
Stocks with market value over $1-billion

Costs		Performance	
Sales Load	6.1%	1-Year Return (1993)	+4%
Redemption Fee	None	3-Year Return (1991–93)	+48%
Tax Load (Estimated)	2%	5-Year Return (1989–93)	+93%
Annual 12b-1 Fee	0.25%	10-Year Return (1984–93)	NA
Annual Expense Ratio	1.46%	Worst-Ever Loss (1990)	20%
Annual Portfolio Turnover	524%	Stock Market Correlation	76%
5-Year Cost Estimate	17%	Up/Down Market Rank	B – C

Benefits		Investment Information	
Investment Objective	Gr. & Icm.	Telephone	800-621-1048
5-Year Projected Return	+7%	Minimum Investment	$1,000
Safety Rating (0-100)	72%	Telephone Switching	1 per 15da; fr
Yield	1.4%	Total Assets	$204 million

Kemper - Environmentl Services
Cos. in environmentally related activities

S&P 500

Fund

Costs		Performance	
Sales Load	6.1%	1-Year Return (1993)	–3%
Redemption Fee	None	3-Year Return (1991–93)	+10%
Tax Load (Estimated)	Neg.	5-Year Return (1989–93)	NA
Annual 12b-1 Fee	0.25%	10-Year Return (1984–93)	NA
Annual Expense Ratio	1.58%	Worst-Ever Loss (1990)	26%
Annual Portfolio Turnover	388%	Stock Market Correlation	51%
5-Year Cost Estimate	15%	Up/Down Market Rank	NA – NA

Benefits		Investment Information	
Investment Objective	Growth	Telephone	800-621-1048
5-Year Projected Return	NA	Minimum Investment	$1,000
Safety Rating (0-100)	54%	Telephone Switching	1 per 15da; fr
Yield	0.0%	Total Assets	$43 million

Kemper - Growth
Growth stocks; long term
★

Costs		Performance	
Sales Load	6.1%	1-Year Return (1993)	+2%
Redemption Fee	None	3-Year Return (1991–93)	+67%
Tax Load (Estimated)	4%	5-Year Return (1989–93)	+127%
Annual 12b-1 Fee	0.25%	10-Year Return (1984–93)	+255%
Annual Expense Ratio	1.03%	Worst-Ever Loss (1987)	36%
Annual Portfolio Turnover	268%	Stock Market Correlation	69%
5-Year Cost Estimate	16%	Up/Down Market Rank	A – E

Benefits		Investment Information	
Investment Objective	Growth	Telephone	800-621-1048
5-Year Projected Return	+21%	Minimum Investment	$1,000
Safety Rating (0-100)	70%	Telephone Switching	1 per 15da; fr
Yield	0.0%	Total Assets	$1.82 billion

Kemper - International
Foreign - diversified stocks

Costs		Performance	
Sales Load	6.1%	1-Year Return (1993)	+36%
Redemption Fee	None	3-Year Return (1991–93)	+41%
Tax Load (Estimated)	3%	5-Year Return (1989–93)	+55%
Annual 12b-1 Fee	0.25%	10-Year Return (1984–93)	+294%
Annual Expense Ratio	1.36%	Worst-Ever Loss (1987)	28%
Annual Portfolio Turnover	312%	Stock Market Correlation	15%
5-Year Cost Estimate	17%	Up/Down Market Rank	E – A

Benefits		Investment Information	
Investment Objective	Gr. & Icm.	Telephone	800-621-1048
5-Year Projected Return	NA	Minimum Investment	$1,000
Safety Rating (0-100)	75%	Telephone Switching	1 per 15da; fr
Yield	0.0%	Total Assets	$255 million

Kemper - Retirement II
Guar ret of invst 2000; stks & zero-coup tres
★

Costs		Performance	
Sales Load	5.3%	1-Year Return (1993)	+13%
Redemption Fee	None	3-Year Return (1991–93)	+64%
Tax Load (Estimated)	4%	5-Year Return (1989–93)	NA
Annual 12b-1 Fee	None	10-Year Return (1984–93)	NA
Annual Expense Ratio	1.01%	Worst-Ever Loss (1992)	7%
Annual Portfolio Turnover	51%	Stock Market Correlation	51%
5-Year Cost Estimate	15%	Up/Down Market Rank	NA – NA

Benefits		Investment Information	
Investment Objective	Growth	Telephone	800-621-1048
5-Year Projected Return	+35%	Minimum Investment	$1,000
Safety Rating (0-100)	81%	Telephone Switching	1 per 15da; fr
Yield	4.3%	Total Assets	$208 million

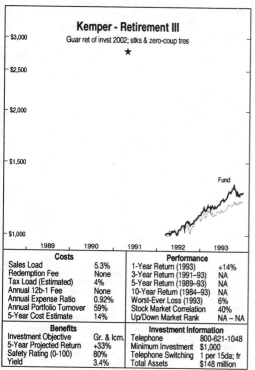

Kemper - Retirement III
Guar ret of invst 2002; stks & zero-coup tres
★

Costs		Performance	
Sales Load	5.3%	1-Year Return (1993)	+14%
Redemption Fee	None	3-Year Return (1991–93)	NA
Tax Load (Estimated)	4%	5-Year Return (1989–93)	NA
Annual 12b-1 Fee	None	10-Year Return (1984–93)	NA
Annual Expense Ratio	0.92%	Worst-Ever Loss (1993)	6%
Annual Portfolio Turnover	59%	Stock Market Correlation	40%
5-Year Cost Estimate	14%	Up/Down Market Rank	NA – NA

Benefits		Investment Information	
Investment Objective	Gr. & Icm.	Telephone	800-621-1048
5-Year Projected Return	+33%	Minimum Investment	$1,000
Safety Rating (0-100)	80%	Telephone Switching	1 per 15da; fr
Yield	3.4%	Total Assets	$148 million

Kemper - Small Cap Equity
Diversified stocks
★

Costs		Performance	
Sales Load	6.1%	1-Year Return (1993)	+17%
Redemption Fee	None	3-Year Return (1991–93)	+98%
Tax Load (Estimated)	4%	5-Year Return (1989–93)	+136%
Annual 12b-1 Fee	0.25%	10-Year Return (1984–93)	+244%
Annual Expense Ratio	1.28%	Worst-Ever Loss (1987)	38%
Annual Portfolio Turnover	198%	Stock Market Correlation	55%
5-Year Cost Estimate	18%	Up/Down Market Rank	A – E

Benefits		Investment Information	
Investment Objective	Growth	Telephone	800-621-1048
5-Year Projected Return	+30%	Minimum Investment	$1,000
Safety Rating (0-100)	68%	Telephone Switching	1 per 15da; fr
Yield	0.0%	Total Assets	$480 million

Kemper - Technology
Technology stocks

Costs		Performance	
Sales Load	6.1%	1-Year Return (1993)	+12%
Redemption Fee	None	3-Year Return (1991–93)	+59%
Tax Load (Estimated)	1%	5-Year Return (1989–93)	+100%
Annual 12b-1 Fee	0.25%	10-Year Return (1984–93)	+202%
Annual Expense Ratio	0.82%	Worst-Ever Loss (1987)	39%
Annual Portfolio Turnover	81%	Stock Market Correlation	51%
5-Year Cost Estimate	12%	Up/Down Market Rank	B – E

Benefits		Investment Information	
Investment Objective	Growth	Telephone	800-621-1048
5-Year Projected Return	NA	Minimum Investment	$1,000
Safety Rating (0-100)	65%	Telephone Switching	1 per 15da; fr
Yield	0.0%	Total Assets	$617 million

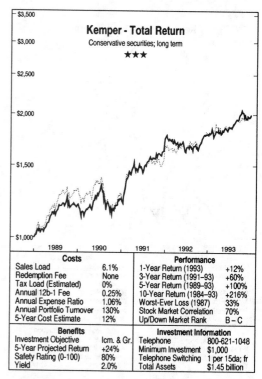

Kemper - Total Return
Conservative securities; long term
★★★

Costs		Performance	
Sales Load	6.1%	1-Year Return (1993)	+12%
Redemption Fee	None	3-Year Return (1991–93)	+60%
Tax Load (Estimated)	0%	5-Year Return (1989–93)	+100%
Annual 12b-1 Fee	0.25%	10-Year Return (1984–93)	+216%
Annual Expense Ratio	1.06%	Worst-Ever Loss (1987)	33%
Annual Portfolio Turnover	130%	Stock Market Correlation	70%
5-Year Cost Estimate	12%	Up/Down Market Rank	B – C

Benefits		Investment Information	
Investment Objective	Icm. & Gr.	Telephone	800-621-1048
5-Year Projected Return	+24%	Minimum Investment	$1,000
Safety Rating (0-100)	80%	Telephone Switching	1 per 15da; fr
Yield	2.0%	Total Assets	$1.45 billion

Kemper Invst - Growth
Diversified secs; stocks; pfds and warrants

Fund

S&P 500

Costs		Performance	
Sales Load	None	1-Year Return (1993)	+4%
Redemption Fee	4.2%	3-Year Return (1991–93)	+60%
Tax Load (Estimated)	3%	5-Year Return (1989–93)	+107%
Annual 12b-1 Fee	1.00%	10-Year Return (1984–93)	NA
Annual Expense Ratio	2.06%	Worst-Ever Loss (1987)	35%
Annual Portfolio Turnover	128%	Stock Market Correlation	68%
5-Year Cost Estimate	16%	Up/Down Market Rank	B – E
Benefits		**Investment Information**	
Investment Objective	Growth	Telephone	800-621-1048
5-Year Projected Return	+16%	Minimum Investment	$1,000
Safety Rating (0-100)	68%	Telephone Switching	1 per 15da; fr
Yield	0.0%	Total Assets	$996 million

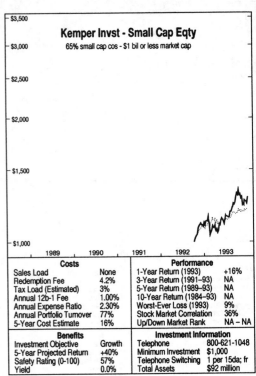

Kemper Invst - Small Cap Eqty
65% small cap cos - $1 bil or less market cap

Costs		Performance	
Sales Load	None	1-Year Return (1993)	+16%
Redemption Fee	4.2%	3-Year Return (1991–93)	NA
Tax Load (Estimated)	3%	5-Year Return (1989–93)	NA
Annual 12b-1 Fee	1.00%	10-Year Return (1984–93)	NA
Annual Expense Ratio	2.30%	Worst-Ever Loss (1993)	9%
Annual Portfolio Turnover	77%	Stock Market Correlation	36%
5-Year Cost Estimate	16%	Up/Down Market Rank	NA – NA
Benefits		**Investment Information**	
Investment Objective	Growth	Telephone	800-621-1048
5-Year Projected Return	+40%	Minimum Investment	$1,000
Safety Rating (0-100)	57%	Telephone Switching	1 per 15da; fr
Yield	0.0%	Total Assets	$92 million

Kemper Invst - Total Return
Diversified stocks and bonds
★★

Costs		Performance	
Sales Load	None	1-Year Return (1993)	+8%
Redemption Fee	4.2%	3-Year Return (1991–93)	+61%
Tax Load (Estimated)	4%	5-Year Return (1989–93)	+93%
Annual 12b-1 Fee	1.00%	10-Year Return (1984–93)	NA
Annual Expense Ratio	1.96%	Worst-Ever Loss (1987)	29%
Annual Portfolio Turnover	76%	Stock Market Correlation	70%
5-Year Cost Estimate	16%	Up/Down Market Rank	B – C
Benefits		**Investment Information**	
Investment Objective	Icm. & Gr.	Telephone	800-621-1048
5-Year Projected Return	+25%	Minimum Investment	$1,000
Safety Rating (0-100)	80%	Telephone Switching	1 per 15da; fr
Yield	2.1%	Total Assets	$1.43 billion

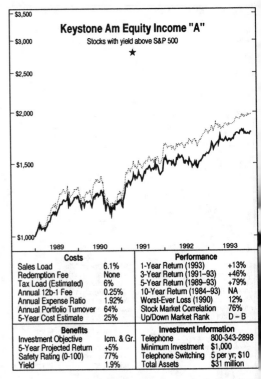

Keystone Am Equity Income "A"
Stocks with yield above S&P 500
★

Costs		Performance	
Sales Load	6.1%	1-Year Return (1993)	+13%
Redemption Fee	None	3-Year Return (1991–93)	+46%
Tax Load (Estimated)	6%	5-Year Return (1989–93)	+79%
Annual 12b-1 Fee	0.25%	10-Year Return (1984–93)	NA
Annual Expense Ratio	1.92%	Worst-Ever Loss (1990)	12%
Annual Portfolio Turnover	64%	Stock Market Correlation	76%
5-Year Cost Estimate	25%	Up/Down Market Rank	D – B
Benefits		**Investment Information**	
Investment Objective	Icm. & Gr.	Telephone	800-343-2898
5-Year Projected Return	+5%	Minimum Investment	$1,000
Safety Rating (0-100)	77%	Telephone Switching	5 per yr; $10
Yield	1.9%	Total Assets	$31 million

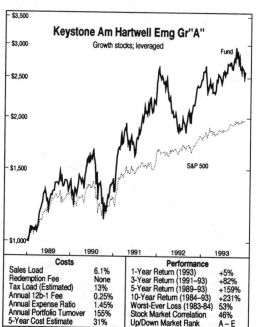

Keystone Am Hartwell Emg Gr"A"
Growth stocks; leveraged

Costs		Performance	
Sales Load	6.1%	1-Year Return (1993)	+5%
Redemption Fee	None	3-Year Return (1991–93)	+82%
Tax Load (Estimated)	13%	5-Year Return (1989–93)	+159%
Annual 12b-1 Fee	0.25%	10-Year Return (1984–93)	+231%
Annual Expense Ratio	1.45%	Worst-Ever Loss (1983-84)	53%
Annual Portfolio Turnover	155%	Stock Market Correlation	46%
5-Year Cost Estimate	31%	Up/Down Market Rank	A – E

Benefits		Investment Information	
Investment Objective	Growth	Telephone	800-343-2898
5-Year Projected Return	+28%	Minimum Investment	$1,000
Safety Rating (0-100)	52%	Telephone Switching	5 per yr; $10
Yield	9.8%	Total Assets	$191 million

Keystone Am Hartwell Grth "A"
Undervalued growth stocks

Costs		Performance	
Sales Load	6.1%	1-Year Return (1993)	+10%
Redemption Fee	None	3-Year Return (1991–93)	+82%
Tax Load (Estimated)	13%	5-Year Return (1989–93)	+108%
Annual 12b-1 Fee	0.25%	10-Year Return (1984–93)	+252%
Annual Expense Ratio	2.10%	Worst-Ever Loss (1981-82)	39%
Annual Portfolio Turnover	42%	Stock Market Correlation	65%
5-Year Cost Estimate	30%	Up/Down Market Rank	A – E

Benefits		Investment Information	
Investment Objective	Growth	Telephone	800-343-2898
5-Year Projected Return	+10%	Minimum Investment	$1,000
Safety Rating (0-100)	61%	Telephone Switching	5 per yr; $10
Yield	0.0%	Total Assets	$26 million

Keystone America Omega
Maximum growth stocks; leveraged
★

Costs		Performance	
Sales Load	6.1%	1-Year Return (1993)	+19%
Redemption Fee	None	3-Year Return (1991–93)	+91%
Tax Load (Estimated)	2%	5-Year Return (1989–93)	+147%
Annual 12b-1 Fee	0.25%	10-Year Return (1984–93)	+351%
Annual Expense Ratio	1.60%	Worst-Ever Loss (1981-82)	45%
Annual Portfolio Turnover	176%	Stock Market Correlation	67%
5-Year Cost Estimate	18%	Up/Down Market Rank	A – E

Benefits		Investment Information	
Investment Objective	Growth	Telephone	800-343-2898
5-Year Projected Return	+30%	Minimum Investment	$1,000
Safety Rating (0-100)	67%	Telephone Switching	5 per yr; $10
Yield	0.0%	Total Assets	$87 million

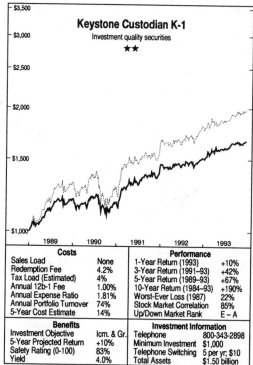

Keystone Custodian K-1
Investment quality securities
★★

Costs		Performance	
Sales Load	None	1-Year Return (1993)	+10%
Redemption Fee	4.2%	3-Year Return (1991–93)	+42%
Tax Load (Estimated)	4%	5-Year Return (1989–93)	+67%
Annual 12b-1 Fee	1.00%	10-Year Return (1984–93)	+190%
Annual Expense Ratio	1.81%	Worst-Ever Loss (1987)	22%
Annual Portfolio Turnover	74%	Stock Market Correlation	85%
5-Year Cost Estimate	14%	Up/Down Market Rank	E – A

Benefits		Investment Information	
Investment Objective	Icm. & Gr.	Telephone	800-343-2898
5-Year Projected Return	+10%	Minimum Investment	$1,000
Safety Rating (0-100)	83%	Telephone Switching	5 per yr; $10
Yield	4.0%	Total Assets	$1.50 billion

Keystone Custodian K-2
Diversified securities

S&P 500

Costs		Performance	
Sales Load	None	1-Year Return (1993)	+13%
Redemption Fee	4.2%	3-Year Return (1991–93)	+73%
Tax Load (Estimated)	0%	5-Year Return (1989–93)	+100%
Annual 12b-1 Fee	1.00%	10-Year Return (1984–93)	+229%
Annual Expense Ratio	1.58%	Worst-Ever Loss (1987)	35%
Annual Portfolio Turnover	74%	Stock Market Correlation	72%
5-Year Cost Estimate	8%	Up/Down Market Rank	B – D

Benefits		Investment Information	
Investment Objective	Growth	Telephone	800-343-2898
5-Year Projected Return	+20%	Minimum Investment	$1,000
Safety Rating (0-100)	70%	Telephone Switching	5 per yr; $10
Yield	0.0%	Total Assets	$396 million

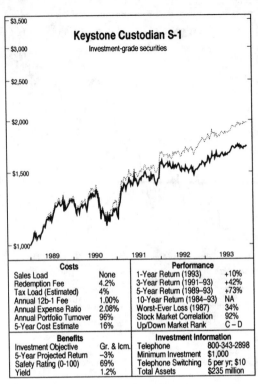

Keystone Custodian S-1
Investment-grade securities

Costs		Performance	
Sales Load	None	1-Year Return (1993)	+10%
Redemption Fee	4.2%	3-Year Return (1991–93)	+42%
Tax Load (Estimated)	4%	5-Year Return (1989–93)	+73%
Annual 12b-1 Fee	1.00%	10-Year Return (1984–93)	NA
Annual Expense Ratio	2.08%	Worst-Ever Loss (1987)	34%
Annual Portfolio Turnover	96%	Stock Market Correlation	92%
5-Year Cost Estimate	16%	Up/Down Market Rank	C – D

Benefits		Investment Information	
Investment Objective	Gr. & Icm.	Telephone	800-343-2898
5-Year Projected Return	–3%	Minimum Investment	$1,000
Safety Rating (0-100)	69%	Telephone Switching	5 per yr; $10
Yield	1.2%	Total Assets	$235 million

Keystone Custodian S-3
Established growth stocks

Costs		Performance	
Sales Load	None	1-Year Return (1993)	+9%
Redemption Fee	4.2%	3-Year Return (1991–93)	+62%
Tax Load (Estimated)	5%	5-Year Return (1989–93)	+85%
Annual 12b-1 Fee	1.00%	10-Year Return (1984–93)	+176%
Annual Expense Ratio	1.69%	Worst-Ever Loss (1987)	38%
Annual Portfolio Turnover	69%	Stock Market Correlation	77%
5-Year Cost Estimate	14%	Up/Down Market Rank	A – E

Benefits		Investment Information	
Investment Objective	Growth	Telephone	800-343-2898
5-Year Projected Return	+9%	Minimum Investment	$1,000
Safety Rating (0-100)	67%	Telephone Switching	5 per yr; $10
Yield	0.3%	Total Assets	$293 million

Keystone Custodian S-4
Emerging and volatile stocks

Costs		Performance	
Sales Load	None	1-Year Return (1993)	+25%
Redemption Fee	4.2%	3-Year Return (1991–93)	+137%
Tax Load (Estimated)	5%	5-Year Return (1989–93)	+176%
Annual 12b-1 Fee	1.00%	10-Year Return (1984–93)	+211%
Annual Expense Ratio	2.04%	Worst-Ever Loss (1981-82)	45%
Annual Portfolio Turnover	78%	Stock Market Correlation	50%
5-Year Cost Estimate	17%	Up/Down Market Rank	A – E

Benefits		Investment Information	
Investment Objective	Growth	Telephone	800-343-2898
5-Year Projected Return	+56%	Minimum Investment	$1,000
Safety Rating (0-100)	59%	Telephone Switching	5 per yr; $10
Yield	0.0%	Total Assets	$1.08 billion

Keystone International
Foreign - diversified stocks

S&P 500

Fund

Costs		Performance	
Sales Load	None	1-Year Return (1993)	+30%
Redemption Fee	4.2%	3-Year Return (1991–93)	+53%
Tax Load (Estimated)	6%	5-Year Return (1989–93)	+21%
Annual 12b-1 Fee	1.00%	10-Year Return (1984–93)	+195%
Annual Expense Ratio	3.63%	Worst-Ever Loss (1987-90)	29%
Annual Portfolio Turnover	68%	Stock Market Correlation	13%
5-Year Cost Estimate	28%	Up/Down Market Rank	E – B

Benefits		Investment Information	
Investment Objective	Gr. & Icm.	Telephone	800-343-2898
5-Year Projected Return	NA	Minimum Investment	$1,000
Safety Rating (0-100)	69%	Telephone Switching	5 per yr; $10
Yield	0.0%	Total Assets	$112 million

Keystone Precious Metals
International gold stocks

Costs		Performance	
Sales Load	None	1-Year Return (1993)	+102%
Redemption Fee	4.2%	3-Year Return (1991–93)	+89%
Tax Load (Estimated)	1%	5-Year Return (1989–93)	+73%
Annual 12b-1 Fee	1.00%	10-Year Return (1984–93)	+89%
Annual Expense Ratio	2.83%	Worst-Ever Loss (1987-92)	49%
Annual Portfolio Turnover	60%	Stock Market Correlation	–1%
5-Year Cost Estimate	17%	Up/Down Market Rank	E – A

Benefits		Investment Information	
Investment Objective	Gr. & Icm.	Telephone	800-343-2898
5-Year Projected Return	NA	Minimum Investment	$1,000
Safety Rating (0-100)	54%	Telephone Switching	5 per yr; $10
Yield	0.0%	Total Assets	$173 million

Kidder Peabody - Equity Income
High-yielding equity securities
★

Costs		Performance	
Sales Load	6.1%	1-Year Return (1993)	+1%
Redemption Fee	None	3-Year Return (1991–93)	+43%
Tax Load (Estimated)	5%	5-Year Return (1989–93)	+87%
Annual 12b-1 Fee	0.50%	10-Year Return (1984–93)	NA
Annual Expense Ratio	1.27%	Worst-Ever Loss (1987)	22%
Annual Portfolio Turnover	43%	Stock Market Correlation	65%
5-Year Cost Estimate	18%	Up/Down Market Rank	D – B

Benefits		Investment Information	
Investment Objective	Icm. & Gr.	Telephone	800-543-3373
5-Year Projected Return	+7%	Minimum Investment	$1,000
Safety Rating (0-100)	76%	Telephone Switching	Unlimited;free
Yield	1.6%	Total Assets	$127 million

Korea
Foreign - Korean stocks

Costs		Performance	
Sales Load	None	1-Year Return (1993)	+72%
Redemption Fee	None	3-Year Return (1991–93)	+104%
Tax Load (Estimated)	19%	5-Year Return (1989–93)	+29%
Annual 12b-1 Fee	None	10-Year Return (1984–93)	NA
Annual Expense Ratio	1.52%	Worst-Ever Loss (1989-92)	70%
Annual Portfolio Turnover	14%	Stock Market Correlation	1%
5-Year Cost Estimate	15%	Up/Down Market Rank	D – E

Benefits		Investment Information	
Investment Objective	Growth	Telephone	800-225-2470
5-Year Projected Return	NA	Minimum Investment	None
Safety Rating (0-100)	18%	Telephone Switching	Via broker
Yield	0.0%	Total Assets	$233 million

EQUITY

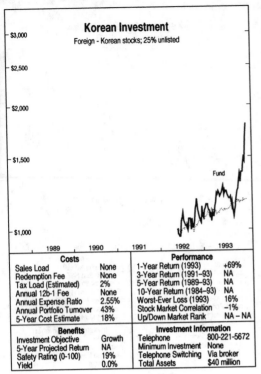

Korean Investment
Foreign - Korean stocks; 25% unlisted

Fund

Costs		Performance	
Sales Load	None	1-Year Return (1993)	+69%
Redemption Fee	None	3-Year Return (1991–93)	NA
Tax Load (Estimated)	2%	5-Year Return (1989–93)	NA
Annual 12b-1 Fee	None	10-Year Return (1984–93)	NA
Annual Expense Ratio	2.55%	Worst-Ever Loss (1993)	16%
Annual Portfolio Turnover	43%	Stock Market Correlation	–1%
5-Year Cost Estimate	18%	Up/Down Market Rank	NA – NA

Benefits		Investment Information	
Investment Objective	Growth	Telephone	800-221-5672
5-Year Projected Return	NA	Minimum Investment	None
Safety Rating (0-100)	19%	Telephone Switching	Via broker
Yield	0.0%	Total Assets	$40 million

Landmark - Balanced
Diversified stocks and bonds
★★

Costs		Performance	
Sales Load	3.6%	1-Year Return (1993)	+8%
Redemption Fee	None	3-Year Return (1991–93)	+50%
Tax Load (Estimated)	1%	5-Year Return (1989–93)	+63%
Annual 12b-1 Fee	0.20%	10-Year Return (1984–93)	NA
Annual Expense Ratio	1.40%	Worst-Ever Loss (1987)	21%
Annual Portfolio Turnover	82%	Stock Market Correlation	78%
5-Year Cost Estimate	12%	Up/Down Market Rank	E – A

Benefits		Investment Information	
Investment Objective	Icm. & Gr.	Telephone	800-846-5300
5-Year Projected Return	+13%	Minimum Investment	$1,000
Safety Rating (0-100)	85%	Telephone Switching	Unlimited;free
Yield	2.3%	Total Assets	$264 million

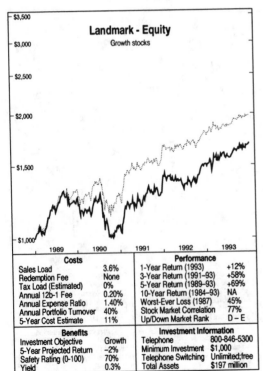

Landmark - Equity
Growth stocks

Costs		Performance	
Sales Load	3.6%	1-Year Return (1993)	+12%
Redemption Fee	None	3-Year Return (1991–93)	+58%
Tax Load (Estimated)	0%	5-Year Return (1989–93)	+69%
Annual 12b-1 Fee	0.20%	10-Year Return (1984–93)	NA
Annual Expense Ratio	1.40%	Worst-Ever Loss (1987)	45%
Annual Portfolio Turnover	40%	Stock Market Correlation	77%
5-Year Cost Estimate	11%	Up/Down Market Rank	D – E

Benefits		Investment Information	
Investment Objective	Growth	Telephone	800-846-5300
5-Year Projected Return	–2%	Minimum Investment	$1,000
Safety Rating (0-100)	70%	Telephone Switching	Unlimited;free
Yield	0.3%	Total Assets	$197 million

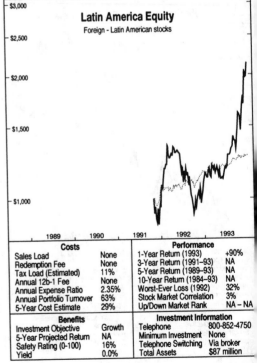

Latin America Equity
Foreign - Latin American stocks

Costs		Performance	
Sales Load	None	1-Year Return (1993)	+90%
Redemption Fee	None	3-Year Return (1991–93)	NA
Tax Load (Estimated)	11%	5-Year Return (1989–93)	NA
Annual 12b-1 Fee	None	10-Year Return (1984–93)	NA
Annual Expense Ratio	2.35%	Worst-Ever Loss (1992)	32%
Annual Portfolio Turnover	63%	Stock Market Correlation	3%
5-Year Cost Estimate	29%	Up/Down Market Rank	NA – NA

Benefits		Investment Information	
Investment Objective	Growth	Telephone	800-852-4750
5-Year Projected Return	NA	Minimum Investment	None
Safety Rating (0-100)	16%	Telephone Switching	Via broker
Yield	0.0%	Total Assets	$87 million

Latin America Investment
Foreign - Latin American secs; non-diversif

Fund

S&P 500

Costs		Performance	
Sales Load	None	1-Year Return (1993)	+77%
Redemption Fee	None	3-Year Return (1991–93)	+378%
Tax Load (Estimated)	5%	5-Year Return (1989–93)	NA
Annual 12b-1 Fee	None	10-Year Return (1984–93)	NA
Annual Expense Ratio	2.61%	Worst-Ever Loss (1992-93)	33%
Annual Portfolio Turnover	120%	Stock Market Correlation	7%
5-Year Cost Estimate	22%	Up/Down Market Rank	NA – NA

Benefits		Investment Information	
Investment Objective	Growth	Telephone	800-852-4750
5-Year Projected Return	NA	Minimum Investment	None
Safety Rating (0-100)	19%	Telephone Switching	Via broker
Yield	0.7%	Total Assets	$77 million

Legg Mason Special Investment
Undervalued neglected stocks
★★★★

Costs		Performance	
Sales Load	None	1-Year Return (1993)	+23%
Redemption Fee	None	3-Year Return (1991–93)	+99%
Tax Load (Estimated)	8%	5-Year Return (1989–93)	+164%
Annual 12b-1 Fee	1.00%	10-Year Return (1984–93)	NA
Annual Expense Ratio	2.04%	Worst-Ever Loss (1987)	37%
Annual Portfolio Turnover	8%	Stock Market Correlation	43%
5-Year Cost Estimate	12%	Up/Down Market Rank	B – D

Benefits		Investment Information	
Investment Objective	Growth	Telephone	800-822-5544
5-Year Projected Return	+53%	Minimum Investment	$1,000
Safety Rating (0-100)	73%	Telephone Switching	4 per yr; free
Yield	0.1%	Total Assets	$425 million

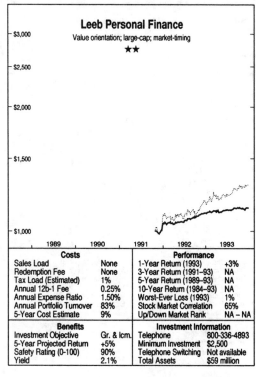

Leeb Personal Finance
Value orientation; large-cap; market-timing
★★

Costs		Performance	
Sales Load	None	1-Year Return (1993)	+3%
Redemption Fee	None	3-Year Return (1991–93)	NA
Tax Load (Estimated)	1%	5-Year Return (1989–93)	NA
Annual 12b-1 Fee	0.25%	10-Year Return (1984–93)	NA
Annual Expense Ratio	1.50%	Worst-Ever Loss (1993)	1%
Annual Portfolio Turnover	83%	Stock Market Correlation	65%
5-Year Cost Estimate	9%	Up/Down Market Rank	NA – NA

Benefits		Investment Information	
Investment Objective	Gr. & Icm.	Telephone	800-336-4893
5-Year Projected Return	+5%	Minimum Investment	$2,500
Safety Rating (0-100)	90%	Telephone Switching	Not available
Yield	2.1%	Total Assets	$59 million

Legg Mason Total Return
Dividend-paying securities
★★

Costs		Performance	
Sales Load	None	1-Year Return (1993)	+14%
Redemption Fee	None	3-Year Return (1991–93)	+83%
Tax Load (Estimated)	4%	5-Year Return (1989–93)	+77%
Annual 12b-1 Fee	1.00%	10-Year Return (1984–93)	NA
Annual Expense Ratio	1.95%	Worst-Ever Loss (1987)	32%
Annual Portfolio Turnover	37%	Stock Market Correlation	63%
5-Year Cost Estimate	13%	Up/Down Market Rank	D – D

Benefits		Investment Information	
Investment Objective	Gr. & Icm.	Telephone	800-822-5544
5-Year Projected Return	+21%	Minimum Investment	$1,000
Safety Rating (0-100)	81%	Telephone Switching	4 per yr; free
Yield	2.4%	Total Assets	$160 million

Legg Mason Value Trust
Undervalued stocks

S&P 500

Fund

| | | 1989 | 1990 | 1991 | 1992 | 1993 |

Costs		Performance	
Sales Load	None	1-Year Return (1993)	+10%
Redemption Fee	None	3-Year Return (1991–93)	+65%
Tax Load (Estimated)	9%	5-Year Return (1989–93)	+65%
Annual 12b-1 Fee	1.00%	10-Year Return (1984–93)	+213%
Annual Expense Ratio	1.86%	Worst-Ever Loss (1987)	34%
Annual Portfolio Turnover	32%	Stock Market Correlation	72%
5-Year Cost Estimate	16%	Up/Down Market Rank	C – C

Benefits		Investment Information	
Investment Objective	Growth	Telephone	800-822-5544
5-Year Projected Return	+4%	Minimum Investment	$1,000
Safety Rating (0-100)	73%	Telephone Switching	4 per yr; free
Yield	0.9%	Total Assets	$882 million

Lexington Global
Foreign & U.S. - diversified stocks

| | | 1989 | 1990 | 1991 | 1992 | 1993 |

Costs		Performance	
Sales Load	None	1-Year Return (1993)	+32%
Redemption Fee	None	3-Year Return (1991–93)	+47%
Tax Load (Estimated)	3%	5-Year Return (1989–93)	+53%
Annual 12b-1 Fee	None	10-Year Return (1984–93)	NA
Annual Expense Ratio	1.52%	Worst-Ever Loss (1990)	22%
Annual Portfolio Turnover	74%	Stock Market Correlation	30%
5-Year Cost Estimate	11%	Up/Down Market Rank	E – B

Benefits		Investment Information	
Investment Objective	Growth	Telephone	800-526-0056
5-Year Projected Return	NA	Minimum Investment	$1,000
Safety Rating (0-100)	70%	Telephone Switching	1 per wk; free
Yield	0.4%	Total Assets	$89 million

Lexington Goldfund
Gold stocks and bullion

| | | 1989 | 1990 | 1991 | 1992 | 1993 |

Costs		Performance	
Sales Load	None	1-Year Return (1993)	+87%
Redemption Fee	None	3-Year Return (1991–93)	+40%
Tax Load (Estimated)	5%	5-Year Return (1989–93)	+37%
Annual 12b-1 Fee	0.25%	10-Year Return (1984–93)	+94%
Annual Expense Ratio	1.77%	Worst-Ever Loss (1987-93)	52%
Annual Portfolio Turnover	18%	Stock Market Correlation	0%
5-Year Cost Estimate	11%	Up/Down Market Rank	E – A

Benefits		Investment Information	
Investment Objective	Growth	Telephone	800-526-0056
5-Year Projected Return	NA	Minimum Investment	$1,000
Safety Rating (0-100)	53%	Telephone Switching	1 per wk; free
Yield	0.2%	Total Assets	$131 million

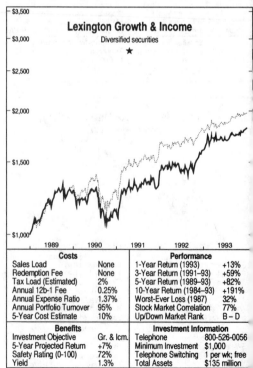

Lexington Growth & Income
Diversified securities
★

| | | 1989 | 1990 | 1991 | 1992 | 1993 |

Costs		Performance	
Sales Load	None	1-Year Return (1993)	+13%
Redemption Fee	None	3-Year Return (1991–93)	+59%
Tax Load (Estimated)	2%	5-Year Return (1989–93)	+82%
Annual 12b-1 Fee	0.25%	10-Year Return (1984–93)	+191%
Annual Expense Ratio	1.37%	Worst-Ever Loss (1987)	32%
Annual Portfolio Turnover	95%	Stock Market Correlation	77%
5-Year Cost Estimate	10%	Up/Down Market Rank	B – D

Benefits		Investment Information	
Investment Objective	Gr. & Icm.	Telephone	800-526-0056
5-Year Projected Return	+7%	Minimum Investment	$1,000
Safety Rating (0-100)	72%	Telephone Switching	1 per wk; free
Yield	1.3%	Total Assets	$135 million

Lexington Strategic Invstmnts
South African gold stocks

Costs		Performance	
Sales Load	6.1%	1-Year Return (1993)	+270%
Redemption Fee	None	3-Year Return (1991–93)	+18%
Tax Load (Estimated)	Neg.	5-Year Return (1989–93)	+9%
Annual 12b-1 Fee	None	10-Year Return (1984–93)	–54%
Annual Expense Ratio	2.50%	Worst-Ever Loss (1984–93)	90%
Annual Portfolio Turnover	0%	Stock Market Correlation	1%
5-Year Cost Estimate	20%	Up/Down Market Rank	E – B

Benefits		Investment Information	
Investment Objective	Gr. & Icm.	Telephone	800-526-0056
5-Year Projected Return	NA	Minimum Investment	$1,000
Safety Rating (0-100)	12%	Telephone Switching	1 per wk; free
Yield	1.3%	Total Assets	$46 million

Lexington Worldwide Emrg Mkts
Foreign & U.S. - emerging markets
★★

Costs		Performance	
Sales Load	None	1-Year Return (1993)	+63%
Redemption Fee	None	3-Year Return (1991–93)	+111%
Tax Load (Estimated)	3%	5-Year Return (1989–93)	+128%
Annual 12b-1 Fee	None	10-Year Return (1984–93)	+241%
Annual Expense Ratio	1.89%	Worst-Ever Loss (1981–82)	37%
Annual Portfolio Turnover	130%	Stock Market Correlation	36%
5-Year Cost Estimate	14%	Up/Down Market Rank	B – E

Benefits		Investment Information	
Investment Objective	Growth	Telephone	800-526-0056
5-Year Projected Return	NA	Minimum Investment	$1,000
Safety Rating (0-100)	75%	Telephone Switching	1 per wk; free
Yield	0.0%	Total Assets	$52 million

Lexington Strategic Silver
Silver stocks

Costs		Performance	
Sales Load	6.1%	1-Year Return (1993)	+77%
Redemption Fee	None	3-Year Return (1991–93)	+34%
Tax Load (Estimated)	Neg.	5-Year Return (1989–93)	+5%
Annual 12b-1 Fee	None	10-Year Return (1984–93)	NA
Annual Expense Ratio	2.60%	Worst-Ever Loss (1987–93)	70%
Annual Portfolio Turnover	19%	Stock Market Correlation	0%
5-Year Cost Estimate	21%	Up/Down Market Rank	E – B

Benefits		Investment Information	
Investment Objective	Growth	Telephone	800-526-0056
5-Year Projected Return	NA	Minimum Investment	$1,000
Safety Rating (0-100)	43%	Telephone Switching	1 per wk; free
Yield	0.0%	Total Assets	$23 million

Liberty All-Star Equity
Five independent portfolio managers
★★

Costs		Performance	
Sales Load	None	1-Year Return (1993)	+10%
Redemption Fee	None	3-Year Return (1991–93)	+93%
Tax Load (Estimated)	8%	5-Year Return (1989–93)	+158%
Annual 12b-1 Fee	None	10-Year Return (1984–93)	NA
Annual Expense Ratio	1.09%	Worst-Ever Loss (1987)	44%
Annual Portfolio Turnover	60%	Stock Market Correlation	20%
5-Year Cost Estimate	17%	Up/Down Market Rank	A – C

Benefits		Investment Information	
Investment Objective	Gr. & Icm.	Telephone	800-542-3863
5-Year Projected Return	+15%	Minimum Investment	None
Safety Rating (0-100)	69%	Telephone Switching	Via broker
Yield	7.4%	Total Assets	$669 million

Liberty American Leaders
High-quality stocks

(S&P 500 / Fund chart, $1,000–$3,000 scale, 1989–1993)

Costs		Performance	
Sales Load	4.7%	1-Year Return (1993)	+12%
Redemption Fee	None	3-Year Return (1991–93)	+64%
Tax Load (Estimated)	5%	5-Year Return (1989–93)	+81%
Annual 12b-1 Fee	0.25%	10-Year Return (1984–93)	+260%
Annual Expense Ratio	1.19%	Worst-Ever Loss (1987)	24%
Annual Portfolio Turnover	39%	Stock Market Correlation	81%
5-Year Cost Estimate	15%	Up/Down Market Rank	D – B

Benefits		Investment Information	
Investment Objective	Gr. & Icm.	Telephone	800-245-4770
5-Year Projected Return	+15%	Minimum Investment	$500
Safety Rating (0-100)	76%	Telephone Switching	Unlimited;free
Yield	1.6%	Total Assets	$201 million

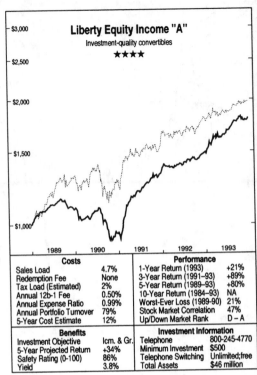

Liberty Equity Income "A"
Investment-quality convertibles
★★★★

(Fund chart, $1,000–$3,000 scale, 1989–1993)

Costs		Performance	
Sales Load	4.7%	1-Year Return (1993)	+21%
Redemption Fee	None	3-Year Return (1991–93)	+89%
Tax Load (Estimated)	2%	5-Year Return (1989–93)	+80%
Annual 12b-1 Fee	0.50%	10-Year Return (1984–93)	NA
Annual Expense Ratio	0.99%	Worst-Ever Loss (1989-90)	21%
Annual Portfolio Turnover	79%	Stock Market Correlation	47%
5-Year Cost Estimate	12%	Up/Down Market Rank	D – A

Benefits		Investment Information	
Investment Objective	Icm. & Gr.	Telephone	800-245-4770
5-Year Projected Return	+34%	Minimum Investment	$500
Safety Rating (0-100)	86%	Telephone Switching	Unlimited;free
Yield	3.8%	Total Assets	$46 million

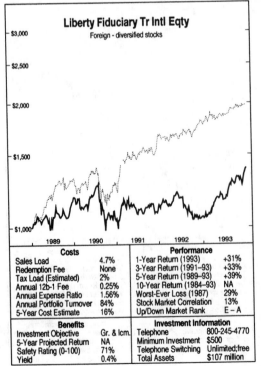

Liberty Fiduciary Tr Intl Eqty
Foreign - diversified stocks

(Fund chart, $1,000–$3,000 scale, 1989–1993)

Costs		Performance	
Sales Load	4.7%	1-Year Return (1993)	+31%
Redemption Fee	None	3-Year Return (1991–93)	+33%
Tax Load (Estimated)	2%	5-Year Return (1989–93)	+39%
Annual 12b-1 Fee	0.25%	10-Year Return (1984–93)	NA
Annual Expense Ratio	1.56%	Worst-Ever Loss (1987)	29%
Annual Portfolio Turnover	84%	Stock Market Correlation	13%
5-Year Cost Estimate	16%	Up/Down Market Rank	E – A

Benefits		Investment Information	
Investment Objective	Gr. & Icm.	Telephone	800-245-4770
5-Year Projected Return	NA	Minimum Investment	$500
Safety Rating (0-100)	71%	Telephone Switching	Unlimited;free
Yield	0.4%	Total Assets	$107 million

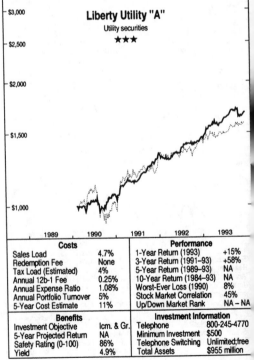

Liberty Utility "A"
Utility securities
★★★

(Fund chart, $1,000–$3,000 scale, 1989–1993)

Costs		Performance	
Sales Load	4.7%	1-Year Return (1993)	+15%
Redemption Fee	None	3-Year Return (1991–93)	+58%
Tax Load (Estimated)	4%	5-Year Return (1989–93)	NA
Annual 12b-1 Fee	0.25%	10-Year Return (1984–93)	NA
Annual Expense Ratio	1.08%	Worst-Ever Loss (1990)	8%
Annual Portfolio Turnover	5%	Stock Market Correlation	45%
5-Year Cost Estimate	11%	Up/Down Market Rank	NA – NA

Benefits		Investment Information	
Investment Objective	Icm. & Gr.	Telephone	800-245-4770
5-Year Projected Return	NA	Minimum Investment	$500
Safety Rating (0-100)	86%	Telephone Switching	Unlimited;free
Yield	4.9%	Total Assets	$955 million

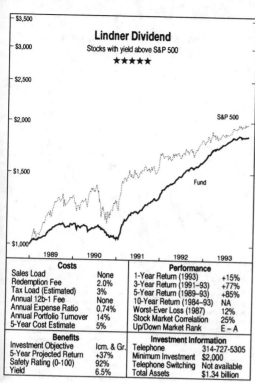

Lindner Dividend

Stocks with yield above S&P 500

★★★★★

Costs		Performance	
Sales Load	None	1-Year Return (1993)	+15%
Redemption Fee	2.0%	3-Year Return (1991–93)	+77%
Tax Load (Estimated)	3%	5-Year Return (1989–93)	+85%
Annual 12b-1 Fee	None	10-Year Return (1984–93)	NA
Annual Expense Ratio	0.74%	Worst-Ever Loss (1987)	12%
Annual Portfolio Turnover	14%	Stock Market Correlation	25%
5-Year Cost Estimate	5%	Up/Down Market Rank	E – A

Benefits		Investment Information	
Investment Objective	Icm. & Gr.	Telephone	314-727-5305
5-Year Projected Return	+37%	Minimum Investment	$2,000
Safety Rating (0-100)	92%	Telephone Switching	Not available
Yield	6.5%	Total Assets	$1.34 billion

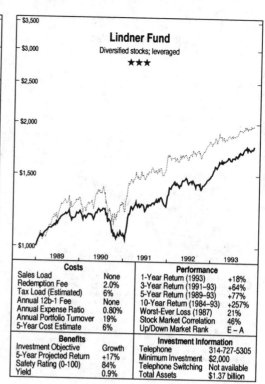

Lindner Fund

Diversified stocks; leveraged

★★★

Costs		Performance	
Sales Load	None	1-Year Return (1993)	+18%
Redemption Fee	2.0%	3-Year Return (1991–93)	+64%
Tax Load (Estimated)	6%	5-Year Return (1989–93)	+77%
Annual 12b-1 Fee	None	10-Year Return (1984–93)	+257%
Annual Expense Ratio	0.80%	Worst-Ever Loss (1987)	21%
Annual Portfolio Turnover	19%	Stock Market Correlation	46%
5-Year Cost Estimate	6%	Up/Down Market Rank	E – A

Benefits		Investment Information	
Investment Objective	Growth	Telephone	314-727-5305
5-Year Projected Return	+17%	Minimum Investment	$2,000
Safety Rating (0-100)	84%	Telephone Switching	Not available
Yield	0.9%	Total Assets	$1.37 billion

LMH

Benjamin Graham fundamental analysis

Costs		Performance	
Sales Load	None	1-Year Return (1993)	+7%
Redemption Fee	None	3-Year Return (1991–93)	+38%
Tax Load (Estimated)	11%	5-Year Return (1989–93)	+26%
Annual 12b-1 Fee	None	10-Year Return (1984–93)	NA
Annual Expense Ratio	2.50%	Worst-Ever Loss (1989-90)	34%
Annual Portfolio Turnover	76%	Stock Market Correlation	69%
5-Year Cost Estimate	28%	Up/Down Market Rank	E – B

Benefits		Investment Information	
Investment Objective	Gr. & Icm.	Telephone	800-338-1579
5-Year Projected Return	–12%	Minimum Investment	$1,000
Safety Rating (0-100)	69%	Telephone Switching	Unlimited; $5
Yield	0.0%	Total Assets	$7 million

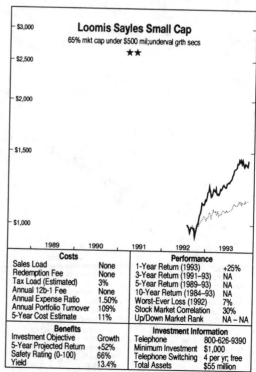

Loomis Sayles Small Cap

65% mkt cap under $500 mil; underval grth secs

★★

Costs		Performance	
Sales Load	None	1-Year Return (1993)	+25%
Redemption Fee	None	3-Year Return (1991–93)	NA
Tax Load (Estimated)	3%	5-Year Return (1989–93)	NA
Annual 12b-1 Fee	None	10-Year Return (1984–93)	NA
Annual Expense Ratio	1.50%	Worst-Ever Loss (1992)	7%
Annual Portfolio Turnover	109%	Stock Market Correlation	30%
5-Year Cost Estimate	11%	Up/Down Market Rank	NA – NA

Benefits		Investment Information	
Investment Objective	Growth	Telephone	800-626-9390
5-Year Projected Return	+52%	Minimum Investment	$1,000
Safety Rating (0-100)	66%	Telephone Switching	4 per yr; free
Yield	13.4%	Total Assets	$55 million

Lord, Abbett Affiliated
Large; undervalued stocks
★

S&P 500

Fund

Costs		Performance	
Sales Load	6.1%	1-Year Return (1993)	+13%
Redemption Fee	None	3-Year Return (1991–93)	+55%
Tax Load (Estimated)	4%	5-Year Return (1989–93)	+81%
Annual 12b-1 Fee	0.25%	10-Year Return (1984–93)	+244%
Annual Expense Ratio	0.60%	Worst-Ever Loss (1987)	31%
Annual Portfolio Turnover	46%	Stock Market Correlation	84%
5-Year Cost Estimate	13%	Up/Down Market Rank	C – C

Benefits		Investment Information	
Investment Objective	Gr. & Icm.	Telephone	800-821-5129
5-Year Projected Return	+5%	Minimum Investment	$250
Safety Rating (0-100)	76%	Telephone Switching	Unlimited;free
Yield	3.1%	Total Assets	$3.89 billion

Lord, Abbett Developing Growth
Emerging growth stocks

Costs		Performance	
Sales Load	6.1%	1-Year Return (1993)	+13%
Redemption Fee	None	3-Year Return (1991–93)	+71%
Tax Load (Estimated)	14%	5-Year Return (1989–93)	+82%
Annual 12b-1 Fee	0.25%	10-Year Return (1984–93)	+70%
Annual Expense Ratio	1.31%	Worst-Ever Loss (1987)	38%
Annual Portfolio Turnover	17%	Stock Market Correlation	49%
5-Year Cost Estimate	18%	Up/Down Market Rank	B – E

Benefits		Investment Information	
Investment Objective	Growth	Telephone	800-821-5129
5-Year Projected Return	+12%	Minimum Investment	$1,000
Safety Rating (0-100)	66%	Telephone Switching	Unlimited;free
Yield	0.0%	Total Assets	$139 million

Lord, Abbett Equity 1990
Large seasoned cos; ret $10 a share May 2000
★★

Costs		Performance	
Sales Load	5.8%	1-Year Return (1993)	+14%
Redemption Fee	None	3-Year Return (1991–93)	+48%
Tax Load (Estimated)	2%	5-Year Return (1989–93)	NA
Annual 12b-1 Fee	0.25%	10-Year Return (1984–93)	NA
Annual Expense Ratio	1.80%	Worst-Ever Loss (1990)	11%
Annual Portfolio Turnover	28%	Stock Market Correlation	72%
5-Year Cost Estimate	17%	Up/Down Market Rank	NA – NA

Benefits		Investment Information	
Investment Objective	Gr. & Icm.	Telephone	800-821-5129
5-Year Projected Return	+17%	Minimum Investment	$1,000
Safety Rating (0-100)	81%	Telephone Switching	Unlimited;free
Yield	2.0%	Total Assets	$58 million

Lord, Abbett Fundamental Value
Undervalued stocks
★★

Costs		Performance	
Sales Load	6.1%	1-Year Return (1993)	+14%
Redemption Fee	None	3-Year Return (1991–93)	+52%
Tax Load (Estimated)	2%	5-Year Return (1989–93)	+96%
Annual 12b-1 Fee	0.25%	10-Year Return (1984–93)	NA
Annual Expense Ratio	1.60%	Worst-Ever Loss (1987)	31%
Annual Portfolio Turnover	82%	Stock Market Correlation	79%
5-Year Cost Estimate	17%	Up/Down Market Rank	C – B

Benefits		Investment Information	
Investment Objective	Gr. & Icm.	Telephone	800-821-5129
5-Year Projected Return	+10%	Minimum Investment	$1,000
Safety Rating (0-100)	77%	Telephone Switching	Unlimited;free
Yield	1.5%	Total Assets	$32 million

Lord, Abbett Global Equity
Foreign & U.S. - diversified stocks

S&P 500

Fund

1989	1990	1991	1992	1993

Costs		Performance	
Sales Load	6.1%	1-Year Return (1993)	+26%
Redemption Fee	None	3-Year Return (1991–93)	+42%
Tax Load (Estimated)	0%	5-Year Return (1989–93)	+47%
Annual 12b-1 Fee	0.25%	10-Year Return (1984–93)	NA
Annual Expense Ratio	1.84%	Worst-Ever Loss (1990)	21%
Annual Portfolio Turnover	137%	Stock Market Correlation	26%
5-Year Cost Estimate	17%	Up/Down Market Rank	E – B

Benefits		Investment Information	
Investment Objective	Growth	Telephone	800-821-5129
5-Year Projected Return	NA	Minimum Investment	$1,000
Safety Rating (0-100)	74%	Telephone Switching	Unlimited;free
Yield	1.2%	Total Assets	$58 million

Lord, Abbett Value Appreciatn
Undervalued stocks
★

1989	1990	1991	1992	1993

Costs		Performance	
Sales Load	6.1%	1-Year Return (1993)	+14%
Redemption Fee	None	3-Year Return (1991–93)	+65%
Tax Load (Estimated)	6%	5-Year Return (1989–93)	+89%
Annual 12b-1 Fee	0.25%	10-Year Return (1984–93)	+225%
Annual Expense Ratio	1.22%	Worst-Ever Loss (1987)	33%
Annual Portfolio Turnover	63%	Stock Market Correlation	73%
5-Year Cost Estimate	20%	Up/Down Market Rank	C – C

Benefits		Investment Information	
Investment Objective	Growth	Telephone	800-821-5129
5-Year Projected Return	+14%	Minimum Investment	$1,000
Safety Rating (0-100)	77%	Telephone Switching	Unlimited;free
Yield	1.6%	Total Assets	$199 million

Lutheran Brotherhood
Stocks of 100 leading companies

1989	1990	1991	1992	1993

Costs		Performance	
Sales Load	5.3%	1-Year Return (1993)	+9%
Redemption Fee	None	3-Year Return (1991–93)	+50%
Tax Load (Estimated)	0%	5-Year Return (1989–93)	+86%
Annual 12b-1 Fee	None	10-Year Return (1984–93)	+226%
Annual Expense Ratio	1.10%	Worst-Ever Loss (1987)	32%
Annual Portfolio Turnover	249%	Stock Market Correlation	89%
5-Year Cost Estimate	11%	Up/Down Market Rank	C – C

Benefits		Investment Information	
Investment Objective	Gr. & Icm.	Telephone	800-328-4552
5-Year Projected Return	+3%	Minimum Investment	$500
Safety Rating (0-100)	71%	Telephone Switching	Unlimited; $10
Yield	2.0%	Total Assets	$517 million

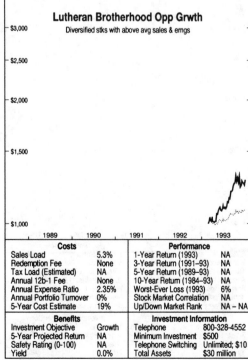

Lutheran Brotherhood Opp Grwth
Diversified stks with above avg sales & erngs

1989	1990	1991	1992	1993

Costs		Performance	
Sales Load	5.3%	1-Year Return (1993)	NA
Redemption Fee	None	3-Year Return (1991–93)	NA
Tax Load (Estimated)	NA	5-Year Return (1989–93)	NA
Annual 12b-1 Fee	None	10-Year Return (1984–93)	NA
Annual Expense Ratio	2.35%	Worst-Ever Loss (1993)	6%
Annual Portfolio Turnover	0%	Stock Market Correlation	NA
5-Year Cost Estimate	19%	Up/Down Market Rank	NA – NA

Benefits		Investment Information	
Investment Objective	Growth	Telephone	800-328-4552
5-Year Projected Return	NA	Minimum Investment	$500
Safety Rating (0-100)	NA	Telephone Switching	Unlimited; $10
Yield	0.0%	Total Assets	$30 million

EQUITY

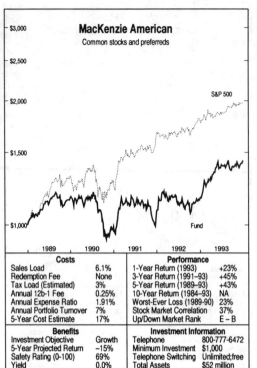

MacKenzie American
Common stocks and preferreds

S&P 500

Fund

Costs		Performance	
Sales Load	6.1%	1-Year Return (1993)	+23%
Redemption Fee	None	3-Year Return (1991–93)	+45%
Tax Load (Estimated)	3%	5-Year Return (1989–93)	+43%
Annual 12b-1 Fee	0.25%	10-Year Return (1984–93)	NA
Annual Expense Ratio	1.91%	Worst-Ever Loss (1989-90)	23%
Annual Portfolio Turnover	7%	Stock Market Correlation	37%
5-Year Cost Estimate	17%	Up/Down Market Rank	E – B

Benefits		Investment Information	
Investment Objective	Growth	Telephone	800-777-6472
5-Year Projected Return	–15%	Minimum Investment	$1,000
Safety Rating (0-100)	69%	Telephone Switching	Unlimited;free
Yield	0.0%	Total Assets	$52 million

MacKenzie Canada
Foreign - Canadian stocks

Costs		Performance	
Sales Load	6.1%	1-Year Return (1993)	+60%
Redemption Fee	None	3-Year Return (1991–93)	+36%
Tax Load (Estimated)	1%	5-Year Return (1989–93)	+18%
Annual 12b-1 Fee	0.40%	10-Year Return (1984–93)	NA
Annual Expense Ratio	2.63%	Worst-Ever Loss (1990-92)	38%
Annual Portfolio Turnover	32%	Stock Market Correlation	3%
5-Year Cost Estimate	22%	Up/Down Market Rank	E – A

Benefits		Investment Information	
Investment Objective	Growth	Telephone	800-777-6472
5-Year Projected Return	NA	Minimum Investment	$1,000
Safety Rating (0-100)	75%	Telephone Switching	Unlimited;free
Yield	0.0%	Total Assets	$34 million

Mackenzie Ivy Emer Growth "A"
Small-medium sized emerging growth stocks

Costs		Performance	
Sales Load	6.1%	1-Year Return (1993)	NA
Redemption Fee	None	3-Year Return (1991–93)	NA
Tax Load (Estimated)	0%	5-Year Return (1989–93)	NA
Annual 12b-1 Fee	0.25%	10-Year Return (1984–93)	NA
Annual Expense Ratio	1.94%	Worst-Ever Loss (1993)	5%
Annual Portfolio Turnover	82%	Stock Market Correlation	NA
5-Year Cost Estimate	17%	Up/Down Market Rank	NA – NA

Benefits		Investment Information	
Investment Objective	Gr. & Icm.	Telephone	800-777-6472
5-Year Projected Return	NA	Minimum Investment	$1,000
Safety Rating (0-100)	NA	Telephone Switching	Unlimited;free
Yield	0.0%	Total Assets	$15 million

Mackenzie Ivy Growth
Diversified stocks

Costs		Performance	
Sales Load	6.1%	1-Year Return (1993)	+12%
Redemption Fee	None	3-Year Return (1991–93)	+54%
Tax Load (Estimated)	1%	5-Year Return (1989–93)	+88%
Annual 12b-1 Fee	0.25%	10-Year Return (1984–93)	+240%
Annual Expense Ratio	1.32%	Worst-Ever Loss (1987)	27%
Annual Portfolio Turnover	78%	Stock Market Correlation	79%
5-Year Cost Estimate	14%	Up/Down Market Rank	C – B

Benefits		Investment Information	
Investment Objective	Growth	Telephone	800-777-6472
5-Year Projected Return	+3%	Minimum Investment	$1,000
Safety Rating (0-100)	71%	Telephone Switching	Unlimited;free
Yield	0.5%	Total Assets	$260 million

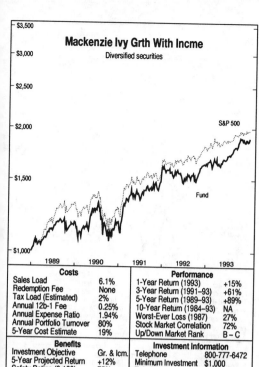

Mackenzie Ivy Grth With Incme
Diversified securities

S&P 500

Fund

Costs		Performance	
Sales Load	6.1%	1-Year Return (1993)	+15%
Redemption Fee	None	3-Year Return (1991–93)	+61%
Tax Load (Estimated)	2%	5-Year Return (1989–93)	+89%
Annual 12b-1 Fee	0.25%	10-Year Return (1984–93)	NA
Annual Expense Ratio	1.94%	Worst-Ever Loss (1987)	27%
Annual Portfolio Turnover	80%	Stock Market Correlation	72%
5-Year Cost Estimate	19%	Up/Down Market Rank	B – C

Benefits		Investment Information	
Investment Objective	Gr. & Icm.	Telephone	800-777-6472
5-Year Projected Return	+12%	Minimum Investment	$1,000
Safety Rating (0-100)	75%	Telephone Switching	Unlimited;free
Yield	1.5%	Total Assets	$28 million

Mackenzie Ivy International
Foreign - diversified stocks

Costs		Performance	
Sales Load	6.1%	1-Year Return (1993)	+48%
Redemption Fee	None	3-Year Return (1991–93)	+73%
Tax Load (Estimated)	5%	5-Year Return (1989–93)	+93%
Annual 12b-1 Fee	0.25%	10-Year Return (1984–93)	NA
Annual Expense Ratio	1.71%	Worst-Ever Loss (1987)	31%
Annual Portfolio Turnover	17%	Stock Market Correlation	13%
5-Year Cost Estimate	17%	Up/Down Market Rank	E – B

Benefits		Investment Information	
Investment Objective	Growth	Telephone	800-777-6472
5-Year Projected Return	NA	Minimum Investment	$1,000
Safety Rating (0-100)	74%	Telephone Switching	Unlimited;free
Yield	0.2%	Total Assets	$123 million

Mackenzie North American
U.S. & Canadian; 60% bonds, 40% stocks

Costs		Performance	
Sales Load	6.1%	1-Year Return (1993)	+14%
Redemption Fee	None	3-Year Return (1991–93)	+40%
Tax Load (Estimated)	Neg.	5-Year Return (1989–93)	+45%
Annual 12b-1 Fee	0.25%	10-Year Return (1984–93)	NA
Annual Expense Ratio	1.72%	Worst-Ever Loss (1989-90)	17%
Annual Portfolio Turnover	149%	Stock Market Correlation	63%
5-Year Cost Estimate	16%	Up/Down Market Rank	E – B

Benefits		Investment Information	
Investment Objective	Icm. & Gr.	Telephone	800-777-6472
5-Year Projected Return	–8%	Minimum Investment	$1,000
Safety Rating (0-100)	80%	Telephone Switching	Unlimited;free
Yield	4.9%	Total Assets	$39 million

MainStay - Cap. Appreciation
Growth companies
★

Costs		Performance	
Sales Load	None	1-Year Return (1993)	+14%
Redemption Fee	5.3%	3-Year Return (1991–93)	+113%
Tax Load (Estimated)	0%	5-Year Return (1989–93)	+180%
Annual 12b-1 Fee	1.00%	10-Year Return (1984–93)	NA
Annual Expense Ratio	1.99%	Worst-Ever Loss (1987)	39%
Annual Portfolio Turnover	157%	Stock Market Correlation	51%
5-Year Cost Estimate	12%	Up/Down Market Rank	A – E

Benefits		Investment Information	
Investment Objective	Growth	Telephone	800-522-4202
5-Year Projected Return	+57%	Minimum Investment	$500
Safety Rating (0-100)	64%	Telephone Switching	See prospectus
Yield	0.0%	Total Assets	$279 million

MainStay - Convertible
Convertible securities
★★★★

S&P 500

Fund

Costs		Performance	
Sales Load	None	1-Year Return (1993)	+24%
Redemption Fee	5.3%	3-Year Return (1991–93)	+109%
Tax Load (Estimated)	Neg.	5-Year Return (1989–93)	+106%
Annual 12b-1 Fee	1.00%	10-Year Return (1984–93)	NA
Annual Expense Ratio	2.27%	Worst-Ever Loss (1987)	17%
Annual Portfolio Turnover	291%	Stock Market Correlation	56%
5-Year Cost Estimate	13%	Up/Down Market Rank	D – B

Benefits		Investment Information	
Investment Objective	Gr. & Icm.	Telephone	800-522-4202
5-Year Projected Return	+45%	Minimum Investment	$500
Safety Rating (0-100)	83%	Telephone Switching	See prospectus
Yield	3.7%	Total Assets	$59 million

MainStay - Global
Foreign & U.S. - diversified stocks

Costs		Performance	
Sales Load	None	1-Year Return (1993)	+25%
Redemption Fee	5.3%	3-Year Return (1991–93)	+29%
Tax Load (Estimated)	0%	5-Year Return (1989–93)	+23%
Annual 12b-1 Fee	1.00%	10-Year Return (1984–93)	NA
Annual Expense Ratio	2.80%	Worst-Ever Loss (1990)	22%
Annual Portfolio Turnover	136%	Stock Market Correlation	31%
5-Year Cost Estimate	16%	Up/Down Market Rank	E – A

Benefits		Investment Information	
Investment Objective	Gr. & Icm.	Telephone	800-522-4202
5-Year Projected Return	NA	Minimum Investment	$500
Safety Rating (0-100)	70%	Telephone Switching	See prospectu
Yield	0.0%	Total Assets	$26 million

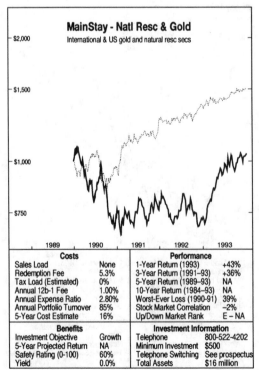

MainStay - Natl Resc & Gold
International & US gold and natural resc secs

Costs		Performance	
Sales Load	None	1-Year Return (1993)	+43%
Redemption Fee	5.3%	3-Year Return (1991–93)	+36%
Tax Load (Estimated)	0%	5-Year Return (1989–93)	NA
Annual 12b-1 Fee	1.00%	10-Year Return (1984–93)	NA
Annual Expense Ratio	2.80%	Worst-Ever Loss (1990-91)	39%
Annual Portfolio Turnover	85%	Stock Market Correlation	-2%
5-Year Cost Estimate	16%	Up/Down Market Rank	E – NA

Benefits		Investment Information	
Investment Objective	Growth	Telephone	800-522-4202
5-Year Projected Return	NA	Minimum Investment	$500
Safety Rating (0-100)	60%	Telephone Switching	See prospectus
Yield	0.0%	Total Assets	$16 million

MainStay - Total Return
Minimum 30% stocks, 30% bonds
★★

Costs		Performance	
Sales Load	None	1-Year Return (1993)	+10%
Redemption Fee	5.3%	3-Year Return (1991–93)	+57%
Tax Load (Estimated)	1%	5-Year Return (1989–93)	+89%
Annual 12b-1 Fee	1.00%	10-Year Return (1984–93)	NA
Annual Expense Ratio	2.01%	Worst-Ever Loss (1992)	12%
Annual Portfolio Turnover	316%	Stock Market Correlation	58%
5-Year Cost Estimate	13%	Up/Down Market Rank	C – B

Benefits		Investment Information	
Investment Objective	Icm. & Gr.	Telephone	800-522-4202
5-Year Projected Return	+29%	Minimum Investment	$500
Safety Rating (0-100)	80%	Telephone Switching	See prospectu
Yield	2.4%	Total Assets	$484 million

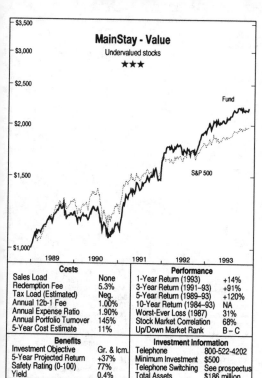

MainStay - Value
Undervalued stocks
★★★

Fund

S&P 500

Costs		**Performance**		
Sales Load	None	1-Year Return (1993)	+14%	
Redemption Fee	5.3%	3-Year Return (1991–93)	+91%	
Tax Load (Estimated)	Neg.	5-Year Return (1989–93)	+120%	
Annual 12b-1 Fee	1.00%	10-Year Return (1984–93)	NA	
Annual Expense Ratio	1.90%	Worst-Ever Loss (1987)	31%	
Annual Portfolio Turnover	145%	Stock Market Correlation	68%	
5-Year Cost Estimate	11%	Up/Down Market Rank	B – C	
Benefits		**Investment Information**		
Investment Objective	Gr. & Icm.	Telephone	800-522-4202	
5-Year Projected Return	+37%	Minimum Investment	$500	
Safety Rating (0-100)	77%	Telephone Switching	See prospectus	
Yield	0.4%	Total Assets	$186 million	

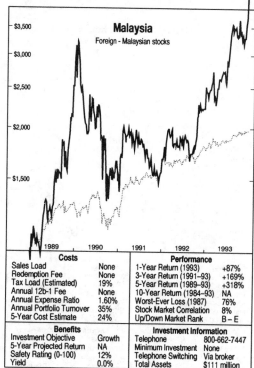

Malaysia
Foreign - Malaysian stocks

Costs		**Performance**		
Sales Load	None	1-Year Return (1993)	+87%	
Redemption Fee	None	3-Year Return (1991–93)	+169%	
Tax Load (Estimated)	19%	5-Year Return (1989–93)	+318%	
Annual 12b-1 Fee	None	10-Year Return (1984–93)	NA	
Annual Expense Ratio	1.60%	Worst-Ever Loss (1987)	76%	
Annual Portfolio Turnover	35%	Stock Market Correlation	8%	
5-Year Cost Estimate	24%	Up/Down Market Rank	B – E	
Benefits		**Investment Information**		
Investment Objective	Growth	Telephone	800-662-7447	
5-Year Projected Return	NA	Minimum Investment	None	
Safety Rating (0-100)	12%	Telephone Switching	Via broker	
Yield	0.0%	Total Assets	$111 million	

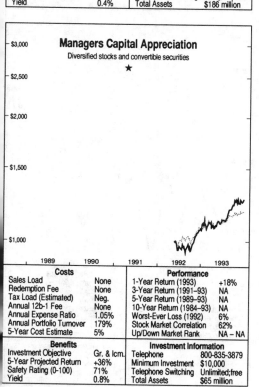

Managers Capital Appreciation
Diversified stocks and convertible securities
★

Costs		**Performance**		
Sales Load	None	1-Year Return (1993)	+18%	
Redemption Fee	None	3-Year Return (1991–93)	NA	
Tax Load (Estimated)	Neg.	5-Year Return (1989–93)	NA	
Annual 12b-1 Fee	None	10-Year Return (1984–93)	NA	
Annual Expense Ratio	1.05%	Worst-Ever Loss (1992)	6%	
Annual Portfolio Turnover	179%	Stock Market Correlation	62%	
5-Year Cost Estimate	5%	Up/Down Market Rank	NA – NA	
Benefits		**Investment Information**		
Investment Objective	Gr. & Icm.	Telephone	800-835-3879	
5-Year Projected Return	+36%	Minimum Investment	$10,000	
Safety Rating (0-100)	71%	Telephone Switching	Unlimited;free	
Yield	0.8%	Total Assets	$65 million	

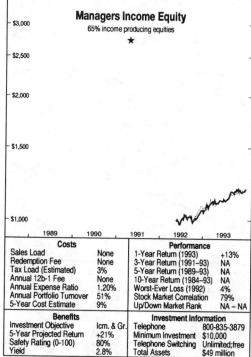

Managers Income Equity
65% income producing equities
★

Costs		**Performance**		
Sales Load	None	1-Year Return (1993)	+13%	
Redemption Fee	None	3-Year Return (1991–93)	NA	
Tax Load (Estimated)	3%	5-Year Return (1989–93)	NA	
Annual 12b-1 Fee	None	10-Year Return (1984–93)	NA	
Annual Expense Ratio	1.20%	Worst-Ever Loss (1992)	4%	
Annual Portfolio Turnover	51%	Stock Market Correlation	79%	
5-Year Cost Estimate	9%	Up/Down Market Rank	NA – NA	
Benefits		**Investment Information**		
Investment Objective	Icm. & Gr.	Telephone	800-835-3879	
5-Year Projected Return	+21%	Minimum Investment	$10,000	
Safety Rating (0-100)	80%	Telephone Switching	Unlimited;free	
Yield	2.8%	Total Assets	$49 million	

EQUITY

Managers Special Equity

High earnings growth; small to med mkt cap

★

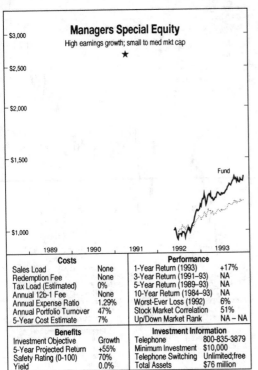

Costs		Performance	
Sales Load	None	1-Year Return (1993)	+17%
Redemption Fee	None	3-Year Return (1991–93)	NA
Tax Load (Estimated)	0%	5-Year Return (1989–93)	NA
Annual 12b-1 Fee	None	10-Year Return (1984–93)	NA
Annual Expense Ratio	1.29%	Worst-Ever Loss (1992)	6%
Annual Portfolio Turnover	47%	Stock Market Correlation	51%
5-Year Cost Estimate	7%	Up/Down Market Rank	NA – NA

Benefits		Investment Information	
Investment Objective	Growth	Telephone	800-835-3879
5-Year Projected Return	+55%	Minimum Investment	$10,000
Safety Rating (0-100)	70%	Telephone Switching	Unlimited;free
Yield	0.0%	Total Assets	$76 million

Marshall Stock

65% established stks; stable erngs & div grth

Costs		Performance	
Sales Load	None	1-Year Return (1993)	+3%
Redemption Fee	None	3-Year Return (1991–93)	NA
Tax Load (Estimated)	0%	5-Year Return (1989–93)	NA
Annual 12b-1 Fee	None	10-Year Return (1984–93)	NA
Annual Expense Ratio	0.98%	Worst-Ever Loss (1993)	7%
Annual Portfolio Turnover	98%	Stock Market Correlation	69%
5-Year Cost Estimate	5%	Up/Down Market Rank	NA – NA

Benefits		Investment Information	
Investment Objective	Gr. & lcm.	Telephone	800-236-8560
5-Year Projected Return	–9%	Minimum Investment	$1,000
Safety Rating (0-100)	65%	Telephone Switching	Unlimited;free
Yield	1.1%	Total Assets	$307 million

Mathers

Diversified stocks

★★★★

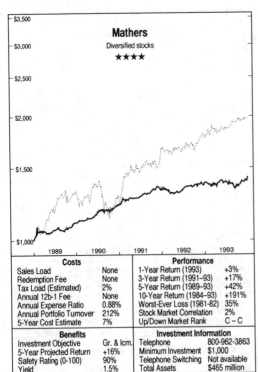

Costs		Performance	
Sales Load	None	1-Year Return (1993)	+3%
Redemption Fee	None	3-Year Return (1991–93)	+17%
Tax Load (Estimated)	2%	5-Year Return (1989–93)	+42%
Annual 12b-1 Fee	None	10-Year Return (1984–93)	+191%
Annual Expense Ratio	0.88%	Worst-Ever Loss (1981-82)	35%
Annual Portfolio Turnover	212%	Stock Market Correlation	2%
5-Year Cost Estimate	7%	Up/Down Market Rank	C – C

Benefits		Investment Information	
Investment Objective	Gr. & lcm.	Telephone	800-962-3863
5-Year Projected Return	+16%	Minimum Investment	$1,000
Safety Rating (0-100)	90%	Telephone Switching	Not available
Yield	1.5%	Total Assets	$465 million

Mentor Growth

Diversified stocks; long term growth

Costs		Performance	
Sales Load	None	1-Year Return (1993)	+16%
Redemption Fee	5.3%	3-Year Return (1991–93)	+101%
Tax Load (Estimated)	8%	5-Year Return (1989–93)	+109%
Annual 12b-1 Fee	1.00%	10-Year Return (1984–93)	NA
Annual Expense Ratio	2.05%	Worst-Ever Loss (1987)	37%
Annual Portfolio Turnover	50%	Stock Market Correlation	51%
5-Year Cost Estimate	20%	Up/Down Market Rank	B – E

Benefits		Investment Information	
Investment Objective	Growth	Telephone	800-321-0038
5-Year Projected Return	+33%	Minimum Investment	$1,000
Safety Rating (0-100)	71%	Telephone Switching	Not available
Yield	0.0%	Total Assets	$169 million

Mentor Strategy
Undervalued stocks, mkt cap above $30-mil

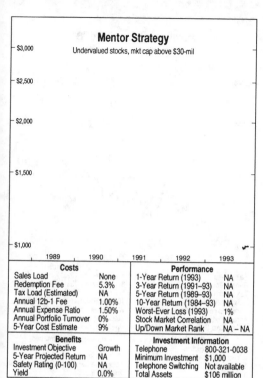

Costs		Performance	
Sales Load	None	1-Year Return (1993)	NA
Redemption Fee	5.3%	3-Year Return (1991–93)	NA
Tax Load (Estimated)	NA	5-Year Return (1989–93)	NA
Annual 12b-1 Fee	1.00%	10-Year Return (1984–93)	NA
Annual Expense Ratio	1.50%	Worst-Ever Loss (1993)	1%
Annual Portfolio Turnover	0%	Stock Market Correlation	NA
5-Year Cost Estimate	9%	Up/Down Market Rank	NA – NA

Benefits		Investment Information	
Investment Objective	Growth	Telephone	800-321-0038
5-Year Projected Return	NA	Minimum Investment	$1,000
Safety Rating (0-100)	NA	Telephone Switching	Not available
Yield	0.0%	Total Assets	$106 million

Merrill Lynch Balanced "B"
Large, high-quality stocks
★★

Costs		Performance	
Sales Load	None	1-Year Return (1993)	+15%
Redemption Fee	4.2%	3-Year Return (1991–93)	+49%
Tax Load (Estimated)	4%	5-Year Return (1989–93)	+69%
Annual 12b-1 Fee	1.00%	10-Year Return (1984–93)	NA
Annual Expense Ratio	1.85%	Worst-Ever Loss (1987)	18%
Annual Portfolio Turnover	67%	Stock Market Correlation	73%
5-Year Cost Estimate	15%	Up/Down Market Rank	E – A

Benefits		Investment Information	
Investment Objective	Icm. & Gr.	Telephone	800-637-3863
5-Year Projected Return	+15%	Minimum Investment	$1,000
Safety Rating (0-100)	83%	Telephone Switching	See prospectus
Yield	2.0%	Total Assets	$882 million

Merrill Lynch Basic Value "A"
Undervalued stocks

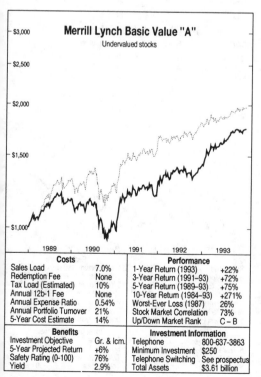

Costs		Performance	
Sales Load	7.0%	1-Year Return (1993)	+22%
Redemption Fee	None	3-Year Return (1991–93)	+72%
Tax Load (Estimated)	10%	5-Year Return (1989–93)	+75%
Annual 12b-1 Fee	None	10-Year Return (1984–93)	+271%
Annual Expense Ratio	0.54%	Worst-Ever Loss (1987)	26%
Annual Portfolio Turnover	21%	Stock Market Correlation	73%
5-Year Cost Estimate	14%	Up/Down Market Rank	C – B

Benefits		Investment Information	
Investment Objective	Gr. & Icm.	Telephone	800-637-3863
5-Year Projected Return	+6%	Minimum Investment	$250
Safety Rating (0-100)	76%	Telephone Switching	See prospectus
Yield	2.9%	Total Assets	$3.61 billion

Merrill Lynch Capital "A"
Diversified securities
★★★

Costs		Performance	
Sales Load	7.0%	1-Year Return (1993)	+14%
Redemption Fee	None	3-Year Return (1991–93)	+54%
Tax Load (Estimated)	2%	5-Year Return (1989–93)	+91%
Annual 12b-1 Fee	None	10-Year Return (1984–93)	+299%
Annual Expense Ratio	0.55%	Worst-Ever Loss (1987)	24%
Annual Portfolio Turnover	59%	Stock Market Correlation	75%
5-Year Cost Estimate	12%	Up/Down Market Rank	D – A

Benefits		Investment Information	
Investment Objective	Gr. & Icm.	Telephone	800-637-3863
5-Year Projected Return	+16%	Minimum Investment	$250
Safety Rating (0-100)	84%	Telephone Switching	See prospectus
Yield	3.4%	Total Assets	$5.14 billion

Merrill Lynch Developing Cap
Foreign - countries with smaller capital mkts
★★

Fund

Costs		Performance	
Sales Load	4.2%	1-Year Return (1993)	+69%
Redemption Fee	2.0%	3-Year Return (1991–93)	+110%
Tax Load (Estimated)	6%	5-Year Return (1989–93)	NA
Annual 12b-1 Fee	1.00%	10-Year Return (1984–93)	NA
Annual Expense Ratio	1.71%	Worst-Ever Loss (1990-91)	26%
Annual Portfolio Turnover	92%	Stock Market Correlation	14%
5-Year Cost Estimate	21%	Up/Down Market Rank	B – B

Benefits		Investment Information	
Investment Objective	Growth	Telephone	800-637-3863
5-Year Projected Return	NA	Minimum Investment	$5,000
Safety Rating (0-100)	76%	Telephone Switching	See prospectus
Yield	0.4%	Total Assets	$182 million

Merrill Lynch EuroFund "B"
Foreign - Western European stocks

Costs		Performance	
Sales Load	None	1-Year Return (1993)	+31%
Redemption Fee	4.2%	3-Year Return (1991–93)	+41%
Tax Load (Estimated)	4%	5-Year Return (1989–93)	+70%
Annual 12b-1 Fee	1.00%	10-Year Return (1984–93)	NA
Annual Expense Ratio	2.12%	Worst-Ever Loss (1987)	29%
Annual Portfolio Turnover	92%	Stock Market Correlation	8%
5-Year Cost Estimate	16%	Up/Down Market Rank	E – A

Benefits		Investment Information	
Investment Objective	Growth	Telephone	800-637-3863
5-Year Projected Return	NA	Minimum Investment	$500
Safety Rating (0-100)	73%	Telephone Switching	See prospectus
Yield	0.0%	Total Assets	$786 million

Merrill Lynch Fd for Tomor "B"
Quality companies; consumer growth

Costs		Performance	
Sales Load	None	1-Year Return (1993)	+10%
Redemption Fee	4.2%	3-Year Return (1991–93)	+52%
Tax Load (Estimated)	2%	5-Year Return (1989–93)	+80%
Annual 12b-1 Fee	1.00%	10-Year Return (1984–93)	NA
Annual Expense Ratio	1.92%	Worst-Ever Loss (1987)	34%
Annual Portfolio Turnover	40%	Stock Market Correlation	73%
5-Year Cost Estimate	12%	Up/Down Market Rank	B – E

Benefits		Investment Information	
Investment Objective	Growth	Telephone	800-637-3863
5-Year Projected Return	+6%	Minimum Investment	$500
Safety Rating (0-100)	71%	Telephone Switching	See prospectus
Yield	0.5%	Total Assets	$419 million

Merrill Lynch Glbl Holdngs "A"
Foreign & U.S. - diversified securities

Costs		Performance	
Sales Load	7.0%	1-Year Return (1993)	+24%
Redemption Fee	None	3-Year Return (1991–93)	+52%
Tax Load (Estimated)	4%	5-Year Return (1989–93)	+62%
Annual 12b-1 Fee	1.00%	10-Year Return (1984–93)	NA
Annual Expense Ratio	1.49%	Worst-Ever Loss (1987)	24%
Annual Portfolio Turnover	79%	Stock Market Correlation	45%
5-Year Cost Estimate	20%	Up/Down Market Rank	E – A

Benefits		Investment Information	
Investment Objective	Gr. & Icm.	Telephone	800-637-3863
5-Year Projected Return	NA	Minimum Investment	$1,000
Safety Rating (0-100)	77%	Telephone Switching	See prospectus
Yield	3.0%	Total Assets	$258 million

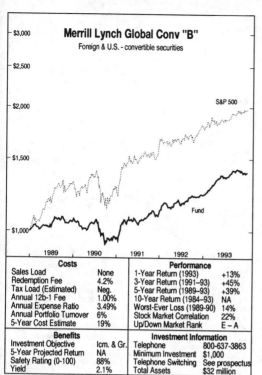

Merrill Lynch Global Conv "B"
Foreign & U.S. - convertible securities

Costs		Performance	
Sales Load	None	1-Year Return (1993)	+13%
Redemption Fee	4.2%	3-Year Return (1991–93)	+45%
Tax Load (Estimated)	Neg.	5-Year Return (1989–93)	+39%
Annual 12b-1 Fee	1.00%	10-Year Return (1984–93)	NA
Annual Expense Ratio	3.49%	Worst-Ever Loss (1989–90)	14%
Annual Portfolio Turnover	6%	Stock Market Correlation	22%
5-Year Cost Estimate	19%	Up/Down Market Rank	E – A

Benefits		Investment Information	
Investment Objective	Icm. & Gr.	Telephone	800-637-3863
5-Year Projected Return	NA	Minimum Investment	$1,000
Safety Rating (0-100)	88%	Telephone Switching	See prospectus
Yield	2.1%	Total Assets	$32 million

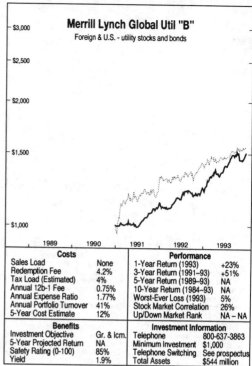

Merrill Lynch Global Util "B"
Foreign & U.S. - utility stocks and bonds

Costs		Performance	
Sales Load	None	1-Year Return (1993)	+23%
Redemption Fee	4.2%	3-Year Return (1991–93)	+51%
Tax Load (Estimated)	4%	5-Year Return (1989–93)	NA
Annual 12b-1 Fee	0.75%	10-Year Return (1984–93)	NA
Annual Expense Ratio	1.77%	Worst-Ever Loss (1993)	5%
Annual Portfolio Turnover	41%	Stock Market Correlation	26%
5-Year Cost Estimate	12%	Up/Down Market Rank	NA – NA

Benefits		Investment Information	
Investment Objective	Gr. & Icm.	Telephone	800-637-3863
5-Year Projected Return	NA	Minimum Investment	$1,000
Safety Rating (0-100)	85%	Telephone Switching	See prospectus
Yield	1.9%	Total Assets	$544 million

Merrill Lynch Gr Inv & Ret "B"
Undervalued stocks

Costs		Performance	
Sales Load	None	1-Year Return (1993)	+31%
Redemption Fee	4.2%	3-Year Return (1991–93)	+77%
Tax Load (Estimated)	0%	5-Year Return (1989–93)	+130%
Annual 12b-1 Fee	1.00%	10-Year Return (1984–93)	NA
Annual Expense Ratio	1.87%	Worst-Ever Loss (1990)	29%
Annual Portfolio Turnover	21%	Stock Market Correlation	41%
5-Year Cost Estimate	10%	Up/Down Market Rank	A – D

Benefits		Investment Information	
Investment Objective	Gr. & Icm.	Telephone	800-637-3863
5-Year Projected Return	+27%	Minimum Investment	$1,000
Safety Rating (0-100)	63%	Telephone Switching	See prospectus
Yield	0.0%	Total Assets	$1.23 billion

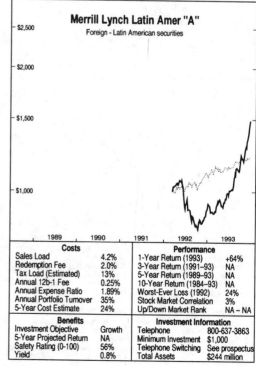

Merrill Lynch Latin Amer "A"
Foreign - Latin American securities

Costs		Performance	
Sales Load	4.2%	1-Year Return (1993)	+64%
Redemption Fee	2.0%	3-Year Return (1991–93)	NA
Tax Load (Estimated)	13%	5-Year Return (1989–93)	NA
Annual 12b-1 Fee	0.25%	10-Year Return (1984–93)	NA
Annual Expense Ratio	1.89%	Worst-Ever Loss (1992)	24%
Annual Portfolio Turnover	35%	Stock Market Correlation	3%
5-Year Cost Estimate	24%	Up/Down Market Rank	NA – NA

Benefits		Investment Information	
Investment Objective	Growth	Telephone	800-637-3863
5-Year Projected Return	NA	Minimum Investment	$1,000
Safety Rating (0-100)	56%	Telephone Switching	See prospectus
Yield	0.8%	Total Assets	$244 million

Merrill Lynch Natural Res "B"
Natural resource securities

S&P 500

Fund

| | 1989 | 1990 | 1991 | 1992 | 1993 |

Costs		Performance	
Sales Load	None	1-Year Return (1993)	+18%
Redemption Fee	4.2%	3-Year Return (1991–93)	+15%
Tax Load (Estimated)	Neg.	5-Year Return (1989–93)	+43%
Annual 12b-1 Fee	1.00%	10-Year Return (1984–93)	NA
Annual Expense Ratio	2.00%	Worst-Ever Loss (1987)	36%
Annual Portfolio Turnover	31%	Stock Market Correlation	14%
5-Year Cost Estimate	11%	Up/Down Market Rank	E – B

Benefits		Investment Information	
Investment Objective	Growth	Telephone	800-637-3863
5-Year Projected Return	NA	Minimum Investment	$500
Safety Rating (0-100)	74%	Telephone Switching	See prospectus
Yield	0.3%	Total Assets	$221 million

Merrill Lynch Pacific "A"
Foreign - Pacific-Basin stocks

| | 1989 | 1990 | 1991 | 1992 | 1993 |

Costs		Performance	
Sales Load	7.0%	1-Year Return (1993)	+34%
Redemption Fee	None	3-Year Return (1991–93)	+45%
Tax Load (Estimated)	4%	5-Year Return (1989–93)	+52%
Annual 12b-1 Fee	None	10-Year Return (1984–93)	+480%
Annual Expense Ratio	0.98%	Worst-Ever Loss (1987)	33%
Annual Portfolio Turnover	14%	Stock Market Correlation	6%
5-Year Cost Estimate	13%	Up/Down Market Rank	E – B

Benefits		Investment Information	
Investment Objective	Growth	Telephone	800-637-3863
5-Year Projected Return	NA	Minimum Investment	$250
Safety Rating (0-100)	69%	Telephone Switching	See prospectus
Yield	0.3%	Total Assets	$868 million

Merrill Lynch Phoenix "A"
Weak undervalued firms
★

| | 1989 | 1990 | 1991 | 1992 | 1993 |

Costs		Performance	
Sales Load	7.0%	1-Year Return (1993)	+30%
Redemption Fee	None	3-Year Return (1991–93)	+125%
Tax Load (Estimated)	4%	5-Year Return (1989–93)	+103%
Annual 12b-1 Fee	None	10-Year Return (1984–93)	+357%
Annual Expense Ratio	1.35%	Worst-Ever Loss (1989-90)	28%
Annual Portfolio Turnover	80%	Stock Market Correlation	37%
5-Year Cost Estimate	19%	Up/Down Market Rank	C – B

Benefits		Investment Information	
Investment Objective	Growth	Telephone	800-637-3863
5-Year Projected Return	+30%	Minimum Investment	$1,000
Safety Rating (0-100)	75%	Telephone Switching	See prospectus
Yield	6.2%	Total Assets	$436 million

Merrill Lynch Specl Value "A"
Small stocks; emerging growth

| | 1989 | 1990 | 1991 | 1992 | 1993 |

Costs		Performance	
Sales Load	7.0%	1-Year Return (1993)	+14%
Redemption Fee	None	3-Year Return (1991–93)	+107%
Tax Load (Estimated)	5%	5-Year Return (1989–93)	+51%
Annual 12b-1 Fee	None	10-Year Return (1984–93)	+80%
Annual Expense Ratio	1.28%	Worst-Ever Loss (1986-90)	46%
Annual Portfolio Turnover	42%	Stock Market Correlation	43%
5-Year Cost Estimate	18%	Up/Down Market Rank	D – D

Benefits		Investment Information	
Investment Objective	Growth	Telephone	800-637-3863
5-Year Projected Return	+9%	Minimum Investment	$250
Safety Rating (0-100)	74%	Telephone Switching	See prospectus
Yield	0.0%	Total Assets	$152 million

Merrill Lynch Stratgc Div "B"
Stocks with yield above S&P 500

S&P 500

Fund

Costs		Performance	
Sales Load	None	1-Year Return (1993)	+7%
Redemption Fee	4.2%	3-Year Return (1991–93)	+32%
Tax Load (Estimated)	6%	5-Year Return (1989–93)	+51%
Annual 12b-1 Fee	1.00%	10-Year Return (1984–93)	NA
Annual Expense Ratio	1.91%	Worst-Ever Loss (1989-90)	13%
Annual Portfolio Turnover	29%	Stock Market Correlation	71%
5-Year Cost Estimate	13%	Up/Down Market Rank	E – B

Benefits		Investment Information	
Investment Objective	Icm. & Gr.	Telephone	800-637-3863
5-Year Projected Return	–7%	Minimum Investment	$1,000
Safety Rating (0-100)	75%	Telephone Switching	See prospectus
Yield	1.8%	Total Assets	$266 million

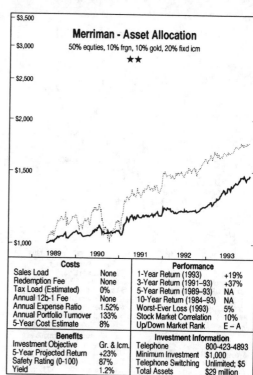

Merriman - Asset Allocation
50% equties, 10% frgn, 10% gold, 20% fixd icm
★★

Costs		Performance	
Sales Load	None	1-Year Return (1993)	+19%
Redemption Fee	None	3-Year Return (1991–93)	+37%
Tax Load (Estimated)	0%	5-Year Return (1989–93)	NA
Annual 12b-1 Fee	None	10-Year Return (1984–93)	NA
Annual Expense Ratio	1.52%	Worst-Ever Loss (1993)	5%
Annual Portfolio Turnover	133%	Stock Market Correlation	10%
5-Year Cost Estimate	8%	Up/Down Market Rank	E – A

Benefits		Investment Information	
Investment Objective	Gr. & Icm.	Telephone	800-423-4893
5-Year Projected Return	+23%	Minimum Investment	$1,000
Safety Rating (0-100)	87%	Telephone Switching	Unlimited; $5
Yield	1.2%	Total Assets	$29 million

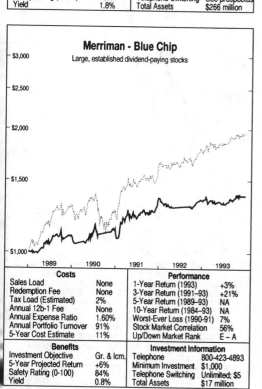

Merriman - Blue Chip
Large, established dividend-paying stocks

Costs		Performance	
Sales Load	None	1-Year Return (1993)	+3%
Redemption Fee	None	3-Year Return (1991–93)	+21%
Tax Load (Estimated)	2%	5-Year Return (1989–93)	NA
Annual 12b-1 Fee	None	10-Year Return (1984–93)	NA
Annual Expense Ratio	1.60%	Worst-Ever Loss (1990-91)	7%
Annual Portfolio Turnover	91%	Stock Market Correlation	56%
5-Year Cost Estimate	11%	Up/Down Market Rank	E – A

Benefits		Investment Information	
Investment Objective	Gr. & Icm.	Telephone	800-423-4893
5-Year Projected Return	+6%	Minimum Investment	$1,000
Safety Rating (0-100)	84%	Telephone Switching	Unlimited; $5
Yield	0.8%	Total Assets	$17 million

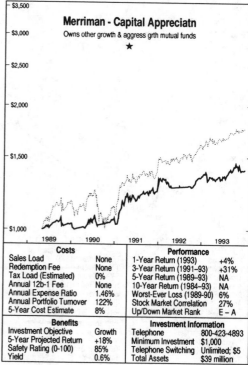

Merriman - Capital Appreciatn
Owns other growth & aggress grth mutual funds
★

Costs		Performance	
Sales Load	None	1-Year Return (1993)	+4%
Redemption Fee	None	3-Year Return (1991–93)	+31%
Tax Load (Estimated)	0%	5-Year Return (1989–93)	NA
Annual 12b-1 Fee	None	10-Year Return (1984–93)	NA
Annual Expense Ratio	1.46%	Worst-Ever Loss (1989-90)	6%
Annual Portfolio Turnover	122%	Stock Market Correlation	27%
5-Year Cost Estimate	8%	Up/Down Market Rank	E – A

Benefits		Investment Information	
Investment Objective	Growth	Telephone	800-423-4893
5-Year Projected Return	+18%	Minimum Investment	$1,000
Safety Rating (0-100)	85%	Telephone Switching	Unlimited; $5
Yield	0.6%	Total Assets	$39 million

MetLife-State St Captl App "A"
Emerging growth and undervalued stocks

Fund

S&P 500

Costs		Performance	
Sales Load	4.7%	1-Year Return (1993)	+23%
Redemption Fee	None	3-Year Return (1991–93)	+134%
Tax Load (Estimated)	Neg.	5-Year Return (1989–93)	+165%
Annual 12b-1 Fee	0.50%	10-Year Return (1984–93)	NA
Annual Expense Ratio	1.50%	Worst-Ever Loss (1987)	36%
Annual Portfolio Turnover	128%	Stock Market Correlation	59%
5-Year Cost Estimate	13%	Up/Down Market Rank	B – D
Benefits		**Investment Information**	
Investment Objective	Growth	Telephone	800-562-0032
5-Year Projected Return	+37%	Minimum Investment	$250
Safety Rating (0-100)	61%	Telephone Switching	Unlimited; $5
Yield	0.0%	Total Assets	$236 million

MetLife-State St Eqty Incm "A"
Stocks with above-average yield
★★

Costs		Performance	
Sales Load	4.7%	1-Year Return (1993)	+23%
Redemption Fee	None	3-Year Return (1991–93)	+63%
Tax Load (Estimated)	2%	5-Year Return (1989–93)	+85%
Annual 12b-1 Fee	0.50%	10-Year Return (1984–93)	NA
Annual Expense Ratio	1.50%	Worst-Ever Loss (1987)	24%
Annual Portfolio Turnover	102%	Stock Market Correlation	55%
5-Year Cost Estimate	15%	Up/Down Market Rank	D – B
Benefits		**Investment Information**	
Investment Objective	Icm. & Gr.	Telephone	800-562-0032
5-Year Projected Return	+12%	Minimum Investment	$250
Safety Rating (0-100)	82%	Telephone Switching	Unlimited; $5
Yield	1.6%	Total Assets	$49 million

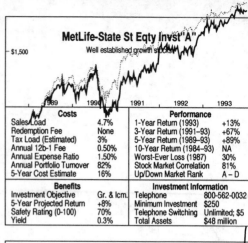

MetLife-State St Eqty Invst "A"
Well established growth stocks

Costs		Performance	
Sales Load	4.7%	1-Year Return (1993)	+13%
Redemption Fee	None	3-Year Return (1991–93)	+67%
Tax Load (Estimated)	3%	5-Year Return (1989–93)	+89%
Annual 12b-1 Fee	0.50%	10-Year Return (1984–93)	NA
Annual Expense Ratio	1.50%	Worst-Ever Loss (1987)	30%
Annual Portfolio Turnover	82%	Stock Market Correlation	81%
5-Year Cost Estimate	16%	Up/Down Market Rank	A – D
Benefits		**Investment Information**	
Investment Objective	Gr. & Icm.	Telephone	800-562-0032
5-Year Projected Return	+8%	Minimum Investment	$250
Safety Rating (0-100)	70%	Telephone Switching	Unlimited; $5
Yield	0.3%	Total Assets	$48 million

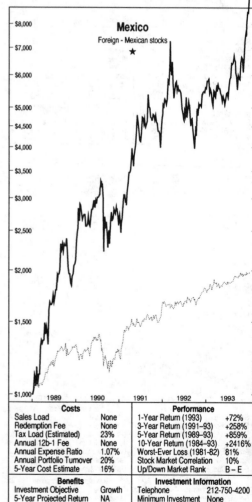

Mexico
Foreign - Mexican stocks
★

Costs		Performance	
Sales Load	None	1-Year Return (1993)	+72%
Redemption Fee	None	3-Year Return (1991–93)	+258%
Tax Load (Estimated)	23%	5-Year Return (1989–93)	+859%
Annual 12b-1 Fee	None	10-Year Return (1984–93)	+2416%
Annual Expense Ratio	1.07%	Worst-Ever Loss (1981-82)	81%
Annual Portfolio Turnover	20%	Stock Market Correlation	10%
5-Year Cost Estimate	16%	Up/Down Market Rank	B – E
Benefits		**Investment Information**	
Investment Objective	Growth	Telephone	212-750-4200
5-Year Projected Return	NA	Minimum Investment	None
Safety Rating (0-100)	23%	Telephone Switching	Via broker
Yield	1.4%	Total Assets	$970 million

Mexico Equity & Income

Foreign - Mexican; 50% conv; 50% stks & bonds — Fund

S&P 500

Costs		Performance	
Sales Load	None	1-Year Return (1993)	+79%
Redemption Fee	None	3-Year Return (1991–93)	+216%
Tax Load (Estimated)	13%	5-Year Return (1989–93)	NA
Annual 12b-1 Fee	None	10-Year Return (1984–93)	NA
Annual Expense Ratio	1.62%	Worst-Ever Loss (1992)	38%
Annual Portfolio Turnover	48%	Stock Market Correlation	5%
5-Year Cost Estimate	23%	Up/Down Market Rank	NA – NA

Benefits		Investment Information	
Investment Objective	Gr. & Icm.	Telephone	212-667-5000
5-Year Projected Return	NA	Minimum Investment	None
Safety Rating (0-100)	20%	Telephone Switching	Via broker
Yield	0.0%	Total Assets	$102 million

MFS - Capital Growth "B"

Small company growth stocks ★

Costs		Performance	
Sales Load	None	1-Year Return (1993)	+4%
Redemption Fee	4.2%	3-Year Return (1991–93)	+47%
Tax Load (Estimated)	3%	5-Year Return (1989–93)	+86%
Annual 12b-1 Fee	1.00%	10-Year Return (1984–93)	NA
Annual Expense Ratio	2.15%	Worst-Ever Loss (1987)	34%
Annual Portfolio Turnover	82%	Stock Market Correlation	83%
5-Year Cost Estimate	16%	Up/Down Market Rank	C – C

Benefits		Investment Information	
Investment Objective	Growth	Telephone	800-225-2606
5-Year Projected Return	+9%	Minimum Investment	$1,000
Safety Rating (0-100)	75%	Telephone Switching	Unlimited;free
Yield	0.0%	Total Assets	$478 million

MFS - Emerging Growth "B"

Emerging growth stocks ★

Costs		Performance	
Sales Load	None	1-Year Return (1993)	+24%
Redemption Fee	4.2%	3-Year Return (1991–93)	+160%
Tax Load (Estimated)	7%	5-Year Return (1989–93)	+222%
Annual 12b-1 Fee	1.00%	10-Year Return (1984–93)	NA
Annual Expense Ratio	2.22%	Worst-Ever Loss (1987)	46%
Annual Portfolio Turnover	56%	Stock Market Correlation	40%
5-Year Cost Estimate	21%	Up/Down Market Rank	A – E

Benefits		Investment Information	
Investment Objective	Growth	Telephone	800-225-2606
5-Year Projected Return	+63%	Minimum Investment	$1,000
Safety Rating (0-100)	57%	Telephone Switching	Unlimited;free
Yield	0.0%	Total Assets	$532 million

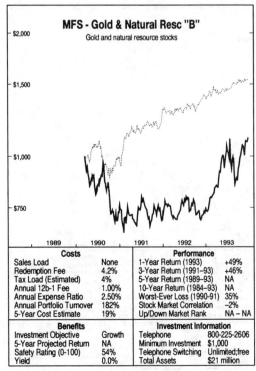

MFS - Gold & Natural Resc "B"

Gold and natural resource stocks

Costs		Performance	
Sales Load	None	1-Year Return (1993)	+49%
Redemption Fee	4.2%	3-Year Return (1991–93)	+46%
Tax Load (Estimated)	4%	5-Year Return (1989–93)	NA
Annual 12b-1 Fee	1.00%	10-Year Return (1984–93)	NA
Annual Expense Ratio	2.50%	Worst-Ever Loss (1990-91)	35%
Annual Portfolio Turnover	182%	Stock Market Correlation	–2%
5-Year Cost Estimate	19%	Up/Down Market Rank	NA – NA

Benefits		Investment Information	
Investment Objective	Growth	Telephone	800-225-2606
5-Year Projected Return	NA	Minimum Investment	$1,000
Safety Rating (0-100)	54%	Telephone Switching	Unlimited;free
Yield	0.0%	Total Assets	$21 million

MFS - Growth Opportunities "A"
Small; growth stocks

S&P 500

Fund

Costs		Performance	
Sales Load	6.1%	1-Year Return (1993)	+16%
Redemption Fee	None	3-Year Return (1991–93)	+50%
Tax Load (Estimated)	5%	5-Year Return (1989–93)	+81%
Annual 12b-1 Fee	0.35%	10-Year Return (1984–93)	+140%
Annual Expense Ratio	0.95%	Worst-Ever Loss (1987)	38%
Annual Portfolio Turnover	66%	Stock Market Correlation	75%
5-Year Cost Estimate	17%	Up/Down Market Rank	A – E

Benefits		Investment Information	
Investment Objective	Growth	Telephone	800-225-2606
5-Year Projected Return	+5%	Minimum Investment	$1,000
Safety Rating (0-100)	74%	Telephone Switching	Unlimited;free
Yield	0.8%	Total Assets	$719 million

MFS - Growth Stock (MIG)
Long term growth stocks

Costs		Performance	
Sales Load	6.1%	1-Year Return (1993)	+14%
Redemption Fee	None	3-Year Return (1991–93)	+80%
Tax Load (Estimated)	5%	5-Year Return (1989–93)	+138%
Annual 12b-1 Fee	0.35%	10-Year Return (1984–93)	+248%
Annual Expense Ratio	0.72%	Worst-Ever Loss (1987)	35%
Annual Portfolio Turnover	16%	Stock Market Correlation	58%
5-Year Cost Estimate	12%	Up/Down Market Rank	A – E

Benefits		Investment Information	
Investment Objective	Growth	Telephone	800-225-2606
5-Year Projected Return	+15%	Minimum Investment	$1,000
Safety Rating (0-100)	62%	Telephone Switching	Unlimited;free
Yield	0.0%	Total Assets	$1.05 billion

MFS - Investors Trust (MIT)
High-quality stocks
★★

Costs		Performance	
Sales Load	6.1%	1-Year Return (1993)	+10%
Redemption Fee	None	3-Year Return (1991–93)	+51%
Tax Load (Estimated)	2%	5-Year Return (1989–93)	+103%
Annual 12b-1 Fee	0.35%	10-Year Return (1984–93)	+259%
Annual Expense Ratio	0.72%	Worst-Ever Loss (1987)	34%
Annual Portfolio Turnover	46%	Stock Market Correlation	90%
5-Year Cost Estimate	12%	Up/Down Market Rank	B – D

Benefits		Investment Information	
Investment Objective	Gr. & Icm.	Telephone	800-225-2606
5-Year Projected Return	+8%	Minimum Investment	$1,000
Safety Rating (0-100)	75%	Telephone Switching	Unlimited;free
Yield	3.4%	Total Assets	$1.61 billion

MFS - Research "A"
Diversified securities
★★

Costs		Performance	
Sales Load	6.1%	1-Year Return (1993)	+22%
Redemption Fee	None	3-Year Return (1991–93)	+79%
Tax Load (Estimated)	Neg.	5-Year Return (1989–93)	+110%
Annual 12b-1 Fee	0.35%	10-Year Return (1984–93)	+236%
Annual Expense Ratio	0.85%	Worst-Ever Loss (1987)	36%
Annual Portfolio Turnover	74%	Stock Market Correlation	61%
5-Year Cost Estimate	11%	Up/Down Market Rank	B – D

Benefits		Investment Information	
Investment Objective	Gr. & Icm.	Telephone	800-225-2606
5-Year Projected Return	+22%	Minimum Investment	$1,000
Safety Rating (0-100)	76%	Telephone Switching	Unlimited;free
Yield	0.3%	Total Assets	$288 million

MFS - Total Return "A"
Long term growth securities
★★★★

S&P 500

Fund

Costs		Performance	
Sales Load	5.0%	1-Year Return (1993)	+13%
Redemption Fee	None	3-Year Return (1991–93)	+51%
Tax Load (Estimated)	3%	5-Year Return (1989–93)	+80%
Annual 12b-1 Fee	0.35%	10-Year Return (1984–93)	+252%
Annual Expense Ratio	0.89%	Worst-Ever Loss (1987)	22%
Annual Portfolio Turnover	74%	Stock Market Correlation	76%
5-Year Cost Estimate	14%	Up/Down Market Rank	E – A
Benefits		**Investment Information**	
Investment Objective	Growth	Telephone	800-225-2606
5-Year Projected Return	+14%	Minimum Investment	$1,000
Safety Rating (0-100)	85%	Telephone Switching	Unlimited;free
Yield	2.1%	Total Assets	$1.66 billion

MFS - Value "A"
Diversified securities
★★

Costs		Performance	
Sales Load	6.1%	1-Year Return (1993)	+25%
Redemption Fee	None	3-Year Return (1991–93)	+83%
Tax Load (Estimated)	Neg.	5-Year Return (1989–93)	+97%
Annual 12b-1 Fee	0.35%	10-Year Return (1984–93)	+217%
Annual Expense Ratio	1.38%	Worst-Ever Loss (1987)	37%
Annual Portfolio Turnover	111%	Stock Market Correlation	53%
5-Year Cost Estimate	14%	Up/Down Market Rank	C – C
Benefits		**Investment Information**	
Investment Objective	Growth	Telephone	800-225-2606
5-Year Projected Return	+17%	Minimum Investment	$1,000
Safety Rating (0-100)	78%	Telephone Switching	Unlimited;free
Yield	0.3%	Total Assets	$131 million

MFS - World Equity "B"
Foreign & U.S. - diversified stocks

Costs		Performance	
Sales Load	None	1-Year Return (1993)	+29%
Redemption Fee	4.2%	3-Year Return (1991–93)	+41%
Tax Load (Estimated)	4%	5-Year Return (1989–93)	+71%
Annual 12b-1 Fee	1.00%	10-Year Return (1984–93)	NA
Annual Expense Ratio	2.67%	Worst-Ever Loss (1987)	24%
Annual Portfolio Turnover	82%	Stock Market Correlation	26%
5-Year Cost Estimate	21%	Up/Down Market Rank	E – A
Benefits		**Investment Information**	
Investment Objective	Growth	Telephone	800-225-2606
5-Year Projected Return	NA	Minimum Investment	$1,000
Safety Rating (0-100)	81%	Telephone Switching	Unlimited;free
Yield	0.1%	Total Assets	$132 million

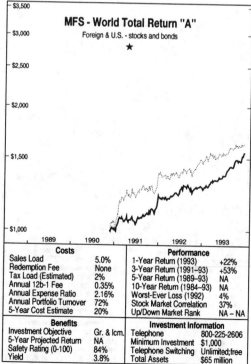

MFS - World Total Return "A"
Foreign & U.S. - stocks and bonds
★

Costs		Performance	
Sales Load	5.0%	1-Year Return (1993)	+22%
Redemption Fee	None	3-Year Return (1991–93)	+53%
Tax Load (Estimated)	2%	5-Year Return (1989–93)	NA
Annual 12b-1 Fee	0.35%	10-Year Return (1984–93)	NA
Annual Expense Ratio	2.16%	Worst-Ever Loss (1992)	4%
Annual Portfolio Turnover	72%	Stock Market Correlation	37%
5-Year Cost Estimate	20%	Up/Down Market Rank	NA – NA
Benefits		**Investment Information**	
Investment Objective	Gr. & Icm.	Telephone	800-225-2606
5-Year Projected Return	NA	Minimum Investment	$1,000
Safety Rating (0-100)	84%	Telephone Switching	Unlimited;free
Yield	3.8%	Total Assets	$65 million

MIM Stock Appreciation
Fundamental and technical analysis
★★★

Fund

S&P 500

(chart years: 1989, 1990, 1991, 1992, 1993; $1,000–$3,000)

Costs		Performance	
Sales Load	None	1-Year Return (1993)	+10%
Redemption Fee	None	3-Year Return (1991–93)	+107%
Tax Load (Estimated)	5%	5-Year Return (1989–93)	NA
Annual 12b-1 Fee	0.95%	10-Year Return (1984–93)	NA
Annual Expense Ratio	2.67%	Worst-Ever Loss (1990)	30%
Annual Portfolio Turnover	216%	Stock Market Correlation	46%
5-Year Cost Estimate	20%	Up/Down Market Rank	A – D

Benefits		Investment Information	
Investment Objective	Growth	Telephone	800-233-1240
5-Year Projected Return	+59%	Minimum Investment	$250
Safety Rating (0-100)	64%	Telephone Switching	Unlimited;free
Yield	0.0%	Total Assets	$58 million

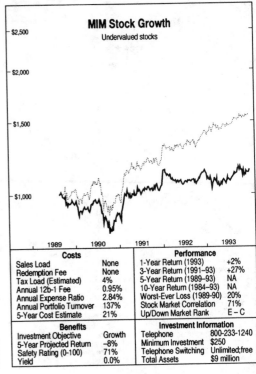

MIM Stock Growth
Undervalued stocks

(chart years: 1989, 1990, 1991, 1992, 1993; $1,000–$2,500)

Costs		Performance	
Sales Load	None	1-Year Return (1993)	+2%
Redemption Fee	None	3-Year Return (1991–93)	+27%
Tax Load (Estimated)	4%	5-Year Return (1989–93)	NA
Annual 12b-1 Fee	0.95%	10-Year Return (1984–93)	NA
Annual Expense Ratio	2.84%	Worst-Ever Loss (1989-90)	20%
Annual Portfolio Turnover	137%	Stock Market Correlation	71%
5-Year Cost Estimate	21%	Up/Down Market Rank	E – C

Benefits		Investment Information	
Investment Objective	Growth	Telephone	800-233-1240
5-Year Projected Return	–8%	Minimum Investment	$250
Safety Rating (0-100)	71%	Telephone Switching	Unlimited;free
Yield	0.0%	Total Assets	$9 million

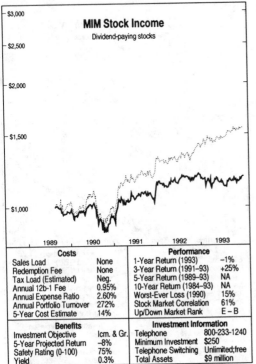

MIM Stock Income
Dividend-paying stocks

(chart years: 1989, 1990, 1991, 1992, 1993; $1,000–$3,000)

Costs		Performance	
Sales Load	None	1-Year Return (1993)	–1%
Redemption Fee	None	3-Year Return (1991–93)	+25%
Tax Load (Estimated)	Neg.	5-Year Return (1989–93)	NA
Annual 12b-1 Fee	0.95%	10-Year Return (1984–93)	NA
Annual Expense Ratio	2.60%	Worst-Ever Loss (1990)	15%
Annual Portfolio Turnover	272%	Stock Market Correlation	61%
5-Year Cost Estimate	14%	Up/Down Market Rank	E – B

Benefits		Investment Information	
Investment Objective	Icm. & Gr.	Telephone	800-233-1240
5-Year Projected Return	–8%	Minimum Investment	$250
Safety Rating (0-100)	75%	Telephone Switching	Unlimited;free
Yield	0.3%	Total Assets	$9 million

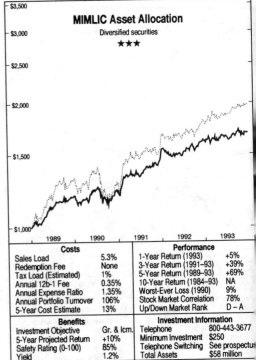

MIMLIC Asset Allocation
Diversified securities
★★★

(chart years: 1989, 1990, 1991, 1992, 1993; $1,000–$3,500)

Costs		Performance	
Sales Load	5.3%	1-Year Return (1993)	+5%
Redemption Fee	None	3-Year Return (1991–93)	+39%
Tax Load (Estimated)	1%	5-Year Return (1989–93)	+69%
Annual 12b-1 Fee	0.35%	10-Year Return (1984–93)	NA
Annual Expense Ratio	1.35%	Worst-Ever Loss (1990)	9%
Annual Portfolio Turnover	106%	Stock Market Correlation	78%
5-Year Cost Estimate	13%	Up/Down Market Rank	D – A

Benefits		Investment Information	
Investment Objective	Gr. & Icm.	Telephone	800-443-3677
5-Year Projected Return	+10%	Minimum Investment	$250
Safety Rating (0-100)	85%	Telephone Switching	See prospectus
Yield	1.2%	Total Assets	$58 million

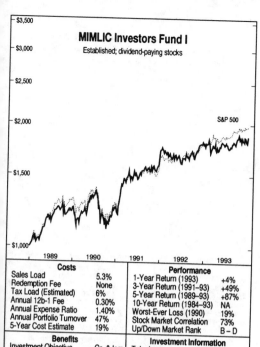

MIMLIC Investors Fund I
Established; dividend-paying stocks

S&P 500

Costs		Performance	
Sales Load	5.3%	1-Year Return (1993)	+4%
Redemption Fee	None	3-Year Return (1991–93)	+49%
Tax Load (Estimated)	6%	5-Year Return (1989–93)	+87%
Annual 12b-1 Fee	0.30%	10-Year Return (1984–93)	NA
Annual Expense Ratio	1.40%	Worst-Ever Loss (1990)	19%
Annual Portfolio Turnover	47%	Stock Market Correlation	73%
5-Year Cost Estimate	19%	Up/Down Market Rank	B – D

Benefits		Investment Information	
Investment Objective	Gr. & Icm.	Telephone	800-443-3677
5-Year Projected Return	+8%	Minimum Investment	$250
Safety Rating (0-100)	72%	Telephone Switching	See prospectus
Yield	0.1%	Total Assets	$29 million

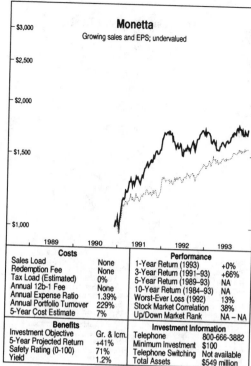

Monetta
Growing sales and EPS; undervalued

Costs		Performance	
Sales Load	None	1-Year Return (1993)	+0%
Redemption Fee	None	3-Year Return (1991–93)	+66%
Tax Load (Estimated)	0%	5-Year Return (1989–93)	NA
Annual 12b-1 Fee	None	10-Year Return (1984–93)	NA
Annual Expense Ratio	1.39%	Worst-Ever Loss (1992)	13%
Annual Portfolio Turnover	229%	Stock Market Correlation	38%
5-Year Cost Estimate	7%	Up/Down Market Rank	NA – NA

Benefits		Investment Information	
Investment Objective	Gr. & Icm.	Telephone	800-666-3882
5-Year Projected Return	+41%	Minimum Investment	$100
Safety Rating (0-100)	71%	Telephone Switching	Not available
Yield	1.2%	Total Assets	$549 million

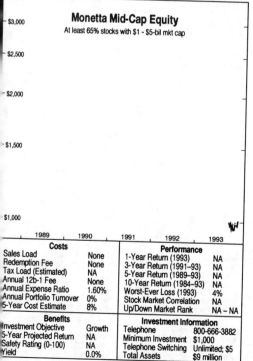

Monetta Mid-Cap Equity
At least 65% stocks with $1 - $5-bil mkt cap

Costs		Performance	
Sales Load	None	1-Year Return (1993)	NA
Redemption Fee	None	3-Year Return (1991–93)	NA
Tax Load (Estimated)	NA	5-Year Return (1989–93)	NA
Annual 12b-1 Fee	None	10-Year Return (1984–93)	NA
Annual Expense Ratio	1.60%	Worst-Ever Loss (1993)	4%
Annual Portfolio Turnover	0%	Stock Market Correlation	NA
5-Year Cost Estimate	8%	Up/Down Market Rank	NA – NA

Benefits		Investment Information	
Investment Objective	Growth	Telephone	800-666-3882
5-Year Projected Return	NA	Minimum Investment	$1,000
Safety Rating (0-100)	NA	Telephone Switching	Unlimited; $5
Yield	0.0%	Total Assets	$9 million

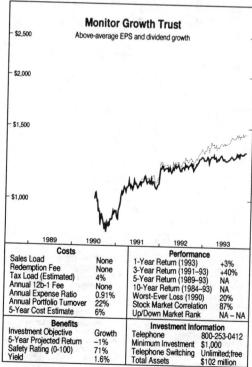

Monitor Growth Trust
Above-average EPS and dividend growth

Costs		Performance	
Sales Load	None	1-Year Return (1993)	+3%
Redemption Fee	None	3-Year Return (1991–93)	+40%
Tax Load (Estimated)	4%	5-Year Return (1989–93)	NA
Annual 12b-1 Fee	None	10-Year Return (1984–93)	NA
Annual Expense Ratio	0.91%	Worst-Ever Loss (1990)	20%
Annual Portfolio Turnover	22%	Stock Market Correlation	87%
5-Year Cost Estimate	6%	Up/Down Market Rank	NA – NA

Benefits		Investment Information	
Investment Objective	Growth	Telephone	800-253-0412
5-Year Projected Return	–1%	Minimum Investment	$1,000
Safety Rating (0-100)	71%	Telephone Switching	Unlimited; free
Yield	1.6%	Total Assets	$102 million

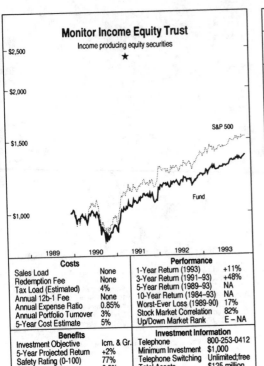

Monitor Income Equity Trust

Income producing equity securities

★

Chart showing S&P 500 and Fund from 1989 to 1993, scaled $1,000 to $2,500.

S&P 500

Fund

Costs		Performance	
Sales Load	None	1-Year Return (1993)	+11%
Redemption Fee	None	3-Year Return (1991–93)	+48%
Tax Load (Estimated)	4%	5-Year Return (1989–93)	NA
Annual 12b-1 Fee	None	10-Year Return (1984–93)	NA
Annual Expense Ratio	0.85%	Worst-Ever Loss (1989-90)	17%
Annual Portfolio Turnover	3%	Stock Market Correlation	82%
5-Year Cost Estimate	5%	Up/Down Market Rank	E – NA

Benefits		Investment Information	
Investment Objective	Icm. & Gr.	Telephone	800-253-0412
5-Year Projected Return	+2%	Minimum Investment	$1,000
Safety Rating (0-100)	77%	Telephone Switching	Unlimited;free
Yield	3.5%	Total Assets	$125 million

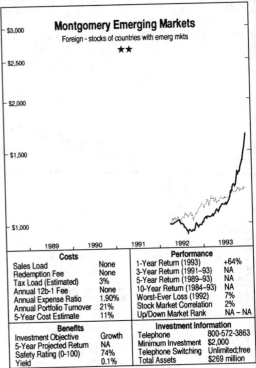

Montgomery Emerging Markets

Foreign - stocks of countries with emerg mkts

★★

Chart from 1989 to 1993, scaled $1,000 to $3,000.

Costs		Performance	
Sales Load	None	1-Year Return (1993)	+64%
Redemption Fee	None	3-Year Return (1991–93)	NA
Tax Load (Estimated)	3%	5-Year Return (1989–93)	NA
Annual 12b-1 Fee	None	10-Year Return (1984–93)	NA
Annual Expense Ratio	1.90%	Worst-Ever Loss (1992)	7%
Annual Portfolio Turnover	21%	Stock Market Correlation	2%
5-Year Cost Estimate	11%	Up/Down Market Rank	NA – NA

Benefits		Investment Information	
Investment Objective	Growth	Telephone	800-572-3863
5-Year Projected Return	NA	Minimum Investment	$2,000
Safety Rating (0-100)	74%	Telephone Switching	Unlimited;free
Yield	0.1%	Total Assets	$269 million

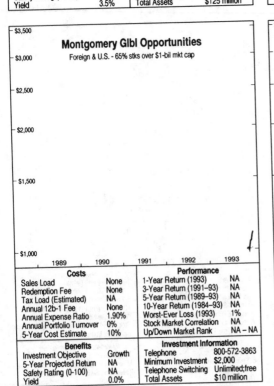

Montgomery Glbl Opportunities

Foreign & U.S. - 65% stks over $1-bil mkt cap

Chart from 1989 to 1993, scaled $1,000 to $3,500.

Costs		Performance	
Sales Load	None	1-Year Return (1993)	NA
Redemption Fee	None	3-Year Return (1991–93)	NA
Tax Load (Estimated)	NA	5-Year Return (1989–93)	NA
Annual 12b-1 Fee	None	10-Year Return (1984–93)	NA
Annual Expense Ratio	1.90%	Worst-Ever Loss (1993)	1%
Annual Portfolio Turnover	0%	Stock Market Correlation	NA
5-Year Cost Estimate	10%	Up/Down Market Rank	NA – NA

Benefits		Investment Information	
Investment Objective	Growth	Telephone	800-572-3863
5-Year Projected Return	NA	Minimum Investment	$2,000
Safety Rating (0-100)	NA	Telephone Switching	Unlimited;free
Yield	0.0%	Total Assets	$10 million

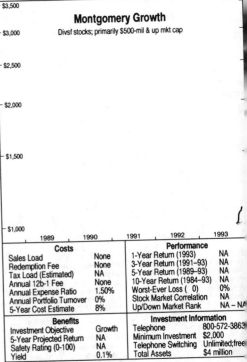

Montgomery Growth

Divsf stocks; primarily $500-mil & up mkt cap

Chart from 1989 to 1993, scaled $1,000 to $3,500.

Costs		Performance	
Sales Load	None	1-Year Return (1993)	NA
Redemption Fee	None	3-Year Return (1991–93)	NA
Tax Load (Estimated)	NA	5-Year Return (1989–93)	NA
Annual 12b-1 Fee	None	10-Year Return (1984–93)	NA
Annual Expense Ratio	1.50%	Worst-Ever Loss (0)	0%
Annual Portfolio Turnover	0%	Stock Market Correlation	NA
5-Year Cost Estimate	8%	Up/Down Market Rank	NA – NA

Benefits		Investment Information	
Investment Objective	Growth	Telephone	800-572-3863
5-Year Projected Return	NA	Minimum Investment	$2,000
Safety Rating (0-100)	NA	Telephone Switching	Unlimited;free
Yield	0.1%	Total Assets	$4 million

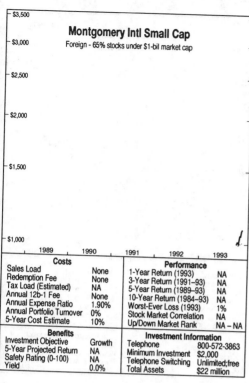

Montgomery Intl Small Cap

Foreign - 65% stocks under $1-bil market cap

Costs		Performance	
Sales Load	None	1-Year Return (1993)	NA
Redemption Fee	None	3-Year Return (1991–93)	NA
Tax Load (Estimated)	NA	5-Year Return (1989–93)	NA
Annual 12b-1 Fee	None	10-Year Return (1984–93)	NA
Annual Expense Ratio	1.90%	Worst-Ever Loss (1993)	1%
Annual Portfolio Turnover	0%	Stock Market Correlation	NA
5-Year Cost Estimate	10%	Up/Down Market Rank	NA – NA

Benefits		Investment Information	
Investment Objective	Growth	Telephone	800-572-3863
5-Year Projected Return	NA	Minimum Investment	$2,000
Safety Rating (0-100)	NA	Telephone Switching	Unlimited;free
Yield	0.0%	Total Assets	$22 million

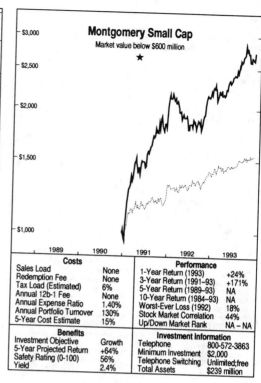

Montgomery Small Cap

Market value below $600 million

★

Costs		Performance	
Sales Load	None	1-Year Return (1993)	+24%
Redemption Fee	None	3-Year Return (1991–93)	+171%
Tax Load (Estimated)	6%	5-Year Return (1989–93)	NA
Annual 12b-1 Fee	None	10-Year Return (1984–93)	NA
Annual Expense Ratio	1.40%	Worst-Ever Loss (1992)	18%
Annual Portfolio Turnover	130%	Stock Market Correlation	44%
5-Year Cost Estimate	15%	Up/Down Market Rank	NA – NA

Benefits		Investment Information	
Investment Objective	Growth	Telephone	800-572-3863
5-Year Projected Return	+64%	Minimum Investment	$2,000
Safety Rating (0-100)	56%	Telephone Switching	Unlimited;free
Yield	2.4%	Total Assets	$239 million

Morgan Grenfell SmallCap

Stocks with $50 to $500-million market value

Costs		Performance	
Sales Load	None	1-Year Return (1993)	–2%
Redemption Fee	None	3-Year Return (1991–93)	+57%
Tax Load (Estimated)	Neg.	5-Year Return (1989–93)	+105%
Annual 12b-1 Fee	None	10-Year Return (1984–93)	NA
Annual Expense Ratio	1.38%	Worst-Ever Loss (1987)	55%
Annual Portfolio Turnover	89%	Stock Market Correlation	16%
5-Year Cost Estimate	9%	Up/Down Market Rank	A – E

Benefits		Investment Information	
Investment Objective	Gr. & Icm.	Telephone	800-888-8060
5-Year Projected Return	+2%	Minimum Investment	None
Safety Rating (0-100)	43%	Telephone Switching	Via broker
Yield	0.0%	Total Assets	$69 million

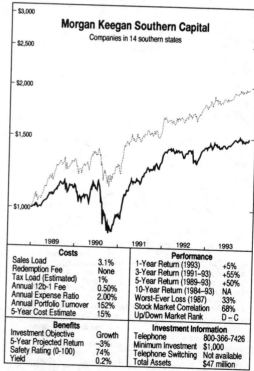

Morgan Keegan Southern Capital

Companies in 14 southern states

Costs		Performance	
Sales Load	3.1%	1-Year Return (1993)	+5%
Redemption Fee	None	3-Year Return (1991–93)	+55%
Tax Load (Estimated)	1%	5-Year Return (1989–93)	+50%
Annual 12b-1 Fee	0.50%	10-Year Return (1984–93)	NA
Annual Expense Ratio	2.00%	Worst-Ever Loss (1987)	33%
Annual Portfolio Turnover	152%	Stock Market Correlation	68%
5-Year Cost Estimate	15%	Up/Down Market Rank	D – C

Benefits		Investment Information	
Investment Objective	Growth	Telephone	800-366-7426
5-Year Projected Return	–3%	Minimum Investment	$1,000
Safety Rating (0-100)	74%	Telephone Switching	Not available
Yield	0.2%	Total Assets	$47 million

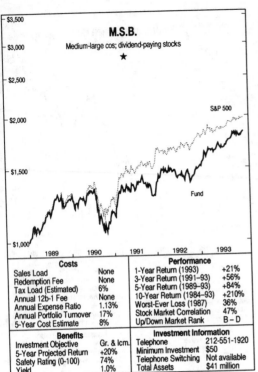

M.S.B.
Medium-large cos; dividend-paying stocks
★

S&P 500

Fund

Costs		Performance	
Sales Load	None	1-Year Return (1993)	+21%
Redemption Fee	None	3-Year Return (1991–93)	+56%
Tax Load (Estimated)	6%	5-Year Return (1989–93)	+84%
Annual 12b-1 Fee	None	10-Year Return (1984–93)	+210%
Annual Expense Ratio	1.13%	Worst-Ever Loss (1987)	36%
Annual Portfolio Turnover	17%	Stock Market Correlation	47%
5-Year Cost Estimate	8%	Up/Down Market Rank	B – D

Benefits		Investment Information	
Investment Objective	Gr. & Icm.	Telephone	212-551-1920
5-Year Projected Return	+20%	Minimum Investment	$50
Safety Rating (0-100)	74%	Telephone Switching	Not available
Yield	1.0%	Total Assets	$41 million

Mutual Benefit
Well managed growth companies
★★

Costs		Performance	
Sales Load	5.0%	1-Year Return (1993)	+9%
Redemption Fee	None	3-Year Return (1991–93)	+53%
Tax Load (Estimated)	6%	5-Year Return (1989–93)	+87%
Annual 12b-1 Fee	None	10-Year Return (1984–93)	NA
Annual Expense Ratio	1.01%	Worst-Ever Loss (1987)	30%
Annual Portfolio Turnover	15%	Stock Market Correlation	74%
5-Year Cost Estimate	12%	Up/Down Market Rank	C – C

Benefits		Investment Information	
Investment Objective	Gr. & Icm.	Telephone	800-323-4726
5-Year Projected Return	+7%	Minimum Investment	$250
Safety Rating (0-100)	79%	Telephone Switching	Not available
Yield	2.0%	Total Assets	$49 million

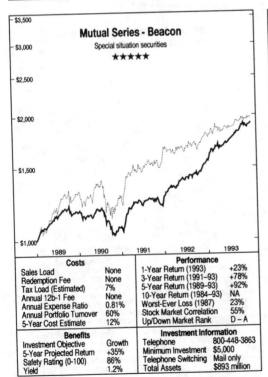

Mutual Series - Beacon
Special situation securities
★★★★★

Costs		Performance	
Sales Load	None	1-Year Return (1993)	+23%
Redemption Fee	None	3-Year Return (1991–93)	+78%
Tax Load (Estimated)	7%	5-Year Return (1989–93)	+92%
Annual 12b-1 Fee	None	10-Year Return (1984–93)	NA
Annual Expense Ratio	0.81%	Worst-Ever Loss (1987)	23%
Annual Portfolio Turnover	60%	Stock Market Correlation	55%
5-Year Cost Estimate	12%	Up/Down Market Rank	D – A

Benefits		Investment Information	
Investment Objective	Growth	Telephone	800-448-3863
5-Year Projected Return	+35%	Minimum Investment	$5,000
Safety Rating (0-100)	86%	Telephone Switching	Mail only
Yield	1.2%	Total Assets	$893 million

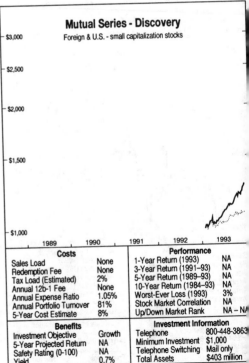

Mutual Series - Discovery
Foreign & U.S. - small capitalization stocks

Costs		Performance	
Sales Load	None	1-Year Return (1993)	NA
Redemption Fee	None	3-Year Return (1991–93)	NA
Tax Load (Estimated)	2%	5-Year Return (1989–93)	NA
Annual 12b-1 Fee	None	10-Year Return (1984–93)	NA
Annual Expense Ratio	1.05%	Worst-Ever Loss (1993)	3%
Annual Portfolio Turnover	81%	Stock Market Correlation	NA
5-Year Cost Estimate	8%	Up/Down Market Rank	NA – NA

Benefits		Investment Information	
Investment Objective	Growth	Telephone	800-448-3863
5-Year Projected Return	NA	Minimum Investment	$1,000
Safety Rating (0-100)	NA	Telephone Switching	Mail only
Yield	0.7%	Total Assets	$403 million

Mutual Series - Qualified Incm
Special situation securities
★★★★★

S&P 500

Fund

$3,000				
$2,500				
$2,000				
$1,500				
$1,000	1989	1990	1991	1992	1993

Costs		Performance	
Sales Load	None	1-Year Return (1993)	+23%
Redemption Fee	None	3-Year Return (1991–93)	+82%
Tax Load (Estimated)	5%	5-Year Return (1989–93)	+88%
Annual 12b-1 Fee	None	10-Year Return (1984–93)	+344%
Annual Expense Ratio	0.82%	Worst-Ever Loss (1987)	24%
Annual Portfolio Turnover	60%	Stock Market Correlation	63%
5-Year Cost Estimate	9%	Up/Down Market Rank	D – A

Benefits		Investment Information	
Investment Objective	Growth	Telephone	800-448-3863
5-Year Projected Return	+35%	Minimum Investment	$1,000
Safety Rating (0-100)	85%	Telephone Switching	Mail only
Yield	1.4%	Total Assets	$1.48 billion

Mutual Series - Shares
Special situation securities
★★★★★

$3,000				
$2,500				
$2,000				
$1,500				
$1,000	1989	1990	1991	1992	1993

Costs		Performance	
Sales Load	None	1-Year Return (1993)	+21%
Redemption Fee	None	3-Year Return (1991–93)	+78%
Tax Load (Estimated)	6%	5-Year Return (1989–93)	+84%
Annual 12b-1 Fee	None	10-Year Return (1984–93)	+334%
Annual Expense Ratio	0.78%	Worst-Ever Loss (1987)	24%
Annual Portfolio Turnover	56%	Stock Market Correlation	66%
5-Year Cost Estimate	10%	Up/Down Market Rank	E – A

Benefits		Investment Information	
Investment Objective	Growth	Telephone	800-448-3863
5-Year Projected Return	+32%	Minimum Investment	$5,000
Safety Rating (0-100)	85%	Telephone Switching	Mail only
Yield	1.7%	Total Assets	$3.42 billion

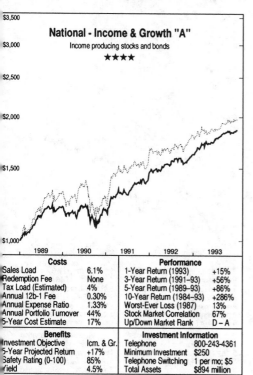

National - Income & Growth "A"
Income producing stocks and bonds
★★★★

$3,500				
$3,000				
$2,500				
$2,000				
$1,500				
$1,000	1989	1990	1991	1992	1993

Costs		Performance	
Sales Load	6.1%	1-Year Return (1993)	+15%
Redemption Fee	None	3-Year Return (1991–93)	+56%
Tax Load (Estimated)	4%	5-Year Return (1989–93)	+86%
Annual 12b-1 Fee	0.30%	10-Year Return (1984–93)	+286%
Annual Expense Ratio	1.33%	Worst-Ever Loss (1987)	13%
Annual Portfolio Turnover	44%	Stock Market Correlation	67%
5-Year Cost Estimate	17%	Up/Down Market Rank	D – A

Benefits		Investment Information	
Investment Objective	Icm. & Gr.	Telephone	800-243-4361
5-Year Projected Return	+17%	Minimum Investment	$250
Safety Rating (0-100)	85%	Telephone Switching	1 per mo; $5
Yield	4.5%	Total Assets	$894 million

National - Stock
Diversified stocks
★

$3,500				
$3,000				
$2,500				
$2,000				
$1,500				
$1,000	1989	1990	1991	1992	1993

Costs		Performance	
Sales Load	6.1%	1-Year Return (1993)	+13%
Redemption Fee	None	3-Year Return (1991–93)	+63%
Tax Load (Estimated)	Neg.	5-Year Return (1989–93)	+93%
Annual 12b-1 Fee	0.30%	10-Year Return (1984–93)	+250%
Annual Expense Ratio	1.36%	Worst-Ever Loss (1987)	32%
Annual Portfolio Turnover	28%	Stock Market Correlation	78%
5-Year Cost Estimate	14%	Up/Down Market Rank	C – C

Benefits		Investment Information	
Investment Objective	Gr. & Icm.	Telephone	800-243-4361
5-Year Projected Return	+8%	Minimum Investment	$250
Safety Rating (0-100)	74%	Telephone Switching	1 per mo; $5
Yield	0.5%	Total Assets	$226 million

EQUITY

National - Worldwide Oppor
Foreign & U.S. - diversified securities

S&P 500

Fund

Costs		Performance	
Sales Load	6.1%	1-Year Return (1993)	+38%
Redemption Fee	None	3-Year Return (1991–93)	+77%
Tax Load (Estimated)	2%	5-Year Return (1989–93)	+49%
Annual 12b-1 Fee	0.30%	10-Year Return (1984–93)	NA
Annual Expense Ratio	2.18%	Worst-Ever Loss (1987)	39%
Annual Portfolio Turnover	95%	Stock Market Correlation	40%
5-Year Cost Estimate	20%	Up/Down Market Rank	E – D

Benefits		Investment Information	
Investment Objective	Growth	Telephone	800-243-4361
5-Year Projected Return	NA	Minimum Investment	$250
Safety Rating (0-100)	75%	Telephone Switching	1 per mo; $5
Yield	0.0%	Total Assets	$95 million

National Industries
Stocks with good earnings and dividend growth

Costs		Performance	
Sales Load	None	1-Year Return (1993)	–1%
Redemption Fee	None	3-Year Return (1991–93)	+30%
Tax Load (Estimated)	7%	5-Year Return (1989–93)	+67%
Annual 12b-1 Fee	None	10-Year Return (1984–93)	+129%
Annual Expense Ratio	1.50%	Worst-Ever Loss (1987)	30%
Annual Portfolio Turnover	20%	Stock Market Correlation	69%
5-Year Cost Estimate	10%	Up/Down Market Rank	D – C

Benefits		Investment Information	
Investment Objective	Gr. & Icm.	Telephone	800-367-7814
5-Year Projected Return	+0%	Minimum Investment	$250
Safety Rating (0-100)	73%	Telephone Switching	Not available
Yield	0.3%	Total Assets	$32 million

Nations Value Inv "A"
Low PE stocks; minimum $300-mil market cap

Costs		Performance	
Sales Load	4.7%	1-Year Return (1993)	+16%
Redemption Fee	None	3-Year Return (1991–93)	+60%
Tax Load (Estimated)	16%	5-Year Return (1989–93)	NA
Annual 12b-1 Fee	0.25%	10-Year Return (1984–93)	NA
Annual Expense Ratio	1.20%	Worst-Ever Loss (1992)	6%
Annual Portfolio Turnover	60%	Stock Market Correlation	77%
5-Year Cost Estimate	32%	Up/Down Market Rank	NA – NA

Benefits		Investment Information	
Investment Objective	Growth	Telephone	800-321-7854
5-Year Projected Return	+17%	Minimum Investment	$1,000
Safety Rating (0-100)	78%	Telephone Switching	Unlimited;free
Yield	1.4%	Total Assets	$39 million

Nationwide Fund
Diversified securities
★

Costs		Performance	
Sales Load	4.7%	1-Year Return (1993)	+7%
Redemption Fee	None	3-Year Return (1991–93)	+43%
Tax Load (Estimated)	7%	5-Year Return (1989–93)	+92%
Annual 12b-1 Fee	None	10-Year Return (1984–93)	+290%
Annual Expense Ratio	0.61%	Worst-Ever Loss (1987)	33%
Annual Portfolio Turnover	21%	Stock Market Correlation	81%
5-Year Cost Estimate	10%	Up/Down Market Rank	C – C

Benefits		Investment Information	
Investment Objective	Icm. & Gr.	Telephone	800-848-0920
5-Year Projected Return	+4%	Minimum Investment	$250
Safety Rating (0-100)	74%	Telephone Switching	Unlimited;free
Yield	2.3%	Total Assets	$736 million

Nationwide Growth
Growth industries

Costs		Performance	
Sales Load	4.7%	1-Year Return (1993)	+11%
Redemption Fee	None	3-Year Return (1991–93)	+61%
Tax Load (Estimated)	5%	5-Year Return (1989–93)	+71%
Annual 12b-1 Fee	None	10-Year Return (1984–93)	+263%
Annual Expense Ratio	0.65%	Worst-Ever Loss (1987)	31%
Annual Portfolio Turnover	6%	Stock Market Correlation	65%
5-Year Cost Estimate	9%	Up/Down Market Rank	C – B
Benefits		**Investment Information**	
Investment Objective	Growth	Telephone	800-848-0920
5-Year Projected Return	+10%	Minimum Investment	$250
Safety Rating (0-100)	77%	Telephone Switching	Unlimited;free
Yield	1.7%	Total Assets	$399 million

Neuberger - Genesis
Under $500 million capitaliztn; undervalued

Costs		Performance	
Sales Load	None	1-Year Return (1993)	+14%
Redemption Fee	None	3-Year Return (1991–93)	+86%
Tax Load (Estimated)	4%	5-Year Return (1989–93)	+83%
Annual 12b-1 Fee	None	10-Year Return (1984–93)	NA
Annual Expense Ratio	1.51%	Worst-Ever Loss (1989-90)	31%
Annual Portfolio Turnover	10%	Stock Market Correlation	50%
5-Year Cost Estimate	9%	Up/Down Market Rank	B – E
Benefits		**Investment Information**	
Investment Objective	Growth	Telephone	800-877-9700
5-Year Projected Return	+22%	Minimum Investment	$1,000
Safety Rating (0-100)	77%	Telephone Switching	Unlimited;free
Yield	0.0%	Total Assets	$119 million

Neuberger - Guardian
Established companies
★★★

Costs		Performance	
Sales Load	None	1-Year Return (1993)	+14%
Redemption Fee	None	3-Year Return (1991–93)	+83%
Tax Load (Estimated)	6%	5-Year Return (1989–93)	+112%
Annual 12b-1 Fee	None	10-Year Return (1984–93)	+303%
Annual Expense Ratio	0.81%	Worst-Ever Loss (1987)	34%
Annual Portfolio Turnover	27%	Stock Market Correlation	84%
5-Year Cost Estimate	7%	Up/Down Market Rank	B – D
Benefits		**Investment Information**	
Investment Objective	Gr. & Icm.	Telephone	800-877-9700
5-Year Projected Return	+29%	Minimum Investment	$1,000
Safety Rating (0-100)	76%	Telephone Switching	Unlimited;free
Yield	0.8%	Total Assets	$1.78 billion

Neuberger - Manhattan
Diversified growth stocks
★

Costs		Performance	
Sales Load	None	1-Year Return (1993)	+10%
Redemption Fee	None	3-Year Return (1991–93)	+70%
Tax Load (Estimated)	1%	5-Year Return (1989–93)	+101%
Annual 12b-1 Fee	None	10-Year Return (1984–93)	+310%
Annual Expense Ratio	1.04%	Worst-Ever Loss (1987)	37%
Annual Portfolio Turnover	76%	Stock Market Correlation	75%
5-Year Cost Estimate	7%	Up/Down Market Rank	A – D
Benefits		**Investment Information**	
Investment Objective	Growth	Telephone	800-877-9700
5-Year Projected Return	+18%	Minimum Investment	$1,000
Safety Rating (0-100)	70%	Telephone Switching	Unlimited;free
Yield	0.0%	Total Assets	$537 million

Neuberger - Partners
Short term trading
★★

Costs		Performance	
Sales Load	None	1-Year Return (1993)	+17%
Redemption Fee	None	3-Year Return (1991–93)	+68%
Tax Load (Estimated)	3%	5-Year Return (1989–93)	+95%
Annual 12b-1 Fee	None	10-Year Return (1984–93)	+286%
Annual Expense Ratio	0.84%	Worst-Ever Loss (1987)	27%
Annual Portfolio Turnover	88%	Stock Market Correlation	74%
5-Year Cost Estimate	7%	Up/Down Market Rank	D – B

Benefits		Investment Information	
Investment Objective	Growth	Telephone	800-877-9700
5-Year Projected Return	+24%	Minimum Investment	$1,000
Safety Rating (0-100)	78%	Telephone Switching	Unlimited;free
Yield	0.0%	Total Assets	$1.18 billion

Neuberger - Prof Invstrs Grwth
Undervalued grth stks; options, futrs; levrgd

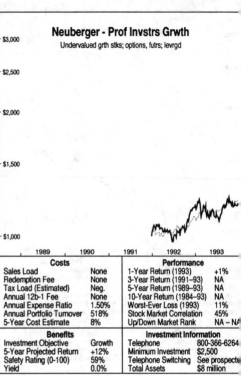

Costs		Performance	
Sales Load	None	1-Year Return (1993)	+1%
Redemption Fee	None	3-Year Return (1991–93)	NA
Tax Load (Estimated)	Neg.	5-Year Return (1989–93)	NA
Annual 12b-1 Fee	None	10-Year Return (1984–93)	NA
Annual Expense Ratio	1.50%	Worst-Ever Loss (1993)	11%
Annual Portfolio Turnover	518%	Stock Market Correlation	45%
5-Year Cost Estimate	8%	Up/Down Market Rank	NA – N

Benefits		Investment Information	
Investment Objective	Growth	Telephone	800-366-6264
5-Year Projected Return	+12%	Minimum Investment	$2,500
Safety Rating (0-100)	59%	Telephone Switching	See prospectus
Yield	0.0%	Total Assets	$8 million

Neuberger - Selectd Sectr Engy
Underval stks; 13 sectors, 90% in 6 or less
★★

Costs		Performance	
Sales Load	None	1-Year Return (1993)	+16%
Redemption Fee	None	3-Year Return (1991–93)	+76%
Tax Load (Estimated)	8%	5-Year Return (1989–93)	+114%
Annual 12b-1 Fee	None	10-Year Return (1984–93)	+255%
Annual Expense Ratio	0.92%	Worst-Ever Loss (1987)	30%
Annual Portfolio Turnover	52%	Stock Market Correlation	81%
5-Year Cost Estimate	13%	Up/Down Market Rank	D – C

Benefits		Investment Information	
Investment Objective	Growth	Telephone	800-877-9700
5-Year Projected Return	NA	Minimum Investment	$1,000
Safety Rating (0-100)	75%	Telephone Switching	Unlimited;free
Yield	0.0%	Total Assets	$574 million

New Age Media
Equity securities of new age media companies

Costs		Performance	
Sales Load	None	1-Year Return (1993)	NA
Redemption Fee	2.0%	3-Year Return (1991–93)	NA
Tax Load (Estimated)	NA	5-Year Return (1989–93)	NA
Annual 12b-1 Fee	None	10-Year Return (1984–93)	NA
Annual Expense Ratio	1.00%	Worst-Ever Loss (1993)	15%
Annual Portfolio Turnover	0%	Stock Market Correlation	NA
5-Year Cost Estimate	7%	Up/Down Market Rank	NA – N

Benefits		Investment Information	
Investment Objective	Growth	Telephone	800-638-5660
5-Year Projected Return	NA	Minimum Investment	None
Safety Rating (0-100)	NA	Telephone Switching	Via broker
Yield	0.0%	Total Assets	$201 million

New Alternatives
Solar and alternative energy stocks

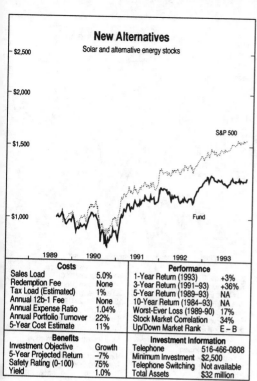

Costs		Performance	
Sales Load	5.0%	1-Year Return (1993)	+3%
Redemption Fee	None	3-Year Return (1991–93)	+36%
Tax Load (Estimated)	1%	5-Year Return (1989–93)	NA
Annual 12b-1 Fee	None	10-Year Return (1984–93)	NA
Annual Expense Ratio	1.04%	Worst-Ever Loss (1989-90)	17%
Annual Portfolio Turnover	22%	Stock Market Correlation	34%
5-Year Cost Estimate	11%	Up/Down Market Rank	E – B

Benefits		Investment Information	
Investment Objective	Growth	Telephone	516-466-0808
5-Year Projected Return	–7%	Minimum Investment	$2,500
Safety Rating (0-100)	75%	Telephone Switching	Not available
Yield	1.0%	Total Assets	$32 million

New Germany
Foreign - small-medium sized German companies

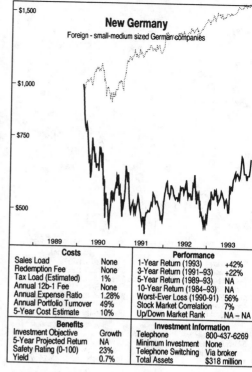

Costs		Performance	
Sales Load	None	1-Year Return (1993)	+42%
Redemption Fee	None	3-Year Return (1991–93)	+22%
Tax Load (Estimated)	1%	5-Year Return (1989–93)	NA
Annual 12b-1 Fee	None	10-Year Return (1984–93)	NA
Annual Expense Ratio	1.28%	Worst-Ever Loss (1990-91)	56%
Annual Portfolio Turnover	49%	Stock Market Correlation	7%
5-Year Cost Estimate	10%	Up/Down Market Rank	NA – NA

Benefits		Investment Information	
Investment Objective	Growth	Telephone	800-437-6269
5-Year Projected Return	NA	Minimum Investment	None
Safety Rating (0-100)	23%	Telephone Switching	Via broker
Yield	0.7%	Total Assets	$318 million

New USA
Entrepreneurially mgd cos; superior grth potl

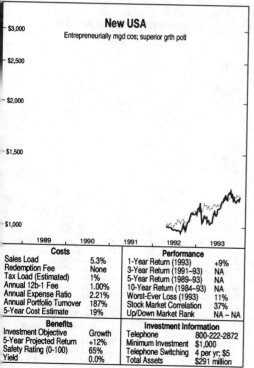

Costs		Performance	
Sales Load	5.3%	1-Year Return (1993)	+9%
Redemption Fee	None	3-Year Return (1991–93)	NA
Tax Load (Estimated)	1%	5-Year Return (1989–93)	NA
Annual 12b-1 Fee	1.00%	10-Year Return (1984–93)	NA
Annual Expense Ratio	2.21%	Worst-Ever Loss (1993)	11%
Annual Portfolio Turnover	187%	Stock Market Correlation	37%
5-Year Cost Estimate	19%	Up/Down Market Rank	NA – NA

Benefits		Investment Information	
Investment Objective	Growth	Telephone	800-222-2872
5-Year Projected Return	+12%	Minimum Investment	$1,000
Safety Rating (0-100)	65%	Telephone Switching	4 per yr; $5
Yield	0.0%	Total Assets	$291 million

Nicholas
Growth stocks
★★

Costs		Performance	
Sales Load	None	1-Year Return (1993)	+5%
Redemption Fee	None	3-Year Return (1991–93)	+69%
Tax Load (Estimated)	1%	5-Year Return (1989–93)	+100%
Annual 12b-1 Fee	None	10-Year Return (1984–93)	+273%
Annual Expense Ratio	0.76%	Worst-Ever Loss (1987)	24%
Annual Portfolio Turnover	32%	Stock Market Correlation	74%
5-Year Cost Estimate	4%	Up/Down Market Rank	C – B

Benefits		Investment Information	
Investment Objective	Gr. & Icm.	Telephone	414-272-6133
5-Year Projected Return	+23%	Minimum Investment	$500
Safety Rating (0-100)	77%	Telephone Switching	4 per yr; $5
Yield	0.6%	Total Assets	$3.12 billion

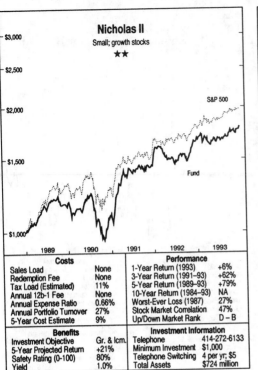

Nicholas II
Small; growth stocks
★★

(chart showing S&P 500 and Fund from 1989 to 1993, scale $1,000–$3,000)

Costs		Performance	
Sales Load	None	1-Year Return (1993)	+6%
Redemption Fee	None	3-Year Return (1991–93)	+62%
Tax Load (Estimated)	11%	5-Year Return (1989–93)	+79%
Annual 12b-1 Fee	None	10-Year Return (1984–93)	NA
Annual Expense Ratio	0.66%	Worst-Ever Loss (1987)	27%
Annual Portfolio Turnover	27%	Stock Market Correlation	47%
5-Year Cost Estimate	9%	Up/Down Market Rank	D – B

Benefits		Investment Information	
Investment Objective	Gr. & Icm.	Telephone	414-272-6133
5-Year Projected Return	+21%	Minimum Investment	$1,000
Safety Rating (0-100)	80%	Telephone Switching	4 per yr; $5
Yield	1.0%	Total Assets	$724 million

Nicholas Limited Edition
Diversified growth stocks
★★★★

(chart from 1989 to 1993, scale $1,000–$3,000)

Costs		Performance	
Sales Load	None	1-Year Return (1993)	+9%
Redemption Fee	None	3-Year Return (1991–93)	+83%
Tax Load (Estimated)	6%	5-Year Return (1989–93)	+111%
Annual 12b-1 Fee	None	10-Year Return (1984–93)	NA
Annual Expense Ratio	0.94%	Worst-Ever Loss (1990)	24%
Annual Portfolio Turnover	28%	Stock Market Correlation	44%
5-Year Cost Estimate	8%	Up/Down Market Rank	C – B

Benefits		Investment Information	
Investment Objective	Growth	Telephone	414-272-6133
5-Year Projected Return	+40%	Minimum Investment	$2,000
Safety Rating (0-100)	78%	Telephone Switching	Not available
Yield	0.5%	Total Assets	$181 million

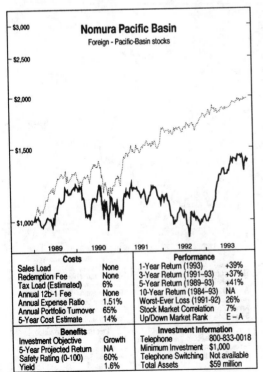

Nomura Pacific Basin
Foreign - Pacific-Basin stocks

(chart from 1989 to 1993, scale $1,000–$3,000)

Costs		Performance	
Sales Load	None	1-Year Return (1993)	+39%
Redemption Fee	None	3-Year Return (1991–93)	+37%
Tax Load (Estimated)	6%	5-Year Return (1989–93)	+41%
Annual 12b-1 Fee	None	10-Year Return (1984–93)	NA
Annual Expense Ratio	1.51%	Worst-Ever Loss (1991-92)	26%
Annual Portfolio Turnover	65%	Stock Market Correlation	7%
5-Year Cost Estimate	14%	Up/Down Market Rank	E – A

Benefits		Investment Information	
Investment Objective	Growth	Telephone	800-833-0018
5-Year Projected Return	NA	Minimum Investment	$1,000
Safety Rating (0-100)	60%	Telephone Switching	Not available
Yield	1.6%	Total Assets	$59 million

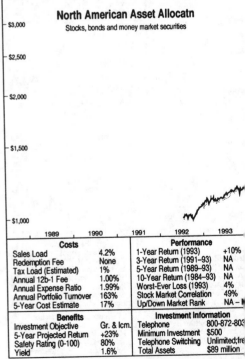

North American Asset Allocatn
Stocks, bonds and money market securities

(chart from 1989 to 1993, scale $1,000–$3,000)

Costs		Performance	
Sales Load	4.2%	1-Year Return (1993)	+10%
Redemption Fee	None	3-Year Return (1991–93)	NA
Tax Load (Estimated)	1%	5-Year Return (1989–93)	NA
Annual 12b-1 Fee	1.00%	10-Year Return (1984–93)	NA
Annual Expense Ratio	1.99%	Worst-Ever Loss (1993)	4%
Annual Portfolio Turnover	163%	Stock Market Correlation	49%
5-Year Cost Estimate	17%	Up/Down Market Rank	NA –

Benefits		Investment Information	
Investment Objective	Gr. & Icm.	Telephone	800-872-80⊃
5-Year Projected Return	+23%	Minimum Investment	$500
Safety Rating (0-100)	80%	Telephone Switching	Unlimited;fre
Yield	1.6%	Total Assets	$89 million

1994 Mutual Fund Buyer's Gui

North American Growth
Diversified growth stocks

S&P 500

Fund

Costs		Performance	
Sales Load	4.2%	1-Year Return (1993)	+11%
Redemption Fee	None	3-Year Return (1991–93)	+65%
Tax Load (Estimated)	3%	5-Year Return (1989–93)	+70%
Annual 12b-1 Fee	1.00%	10-Year Return (1984–93)	NA
Annual Expense Ratio	1.99%	Worst-Ever Loss (1989-90)	31%
Annual Portfolio Turnover	40%	Stock Market Correlation	67%
5-Year Cost Estimate	18%	Up/Down Market Rank	B – E

Benefits		Investment Information	
Investment Objective	Gr. & Icm.	Telephone	800-872-8037
5-Year Projected Return	–1%	Minimum Investment	$500
Safety Rating (0-100)	69%	Telephone Switching	Unlimited;free
Yield	0.2%	Total Assets	$48 million

Northeast Investors Growth
Diversified securities; leveraged

Costs		Performance	
Sales Load	None	1-Year Return (1993)	+2%
Redemption Fee	None	3-Year Return (1991–93)	+39%
Tax Load (Estimated)	2%	5-Year Return (1989–93)	+88%
Annual 12b-1 Fee	None	10-Year Return (1984–93)	+274%
Annual Expense Ratio	1.50%	Worst-Ever Loss (1987)	34%
Annual Portfolio Turnover	23%	Stock Market Correlation	76%
5-Year Cost Estimate	9%	Up/Down Market Rank	C – D

Benefits		Investment Information	
Investment Objective	Gr. & Icm.	Telephone	800-225-6704
5-Year Projected Return	+7%	Minimum Investment	$1,000
Safety Rating (0-100)	70%	Telephone Switching	Unlimited;free
Yield	0.8%	Total Assets	$39 million

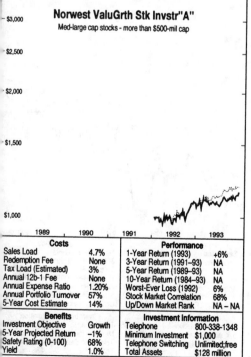

Norwest ValuGrth Stk Invstr"A"
Med-large cap stocks - more than $500-mil cap

Costs		Performance	
Sales Load	4.7%	1-Year Return (1993)	+6%
Redemption Fee	None	3-Year Return (1991–93)	NA
Tax Load (Estimated)	3%	5-Year Return (1989–93)	NA
Annual 12b-1 Fee	None	10-Year Return (1984–93)	NA
Annual Expense Ratio	1.20%	Worst-Ever Loss (1992)	6%
Annual Portfolio Turnover	57%	Stock Market Correlation	68%
5-Year Cost Estimate	14%	Up/Down Market Rank	NA – NA

Benefits		Investment Information	
Investment Objective	Growth	Telephone	800-338-1348
5-Year Projected Return	–1%	Minimum Investment	$1,000
Safety Rating (0-100)	68%	Telephone Switching	Unlimited;free
Yield	1.0%	Total Assets	$128 million

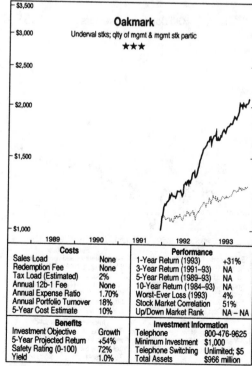

Oakmark
Underval stks; qlty of mgmt & mgmt stk partic
★★★

Costs		Performance	
Sales Load	None	1-Year Return (1993)	+31%
Redemption Fee	None	3-Year Return (1991–93)	NA
Tax Load (Estimated)	2%	5-Year Return (1989–93)	NA
Annual 12b-1 Fee	None	10-Year Return (1984–93)	NA
Annual Expense Ratio	1.70%	Worst-Ever Loss (1993)	4%
Annual Portfolio Turnover	18%	Stock Market Correlation	51%
5-Year Cost Estimate	10%	Up/Down Market Rank	NA – NA

Benefits		Investment Information	
Investment Objective	Growth	Telephone	800-476-9625
5-Year Projected Return	+54%	Minimum Investment	$1,000
Safety Rating (0-100)	72%	Telephone Switching	Unlimited; $5
Yield	1.0%	Total Assets	$966 million

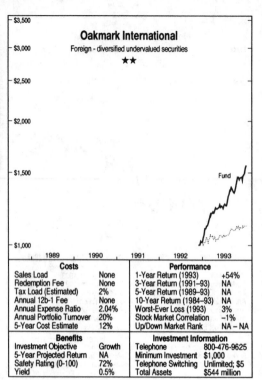

Oakmark International
Foreign - diversified undervalued securities
★★

Fund

Costs		Performance	
Sales Load	None	1-Year Return (1993)	+54%
Redemption Fee	None	3-Year Return (1991–93)	NA
Tax Load (Estimated)	2%	5-Year Return (1989–93)	NA
Annual 12b-1 Fee	None	10-Year Return (1984–93)	NA
Annual Expense Ratio	2.04%	Worst-Ever Loss (1993)	3%
Annual Portfolio Turnover	20%	Stock Market Correlation	–1%
5-Year Cost Estimate	12%	Up/Down Market Rank	NA – NA

Benefits		Investment Information	
Investment Objective	Growth	Telephone	800-476-9625
5-Year Projected Return	NA	Minimum Investment	$1,000
Safety Rating (0-100)	72%	Telephone Switching	Unlimited; $5
Yield	0.5%	Total Assets	$544 million

Oberweis Emerging Growth
Small and undervalued growth stocks

Costs		Performance	
Sales Load	None	1-Year Return (1993)	+10%
Redemption Fee	None	3-Year Return (1991–93)	+133%
Tax Load (Estimated)	2%	5-Year Return (1989–93)	+191%
Annual 12b-1 Fee	0.50%	10-Year Return (1984–93)	NA
Annual Expense Ratio	1.99%	Worst-Ever Loss (1987)	48%
Annual Portfolio Turnover	63%	Stock Market Correlation	44%
5-Year Cost Estimate	12%	Up/Down Market Rank	A – E

Benefits		Investment Information	
Investment Objective	Growth	Telephone	800-245-731
5-Year Projected Return	+60%	Minimum Investment	$1,000
Safety Rating (0-100)	55%	Telephone Switching	Not available
Yield	0.0%	Total Assets	$99 million

Old Dominion Investors
Dividend-paying NYSE and AMEX listed stocks

Costs		Performance	
Sales Load	6.1%	1-Year Return (1993)	+10%
Redemption Fee	None	3-Year Return (1991–93)	+46%
Tax Load (Estimated)	Neg.	5-Year Return (1989–93)	NA
Annual 12b-1 Fee	0.25%	10-Year Return (1984–93)	NA
Annual Expense Ratio	1.33%	Worst-Ever Loss (1989-90)	27%
Annual Portfolio Turnover	62%	Stock Market Correlation	69%
5-Year Cost Estimate	13%	Up/Down Market Rank	D – D

Benefits		Investment Information	
Investment Objective	Icm. & Gr.	Telephone	800-441-6580
5-Year Projected Return	–15%	Minimum Investment	$200
Safety Rating (0-100)	69%	Telephone Switching	Unlimited; $5
Yield	5.8%	Total Assets	$7 million

Olympic Equity Income
Stocks with above-average yields

Costs		Performance	
Sales Load	None	1-Year Return (1993)	+16%
Redemption Fee	None	3-Year Return (1991–93)	+78%
Tax Load (Estimated)	4%	5-Year Return (1989–93)	+80%
Annual 12b-1 Fee	None	10-Year Return (1984–93)	NA
Annual Expense Ratio	1.00%	Worst-Ever Loss (1989-90)	34%
Annual Portfolio Turnover	32%	Stock Market Correlation	69%
5-Year Cost Estimate	7%	Up/Down Market Rank	C – E

Benefits		Investment Information	
Investment Objective	Icm. & Gr.	Telephone	800-346-7301
5-Year Projected Return	+8%	Minimum Investment	$10,000
Safety Rating (0-100)	70%	Telephone Switching	Not available
Yield	2.8%	Total Assets	$88 million

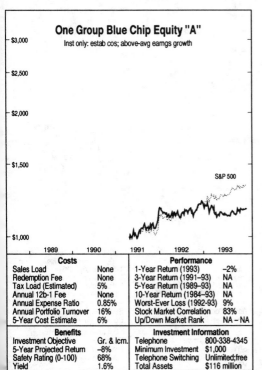

One Group Blue Chip Equity "A"

Inst only: estab cos; above-avg earngs growth

S&P 500

Costs		Performance	
Sales Load	None	1-Year Return (1993)	–2%
Redemption Fee	None	3-Year Return (1991–93)	NA
Tax Load (Estimated)	5%	5-Year Return (1989–93)	NA
Annual 12b-1 Fee	None	10-Year Return (1984–93)	NA
Annual Expense Ratio	0.85%	Worst-Ever Loss (1992-93)	9%
Annual Portfolio Turnover	16%	Stock Market Correlation	83%
5-Year Cost Estimate	6%	Up/Down Market Rank	NA – NA

Benefits		Investment Information	
Investment Objective	Gr. & Icm.	Telephone	800-338-4345
5-Year Projected Return	–8%	Minimum Investment	$1,000
Safety Rating (0-100)	68%	Telephone Switching	Unlimited;free
Yield	1.6%	Total Assets	$116 million

One Group Disciplined Value "A"

Inst only: div-pay low PE & price-book stks

Costs		Performance	
Sales Load	None	1-Year Return (1993)	+13%
Redemption Fee	None	3-Year Return (1991–93)	+62%
Tax Load (Estimated)	0%	5-Year Return (1989–93)	NA
Annual 12b-1 Fee	None	10-Year Return (1984–93)	NA
Annual Expense Ratio	0.85%	Worst-Ever Loss (1989-90)	26%
Annual Portfolio Turnover	80%	Stock Market Correlation	75%
5-Year Cost Estimate	5%	Up/Down Market Rank	D – D

Benefits		Investment Information	
Investment Objective	Gr. & Icm.	Telephone	800-338-4345
5-Year Projected Return	+6%	Minimum Investment	$1,000
Safety Rating (0-100)	73%	Telephone Switching	Unlimited;free
Yield	2.0%	Total Assets	$257 million

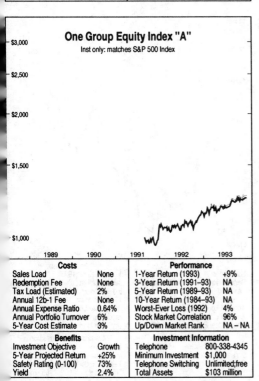

One Group Equity Index "A"

Inst only: matches S&P 500 Index

Costs		Performance	
Sales Load	None	1-Year Return (1993)	+9%
Redemption Fee	None	3-Year Return (1991–93)	NA
Tax Load (Estimated)	2%	5-Year Return (1989–93)	NA
Annual 12b-1 Fee	None	10-Year Return (1984–93)	NA
Annual Expense Ratio	0.64%	Worst-Ever Loss (1992)	4%
Annual Portfolio Turnover	6%	Stock Market Correlation	96%
5-Year Cost Estimate	3%	Up/Down Market Rank	NA – NA

Benefits		Investment Information	
Investment Objective	Growth	Telephone	800-338-4345
5-Year Projected Return	+25%	Minimum Investment	$1,000
Safety Rating (0-100)	73%	Telephone Switching	Unlimited;free
Yield	2.4%	Total Assets	$103 million

One Group Income Equity "A"

Inst only: yld above S&P 500;good fundamentls

★★

Costs		Performance	
Sales Load	None	1-Year Return (1993)	+11%
Redemption Fee	None	3-Year Return (1991–93)	+47%
Tax Load (Estimated)	4%	5-Year Return (1989–93)	NA
Annual 12b-1 Fee	None	10-Year Return (1984–93)	NA
Annual Expense Ratio	0.85%	Worst-Ever Loss (1990)	14%
Annual Portfolio Turnover	3%	Stock Market Correlation	86%
5-Year Cost Estimate	5%	Up/Down Market Rank	D – B

Benefits		Investment Information	
Investment Objective	Icm. & Gr.	Telephone	800-338-4345
5-Year Projected Return	+10%	Minimum Investment	$1,000
Safety Rating (0-100)	78%	Telephone Switching	Unlimited;free
Yield	3.2%	Total Assets	$189 million

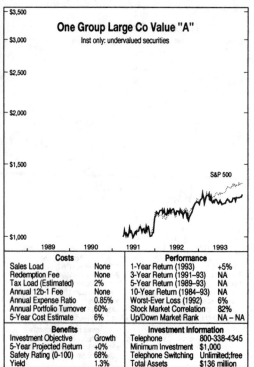

One Group Large Co Value "A"
Inst only: undervalued securities

S&P 500

Costs		Performance	
Sales Load	None	1-Year Return (1993)	+5%
Redemption Fee	None	3-Year Return (1991–93)	NA
Tax Load (Estimated)	2%	5-Year Return (1989–93)	NA
Annual 12b-1 Fee	None	10-Year Return (1984–93)	NA
Annual Expense Ratio	0.85%	Worst-Ever Loss (1992)	6%
Annual Portfolio Turnover	60%	Stock Market Correlation	82%
5-Year Cost Estimate	6%	Up/Down Market Rank	NA – NA

Benefits		Investment Information	
Investment Objective	Growth	Telephone	800-338-4345
5-Year Projected Return	+0%	Minimum Investment	$1,000
Safety Rating (0-100)	68%	Telephone Switching	Unlimited;free
Yield	1.3%	Total Assets	$136 million

One Group Small Co Growth "A"
Inst only: above-average EPS growth forecast
★★

Costs		Performance	
Sales Load	None	1-Year Return (1993)	+13%
Redemption Fee	None	3-Year Return (1991–93)	+76%
Tax Load (Estimated)	2%	5-Year Return (1989–93)	NA
Annual 12b-1 Fee	None	10-Year Return (1984–93)	NA
Annual Expense Ratio	0.85%	Worst-Ever Loss (1990)	24%
Annual Portfolio Turnover	57%	Stock Market Correlation	64%
5-Year Cost Estimate	6%	Up/Down Market Rank	A – D

Benefits		Investment Information	
Investment Objective	Growth	Telephone	800-338-4345
5-Year Projected Return	+33%	Minimum Investment	$1,000
Safety Rating (0-100)	70%	Telephone Switching	Unlimited free
Yield	0.4%	Total Assets	$269 million

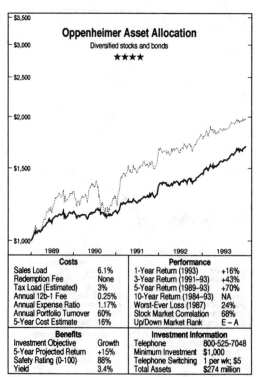

Oppenheimer Asset Allocation
Diversified stocks and bonds
★★★★

Costs		Performance	
Sales Load	6.1%	1-Year Return (1993)	+16%
Redemption Fee	None	3-Year Return (1991–93)	+43%
Tax Load (Estimated)	3%	5-Year Return (1989–93)	+70%
Annual 12b-1 Fee	0.25%	10-Year Return (1984–93)	NA
Annual Expense Ratio	1.17%	Worst-Ever Loss (1987)	24%
Annual Portfolio Turnover	60%	Stock Market Correlation	68%
5-Year Cost Estimate	16%	Up/Down Market Rank	E – A

Benefits		Investment Information	
Investment Objective	Growth	Telephone	800-525-7048
5-Year Projected Return	+15%	Minimum Investment	$1,000
Safety Rating (0-100)	88%	Telephone Switching	1 per wk; $5
Yield	3.4%	Total Assets	$274 million

Oppenheimer Discovery
Growth stocks
★

Costs		Performance	
Sales Load	6.1%	1-Year Return (1993)	+18%
Redemption Fee	None	3-Year Return (1991–93)	+137%
Tax Load (Estimated)	1%	5-Year Return (1989–93)	+170%
Annual 12b-1 Fee	0.25%	10-Year Return (1984–93)	NA
Annual Expense Ratio	1.52%	Worst-Ever Loss (1987)	34%
Annual Portfolio Turnover	68%	Stock Market Correlation	49%
5-Year Cost Estimate	16%	Up/Down Market Rank	A – D

Benefits		Investment Information	
Investment Objective	Growth	Telephone	800-525-7048
5-Year Projected Return	+41%	Minimum Investment	$1,000
Safety Rating (0-100)	66%	Telephone Switching	1 per wk; $5
Yield	0.0%	Total Assets	$550 million

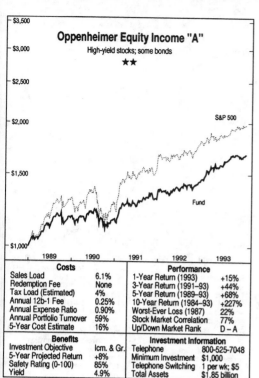

Oppenheimer Equity Income "A"

High-yield stocks; some bonds

★★

Costs		Performance	
Sales Load	6.1%	1-Year Return (1993)	+15%
Redemption Fee	None	3-Year Return (1991–93)	+44%
Tax Load (Estimated)	4%	5-Year Return (1989–93)	+68%
Annual 12b-1 Fee	0.25%	10-Year Return (1984–93)	+227%
Annual Expense Ratio	0.90%	Worst-Ever Loss (1987)	22%
Annual Portfolio Turnover	59%	Stock Market Correlation	77%
5-Year Cost Estimate	16%	Up/Down Market Rank	D – A
Benefits		**Investment Information**	
Investment Objective	Icm. & Gr.	Telephone	800-525-7048
5-Year Projected Return	+8%	Minimum Investment	$1,000
Safety Rating (0-100)	85%	Telephone Switching	1 per wk; $5
Yield	4.9%	Total Assets	$1.85 billion

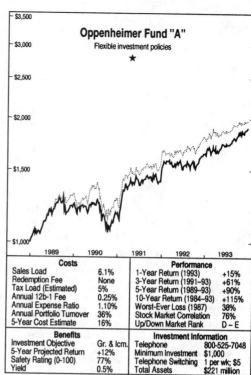

Oppenheimer Fund "A"

Flexible investment policies

★

Costs		Performance	
Sales Load	6.1%	1-Year Return (1993)	+15%
Redemption Fee	None	3-Year Return (1991–93)	+61%
Tax Load (Estimated)	5%	5-Year Return (1989–93)	+90%
Annual 12b-1 Fee	0.25%	10-Year Return (1984–93)	+115%
Annual Expense Ratio	1.10%	Worst-Ever Loss (1987)	38%
Annual Portfolio Turnover	36%	Stock Market Correlation	76%
5-Year Cost Estimate	16%	Up/Down Market Rank	D – E
Benefits		**Investment Information**	
Investment Objective	Gr. & Icm.	Telephone	800-525-7048
5-Year Projected Return	+12%	Minimum Investment	$1,000
Safety Rating (0-100)	77%	Telephone Switching	1 per wk; $5
Yield	0.5%	Total Assets	$221 million

Oppenheimer Global "A"

Foreign & U.S. - diversified stocks

Costs		Performance	
Sales Load	6.1%	1-Year Return (1993)	+43%
Redemption Fee	None	3-Year Return (1991–93)	+56%
Tax Load (Estimated)	3%	5-Year Return (1989–93)	+109%
Annual 12b-1 Fee	0.25%	10-Year Return (1984–93)	+324%
Annual Expense Ratio	1.36%	Worst-Ever Loss (1987)	39%
Annual Portfolio Turnover	20%	Stock Market Correlation	17%
5-Year Cost Estimate	15%	Up/Down Market Rank	C – C
Benefits		**Investment Information**	
Investment Objective	Growth	Telephone	800-525-7048
5-Year Projected Return	NA	Minimum Investment	$1,000
Safety Rating (0-100)	73%	Telephone Switching	1 per wk; $5
Yield	0.7%	Total Assets	$1.38 billion

Oppenheimer Global Bio-Tech

Foreign & U.S. - biotechnology stocks

Costs		Performance	
Sales Load	6.1%	1-Year Return (1993)	–1%
Redemption Fee	None	3-Year Return (1991–93)	+69%
Tax Load (Estimated)	1%	5-Year Return (1989–93)	NA
Annual 12b-1 Fee	0.25%	10-Year Return (1984–93)	NA
Annual Expense Ratio	1.39%	Worst-Ever Loss (1992-93)	47%
Annual Portfolio Turnover	3%	Stock Market Correlation	18%
5-Year Cost Estimate	14%	Up/Down Market Rank	NA – NA
Benefits		**Investment Information**	
Investment Objective	Growth	Telephone	800-525-7048
5-Year Projected Return	NA	Minimum Investment	$1,000
Safety Rating (0-100)	46%	Telephone Switching	1 per wk; $5
Yield	0.7%	Total Assets	$196 million

Oppenheimer Global Environment
Foreign & U.S. - environmental companies

S&P 500

Fund

Costs		Performance	
Sales Load	6.1%	1-Year Return (1993)	+12%
Redemption Fee	None	3-Year Return (1991–93)	+2%
Tax Load (Estimated)	Neg.	5-Year Return (1989–93)	NA
Annual 12b-1 Fee	0.25%	10-Year Return (1984–93)	NA
Annual Expense Ratio	1.68%	Worst-Ever Loss (1990-92)	29%
Annual Portfolio Turnover	135%	Stock Market Correlation	38%
5-Year Cost Estimate	15%	Up/Down Market Rank	NA – NA

Benefits		Investment Information	
Investment Objective	Growth	Telephone	800-525-7048
5-Year Projected Return	NA	Minimum Investment	$1,000
Safety Rating (0-100)	61%	Telephone Switching	1 per wk; $5
Yield	0.2%	Total Assets	$44 million

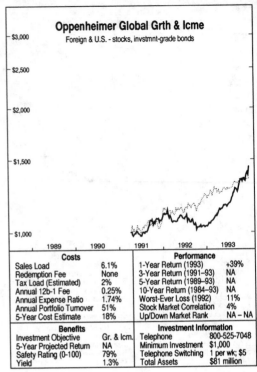

Oppenheimer Global Grth & Icme
Foreign & U.S. - stocks, invstmnt-grade bonds

Costs		Performance	
Sales Load	6.1%	1-Year Return (1993)	+39%
Redemption Fee	None	3-Year Return (1991–93)	NA
Tax Load (Estimated)	2%	5-Year Return (1989–93)	NA
Annual 12b-1 Fee	0.25%	10-Year Return (1984–93)	NA
Annual Expense Ratio	1.74%	Worst-Ever Loss (1992)	11%
Annual Portfolio Turnover	51%	Stock Market Correlation	4%
5-Year Cost Estimate	18%	Up/Down Market Rank	NA – NA

Benefits		Investment Information	
Investment Objective	Gr. & Icm.	Telephone	800-525-7048
5-Year Projected Return	NA	Minimum Investment	$1,000
Safety Rating (0-100)	79%	Telephone Switching	1 per wk; $5
Yield	1.3%	Total Assets	$81 million

Oppenheimer Gold & Specl Miner
International gold and silver stocks

Costs		Performance	
Sales Load	6.1%	1-Year Return (1993)	+62%
Redemption Fee	None	3-Year Return (1991–93)	+46%
Tax Load (Estimated)	Neg.	5-Year Return (1989–93)	+44%
Annual 12b-1 Fee	0.25%	10-Year Return (1984–93)	+155%
Annual Expense Ratio	1.38%	Worst-Ever Loss (1990-92)	43%
Annual Portfolio Turnover	0%	Stock Market Correlation	–1%
5-Year Cost Estimate	14%	Up/Down Market Rank	E – A

Benefits		Investment Information	
Investment Objective	Growth	Telephone	800-525-7048
5-Year Projected Return	NA	Minimum Investment	$1,000
Safety Rating (0-100)	61%	Telephone Switching	1 per wk; $5
Yield	0.4%	Total Assets	$162 million

Oppenheimer Main Str Inc & Gr
Income producing stocks and bonds
★★★★

Costs		Performance	
Sales Load	6.1%	1-Year Return (1993)	+35%
Redemption Fee	None	3-Year Return (1991–93)	+195%
Tax Load (Estimated)	1%	5-Year Return (1989–93)	NA
Annual 12b-1 Fee	0.25%	10-Year Return (1984–93)	NA
Annual Expense Ratio	1.25%	Worst-Ever Loss (1990)	16%
Annual Portfolio Turnover	273%	Stock Market Correlation	45%
5-Year Cost Estimate	14%	Up/Down Market Rank	B – NA

Benefits		Investment Information	
Investment Objective	Icm. & Gr.	Telephone	800-525-7048
5-Year Projected Return	+46%	Minimum Investment	$1,000
Safety Rating (0-100)	71%	Telephone Switching	1 per wk; $5
Yield	1.3%	Total Assets	$72 million

Oppenheimer Special "A"
Market timing

Costs		Performance	
Sales Load	6.1%	1-Year Return (1993)	+3%
Redemption Fee	None	3-Year Return (1991–93)	+68%
Tax Load (Estimated)	9%	5-Year Return (1989–93)	+98%
Annual 12b-1 Fee	0.25%	10-Year Return (1984–93)	+154%
Annual Expense Ratio	1.06%	Worst-Ever Loss (1987)	27%
Annual Portfolio Turnover	23%	Stock Market Correlation	72%
5-Year Cost Estimate	16%	Up/Down Market Rank	B – D

Benefits		Investment Information	
Investment Objective	Growth	Telephone	800-525-7048
5-Year Projected Return	+13%	Minimum Investment	$1,000
Safety Rating (0-100)	70%	Telephone Switching	1 per wk; $5
Yield	0.6%	Total Assets	$736 million

Oppenheimer Target
Diversified growth stocks

Costs		Performance	
Sales Load	6.1%	1-Year Return (1993)	+4%
Redemption Fee	None	3-Year Return (1991–93)	+62%
Tax Load (Estimated)	3%	5-Year Return (1989–93)	+88%
Annual 12b-1 Fee	0.25%	10-Year Return (1984–93)	+136%
Annual Expense Ratio	1.09%	Worst-Ever Loss (1987)	41%
Annual Portfolio Turnover	40%	Stock Market Correlation	71%
5-Year Cost Estimate	14%	Up/Down Market Rank	D – D

Benefits		Investment Information	
Investment Objective	Growth	Telephone	800-525-7048
5-Year Projected Return	+10%	Minimum Investment	$1,000
Safety Rating (0-100)	69%	Telephone Switching	1 per wk; $5
Yield	0.5%	Total Assets	$376 million

Oppenheimer Time
Diversified growth stocks

Costs		Performance	
Sales Load	6.1%	1-Year Return (1993)	+20%
Redemption Fee	None	3-Year Return (1991–93)	+69%
Tax Load (Estimated)	5%	5-Year Return (1989–93)	+101%
Annual 12b-1 Fee	0.25%	10-Year Return (1984–93)	+230%
Annual Expense Ratio	1.00%	Worst-Ever Loss (1987)	32%
Annual Portfolio Turnover	62%	Stock Market Correlation	57%
5-Year Cost Estimate	18%	Up/Down Market Rank	A – C

Benefits		Investment Information	
Investment Objective	Growth	Telephone	800-525-7048
5-Year Projected Return	+14%	Minimum Investment	$1,000
Safety Rating (0-100)	73%	Telephone Switching	1 per wk; $5
Yield	0.0%	Total Assets	$400 million

Oppenheimer Total Return "A"
Diversified securities
★★

Costs		Performance	
Sales Load	6.1%	1-Year Return (1993)	+21%
Redemption Fee	None	3-Year Return (1991–93)	+86%
Tax Load (Estimated)	1%	5-Year Return (1989–93)	+114%
Annual 12b-1 Fee	0.25%	10-Year Return (1984–93)	+323%
Annual Expense Ratio	0.96%	Worst-Ever Loss (1987)	29%
Annual Portfolio Turnover	136%	Stock Market Correlation	67%
5-Year Cost Estimate	12%	Up/Down Market Rank	B – C

Benefits		Investment Information	
Investment Objective	Gr. & Icm.	Telephone	800-525-7048
5-Year Projected Return	+30%	Minimum Investment	$1,000
Safety Rating (0-100)	76%	Telephone Switching	1 per wk; $5
Yield	2.3%	Total Assets	$1.18 billion

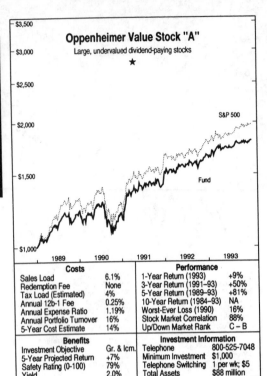

Oppenheimer Value Stock "A"

Large, undervalued dividend-paying stocks

★

S&P 500

Fund

Costs		Performance	
Sales Load	6.1%	1-Year Return (1993)	+9%
Redemption Fee	None	3-Year Return (1991–93)	+50%
Tax Load (Estimated)	4%	5-Year Return (1989–93)	+81%
Annual 12b-1 Fee	0.25%	10-Year Return (1984–93)	NA
Annual Expense Ratio	1.19%	Worst-Ever Loss (1990)	16%
Annual Portfolio Turnover	16%	Stock Market Correlation	88%
5-Year Cost Estimate	14%	Up/Down Market Rank	C – B

Benefits		Investment Information	
Investment Objective	Gr. & Icm.	Telephone	800-525-7048
5-Year Projected Return	+7%	Minimum Investment	$1,000
Safety Rating (0-100)	79%	Telephone Switching	1 per wk; $5
Yield	2.0%	Total Assets	$88 million

Overland Asset Allocation

S&P 500 stocks, Treas bonds & money mkt secs

★★★★

Costs		Performance	
Sales Load	4.7%	1-Year Return (1993)	+13%
Redemption Fee	None	3-Year Return (1991–93)	+47%
Tax Load (Estimated)	2%	5-Year Return (1989–93)	NA
Annual 12b-1 Fee	0.25%	10-Year Return (1984–93)	NA
Annual Expense Ratio	1.25%	Worst-Ever Loss (1992)	7%
Annual Portfolio Turnover	50%	Stock Market Correlation	67%
5-Year Cost Estimate	14%	Up/Down Market Rank	NA – NA

Benefits		Investment Information	
Investment Objective	Growth	Telephone	800-552-9612
5-Year Projected Return	+27%	Minimum Investment	$1,000
Safety Rating (0-100)	87%	Telephone Switching	Unlimited;free
Yield	2.6%	Total Assets	$51 million

Pacific Horizon Aggres Growth

Small capitalization stocks

Costs		Performance	
Sales Load	4.7%	1-Year Return (1993)	+7%
Redemption Fee	None	3-Year Return (1991–93)	+80%
Tax Load (Estimated)	10%	5-Year Return (1989–93)	+159%
Annual 12b-1 Fee	0.25%	10-Year Return (1984–93)	NA
Annual Expense Ratio	1.49%	Worst-Ever Loss (1990)	30%
Annual Portfolio Turnover	32%	Stock Market Correlation	53%
5-Year Cost Estimate	19%	Up/Down Market Rank	A – D

Benefits		Investment Information	
Investment Objective	Growth	Telephone	800-332-3863
5-Year Projected Return	+31%	Minimum Investment	$1,000
Safety Rating (0-100)	59%	Telephone Switching	Unlimited;free
Yield	0.0%	Total Assets	$180 million

Pacifica Balanced

30-70% stocks; 30-70% investment-grade bonds

★★★★

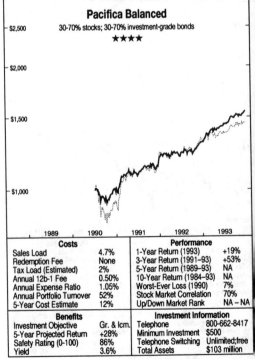

Costs		Performance	
Sales Load	4.7%	1-Year Return (1993)	+19%
Redemption Fee	None	3-Year Return (1991–93)	+53%
Tax Load (Estimated)	2%	5-Year Return (1989–93)	NA
Annual 12b-1 Fee	0.50%	10-Year Return (1984–93)	NA
Annual Expense Ratio	1.05%	Worst-Ever Loss (1990)	7%
Annual Portfolio Turnover	52%	Stock Market Correlation	70%
5-Year Cost Estimate	12%	Up/Down Market Rank	NA – NA

Benefits		Investment Information	
Investment Objective	Gr. & Icm.	Telephone	800-662-8417
5-Year Projected Return	+28%	Minimum Investment	$500
Safety Rating (0-100)	86%	Telephone Switching	Unlimited;free
Yield	3.6%	Total Assets	$103 million

Pacifica Equity Value

Foreign & U.S. - diversified securities

★

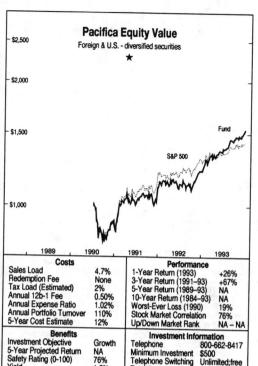

Fund

S&P 500

Costs		Performance	
Sales Load	4.7%	1-Year Return (1993)	+26%
Redemption Fee	None	3-Year Return (1991–93)	+67%
Tax Load (Estimated)	2%	5-Year Return (1989–93)	NA
Annual 12b-1 Fee	0.50%	10-Year Return (1984–93)	NA
Annual Expense Ratio	1.02%	Worst-Ever Loss (1990)	19%
Annual Portfolio Turnover	110%	Stock Market Correlation	76%
5-Year Cost Estimate	12%	Up/Down Market Rank	NA – NA

Benefits		Investment Information	
Investment Objective	Growth	Telephone	800-662-8417
5-Year Projected Return	NA	Minimum Investment	$500
Safety Rating (0-100)	76%	Telephone Switching	Unlimited;free
Yield	1.8%	Total Assets	$140 million

Paine Webber Asset Alloc "B"

Mix of stocks, bonds and Treasury bills

★★★

Costs		Performance	
Sales Load	None	1-Year Return (1993)	+15%
Redemption Fee	5.3%	3-Year Return (1991–93)	+42%
Tax Load (Estimated)	4%	5-Year Return (1989–93)	+61%
Annual 12b-1 Fee	1.00%	10-Year Return (1984–93)	NA
Annual Expense Ratio	1.98%	Worst-Ever Loss (1987)	12%
Annual Portfolio Turnover	33%	Stock Market Correlation	69%
5-Year Cost Estimate	14%	Up/Down Market Rank	E – A

Benefits		Investment Information	
Investment Objective	Gr. & Icm.	Telephone	800-457-0849
5-Year Projected Return	+20%	Minimum Investment	$1,000
Safety Rating (0-100)	88%	Telephone Switching	Unlimited; $5
Yield	1.0%	Total Assets	$309 million

Paine Webber Atlas Glbl Gr "A"

Foreign & U.S. - diversified securities

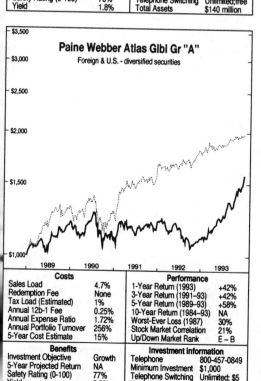

Costs		Performance	
Sales Load	4.7%	1-Year Return (1993)	+42%
Redemption Fee	None	3-Year Return (1991–93)	+42%
Tax Load (Estimated)	1%	5-Year Return (1989–93)	+58%
Annual 12b-1 Fee	0.25%	10-Year Return (1984–93)	NA
Annual Expense Ratio	1.72%	Worst-Ever Loss (1987)	30%
Annual Portfolio Turnover	256%	Stock Market Correlation	21%
5-Year Cost Estimate	15%	Up/Down Market Rank	E – B

Benefits		Investment Information	
Investment Objective	Growth	Telephone	800-457-0849
5-Year Projected Return	NA	Minimum Investment	$1,000
Safety Rating (0-100)	77%	Telephone Switching	Unlimited; $5
Yield	0.3%	Total Assets	$257 million

Paine Webber Blue Chip "B"

Diversified growth stocks

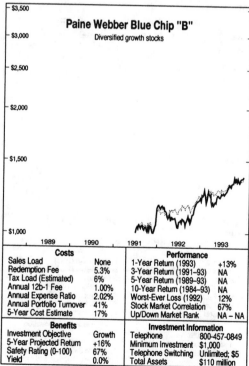

Costs		Performance	
Sales Load	None	1-Year Return (1993)	+13%
Redemption Fee	5.3%	3-Year Return (1991–93)	NA
Tax Load (Estimated)	6%	5-Year Return (1989–93)	NA
Annual 12b-1 Fee	1.00%	10-Year Return (1984–93)	NA
Annual Expense Ratio	2.02%	Worst-Ever Loss (1992)	12%
Annual Portfolio Turnover	41%	Stock Market Correlation	67%
5-Year Cost Estimate	17%	Up/Down Market Rank	NA – NA

Benefits		Investment Information	
Investment Objective	Growth	Telephone	800-457-0849
5-Year Projected Return	+16%	Minimum Investment	$1,000
Safety Rating (0-100)	67%	Telephone Switching	Unlimited; $5
Yield	0.0%	Total Assets	$110 million

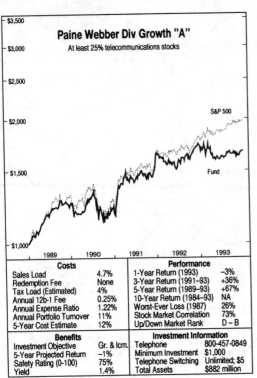

Paine Webber Div Growth "A"
At least 25% telecommunications stocks

S&P 500

Fund

Costs		Performance	
Sales Load	4.7%	1-Year Return (1993)	–3%
Redemption Fee	None	3-Year Return (1991–93)	+36%
Tax Load (Estimated)	4%	5-Year Return (1989–93)	+67%
Annual 12b-1 Fee	0.25%	10-Year Return (1984–93)	NA
Annual Expense Ratio	1.22%	Worst-Ever Loss (1987)	26%
Annual Portfolio Turnover	11%	Stock Market Correlation	73%
5-Year Cost Estimate	12%	Up/Down Market Rank	D – B

Benefits		Investment Information	
Investment Objective	Gr. & Icm.	Telephone	800-457-0849
5-Year Projected Return	–1%	Minimum Investment	$1,000
Safety Rating (0-100)	75%	Telephone Switching	Unlimited; $5
Yield	1.4%	Total Assets	$882 million

Paine Webber Europe Growth "A"
Foreign - European stocks

Costs		Performance	
Sales Load	4.7%	1-Year Return (1993)	+33%
Redemption Fee	None	3-Year Return (1991–93)	+20%
Tax Load (Estimated)	Neg.	5-Year Return (1989–93)	NA
Annual 12b-1 Fee	0.25%	10-Year Return (1984–93)	NA
Annual Expense Ratio	2.05%	Worst-Ever Loss (1990-92)	31%
Annual Portfolio Turnover	69%	Stock Market Correlation	7%
5-Year Cost Estimate	16%	Up/Down Market Rank	NA – NA

Benefits		Investment Information	
Investment Objective	Growth	Telephone	800-457-0849
5-Year Projected Return	NA	Minimum Investment	$1,000
Safety Rating (0-100)	68%	Telephone Switching	Unlimited; $5
Yield	0.2%	Total Assets	$134 million

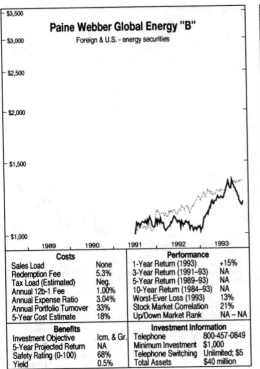

Paine Webber Global Energy "B"
Foreign & U.S. - energy securities

Costs		Performance	
Sales Load	None	1-Year Return (1993)	+15%
Redemption Fee	5.3%	3-Year Return (1991–93)	NA
Tax Load (Estimated)	Neg.	5-Year Return (1989–93)	NA
Annual 12b-1 Fee	1.00%	10-Year Return (1984–93)	NA
Annual Expense Ratio	3.04%	Worst-Ever Loss (1993)	13%
Annual Portfolio Turnover	33%	Stock Market Correlation	21%
5-Year Cost Estimate	18%	Up/Down Market Rank	NA – NA

Benefits		Investment Information	
Investment Objective	Icm. & Gr.	Telephone	800-457-0849
5-Year Projected Return	NA	Minimum Investment	$1,000
Safety Rating (0-100)	68%	Telephone Switching	Unlimited; $5
Yield	0.5%	Total Assets	$40 million

Paine Webber Glb Gr & Icm "A"
Foreign & U.S. - corporate and govt secs
★★

Costs		Performance	
Sales Load	4.7%	1-Year Return (1993)	+35%
Redemption Fee	None	3-Year Return (1991–93)	+44%
Tax Load (Estimated)	1%	5-Year Return (1989–93)	NA
Annual 12b-1 Fee	0.25%	10-Year Return (1984–93)	NA
Annual Expense Ratio	1.72%	Worst-Ever Loss (1990)	8%
Annual Portfolio Turnover	75%	Stock Market Correlation	15%
5-Year Cost Estimate	15%	Up/Down Market Rank	E – A

Benefits		Investment Information	
Investment Objective	Gr. & Icm.	Telephone	800-457-0849
5-Year Projected Return	NA	Minimum Investment	$1,000
Safety Rating (0-100)	85%	Telephone Switching	Unlimited; $5
Yield	1.4%	Total Assets	$80 million

Paine Webber Growth "A"
Diversified stocks
★★

Fund

S&P 500

Costs		Performance	
Sales Load	4.7%	1-Year Return (1993)	+20%
Redemption Fee	None	3-Year Return (1991–93)	+84%
Tax Load (Estimated)	4%	5-Year Return (1989–93)	+128%
Annual 12b-1 Fee	0.25%	10-Year Return (1984–93)	NA
Annual Expense Ratio	1.43%	Worst-Ever Loss (1987)	35%
Annual Portfolio Turnover	46%	Stock Market Correlation	60%
5-Year Cost Estimate	16%	Up/Down Market Rank	B – D

Benefits		Investment Information	
Investment Objective	Growth	Telephone	800-457-0849
5-Year Projected Return	+22%	Minimum Investment	$1,000
Safety Rating (0-100)	73%	Telephone Switching	Unlimited; $5
Yield	0.0%	Total Assets	$207 million

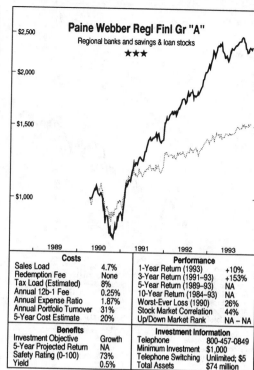

Paine Webber Regl Finl Gr "A"
Regional banks and savings & loan stocks
★★★

Costs		Performance	
Sales Load	4.7%	1-Year Return (1993)	+10%
Redemption Fee	None	3-Year Return (1991–93)	+153%
Tax Load (Estimated)	8%	5-Year Return (1989–93)	NA
Annual 12b-1 Fee	0.25%	10-Year Return (1984–93)	NA
Annual Expense Ratio	1.87%	Worst-Ever Loss (1990)	26%
Annual Portfolio Turnover	31%	Stock Market Correlation	44%
5-Year Cost Estimate	20%	Up/Down Market Rank	NA – NA

Benefits		Investment Information	
Investment Objective	Growth	Telephone	800-457-0849
5-Year Projected Return	NA	Minimum Investment	$1,000
Safety Rating (0-100)	73%	Telephone Switching	Unlimited; $5
Yield	0.5%	Total Assets	$74 million

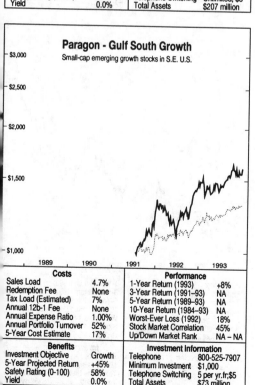

Paragon - Gulf South Growth
Small-cap emerging growth stocks in S.E. U.S.

Costs		Performance	
Sales Load	4.7%	1-Year Return (1993)	+8%
Redemption Fee	None	3-Year Return (1991–93)	NA
Tax Load (Estimated)	7%	5-Year Return (1989–93)	NA
Annual 12b-1 Fee	None	10-Year Return (1984–93)	NA
Annual Expense Ratio	1.00%	Worst-Ever Loss (1992)	18%
Annual Portfolio Turnover	52%	Stock Market Correlation	45%
5-Year Cost Estimate	17%	Up/Down Market Rank	NA – NA

Benefits		Investment Information	
Investment Objective	Growth	Telephone	800-525-7907
5-Year Projected Return	+45%	Minimum Investment	$1,000
Safety Rating (0-100)	58%	Telephone Switching	5 per yr.fr;$5
Yield	0.0%	Total Assets	$73 million

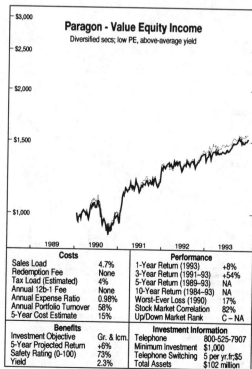

Paragon - Value Equity Income
Diversified secs; low PE, above-average yield

Costs		Performance	
Sales Load	4.7%	1-Year Return (1993)	+8%
Redemption Fee	None	3-Year Return (1991–93)	+54%
Tax Load (Estimated)	4%	5-Year Return (1989–93)	NA
Annual 12b-1 Fee	None	10-Year Return (1984–93)	NA
Annual Expense Ratio	0.98%	Worst-Ever Loss (1990)	17%
Annual Portfolio Turnover	58%	Stock Market Correlation	82%
5-Year Cost Estimate	15%	Up/Down Market Rank	C – NA

Benefits		Investment Information	
Investment Objective	Gr. & Icm.	Telephone	800-525-7907
5-Year Projected Return	+6%	Minimum Investment	$1,000
Safety Rating (0-100)	73%	Telephone Switching	5 per yr.fr;$5
Yield	2.3%	Total Assets	$102 million

Paragon - Value Growth
Undervalued; potential for earnings growth
★★

Fund

S&P 500

Costs		Performance	
Sales Load	4.7%	1-Year Return (1993)	+7%
Redemption Fee	None	3-Year Return (1991–93)	+68%
Tax Load (Estimated)	8%	5-Year Return (1989–93)	NA
Annual 12b-1 Fee	None	10-Year Return (1984–93)	NA
Annual Expense Ratio	0.97%	Worst-Ever Loss (1990)	18%
Annual Portfolio Turnover	84%	Stock Market Correlation	81%
5-Year Cost Estimate	19%	Up/Down Market Rank	B – NA

Benefits		Investment Information	
Investment Objective	Gr. & Icm.	Telephone	800-525-7907
5-Year Projected Return	+23%	Minimum Investment	$1,000
Safety Rating (0-100)	74%	Telephone Switching	5 per yr.fr;$5
Yield	1.0%	Total Assets	$167 million

Parkstone "C" - Equity
Sound management; strong financials
★★

Costs		Performance	
Sales Load	None	1-Year Return (1993)	+13%
Redemption Fee	None	3-Year Return (1991–93)	+66%
Tax Load (Estimated)	0%	5-Year Return (1989–93)	+116%
Annual 12b-1 Fee	0.25%	10-Year Return (1984–93)	NA
Annual Expense Ratio	1.37%	Worst-Ever Loss (1990)	13%
Annual Portfolio Turnover	66%	Stock Market Correlation	53%
5-Year Cost Estimate	7%	Up/Down Market Rank	B – C

Benefits		Investment Information	
Investment Objective	Gr. & Icm.	Telephone	800-451-8377
5-Year Projected Return	+31%	Minimum Investment	$1,000
Safety Rating (0-100)	74%	Telephone Switching	Unlimited;free
Yield	0.0%	Total Assets	$651 million

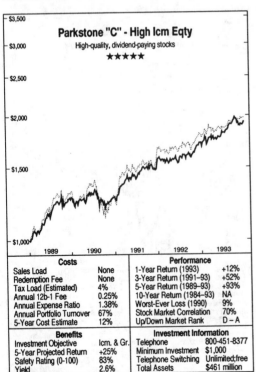

Parkstone "C" - High Icm Eqty
High-quality, dividend-paying stocks
★★★★★

Costs		Performance	
Sales Load	None	1-Year Return (1993)	+12%
Redemption Fee	None	3-Year Return (1991–93)	+52%
Tax Load (Estimated)	4%	5-Year Return (1989–93)	+93%
Annual 12b-1 Fee	0.25%	10-Year Return (1984–93)	NA
Annual Expense Ratio	1.38%	Worst-Ever Loss (1990)	9%
Annual Portfolio Turnover	67%	Stock Market Correlation	70%
5-Year Cost Estimate	12%	Up/Down Market Rank	D – A

Benefits		Investment Information	
Investment Objective	Icm. & Gr.	Telephone	800-451-8377
5-Year Projected Return	+25%	Minimum Investment	$1,000
Safety Rating (0-100)	83%	Telephone Switching	Unlimited;free
Yield	2.6%	Total Assets	$461 million

Parkstone "C" - Small Cap
Diversified small-medium sized companies
★

Costs		Performance	
Sales Load	None	1-Year Return (1993)	+22%
Redemption Fee	None	3-Year Return (1991–93)	+109%
Tax Load (Estimated)	8%	5-Year Return (1989–93)	NA
Annual 12b-1 Fee	0.25%	10-Year Return (1984–93)	NA
Annual Expense Ratio	1.38%	Worst-Ever Loss (1990)	31%
Annual Portfolio Turnover	66%	Stock Market Correlation	40%
5-Year Cost Estimate	17%	Up/Down Market Rank	A – E

Benefits		Investment Information	
Investment Objective	Gr. & Icm.	Telephone	800-451-8377
5-Year Projected Return	+52%	Minimum Investment	$1,000
Safety Rating (0-100)	61%	Telephone Switching	Unlimited;free
Yield	0.0%	Total Assets	$339 million

Parnassus
Stocks of socially responsible companies

S&P 500

Fund

Costs		Performance	
Sales Load	3.6%	1-Year Return (1993)	+17%
Redemption Fee	None	3-Year Return (1991–93)	+143%
Tax Load (Estimated)	3%	5-Year Return (1989–93)	+97%
Annual 12b-1 Fee	None	10-Year Return (1984–93)	NA
Annual Expense Ratio	1.47%	Worst-Ever Loss (1989-90)	37%
Annual Portfolio Turnover	25%	Stock Market Correlation	42%
5-Year Cost Estimate	13%	Up/Down Market Rank	A – E
Benefits		**Investment Information**	
Investment Objective	Gr. & Icm.	Telephone	800-999-3505
5-Year Projected Return	+34%	Minimum Investment	$2,000
Safety Rating (0-100)	68%	Telephone Switching	Not available
Yield	0.1%	Total Assets	$83 million

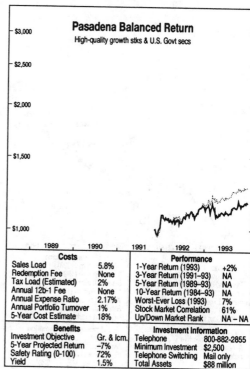

Pasadena Balanced Return
High-quality growth stks & U.S. Govt secs

Costs		Performance	
Sales Load	5.8%	1-Year Return (1993)	+2%
Redemption Fee	None	3-Year Return (1991–93)	NA
Tax Load (Estimated)	2%	5-Year Return (1989–93)	NA
Annual 12b-1 Fee	None	10-Year Return (1984–93)	NA
Annual Expense Ratio	2.17%	Worst-Ever Loss (1993)	7%
Annual Portfolio Turnover	1%	Stock Market Correlation	61%
5-Year Cost Estimate	18%	Up/Down Market Rank	NA – NA
Benefits		**Investment Information**	
Investment Objective	Gr. & Icm.	Telephone	800-882-2855
5-Year Projected Return	–7%	Minimum Investment	$2,500
Safety Rating (0-100)	72%	Telephone Switching	Mail only
Yield	1.5%	Total Assets	$88 million

Pasadena Growth
70% large capitalization stocks

Costs		Performance	
Sales Load	5.8%	1-Year Return (1993)	–6%
Redemption Fee	None	3-Year Return (1991–93)	+62%
Tax Load (Estimated)	5%	5-Year Return (1989–93)	+113%
Annual 12b-1 Fee	None	10-Year Return (1984–93)	NA
Annual Expense Ratio	1.60%	Worst-Ever Loss (1987)	38%
Annual Portfolio Turnover	22%	Stock Market Correlation	66%
5-Year Cost Estimate	17%	Up/Down Market Rank	B – E
Benefits		**Investment Information**	
Investment Objective	Growth	Telephone	800-882-2855
5-Year Projected Return	+3%	Minimum Investment	$2,500
Safety Rating (0-100)	61%	Telephone Switching	Mail only
Yield	0.0%	Total Assets	$573 million

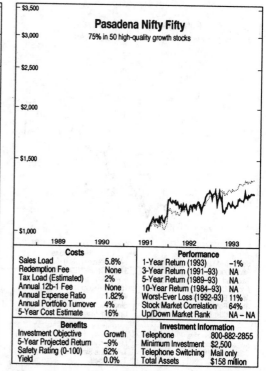

Pasadena Nifty Fifty
75% in 50 high-quality growth stocks

Costs		Performance	
Sales Load	5.8%	1-Year Return (1993)	–1%
Redemption Fee	None	3-Year Return (1991–93)	NA
Tax Load (Estimated)	2%	5-Year Return (1989–93)	NA
Annual 12b-1 Fee	None	10-Year Return (1984–93)	NA
Annual Expense Ratio	1.82%	Worst-Ever Loss (1992-93)	11%
Annual Portfolio Turnover	4%	Stock Market Correlation	64%
5-Year Cost Estimate	16%	Up/Down Market Rank	NA – NA
Benefits		**Investment Information**	
Investment Objective	Growth	Telephone	800-882-2855
5-Year Projected Return	–9%	Minimum Investment	$2,500
Safety Rating (0-100)	62%	Telephone Switching	Mail only
Yield	0.0%	Total Assets	$158 million

Patriot Premium Dividend I
Dividend-paying common and inv-grade pfds

Costs		Performance	
Sales Load	None	1-Year Return (1993)	+8%
Redemption Fee	None	3-Year Return (1991–93)	+74%
Tax Load (Estimated)	2%	5-Year Return (1989–93)	+82%
Annual 12b-1 Fee	None	10-Year Return (1984–93)	NA
Annual Expense Ratio	1.37%	Worst-Ever Loss (1990)	27%
Annual Portfolio Turnover	98%	Stock Market Correlation	1%
5-Year Cost Estimate	11%	Up/Down Market Rank	E – A

Benefits		Investment Information	
Investment Objective	Icm. & Gr.	Telephone	800-843-0090
5-Year Projected Return	+23%	Minimum Investment	None
Safety Rating (0-100)	64%	Telephone Switching	Via broker
Yield	18.4%	Total Assets	$224 million

Patriot Premium Dividend II
Dividend-paying common and inv-grade pfds

Costs		Performance	
Sales Load	None	1-Year Return (1993)	+14%
Redemption Fee	None	3-Year Return (1991–93)	+79%
Tax Load (Estimated)	3%	5-Year Return (1989–93)	NA
Annual 12b-1 Fee	None	10-Year Return (1984–93)	NA
Annual Expense Ratio	1.33%	Worst-Ever Loss (1989-90)	24%
Annual Portfolio Turnover	146%	Stock Market Correlation	3%
5-Year Cost Estimate	12%	Up/Down Market Rank	E – NA

Benefits		Investment Information	
Investment Objective	Icm. & Gr.	Telephone	800-843-0090
5-Year Projected Return	+35%	Minimum Investment	None
Safety Rating (0-100)	62%	Telephone Switching	Via broker
Yield	14.8%	Total Assets	$293 million

Patriot Select Dividend Trust
Dividend-paying common and inv-grade pfds

Costs		Performance	
Sales Load	None	1-Year Return (1993)	–6%
Redemption Fee	None	3-Year Return (1991–93)	+53%
Tax Load (Estimated)	2%	5-Year Return (1989–93)	NA
Annual 12b-1 Fee	None	10-Year Return (1984–93)	NA
Annual Expense Ratio	1.69%	Worst-Ever Loss (1993)	21%
Annual Portfolio Turnover	41%	Stock Market Correlation	1%
5-Year Cost Estimate	13%	Up/Down Market Rank	NA – NA

Benefits		Investment Information	
Investment Objective	Icm. & Gr.	Telephone	800-843-0090
5-Year Projected Return	+38%	Minimum Investment	None
Safety Rating (0-100)	68%	Telephone Switching	Via broker
Yield	14.4%	Total Assets	$248 million

Pax World
Stocks of socially responsible companies
★★★

Costs		Performance	
Sales Load	None	1-Year Return (1993)	–1%
Redemption Fee	None	3-Year Return (1991–93)	+20%
Tax Load (Estimated)	1%	5-Year Return (1989–93)	+66%
Annual 12b-1 Fee	0.25%	10-Year Return (1984–93)	+178%
Annual Expense Ratio	1.03%	Worst-Ever Loss (1987)	21%
Annual Portfolio Turnover	15%	Stock Market Correlation	55%
5-Year Cost Estimate	6%	Up/Down Market Rank	D – A

Benefits		Investment Information	
Investment Objective	Icm. & Gr.	Telephone	800-767-1729
5-Year Projected Return	+11%	Minimum Investment	$250
Safety Rating (0-100)	84%	Telephone Switching	Not available
Yield	3.7%	Total Assets	$489 million

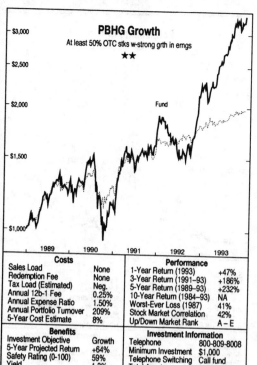

PBHG Growth
At least 50% OTC stks w-strong grth in erngs
★★

Fund

Costs		Performance	
Sales Load	None	1-Year Return (1993)	+47%
Redemption Fee	None	3-Year Return (1991–93)	+186%
Tax Load (Estimated)	Neg.	5-Year Return (1989–93)	+232%
Annual 12b-1 Fee	0.25%	10-Year Return (1984–93)	NA
Annual Expense Ratio	1.50%	Worst-Ever Loss (1987)	41%
Annual Portfolio Turnover	209%	Stock Market Correlation	42%
5-Year Cost Estimate	8%	Up/Down Market Rank	A – E

Benefits		Investment Information	
Investment Objective	Growth	Telephone	800-809-8008
5-Year Projected Return	+64%	Minimum Investment	$1,000
Safety Rating (0-100)	59%	Telephone Switching	Call fund
Yield	1.3%	Total Assets	$16 million

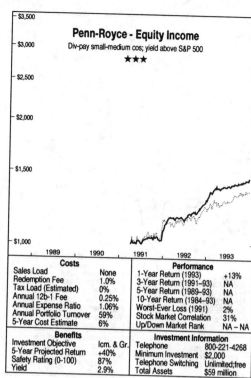

Penn-Royce - Equity Income
Div-pay small-medium cos; yield above S&P 500
★★★

Costs		Performance	
Sales Load	None	1-Year Return (1993)	+13%
Redemption Fee	1.0%	3-Year Return (1991–93)	NA
Tax Load (Estimated)	0%	5-Year Return (1989–93)	NA
Annual 12b-1 Fee	0.25%	10-Year Return (1984–93)	NA
Annual Expense Ratio	1.06%	Worst-Ever Loss (1991)	2%
Annual Portfolio Turnover	59%	Stock Market Correlation	31%
5-Year Cost Estimate	6%	Up/Down Market Rank	NA – NA

Benefits		Investment Information	
Investment Objective	Icm. & Gr.	Telephone	800-221-4268
5-Year Projected Return	+40%	Minimum Investment	$2,000
Safety Rating (0-100)	87%	Telephone Switching	Unlimited;free
Yield	2.9%	Total Assets	$59 million

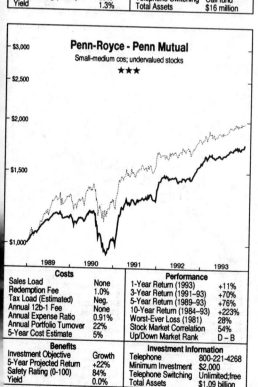

Penn-Royce - Penn Mutual
Small-medium cos; undervalued stocks
★★★

Costs		Performance	
Sales Load	None	1-Year Return (1993)	+11%
Redemption Fee	1.0%	3-Year Return (1991–93)	+70%
Tax Load (Estimated)	Neg.	5-Year Return (1989–93)	+76%
Annual 12b-1 Fee	None	10-Year Return (1984–93)	+223%
Annual Expense Ratio	0.91%	Worst-Ever Loss (1981)	28%
Annual Portfolio Turnover	22%	Stock Market Correlation	54%
5-Year Cost Estimate	5%	Up/Down Market Rank	D – B

Benefits		Investment Information	
Investment Objective	Growth	Telephone	800-221-4268
5-Year Projected Return	+22%	Minimum Investment	$2,000
Safety Rating (0-100)	84%	Telephone Switching	Unlimited;free
Yield	0.0%	Total Assets	$1.09 billion

Penn-Royce - Premier
Ltd portfolio of div-paying stks and converts

Costs		Performance	
Sales Load	None	1-Year Return (1993)	NA
Redemption Fee	1.0%	3-Year Return (1991–93)	NA
Tax Load (Estimated)	2%	5-Year Return (1989–93)	NA
Annual 12b-1 Fee	None	10-Year Return (1984–93)	NA
Annual Expense Ratio	1.99%	Worst-Ever Loss (1993)	1%
Annual Portfolio Turnover	136%	Stock Market Correlation	NA
5-Year Cost Estimate	13%	Up/Down Market Rank	NA – NA

Benefits		Investment Information	
Investment Objective	Gr. & Icm.	Telephone	800-221-4268
5-Year Projected Return	NA	Minimum Investment	$2,000
Safety Rating (0-100)	NA	Telephone Switching	Unlimited;free
Yield	2.3%	Total Assets	$25 million

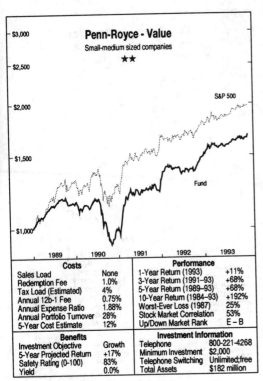

Penn-Royce - Value
Small-medium sized companies
★★

S&P 500

Fund

Costs		Performance	
Sales Load	None	1-Year Return (1993)	+11%
Redemption Fee	1.0%	3-Year Return (1991–93)	+68%
Tax Load (Estimated)	4%	5-Year Return (1989–93)	+68%
Annual 12b-1 Fee	0.75%	10-Year Return (1984–93)	+192%
Annual Expense Ratio	1.88%	Worst-Ever Loss (1987)	25%
Annual Portfolio Turnover	28%	Stock Market Correlation	53%
5-Year Cost Estimate	12%	Up/Down Market Rank	E – B

Benefits		Investment Information	
Investment Objective	Growth	Telephone	800-221-4268
5-Year Projected Return	+17%	Minimum Investment	$2,000
Safety Rating (0-100)	83%	Telephone Switching	Unlimited;free
Yield	0.0%	Total Assets	$182 million

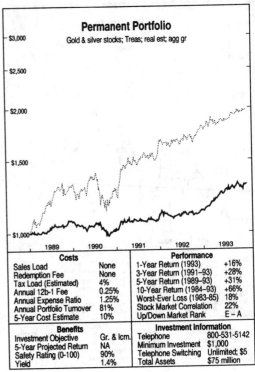

Permanent Portfolio
Gold & silver stocks; Treas; real est; agg gr

Costs		Performance	
Sales Load	None	1-Year Return (1993)	+16%
Redemption Fee	None	3-Year Return (1991–93)	+28%
Tax Load (Estimated)	4%	5-Year Return (1989–93)	+31%
Annual 12b-1 Fee	0.25%	10-Year Return (1984–93)	+66%
Annual Expense Ratio	1.25%	Worst-Ever Loss (1983-85)	18%
Annual Portfolio Turnover	81%	Stock Market Correlation	22%
5-Year Cost Estimate	10%	Up/Down Market Rank	E – A

Benefits		Investment Information	
Investment Objective	Gr. & Icm.	Telephone	800-531-5142
5-Year Projected Return	NA	Minimum Investment	$1,000
Safety Rating (0-100)	90%	Telephone Switching	Unlimited; $5
Yield	1.4%	Total Assets	$75 million

Perritt Capital Growth
Companies with market values of $3-$200 mil

Costs		Performance	
Sales Load	None	1-Year Return (1993)	+5%
Redemption Fee	None	3-Year Return (1991–93)	+56%
Tax Load (Estimated)	2%	5-Year Return (1989–93)	+32%
Annual 12b-1 Fee	None	10-Year Return (1984–93)	NA
Annual Expense Ratio	2.30%	Worst-Ever Loss (1989-90)	25%
Annual Portfolio Turnover	4%	Stock Market Correlation	28%
5-Year Cost Estimate	12%	Up/Down Market Rank	E – C

Benefits		Investment Information	
Investment Objective	Growth	Telephone	800-338-1579
5-Year Projected Return	+3%	Minimum Investment	$1,000
Safety Rating (0-100)	76%	Telephone Switching	Not available
Yield	0.0%	Total Assets	$7 million

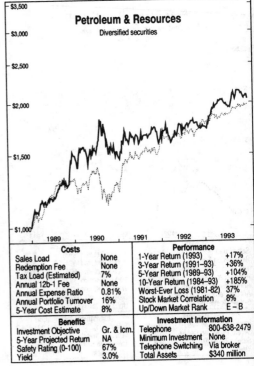

Petroleum & Resources
Diversified securities

Costs		Performance	
Sales Load	None	1-Year Return (1993)	+17%
Redemption Fee	None	3-Year Return (1991–93)	+36%
Tax Load (Estimated)	7%	5-Year Return (1989–93)	+104%
Annual 12b-1 Fee	None	10-Year Return (1984–93)	+185%
Annual Expense Ratio	0.81%	Worst-Ever Loss (1981-82)	37%
Annual Portfolio Turnover	16%	Stock Market Correlation	8%
5-Year Cost Estimate	8%	Up/Down Market Rank	E – B

Benefits		Investment Information	
Investment Objective	Gr. & Icm.	Telephone	800-638-2479
5-Year Projected Return	NA	Minimum Investment	None
Safety Rating (0-100)	67%	Telephone Switching	Via broker
Yield	3.0%	Total Assets	$340 million

EQUITY

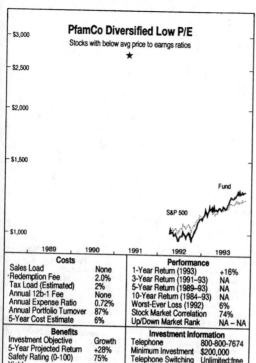

PfamCo Diversified Low P/E
Stocks with below avg price to earngs ratios
★

Costs		Performance	
Sales Load	None	1-Year Return (1993)	+16%
Redemption Fee	2.0%	3-Year Return (1991–93)	NA
Tax Load (Estimated)	2%	5-Year Return (1989–93)	NA
Annual 12b-1 Fee	None	10-Year Return (1984–93)	NA
Annual Expense Ratio	0.72%	Worst-Ever Loss (1992)	6%
Annual Portfolio Turnover	87%	Stock Market Correlation	74%
5-Year Cost Estimate	6%	Up/Down Market Rank	NA – NA
Benefits		Investment Information	
Investment Objective	Growth	Telephone	800-800-7674
5-Year Projected Return	+28%	Minimum Investment	$200,000
Safety Rating (0-100)	75%	Telephone Switching	Unlimited;free
Yield	5.6%	Total Assets	$22 million

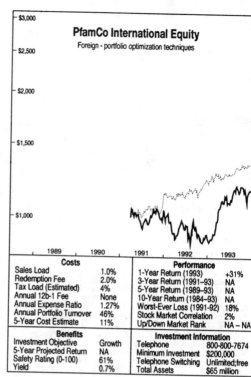

PfamCo International Equity
Foreign - portfolio optimization techniques

Costs		Performance	
Sales Load	1.0%	1-Year Return (1993)	+31%
Redemption Fee	2.0%	3-Year Return (1991–93)	NA
Tax Load (Estimated)	4%	5-Year Return (1989–93)	NA
Annual 12b-1 Fee	None	10-Year Return (1984–93)	NA
Annual Expense Ratio	1.27%	Worst-Ever Loss (1991-92)	18%
Annual Portfolio Turnover	46%	Stock Market Correlation	2%
5-Year Cost Estimate	11%	Up/Down Market Rank	NA – NA
Benefits		Investment Information	
Investment Objective	Growth	Telephone	800-800-7674
5-Year Projected Return	NA	Minimum Investment	$200,000
Safety Rating (0-100)	61%	Telephone Switching	Unlimited;free
Yield	0.7%	Total Assets	$65 million

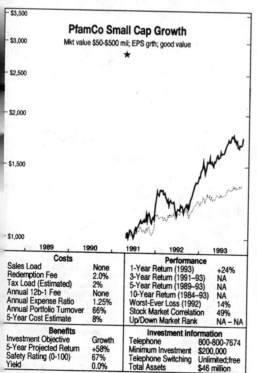

PfamCo Small Cap Growth
Mkt value $50-$500 mil; EPS grth; good value
★

Costs		Performance	
Sales Load	None	1-Year Return (1993)	+24%
Redemption Fee	2.0%	3-Year Return (1991–93)	NA
Tax Load (Estimated)	2%	5-Year Return (1989–93)	NA
Annual 12b-1 Fee	None	10-Year Return (1984–93)	NA
Annual Expense Ratio	1.25%	Worst-Ever Loss (1992)	14%
Annual Portfolio Turnover	66%	Stock Market Correlation	49%
5-Year Cost Estimate	8%	Up/Down Market Rank	NA – NA
Benefits		Investment Information	
Investment Objective	Growth	Telephone	800-800-7674
5-Year Projected Return	+58%	Minimum Investment	$200,000
Safety Rating (0-100)	67%	Telephone Switching	Unlimited;free
Yield	0.0%	Total Assets	$46 million

Philadelphia
Diversified securities
★

Costs		Performance	
Sales Load	None	1-Year Return (1993)	+18%
Redemption Fee	None	3-Year Return (1991–93)	+49%
Tax Load (Estimated)	5%	5-Year Return (1989–93)	+75%
Annual 12b-1 Fee	0.50%	10-Year Return (1984–93)	+154%
Annual Expense Ratio	1.79%	Worst-Ever Loss (1987)	29%
Annual Portfolio Turnover	28%	Stock Market Correlation	58%
5-Year Cost Estimate	12%	Up/Down Market Rank	D – C
Benefits		Investment Information	
Investment Objective	Gr. & Icm.	Telephone	800-749-9933
5-Year Projected Return	+3%	Minimum Investment	$1,000
Safety Rating (0-100)	76%	Telephone Switching	Not available
Yield	1.9%	Total Assets	$99 million

EQUITY

Phoenix Balanced
Income producing securities
★★★★

Fund

S&P 500

Costs		Performance	
Sales Load	5.0%	1-Year Return (1993)	+7%
Redemption Fee	None	3-Year Return (1991–93)	+44%
Tax Load (Estimated)	1%	5-Year Return (1989–93)	+93%
Annual 12b-1 Fee	0.25%	10-Year Return (1984–93)	+287%
Annual Expense Ratio	0.98%	Worst-Ever Loss (1987)	17%
Annual Portfolio Turnover	172%	Stock Market Correlation	78%
5-Year Cost Estimate	12%	Up/Down Market Rank	E – A

Benefits		Investment Information	
Investment Objective	Icm. & Gr.	Telephone	800-243-4361
5-Year Projected Return	+19%	Minimum Investment	$500
Safety Rating (0-100)	85%	Telephone Switching	Unlimited;free
Yield	3.7%	Total Assets	$3.05 billion

Phoenix Capital Appreciation
Diversified stocks; growth potential
★★★

Costs		Performance	
Sales Load	5.0%	1-Year Return (1993)	+10%
Redemption Fee	None	3-Year Return (1991–93)	+76%
Tax Load (Estimated)	2%	5-Year Return (1989–93)	NA
Annual 12b-1 Fee	0.25%	10-Year Return (1984–93)	NA
Annual Expense Ratio	1.40%	Worst-Ever Loss (1990)	14%
Annual Portfolio Turnover	202%	Stock Market Correlation	72%
5-Year Cost Estimate	15%	Up/Down Market Rank	NA – NA

Benefits		Investment Information	
Investment Objective	Growth	Telephone	800-243-4361
5-Year Projected Return	+41%	Minimum Investment	$500
Safety Rating (0-100)	75%	Telephone Switching	Unlimited;free
Yield	0.6%	Total Assets	$389 million

Phoenix Convertible
Convertible securities; leveraged
★★★★

Costs		Performance	
Sales Load	5.0%	1-Year Return (1993)	+9%
Redemption Fee	None	3-Year Return (1991–93)	+38%
Tax Load (Estimated)	0%	5-Year Return (1989–93)	+73%
Annual 12b-1 Fee	0.25%	10-Year Return (1984–93)	+200%
Annual Expense Ratio	1.20%	Worst-Ever Loss (1987)	18%
Annual Portfolio Turnover	95%	Stock Market Correlation	60%
5-Year Cost Estimate	12%	Up/Down Market Rank	E – A

Benefits		Investment Information	
Investment Objective	Gr. & Icm.	Telephone	800-243-4361
5-Year Projected Return	+14%	Minimum Investment	$500
Safety Rating (0-100)	89%	Telephone Switching	Unlimited;free
Yield	2.8%	Total Assets	$243 million

Phoenix Growth
Diversified growth stocks
★★

Costs		Performance	
Sales Load	5.0%	1-Year Return (1993)	+4%
Redemption Fee	None	3-Year Return (1991–93)	+39%
Tax Load (Estimated)	1%	5-Year Return (1989–93)	+88%
Annual 12b-1 Fee	0.25%	10-Year Return (1984–93)	+289%
Annual Expense Ratio	1.17%	Worst-Ever Loss (1987)	26%
Annual Portfolio Turnover	231%	Stock Market Correlation	83%
5-Year Cost Estimate	13%	Up/Down Market Rank	B – B

Benefits		Investment Information	
Investment Objective	Growth	Telephone	800-243-4361
5-Year Projected Return	+9%	Minimum Investment	$500
Safety Rating (0-100)	79%	Telephone Switching	Unlimited;free
Yield	1.5%	Total Assets	$2.61 billion

Phoenix International
Foreign - equity securities

S&P 500

| | 1989 | 1990 | 1991 | 1992 | 1993 |

Costs		Performance	
Sales Load	5.0%	1-Year Return (1993)	+38%
Redemption Fee	None	3-Year Return (1991–93)	+33%
Tax Load (Estimated)	2%	5-Year Return (1989–93)	NA
Annual 12b-1 Fee	0.25%	10-Year Return (1984–93)	NA
Annual Expense Ratio	1.97%	Worst-Ever Loss (1990)	23%
Annual Portfolio Turnover	256%	Stock Market Correlation	10%
5-Year Cost Estimate	18%	Up/Down Market Rank	NA – NA

Benefits		Investment Information	
Investment Objective	Growth	Telephone	800-243-4361
5-Year Projected Return	NA	Minimum Investment	$500
Safety Rating (0-100)	69%	Telephone Switching	Unlimited;free
Yield	0.0%	Total Assets	$65 million

Phoenix Stock
Leveraged stocks

| | 1989 | 1990 | 1991 | 1992 | 1993 |

Costs		Performance	
Sales Load	5.0%	1-Year Return (1993)	+12%
Redemption Fee	None	3-Year Return (1991–93)	+56%
Tax Load (Estimated)	1%	5-Year Return (1989–93)	+79%
Annual 12b-1 Fee	0.25%	10-Year Return (1984–93)	NA
Annual Expense Ratio	1.25%	Worst-Ever Loss (1987)	30%
Annual Portfolio Turnover	189%	Stock Market Correlation	77%
5-Year Cost Estimate	13%	Up/Down Market Rank	C – D

Benefits		Investment Information	
Investment Objective	Growth	Telephone	800-243-4361
5-Year Projected Return	+1%	Minimum Investment	$500
Safety Rating (0-100)	70%	Telephone Switching	Unlimited;free
Yield	2.0%	Total Assets	$142 million

Phoenix Total Return
Investment quality securities
★★★★

| | 1989 | 1990 | 1991 | 1992 | 1993 |

Costs		Performance	
Sales Load	5.0%	1-Year Return (1993)	+10%
Redemption Fee	None	3-Year Return (1991–93)	+57%
Tax Load (Estimated)	Neg.	5-Year Return (1989–93)	+94%
Annual 12b-1 Fee	0.25%	10-Year Return (1984–93)	NA
Annual Expense Ratio	1.36%	Worst-Ever Loss (1987)	21%
Annual Portfolio Turnover	290%	Stock Market Correlation	73%
5-Year Cost Estimate	12%	Up/Down Market Rank	D – B

Benefits		Investment Information	
Investment Objective	Gr. & Icm.	Telephone	800-243-4361
5-Year Projected Return	+27%	Minimum Investment	$500
Safety Rating (0-100)	84%	Telephone Switching	Unlimited;free
Yield	0.8%	Total Assets	$93 million

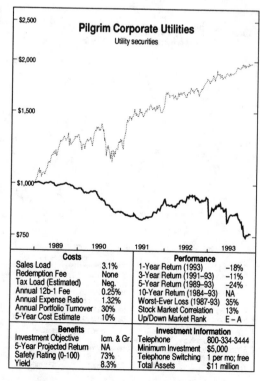

Pilgrim Corporate Utilities
Utility securities

| | 1989 | 1990 | 1991 | 1992 | 1993 |

Costs		Performance	
Sales Load	3.1%	1-Year Return (1993)	–18%
Redemption Fee	None	3-Year Return (1991–93)	–11%
Tax Load (Estimated)	Neg.	5-Year Return (1989–93)	–24%
Annual 12b-1 Fee	0.25%	10-Year Return (1984–93)	NA
Annual Expense Ratio	1.32%	Worst-Ever Loss (1987-93)	35%
Annual Portfolio Turnover	30%	Stock Market Correlation	13%
5-Year Cost Estimate	10%	Up/Down Market Rank	E – A

Benefits		Investment Information	
Investment Objective	Icm. & Gr.	Telephone	800-334-3444
5-Year Projected Return	NA	Minimum Investment	$5,000
Safety Rating (0-100)	73%	Telephone Switching	1 per mo; free
Yield	8.3%	Total Assets	$11 million

EQUITY

Pilgrim Magnacap
Companies with dividend increases

Costs		Performance	
Sales Load	5.3%	1-Year Return (1993)	+9%
Redemption Fee	None	3-Year Return (1991–93)	+48%
Tax Load (Estimated)	10%	5-Year Return (1989–93)	+75%
Annual 12b-1 Fee	0.30%	10-Year Return (1984–93)	+271%
Annual Expense Ratio	1.53%	Worst-Ever Loss (1987)	32%
Annual Portfolio Turnover	36%	Stock Market Correlation	78%
5-Year Cost Estimate	21%	Up/Down Market Rank	C – C

Benefits		Investment Information	
Investment Objective	Gr. & Icm.	Telephone	800-334-3444
5-Year Projected Return	+1%	Minimum Investment	$1,000
Safety Rating (0-100)	73%	Telephone Switching	1 per mo; free
Yield	4.6%	Total Assets	$202 million

Pilgrim Regional Bankshares
Regional bank stocks

Costs		Performance	
Sales Load	None	1-Year Return (1993)	+2%
Redemption Fee	None	3-Year Return (1991–93)	+96%
Tax Load (Estimated)	8%	5-Year Return (1989–93)	+123%
Annual 12b-1 Fee	None	10-Year Return (1984–93)	NA
Annual Expense Ratio	1.44%	Worst-Ever Loss (1987)	39%
Annual Portfolio Turnover	20%	Stock Market Correlation	7%
5-Year Cost Estimate	13%	Up/Down Market Rank	C – C

Benefits		Investment Information	
Investment Objective	Gr. & Icm.	Telephone	800-331-1080
5-Year Projected Return	NA	Minimum Investment	None
Safety Rating (0-100)	59%	Telephone Switching	Via broker
Yield	3.7%	Total Assets	$177 million

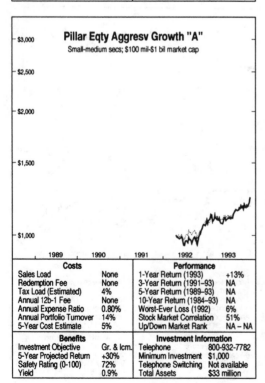

Pillar Eqty Aggresv Growth "A"
Small-medium secs; $100 mil-$1 bil market cap

Costs		Performance	
Sales Load	None	1-Year Return (1993)	+13%
Redemption Fee	None	3-Year Return (1991–93)	NA
Tax Load (Estimated)	4%	5-Year Return (1989–93)	NA
Annual 12b-1 Fee	None	10-Year Return (1984–93)	NA
Annual Expense Ratio	0.80%	Worst-Ever Loss (1992)	6%
Annual Portfolio Turnover	14%	Stock Market Correlation	51%
5-Year Cost Estimate	5%	Up/Down Market Rank	NA – NA

Benefits		Investment Information	
Investment Objective	Gr. & Icm.	Telephone	800-932-7782
5-Year Projected Return	+30%	Minimum Investment	$1,000
Safety Rating (0-100)	72%	Telephone Switching	Not available
Yield	0.9%	Total Assets	$33 million

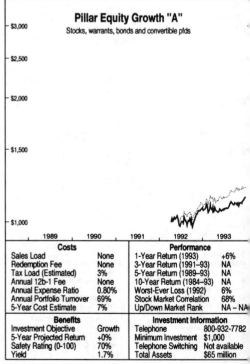

Pillar Equity Growth "A"
Stocks, warrants, bonds and convertible pfds

Costs		Performance	
Sales Load	None	1-Year Return (1993)	+6%
Redemption Fee	None	3-Year Return (1991–93)	NA
Tax Load (Estimated)	3%	5-Year Return (1989–93)	NA
Annual 12b-1 Fee	None	10-Year Return (1984–93)	NA
Annual Expense Ratio	0.80%	Worst-Ever Loss (1992)	6%
Annual Portfolio Turnover	69%	Stock Market Correlation	68%
5-Year Cost Estimate	7%	Up/Down Market Rank	NA – NA

Benefits		Investment Information	
Investment Objective	Growth	Telephone	800-932-7782
5-Year Projected Return	+0%	Minimum Investment	$1,000
Safety Rating (0-100)	70%	Telephone Switching	Not available
Yield	1.7%	Total Assets	$65 million

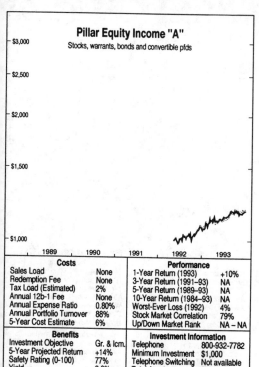

Pillar Equity Income "A"
Stocks, warrants, bonds and convertible pfds

Costs		Performance	
Sales Load	None	1-Year Return (1993)	+10%
Redemption Fee	None	3-Year Return (1991–93)	NA
Tax Load (Estimated)	2%	5-Year Return (1989–93)	NA
Annual 12b-1 Fee	None	10-Year Return (1984–93)	NA
Annual Expense Ratio	0.80%	Worst-Ever Loss (1992)	4%
Annual Portfolio Turnover	88%	Stock Market Correlation	79%
5-Year Cost Estimate	6%	Up/Down Market Rank	NA – NA
Benefits		**Investment Information**	
Investment Objective	Gr. & Icm.	Telephone	800-932-7782
5-Year Projected Return	+14%	Minimum Investment	$1,000
Safety Rating (0-100)	77%	Telephone Switching	Not available
Yield	2.6%	Total Assets	$39 million

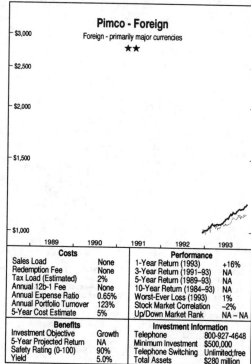

Pimco - Foreign
Foreign - primarily major currencies
★★

Costs		Performance	
Sales Load	None	1-Year Return (1993)	+16%
Redemption Fee	None	3-Year Return (1991–93)	NA
Tax Load (Estimated)	2%	5-Year Return (1989–93)	NA
Annual 12b-1 Fee	None	10-Year Return (1984–93)	NA
Annual Expense Ratio	0.65%	Worst-Ever Loss (1993)	1%
Annual Portfolio Turnover	123%	Stock Market Correlation	–2%
5-Year Cost Estimate	5%	Up/Down Market Rank	NA – NA
Benefits		**Investment Information**	
Investment Objective	Growth	Telephone	800-927-4648
5-Year Projected Return	NA	Minimum Investment	$500,000
Safety Rating (0-100)	90%	Telephone Switching	Unlimited;free
Yield	5.0%	Total Assets	$280 million

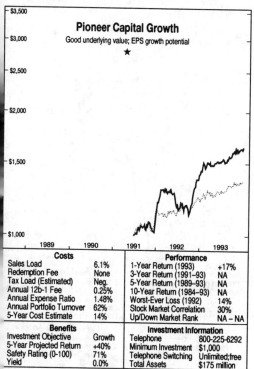

Pioneer Capital Growth
Good underlying value; EPS growth potential
★

Costs		Performance	
Sales Load	6.1%	1-Year Return (1993)	+17%
Redemption Fee	None	3-Year Return (1991–93)	NA
Tax Load (Estimated)	Neg.	5-Year Return (1989–93)	NA
Annual 12b-1 Fee	0.25%	10-Year Return (1984–93)	NA
Annual Expense Ratio	1.48%	Worst-Ever Loss (1992)	14%
Annual Portfolio Turnover	62%	Stock Market Correlation	30%
5-Year Cost Estimate	14%	Up/Down Market Rank	NA – NA
Benefits		**Investment Information**	
Investment Objective	Growth	Telephone	800-225-6292
5-Year Projected Return	+40%	Minimum Investment	$1,000
Safety Rating (0-100)	71%	Telephone Switching	Unlimited;free
Yield	0.0%	Total Assets	$175 million

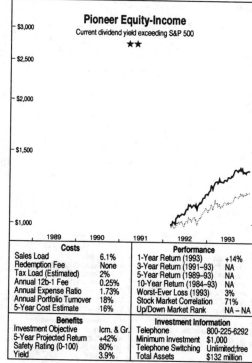

Pioneer Equity-Income
Current dividend yield exceeding S&P 500
★★

Costs		Performance	
Sales Load	6.1%	1-Year Return (1993)	+14%
Redemption Fee	None	3-Year Return (1991–93)	NA
Tax Load (Estimated)	2%	5-Year Return (1989–93)	NA
Annual 12b-1 Fee	0.25%	10-Year Return (1984–93)	NA
Annual Expense Ratio	1.73%	Worst-Ever Loss (1993)	3%
Annual Portfolio Turnover	18%	Stock Market Correlation	71%
5-Year Cost Estimate	16%	Up/Down Market Rank	NA – NA
Benefits		**Investment Information**	
Investment Objective	Icm. & Gr.	Telephone	800-225-6292
5-Year Projected Return	+42%	Minimum Investment	$1,000
Safety Rating (0-100)	80%	Telephone Switching	Unlimited;free
Yield	3.9%	Total Assets	$132 million

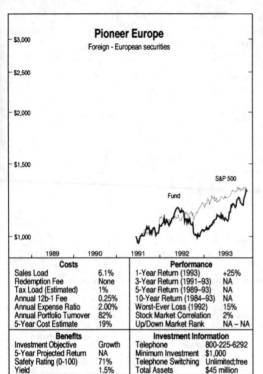

Pioneer Europe
Foreign - European securities

Costs		Performance	
Sales Load	6.1%	1-Year Return (1993)	+25%
Redemption Fee	None	3-Year Return (1991–93)	NA
Tax Load (Estimated)	1%	5-Year Return (1989–93)	NA
Annual 12b-1 Fee	0.25%	10-Year Return (1984–93)	NA
Annual Expense Ratio	2.00%	Worst-Ever Loss (1992)	15%
Annual Portfolio Turnover	82%	Stock Market Correlation	2%
5-Year Cost Estimate	19%	Up/Down Market Rank	NA – NA

Benefits		Investment Information	
Investment Objective	Growth	Telephone	800-225-6292
5-Year Projected Return	NA	Minimum Investment	$1,000
Safety Rating (0-100)	71%	Telephone Switching	Unlimited;free
Yield	1.5%	Total Assets	$45 million

Pioneer Fund
Diversified stocks
★

Costs		Performance	
Sales Load	6.1%	1-Year Return (1993)	+14%
Redemption Fee	None	3-Year Return (1991–93)	+59%
Tax Load (Estimated)	8%	5-Year Return (1989–93)	+76%
Annual 12b-1 Fee	0.25%	10-Year Return (1984–93)	+204%
Annual Expense Ratio	0.98%	Worst-Ever Loss (1987)	32%
Annual Portfolio Turnover	13%	Stock Market Correlation	85%
5-Year Cost Estimate	13%	Up/Down Market Rank	C – D

Benefits		Investment Information	
Investment Objective	Icm. & Gr.	Telephone	800-225-6292
5-Year Projected Return	+3%	Minimum Investment	$500
Safety Rating (0-100)	77%	Telephone Switching	Unlimited;free
Yield	2.0%	Total Assets	$1.97 billion

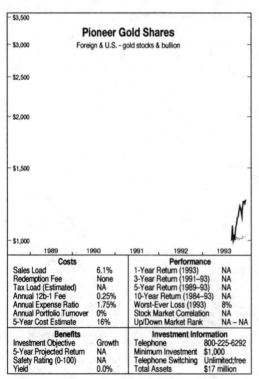

Pioneer Gold Shares
Foreign & U.S. - gold stocks & bullion

Costs		Performance	
Sales Load	6.1%	1-Year Return (1993)	NA
Redemption Fee	None	3-Year Return (1991–93)	NA
Tax Load (Estimated)	NA	5-Year Return (1989–93)	NA
Annual 12b-1 Fee	0.25%	10-Year Return (1984–93)	NA
Annual Expense Ratio	1.75%	Worst-Ever Loss (1993)	8%
Annual Portfolio Turnover	0%	Stock Market Correlation	NA
5-Year Cost Estimate	16%	Up/Down Market Rank	NA – NA

Benefits		Investment Information	
Investment Objective	Growth	Telephone	800-225-6292
5-Year Projected Return	NA	Minimum Investment	$1,000
Safety Rating (0-100)	NA	Telephone Switching	Unlimited;free
Yield	0.0%	Total Assets	$17 million

Pioneer Growth Shares
Companies with good earnings growth

Costs		Performance	
Sales Load	6.1%	1-Year Return (1993)	+9%
Redemption Fee	None	3-Year Return (1991–93)	+78%
Tax Load (Estimated)	8%	5-Year Return (1989–93)	+119%
Annual 12b-1 Fee	0.25%	10-Year Return (1984–93)	NA
Annual Expense Ratio	1.32%	Worst-Ever Loss (1990)	34%
Annual Portfolio Turnover	24%	Stock Market Correlation	43%
5-Year Cost Estimate	17%	Up/Down Market Rank	A – D

Benefits		Investment Information	
Investment Objective	Growth	Telephone	800-225-6292
5-Year Projected Return	+15%	Minimum Investment	$1,000
Safety Rating (0-100)	61%	Telephone Switching	Unlimited;free
Yield	0.0%	Total Assets	$127 million

Pioneer II
Diversified stocks
★

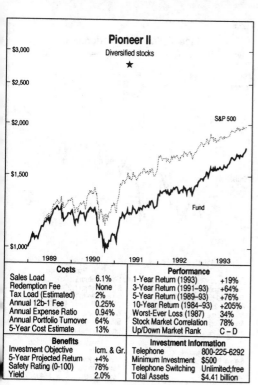

S&P 500

Fund

| 1989 | 1990 | 1991 | 1992 | 1993 |

Costs		Performance	
Sales Load	6.1%	1-Year Return (1993)	+19%
Redemption Fee	None	3-Year Return (1991–93)	+64%
Tax Load (Estimated)	2%	5-Year Return (1989–93)	+76%
Annual 12b-1 Fee	0.25%	10-Year Return (1984–93)	+205%
Annual Expense Ratio	0.94%	Worst-Ever Loss (1987)	34%
Annual Portfolio Turnover	64%	Stock Market Correlation	78%
5-Year Cost Estimate	13%	Up/Down Market Rank	C – D

Benefits		Investment Information	
Investment Objective	Icm. & Gr.	Telephone	800-225-6292
5-Year Projected Return	+4%	Minimum Investment	$500
Safety Rating (0-100)	78%	Telephone Switching	Unlimited;free
Yield	2.0%	Total Assets	$4.41 billion

Pioneer Three
Diversified stocks
★★

| 1989 | 1990 | 1991 | 1992 | 1993 |

Costs		Performance	
Sales Load	6.1%	1-Year Return (1993)	+16%
Redemption Fee	None	3-Year Return (1991–93)	+90%
Tax Load (Estimated)	5%	5-Year Return (1989–93)	+100%
Annual 12b-1 Fee	0.25%	10-Year Return (1984–93)	+245%
Annual Expense Ratio	0.86%	Worst-Ever Loss (1987)	36%
Annual Portfolio Turnover	18%	Stock Market Correlation	54%
5-Year Cost Estimate	13%	Up/Down Market Rank	D – C

Benefits		Investment Information	
Investment Objective	Icm. & Gr.	Telephone	800-225-6292
5-Year Projected Return	+24%	Minimum Investment	$1,000
Safety Rating (0-100)	79%	Telephone Switching	Unlimited;free
Yield	1.3%	Total Assets	$1.01 billion

Piper Jaffray Balanced
Dividend-paying stocks; high-grade bonds
★★

| 1989 | 1990 | 1991 | 1992 | 1993 |

Costs		Performance	
Sales Load	4.2%	1-Year Return (1993)	+7%
Redemption Fee	None	3-Year Return (1991–93)	+51%
Tax Load (Estimated)	2%	5-Year Return (1989–93)	+73%
Annual 12b-1 Fee	0.50%	10-Year Return (1984–93)	NA
Annual Expense Ratio	1.32%	Worst-Ever Loss (1987)	18%
Annual Portfolio Turnover	41%	Stock Market Correlation	83%
5-Year Cost Estimate	13%	Up/Down Market Rank	D – A

Benefits		Investment Information	
Investment Objective	Icm. & Gr.	Telephone	800-333-6000
5-Year Projected Return	+11%	Minimum Investment	$250
Safety Rating (0-100)	84%	Telephone Switching	4 per yr.fr;$5
Yield	2.9%	Total Assets	$56 million

Piper Jaffray Emerging Growth
Emerging growth stocks; small-med sized cos
★

| 1989 | 1990 | 1991 | 1992 | 1993 |

Costs		Performance	
Sales Load	4.2%	1-Year Return (1993)	+18%
Redemption Fee	None	3-Year Return (1991–93)	+110%
Tax Load (Estimated)	9%	5-Year Return (1989–93)	NA
Annual 12b-1 Fee	0.50%	10-Year Return (1984–93)	NA
Annual Expense Ratio	1.32%	Worst-Ever Loss (1990)	26%
Annual Portfolio Turnover	30%	Stock Market Correlation	59%
5-Year Cost Estimate	16%	Up/Down Market Rank	NA – NA

Benefits		Investment Information	
Investment Objective	Growth	Telephone	800-333-6000
5-Year Projected Return	+40%	Minimum Investment	$250
Safety Rating (0-100)	65%	Telephone Switching	4 per yr.fr;$5
Yield	0.0%	Total Assets	$180 million

Piper Jaffray Pacific Eurpn Gr
Foreign - Pacific-Basin and European

S&P 500

Fund

Costs		Performance	
Sales Load	4.2%	1-Year Return (1993)	+51%
Redemption Fee	None	3-Year Return (1991–93)	+67%
Tax Load (Estimated)	5%	5-Year Return (1989–93)	NA
Annual 12b-1 Fee	0.50%	10-Year Return (1984–93)	NA
Annual Expense Ratio	2.25%	Worst-Ever Loss (1990)	91%
Annual Portfolio Turnover	31%	Stock Market Correlation	6%
5-Year Cost Estimate	20%	Up/Down Market Rank	NA – NA

Benefits		Investment Information	
Investment Objective	Growth	Telephone	800-866-7778
5-Year Projected Return	NA	Minimum Investment	$250
Safety Rating (0-100)	70%	Telephone Switching	4 per yr.fr;$5
Yield	0.0%	Total Assets	$103 million

Piper Jaffray Sectr Performnce
Fundamental and technical analysis
★

Costs		Performance	
Sales Load	4.2%	1-Year Return (1993)	+11%
Redemption Fee	None	3-Year Return (1991–93)	+74%
Tax Load (Estimated)	2%	5-Year Return (1989–93)	+121%
Annual 12b-1 Fee	0.50%	10-Year Return (1984–93)	NA
Annual Expense Ratio	1.32%	Worst-Ever Loss (1987)	37%
Annual Portfolio Turnover	154%	Stock Market Correlation	44%
5-Year Cost Estimate	14%	Up/Down Market Rank	B – D

Benefits		Investment Information	
Investment Objective	Growth	Telephone	800-866-7778
5-Year Projected Return	NA	Minimum Investment	$250
Safety Rating (0-100)	73%	Telephone Switching	4 per yr.fr;$5
Yield	0.2%	Total Assets	$54 million

Piper Jaffray Value
Large; low PE growth stocks
★★

Costs		Performance	
Sales Load	4.2%	1-Year Return (1993)	+5%
Redemption Fee	None	3-Year Return (1991–93)	+60%
Tax Load (Estimated)	7%	5-Year Return (1989–93)	+125%
Annual 12b-1 Fee	0.50%	10-Year Return (1984–93)	NA
Annual Expense Ratio	1.32%	Worst-Ever Loss (1987)	31%
Annual Portfolio Turnover	45%	Stock Market Correlation	80%
5-Year Cost Estimate	17%	Up/Down Market Rank	A – D

Benefits		Investment Information	
Investment Objective	Gr. & Icm.	Telephone	800-866-7778
5-Year Projected Return	+17%	Minimum Investment	$250
Safety Rating (0-100)	72%	Telephone Switching	4 per yr.fr;$5
Yield	0.6%	Total Assets	$251 million

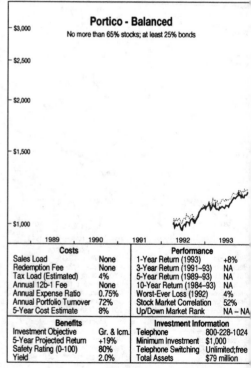

Portico - Balanced
No more than 65% stocks; at least 25% bonds

Costs		Performance	
Sales Load	None	1-Year Return (1993)	+8%
Redemption Fee	None	3-Year Return (1991–93)	NA
Tax Load (Estimated)	4%	5-Year Return (1989–93)	NA
Annual 12b-1 Fee	None	10-Year Return (1984–93)	NA
Annual Expense Ratio	0.75%	Worst-Ever Loss (1992)	4%
Annual Portfolio Turnover	72%	Stock Market Correlation	52%
5-Year Cost Estimate	8%	Up/Down Market Rank	NA – NA

Benefits		Investment Information	
Investment Objective	Gr. & Icm.	Telephone	800-228-1024
5-Year Projected Return	+19%	Minimum Investment	$1,000
Safety Rating (0-100)	80%	Telephone Switching	Unlimited;free
Yield	2.0%	Total Assets	$79 million

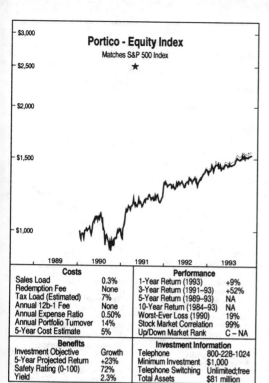

Portico - Equity Index
Matches S&P 500 Index
★

Costs		Performance	
Sales Load	0.3%	1-Year Return (1993)	+9%
Redemption Fee	None	3-Year Return (1991–93)	+52%
Tax Load (Estimated)	7%	5-Year Return (1989–93)	NA
Annual 12b-1 Fee	None	10-Year Return (1984–93)	NA
Annual Expense Ratio	0.50%	Worst-Ever Loss (1990)	19%
Annual Portfolio Turnover	14%	Stock Market Correlation	99%
5-Year Cost Estimate	5%	Up/Down Market Rank	C – NA

Benefits		Investment Information	
Investment Objective	Growth	Telephone	800-228-1024
5-Year Projected Return	+23%	Minimum Investment	$1,000
Safety Rating (0-100)	72%	Telephone Switching	Unlimited;free
Yield	2.3%	Total Assets	$81 million

Portico - Growth & Income
Portfolio yield greater than S&P 500
★

Costs		Performance	
Sales Load	None	1-Year Return (1993)	+7%
Redemption Fee	None	3-Year Return (1991–93)	+37%
Tax Load (Estimated)	3%	5-Year Return (1989–93)	NA
Annual 12b-1 Fee	None	10-Year Return (1984–93)	NA
Annual Expense Ratio	0.90%	Worst-Ever Loss (1990)	12%
Annual Portfolio Turnover	86%	Stock Market Correlation	84%
5-Year Cost Estimate	8%	Up/Down Market Rank	E – NA

Benefits		Investment Information	
Investment Objective	Gr. & Icm.	Telephone	800-228-1024
5-Year Projected Return	+8%	Minimum Investment	$1,000
Safety Rating (0-100)	79%	Telephone Switching	Unlimited;free
Yield	2.2%	Total Assets	$159 million

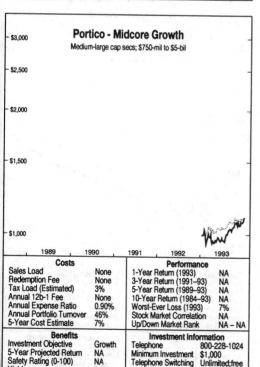

Portico - Midcore Growth
Medium-large cap secs; $750-mil to $5-bil

Costs		Performance	
Sales Load	None	1-Year Return (1993)	NA
Redemption Fee	None	3-Year Return (1991–93)	NA
Tax Load (Estimated)	3%	5-Year Return (1989–93)	NA
Annual 12b-1 Fee	None	10-Year Return (1984–93)	NA
Annual Expense Ratio	0.90%	Worst-Ever Loss (1993)	7%
Annual Portfolio Turnover	46%	Stock Market Correlation	NA
5-Year Cost Estimate	7%	Up/Down Market Rank	NA – NA

Benefits		Investment Information	
Investment Objective	Growth	Telephone	800-228-1024
5-Year Projected Return	NA	Minimum Investment	$1,000
Safety Rating (0-100)	NA	Telephone Switching	Unlimited;free
Yield	0.5%	Total Assets	$75 million

Portico - Special Growth
$500-mil - $2-bil mkt cap; good fundamentals
★★★

Costs		Performance	
Sales Load	None	1-Year Return (1993)	+8%
Redemption Fee	None	3-Year Return (1991–93)	+83%
Tax Load (Estimated)	6%	5-Year Return (1989–93)	NA
Annual 12b-1 Fee	None	10-Year Return (1984–93)	NA
Annual Expense Ratio	0.90%	Worst-Ever Loss (1990)	19%
Annual Portfolio Turnover	59%	Stock Market Correlation	52%
5-Year Cost Estimate	11%	Up/Down Market Rank	A – NA

Benefits		Investment Information	
Investment Objective	Growth	Telephone	800-228-1024
5-Year Projected Return	+42%	Minimum Investment	$1,000
Safety Rating (0-100)	71%	Telephone Switching	Unlimited;free
Yield	0.2%	Total Assets	$328 million

Portugal
Foreign - Portuguese stocks

Fund

Costs		Performance	
Sales Load	None	1-Year Return (1993)	+77%
Redemption Fee	None	3-Year Return (1991–93)	+55%
Tax Load (Estimated)	3%	5-Year Return (1989–93)	NA
Annual 12b-1 Fee	None	10-Year Return (1984–93)	NA
Annual Expense Ratio	1.92%	Worst-Ever Loss (1990-92)	62%
Annual Portfolio Turnover	2%	Stock Market Correlation	4%
5-Year Cost Estimate	13%	Up/Down Market Rank	E – NA

Benefits		Investment Information	
Investment Objective	Gr. & Icm.	Telephone	212-832-2626
5-Year Projected Return	NA	Minimum Investment	None
Safety Rating (0-100)	15%	Telephone Switching	Via broker
Yield	0.0%	Total Assets	$53 million

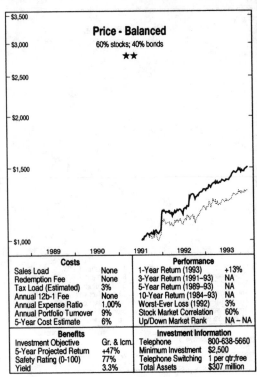

Price - Balanced
60% stocks; 40% bonds
★★

Costs		Performance	
Sales Load	None	1-Year Return (1993)	+13%
Redemption Fee	None	3-Year Return (1991–93)	NA
Tax Load (Estimated)	3%	5-Year Return (1989–93)	NA
Annual 12b-1 Fee	None	10-Year Return (1984–93)	NA
Annual Expense Ratio	1.00%	Worst-Ever Loss (1992)	3%
Annual Portfolio Turnover	9%	Stock Market Correlation	60%
5-Year Cost Estimate	6%	Up/Down Market Rank	NA – NA

Benefits		Investment Information	
Investment Objective	Gr. & Icm.	Telephone	800-638-5660
5-Year Projected Return	+47%	Minimum Investment	$2,500
Safety Rating (0-100)	77%	Telephone Switching	1 per qtr;free
Yield	3.3%	Total Assets	$307 million

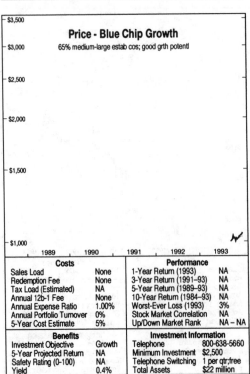

Price - Blue Chip Growth
65% medium-large estab cos; good grth potentl

Costs		Performance	
Sales Load	None	1-Year Return (1993)	NA
Redemption Fee	None	3-Year Return (1991–93)	NA
Tax Load (Estimated)	NA	5-Year Return (1989–93)	NA
Annual 12b-1 Fee	None	10-Year Return (1984–93)	NA
Annual Expense Ratio	1.00%	Worst-Ever Loss (1993)	3%
Annual Portfolio Turnover	0%	Stock Market Correlation	NA
5-Year Cost Estimate	5%	Up/Down Market Rank	NA – NA

Benefits		Investment Information	
Investment Objective	Growth	Telephone	800-638-5660
5-Year Projected Return	NA	Minimum Investment	$2,500
Safety Rating (0-100)	NA	Telephone Switching	1 per qtr;free
Yield	0.4%	Total Assets	$22 million

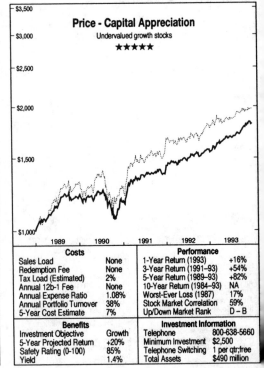

Price - Capital Appreciation
Undervalued growth stocks
★★★★★

Costs		Performance	
Sales Load	None	1-Year Return (1993)	+16%
Redemption Fee	None	3-Year Return (1991–93)	+54%
Tax Load (Estimated)	2%	5-Year Return (1989–93)	+82%
Annual 12b-1 Fee	None	10-Year Return (1984–93)	NA
Annual Expense Ratio	1.08%	Worst-Ever Loss (1987)	17%
Annual Portfolio Turnover	38%	Stock Market Correlation	59%
5-Year Cost Estimate	7%	Up/Down Market Rank	D – B

Benefits		Investment Information	
Investment Objective	Growth	Telephone	800-638-5660
5-Year Projected Return	+20%	Minimum Investment	$2,500
Safety Rating (0-100)	85%	Telephone Switching	1 per qtr;free
Yield	1.4%	Total Assets	$490 million

EQUITY

Price - Dividend Growth
65% div-paying stocks with growth potential

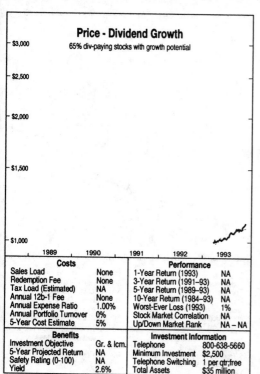

Costs		Performance	
Sales Load	None	1-Year Return (1993)	NA
Redemption Fee	None	3-Year Return (1991–93)	NA
Tax Load (Estimated)	NA	5-Year Return (1989–93)	NA
Annual 12b-1 Fee	None	10-Year Return (1984–93)	NA
Annual Expense Ratio	1.00%	Worst-Ever Loss (1993)	1%
Annual Portfolio Turnover	0%	Stock Market Correlation	NA
5-Year Cost Estimate	5%	Up/Down Market Rank	NA – NA

Benefits		Investment Information	
Investment Objective	Gr. & Icm.	Telephone	800-638-5660
5-Year Projected Return	NA	Minimum Investment	$2,500
Safety Rating (0-100)	NA	Telephone Switching	1 per qtr;free
Yield	2.6%	Total Assets	$35 million

Price - Equity Income
Dividend-paying quality stocks
★★

Costs		Performance	
Sales Load	None	1-Year Return (1993)	+15%
Redemption Fee	None	3-Year Return (1991–93)	+64%
Tax Load (Estimated)	2%	5-Year Return (1989–93)	+74%
Annual 12b-1 Fee	None	10-Year Return (1984–93)	NA
Annual Expense Ratio	0.97%	Worst-Ever Loss (1987)	22%
Annual Portfolio Turnover	30%	Stock Market Correlation	83%
5-Year Cost Estimate	6%	Up/Down Market Rank	D – B

Benefits		Investment Information	
Investment Objective	Icm. & Gr.	Telephone	800-638-5660
5-Year Projected Return	+19%	Minimum Investment	$2,500
Safety Rating (0-100)	82%	Telephone Switching	1 per qtr;free
Yield	3.3%	Total Assets	$2.69 billion

Price - European Stock
Foreign - diversified European stocks

Costs		Performance	
Sales Load	None	1-Year Return (1993)	+27%
Redemption Fee	None	3-Year Return (1991–93)	+29%
Tax Load (Estimated)	1%	5-Year Return (1989–93)	NA
Annual 12b-1 Fee	None	10-Year Return (1984–93)	NA
Annual Expense Ratio	1.48%	Worst-Ever Loss (1990-91)	21%
Annual Portfolio Turnover	52%	Stock Market Correlation	8%
5-Year Cost Estimate	9%	Up/Down Market Rank	NA – NA

Benefits		Investment Information	
Investment Objective	Gr. & Icm.	Telephone	800-638-5660
5-Year Projected Return	NA	Minimum Investment	$2,500
Safety Rating (0-100)	70%	Telephone Switching	1 per qtr;free
Yield	0.3%	Total Assets	$233 million

Price - Foreign Equity
Inst only: foreign - established companies

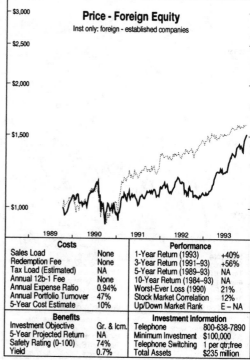

Costs		Performance	
Sales Load	None	1-Year Return (1993)	+40%
Redemption Fee	None	3-Year Return (1991–93)	+56%
Tax Load (Estimated)	NA	5-Year Return (1989–93)	NA
Annual 12b-1 Fee	None	10-Year Return (1984–93)	NA
Annual Expense Ratio	0.94%	Worst-Ever Loss (1990)	21%
Annual Portfolio Turnover	47%	Stock Market Correlation	12%
5-Year Cost Estimate	10%	Up/Down Market Rank	E – NA

Benefits		Investment Information	
Investment Objective	Gr. & Icm.	Telephone	800-638-7890
5-Year Projected Return	NA	Minimum Investment	$100,000
Safety Rating (0-100)	74%	Telephone Switching	1 per qtr;free
Yield	0.7%	Total Assets	$235 million

Price - Growth
Established growth stocks
★★

(Chart showing S&P 500 and Fund, 1989–1993, scale $1,000–$3,500)

Costs		Performance	
Sales Load	None	1-Year Return (1993)	+16%
Redemption Fee	None	3-Year Return (1991–93)	+64%
Tax Load (Estimated)	11%	5-Year Return (1989–93)	+97%
Annual 12b-1 Fee	None	10-Year Return (1984–93)	+251%
Annual Expense Ratio	0.83%	Worst-Ever Loss (1987)	33%
Annual Portfolio Turnover	27%	Stock Market Correlation	73%
5-Year Cost Estimate	9%	Up/Down Market Rank	C – D

Benefits		Investment Information	
Investment Objective	Growth	Telephone	800-638-5660
5-Year Projected Return	+17%	Minimum Investment	$2,500
Safety Rating (0-100)	75%	Telephone Switching	1 per qtr;free
Yield	0.7%	Total Assets	$1.85 billion

Price - Growth & Income
High-yield growth securities
★

(Chart, 1989–1993, scale $1,000–$3,000)

Costs		Performance	
Sales Load	None	1-Year Return (1993)	+13%
Redemption Fee	None	3-Year Return (1991–93)	+71%
Tax Load (Estimated)	5%	5-Year Return (1989–93)	+82%
Annual 12b-1 Fee	None	10-Year Return (1984–93)	+186%
Annual Expense Ratio	0.85%	Worst-Ever Loss (1987)	32%
Annual Portfolio Turnover	30%	Stock Market Correlation	76%
5-Year Cost Estimate	7%	Up/Down Market Rank	C – D

Benefits		Investment Information	
Investment Objective	Gr. & Icm.	Telephone	800-638-5660
5-Year Projected Return	+15%	Minimum Investment	$2,500
Safety Rating (0-100)	77%	Telephone Switching	1 per qtr;free
Yield	2.9%	Total Assets	$1.10 billion

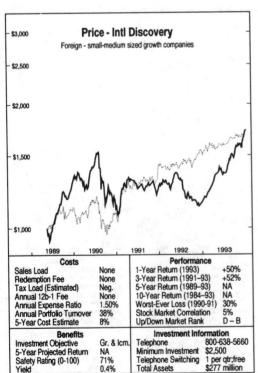

Price - Intl Discovery
Foreign - small-medium sized growth companies

(Chart, 1989–1993, scale $1,000–$3,000)

Costs		Performance	
Sales Load	None	1-Year Return (1993)	+50%
Redemption Fee	None	3-Year Return (1991–93)	+52%
Tax Load (Estimated)	Neg.	5-Year Return (1989–93)	NA
Annual 12b-1 Fee	None	10-Year Return (1984–93)	NA
Annual Expense Ratio	1.50%	Worst-Ever Loss (1990-91)	30%
Annual Portfolio Turnover	38%	Stock Market Correlation	5%
5-Year Cost Estimate	8%	Up/Down Market Rank	D – B

Benefits		Investment Information	
Investment Objective	Gr. & Icm.	Telephone	800-638-5660
5-Year Projected Return	NA	Minimum Investment	$2,500
Safety Rating (0-100)	71%	Telephone Switching	1 per qtr;free
Yield	0.4%	Total Assets	$277 million

Price - International Stock
Foreign - diversified stocks

(Chart, 1989–1993, scale $1,000–$3,500)

Costs		Performance	
Sales Load	None	1-Year Return (1993)	+40%
Redemption Fee	None	3-Year Return (1991–93)	+57%
Tax Load (Estimated)	3%	5-Year Return (1989–93)	+77%
Annual 12b-1 Fee	None	10-Year Return (1984–93)	+396%
Annual Expense Ratio	1.05%	Worst-Ever Loss (1987)	28%
Annual Portfolio Turnover	38%	Stock Market Correlation	12%
5-Year Cost Estimate	7%	Up/Down Market Rank	E – B

Benefits		Investment Information	
Investment Objective	Gr. & Icm.	Telephone	800-638-5660
5-Year Projected Return	NA	Minimum Investment	$2,500
Safety Rating (0-100)	74%	Telephone Switching	1 per qtr;free
Yield	0.7%	Total Assets	$3.51 billion

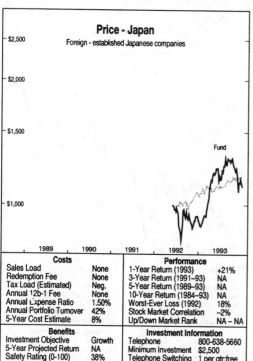

Price - Japan
Foreign - established Japanese companies

Costs		Performance	
Sales Load	None	1-Year Return (1993)	+21%
Redemption Fee	None	3-Year Return (1991–93)	NA
Tax Load (Estimated)	Neg.	5-Year Return (1989–93)	NA
Annual 12b-1 Fee	None	10-Year Return (1984–93)	NA
Annual Expense Ratio	1.50%	Worst-Ever Loss (1992)	18%
Annual Portfolio Turnover	42%	Stock Market Correlation	-2%
5-Year Cost Estimate	8%	Up/Down Market Rank	NA – NA

Benefits		Investment Information	
Investment Objective	Growth	Telephone	800-638-5660
5-Year Projected Return	NA	Minimum Investment	$2,500
Safety Rating (0-100)	38%	Telephone Switching	1 per qtr;free
Yield	0.0%	Total Assets	$45 million

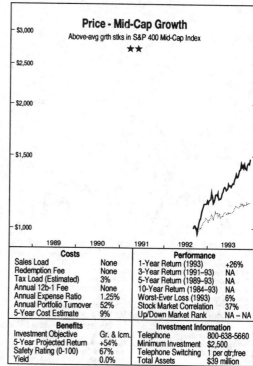

Price - Mid-Cap Growth
Above-avg grth stks in S&P 400 Mid-Cap Index
★★

Costs		Performance	
Sales Load	None	1-Year Return (1993)	+26%
Redemption Fee	None	3-Year Return (1991–93)	NA
Tax Load (Estimated)	3%	5-Year Return (1989–93)	NA
Annual 12b-1 Fee	None	10-Year Return (1984–93)	NA
Annual Expense Ratio	1.25%	Worst-Ever Loss (1993)	6%
Annual Portfolio Turnover	52%	Stock Market Correlation	37%
5-Year Cost Estimate	9%	Up/Down Market Rank	NA – NA

Benefits		Investment Information	
Investment Objective	Gr. & Icm.	Telephone	800-638-5660
5-Year Projected Return	+54%	Minimum Investment	$2,500
Safety Rating (0-100)	67%	Telephone Switching	1 per qtr;free
Yield	0.0%	Total Assets	$39 million

Price - New America
Service related growth stocks
★

Costs		Performance	
Sales Load	None	1-Year Return (1993)	+17%
Redemption Fee	None	3-Year Return (1991–93)	+109%
Tax Load (Estimated)	7%	5-Year Return (1989–93)	+154%
Annual 12b-1 Fee	None	10-Year Return (1984–93)	NA
Annual Expense Ratio	1.25%	Worst-Ever Loss (1987)	38%
Annual Portfolio Turnover	26%	Stock Market Correlation	60%
5-Year Cost Estimate	10%	Up/Down Market Rank	A – E

Benefits		Investment Information	
Investment Objective	Growth	Telephone	800-638-5660
5-Year Projected Return	+34%	Minimum Investment	$2,500
Safety Rating (0-100)	67%	Telephone Switching	1 per qtr;free
Yield	0.0%	Total Assets	$555 million

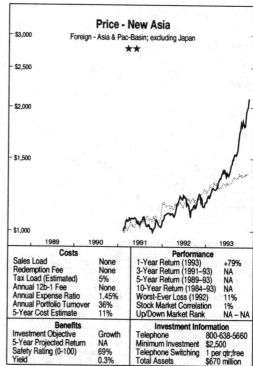

Price - New Asia
Foreign - Asia & Pac-Basin; excluding Japan
★★

Costs		Performance	
Sales Load	None	1-Year Return (1993)	+79%
Redemption Fee	None	3-Year Return (1991–93)	NA
Tax Load (Estimated)	5%	5-Year Return (1989–93)	NA
Annual 12b-1 Fee	None	10-Year Return (1984–93)	NA
Annual Expense Ratio	1.45%	Worst-Ever Loss (1992)	11%
Annual Portfolio Turnover	36%	Stock Market Correlation	1%
5-Year Cost Estimate	11%	Up/Down Market Rank	NA – NA

Benefits		Investment Information	
Investment Objective	Growth	Telephone	800-638-5660
5-Year Projected Return	NA	Minimum Investment	$2,500
Safety Rating (0-100)	69%	Telephone Switching	1 per qtr;free
Yield	0.3%	Total Assets	$670 million

Price - New Era
Natural resource and growth stocks

S&P 500

Fund

Costs		Performance	
Sales Load	None	1-Year Return (1993)	+15%
Redemption Fee	None	3-Year Return (1991–93)	+35%
Tax Load (Estimated)	7%	5-Year Return (1989–93)	+53%
Annual 12b-1 Fee	None	10-Year Return (1984–93)	+195%
Annual Expense Ratio	0.81%	Worst-Ever Loss (1981-82)	38%
Annual Portfolio Turnover	17%	Stock Market Correlation	46%
5-Year Cost Estimate	6%	Up/Down Market Rank	D – C

Benefits		Investment Information	
Investment Objective	Growth	Telephone	800-638-5660
5-Year Projected Return	–9%	Minimum Investment	$2,500
Safety Rating (0-100)	73%	Telephone Switching	1 per qtr;free
Yield	1.9%	Total Assets	$748 million

Price - New Horizons
Small; growth stocks
★

Costs		Performance	
Sales Load	None	1-Year Return (1993)	+22%
Redemption Fee	None	3-Year Return (1991–93)	+105%
Tax Load (Estimated)	8%	5-Year Return (1989–93)	+134%
Annual 12b-1 Fee	None	10-Year Return (1984–93)	+177%
Annual Expense Ratio	0.93%	Worst-Ever Loss (1987)	40%
Annual Portfolio Turnover	50%	Stock Market Correlation	52%
5-Year Cost Estimate	13%	Up/Down Market Rank	A – E

Benefits		Investment Information	
Investment Objective	Growth	Telephone	800-638-5660
5-Year Projected Return	+35%	Minimum Investment	$2,500
Safety Rating (0-100)	66%	Telephone Switching	1 per qtr;free
Yield	0.0%	Total Assets	$1.52 billion

Price - OTC
Over-the-counter securities
★

Costs		Performance	
Sales Load	None	1-Year Return (1993)	+18%
Redemption Fee	None	3-Year Return (1991–93)	+87%
Tax Load (Estimated)	6%	5-Year Return (1989–93)	+77%
Annual 12b-1 Fee	None	10-Year Return (1984–93)	+173%
Annual Expense Ratio	1.25%	Worst-Ever Loss (1987)	33%
Annual Portfolio Turnover	31%	Stock Market Correlation	39%
5-Year Cost Estimate	10%	Up/Down Market Rank	E – B

Benefits		Investment Information	
Investment Objective	Growth	Telephone	800-638-5660
5-Year Projected Return	+19%	Minimum Investment	$2,500
Safety Rating (0-100)	78%	Telephone Switching	1 per qtr;free
Yield	0.0%	Total Assets	$201 million

Price - Science & Technology
Science and technology stocks
★

Costs		Performance	
Sales Load	None	1-Year Return (1993)	+24%
Redemption Fee	None	3-Year Return (1991–93)	+136%
Tax Load (Estimated)	3%	5-Year Return (1989–93)	+228%
Annual 12b-1 Fee	None	10-Year Return (1984–93)	NA
Annual Expense Ratio	1.25%	Worst-Ever Loss (1990)	35%
Annual Portfolio Turnover	144%	Stock Market Correlation	42%
5-Year Cost Estimate	9%	Up/Down Market Rank	A – D

Benefits		Investment Information	
Investment Objective	Growth	Telephone	800-638-5660
5-Year Projected Return	NA	Minimum Investment	$2,500
Safety Rating (0-100)	58%	Telephone Switching	1 per qtr;free
Yield	0.0%	Total Assets	$406 million

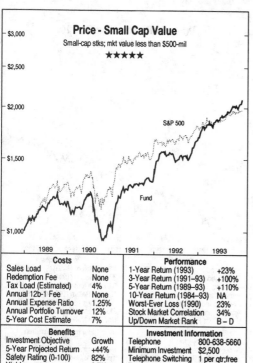

Price - Small Cap Value
Small-cap stks; mkt value less than $500-mil
★★★★★

(chart showing S&P 500 and Fund, 1989–1993, $1,000–$3,000)

Costs		Performance	
Sales Load	None	1-Year Return (1993)	+23%
Redemption Fee	None	3-Year Return (1991–93)	+100%
Tax Load (Estimated)	4%	5-Year Return (1989–93)	+110%
Annual 12b-1 Fee	None	10-Year Return (1984–93)	NA
Annual Expense Ratio	1.25%	Worst-Ever Loss (1990)	23%
Annual Portfolio Turnover	12%	Stock Market Correlation	34%
5-Year Cost Estimate	7%	Up/Down Market Rank	B – D

Benefits		Investment Information	
Investment Objective	Growth	Telephone	800-638-5660
5-Year Projected Return	+44%	Minimum Investment	$2,500
Safety Rating (0-100)	82%	Telephone Switching	1 per qtr;free
Yield	0.7%	Total Assets	$423 million

Price - Spectrum Growth
Owns other Price equity funds
★

(chart 1989–1993, $1,000–$3,000)

Costs		Performance	
Sales Load	None	1-Year Return (1993)	+21%
Redemption Fee	None	3-Year Return (1991–93)	+61%
Tax Load (Estimated)	1%	5-Year Return (1989–93)	NA
Annual 12b-1 Fee	None	10-Year Return (1984–93)	NA
Annual Expense Ratio	0.93%	Worst-Ever Loss (1992)	6%
Annual Portfolio Turnover	8%	Stock Market Correlation	68%
5-Year Cost Estimate	5%	Up/Down Market Rank	NA – NA

Benefits		Investment Information	
Investment Objective	Growth	Telephone	800-638-5660
5-Year Projected Return	+26%	Minimum Investment	$2,500
Safety Rating (0-100)	77%	Telephone Switching	1 per qtr;free
Yield	1.3%	Total Assets	$496 million

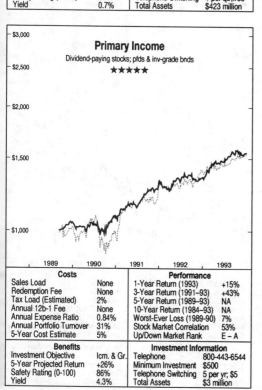

Primary Income
Dividend-paying stocks; pfds & inv-grade bnds
★★★★★

(chart 1989–1993, $1,000–$3,000)

Costs		Performance	
Sales Load	None	1-Year Return (1993)	+15%
Redemption Fee	None	3-Year Return (1991–93)	+43%
Tax Load (Estimated)	2%	5-Year Return (1989–93)	NA
Annual 12b-1 Fee	None	10-Year Return (1984–93)	NA
Annual Expense Ratio	0.84%	Worst-Ever Loss (1989-90)	7%
Annual Portfolio Turnover	31%	Stock Market Correlation	53%
5-Year Cost Estimate	5%	Up/Down Market Rank	E – A

Benefits		Investment Information	
Investment Objective	Icm. & Gr.	Telephone	800-443-6544
5-Year Projected Return	+26%	Minimum Investment	$500
Safety Rating (0-100)	86%	Telephone Switching	5 per yr; $5
Yield	4.3%	Total Assets	$3 million

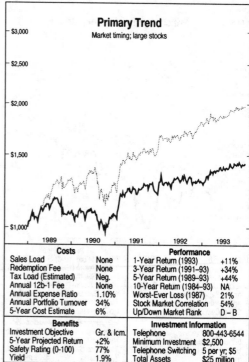

Primary Trend
Market timing; large stocks

(chart 1989–1993, $1,000–$3,000)

Costs		Performance	
Sales Load	None	1-Year Return (1993)	+11%
Redemption Fee	None	3-Year Return (1991–93)	+34%
Tax Load (Estimated)	Neg.	5-Year Return (1989–93)	+44%
Annual 12b-1 Fee	None	10-Year Return (1984–93)	NA
Annual Expense Ratio	1.10%	Worst-Ever Loss (1987)	21%
Annual Portfolio Turnover	34%	Stock Market Correlation	54%
5-Year Cost Estimate	6%	Up/Down Market Rank	D – B

Benefits		Investment Information	
Investment Objective	Gr. & Icm.	Telephone	800-443-6544
5-Year Projected Return	+2%	Minimum Investment	$2,500
Safety Rating (0-100)	77%	Telephone Switching	5 per yr; $5
Yield	1.9%	Total Assets	$25 million

Principal Preserv Div Achivrs
Dividend growth stocks

S&P 500

Fund

Costs		Performance	
Sales Load	4.7%	1-Year Return (1993)	–5%
Redemption Fee	None	3-Year Return (1991–93)	+36%
Tax Load (Estimated)	3%	5-Year Return (1989–93)	+64%
Annual 12b-1 Fee	0.25%	10-Year Return (1984–93)	NA
Annual Expense Ratio	1.30%	Worst-Ever Loss (1987)	27%
Annual Portfolio Turnover	107%	Stock Market Correlation	83%
5-Year Cost Estimate	16%	Up/Down Market Rank	D – B
Benefits		Investment Information	
Investment Objective	Gr. & Icm.	Telephone	800-826-4600
5-Year Projected Return	+0%	Minimum Investment	$1,000
Safety Rating (0-100)	73%	Telephone Switching	Unlimited; $5
Yield	1.0%	Total Assets	$26 million

Principal Preservation S&P 100
S&P 100; call writing

Costs		Performance	
Sales Load	4.7%	1-Year Return (1993)	+15%
Redemption Fee	None	3-Year Return (1991–93)	+54%
Tax Load (Estimated)	6%	5-Year Return (1989–93)	+86%
Annual 12b-1 Fee	0.25%	10-Year Return (1984–93)	NA
Annual Expense Ratio	1.28%	Worst-Ever Loss (1987)	34%
Annual Portfolio Turnover	4%	Stock Market Correlation	82%
5-Year Cost Estimate	12%	Up/Down Market Rank	B – C
Benefits		Investment Information	
Investment Objective	Gr. & Icm.	Telephone	800-826-4600
5-Year Projected Return	+5%	Minimum Investment	$1,000
Safety Rating (0-100)	72%	Telephone Switching	Unlimited; $5
Yield	1.4%	Total Assets	$36 million

Princor Capital Accumulatn
Long term earnings growth

Costs		Performance	
Sales Load	5.3%	1-Year Return (1993)	+8%
Redemption Fee	None	3-Year Return (1991–93)	+61%
Tax Load (Estimated)	1%	5-Year Return (1989–93)	+65%
Annual 12b-1 Fee	0.25%	10-Year Return (1984–93)	NA
Annual Expense Ratio	0.93%	Worst-Ever Loss (1987)	33%
Annual Portfolio Turnover	28%	Stock Market Correlation	82%
5-Year Cost Estimate	11%	Up/Down Market Rank	C – D
Benefits		Investment Information	
Investment Objective	Gr. & Icm.	Telephone	800-247-4123
5-Year Projected Return	+2%	Minimum Investment	$300
Safety Rating (0-100)	74%	Telephone Switching	Unlimited;free
Yield	2.1%	Total Assets	$239 million

Princor Emerging Growth
Emerging and other growth companies
★★★

Costs		Performance	
Sales Load	5.3%	1-Year Return (1993)	+12%
Redemption Fee	None	3-Year Return (1991–93)	+97%
Tax Load (Estimated)	7%	5-Year Return (1989–93)	NA
Annual 12b-1 Fee	0.25%	10-Year Return (1984–93)	NA
Annual Expense Ratio	1.74%	Worst-Ever Loss (1990)	24%
Annual Portfolio Turnover	5%	Stock Market Correlation	39%
5-Year Cost Estimate	16%	Up/Down Market Rank	A – D
Benefits		Investment Information	
Investment Objective	Growth	Telephone	800-247-4123
5-Year Projected Return	+37%	Minimum Investment	$300
Safety Rating (0-100)	76%	Telephone Switching	Unlimited;free
Yield	0.2%	Total Assets	$43 million

Princor Growth
Earnings and capital growth
★

Costs		Performance	
Sales Load	5.3%	1-Year Return (1993)	+7%
Redemption Fee	None	3-Year Return (1991–93)	+85%
Tax Load (Estimated)	7%	5-Year Return (1989–93)	+116%
Annual 12b-1 Fee	0.25%	10-Year Return (1984–93)	NA
Annual Expense Ratio	1.19%	Worst-Ever Loss (1987)	37%
Annual Portfolio Turnover	12%	Stock Market Correlation	66%
5-Year Cost Estimate	13%	Up/Down Market Rank	B – E

Benefits		Investment Information	
Investment Objective	Gr. & Icm.	Telephone	800-247-4123
5-Year Projected Return	+29%	Minimum Investment	$300
Safety Rating (0-100)	74%	Telephone Switching	Unlimited;free
Yield	1.3%	Total Assets	$76 million

Princor Managed
Diversified stocks; market timing
★★

Costs		Performance	
Sales Load	5.3%	1-Year Return (1993)	+9%
Redemption Fee	None	3-Year Return (1991–93)	+59%
Tax Load (Estimated)	2%	5-Year Return (1989–93)	NA
Annual 12b-1 Fee	0.25%	10-Year Return (1984–93)	NA
Annual Expense Ratio	1.29%	Worst-Ever Loss (1989-90)	14%
Annual Portfolio Turnover	45%	Stock Market Correlation	76%
5-Year Cost Estimate	14%	Up/Down Market Rank	D – B

Benefits		Investment Information	
Investment Objective	Icm. & Gr.	Telephone	800-247-4123
5-Year Projected Return	+15%	Minimum Investment	$300
Safety Rating (0-100)	85%	Telephone Switching	Unlimited;free
Yield	2.7%	Total Assets	$40 million

Prudent Speculator
Diversified; undervalued small stocks

Costs		Performance	
Sales Load	None	1-Year Return (1993)	+5%
Redemption Fee	None	3-Year Return (1991–93)	+73%
Tax Load (Estimated)	9%	5-Year Return (1989–93)	+5%
Annual 12b-1 Fee	0.25%	10-Year Return (1984–93)	NA
Annual Expense Ratio	3.83%	Worst-Ever Loss (1987-90)	64%
Annual Portfolio Turnover	72%	Stock Market Correlation	33%
5-Year Cost Estimate	33%	Up/Down Market Rank	C – E

Benefits		Investment Information	
Investment Objective	Growth	Telephone	800-444-4778
5-Year Projected Return	–4%	Minimum Investment	$250
Safety Rating (0-100)	44%	Telephone Switching	Unlimited;free
Yield	0.0%	Total Assets	$4 million

Prudential Equity "B"
Established financially sound companies
★★

Costs		Performance	
Sales Load	None	1-Year Return (1993)	+21%
Redemption Fee	5.3%	3-Year Return (1991–93)	+69%
Tax Load (Estimated)	1%	5-Year Return (1989–93)	+113%
Annual 12b-1 Fee	1.00%	10-Year Return (1984–93)	+295%
Annual Expense Ratio	1.74%	Worst-Ever Loss (1987)	35%
Annual Portfolio Turnover	28%	Stock Market Correlation	72%
5-Year Cost Estimate	11%	Up/Down Market Rank	B – C

Benefits		Investment Information	
Investment Objective	Growth	Telephone	800-225-1852
5-Year Projected Return	+20%	Minimum Investment	$1,000
Safety Rating (0-100)	75%	Telephone Switching	Unlimited;free
Yield	0.8%	Total Assets	$1.77 billion

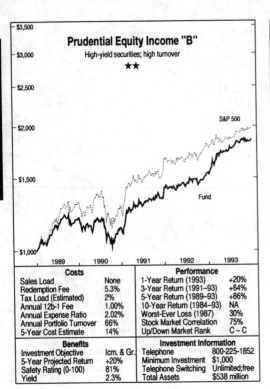

Prudential Equity Income "B"

High-yield securities; high turnover

★★

(Chart shows S&P 500 and Fund lines, 1989–1993, $1,000–$3,500 scale)

Costs		Performance	
Sales Load	None	1-Year Return (1993)	+20%
Redemption Fee	5.3%	3-Year Return (1991–93)	+64%
Tax Load (Estimated)	2%	5-Year Return (1989–93)	+86%
Annual 12b-1 Fee	1.00%	10-Year Return (1984–93)	NA
Annual Expense Ratio	2.02%	Worst-Ever Loss (1987)	30%
Annual Portfolio Turnover	66%	Stock Market Correlation	75%
5-Year Cost Estimate	14%	Up/Down Market Rank	C – C

Benefits		Investment Information	
Investment Objective	Icm. & Gr.	Telephone	800-225-1852
5-Year Projected Return	+20%	Minimum Investment	$1,000
Safety Rating (0-100)	81%	Telephone Switching	Unlimited;free
Yield	2.3%	Total Assets	$538 million

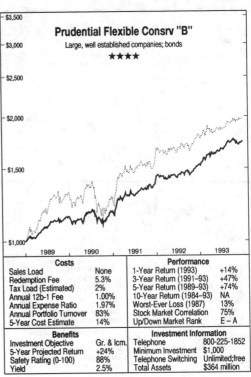

Prudential Flexible Consrv "B"

Large, well established companies; bonds

★★★★

(Chart shows index and fund lines, 1989–1993, $1,000–$3,500 scale)

Costs		Performance	
Sales Load	None	1-Year Return (1993)	+14%
Redemption Fee	5.3%	3-Year Return (1991–93)	+47%
Tax Load (Estimated)	2%	5-Year Return (1989–93)	+74%
Annual 12b-1 Fee	1.00%	10-Year Return (1984–93)	NA
Annual Expense Ratio	1.97%	Worst-Ever Loss (1987)	13%
Annual Portfolio Turnover	83%	Stock Market Correlation	75%
5-Year Cost Estimate	14%	Up/Down Market Rank	E – A

Benefits		Investment Information	
Investment Objective	Gr. & Icm.	Telephone	800-225-1852
5-Year Projected Return	+24%	Minimum Investment	$1,000
Safety Rating (0-100)	88%	Telephone Switching	Unlimited;free
Yield	2.5%	Total Assets	$364 million

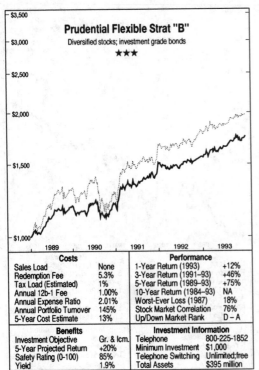

Prudential Flexible Strat "B"

Diversified stocks; investment grade bonds

★★★

(Chart shows index and fund lines, 1989–1993, $1,000–$3,500 scale)

Costs		Performance	
Sales Load	None	1-Year Return (1993)	+12%
Redemption Fee	5.3%	3-Year Return (1991–93)	+46%
Tax Load (Estimated)	1%	5-Year Return (1989–93)	+75%
Annual 12b-1 Fee	1.00%	10-Year Return (1984–93)	NA
Annual Expense Ratio	2.01%	Worst-Ever Loss (1987)	18%
Annual Portfolio Turnover	145%	Stock Market Correlation	76%
5-Year Cost Estimate	13%	Up/Down Market Rank	D – A

Benefits		Investment Information	
Investment Objective	Gr. & Icm.	Telephone	800-225-1852
5-Year Projected Return	+20%	Minimum Investment	$1,000
Safety Rating (0-100)	85%	Telephone Switching	Unlimited;free
Yield	1.9%	Total Assets	$395 million

Prudential Global "B"

Foreign & U.S. - diversified securities

(Chart shows index and fund lines, 1989–1993, $1,000–$3,000 scale)

Costs		Performance	
Sales Load	None	1-Year Return (1993)	+48%
Redemption Fee	5.3%	3-Year Return (1991–93)	+62%
Tax Load (Estimated)	3%	5-Year Return (1989–93)	+51%
Annual 12b-1 Fee	1.00%	10-Year Return (1984–93)	NA
Annual Expense Ratio	2.40%	Worst-Ever Loss (1987)	27%
Annual Portfolio Turnover	76%	Stock Market Correlation	24%
5-Year Cost Estimate	17%	Up/Down Market Rank	E – A

Benefits		Investment Information	
Investment Objective	Gr. & Icm.	Telephone	800-225-1852
5-Year Projected Return	NA	Minimum Investment	$1,000
Safety Rating (0-100)	75%	Telephone Switching	Unlimited;free
Yield	0.0%	Total Assets	$241 million

Prudential Global Genesis "B"
Foreign - under $.5-billion market value

Chart shows values from $1,000 to $3,000 across years 1989–1993, with S&P 500 and Fund lines.

Costs		Performance	
Sales Load	None	1-Year Return (1993)	+60%
Redemption Fee	5.3%	3-Year Return (1991–93)	+84%
Tax Load (Estimated)	5%	5-Year Return (1989–93)	+98%
Annual 12b-1 Fee	1.00%	10-Year Return (1984–93)	NA
Annual Expense Ratio	3.29%	Worst-Ever Loss (1990-91)	28%
Annual Portfolio Turnover	67%	Stock Market Correlation	21%
5-Year Cost Estimate	26%	Up/Down Market Rank	C – C

Benefits		Investment Information	
Investment Objective	Growth	Telephone	800-225-1852
5-Year Projected Return	NA	Minimum Investment	$1,000
Safety Rating (0-100)	74%	Telephone Switching	Unlimited;free
Yield	0.3%	Total Assets	$52 million

Prudential Globl Resources "B"
Foreign & U.S. - natural resource stocks

Chart shows values from $1,000 to $3,500 across years 1989–1993.

Costs		Performance	
Sales Load	None	1-Year Return (1993)	+30%
Redemption Fee	5.3%	3-Year Return (1991–93)	+36%
Tax Load (Estimated)	5%	5-Year Return (1989–93)	+44%
Annual 12b-1 Fee	1.00%	10-Year Return (1984–93)	NA
Annual Expense Ratio	3.18%	Worst-Ever Loss (1987)	25%
Annual Portfolio Turnover	50%	Stock Market Correlation	15%
5-Year Cost Estimate	23%	Up/Down Market Rank	E – A

Benefits		Investment Information	
Investment Objective	Growth	Telephone	800-225-1852
5-Year Projected Return	NA	Minimum Investment	$1,000
Safety Rating (0-100)	71%	Telephone Switching	Unlimited;free
Yield	0.0%	Total Assets	$48 million

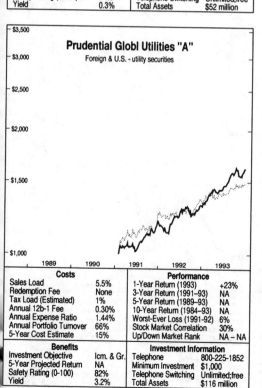

Prudential Globl Utilities "A"
Foreign & U.S. - utility securities

Chart shows values from $1,000 to $3,500 across years 1989–1993.

Costs		Performance	
Sales Load	5.5%	1-Year Return (1993)	+23%
Redemption Fee	None	3-Year Return (1991–93)	NA
Tax Load (Estimated)	1%	5-Year Return (1989–93)	NA
Annual 12b-1 Fee	0.30%	10-Year Return (1984–93)	NA
Annual Expense Ratio	1.44%	Worst-Ever Loss (1991-92)	6%
Annual Portfolio Turnover	66%	Stock Market Correlation	30%
5-Year Cost Estimate	15%	Up/Down Market Rank	NA – NA

Benefits		Investment Information	
Investment Objective	Icm. & Gr.	Telephone	800-225-1852
5-Year Projected Return	NA	Minimum Investment	$1,000
Safety Rating (0-100)	82%	Telephone Switching	Unlimited;free
Yield	3.2%	Total Assets	$116 million

Prudential Growth "B"
Brokerage recommended stocks

Chart shows values from $1,000 to $3,500 across years 1989–1993.

Costs		Performance	
Sales Load	None	1-Year Return (1993)	+8%
Redemption Fee	5.3%	3-Year Return (1991–93)	+39%
Tax Load (Estimated)	2%	5-Year Return (1989–93)	+53%
Annual 12b-1 Fee	1.00%	10-Year Return (1984–93)	+168%
Annual Expense Ratio	2.09%	Worst-Ever Loss (1987)	34%
Annual Portfolio Turnover	99%	Stock Market Correlation	75%
5-Year Cost Estimate	15%	Up/Down Market Rank	B – D

Benefits		Investment Information	
Investment Objective	Gr. & Icm.	Telephone	800-225-1852
5-Year Projected Return	–8%	Minimum Investment	$1,000
Safety Rating (0-100)	67%	Telephone Switching	Unlimited;free
Yield	0.0%	Total Assets	$224 million

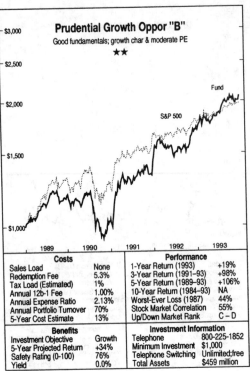

Prudential Growth Oppor "B"
Good fundamentals; growth char & moderate PE
★★

(Chart showing Fund vs S&P 500, 1989–1993, scale $1,000–$3,000)

Costs		Performance	
Sales Load	None	1-Year Return (1993)	+19%
Redemption Fee	5.3%	3-Year Return (1991–93)	+98%
Tax Load (Estimated)	1%	5-Year Return (1989–93)	+106%
Annual 12b-1 Fee	1.00%	10-Year Return (1984–93)	NA
Annual Expense Ratio	2.13%	Worst-Ever Loss (1987)	44%
Annual Portfolio Turnover	70%	Stock Market Correlation	55%
5-Year Cost Estimate	13%	Up/Down Market Rank	C – D

Benefits		Investment Information	
Investment Objective	Growth	Telephone	800-225-1852
5-Year Projected Return	+34%	Minimum Investment	$1,000
Safety Rating (0-100)	76%	Telephone Switching	Unlimited;free
Yield	0.0%	Total Assets	$459 million

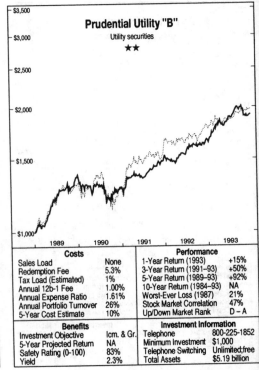

Prudential IncomeVertible "B"
65% conv secs; 35% stocks, bonds, money mkts
★★★

(Chart, 1989–1993, scale $1,000–$3,500)

Costs		Performance	
Sales Load	None	1-Year Return (1993)	+12%
Redemption Fee	5.3%	3-Year Return (1991–93)	+44%
Tax Load (Estimated)	1%	5-Year Return (1989–93)	+64%
Annual 12b-1 Fee	1.00%	10-Year Return (1984–93)	NA
Annual Expense Ratio	2.14%	Worst-Ever Loss (1987)	16%
Annual Portfolio Turnover	109%	Stock Market Correlation	72%
5-Year Cost Estimate	14%	Up/Down Market Rank	E – A

Benefits		Investment Information	
Investment Objective	Icm. & Gr.	Telephone	800-225-1852
5-Year Projected Return	+10%	Minimum Investment	$1,000
Safety Rating (0-100)	85%	Telephone Switching	Unlimited;free
Yield	3.1%	Total Assets	$346 million

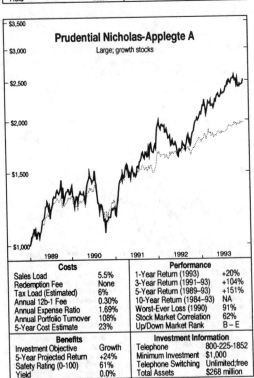

Prudential Nicholas-Applegte A
Large; growth stocks

(Chart, 1989–1993, scale $1,000–$3,500)

Costs		Performance	
Sales Load	5.5%	1-Year Return (1993)	+20%
Redemption Fee	None	3-Year Return (1991–93)	+104%
Tax Load (Estimated)	6%	5-Year Return (1989–93)	+151%
Annual 12b-1 Fee	0.30%	10-Year Return (1984–93)	NA
Annual Expense Ratio	1.69%	Worst-Ever Loss (1990)	91%
Annual Portfolio Turnover	108%	Stock Market Correlation	62%
5-Year Cost Estimate	23%	Up/Down Market Rank	B – E

Benefits		Investment Information	
Investment Objective	Growth	Telephone	800-225-1852
5-Year Projected Return	+24%	Minimum Investment	$1,000
Safety Rating (0-100)	61%	Telephone Switching	Unlimited;free
Yield	0.0%	Total Assets	$268 million

Prudential Utility "B"
Utility securities
★★

(Chart, 1989–1993, scale $1,000–$3,500)

Costs		Performance	
Sales Load	None	1-Year Return (1993)	+15%
Redemption Fee	5.3%	3-Year Return (1991–93)	+50%
Tax Load (Estimated)	1%	5-Year Return (1989–93)	+92%
Annual 12b-1 Fee	1.00%	10-Year Return (1984–93)	NA
Annual Expense Ratio	1.61%	Worst-Ever Loss (1990)	21%
Annual Portfolio Turnover	26%	Stock Market Correlation	47%
5-Year Cost Estimate	10%	Up/Down Market Rank	D – A

Benefits		Investment Information	
Investment Objective	Icm. & Gr.	Telephone	800-225-1852
5-Year Projected Return	NA	Minimum Investment	$1,000
Safety Rating (0-100)	83%	Telephone Switching	Unlimited;free
Yield	2.3%	Total Assets	$5.19 billion

Putnam Convertbl Income Growth

At least 65% convertible secs; stks,pfds,bnds
★★★

S&P 500

Fund

Costs		Performance	
Sales Load	6.1%	1-Year Return (1993)	+17%
Redemption Fee	None	3-Year Return (1991–93)	+83%
Tax Load (Estimated)	4%	5-Year Return (1989–93)	+92%
Annual 12b-1 Fee	0.35%	10-Year Return (1984–93)	+216%
Annual Expense Ratio	1.11%	Worst-Ever Loss (1987)	28%
Annual Portfolio Turnover	60%	Stock Market Correlation	67%
5-Year Cost Estimate	17%	Up/Down Market Rank	E – A

Benefits		Investment Information	
Investment Objective	Icm. & Gr.	Telephone	800-225-1581
5-Year Projected Return	+24%	Minimum Investment	$500
Safety Rating (0-100)	84%	Telephone Switching	Unlimited;free
Yield	4.9%	Total Assets	$700 million

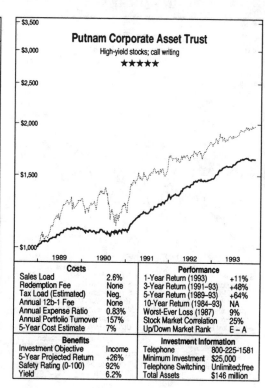

Putnam Corporate Asset Trust

High-yield stocks; call writing
★★★★★

Costs		Performance	
Sales Load	2.6%	1-Year Return (1993)	+11%
Redemption Fee	None	3-Year Return (1991–93)	+48%
Tax Load (Estimated)	Neg.	5-Year Return (1989–93)	+64%
Annual 12b-1 Fee	None	10-Year Return (1984–93)	NA
Annual Expense Ratio	0.83%	Worst-Ever Loss (1987)	9%
Annual Portfolio Turnover	157%	Stock Market Correlation	25%
5-Year Cost Estimate	7%	Up/Down Market Rank	E – A

Benefits		Investment Information	
Investment Objective	Income	Telephone	800-225-1581
5-Year Projected Return	+26%	Minimum Investment	$25,000
Safety Rating (0-100)	92%	Telephone Switching	Unlimited;free
Yield	6.2%	Total Assets	$146 million

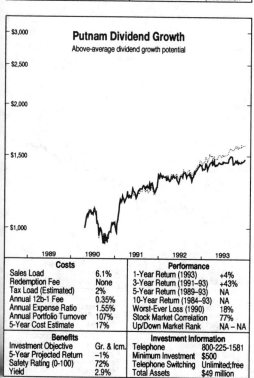

Putnam Dividend Growth

Above-average dividend growth potential

Costs		Performance	
Sales Load	6.1%	1-Year Return (1993)	+4%
Redemption Fee	None	3-Year Return (1991–93)	+43%
Tax Load (Estimated)	2%	5-Year Return (1989–93)	NA
Annual 12b-1 Fee	0.35%	10-Year Return (1984–93)	NA
Annual Expense Ratio	1.55%	Worst-Ever Loss (1990)	18%
Annual Portfolio Turnover	107%	Stock Market Correlation	77%
5-Year Cost Estimate	17%	Up/Down Market Rank	NA – NA

Benefits		Investment Information	
Investment Objective	Gr. & Icm.	Telephone	800-225-1581
5-Year Projected Return	–1%	Minimum Investment	$500
Safety Rating (0-100)	72%	Telephone Switching	Unlimited;free
Yield	2.9%	Total Assets	$49 million

Putnam Dividend Income

Investment-grade dividend-paying stocks

Costs		Performance	
Sales Load	None	1-Year Return (1993)	–2%
Redemption Fee	None	3-Year Return (1991–93)	+52%
Tax Load (Estimated)	2%	5-Year Return (1989–93)	NA
Annual 12b-1 Fee	None	10-Year Return (1984–93)	NA
Annual Expense Ratio	1.64%	Worst-Ever Loss (1989-90)	20%
Annual Portfolio Turnover	133%	Stock Market Correlation	0%
5-Year Cost Estimate	13%	Up/Down Market Rank	E – NA

Benefits		Investment Information	
Investment Objective	Income	Telephone	800-225-1581
5-Year Projected Return	+33%	Minimum Investment	None
Safety Rating (0-100)	68%	Telephone Switching	Via broker
Yield	11.0%	Total Assets	$200 million

Putnam Energy Resources
Oil and energy resource securities

S&P 500

Fund

Costs		Performance	
Sales Load	6.1%	1-Year Return (1993)	+13%
Redemption Fee	None	3-Year Return (1991–93)	+30%
Tax Load (Estimated)	Neg.	5-Year Return (1989–93)	+66%
Annual 12b-1 Fee	0.35%	10-Year Return (1984–93)	+131%
Annual Expense Ratio	1.58%	Worst-Ever Loss (1981-82)	57%
Annual Portfolio Turnover	85%	Stock Market Correlation	31%
5-Year Cost Estimate	15%	Up/Down Market Rank	C – C

Benefits		Investment Information	
Investment Objective	Growth	Telephone	800-225-1581
5-Year Projected Return	NA	Minimum Investment	$500
Safety Rating (0-100)	67%	Telephone Switching	Unlimited;free
Yield	1.3%	Total Assets	$135 million

Putnam Equity Income "A"
65% income producing stocks, pfds, converts

Costs		Performance	
Sales Load	6.1%	1-Year Return (1993)	+17%
Redemption Fee	None	3-Year Return (1991–93)	+52%
Tax Load (Estimated)	5%	5-Year Return (1989–93)	+69%
Annual 12b-1 Fee	0.25%	10-Year Return (1984–93)	+175%
Annual Expense Ratio	1.27%	Worst-Ever Loss (1987)	35%
Annual Portfolio Turnover	198%	Stock Market Correlation	79%
5-Year Cost Estimate	19%	Up/Down Market Rank	D – C

Benefits		Investment Information	
Investment Objective	Income	Telephone	800-225-1581
5-Year Projected Return	+5%	Minimum Investment	$500
Safety Rating (0-100)	77%	Telephone Switching	Unlimited;free
Yield	3.7%	Total Assets	$318 million

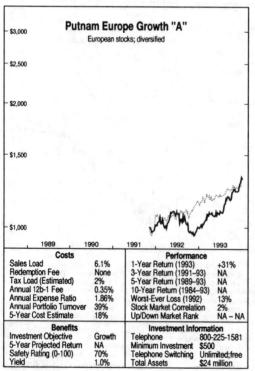

Putnam Europe Growth "A"
European stocks; diversified

Costs		Performance	
Sales Load	6.1%	1-Year Return (1993)	+31%
Redemption Fee	None	3-Year Return (1991–93)	NA
Tax Load (Estimated)	2%	5-Year Return (1989–93)	NA
Annual 12b-1 Fee	0.35%	10-Year Return (1984–93)	NA
Annual Expense Ratio	1.86%	Worst-Ever Loss (1992)	13%
Annual Portfolio Turnover	39%	Stock Market Correlation	2%
5-Year Cost Estimate	18%	Up/Down Market Rank	NA – NA

Benefits		Investment Information	
Investment Objective	Growth	Telephone	800-225-1581
5-Year Projected Return	NA	Minimum Investment	$500
Safety Rating (0-100)	70%	Telephone Switching	Unlimited;free
Yield	1.0%	Total Assets	$24 million

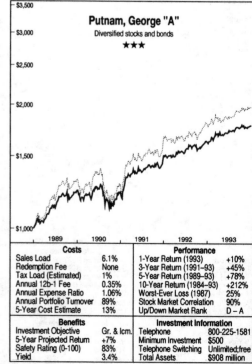

Putnam, George "A"
Diversified stocks and bonds
★★★

Costs		Performance	
Sales Load	6.1%	1-Year Return (1993)	+10%
Redemption Fee	None	3-Year Return (1991–93)	+45%
Tax Load (Estimated)	1%	5-Year Return (1989–93)	+78%
Annual 12b-1 Fee	0.35%	10-Year Return (1984–93)	+212%
Annual Expense Ratio	1.06%	Worst-Ever Loss (1987)	25%
Annual Portfolio Turnover	89%	Stock Market Correlation	90%
5-Year Cost Estimate	13%	Up/Down Market Rank	D – A

Benefits		Investment Information	
Investment Objective	Gr. & Icm.	Telephone	800-225-1581
5-Year Projected Return	+7%	Minimum Investment	$500
Safety Rating (0-100)	83%	Telephone Switching	Unlimited;free
Yield	3.4%	Total Assets	$908 million

Putnam Global Growth "A"
Foreign - diversified stocks

S&P 500

Fund

Costs		Performance	
Sales Load	6.1%	1-Year Return (1993)	+32%
Redemption Fee	None	3-Year Return (1991–93)	+56%
Tax Load (Estimated)	4%	5-Year Return (1989–93)	+76%
Annual 12b-1 Fee	0.35%	10-Year Return (1984–93)	+372%
Annual Expense Ratio	1.57%	Worst-Ever Loss (1987)	29%
Annual Portfolio Turnover	62%	Stock Market Correlation	29%
5-Year Cost Estimate	19%	Up/Down Market Rank	D – B

Benefits		Investment Information	
Investment Objective	Growth	Telephone	800-225-1581
5-Year Projected Return	NA	Minimum Investment	$500
Safety Rating (0-100)	76%	Telephone Switching	Unlimited;free
Yield	0.1%	Total Assets	$1.02 billion

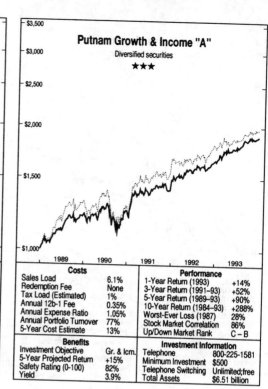

Putnam Growth & Income "A"
Diversified securities
★★★

Costs		Performance	
Sales Load	6.1%	1-Year Return (1993)	+14%
Redemption Fee	None	3-Year Return (1991–93)	+52%
Tax Load (Estimated)	1%	5-Year Return (1989–93)	+90%
Annual 12b-1 Fee	0.35%	10-Year Return (1984–93)	+288%
Annual Expense Ratio	1.05%	Worst-Ever Loss (1987)	28%
Annual Portfolio Turnover	77%	Stock Market Correlation	86%
5-Year Cost Estimate	13%	Up/Down Market Rank	C – B

Benefits		Investment Information	
Investment Objective	Gr. & Icm.	Telephone	800-225-1581
5-Year Projected Return	+15%	Minimum Investment	$500
Safety Rating (0-100)	82%	Telephone Switching	Unlimited;free
Yield	3.9%	Total Assets	$6.51 billion

Putnam Health Sciences "A"
Health-care stocks

Costs		Performance	
Sales Load	6.1%	1-Year Return (1993)	+0%
Redemption Fee	None	3-Year Return (1991–93)	+33%
Tax Load (Estimated)	5%	5-Year Return (1989–93)	+118%
Annual 12b-1 Fee	0.35%	10-Year Return (1984–93)	+304%
Annual Expense Ratio	1.21%	Worst-Ever Loss (1987)	35%
Annual Portfolio Turnover	27%	Stock Market Correlation	40%
5-Year Cost Estimate	15%	Up/Down Market Rank	B – D

Benefits		Investment Information	
Investment Objective	Growth	Telephone	800-225-1581
5-Year Projected Return	NA	Minimum Investment	$500
Safety Rating (0-100)	66%	Telephone Switching	Unlimited;free
Yield	0.9%	Total Assets	$785 million

Putnam Investors "A"
High-quality stocks; long term
★

Costs		Performance	
Sales Load	6.1%	1-Year Return (1993)	+18%
Redemption Fee	None	3-Year Return (1991–93)	+63%
Tax Load (Estimated)	Neg.	5-Year Return (1989–93)	+112%
Annual 12b-1 Fee	0.35%	10-Year Return (1984–93)	+253%
Annual Expense Ratio	1.03%	Worst-Ever Loss (1987)	35%
Annual Portfolio Turnover	100%	Stock Market Correlation	83%
5-Year Cost Estimate	12%	Up/Down Market Rank	A – E

Benefits		Investment Information	
Investment Objective	Gr. & Icm.	Telephone	800-225-1581
5-Year Projected Return	+10%	Minimum Investment	$500
Safety Rating (0-100)	70%	Telephone Switching	Unlimited;free
Yield	1.2%	Total Assets	$844 million

Putnam Managed Income Trust
Dividend-paying stocks; inv-grade bonds
★

(chart: S&P 500, Fund; years 1989–1993; $1,000–$3,500)

Costs		Performance	
Sales Load	6.1%	1-Year Return (1993)	+12%
Redemption Fee	None	3-Year Return (1991–93)	+52%
Tax Load (Estimated)	4%	5-Year Return (1989–93)	+76%
Annual 12b-1 Fee	0.35%	10-Year Return (1984–93)	NA
Annual Expense Ratio	1.14%	Worst-Ever Loss (1987)	30%
Annual Portfolio Turnover	135%	Stock Market Correlation	72%
5-Year Cost Estimate	16%	Up/Down Market Rank	B – D

Benefits		Investment Information	
Investment Objective	Income	Telephone	800-225-1581
5-Year Projected Return	+6%	Minimum Investment	$500
Safety Rating (0-100)	80%	Telephone Switching	Unlimited;free
Yield	6.3%	Total Assets	$562 million

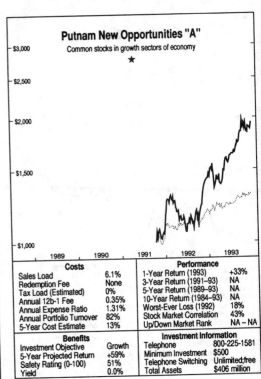

Putnam New Opportunities "A"
Common stocks in growth sectors of economy
★

(chart: years 1989–1993; $1,000–$3,000)

Costs		Performance	
Sales Load	6.1%	1-Year Return (1993)	+33%
Redemption Fee	None	3-Year Return (1991–93)	NA
Tax Load (Estimated)	0%	5-Year Return (1989–93)	NA
Annual 12b-1 Fee	0.35%	10-Year Return (1984–93)	NA
Annual Expense Ratio	1.31%	Worst-Ever Loss (1992)	18%
Annual Portfolio Turnover	82%	Stock Market Correlation	43%
5-Year Cost Estimate	13%	Up/Down Market Rank	NA – NA

Benefits		Investment Information	
Investment Objective	Growth	Telephone	800-225-1581
5-Year Projected Return	+59%	Minimum Investment	$500
Safety Rating (0-100)	51%	Telephone Switching	Unlimited;free
Yield	0.0%	Total Assets	$406 million

Putnam OTC Emerging Growth
Small-medium sized OTC growth stocks

(chart: years 1989–1993; $1,000–$3,000)

Costs		Performance	
Sales Load	6.1%	1-Year Return (1993)	+32%
Redemption Fee	None	3-Year Return (1991–93)	+110%
Tax Load (Estimated)	3%	5-Year Return (1989–93)	+144%
Annual 12b-1 Fee	0.35%	10-Year Return (1984–93)	NA
Annual Expense Ratio	1.34%	Worst-Ever Loss (1987)	42%
Annual Portfolio Turnover	133%	Stock Market Correlation	52%
5-Year Cost Estimate	17%	Up/Down Market Rank	A – E

Benefits		Investment Information	
Investment Objective	Growth	Telephone	800-225-1581
5-Year Projected Return	+34%	Minimum Investment	$500
Safety Rating (0-100)	65%	Telephone Switching	Unlimited;free
Yield	0.0%	Total Assets	$382 million

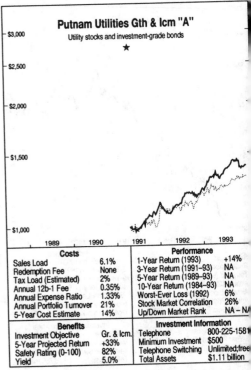

Putnam Utilities Gth & Icm "A"
Utility stocks and investment-grade bonds
★

(chart: years 1989–1993; $1,000–$3,000)

Costs		Performance	
Sales Load	6.1%	1-Year Return (1993)	+14%
Redemption Fee	None	3-Year Return (1991–93)	NA
Tax Load (Estimated)	2%	5-Year Return (1989–93)	NA
Annual 12b-1 Fee	0.35%	10-Year Return (1984–93)	NA
Annual Expense Ratio	1.33%	Worst-Ever Loss (1992)	6%
Annual Portfolio Turnover	21%	Stock Market Correlation	26%
5-Year Cost Estimate	14%	Up/Down Market Rank	NA – NA

Benefits		Investment Information	
Investment Objective	Gr. & Icm.	Telephone	800-225-1581
5-Year Projected Return	+33%	Minimum Investment	$500
Safety Rating (0-100)	82%	Telephone Switching	Unlimited;free
Yield	5.0%	Total Assets	$1.11 billion

Putnam Vista
Undervalued stocks
★★

Costs		Performance	
Sales Load	6.1%	1-Year Return (1993)	+17%
Redemption Fee	None	3-Year Return (1991–93)	+90%
Tax Load (Estimated)	1%	5-Year Return (1989–93)	+122%
Annual 12b-1 Fee	0.35%	10-Year Return (1984–93)	+266%
Annual Expense Ratio	1.11%	Worst-Ever Loss (1987)	32%
Annual Portfolio Turnover	133%	Stock Market Correlation	70%
5-Year Cost Estimate	13%	Up/Down Market Rank	A – D
Benefits		**Investment Information**	
Investment Objective	Growth	Telephone	800-225-1581
5-Year Projected Return	+26%	Minimum Investment	$500
Safety Rating (0-100)	77%	Telephone Switching	Unlimited;free
Yield	0.9%	Total Assets	$494 million

Putnam Voyager "A"
Short term trading; leveraged
★

Costs		Performance	
Sales Load	6.1%	1-Year Return (1993)	+18%
Redemption Fee	None	3-Year Return (1991–93)	+95%
Tax Load (Estimated)	5%	5-Year Return (1989–93)	+156%
Annual 12b-1 Fee	0.35%	10-Year Return (1984–93)	+392%
Annual Expense Ratio	1.20%	Worst-Ever Loss (1987)	37%
Annual Portfolio Turnover	56%	Stock Market Correlation	66%
5-Year Cost Estimate	18%	Up/Down Market Rank	A – E
Benefits		**Investment Information**	
Investment Objective	Growth	Telephone	800-225-1581
5-Year Projected Return	+29%	Minimum Investment	$500
Safety Rating (0-100)	68%	Telephone Switching	Unlimited;free
Yield	0.0%	Total Assets	$3.06 billion

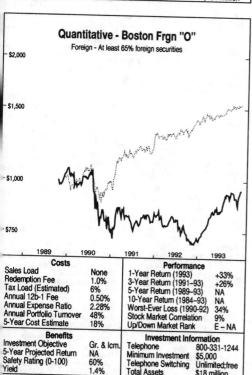

Quantitative - Boston Frgn "O"
Foreign - At least 65% foreign securities

Costs		Performance	
Sales Load	None	1-Year Return (1993)	+33%
Redemption Fee	1.0%	3-Year Return (1991–93)	+26%
Tax Load (Estimated)	6%	5-Year Return (1989–93)	NA
Annual 12b-1 Fee	0.50%	10-Year Return (1984–93)	NA
Annual Expense Ratio	2.28%	Worst-Ever Loss (1990-92)	34%
Annual Portfolio Turnover	48%	Stock Market Correlation	9%
5-Year Cost Estimate	18%	Up/Down Market Rank	E – NA
Benefits		**Investment Information**	
Investment Objective	Gr. & Icm.	Telephone	800-331-1244
5-Year Projected Return	NA	Minimum Investment	$5,000
Safety Rating (0-100)	60%	Telephone Switching	Unlimited;free
Yield	1.4%	Total Assets	$18 million

Quest For Value Capital
Div-pay stks & int bearing secs; liq Jan 1997
★

Costs		Performance	
Sales Load	None	1-Year Return (1993)	+4%
Redemption Fee	None	3-Year Return (1991–93)	+111%
Tax Load (Estimated)	9%	5-Year Return (1989–93)	+201%
Annual 12b-1 Fee	None	10-Year Return (1984–93)	NA
Annual Expense Ratio	None	Worst-Ever Loss (1987)	60%
Annual Portfolio Turnover	56%	Stock Market Correlation	38%
5-Year Cost Estimate	11%	Up/Down Market Rank	B – D
Benefits		**Investment Information**	
Investment Objective	Growth	Telephone	800-232-3863
5-Year Projected Return	+20%	Minimum Investment	None
Safety Rating (0-100)	59%	Telephone Switching	Via broker
Yield	0.0%	Total Assets	$495 million

Quest For Value Fund
Undervalued stocks
★

S&P 500

Fund

Costs		Performance	
Sales Load	5.8%	1-Year Return (1993)	+7%
Redemption Fee	None	3-Year Return (1991–93)	+67%
Tax Load (Estimated)	3%	5-Year Return (1989–93)	+86%
Annual 12b-1 Fee	0.50%	10-Year Return (1984–93)	NA
Annual Expense Ratio	1.75%	Worst-Ever Loss (1987)	29%
Annual Portfolio Turnover	34%	Stock Market Correlation	75%
5-Year Cost Estimate	18%	Up/Down Market Rank	C – C

Benefits		Investment Information	
Investment Objective	Growth	Telephone	800-232-3863
5-Year Projected Return	+10%	Minimum Investment	$1,000
Safety Rating (0-100)	76%	Telephone Switching	Unlimited; $5
Yield	0.3%	Total Assets	$244 million

Quest For Value Global Equity
Foreign - diversified securities

Costs		Performance	
Sales Load	5.8%	1-Year Return (1993)	+24%
Redemption Fee	None	3-Year Return (1991–93)	+47%
Tax Load (Estimated)	1%	5-Year Return (1989–93)	NA
Annual 12b-1 Fee	0.50%	10-Year Return (1984–93)	NA
Annual Expense Ratio	1.76%	Worst-Ever Loss (1990)	19%
Annual Portfolio Turnover	62%	Stock Market Correlation	21%
5-Year Cost Estimate	17%	Up/Down Market Rank	NA – NA

Benefits		Investment Information	
Investment Objective	Growth	Telephone	800-232-3863
5-Year Projected Return	NA	Minimum Investment	$1,000
Safety Rating (0-100)	72%	Telephone Switching	Unlimited; $5
Yield	0.0%	Total Assets	$140 million

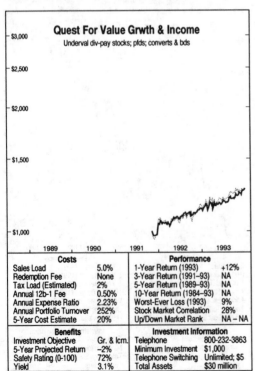

Quest For Value Grwth & Income
Underval div-pay stocks; pfds; converts & bds

Costs		Performance	
Sales Load	5.0%	1-Year Return (1993)	+12%
Redemption Fee	None	3-Year Return (1991–93)	NA
Tax Load (Estimated)	2%	5-Year Return (1989–93)	NA
Annual 12b-1 Fee	0.50%	10-Year Return (1984–93)	NA
Annual Expense Ratio	2.23%	Worst-Ever Loss (1993)	9%
Annual Portfolio Turnover	252%	Stock Market Correlation	28%
5-Year Cost Estimate	20%	Up/Down Market Rank	NA – NA

Benefits		Investment Information	
Investment Objective	Gr. & Icm.	Telephone	800-232-3863
5-Year Projected Return	–2%	Minimum Investment	$1,000
Safety Rating (0-100)	72%	Telephone Switching	Unlimited; $5
Yield	3.1%	Total Assets	$30 million

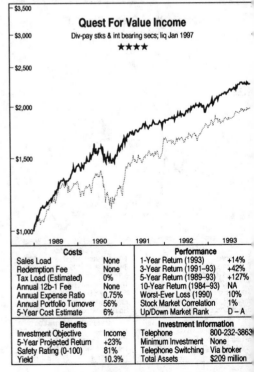

Quest For Value Income
Div-pay stks & int bearing secs; liq Jan 1997
★★★★

Costs		Performance	
Sales Load	None	1-Year Return (1993)	+14%
Redemption Fee	None	3-Year Return (1991–93)	+42%
Tax Load (Estimated)	0%	5-Year Return (1989–93)	+127%
Annual 12b-1 Fee	None	10-Year Return (1984–93)	NA
Annual Expense Ratio	0.75%	Worst-Ever Loss (1990)	10%
Annual Portfolio Turnover	56%	Stock Market Correlation	1%
5-Year Cost Estimate	6%	Up/Down Market Rank	D – A

Benefits		Investment Information	
Investment Objective	Income	Telephone	800-232-3863
5-Year Projected Return	+23%	Minimum Investment	None
Safety Rating (0-100)	81%	Telephone Switching	Via broker
Yield	10.3%	Total Assets	$209 million

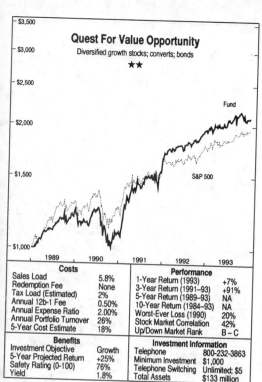

Quest For Value Opportunity
Diversified growth stocks; converts; bonds
★★

Costs		Performance	
Sales Load	5.8%	1-Year Return (1993)	+7%
Redemption Fee	None	3-Year Return (1991–93)	+91%
Tax Load (Estimated)	2%	5-Year Return (1989–93)	NA
Annual 12b-1 Fee	0.50%	10-Year Return (1984–93)	NA
Annual Expense Ratio	2.00%	Worst-Ever Loss (1990)	20%
Annual Portfolio Turnover	26%	Stock Market Correlation	42%
5-Year Cost Estimate	18%	Up/Down Market Rank	B – C

Benefits		Investment Information	
Investment Objective	Growth	Telephone	800-232-3863
5-Year Projected Return	+25%	Minimum Investment	$1,000
Safety Rating (0-100)	76%	Telephone Switching	Unlimited; $5
Yield	1.8%	Total Assets	$133 million

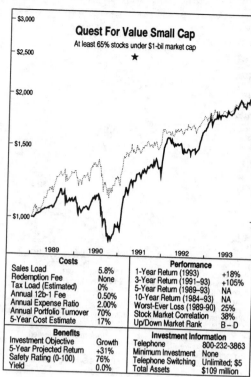

Quest For Value Small Cap
At least 65% stocks under $1-bil market cap
★

Costs		Performance	
Sales Load	5.8%	1-Year Return (1993)	+18%
Redemption Fee	None	3-Year Return (1991–93)	+105%
Tax Load (Estimated)	0%	5-Year Return (1989–93)	NA
Annual 12b-1 Fee	0.50%	10-Year Return (1984–93)	NA
Annual Expense Ratio	2.00%	Worst-Ever Loss (1989-90)	25%
Annual Portfolio Turnover	70%	Stock Market Correlation	38%
5-Year Cost Estimate	17%	Up/Down Market Rank	B – D

Benefits		Investment Information	
Investment Objective	Growth	Telephone	800-232-3863
5-Year Projected Return	+31%	Minimum Investment	None
Safety Rating (0-100)	76%	Telephone Switching	Unlimited; $5
Yield	0.0%	Total Assets	$109 million

Rainbow
Growth stocks; non-diversified

Costs		Performance	
Sales Load	None	1-Year Return (1993)	–5%
Redemption Fee	None	3-Year Return (1991–93)	+28%
Tax Load (Estimated)	0%	5-Year Return (1989–93)	+26%
Annual 12b-1 Fee	None	10-Year Return (1984–93)	+87%
Annual Expense Ratio	2.66%	Worst-Ever Loss (1981-82)	33%
Annual Portfolio Turnover	81%	Stock Market Correlation	55%
5-Year Cost Estimate	15%	Up/Down Market Rank	D – D

Benefits		Investment Information	
Investment Objective	Growth	Telephone	212-983-2980
5-Year Projected Return	–9%	Minimum Investment	$300
Safety Rating (0-100)	66%	Telephone Switching	Mail only
Yield	0.0%	Total Assets	$2 million

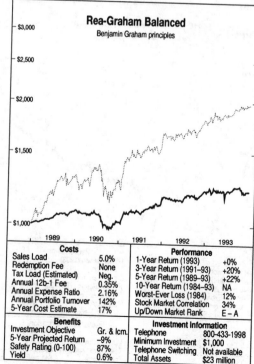

Rea-Graham Balanced
Benjamin Graham principles

Costs		Performance	
Sales Load	5.0%	1-Year Return (1993)	+0%
Redemption Fee	None	3-Year Return (1991–93)	+20%
Tax Load (Estimated)	Neg.	5-Year Return (1989–93)	+22%
Annual 12b-1 Fee	0.35%	10-Year Return (1984–93)	NA
Annual Expense Ratio	2.16%	Worst-Ever Loss (1984)	12%
Annual Portfolio Turnover	142%	Stock Market Correlation	34%
5-Year Cost Estimate	17%	Up/Down Market Rank	E – A

Benefits		Investment Information	
Investment Objective	Gr. & Icm.	Telephone	800-433-1998
5-Year Projected Return	–9%	Minimum Investment	$1,000
Safety Rating (0-100)	87%	Telephone Switching	Not available
Yield	0.6%	Total Assets	$23 million

EQUITY

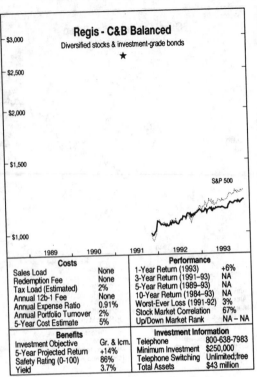

Regis - C&B Balanced
Diversified stocks & investment-grade bonds
★

S&P 500

Costs		Performance	
Sales Load	None	1-Year Return (1993)	+6%
Redemption Fee	None	3-Year Return (1991–93)	NA
Tax Load (Estimated)	2%	5-Year Return (1989–93)	NA
Annual 12b-1 Fee	None	10-Year Return (1984–93)	NA
Annual Expense Ratio	0.91%	Worst-Ever Loss (1991-92)	3%
Annual Portfolio Turnover	2%	Stock Market Correlation	67%
5-Year Cost Estimate	5%	Up/Down Market Rank	NA – NA

Benefits		Investment Information	
Investment Objective	Gr. & Icm.	Telephone	800-638-7983
5-Year Projected Return	+14%	Minimum Investment	$250,000
Safety Rating (0-100)	86%	Telephone Switching	Unlimited;free
Yield	3.7%	Total Assets	$43 million

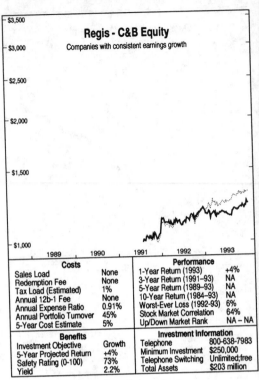

Regis - C&B Equity
Companies with consistent earnings growth

Costs		Performance	
Sales Load	None	1-Year Return (1993)	+4%
Redemption Fee	None	3-Year Return (1991–93)	NA
Tax Load (Estimated)	1%	5-Year Return (1989–93)	NA
Annual 12b-1 Fee	None	10-Year Return (1984–93)	NA
Annual Expense Ratio	0.91%	Worst-Ever Loss (1992-93)	6%
Annual Portfolio Turnover	45%	Stock Market Correlation	64%
5-Year Cost Estimate	5%	Up/Down Market Rank	NA – NA

Benefits		Investment Information	
Investment Objective	Growth	Telephone	800-638-7983
5-Year Projected Return	+4%	Minimum Investment	$250,000
Safety Rating (0-100)	73%	Telephone Switching	Unlimited;free
Yield	2.2%	Total Assets	$203 million

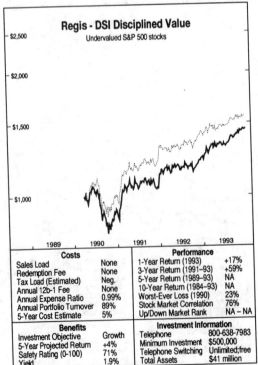

Regis - DSI Disciplined Value
Undervalued S&P 500 stocks

Costs		Performance	
Sales Load	None	1-Year Return (1993)	+17%
Redemption Fee	None	3-Year Return (1991–93)	+59%
Tax Load (Estimated)	Neg.	5-Year Return (1989–93)	NA
Annual 12b-1 Fee	None	10-Year Return (1984–93)	NA
Annual Expense Ratio	0.99%	Worst-Ever Loss (1990)	23%
Annual Portfolio Turnover	89%	Stock Market Correlation	76%
5-Year Cost Estimate	5%	Up/Down Market Rank	NA – NA

Benefits		Investment Information	
Investment Objective	Growth	Telephone	800-638-7983
5-Year Projected Return	+4%	Minimum Investment	$500,000
Safety Rating (0-100)	71%	Telephone Switching	Unlimited;free
Yield	1.9%	Total Assets	$41 million

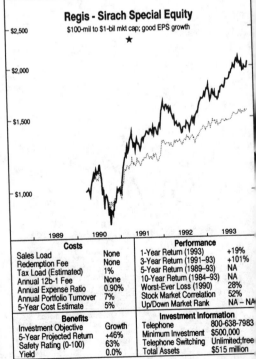

Regis - Sirach Special Equity
$100-mil to $1-bil mkt cap; good EPS growth
★

Costs		Performance	
Sales Load	None	1-Year Return (1993)	+19%
Redemption Fee	None	3-Year Return (1991–93)	+101%
Tax Load (Estimated)	1%	5-Year Return (1989–93)	NA
Annual 12b-1 Fee	None	10-Year Return (1984–93)	NA
Annual Expense Ratio	0.90%	Worst-Ever Loss (1990)	28%
Annual Portfolio Turnover	7%	Stock Market Correlation	52%
5-Year Cost Estimate	5%	Up/Down Market Rank	NA – NA

Benefits		Investment Information	
Investment Objective	Growth	Telephone	800-638-7983
5-Year Projected Return	+46%	Minimum Investment	$500,000
Safety Rating (0-100)	63%	Telephone Switching	Unlimited;free
Yield	0.0%	Total Assets	$515 million

Reich & Tang Equity
Undervalued stocks
★★

Costs		Performance	
Sales Load	None	1-Year Return (1993)	+14%
Redemption Fee	None	3-Year Return (1991–93)	+63%
Tax Load (Estimated)	5%	5-Year Return (1989–93)	+81%
Annual 12b-1 Fee	0.05%	10-Year Return (1984–93)	NA
Annual Expense Ratio	1.15%	Worst-Ever Loss (1987)	28%
Annual Portfolio Turnover	32%	Stock Market Correlation	51%
5-Year Cost Estimate	9%	Up/Down Market Rank	C – C
Benefits		**Investment Information**	
Investment Objective	Growth	Telephone	800-221-3079
5-Year Projected Return	+26%	Minimum Investment	$5,000
Safety Rating (0-100)	77%	Telephone Switching	Unlimited;free
Yield	1.2%	Total Assets	$109 million

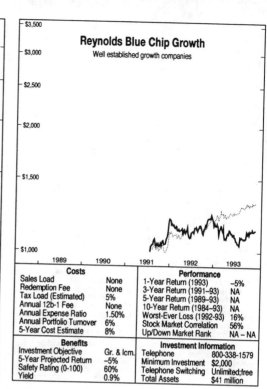

Reynolds Blue Chip Growth
Well established growth companies

Costs		Performance	
Sales Load	None	1-Year Return (1993)	–5%
Redemption Fee	None	3-Year Return (1991–93)	NA
Tax Load (Estimated)	5%	5-Year Return (1989–93)	NA
Annual 12b-1 Fee	None	10-Year Return (1984–93)	NA
Annual Expense Ratio	1.50%	Worst-Ever Loss (1992-93)	16%
Annual Portfolio Turnover	6%	Stock Market Correlation	56%
5-Year Cost Estimate	8%	Up/Down Market Rank	NA – NA
Benefits		**Investment Information**	
Investment Objective	Gr. & Icm.	Telephone	800-338-1579
5-Year Projected Return	–5%	Minimum Investment	$2,000
Safety Rating (0-100)	60%	Telephone Switching	Unlimited;free
Yield	0.9%	Total Assets	$41 million

Rightime
Owns other mutual funds; market timing

Costs		Performance	
Sales Load	None	1-Year Return (1993)	+8%
Redemption Fee	None	3-Year Return (1991–93)	+46%
Tax Load (Estimated)	Neg.	5-Year Return (1989–93)	+64%
Annual 12b-1 Fee	0.75%	10-Year Return (1984–93)	NA
Annual Expense Ratio	2.46%	Worst-Ever Loss (1986)	14%
Annual Portfolio Turnover	0%	Stock Market Correlation	42%
5-Year Cost Estimate	13%	Up/Down Market Rank	E – A
Benefits		**Investment Information**	
Investment Objective	Gr. & Icm.	Telephone	800-242-1421
5-Year Projected Return	+21%	Minimum Investment	$2,000
Safety Rating (0-100)	78%	Telephone Switching	Unlimited;free
Yield	0.0%	Total Assets	$173 million

Rightime Blue Chip
Well known and established companies

Costs		Performance	
Sales Load	5.0%	1-Year Return (1993)	+7%
Redemption Fee	None	3-Year Return (1991–93)	+38%
Tax Load (Estimated)	4%	5-Year Return (1989–93)	+67%
Annual 12b-1 Fee	0.50%	10-Year Return (1984–93)	NA
Annual Expense Ratio	2.20%	Worst-Ever Loss (1990)	8%
Annual Portfolio Turnover	1%	Stock Market Correlation	73%
5-Year Cost Estimate	17%	Up/Down Market Rank	E – A
Benefits		**Investment Information**	
Investment Objective	Gr. & Icm.	Telephone	800-242-1421
5-Year Projected Return	+8%	Minimum Investment	$2,000
Safety Rating (0-100)	78%	Telephone Switching	Unlimited;free
Yield	0.7%	Total Assets	$225 million

Rightime Growth
Diversified growth stocks

S&P 500

Fund

| $3,000 |
| $2,500 |
| $2,000 |
| $1,500 |
| $1,000 |

1989 1990 1991 1992 1993

Costs		Performance	
Sales Load	5.0%	1-Year Return (1993)	–5%
Redemption Fee	None	3-Year Return (1991–93)	+30%
Tax Load (Estimated)	Neg.	5-Year Return (1989–93)	+34%
Annual 12b-1 Fee	0.50%	10-Year Return (1984–93)	NA
Annual Expense Ratio	2.34%	Worst-Ever Loss (1989-91)	22%
Annual Portfolio Turnover	185%	Stock Market Correlation	62%
5-Year Cost Estimate	18%	Up/Down Market Rank	E – C

Benefits		Investment Information	
Investment Objective	Growth	Telephone	800-242-1421
5-Year Projected Return	–16%	Minimum Investment	$2,000
Safety Rating (0-100)	71%	Telephone Switching	Unlimited;free
Yield	0.0%	Total Assets	$39 million

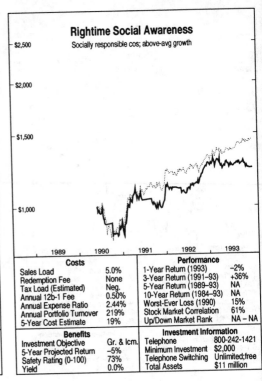

Rightime Social Awareness
Socially responsible cos; above-avg growth

| $2,500 |
| $2,000 |
| $1,500 |
| $1,000 |

1989 1990 1991 1992 1993

Costs		Performance	
Sales Load	5.0%	1-Year Return (1993)	–2%
Redemption Fee	None	3-Year Return (1991–93)	+36%
Tax Load (Estimated)	Neg.	5-Year Return (1989–93)	NA
Annual 12b-1 Fee	0.50%	10-Year Return (1984–93)	NA
Annual Expense Ratio	2.44%	Worst-Ever Loss (1990)	15%
Annual Portfolio Turnover	219%	Stock Market Correlation	61%
5-Year Cost Estimate	19%	Up/Down Market Rank	NA – NA

Benefits		Investment Information	
Investment Objective	Gr. & Icm.	Telephone	800-242-1421
5-Year Projected Return	–5%	Minimum Investment	$2,000
Safety Rating (0-100)	73%	Telephone Switching	Unlimited;free
Yield	0.0%	Total Assets	$11 million

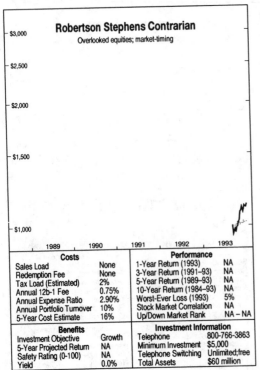

Robertson Stephens Contrarian
Overlooked equities; market-timing

| $3,000 |
| $2,500 |
| $2,000 |
| $1,500 |
| $1,000 |

1989 1990 1991 1992 1993

Costs		Performance	
Sales Load	None	1-Year Return (1993)	NA
Redemption Fee	None	3-Year Return (1991–93)	NA
Tax Load (Estimated)	2%	5-Year Return (1989–93)	NA
Annual 12b-1 Fee	0.75%	10-Year Return (1984–93)	NA
Annual Expense Ratio	2.90%	Worst-Ever Loss (1993)	5%
Annual Portfolio Turnover	10%	Stock Market Correlation	NA
5-Year Cost Estimate	16%	Up/Down Market Rank	NA – NA

Benefits		Investment Information	
Investment Objective	Growth	Telephone	800-766-3863
5-Year Projected Return	NA	Minimum Investment	$5,000
Safety Rating (0-100)	NA	Telephone Switching	Unlimited;free
Yield	0.0%	Total Assets	$60 million

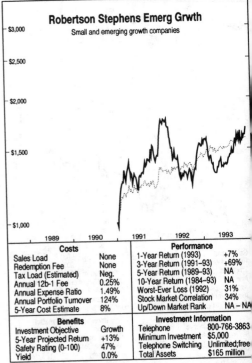

Robertson Stephens Emerg Grwth
Small and emerging growth companies

| $3,000 |
| $2,500 |
| $2,000 |
| $1,500 |
| $1,000 |

1989 1990 1991 1992 1993

Costs		Performance	
Sales Load	None	1-Year Return (1993)	+7%
Redemption Fee	None	3-Year Return (1991–93)	+69%
Tax Load (Estimated)	Neg.	5-Year Return (1989–93)	NA
Annual 12b-1 Fee	0.25%	10-Year Return (1984–93)	NA
Annual Expense Ratio	1.49%	Worst-Ever Loss (1992)	31%
Annual Portfolio Turnover	124%	Stock Market Correlation	34%
5-Year Cost Estimate	8%	Up/Down Market Rank	NA – NA

Benefits		Investment Information	
Investment Objective	Growth	Telephone	800-766-3863
5-Year Projected Return	+13%	Minimum Investment	$5,000
Safety Rating (0-100)	47%	Telephone Switching	Unlimited;free
Yield	0.0%	Total Assets	$165 million

ROC Taiwan
Foreign - Taiwan stocks

S&P 500

$1,500

$1,000

$750

Fund

$500

1989   1990   1991   1992   1993

Costs		Performance	
Sales Load	None	1-Year Return (1993)	+59%
Redemption Fee	None	3-Year Return (1991–93)	+100%
Tax Load (Estimated)	Neg.	5-Year Return (1989–93)	NA
Annual 12b-1 Fee	None	10-Year Return (1984–93)	NA
Annual Expense Ratio	1.98%	Worst-Ever Loss (1989-90)	67%
Annual Portfolio Turnover	27%	Stock Market Correlation	3%
5-Year Cost Estimate	13%	Up/Down Market Rank	D – C

Benefits		Investment Information	
Investment Objective	Growth	Telephone	800-343-9567
5-Year Projected Return	NA	Minimum Investment	None
Safety Rating (0-100)	7%	Telephone Switching	Via broker
Yield	1.1%	Total Assets	$243 million

Rochester Tax Managed
High-yield and growth securities

$3,000

$2,500

$2,000

$1,500

$1,000

1989   1990   1991   1992   1993

Costs		Performance	
Sales Load	6.7%	1-Year Return (1993)	+6%
Redemption Fee	None	3-Year Return (1991–93)	+49%
Tax Load (Estimated)	0%	5-Year Return (1989–93)	+41%
Annual 12b-1 Fee	0.25%	10-Year Return (1984–93)	NA
Annual Expense Ratio	1.67%	Worst-Ever Loss (1989-90)	28%
Annual Portfolio Turnover	20%	Stock Market Correlation	57%
5-Year Cost Estimate	16%	Up/Down Market Rank	D – C

Benefits		Investment Information	
Investment Objective	Icm. & Gr.	Telephone	716-383-1300
5-Year Projected Return	–8%	Minimum Investment	$2,000
Safety Rating (0-100)	72%	Telephone Switching	Unlimited;free
Yield	0.0%	Total Assets	$14 million

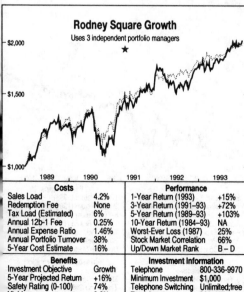

Rodney Square Growth
Uses 3 independent portfolio managers
★

$2,000

$1,500

$1,000

1989   1990   1991   1992   1993

Costs		Performance	
Sales Load	4.2%	1-Year Return (1993)	+15%
Redemption Fee	None	3-Year Return (1991–93)	+72%
Tax Load (Estimated)	6%	5-Year Return (1989–93)	+103%
Annual 12b-1 Fee	0.25%	10-Year Return (1984–93)	NA
Annual Expense Ratio	1.46%	Worst-Ever Loss (1987)	25%
Annual Portfolio Turnover	38%	Stock Market Correlation	66%
5-Year Cost Estimate	16%	Up/Down Market Rank	B – D

Benefits		Investment Information	
Investment Objective	Growth	Telephone	800-336-9970
5-Year Projected Return	+16%	Minimum Investment	$1,000
Safety Rating (0-100)	74%	Telephone Switching	Unlimited;free
Yield	0.0%	Total Assets	$62 million

Rodney Square Intl Equity
Foreign - diversified stocks

$3,000

$2,500

$2,000

$1,500

$1,000

1989   1990   1991   1992   1993

Costs		Performance	
Sales Load	4.2%	1-Year Return (1993)	+35%
Redemption Fee	None	3-Year Return (1991–93)	+32%
Tax Load (Estimated)	3%	5-Year Return (1989–93)	+34%
Annual 12b-1 Fee	0.25%	10-Year Return (1984–93)	NA
Annual Expense Ratio	1.75%	Worst-Ever Loss (1990)	27%
Annual Portfolio Turnover	162%	Stock Market Correlation	10%
5-Year Cost Estimate	17%	Up/Down Market Rank	E – B

Benefits		Investment Information	
Investment Objective	Growth	Telephone	800-336-9970
5-Year Projected Return	NA	Minimum Investment	$1,000
Safety Rating (0-100)	68%	Telephone Switching	Unlimited;free
Yield	0.0%	Total Assets	$14 million

Royce Value Trust
$15 - $300-million market value stocks

Costs		Performance	
Sales Load	None	1-Year Return (1993)	+13%
Redemption Fee	None	3-Year Return (1991–93)	+90%
Tax Load (Estimated)	3%	5-Year Return (1989–93)	+108%
Annual 12b-1 Fee	None	10-Year Return (1984–93)	NA
Annual Expense Ratio	1.35%	Worst-Ever Loss (1987)	41%
Annual Portfolio Turnover	28%	Stock Market Correlation	19%
5-Year Cost Estimate	11%	Up/Down Market Rank	C – C

Benefits		Investment Information	
Investment Objective	Growth	Telephone	800-221-4268
5-Year Projected Return	+27%	Minimum Investment	None
Safety Rating (0-100)	67%	Telephone Switching	Via broker
Yield	0.0%	Total Assets	$222 million

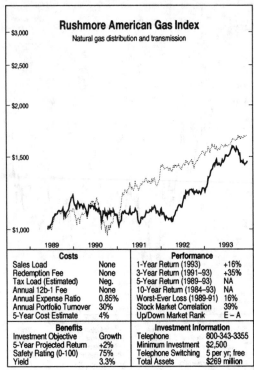

Rushmore American Gas Index
Natural gas distribution and transmission

Costs		Performance	
Sales Load	None	1-Year Return (1993)	+16%
Redemption Fee	None	3-Year Return (1991–93)	+35%
Tax Load (Estimated)	Neg.	5-Year Return (1989–93)	NA
Annual 12b-1 Fee	None	10-Year Return (1984–93)	NA
Annual Expense Ratio	0.85%	Worst-Ever Loss (1989-91)	16%
Annual Portfolio Turnover	30%	Stock Market Correlation	39%
5-Year Cost Estimate	4%	Up/Down Market Rank	E – A

Benefits		Investment Information	
Investment Objective	Growth	Telephone	800-343-3355
5-Year Projected Return	+2%	Minimum Investment	$2,500
Safety Rating (0-100)	75%	Telephone Switching	5 per yr; free
Yield	3.3%	Total Assets	$269 million

Rushmore OTC Index Plus
Matches NASDAQ 100 Index

Costs		Performance	
Sales Load	None	1-Year Return (1993)	+13%
Redemption Fee	None	3-Year Return (1991–93)	+77%
Tax Load (Estimated)	5%	5-Year Return (1989–93)	+68%
Annual 12b-1 Fee	None	10-Year Return (1984–93)	NA
Annual Expense Ratio	0.87%	Worst-Ever Loss (1987)	40%
Annual Portfolio Turnover	327%	Stock Market Correlation	54%
5-Year Cost Estimate	10%	Up/Down Market Rank	B – E

Benefits		Investment Information	
Investment Objective	Growth	Telephone	800-343-3355
5-Year Projected Return	+4%	Minimum Investment	$2,500
Safety Rating (0-100)	59%	Telephone Switching	1 per 3mo;free
Yield	1.6%	Total Assets	$6 million

Rushmore Stock Index Plus
100 largest NYSE stocks

Costs		Performance	
Sales Load	None	1-Year Return (1993)	+10%
Redemption Fee	None	3-Year Return (1991–93)	+42%
Tax Load (Estimated)	0%	5-Year Return (1989–93)	+69%
Annual 12b-1 Fee	None	10-Year Return (1984–93)	NA
Annual Expense Ratio	0.99%	Worst-Ever Loss (1987)	30%
Annual Portfolio Turnover	40%	Stock Market Correlation	86%
5-Year Cost Estimate	5%	Up/Down Market Rank	B – D

Benefits		Investment Information	
Investment Objective	Growth	Telephone	800-343-3355
5-Year Projected Return	-2%	Minimum Investment	$2,500
Safety Rating (0-100)	70%	Telephone Switching	1 per 3mo;free
Yield	2.0%	Total Assets	$9 million

Safeco Equity
Large; strong companies
★★

		1989	1990	1991	1992	1993

Fund

Costs		Performance	
Sales Load	None	1-Year Return (1993)	+31%
Redemption Fee	None	3-Year Return (1991–93)	+83%
Tax Load (Estimated)	3%	5-Year Return (1989–93)	+127%
Annual 12b-1 Fee	None	10-Year Return (1984–93)	+318%
Annual Expense Ratio	0.96%	Worst-Ever Loss (1987)	37%
Annual Portfolio Turnover	53%	Stock Market Correlation	64%
5-Year Cost Estimate	8%	Up/Down Market Rank	C – D

Benefits		Investment Information	
Investment Objective	Gr. & Icm.	Telephone	800-426-6730
5-Year Projected Return	+26%	Minimum Investment	$1,000
Safety Rating (0-100)	72%	Telephone Switching	Unlimited;free
Yield	1.4%	Total Assets	$144 million

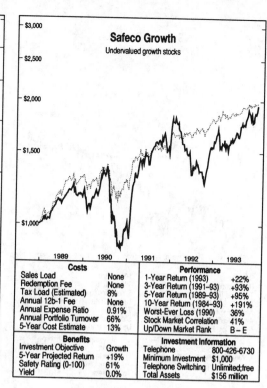

Safeco Growth
Undervalued growth stocks

		1989	1990	1991	1992	1993

Costs		Performance	
Sales Load	None	1-Year Return (1993)	+22%
Redemption Fee	None	3-Year Return (1991–93)	+93%
Tax Load (Estimated)	8%	5-Year Return (1989–93)	+95%
Annual 12b-1 Fee	None	10-Year Return (1984–93)	+191%
Annual Expense Ratio	0.91%	Worst-Ever Loss (1990)	36%
Annual Portfolio Turnover	66%	Stock Market Correlation	41%
5-Year Cost Estimate	13%	Up/Down Market Rank	B – E

Benefits		Investment Information	
Investment Objective	Growth	Telephone	800-426-6730
5-Year Projected Return	+19%	Minimum Investment	$1,000
Safety Rating (0-100)	61%	Telephone Switching	Unlimited;free
Yield	0.0%	Total Assets	$156 million

Safeco Income
Common and preferred stocks
★★

		1989	1990	1991	1992	1993

Costs		Performance	
Sales Load	None	1-Year Return (1993)	+13%
Redemption Fee	None	3-Year Return (1991–93)	+55%
Tax Load (Estimated)	5%	5-Year Return (1989–93)	+65%
Annual 12b-1 Fee	None	10-Year Return (1984–93)	+220%
Annual Expense Ratio	0.90%	Worst-Ever Loss (1987)	27%
Annual Portfolio Turnover	22%	Stock Market Correlation	80%
5-Year Cost Estimate	6%	Up/Down Market Rank	E – B

Benefits		Investment Information	
Investment Objective	Icm. & Gr.	Telephone	800-426-6730
5-Year Projected Return	+9%	Minimum Investment	$1,000
Safety Rating (0-100)	82%	Telephone Switching	Unlimited;free
Yield	4.5%	Total Assets	$203 million

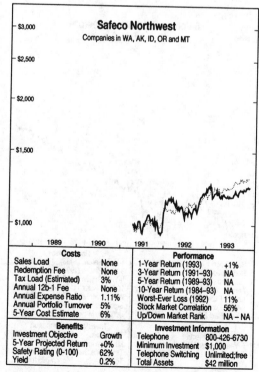

Safeco Northwest
Companies in WA, AK, ID, OR and MT

		1989	1990	1991	1992	1993

Costs		Performance	
Sales Load	None	1-Year Return (1993)	+1%
Redemption Fee	None	3-Year Return (1991–93)	NA
Tax Load (Estimated)	3%	5-Year Return (1989–93)	NA
Annual 12b-1 Fee	None	10-Year Return (1984–93)	NA
Annual Expense Ratio	1.11%	Worst-Ever Loss (1992)	11%
Annual Portfolio Turnover	5%	Stock Market Correlation	56%
5-Year Cost Estimate	6%	Up/Down Market Rank	NA – NA

Benefits		Investment Information	
Investment Objective	Growth	Telephone	800-426-6730
5-Year Projected Return	+0%	Minimum Investment	$1,000
Safety Rating (0-100)	62%	Telephone Switching	Unlimited;free
Yield	0.2%	Total Assets	$42 million

Salomon Brothers
Diversified securities

(S&P 500 labeled on chart)

Costs		Performance	
Sales Load	None	1-Year Return (1993)	+4%
Redemption Fee	None	3-Year Return (1991–93)	+54%
Tax Load (Estimated)	5%	5-Year Return (1989–93)	+83%
Annual 12b-1 Fee	None	10-Year Return (1984–93)	+145%
Annual Expense Ratio	0.43%	Worst-Ever Loss (1987)	29%
Annual Portfolio Turnover	90%	Stock Market Correlation	24%
5-Year Cost Estimate	10%	Up/Down Market Rank	D – B

Benefits		Investment Information	
Investment Objective	Growth	Telephone	800-725-6666
5-Year Projected Return	–5%	Minimum Investment	None
Safety Rating (0-100)	65%	Telephone Switching	Via broker
Yield	2.0%	Total Assets	$1.13 billion

Salomon Brothers - Capital
Non-diversified securities
★

Costs		Performance	
Sales Load	None	1-Year Return (1993)	+17%
Redemption Fee	None	3-Year Return (1991–93)	+64%
Tax Load (Estimated)	5%	5-Year Return (1989–93)	+107%
Annual 12b-1 Fee	None	10-Year Return (1984–93)	+170%
Annual Expense Ratio	1.34%	Worst-Ever Loss (1987)	45%
Annual Portfolio Turnover	92%	Stock Market Correlation	67%
5-Year Cost Estimate	13%	Up/Down Market Rank	B – E

Benefits		Investment Information	
Investment Objective	Growth	Telephone	800-725-6666
5-Year Projected Return	+15%	Minimum Investment	$1,000
Safety Rating (0-100)	68%	Telephone Switching	Unlimited;free
Yield	0.2%	Total Assets	$114 million

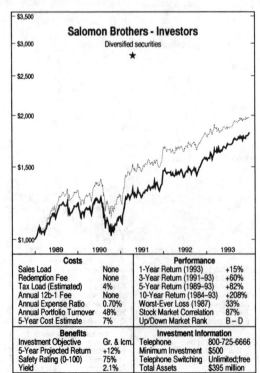

Salomon Brothers - Investors
Diversified securities
★

Costs		Performance	
Sales Load	None	1-Year Return (1993)	+15%
Redemption Fee	None	3-Year Return (1991–93)	+60%
Tax Load (Estimated)	4%	5-Year Return (1989–93)	+82%
Annual 12b-1 Fee	None	10-Year Return (1984–93)	+208%
Annual Expense Ratio	0.70%	Worst-Ever Loss (1987)	33%
Annual Portfolio Turnover	48%	Stock Market Correlation	87%
5-Year Cost Estimate	7%	Up/Down Market Rank	B – D

Benefits		Investment Information	
Investment Objective	Gr. & Icm.	Telephone	800-725-6666
5-Year Projected Return	+12%	Minimum Investment	$500
Safety Rating (0-100)	75%	Telephone Switching	Unlimited;free
Yield	2.1%	Total Assets	$395 million

Salomon Brothers - Opportunity
Diversified securities
★

Costs		Performance	
Sales Load	None	1-Year Return (1993)	+13%
Redemption Fee	None	3-Year Return (1991–93)	+68%
Tax Load (Estimated)	9%	5-Year Return (1989–93)	+71%
Annual 12b-1 Fee	None	10-Year Return (1984–93)	NA
Annual Expense Ratio	1.25%	Worst-Ever Loss (1989–90)	31%
Annual Portfolio Turnover	11%	Stock Market Correlation	72%
5-Year Cost Estimate	8%	Up/Down Market Rank	C – C

Benefits		Investment Information	
Investment Objective	Gr. & Icm.	Telephone	800-725-6666
5-Year Projected Return	+9%	Minimum Investment	$1,000
Safety Rating (0-100)	76%	Telephone Switching	Unlimited;free
Yield	2.1%	Total Assets	$117 million

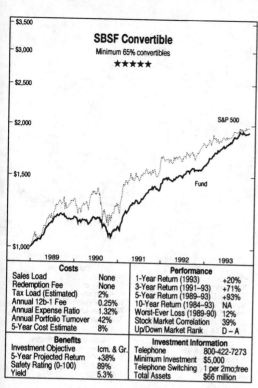

SBSF Convertible
Minimum 65% convertibles
★★★★★

(Chart showing Fund and S&P 500 lines, 1989–1993, scale $1,000–$3,500)

Costs		Performance	
Sales Load	None	1-Year Return (1993)	+20%
Redemption Fee	None	3-Year Return (1991–93)	+71%
Tax Load (Estimated)	2%	5-Year Return (1989–93)	+93%
Annual 12b-1 Fee	0.25%	10-Year Return (1984–93)	NA
Annual Expense Ratio	1.32%	Worst-Ever Loss (1989-90)	12%
Annual Portfolio Turnover	42%	Stock Market Correlation	39%
5-Year Cost Estimate	8%	Up/Down Market Rank	D – A

Benefits		Investment Information	
Investment Objective	Icm. & Gr.	Telephone	800-422-7273
5-Year Projected Return	+38%	Minimum Investment	$5,000
Safety Rating (0-100)	89%	Telephone Switching	1 per 2mo;free
Yield	5.3%	Total Assets	$66 million

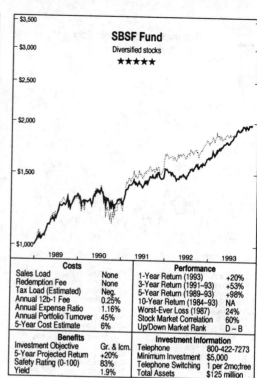

SBSF Fund
Diversified stocks
★★★★★

(Chart 1989–1993, scale $1,000–$3,500)

Costs		Performance	
Sales Load	None	1-Year Return (1993)	+20%
Redemption Fee	None	3-Year Return (1991–93)	+53%
Tax Load (Estimated)	Neg.	5-Year Return (1989–93)	+98%
Annual 12b-1 Fee	0.25%	10-Year Return (1984–93)	NA
Annual Expense Ratio	1.16%	Worst-Ever Loss (1987)	24%
Annual Portfolio Turnover	45%	Stock Market Correlation	60%
5-Year Cost Estimate	6%	Up/Down Market Rank	D – B

Benefits		Investment Information	
Investment Objective	Gr. & Icm.	Telephone	800-422-7273
5-Year Projected Return	+20%	Minimum Investment	$5,000
Safety Rating (0-100)	83%	Telephone Switching	1 per 2mo;free
Yield	1.9%	Total Assets	$125 million

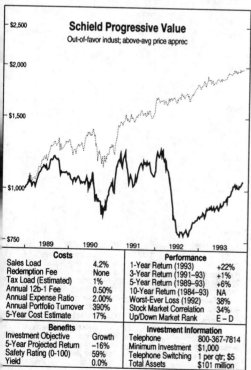

Schield Progressive Value
Out-of-favor indust; above-avg price apprec

(Chart 1989–1993, scale $750–$2,500)

Costs		Performance	
Sales Load	4.2%	1-Year Return (1993)	+22%
Redemption Fee	None	3-Year Return (1991–93)	+1%
Tax Load (Estimated)	1%	5-Year Return (1989–93)	+6%
Annual 12b-1 Fee	0.50%	10-Year Return (1984–93)	NA
Annual Expense Ratio	2.00%	Worst-Ever Loss (1992)	38%
Annual Portfolio Turnover	390%	Stock Market Correlation	34%
5-Year Cost Estimate	17%	Up/Down Market Rank	E – D

Benefits		Investment Information	
Investment Objective	Growth	Telephone	800-367-7814
5-Year Projected Return	–16%	Minimum Investment	$1,000
Safety Rating (0-100)	59%	Telephone Switching	1 per qtr; $5
Yield	0.0%	Total Assets	$101 million

Schroder – Capital U.S. Equity
Common stocks and convertible securities
★★

(Chart 1989–1993, scale $1,000–$3,500)

Costs		Performance	
Sales Load	None	1-Year Return (1993)	+12%
Redemption Fee	None	3-Year Return (1991–93)	+79%
Tax Load (Estimated)	0%	5-Year Return (1989–93)	+112%
Annual 12b-1 Fee	None	10-Year Return (1984–93)	NA
Annual Expense Ratio	1.40%	Worst-Ever Loss (1987)	34%
Annual Portfolio Turnover	31%	Stock Market Correlation	81%
5-Year Cost Estimate	7%	Up/Down Market Rank	A – E

Benefits		Investment Information	
Investment Objective	Growth	Telephone	800-344-8332
5-Year Projected Return	+30%	Minimum Investment	$500
Safety Rating (0-100)	75%	Telephone Switching	Not available
Yield	0.6%	Total Assets	$21 million

Schroder - International Eqty
Foreign - diversified stocks

Costs		Performance	
Sales Load	None	1-Year Return (1993)	+46%
Redemption Fee	None	3-Year Return (1991–93)	+46%
Tax Load (Estimated)	2%	5-Year Return (1989–93)	+59%
Annual 12b-1 Fee	0.50%	10-Year Return (1984–93)	NA
Annual Expense Ratio	1.07%	Worst-Ever Loss (1987)	26%
Annual Portfolio Turnover	51%	Stock Market Correlation	9%
5-Year Cost Estimate	7%	Up/Down Market Rank	E – A

Benefits		Investment Information	
Investment Objective	Growth	Telephone	800-344-8332
5-Year Projected Return	NA	Minimum Investment	$2,500
Safety Rating (0-100)	70%	Telephone Switching	Not available
Yield	0.3%	Total Assets	$290 million

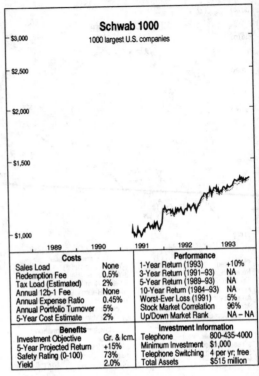

Schwab 1000
1000 largest U.S. companies

Costs		Performance	
Sales Load	None	1-Year Return (1993)	+10%
Redemption Fee	0.5%	3-Year Return (1991–93)	NA
Tax Load (Estimated)	2%	5-Year Return (1989–93)	NA
Annual 12b-1 Fee	None	10-Year Return (1984–93)	NA
Annual Expense Ratio	0.45%	Worst-Ever Loss (1991)	5%
Annual Portfolio Turnover	5%	Stock Market Correlation	96%
5-Year Cost Estimate	2%	Up/Down Market Rank	NA – NA

Benefits		Investment Information	
Investment Objective	Gr. & Icm.	Telephone	800-435-4000
5-Year Projected Return	+15%	Minimum Investment	$1,000
Safety Rating (0-100)	73%	Telephone Switching	4 per yr; free
Yield	2.0%	Total Assets	$515 million

Schwab International Index
Foreign - large stks from major mkt countries

Costs		Performance	
Sales Load	None	1-Year Return (1993)	NA
Redemption Fee	0.8%	3-Year Return (1991–93)	NA
Tax Load (Estimated)	NA	5-Year Return (1989–93)	NA
Annual 12b-1 Fee	None	10-Year Return (1984–93)	NA
Annual Expense Ratio	0.60%	Worst-Ever Loss (1993)	7%
Annual Portfolio Turnover	0%	Stock Market Correlation	NA
5-Year Cost Estimate	3%	Up/Down Market Rank	NA – NA

Benefits		Investment Information	
Investment Objective	Growth	Telephone	800-435-4000
5-Year Projected Return	NA	Minimum Investment	$1,000
Safety Rating (0-100)	NA	Telephone Switching	4 per yr; free
Yield	0.2%	Total Assets	$96 million

Scudder Balanced
50-75% seasoned equities; 25-50% inv-gr bonds

Costs		Performance	
Sales Load	None	1-Year Return (1993)	NA
Redemption Fee	None	3-Year Return (1991–93)	NA
Tax Load (Estimated)	1%	5-Year Return (1989–93)	NA
Annual 12b-1 Fee	None	10-Year Return (1984–93)	NA
Annual Expense Ratio	1.00%	Worst-Ever Loss (1993)	5%
Annual Portfolio Turnover	87%	Stock Market Correlation	NA
5-Year Cost Estimate	6%	Up/Down Market Rank	NA – NA

Benefits		Investment Information	
Investment Objective	Gr. & Icm.	Telephone	800-225-2470
5-Year Projected Return	NA	Minimum Investment	$1,000
Safety Rating (0-100)	NA	Telephone Switching	4 per yr; free
Yield	2.1%	Total Assets	$59 million

EQUITY

Scudder Capital Growth
Diversified growth stocks
★

S&P 500

Fund

1989	1990	1991	1992	1993

Costs		Performance	
Sales Load	None	1-Year Return (1993)	+20%
Redemption Fee	None	3-Year Return (1991–93)	+84%
Tax Load (Estimated)	0%	5-Year Return (1989–93)	+104%
Annual 12b-1 Fee	None	10-Year Return (1984–93)	+321%
Annual Expense Ratio	0.98%	Worst-Ever Loss (1987)	37%
Annual Portfolio Turnover	103%	Stock Market Correlation	69%
5-Year Cost Estimate	5%	Up/Down Market Rank	B – D

Benefits		Investment Information	
Investment Objective	Growth	Telephone	800-225-2470
5-Year Projected Return	+14%	Minimum Investment	$1,000
Safety Rating (0-100)	67%	Telephone Switching	4 per yr; free
Yield	0.0%	Total Assets	$1.37 billion

Scudder Development
Emerging growth stocks
★

1989	1990	1991	1992	1993

Costs		Performance	
Sales Load	None	1-Year Return (1993)	+9%
Redemption Fee	None	3-Year Return (1991–93)	+84%
Tax Load (Estimated)	7%	5-Year Return (1989–93)	+130%
Annual 12b-1 Fee	None	10-Year Return (1984–93)	+190%
Annual Expense Ratio	1.28%	Worst-Ever Loss (1987)	41%
Annual Portfolio Turnover	35%	Stock Market Correlation	48%
5-Year Cost Estimate	11%	Up/Down Market Rank	C – D

Benefits		Investment Information	
Investment Objective	Growth	Telephone	800-225-2470
5-Year Projected Return	+33%	Minimum Investment	$1,000
Safety Rating (0-100)	64%	Telephone Switching	4 per yr; free
Yield	0.0%	Total Assets	$803 million

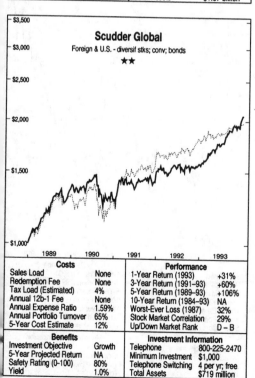

Scudder Global
Foreign & U.S. - diversif stks; conv; bonds
★★

1989	1990	1991	1992	1993

Costs		Performance	
Sales Load	None	1-Year Return (1993)	+31%
Redemption Fee	None	3-Year Return (1991–93)	+60%
Tax Load (Estimated)	4%	5-Year Return (1989–93)	+106%
Annual 12b-1 Fee	None	10-Year Return (1984–93)	NA
Annual Expense Ratio	1.59%	Worst-Ever Loss (1987)	32%
Annual Portfolio Turnover	65%	Stock Market Correlation	29%
5-Year Cost Estimate	12%	Up/Down Market Rank	D – B

Benefits		Investment Information	
Investment Objective	Growth	Telephone	800-225-2470
5-Year Projected Return	NA	Minimum Investment	$1,000
Safety Rating (0-100)	80%	Telephone Switching	4 per yr; free
Yield	1.0%	Total Assets	$719 million

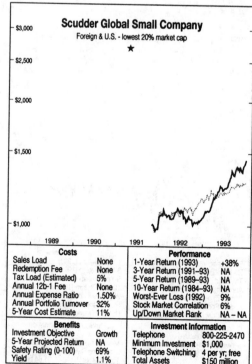

Scudder Global Small Company
Foreign & U.S. - lowest 20% market cap
★

1989	1990	1991	1992	1993

Costs		Performance	
Sales Load	None	1-Year Return (1993)	+38%
Redemption Fee	None	3-Year Return (1991–93)	NA
Tax Load (Estimated)	5%	5-Year Return (1989–93)	NA
Annual 12b-1 Fee	None	10-Year Return (1984–93)	NA
Annual Expense Ratio	1.50%	Worst-Ever Loss (1992)	9%
Annual Portfolio Turnover	32%	Stock Market Correlation	6%
5-Year Cost Estimate	11%	Up/Down Market Rank	NA – NA

Benefits		Investment Information	
Investment Objective	Growth	Telephone	800-225-2470
5-Year Projected Return	NA	Minimum Investment	$1,000
Safety Rating (0-100)	69%	Telephone Switching	4 per yr; free
Yield	1.1%	Total Assets	$150 million

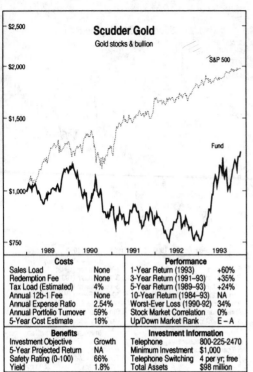

Scudder Gold
Gold stocks & bullion

S&P 500

Fund

Costs		Performance	
Sales Load	None	1-Year Return (1993)	+60%
Redemption Fee	None	3-Year Return (1991–93)	+35%
Tax Load (Estimated)	4%	5-Year Return (1989–93)	+24%
Annual 12b-1 Fee	None	10-Year Return (1984–93)	NA
Annual Expense Ratio	2.54%	Worst-Ever Loss (1990-92)	34%
Annual Portfolio Turnover	59%	Stock Market Correlation	0%
5-Year Cost Estimate	18%	Up/Down Market Rank	E – A

Benefits		Investment Information	
Investment Objective	Growth	Telephone	800-225-2470
5-Year Projected Return	NA	Minimum Investment	$1,000
Safety Rating (0-100)	66%	Telephone Switching	4 per yr; free
Yield	1.8%	Total Assets	$98 million

Scudder Growth & Income
Dividend-paying growth stocks
★★★★

Costs		Performance	
Sales Load	None	1-Year Return (1993)	+16%
Redemption Fee	None	3-Year Return (1991–93)	+62%
Tax Load (Estimated)	5%	5-Year Return (1989–93)	+100%
Annual 12b-1 Fee	None	10-Year Return (1984–93)	+253%
Annual Expense Ratio	0.92%	Worst-Ever Loss (1987)	26%
Annual Portfolio Turnover	42%	Stock Market Correlation	75%
5-Year Cost Estimate	8%	Up/Down Market Rank	C – C

Benefits		Investment Information	
Investment Objective	Gr. & Icm.	Telephone	800-225-2470
5-Year Projected Return	+23%	Minimum Investment	$1,000
Safety Rating (0-100)	80%	Telephone Switching	4 per yr; free
Yield	2.9%	Total Assets	$1.53 billion

Scudder International
Foreign - diversified securities

Costs		Performance	
Sales Load	None	1-Year Return (1993)	+37%
Redemption Fee	None	3-Year Return (1991–93)	+49%
Tax Load (Estimated)	3%	5-Year Return (1989–93)	+72%
Annual 12b-1 Fee	None	10-Year Return (1984–93)	+357%
Annual Expense Ratio	1.26%	Worst-Ever Loss (1987)	32%
Annual Portfolio Turnover	29%	Stock Market Correlation	13%
5-Year Cost Estimate	8%	Up/Down Market Rank	E – B

Benefits		Investment Information	
Investment Objective	Growth	Telephone	800-225-2470
5-Year Projected Return	NA	Minimum Investment	$1,000
Safety Rating (0-100)	76%	Telephone Switching	4 per yr; free
Yield	0.9%	Total Assets	$1.64 billion

Scudder New Asia
Foreign - Asia basin; diversified securities

Costs		Performance	
Sales Load	None	1-Year Return (1993)	+96%
Redemption Fee	None	3-Year Return (1991–93)	+144%
Tax Load (Estimated)	14%	5-Year Return (1989–93)	+313%
Annual 12b-1 Fee	None	10-Year Return (1984–93)	NA
Annual Expense Ratio	1.76%	Worst-Ever Loss (1987)	52%
Annual Portfolio Turnover	19%	Stock Market Correlation	13%
5-Year Cost Estimate	17%	Up/Down Market Rank	A – C

Benefits		Investment Information	
Investment Objective	Growth	Telephone	800-225-2470
5-Year Projected Return	NA	Minimum Investment	None
Safety Rating (0-100)	37%	Telephone Switching	Via broker
Yield	1.0%	Total Assets	$139 million

Scudder New Europe
Forgn - stks in small & emerging Europn mkts

Costs		Performance	
Sales Load	None	1-Year Return (1993)	+41%
Redemption Fee	None	3-Year Return (1991–93)	+38%
Tax Load (Estimated)	Neg.	5-Year Return (1989–93)	NA
Annual 12b-1 Fee	None	10-Year Return (1984–93)	NA
Annual Expense Ratio	1.76%	Worst-Ever Loss (1990)	36%
Annual Portfolio Turnover	34%	Stock Market Correlation	5%
5-Year Cost Estimate	11%	Up/Down Market Rank	NA – NA

Benefits		Investment Information	
Investment Objective	Growth	Telephone	800-225-2470
5-Year Projected Return	NA	Minimum Investment	None
Safety Rating (0-100)	46%	Telephone Switching	Via broker
Yield	0.0%	Total Assets	$170 million

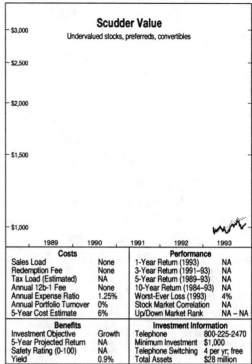

Scudder Value
Undervalued stocks, preferreds, convertibles

Costs		Performance	
Sales Load	None	1-Year Return (1993)	NA
Redemption Fee	None	3-Year Return (1991–93)	NA
Tax Load (Estimated)	NA	5-Year Return (1989–93)	NA
Annual 12b-1 Fee	None	10-Year Return (1984–93)	NA
Annual Expense Ratio	1.25%	Worst-Ever Loss (1993)	4%
Annual Portfolio Turnover	0%	Stock Market Correlation	NA
5-Year Cost Estimate	6%	Up/Down Market Rank	NA – NA

Benefits		Investment Information	
Investment Objective	Growth	Telephone	800-225-2470
5-Year Projected Return	NA	Minimum Investment	$1,000
Safety Rating (0-100)	NA	Telephone Switching	4 per yr; free
Yield	0.9%	Total Assets	$28 million

Seafirst IRA - Asset Allocatn
Stocks, bonds, money market
★★

Costs		Performance	
Sales Load	None	1-Year Return (1993)	+10%
Redemption Fee	None	3-Year Return (1991–93)	+39%
Tax Load (Estimated)	0%	5-Year Return (1989–93)	NA
Annual 12b-1 Fee	None	10-Year Return (1984–93)	NA
Annual Expense Ratio	0.95%	Worst-Ever Loss (1990)	10%
Annual Portfolio Turnover	126%	Stock Market Correlation	51%
5-Year Cost Estimate	5%	Up/Down Market Rank	NA – NA

Benefits		Investment Information	
Investment Objective	Gr. & Icm.	Telephone	800-323-9919
5-Year Projected Return	+19%	Minimum Investment	$500
Safety Rating (0-100)	84%	Telephone Switching	Unlimited;free
Yield	3.3%	Total Assets	$146 million

Seafirst IRA - Blue Chip
100 stks in DJIA, Maj Mkt Idx or S&P 500

Costs		Performance	
Sales Load	None	1-Year Return (1993)	+12%
Redemption Fee	None	3-Year Return (1991–93)	+46%
Tax Load (Estimated)	0%	5-Year Return (1989–93)	NA
Annual 12b-1 Fee	None	10-Year Return (1984–93)	NA
Annual Expense Ratio	0.95%	Worst-Ever Loss (1990)	20%
Annual Portfolio Turnover	41%	Stock Market Correlation	52%
5-Year Cost Estimate	5%	Up/Down Market Rank	NA – NA

Benefits		Investment Information	
Investment Objective	Growth	Telephone	800-323-9919
5-Year Projected Return	+8%	Minimum Investment	$500
Safety Rating (0-100)	70%	Telephone Switching	Unlimited;free
Yield	0.8%	Total Assets	$121 million

Security Equity
Diversified stocks
★

Costs		Performance	
Sales Load	6.1%	1-Year Return (1993)	+13%
Redemption Fee	None	3-Year Return (1991–93)	+69%
Tax Load (Estimated)	3%	5-Year Return (1989–93)	+110%
Annual 12b-1 Fee	0.25%	10-Year Return (1984–93)	+266%
Annual Expense Ratio	1.06%	Worst-Ever Loss (1987)	35%
Annual Portfolio Turnover	95%	Stock Market Correlation	84%
5-Year Cost Estimate	15%	Up/Down Market Rank	A – E

Benefits		Investment Information	
Investment Objective	Growth	Telephone	800-888-2461
5-Year Projected Return	+14%	Minimum Investment	$100
Safety Rating (0-100)	73%	Telephone Switching	Unlimited;free
Yield	0.2%	Total Assets	$382 million

Security Growth & Income
Divsf stocks; grth & future divid potential
★

Costs		Performance	
Sales Load	6.1%	1-Year Return (1993)	+8%
Redemption Fee	None	3-Year Return (1991–93)	+38%
Tax Load (Estimated)	5%	5-Year Return (1989–93)	+61%
Annual 12b-1 Fee	0.25%	10-Year Return (1984–93)	+133%
Annual Expense Ratio	1.27%	Worst-Ever Loss (1987)	27%
Annual Portfolio Turnover	135%	Stock Market Correlation	71%
5-Year Cost Estimate	19%	Up/Down Market Rank	D – B

Benefits		Investment Information	
Investment Objective	Gr. & Icm.	Telephone	800-888-2461
5-Year Projected Return	+5%	Minimum Investment	$100
Safety Rating (0-100)	81%	Telephone Switching	Unlimited;free
Yield	2.9%	Total Assets	$81 million

Security Ultra
Growth stocks; leveraged; trading

Costs		Performance	
Sales Load	6.1%	1-Year Return (1993)	+10%
Redemption Fee	None	3-Year Return (1991–93)	+89%
Tax Load (Estimated)	9%	5-Year Return (1989–93)	+53%
Annual 12b-1 Fee	0.25%	10-Year Return (1984–93)	+112%
Annual Expense Ratio	1.32%	Worst-Ever Loss (1987-90)	47%
Annual Portfolio Turnover	101%	Stock Market Correlation	45%
5-Year Cost Estimate	25%	Up/Down Market Rank	B – E

Benefits		Investment Information	
Investment Objective	Growth	Telephone	800-888-2461
5-Year Projected Return	–10%	Minimum Investment	$100
Safety Rating (0-100)	57%	Telephone Switching	Unlimited;free
Yield	14.6%	Total Assets	$70 million

SEI Capital Appreciation
Institutional only; diversified stocks
★★★

Costs		Performance	
Sales Load	None	1-Year Return (1993)	+9%
Redemption Fee	None	3-Year Return (1991–93)	+59%
Tax Load (Estimated)	0%	5-Year Return (1989–93)	NA
Annual 12b-1 Fee	0.30%	10-Year Return (1984–93)	NA
Annual Expense Ratio	0.75%	Worst-Ever Loss (1990)	17%
Annual Portfolio Turnover	58%	Stock Market Correlation	86%
5-Year Cost Estimate	4%	Up/Down Market Rank	B – C

Benefits		Investment Information	
Investment Objective	Growth	Telephone	800-342-5734
5-Year Projected Return	+21%	Minimum Investment	None
Safety Rating (0-100)	76%	Telephone Switching	Unlimited;free
Yield	1.9%	Total Assets	$758 million

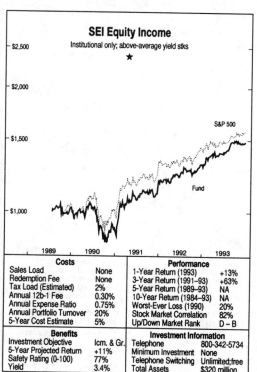

SEI Equity Income

Institutional only; above-average yield stks

★

Costs		Performance	
Sales Load	None	1-Year Return (1993)	+13%
Redemption Fee	None	3-Year Return (1991–93)	+63%
Tax Load (Estimated)	2%	5-Year Return (1989–93)	NA
Annual 12b-1 Fee	0.30%	10-Year Return (1984–93)	NA
Annual Expense Ratio	0.75%	Worst-Ever Loss (1990)	20%
Annual Portfolio Turnover	20%	Stock Market Correlation	82%
5-Year Cost Estimate	5%	Up/Down Market Rank	D – B

Benefits		Investment Information	
Investment Objective	Icm. & Gr.	Telephone	800-342-5734
5-Year Projected Return	+11%	Minimum Investment	None
Safety Rating (0-100)	77%	Telephone Switching	Unlimited;free
Yield	3.4%	Total Assets	$320 million

SEI S&P 500 Equity Index

Institutional only; matches S&P 500 Index

★

Costs		Performance	
Sales Load	None	1-Year Return (1993)	+10%
Redemption Fee	None	3-Year Return (1991–93)	+54%
Tax Load (Estimated)	3%	5-Year Return (1989–93)	NA
Annual 12b-1 Fee	0.50%	10-Year Return (1984–93)	NA
Annual Expense Ratio	0.25%	Worst-Ever Loss (1990)	19%
Annual Portfolio Turnover	1%	Stock Market Correlation	98%
5-Year Cost Estimate	1%	Up/Down Market Rank	C – C

Benefits		Investment Information	
Investment Objective	Growth	Telephone	800-342-5734
5-Year Projected Return	+23%	Minimum Investment	None
Safety Rating (0-100)	72%	Telephone Switching	Unlimited;free
Yield	2.1%	Total Assets	$509 million

SEI Value

Inst only; high yld, low PE, good fundamentls

Costs		Performance	
Sales Load	None	1-Year Return (1993)	+2%
Redemption Fee	None	3-Year Return (1991–93)	+39%
Tax Load (Estimated)	1%	5-Year Return (1989–93)	NA
Annual 12b-1 Fee	0.30%	10-Year Return (1984–93)	NA
Annual Expense Ratio	0.75%	Worst-Ever Loss (1990)	23%
Annual Portfolio Turnover	32%	Stock Market Correlation	84%
5-Year Cost Estimate	5%	Up/Down Market Rank	C – D

Benefits		Investment Information	
Investment Objective	Growth	Telephone	800-342-5734
5-Year Projected Return	–6%	Minimum Investment	None
Safety Rating (0-100)	66%	Telephone Switching	Unlimited;free
Yield	2.7%	Total Assets	$214 million

Selected American Shares

Diversified securities; large firms

★

Costs		Performance	
Sales Load	None	1-Year Return (1993)	+5%
Redemption Fee	None	3-Year Return (1991–93)	+63%
Tax Load (Estimated)	3%	5-Year Return (1989–93)	+88%
Annual 12b-1 Fee	0.25%	10-Year Return (1984–93)	+313%
Annual Expense Ratio	1.17%	Worst-Ever Loss (1987)	28%
Annual Portfolio Turnover	114%	Stock Market Correlation	71%
5-Year Cost Estimate	9%	Up/Down Market Rank	C – C

Benefits		Investment Information	
Investment Objective	Gr. & Icm.	Telephone	800-243-1575
5-Year Projected Return	+18%	Minimum Investment	$1,000
Safety Rating (0-100)	73%	Telephone Switching	Unlimited;free
Yield	1.8%	Total Assets	$473 million

Selected Special Shares
Undervalued securities

(Chart shows Fund vs S&P 500, 1989–1993, $1,000–$3,500)

Costs		Performance	
Sales Load	None	1-Year Return (1993)	+11%
Redemption Fee	None	3-Year Return (1991–93)	+52%
Tax Load (Estimated)	6%	5-Year Return (1989–93)	+82%
Annual 12b-1 Fee	0.25%	10-Year Return (1984–93)	+178%
Annual Expense Ratio	1.41%	Worst-Ever Loss (1987)	36%
Annual Portfolio Turnover	96%	Stock Market Correlation	51%
5-Year Cost Estimate	14%	Up/Down Market Rank	C – D

Benefits		Investment Information	
Investment Objective	Growth	Telephone	800-243-1575
5-Year Projected Return	+11%	Minimum Investment	$1,000
Safety Rating (0-100)	70%	Telephone Switching	Unlimited;free
Yield	0.0%	Total Assets	$63 million

Seligman Capital "A"
Diversified securities
★

(Chart shows Fund vs S&P 500, 1989–1993, $1,000–$3,500)

Costs		Performance	
Sales Load	5.0%	1-Year Return (1993)	+5%
Redemption Fee	None	3-Year Return (1991–93)	+82%
Tax Load (Estimated)	2%	5-Year Return (1989–93)	+145%
Annual 12b-1 Fee	0.25%	10-Year Return (1984–93)	+220%
Annual Expense Ratio	1.21%	Worst-Ever Loss (1987)	40%
Annual Portfolio Turnover	27%	Stock Market Correlation	68%
5-Year Cost Estimate	13%	Up/Down Market Rank	A – E

Benefits		Investment Information	
Investment Objective	Growth	Telephone	800-221-2450
5-Year Projected Return	+28%	Minimum Investment	$1,000
Safety Rating (0-100)	69%	Telephone Switching	Unlimited;free
Yield	0.0%	Total Assets	$207 million

Seligman Common Stock "A"
Diversified stocks
★

(Chart shows Fund vs S&P 500, 1989–1993, $1,000–$3,500)

Costs		Performance	
Sales Load	5.0%	1-Year Return (1993)	+15%
Redemption Fee	None	3-Year Return (1991–93)	+64%
Tax Load (Estimated)	7%	5-Year Return (1989–93)	+99%
Annual 12b-1 Fee	0.25%	10-Year Return (1984–93)	+254%
Annual Expense Ratio	1.00%	Worst-Ever Loss (1987)	31%
Annual Portfolio Turnover	46%	Stock Market Correlation	84%
5-Year Cost Estimate	17%	Up/Down Market Rank	B – C

Benefits		Investment Information	
Investment Objective	Icm. & Gr.	Telephone	800-221-2450
5-Year Projected Return	+12%	Minimum Investment	$1,000
Safety Rating (0-100)	76%	Telephone Switching	Unlimited;free
Yield	2.9%	Total Assets	$558 million

Seligman Communications "A"
Communications and information stocks

(Chart shows Fund vs S&P 500, 1989–1993, $1,000–$3,000)

Costs		Performance	
Sales Load	5.0%	1-Year Return (1993)	+36%
Redemption Fee	None	3-Year Return (1991–93)	+152%
Tax Load (Estimated)	3%	5-Year Return (1989–93)	+192%
Annual 12b-1 Fee	0.25%	10-Year Return (1984–93)	NA
Annual Expense Ratio	1.76%	Worst-Ever Loss (1990)	41%
Annual Portfolio Turnover	151%	Stock Market Correlation	42%
5-Year Cost Estimate	18%	Up/Down Market Rank	A – E

Benefits		Investment Information	
Investment Objective	Growth	Telephone	800-221-2450
5-Year Projected Return	NA	Minimum Investment	$1,000
Safety Rating (0-100)	54%	Telephone Switching	Unlimited;free
Yield	0.0%	Total Assets	$81 million

Seligman Growth "A"
Diversified stocks

Costs		Performance	
Sales Load	5.0%	1-Year Return (1993)	+6%
Redemption Fee	None	3-Year Return (1991–93)	+64%
Tax Load (Estimated)	4%	5-Year Return (1989–93)	+106%
Annual 12b-1 Fee	0.25%	10-Year Return (1984–93)	+213%
Annual Expense Ratio	1.02%	Worst-Ever Loss (1987)	37%
Annual Portfolio Turnover	103%	Stock Market Correlation	72%
5-Year Cost Estimate	15%	Up/Down Market Rank	A – E
Benefits		**Investment Information**	
Investment Objective	Gr. & Icm.	Telephone	800-221-2450
5-Year Projected Return	+8%	Minimum Investment	$1,000
Safety Rating (0-100)	67%	Telephone Switching	Unlimited;free
Yield	0.2%	Total Assets	$599 million

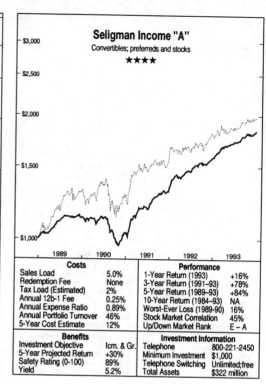

Seligman Income "A"
Convertibles; preferreds and stocks
★★★★

Costs		Performance	
Sales Load	5.0%	1-Year Return (1993)	+16%
Redemption Fee	None	3-Year Return (1991–93)	+78%
Tax Load (Estimated)	2%	5-Year Return (1989–93)	+84%
Annual 12b-1 Fee	0.25%	10-Year Return (1984–93)	NA
Annual Expense Ratio	0.89%	Worst-Ever Loss (1989-90)	16%
Annual Portfolio Turnover	46%	Stock Market Correlation	45%
5-Year Cost Estimate	12%	Up/Down Market Rank	E – A
Benefits		**Investment Information**	
Investment Objective	Icm. & Gr.	Telephone	800-221-2450
5-Year Projected Return	+30%	Minimum Investment	$1,000
Safety Rating (0-100)	89%	Telephone Switching	Unlimited;free
Yield	5.2%	Total Assets	$322 million

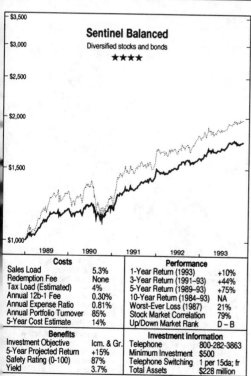

Sentinel Balanced
Diversified stocks and bonds
★★★★

Costs		Performance	
Sales Load	5.3%	1-Year Return (1993)	+10%
Redemption Fee	None	3-Year Return (1991–93)	+44%
Tax Load (Estimated)	4%	5-Year Return (1989–93)	+75%
Annual 12b-1 Fee	0.30%	10-Year Return (1984–93)	NA
Annual Expense Ratio	0.81%	Worst-Ever Loss (1987)	21%
Annual Portfolio Turnover	85%	Stock Market Correlation	79%
5-Year Cost Estimate	14%	Up/Down Market Rank	D – B
Benefits		**Investment Information**	
Investment Objective	Icm. & Gr.	Telephone	800-282-3863
5-Year Projected Return	+15%	Minimum Investment	$500
Safety Rating (0-100)	87%	Telephone Switching	1 per 15da; fr
Yield	3.7%	Total Assets	$228 million

Sentinel Common Stock
Well established companies
★

Costs		Performance	
Sales Load	5.3%	1-Year Return (1993)	+9%
Redemption Fee	None	3-Year Return (1991–93)	+51%
Tax Load (Estimated)	12%	5-Year Return (1989–93)	+86%
Annual 12b-1 Fee	0.30%	10-Year Return (1984–93)	+280%
Annual Expense Ratio	0.99%	Worst-Ever Loss (1987)	32%
Annual Portfolio Turnover	11%	Stock Market Correlation	89%
5-Year Cost Estimate	13%	Up/Down Market Rank	C – B
Benefits		**Investment Information**	
Investment Objective	Gr. & Icm.	Telephone	800-282-3863
5-Year Projected Return	+6%	Minimum Investment	$500
Safety Rating (0-100)	74%	Telephone Switching	1 per 15da; fr
Yield	2.6%	Total Assets	$910 million

EQUITY

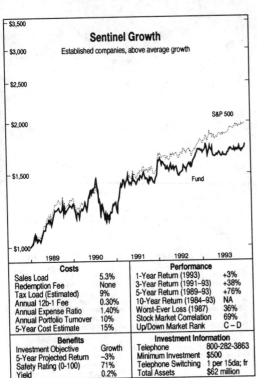

Sentinel Growth
Established companies, above average growth

S&P 500
Fund

Costs		Performance	
Sales Load	5.3%	1-Year Return (1993)	+3%
Redemption Fee	None	3-Year Return (1991–93)	+38%
Tax Load (Estimated)	9%	5-Year Return (1989–93)	+76%
Annual 12b-1 Fee	0.30%	10-Year Return (1984–93)	NA
Annual Expense Ratio	1.40%	Worst-Ever Loss (1987)	36%
Annual Portfolio Turnover	10%	Stock Market Correlation	69%
5-Year Cost Estimate	15%	Up/Down Market Rank	C – D

Benefits		Investment Information	
Investment Objective	Growth	Telephone	800-282-3863
5-Year Projected Return	–3%	Minimum Investment	$500
Safety Rating (0-100)	71%	Telephone Switching	1 per 15da; fr
Yield	0.2%	Total Assets	$62 million

Sentinel World
Foreign - diversified stocks

Costs		Performance	
Sales Load	5.3%	1-Year Return (1993)	+37%
Redemption Fee	None	3-Year Return (1991–93)	+39%
Tax Load (Estimated)	1%	5-Year Return (1989–93)	+27%
Annual 12b-1 Fee	0.30%	10-Year Return (1984–93)	NA
Annual Expense Ratio	2.00%	Worst-Ever Loss (1987)	32%
Annual Portfolio Turnover	143%	Stock Market Correlation	9%
5-Year Cost Estimate	18%	Up/Down Market Rank	E – B

Benefits		Investment Information	
Investment Objective	Growth	Telephone	800-282-3863
5-Year Projected Return	NA	Minimum Investment	$500
Safety Rating (0-100)	69%	Telephone Switching	1 per 15da; fr
Yield	0.2%	Total Assets	$12 million

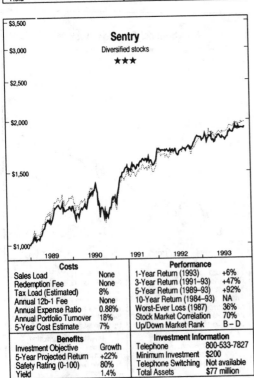

Sentry
Diversified stocks
★★★

Costs		Performance	
Sales Load	None	1-Year Return (1993)	+6%
Redemption Fee	None	3-Year Return (1991–93)	+47%
Tax Load (Estimated)	8%	5-Year Return (1989–93)	+92%
Annual 12b-1 Fee	None	10-Year Return (1984–93)	NA
Annual Expense Ratio	0.88%	Worst-Ever Loss (1987)	36%
Annual Portfolio Turnover	18%	Stock Market Correlation	70%
5-Year Cost Estimate	7%	Up/Down Market Rank	B – D

Benefits		Investment Information	
Investment Objective	Growth	Telephone	800-533-7827
5-Year Projected Return	+22%	Minimum Investment	$200
Safety Rating (0-100)	80%	Telephone Switching	Not available
Yield	1.4%	Total Assets	$77 million

Sequoia
Undervalued stocks
★★★★

Costs		Performance	
Sales Load	None	1-Year Return (1993)	+11%
Redemption Fee	None	3-Year Return (1991–93)	+70%
Tax Load (Estimated)	8%	5-Year Return (1989–93)	+109%
Annual 12b-1 Fee	None	10-Year Return (1984–93)	+328%
Annual Expense Ratio	1.00%	Worst-Ever Loss (1990)	20%
Annual Portfolio Turnover	26%	Stock Market Correlation	49%
5-Year Cost Estimate	9%	Up/Down Market Rank	D – A

Benefits		Investment Information	
Investment Objective	Growth	Telephone	212-245-4500
5-Year Projected Return	+27%	Minimum Investment	$10,000
Safety Rating (0-100)	79%	Telephone Switching	Not available
Yield	1.2%	Total Assets	$1.56 billion

Sierra Growth
Diversified stocks

S&P 500

Fund

	Costs		Performance	
Sales Load	None	1-Year Return (1993)	+5%
Redemption Fee	None	3-Year Return (1991–93)	+54%
Tax Load (Estimated)	Neg.	5-Year Return (1989–93)	+66%
Annual 12b-1 Fee	None	10-Year Return (1984–93)	+67%
Annual Expense Ratio	3.03%	Worst-Ever Loss (1987)	43%
Annual Portfolio Turnover	49%	Stock Market Correlation	41%
5-Year Cost Estimate	17%	Up/Down Market Rank	D – E

	Benefits		Investment Information	
Investment Objective	Gr. & Icm.	Telephone	800-367-7814
5-Year Projected Return	+11%	Minimum Investment	$1,000
Safety Rating (0-100)	63%	Telephone Switching	Not available
Yield	0.0%	Total Assets	$3 million

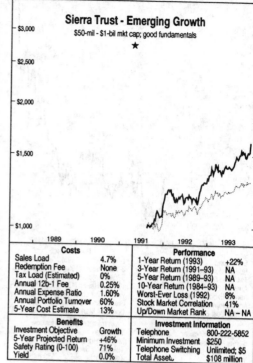

Sierra Trust - Emerging Growth
$50-mil - $1-bil mkt cap; good fundamentals
★

	Costs		Performance	
Sales Load	4.7%	1-Year Return (1993)	+22%
Redemption Fee	None	3-Year Return (1991–93)	NA
Tax Load (Estimated)	0%	5-Year Return (1989–93)	NA
Annual 12b-1 Fee	0.25%	10-Year Return (1984–93)	NA
Annual Expense Ratio	1.60%	Worst-Ever Loss (1992)	8%
Annual Portfolio Turnover	60%	Stock Market Correlation	41%
5-Year Cost Estimate	13%	Up/Down Market Rank	NA – NA

	Benefits		Investment Information	
Investment Objective	Growth	Telephone	800-222-5852
5-Year Projected Return	+46%	Minimum Investment	$250
Safety Rating (0-100)	71%	Telephone Switching	Unlimited; $5
Yield	0.0%	Total Assets	$108 million

Sierra Trust - Growth & Income
Dividend-paying stocks and high-grade bonds

	Costs		Performance	
Sales Load	4.7%	1-Year Return (1993)	+11%
Redemption Fee	None	3-Year Return (1991–93)	+45%
Tax Load (Estimated)	Neg.	5-Year Return (1989–93)	NA
Annual 12b-1 Fee	0.25%	10-Year Return (1984–93)	NA
Annual Expense Ratio	1.50%	Worst-Ever Loss (1990)	18%
Annual Portfolio Turnover	16%	Stock Market Correlation	82%
5-Year Cost Estimate	13%	Up/Down Market Rank	D – NA

	Benefits		Investment Information	
Investment Objective	Gr. & Icm.	Telephone	800-222-5852
5-Year Projected Return	+0%	Minimum Investment	$250
Safety Rating (0-100)	73%	Telephone Switching	Unlimited; $5
Yield	0.6%	Total Assets	$94 million

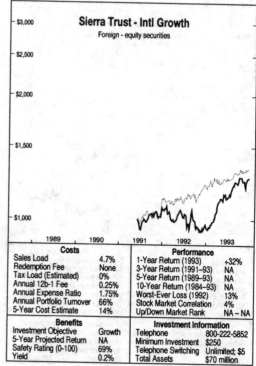

Sierra Trust - Intl Growth
Foreign - equity securities

	Costs		Performance	
Sales Load	4.7%	1-Year Return (1993)	+32%
Redemption Fee	None	3-Year Return (1991–93)	NA
Tax Load (Estimated)	0%	5-Year Return (1989–93)	NA
Annual 12b-1 Fee	0.25%	10-Year Return (1984–93)	NA
Annual Expense Ratio	1.75%	Worst-Ever Loss (1992)	13%
Annual Portfolio Turnover	66%	Stock Market Correlation	4%
5-Year Cost Estimate	14%	Up/Down Market Rank	NA – NA

	Benefits		Investment Information	
Investment Objective	Growth	Telephone	800-222-5852
5-Year Projected Return	NA	Minimum Investment	$250
Safety Rating (0-100)	69%	Telephone Switching	Unlimited; $5
Yield	0.2%	Total Assets	$70 million

Singapore
Foreign - Singapore stocks

Fund

S&P 500

Costs		Performance	
Sales Load	None	1-Year Return (1993)	+166%
Redemption Fee	None	3-Year Return (1991–93)	+210%
Tax Load (Estimated)	6%	5-Year Return (1989–93)	NA
Annual 12b-1 Fee	None	10-Year Return (1984–93)	NA
Annual Expense Ratio	2.53%	Worst-Ever Loss (1990)	26%
Annual Portfolio Turnover	21%	Stock Market Correlation	7%
5-Year Cost Estimate	18%	Up/Down Market Rank	NA – NA

Benefits		Investment Information	
Investment Objective	Growth	Telephone	800-933-3440
5-Year Projected Return	NA	Minimum Investment	None
Safety Rating (0-100)	34%	Telephone Switching	Via broker
Yield	3.0%	Total Assets	$59 million

SIT - Growth
Small-medium sized growth stocks
★

Costs		Performance	
Sales Load	None	1-Year Return (1993)	+9%
Redemption Fee	None	3-Year Return (1991–93)	+76%
Tax Load (Estimated)	2%	5-Year Return (1989–93)	+133%
Annual 12b-1 Fee	None	10-Year Return (1984–93)	NA
Annual Expense Ratio	0.83%	Worst-Ever Loss (1987)	36%
Annual Portfolio Turnover	45%	Stock Market Correlation	56%
5-Year Cost Estimate	6%	Up/Down Market Rank	A – E

Benefits		Investment Information	
Investment Objective	Growth	Telephone	800-332-5580
5-Year Projected Return	+26%	Minimum Investment	$2,000
Safety Rating (0-100)	69%	Telephone Switching	4 per yr; free
Yield	0.1%	Total Assets	$329 million

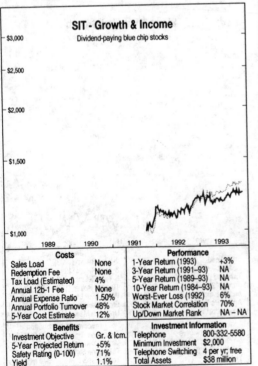

SIT - Growth & Income
Dividend-paying blue chip stocks

Costs		Performance	
Sales Load	None	1-Year Return (1993)	+3%
Redemption Fee	None	3-Year Return (1991–93)	NA
Tax Load (Estimated)	4%	5-Year Return (1989–93)	NA
Annual 12b-1 Fee	None	10-Year Return (1984–93)	NA
Annual Expense Ratio	1.50%	Worst-Ever Loss (1992)	6%
Annual Portfolio Turnover	48%	Stock Market Correlation	70%
5-Year Cost Estimate	12%	Up/Down Market Rank	NA – NA

Benefits		Investment Information	
Investment Objective	Gr. & Icm.	Telephone	800-332-5580
5-Year Projected Return	+5%	Minimum Investment	$2,000
Safety Rating (0-100)	71%	Telephone Switching	4 per yr; free
Yield	1.1%	Total Assets	$38 million

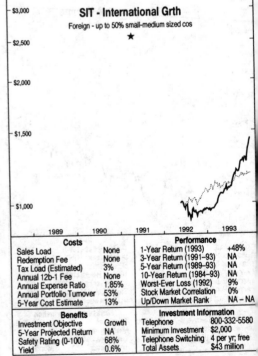

SIT - International Grth
Foreign - up to 50% small-medium sized cos
★

Costs		Performance	
Sales Load	None	1-Year Return (1993)	+48%
Redemption Fee	None	3-Year Return (1991–93)	NA
Tax Load (Estimated)	3%	5-Year Return (1989–93)	NA
Annual 12b-1 Fee	None	10-Year Return (1984–93)	NA
Annual Expense Ratio	1.85%	Worst-Ever Loss (1992)	9%
Annual Portfolio Turnover	53%	Stock Market Correlation	0%
5-Year Cost Estimate	13%	Up/Down Market Rank	NA – NA

Benefits		Investment Information	
Investment Objective	Growth	Telephone	800-332-5580
5-Year Projected Return	NA	Minimum Investment	$2,000
Safety Rating (0-100)	68%	Telephone Switching	4 per yr; free
Yield	0.6%	Total Assets	$43 million

Skyline Special Equities

65% small company stocks - under $400-mil cap

★★★★★

Fund

S&P 500

Costs		Performance	
Sales Load	None	1-Year Return (1993)	+23%
Redemption Fee	None	3-Year Return (1991–93)	+158%
Tax Load (Estimated)	Neg.	5-Year Return (1989–93)	+190%
Annual 12b-1 Fee	None	10-Year Return (1984–93)	NA
Annual Expense Ratio	1.51%	Worst-Ever Loss (1990)	28%
Annual Portfolio Turnover	120%	Stock Market Correlation	46%
5-Year Cost Estimate	8%	Up/Down Market Rank	A – E

Benefits		Investment Information	
Investment Objective	Growth	Telephone	800-458-5222
5-Year Projected Return	+53%	Minimum Investment	$1,000
Safety Rating (0-100)	74%	Telephone Switching	2 per mo; free
Yield	0.0%	Total Assets	$216 million

Smith Barney Equity "A"

Diversified stocks

Costs		Performance	
Sales Load	4.7%	1-Year Return (1993)	+18%
Redemption Fee	None	3-Year Return (1991–93)	+47%
Tax Load (Estimated)	1%	5-Year Return (1989–93)	+87%
Annual 12b-1 Fee	0.25%	10-Year Return (1984–93)	+214%
Annual Expense Ratio	0.99%	Worst-Ever Loss (1987)	28%
Annual Portfolio Turnover	93%	Stock Market Correlation	77%
5-Year Cost Estimate	11%	Up/Down Market Rank	C – C

Benefits		Investment Information	
Investment Objective	Gr. & Icm.	Telephone	800-544-7835
5-Year Projected Return	+2%	Minimum Investment	$3,000
Safety Rating (0-100)	71%	Telephone Switching	Unlimited; $5
Yield	1.1%	Total Assets	$88 million

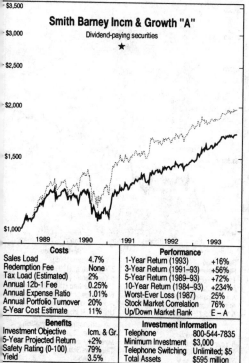

Smith Barney Incm & Growth "A"

Dividend-paying securities

★

Costs		Performance	
Sales Load	4.7%	1-Year Return (1993)	+16%
Redemption Fee	None	3-Year Return (1991–93)	+56%
Tax Load (Estimated)	2%	5-Year Return (1989–93)	+72%
Annual 12b-1 Fee	0.25%	10-Year Return (1984–93)	+234%
Annual Expense Ratio	1.01%	Worst-Ever Loss (1987)	25%
Annual Portfolio Turnover	20%	Stock Market Correlation	76%
5-Year Cost Estimate	11%	Up/Down Market Rank	E – A

Benefits		Investment Information	
Investment Objective	Icm. & Gr.	Telephone	800-544-7835
5-Year Projected Return	+2%	Minimum Investment	$3,000
Safety Rating (0-100)	79%	Telephone Switching	Unlimited; $5
Yield	3.5%	Total Assets	$595 million

Smith Barney Intl "A"

Foreign - stks of well established companies

★

Costs		Performance	
Sales Load	4.7%	1-Year Return (1993)	+53%
Redemption Fee	None	3-Year Return (1991–93)	+103%
Tax Load (Estimated)	3%	5-Year Return (1989–93)	+136%
Annual 12b-1 Fee	0.25%	10-Year Return (1984–93)	NA
Annual Expense Ratio	1.60%	Worst-Ever Loss (1987)	37%
Annual Portfolio Turnover	13%	Stock Market Correlation	14%
5-Year Cost Estimate	14%	Up/Down Market Rank	E – B

Benefits		Investment Information	
Investment Objective	Gr. & Icm.	Telephone	800-544-7835
5-Year Projected Return	NA	Minimum Investment	$3,000
Safety Rating (0-100)	72%	Telephone Switching	Unlimited; $5
Yield	0.0%	Total Assets	$127 million

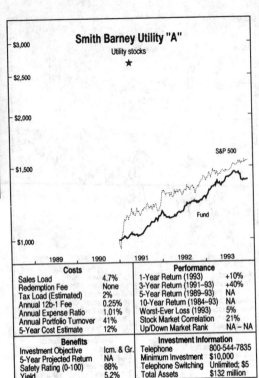

Smith Barney Utility "A"

Utility stocks

★

S&P 500

Fund

Costs		Performance	
Sales Load	4.7%	1-Year Return (1993)	+10%
Redemption Fee	None	3-Year Return (1991–93)	+40%
Tax Load (Estimated)	2%	5-Year Return (1989–93)	NA
Annual 12b-1 Fee	0.25%	10-Year Return (1984–93)	NA
Annual Expense Ratio	1.01%	Worst-Ever Loss (1993)	5%
Annual Portfolio Turnover	41%	Stock Market Correlation	21%
5-Year Cost Estimate	12%	Up/Down Market Rank	NA – NA
Benefits		**Investment Information**	
Investment Objective	Icm. & Gr.	Telephone	800-544-7835
5-Year Projected Return	NA	Minimum Investment	$10,000
Safety Rating (0-100)	88%	Telephone Switching	Unlimited; $5
Yield	5.2%	Total Assets	$132 million

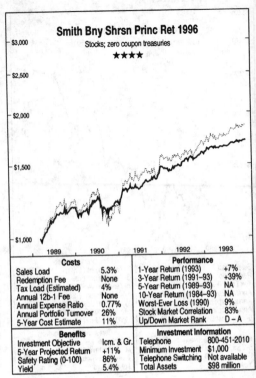

Smith Bny Shrsn Princ Ret 1996

Stocks; zero coupon treasuries

★★★★

Costs		Performance	
Sales Load	5.3%	1-Year Return (1993)	+7%
Redemption Fee	None	3-Year Return (1991–93)	+39%
Tax Load (Estimated)	4%	5-Year Return (1989–93)	NA
Annual 12b-1 Fee	None	10-Year Return (1984–93)	NA
Annual Expense Ratio	0.77%	Worst-Ever Loss (1990)	9%
Annual Portfolio Turnover	26%	Stock Market Correlation	83%
5-Year Cost Estimate	11%	Up/Down Market Rank	D – A
Benefits		**Investment Information**	
Investment Objective	Icm. & Gr.	Telephone	800-451-2010
5-Year Projected Return	+11%	Minimum Investment	$1,000
Safety Rating (0-100)	86%	Telephone Switching	Not available
Yield	5.4%	Total Assets	$98 million

Smith Bny Shrsn A - Agg Growth

High earnings growth stocks

Costs		Performance	
Sales Load	5.3%	1-Year Return (1993)	+21%
Redemption Fee	None	3-Year Return (1991–93)	+76%
Tax Load (Estimated)	13%	5-Year Return (1989–93)	+134%
Annual 12b-1 Fee	0.25%	10-Year Return (1984–93)	+264%
Annual Expense Ratio	1.34%	Worst-Ever Loss (1987)	47%
Annual Portfolio Turnover	13%	Stock Market Correlation	46%
5-Year Cost Estimate	16%	Up/Down Market Rank	A – E
Benefits		**Investment Information**	
Investment Objective	Growth	Telephone	800-451-2010
5-Year Projected Return	+11%	Minimum Investment	$1,000
Safety Rating (0-100)	56%	Telephone Switching	Unlimited;free
Yield	0.0%	Total Assets	$178 million

Smith Bny Shrsn A - Appreciatn

Diversified stocks

★★

Costs		Performance	
Sales Load	5.3%	1-Year Return (1993)	+8%
Redemption Fee	None	3-Year Return (1991–93)	+46%
Tax Load (Estimated)	6%	5-Year Return (1989–93)	+98%
Annual 12b-1 Fee	0.25%	10-Year Return (1984–93)	+287%
Annual Expense Ratio	1.05%	Worst-Ever Loss (1987)	29%
Annual Portfolio Turnover	23%	Stock Market Correlation	94%
5-Year Cost Estimate	14%	Up/Down Market Rank	B – C
Benefits		**Investment Information**	
Investment Objective	Growth	Telephone	800-451-2010
5-Year Projected Return	+4%	Minimum Investment	$1,000
Safety Rating (0-100)	75%	Telephone Switching	Unlimited;free
Yield	1.4%	Total Assets	$2.85 billion

Smith Bny Shrsn A - Fund Value
Undervalued securities
★★

S&P 500

Fund

Costs		Performance	
Sales Load	5.3%	1-Year Return (1993)	+20%
Redemption Fee	None	3-Year Return (1991–93)	+81%
Tax Load (Estimated)	4%	5-Year Return (1989–93)	+97%
Annual 12b-1 Fee	0.25%	10-Year Return (1984–93)	+252%
Annual Expense Ratio	1.51%	Worst-Ever Loss (1987)	31%
Annual Portfolio Turnover	111%	Stock Market Correlation	62%
5-Year Cost Estimate	18%	Up/Down Market Rank	C – C

Benefits		Investment Information	
Investment Objective	Gr. & Icm.	Telephone	800-451-2010
5-Year Projected Return	+18%	Minimum Investment	$1,000
Safety Rating (0-100)	78%	Telephone Switching	Unlimited;free
Yield	1.0%	Total Assets	$236 million

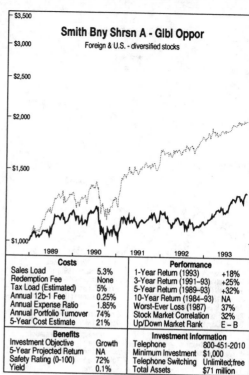

Smith Bny Shrsn A - Glbl Oppor
Foreign & U.S. - diversified stocks

Costs		Performance	
Sales Load	5.3%	1-Year Return (1993)	+18%
Redemption Fee	None	3-Year Return (1991–93)	+25%
Tax Load (Estimated)	5%	5-Year Return (1989–93)	+32%
Annual 12b-1 Fee	0.25%	10-Year Return (1984–93)	NA
Annual Expense Ratio	1.85%	Worst-Ever Loss (1987)	37%
Annual Portfolio Turnover	74%	Stock Market Correlation	32%
5-Year Cost Estimate	21%	Up/Down Market Rank	E – B

Benefits		Investment Information	
Investment Objective	Growth	Telephone	800-451-2010
5-Year Projected Return	NA	Minimum Investment	$1,000
Safety Rating (0-100)	72%	Telephone Switching	Unlimited;free
Yield	0.1%	Total Assets	$71 million

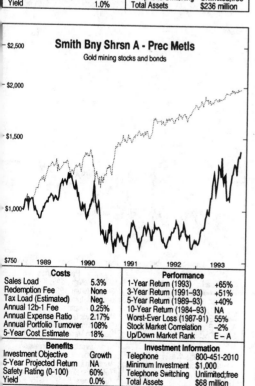

Smith Bny Shrsn A - Prec Metls
Gold mining stocks and bonds

Costs		Performance	
Sales Load	5.3%	1-Year Return (1993)	+65%
Redemption Fee	None	3-Year Return (1991–93)	+51%
Tax Load (Estimated)	Neg.	5-Year Return (1989–93)	+40%
Annual 12b-1 Fee	0.25%	10-Year Return (1984–93)	NA
Annual Expense Ratio	2.17%	Worst-Ever Loss (1987-91)	55%
Annual Portfolio Turnover	108%	Stock Market Correlation	–2%
5-Year Cost Estimate	18%	Up/Down Market Rank	E – A

Benefits		Investment Information	
Investment Objective	Growth	Telephone	800-451-2010
5-Year Projected Return	NA	Minimum Investment	$1,000
Safety Rating (0-100)	60%	Telephone Switching	Unlimited;free
Yield	0.0%	Total Assets	$68 million

Smith Bny Shrsn A - Telecom Gr
Telecommunications stocks

Costs		Performance	
Sales Load	5.3%	1-Year Return (1993)	+35%
Redemption Fee	None	3-Year Return (1991–93)	+95%
Tax Load (Estimated)	4%	5-Year Return (1989–93)	+131%
Annual 12b-1 Fee	0.25%	10-Year Return (1984–93)	NA
Annual Expense Ratio	1.45%	Worst-Ever Loss (1987)	36%
Annual Portfolio Turnover	16%	Stock Market Correlation	55%
5-Year Cost Estimate	14%	Up/Down Market Rank	A – E

Benefits		Investment Information	
Investment Objective	Growth	Telephone	800-451-2010
5-Year Projected Return	NA	Minimum Investment	$1,000
Safety Rating (0-100)	70%	Telephone Switching	Unlimited;free
Yield	0.0%	Total Assets	$143 million

Smith Bny Shrsn B - Convertble

Convertible securities; warrants; options

★★★

S&P 500

Fund

Costs		Performance	
Sales Load	None	1-Year Return (1993)	+13%
Redemption Fee	5.3%	3-Year Return (1991–93)	+59%
Tax Load (Estimated)	2%	5-Year Return (1989–93)	+60%
Annual 12b-1 Fee	0.75%	10-Year Return (1984–93)	NA
Annual Expense Ratio	2.00%	Worst-Ever Loss (1989-90)	16%
Annual Portfolio Turnover	95%	Stock Market Correlation	57%
5-Year Cost Estimate	13%	Up/Down Market Rank	E – A
Benefits		**Investment Information**	
Investment Objective	Icm. & Gr.	Telephone	800-451-2010
5-Year Projected Return	+21%	Minimum Investment	$1,000
Safety Rating (0-100)	88%	Telephone Switching	Unlimited;free
Yield	4.4%	Total Assets	$78 million

Smith Bny Shrsn B - Dirct Valu

Undervalued stocks

Costs		Performance	
Sales Load	None	1-Year Return (1993)	+9%
Redemption Fee	5.3%	3-Year Return (1991–93)	+45%
Tax Load (Estimated)	4%	5-Year Return (1989–93)	+67%
Annual 12b-1 Fee	1.00%	10-Year Return (1984–93)	NA
Annual Expense Ratio	1.83%	Worst-Ever Loss (1987)	30%
Annual Portfolio Turnover	47%	Stock Market Correlation	58%
5-Year Cost Estimate	13%	Up/Down Market Rank	C – C
Benefits		**Investment Information**	
Investment Objective	Gr. & Icm.	Telephone	800-451-2010
5-Year Projected Return	–4%	Minimum Investment	$1,000
Safety Rating (0-100)	67%	Telephone Switching	Unlimited;free
Yield	0.1%	Total Assets	$161 million

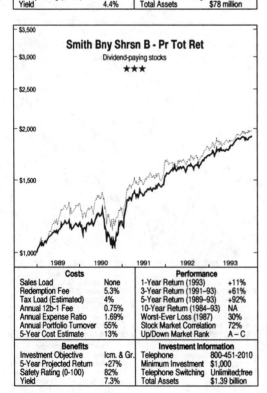

Smith Bny Shrsn B - Pr Tot Ret

Dividend-paying stocks

★★★

Costs		Performance	
Sales Load	None	1-Year Return (1993)	+11%
Redemption Fee	5.3%	3-Year Return (1991–93)	+61%
Tax Load (Estimated)	4%	5-Year Return (1989–93)	+92%
Annual 12b-1 Fee	0.75%	10-Year Return (1984–93)	NA
Annual Expense Ratio	1.69%	Worst-Ever Loss (1987)	30%
Annual Portfolio Turnover	55%	Stock Market Correlation	72%
5-Year Cost Estimate	13%	Up/Down Market Rank	A – C
Benefits		**Investment Information**	
Investment Objective	Icm. & Gr.	Telephone	800-451-2010
5-Year Projected Return	+27%	Minimum Investment	$1,000
Safety Rating (0-100)	82%	Telephone Switching	Unlimited;free
Yield	7.3%	Total Assets	$1.39 billion

Smith Bny Shrsn B - Sectr Anal

Stocks in selected industries

Costs		Performance	
Sales Load	None	1-Year Return (1993)	+5%
Redemption Fee	5.3%	3-Year Return (1991–93)	+47%
Tax Load (Estimated)	1%	5-Year Return (1989–93)	+66%
Annual 12b-1 Fee	1.00%	10-Year Return (1984–93)	NA
Annual Expense Ratio	2.16%	Worst-Ever Loss (1989-90)	21%
Annual Portfolio Turnover	166%	Stock Market Correlation	79%
5-Year Cost Estimate	12%	Up/Down Market Rank	E – B
Benefits		**Investment Information**	
Investment Objective	Growth	Telephone	800-451-201
5-Year Projected Return	NA	Minimum Investment	$1,000
Safety Rating (0-100)	68%	Telephone Switching	Unlimited;free
Yield	0.1%	Total Assets	$154 million

Smith Bny Shrsn B - Spcl Eqtys
Emerging growth stocks

Costs		Performance	
Sales Load	None	1-Year Return (1993)	+32%
Redemption Fee	5.3%	3-Year Return (1991–93)	+107%
Tax Load (Estimated)	4%	5-Year Return (1989–93)	+81%
Annual 12b-1 Fee	1.00%	10-Year Return (1984–93)	+134%
Annual Expense Ratio	2.30%	Worst-Ever Loss (1987)	40%
Annual Portfolio Turnover	164%	Stock Market Correlation	35%
5-Year Cost Estimate	17%	Up/Down Market Rank	C – E

Benefits		Investment Information	
Investment Objective	Growth	Telephone	800-451-2010
5-Year Projected Return	+20%	Minimum Investment	$1,000
Safety Rating (0-100)	61%	Telephone Switching	Unlimited;free
Yield	0.0%	Total Assets	$116 million

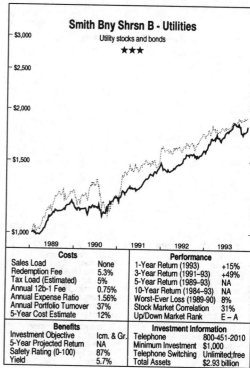

Smith Bny Shrsn B - Utilities
Utility stocks and bonds
★★★

Costs		Performance	
Sales Load	None	1-Year Return (1993)	+15%
Redemption Fee	5.3%	3-Year Return (1991–93)	+49%
Tax Load (Estimated)	5%	5-Year Return (1989–93)	NA
Annual 12b-1 Fee	0.75%	10-Year Return (1984–93)	NA
Annual Expense Ratio	1.56%	Worst-Ever Loss (1989-90)	8%
Annual Portfolio Turnover	37%	Stock Market Correlation	31%
5-Year Cost Estimate	12%	Up/Down Market Rank	E – A

Benefits		Investment Information	
Investment Objective	Icm. & Gr.	Telephone	800-451-2010
5-Year Projected Return	NA	Minimum Investment	$1,000
Safety Rating (0-100)	87%	Telephone Switching	Unlimited;free
Yield	5.7%	Total Assets	$2.93 billion

Society Diversified Stock
Foreign & U.S. - established undervalued secs
★

Costs		Performance	
Sales Load	4.2%	1-Year Return (1993)	+10%
Redemption Fee	None	3-Year Return (1991–93)	+50%
Tax Load (Estimated)	0%	5-Year Return (1989–93)	NA
Annual 12b-1 Fee	None	10-Year Return (1984–93)	NA
Annual Expense Ratio	0.91%	Worst-Ever Loss (1990)	17%
Annual Portfolio Turnover	51%	Stock Market Correlation	85%
5-Year Cost Estimate	9%	Up/Down Market Rank	C – NA

Benefits		Investment Information	
Investment Objective	Growth	Telephone	800-362-5365
5-Year Projected Return	+9%	Minimum Investment	$1,000
Safety Rating (0-100)	74%	Telephone Switching	Unlimited;free
Yield	1.9%	Total Assets	$33 million

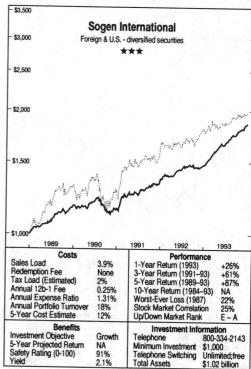

Sogen International
Foreign & U.S. - diversified securities
★★★

Costs		Performance	
Sales Load	3.9%	1-Year Return (1993)	+26%
Redemption Fee	None	3-Year Return (1991–93)	+61%
Tax Load (Estimated)	2%	5-Year Return (1989–93)	+87%
Annual 12b-1 Fee	0.25%	10-Year Return (1984–93)	NA
Annual Expense Ratio	1.31%	Worst-Ever Loss (1987)	22%
Annual Portfolio Turnover	18%	Stock Market Correlation	25%
5-Year Cost Estimate	12%	Up/Down Market Rank	E – A

Benefits		Investment Information	
Investment Objective	Growth	Telephone	800-334-2143
5-Year Projected Return	NA	Minimum Investment	$1,000
Safety Rating (0-100)	91%	Telephone Switching	Unlimited;free
Yield	2.1%	Total Assets	$1.02 billion

EQUITY

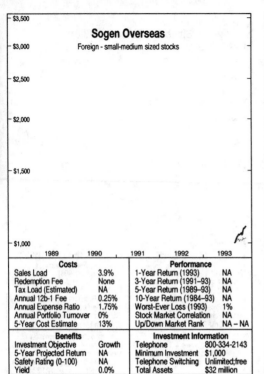

Sogen Overseas
Foreign - small-medium sized stocks

Costs		Performance	
Sales Load	3.9%	1-Year Return (1993)	NA
Redemption Fee	None	3-Year Return (1991–93)	NA
Tax Load (Estimated)	NA	5-Year Return (1989–93)	NA
Annual 12b-1 Fee	0.25%	10-Year Return (1984–93)	NA
Annual Expense Ratio	1.75%	Worst-Ever Loss (1993)	1%
Annual Portfolio Turnover	0%	Stock Market Correlation	NA
5-Year Cost Estimate	13%	Up/Down Market Rank	NA – NA

Benefits		Investment Information	
Investment Objective	Growth	Telephone	800-334-2143
5-Year Projected Return	NA	Minimum Investment	$1,000
Safety Rating (0-100)	NA	Telephone Switching	Unlimited;free
Yield	0.0%	Total Assets	$32 million

Sound Shore
Stocks with good fundamental value
★★

Costs		Performance	
Sales Load	None	1-Year Return (1993)	+12%
Redemption Fee	None	3-Year Return (1991–93)	+78%
Tax Load (Estimated)	3%	5-Year Return (1989–93)	+95%
Annual 12b-1 Fee	None	10-Year Return (1984–93)	NA
Annual Expense Ratio	1.37%	Worst-Ever Loss (1987)	28%
Annual Portfolio Turnover	101%	Stock Market Correlation	62%
5-Year Cost Estimate	10%	Up/Down Market Rank	C – C

Benefits		Investment Information	
Investment Objective	Gr. & Icm.	Telephone	800-551-1980
5-Year Projected Return	+21%	Minimum Investment	$10,000
Safety Rating (0-100)	78%	Telephone Switching	Unlimited;free
Yield	0.9%	Total Assets	$53 million

Source Capital
Diversified securities

Costs		Performance	
Sales Load	None	1-Year Return (1993)	–2%
Redemption Fee	None	3-Year Return (1991–93)	+52%
Tax Load (Estimated)	7%	5-Year Return (1989–93)	+79%
Annual 12b-1 Fee	None	10-Year Return (1984–93)	+243%
Annual Expense Ratio	0.98%	Worst-Ever Loss (1987)	29%
Annual Portfolio Turnover	76%	Stock Market Correlation	7%
5-Year Cost Estimate	15%	Up/Down Market Rank	D – A

Benefits		Investment Information	
Investment Objective	Gr. & Icm.	Telephone	800-982-4372
5-Year Projected Return	+7%	Minimum Investment	None
Safety Rating (0-100)	72%	Telephone Switching	Via broker
Yield	8.6%	Total Assets	$335 million

Southeastern Asset Mgmt Value
Undervalued stocks; over $500-mil market cap
★★★

Costs		Performance	
Sales Load	None	1-Year Return (1993)	+22%
Redemption Fee	None	3-Year Return (1991–93)	+105%
Tax Load (Estimated)	4%	5-Year Return (1989–93)	NA
Annual 12b-1 Fee	None	10-Year Return (1984–93)	NA
Annual Expense Ratio	1.29%	Worst-Ever Loss (1989-90)	31%
Annual Portfolio Turnover	13%	Stock Market Correlation	51%
5-Year Cost Estimate	8%	Up/Down Market Rank	C – D

Benefits		Investment Information	
Investment Objective	Growth	Telephone	800-445-9469
5-Year Projected Return	+34%	Minimum Investment	$50,000
Safety Rating (0-100)	76%	Telephone Switching	Not available
Yield	0.5%	Total Assets	$325 million

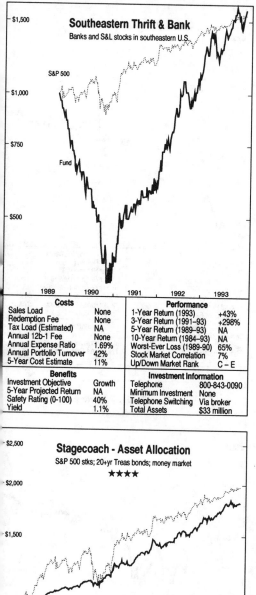

Southeastern Thrift & Bank
Banks and S&L stocks in southeastern U.S.

S&P 500

Fund

Costs		Performance	
Sales Load	None	1-Year Return (1993)	+43%
Redemption Fee	None	3-Year Return (1991–93)	+298%
Tax Load (Estimated)	NA	5-Year Return (1989–93)	NA
Annual 12b-1 Fee	None	10-Year Return (1984–93)	NA
Annual Expense Ratio	1.69%	Worst-Ever Loss (1989–90)	65%
Annual Portfolio Turnover	42%	Stock Market Correlation	7%
5-Year Cost Estimate	11%	Up/Down Market Rank	C – E

Benefits		Investment Information	
Investment Objective	Growth	Telephone	800-843-0090
5-Year Projected Return	NA	Minimum Investment	None
Safety Rating (0-100)	40%	Telephone Switching	Via broker
Yield	1.1%	Total Assets	$33 million

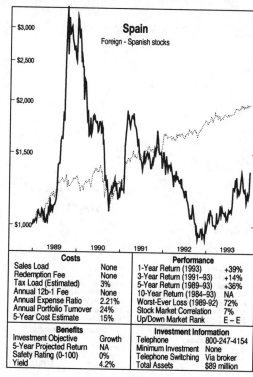

Spain
Foreign - Spanish stocks

Costs		Performance	
Sales Load	None	1-Year Return (1993)	+39%
Redemption Fee	None	3-Year Return (1991–93)	+14%
Tax Load (Estimated)	3%	5-Year Return (1989–93)	+36%
Annual 12b-1 Fee	None	10-Year Return (1984–93)	NA
Annual Expense Ratio	2.21%	Worst-Ever Loss (1989–92)	72%
Annual Portfolio Turnover	24%	Stock Market Correlation	7%
5-Year Cost Estimate	15%	Up/Down Market Rank	E – E

Benefits		Investment Information	
Investment Objective	Growth	Telephone	800-247-4154
5-Year Projected Return	NA	Minimum Investment	None
Safety Rating (0-100)	0%	Telephone Switching	Via broker
Yield	4.2%	Total Assets	$89 million

Stagecoach - Asset Allocation
S&P 500 stks; 20+yr Treas bonds; money market
★★★★

Costs		Performance	
Sales Load	4.7%	1-Year Return (1993)	+15%
Redemption Fee	None	3-Year Return (1991–93)	+50%
Tax Load (Estimated)	2%	5-Year Return (1989–93)	+80%
Annual 12b-1 Fee	0.25%	10-Year Return (1984–93)	NA
Annual Expense Ratio	0.95%	Worst-Ever Loss (1988)	6%
Annual Portfolio Turnover	5%	Stock Market Correlation	48%
5-Year Cost Estimate	10%	Up/Down Market Rank	E – A

Benefits		Investment Information	
Investment Objective	Growth	Telephone	800-222-8222
5-Year Projected Return	+32%	Minimum Investment	$1,000
Safety Rating (0-100)	89%	Telephone Switching	Unlimited;free
Yield	4.2%	Total Assets	$901 million

Stagecoach - Corporate Stock
Matches S&P 500 Index
★

Costs		Performance	
Sales Load	None	1-Year Return (1993)	+9%
Redemption Fee	None	3-Year Return (1991–93)	+48%
Tax Load (Estimated)	7%	5-Year Return (1989–93)	+83%
Annual 12b-1 Fee	0.25%	10-Year Return (1984–93)	NA
Annual Expense Ratio	0.93%	Worst-Ever Loss (1990)	19%
Annual Portfolio Turnover	4%	Stock Market Correlation	97%
5-Year Cost Estimate	5%	Up/Down Market Rank	C – C

Benefits		Investment Information	
Investment Objective	Growth	Telephone	800-222-8222
5-Year Projected Return	+19%	Minimum Investment	$1,000
Safety Rating (0-100)	71%	Telephone Switching	Unlimited;free
Yield	1.8%	Total Assets	$259 million

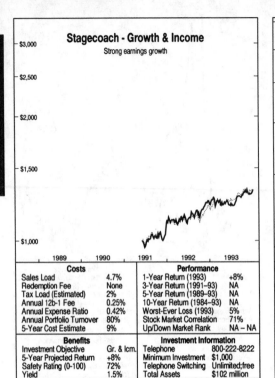

Stagecoach - Growth & Income
Strong earnings growth

Costs			Performance	
Sales Load	4.7%	1-Year Return (1993)	+8%
Redemption Fee	None	3-Year Return (1991–93)	NA
Tax Load (Estimated)	2%	5-Year Return (1989–93)	NA
Annual 12b-1 Fee	0.25%	10-Year Return (1984–93)	NA
Annual Expense Ratio	0.42%	Worst-Ever Loss (1993)	5%
Annual Portfolio Turnover	80%	Stock Market Correlation	71%
5-Year Cost Estimate	9%	Up/Down Market Rank	NA – NA

Benefits			Investment Information	
Investment Objective	Gr. & Icm.	Telephone	800-222-8222
5-Year Projected Return	+8%	Minimum Investment	$1,000
Safety Rating (0-100)	72%	Telephone Switching	Unlimited;free
Yield	1.5%	Total Assets	$102 million

State Bond - Common Stock
Diversified securities
★

Costs			Performance	
Sales Load	5.0%	1-Year Return (1993)	+2%
Redemption Fee	None	3-Year Return (1991–93)	+36%
Tax Load (Estimated)	11%	5-Year Return (1989–93)	+96%
Annual 12b-1 Fee	0.25%	10-Year Return (1984–93)	NA
Annual Expense Ratio	1.21%	Worst-Ever Loss (1987)	34%
Annual Portfolio Turnover	8%	Stock Market Correlation	82%
5-Year Cost Estimate	13%	Up/Down Market Rank	A – D

Benefits			Investment Information	
Investment Objective	Gr. & Icm.	Telephone	800-328-4735
5-Year Projected Return	–1%	Minimum Investment	$250
Safety Rating (0-100)	70%	Telephone Switching	Unlimited; $5
Yield	1.2%	Total Assets	$45 million

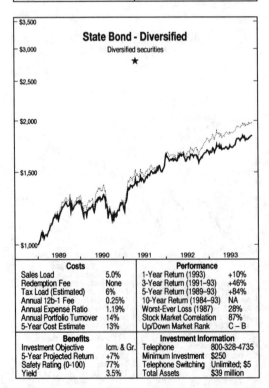

State Bond - Diversified
Diversified securities
★

Costs			Performance	
Sales Load	5.0%	1-Year Return (1993)	+10%
Redemption Fee	None	3-Year Return (1991–93)	+46%
Tax Load (Estimated)	6%	5-Year Return (1989–93)	+84%
Annual 12b-1 Fee	0.25%	10-Year Return (1984–93)	NA
Annual Expense Ratio	1.19%	Worst-Ever Loss (1987)	28%
Annual Portfolio Turnover	14%	Stock Market Correlation	87%
5-Year Cost Estimate	13%	Up/Down Market Rank	C – B

Benefits			Investment Information	
Investment Objective	Icm. & Gr.	Telephone	800-328-4735
5-Year Projected Return	+7%	Minimum Investment	$250
Safety Rating (0-100)	77%	Telephone Switching	Unlimited; $5
Yield	3.5%	Total Assets	$39 million

State Bond - Progress
Short-intermediate term outlook

Costs			Performance	
Sales Load	5.0%	1-Year Return (1993)	+2%
Redemption Fee	None	3-Year Return (1991–93)	+50%
Tax Load (Estimated)	7%	5-Year Return (1989–93)	+87%
Annual 12b-1 Fee	0.25%	10-Year Return (1984–93)	NA
Annual Expense Ratio	1.42%	Worst-Ever Loss (1987)	33%
Annual Portfolio Turnover	9%	Stock Market Correlation	60%
5-Year Cost Estimate	14%	Up/Down Market Rank	B – D

Benefits			Investment Information	
Investment Objective	Gr. & Icm.	Telephone	800-328-473!
5-Year Projected Return	+6%	Minimum Investment	$250
Safety Rating (0-100)	71%	Telephone Switching	Unlimited; $5
Yield	0.2%	Total Assets	$10 million

State Farm Balanced
For State Farm employees only
★★★★★

Costs		Performance	
Sales Load	None	1-Year Return (1993)	+3%
Redemption Fee	None	3-Year Return (1991–93)	+52%
Tax Load (Estimated)	9%	5-Year Return (1989–93)	+110%
Annual 12b-1 Fee	None	10-Year Return (1984–93)	NA
Annual Expense Ratio	0.22%	Worst-Ever Loss (1987)	19%
Annual Portfolio Turnover	1%	Stock Market Correlation	76%
5-Year Cost Estimate	1%	Up/Down Market Rank	C – A

Benefits		Investment Information	
Investment Objective	Gr. & Icm.	Telephone	309-766-2029
5-Year Projected Return	+32%	Minimum Investment	$1,000
Safety Rating (0-100)	83%	Telephone Switching	Unlimited;free
Yield	3.1%	Total Assets	$316 million

State Farm Growth
For State Farm employees
★★

Costs		Performance	
Sales Load	None	1-Year Return (1993)	+1%
Redemption Fee	None	3-Year Return (1991–93)	+46%
Tax Load (Estimated)	16%	5-Year Return (1989–93)	+101%
Annual 12b-1 Fee	None	10-Year Return (1984–93)	+263%
Annual Expense Ratio	0.16%	Worst-Ever Loss (1987)	27%
Annual Portfolio Turnover	1%	Stock Market Correlation	76%
5-Year Cost Estimate	1%	Up/Down Market Rank	C – C

Benefits		Investment Information	
Investment Objective	Growth	Telephone	309-766-2029
5-Year Projected Return	+15%	Minimum Investment	$1,000
Safety Rating (0-100)	75%	Telephone Switching	Unlimited;free
Yield	2.0%	Total Assets	$721 million

State Street Research Exchange
Diversified securities

Costs		Performance	
Sales Load	4.7%	1-Year Return (1993)	–1%
Redemption Fee	None	3-Year Return (1991–93)	+38%
Tax Load (Estimated)	23%	5-Year Return (1989–93)	+81%
Annual 12b-1 Fee	None	10-Year Return (1984–93)	NA
Annual Expense Ratio	0.59%	Worst-Ever Loss (1987)	33%
Annual Portfolio Turnover	6%	Stock Market Correlation	86%
5-Year Cost Estimate	10%	Up/Down Market Rank	A – D

Benefits		Investment Information	
Investment Objective	Gr. & Icm.	Telephone	800-233-2089
5-Year Projected Return	–6%	Minimum Investment	$250
Safety Rating (0-100)	67%	Telephone Switching	Unlimited; $5
Yield	1.4%	Total Assets	$210 million

MetLife-State St Glbl Engy "A"
Foreign & U.S. - energy stocks

Costs		Performance	
Sales Load	4.7%	1-Year Return (1993)	+32%
Redemption Fee	None	3-Year Return (1991–93)	+16%
Tax Load (Estimated)	Neg.	5-Year Return (1989–93)	NA
Annual 12b-1 Fee	0.50%	10-Year Return (1984–93)	NA
Annual Expense Ratio	1.75%	Worst-Ever Loss (1990-92)	40%
Annual Portfolio Turnover	47%	Stock Market Correlation	6%
5-Year Cost Estimate	14%	Up/Down Market Rank	NA – NA

Benefits		Investment Information	
Investment Objective	Growth	Telephone	800-562-2089
5-Year Projected Return	NA	Minimum Investment	$250
Safety Rating (0-100)	53%	Telephone Switching	Unlimited; $5
Yield	0.0%	Total Assets	$35 million

EQUITY

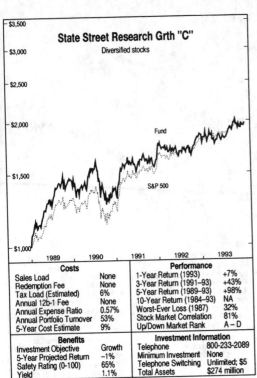

State Street Research Grth "C"
Diversified stocks

Fund

S&P 500

Costs		Performance	
Sales Load	None	1-Year Return (1993)	+7%
Redemption Fee	None	3-Year Return (1991–93)	+43%
Tax Load (Estimated)	6%	5-Year Return (1989–93)	+98%
Annual 12b-1 Fee	None	10-Year Return (1984–93)	NA
Annual Expense Ratio	0.57%	Worst-Ever Loss (1987)	32%
Annual Portfolio Turnover	53%	Stock Market Correlation	81%
5-Year Cost Estimate	9%	Up/Down Market Rank	A – D
Benefits		**Investment Information**	
Investment Objective	Growth	Telephone	800-233-2089
5-Year Projected Return	–1%	Minimum Investment	None
Safety Rating (0-100)	65%	Telephone Switching	Unlimited; $5
Yield	1.1%	Total Assets	$274 million

State Street Research Invs "C"
Diversified securities
★

Costs		Performance	
Sales Load	None	1-Year Return (1993)	+10%
Redemption Fee	None	3-Year Return (1991–93)	+50%
Tax Load (Estimated)	14%	5-Year Return (1989–93)	+96%
Annual 12b-1 Fee	None	10-Year Return (1984–93)	+245%
Annual Expense Ratio	0.51%	Worst-Ever Loss (1987)	32%
Annual Portfolio Turnover	20%	Stock Market Correlation	90%
5-Year Cost Estimate	7%	Up/Down Market Rank	B – D
Benefits		**Investment Information**	
Investment Objective	Gr. & Icm.	Telephone	800-233-2089
5-Year Projected Return	+10%	Minimum Investment	None
Safety Rating (0-100)	71%	Telephone Switching	Unlimited; $5
Yield	1.4%	Total Assets	$875 million

Steadman American Industry
Non-diversified securities

Costs		Performance	
Sales Load	None	1-Year Return (1993)	+9%
Redemption Fee	None	3-Year Return (1991–93)	+3%
Tax Load (Estimated)	NA	5-Year Return (1989–93)	–25%
Annual 12b-1 Fee	0.25%	10-Year Return (1984–93)	–55%
Annual Expense Ratio	13.42%	Worst-Ever Loss (1983-92)	71%
Annual Portfolio Turnover	0%	Stock Market Correlation	43%
5-Year Cost Estimate	106%	Up/Down Market Rank	E – E
Benefits		**Investment Information**	
Investment Objective	Gr. & Icm.	Telephone	800-424-8570
5-Year Projected Return	–1%	Minimum Investment	$500
Safety Rating (0-100)	40%	Telephone Switching	Not available
Yield	0.0%	Total Assets	$3 million

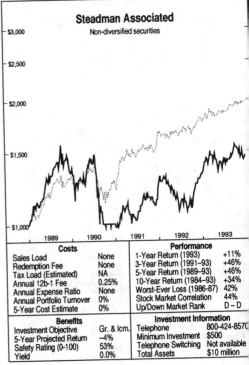

Steadman Associated
Non-diversified securities

Costs		Performance	
Sales Load	None	1-Year Return (1993)	+11%
Redemption Fee	None	3-Year Return (1991–93)	+46%
Tax Load (Estimated)	NA	5-Year Return (1989–93)	+46%
Annual 12b-1 Fee	0.25%	10-Year Return (1984–93)	+34%
Annual Expense Ratio	None	Worst-Ever Loss (1986-87)	42%
Annual Portfolio Turnover	0%	Stock Market Correlation	44%
5-Year Cost Estimate	0%	Up/Down Market Rank	D – D
Benefits		**Investment Information**	
Investment Objective	Gr. & Icm.	Telephone	800-424-8570
5-Year Projected Return	–4%	Minimum Investment	$500
Safety Rating (0-100)	53%	Telephone Switching	Not available
Yield	0.0%	Total Assets	$10 million

Steadman Investment
Non-diversified securities

S&P 500

Fund

| | | 1989 | 1990 | 1991 | 1992 | 1993 |

Costs		Performance	
Sales Load	None	1-Year Return (1993)	+3%
Redemption Fee	None	3-Year Return (1991–93)	+27%
Tax Load (Estimated)	NA	5-Year Return (1989–93)	+16%
Annual 12b-1 Fee	0.25%	10-Year Return (1984–93)	–7%
Annual Expense Ratio	None	Worst-Ever Loss (1987-90)	44%
Annual Portfolio Turnover	0%	Stock Market Correlation	47%
5-Year Cost Estimate	0%	Up/Down Market Rank	E – E
Benefits		**Investment Information**	
Investment Objective	Gr. & Icm.	Telephone	800-424-8570
5-Year Projected Return	–3%	Minimum Investment	$500
Safety Rating (0-100)	55%	Telephone Switching	Not available
Yield	0.0%	Total Assets	$4 million

Steadman Oceanographc Tch & Gr
High technology securities

| | | 1989 | 1990 | 1991 | 1992 | 1993 |

Costs		Performance	
Sales Load	None	1-Year Return (1993)	–8%
Redemption Fee	None	3-Year Return (1991–93)	+12%
Tax Load (Estimated)	NA	5-Year Return (1989–93)	–18%
Annual 12b-1 Fee	0.25%	10-Year Return (1984–93)	–62%
Annual Expense Ratio	None	Worst-Ever Loss (1983-91)	74%
Annual Portfolio Turnover	0%	Stock Market Correlation	36%
5-Year Cost Estimate	0%	Up/Down Market Rank	E – E
Benefits		**Investment Information**	
Investment Objective	Gr. & Icm.	Telephone	800-424-8570
5-Year Projected Return	NA	Minimum Investment	$500
Safety Rating (0-100)	22%	Telephone Switching	Not available
Yield	0.0%	Total Assets	$3 million

Stein Roe Capital Opportunity
Diversified stocks

| | | 1989 | 1990 | 1991 | 1992 | 1993 |

Costs		Performance	
Sales Load	None	1-Year Return (1993)	+28%
Redemption Fee	None	3-Year Return (1991–93)	+113%
Tax Load (Estimated)	9%	5-Year Return (1989–93)	+107%
Annual 12b-1 Fee	None	10-Year Return (1984–93)	+162%
Annual Expense Ratio	1.06%	Worst-Ever Loss (1989-90)	43%
Annual Portfolio Turnover	55%	Stock Market Correlation	53%
5-Year Cost Estimate	15%	Up/Down Market Rank	A – E
Benefits		**Investment Information**	
Investment Objective	Growth	Telephone	800-338-2550
5-Year Projected Return	+9%	Minimum Investment	$1,000
Safety Rating (0-100)	61%	Telephone Switching	4 per yr; free
Yield	0.0%	Total Assets	$137 million

Stein Roe Prime Equities
Stocks with market value over $1-billion
★★★★

| | | 1989 | 1990 | 1991 | 1992 | 1993 |

Costs		Performance	
Sales Load	None	1-Year Return (1993)	+13%
Redemption Fee	None	3-Year Return (1991–93)	+64%
Tax Load (Estimated)	6%	5-Year Return (1989–93)	+112%
Annual 12b-1 Fee	None	10-Year Return (1984–93)	NA
Annual Expense Ratio	0.97%	Worst-Ever Loss (1987)	29%
Annual Portfolio Turnover	50%	Stock Market Correlation	73%
5-Year Cost Estimate	10%	Up/Down Market Rank	B – B
Benefits		**Investment Information**	
Investment Objective	Growth	Telephone	800-338-2550
5-Year Projected Return	+25%	Minimum Investment	$1,000
Safety Rating (0-100)	78%	Telephone Switching	4 per yr; free
Yield	1.1%	Total Assets	$98 million

Stein Roe Special
Diversified stocks
★★★★★

Fund

S&P 500

	1989	1990	1991	1992	1993

Costs		Performance	
Sales Load	None	1-Year Return (1993)	+20%
Redemption Fee	None	3-Year Return (1991–93)	+84%
Tax Load (Estimated)	7%	5-Year Return (1989–93)	+139%
Annual 12b-1 Fee	None	10-Year Return (1984–93)	+340%
Annual Expense Ratio	0.99%	Worst-Ever Loss (1987)	34%
Annual Portfolio Turnover	42%	Stock Market Correlation	65%
5-Year Cost Estimate	10%	Up/Down Market Rank	A – D

Benefits		Investment Information	
Investment Objective	Growth	Telephone	800-338-2550
5-Year Projected Return	+32%	Minimum Investment	$1,000
Safety Rating (0-100)	76%	Telephone Switching	4 per yr; free
Yield	0.9%	Total Assets	$1.05 billion

Stein Roe Stock
Diversified stocks
★★

	1989	1990	1991	1992	1993

Costs		Performance	
Sales Load	None	1-Year Return (1993)	+3%
Redemption Fee	None	3-Year Return (1991–93)	+63%
Tax Load (Estimated)	8%	5-Year Return (1989–93)	+122%
Annual 12b-1 Fee	None	10-Year Return (1984–93)	+211%
Annual Expense Ratio	0.92%	Worst-Ever Loss (1987)	37%
Annual Portfolio Turnover	29%	Stock Market Correlation	72%
5-Year Cost Estimate	9%	Up/Down Market Rank	A – E

Benefits		Investment Information	
Investment Objective	Growth	Telephone	800-338-2550
5-Year Projected Return	+24%	Minimum Investment	$1,000
Safety Rating (0-100)	73%	Telephone Switching	4 per yr; free
Yield	0.6%	Total Assets	$378 million

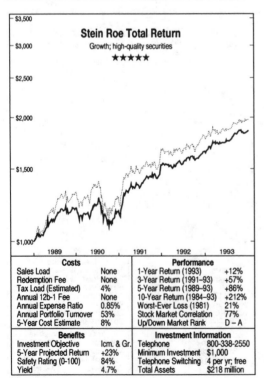

Stein Roe Total Return
Growth; high-quality securities
★★★★★

	1989	1990	1991	1992	1993

Costs		Performance	
Sales Load	None	1-Year Return (1993)	+12%
Redemption Fee	None	3-Year Return (1991–93)	+57%
Tax Load (Estimated)	4%	5-Year Return (1989–93)	+86%
Annual 12b-1 Fee	None	10-Year Return (1984–93)	+212%
Annual Expense Ratio	0.85%	Worst-Ever Loss (1981)	21%
Annual Portfolio Turnover	53%	Stock Market Correlation	77%
5-Year Cost Estimate	8%	Up/Down Market Rank	D – A

Benefits		Investment Information	
Investment Objective	Icm. & Gr.	Telephone	800-338-2550
5-Year Projected Return	+23%	Minimum Investment	$1,000
Safety Rating (0-100)	84%	Telephone Switching	4 per yr; free
Yield	4.7%	Total Assets	$218 million

Stratton Growth
Undervalued; quality stocks

	1989	1990	1991	1992	1993

Costs		Performance	
Sales Load	None	1-Year Return (1993)	+6%
Redemption Fee	None	3-Year Return (1991–93)	+39%
Tax Load (Estimated)	5%	5-Year Return (1989–93)	+61%
Annual 12b-1 Fee	None	10-Year Return (1984–93)	+157%
Annual Expense Ratio	1.39%	Worst-Ever Loss (1987)	32%
Annual Portfolio Turnover	35%	Stock Market Correlation	70%
5-Year Cost Estimate	10%	Up/Down Market Rank	C – D

Benefits		Investment Information	
Investment Objective	Gr. & Icm.	Telephone	800-634-5726
5-Year Projected Return	+1%	Minimum Investment	$2,000
Safety Rating (0-100)	77%	Telephone Switching	Unlimited;free
Yield	2.6%	Total Assets	$26 million

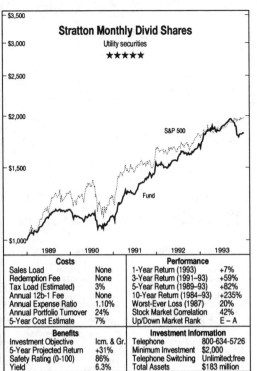

Stratton Monthly Divid Shares
Utility securities
★★★★★

(Chart shows Fund vs S&P 500, 1989–1993)

Costs		Performance	
Sales Load	None	1-Year Return (1993)	+7%
Redemption Fee	None	3-Year Return (1991–93)	+59%
Tax Load (Estimated)	3%	5-Year Return (1989–93)	+82%
Annual 12b-1 Fee	None	10-Year Return (1984–93)	+235%
Annual Expense Ratio	1.10%	Worst-Ever Loss (1987)	20%
Annual Portfolio Turnover	24%	Stock Market Correlation	42%
5-Year Cost Estimate	7%	Up/Down Market Rank	E – A

Benefits		Investment Information	
Investment Objective	Icm. & Gr.	Telephone	800-634-5726
5-Year Projected Return	+31%	Minimum Investment	$2,000
Safety Rating (0-100)	86%	Telephone Switching	Unlimited;free
Yield	6.3%	Total Assets	$183 million

Stratton Small-Cap Yield
Div-pay stks not in S&P; under $500-mil cap

Costs		Performance	
Sales Load	None	1-Year Return (1993)	NA
Redemption Fee	None	3-Year Return (1991–93)	NA
Tax Load (Estimated)	2%	5-Year Return (1989–93)	NA
Annual 12b-1 Fee	None	10-Year Return (1984–93)	NA
Annual Expense Ratio	1.78%	Worst-Ever Loss (1993)	0%
Annual Portfolio Turnover	5%	Stock Market Correlation	NA
5-Year Cost Estimate	10%	Up/Down Market Rank	NA – NA

Benefits		Investment Information	
Investment Objective	Gr. & Icm.	Telephone	800-634-5726
5-Year Projected Return	NA	Minimum Investment	$500
Safety Rating (0-100)	NA	Telephone Switching	Unlimited;free
Yield	1.0%	Total Assets	$8 million

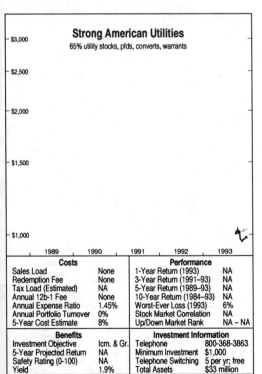

Strong American Utilities
65% utility stocks, pfds, converts, warrants

(Chart, 1989–1993)

Costs		Performance	
Sales Load	None	1-Year Return (1993)	NA
Redemption Fee	None	3-Year Return (1991–93)	NA
Tax Load (Estimated)	NA	5-Year Return (1989–93)	NA
Annual 12b-1 Fee	None	10-Year Return (1984–93)	NA
Annual Expense Ratio	1.45%	Worst-Ever Loss (1993)	6%
Annual Portfolio Turnover	0%	Stock Market Correlation	NA
5-Year Cost Estimate	8%	Up/Down Market Rank	NA – NA

Benefits		Investment Information	
Investment Objective	Icm. & Gr.	Telephone	800-368-3863
5-Year Projected Return	NA	Minimum Investment	$1,000
Safety Rating (0-100)	NA	Telephone Switching	5 per yr; free
Yield	1.9%	Total Assets	$33 million

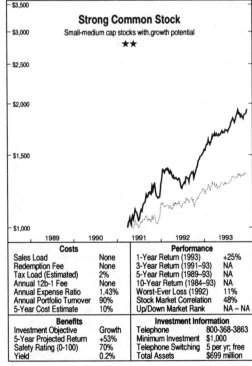

Strong Common Stock
Small-medium cap stocks with growth potential
★★

(Chart, 1989–1993)

Costs		Performance	
Sales Load	None	1-Year Return (1993)	+25%
Redemption Fee	None	3-Year Return (1991–93)	NA
Tax Load (Estimated)	2%	5-Year Return (1989–93)	NA
Annual 12b-1 Fee	None	10-Year Return (1984–93)	NA
Annual Expense Ratio	1.43%	Worst-Ever Loss (1992)	11%
Annual Portfolio Turnover	90%	Stock Market Correlation	48%
5-Year Cost Estimate	10%	Up/Down Market Rank	NA – NA

Benefits		Investment Information	
Investment Objective	Growth	Telephone	800-368-3863
5-Year Projected Return	+53%	Minimum Investment	$1,000
Safety Rating (0-100)	70%	Telephone Switching	5 per yr; free
Yield	0.2%	Total Assets	$699 million

EQUITY

Strong Discovery
Diversified small-cap cos equities; govts
★★★

Fund

S&P 500

Costs		Performance	
Sales Load	None	1-Year Return (1993)	+22%
Redemption Fee	None	3-Year Return (1991–93)	+109%
Tax Load (Estimated)	3%	5-Year Return (1989–93)	+152%
Annual 12b-1 Fee	None	10-Year Return (1984–93)	NA
Annual Expense Ratio	1.51%	Worst-Ever Loss (1992)	20%
Annual Portfolio Turnover	777%	Stock Market Correlation	45%
5-Year Cost Estimate	12%	Up/Down Market Rank	A – D

Benefits		Investment Information	
Investment Objective	Growth	Telephone	800-368-3863
5-Year Projected Return	+56%	Minimum Investment	$1,000
Safety Rating (0-100)	71%	Telephone Switching	5 per yr; free
Yield	2.8%	Total Assets	$247 million

Strong International
Foreign - growth securities

Costs		Performance	
Sales Load	None	1-Year Return (1993)	+48%
Redemption Fee	None	3-Year Return (1991–93)	NA
Tax Load (Estimated)	1%	5-Year Return (1989–93)	NA
Annual 12b-1 Fee	None	10-Year Return (1984–93)	NA
Annual Expense Ratio	2.00%	Worst-Ever Loss (1992)	15%
Annual Portfolio Turnover	25%	Stock Market Correlation	–3%
5-Year Cost Estimate	11%	Up/Down Market Rank	NA – NA

Benefits		Investment Information	
Investment Objective	Growth	Telephone	800-368-3863
5-Year Projected Return	NA	Minimum Investment	$1,000
Safety Rating (0-100)	63%	Telephone Switching	5 per yr; free
Yield	0.1%	Total Assets	$54 million

Strong Investment
40% stocks; 40% bonds; 20% money markets
★★★★

Costs		Performance	
Sales Load	None	1-Year Return (1993)	+14%
Redemption Fee	None	3-Year Return (1991–93)	+41%
Tax Load (Estimated)	1%	5-Year Return (1989–93)	+61%
Annual 12b-1 Fee	None	10-Year Return (1984–93)	+171%
Annual Expense Ratio	1.20%	Worst-Ever Loss (1987)	11%
Annual Portfolio Turnover	332%	Stock Market Correlation	55%
5-Year Cost Estimate	7%	Up/Down Market Rank	E – A

Benefits		Investment Information	
Investment Objective	Gr. & Icm.	Telephone	800-368-3863
5-Year Projected Return	+25%	Minimum Investment	$250
Safety Rating (0-100)	89%	Telephone Switching	5 per yr; free
Yield	4.3%	Total Assets	$239 million

Strong Opportunity
At least 70% equities; small-medium cap cos
★★

Costs		Performance	
Sales Load	None	1-Year Return (1993)	+21%
Redemption Fee	None	3-Year Return (1991–93)	+87%
Tax Load (Estimated)	4%	5-Year Return (1989–93)	+97%
Annual 12b-1 Fee	None	10-Year Return (1984–93)	NA
Annual Expense Ratio	1.50%	Worst-Ever Loss (1987)	27%
Annual Portfolio Turnover	105%	Stock Market Correlation	56%
5-Year Cost Estimate	12%	Up/Down Market Rank	C – B

Benefits		Investment Information	
Investment Objective	Growth	Telephone	800-368-3863
5-Year Projected Return	+31%	Minimum Investment	$1,000
Safety Rating (0-100)	78%	Telephone Switching	5 per yr; free
Yield	1.2%	Total Assets	$394 million

Strong Total Return
Stocks, corp bonds, govts, money markets

S&P 500

Fund

Costs		Performance	
Sales Load	None	1-Year Return (1993)	+23%
Redemption Fee	None	3-Year Return (1991–93)	+65%
Tax Load (Estimated)	6%	5-Year Return (1989–93)	+57%
Annual 12b-1 Fee	None	10-Year Return (1984–93)	+219%
Annual Expense Ratio	1.27%	Worst-Ever Loss (1987)	21%
Annual Portfolio Turnover	246%	Stock Market Correlation	52%
5-Year Cost Estimate	13%	Up/Down Market Rank	E – A

Benefits		Investment Information	
Investment Objective	Gr. & Icm.	Telephone	800-368-3863
5-Year Projected Return	+24%	Minimum Investment	$250
Safety Rating (0-100)	78%	Telephone Switching	5 per yr; free
Yield	1.4%	Total Assets	$584 million

SunAmerica - Balanced Asts "B"
Medium-large undervalued stocks
★★

Costs		Performance	
Sales Load	None	1-Year Return (1993)	+14%
Redemption Fee	4.2%	3-Year Return (1991–93)	+53%
Tax Load (Estimated)	Neg.	5-Year Return (1989–93)	+78%
Annual 12b-1 Fee	1.00%	10-Year Return (1984–93)	NA
Annual Expense Ratio	2.22%	Worst-Ever Loss (1987)	24%
Annual Portfolio Turnover	251%	Stock Market Correlation	73%
5-Year Cost Estimate	16%	Up/Down Market Rank	D – B

Benefits		Investment Information	
Investment Objective	Gr. & Icm.	Telephone	800-858-8850
5-Year Projected Return	+13%	Minimum Investment	$500
Safety Rating (0-100)	82%	Telephone Switching	Unlimited; $5
Yield	1.7%	Total Assets	$127 million

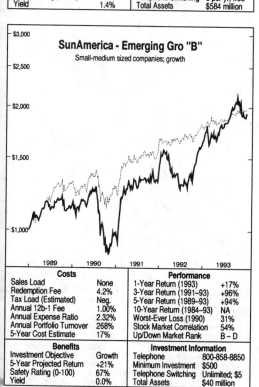

SunAmerica - Emerging Gro "B"
Small-medium sized companies; growth

Costs		Performance	
Sales Load	None	1-Year Return (1993)	+17%
Redemption Fee	4.2%	3-Year Return (1991–93)	+96%
Tax Load (Estimated)	Neg.	5-Year Return (1989–93)	+94%
Annual 12b-1 Fee	1.00%	10-Year Return (1984–93)	NA
Annual Expense Ratio	2.32%	Worst-Ever Loss (1990)	31%
Annual Portfolio Turnover	268%	Stock Market Correlation	54%
5-Year Cost Estimate	17%	Up/Down Market Rank	B – D

Benefits		Investment Information	
Investment Objective	Growth	Telephone	800-858-8850
5-Year Projected Return	+21%	Minimum Investment	$500
Safety Rating (0-100)	67%	Telephone Switching	Unlimited; $5
Yield	0.0%	Total Assets	$40 million

SunAmerica - Growth "A"
Diversified growth

Costs		Performance	
Sales Load	6.1%	1-Year Return (1993)	+11%
Redemption Fee	None	3-Year Return (1991–93)	+78%
Tax Load (Estimated)	Neg.	5-Year Return (1989–93)	+95%
Annual 12b-1 Fee	0.35%	10-Year Return (1984–93)	NA
Annual Expense Ratio	1.57%	Worst-Ever Loss (1987)	35%
Annual Portfolio Turnover	98%	Stock Market Correlation	57%
5-Year Cost Estimate	15%	Up/Down Market Rank	A – D

Benefits		Investment Information	
Investment Objective	Growth	Telephone	800-858-8850
5-Year Projected Return	+10%	Minimum Investment	$500
Safety Rating (0-100)	70%	Telephone Switching	Unlimited; $5
Yield	0.0%	Total Assets	$35 million

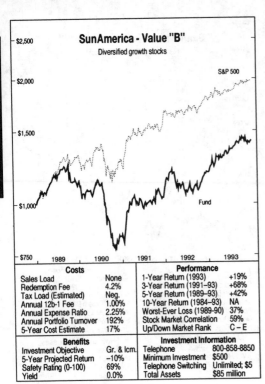

SunAmerica - Value "B"
Diversified growth stocks

S&P 500

Fund

Costs		Performance	
Sales Load	None	1-Year Return (1993)	+19%
Redemption Fee	4.2%	3-Year Return (1991–93)	+68%
Tax Load (Estimated)	Neg.	5-Year Return (1989–93)	+42%
Annual 12b-1 Fee	1.00%	10-Year Return (1984–93)	NA
Annual Expense Ratio	2.25%	Worst-Ever Loss (1989–90)	37%
Annual Portfolio Turnover	192%	Stock Market Correlation	59%
5-Year Cost Estimate	17%	Up/Down Market Rank	C – E

Benefits		Investment Information	
Investment Objective	Gr. & Icm.	Telephone	800-858-8850
5-Year Projected Return	–10%	Minimum Investment	$500
Safety Rating (0-100)	69%	Telephone Switching	Unlimited; $5
Yield	0.0%	Total Assets	$85 million

Swiss Helvetia
Foreign - Swiss stocks

Costs		Performance	
Sales Load	None	1-Year Return (1993)	+67%
Redemption Fee	None	3-Year Return (1991–93)	+95%
Tax Load (Estimated)	10%	5-Year Return (1989–93)	+142%
Annual 12b-1 Fee	None	10-Year Return (1984–93)	NA
Annual Expense Ratio	1.53%	Worst-Ever Loss (1987)	39%
Annual Portfolio Turnover	11%	Stock Market Correlation	7%
5-Year Cost Estimate	12%	Up/Down Market Rank	D – C

Benefits		Investment Information	
Investment Objective	Growth	Telephone	212-867-7660
5-Year Projected Return	NA	Minimum Investment	None
Safety Rating (0-100)	46%	Telephone Switching	Via broker
Yield	0.4%	Total Assets	$132 million

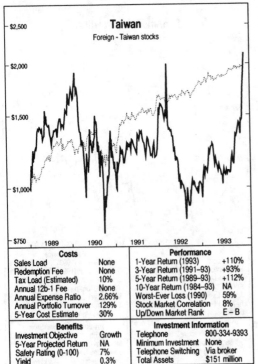

Taiwan
Foreign - Taiwan stocks

Costs		Performance	
Sales Load	None	1-Year Return (1993)	+110%
Redemption Fee	None	3-Year Return (1991–93)	+93%
Tax Load (Estimated)	10%	5-Year Return (1989–93)	+112%
Annual 12b-1 Fee	None	10-Year Return (1984–93)	NA
Annual Expense Ratio	2.66%	Worst-Ever Loss (1990)	59%
Annual Portfolio Turnover	129%	Stock Market Correlation	8%
5-Year Cost Estimate	30%	Up/Down Market Rank	E – B

Benefits		Investment Information	
Investment Objective	Growth	Telephone	800-334-9393
5-Year Projected Return	NA	Minimum Investment	None
Safety Rating (0-100)	7%	Telephone Switching	Via broker
Yield	0.3%	Total Assets	$151 million

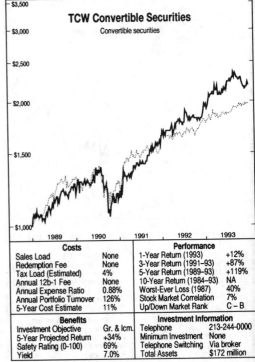

TCW Convertible Securities
Convertible securities

Costs		Performance	
Sales Load	None	1-Year Return (1993)	+12%
Redemption Fee	None	3-Year Return (1991–93)	+87%
Tax Load (Estimated)	4%	5-Year Return (1989–93)	+119%
Annual 12b-1 Fee	None	10-Year Return (1984–93)	NA
Annual Expense Ratio	0.88%	Worst-Ever Loss (1987)	40%
Annual Portfolio Turnover	126%	Stock Market Correlation	7%
5-Year Cost Estimate	11%	Up/Down Market Rank	C – B

Benefits		Investment Information	
Investment Objective	Gr. & Icm.	Telephone	213-244-0000
5-Year Projected Return	+34%	Minimum Investment	None
Safety Rating (0-100)	69%	Telephone Switching	Via broker
Yield	7.0%	Total Assets	$172 million

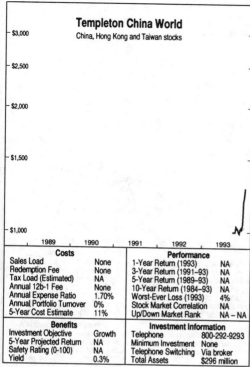

Templeton China World
China, Hong Kong and Taiwan stocks

Costs		Performance	
Sales Load	None	1-Year Return (1993)	NA
Redemption Fee	None	3-Year Return (1991–93)	NA
Tax Load (Estimated)	NA	5-Year Return (1989–93)	NA
Annual 12b-1 Fee	None	10-Year Return (1984–93)	NA
Annual Expense Ratio	1.70%	Worst-Ever Loss (1993)	4%
Annual Portfolio Turnover	0%	Stock Market Correlation	NA
5-Year Cost Estimate	11%	Up/Down Market Rank	NA – NA
Benefits		**Investment Information**	
Investment Objective	Growth	Telephone	800-292-9293
5-Year Projected Return	NA	Minimum Investment	None
Safety Rating (0-100)	NA	Telephone Switching	Via broker
Yield	0.3%	Total Assets	$296 million

Templeton Emerging Markets
Foreign - small nation stocks
★

Costs		Performance	
Sales Load	None	1-Year Return (1993)	+102%
Redemption Fee	None	3-Year Return (1991–93)	+284%
Tax Load (Estimated)	15%	5-Year Return (1989–93)	+629%
Annual 12b-1 Fee	None	10-Year Return (1984–93)	NA
Annual Expense Ratio	1.91%	Worst-Ever Loss (1987)	51%
Annual Portfolio Turnover	22%	Stock Market Correlation	10%
5-Year Cost Estimate	19%	Up/Down Market Rank	A – B
Benefits		**Investment Information**	
Investment Objective	Growth	Telephone	800-292-9293
5-Year Projected Return	NA	Minimum Investment	None
Safety Rating (0-100)	35%	Telephone Switching	Via broker
Yield	1.0%	Total Assets	$226 million

Templeton Foreign
Foreign - diversified stocks
★★

Costs		Performance	
Sales Load	6.1%	1-Year Return (1993)	+37%
Redemption Fee	None	3-Year Return (1991–93)	+62%
Tax Load (Estimated)	6%	5-Year Return (1989–93)	+105%
Annual 12b-1 Fee	0.25%	10-Year Return (1984–93)	+404%
Annual Expense Ratio	1.26%	Worst-Ever Loss (1987)	26%
Annual Portfolio Turnover	21%	Stock Market Correlation	14%
5-Year Cost Estimate	16%	Up/Down Market Rank	D – A
Benefits		**Investment Information**	
Investment Objective	Growth	Telephone	800-292-9293
5-Year Projected Return	NA	Minimum Investment	$100
Safety Rating (0-100)	80%	Telephone Switching	Unlimited;free
Yield	1.3%	Total Assets	$2.66 billion

Templeton Global Opportunities
Foreign & U.S. - diversified securities
★★

Costs		Performance	
Sales Load	6.1%	1-Year Return (1993)	+38%
Redemption Fee	None	3-Year Return (1991–93)	+97%
Tax Load (Estimated)	7%	5-Year Return (1989–93)	NA
Annual 12b-1 Fee	0.25%	10-Year Return (1984–93)	NA
Annual Expense Ratio	1.63%	Worst-Ever Loss (1990-91)	21%
Annual Portfolio Turnover	5%	Stock Market Correlation	38%
5-Year Cost Estimate	16%	Up/Down Market Rank	NA – NA
Benefits		**Investment Information**	
Investment Objective	Growth	Telephone	800-292-9293
5-Year Projected Return	NA	Minimum Investment	$100
Safety Rating (0-100)	76%	Telephone Switching	Unlimited;free
Yield	0.8%	Total Assets	$336 million

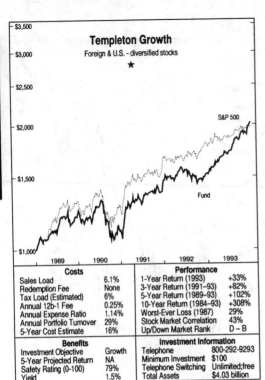

Templeton Growth
Foreign & U.S. - diversified stocks
★

S&P 500

Fund

Costs		Performance	
Sales Load	6.1%	1-Year Return (1993)	+33%
Redemption Fee	None	3-Year Return (1991–93)	+82%
Tax Load (Estimated)	6%	5-Year Return (1989–93)	+102%
Annual 12b-1 Fee	0.25%	10-Year Return (1984–93)	+308%
Annual Expense Ratio	1.14%	Worst-Ever Loss (1987)	29%
Annual Portfolio Turnover	29%	Stock Market Correlation	43%
5-Year Cost Estimate	16%	Up/Down Market Rank	D – B

Benefits		Investment Information	
Investment Objective	Growth	Telephone	800-292-9293
5-Year Projected Return	NA	Minimum Investment	$100
Safety Rating (0-100)	79%	Telephone Switching	Unlimited;free
Yield	1.5%	Total Assets	$4.03 billion

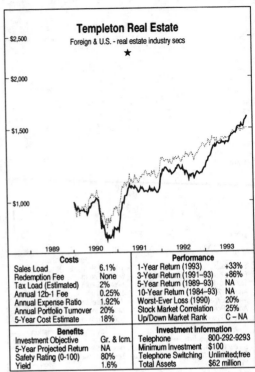

Templeton Real Estate
Foreign & U.S. - real estate industry secs
★

Costs		Performance	
Sales Load	6.1%	1-Year Return (1993)	+33%
Redemption Fee	None	3-Year Return (1991–93)	+86%
Tax Load (Estimated)	2%	5-Year Return (1989–93)	NA
Annual 12b-1 Fee	0.25%	10-Year Return (1984–93)	NA
Annual Expense Ratio	1.92%	Worst-Ever Loss (1990)	20%
Annual Portfolio Turnover	20%	Stock Market Correlation	25%
5-Year Cost Estimate	18%	Up/Down Market Rank	C – NA

Benefits		Investment Information	
Investment Objective	Gr. & Icm.	Telephone	800-292-9293
5-Year Projected Return	NA	Minimum Investment	$100
Safety Rating (0-100)	80%	Telephone Switching	Unlimited;free
Yield	1.6%	Total Assets	$62 million

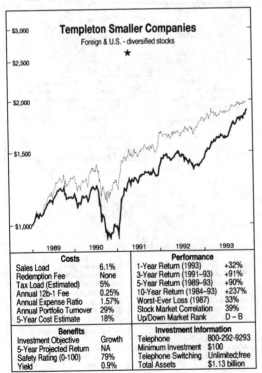

Templeton Smaller Companies
Foreign & U.S. - diversified stocks
★

Costs		Performance	
Sales Load	6.1%	1-Year Return (1993)	+32%
Redemption Fee	None	3-Year Return (1991–93)	+91%
Tax Load (Estimated)	5%	5-Year Return (1989–93)	+90%
Annual 12b-1 Fee	0.25%	10-Year Return (1984–93)	+237%
Annual Expense Ratio	1.57%	Worst-Ever Loss (1987)	33%
Annual Portfolio Turnover	29%	Stock Market Correlation	39%
5-Year Cost Estimate	18%	Up/Down Market Rank	D – B

Benefits		Investment Information	
Investment Objective	Growth	Telephone	800-292-9293
5-Year Projected Return	NA	Minimum Investment	$100
Safety Rating (0-100)	79%	Telephone Switching	Unlimited;free
Yield	0.9%	Total Assets	$1.13 billion

Templeton World
Foreign & U.S. - diversified stocks

Costs		Performance	
Sales Load	6.1%	1-Year Return (1993)	+34%
Redemption Fee	None	3-Year Return (1991–93)	+79%
Tax Load (Estimated)	6%	5-Year Return (1989–93)	+85%
Annual 12b-1 Fee	0.25%	10-Year Return (1984–93)	+269%
Annual Expense Ratio	1.10%	Worst-Ever Loss (1987)	28%
Annual Portfolio Turnover	24%	Stock Market Correlation	46%
5-Year Cost Estimate	15%	Up/Down Market Rank	C – C

Benefits		Investment Information	
Investment Objective	Growth	Telephone	800-292-9293
5-Year Projected Return	NA	Minimum Investment	$100
Safety Rating (0-100)	77%	Telephone Switching	Unlimited;free
Yield	1.7%	Total Assets	$4.62 billion

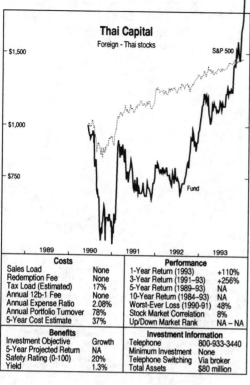

Thai Capital
Foreign - Thai stocks

S&P 500

Fund

| | | 1989 | 1990 | 1991 | 1992 | 1993 |

Costs			Performance	
Sales Load	None	1-Year Return (1993)	+110%
Redemption Fee	None	3-Year Return (1991–93)	+256%
Tax Load (Estimated)	17%	5-Year Return (1989–93)	NA
Annual 12b-1 Fee	None	10-Year Return (1984–93)	NA
Annual Expense Ratio	2.08%	Worst-Ever Loss (1990-91)	48%
Annual Portfolio Turnover	78%	Stock Market Correlation	8%
5-Year Cost Estimate	37%	Up/Down Market Rank	NA – NA

Benefits			Investment Information	
Investment Objective	Growth	Telephone	800-933-3440
5-Year Projected Return	NA	Minimum Investment	None
Safety Rating (0-100)	20%	Telephone Switching	Via broker
Yield	1.3%	Total Assets	$80 million

Thai Fund
Foreign - Thai stocks

| | | 1989 | 1990 | 1991 | 1992 | 1993 |

Costs			Performance	
Sales Load	None	1-Year Return (1993)	+105%
Redemption Fee	None	3-Year Return (1991–93)	+159%
Tax Load (Estimated)	28%	5-Year Return (1989–93)	+340%
Annual 12b-1 Fee	None	10-Year Return (1984–93)	NA
Annual Expense Ratio	1.27%	Worst-Ever Loss (1990)	58%
Annual Portfolio Turnover	11%	Stock Market Correlation	4%
5-Year Cost Estimate	15%	Up/Down Market Rank	D – C

Benefits			Investment Information	
Investment Objective	Growth	Telephone	800-221-6726
5-Year Projected Return	NA	Minimum Investment	None
Safety Rating (0-100)	12%	Telephone Switching	Via broker
Yield	0.0%	Total Assets	$232 million

Thomson - Equity Income "B"
Minimum 65% convertible securities
★

| | | 1989 | 1990 | 1991 | 1992 | 1993 |

Costs			Performance	
Sales Load	None	1-Year Return (1993)	+21%
Redemption Fee	1.0%	3-Year Return (1991–93)	+74%
Tax Load (Estimated)	2%	5-Year Return (1989–93)	+64%
Annual 12b-1 Fee	1.00%	10-Year Return (1984–93)	NA
Annual Expense Ratio	2.10%	Worst-Ever Loss (1989-90)	23%
Annual Portfolio Turnover	149%	Stock Market Correlation	58%
5-Year Cost Estimate	14%	Up/Down Market Rank	D – C

Benefits			Investment Information	
Investment Objective	Icm. & Gr.	Telephone	800-628-1237
5-Year Projected Return	+20%	Minimum Investment	$1,000
Safety Rating (0-100)	82%	Telephone Switching	Unlimited;free
Yield	1.9%	Total Assets	$93 million

Thomson - Growth "B"
Diversified growth stocks
★ ★

| | | 1989 | 1990 | 1991 | 1992 | 1993 |

Costs			Performance	
Sales Load	None	1-Year Return (1993)	+9%
Redemption Fee	1.0%	3-Year Return (1991–93)	+58%
Tax Load (Estimated)	2%	5-Year Return (1989–93)	+118%
Annual 12b-1 Fee	1.00%	10-Year Return (1984–93)	NA
Annual Expense Ratio	1.90%	Worst-Ever Loss (1987)	34%
Annual Portfolio Turnover	92%	Stock Market Correlation	72%
5-Year Cost Estimate	12%	Up/Down Market Rank	A – E

Benefits			Investment Information	
Investment Objective	Gr. & Icm.	Telephone	800-628-1237
5-Year Projected Return	+20%	Minimum Investment	$1,000
Safety Rating (0-100)	71%	Telephone Switching	Unlimited;free
Yield	0.0%	Total Assets	$1.16 billion

EQUITY

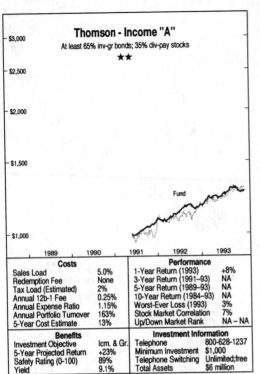

Thomson - Income "A"

At least 65% inv-gr bonds; 35% div-pay stocks

★★

Fund

Costs		Performance	
Sales Load	5.0%	1-Year Return (1993)	+8%
Redemption Fee	None	3-Year Return (1991–93)	NA
Tax Load (Estimated)	2%	5-Year Return (1989–93)	NA
Annual 12b-1 Fee	0.25%	10-Year Return (1984–93)	NA
Annual Expense Ratio	1.15%	Worst-Ever Loss (1993)	3%
Annual Portfolio Turnover	163%	Stock Market Correlation	7%
5-Year Cost Estimate	13%	Up/Down Market Rank	NA – NA

Benefits		Investment Information	
Investment Objective	Icm. & Gr.	Telephone	800-628-1237
5-Year Projected Return	+23%	Minimum Investment	$1,000
Safety Rating (0-100)	89%	Telephone Switching	Unlimited;free
Yield	9.1%	Total Assets	$6 million

Thomson - International "A"

Foreign & U.S. - stocks and bonds

Costs		Performance	
Sales Load	5.8%	1-Year Return (1993)	+34%
Redemption Fee	None	3-Year Return (1991–93)	NA
Tax Load (Estimated)	1%	5-Year Return (1989–93)	NA
Annual 12b-1 Fee	0.25%	10-Year Return (1984–93)	NA
Annual Expense Ratio	1.85%	Worst-Ever Loss (1992)	10%
Annual Portfolio Turnover	160%	Stock Market Correlation	19%
5-Year Cost Estimate	17%	Up/Down Market Rank	NA – NA

Benefits		Investment Information	
Investment Objective	Gr. & Icm.	Telephone	800-628-1237
5-Year Projected Return	NA	Minimum Investment	$1,000
Safety Rating (0-100)	71%	Telephone Switching	Unlimited;free
Yield	0.0%	Total Assets	$5 million

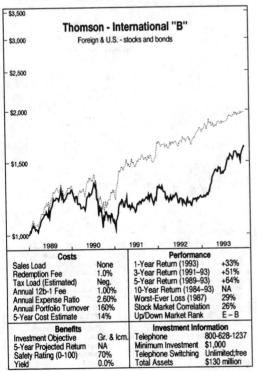

Thomson - International "B"

Foreign & U.S. - stocks and bonds

Costs		Performance	
Sales Load	None	1-Year Return (1993)	+33%
Redemption Fee	1.0%	3-Year Return (1991–93)	+51%
Tax Load (Estimated)	Neg.	5-Year Return (1989–93)	+64%
Annual 12b-1 Fee	1.00%	10-Year Return (1984–93)	NA
Annual Expense Ratio	2.60%	Worst-Ever Loss (1987)	29%
Annual Portfolio Turnover	160%	Stock Market Correlation	26%
5-Year Cost Estimate	14%	Up/Down Market Rank	E – B

Benefits		Investment Information	
Investment Objective	Gr. & Icm.	Telephone	800-628-1237
5-Year Projected Return	NA	Minimum Investment	$1,000
Safety Rating (0-100)	70%	Telephone Switching	Unlimited;free
Yield	0.0%	Total Assets	$130 million

Thomson - Opportunity "B"

Neglected stocks; turnarounds; high EPS grth

★★★★

Costs		Performance	
Sales Load	None	1-Year Return (1993)	+36%
Redemption Fee	1.0%	3-Year Return (1991–93)	+194%
Tax Load (Estimated)	1%	5-Year Return (1989–93)	+256%
Annual 12b-1 Fee	1.00%	10-Year Return (1984–93)	NA
Annual Expense Ratio	2.00%	Worst-Ever Loss (1987)	38%
Annual Portfolio Turnover	94%	Stock Market Correlation	44%
5-Year Cost Estimate	11%	Up/Down Market Rank	A – E

Benefits		Investment Information	
Investment Objective	Growth	Telephone	800-628-1237
5-Year Projected Return	+64%	Minimum Investment	$1,000
Safety Rating (0-100)	63%	Telephone Switching	Unlimited;free
Yield	0.0%	Total Assets	$680 million

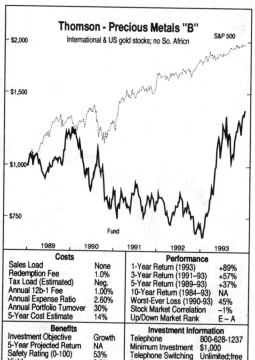

Thomson - Precious Metals "B"
International & US gold stocks; no So. Africn

Costs		Performance	
Sales Load	None	1-Year Return (1993)	+89%
Redemption Fee	1.0%	3-Year Return (1991–93)	+57%
Tax Load (Estimated)	Neg.	5-Year Return (1989–93)	+37%
Annual 12b-1 Fee	1.00%	10-Year Return (1984–93)	NA
Annual Expense Ratio	2.60%	Worst-Ever Loss (1990-93)	45%
Annual Portfolio Turnover	30%	Stock Market Correlation	−1%
5-Year Cost Estimate	14%	Up/Down Market Rank	E – A

Benefits		Investment Information	
Investment Objective	Growth	Telephone	800-628-1237
5-Year Projected Return	NA	Minimum Investment	$1,000
Safety Rating (0-100)	53%	Telephone Switching	Unlimited;free
Yield	0.0%	Total Assets	$28 million

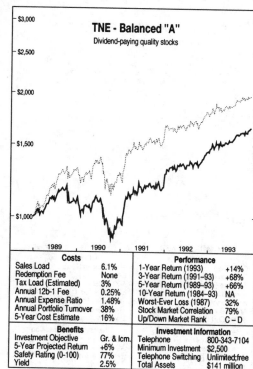

TNE - Balanced "A"
Dividend-paying quality stocks

Costs		Performance	
Sales Load	6.1%	1-Year Return (1993)	+14%
Redemption Fee	None	3-Year Return (1991–93)	+68%
Tax Load (Estimated)	3%	5-Year Return (1989–93)	+66%
Annual 12b-1 Fee	0.25%	10-Year Return (1984–93)	NA
Annual Expense Ratio	1.48%	Worst-Ever Loss (1987)	32%
Annual Portfolio Turnover	38%	Stock Market Correlation	79%
5-Year Cost Estimate	16%	Up/Down Market Rank	C – D

Benefits		Investment Information	
Investment Objective	Gr. & Icm.	Telephone	800-343-7104
5-Year Projected Return	+6%	Minimum Investment	$2,500
Safety Rating (0-100)	77%	Telephone Switching	Unlimited;free
Yield	2.5%	Total Assets	$141 million

TNE - Growth "A"
Established growth stocks

Costs		Performance	
Sales Load	7.0%	1-Year Return (1993)	+11%
Redemption Fee	None	3-Year Return (1991–93)	+63%
Tax Load (Estimated)	3%	5-Year Return (1989–93)	+109%
Annual 12b-1 Fee	0.25%	10-Year Return (1984–93)	+276%
Annual Expense Ratio	1.15%	Worst-Ever Loss (1987)	45%
Annual Portfolio Turnover	130%	Stock Market Correlation	61%
5-Year Cost Estimate	17%	Up/Down Market Rank	A – D

Benefits		Investment Information	
Investment Objective	Growth	Telephone	800-343-7104
5-Year Projected Return	+19%	Minimum Investment	$2,500
Safety Rating (0-100)	67%	Telephone Switching	Unlimited;free
Yield	0.1%	Total Assets	$1.19 billion

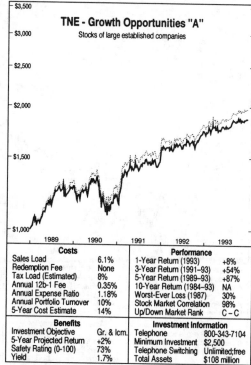

TNE - Growth Opportunities "A"
Stocks of large established companies

Costs		Performance	
Sales Load	6.1%	1-Year Return (1993)	+8%
Redemption Fee	None	3-Year Return (1991–93)	+54%
Tax Load (Estimated)	8%	5-Year Return (1989–93)	+87%
Annual 12b-1 Fee	0.35%	10-Year Return (1984–93)	NA
Annual Expense Ratio	1.18%	Worst-Ever Loss (1987)	30%
Annual Portfolio Turnover	10%	Stock Market Correlation	98%
5-Year Cost Estimate	14%	Up/Down Market Rank	C – C

Benefits		Investment Information	
Investment Objective	Gr. & Icm.	Telephone	800-343-7104
5-Year Projected Return	+2%	Minimum Investment	$2,500
Safety Rating (0-100)	73%	Telephone Switching	Unlimited;free
Yield	1.7%	Total Assets	$108 million

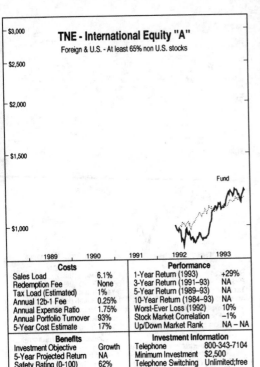

TNE - International Equity "A"
Foreign & U.S. - At least 65% non U.S. stocks

Fund

Costs			Performance	
Sales Load	6.1%	1-Year Return (1993)	+29%
Redemption Fee	None	3-Year Return (1991–93)	NA
Tax Load (Estimated)	1%	5-Year Return (1989–93)	NA
Annual 12b-1 Fee	0.25%	10-Year Return (1984–93)	NA
Annual Expense Ratio	1.75%	Worst-Ever Loss (1992)	10%
Annual Portfolio Turnover	93%	Stock Market Correlation	–1%
5-Year Cost Estimate	17%	Up/Down Market Rank	NA – NA

Benefits		Investment Information	
Investment Objective	Growth	Telephone	800-343-7104
5-Year Projected Return	NA	Minimum Investment	$2,500
Safety Rating (0-100)	62%	Telephone Switching	Unlimited;free
Yield	0.7%	Total Assets	$57 million

TNE - Value "A"
Retirement plans only

Costs			Performance	
Sales Load	6.1%	1-Year Return (1993)	+17%
Redemption Fee	None	3-Year Return (1991–93)	+73%
Tax Load (Estimated)	4%	5-Year Return (1989–93)	+84%
Annual 12b-1 Fee	0.25%	10-Year Return (1984–93)	NA
Annual Expense Ratio	1.32%	Worst-Ever Loss (1987)	43%
Annual Portfolio Turnover	44%	Stock Market Correlation	78%
5-Year Cost Estimate	17%	Up/Down Market Rank	C – E

Benefits		Investment Information	
Investment Objective	Gr. & Icm.	Telephone	800-343-7104
5-Year Projected Return	+1%	Minimum Investment	$2,500
Safety Rating (0-100)	66%	Telephone Switching	Unlimited;free
Yield	0.9%	Total Assets	$178 million

Tower Capital Appreciation
Diversified stocks; good fundamentals

Costs			Performance	
Sales Load	4.7%	1-Year Return (1993)	+14%
Redemption Fee	None	3-Year Return (1991–93)	+50%
Tax Load (Estimated)	Neg.	5-Year Return (1989–93)	NA
Annual 12b-1 Fee	0.25%	10-Year Return (1984–93)	NA
Annual Expense Ratio	0.83%	Worst-Ever Loss (1990)	19%
Annual Portfolio Turnover	54%	Stock Market Correlation	91%
5-Year Cost Estimate	9%	Up/Down Market Rank	NA – NA

Benefits		Investment Information	
Investment Objective	Gr. & Icm.	Telephone	800-999-0124
5-Year Projected Return	+4%	Minimum Investment	$1,000
Safety Rating (0-100)	73%	Telephone Switching	Unlimited;free
Yield	2.0%	Total Assets	$141 million

Transamerica - Capital Apprec
Foreign & U.S. - diversified equities

Costs			Performance	
Sales Load	5.0%	1-Year Return (1993)	+6%
Redemption Fee	None	3-Year Return (1991–93)	+55%
Tax Load (Estimated)	3%	5-Year Return (1989–93)	+75%
Annual 12b-1 Fee	0.25%	10-Year Return (1984–93)	NA
Annual Expense Ratio	1.41%	Worst-Ever Loss (1990)	39%
Annual Portfolio Turnover	70%	Stock Market Correlation	42%
5-Year Cost Estimate	16%	Up/Down Market Rank	A – E

Benefits		Investment Information	
Investment Objective	Growth	Telephone	800-472-3863
5-Year Projected Return	+1%	Minimum Investment	$1,000
Safety Rating (0-100)	56%	Telephone Switching	Unlimited;free
Yield	0.0%	Total Assets	$83 million

Transamerica - Grwth & Icm "A"
Diversified securities
★

S&P 500

Fund

	Costs		Performance	
Sales Load	5.0%	1-Year Return (1993)	+10%
Redemption Fee	None	3-Year Return (1991–93)	+54%
Tax Load (Estimated)	1%	5-Year Return (1989–93)	+88%
Annual 12b-1 Fee	0.25%	10-Year Return (1984–93)	NA
Annual Expense Ratio	1.34%	Worst-Ever Loss (1990-91)	23%
Annual Portfolio Turnover	140%	Stock Market Correlation	82%
5-Year Cost Estimate	14%	Up/Down Market Rank	C – B
	Benefits		Investment Information	
Investment Objective	Icm. & Gr.	Telephone	800-472-3863
5-Year Projected Return	+9%	Minimum Investment	$1,000
Safety Rating (0-100)	77%	Telephone Switching	Unlimited;free
Yield	3.3%	Total Assets	$181 million

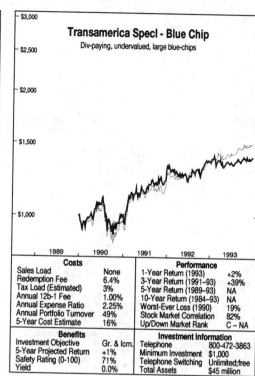

Transamerica Specl - Blue Chip
Div-paying, undervalued, large blue-chips

	Costs		Performance	
Sales Load	None	1-Year Return (1993)	+2%
Redemption Fee	6.4%	3-Year Return (1991–93)	+39%
Tax Load (Estimated)	3%	5-Year Return (1989–93)	NA
Annual 12b-1 Fee	1.00%	10-Year Return (1984–93)	NA
Annual Expense Ratio	2.25%	Worst-Ever Loss (1990)	19%
Annual Portfolio Turnover	49%	Stock Market Correlation	82%
5-Year Cost Estimate	16%	Up/Down Market Rank	C – NA
	Benefits		Investment Information	
Investment Objective	Gr. & Icm.	Telephone	800-472-3863
5-Year Projected Return	+1%	Minimum Investment	$1,000
Safety Rating (0-100)	71%	Telephone Switching	Unlimited;free
Yield	0.0%	Total Assets	$45 million

Transamerica Spl - Emg Gth "B"
Stocks with $500-mil - $1-bil market cap

	Costs		Performance	
Sales Load	None	1-Year Return (1993)	+12%
Redemption Fee	6.4%	3-Year Return (1991–93)	+99%
Tax Load (Estimated)	5%	5-Year Return (1989–93)	NA
Annual 12b-1 Fee	1.00%	10-Year Return (1984–93)	NA
Annual Expense Ratio	2.42%	Worst-Ever Loss (1990)	32%
Annual Portfolio Turnover	48%	Stock Market Correlation	54%
5-Year Cost Estimate	18%	Up/Down Market Rank	A – NA
	Benefits		Investment Information	
Investment Objective	Growth	Telephone	800-472-3863
5-Year Projected Return	+40%	Minimum Investment	$1,000
Safety Rating (0-100)	62%	Telephone Switching	Unlimited;free
Yield	0.0%	Total Assets	$284 million

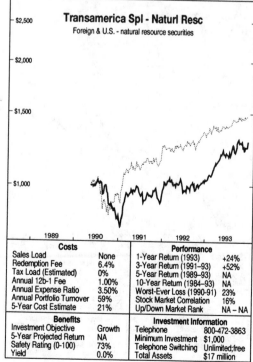

Transamerica Spl - Naturl Resc
Foreign & U.S. - natural resource securities

	Costs		Performance	
Sales Load	None	1-Year Return (1993)	+24%
Redemption Fee	6.4%	3-Year Return (1991–93)	+52%
Tax Load (Estimated)	0%	5-Year Return (1989–93)	NA
Annual 12b-1 Fee	1.00%	10-Year Return (1984–93)	NA
Annual Expense Ratio	3.50%	Worst-Ever Loss (1990-91)	23%
Annual Portfolio Turnover	59%	Stock Market Correlation	16%
5-Year Cost Estimate	21%	Up/Down Market Rank	NA – NA
	Benefits		Investment Information	
Investment Objective	Growth	Telephone	800-472-3863
5-Year Projected Return	NA	Minimum Investment	$1,000
Safety Rating (0-100)	73%	Telephone Switching	Unlimited;free
Yield	0.0%	Total Assets	$17 million

Tri-Continental
Diversified securities

Costs		Performance	
Sales Load	None	1-Year Return (1993)	+3%
Redemption Fee	None	3-Year Return (1991–93)	+41%
Tax Load (Estimated)	5%	5-Year Return (1989–93)	+101%
Annual 12b-1 Fee	None	10-Year Return (1984–93)	+219%
Annual Expense Ratio	0.68%	Worst-Ever Loss (1987)	29%
Annual Portfolio Turnover	60%	Stock Market Correlation	38%
5-Year Cost Estimate	11%	Up/Down Market Rank	D – A

Benefits		Investment Information	
Investment Objective	Gr. & Icm.	Telephone	800-221-2450
5-Year Projected Return	+2%	Minimum Investment	None
Safety Rating (0-100)	66%	Telephone Switching	Via broker
Yield	3.4%	Total Assets	$2.17 billion

Turkish Investment
Foreign - Turkish stocks

Costs		Performance	
Sales Load	None	1-Year Return (1993)	+171%
Redemption Fee	None	3-Year Return (1991–93)	+118%
Tax Load (Estimated)	Neg.	5-Year Return (1989–93)	NA
Annual 12b-1 Fee	None	10-Year Return (1984–93)	NA
Annual Expense Ratio	2.55%	Worst-Ever Loss (1990-92)	65%
Annual Portfolio Turnover	45%	Stock Market Correlation	2%
5-Year Cost Estimate	16%	Up/Down Market Rank	E – NA

Benefits		Investment Information	
Investment Objective	Growth	Telephone	800-332-5577
5-Year Projected Return	NA	Minimum Investment	None
Safety Rating (0-100)	9%	Telephone Switching	Via broker
Yield	0.0%	Total Assets	$59 million

Twentieth Century Balanced
60% stocks, 40% bonds
★★

Costs		Performance	
Sales Load	None	1-Year Return (1993)	+7%
Redemption Fee	None	3-Year Return (1991–93)	+48%
Tax Load (Estimated)	2%	5-Year Return (1989–93)	+89%
Annual 12b-1 Fee	None	10-Year Return (1984–93)	NA
Annual Expense Ratio	1.00%	Worst-Ever Loss (1990)	16%
Annual Portfolio Turnover	107%	Stock Market Correlation	66%
5-Year Cost Estimate	7%	Up/Down Market Rank	B – B

Benefits		Investment Information	
Investment Objective	Gr. & Icm.	Telephone	800-345-2021
5-Year Projected Return	+18%	Minimum Investment	$1,000
Safety Rating (0-100)	78%	Telephone Switching	4 per yr; free
Yield	2.4%	Total Assets	$693 million

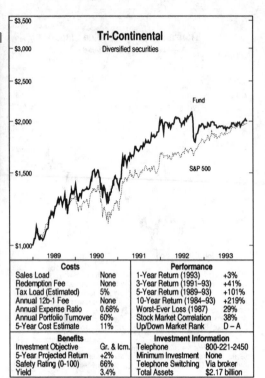

Twentieth Century Giftrust
For trust accounts only
★★

Costs		Performance	
Sales Load	None	1-Year Return (1993)	+31%
Redemption Fee	None	3-Year Return (1991–93)	+187%
Tax Load (Estimated)	3%	5-Year Return (1989–93)	+258%
Annual 12b-1 Fee	None	10-Year Return (1984–93)	+636%
Annual Expense Ratio	1.00%	Worst-Ever Loss (1987)	48%
Annual Portfolio Turnover	147%	Stock Market Correlation	43%
5-Year Cost Estimate	9%	Up/Down Market Rank	A – E

Benefits		Investment Information	
Investment Objective	Growth	Telephone	800-345-2021
5-Year Projected Return	+65%	Minimum Investment	$250
Safety Rating (0-100)	57%	Telephone Switching	Not available
Yield	0.0%	Total Assets	$136 million

Twentieth Century Growth
Large established growth stocks

Fund

S&P 500

Costs		Performance	
Sales Load	None	1-Year Return (1993)	+4%
Redemption Fee	None	3-Year Return (1991–93)	+68%
Tax Load (Estimated)	4%	5-Year Return (1989–93)	+131%
Annual 12b-1 Fee	None	10-Year Return (1984–93)	+279%
Annual Expense Ratio	1.00%	Worst-Ever Loss (1987)	41%
Annual Portfolio Turnover	103%	Stock Market Correlation	63%
5-Year Cost Estimate	10%	Up/Down Market Rank	A – E

Benefits		Investment Information	
Investment Objective	Growth	Telephone	800-345-2021
5-Year Projected Return	+17%	Minimum Investment	$1,000
Safety Rating (0-100)	62%	Telephone Switching	4 per yr; free
Yield	0.2%	Total Assets	$4.72 billion

Twentieth Century Heritage
Dividend-paying growth stocks
★★

Costs		Performance	
Sales Load	None	1-Year Return (1993)	+20%
Redemption Fee	None	3-Year Return (1991–93)	+82%
Tax Load (Estimated)	3%	5-Year Return (1989–93)	+123%
Annual 12b-1 Fee	None	10-Year Return (1984–93)	NA
Annual Expense Ratio	1.00%	Worst-Ever Loss (1990)	24%
Annual Portfolio Turnover	114%	Stock Market Correlation	61%
5-Year Cost Estimate	8%	Up/Down Market Rank	A – D

Benefits		Investment Information	
Investment Objective	Growth	Telephone	800-345-2021
5-Year Projected Return	+24%	Minimum Investment	$1,000
Safety Rating (0-100)	71%	Telephone Switching	4 per yr; free
Yield	0.6%	Total Assets	$667 million

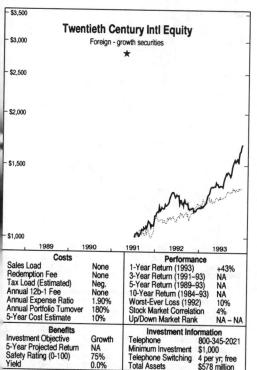

Twentieth Century Intl Equity
Foreign - growth securities
★

Costs		Performance	
Sales Load	None	1-Year Return (1993)	+43%
Redemption Fee	None	3-Year Return (1991–93)	NA
Tax Load (Estimated)	Neg.	5-Year Return (1989–93)	NA
Annual 12b-1 Fee	None	10-Year Return (1984–93)	NA
Annual Expense Ratio	1.90%	Worst-Ever Loss (1992)	10%
Annual Portfolio Turnover	180%	Stock Market Correlation	4%
5-Year Cost Estimate	10%	Up/Down Market Rank	NA – NA

Benefits		Investment Information	
Investment Objective	Growth	Telephone	800-345-2021
5-Year Projected Return	NA	Minimum Investment	$1,000
Safety Rating (0-100)	75%	Telephone Switching	4 per yr; free
Yield	0.0%	Total Assets	$578 million

Twentieth Century Select
Dividend-paying; large growth stocks
★

Costs		Performance	
Sales Load	None	1-Year Return (1993)	+15%
Redemption Fee	None	3-Year Return (1991–93)	+44%
Tax Load (Estimated)	3%	5-Year Return (1989–93)	+100%
Annual 12b-1 Fee	None	10-Year Return (1984–93)	+233%
Annual Expense Ratio	1.00%	Worst-Ever Loss (1987)	36%
Annual Portfolio Turnover	82%	Stock Market Correlation	82%
5-Year Cost Estimate	9%	Up/Down Market Rank	A – E

Benefits		Investment Information	
Investment Objective	Growth	Telephone	800-345-2021
5-Year Projected Return	+7%	Minimum Investment	$1,000
Safety Rating (0-100)	68%	Telephone Switching	4 per yr; free
Yield	1.1%	Total Assets	$5.05 billion

EQUITY

Twentieth Century Ultra
Medium-small capitalization growth stocks

★

Fund

Costs		Performance	
Sales Load	None	1-Year Return (1993)	+22%
Redemption Fee	None	3-Year Return (1991–93)	+130%
Tax Load (Estimated)	5%	5-Year Return (1989–93)	+244%
Annual 12b-1 Fee	None	10-Year Return (1984–93)	+367%
Annual Expense Ratio	1.00%	Worst-Ever Loss (1987)	47%
Annual Portfolio Turnover	57%	Stock Market Correlation	44%
5-Year Cost Estimate	11%	Up/Down Market Rank	A – E

Benefits		Investment Information	
Investment Objective	Growth	Telephone	800-345-2021
5-Year Projected Return	+68%	Minimum Investment	$1,000
Safety Rating (0-100)	55%	Telephone Switching	4 per yr; free
Yield	0.0%	Total Assets	$7.49 billion

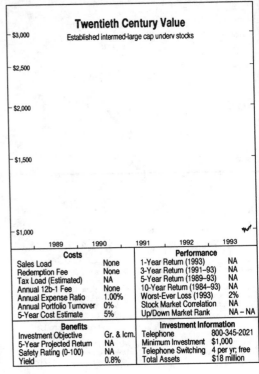

Twentieth Century Value
Established intermed-large cap underv stocks

Costs		Performance	
Sales Load	None	1-Year Return (1993)	NA
Redemption Fee	None	3-Year Return (1991–93)	NA
Tax Load (Estimated)	NA	5-Year Return (1989–93)	NA
Annual 12b-1 Fee	None	10-Year Return (1984–93)	NA
Annual Expense Ratio	1.00%	Worst-Ever Loss (1993)	2%
Annual Portfolio Turnover	0%	Stock Market Correlation	NA
5-Year Cost Estimate	5%	Up/Down Market Rank	NA – NA

Benefits		Investment Information	
Investment Objective	Gr. & Icm.	Telephone	800-345-2021
5-Year Projected Return	NA	Minimum Investment	$1,000
Safety Rating (0-100)	NA	Telephone Switching	4 per yr; free
Yield	0.8%	Total Assets	$18 million

Twentieth Century Vista
Small capitalization growth stocks

Costs		Performance	
Sales Load	None	1-Year Return (1993)	+5%
Redemption Fee	None	3-Year Return (1991–93)	+79%
Tax Load (Estimated)	1%	5-Year Return (1989–93)	+130%
Annual 12b-1 Fee	None	10-Year Return (1984–93)	+223%
Annual Expense Ratio	1.00%	Worst-Ever Loss (1987)	51%
Annual Portfolio Turnover	108%	Stock Market Correlation	52%
5-Year Cost Estimate	7%	Up/Down Market Rank	A – E

Benefits		Investment Information	
Investment Objective	Growth	Telephone	800-345-2021
5-Year Projected Return	+8%	Minimum Investment	$1,000
Safety Rating (0-100)	51%	Telephone Switching	4 per yr; free
Yield	0.0%	Total Assets	$848 million

United - Accumulative
Large; well known companies

Costs		Performance	
Sales Load	6.1%	1-Year Return (1993)	+9%
Redemption Fee	None	3-Year Return (1991–93)	+54%
Tax Load (Estimated)	1%	5-Year Return (1989–93)	+77%
Annual 12b-1 Fee	0.25%	10-Year Return (1984–93)	+246%
Annual Expense Ratio	0.88%	Worst-Ever Loss (1987)	25%
Annual Portfolio Turnover	280%	Stock Market Correlation	74%
5-Year Cost Estimate	12%	Up/Down Market Rank	C – B

Benefits		Investment Information	
Investment Objective	Gr. & Icm.	Telephone	800-366-5465
5-Year Projected Return	–2%	Minimum Investment	$500
Safety Rating (0-100)	73%	Telephone Switching	Mail only
Yield	1.5%	Total Assets	$1.03 billion

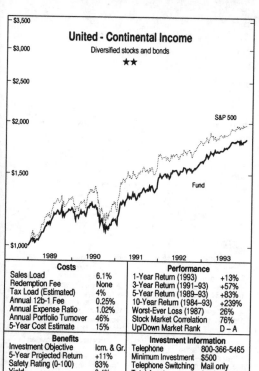

United - Continental Income
Diversified stocks and bonds
★★

S&P 500

Fund

1989 1990 1991 1992 1993

Costs		Performance	
Sales Load	6.1%	1-Year Return (1993)	+13%
Redemption Fee	None	3-Year Return (1991–93)	+57%
Tax Load (Estimated)	4%	5-Year Return (1989–93)	+83%
Annual 12b-1 Fee	0.25%	10-Year Return (1984–93)	+239%
Annual Expense Ratio	1.02%	Worst-Ever Loss (1987)	26%
Annual Portfolio Turnover	46%	Stock Market Correlation	76%
5-Year Cost Estimate	15%	Up/Down Market Rank	D – A

Benefits		Investment Information	
Investment Objective	Icm. & Gr.	Telephone	800-366-5465
5-Year Projected Return	+11%	Minimum Investment	$500
Safety Rating (0-100)	83%	Telephone Switching	Mail only
Yield	3.4%	Total Assets	$416 million

United - Gold & Government
Gold and government securities

1989 1990 1991 1992 1993

Costs		Performance	
Sales Load	6.1%	1-Year Return (1993)	+76%
Redemption Fee	None	3-Year Return (1991–93)	+55%
Tax Load (Estimated)	Neg.	5-Year Return (1989–93)	+44%
Annual 12b-1 Fee	0.25%	10-Year Return (1984–93)	NA
Annual Expense Ratio	2.18%	Worst-Ever Loss (1987-92)	46%
Annual Portfolio Turnover	83%	Stock Market Correlation	–1%
5-Year Cost Estimate	18%	Up/Down Market Rank	E – A

Benefits		Investment Information	
Investment Objective	Gr. & Icm.	Telephone	800-366-5465
5-Year Projected Return	NA	Minimum Investment	$500
Safety Rating (0-100)	66%	Telephone Switching	Mail only
Yield	0.4%	Total Assets	$42 million

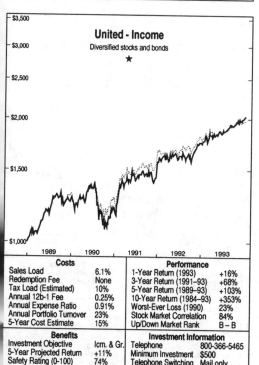

United - Income
Diversified stocks and bonds
★

1989 1990 1991 1992 1993

Costs		Performance	
Sales Load	6.1%	1-Year Return (1993)	+16%
Redemption Fee	None	3-Year Return (1991–93)	+68%
Tax Load (Estimated)	10%	5-Year Return (1989–93)	+103%
Annual 12b-1 Fee	0.25%	10-Year Return (1984–93)	+353%
Annual Expense Ratio	0.91%	Worst-Ever Loss (1990)	23%
Annual Portfolio Turnover	23%	Stock Market Correlation	84%
5-Year Cost Estimate	15%	Up/Down Market Rank	B – B

Benefits		Investment Information	
Investment Objective	Icm. & Gr.	Telephone	800-366-5465
5-Year Projected Return	+11%	Minimum Investment	$500
Safety Rating (0-100)	74%	Telephone Switching	Mail only
Yield	1.6%	Total Assets	$2.90 billion

United - International Growth
Foreign & U.S. - diversified stocks

1989 1990 1991 1992 1993

Costs		Performance	
Sales Load	6.1%	1-Year Return (1993)	+46%
Redemption Fee	None	3-Year Return (1991–93)	+72%
Tax Load (Estimated)	5%	5-Year Return (1989–93)	+69%
Annual 12b-1 Fee	0.25%	10-Year Return (1984–93)	+283%
Annual Expense Ratio	1.44%	Worst-Ever Loss (1987)	22%
Annual Portfolio Turnover	94%	Stock Market Correlation	12%
5-Year Cost Estimate	20%	Up/Down Market Rank	E – A

Benefits		Investment Information	
Investment Objective	Growth	Telephone	800-366-5465
5-Year Projected Return	NA	Minimum Investment	$500
Safety Rating (0-100)	75%	Telephone Switching	Mail only
Yield	0.5%	Total Assets	$393 million

United - New Concepts
Emerging growth stocks
★★

(chart labels: Fund, S&P 500; y-axis $1,000–$3,000; x-axis 1989–1993)

Costs		Performance	
Sales Load	6.1%	1-Year Return (1993)	+11%
Redemption Fee	None	3-Year Return (1991–93)	+118%
Tax Load (Estimated)	10%	5-Year Return (1989–93)	+141%
Annual 12b-1 Fee	0.25%	10-Year Return (1984–93)	NA
Annual Expense Ratio	1.44%	Worst-Ever Loss (1987)	36%
Annual Portfolio Turnover	39%	Stock Market Correlation	44%
5-Year Cost Estimate	22%	Up/Down Market Rank	C – D

Benefits		Investment Information	
Investment Objective	Growth	Telephone	800-366-5465
5-Year Projected Return	+46%	Minimum Investment	$500
Safety Rating (0-100)	71%	Telephone Switching	Mail only
Yield	0.0%	Total Assets	$204 million

United - Retirement Shares
Diversified stocks and bonds
★★★

(chart: y-axis $1,000–$3,500; x-axis 1989–1993)

Costs		Performance	
Sales Load	6.1%	1-Year Return (1993)	+13%
Redemption Fee	None	3-Year Return (1991–93)	+55%
Tax Load (Estimated)	5%	5-Year Return (1989–93)	+96%
Annual 12b-1 Fee	0.25%	10-Year Return (1984–93)	+222%
Annual Expense Ratio	1.05%	Worst-Ever Loss (1987)	24%
Annual Portfolio Turnover	31%	Stock Market Correlation	76%
5-Year Cost Estimate	15%	Up/Down Market Rank	E – A

Benefits		Investment Information	
Investment Objective	Gr. & Icm.	Telephone	800-366-5465
5-Year Projected Return	+18%	Minimum Investment	$500
Safety Rating (0-100)	83%	Telephone Switching	Mail only
Yield	2.5%	Total Assets	$405 million

United - Science & Technology
Science and energy securities

(chart: y-axis $1,000–$3,500; x-axis 1989–1993)

Costs		Performance	
Sales Load	6.1%	1-Year Return (1993)	+8%
Redemption Fee	None	3-Year Return (1991–93)	+66%
Tax Load (Estimated)	9%	5-Year Return (1989–93)	+104%
Annual 12b-1 Fee	0.25%	10-Year Return (1984–93)	+258%
Annual Expense Ratio	1.14%	Worst-Ever Loss (1987)	33%
Annual Portfolio Turnover	82%	Stock Market Correlation	52%
5-Year Cost Estimate	23%	Up/Down Market Rank	C – C

Benefits		Investment Information	
Investment Objective	Growth	Telephone	800-366-5465
5-Year Projected Return	NA	Minimum Investment	$500
Safety Rating (0-100)	68%	Telephone Switching	Mail only
Yield	0.1%	Total Assets	$428 million

United - Vanguard
Diversified stocks and bonds

(chart: y-axis $1,000–$3,500; x-axis 1989–1993)

Costs		Performance	
Sales Load	6.1%	1-Year Return (1993)	+14%
Redemption Fee	None	3-Year Return (1991–93)	+50%
Tax Load (Estimated)	7%	5-Year Return (1989–93)	+72%
Annual 12b-1 Fee	0.25%	10-Year Return (1984–93)	+227%
Annual Expense Ratio	1.22%	Worst-Ever Loss (1987)	32%
Annual Portfolio Turnover	62%	Stock Market Correlation	60%
5-Year Cost Estimate	22%	Up/Down Market Rank	C – C

Benefits		Investment Information	
Investment Objective	Growth	Telephone	800-366-5465
5-Year Projected Return	+3%	Minimum Investment	$500
Safety Rating (0-100)	71%	Telephone Switching	Mail only
Yield	0.1%	Total Assets	$900 million

United Kingdom
Foreign - United Kingdom stocks

S&P 500

Fund

Costs		Performance	
Sales Load	None	1-Year Return (1993)	+54%
Redemption Fee	None	3-Year Return (1991–93)	+83%
Tax Load (Estimated)	5%	5-Year Return (1989–93)	+96%
Annual 12b-1 Fee	None	10-Year Return (1984–93)	NA
Annual Expense Ratio	1.65%	Worst-Ever Loss (1987)	50%
Annual Portfolio Turnover	46%	Stock Market Correlation	10%
5-Year Cost Estimate	16%	Up/Down Market Rank	D – B

Benefits		Investment Information	
Investment Objective	Growth	Telephone	800-524-4458
5-Year Projected Return	NA	Minimum Investment	None
Safety Rating (0-100)	44%	Telephone Switching	Via broker
Yield	6.1%	Total Assets	$42 million

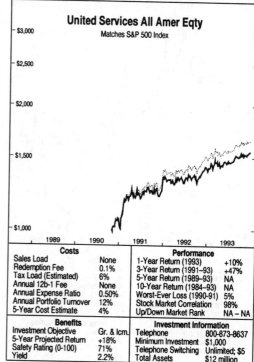

United Services All Amer Eqty
Matches S&P 500 Index

Costs		Performance	
Sales Load	None	1-Year Return (1993)	+10%
Redemption Fee	0.1%	3-Year Return (1991–93)	+47%
Tax Load (Estimated)	6%	5-Year Return (1989–93)	NA
Annual 12b-1 Fee	None	10-Year Return (1984–93)	NA
Annual Expense Ratio	0.50%	Worst-Ever Loss (1990-91)	5%
Annual Portfolio Turnover	12%	Stock Market Correlation	98%
5-Year Cost Estimate	4%	Up/Down Market Rank	NA – NA

Benefits		Investment Information	
Investment Objective	Gr. & Icm.	Telephone	800-873-8637
5-Year Projected Return	+18%	Minimum Investment	$1,000
Safety Rating (0-100)	71%	Telephone Switching	Unlimited; $5
Yield	2.2%	Total Assets	$12 million

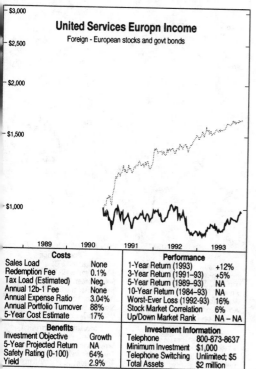

United Services Europn Income
Foreign - European stocks and govt bonds

Costs		Performance	
Sales Load	None	1-Year Return (1993)	+12%
Redemption Fee	0.1%	3-Year Return (1991–93)	+5%
Tax Load (Estimated)	Neg.	5-Year Return (1989–93)	NA
Annual 12b-1 Fee	None	10-Year Return (1984–93)	NA
Annual Expense Ratio	3.04%	Worst-Ever Loss (1992-93)	16%
Annual Portfolio Turnover	88%	Stock Market Correlation	6%
5-Year Cost Estimate	17%	Up/Down Market Rank	NA – NA

Benefits		Investment Information	
Investment Objective	Growth	Telephone	800-873-8637
5-Year Projected Return	NA	Minimum Investment	$1,000
Safety Rating (0-100)	64%	Telephone Switching	Unlimited; $5
Yield	2.9%	Total Assets	$2 million

United Services Global Resourc
Gold stocks; no South African gold

Costs		Performance	
Sales Load	None	1-Year Return (1993)	+20%
Redemption Fee	0.1%	3-Year Return (1991–93)	+23%
Tax Load (Estimated)	4%	5-Year Return (1989–93)	+26%
Annual 12b-1 Fee	None	10-Year Return (1984–93)	+13%
Annual Expense Ratio	2.36%	Worst-Ever Loss (1987-88)	52%
Annual Portfolio Turnover	120%	Stock Market Correlation	15%
5-Year Cost Estimate	17%	Up/Down Market Rank	E – B

Benefits		Investment Information	
Investment Objective	Growth	Telephone	800-873-8637
5-Year Projected Return	NA	Minimum Investment	$1,000
Safety Rating (0-100)	68%	Telephone Switching	Unlimited; $5
Yield	0.2%	Total Assets	$24 million

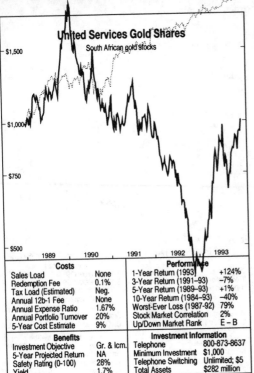

United Services Gold Shares
South African gold stocks

Costs		Performance	
Sales Load	None	1-Year Return (1993)	+124%
Redemption Fee	0.1%	3-Year Return (1991–93)	−7%
Tax Load (Estimated)	Neg.	5-Year Return (1989–93)	+1%
Annual 12b-1 Fee	None	10-Year Return (1984–93)	−40%
Annual Expense Ratio	1.67%	Worst-Ever Loss (1987-92)	79%
Annual Portfolio Turnover	20%	Stock Market Correlation	2%
5-Year Cost Estimate	9%	Up/Down Market Rank	E – B

Benefits		Investment Information	
Investment Objective	Gr. & Icm.	Telephone	800-873-8637
5-Year Projected Return	NA	Minimum Investment	$1,000
Safety Rating (0-100)	28%	Telephone Switching	Unlimited; $5
Yield	1.7%	Total Assets	$282 million

United Services Growth
Diversified securities

Costs		Performance	
Sales Load	None	1-Year Return (1993)	+13%
Redemption Fee	0.1%	3-Year Return (1991–93)	+27%
Tax Load (Estimated)	6%	5-Year Return (1989–93)	+32%
Annual 12b-1 Fee	None	10-Year Return (1984–93)	+30%
Annual Expense Ratio	2.40%	Worst-Ever Loss (1987)	37%
Annual Portfolio Turnover	99%	Stock Market Correlation	38%
5-Year Cost Estimate	20%	Up/Down Market Rank	E – D

Benefits		Investment Information	
Investment Objective	Growth	Telephone	800-873-8637
5-Year Projected Return	−9%	Minimum Investment	$1,000
Safety Rating (0-100)	57%	Telephone Switching	Unlimited; $5
Yield	0.0%	Total Assets	$4 million

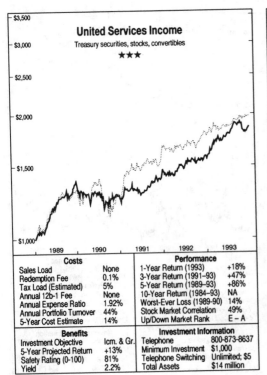

United Services Income
Treasury securities, stocks, convertibles
★★★

Costs		Performance	
Sales Load	None	1-Year Return (1993)	+18%
Redemption Fee	0.1%	3-Year Return (1991–93)	+47%
Tax Load (Estimated)	5%	5-Year Return (1989–93)	+86%
Annual 12b-1 Fee	None	10-Year Return (1984–93)	NA
Annual Expense Ratio	1.92%	Worst-Ever Loss (1989-90)	14%
Annual Portfolio Turnover	44%	Stock Market Correlation	49%
5-Year Cost Estimate	14%	Up/Down Market Rank	E – A

Benefits		Investment Information	
Investment Objective	Icm. & Gr.	Telephone	800-873-8637
5-Year Projected Return	+13%	Minimum Investment	$1,000
Safety Rating (0-100)	81%	Telephone Switching	Unlimited; $5
Yield	2.2%	Total Assets	$14 million

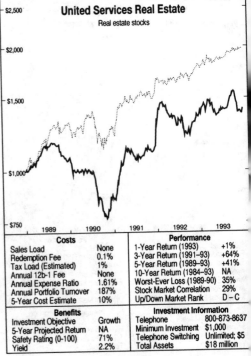

United Services Real Estate
Real estate stocks

Costs		Performance	
Sales Load	None	1-Year Return (1993)	+1%
Redemption Fee	0.1%	3-Year Return (1991–93)	+64%
Tax Load (Estimated)	1%	5-Year Return (1989–93)	+41%
Annual 12b-1 Fee	None	10-Year Return (1984–93)	NA
Annual Expense Ratio	1.61%	Worst-Ever Loss (1989-90)	35%
Annual Portfolio Turnover	187%	Stock Market Correlation	29%
5-Year Cost Estimate	10%	Up/Down Market Rank	D – C

Benefits		Investment Information	
Investment Objective	Growth	Telephone	800-873-8637
5-Year Projected Return	NA	Minimum Investment	$1,000
Safety Rating (0-100)	71%	Telephone Switching	Unlimited; $5
Yield	2.2%	Total Assets	$18 million

United Services World Gold

Gold stocks; no South African gold

S&P 500

Costs		Performance	
Sales Load	None	1-Year Return (1993)	+90%
Redemption Fee	0.1%	3-Year Return (1991–93)	+75%
Tax Load (Estimated)	0%	5-Year Return (1989–93)	+47%
Annual 12b-1 Fee	None	10-Year Return (1984–93)	NA
Annual Expense Ratio	2.22%	Worst-Ever Loss (1987-92)	62%
Annual Portfolio Turnover	26%	Stock Market Correlation	–1%
5-Year Cost Estimate	12%	Up/Down Market Rank	E – A
Benefits		**Investment Information**	
Investment Objective	Growth	Telephone	800-873-8637
5-Year Projected Return	NA	Minimum Investment	$1,000
Safety Rating (0-100)	53%	Telephone Switching	Unlimited; $5
Yield	0.0%	Total Assets	$154 million

USAA Aggressive Growth

Emerging growth stocks

Costs		Performance	
Sales Load	None	1-Year Return (1993)	+8%
Redemption Fee	None	3-Year Return (1991–93)	+70%
Tax Load (Estimated)	3%	5-Year Return (1989–93)	+74%
Annual 12b-1 Fee	None	10-Year Return (1984–93)	+112%
Annual Expense Ratio	0.86%	Worst-Ever Loss (1987)	38%
Annual Portfolio Turnover	113%	Stock Market Correlation	56%
5-Year Cost Estimate	8%	Up/Down Market Rank	B – E
Benefits		**Investment Information**	
Investment Objective	Growth	Telephone	800-531-8181
5-Year Projected Return	+5%	Minimum Investment	$1,000
Safety Rating (0-100)	60%	Telephone Switching	6 per yr; $5
Yield	0.1%	Total Assets	$268 million

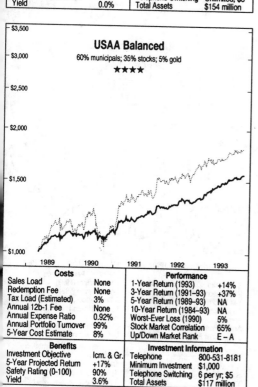

USAA Balanced

60% municipals; 35% stocks; 5% gold

★★★★

Costs		Performance	
Sales Load	None	1-Year Return (1993)	+14%
Redemption Fee	None	3-Year Return (1991–93)	+37%
Tax Load (Estimated)	3%	5-Year Return (1989–93)	NA
Annual 12b-1 Fee	None	10-Year Return (1984–93)	NA
Annual Expense Ratio	0.92%	Worst-Ever Loss (1990)	5%
Annual Portfolio Turnover	99%	Stock Market Correlation	65%
5-Year Cost Estimate	8%	Up/Down Market Rank	E – A
Benefits		**Investment Information**	
Investment Objective	Icm. & Gr.	Telephone	800-531-8181
5-Year Projected Return	+17%	Minimum Investment	$1,000
Safety Rating (0-100)	90%	Telephone Switching	6 per yr; $5
Yield	3.6%	Total Assets	$117 million

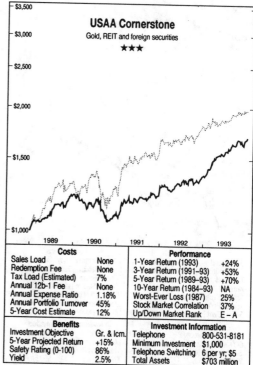

USAA Cornerstone

Gold, REIT and foreign securities

★★★

Costs		Performance	
Sales Load	None	1-Year Return (1993)	+24%
Redemption Fee	None	3-Year Return (1991–93)	+53%
Tax Load (Estimated)	7%	5-Year Return (1989–93)	+70%
Annual 12b-1 Fee	None	10-Year Return (1984–93)	NA
Annual Expense Ratio	1.18%	Worst-Ever Loss (1987)	25%
Annual Portfolio Turnover	45%	Stock Market Correlation	37%
5-Year Cost Estimate	12%	Up/Down Market Rank	E – A
Benefits		**Investment Information**	
Investment Objective	Gr. & Icm.	Telephone	800-531-8181
5-Year Projected Return	+15%	Minimum Investment	$1,000
Safety Rating (0-100)	86%	Telephone Switching	6 per yr; $5
Yield	2.5%	Total Assets	$703 million

USAA Gold
International gold stocks

S&P 500

Fund

| 1989 | 1990 | 1991 | 1992 | 1993 |

Costs		Performance	
Sales Load	None	1-Year Return (1993)	+58%
Redemption Fee	None	3-Year Return (1991–93)	+39%
Tax Load (Estimated)	Neg.	5-Year Return (1989–93)	+21%
Annual 12b-1 Fee	None	10-Year Return (1984–93)	NA
Annual Expense Ratio	1.43%	Worst-Ever Loss (1987–93)	64%
Annual Portfolio Turnover	81%	Stock Market Correlation	–1%
5-Year Cost Estimate	7%	Up/Down Market Rank	E – A

Benefits		Investment Information	
Investment Objective	Growth	Telephone	800-531-8181
5-Year Projected Return	NA	Minimum Investment	$1,000
Safety Rating (0-100)	54%	Telephone Switching	6 per yr; $5
Yield	0.1%	Total Assets	$172 million

USAA Growth
Diversified growth stocks
★

| 1989 | 1990 | 1991 | 1992 | 1993 |

Costs		Performance	
Sales Load	None	1-Year Return (1993)	+7%
Redemption Fee	None	3-Year Return (1991–93)	+51%
Tax Load (Estimated)	3%	5-Year Return (1989–93)	+92%
Annual 12b-1 Fee	None	10-Year Return (1984–93)	+164%
Annual Expense Ratio	1.07%	Worst-Ever Loss (1987)	30%
Annual Portfolio Turnover	96%	Stock Market Correlation	88%
5-Year Cost Estimate	9%	Up/Down Market Rank	B – D

Benefits		Investment Information	
Investment Objective	Gr. & Icm.	Telephone	800-531-8181
5-Year Projected Return	+15%	Minimum Investment	$1,000
Safety Rating (0-100)	73%	Telephone Switching	6 per yr; $5
Yield	0.9%	Total Assets	$599 million

USAA Income Stock
Above-average yield; large stocks
★★★★

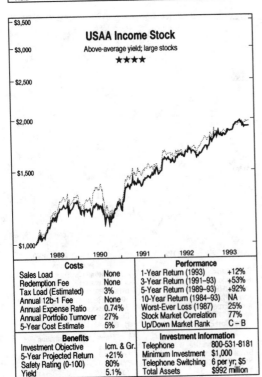

| 1989 | 1990 | 1991 | 1992 | 1993 |

Costs		Performance	
Sales Load	None	1-Year Return (1993)	+12%
Redemption Fee	None	3-Year Return (1991–93)	+53%
Tax Load (Estimated)	3%	5-Year Return (1989–93)	+92%
Annual 12b-1 Fee	None	10-Year Return (1984–93)	NA
Annual Expense Ratio	0.74%	Worst-Ever Loss (1987)	25%
Annual Portfolio Turnover	27%	Stock Market Correlation	77%
5-Year Cost Estimate	5%	Up/Down Market Rank	C – B

Benefits		Investment Information	
Investment Objective	Icm. & Gr.	Telephone	800-531-8181
5-Year Projected Return	+21%	Minimum Investment	$1,000
Safety Rating (0-100)	80%	Telephone Switching	6 per yr; $5
Yield	5.1%	Total Assets	$992 million

USAA International
Foreign - high market value stocks

| 1989 | 1990 | 1991 | 1992 | 1993 |

Costs		Performance	
Sales Load	None	1-Year Return (1993)	+40%
Redemption Fee	None	3-Year Return (1991–93)	+58%
Tax Load (Estimated)	4%	5-Year Return (1989–93)	+68%
Annual 12b-1 Fee	None	10-Year Return (1984–93)	NA
Annual Expense Ratio	1.69%	Worst-Ever Loss (1990)	22%
Annual Portfolio Turnover	53%	Stock Market Correlation	14%
5-Year Cost Estimate	13%	Up/Down Market Rank	E – A

Benefits		Investment Information	
Investment Objective	Growth	Telephone	800-531-8181
5-Year Projected Return	NA	Minimum Investment	$1,000
Safety Rating (0-100)	76%	Telephone Switching	6 per yr; $5
Yield	0.0%	Total Assets	$83 million

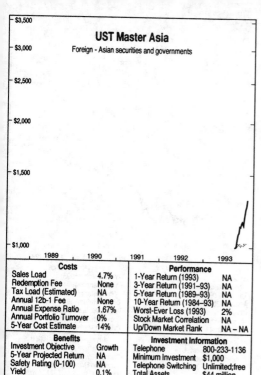

UST Master Asia

Foreign - Asian securities and governments

Costs		Performance	
Sales Load	4.7%	1-Year Return (1993)	NA
Redemption Fee	None	3-Year Return (1991–93)	NA
Tax Load (Estimated)	NA	5-Year Return (1989–93)	NA
Annual 12b-1 Fee	None	10-Year Return (1984–93)	NA
Annual Expense Ratio	1.67%	Worst-Ever Loss (1993)	2%
Annual Portfolio Turnover	0%	Stock Market Correlation	NA
5-Year Cost Estimate	14%	Up/Down Market Rank	NA – NA

Benefits		Investment Information	
Investment Objective	Growth	Telephone	800-233-1136
5-Year Projected Return	NA	Minimum Investment	$1,000
Safety Rating (0-100)	NA	Telephone Switching	Unlimited;free
Yield	0.1%	Total Assets	$44 million

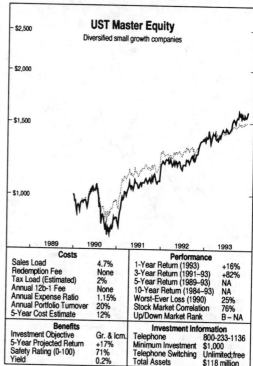

UST Master Equity

Diversified small growth companies

Costs		Performance	
Sales Load	4.7%	1-Year Return (1993)	+16%
Redemption Fee	None	3-Year Return (1991–93)	+82%
Tax Load (Estimated)	2%	5-Year Return (1989–93)	NA
Annual 12b-1 Fee	None	10-Year Return (1984–93)	NA
Annual Expense Ratio	1.15%	Worst-Ever Loss (1990)	25%
Annual Portfolio Turnover	20%	Stock Market Correlation	76%
5-Year Cost Estimate	12%	Up/Down Market Rank	B – NA

Benefits		Investment Information	
Investment Objective	Gr. & Icm.	Telephone	800-233-1136
5-Year Projected Return	+17%	Minimum Investment	$1,000
Safety Rating (0-100)	71%	Telephone Switching	Unlimited;free
Yield	0.2%	Total Assets	$118 million

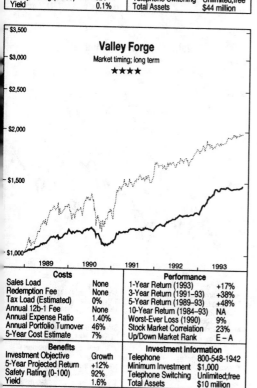

Valley Forge

Market timing; long term

★★★★

Costs		Performance	
Sales Load	None	1-Year Return (1993)	+17%
Redemption Fee	None	3-Year Return (1991–93)	+38%
Tax Load (Estimated)	0%	5-Year Return (1989–93)	+48%
Annual 12b-1 Fee	None	10-Year Return (1984–93)	NA
Annual Expense Ratio	1.40%	Worst-Ever Loss (1990)	9%
Annual Portfolio Turnover	46%	Stock Market Correlation	23%
5-Year Cost Estimate	7%	Up/Down Market Rank	E – A

Benefits		Investment Information	
Investment Objective	Growth	Telephone	800-548-1942
5-Year Projected Return	+12%	Minimum Investment	$1,000
Safety Rating (0-100)	92%	Telephone Switching	Unlimited;free
Yield	1.6%	Total Assets	$10 million

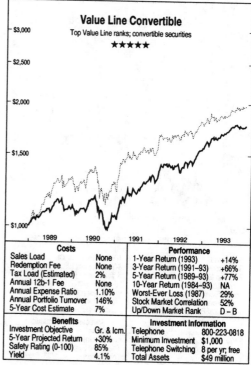

Value Line Convertible

Top Value Line ranks; convertible securities

★★★★★

Costs		Performance	
Sales Load	None	1-Year Return (1993)	+14%
Redemption Fee	None	3-Year Return (1991–93)	+66%
Tax Load (Estimated)	2%	5-Year Return (1989–93)	+77%
Annual 12b-1 Fee	None	10-Year Return (1984–93)	NA
Annual Expense Ratio	1.10%	Worst-Ever Loss (1987)	29%
Annual Portfolio Turnover	146%	Stock Market Correlation	52%
5-Year Cost Estimate	7%	Up/Down Market Rank	D – B

Benefits		Investment Information	
Investment Objective	Gr. & Icm.	Telephone	800-223-0818
5-Year Projected Return	+30%	Minimum Investment	$1,000
Safety Rating (0-100)	85%	Telephone Switching	8 per yr; free
Yield	4.1%	Total Assets	$49 million

Value Line Fund

Top Value Line ranks
★

Costs		Performance	
Sales Load	None	1-Year Return (1993)	+7%
Redemption Fee	None	3-Year Return (1991–93)	+66%
Tax Load (Estimated)	7%	5-Year Return (1989–93)	+117%
Annual 12b-1 Fee	None	10-Year Return (1984–93)	+235%
Annual Expense Ratio	0.84%	Worst-Ever Loss (1983-84)	35%
Annual Portfolio Turnover	88%	Stock Market Correlation	65%
5-Year Cost Estimate	12%	Up/Down Market Rank	B – D

Benefits		Investment Information	
Investment Objective	Gr. & Icm.	Telephone	800-223-0818
5-Year Projected Return	+25%	Minimum Investment	$1,000
Safety Rating (0-100)	70%	Telephone Switching	8 per yr; free
Yield	0.3%	Total Assets	$353 million

Value Line Income

Top Value Line ranks
★★★★

Costs		Performance	
Sales Load	None	1-Year Return (1993)	+8%
Redemption Fee	None	3-Year Return (1991–93)	+41%
Tax Load (Estimated)	2%	5-Year Return (1989–93)	+76%
Annual 12b-1 Fee	None	10-Year Return (1984–93)	+186%
Annual Expense Ratio	0.89%	Worst-Ever Loss (1987)	24%
Annual Portfolio Turnover	166%	Stock Market Correlation	71%
5-Year Cost Estimate	7%	Up/Down Market Rank	E – A

Benefits		Investment Information	
Investment Objective	Icm. & Gr.	Telephone	800-223-0818
5-Year Projected Return	+16%	Minimum Investment	$1,000
Safety Rating (0-100)	84%	Telephone Switching	8 per yr; free
Yield	2.5%	Total Assets	$174 million

Value Line Leveraged Growth

Top Value Line ranks; leveraged
★

Costs		Performance	
Sales Load	None	1-Year Return (1993)	+16%
Redemption Fee	None	3-Year Return (1991–93)	+66%
Tax Load (Estimated)	6%	5-Year Return (1989–93)	+116%
Annual 12b-1 Fee	None	10-Year Return (1984–93)	+237%
Annual Expense Ratio	0.93%	Worst-Ever Loss (1987)	37%
Annual Portfolio Turnover	118%	Stock Market Correlation	69%
5-Year Cost Estimate	12%	Up/Down Market Rank	B – D

Benefits		Investment Information	
Investment Objective	Growth	Telephone	800-223-0818
5-Year Projected Return	+21%	Minimum Investment	$1,000
Safety Rating (0-100)	68%	Telephone Switching	8 per yr; free
Yield	0.2%	Total Assets	$315 million

Value Line Special Situations

Top Value Line ranks

Costs		Performance	
Sales Load	None	1-Year Return (1993)	+13%
Redemption Fee	None	3-Year Return (1991–93)	+49%
Tax Load (Estimated)	7%	5-Year Return (1989–93)	+73%
Annual 12b-1 Fee	None	10-Year Return (1984–93)	+54%
Annual Expense Ratio	1.09%	Worst-Ever Loss (1987)	42%
Annual Portfolio Turnover	43%	Stock Market Correlation	45%
5-Year Cost Estimate	12%	Up/Down Market Rank	B – E

Benefits		Investment Information	
Investment Objective	Growth	Telephone	800-223-0818
5-Year Projected Return	+5%	Minimum Investment	$1,000
Safety Rating (0-100)	63%	Telephone Switching	8 per yr; free
Yield	0.0%	Total Assets	$90 million

Van Eck - Gold Resources
Gold stocks; no South African gold

S&P 500

Fund

Costs		Performance	
Sales Load	6.1%	1-Year Return (1993)	+78%
Redemption Fee	None	3-Year Return (1991–93)	+63%
Tax Load (Estimated)	Neg.	5-Year Return (1989–93)	+43%
Annual 12b-1 Fee	0.25%	10-Year Return (1984–93)	NA
Annual Expense Ratio	1.57%	Worst-Ever Loss (1987-92)	58%
Annual Portfolio Turnover	10%	Stock Market Correlation	–1%
5-Year Cost Estimate	15%	Up/Down Market Rank	E – A

Benefits		Investment Information	
Investment Objective	Growth	Telephone	800-221-2220
5-Year Projected Return	NA	Minimum Investment	$1,000
Safety Rating (0-100)	54%	Telephone Switching	Unlimited;free
Yield	0.0%	Total Assets	$192 million

Van Eck - Intl Investors
International gold stocks

Costs		Performance	
Sales Load	6.1%	1-Year Return (1993)	+113%
Redemption Fee	None	3-Year Return (1991–93)	+55%
Tax Load (Estimated)	3%	5-Year Return (1989–93)	+71%
Annual 12b-1 Fee	None	10-Year Return (1984–93)	+81%
Annual Expense Ratio	1.18%	Worst-Ever Loss (1990-92)	55%
Annual Portfolio Turnover	2%	Stock Market Correlation	0%
5-Year Cost Estimate	13%	Up/Down Market Rank	E – B

Benefits		Investment Information	
Investment Objective	Gr. & Icm.	Telephone	800-221-2220
5-Year Projected Return	NA	Minimum Investment	$1,000
Safety Rating (0-100)	45%	Telephone Switching	Unlimited;free
Yield	0.8%	Total Assets	$598 million

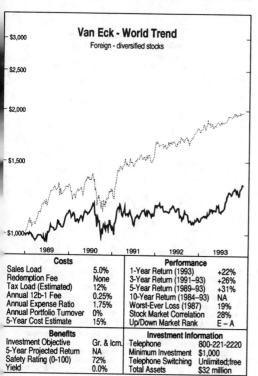

Van Eck - World Trend
Foreign - diversified stocks

Costs		Performance	
Sales Load	5.0%	1-Year Return (1993)	+22%
Redemption Fee	None	3-Year Return (1991–93)	+26%
Tax Load (Estimated)	12%	5-Year Return (1989–93)	+31%
Annual 12b-1 Fee	0.25%	10-Year Return (1984–93)	NA
Annual Expense Ratio	1.75%	Worst-Ever Loss (1987)	19%
Annual Portfolio Turnover	0%	Stock Market Correlation	28%
5-Year Cost Estimate	15%	Up/Down Market Rank	E – A

Benefits		Investment Information	
Investment Objective	Gr. & Icm.	Telephone	800-221-2220
5-Year Projected Return	NA	Minimum Investment	$1,000
Safety Rating (0-100)	72%	Telephone Switching	Unlimited;free
Yield	0.0%	Total Assets	$32 million

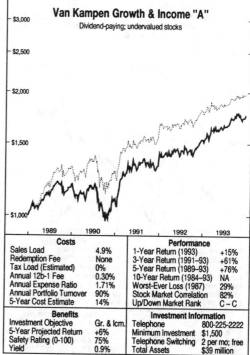

Van Kampen Growth & Income "A"
Dividend-paying; undervalued stocks

Costs		Performance	
Sales Load	4.9%	1-Year Return (1993)	+15%
Redemption Fee	None	3-Year Return (1991–93)	+61%
Tax Load (Estimated)	0%	5-Year Return (1989–93)	+76%
Annual 12b-1 Fee	0.30%	10-Year Return (1984–93)	NA
Annual Expense Ratio	1.71%	Worst-Ever Loss (1987)	29%
Annual Portfolio Turnover	90%	Stock Market Correlation	82%
5-Year Cost Estimate	14%	Up/Down Market Rank	C – C

Benefits		Investment Information	
Investment Objective	Gr. & Icm.	Telephone	800-225-2222
5-Year Projected Return	+6%	Minimum Investment	$1,500
Safety Rating (0-100)	75%	Telephone Switching	2 per mo; free
Yield	0.9%	Total Assets	$39 million

EQUITY

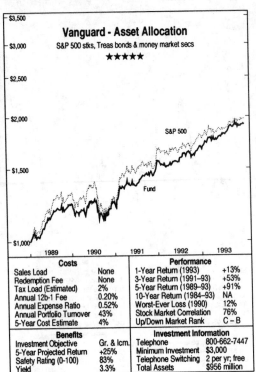

Vanguard - Asset Allocation
S&P 500 stks, Treas bonds & money market secs
★★★★★

(chart showing S&P 500 and Fund lines, 1989–1993, scale $1,000–$3,500)

Costs		Performance	
Sales Load	None	1-Year Return (1993)	+13%
Redemption Fee	None	3-Year Return (1991–93)	+53%
Tax Load (Estimated)	2%	5-Year Return (1989–93)	+91%
Annual 12b-1 Fee	0.20%	10-Year Return (1984–93)	NA
Annual Expense Ratio	0.52%	Worst-Ever Loss (1990)	12%
Annual Portfolio Turnover	43%	Stock Market Correlation	76%
5-Year Cost Estimate	4%	Up/Down Market Rank	C – B

Benefits		Investment Information	
Investment Objective	Gr. & Icm.	Telephone	800-662-7447
5-Year Projected Return	+25%	Minimum Investment	$3,000
Safety Rating (0-100)	83%	Telephone Switching	2 per yr; free
Yield	3.3%	Total Assets	$956 million

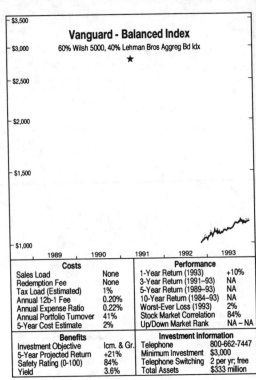

Vanguard - Balanced Index
60% Wilsh 5000, 40% Lehman Bros Aggreg Bd Idx
★

(chart, 1989–1993, scale $1,000–$3,500)

Costs		Performance	
Sales Load	None	1-Year Return (1993)	+10%
Redemption Fee	None	3-Year Return (1991–93)	NA
Tax Load (Estimated)	1%	5-Year Return (1989–93)	NA
Annual 12b-1 Fee	0.20%	10-Year Return (1984–93)	NA
Annual Expense Ratio	0.22%	Worst-Ever Loss (1993)	2%
Annual Portfolio Turnover	41%	Stock Market Correlation	84%
5-Year Cost Estimate	2%	Up/Down Market Rank	NA – NA

Benefits		Investment Information	
Investment Objective	Icm. & Gr.	Telephone	800-662-7447
5-Year Projected Return	+21%	Minimum Investment	$3,000
Safety Rating (0-100)	84%	Telephone Switching	2 per yr; free
Yield	3.6%	Total Assets	$333 million

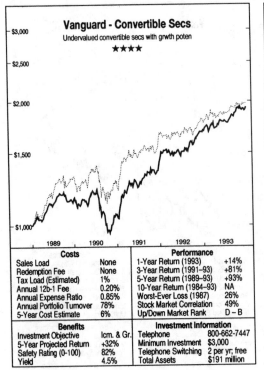

Vanguard - Convertible Secs
Undervalued convertible secs with grwth poten
★★★★

(chart, 1989–1993, scale $1,000–$3,000)

Costs		Performance	
Sales Load	None	1-Year Return (1993)	+14%
Redemption Fee	None	3-Year Return (1991–93)	+81%
Tax Load (Estimated)	1%	5-Year Return (1989–93)	+93%
Annual 12b-1 Fee	0.20%	10-Year Return (1984–93)	NA
Annual Expense Ratio	0.85%	Worst-Ever Loss (1987)	26%
Annual Portfolio Turnover	78%	Stock Market Correlation	49%
5-Year Cost Estimate	6%	Up/Down Market Rank	D – B

Benefits		Investment Information	
Investment Objective	Icm. & Gr.	Telephone	800-662-7447
5-Year Projected Return	+32%	Minimum Investment	$3,000
Safety Rating (0-100)	82%	Telephone Switching	2 per yr; free
Yield	4.5%	Total Assets	$191 million

Vanguard - Equity Income
Stocks with above average dividend yield
★

(chart, 1989–1993, scale $1,000–$3,500)

Costs		Performance	
Sales Load	None	1-Year Return (1993)	+15%
Redemption Fee	None	3-Year Return (1991–93)	+57%
Tax Load (Estimated)	3%	5-Year Return (1989–93)	+75%
Annual 12b-1 Fee	0.20%	10-Year Return (1984–93)	NA
Annual Expense Ratio	0.44%	Worst-Ever Loss (1989-90)	21%
Annual Portfolio Turnover	16%	Stock Market Correlation	82%
5-Year Cost Estimate	3%	Up/Down Market Rank	D – C

Benefits		Investment Information	
Investment Objective	Icm. & Gr.	Telephone	800-662-7447
5-Year Projected Return	+5%	Minimum Investment	$3,000
Safety Rating (0-100)	75%	Telephone Switching	2 per yr; free
Yield	4.5%	Total Assets	$1.12 billion

Vanguard - Eqty Index European
Matches MSCI Europe Index; 13 countries secs

$2,500
$2,000
$1,500
$1,000

S&P 500
Fund

1989 1990 1991 1992 1993

Costs		Performance	
Sales Load	1.0%	1-Year Return (1993)	+29%
Redemption Fee	None	3-Year Return (1991–93)	+40%
Tax Load (Estimated)	1%	5-Year Return (1989–93)	NA
Annual 12b-1 Fee	0.20%	10-Year Return (1984–93)	NA
Annual Expense Ratio	0.32%	Worst-Ever Loss (1990)	21%
Annual Portfolio Turnover	4%	Stock Market Correlation	8%
5-Year Cost Estimate	3%	Up/Down Market Rank	NA – NA

Benefits		Investment Information	
Investment Objective	Gr. & Icm.	Telephone	800-662-7447
5-Year Projected Return	NA	Minimum Investment	$3,000
Safety Rating (0-100)	68%	Telephone Switching	Mail only
Yield	1.4%	Total Assets	$495 million

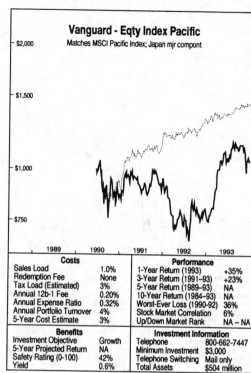

Vanguard - Eqty Index Pacific
Matches MSCI Pacific Index; Japan mjr compont

$2,000
$1,500
$1,000
$750

1989 1990 1991 1992 1993

Costs		Performance	
Sales Load	1.0%	1-Year Return (1993)	+35%
Redemption Fee	None	3-Year Return (1991–93)	+23%
Tax Load (Estimated)	3%	5-Year Return (1989–93)	NA
Annual 12b-1 Fee	0.20%	10-Year Return (1984–93)	NA
Annual Expense Ratio	0.32%	Worst-Ever Loss (1990-92)	36%
Annual Portfolio Turnover	4%	Stock Market Correlation	6%
5-Year Cost Estimate	3%	Up/Down Market Rank	NA – NA

Benefits		Investment Information	
Investment Objective	Growth	Telephone	800-662-7447
5-Year Projected Return	NA	Minimum Investment	$3,000
Safety Rating (0-100)	42%	Telephone Switching	Mail only
Yield	0.6%	Total Assets	$504 million

Vanguard - Explorer
Companies with good management
★

$2,500
$2,000
$1,500
$1,000

1989 1990 1991 1992 1993

Costs		Performance	
Sales Load	None	1-Year Return (1993)	+15%
Redemption Fee	None	3-Year Return (1991–93)	+103%
Tax Load (Estimated)	2%	5-Year Return (1989–93)	+98%
Annual 12b-1 Fee	0.20%	10-Year Return (1984–93)	+109%
Annual Expense Ratio	0.69%	Worst-Ever Loss (1983-87)	35%
Annual Portfolio Turnover	47%	Stock Market Correlation	46%
5-Year Cost Estimate	5%	Up/Down Market Rank	C – D

Benefits		Investment Information	
Investment Objective	Growth	Telephone	800-662-7447
5-Year Projected Return	+39%	Minimum Investment	$3,000
Safety Rating (0-100)	74%	Telephone Switching	Mail only
Yield	0.3%	Total Assets	$747 million

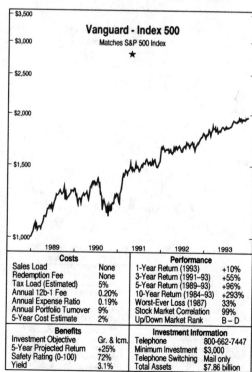

Vanguard - Index 500
Matches S&P 500 Index
★

$3,500
$3,000
$2,500
$2,000
$1,500
$1,000

1989 1990 1991 1992 1993

Costs		Performance	
Sales Load	None	1-Year Return (1993)	+10%
Redemption Fee	None	3-Year Return (1991–93)	+55%
Tax Load (Estimated)	5%	5-Year Return (1989–93)	+96%
Annual 12b-1 Fee	0.20%	10-Year Return (1984–93)	+293%
Annual Expense Ratio	0.19%	Worst-Ever Loss (1987)	33%
Annual Portfolio Turnover	9%	Stock Market Correlation	99%
5-Year Cost Estimate	2%	Up/Down Market Rank	B – D

Benefits		Investment Information	
Investment Objective	Gr. & Icm.	Telephone	800-662-7447
5-Year Projected Return	+25%	Minimum Investment	$3,000
Safety Rating (0-100)	72%	Telephone Switching	Mail only
Yield	3.1%	Total Assets	$7.86 billion

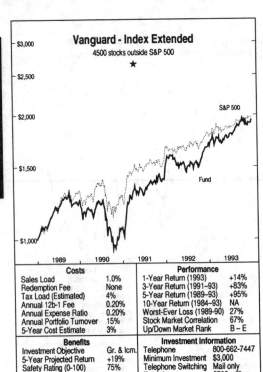

Vanguard - Index Extended
4500 stocks outside S&P 500
★

Costs		Performance	
Sales Load	1.0%	1-Year Return (1993)	+14%
Redemption Fee	None	3-Year Return (1991–93)	+83%
Tax Load (Estimated)	4%	5-Year Return (1989–93)	+95%
Annual 12b-1 Fee	0.20%	10-Year Return (1984–93)	NA
Annual Expense Ratio	0.20%	Worst-Ever Loss (1989-90)	27%
Annual Portfolio Turnover	15%	Stock Market Correlation	67%
5-Year Cost Estimate	3%	Up/Down Market Rank	B – E

Benefits		Investment Information	
Investment Objective	Gr. & Icm.	Telephone	800-662-7447
5-Year Projected Return	+19%	Minimum Investment	$3,000
Safety Rating (0-100)	75%	Telephone Switching	Mail only
Yield	1.2%	Total Assets	$725 million

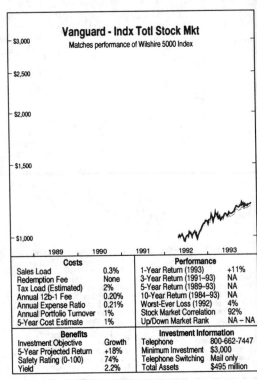

Vanguard - Indx Totl Stock Mkt
Matches performance of Wilshire 5000 Index

Costs		Performance	
Sales Load	0.3%	1-Year Return (1993)	+11%
Redemption Fee	None	3-Year Return (1991–93)	NA
Tax Load (Estimated)	2%	5-Year Return (1989–93)	NA
Annual 12b-1 Fee	0.20%	10-Year Return (1984–93)	NA
Annual Expense Ratio	0.21%	Worst-Ever Loss (1992)	4%
Annual Portfolio Turnover	1%	Stock Market Correlation	92%
5-Year Cost Estimate	1%	Up/Down Market Rank	NA – NA

Benefits		Investment Information	
Investment Objective	Growth	Telephone	800-662-7447
5-Year Projected Return	+18%	Minimum Investment	$3,000
Safety Rating (0-100)	74%	Telephone Switching	Mail only
Yield	2.2%	Total Assets	$495 million

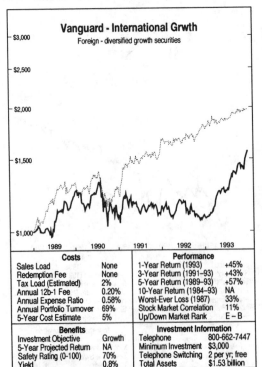

Vanguard - International Grwth
Foreign - diversified growth securities

Costs		Performance	
Sales Load	None	1-Year Return (1993)	+45%
Redemption Fee	None	3-Year Return (1991–93)	+43%
Tax Load (Estimated)	2%	5-Year Return (1989–93)	+57%
Annual 12b-1 Fee	0.20%	10-Year Return (1984–93)	NA
Annual Expense Ratio	0.58%	Worst-Ever Loss (1987)	33%
Annual Portfolio Turnover	69%	Stock Market Correlation	11%
5-Year Cost Estimate	5%	Up/Down Market Rank	E – B

Benefits		Investment Information	
Investment Objective	Growth	Telephone	800-662-7447
5-Year Projected Return	NA	Minimum Investment	$3,000
Safety Rating (0-100)	70%	Telephone Switching	2 per yr; free
Yield	0.8%	Total Assets	$1.53 billion

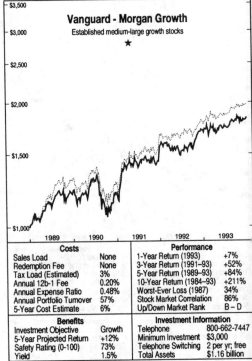

Vanguard - Morgan Growth
Established medium-large growth stocks
★

Costs		Performance	
Sales Load	None	1-Year Return (1993)	+7%
Redemption Fee	None	3-Year Return (1991–93)	+52%
Tax Load (Estimated)	3%	5-Year Return (1989–93)	+84%
Annual 12b-1 Fee	0.20%	10-Year Return (1984–93)	+211%
Annual Expense Ratio	0.48%	Worst-Ever Loss (1987)	34%
Annual Portfolio Turnover	57%	Stock Market Correlation	86%
5-Year Cost Estimate	6%	Up/Down Market Rank	B – D

Benefits		Investment Information	
Investment Objective	Growth	Telephone	800-662-7447
5-Year Projected Return	+12%	Minimum Investment	$3,000
Safety Rating (0-100)	73%	Telephone Switching	2 per yr; free
Yield	1.5%	Total Assets	$1.16 billion

Vanguard - Primecap

Stocks with earnings growth; hi-quality mgmt

★

Costs		Performance	
Sales Load	None	1-Year Return (1993)	+18%
Redemption Fee	None	3-Year Return (1991–93)	+66%
Tax Load (Estimated)	8%	5-Year Return (1989–93)	+96%
Annual 12b-1 Fee	0.20%	10-Year Return (1984–93)	NA
Annual Expense Ratio	0.68%	Worst-Ever Loss (1987)	37%
Annual Portfolio Turnover	18%	Stock Market Correlation	63%
5-Year Cost Estimate	6%	Up/Down Market Rank	A – E

Benefits		Investment Information	
Investment Objective	Growth	Telephone	800-662-7447
5-Year Projected Return	+22%	Minimum Investment	$3,000
Safety Rating (0-100)	71%	Telephone Switching	2 per yr; free
Yield	0.4%	Total Assets	$772 million

Vanguard - Quantitative

Total return greater than S&P 500

★★

Costs		Performance	
Sales Load	None	1-Year Return (1993)	+14%
Redemption Fee	None	3-Year Return (1991–93)	+59%
Tax Load (Estimated)	4%	5-Year Return (1989–93)	+104%
Annual 12b-1 Fee	0.20%	10-Year Return (1984–93)	NA
Annual Expense Ratio	0.40%	Worst-Ever Loss (1987)	33%
Annual Portfolio Turnover	79%	Stock Market Correlation	96%
5-Year Cost Estimate	6%	Up/Down Market Rank	A – D

Benefits		Investment Information	
Investment Objective	Gr. & Icm.	Telephone	800-662-7447
5-Year Projected Return	+17%	Minimum Investment	$3,000
Safety Rating (0-100)	74%	Telephone Switching	Mail only
Yield	2.4%	Total Assets	$490 million

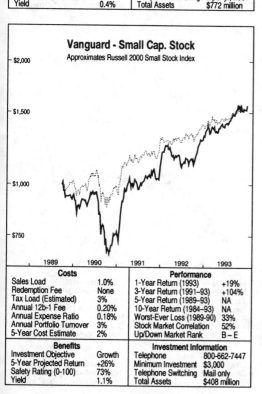

Vanguard - Small Cap. Stock

Approximates Russell 2000 Small Stock Index

Costs		Performance	
Sales Load	1.0%	1-Year Return (1993)	+19%
Redemption Fee	None	3-Year Return (1991–93)	+104%
Tax Load (Estimated)	3%	5-Year Return (1989–93)	NA
Annual 12b-1 Fee	0.20%	10-Year Return (1984–93)	NA
Annual Expense Ratio	0.18%	Worst-Ever Loss (1989-90)	33%
Annual Portfolio Turnover	3%	Stock Market Correlation	52%
5-Year Cost Estimate	2%	Up/Down Market Rank	B – E

Benefits		Investment Information	
Investment Objective	Growth	Telephone	800-662-7447
5-Year Projected Return	+26%	Minimum Investment	$3,000
Safety Rating (0-100)	73%	Telephone Switching	Mail only
Yield	1.1%	Total Assets	$408 million

Vanguard - Star

Combination of 9 Vanguard funds

★★★★

Costs		Performance	
Sales Load	None	1-Year Return (1993)	+11%
Redemption Fee	None	3-Year Return (1991–93)	+52%
Tax Load (Estimated)	2%	5-Year Return (1989–93)	+74%
Annual 12b-1 Fee	0.20%	10-Year Return (1984–93)	NA
Annual Expense Ratio	0.37%	Worst-Ever Loss (1987)	19%
Annual Portfolio Turnover	3%	Stock Market Correlation	85%
5-Year Cost Estimate	2%	Up/Down Market Rank	D – B

Benefits		Investment Information	
Investment Objective	Gr. & Icm.	Telephone	800-662-7447
5-Year Projected Return	+17%	Minimum Investment	$500
Safety Rating (0-100)	84%	Telephone Switching	2 per yr; free
Yield	3.5%	Total Assets	$3.47 billion

EQUITY

Vanguard - Trustees Eqty Intl
Foreign - undervalued stocks

S&P 500

Fund

Costs		Performance	
Sales Load	None	1-Year Return (1993)	+30%
Redemption Fee	None	3-Year Return (1991–93)	+31%
Tax Load (Estimated)	5%	5-Year Return (1989–93)	+43%
Annual 12b-1 Fee	0.20%	10-Year Return (1984–93)	+350%
Annual Expense Ratio	0.42%	Worst-Ever Loss (1990-91)	22%
Annual Portfolio Turnover	49%	Stock Market Correlation	9%
5-Year Cost Estimate	7%	Up/Down Market Rank	E – A

Benefits		Investment Information	
Investment Objective	Gr. & Icm.	Telephone	800-662-7447
5-Year Projected Return	NA	Minimum Investment	$10,000
Safety Rating (0-100)	72%	Telephone Switching	2 per yr; free
Yield	2.6%	Total Assets	$935 million

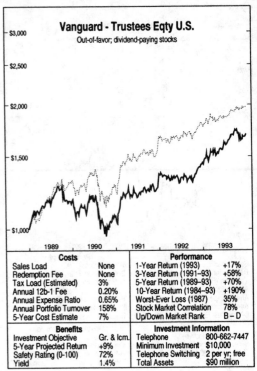

Vanguard - Trustees Eqty U.S.
Out-of-favor; dividend-paying stocks

Costs		Performance	
Sales Load	None	1-Year Return (1993)	+17%
Redemption Fee	None	3-Year Return (1991–93)	+58%
Tax Load (Estimated)	3%	5-Year Return (1989–93)	+70%
Annual 12b-1 Fee	0.20%	10-Year Return (1984–93)	+190%
Annual Expense Ratio	0.65%	Worst-Ever Loss (1987)	35%
Annual Portfolio Turnover	158%	Stock Market Correlation	78%
5-Year Cost Estimate	7%	Up/Down Market Rank	B – D

Benefits		Investment Information	
Investment Objective	Gr. & Icm.	Telephone	800-662-7447
5-Year Projected Return	+9%	Minimum Investment	$10,000
Safety Rating (0-100)	72%	Telephone Switching	2 per yr; free
Yield	1.4%	Total Assets	$90 million

Vanguard - U.S. Growth
Established growth stocks; good fundamentals
★★

Costs		Performance	
Sales Load	None	1-Year Return (1993)	–1%
Redemption Fee	None	3-Year Return (1991–93)	+49%
Tax Load (Estimated)	4%	5-Year Return (1989–93)	+114%
Annual 12b-1 Fee	0.20%	10-Year Return (1984–93)	+231%
Annual Expense Ratio	0.49%	Worst-Ever Loss (1987)	35%
Annual Portfolio Turnover	38%	Stock Market Correlation	76%
5-Year Cost Estimate	5%	Up/Down Market Rank	A – E

Benefits		Investment Information	
Investment Objective	Growth	Telephone	800-662-7447
5-Year Projected Return	+14%	Minimum Investment	$3,000
Safety Rating (0-100)	70%	Telephone Switching	2 per yr; free
Yield	1.4%	Total Assets	$1.93 billion

Vanguard - VSP Energy
Exploratn & prodctn of oil, natrl gas & coal

Costs		Performance	
Sales Load	None	1-Year Return (1993)	+26%
Redemption Fee	1.0%	3-Year Return (1991–93)	+35%
Tax Load (Estimated)	Neg.	5-Year Return (1989–93)	+90%
Annual 12b-1 Fee	0.20%	10-Year Return (1984–93)	NA
Annual Expense Ratio	0.21%	Worst-Ever Loss (1987)	32%
Annual Portfolio Turnover	37%	Stock Market Correlation	21%
5-Year Cost Estimate	1%	Up/Down Market Rank	D – B

Benefits		Investment Information	
Investment Objective	Growth	Telephone	800-662-7447
5-Year Projected Return	NA	Minimum Investment	$3,000
Safety Rating (0-100)	69%	Telephone Switching	2 per yr; free
Yield	1.9%	Total Assets	$267 million

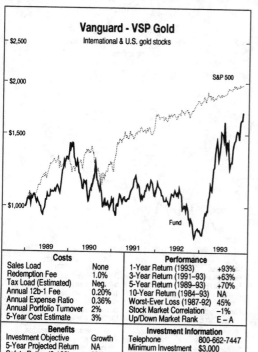

Vanguard - VSP Gold
International & U.S. gold stocks

S&P 500

Fund

Costs		Performance	
Sales Load	None	1-Year Return (1993)	+93%
Redemption Fee	1.0%	3-Year Return (1991–93)	+63%
Tax Load (Estimated)	Neg.	5-Year Return (1989–93)	+70%
Annual 12b-1 Fee	0.20%	10-Year Return (1984–93)	NA
Annual Expense Ratio	0.36%	Worst-Ever Loss (1987-92)	45%
Annual Portfolio Turnover	2%	Stock Market Correlation	–1%
5-Year Cost Estimate	3%	Up/Down Market Rank	E – A

Benefits		Investment Information	
Investment Objective	Growth	Telephone	800-662-7447
5-Year Projected Return	NA	Minimum Investment	$3,000
Safety Rating (0-100)	58%	Telephone Switching	2 per yr; free
Yield	1.5%	Total Assets	$385 million

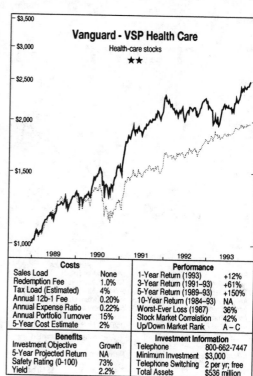

Vanguard - VSP Health Care
Health-care stocks
★★

Costs		Performance	
Sales Load	None	1-Year Return (1993)	+12%
Redemption Fee	1.0%	3-Year Return (1991–93)	+61%
Tax Load (Estimated)	4%	5-Year Return (1989–93)	+150%
Annual 12b-1 Fee	0.20%	10-Year Return (1984–93)	NA
Annual Expense Ratio	0.22%	Worst-Ever Loss (1987)	36%
Annual Portfolio Turnover	15%	Stock Market Correlation	42%
5-Year Cost Estimate	2%	Up/Down Market Rank	A – C

Benefits		Investment Information	
Investment Objective	Growth	Telephone	800-662-7447
5-Year Projected Return	NA	Minimum Investment	$3,000
Safety Rating (0-100)	73%	Telephone Switching	2 per yr; free
Yield	2.2%	Total Assets	$536 million

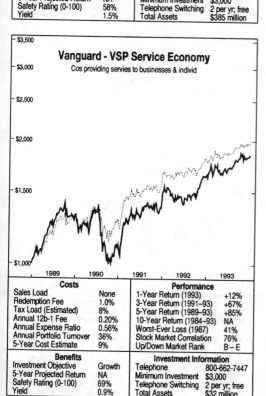

Vanguard - VSP Service Economy
Cos providing servies to businesses & individ

Costs		Performance	
Sales Load	None	1-Year Return (1993)	+12%
Redemption Fee	1.0%	3-Year Return (1991–93)	+67%
Tax Load (Estimated)	8%	5-Year Return (1989–93)	+85%
Annual 12b-1 Fee	0.20%	10-Year Return (1984–93)	NA
Annual Expense Ratio	0.56%	Worst-Ever Loss (1987)	41%
Annual Portfolio Turnover	36%	Stock Market Correlation	76%
5-Year Cost Estimate	9%	Up/Down Market Rank	B – E

Benefits		Investment Information	
Investment Objective	Growth	Telephone	800-662-7447
5-Year Projected Return	NA	Minimum Investment	$3,000
Safety Rating (0-100)	69%	Telephone Switching	2 per yr; free
Yield	0.9%	Total Assets	$32 million

Vanguard - VSP Technology
High growth industries; technology stocks

Costs		Performance	
Sales Load	None	1-Year Return (1993)	+11%
Redemption Fee	1.0%	3-Year Return (1991–93)	+86%
Tax Load (Estimated)	1%	5-Year Return (1989–93)	+99%
Annual 12b-1 Fee	0.20%	10-Year Return (1984–93)	NA
Annual Expense Ratio	0.25%	Worst-Ever Loss (1987)	44%
Annual Portfolio Turnover	65%	Stock Market Correlation	43%
5-Year Cost Estimate	2%	Up/Down Market Rank	B – E

Benefits		Investment Information	
Investment Objective	Growth	Telephone	800-662-7447
5-Year Projected Return	NA	Minimum Investment	$3,000
Safety Rating (0-100)	66%	Telephone Switching	2 per yr; free
Yield	0.7%	Total Assets	$56 million

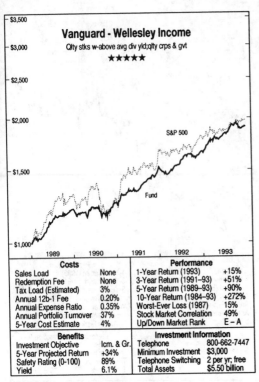

Vanguard - Wellesley Income
Qlty stks w-above avg div yld;qlty crps & gvt
★★★★★

S&P 500

Fund

Costs		Performance	
Sales Load	None	1-Year Return (1993)	+15%
Redemption Fee	None	3-Year Return (1991–93)	+51%
Tax Load (Estimated)	3%	5-Year Return (1989–93)	+90%
Annual 12b-1 Fee	0.20%	10-Year Return (1984–93)	+272%
Annual Expense Ratio	0.35%	Worst-Ever Loss (1987)	15%
Annual Portfolio Turnover	37%	Stock Market Correlation	49%
5-Year Cost Estimate	4%	Up/Down Market Rank	E – A

Benefits		Investment Information	
Investment Objective	Icm. & Gr.	Telephone	800-662-7447
5-Year Projected Return	+34%	Minimum Investment	$3,000
Safety Rating (0-100)	89%	Telephone Switching	2 per yr; free
Yield	6.1%	Total Assets	$5.50 billion

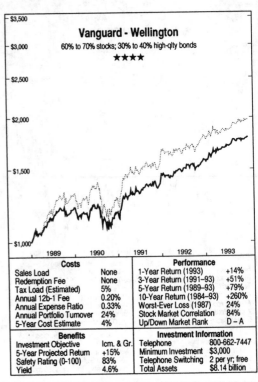

Vanguard - Wellington
60% to 70% stocks; 30% to 40% high-qlty bonds
★★★★

Costs		Performance	
Sales Load	None	1-Year Return (1993)	+14%
Redemption Fee	None	3-Year Return (1991–93)	+51%
Tax Load (Estimated)	5%	5-Year Return (1989–93)	+79%
Annual 12b-1 Fee	0.20%	10-Year Return (1984–93)	+260%
Annual Expense Ratio	0.33%	Worst-Ever Loss (1987)	24%
Annual Portfolio Turnover	24%	Stock Market Correlation	84%
5-Year Cost Estimate	4%	Up/Down Market Rank	D – A

Benefits		Investment Information	
Investment Objective	Icm. & Gr.	Telephone	800-662-7447
5-Year Projected Return	+15%	Minimum Investment	$3,000
Safety Rating (0-100)	83%	Telephone Switching	2 per yr; free
Yield	4.6%	Total Assets	$8.14 billion

Vanguard - Windsor
Undervalued stocks

Costs		Performance	
Sales Load	None	1-Year Return (1993)	+19%
Redemption Fee	None	3-Year Return (1991–93)	+80%
Tax Load (Estimated)	2%	5-Year Return (1989–93)	+75%
Annual 12b-1 Fee	0.20%	10-Year Return (1984–93)	+318%
Annual Expense Ratio	0.26%	Worst-Ever Loss (1989-90)	32%
Annual Portfolio Turnover	22%	Stock Market Correlation	62%
5-Year Cost Estimate	2%	Up/Down Market Rank	B – C

Benefits		Investment Information	
Investment Objective	Gr. & Icm.	Telephone	800-662-7447
5-Year Projected Return	+13%	Minimum Investment	$3,000
Safety Rating (0-100)	73%	Telephone Switching	2 per yr; free
Yield	2.7%	Total Assets	$10.60 billion

Vanguard - Windsor II
Value stks; PE lower than mkt, div yld higher
★

Costs		Performance	
Sales Load	None	1-Year Return (1993)	+14%
Redemption Fee	None	3-Year Return (1991–93)	+64%
Tax Load (Estimated)	3%	5-Year Return (1989–93)	+88%
Annual 12b-1 Fee	0.20%	10-Year Return (1984–93)	NA
Annual Expense Ratio	0.41%	Worst-Ever Loss (1987)	29%
Annual Portfolio Turnover	34%	Stock Market Correlation	85%
5-Year Cost Estimate	4%	Up/Down Market Rank	B – C

Benefits		Investment Information	
Investment Objective	Gr. & Icm.	Telephone	800-662-7447
5-Year Projected Return	+11%	Minimum Investment	$3,000
Safety Rating (0-100)	74%	Telephone Switching	2 per yr; free
Yield	3.0%	Total Assets	$7.26 billion

Venture - New York Venture
Diversified stocks
★★★

Fund

S&P 500

Costs		Performance	
Sales Load	5.0%	1-Year Return (1993)	+16%
Redemption Fee	None	3-Year Return (1991–93)	+83%
Tax Load (Estimated)	8%	5-Year Return (1989–93)	+150%
Annual 12b-1 Fee	0.25%	10-Year Return (1984–93)	+425%
Annual Expense Ratio	0.89%	Worst-Ever Loss (1987)	29%
Annual Portfolio Turnover	24%	Stock Market Correlation	76%
5-Year Cost Estimate	13%	Up/Down Market Rank	A – C
Benefits		**Investment Information**	
Investment Objective	Growth	Telephone	800-279-0279
5-Year Projected Return	+29%	Minimum Investment	$1,000
Safety Rating (0-100)	75%	Telephone Switching	Unlimited; $5
Yield	2.2%	Total Assets	$632 million

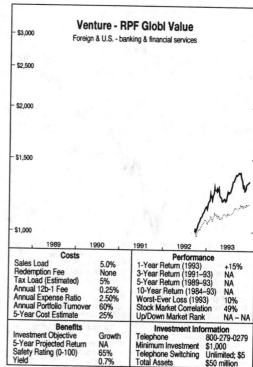

Venture - RPF Globl Value
Foreign & U.S. - banking & financial services

Costs		Performance	
Sales Load	5.0%	1-Year Return (1993)	+15%
Redemption Fee	None	3-Year Return (1991–93)	NA
Tax Load (Estimated)	5%	5-Year Return (1989–93)	NA
Annual 12b-1 Fee	0.25%	10-Year Return (1984–93)	NA
Annual Expense Ratio	2.50%	Worst-Ever Loss (1993)	10%
Annual Portfolio Turnover	60%	Stock Market Correlation	49%
5-Year Cost Estimate	25%	Up/Down Market Rank	NA – NA
Benefits		**Investment Information**	
Investment Objective	Growth	Telephone	800-279-0279
5-Year Projected Return	NA	Minimum Investment	$1,000
Safety Rating (0-100)	65%	Telephone Switching	Unlimited; $5
Yield	0.7%	Total Assets	$50 million

Venture - RPF Growth
Diversified stocks

Costs		Performance	
Sales Load	None	1-Year Return (1993)	+11%
Redemption Fee	4.2%	3-Year Return (1991–93)	+52%
Tax Load (Estimated)	10%	5-Year Return (1989–93)	+104%
Annual 12b-1 Fee	1.00%	10-Year Return (1984–93)	NA
Annual Expense Ratio	2.55%	Worst-Ever Loss (1987)	33%
Annual Portfolio Turnover	24%	Stock Market Correlation	55%
5-Year Cost Estimate	19%	Up/Down Market Rank	B – D
Benefits		**Investment Information**	
Investment Objective	Growth	Telephone	800-279-0279
5-Year Projected Return	+9%	Minimum Investment	$1,000
Safety Rating (0-100)	66%	Telephone Switching	Unlimited; $5
Yield	0.3%	Total Assets	$45 million

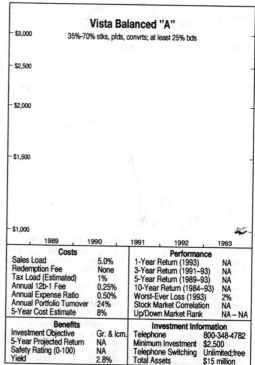

Vista Balanced "A"
35%-70% stks, pfds, convrts; at least 25% bds

Costs		Performance	
Sales Load	5.0%	1-Year Return (1993)	NA
Redemption Fee	None	3-Year Return (1991–93)	NA
Tax Load (Estimated)	1%	5-Year Return (1989–93)	NA
Annual 12b-1 Fee	0.25%	10-Year Return (1984–93)	NA
Annual Expense Ratio	0.50%	Worst-Ever Loss (1993)	2%
Annual Portfolio Turnover	24%	Stock Market Correlation	NA
5-Year Cost Estimate	8%	Up/Down Market Rank	NA – NA
Benefits		**Investment Information**	
Investment Objective	Gr. & Icm.	Telephone	800-348-4782
5-Year Projected Return	NA	Minimum Investment	$2,500
Safety Rating (0-100)	NA	Telephone Switching	Unlimited;free
Yield	2.8%	Total Assets	$15 million

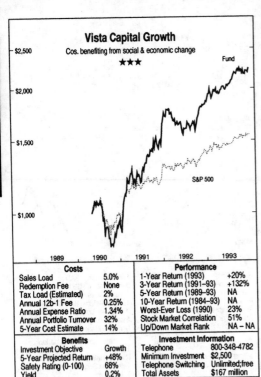

Vista Capital Growth

Cos. benefiting from social & economic change

★★★

Costs		Performance	
Sales Load	5.0%	1-Year Return (1993)	+20%
Redemption Fee	None	3-Year Return (1991–93)	+132%
Tax Load (Estimated)	2%	5-Year Return (1989–93)	NA
Annual 12b-1 Fee	0.25%	10-Year Return (1984–93)	NA
Annual Expense Ratio	1.34%	Worst-Ever Loss (1990)	23%
Annual Portfolio Turnover	32%	Stock Market Correlation	51%
5-Year Cost Estimate	14%	Up/Down Market Rank	NA – NA

Benefits		Investment Information	
Investment Objective	Growth	Telephone	800-348-4782
5-Year Projected Return	+48%	Minimum Investment	$2,500
Safety Rating (0-100)	68%	Telephone Switching	Unlimited;free
Yield	0.2%	Total Assets	$167 million

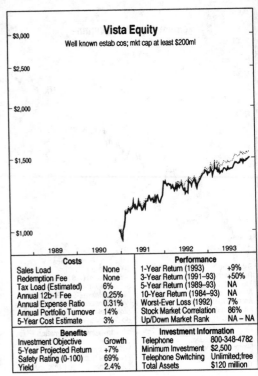

Vista Equity

Well known estab cos; mkt cap at least $200ml

Costs		Performance	
Sales Load	None	1-Year Return (1993)	+9%
Redemption Fee	None	3-Year Return (1991–93)	+50%
Tax Load (Estimated)	6%	5-Year Return (1989–93)	NA
Annual 12b-1 Fee	0.25%	10-Year Return (1984–93)	NA
Annual Expense Ratio	0.31%	Worst-Ever Loss (1992)	7%
Annual Portfolio Turnover	14%	Stock Market Correlation	86%
5-Year Cost Estimate	3%	Up/Down Market Rank	NA – NA

Benefits		Investment Information	
Investment Objective	Growth	Telephone	800-348-4782
5-Year Projected Return	+7%	Minimum Investment	$2,500
Safety Rating (0-100)	69%	Telephone Switching	Unlimited;free
Yield	2.4%	Total Assets	$120 million

Vista Growth & Income "A"

Div-paying out-of-favor stks; small-med cap

★★★

Costs		Performance	
Sales Load	5.0%	1-Year Return (1993)	+13%
Redemption Fee	None	3-Year Return (1991–93)	+107%
Tax Load (Estimated)	2%	5-Year Return (1989–93)	NA
Annual 12b-1 Fee	0.75%	10-Year Return (1984–93)	NA
Annual Expense Ratio	1.40%	Worst-Ever Loss (1990)	19%
Annual Portfolio Turnover	34%	Stock Market Correlation	69%
5-Year Cost Estimate	14%	Up/Down Market Rank	NA – NA

Benefits		Investment Information	
Investment Objective	Gr. & Icm.	Telephone	800-348-4782
5-Year Projected Return	+42%	Minimum Investment	$2,500
Safety Rating (0-100)	73%	Telephone Switching	Unlimited;free
Yield	1.1%	Total Assets	$808 million

Vista Growth Fd Of Washington

Maryland, Virginia, D.C. area stocks

Costs		Performance	
Sales Load	5.0%	1-Year Return (1993)	+13%
Redemption Fee	None	3-Year Return (1991–93)	+67%
Tax Load (Estimated)	10%	5-Year Return (1989–93)	+58%
Annual 12b-1 Fee	0.25%	10-Year Return (1984–93)	NA
Annual Expense Ratio	1.55%	Worst-Ever Loss (1989-90)	33%
Annual Portfolio Turnover	15%	Stock Market Correlation	63%
5-Year Cost Estimate	16%	Up/Down Market Rank	D – C

Benefits		Investment Information	
Investment Objective	Growth	Telephone	800-348-4782
5-Year Projected Return	–3%	Minimum Investment	$2,500
Safety Rating (0-100)	72%	Telephone Switching	Unlimited;free
Yield	0.9%	Total Assets	$40 million

Voyager - Growth Stock
80% common stocks; 20% bonds

(Chart labels: Fund, S&P 500)

Costs		Performance	
Sales Load	5.0%	1-Year Return (1993)	–5%
Redemption Fee	None	3-Year Return (1991–93)	+61%
Tax Load (Estimated)	Neg.	5-Year Return (1989–93)	+93%
Annual 12b-1 Fee	1.00%	10-Year Return (1984–93)	NA
Annual Expense Ratio	1.90%	Worst-Ever Loss (1987)	34%
Annual Portfolio Turnover	17%	Stock Market Correlation	66%
5-Year Cost Estimate	16%	Up/Down Market Rank	A – E

Benefits		Investment Information	
Investment Objective	Growth	Telephone	800-553-2143
5-Year Projected Return	+8%	Minimum Investment	$1,000
Safety Rating (0-100)	70%	Telephone Switching	4 per yr; free
Yield	0.0%	Total Assets	$32 million

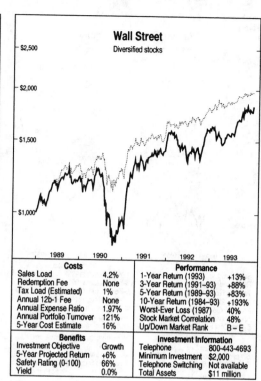

Wall Street
Diversified stocks

Costs		Performance	
Sales Load	4.2%	1-Year Return (1993)	+13%
Redemption Fee	None	3-Year Return (1991–93)	+88%
Tax Load (Estimated)	1%	5-Year Return (1989–93)	+83%
Annual 12b-1 Fee	None	10-Year Return (1984–93)	+193%
Annual Expense Ratio	1.97%	Worst-Ever Loss (1987)	40%
Annual Portfolio Turnover	121%	Stock Market Correlation	48%
5-Year Cost Estimate	16%	Up/Down Market Rank	B – E

Benefits		Investment Information	
Investment Objective	Growth	Telephone	800-443-4693
5-Year Projected Return	+6%	Minimum Investment	$2,000
Safety Rating (0-100)	66%	Telephone Switching	Not available
Yield	0.0%	Total Assets	$11 million

Warburg Pincus Capital Apprec
80% common stocks; 20% corps & preferreds
★

Costs		Performance	
Sales Load	None	1-Year Return (1993)	+16%
Redemption Fee	None	3-Year Return (1991–93)	+57%
Tax Load (Estimated)	3%	5-Year Return (1989–93)	+89%
Annual 12b-1 Fee	None	10-Year Return (1984–93)	NA
Annual Expense Ratio	1.06%	Worst-Ever Loss (1990)	18%
Annual Portfolio Turnover	40%	Stock Market Correlation	75%
5-Year Cost Estimate	7%	Up/Down Market Rank	B – D

Benefits		Investment Information	
Investment Objective	Growth	Telephone	800-888-6878
5-Year Projected Return	+15%	Minimum Investment	$2,500
Safety Rating (0-100)	74%	Telephone Switching	3 per mo; free
Yield	2.2%	Total Assets	$153 million

Warburg Pincus Emerging Growth
Divsf stocks or warrants; emerging growth cos
★

Costs		Performance	
Sales Load	None	1-Year Return (1993)	+18%
Redemption Fee	None	3-Year Return (1991–93)	+107%
Tax Load (Estimated)	1%	5-Year Return (1989–93)	+133%
Annual 12b-1 Fee	None	10-Year Return (1984–93)	NA
Annual Expense Ratio	1.24%	Worst-Ever Loss (1989-90)	24%
Annual Portfolio Turnover	94%	Stock Market Correlation	44%
5-Year Cost Estimate	7%	Up/Down Market Rank	A – D

Benefits		Investment Information	
Investment Objective	Growth	Telephone	800-888-6878
5-Year Projected Return	+38%	Minimum Investment	$2,500
Safety Rating (0-100)	69%	Telephone Switching	3 per mo; free
Yield	1.1%	Total Assets	$150 million

EQUITY

Warburg Pincus Intl Equity
Foreign - financially strong companies
★★

Costs		Performance	
Sales Load	None	1-Year Return (1993)	+51%
Redemption Fee	None	3-Year Return (1991–93)	+74%
Tax Load (Estimated)	2%	5-Year Return (1989–93)	NA
Annual 12b-1 Fee	None	10-Year Return (1984–93)	NA
Annual Expense Ratio	1.49%	Worst-Ever Loss (1990)	19%
Annual Portfolio Turnover	33%	Stock Market Correlation	13%
5-Year Cost Estimate	9%	Up/Down Market Rank	D – A

Benefits		Investment Information	
Investment Objective	Growth	Telephone	800-888-6878
5-Year Projected Return	NA	Minimum Investment	$2,500
Safety Rating (0-100)	75%	Telephone Switching	3 per mo; free
Yield	0.4%	Total Assets	$315 million

Weiss Peck Greer - Growth
Lesser known; emerging growth stocks

Costs		Performance	
Sales Load	None	1-Year Return (1993)	+15%
Redemption Fee	None	3-Year Return (1991–93)	+91%
Tax Load (Estimated)	2%	5-Year Return (1989–93)	+109%
Annual 12b-1 Fee	None	10-Year Return (1984–93)	NA
Annual Expense Ratio	0.96%	Worst-Ever Loss (1987)	42%
Annual Portfolio Turnover	93%	Stock Market Correlation	50%
5-Year Cost Estimate	8%	Up/Down Market Rank	A – E

Benefits		Investment Information	
Investment Objective	Growth	Telephone	800-223-3332
5-Year Projected Return	+24%	Minimum Investment	$2,500
Safety Rating (0-100)	65%	Telephone Switching	6 per yr; free
Yield	0.0%	Total Assets	$166 million

Weiss Peck Greer - Grwth & Icm
75% stocks, 25% debt securities
★

Costs		Performance	
Sales Load	None	1-Year Return (1993)	+10%
Redemption Fee	None	3-Year Return (1991–93)	+75%
Tax Load (Estimated)	4%	5-Year Return (1989–93)	+105%
Annual 12b-1 Fee	None	10-Year Return (1984–93)	+242%
Annual Expense Ratio	1.36%	Worst-Ever Loss (1987)	35%
Annual Portfolio Turnover	90%	Stock Market Correlation	75%
5-Year Cost Estimate	12%	Up/Down Market Rank	A – D

Benefits		Investment Information	
Investment Objective	Gr. & Icm.	Telephone	800-223-3332
5-Year Projected Return	+17%	Minimum Investment	$2,500
Safety Rating (0-100)	71%	Telephone Switching	6 per yr; free
Yield	3.9%	Total Assets	$60 million

Weiss Peck Greer - Tudor
Small-med stks with steady erngs;50% spcl sit

Costs		Performance	
Sales Load	None	1-Year Return (1993)	+11%
Redemption Fee	None	3-Year Return (1991–93)	+70%
Tax Load (Estimated)	5%	5-Year Return (1989–93)	+101%
Annual 12b-1 Fee	None	10-Year Return (1984–93)	+232%
Annual Expense Ratio	1.23%	Worst-Ever Loss (1987)	42%
Annual Portfolio Turnover	124%	Stock Market Correlation	49%
5-Year Cost Estimate	12%	Up/Down Market Rank	A – E

Benefits		Investment Information	
Investment Objective	Growth	Telephone	800-223-3332
5-Year Projected Return	+19%	Minimum Investment	$2,500
Safety Rating (0-100)	66%	Telephone Switching	6 per yr; free
Yield	0.0%	Total Assets	$267 million

Westcore Basic Value
Low PE, 10-year EPS growth

S&P 500

Fund

| | 1989 | 1990 | 1991 | 1992 | 1993 |

Costs		Performance	
Sales Load	None	1-Year Return (1993)	+5%
Redemption Fee	None	3-Year Return (1991–93)	+50%
Tax Load (Estimated)	5%	5-Year Return (1989–93)	+58%
Annual 12b-1 Fee	None	10-Year Return (1984–93)	NA
Annual Expense Ratio	0.96%	Worst-Ever Loss (1989-90)	27%
Annual Portfolio Turnover	37%	Stock Market Correlation	83%
5-Year Cost Estimate	8%	Up/Down Market Rank	D – D

Benefits		Investment Information	
Investment Objective	Gr. & Icm.	Telephone	800-392-2673
5-Year Projected Return	–4%	Minimum Investment	$1,000
Safety Rating (0-100)	72%	Telephone Switching	Unlimited;free
Yield	2.2%	Total Assets	$100 million

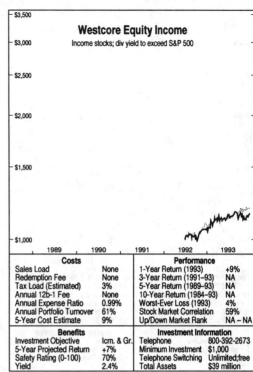

Westcore Equity Income
Income stocks; div yield to exceed S&P 500

| | 1989 | 1990 | 1991 | 1992 | 1993 |

Costs		Performance	
Sales Load	None	1-Year Return (1993)	+9%
Redemption Fee	None	3-Year Return (1991–93)	NA
Tax Load (Estimated)	3%	5-Year Return (1989–93)	NA
Annual 12b-1 Fee	None	10-Year Return (1984–93)	NA
Annual Expense Ratio	0.99%	Worst-Ever Loss (1993)	4%
Annual Portfolio Turnover	61%	Stock Market Correlation	59%
5-Year Cost Estimate	9%	Up/Down Market Rank	NA – NA

Benefits		Investment Information	
Investment Objective	Icm. & Gr.	Telephone	800-392-2673
5-Year Projected Return	+7%	Minimum Investment	$1,000
Safety Rating (0-100)	70%	Telephone Switching	Unlimited;free
Yield	2.4%	Total Assets	$39 million

Westcore Midco Growth
Medium-sized growth stocks
★★

| | 1989 | 1990 | 1991 | 1992 | 1993 |

Costs		Performance	
Sales Load	None	1-Year Return (1993)	+17%
Redemption Fee	None	3-Year Return (1991–93)	+109%
Tax Load (Estimated)	5%	5-Year Return (1989–93)	+182%
Annual 12b-1 Fee	None	10-Year Return (1984–93)	NA
Annual Expense Ratio	0.83%	Worst-Ever Loss (1990)	25%
Annual Portfolio Turnover	56%	Stock Market Correlation	62%
5-Year Cost Estimate	10%	Up/Down Market Rank	A – E

Benefits		Investment Information	
Investment Objective	Growth	Telephone	800-392-2673
5-Year Projected Return	+57%	Minimum Investment	$1,000
Safety Rating (0-100)	68%	Telephone Switching	Unlimited;free
Yield	0.0%	Total Assets	$271 million

Westcore Modern Value Equity
Undervalued; large dividend-paying stocks

| | 1989 | 1990 | 1991 | 1992 | 1993 |

Costs		Performance	
Sales Load	4.7%	1-Year Return (1993)	+12%
Redemption Fee	None	3-Year Return (1991–93)	+54%
Tax Load (Estimated)	3%	5-Year Return (1989–93)	+85%
Annual 12b-1 Fee	None	10-Year Return (1984–93)	NA
Annual Expense Ratio	0.99%	Worst-Ever Loss (1990)	22%
Annual Portfolio Turnover	86%	Stock Market Correlation	83%
5-Year Cost Estimate	14%	Up/Down Market Rank	B – D

Benefits		Investment Information	
Investment Objective	Gr. & Icm.	Telephone	800-392-2673
5-Year Projected Return	+9%	Minimum Investment	$1,000
Safety Rating (0-100)	72%	Telephone Switching	Unlimited;free
Yield	3.2%	Total Assets	$31 million

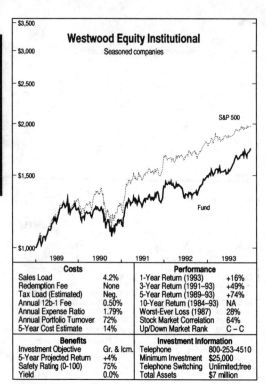

Westwood Equity Institutional
Seasoned companies

S&P 500

Fund

Costs		Performance	
Sales Load	4.2%	1-Year Return (1993)	+16%
Redemption Fee	None	3-Year Return (1991–93)	+49%
Tax Load (Estimated)	Neg.	5-Year Return (1989–93)	+74%
Annual 12b-1 Fee	0.50%	10-Year Return (1984–93)	NA
Annual Expense Ratio	1.79%	Worst-Ever Loss (1987)	28%
Annual Portfolio Turnover	72%	Stock Market Correlation	64%
5-Year Cost Estimate	14%	Up/Down Market Rank	C – C

Benefits		Investment Information	
Investment Objective	Gr. & Icm.	Telephone	800-253-4510
5-Year Projected Return	+4%	Minimum Investment	$25,000
Safety Rating (0-100)	75%	Telephone Switching	Unlimited;free
Yield	0.0%	Total Assets	$7 million

William Blair Growth Shares
Diversified growth stocks
★★★

Costs		Performance	
Sales Load	None	1-Year Return (1993)	+16%
Redemption Fee	None	3-Year Return (1991–93)	+79%
Tax Load (Estimated)	6%	5-Year Return (1989–93)	+129%
Annual 12b-1 Fee	None	10-Year Return (1984–93)	+244%
Annual Expense Ratio	0.83%	Worst-Ever Loss (1987)	30%
Annual Portfolio Turnover	80%	Stock Market Correlation	59%
5-Year Cost Estimate	11%	Up/Down Market Rank	B – D

Benefits		Investment Information	
Investment Objective	Gr. & Icm.	Telephone	800-742-7272
5-Year Projected Return	+33%	Minimum Investment	$1,000
Safety Rating (0-100)	74%	Telephone Switching	4 per yr; free
Yield	0.4%	Total Assets	$134 million

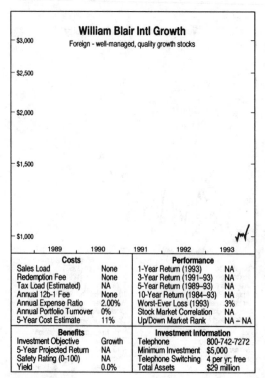

William Blair Intl Growth
Foreign - well-managed, quality growth stocks

Costs		Performance	
Sales Load	None	1-Year Return (1993)	NA
Redemption Fee	None	3-Year Return (1991–93)	NA
Tax Load (Estimated)	NA	5-Year Return (1989–93)	NA
Annual 12b-1 Fee	None	10-Year Return (1984–93)	NA
Annual Expense Ratio	2.00%	Worst-Ever Loss (1993)	3%
Annual Portfolio Turnover	0%	Stock Market Correlation	NA
5-Year Cost Estimate	11%	Up/Down Market Rank	NA – NA

Benefits		Investment Information	
Investment Objective	Growth	Telephone	800-742-7272
5-Year Projected Return	NA	Minimum Investment	$5,000
Safety Rating (0-100)	NA	Telephone Switching	4 per yr; free
Yield	0.0%	Total Assets	$29 million

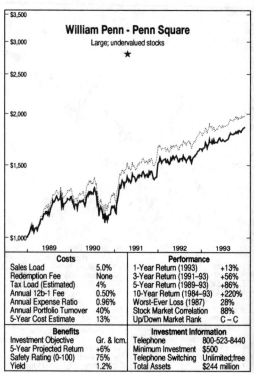

William Penn - Penn Square
Large; undervalued stocks
★

Costs		Performance	
Sales Load	5.0%	1-Year Return (1993)	+13%
Redemption Fee	None	3-Year Return (1991–93)	+56%
Tax Load (Estimated)	4%	5-Year Return (1989–93)	+86%
Annual 12b-1 Fee	0.50%	10-Year Return (1984–93)	+220%
Annual Expense Ratio	0.96%	Worst-Ever Loss (1987)	28%
Annual Portfolio Turnover	40%	Stock Market Correlation	88%
5-Year Cost Estimate	13%	Up/Down Market Rank	C – C

Benefits		Investment Information	
Investment Objective	Gr. & Icm.	Telephone	800-523-8440
5-Year Projected Return	+6%	Minimum Investment	$500
Safety Rating (0-100)	75%	Telephone Switching	Unlimited;free
Yield	1.2%	Total Assets	$244 million

Wood Strut - Winthrop Agg Grth
Small; undervalued stocks
★★

Fund
S&P 500

Costs		Performance	
Sales Load	None	1-Year Return (1993)	+22%
Redemption Fee	4.2%	3-Year Return (1991–93)	+117%
Tax Load (Estimated)	0%	5-Year Return (1989–93)	+119%
Annual 12b-1 Fee	0.50%	10-Year Return (1984–93)	+251%
Annual Expense Ratio	1.50%	Worst-Ever Loss (1987)	39%
Annual Portfolio Turnover	186%	Stock Market Correlation	56%
5-Year Cost Estimate	8%	Up/Down Market Rank	B – E

Benefits		Investment Information	
Investment Objective	Growth	Telephone	800-225-8011
5-Year Projected Return	+46%	Minimum Investment	$1,000
Safety Rating (0-100)	77%	Telephone Switching	Unlimited;free
Yield	0.2%	Total Assets	$69 million

Wood Strut - Winthrop Growth
At least 65% diversified growth stocks

Costs		Performance	
Sales Load	None	1-Year Return (1993)	+14%
Redemption Fee	4.2%	3-Year Return (1991–93)	+49%
Tax Load (Estimated)	0%	5-Year Return (1989–93)	+74%
Annual 12b-1 Fee	0.50%	10-Year Return (1984–93)	+162%
Annual Expense Ratio	1.26%	Worst-Ever Loss (1987)	34%
Annual Portfolio Turnover	74%	Stock Market Correlation	79%
5-Year Cost Estimate	7%	Up/Down Market Rank	D – D

Benefits		Investment Information	
Investment Objective	Growth	Telephone	800-225-8011
5-Year Projected Return	+3%	Minimum Investment	$1,000
Safety Rating (0-100)	71%	Telephone Switching	Unlimited;free
Yield	0.5%	Total Assets	$50 million

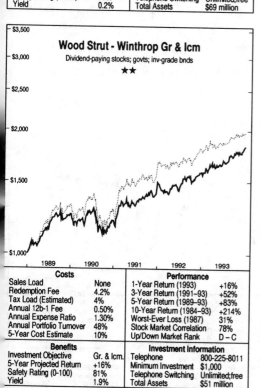

Wood Strut - Winthrop Gr & Icm
Dividend-paying stocks; govts; inv-grade bnds
★★

Costs		Performance	
Sales Load	None	1-Year Return (1993)	+16%
Redemption Fee	4.2%	3-Year Return (1991–93)	+52%
Tax Load (Estimated)	4%	5-Year Return (1989–93)	+83%
Annual 12b-1 Fee	0.50%	10-Year Return (1984–93)	+214%
Annual Expense Ratio	1.30%	Worst-Ever Loss (1987)	31%
Annual Portfolio Turnover	48%	Stock Market Correlation	78%
5-Year Cost Estimate	10%	Up/Down Market Rank	D – C

Benefits		Investment Information	
Investment Objective	Gr. & Icm.	Telephone	800-225-8011
5-Year Projected Return	+16%	Minimum Investment	$1,000
Safety Rating (0-100)	81%	Telephone Switching	Unlimited;free
Yield	1.9%	Total Assets	$51 million

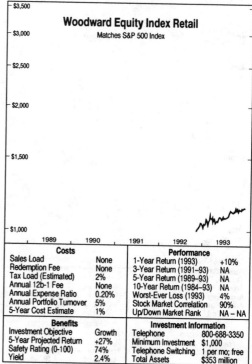

Woodward Equity Index Retail
Matches S&P 500 Index

Costs		Performance	
Sales Load	None	1-Year Return (1993)	+10%
Redemption Fee	None	3-Year Return (1991–93)	NA
Tax Load (Estimated)	2%	5-Year Return (1989–93)	NA
Annual 12b-1 Fee	None	10-Year Return (1984–93)	NA
Annual Expense Ratio	0.20%	Worst-Ever Loss (1993)	4%
Annual Portfolio Turnover	5%	Stock Market Correlation	90%
5-Year Cost Estimate	1%	Up/Down Market Rank	NA – NA

Benefits		Investment Information	
Investment Objective	Growth	Telephone	800-688-3350
5-Year Projected Return	+27%	Minimum Investment	$1,000
Safety Rating (0-100)	74%	Telephone Switching	1 per mo; free
Yield	2.4%	Total Assets	$353 million

World - Vontobel EuroPacific
Foreign - diversified stocks

(Chart: S&P 500 and Fund, $1,000–$3,000 scale, 1989–1993)

Costs		Performance	
Sales Load	None	1-Year Return (1993)	+41%
Redemption Fee	None	3-Year Return (1991–93)	+63%
Tax Load (Estimated)	2%	5-Year Return (1989–93)	+58%
Annual 12b-1 Fee	None	10-Year Return (1984–93)	NA
Annual Expense Ratio	1.98%	Worst-Ever Loss (1987)	26%
Annual Portfolio Turnover	13%	Stock Market Correlation	15%
5-Year Cost Estimate	11%	Up/Down Market Rank	E – A

Benefits		Investment Information	
Investment Objective	Growth	Telephone	800-527-9500
5-Year Projected Return	NA	Minimum Investment	$1,000
Safety Rating (0-100)	74%	Telephone Switching	Not available
Yield	0.0%	Total Assets	$101 million

Worldwide Value
Foreign & U.S. - stocks

(Chart: $1,000–$2,500 scale, 1989–1993)

Costs		Performance	
Sales Load	None	1-Year Return (1993)	+39%
Redemption Fee	None	3-Year Return (1991–93)	+40%
Tax Load (Estimated)	Neg.	5-Year Return (1989–93)	+25%
Annual 12b-1 Fee	None	10-Year Return (1984–93)	NA
Annual Expense Ratio	2.20%	Worst-Ever Loss (1986-87)	43%
Annual Portfolio Turnover	148%	Stock Market Correlation	4%
5-Year Cost Estimate	14%	Up/Down Market Rank	D – B

Benefits		Investment Information	
Investment Objective	Growth	Telephone	800-368-2558
5-Year Projected Return	NA	Minimum Investment	None
Safety Rating (0-100)	61%	Telephone Switching	Via broker
Yield	0.6%	Total Assets	$45 million

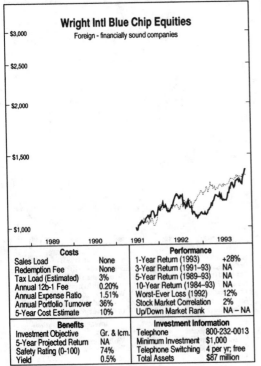

Wright Intl Blue Chip Equities
Foreign - financially sound companies

(Chart: $1,000–$3,000 scale, 1989–1993)

Costs		Performance	
Sales Load	None	1-Year Return (1993)	+28%
Redemption Fee	None	3-Year Return (1991–93)	NA
Tax Load (Estimated)	3%	5-Year Return (1989–93)	NA
Annual 12b-1 Fee	0.20%	10-Year Return (1984–93)	NA
Annual Expense Ratio	1.51%	Worst-Ever Loss (1992)	12%
Annual Portfolio Turnover	36%	Stock Market Correlation	2%
5-Year Cost Estimate	10%	Up/Down Market Rank	NA – NA

Benefits		Investment Information	
Investment Objective	Gr. & Icm.	Telephone	800-232-0013
5-Year Projected Return	NA	Minimum Investment	$1,000
Safety Rating (0-100)	74%	Telephone Switching	4 per yr; free
Yield	0.5%	Total Assets	$87 million

Wright Junior Blue Chip
Rapid growth; $25-$300 million market cap

(Chart: $750–$2,500 scale, 1989–1993)

Costs		Performance	
Sales Load	None	1-Year Return (1993)	+8%
Redemption Fee	None	3-Year Return (1991–93)	+53%
Tax Load (Estimated)	4%	5-Year Return (1989–93)	NA
Annual 12b-1 Fee	0.20%	10-Year Return (1984–93)	NA
Annual Expense Ratio	1.07%	Worst-Ever Loss (1990)	27%
Annual Portfolio Turnover	58%	Stock Market Correlation	52%
5-Year Cost Estimate	10%	Up/Down Market Rank	B – NA

Benefits		Investment Information	
Investment Objective	Gr. & Icm.	Telephone	800-232-0013
5-Year Projected Return	+5%	Minimum Investment	$1,000
Safety Rating (0-100)	70%	Telephone Switching	Unlimited;free
Yield	0.5%	Total Assets	$68 million

Wright Quality Core Equities
300 high-quality, established profitable cos
★

Costs		Performance	
Sales Load	None	1-Year Return (1993)	+1%
Redemption Fee	None	3-Year Return (1991–93)	+52%
Tax Load (Estimated)	5%	5-Year Return (1989–93)	NA
Annual 12b-1 Fee	0.20%	10-Year Return (1984–93)	NA
Annual Expense Ratio	1.01%	Worst-Ever Loss (1990)	22%
Annual Portfolio Turnover	76%	Stock Market Correlation	84%
5-Year Cost Estimate	10%	Up/Down Market Rank	B – NA

Benefits		Investment Information	
Investment Objective	Gr. & Icm.	Telephone	800-232-0013
5-Year Projected Return	+10%	Minimum Investment	$1,000
Safety Rating (0-100)	72%	Telephone Switching	Unlimited;free
Yield	1.3%	Total Assets	$84 million

Wright Selectd Blue Chip Eqtys
Well established, high-quality companies
★

Costs		Performance	
Sales Load	None	1-Year Return (1993)	+2%
Redemption Fee	None	3-Year Return (1991–93)	+45%
Tax Load (Estimated)	3%	5-Year Return (1989–93)	NA
Annual 12b-1 Fee	0.20%	10-Year Return (1984–93)	NA
Annual Expense Ratio	1.02%	Worst-Ever Loss (1990)	18%
Annual Portfolio Turnover	24%	Stock Market Correlation	79%
5-Year Cost Estimate	7%	Up/Down Market Rank	C – NA

Benefits		Investment Information	
Investment Objective	Gr. & Icm.	Telephone	800-232-0013
5-Year Projected Return	+7%	Minimum Investment	$1,000
Safety Rating (0-100)	73%	Telephone Switching	Unlimited;free
Yield	1.1%	Total Assets	$171 million

Yamaichi Global
Foreign & U.S. - diversified stocks

Costs		Performance	
Sales Load	5.0%	1-Year Return (1993)	+34%
Redemption Fee	None	3-Year Return (1991–93)	+49%
Tax Load (Estimated)	Neg.	5-Year Return (1989–93)	+37%
Annual 12b-1 Fee	0.40%	10-Year Return (1984–93)	NA
Annual Expense Ratio	1.94%	Worst-Ever Loss (1989-90)	25%
Annual Portfolio Turnover	58%	Stock Market Correlation	34%
5-Year Cost Estimate	16%	Up/Down Market Rank	E – B

Benefits		Investment Information	
Investment Objective	Growth	Telephone	800-327-6143
5-Year Projected Return	NA	Minimum Investment	$2,500
Safety Rating (0-100)	69%	Telephone Switching	Unlimited;free
Yield	1.0%	Total Assets	$37 million

Z-Seven
Growth stocks; long term

Costs		Performance	
Sales Load	None	1-Year Return (1993)	+11%
Redemption Fee	None	3-Year Return (1991–93)	+51%
Tax Load (Estimated)	4%	5-Year Return (1989–93)	+24%
Annual 12b-1 Fee	None	10-Year Return (1984–93)	NA
Annual Expense Ratio	2.35%	Worst-Ever Loss (1987-90)	55%
Annual Portfolio Turnover	31%	Stock Market Correlation	3%
5-Year Cost Estimate	18%	Up/Down Market Rank	E – C

Benefits		Investment Information	
Investment Objective	Growth	Telephone	602-897-6214
5-Year Projected Return	+2%	Minimum Investment	None
Safety Rating (0-100)	50%	Telephone Switching	Via broker
Yield	1.0%	Total Assets	$25 million

Zweig
Blue chip stocks; hedging
★

Fund

S&P 500

Costs		Performance	
Sales Load	None	1-Year Return (1993)	+16%
Redemption Fee	None	3-Year Return (1991–93)	+60%
Tax Load (Estimated)	9%	5-Year Return (1989–93)	+111%
Annual 12b-1 Fee	None	10-Year Return (1984–93)	NA
Annual Expense Ratio	1.25%	Worst-Ever Loss (1987)	18%
Annual Portfolio Turnover	144%	Stock Market Correlation	16%
5-Year Cost Estimate	19%	Up/Down Market Rank	C – B

Benefits		Investment Information	
Investment Objective	Growth	Telephone	800-272-2700
5-Year Projected Return	+17%	Minimum Investment	None
Safety Rating (0-100)	72%	Telephone Switching	Via broker
Yield	6.4%	Total Assets	$506 million

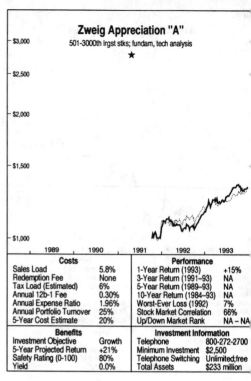

Zweig Appreciation "A"
501-3000th lrgst stks; fundam, tech analysis
★

Costs		Performance	
Sales Load	5.8%	1-Year Return (1993)	+15%
Redemption Fee	None	3-Year Return (1991–93)	NA
Tax Load (Estimated)	6%	5-Year Return (1989–93)	NA
Annual 12b-1 Fee	0.30%	10-Year Return (1984–93)	NA
Annual Expense Ratio	1.96%	Worst-Ever Loss (1992)	7%
Annual Portfolio Turnover	25%	Stock Market Correlation	66%
5-Year Cost Estimate	20%	Up/Down Market Rank	NA – NA

Benefits		Investment Information	
Investment Objective	Growth	Telephone	800-272-2700
5-Year Projected Return	+21%	Minimum Investment	$2,500
Safety Rating (0-100)	80%	Telephone Switching	Unlimited;free
Yield	0.0%	Total Assets	$233 million

Zweig Priority Selection "A"
6-12 months growth prospects
★

Costs		Performance	
Sales Load	5.8%	1-Year Return (1993)	+14%
Redemption Fee	None	3-Year Return (1991–93)	+48%
Tax Load (Estimated)	0%	5-Year Return (1989–93)	+97%
Annual 12b-1 Fee	0.30%	10-Year Return (1984–93)	NA
Annual Expense Ratio	1.65%	Worst-Ever Loss (1990)	16%
Annual Portfolio Turnover	161%	Stock Market Correlation	77%
5-Year Cost Estimate	15%	Up/Down Market Rank	C – B

Benefits		Investment Information	
Investment Objective	Growth	Telephone	800-272-2700
5-Year Projected Return	+6%	Minimum Investment	$1,000
Safety Rating (0-100)	74%	Telephone Switching	Unlimited;free
Yield	0.0%	Total Assets	$60 million

Zweig Strategy "A"
Blue chips selected with model; mkt timing
★★

Costs		Performance	
Sales Load	5.8%	1-Year Return (1993)	+15%
Redemption Fee	None	3-Year Return (1991–93)	+53%
Tax Load (Estimated)	Neg.	5-Year Return (1989–93)	NA
Annual 12b-1 Fee	0.30%	10-Year Return (1984–93)	NA
Annual Expense Ratio	1.63%	Worst-Ever Loss (1990)	9%
Annual Portfolio Turnover	200%	Stock Market Correlation	67%
5-Year Cost Estimate	15%	Up/Down Market Rank	D – NA

Benefits		Investment Information	
Investment Objective	Growth	Telephone	800-272-2700
5-Year Projected Return	+15%	Minimum Investment	$1,000
Safety Rating (0-100)	81%	Telephone Switching	Unlimited;free
Yield	0.7%	Total Assets	$540 million

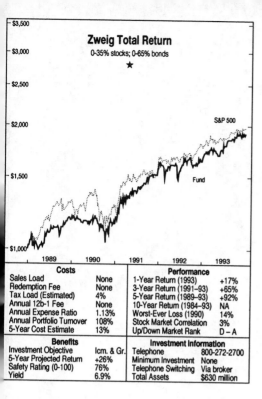

Zweig Total Return
0-35% stocks; 0-65% bonds
★

S&P 500

Fund

$3,500		
$3,000		
$2,500		
$2,000		
$1,500		
$1,000		

1989 1990 1991 1992 1993

Costs		Performance	
Sales Load	None	1-Year Return (1993)	+17%
Redemption Fee	None	3-Year Return (1991–93)	+65%
Tax Load (Estimated)	4%	5-Year Return (1989–93)	+92%
Annual 12b-1 Fee	None	10-Year Return (1984–93)	NA
Annual Expense Ratio	1.13%	Worst-Ever Loss (1990)	14%
Annual Portfolio Turnover	108%	Stock Market Correlation	3%
5-Year Cost Estimate	13%	Up/Down Market Rank	D – A

Benefits		Investment Information	
Investment Objective	Icm. & Gr.	Telephone	800-272-2700
5-Year Projected Return	+26%	Minimum Investment	None
Safety Rating (0-100)	76%	Telephone Switching	Via broker
Yield	6.9%	Total Assets	$630 million

EQUITY

Chapter Nine

The Buyer's Guide to Bond Funds

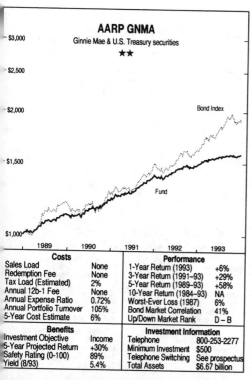

AARP GNMA
Ginnie Mae & U.S. Treasury securities
★★

Bond Index

Fund

Costs		Performance	
Sales Load	None	1-Year Return (1993)	+6%
Redemption Fee	None	3-Year Return (1991–93)	+29%
Tax Load (Estimated)	2%	5-Year Return (1989–93)	+58%
Annual 12b-1 Fee	None	10-Year Return (1984–93)	NA
Annual Expense Ratio	0.72%	Worst-Ever Loss (1987)	6%
Annual Portfolio Turnover	105%	Bond Market Correlation	41%
5-Year Cost Estimate	6%	Up/Down Market Rank	D – B

Benefits		Investment Information	
Investment Objective	Income	Telephone	800-253-2277
5-Year Projected Return	+30%	Minimum Investment	$500
Safety Rating (0-100)	89%	Telephone Switching	See prospectus
Yield (8/93)	5.4%	Total Assets	$6.67 billion

AARP High Quality Bond
Corporate and government bonds
★

Costs		Performance	
Sales Load	None	1-Year Return (1993)	+11%
Redemption Fee	None	3-Year Return (1991–93)	+36%
Tax Load (Estimated)	3%	5-Year Return (1989–93)	+65%
Annual 12b-1 Fee	None	10-Year Return (1984–93)	NA
Annual Expense Ratio	1.15%	Worst-Ever Loss (1987)	9%
Annual Portfolio Turnover	101%	Bond Market Correlation	67%
5-Year Cost Estimate	9%	Up/Down Market Rank	B – D

Benefits		Investment Information	
Investment Objective	Income	Telephone	800-253-2277
5-Year Projected Return	+27%	Minimum Investment	$500
Safety Rating (0-100)	86%	Telephone Switching	See prospectus
Yield (12/93)	4.9%	Total Assets	$589 million

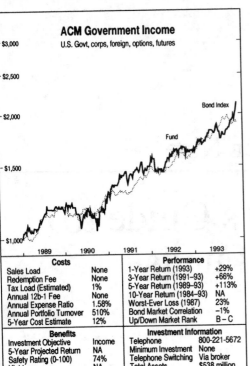

ACM Government Income
U.S. Govt, corps, foreign, options, futures

Costs		Performance	
Sales Load	None	1-Year Return (1993)	+29%
Redemption Fee	None	3-Year Return (1991–93)	+66%
Tax Load (Estimated)	1%	5-Year Return (1989–93)	+113%
Annual 12b-1 Fee	None	10-Year Return (1984–93)	NA
Annual Expense Ratio	1.58%	Worst-Ever Loss (1987)	23%
Annual Portfolio Turnover	510%	Bond Market Correlation	–1%
5-Year Cost Estimate	12%	Up/Down Market Rank	B – C

Benefits		Investment Information	
Investment Objective	Income	Telephone	800-221-5672
5-Year Projected Return	NA	Minimum Investment	None
Safety Rating (0-100)	74%	Telephone Switching	Via broker
Yield	NA	Total Assets	$538 million

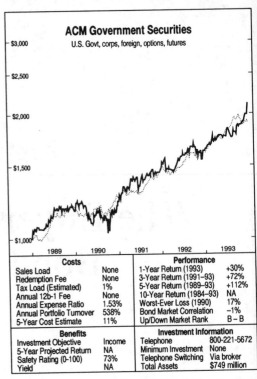

ACM Government Securities
U.S. Govt, corps, foreign, options, futures

Costs		Performance	
Sales Load	None	1-Year Return (1993)	+30%
Redemption Fee	None	3-Year Return (1991–93)	+72%
Tax Load (Estimated)	1%	5-Year Return (1989–93)	+112%
Annual 12b-1 Fee	None	10-Year Return (1984–93)	NA
Annual Expense Ratio	1.53%	Worst-Ever Loss (1990)	17%
Annual Portfolio Turnover	538%	Bond Market Correlation	–1%
5-Year Cost Estimate	11%	Up/Down Market Rank	B – B

Benefits		Investment Information	
Investment Objective	Income	Telephone	800-221-5672
5-Year Projected Return	NA	Minimum Investment	None
Safety Rating (0-100)	73%	Telephone Switching	Via broker
Yield	NA	Total Assets	$749 million

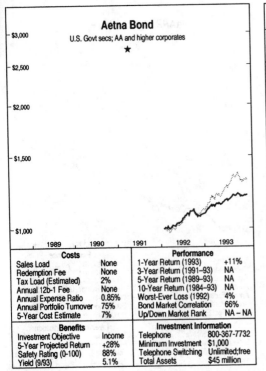

Aetna Bond
U.S. Govt secs; AA and higher corporates
★

Costs		Performance	
Sales Load	None	1-Year Return (1993)	+11%
Redemption Fee	None	3-Year Return (1991–93)	NA
Tax Load (Estimated)	2%	5-Year Return (1989–93)	NA
Annual 12b-1 Fee	None	10-Year Return (1984–93)	NA
Annual Expense Ratio	0.85%	Worst-Ever Loss (1992)	4%
Annual Portfolio Turnover	75%	Bond Market Correlation	66%
5-Year Cost Estimate	7%	Up/Down Market Rank	NA – NA

Benefits		Investment Information	
Investment Objective	Income	Telephone	800-367-7732
5-Year Projected Return	+28%	Minimum Investment	$1,000
Safety Rating (0-100)	88%	Telephone Switching	Unlimited;free
Yield (9/93)	5.1%	Total Assets	$45 million

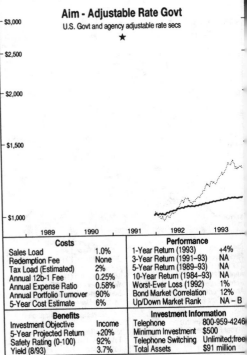

Aim - Adjustable Rate Govt
U.S. Govt and agency adjustable rate secs
★

Costs		Performance	
Sales Load	1.0%	1-Year Return (1993)	+4%
Redemption Fee	None	3-Year Return (1991–93)	NA
Tax Load (Estimated)	2%	5-Year Return (1989–93)	NA
Annual 12b-1 Fee	0.25%	10-Year Return (1984–93)	NA
Annual Expense Ratio	0.58%	Worst-Ever Loss (1992)	1%
Annual Portfolio Turnover	90%	Bond Market Correlation	12%
5-Year Cost Estimate	6%	Up/Down Market Rank	NA – B

Benefits		Investment Information	
Investment Objective	Income	Telephone	800-959-4246
5-Year Projected Return	+20%	Minimum Investment	$500
Safety Rating (0-100)	92%	Telephone Switching	Unlimited;free
Yield (8/93)	3.7%	Total Assets	$91 million

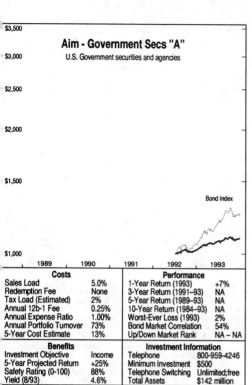

Aim - Government Secs "A"
U.S. Government securities and agencies

Bond Index

| 1989 | 1990 | 1991 | 1992 | 1993 |

Costs		Performance	
Sales Load	5.0%	1-Year Return (1993)	+7%
Redemption Fee	None	3-Year Return (1991–93)	NA
Tax Load (Estimated)	2%	5-Year Return (1989–93)	NA
Annual 12b-1 Fee	0.25%	10-Year Return (1984–93)	NA
Annual Expense Ratio	1.00%	Worst-Ever Loss (1993)	2%
Annual Portfolio Turnover	73%	Bond Market Correlation	54%
5-Year Cost Estimate	13%	Up/Down Market Rank	NA – NA

Benefits		Investment Information	
Investment Objective	Income	Telephone	800-959-4246
5-Year Projected Return	+25%	Minimum Investment	$500
Safety Rating (0-100)	88%	Telephone Switching	Unlimited;free
Yield (8/93)	4.6%	Total Assets	$142 million

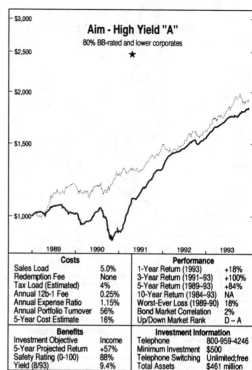

Aim - High Yield "A"
80% BB-rated and lower corporates
★

| 1989 | 1990 | 1991 | 1992 | 1993 |

Costs		Performance	
Sales Load	5.0%	1-Year Return (1993)	+18%
Redemption Fee	None	3-Year Return (1991–93)	+100%
Tax Load (Estimated)	4%	5-Year Return (1989–93)	+84%
Annual 12b-1 Fee	0.25%	10-Year Return (1984–93)	NA
Annual Expense Ratio	1.15%	Worst-Ever Loss (1989-90)	18%
Annual Portfolio Turnover	56%	Bond Market Correlation	2%
5-Year Cost Estimate	16%	Up/Down Market Rank	D – A

Benefits		Investment Information	
Investment Objective	Income	Telephone	800-959-4246
5-Year Projected Return	+57%	Minimum Investment	$500
Safety Rating (0-100)	88%	Telephone Switching	Unlimited;free
Yield (8/93)	9.4%	Total Assets	$461 million

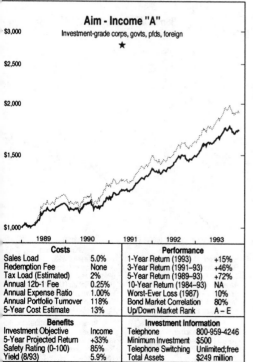

Aim - Income "A"
Investment-grade corps, govts, pfds, foreign
★

| 1989 | 1990 | 1991 | 1992 | 1993 |

Costs		Performance	
Sales Load	5.0%	1-Year Return (1993)	+15%
Redemption Fee	None	3-Year Return (1991–93)	+46%
Tax Load (Estimated)	2%	5-Year Return (1989–93)	+72%
Annual 12b-1 Fee	0.25%	10-Year Return (1984–93)	NA
Annual Expense Ratio	1.00%	Worst-Ever Loss (1987)	10%
Annual Portfolio Turnover	118%	Bond Market Correlation	80%
5-Year Cost Estimate	13%	Up/Down Market Rank	A – E

Benefits		Investment Information	
Investment Objective	Income	Telephone	800-959-4246
5-Year Projected Return	+33%	Minimum Investment	$500
Safety Rating (0-100)	85%	Telephone Switching	Unlimited;free
Yield (8/93)	5.9%	Total Assets	$249 million

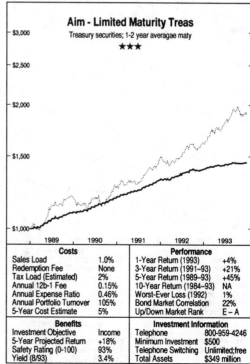

Aim - Limited Maturity Treas
Treasury securities; 1-2 year averagae maty
★★★

| 1989 | 1990 | 1991 | 1992 | 1993 |

Costs		Performance	
Sales Load	1.0%	1-Year Return (1993)	+4%
Redemption Fee	None	3-Year Return (1991–93)	+21%
Tax Load (Estimated)	2%	5-Year Return (1989–93)	+45%
Annual 12b-1 Fee	0.15%	10-Year Return (1984–93)	NA
Annual Expense Ratio	0.46%	Worst-Ever Loss (1992)	1%
Annual Portfolio Turnover	105%	Bond Market Correlation	22%
5-Year Cost Estimate	5%	Up/Down Market Rank	E – A

Benefits		Investment Information	
Investment Objective	Income	Telephone	800-959-4246
5-Year Projected Return	+18%	Minimum Investment	$500
Safety Rating (0-100)	93%	Telephone Switching	Unlimited;free
Yield (8/93)	3.4%	Total Assets	$349 million

B O N D

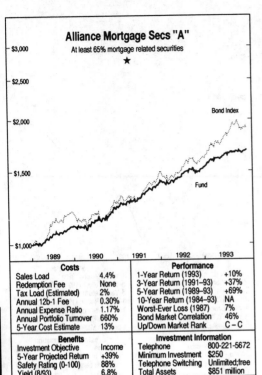

Alliance Mortgage Secs "A"
At least 65% mortgage related securities
★

Bond Index

Fund

Costs		Performance	
Sales Load	4.4%	1-Year Return (1993)	+10%
Redemption Fee	None	3-Year Return (1991–93)	+37%
Tax Load (Estimated)	2%	5-Year Return (1989–93)	+69%
Annual 12b-1 Fee	0.30%	10-Year Return (1984–93)	NA
Annual Expense Ratio	1.17%	Worst-Ever Loss (1987)	7%
Annual Portfolio Turnover	660%	Bond Market Correlation	46%
5-Year Cost Estimate	13%	Up/Down Market Rank	C – C

Benefits		Investment Information	
Investment Objective	Income	Telephone	800-221-5672
5-Year Projected Return	+39%	Minimum Investment	$250
Safety Rating (0-100)	88%	Telephone Switching	Unlimited;free
Yield (8/93)	6.8%	Total Assets	$851 million

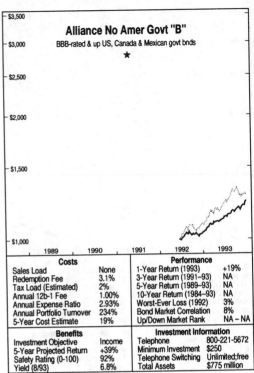

Alliance No Amer Govt "B"
BBB-rated & up US, Canada & Mexican govt bnds
★

Costs		Performance	
Sales Load	None	1-Year Return (1993)	+19%
Redemption Fee	3.1%	3-Year Return (1991–93)	NA
Tax Load (Estimated)	2%	5-Year Return (1989–93)	NA
Annual 12b-1 Fee	1.00%	10-Year Return (1984–93)	NA
Annual Expense Ratio	2.93%	Worst-Ever Loss (1992)	3%
Annual Portfolio Turnover	234%	Bond Market Correlation	8%
5-Year Cost Estimate	19%	Up/Down Market Rank	NA – NA

Benefits		Investment Information	
Investment Objective	Income	Telephone	800-221-5672
5-Year Projected Return	+39%	Minimum Investment	$250
Safety Rating (0-100)	92%	Telephone Switching	Unlimited;free
Yield (8/93)	6.8%	Total Assets	$775 million

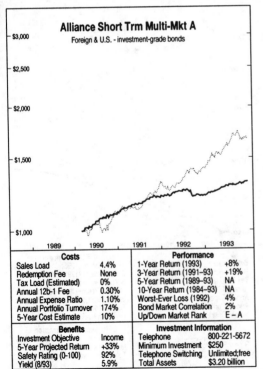

Alliance Short Trm Multi-Mkt A
Foreign & U.S. - investment-grade bonds

Costs		Performance	
Sales Load	4.4%	1-Year Return (1993)	+8%
Redemption Fee	None	3-Year Return (1991–93)	+19%
Tax Load (Estimated)	0%	5-Year Return (1989–93)	NA
Annual 12b-1 Fee	0.30%	10-Year Return (1984–93)	NA
Annual Expense Ratio	1.10%	Worst-Ever Loss (1992)	4%
Annual Portfolio Turnover	174%	Bond Market Correlation	2%
5-Year Cost Estimate	10%	Up/Down Market Rank	E – A

Benefits		Investment Information	
Investment Objective	Income	Telephone	800-221-5672
5-Year Projected Return	+33%	Minimum Investment	$250
Safety Rating (0-100)	92%	Telephone Switching	Unlimited;free
Yield (8/93)	5.9%	Total Assets	$3.20 billion

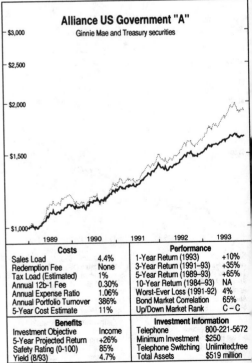

Alliance US Government "A"
Ginnie Mae and Treasury securities

Costs		Performance	
Sales Load	4.4%	1-Year Return (1993)	+10%
Redemption Fee	None	3-Year Return (1991–93)	+35%
Tax Load (Estimated)	1%	5-Year Return (1989–93)	+65%
Annual 12b-1 Fee	0.30%	10-Year Return (1984–93)	NA
Annual Expense Ratio	1.06%	Worst-Ever Loss (1991-92)	4%
Annual Portfolio Turnover	386%	Bond Market Correlation	65%
5-Year Cost Estimate	11%	Up/Down Market Rank	C – C

Benefits		Investment Information	
Investment Objective	Income	Telephone	800-221-5672
5-Year Projected Return	+26%	Minimum Investment	$250
Safety Rating (0-100)	85%	Telephone Switching	Unlimited;free
Yield (8/93)	4.7%	Total Assets	$519 million

BOND

1994 Mutual Fund Buyer's Guide

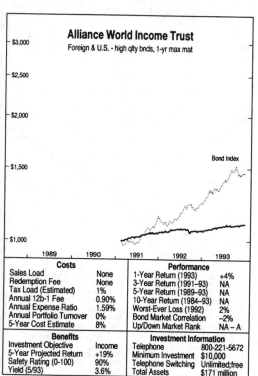

Alliance World Income Trust
Foreign & U.S. - high qlty bnds, 1-yr max mat

Costs		Performance	
Sales Load	None	1-Year Return (1993)	+4%
Redemption Fee	None	3-Year Return (1991–93)	NA
Tax Load (Estimated)	1%	5-Year Return (1989–93)	NA
Annual 12b-1 Fee	0.90%	10-Year Return (1984–93)	NA
Annual Expense Ratio	1.59%	Worst-Ever Loss (1992)	2%
Annual Portfolio Turnover	0%	Bond Market Correlation	–2%
5-Year Cost Estimate	8%	Up/Down Market Rank	NA – A

Benefits		Investment Information	
Investment Objective	Income	Telephone	800-221-5672
5-Year Projected Return	+19%	Minimum Investment	$10,000
Safety Rating (0-100)	90%	Telephone Switching	Unlimited;free
Yield (5/93)	3.6%	Total Assets	$171 million

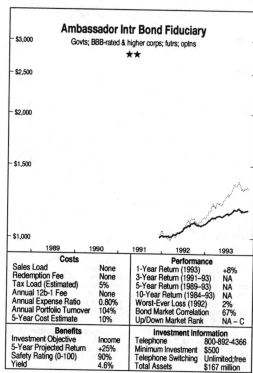

Ambassador Intr Bond Fiduciary
Govts; BBB-rated & higher corps; futrs; optns
★★

Costs		Performance	
Sales Load	None	1-Year Return (1993)	+8%
Redemption Fee	None	3-Year Return (1991–93)	NA
Tax Load (Estimated)	5%	5-Year Return (1989–93)	NA
Annual 12b-1 Fee	None	10-Year Return (1984–93)	NA
Annual Expense Ratio	0.80%	Worst-Ever Loss (1992)	2%
Annual Portfolio Turnover	104%	Bond Market Correlation	67%
5-Year Cost Estimate	10%	Up/Down Market Rank	NA – C

Benefits		Investment Information	
Investment Objective	Income	Telephone	800-892-4366
5-Year Projected Return	+25%	Minimum Investment	$500
Safety Rating (0-100)	90%	Telephone Switching	Unlimited;free
Yield	4.6%	Total Assets	$167 million

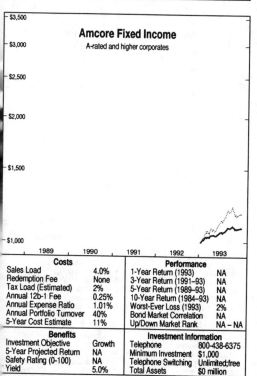

Amcore Fixed Income
A-rated and higher corporates

Costs		Performance	
Sales Load	4.0%	1-Year Return (1993)	NA
Redemption Fee	None	3-Year Return (1991–93)	NA
Tax Load (Estimated)	2%	5-Year Return (1989–93)	NA
Annual 12b-1 Fee	0.25%	10-Year Return (1984–93)	NA
Annual Expense Ratio	1.01%	Worst-Ever Loss (1993)	2%
Annual Portfolio Turnover	40%	Bond Market Correlation	NA
5-Year Cost Estimate	11%	Up/Down Market Rank	NA – NA

Benefits		Investment Information	
Investment Objective	Growth	Telephone	800-438-6375
5-Year Projected Return	NA	Minimum Investment	$1,000
Safety Rating (0-100)	NA	Telephone Switching	Unlimited;free
Yield	5.0%	Total Assets	$0 million

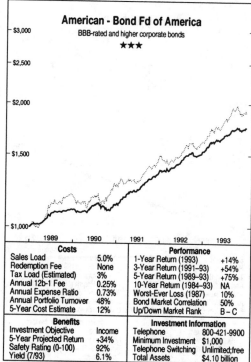

American - Bond Fd of America
BBB-rated and higher corporate bonds
★★★

Costs		Performance	
Sales Load	5.0%	1-Year Return (1993)	+14%
Redemption Fee	None	3-Year Return (1991–93)	+54%
Tax Load (Estimated)	3%	5-Year Return (1989–93)	+75%
Annual 12b-1 Fee	0.25%	10-Year Return (1984–93)	NA
Annual Expense Ratio	0.73%	Worst-Ever Loss (1987)	10%
Annual Portfolio Turnover	48%	Bond Market Correlation	50%
5-Year Cost Estimate	12%	Up/Down Market Rank	B – C

Benefits		Investment Information	
Investment Objective	Income	Telephone	800-421-9900
5-Year Projected Return	+34%	Minimum Investment	$1,000
Safety Rating (0-100)	92%	Telephone Switching	Unlimited;free
Yield (7/93)	6.1%	Total Assets	$4.10 billion

BOND

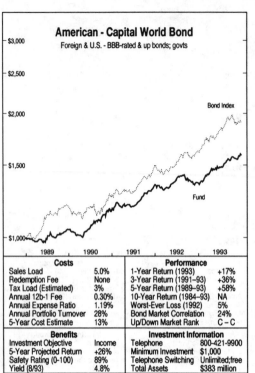

American - Capital World Bond
Foreign & U.S. - BBB-rated & up bonds; govts

Bond Index

Fund

Costs		Performance	
Sales Load	5.0%	1-Year Return (1993)	+17%
Redemption Fee	None	3-Year Return (1991–93)	+36%
Tax Load (Estimated)	3%	5-Year Return (1989–93)	+58%
Annual 12b-1 Fee	0.30%	10-Year Return (1984–93)	NA
Annual Expense Ratio	1.19%	Worst-Ever Loss (1992)	5%
Annual Portfolio Turnover	28%	Bond Market Correlation	24%
5-Year Cost Estimate	13%	Up/Down Market Rank	C – C

Benefits		Investment Information	
Investment Objective	Income	Telephone	800-421-9900
5-Year Projected Return	+26%	Minimum Investment	$1,000
Safety Rating (0-100)	89%	Telephone Switching	Unlimited;free
Yield (8/93)	4.8%	Total Assets	$383 million

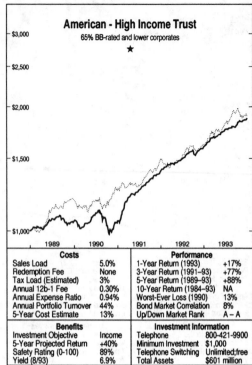

American - High Income Trust
65% BB-rated and lower corporates
★

Costs		Performance	
Sales Load	5.0%	1-Year Return (1993)	+17%
Redemption Fee	None	3-Year Return (1991–93)	+77%
Tax Load (Estimated)	3%	5-Year Return (1989–93)	+88%
Annual 12b-1 Fee	0.30%	10-Year Return (1984–93)	NA
Annual Expense Ratio	0.94%	Worst-Ever Loss (1990)	13%
Annual Portfolio Turnover	44%	Bond Market Correlation	8%
5-Year Cost Estimate	13%	Up/Down Market Rank	A – A

Benefits		Investment Information	
Investment Objective	Income	Telephone	800-421-9900
5-Year Projected Return	+40%	Minimum Investment	$1,000
Safety Rating (0-100)	89%	Telephone Switching	Unlimited;free
Yield (8/93)	6.9%	Total Assets	$601 million

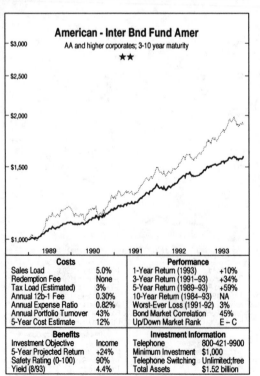

American - Inter Bnd Fund Amer
AA and higher corporates; 3-10 year maturity
★★

Costs		Performance	
Sales Load	5.0%	1-Year Return (1993)	+10%
Redemption Fee	None	3-Year Return (1991–93)	+34%
Tax Load (Estimated)	3%	5-Year Return (1989–93)	+59%
Annual 12b-1 Fee	0.30%	10-Year Return (1984–93)	NA
Annual Expense Ratio	0.82%	Worst-Ever Loss (1991-92)	3%
Annual Portfolio Turnover	43%	Bond Market Correlation	45%
5-Year Cost Estimate	12%	Up/Down Market Rank	E – C

Benefits		Investment Information	
Investment Objective	Income	Telephone	800-421-9900
5-Year Projected Return	+24%	Minimum Investment	$1,000
Safety Rating (0-100)	90%	Telephone Switching	Unlimited;free
Yield (8/93)	4.4%	Total Assets	$1.52 billion

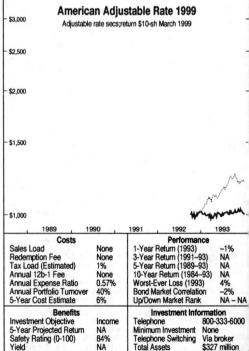

American Adjustable Rate 1999
Adjustable rate secs;return $10-sh March 1999

Costs		Performance	
Sales Load	None	1-Year Return (1993)	–1%
Redemption Fee	None	3-Year Return (1991–93)	NA
Tax Load (Estimated)	1%	5-Year Return (1989–93)	NA
Annual 12b-1 Fee	None	10-Year Return (1984–93)	NA
Annual Expense Ratio	0.57%	Worst-Ever Loss (1993)	4%
Annual Portfolio Turnover	40%	Bond Market Correlation	–2%
5-Year Cost Estimate	6%	Up/Down Market Rank	NA – NA

Benefits		Investment Information	
Investment Objective	Income	Telephone	800-333-6000
5-Year Projected Return	NA	Minimum Investment	None
Safety Rating (0-100)	84%	Telephone Switching	Via broker
Yield	NA	Total Assets	$327 million

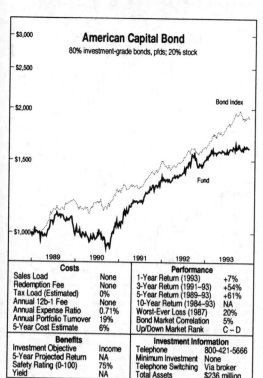

American Capital Bond
80% investment-grade bonds, pfds; 20% stock

Bond Index

Fund

Costs		Performance	
Sales Load	None	1-Year Return (1993)	+7%
Redemption Fee	None	3-Year Return (1991–93)	+54%
Tax Load (Estimated)	0%	5-Year Return (1989–93)	+61%
Annual 12b-1 Fee	None	10-Year Return (1984–93)	NA
Annual Expense Ratio	0.71%	Worst-Ever Loss (1987)	20%
Annual Portfolio Turnover	19%	Bond Market Correlation	5%
5-Year Cost Estimate	6%	Up/Down Market Rank	C – D

Benefits		Investment Information	
Investment Objective	Income	Telephone	800-421-5666
5-Year Projected Return	NA	Minimum Investment	None
Safety Rating (0-100)	75%	Telephone Switching	Via broker
Yield	NA	Total Assets	$236 million

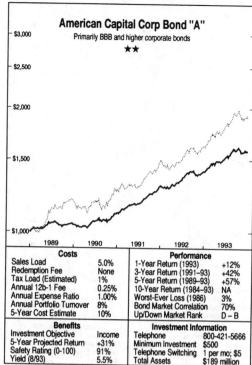

American Capital Corp Bond "A"
Primarily BBB and higher corporate bonds
★★

Costs		Performance	
Sales Load	5.0%	1-Year Return (1993)	+12%
Redemption Fee	None	3-Year Return (1991–93)	+42%
Tax Load (Estimated)	1%	5-Year Return (1989–93)	+57%
Annual 12b-1 Fee	0.25%	10-Year Return (1984–93)	NA
Annual Expense Ratio	1.00%	Worst-Ever Loss (1986)	3%
Annual Portfolio Turnover	8%	Bond Market Correlation	70%
5-Year Cost Estimate	10%	Up/Down Market Rank	D – B

Benefits		Investment Information	
Investment Objective	Income	Telephone	800-421-5666
5-Year Projected Return	+31%	Minimum Investment	$500
Safety Rating (0-100)	91%	Telephone Switching	1 per mo; $5
Yield (8/93)	5.5%	Total Assets	$189 million

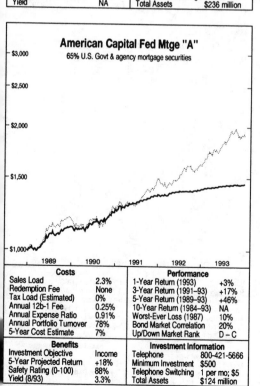

American Capital Fed Mtge "A"
65% U.S. Govt & agency mortgage securities

Costs		Performance	
Sales Load	2.3%	1-Year Return (1993)	+3%
Redemption Fee	None	3-Year Return (1991–93)	+17%
Tax Load (Estimated)	0%	5-Year Return (1989–93)	+46%
Annual 12b-1 Fee	0.25%	10-Year Return (1984–93)	NA
Annual Expense Ratio	0.91%	Worst-Ever Loss (1987)	10%
Annual Portfolio Turnover	78%	Bond Market Correlation	20%
5-Year Cost Estimate	7%	Up/Down Market Rank	D – C

Benefits		Investment Information	
Investment Objective	Income	Telephone	800-421-5666
5-Year Projected Return	+18%	Minimum Investment	$500
Safety Rating (0-100)	88%	Telephone Switching	1 per mo; $5
Yield (8/93)	3.3%	Total Assets	$124 million

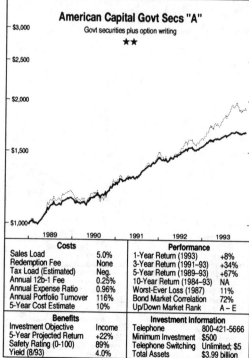

American Capital Govt Secs "A"
Govt securities plus option writing
★★

Costs		Performance	
Sales Load	5.0%	1-Year Return (1993)	+8%
Redemption Fee	None	3-Year Return (1991–93)	+34%
Tax Load (Estimated)	Neg.	5-Year Return (1989–93)	+67%
Annual 12b-1 Fee	0.25%	10-Year Return (1984–93)	NA
Annual Expense Ratio	0.96%	Worst-Ever Loss (1987)	11%
Annual Portfolio Turnover	116%	Bond Market Correlation	72%
5-Year Cost Estimate	10%	Up/Down Market Rank	A – E

Benefits		Investment Information	
Investment Objective	Income	Telephone	800-421-5666
5-Year Projected Return	+22%	Minimum Investment	$500
Safety Rating (0-100)	89%	Telephone Switching	Unlimited; $5
Yield (8/93)	4.0%	Total Assets	$3.99 billion

BOND

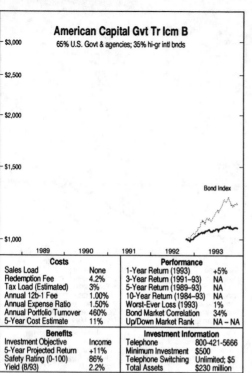

American Capital Gvt Tr Icm B
65% U.S. Govt & agencies; 35% hi-gr intl bnds

Bond Index

Costs		Performance	
Sales Load	None	1-Year Return (1993)	+5%
Redemption Fee	4.2%	3-Year Return (1991–93)	NA
Tax Load (Estimated)	3%	5-Year Return (1989–93)	NA
Annual 12b-1 Fee	1.00%	10-Year Return (1984–93)	NA
Annual Expense Ratio	1.50%	Worst-Ever Loss (1993)	1%
Annual Portfolio Turnover	460%	Bond Market Correlation	34%
5-Year Cost Estimate	11%	Up/Down Market Rank	NA – NA

Benefits		Investment Information	
Investment Objective	Income	Telephone	800-421-5666
5-Year Projected Return	+11%	Minimum Investment	$500
Safety Rating (0-100)	86%	Telephone Switching	Unlimited; $5
Yield (8/93)	2.2%	Total Assets	$230 million

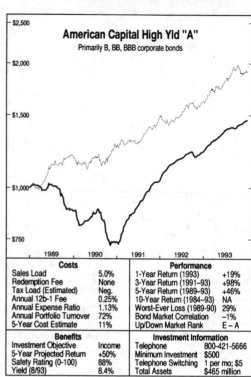

American Capital High Yld "A"
Primarily B, BB, BBB corporate bonds

Costs		Performance	
Sales Load	5.0%	1-Year Return (1993)	+19%
Redemption Fee	None	3-Year Return (1991–93)	+98%
Tax Load (Estimated)	Neg.	5-Year Return (1989–93)	+46%
Annual 12b-1 Fee	0.25%	10-Year Return (1984–93)	NA
Annual Expense Ratio	1.13%	Worst-Ever Loss (1989-90)	29%
Annual Portfolio Turnover	72%	Bond Market Correlation	–1%
5-Year Cost Estimate	11%	Up/Down Market Rank	E – A

Benefits		Investment Information	
Investment Objective	Income	Telephone	800-421-5666
5-Year Projected Return	+50%	Minimum Investment	$500
Safety Rating (0-100)	88%	Telephone Switching	1 per mo; $5
Yield (8/93)	8.4%	Total Assets	$465 million

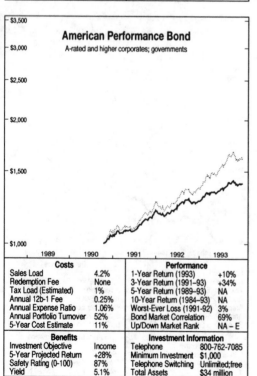

American Performance Bond
A-rated and higher corporates; governments

Costs		Performance	
Sales Load	4.2%	1-Year Return (1993)	+10%
Redemption Fee	None	3-Year Return (1991–93)	+34%
Tax Load (Estimated)	1%	5-Year Return (1989–93)	NA
Annual 12b-1 Fee	0.25%	10-Year Return (1984–93)	NA
Annual Expense Ratio	1.06%	Worst-Ever Loss (1991-92)	3%
Annual Portfolio Turnover	52%	Bond Market Correlation	69%
5-Year Cost Estimate	11%	Up/Down Market Rank	NA – E

Benefits		Investment Information	
Investment Objective	Income	Telephone	800-762-7085
5-Year Projected Return	+28%	Minimum Investment	$1,000
Safety Rating (0-100)	87%	Telephone Switching	Unlimited;free
Yield	5.1%	Total Assets	$34 million

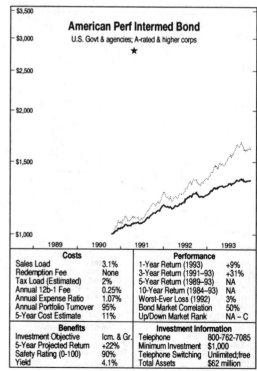

American Perf Intermed Bond
U.S. Govt & agencies; A-rated & higher corps
★

Costs		Performance	
Sales Load	3.1%	1-Year Return (1993)	+9%
Redemption Fee	None	3-Year Return (1991–93)	+31%
Tax Load (Estimated)	2%	5-Year Return (1989–93)	NA
Annual 12b-1 Fee	0.25%	10-Year Return (1984–93)	NA
Annual Expense Ratio	1.07%	Worst-Ever Loss (1992)	3%
Annual Portfolio Turnover	95%	Bond Market Correlation	50%
5-Year Cost Estimate	11%	Up/Down Market Rank	NA – C

Benefits		Investment Information	
Investment Objective	Icm. & Gr.	Telephone	800-762-7085
5-Year Projected Return	+22%	Minimum Investment	$1,000
Safety Rating (0-100)	90%	Telephone Switching	Unlimited;free
Yield	4.1%	Total Assets	$62 million

B
O
N
D

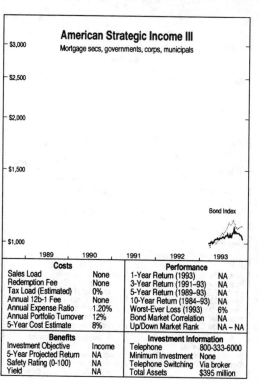

American Strategic Income III
Mortgage secs, governments, corps, municipals

Bond Index

Costs		Performance	
Sales Load	None	1-Year Return (1993)	NA
Redemption Fee	None	3-Year Return (1991–93)	NA
Tax Load (Estimated)	0%	5-Year Return (1989–93)	NA
Annual 12b-1 Fee	None	10-Year Return (1984–93)	NA
Annual Expense Ratio	1.20%	Worst-Ever Loss (1993)	6%
Annual Portfolio Turnover	12%	Bond Market Correlation	NA
5-Year Cost Estimate	8%	Up/Down Market Rank	NA – NA

Benefits		Investment Information	
Investment Objective	Income	Telephone	800-333-6000
5-Year Projected Return	NA	Minimum Investment	None
Safety Rating (0-100)	NA	Telephone Switching	Via broker
Yield	NA	Total Assets	$395 million

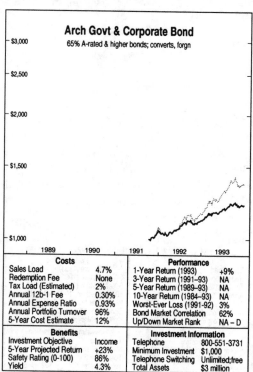

Arch Govt & Corporate Bond
65% A-rated & higher bonds; converts, forgn

Costs		Performance	
Sales Load	4.7%	1-Year Return (1993)	+9%
Redemption Fee	None	3-Year Return (1991–93)	NA
Tax Load (Estimated)	2%	5-Year Return (1989–93)	NA
Annual 12b-1 Fee	0.30%	10-Year Return (1984–93)	NA
Annual Expense Ratio	0.93%	Worst-Ever Loss (1991-92)	3%
Annual Portfolio Turnover	96%	Bond Market Correlation	62%
5-Year Cost Estimate	12%	Up/Down Market Rank	NA – D

Benefits		Investment Information	
Investment Objective	Income	Telephone	800-551-3731
5-Year Projected Return	+23%	Minimum Investment	$1,000
Safety Rating (0-100)	86%	Telephone Switching	Unlimited;free
Yield	4.3%	Total Assets	$3 million

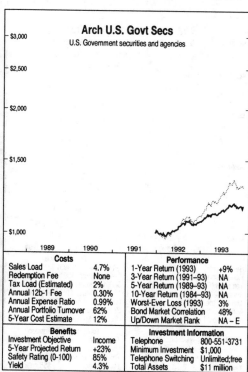

Arch U.S. Govt Secs
U.S. Government securities and agencies

Costs		Performance	
Sales Load	4.7%	1-Year Return (1993)	+9%
Redemption Fee	None	3-Year Return (1991–93)	NA
Tax Load (Estimated)	2%	5-Year Return (1989–93)	NA
Annual 12b-1 Fee	0.30%	10-Year Return (1984–93)	NA
Annual Expense Ratio	0.99%	Worst-Ever Loss (1993)	3%
Annual Portfolio Turnover	62%	Bond Market Correlation	48%
5-Year Cost Estimate	12%	Up/Down Market Rank	NA – E

Benefits		Investment Information	
Investment Objective	Income	Telephone	800-551-3731
5-Year Projected Return	+23%	Minimum Investment	$1,000
Safety Rating (0-100)	85%	Telephone Switching	Unlimited;free
Yield	4.3%	Total Assets	$11 million

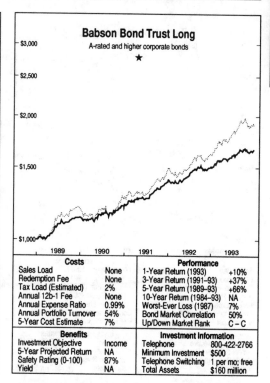

Babson Bond Trust Long
A-rated and higher corporate bonds
★

Costs		Performance	
Sales Load	None	1-Year Return (1993)	+10%
Redemption Fee	None	3-Year Return (1991–93)	+37%
Tax Load (Estimated)	2%	5-Year Return (1989–93)	+66%
Annual 12b-1 Fee	None	10-Year Return (1984–93)	NA
Annual Expense Ratio	0.99%	Worst-Ever Loss (1987)	7%
Annual Portfolio Turnover	54%	Bond Market Correlation	50%
5-Year Cost Estimate	7%	Up/Down Market Rank	C – C

Benefits		Investment Information	
Investment Objective	Income	Telephone	800-422-2766
5-Year Projected Return	NA	Minimum Investment	$500
Safety Rating (0-100)	87%	Telephone Switching	1 per mo; free
Yield	NA	Total Assets	$160 million

BOND

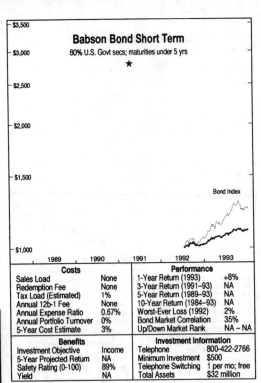

Babson Bond Short Term

80% U.S. Govt secs; maturities under 5 yrs

★

(chart: Bond Index)

Costs		Performance	
Sales Load	None	1-Year Return (1993)	+8%
Redemption Fee	None	3-Year Return (1991–93)	NA
Tax Load (Estimated)	1%	5-Year Return (1989–93)	NA
Annual 12b-1 Fee	None	10-Year Return (1984–93)	NA
Annual Expense Ratio	0.67%	Worst-Ever Loss (1992)	2%
Annual Portfolio Turnover	0%	Bond Market Correlation	35%
5-Year Cost Estimate	3%	Up/Down Market Rank	NA – NA

Benefits		Investment Information	
Investment Objective	Income	Telephone	800-422-2766
5-Year Projected Return	NA	Minimum Investment	$500
Safety Rating (0-100)	89%	Telephone Switching	1 per mo; free
Yield	NA	Total Assets	$32 million

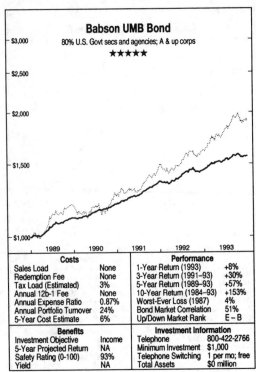

Babson UMB Bond

80% U.S. Govt secs and agencies; A & up corps

★★★★★

Costs		Performance	
Sales Load	None	1-Year Return (1993)	+8%
Redemption Fee	None	3-Year Return (1991–93)	+30%
Tax Load (Estimated)	3%	5-Year Return (1989–93)	+57%
Annual 12b-1 Fee	None	10-Year Return (1984–93)	+153%
Annual Expense Ratio	0.87%	Worst-Ever Loss (1987)	4%
Annual Portfolio Turnover	24%	Bond Market Correlation	51%
5-Year Cost Estimate	6%	Up/Down Market Rank	E – B

Benefits		Investment Information	
Investment Objective	Income	Telephone	800-422-2766
5-Year Projected Return	NA	Minimum Investment	$1,000
Safety Rating (0-100)	93%	Telephone Switching	1 per mo; free
Yield	NA	Total Assets	$0 million

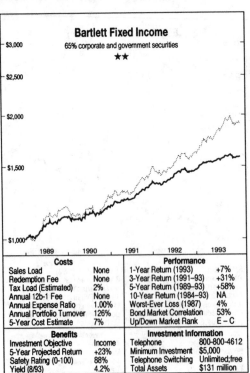

Bartlett Fixed Income

65% corporate and government securities

★★

Costs		Performance	
Sales Load	None	1-Year Return (1993)	+7%
Redemption Fee	None	3-Year Return (1991–93)	+31%
Tax Load (Estimated)	2%	5-Year Return (1989–93)	+58%
Annual 12b-1 Fee	None	10-Year Return (1984–93)	NA
Annual Expense Ratio	1.00%	Worst-Ever Loss (1987)	4%
Annual Portfolio Turnover	126%	Bond Market Correlation	53%
5-Year Cost Estimate	7%	Up/Down Market Rank	E – C

Benefits		Investment Information	
Investment Objective	Income	Telephone	800-800-4612
5-Year Projected Return	+23%	Minimum Investment	$5,000
Safety Rating (0-100)	88%	Telephone Switching	Unlimited; free
Yield (8/93)	4.2%	Total Assets	$131 million

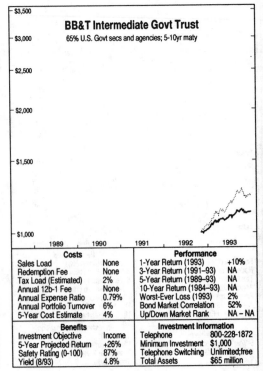

BB&T Intermediate Govt Trust

65% U.S. Govt secs and agencies; 5-10yr maty

Costs		Performance	
Sales Load	None	1-Year Return (1993)	+10%
Redemption Fee	None	3-Year Return (1991–93)	NA
Tax Load (Estimated)	2%	5-Year Return (1989–93)	NA
Annual 12b-1 Fee	None	10-Year Return (1984–93)	NA
Annual Expense Ratio	0.79%	Worst-Ever Loss (1993)	2%
Annual Portfolio Turnover	6%	Bond Market Correlation	52%
5-Year Cost Estimate	4%	Up/Down Market Rank	NA – NA

Benefits		Investment Information	
Investment Objective	Income	Telephone	800-228-1872
5-Year Projected Return	+26%	Minimum Investment	$1,000
Safety Rating (0-100)	87%	Telephone Switching	Unlimited; free
Yield (8/93)	4.8%	Total Assets	$65 million

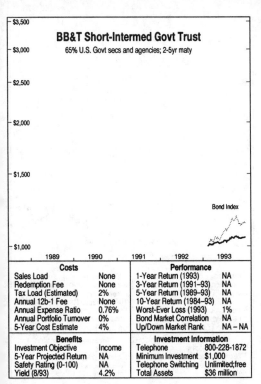

BB&T Short-Intermed Govt Trust

65% U.S. Govt secs and agencies; 2-5yr maty

Bond Index

Costs		Performance	
Sales Load	None	1-Year Return (1993)	NA
Redemption Fee	None	3-Year Return (1991–93)	NA
Tax Load (Estimated)	2%	5-Year Return (1989–93)	NA
Annual 12b-1 Fee	None	10-Year Return (1984–93)	NA
Annual Expense Ratio	0.76%	Worst-Ever Loss (1993)	1%
Annual Portfolio Turnover	0%	Bond Market Correlation	NA
5-Year Cost Estimate	4%	Up/Down Market Rank	NA – NA

Benefits		Investment Information	
Investment Objective	Income	Telephone	800-228-1872
5-Year Projected Return	NA	Minimum Investment	$1,000
Safety Rating (0-100)	NA	Telephone Switching	Unlimited;free
Yield (8/93)	4.2%	Total Assets	$36 million

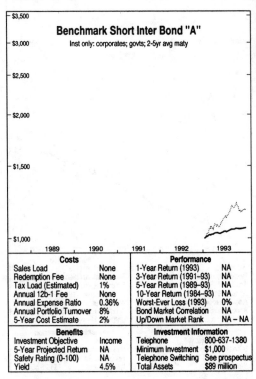

Benchmark Bond "A"

Inst only: corporates; govts; 2-5yr avg maty

Costs		Performance	
Sales Load	None	1-Year Return (1993)	NA
Redemption Fee	None	3-Year Return (1991–93)	NA
Tax Load (Estimated)	1%	5-Year Return (1989–93)	NA
Annual 12b-1 Fee	None	10-Year Return (1984–93)	NA
Annual Expense Ratio	0.36%	Worst-Ever Loss (1993)	3%
Annual Portfolio Turnover	60%	Bond Market Correlation	NA
5-Year Cost Estimate	3%	Up/Down Market Rank	NA – NA

Benefits		Investment Information	
Investment Objective	Income	Telephone	800-637-1380
5-Year Projected Return	NA	Minimum Investment	$1,000
Safety Rating (0-100)	NA	Telephone Switching	See prospectus
Yield (8/93)	7.6%	Total Assets	$190 million

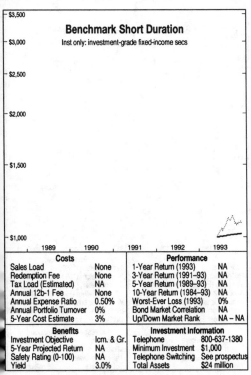

Benchmark Short Duration

Inst only: investment-grade fixed-income secs

Costs		Performance	
Sales Load	None	1-Year Return (1993)	NA
Redemption Fee	None	3-Year Return (1991–93)	NA
Tax Load (Estimated)	NA	5-Year Return (1989–93)	NA
Annual 12b-1 Fee	None	10-Year Return (1984–93)	NA
Annual Expense Ratio	0.50%	Worst-Ever Loss (1993)	0%
Annual Portfolio Turnover	0%	Bond Market Correlation	NA
5-Year Cost Estimate	3%	Up/Down Market Rank	NA – NA

Benefits		Investment Information	
Investment Objective	Icm. & Gr.	Telephone	800-637-1380
5-Year Projected Return	NA	Minimum Investment	$1,000
Safety Rating (0-100)	NA	Telephone Switching	See prospectus
Yield	3.0%	Total Assets	$24 million

Benchmark Short Inter Bond "A"

Inst only: corporates; govts; 2-5yr avg maty

Costs		Performance	
Sales Load	None	1-Year Return (1993)	NA
Redemption Fee	None	3-Year Return (1991–93)	NA
Tax Load (Estimated)	1%	5-Year Return (1989–93)	NA
Annual 12b-1 Fee	None	10-Year Return (1984–93)	NA
Annual Expense Ratio	0.36%	Worst-Ever Loss (1993)	0%
Annual Portfolio Turnover	8%	Bond Market Correlation	NA
5-Year Cost Estimate	2%	Up/Down Market Rank	NA – NA

Benefits		Investment Information	
Investment Objective	Income	Telephone	800-637-1380
5-Year Projected Return	NA	Minimum Investment	$1,000
Safety Rating (0-100)	NA	Telephone Switching	See prospectus
Yield	4.5%	Total Assets	$89 million

BOND

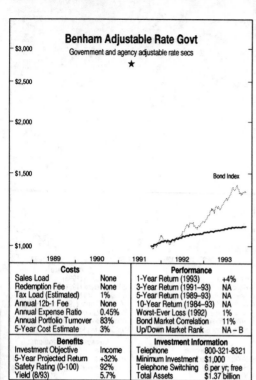

Benham Adjustable Rate Govt

Government and agency adjustable rate secs

★

Costs		Performance	
Sales Load	None	1-Year Return (1993)	+4%
Redemption Fee	None	3-Year Return (1991–93)	NA
Tax Load (Estimated)	1%	5-Year Return (1989–93)	NA
Annual 12b-1 Fee	None	10-Year Return (1984–93)	NA
Annual Expense Ratio	0.45%	Worst-Ever Loss (1992)	1%
Annual Portfolio Turnover	83%	Bond Market Correlation	11%
5-Year Cost Estimate	3%	Up/Down Market Rank	NA – B

Benefits		Investment Information	
Investment Objective	Income	Telephone	800-321-8321
5-Year Projected Return	+32%	Minimum Investment	$1,000
Safety Rating (0-100)	92%	Telephone Switching	6 per yr; free
Yield (8/93)	5.7%	Total Assets	$1.37 billion

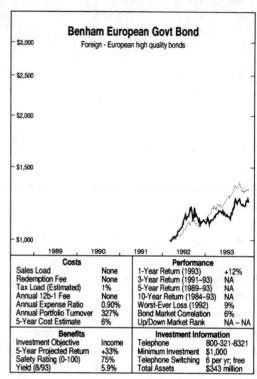

Benham European Govt Bond

Foreign - European high quality bonds

Costs		Performance	
Sales Load	None	1-Year Return (1993)	+12%
Redemption Fee	None	3-Year Return (1991–93)	NA
Tax Load (Estimated)	1%	5-Year Return (1989–93)	NA
Annual 12b-1 Fee	None	10-Year Return (1984–93)	NA
Annual Expense Ratio	0.90%	Worst-Ever Loss (1992)	9%
Annual Portfolio Turnover	327%	Bond Market Correlation	6%
5-Year Cost Estimate	6%	Up/Down Market Rank	NA – NA

Benefits		Investment Information	
Investment Objective	Income	Telephone	800-321-8321
5-Year Projected Return	+33%	Minimum Investment	$1,000
Safety Rating (0-100)	75%	Telephone Switching	6 per yr; free
Yield (8/93)	5.9%	Total Assets	$343 million

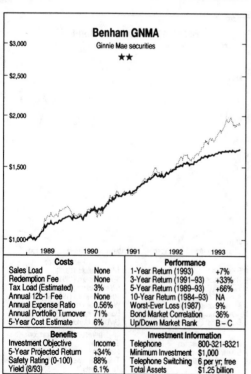

Benham GNMA

Ginnie Mae securities

★★

Costs		Performance	
Sales Load	None	1-Year Return (1993)	+7%
Redemption Fee	None	3-Year Return (1991–93)	+33%
Tax Load (Estimated)	3%	5-Year Return (1989–93)	+66%
Annual 12b-1 Fee	None	10-Year Return (1984–93)	NA
Annual Expense Ratio	0.56%	Worst-Ever Loss (1987)	9%
Annual Portfolio Turnover	71%	Bond Market Correlation	36%
5-Year Cost Estimate	6%	Up/Down Market Rank	B – C

Benefits		Investment Information	
Investment Objective	Income	Telephone	800-321-8321
5-Year Projected Return	+34%	Minimum Investment	$1,000
Safety Rating (0-100)	88%	Telephone Switching	6 per yr; free
Yield (8/93)	6.1%	Total Assets	$1.25 billion

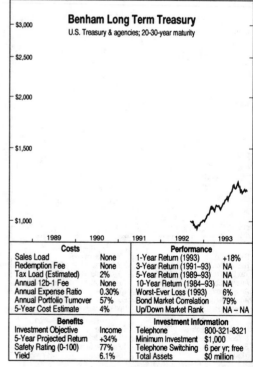

Benham Long Term Treasury

U.S. Treasury & agencies; 20-30-year maturity

Costs		Performance	
Sales Load	None	1-Year Return (1993)	+18%
Redemption Fee	None	3-Year Return (1991–93)	NA
Tax Load (Estimated)	2%	5-Year Return (1989–93)	NA
Annual 12b-1 Fee	None	10-Year Return (1984–93)	NA
Annual Expense Ratio	0.30%	Worst-Ever Loss (1993)	6%
Annual Portfolio Turnover	57%	Bond Market Correlation	79%
5-Year Cost Estimate	4%	Up/Down Market Rank	NA – NA

Benefits		Investment Information	
Investment Objective	Income	Telephone	800-321-8321
5-Year Projected Return	+34%	Minimum Investment	$1,000
Safety Rating (0-100)	77%	Telephone Switching	6 per yr; free
Yield	6.1%	Total Assets	$0 million

BOND

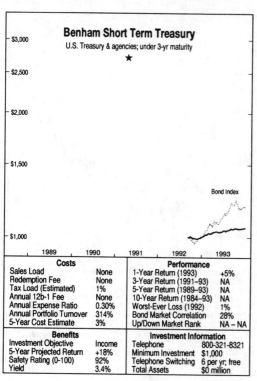

Benham Short Term Treasury

U.S. Treasury & agencies; under 3-yr maturity

★

Bond Index

Costs		Performance	
Sales Load	None	1-Year Return (1993)	+5%
Redemption Fee	None	3-Year Return (1991–93)	NA
Tax Load (Estimated)	1%	5-Year Return (1989–93)	NA
Annual 12b-1 Fee	None	10-Year Return (1984–93)	NA
Annual Expense Ratio	0.30%	Worst-Ever Loss (1992)	1%
Annual Portfolio Turnover	314%	Bond Market Correlation	28%
5-Year Cost Estimate	3%	Up/Down Market Rank	NA – NA

Benefits		Investment Information	
Investment Objective	Income	Telephone	800-321-8321
5-Year Projected Return	+18%	Minimum Investment	$1,000
Safety Rating (0-100)	92%	Telephone Switching	6 per yr; free
Yield	3.4%	Total Assets	$0 million

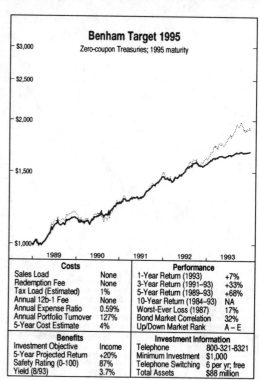

Benham Target 1995

Zero-coupon Treasuries; 1995 maturity

Costs		Performance	
Sales Load	None	1-Year Return (1993)	+7%
Redemption Fee	None	3-Year Return (1991–93)	+33%
Tax Load (Estimated)	1%	5-Year Return (1989–93)	+68%
Annual 12b-1 Fee	None	10-Year Return (1984–93)	NA
Annual Expense Ratio	0.59%	Worst-Ever Loss (1987)	17%
Annual Portfolio Turnover	127%	Bond Market Correlation	32%
5-Year Cost Estimate	4%	Up/Down Market Rank	A – E

Benefits		Investment Information	
Investment Objective	Income	Telephone	800-321-8321
5-Year Projected Return	+20%	Minimum Investment	$1,000
Safety Rating (0-100)	87%	Telephone Switching	6 per yr; free
Yield (8/93)	3.7%	Total Assets	$88 million

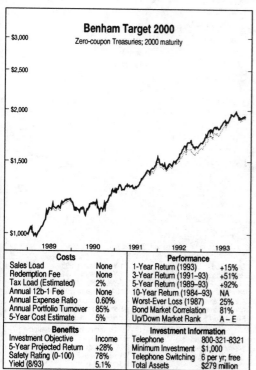

Benham Target 2000

Zero-coupon Treasuries; 2000 maturity

Costs		Performance	
Sales Load	None	1-Year Return (1993)	+15%
Redemption Fee	None	3-Year Return (1991–93)	+51%
Tax Load (Estimated)	2%	5-Year Return (1989–93)	+92%
Annual 12b-1 Fee	None	10-Year Return (1984–93)	NA
Annual Expense Ratio	0.60%	Worst-Ever Loss (1987)	25%
Annual Portfolio Turnover	85%	Bond Market Correlation	81%
5-Year Cost Estimate	5%	Up/Down Market Rank	A – E

Benefits		Investment Information	
Investment Objective	Income	Telephone	800-321-8321
5-Year Projected Return	+28%	Minimum Investment	$1,000
Safety Rating (0-100)	78%	Telephone Switching	6 per yr; free
Yield (8/93)	5.1%	Total Assets	$279 million

Benham Target 2005

Zero-coupon Treasuries; 2005 maturity

Costs		Performance	
Sales Load	None	1-Year Return (1993)	+22%
Redemption Fee	None	3-Year Return (1991–93)	+62%
Tax Load (Estimated)	6%	5-Year Return (1989–93)	+108%
Annual 12b-1 Fee	None	10-Year Return (1984–93)	NA
Annual Expense Ratio	0.62%	Worst-Ever Loss (1987)	31%
Annual Portfolio Turnover	68%	Bond Market Correlation	85%
5-Year Cost Estimate	10%	Up/Down Market Rank	A – E

Benefits		Investment Information	
Investment Objective	Income	Telephone	800-321-8321
5-Year Projected Return	+34%	Minimum Investment	$1,000
Safety Rating (0-100)	67%	Telephone Switching	6 per yr; free
Yield (8/93)	6.0%	Total Assets	$156 million

Benham Target 2010
Zero-coupon Treasuries; 2010 maturity

Costs		Performance	
Sales Load	None	1-Year Return (1993)	+26%
Redemption Fee	None	3-Year Return (1991–93)	+68%
Tax Load (Estimated)	3%	5-Year Return (1989–93)	+115%
Annual 12b-1 Fee	None	10-Year Return (1984–93)	NA
Annual Expense Ratio	0.66%	Worst-Ever Loss (1987)	39%
Annual Portfolio Turnover	171%	Bond Market Correlation	83%
5-Year Cost Estimate	7%	Up/Down Market Rank	A – E

Benefits		Investment Information	
Investment Objective	Income	Telephone	800-321-8321
5-Year Projected Return	+36%	Minimum Investment	$1,000
Safety Rating (0-100)	56%	Telephone Switching	6 per yr; free
Yield (8/93)	6.3%	Total Assets	$59 million

Benham Target 2015
Zero-coupon Treasuries; 2015 maturity

Costs		Performance	
Sales Load	None	1-Year Return (1993)	+31%
Redemption Fee	None	3-Year Return (1991–93)	+72%
Tax Load (Estimated)	10%	5-Year Return (1989–93)	+122%
Annual 12b-1 Fee	None	10-Year Return (1984–93)	NA
Annual Expense Ratio	0.63%	Worst-Ever Loss (1989-90)	25%
Annual Portfolio Turnover	156%	Bond Market Correlation	82%
5-Year Cost Estimate	14%	Up/Down Market Rank	A – E

Benefits		Investment Information	
Investment Objective	Income	Telephone	800-321-8321
5-Year Projected Return	+36%	Minimum Investment	$1,000
Safety Rating (0-100)	43%	Telephone Switching	6 per yr; free
Yield (8/93)	6.4%	Total Assets	$85 million

Benham Target 2020
Zero-coupon Treasuries; 2020 maturity

Costs		Performance	
Sales Load	None	1-Year Return (1993)	+36%
Redemption Fee	None	3-Year Return (1991–93)	+72%
Tax Load (Estimated)	3%	5-Year Return (1989–93)	NA
Annual 12b-1 Fee	None	10-Year Return (1984–93)	NA
Annual Expense Ratio	0.70%	Worst-Ever Loss (1990)	19%
Annual Portfolio Turnover	130%	Bond Market Correlation	80%
5-Year Cost Estimate	7%	Up/Down Market Rank	A – E

Benefits		Investment Information	
Investment Objective	Income	Telephone	800-321-8321
5-Year Projected Return	+36%	Minimum Investment	$1,000
Safety Rating (0-100)	36%	Telephone Switching	6 per yr; free
Yield (8/93)	6.3%	Total Assets	$47 million

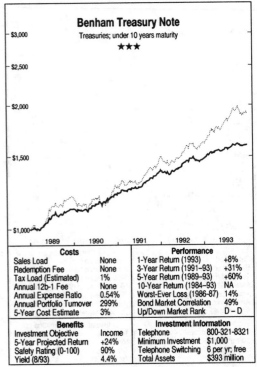

Benham Treasury Note
Treasuries; under 10 years maturity
★★★

Costs		Performance	
Sales Load	None	1-Year Return (1993)	+8%
Redemption Fee	None	3-Year Return (1991–93)	+31%
Tax Load (Estimated)	1%	5-Year Return (1989–93)	+60%
Annual 12b-1 Fee	None	10-Year Return (1984–93)	NA
Annual Expense Ratio	0.54%	Worst-Ever Loss (1986-87)	14%
Annual Portfolio Turnover	299%	Bond Market Correlation	49%
5-Year Cost Estimate	3%	Up/Down Market Rank	D – D

Benefits		Investment Information	
Investment Objective	Income	Telephone	800-321-8321
5-Year Projected Return	+24%	Minimum Investment	$1,000
Safety Rating (0-100)	90%	Telephone Switching	6 per yr; free
Yield (8/93)	4.4%	Total Assets	$393 million

BOND

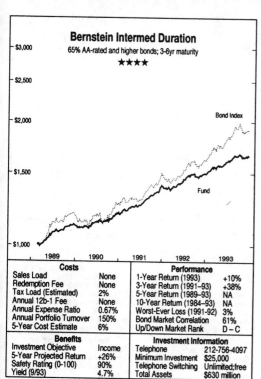

Bernstein Intermed Duration
65% AA-rated and higher bonds; 3-6yr maturity
★★★★

Bond Index

Fund

Costs		Performance	
Sales Load	None	1-Year Return (1993)	+10%
Redemption Fee	None	3-Year Return (1991–93)	+38%
Tax Load (Estimated)	2%	5-Year Return (1989–93)	NA
Annual 12b-1 Fee	None	10-Year Return (1984–93)	NA
Annual Expense Ratio	0.67%	Worst-Ever Loss (1991-92)	3%
Annual Portfolio Turnover	150%	Bond Market Correlation	61%
5-Year Cost Estimate	6%	Up/Down Market Rank	D – C
Benefits		**Investment Information**	
Investment Objective	Income	Telephone	212-756-4097
5-Year Projected Return	+26%	Minimum Investment	$25,000
Safety Rating (0-100)	90%	Telephone Switching	Unlimited;free
Yield (9/93)	4.7%	Total Assets	$630 million

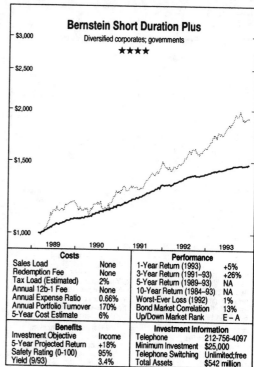

Bernstein Short Duration Plus
Diversified corporates; governments
★★★★

Costs		Performance	
Sales Load	None	1-Year Return (1993)	+5%
Redemption Fee	None	3-Year Return (1991–93)	+26%
Tax Load (Estimated)	2%	5-Year Return (1989–93)	NA
Annual 12b-1 Fee	None	10-Year Return (1984–93)	NA
Annual Expense Ratio	0.66%	Worst-Ever Loss (1992)	1%
Annual Portfolio Turnover	170%	Bond Market Correlation	13%
5-Year Cost Estimate	6%	Up/Down Market Rank	E – A
Benefits		**Investment Information**	
Investment Objective	Income	Telephone	212-756-4097
5-Year Projected Return	+18%	Minimum Investment	$25,000
Safety Rating (0-100)	95%	Telephone Switching	Unlimited;free
Yield (9/93)	3.4%	Total Assets	$542 million

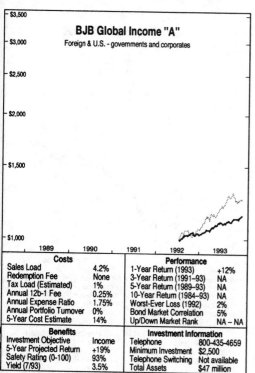

BJB Global Income "A"
Foreign & U.S. - governments and corporates

Costs		Performance	
Sales Load	4.2%	1-Year Return (1993)	+12%
Redemption Fee	None	3-Year Return (1991–93)	NA
Tax Load (Estimated)	1%	5-Year Return (1989–93)	NA
Annual 12b-1 Fee	0.25%	10-Year Return (1984–93)	NA
Annual Expense Ratio	1.75%	Worst-Ever Loss (1992)	2%
Annual Portfolio Turnover	0%	Bond Market Correlation	5%
5-Year Cost Estimate	14%	Up/Down Market Rank	NA – NA
Benefits		**Investment Information**	
Investment Objective	Income	Telephone	800-435-4659
5-Year Projected Return	+19%	Minimum Investment	$2,500
Safety Rating (0-100)	93%	Telephone Switching	Not available
Yield (7/93)	3.5%	Total Assets	$47 million

Blackrock 2001 Term
High-qlty corps, govts & agen; retn $10 2001

Costs		Performance	
Sales Load	None	1-Year Return (1993)	+10%
Redemption Fee	None	3-Year Return (1991–93)	NA
Tax Load (Estimated)	0%	5-Year Return (1989–93)	NA
Annual 12b-1 Fee	None	10-Year Return (1984–93)	NA
Annual Expense Ratio	0.64%	Worst-Ever Loss (1992)	9%
Annual Portfolio Turnover	210%	Bond Market Correlation	–3%
5-Year Cost Estimate	5%	Up/Down Market Rank	NA – NA
Benefits		**Investment Information**	
Investment Objective	Income	Telephone	800-227-7236
5-Year Projected Return	NA	Minimum Investment	None
Safety Rating (0-100)	69%	Telephone Switching	Via broker
Yield	NA	Total Assets	$1.37 billion

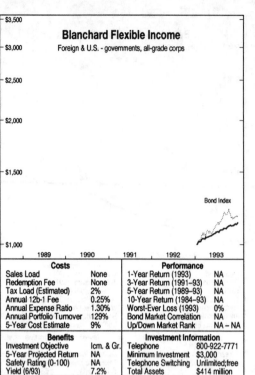

Blanchard Flexible Income
Foreign & U.S. - governments, all-grade corps

Costs		Performance	
Sales Load	None	1-Year Return (1993)	NA
Redemption Fee	None	3-Year Return (1991–93)	NA
Tax Load (Estimated)	2%	5-Year Return (1989–93)	NA
Annual 12b-1 Fee	0.25%	10-Year Return (1984–93)	NA
Annual Expense Ratio	1.30%	Worst-Ever Loss (1993)	0%
Annual Portfolio Turnover	129%	Bond Market Correlation	NA
5-Year Cost Estimate	9%	Up/Down Market Rank	NA – NA

Benefits		Investment Information	
Investment Objective	Icm. & Gr.	Telephone	800-922-7771
5-Year Projected Return	NA	Minimum Investment	$3,000
Safety Rating (0-100)	NA	Telephone Switching	Unlimited;free
Yield (6/93)	7.2%	Total Assets	$414 million

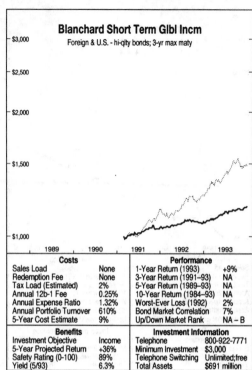

Blanchard Short Term Glbl Incm
Foreign & U.S. - hi-qlty bonds; 3-yr max maty

Costs		Performance	
Sales Load	None	1-Year Return (1993)	+9%
Redemption Fee	None	3-Year Return (1991–93)	NA
Tax Load (Estimated)	2%	5-Year Return (1989–93)	NA
Annual 12b-1 Fee	0.25%	10-Year Return (1984–93)	NA
Annual Expense Ratio	1.32%	Worst-Ever Loss (1992)	2%
Annual Portfolio Turnover	610%	Bond Market Correlation	7%
5-Year Cost Estimate	9%	Up/Down Market Rank	NA – B

Benefits		Investment Information	
Investment Objective	Income	Telephone	800-922-7771
5-Year Projected Return	+36%	Minimum Investment	$3,000
Safety Rating (0-100)	89%	Telephone Switching	Unlimited;free
Yield (5/93)	6.3%	Total Assets	$691 million

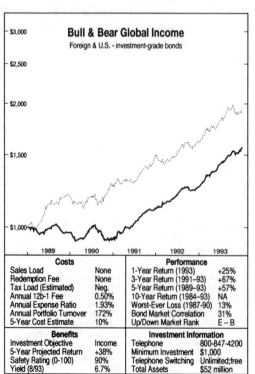

Bull & Bear Global Income
Foreign & U.S. - investment-grade bonds

Costs		Performance	
Sales Load	None	1-Year Return (1993)	+25%
Redemption Fee	None	3-Year Return (1991–93)	+67%
Tax Load (Estimated)	Neg.	5-Year Return (1989–93)	+57%
Annual 12b-1 Fee	0.50%	10-Year Return (1984–93)	NA
Annual Expense Ratio	1.93%	Worst-Ever Loss (1987-90)	13%
Annual Portfolio Turnover	172%	Bond Market Correlation	31%
5-Year Cost Estimate	10%	Up/Down Market Rank	E – B

Benefits		Investment Information	
Investment Objective	Income	Telephone	800-847-4200
5-Year Projected Return	+38%	Minimum Investment	$1,000
Safety Rating (0-100)	90%	Telephone Switching	Unlimited;free
Yield (8/93)	6.7%	Total Assets	$52 million

Bunker Hill Income Securities
75% investment-grade corporates, pfds, levrg

Costs		Performance	
Sales Load	None	1-Year Return (1993)	+8%
Redemption Fee	None	3-Year Return (1991–93)	+54%
Tax Load (Estimated)	Neg.	5-Year Return (1989–93)	+59%
Annual 12b-1 Fee	None	10-Year Return (1984–93)	NA
Annual Expense Ratio	1.06%	Worst-Ever Loss (1989-90)	27%
Annual Portfolio Turnover	252%	Bond Market Correlation	0%
5-Year Cost Estimate	8%	Up/Down Market Rank	B – D

Benefits		Investment Information	
Investment Objective	Income	Telephone	800-332-3863
5-Year Projected Return	NA	Minimum Investment	None
Safety Rating (0-100)	71%	Telephone Switching	Via broker
Yield	NA	Total Assets	$46 million

1994 Mutual Fund Buyer's Guide

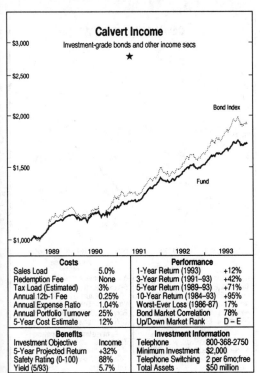

Calvert Income
Investment-grade bonds and other income secs
★

Bond Index

Fund

Costs		Performance	
Sales Load	5.0%	1-Year Return (1993)	+12%
Redemption Fee	None	3-Year Return (1991–93)	+42%
Tax Load (Estimated)	3%	5-Year Return (1989–93)	+71%
Annual 12b-1 Fee	0.25%	10-Year Return (1984–93)	+95%
Annual Expense Ratio	1.04%	Worst-Ever Loss (1986–87)	17%
Annual Portfolio Turnover	25%	Bond Market Correlation	78%
5-Year Cost Estimate	12%	Up/Down Market Rank	D – E

Benefits		Investment Information	
Investment Objective	Income	Telephone	800-368-2750
5-Year Projected Return	+32%	Minimum Investment	$2,000
Safety Rating (0-100)	88%	Telephone Switching	2 per 6mo;free
Yield (5/93)	5.7%	Total Assets	$50 million

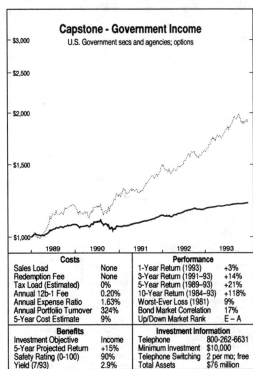

Capstone - Government Income
U.S. Government secs and agencies; options

Costs		Performance	
Sales Load	None	1-Year Return (1993)	+3%
Redemption Fee	None	3-Year Return (1991–93)	+14%
Tax Load (Estimated)	0%	5-Year Return (1989–93)	+21%
Annual 12b-1 Fee	0.20%	10-Year Return (1984–93)	+118%
Annual Expense Ratio	1.63%	Worst-Ever Loss (1981)	9%
Annual Portfolio Turnover	324%	Bond Market Correlation	17%
5-Year Cost Estimate	9%	Up/Down Market Rank	E – A

Benefits		Investment Information	
Investment Objective	Income	Telephone	800-262-6631
5-Year Projected Return	+15%	Minimum Investment	$10,000
Safety Rating (0-100)	90%	Telephone Switching	2 per mo; free
Yield (7/93)	2.9%	Total Assets	$76 million

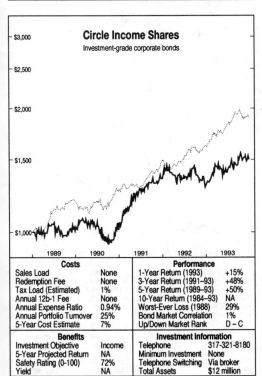

Circle Income Shares
Investment-grade corporate bonds

Costs		Performance	
Sales Load	None	1-Year Return (1993)	+15%
Redemption Fee	None	3-Year Return (1991–93)	+48%
Tax Load (Estimated)	1%	5-Year Return (1989–93)	+50%
Annual 12b-1 Fee	None	10-Year Return (1984–93)	NA
Annual Expense Ratio	0.94%	Worst-Ever Loss (1988)	29%
Annual Portfolio Turnover	25%	Bond Market Correlation	1%
5-Year Cost Estimate	7%	Up/Down Market Rank	D – C

Benefits		Investment Information	
Investment Objective	Income	Telephone	317-321-8180
5-Year Projected Return	NA	Minimum Investment	None
Safety Rating (0-100)	72%	Telephone Switching	Via broker
Yield	NA	Total Assets	$12 million

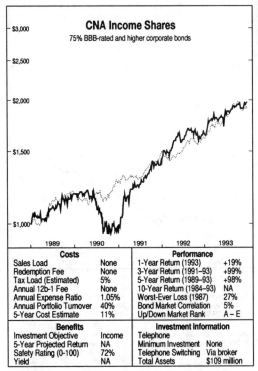

CNA Income Shares
75% BBB-rated and higher corporate bonds

Costs		Performance	
Sales Load	None	1-Year Return (1993)	+19%
Redemption Fee	None	3-Year Return (1991–93)	+99%
Tax Load (Estimated)	5%	5-Year Return (1989–93)	+98%
Annual 12b-1 Fee	None	10-Year Return (1984–93)	NA
Annual Expense Ratio	1.05%	Worst-Ever Loss (1987)	27%
Annual Portfolio Turnover	40%	Bond Market Correlation	5%
5-Year Cost Estimate	11%	Up/Down Market Rank	A – E

Benefits		Investment Information	
Investment Objective	Income	Telephone	
5-Year Projected Return	NA	Minimum Investment	None
Safety Rating (0-100)	72%	Telephone Switching	Via broker
Yield	NA	Total Assets	$109 million

B
O
N
D

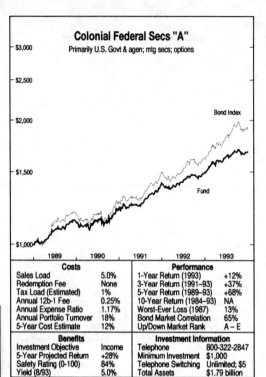

Colonial Federal Secs "A"
Primarily U.S. Govt & agen; mtg secs; options

(Chart labels: Bond Index, Fund; y-axis $1,000 to $3,000; x-axis 1989–1993)

Costs		Performance	
Sales Load	5.0%	1-Year Return (1993)	+12%
Redemption Fee	None	3-Year Return (1991–93)	+37%
Tax Load (Estimated)	1%	5-Year Return (1989–93)	+68%
Annual 12b-1 Fee	0.25%	10-Year Return (1984–93)	NA
Annual Expense Ratio	1.17%	Worst-Ever Loss (1987)	13%
Annual Portfolio Turnover	18%	Bond Market Correlation	65%
5-Year Cost Estimate	12%	Up/Down Market Rank	A – E

Benefits		Investment Information	
Investment Objective	Income	Telephone	800-322-2847
5-Year Projected Return	+28%	Minimum Investment	$1,000
Safety Rating (0-100)	84%	Telephone Switching	Unlimited; $5
Yield (8/93)	5.0%	Total Assets	$1.79 billion

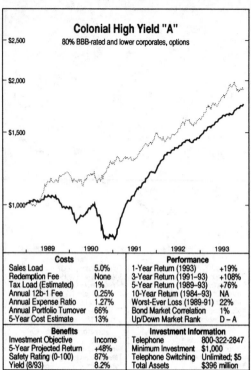

Colonial High Yield "A"
80% BBB-rated and lower corporates, options

(y-axis $1,000 to $2,500; x-axis 1989–1993)

Costs		Performance	
Sales Load	5.0%	1-Year Return (1993)	+19%
Redemption Fee	None	3-Year Return (1991–93)	+108%
Tax Load (Estimated)	1%	5-Year Return (1989–93)	+76%
Annual 12b-1 Fee	0.25%	10-Year Return (1984–93)	NA
Annual Expense Ratio	1.27%	Worst-Ever Loss (1989-91)	22%
Annual Portfolio Turnover	66%	Bond Market Correlation	1%
5-Year Cost Estimate	13%	Up/Down Market Rank	D – A

Benefits		Investment Information	
Investment Objective	Income	Telephone	800-322-2847
5-Year Projected Return	+48%	Minimum Investment	$1,000
Safety Rating (0-100)	87%	Telephone Switching	Unlimited; $5
Yield (8/93)	8.2%	Total Assets	$396 million

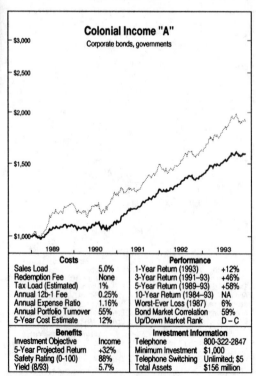

Colonial Income "A"
Corporate bonds, governments

(y-axis $1,000 to $3,000; x-axis 1989–1993)

Costs		Performance	
Sales Load	5.0%	1-Year Return (1993)	+12%
Redemption Fee	None	3-Year Return (1991–93)	+46%
Tax Load (Estimated)	1%	5-Year Return (1989–93)	+58%
Annual 12b-1 Fee	0.25%	10-Year Return (1984–93)	NA
Annual Expense Ratio	1.16%	Worst-Ever Loss (1987)	6%
Annual Portfolio Turnover	55%	Bond Market Correlation	59%
5-Year Cost Estimate	12%	Up/Down Market Rank	D – C

Benefits		Investment Information	
Investment Objective	Income	Telephone	800-322-2847
5-Year Projected Return	+32%	Minimum Investment	$1,000
Safety Rating (0-100)	88%	Telephone Switching	Unlimited; $5
Yield (8/93)	5.7%	Total Assets	$156 million

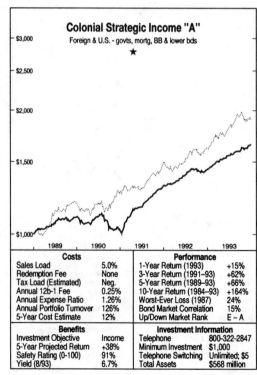

Colonial Strategic Income "A"
Foreign & U.S. - govts, mortg, BB & lower bds
★

(y-axis $1,000 to $3,000; x-axis 1989–1993)

Costs		Performance	
Sales Load	5.0%	1-Year Return (1993)	+15%
Redemption Fee	None	3-Year Return (1991–93)	+62%
Tax Load (Estimated)	Neg.	5-Year Return (1989–93)	+66%
Annual 12b-1 Fee	0.25%	10-Year Return (1984–93)	+164%
Annual Expense Ratio	1.26%	Worst-Ever Loss (1987)	24%
Annual Portfolio Turnover	126%	Bond Market Correlation	15%
5-Year Cost Estimate	12%	Up/Down Market Rank	E – A

Benefits		Investment Information	
Investment Objective	Income	Telephone	800-322-2847
5-Year Projected Return	+38%	Minimum Investment	$1,000
Safety Rating (0-100)	91%	Telephone Switching	Unlimited; $5
Yield (8/93)	6.7%	Total Assets	$568 million

BOND

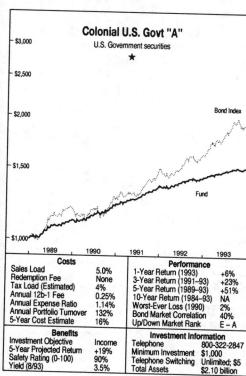

Colonial U.S. Govt "A"
U.S. Government securities
★

Bond Index

Fund

Costs		Performance	
Sales Load	5.0%	1-Year Return (1993)	+6%
Redemption Fee	None	3-Year Return (1991–93)	+23%
Tax Load (Estimated)	4%	5-Year Return (1989–93)	+51%
Annual 12b-1 Fee	0.25%	10-Year Return (1984–93)	NA
Annual Expense Ratio	1.14%	Worst-Ever Loss (1990)	2%
Annual Portfolio Turnover	132%	Bond Market Correlation	40%
5-Year Cost Estimate	16%	Up/Down Market Rank	E – A

Benefits		Investment Information	
Investment Objective	Income	Telephone	800-322-2847
5-Year Projected Return	+19%	Minimum Investment	$1,000
Safety Rating (0-100)	90%	Telephone Switching	Unlimited; $5
Yield (8/93)	3.5%	Total Assets	$2.10 billion

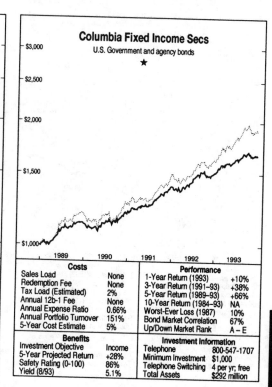

Columbia Fixed Income Secs
U.S. Government and agency bonds
★

Costs		Performance	
Sales Load	None	1-Year Return (1993)	+10%
Redemption Fee	None	3-Year Return (1991–93)	+38%
Tax Load (Estimated)	2%	5-Year Return (1989–93)	+66%
Annual 12b-1 Fee	None	10-Year Return (1984–93)	NA
Annual Expense Ratio	0.66%	Worst-Ever Loss (1987)	10%
Annual Portfolio Turnover	151%	Bond Market Correlation	67%
5-Year Cost Estimate	5%	Up/Down Market Rank	A – E

Benefits		Investment Information	
Investment Objective	Income	Telephone	800-547-1707
5-Year Projected Return	+28%	Minimum Investment	$1,000
Safety Rating (0-100)	86%	Telephone Switching	4 per yr; free
Yield (8/93)	5.1%	Total Assets	$292 million

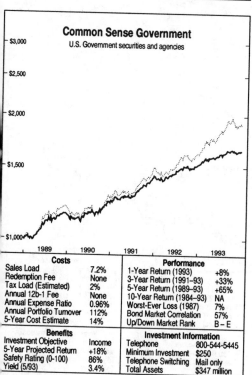

Common Sense Government
U.S. Government securities and agencies

Costs		Performance	
Sales Load	7.2%	1-Year Return (1993)	+8%
Redemption Fee	None	3-Year Return (1991–93)	+33%
Tax Load (Estimated)	2%	5-Year Return (1989–93)	+65%
Annual 12b-1 Fee	None	10-Year Return (1984–93)	NA
Annual Expense Ratio	0.96%	Worst-Ever Loss (1987)	7%
Annual Portfolio Turnover	112%	Bond Market Correlation	57%
5-Year Cost Estimate	14%	Up/Down Market Rank	B – E

Benefits		Investment Information	
Investment Objective	Income	Telephone	800-544-5445
5-Year Projected Return	+18%	Minimum Investment	$250
Safety Rating (0-100)	86%	Telephone Switching	Mail only
Yield (5/93)	3.4%	Total Assets	$347 million

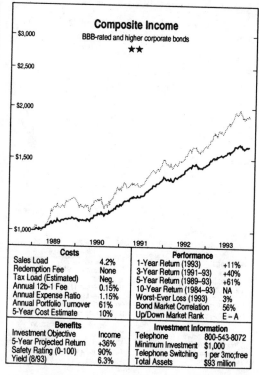

Composite Income
BBB-rated and higher corporate bonds
★★

Costs		Performance	
Sales Load	4.2%	1-Year Return (1993)	+11%
Redemption Fee	None	3-Year Return (1991–93)	+40%
Tax Load (Estimated)	Neg.	5-Year Return (1989–93)	+61%
Annual 12b-1 Fee	0.15%	10-Year Return (1984–93)	NA
Annual Expense Ratio	1.15%	Worst-Ever Loss (1993)	3%
Annual Portfolio Turnover	61%	Bond Market Correlation	56%
5-Year Cost Estimate	10%	Up/Down Market Rank	E – A

Benefits		Investment Information	
Investment Objective	Income	Telephone	800-543-8072
5-Year Projected Return	+36%	Minimum Investment	$1,000
Safety Rating (0-100)	90%	Telephone Switching	1 per 3mo; free
Yield (8/93)	6.3%	Total Assets	$93 million

B
O
N
D

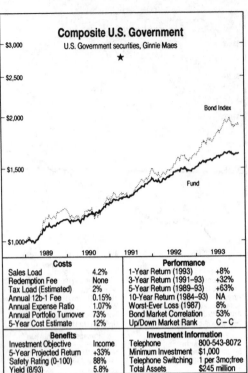

Composite U.S. Government
U.S. Government securities, Ginnie Maes
★

Chart y-axis: $3,000 / $2,500 / $2,000 / $1,500 / $1,000. Labeled "Bond Index" and "Fund". X-axis: 1989, 1990, 1991, 1992, 1993.

Costs		Performance	
Sales Load	4.2%	1-Year Return (1993)	+8%
Redemption Fee	None	3-Year Return (1991–93)	+32%
Tax Load (Estimated)	2%	5-Year Return (1989–93)	+63%
Annual 12b-1 Fee	0.15%	10-Year Return (1984–93)	NA
Annual Expense Ratio	1.07%	Worst-Ever Loss (1987)	8%
Annual Portfolio Turnover	73%	Bond Market Correlation	53%
5-Year Cost Estimate	12%	Up/Down Market Rank	C – C

Benefits		Investment Information	
Investment Objective	Income	Telephone	800-543-8072
5-Year Projected Return	+33%	Minimum Investment	$1,000
Safety Rating (0-100)	88%	Telephone Switching	1 per 3mo;free
Yield (8/93)	5.8%	Total Assets	$245 million

Convertible Holdings Income
Convertible securities; liquidate July 1997

Chart y-axis: $3,000 / $2,500 / $2,000 / $1,500 / $1,000. X-axis: 1989, 1990, 1991, 1992, 1993.

Costs		Performance	
Sales Load	None	1-Year Return (1993)	+3%
Redemption Fee	None	3-Year Return (1991–93)	+41%
Tax Load (Estimated)	0%	5-Year Return (1989–93)	+77%
Annual 12b-1 Fee	None	10-Year Return (1984–93)	NA
Annual Expense Ratio	0.80%	Worst-Ever Loss (1987)	24%
Annual Portfolio Turnover	94%	Bond Market Correlation	–2%
5-Year Cost Estimate	6%	Up/Down Market Rank	E – A

Benefits		Investment Information	
Investment Objective	Income	Telephone	800-426-5523
5-Year Projected Return	NA	Minimum Investment	None
Safety Rating (0-100)	77%	Telephone Switching	Via broker
Yield	NA	Total Assets	$298 million

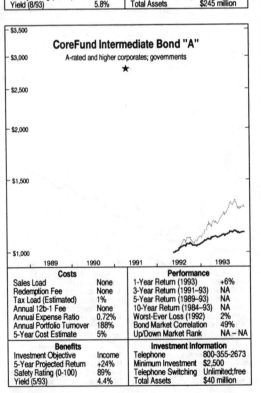

CoreFund Intermediate Bond "A"
A-rated and higher corporates; governments
★

Chart y-axis: $3,500 / $3,000 / $2,500 / $2,000 / $1,500 / $1,000. X-axis: 1989, 1990, 1991, 1992, 1993.

Costs		Performance	
Sales Load	None	1-Year Return (1993)	+6%
Redemption Fee	None	3-Year Return (1991–93)	NA
Tax Load (Estimated)	1%	5-Year Return (1989–93)	NA
Annual 12b-1 Fee	None	10-Year Return (1984–93)	NA
Annual Expense Ratio	0.72%	Worst-Ever Loss (1992)	2%
Annual Portfolio Turnover	188%	Bond Market Correlation	49%
5-Year Cost Estimate	5%	Up/Down Market Rank	NA – NA

Benefits		Investment Information	
Investment Objective	Income	Telephone	800-355-2673
5-Year Projected Return	+24%	Minimum Investment	$2,500
Safety Rating (0-100)	89%	Telephone Switching	Unlimited;free
Yield (5/93)	4.4%	Total Assets	$40 million

Current Income Shares
Investment-grade bonds, leveraged

Chart y-axis: $3,000 / $2,500 / $2,000 / $1,500 / $1,000. X-axis: 1989, 1990, 1991, 1992, 1993.

Costs		Performance	
Sales Load	None	1-Year Return (1993)	+9%
Redemption Fee	None	3-Year Return (1991–93)	+34%
Tax Load (Estimated)	3%	5-Year Return (1989–93)	+60%
Annual 12b-1 Fee	None	10-Year Return (1984–93)	NA
Annual Expense Ratio	0.90%	Worst-Ever Loss (1987)	16%
Annual Portfolio Turnover	115%	Bond Market Correlation	–2%
5-Year Cost Estimate	10%	Up/Down Market Rank	C – B

Benefits		Investment Information	
Investment Objective	Income	Telephone	213-236-7098
5-Year Projected Return	NA	Minimum Investment	None
Safety Rating (0-100)	74%	Telephone Switching	Via broker
Yield	NA	Total Assets	$49 million

BOND

Dean Witter American Value
Undervalued industries

(Chart showing "Fund" and "Bond Index" lines, 1989–1993, $1,000–$3,000 scale)

Costs		Performance	
Sales Load	None	1-Year Return (1993)	+19%
Redemption Fee	5.3%	3-Year Return (1991–93)	+93%
Tax Load (Estimated)	2%	5-Year Return (1989–93)	+139%
Annual 12b-1 Fee	1.00%	10-Year Return (1984–93)	NA
Annual Expense Ratio	1.72%	Worst-Ever Loss (1987)	29%
Annual Portfolio Turnover	330%	Bond Market Correlation	18%
5-Year Cost Estimate	12%	Up/Down Market Rank	A – E

Benefits		Investment Information	
Investment Objective	Growth	Telephone	800-869-3863
5-Year Projected Return	NA	Minimum Investment	$1,000
Safety Rating (0-100)	70%	Telephone Switching	See prospectus
Yield	NA	Total Assets	$947 million

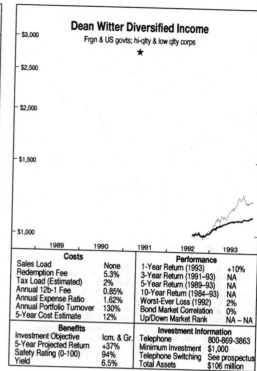

Dean Witter Diversified Income
Frgn & US govts; hi-qlty & low qlty corps
★

(Chart, 1989–1993, $1,000–$3,000 scale)

Costs		Performance	
Sales Load	None	1-Year Return (1993)	+10%
Redemption Fee	5.3%	3-Year Return (1991–93)	NA
Tax Load (Estimated)	2%	5-Year Return (1989–93)	NA
Annual 12b-1 Fee	0.85%	10-Year Return (1984–93)	NA
Annual Expense Ratio	1.62%	Worst-Ever Loss (1992)	2%
Annual Portfolio Turnover	130%	Bond Market Correlation	0%
5-Year Cost Estimate	12%	Up/Down Market Rank	NA – NA

Benefits		Investment Information	
Investment Objective	Icm. & Gr.	Telephone	800-869-3863
5-Year Projected Return	+37%	Minimum Investment	$1,000
Safety Rating (0-100)	94%	Telephone Switching	See prospectus
Yield	6.5%	Total Assets	$106 million

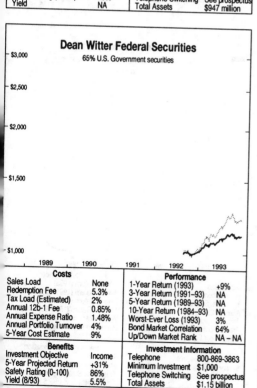

Dean Witter Federal Securities
65% U.S. Government securities

(Chart, 1989–1993, $1,000–$3,000 scale)

Costs		Performance	
Sales Load	None	1-Year Return (1993)	+9%
Redemption Fee	5.3%	3-Year Return (1991–93)	NA
Tax Load (Estimated)	2%	5-Year Return (1989–93)	NA
Annual 12b-1 Fee	0.85%	10-Year Return (1984–93)	NA
Annual Expense Ratio	1.48%	Worst-Ever Loss (1993)	3%
Annual Portfolio Turnover	4%	Bond Market Correlation	64%
5-Year Cost Estimate	9%	Up/Down Market Rank	NA – NA

Benefits		Investment Information	
Investment Objective	Income	Telephone	800-869-3863
5-Year Projected Return	+31%	Minimum Investment	$1,000
Safety Rating (0-100)	86%	Telephone Switching	See prospectus
Yield (8/93)	5.5%	Total Assets	$1.15 billion

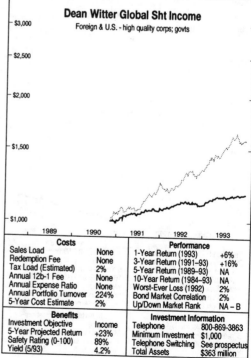

Dean Witter Global Sht Income
Foreign & U.S. - high quality corps; govts

(Chart, 1989–1993, $1,000–$3,000 scale)

Costs		Performance	
Sales Load	None	1-Year Return (1993)	+6%
Redemption Fee	None	3-Year Return (1991–93)	+16%
Tax Load (Estimated)	2%	5-Year Return (1989–93)	NA
Annual 12b-1 Fee	None	10-Year Return (1984–93)	NA
Annual Expense Ratio	None	Worst-Ever Loss (1992)	2%
Annual Portfolio Turnover	224%	Bond Market Correlation	2%
5-Year Cost Estimate	2%	Up/Down Market Rank	NA – B

Benefits		Investment Information	
Investment Objective	Income	Telephone	800-869-3863
5-Year Projected Return	+23%	Minimum Investment	$1,000
Safety Rating (0-100)	89%	Telephone Switching	See prospectus
Yield (5/93)	4.2%	Total Assets	$363 million

BOND

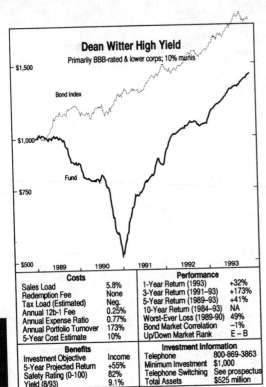

Dean Witter High Yield
Primarily BBB-rated & lower corps; 10% munis

Bond Index

Fund

Costs		Performance	
Sales Load	5.8%	1-Year Return (1993)	+32%
Redemption Fee	None	3-Year Return (1991–93)	+173%
Tax Load (Estimated)	Neg.	5-Year Return (1989–93)	+41%
Annual 12b-1 Fee	0.25%	10-Year Return (1984–93)	NA
Annual Expense Ratio	0.77%	Worst-Ever Loss (1989-90)	49%
Annual Portfolio Turnover	173%	Bond Market Correlation	–1%
5-Year Cost Estimate	10%	Up/Down Market Rank	E – B

Benefits		Investment Information	
Investment Objective	Income	Telephone	800-869-3863
5-Year Projected Return	+55%	Minimum Investment	$1,000
Safety Rating (0-100)	82%	Telephone Switching	See prospectus
Yield (8/93)	9.1%	Total Assets	$525 million

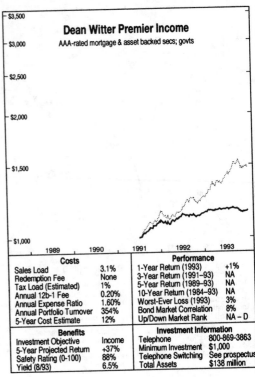

Dean Witter Premier Income
AAA-rated mortgage & asset backed secs; govts

Costs		Performance	
Sales Load	3.1%	1-Year Return (1993)	+1%
Redemption Fee	None	3-Year Return (1991–93)	NA
Tax Load (Estimated)	1%	5-Year Return (1989–93)	NA
Annual 12b-1 Fee	0.20%	10-Year Return (1984–93)	NA
Annual Expense Ratio	1.60%	Worst-Ever Loss (1993)	3%
Annual Portfolio Turnover	354%	Bond Market Correlation	8%
5-Year Cost Estimate	12%	Up/Down Market Rank	NA – D

Benefits		Investment Information	
Investment Objective	Income	Telephone	800-869-3863
5-Year Projected Return	+37%	Minimum Investment	$1,000
Safety Rating (0-100)	88%	Telephone Switching	See prospectus
Yield (8/93)	6.5%	Total Assets	$138 million

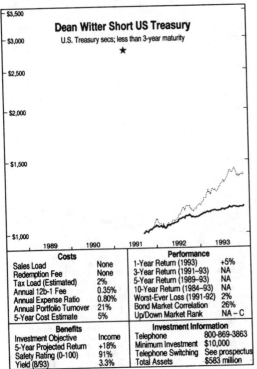

Dean Witter Short US Treasury
U.S. Treasury secs; less than 3-year maturity
★

Costs		Performance	
Sales Load	None	1-Year Return (1993)	+5%
Redemption Fee	None	3-Year Return (1991–93)	NA
Tax Load (Estimated)	2%	5-Year Return (1989–93)	NA
Annual 12b-1 Fee	0.35%	10-Year Return (1984–93)	NA
Annual Expense Ratio	0.80%	Worst-Ever Loss (1991-92)	2%
Annual Portfolio Turnover	21%	Bond Market Correlation	26%
5-Year Cost Estimate	5%	Up/Down Market Rank	NA – C

Benefits		Investment Information	
Investment Objective	Income	Telephone	800-869-3863
5-Year Projected Return	+18%	Minimum Investment	$10,000
Safety Rating (0-100)	91%	Telephone Switching	See prospectus
Yield (8/93)	3.3%	Total Assets	$583 million

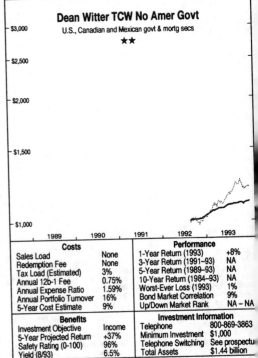

Dean Witter TCW No Amer Govt
U.S., Canadian and Mexican govt & mortg secs
★★

Costs		Performance	
Sales Load	None	1-Year Return (1993)	+8%
Redemption Fee	None	3-Year Return (1991–93)	NA
Tax Load (Estimated)	3%	5-Year Return (1989–93)	NA
Annual 12b-1 Fee	0.75%	10-Year Return (1984–93)	NA
Annual Expense Ratio	1.59%	Worst-Ever Loss (1993)	1%
Annual Portfolio Turnover	16%	Bond Market Correlation	9%
5-Year Cost Estimate	9%	Up/Down Market Rank	NA – NA

Benefits		Investment Information	
Investment Objective	Income	Telephone	800-869-3863
5-Year Projected Return	+37%	Minimum Investment	$1,000
Safety Rating (0-100)	96%	Telephone Switching	See prospectus
Yield (8/93)	6.5%	Total Assets	$1.44 billion

B O N D

1994 Mutual Fund Buyer's Guide

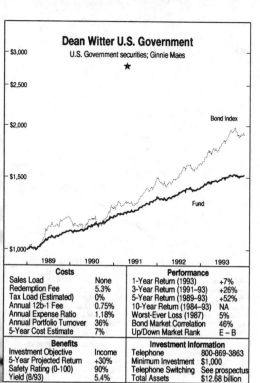

Dean Witter U.S. Government
U.S. Government securities; Ginnie Maes
★

Bond Index

Fund

1989 1990 1991 1992 1993

Costs		Performance	
Sales Load	None	1-Year Return (1993)	+7%
Redemption Fee	5.3%	3-Year Return (1991–93)	+26%
Tax Load (Estimated)	0%	5-Year Return (1989–93)	+52%
Annual 12b-1 Fee	0.75%	10-Year Return (1984–93)	NA
Annual Expense Ratio	1.18%	Worst-Ever Loss (1987)	5%
Annual Portfolio Turnover	36%	Bond Market Correlation	46%
5-Year Cost Estimate	7%	Up/Down Market Rank	E – B

Benefits		Investment Information	
Investment Objective	Income	Telephone	800-869-3863
5-Year Projected Return	+30%	Minimum Investment	$1,000
Safety Rating (0-100)	90%	Telephone Switching	See prospectus
Yield (8/93)	5.4%	Total Assets	$12.68 billion

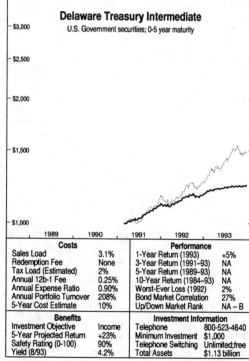

Dean Witter Worldwide Income
Foreign & U.S. - fixed-income securities

1989 1990 1991 1992 1993

Costs		Performance	
Sales Load	None	1-Year Return (1993)	+9%
Redemption Fee	5.3%	3-Year Return (1991–93)	+14%
Tax Load (Estimated)	2%	5-Year Return (1989–93)	NA
Annual 12b-1 Fee	0.85%	10-Year Return (1984–93)	NA
Annual Expense Ratio	1.76%	Worst-Ever Loss (1991)	9%
Annual Portfolio Turnover	254%	Bond Market Correlation	12%
5-Year Cost Estimate	13%	Up/Down Market Rank	D – A

Benefits		Investment Information	
Investment Objective	Income	Telephone	800-869-3863
5-Year Projected Return	+22%	Minimum Investment	$1,000
Safety Rating (0-100)	85%	Telephone Switching	See prospectus
Yield (8/93)	4.1%	Total Assets	$285 million

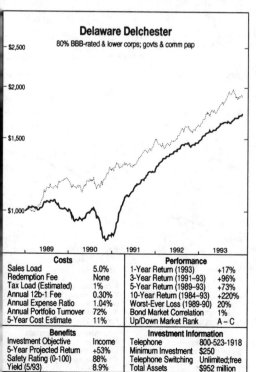

Delaware Delchester
80% BBB-rated & lower corps; govts & comm pap

1989 1990 1991 1992 1993

Costs		Performance	
Sales Load	5.0%	1-Year Return (1993)	+17%
Redemption Fee	None	3-Year Return (1991–93)	+96%
Tax Load (Estimated)	1%	5-Year Return (1989–93)	+73%
Annual 12b-1 Fee	0.30%	10-Year Return (1984–93)	+220%
Annual Expense Ratio	1.04%	Worst-Ever Loss (1989-90)	20%
Annual Portfolio Turnover	72%	Bond Market Correlation	1%
5-Year Cost Estimate	11%	Up/Down Market Rank	A – C

Benefits		Investment Information	
Investment Objective	Income	Telephone	800-523-1918
5-Year Projected Return	+53%	Minimum Investment	$250
Safety Rating (0-100)	88%	Telephone Switching	Unlimited;free
Yield (5/93)	8.9%	Total Assets	$952 million

Delaware Treasury Intermediate
U.S. Government securities; 0-5 year maturity

1989 1990 1991 1992 1993

Costs		Performance	
Sales Load	3.1%	1-Year Return (1993)	+5%
Redemption Fee	None	3-Year Return (1991–93)	NA
Tax Load (Estimated)	2%	5-Year Return (1989–93)	NA
Annual 12b-1 Fee	0.25%	10-Year Return (1984–93)	NA
Annual Expense Ratio	0.90%	Worst-Ever Loss (1992)	2%
Annual Portfolio Turnover	208%	Bond Market Correlation	27%
5-Year Cost Estimate	10%	Up/Down Market Rank	NA – B

Benefits		Investment Information	
Investment Objective	Income	Telephone	800-523-4640
5-Year Projected Return	+23%	Minimum Investment	$1,000
Safety Rating (0-100)	90%	Telephone Switching	Unlimited;free
Yield (8/93)	4.2%	Total Assets	$1.13 billion

BOND

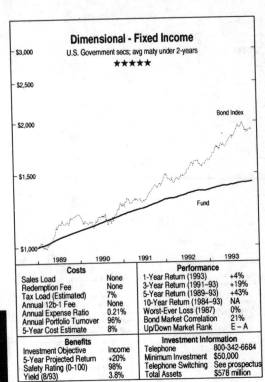

Dimensional - Fixed Income
U.S. Government secs; avg maty under 2-years
★★★★★

Bond Index

Fund

Costs		Performance	
Sales Load	None	1-Year Return (1993)	+4%
Redemption Fee	None	3-Year Return (1991–93)	+19%
Tax Load (Estimated)	7%	5-Year Return (1989–93)	+43%
Annual 12b-1 Fee	None	10-Year Return (1984–93)	NA
Annual Expense Ratio	0.21%	Worst-Ever Loss (1987)	0%
Annual Portfolio Turnover	96%	Bond Market Correlation	21%
5-Year Cost Estimate	8%	Up/Down Market Rank	E – A

Benefits		Investment Information	
Investment Objective	Income	Telephone	800-342-6684
5-Year Projected Return	+20%	Minimum Investment	$50,000
Safety Rating (0-100)	98%	Telephone Switching	See prospectus
Yield (8/93)	3.8%	Total Assets	$578 million

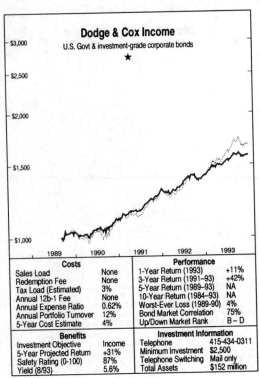

Dodge & Cox Income
U.S. Govt & investment-grade corporate bonds
★

Costs		Performance	
Sales Load	None	1-Year Return (1993)	+11%
Redemption Fee	None	3-Year Return (1991–93)	+42%
Tax Load (Estimated)	3%	5-Year Return (1989–93)	NA
Annual 12b-1 Fee	None	10-Year Return (1984–93)	NA
Annual Expense Ratio	0.62%	Worst-Ever Loss (1989-90)	4%
Annual Portfolio Turnover	12%	Bond Market Correlation	75%
5-Year Cost Estimate	4%	Up/Down Market Rank	B – D

Benefits		Investment Information	
Investment Objective	Income	Telephone	415-434-0311
5-Year Projected Return	+31%	Minimum Investment	$2,500
Safety Rating (0-100)	87%	Telephone Switching	Mail only
Yield (8/93)	5.6%	Total Assets	$152 million

Dreyfus A Bonds Plus
80% A-rated and higher corps; government secs
★★

Costs		Performance	
Sales Load	None	1-Year Return (1993)	+15%
Redemption Fee	None	3-Year Return (1991–93)	+48%
Tax Load (Estimated)	3%	5-Year Return (1989–93)	+75%
Annual 12b-1 Fee	None	10-Year Return (1984–93)	NA
Annual Expense Ratio	0.93%	Worst-Ever Loss (1987)	13%
Annual Portfolio Turnover	67%	Bond Market Correlation	81%
5-Year Cost Estimate	8%	Up/Down Market Rank	A – E

Benefits		Investment Information	
Investment Objective	Income	Telephone	800-645-6561
5-Year Projected Return	+34%	Minimum Investment	$2,500
Safety Rating (0-100)	87%	Telephone Switching	Unlimited;free
Yield (8/93)	6.0%	Total Assets	$620 million

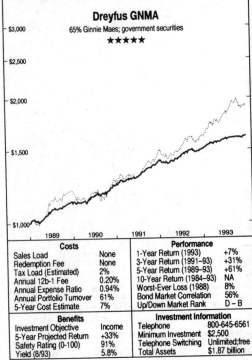

Dreyfus GNMA
65% Ginnie Maes; government securities
★★★★★

Costs		Performance	
Sales Load	None	1-Year Return (1993)	+7%
Redemption Fee	None	3-Year Return (1991–93)	+31%
Tax Load (Estimated)	2%	5-Year Return (1989–93)	+61%
Annual 12b-1 Fee	0.20%	10-Year Return (1984–93)	NA
Annual Expense Ratio	0.94%	Worst-Ever Loss (1988)	8%
Annual Portfolio Turnover	61%	Bond Market Correlation	56%
5-Year Cost Estimate	7%	Up/Down Market Rank	D – B

Benefits		Investment Information	
Investment Objective	Income	Telephone	800-645-6561
5-Year Projected Return	+33%	Minimum Investment	$2,500
Safety Rating (0-100)	91%	Telephone Switching	Unlimited;free
Yield (8/93)	5.8%	Total Assets	$1.87 billion

BOND

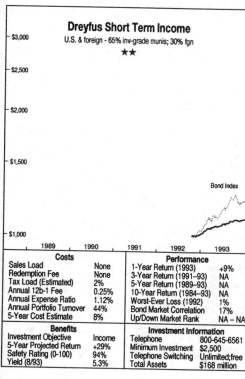

Dreyfus Short Term Income

U.S. & foreign - 65% inv-grade munis; 30% fgn
★★

Bond Index

Costs		Performance	
Sales Load	None	1-Year Return (1993)	+9%
Redemption Fee	None	3-Year Return (1991–93)	NA
Tax Load (Estimated)	2%	5-Year Return (1989–93)	NA
Annual 12b-1 Fee	0.25%	10-Year Return (1984–93)	NA
Annual Expense Ratio	1.12%	Worst-Ever Loss (1992)	1%
Annual Portfolio Turnover	44%	Bond Market Correlation	17%
5-Year Cost Estimate	8%	Up/Down Market Rank	NA – NA

Benefits		Investment Information	
Investment Objective	Income	Telephone	800-645-6561
5-Year Projected Return	+29%	Minimum Investment	$2,500
Safety Rating (0-100)	94%	Telephone Switching	Unlimited;free
Yield (8/93)	5.3%	Total Assets	$168 million

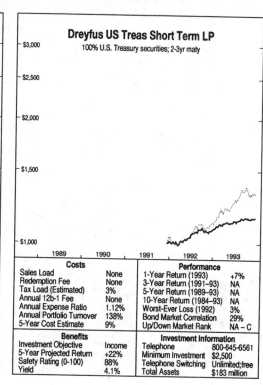

Dreyfus US Treas Short Term LP

100% U.S. Treasury securities; 2-3yr maty

Costs		Performance	
Sales Load	None	1-Year Return (1993)	+7%
Redemption Fee	None	3-Year Return (1991–93)	NA
Tax Load (Estimated)	3%	5-Year Return (1989–93)	NA
Annual 12b-1 Fee	None	10-Year Return (1984–93)	NA
Annual Expense Ratio	1.12%	Worst-Ever Loss (1992)	3%
Annual Portfolio Turnover	138%	Bond Market Correlation	29%
5-Year Cost Estimate	9%	Up/Down Market Rank	NA – C

Benefits		Investment Information	
Investment Objective	Income	Telephone	800-645-6561
5-Year Projected Return	+22%	Minimum Investment	$2,500
Safety Rating (0-100)	88%	Telephone Switching	Unlimited;free
Yield	4.1%	Total Assets	$183 million

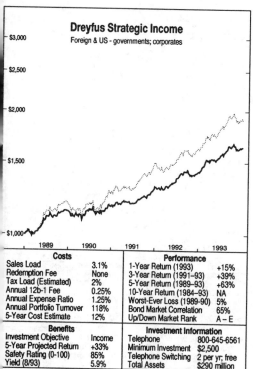

Dreyfus Strategic Income

Foreign & US - governments; corporates

Costs		Performance	
Sales Load	3.1%	1-Year Return (1993)	+15%
Redemption Fee	None	3-Year Return (1991–93)	+39%
Tax Load (Estimated)	2%	5-Year Return (1989–93)	+63%
Annual 12b-1 Fee	0.25%	10-Year Return (1984–93)	NA
Annual Expense Ratio	1.25%	Worst-Ever Loss (1989-90)	5%
Annual Portfolio Turnover	118%	Bond Market Correlation	65%
5-Year Cost Estimate	12%	Up/Down Market Rank	A – E

Benefits		Investment Information	
Investment Objective	Income	Telephone	800-645-6561
5-Year Projected Return	+33%	Minimum Investment	$2,500
Safety Rating (0-100)	85%	Telephone Switching	2 per yr; free
Yield (8/93)	5.9%	Total Assets	$290 million

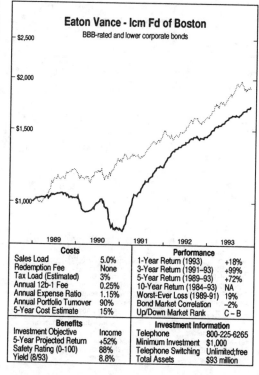

Eaton Vance - Icm Fd of Boston

BBB-rated and lower corporate bonds

Costs		Performance	
Sales Load	5.0%	1-Year Return (1993)	+18%
Redemption Fee	None	3-Year Return (1991–93)	+99%
Tax Load (Estimated)	3%	5-Year Return (1989–93)	+72%
Annual 12b-1 Fee	0.25%	10-Year Return (1984–93)	NA
Annual Expense Ratio	1.15%	Worst-Ever Loss (1989-91)	19%
Annual Portfolio Turnover	90%	Bond Market Correlation	-2%
5-Year Cost Estimate	15%	Up/Down Market Rank	C – B

Benefits		Investment Information	
Investment Objective	Income	Telephone	800-225-6265
5-Year Projected Return	+52%	Minimum Investment	$1,000
Safety Rating (0-100)	88%	Telephone Switching	Unlimited;free
Yield (8/93)	8.8%	Total Assets	$93 million

BOND

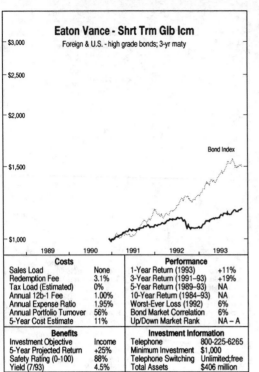

Eaton Vance - Shrt Trm Glb Icm

Foreign & U.S. - high grade bonds; 3-yr maty

Bond Index

Costs		Performance	
Sales Load	None	1-Year Return (1993)	+11%
Redemption Fee	3.1%	3-Year Return (1991–93)	+19%
Tax Load (Estimated)	0%	5-Year Return (1989–93)	NA
Annual 12b-1 Fee	1.00%	10-Year Return (1984–93)	NA
Annual Expense Ratio	1.95%	Worst-Ever Loss (1992)	6%
Annual Portfolio Turnover	56%	Bond Market Correlation	6%
5-Year Cost Estimate	11%	Up/Down Market Rank	NA – A

Benefits		Investment Information	
Investment Objective	Income	Telephone	800-225-6265
5-Year Projected Return	+25%	Minimum Investment	$1,000
Safety Rating (0-100)	88%	Telephone Switching	Unlimited;free
Yield (7/93)	4.5%	Total Assets	$406 million

Eaton Vance - Trad Govt Oblig

100% U.S. Government securities; leveraged

★★★

Costs		Performance	
Sales Load	5.0%	1-Year Return (1993)	+9%
Redemption Fee	None	3-Year Return (1991–93)	+32%
Tax Load (Estimated)	1%	5-Year Return (1989–93)	+63%
Annual 12b-1 Fee	0.25%	10-Year Return (1984–93)	NA
Annual Expense Ratio	1.41%	Worst-Ever Loss (1986)	5%
Annual Portfolio Turnover	26%	Bond Market Correlation	65%
5-Year Cost Estimate	13%	Up/Down Market Rank	D – B

Benefits		Investment Information	
Investment Objective	Income	Telephone	800-225-6265
5-Year Projected Return	+24%	Minimum Investment	$1,000
Safety Rating (0-100)	91%	Telephone Switching	Unlimited;free
Yield (8/93)	4.4%	Total Assets	$513 million

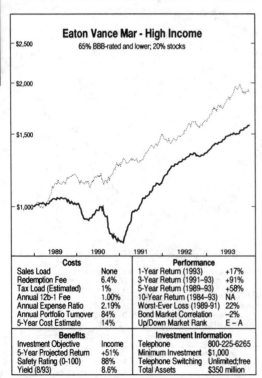

Eaton Vance Mar - High Income

65% BBB-rated and lower; 20% stocks

Costs		Performance	
Sales Load	None	1-Year Return (1993)	+17%
Redemption Fee	6.4%	3-Year Return (1991–93)	+91%
Tax Load (Estimated)	1%	5-Year Return (1989–93)	+58%
Annual 12b-1 Fee	1.00%	10-Year Return (1984–93)	NA
Annual Expense Ratio	2.19%	Worst-Ever Loss (1989-91)	22%
Annual Portfolio Turnover	84%	Bond Market Correlation	–2%
5-Year Cost Estimate	14%	Up/Down Market Rank	E – A

Benefits		Investment Information	
Investment Objective	Income	Telephone	800-225-6265
5-Year Projected Return	+51%	Minimum Investment	$1,000
Safety Rating (0-100)	88%	Telephone Switching	Unlimited;free
Yield (8/93)	8.6%	Total Assets	$350 million

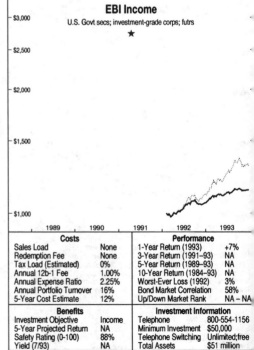

EBI Income

U.S. Govt secs; investment-grade corps; futrs

★

Costs		Performance	
Sales Load	None	1-Year Return (1993)	+7%
Redemption Fee	None	3-Year Return (1991–93)	NA
Tax Load (Estimated)	0%	5-Year Return (1989–93)	NA
Annual 12b-1 Fee	1.00%	10-Year Return (1984–93)	NA
Annual Expense Ratio	2.25%	Worst-Ever Loss (1992)	3%
Annual Portfolio Turnover	16%	Bond Market Correlation	58%
5-Year Cost Estimate	12%	Up/Down Market Rank	NA – NA

Benefits		Investment Information	
Investment Objective	Income	Telephone	800-554-1156
5-Year Projected Return	NA	Minimum Investment	$50,000
Safety Rating (0-100)	88%	Telephone Switching	Unlimited;free
Yield (7/93)	NA	Total Assets	$51 million

Eighteen Thirty-Eight Bond-Deb
75% BBB-rated & higher corps; pfds; leveraged

Costs		Performance	
Sales Load	None	1-Year Return (1993)	+8%
Redemption Fee	None	3-Year Return (1991–93)	+43%
Tax Load (Estimated)	3%	5-Year Return (1989–93)	+101%
Annual 12b-1 Fee	None	10-Year Return (1984–93)	NA
Annual Expense Ratio	0.95%	Worst-Ever Loss (1987)	25%
Annual Portfolio Turnover	73%	Bond Market Correlation	0%
5-Year Cost Estimate	10%	Up/Down Market Rank	A – D

Benefits		Investment Information	
Investment Objective	Income	Telephone	NONE
5-Year Projected Return	NA	Minimum Investment	None
Safety Rating (0-100)	73%	Telephone Switching	Via broker
Yield	NA	Total Assets	$74 million

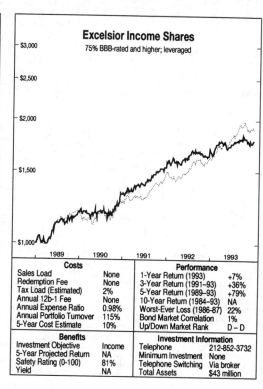

Excelsior Income Shares
75% BBB-rated and higher; leveraged

Costs		Performance	
Sales Load	None	1-Year Return (1993)	+7%
Redemption Fee	None	3-Year Return (1991–93)	+36%
Tax Load (Estimated)	2%	5-Year Return (1989–93)	+79%
Annual 12b-1 Fee	None	10-Year Return (1984–93)	NA
Annual Expense Ratio	0.98%	Worst-Ever Loss (1986-87)	22%
Annual Portfolio Turnover	115%	Bond Market Correlation	1%
5-Year Cost Estimate	10%	Up/Down Market Rank	D – D

Benefits		Investment Information	
Investment Objective	Income	Telephone	212-852-3732
5-Year Projected Return	NA	Minimum Investment	None
Safety Rating (0-100)	81%	Telephone Switching	Via broker
Yield	NA	Total Assets	$43 million

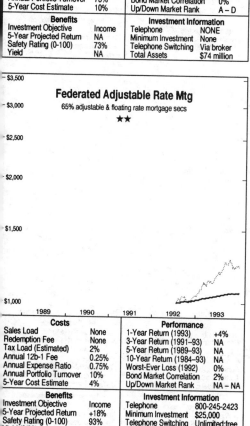

Federated Adjustable Rate Mtg
65% adjustable & floating rate mortgage secs
★★

Costs		Performance	
Sales Load	None	1-Year Return (1993)	+4%
Redemption Fee	None	3-Year Return (1991–93)	NA
Tax Load (Estimated)	2%	5-Year Return (1989–93)	NA
Annual 12b-1 Fee	0.25%	10-Year Return (1984–93)	NA
Annual Expense Ratio	0.75%	Worst-Ever Loss (1992)	0%
Annual Portfolio Turnover	10%	Bond Market Correlation	2%
5-Year Cost Estimate	4%	Up/Down Market Rank	NA – NA

Benefits		Investment Information	
Investment Objective	Income	Telephone	800-245-2423
5-Year Projected Return	+18%	Minimum Investment	$25,000
Safety Rating (0-100)	93%	Telephone Switching	Unlimited;free
Yield (8/93)	3.4%	Total Assets	$2.18 billion

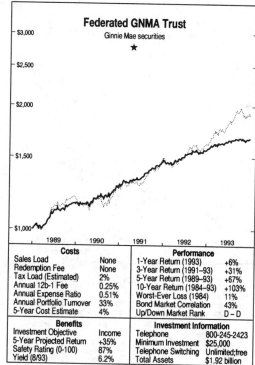

Federated GNMA Trust
Ginnie Mae securities
★

Costs		Performance	
Sales Load	None	1-Year Return (1993)	+6%
Redemption Fee	None	3-Year Return (1991–93)	+31%
Tax Load (Estimated)	2%	5-Year Return (1989–93)	+67%
Annual 12b-1 Fee	0.25%	10-Year Return (1984–93)	+103%
Annual Expense Ratio	0.51%	Worst-Ever Loss (1984)	11%
Annual Portfolio Turnover	33%	Bond Market Correlation	43%
5-Year Cost Estimate	4%	Up/Down Market Rank	D – D

Benefits		Investment Information	
Investment Objective	Income	Telephone	800-245-2423
5-Year Projected Return	+35%	Minimum Investment	$25,000
Safety Rating (0-100)	87%	Telephone Switching	Unlimited;free
Yield (8/93)	6.2%	Total Assets	$1.92 billion

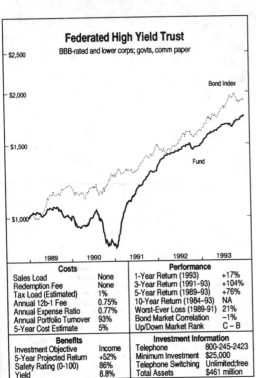

Federated High Yield Trust

BBB-rated and lower corps; govts, comm paper

Bond Index

Fund

Costs		Performance	
Sales Load	None	1-Year Return (1993)	+17%
Redemption Fee	None	3-Year Return (1991–93)	+104%
Tax Load (Estimated)	1%	5-Year Return (1989–93)	+76%
Annual 12b-1 Fee	0.75%	10-Year Return (1984–93)	NA
Annual Expense Ratio	0.77%	Worst-Ever Loss (1989–91)	21%
Annual Portfolio Turnover	93%	Bond Market Correlation	–1%
5-Year Cost Estimate	5%	Up/Down Market Rank	C – B

Benefits		Investment Information	
Investment Objective	Income	Telephone	800-245-2423
5-Year Projected Return	+52%	Minimum Investment	$25,000
Safety Rating (0-100)	86%	Telephone Switching	Unlimited;free
Yield	8.8%	Total Assets	$461 million

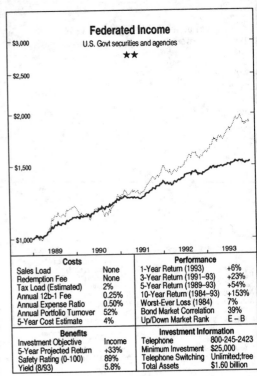

Federated Income

U.S. Govt securities and agencies
★★

Costs		Performance	
Sales Load	None	1-Year Return (1993)	+6%
Redemption Fee	None	3-Year Return (1991–93)	+23%
Tax Load (Estimated)	2%	5-Year Return (1989–93)	+54%
Annual 12b-1 Fee	0.25%	10-Year Return (1984–93)	+153%
Annual Expense Ratio	0.50%	Worst-Ever Loss (1984)	7%
Annual Portfolio Turnover	52%	Bond Market Correlation	39%
5-Year Cost Estimate	4%	Up/Down Market Rank	E – B

Benefits		Investment Information	
Investment Objective	Income	Telephone	800-245-2423
5-Year Projected Return	+33%	Minimum Investment	$25,000
Safety Rating (0-100)	89%	Telephone Switching	Unlimited;free
Yield (8/93)	5.8%	Total Assets	$1.60 billion

B
O
N
D

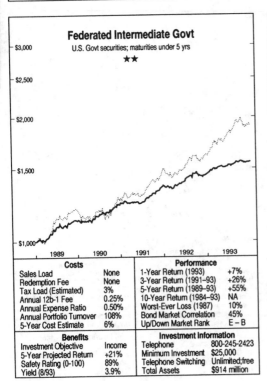

Federated Intermediate Govt

U.S. Govt securities; maturities under 5 yrs
★★

Costs		Performance	
Sales Load	None	1-Year Return (1993)	+7%
Redemption Fee	None	3-Year Return (1991–93)	+26%
Tax Load (Estimated)	3%	5-Year Return (1989–93)	+55%
Annual 12b-1 Fee	0.25%	10-Year Return (1984–93)	NA
Annual Expense Ratio	0.50%	Worst-Ever Loss (1987)	10%
Annual Portfolio Turnover	108%	Bond Market Correlation	45%
5-Year Cost Estimate	6%	Up/Down Market Rank	E – B

Benefits		Investment Information	
Investment Objective	Income	Telephone	800-245-2423
5-Year Projected Return	+21%	Minimum Investment	$25,000
Safety Rating (0-100)	89%	Telephone Switching	Unlimited;free
Yield (8/93)	3.9%	Total Assets	$914 million

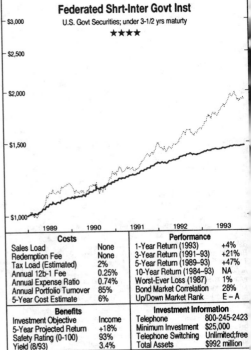

Federated Shrt-Inter Govt Inst

U.S. Govt Securities; under 3-1/2 yrs maturty
★★★★

Costs		Performance	
Sales Load	None	1-Year Return (1993)	+4%
Redemption Fee	None	3-Year Return (1991–93)	+21%
Tax Load (Estimated)	2%	5-Year Return (1989–93)	+47%
Annual 12b-1 Fee	0.25%	10-Year Return (1984–93)	NA
Annual Expense Ratio	0.74%	Worst-Ever Loss (1987)	1%
Annual Portfolio Turnover	85%	Bond Market Correlation	28%
5-Year Cost Estimate	6%	Up/Down Market Rank	E – A

Benefits		Investment Information	
Investment Objective	Income	Telephone	800-245-2423
5-Year Projected Return	+18%	Minimum Investment	$25,000
Safety Rating (0-100)	93%	Telephone Switching	Unlimited;free
Yield (8/93)	3.4%	Total Assets	$992 million

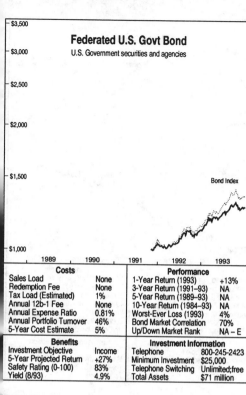

Federated U.S. Govt Bond
U.S. Government securities and agencies

Bond Index

Costs		Performance	
Sales Load	None	1-Year Return (1993)	+13%
Redemption Fee	None	3-Year Return (1991–93)	NA
Tax Load (Estimated)	1%	5-Year Return (1989–93)	NA
Annual 12b-1 Fee	None	10-Year Return (1984–93)	NA
Annual Expense Ratio	0.81%	Worst-Ever Loss (1993)	4%
Annual Portfolio Turnover	46%	Bond Market Correlation	70%
5-Year Cost Estimate	5%	Up/Down Market Rank	NA – E

Benefits		Investment Information	
Investment Objective	Income	Telephone	800-245-2423
5-Year Projected Return	+27%	Minimum Investment	$25,000
Safety Rating (0-100)	83%	Telephone Switching	Unlimited;free
Yield (8/93)	4.9%	Total Assets	$71 million

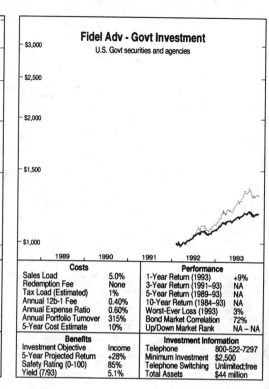

Fidel Adv - Govt Investment
U.S. Govt securities and agencies

Costs		Performance	
Sales Load	5.0%	1-Year Return (1993)	+9%
Redemption Fee	None	3-Year Return (1991–93)	NA
Tax Load (Estimated)	1%	5-Year Return (1989–93)	NA
Annual 12b-1 Fee	0.40%	10-Year Return (1984–93)	NA
Annual Expense Ratio	0.60%	Worst-Ever Loss (1993)	3%
Annual Portfolio Turnover	315%	Bond Market Correlation	72%
5-Year Cost Estimate	10%	Up/Down Market Rank	NA – NA

Benefits		Investment Information	
Investment Objective	Income	Telephone	800-522-7297
5-Year Projected Return	+28%	Minimum Investment	$2,500
Safety Rating (0-100)	85%	Telephone Switching	Unlimited;free
Yield (7/93)	5.1%	Total Assets	$44 million

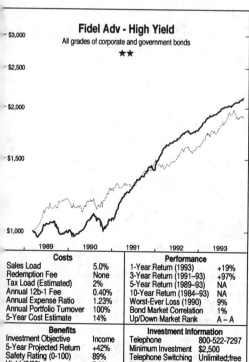

Fidel Adv - High Yield
All grades of corporate and government bonds
★★

Costs		Performance	
Sales Load	5.0%	1-Year Return (1993)	+19%
Redemption Fee	None	3-Year Return (1991–93)	+97%
Tax Load (Estimated)	2%	5-Year Return (1989–93)	NA
Annual 12b-1 Fee	0.40%	10-Year Return (1984–93)	NA
Annual Expense Ratio	1.23%	Worst-Ever Loss (1990)	9%
Annual Portfolio Turnover	100%	Up/Down Market Rank	A – A
5-Year Cost Estimate	14%		

Benefits		Investment Information	
Investment Objective	Income	Telephone	800-522-7297
5-Year Projected Return	+42%	Minimum Investment	$2,500
Safety Rating (0-100)	89%	Telephone Switching	Unlimited;free
Yield (8/93)	7.2%	Total Assets	$377 million

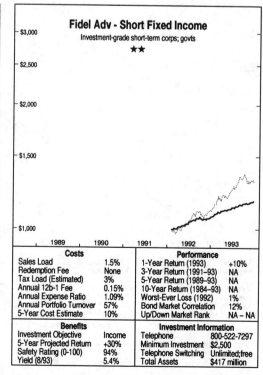

Fidel Adv - Short Fixed Income
Investment-grade short-term corps; govts
★★

Costs		Performance	
Sales Load	1.5%	1-Year Return (1993)	+10%
Redemption Fee	None	3-Year Return (1991–93)	NA
Tax Load (Estimated)	3%	5-Year Return (1989–93)	NA
Annual 12b-1 Fee	0.15%	10-Year Return (1984–93)	NA
Annual Expense Ratio	1.09%	Worst-Ever Loss (1992)	1%
Annual Portfolio Turnover	57%	Bond Market Correlation	12%
5-Year Cost Estimate	10%	Up/Down Market Rank	NA – NA

Benefits		Investment Information	
Investment Objective	Income	Telephone	800-522-7297
5-Year Projected Return	+30%	Minimum Investment	$2,500
Safety Rating (0-100)	94%	Telephone Switching	Unlimited;free
Yield (8/93)	5.4%	Total Assets	$417 million

BOND

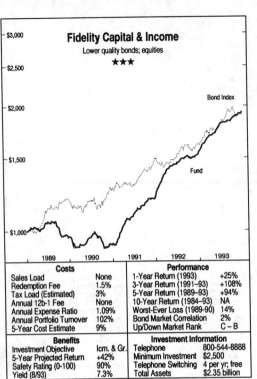

Fidelity Capital & Income
Lower quality bonds; equities
★★★

Bond Index

Fund

Costs		Performance	
Sales Load	None	1-Year Return (1993)	+25%
Redemption Fee	1.5%	3-Year Return (1991–93)	+108%
Tax Load (Estimated)	3%	5-Year Return (1989–93)	+94%
Annual 12b-1 Fee	None	10-Year Return (1984–93)	NA
Annual Expense Ratio	1.09%	Worst-Ever Loss (1989–90)	14%
Annual Portfolio Turnover	102%	Bond Market Correlation	2%
5-Year Cost Estimate	9%	Up/Down Market Rank	C – B

Benefits		Investment Information	
Investment Objective	Icm. & Gr.	Telephone	800-544-8888
5-Year Projected Return	+42%	Minimum Investment	$2,500
Safety Rating (0-100)	90%	Telephone Switching	4 per yr; free
Yield (8/93)	7.3%	Total Assets	$2.35 billion

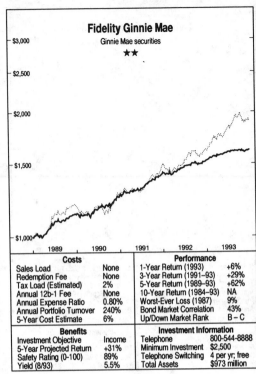

Fidelity Ginnie Mae
Ginnie Mae securities
★★

Costs		Performance	
Sales Load	None	1-Year Return (1993)	+6%
Redemption Fee	None	3-Year Return (1991–93)	+29%
Tax Load (Estimated)	2%	5-Year Return (1989–93)	+62%
Annual 12b-1 Fee	None	10-Year Return (1984–93)	NA
Annual Expense Ratio	0.80%	Worst-Ever Loss (1987)	9%
Annual Portfolio Turnover	240%	Bond Market Correlation	43%
5-Year Cost Estimate	6%	Up/Down Market Rank	B – C

Benefits		Investment Information	
Investment Objective	Income	Telephone	800-544-8888
5-Year Projected Return	+31%	Minimum Investment	$2,500
Safety Rating (0-100)	89%	Telephone Switching	4 per yr; free
Yield (8/93)	5.5%	Total Assets	$973 million

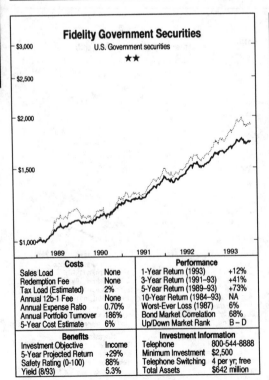

Fidelity Government Securities
U.S. Government securities
★★

Costs		Performance	
Sales Load	None	1-Year Return (1993)	+12%
Redemption Fee	None	3-Year Return (1991–93)	+41%
Tax Load (Estimated)	2%	5-Year Return (1989–93)	+73%
Annual 12b-1 Fee	None	10-Year Return (1984–93)	NA
Annual Expense Ratio	0.70%	Worst-Ever Loss (1987)	6%
Annual Portfolio Turnover	186%	Bond Market Correlation	68%
5-Year Cost Estimate	6%	Up/Down Market Rank	B – D

Benefits		Investment Information	
Investment Objective	Income	Telephone	800-544-8888
5-Year Projected Return	+29%	Minimum Investment	$2,500
Safety Rating (0-100)	88%	Telephone Switching	4 per yr; free
Yield (8/93)	5.3%	Total Assets	$642 million

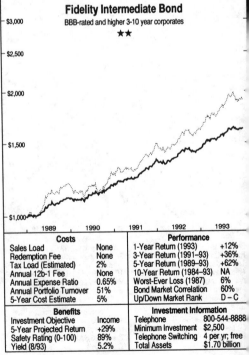

Fidelity Intermediate Bond
BBB-rated and higher 3-10 year corporates
★★

Costs		Performance	
Sales Load	None	1-Year Return (1993)	+12%
Redemption Fee	None	3-Year Return (1991–93)	+36%
Tax Load (Estimated)	2%	5-Year Return (1989–93)	+62%
Annual 12b-1 Fee	None	10-Year Return (1984–93)	NA
Annual Expense Ratio	0.65%	Worst-Ever Loss (1987)	6%
Annual Portfolio Turnover	51%	Bond Market Correlation	60%
5-Year Cost Estimate	5%	Up/Down Market Rank	D – C

Benefits		Investment Information	
Investment Objective	Income	Telephone	800-544-8888
5-Year Projected Return	+29%	Minimum Investment	$2,500
Safety Rating (0-100)	89%	Telephone Switching	4 per yr; free
Yield (8/93)	5.2%	Total Assets	$1.70 billion

BOND

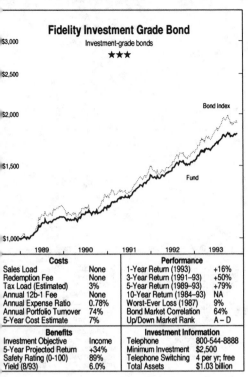

Fidelity Investment Grade Bond
Investment-grade bonds
★★★

Costs		Performance	
Sales Load	None	1-Year Return (1993)	+16%
Redemption Fee	None	3-Year Return (1991–93)	+50%
Tax Load (Estimated)	3%	5-Year Return (1989–93)	+79%
Annual 12b-1 Fee	None	10-Year Return (1984–93)	NA
Annual Expense Ratio	0.78%	Worst-Ever Loss (1987)	9%
Annual Portfolio Turnover	74%	Bond Market Correlation	64%
5-Year Cost Estimate	7%	Up/Down Market Rank	A – D

Benefits		Investment Information	
Investment Objective	Income	Telephone	800-544-8888
5-Year Projected Return	+34%	Minimum Investment	$2,500
Safety Rating (0-100)	89%	Telephone Switching	4 per yr; free
Yield (8/93)	6.0%	Total Assets	$1.03 billion

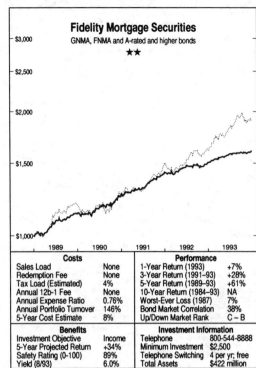

Fidelity Mortgage Securities
GNMA, FNMA and A-rated and higher bonds
★★

Costs		Performance	
Sales Load	None	1-Year Return (1993)	+7%
Redemption Fee	None	3-Year Return (1991–93)	+28%
Tax Load (Estimated)	4%	5-Year Return (1989–93)	+61%
Annual 12b-1 Fee	None	10-Year Return (1984–93)	NA
Annual Expense Ratio	0.76%	Worst-Ever Loss (1987)	7%
Annual Portfolio Turnover	146%	Bond Market Correlation	38%
5-Year Cost Estimate	8%	Up/Down Market Rank	C – B

Benefits		Investment Information	
Investment Objective	Income	Telephone	800-544-8888
5-Year Projected Return	+34%	Minimum Investment	$2,500
Safety Rating (0-100)	89%	Telephone Switching	4 per yr; free
Yield (8/93)	6.0%	Total Assets	$422 million

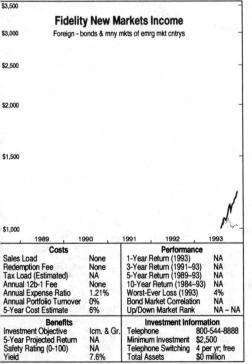

Fidelity New Markets Income
Foreign - bonds & mny mkts of emrg mkt cntrys

Costs		Performance	
Sales Load	None	1-Year Return (1993)	NA
Redemption Fee	None	3-Year Return (1991–93)	NA
Tax Load (Estimated)	NA	5-Year Return (1989–93)	NA
Annual 12b-1 Fee	None	10-Year Return (1984–93)	NA
Annual Expense Ratio	1.21%	Worst-Ever Loss (1993)	4%
Annual Portfolio Turnover	0%	Bond Market Correlation	NA
5-Year Cost Estimate	6%	Up/Down Market Rank	NA – NA

Benefits		Investment Information	
Investment Objective	Icm. & Gr.	Telephone	800-544-8888
5-Year Projected Return	NA	Minimum Investment	$2,500
Safety Rating (0-100)	NA	Telephone Switching	4 per yr; free
Yield	7.6%	Total Assets	$0 million

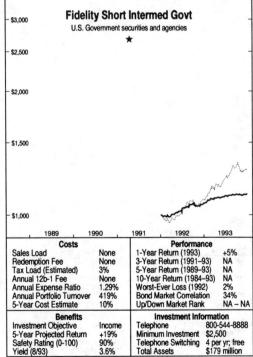

Fidelity Short Intermed Govt
U.S. Government securities and agencies
★

Costs		Performance	
Sales Load	None	1-Year Return (1993)	+5%
Redemption Fee	None	3-Year Return (1991–93)	NA
Tax Load (Estimated)	3%	5-Year Return (1989–93)	NA
Annual 12b-1 Fee	None	10-Year Return (1984–93)	NA
Annual Expense Ratio	1.29%	Worst-Ever Loss (1992)	2%
Annual Portfolio Turnover	419%	Bond Market Correlation	34%
5-Year Cost Estimate	10%	Up/Down Market Rank	NA – NA

Benefits		Investment Information	
Investment Objective	Income	Telephone	800-544-8888
5-Year Projected Return	+19%	Minimum Investment	$2,500
Safety Rating (0-100)	90%	Telephone Switching	4 per yr; free
Yield (8/93)	3.6%	Total Assets	$179 million

B
O
N
D

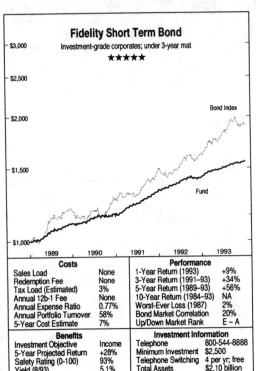

Fidelity Short Term Bond
Investment-grade corporates; under 3-year mat
★★★★★

Bond Index

Fund

$3,000	
$2,500	
$2,000	
$1,500	
$1,000	

1989 1990 1991 1992 1993

Costs		Performance	
Sales Load	None	1-Year Return (1993)	+9%
Redemption Fee	None	3-Year Return (1991–93)	+34%
Tax Load (Estimated)	3%	5-Year Return (1989–93)	+56%
Annual 12b-1 Fee	None	10-Year Return (1984–93)	NA
Annual Expense Ratio	0.77%	Worst-Ever Loss (1987)	2%
Annual Portfolio Turnover	58%	Bond Market Correlation	20%
5-Year Cost Estimate	7%	Up/Down Market Rank	E – A

Benefits		Investment Information	
Investment Objective	Income	Telephone	800-544-8888
5-Year Projected Return	+28%	Minimum Investment	$2,500
Safety Rating (0-100)	93%	Telephone Switching	4 per yr; free
Yield (8/93)	5.1%	Total Assets	$2.10 billion

Fidelity Short Term World
Foreign & U.S. - hi-qlty bonds & money market
★

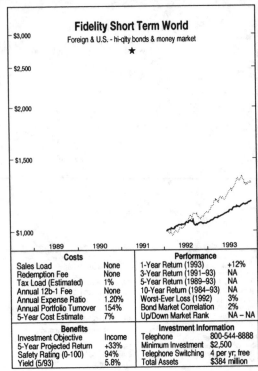

$3,000	
$2,500	
$2,000	
$1,500	
$1,000	

1989 1990 1991 1992 1993

Costs		Performance	
Sales Load	None	1-Year Return (1993)	+12%
Redemption Fee	None	3-Year Return (1991–93)	NA
Tax Load (Estimated)	1%	5-Year Return (1989–93)	NA
Annual 12b-1 Fee	None	10-Year Return (1984–93)	NA
Annual Expense Ratio	1.20%	Worst-Ever Loss (1992)	3%
Annual Portfolio Turnover	154%	Bond Market Correlation	2%
5-Year Cost Estimate	7%	Up/Down Market Rank	NA – NA

Benefits		Investment Information	
Investment Objective	Income	Telephone	800-544-8888
5-Year Projected Return	+33%	Minimum Investment	$2,500
Safety Rating (0-100)	94%	Telephone Switching	4 per yr; free
Yield (5/93)	5.8%	Total Assets	$384 million

Fidelity Spartan Bnd Strategst
At least 65% BBB & up taxable & tax-fr; govts

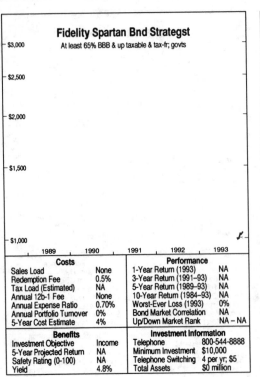

$3,000	
$2,500	
$2,000	
$1,500	
$1,000	

1989 1990 1991 1992 1993

Costs		Performance	
Sales Load	None	1-Year Return (1993)	NA
Redemption Fee	0.5%	3-Year Return (1991–93)	NA
Tax Load (Estimated)	NA	5-Year Return (1989–93)	NA
Annual 12b-1 Fee	None	10-Year Return (1984–93)	NA
Annual Expense Ratio	0.70%	Worst-Ever Loss (1993)	0%
Annual Portfolio Turnover	0%	Bond Market Correlation	NA
5-Year Cost Estimate	4%	Up/Down Market Rank	NA – NA

Benefits		Investment Information	
Investment Objective	Income	Telephone	800-544-8888
5-Year Projected Return	NA	Minimum Investment	$10,000
Safety Rating (0-100)	NA	Telephone Switching	4 per yr; $5
Yield	4.8%	Total Assets	$0 million

Fidelity Spartan GNMA
At least 65% Ginnie Maes; foreign
★

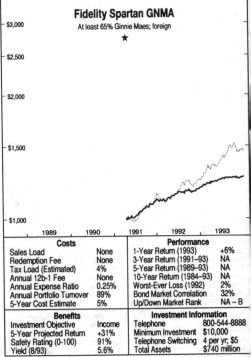

$3,000	
$2,500	
$2,000	
$1,500	
$1,000	

1989 1990 1991 1992 1993

Costs		Performance	
Sales Load	None	1-Year Return (1993)	+6%
Redemption Fee	None	3-Year Return (1991–93)	NA
Tax Load (Estimated)	4%	5-Year Return (1989–93)	NA
Annual 12b-1 Fee	None	10-Year Return (1984–93)	NA
Annual Expense Ratio	0.25%	Worst-Ever Loss (1992)	2%
Annual Portfolio Turnover	89%	Bond Market Correlation	32%
5-Year Cost Estimate	5%	Up/Down Market Rank	NA – B

Benefits		Investment Information	
Investment Objective	Income	Telephone	800-544-8888
5-Year Projected Return	+31%	Minimum Investment	$10,000
Safety Rating (0-100)	91%	Telephone Switching	4 per yr; $5
Yield (8/93)	5.6%	Total Assets	$740 million

BOND

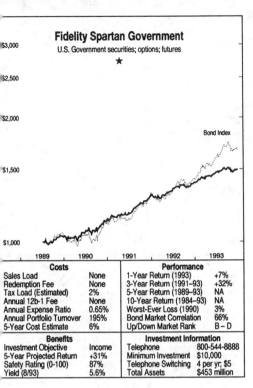

Fidelity Spartan Government
U.S. Government securities; options; futures
★

Bond Index

$3,000				
$2,500				
$2,000				
$1,500				
$1,000				
	1989	1990	1991	1992	1993

Costs		Performance	
Sales Load	None	1-Year Return (1993)	+7%
Redemption Fee	None	3-Year Return (1991–93)	+32%
Tax Load (Estimated)	2%	5-Year Return (1989–93)	NA
Annual 12b-1 Fee	None	10-Year Return (1984–93)	NA
Annual Expense Ratio	0.65%	Worst-Ever Loss (1990)	3%
Annual Portfolio Turnover	195%	Bond Market Correlation	66%
5-Year Cost Estimate	6%	Up/Down Market Rank	B – D

Benefits		Investment Information	
Investment Objective	Income	Telephone	800-544-8888
5-Year Projected Return	+31%	Minimum Investment	$10,000
Safety Rating (0-100)	87%	Telephone Switching	4 per yr; $5
Yield (8/93)	5.6%	Total Assets	$453 million

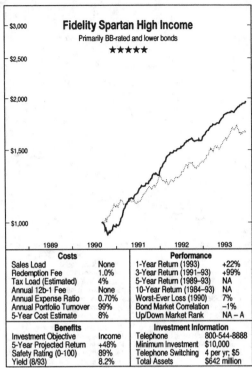

Fidelity Spartan High Income
Primarily BB-rated and lower bonds
★★★★★

$3,000				
$2,500				
$2,000				
$1,500				
$1,000				
	1989	1990	1991	1992	1993

Costs		Performance	
Sales Load	None	1-Year Return (1993)	+22%
Redemption Fee	1.0%	3-Year Return (1991–93)	+99%
Tax Load (Estimated)	4%	5-Year Return (1989–93)	NA
Annual 12b-1 Fee	None	10-Year Return (1984–93)	NA
Annual Expense Ratio	0.70%	Worst-Ever Loss (1990)	7%
Annual Portfolio Turnover	99%	Bond Market Correlation	−1%
5-Year Cost Estimate	8%	Up/Down Market Rank	NA – A

Benefits		Investment Information	
Investment Objective	Income	Telephone	800-544-8888
5-Year Projected Return	+48%	Minimum Investment	$10,000
Safety Rating (0-100)	89%	Telephone Switching	4 per yr; $5
Yield (8/93)	8.2%	Total Assets	$642 million

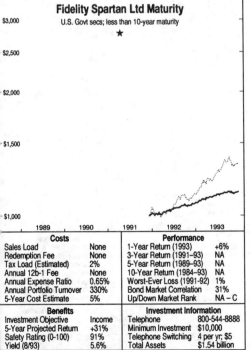

Fidelity Spartan Ltd Maturity
U.S. Govt secs; less than 10-year maturity
★

$3,000				
$2,500				
$2,000				
$1,500				
$1,000				
	1989	1990	1991	1992	1993

Costs		Performance	
Sales Load	None	1-Year Return (1993)	+6%
Redemption Fee	None	3-Year Return (1991–93)	NA
Tax Load (Estimated)	2%	5-Year Return (1989–93)	NA
Annual 12b-1 Fee	None	10-Year Return (1984–93)	NA
Annual Expense Ratio	0.65%	Worst-Ever Loss (1991-92)	1%
Annual Portfolio Turnover	330%	Bond Market Correlation	31%
5-Year Cost Estimate	5%	Up/Down Market Rank	NA – C

Benefits		Investment Information	
Investment Objective	Income	Telephone	800-544-8888
5-Year Projected Return	+31%	Minimum Investment	$10,000
Safety Rating (0-100)	91%	Telephone Switching	4 per yr; $5
Yield (8/93)	5.6%	Total Assets	$1.54 billion

First Australia Prime Income
AA-rated & higher Australian bonds; leveraged

$3,000				
$2,500				
$2,000				
$1,500				
$1,000				
	1989	1990	1991	1992	1993

Costs		Performance	
Sales Load	None	1-Year Return (1993)	+15%
Redemption Fee	None	3-Year Return (1991–93)	+62%
Tax Load (Estimated)	6%	5-Year Return (1989–93)	+107%
Annual 12b-1 Fee	None	10-Year Return (1984–93)	NA
Annual Expense Ratio	2.54%	Worst-Ever Loss (1986-88)	31%
Annual Portfolio Turnover	32%	Bond Market Correlation	−1%
5-Year Cost Estimate	20%	Up/Down Market Rank	E – A

Benefits		Investment Information	
Investment Objective	Income	Telephone	800-451-6788
5-Year Projected Return	NA	Minimum Investment	None
Safety Rating (0-100)	72%	Telephone Switching	Via broker
Yield	NA	Total Assets	$1.07 billion

B O N D

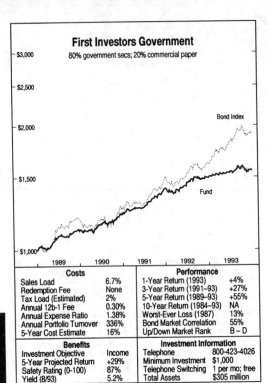

First Investors Government

80% government secs; 20% commercial paper

Bond Index

Fund

Costs		Performance	
Sales Load	6.7%	1-Year Return (1993)	+4%
Redemption Fee	None	3-Year Return (1991–93)	+27%
Tax Load (Estimated)	2%	5-Year Return (1989–93)	+55%
Annual 12b-1 Fee	0.30%	10-Year Return (1984–93)	NA
Annual Expense Ratio	1.38%	Worst-Ever Loss (1987)	13%
Annual Portfolio Turnover	336%	Bond Market Correlation	55%
5-Year Cost Estimate	16%	Up/Down Market Rank	B – D

Benefits		Investment Information	
Investment Objective	Income	Telephone	800-423-4026
5-Year Projected Return	+29%	Minimum Investment	$1,000
Safety Rating (0-100)	87%	Telephone Switching	1 per mo; free
Yield (8/93)	5.2%	Total Assets	$305 million

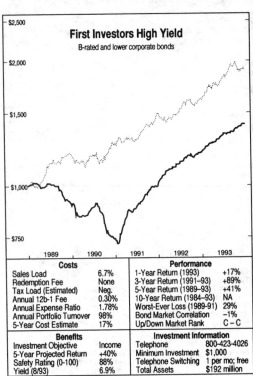

First Investors High Yield

B-rated and lower corporate bonds

Costs		Performance	
Sales Load	6.7%	1-Year Return (1993)	+17%
Redemption Fee	None	3-Year Return (1991–93)	+89%
Tax Load (Estimated)	Neg.	5-Year Return (1989–93)	+41%
Annual 12b-1 Fee	0.30%	10-Year Return (1984–93)	NA
Annual Expense Ratio	1.78%	Worst-Ever Loss (1989-91)	29%
Annual Portfolio Turnover	98%	Bond Market Correlation	–1%
5-Year Cost Estimate	17%	Up/Down Market Rank	C – C

Benefits		Investment Information	
Investment Objective	Income	Telephone	800-423-4026
5-Year Projected Return	+40%	Minimum Investment	$1,000
Safety Rating (0-100)	88%	Telephone Switching	1 per mo; free
Yield (8/93)	6.9%	Total Assets	$192 million

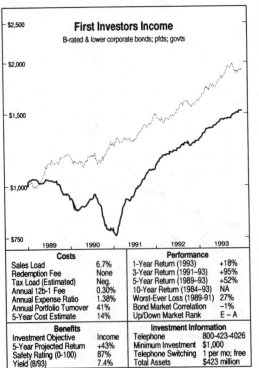

First Investors Income

B-rated & lower corporate bonds; pfds; govts

Costs		Performance	
Sales Load	6.7%	1-Year Return (1993)	+18%
Redemption Fee	None	3-Year Return (1991–93)	+95%
Tax Load (Estimated)	Neg.	5-Year Return (1989–93)	+52%
Annual 12b-1 Fee	0.30%	10-Year Return (1984–93)	NA
Annual Expense Ratio	1.38%	Worst-Ever Loss (1989-91)	27%
Annual Portfolio Turnover	41%	Bond Market Correlation	–1%
5-Year Cost Estimate	14%	Up/Down Market Rank	E – A

Benefits		Investment Information	
Investment Objective	Income	Telephone	800-423-4026
5-Year Projected Return	+43%	Minimum Investment	$1,000
Safety Rating (0-100)	87%	Telephone Switching	1 per mo; free
Yield (8/93)	7.4%	Total Assets	$423 million

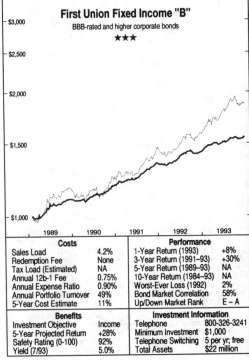

First Union Fixed Income "B"

BBB-rated and higher corporate bonds

★★★

Costs		Performance	
Sales Load	4.2%	1-Year Return (1993)	+8%
Redemption Fee	None	3-Year Return (1991–93)	+30%
Tax Load (Estimated)	NA	5-Year Return (1989–93)	NA
Annual 12b-1 Fee	0.75%	10-Year Return (1984–93)	NA
Annual Expense Ratio	0.90%	Worst-Ever Loss (1992)	2%
Annual Portfolio Turnover	49%	Bond Market Correlation	58%
5-Year Cost Estimate	11%	Up/Down Market Rank	E – A

Benefits		Investment Information	
Investment Objective	Income	Telephone	800-326-3241
5-Year Projected Return	+28%	Minimum Investment	$1,000
Safety Rating (0-100)	92%	Telephone Switching	5 per yr; free
Yield (7/93)	5.0%	Total Assets	$22 million

1994 Mutual Fund Buyer's Guide

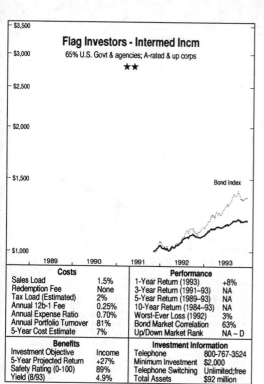

Flag Investors - Intermed Incm

65% U.S. Govt & agencies; A-rated & up corps
★★

Bond Index

Costs		Performance	
Sales Load	1.5%	1-Year Return (1993)	+8%
Redemption Fee	None	3-Year Return (1991–93)	NA
Tax Load (Estimated)	2%	5-Year Return (1989–93)	NA
Annual 12b-1 Fee	0.25%	10-Year Return (1984–93)	NA
Annual Expense Ratio	0.70%	Worst-Ever Loss (1992)	3%
Annual Portfolio Turnover	81%	Bond Market Correlation	63%
5-Year Cost Estimate	7%	Up/Down Market Rank	NA – D

Benefits		Investment Information	
Investment Objective	Income	Telephone	800-767-3524
5-Year Projected Return	+27%	Minimum Investment	$2,000
Safety Rating (0-100)	89%	Telephone Switching	Unlimited;free
Yield (8/93)	4.9%	Total Assets	$92 million

Flag Investors - Tot Rt Tres A

U.S. Treasury securities

Costs		Performance	
Sales Load	4.7%	1-Year Return (1993)	+13%
Redemption Fee	None	3-Year Return (1991–93)	+37%
Tax Load (Estimated)	3%	5-Year Return (1989–93)	+63%
Annual 12b-1 Fee	0.25%	10-Year Return (1984–93)	NA
Annual Expense Ratio	0.77%	Worst-Ever Loss (1990)	6%
Annual Portfolio Turnover	191%	Bond Market Correlation	85%
5-Year Cost Estimate	12%	Up/Down Market Rank	A – E

Benefits		Investment Information	
Investment Objective	Income	Telephone	800-767-3524
5-Year Projected Return	+24%	Minimum Investment	$2,000
Safety Rating (0-100)	81%	Telephone Switching	Unlimited;free
Yield (8/93)	4.4%	Total Assets	$191 million

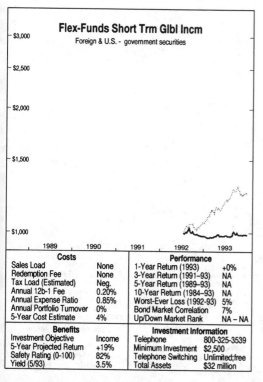

Flex-Funds Short Trm Glbl Incm

Foreign & U.S. - government securities

Costs		Performance	
Sales Load	None	1-Year Return (1993)	+0%
Redemption Fee	None	3-Year Return (1991–93)	NA
Tax Load (Estimated)	Neg.	5-Year Return (1989–93)	NA
Annual 12b-1 Fee	0.20%	10-Year Return (1984–93)	NA
Annual Expense Ratio	0.85%	Worst-Ever Loss (1992-93)	5%
Annual Portfolio Turnover	0%	Bond Market Correlation	7%
5-Year Cost Estimate	4%	Up/Down Market Rank	NA – NA

Benefits		Investment Information	
Investment Objective	Income	Telephone	800-325-3539
5-Year Projected Return	+19%	Minimum Investment	$2,500
Safety Rating (0-100)	82%	Telephone Switching	Unlimited;free
Yield (5/93)	3.5%	Total Assets	$32 million

Fort Dearborn Income Secs

75% investment-grade corps; pfds; foreign

Costs		Performance	
Sales Load	None	1-Year Return (1993)	+9%
Redemption Fee	None	3-Year Return (1991–93)	+35%
Tax Load (Estimated)	8%	5-Year Return (1989–93)	+70%
Annual 12b-1 Fee	None	10-Year Return (1984–93)	NA
Annual Expense Ratio	0.62%	Worst-Ever Loss (1987)	20%
Annual Portfolio Turnover	33%	Bond Market Correlation	–1%
5-Year Cost Estimate	10%	Up/Down Market Rank	A – E

Benefits		Investment Information	
Investment Objective	Income	Telephone	312-346-0676
5-Year Projected Return	NA	Minimum Investment	None
Safety Rating (0-100)	72%	Telephone Switching	Via broker
Yield	NA	Total Assets	$115 million

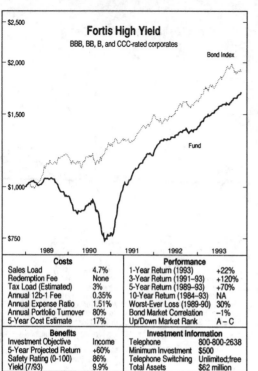

Fortis High Yield
BBB, BB, B, and CCC-rated corporates

Bond Index

Fund

Costs		Performance	
Sales Load	4.7%	1-Year Return (1993)	+22%
Redemption Fee	None	3-Year Return (1991–93)	+120%
Tax Load (Estimated)	3%	5-Year Return (1989–93)	+70%
Annual 12b-1 Fee	0.35%	10-Year Return (1984–93)	NA
Annual Expense Ratio	1.51%	Worst-Ever Loss (1989-90)	30%
Annual Portfolio Turnover	80%	Bond Market Correlation	–1%
5-Year Cost Estimate	17%	Up/Down Market Rank	A – C

Benefits		Investment Information	
Investment Objective	Income	Telephone	800-800-2638
5-Year Projected Return	+60%	Minimum Investment	$500
Safety Rating (0-100)	86%	Telephone Switching	Unlimited;free
Yield (7/93)	9.9%	Total Assets	$62 million

Fortis U.S. Government
At least 65% government securities
★

Costs		Performance	
Sales Load	4.7%	1-Year Return (1993)	+9%
Redemption Fee	None	3-Year Return (1991–93)	+31%
Tax Load (Estimated)	3%	5-Year Return (1989–93)	+63%
Annual 12b-1 Fee	None	10-Year Return (1984–93)	NA
Annual Expense Ratio	0.78%	Worst-Ever Loss (1987)	5%
Annual Portfolio Turnover	128%	Bond Market Correlation	49%
5-Year Cost Estimate	12%	Up/Down Market Rank	C – C

Benefits		Investment Information	
Investment Objective	Income	Telephone	800-800-2638
5-Year Projected Return	+26%	Minimum Investment	$500
Safety Rating (0-100)	88%	Telephone Switching	Unlimited;free
Yield (8/93)	4.7%	Total Assets	$646 million

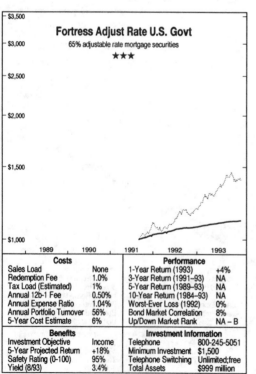

Fortress Adjust Rate U.S. Govt
65% adjustable rate mortgage securities
★★★

Costs		Performance	
Sales Load	None	1-Year Return (1993)	+4%
Redemption Fee	1.0%	3-Year Return (1991–93)	NA
Tax Load (Estimated)	1%	5-Year Return (1989–93)	NA
Annual 12b-1 Fee	0.50%	10-Year Return (1984–93)	NA
Annual Expense Ratio	1.04%	Worst-Ever Loss (1992)	0%
Annual Portfolio Turnover	56%	Bond Market Correlation	8%
5-Year Cost Estimate	6%	Up/Down Market Rank	NA – B

Benefits		Investment Information	
Investment Objective	Income	Telephone	800-245-5051
5-Year Projected Return	+18%	Minimum Investment	$1,500
Safety Rating (0-100)	95%	Telephone Switching	Unlimited;free
Yield (8/93)	3.4%	Total Assets	$999 million

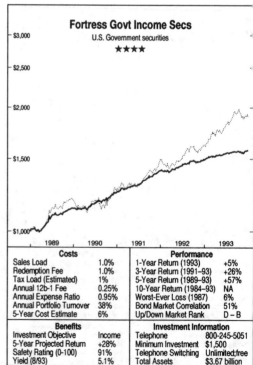

Fortress Govt Income Secs
U.S. Government securities
★★★★

Costs		Performance	
Sales Load	1.0%	1-Year Return (1993)	+5%
Redemption Fee	1.0%	3-Year Return (1991–93)	+26%
Tax Load (Estimated)	1%	5-Year Return (1989–93)	+57%
Annual 12b-1 Fee	0.25%	10-Year Return (1984–93)	NA
Annual Expense Ratio	0.95%	Worst-Ever Loss (1987)	6%
Annual Portfolio Turnover	38%	Bond Market Correlation	51%
5-Year Cost Estimate	6%	Up/Down Market Rank	D – B

Benefits		Investment Information	
Investment Objective	Income	Telephone	800-245-5051
5-Year Projected Return	+28%	Minimum Investment	$1,500
Safety Rating (0-100)	91%	Telephone Switching	Unlimited;free
Yield (8/93)	5.1%	Total Assets	$3.67 billion

BOND

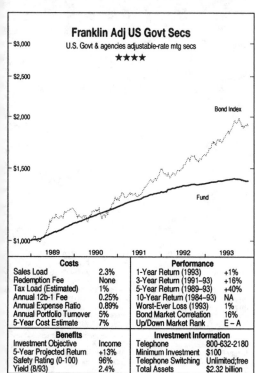

Franklin Adj US Govt Secs

U.S. Govt & agencies adjustable-rate mtg secs
★★★★

Bond Index

Fund

Costs		Performance	
Sales Load	2.3%	1-Year Return (1993)	+1%
Redemption Fee	None	3-Year Return (1991–93)	+16%
Tax Load (Estimated)	1%	5-Year Return (1989–93)	+40%
Annual 12b-1 Fee	0.25%	10-Year Return (1984–93)	NA
Annual Expense Ratio	0.89%	Worst-Ever Loss (1993)	1%
Annual Portfolio Turnover	5%	Bond Market Correlation	16%
5-Year Cost Estimate	7%	Up/Down Market Rank	E – A

Benefits		Investment Information	
Investment Objective	Income	Telephone	800-632-2180
5-Year Projected Return	+13%	Minimum Investment	$100
Safety Rating (0-100)	96%	Telephone Switching	Unlimited;free
Yield (8/93)	2.4%	Total Assets	$2.32 billion

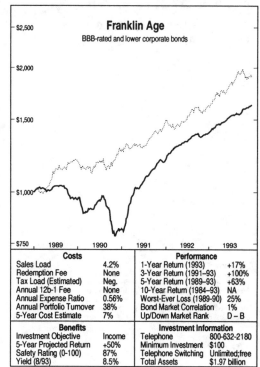

Franklin Age

BBB-rated and lower corporate bonds

Costs		Performance	
Sales Load	4.2%	1-Year Return (1993)	+17%
Redemption Fee	None	3-Year Return (1991–93)	+100%
Tax Load (Estimated)	Neg.	5-Year Return (1989–93)	+63%
Annual 12b-1 Fee	None	10-Year Return (1984–93)	NA
Annual Expense Ratio	0.56%	Worst-Ever Loss (1989-90)	25%
Annual Portfolio Turnover	38%	Bond Market Correlation	1%
5-Year Cost Estimate	7%	Up/Down Market Rank	D – B

Benefits		Investment Information	
Investment Objective	Income	Telephone	800-632-2180
5-Year Projected Return	+50%	Minimum Investment	$100
Safety Rating (0-100)	87%	Telephone Switching	Unlimited;free
Yield (8/93)	8.5%	Total Assets	$1.97 billion

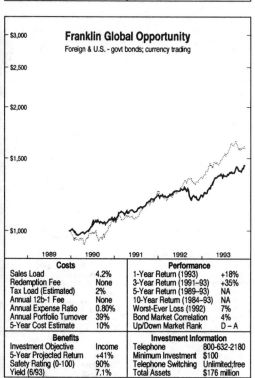

Franklin Global Opportunity

Foreign & U.S. - govt bonds; currency trading

Costs		Performance	
Sales Load	4.2%	1-Year Return (1993)	+18%
Redemption Fee	None	3-Year Return (1991–93)	+35%
Tax Load (Estimated)	2%	5-Year Return (1989–93)	NA
Annual 12b-1 Fee	None	10-Year Return (1984–93)	NA
Annual Expense Ratio	0.80%	Worst-Ever Loss (1992)	7%
Annual Portfolio Turnover	39%	Bond Market Correlation	4%
5-Year Cost Estimate	10%	Up/Down Market Rank	D – A

Benefits		Investment Information	
Investment Objective	Income	Telephone	800-632-2180
5-Year Projected Return	+41%	Minimum Investment	$100
Safety Rating (0-100)	90%	Telephone Switching	Unlimited;free
Yield (6/93)	7.1%	Total Assets	$176 million

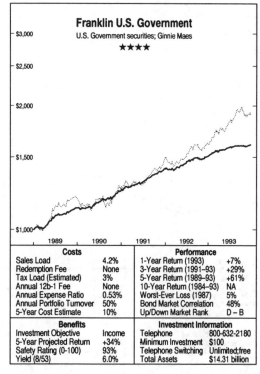

Franklin U.S. Government

U.S. Government securities; Ginnie Maes
★★★★

Costs		Performance	
Sales Load	4.2%	1-Year Return (1993)	+7%
Redemption Fee	None	3-Year Return (1991–93)	+29%
Tax Load (Estimated)	3%	5-Year Return (1989–93)	+61%
Annual 12b-1 Fee	None	10-Year Return (1984–93)	NA
Annual Expense Ratio	0.53%	Worst-Ever Loss (1987)	5%
Annual Portfolio Turnover	50%	Bond Market Correlation	48%
5-Year Cost Estimate	10%	Up/Down Market Rank	D – B

Benefits		Investment Information	
Investment Objective	Income	Telephone	800-632-2180
5-Year Projected Return	+34%	Minimum Investment	$100
Safety Rating (0-100)	93%	Telephone Switching	Unlimited;free
Yield (8/53)	6.0%	Total Assets	$14.31 billion

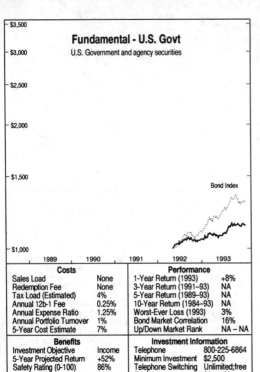

Fundamental - U.S. Govt
U.S. Government and agency securities

Bond Index

Costs		Performance	
Sales Load	None	1-Year Return (1993)	+8%
Redemption Fee	None	3-Year Return (1991–93)	NA
Tax Load (Estimated)	4%	5-Year Return (1989–93)	NA
Annual 12b-1 Fee	0.25%	10-Year Return (1984–93)	NA
Annual Expense Ratio	1.25%	Worst-Ever Loss (1993)	3%
Annual Portfolio Turnover	1%	Bond Market Correlation	16%
5-Year Cost Estimate	7%	Up/Down Market Rank	NA – NA

Benefits		Investment Information	
Investment Objective	Income	Telephone	800-225-6864
5-Year Projected Return	+52%	Minimum Investment	$2,500
Safety Rating (0-100)	86%	Telephone Switching	Unlimited;free
Yield (5/93)	8.7%	Total Assets	$61 million

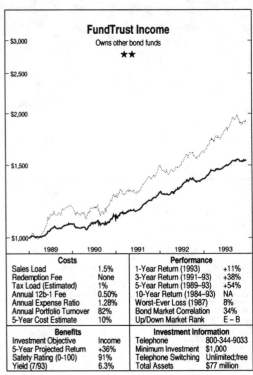

FundTrust Income
Owns other bond funds
★★

Costs		Performance	
Sales Load	1.5%	1-Year Return (1993)	+11%
Redemption Fee	None	3-Year Return (1991–93)	+38%
Tax Load (Estimated)	1%	5-Year Return (1989–93)	+54%
Annual 12b-1 Fee	0.50%	10-Year Return (1984–93)	NA
Annual Expense Ratio	1.28%	Worst-Ever Loss (1987)	8%
Annual Portfolio Turnover	82%	Bond Market Correlation	34%
5-Year Cost Estimate	10%	Up/Down Market Rank	E – B

Benefits		Investment Information	
Investment Objective	Income	Telephone	800-344-9033
5-Year Projected Return	+36%	Minimum Investment	$1,000
Safety Rating (0-100)	91%	Telephone Switching	Unlimited;free
Yield (7/93)	6.3%	Total Assets	$77 million

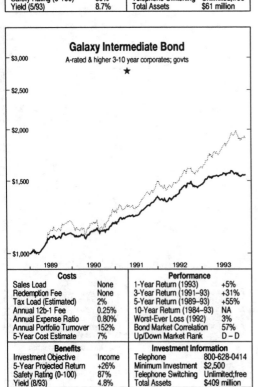

Galaxy Intermediate Bond
A-rated & higher 3-10 year corporates; govts
★

Costs		Performance	
Sales Load	None	1-Year Return (1993)	+5%
Redemption Fee	None	3-Year Return (1991–93)	+31%
Tax Load (Estimated)	2%	5-Year Return (1989–93)	+55%
Annual 12b-1 Fee	0.25%	10-Year Return (1984–93)	NA
Annual Expense Ratio	0.80%	Worst-Ever Loss (1992)	3%
Annual Portfolio Turnover	152%	Bond Market Correlation	57%
5-Year Cost Estimate	7%	Up/Down Market Rank	D – D

Benefits		Investment Information	
Investment Objective	Income	Telephone	800-628-0414
5-Year Projected Return	+26%	Minimum Investment	$2,500
Safety Rating (0-100)	87%	Telephone Switching	Unlimited;free
Yield (8/93)	4.8%	Total Assets	$409 million

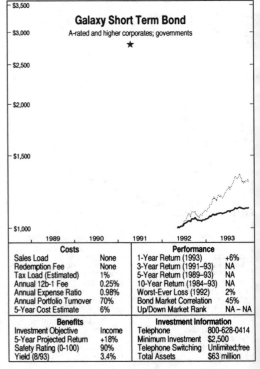

Galaxy Short Term Bond
A-rated and higher corporates; governments
★

Costs		Performance	
Sales Load	None	1-Year Return (1993)	+6%
Redemption Fee	None	3-Year Return (1991–93)	NA
Tax Load (Estimated)	1%	5-Year Return (1989–93)	NA
Annual 12b-1 Fee	0.25%	10-Year Return (1984–93)	NA
Annual Expense Ratio	0.98%	Worst-Ever Loss (1992)	2%
Annual Portfolio Turnover	70%	Bond Market Correlation	45%
5-Year Cost Estimate	6%	Up/Down Market Rank	NA – NA

Benefits		Investment Information	
Investment Objective	Income	Telephone	800-628-0414
5-Year Projected Return	+18%	Minimum Investment	$2,500
Safety Rating (0-100)	90%	Telephone Switching	Unlimited;free
Yield (8/93)	3.4%	Total Assets	$63 million

B O N D

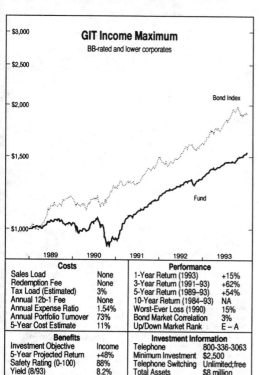

GIT Income Maximum
BB-rated and lower corporates

(chart showing Bond Index and Fund lines, 1989–1993, $1,000–$3,000 scale)

Costs		Performance	
Sales Load	None	1-Year Return (1993)	+15%
Redemption Fee	None	3-Year Return (1991–93)	+62%
Tax Load (Estimated)	3%	5-Year Return (1989–93)	+54%
Annual 12b-1 Fee	None	10-Year Return (1984–93)	NA
Annual Expense Ratio	1.54%	Worst-Ever Loss (1990)	15%
Annual Portfolio Turnover	73%	Bond Market Correlation	3%
5-Year Cost Estimate	11%	Up/Down Market Rank	E – A

Benefits		Investment Information	
Investment Objective	Income	Telephone	800-336-3063
5-Year Projected Return	+48%	Minimum Investment	$2,500
Safety Rating (0-100)	88%	Telephone Switching	Unlimited;free
Yield (8/93)	8.2%	Total Assets	$8 million

Global Government Plus
Foreign & U.S. - government bonds

(chart 1989–1993, $1,000–$3,000 scale)

Costs		Performance	
Sales Load	None	1-Year Return (1993)	+11%
Redemption Fee	None	3-Year Return (1991–93)	+31%
Tax Load (Estimated)	1%	5-Year Return (1989–93)	+32%
Annual 12b-1 Fee	None	10-Year Return (1984–93)	NA
Annual Expense Ratio	1.83%	Worst-Ever Loss (1989-90)	17%
Annual Portfolio Turnover	318%	Bond Market Correlation	3%
5-Year Cost Estimate	13%	Up/Down Market Rank	D – C

Benefits		Investment Information	
Investment Objective	Income	Telephone	800-451-6788
5-Year Projected Return	NA	Minimum Investment	None
Safety Rating (0-100)	63%	Telephone Switching	Via broker
Yield	NA	Total Assets	$358 million

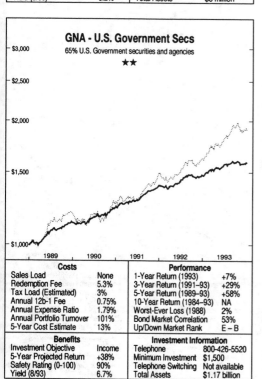

GNA - U.S. Government Secs
65% U.S. Government securities and agencies
★★

(chart 1989–1993, $1,000–$3,000 scale)

Costs		Performance	
Sales Load	None	1-Year Return (1993)	+7%
Redemption Fee	5.3%	3-Year Return (1991–93)	+29%
Tax Load (Estimated)	3%	5-Year Return (1989–93)	+58%
Annual 12b-1 Fee	0.75%	10-Year Return (1984–93)	NA
Annual Expense Ratio	1.79%	Worst-Ever Loss (1988)	2%
Annual Portfolio Turnover	101%	Bond Market Correlation	53%
5-Year Cost Estimate	13%	Up/Down Market Rank	E – B

Benefits		Investment Information	
Investment Objective	Income	Telephone	800-426-5520
5-Year Projected Return	+38%	Minimum Investment	$1,500
Safety Rating (0-100)	90%	Telephone Switching	Not available
Yield (8/93)	6.7%	Total Assets	$1.17 billion

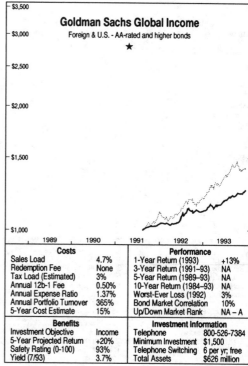

Goldman Sachs Global Income
Foreign & U.S. - AA-rated and higher bonds
★

(chart 1991–1993, $1,000–$3,500 scale)

Costs		Performance	
Sales Load	4.7%	1-Year Return (1993)	+13%
Redemption Fee	None	3-Year Return (1991–93)	NA
Tax Load (Estimated)	3%	5-Year Return (1989–93)	NA
Annual 12b-1 Fee	0.50%	10-Year Return (1984–93)	NA
Annual Expense Ratio	1.37%	Worst-Ever Loss (1992)	3%
Annual Portfolio Turnover	365%	Bond Market Correlation	10%
5-Year Cost Estimate	15%	Up/Down Market Rank	NA – A

Benefits		Investment Information	
Investment Objective	Income	Telephone	800-526-7384
5-Year Projected Return	+20%	Minimum Investment	$1,500
Safety Rating (0-100)	93%	Telephone Switching	6 per yr; free
Yield (7/93)	3.7%	Total Assets	$626 million

B O N D

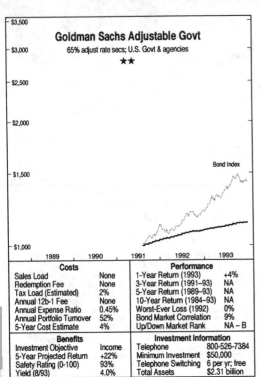

Goldman Sachs Adjustable Govt
65% adjust rate secs; U.S. Govt & agencies
★★

Bond Index

Costs		Performance	
Sales Load	None	1-Year Return (1993)	+4%
Redemption Fee	None	3-Year Return (1991–93)	NA
Tax Load (Estimated)	2%	5-Year Return (1989–93)	NA
Annual 12b-1 Fee	None	10-Year Return (1984–93)	NA
Annual Expense Ratio	0.45%	Worst-Ever Loss (1992)	0%
Annual Portfolio Turnover	52%	Bond Market Correlation	9%
5-Year Cost Estimate	4%	Up/Down Market Rank	NA – B

Benefits		Investment Information	
Investment Objective	Income	Telephone	800-526-7384
5-Year Projected Return	+22%	Minimum Investment	$50,000
Safety Rating (0-100)	93%	Telephone Switching	6 per yr; free
Yield (8/93)	4.0%	Total Assets	$2.31 billion

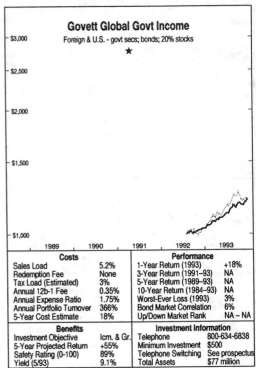

Govett Global Govt Income
Foreign & U.S. - govt secs; bonds; 20% stocks
★

Costs		Performance	
Sales Load	5.2%	1-Year Return (1993)	+18%
Redemption Fee	None	3-Year Return (1991–93)	NA
Tax Load (Estimated)	3%	5-Year Return (1989–93)	NA
Annual 12b-1 Fee	0.35%	10-Year Return (1984–93)	NA
Annual Expense Ratio	1.75%	Worst-Ever Loss (1993)	3%
Annual Portfolio Turnover	366%	Bond Market Correlation	6%
5-Year Cost Estimate	18%	Up/Down Market Rank	NA – NA

Benefits		Investment Information	
Investment Objective	Icm. & Gr.	Telephone	800-634-6838
5-Year Projected Return	+55%	Minimum Investment	$500
Safety Rating (0-100)	89%	Telephone Switching	See prospectus
Yield (5/93)	9.1%	Total Assets	$77 million

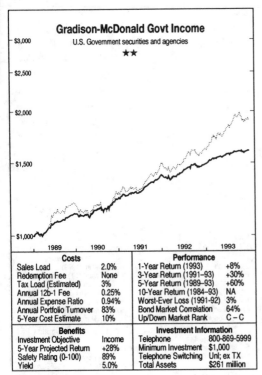

Gradison-McDonald Govt Income
U.S. Government securities and agencies
★★

Costs		Performance	
Sales Load	2.0%	1-Year Return (1993)	+8%
Redemption Fee	None	3-Year Return (1991–93)	+30%
Tax Load (Estimated)	3%	5-Year Return (1989–93)	+60%
Annual 12b-1 Fee	0.25%	10-Year Return (1984–93)	NA
Annual Expense Ratio	0.94%	Worst-Ever Loss (1991-92)	3%
Annual Portfolio Turnover	83%	Bond Market Correlation	64%
5-Year Cost Estimate	10%	Up/Down Market Rank	C – C

Benefits		Investment Information	
Investment Objective	Income	Telephone	800-869-5999
5-Year Projected Return	+28%	Minimum Investment	$1,000
Safety Rating (0-100)	89%	Telephone Switching	Unl; ex TX
Yield	5.0%	Total Assets	$261 million

G.T. Global Govt Income "A"
Foreign & U.S. - government securities

Costs		Performance	
Sales Load	5.0%	1-Year Return (1993)	+25%
Redemption Fee	None	3-Year Return (1991–93)	+45%
Tax Load (Estimated)	0%	5-Year Return (1989–93)	+76%
Annual 12b-1 Fee	0.35%	10-Year Return (1984–93)	NA
Annual Expense Ratio	1.59%	Worst-Ever Loss (1992)	4%
Annual Portfolio Turnover	529%	Bond Market Correlation	26%
5-Year Cost Estimate	14%	Up/Down Market Rank	B – A

Benefits		Investment Information	
Investment Objective	Income	Telephone	800-824-1580
5-Year Projected Return	+33%	Minimum Investment	$500
Safety Rating (0-100)	90%	Telephone Switching	See prospectus
Yield (6/93)	5.9%	Total Assets	$698 million

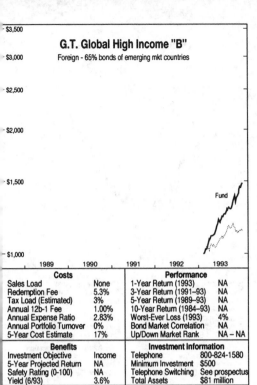

G.T. Global High Income "B"
Foreign - 65% bonds of emerging mkt countries

Fund

Costs		Performance	
Sales Load	None	1-Year Return (1993)	NA
Redemption Fee	5.3%	3-Year Return (1991–93)	NA
Tax Load (Estimated)	3%	5-Year Return (1989–93)	NA
Annual 12b-1 Fee	1.00%	10-Year Return (1984–93)	NA
Annual Expense Ratio	2.83%	Worst-Ever Loss (1993)	4%
Annual Portfolio Turnover	0%	Bond Market Correlation	NA
5-Year Cost Estimate	17%	Up/Down Market Rank	NA – NA

Benefits		Investment Information	
Investment Objective	Income	Telephone	800-824-1580
5-Year Projected Return	NA	Minimum Investment	$500
Safety Rating (0-100)	NA	Telephone Switching	See prospectus
Yield (6/93)	3.6%	Total Assets	$81 million

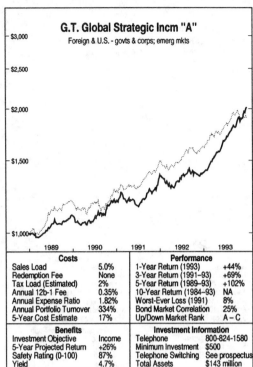

G.T. Global Strategic Incm "A"
Foreign & U.S. - govts & corps; emerg mkts

Costs		Performance	
Sales Load	5.0%	1-Year Return (1993)	+44%
Redemption Fee	None	3-Year Return (1991–93)	+69%
Tax Load (Estimated)	2%	5-Year Return (1989–93)	+102%
Annual 12b-1 Fee	0.35%	10-Year Return (1984–93)	NA
Annual Expense Ratio	1.82%	Worst-Ever Loss (1991)	8%
Annual Portfolio Turnover	334%	Bond Market Correlation	25%
5-Year Cost Estimate	17%	Up/Down Market Rank	A – C

Benefits		Investment Information	
Investment Objective	Income	Telephone	800-824-1580
5-Year Projected Return	+26%	Minimum Investment	$500
Safety Rating (0-100)	87%	Telephone Switching	See prospectus
Yield	4.7%	Total Assets	$143 million

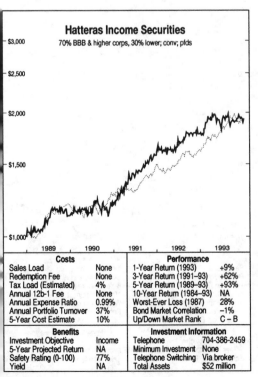

Hatteras Income Securities
70% BBB & higher corps, 30% lower; conv; pfds

Costs		Performance	
Sales Load	None	1-Year Return (1993)	+9%
Redemption Fee	None	3-Year Return (1991–93)	+62%
Tax Load (Estimated)	4%	5-Year Return (1989–93)	+93%
Annual 12b-1 Fee	None	10-Year Return (1984–93)	NA
Annual Expense Ratio	0.99%	Worst-Ever Loss (1987)	28%
Annual Portfolio Turnover	37%	Bond Market Correlation	–1%
5-Year Cost Estimate	10%	Up/Down Market Rank	C – B

Benefits		Investment Information	
Investment Objective	Income	Telephone	704-386-2459
5-Year Projected Return	NA	Minimum Investment	None
Safety Rating (0-100)	77%	Telephone Switching	Via broker
Yield	NA	Total Assets	$52 million

Heartland U.S. Government
U.S. Government securities
★

Costs		Performance	
Sales Load	None	1-Year Return (1993)	+18%
Redemption Fee	3.1%	3-Year Return (1991–93)	+51%
Tax Load (Estimated)	0%	5-Year Return (1989–93)	+85%
Annual 12b-1 Fee	0.30%	10-Year Return (1984–93)	NA
Annual Expense Ratio	1.07%	Worst-Ever Loss (1992)	5%
Annual Portfolio Turnover	185%	Bond Market Correlation	73%
5-Year Cost Estimate	6%	Up/Down Market Rank	A – E

Benefits		Investment Information	
Investment Objective	Income	Telephone	800-432-7856
5-Year Projected Return	+29%	Minimum Investment	$1,000
Safety Rating (0-100)	85%	Telephone Switching	Unlimited;free
Yield (5/93)	5.3%	Total Assets	$45 million

BOND

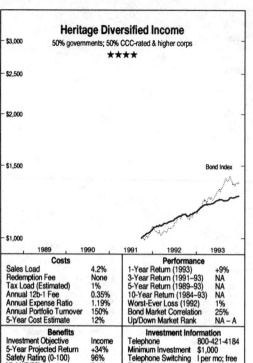

Heritage Diversified Income
50% governments; 50% CCC-rated & higher corps
★★★★

Bond Index

		1989	1990	1991	1992	1993

Costs		Performance	
Sales Load	4.2%	1-Year Return (1993)	+9%
Redemption Fee	None	3-Year Return (1991–93)	NA
Tax Load (Estimated)	1%	5-Year Return (1989–93)	NA
Annual 12b-1 Fee	0.35%	10-Year Return (1984–93)	NA
Annual Expense Ratio	1.19%	Worst-Ever Loss (1992)	1%
Annual Portfolio Turnover	150%	Bond Market Correlation	25%
5-Year Cost Estimate	12%	Up/Down Market Rank	NA – A

Benefits		Investment Information	
Investment Objective	Income	Telephone	800-421-4184
5-Year Projected Return	+34%	Minimum Investment	$1,000
Safety Rating (0-100)	96%	Telephone Switching	1 per mo; free
Yield (8/93)	6.1%	Total Assets	$42 million

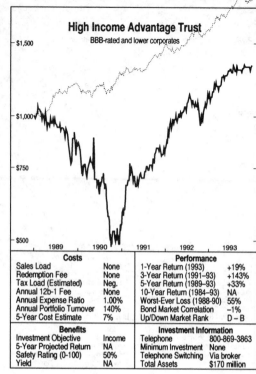

High Income Advantage Trust
BBB-rated and lower corporates

		1989	1990	1991	1992	1993

Costs		Performance	
Sales Load	None	1-Year Return (1993)	+19%
Redemption Fee	None	3-Year Return (1991–93)	+143%
Tax Load (Estimated)	Neg.	5-Year Return (1989–93)	+33%
Annual 12b-1 Fee	None	10-Year Return (1984–93)	NA
Annual Expense Ratio	1.00%	Worst-Ever Loss (1988-90)	55%
Annual Portfolio Turnover	140%	Bond Market Correlation	–1%
5-Year Cost Estimate	7%	Up/Down Market Rank	D – B

Benefits		Investment Information	
Investment Objective	Income	Telephone	800-869-3863
5-Year Projected Return	NA	Minimum Investment	None
Safety Rating (0-100)	50%	Telephone Switching	Via broker
Yield	NA	Total Assets	$170 million

High Income Advantage Trust II
BBB-rated and lower corporates

		1989	1990	1991	1992	1993

Costs		Performance	
Sales Load	None	1-Year Return (1993)	+25%
Redemption Fee	None	3-Year Return (1991–93)	+179%
Tax Load (Estimated)	Neg.	5-Year Return (1989–93)	+49%
Annual 12b-1 Fee	None	10-Year Return (1984–93)	NA
Annual Expense Ratio	0.98%	Worst-Ever Loss (1988-91)	52%
Annual Portfolio Turnover	138%	Bond Market Correlation	0%
5-Year Cost Estimate	7%	Up/Down Market Rank	B – C

Benefits		Investment Information	
Investment Objective	Income	Telephone	800-869-3863
5-Year Projected Return	NA	Minimum Investment	None
Safety Rating (0-100)	50%	Telephone Switching	Via broker
Yield	NA	Total Assets	$223 million

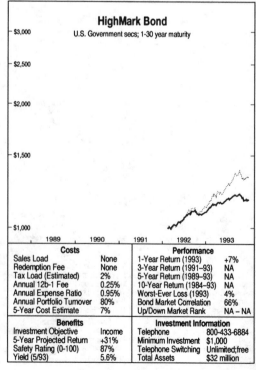

HighMark Bond
U.S. Government secs; 1-30 year maturity

		1989	1990	1991	1992	1993

Costs		Performance	
Sales Load	None	1-Year Return (1993)	+7%
Redemption Fee	None	3-Year Return (1991–93)	NA
Tax Load (Estimated)	2%	5-Year Return (1989–93)	NA
Annual 12b-1 Fee	0.25%	10-Year Return (1984–93)	NA
Annual Expense Ratio	0.95%	Worst-Ever Loss (1993)	4%
Annual Portfolio Turnover	80%	Bond Market Correlation	66%
5-Year Cost Estimate	7%	Up/Down Market Rank	NA – NA

Benefits		Investment Information	
Investment Objective	Income	Telephone	800-433-6884
5-Year Projected Return	+31%	Minimum Investment	$1,000
Safety Rating (0-100)	87%	Telephone Switching	Unlimited; free
Yield (5/93)	5.6%	Total Assets	$32 million

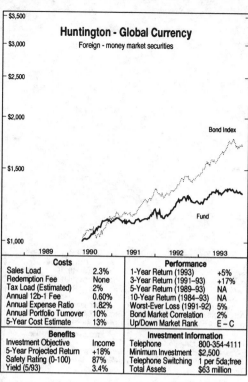

Huntington - Global Currency
Foreign - money market securities

Bond Index

Fund

Costs			Performance	
Sales Load	2.3%	1-Year Return (1993)	+5%
Redemption Fee	None	3-Year Return (1991–93)	+17%
Tax Load (Estimated)	2%	5-Year Return (1989–93)	NA
Annual 12b-1 Fee	0.60%	10-Year Return (1984–93)	NA
Annual Expense Ratio	1.82%	Worst-Ever Loss (1991-92)	5%
Annual Portfolio Turnover	10%	Bond Market Correlation	2%
5-Year Cost Estimate	13%	Up/Down Market Rank	E – C

Benefits		Investment Information	
Investment Objective	Income	Telephone	800-354-4111
5-Year Projected Return	+18%	Minimum Investment	$2,500
Safety Rating (0-100)	87%	Telephone Switching	1 per 5da;free
Yield (5/93)	3.4%	Total Assets	$63 million

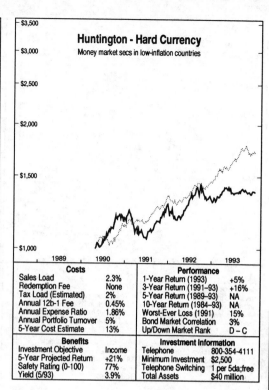

Huntington - Hard Currency
Money market secs in low-inflation countries

Costs			Performance	
Sales Load	2.3%	1-Year Return (1993)	+5%
Redemption Fee	None	3-Year Return (1991–93)	+16%
Tax Load (Estimated)	2%	5-Year Return (1989–93)	NA
Annual 12b-1 Fee	0.45%	10-Year Return (1984–93)	NA
Annual Expense Ratio	1.86%	Worst-Ever Loss (1991)	15%
Annual Portfolio Turnover	5%	Bond Market Correlation	3%
5-Year Cost Estimate	13%	Up/Down Market Rank	D – C

Benefits		Investment Information	
Investment Objective	Income	Telephone	800-354-4111
5-Year Projected Return	+21%	Minimum Investment	$2,500
Safety Rating (0-100)	77%	Telephone Switching	1 per 5da;free
Yield (5/93)	3.9%	Total Assets	$40 million

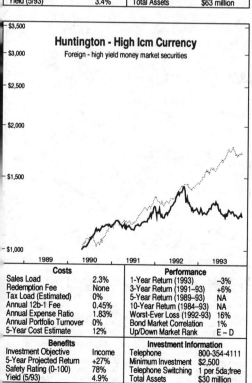

Huntington - High Icm Currency
Foreign - high yield money market securities

Costs			Performance	
Sales Load	2.3%	1-Year Return (1993)	–3%
Redemption Fee	None	3-Year Return (1991–93)	+6%
Tax Load (Estimated)	0%	5-Year Return (1989–93)	NA
Annual 12b-1 Fee	0.45%	10-Year Return (1984–93)	NA
Annual Expense Ratio	1.83%	Worst-Ever Loss (1992-93)	16%
Annual Portfolio Turnover	0%	Bond Market Correlation	1%
5-Year Cost Estimate	12%	Up/Down Market Rank	E – D

Benefits		Investment Information	
Investment Objective	Income	Telephone	800-354-4111
5-Year Projected Return	+27%	Minimum Investment	$2,500
Safety Rating (0-100)	78%	Telephone Switching	1 per 5da;free
Yield (5/93)	4.9%	Total Assets	$30 million

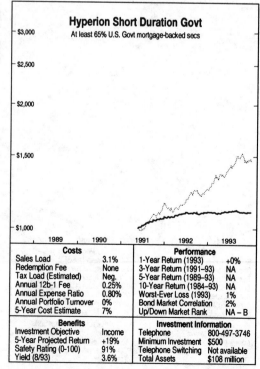

Hyperion Short Duration Govt
At least 65% U.S. Govt mortgage-backed secs

Costs			Performance	
Sales Load	3.1%	1-Year Return (1993)	+0%
Redemption Fee	None	3-Year Return (1991–93)	NA
Tax Load (Estimated)	Neg.	5-Year Return (1989–93)	NA
Annual 12b-1 Fee	0.25%	10-Year Return (1984–93)	NA
Annual Expense Ratio	0.80%	Worst-Ever Loss (1993)	1%
Annual Portfolio Turnover	0%	Bond Market Correlation	2%
5-Year Cost Estimate	7%	Up/Down Market Rank	NA – B

Benefits		Investment Information	
Investment Objective	Income	Telephone	800-497-3746
5-Year Projected Return	+19%	Minimum Investment	$500
Safety Rating (0-100)	91%	Telephone Switching	Not available
Yield (8/93)	3.6%	Total Assets	$108 million

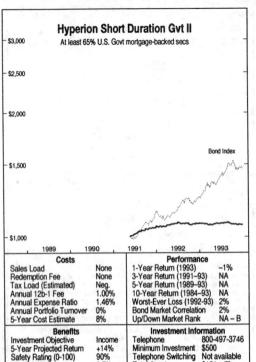

Hyperion Short Duration Gvt II
At least 65% U.S. Govt mortgage-backed secs

Bond Index

Costs		Performance	
Sales Load	None	1-Year Return (1993)	–1%
Redemption Fee	None	3-Year Return (1991–93)	NA
Tax Load (Estimated)	Neg.	5-Year Return (1989–93)	NA
Annual 12b-1 Fee	1.00%	10-Year Return (1984–93)	NA
Annual Expense Ratio	1.46%	Worst-Ever Loss (1992–93)	2%
Annual Portfolio Turnover	0%	Bond Market Correlation	2%
5-Year Cost Estimate	8%	Up/Down Market Rank	NA – B

Benefits		Investment Information	
Investment Objective	Income	Telephone	800-497-3746
5-Year Projected Return	+14%	Minimum Investment	$500
Safety Rating (0-100)	90%	Telephone Switching	Not available
Yield (8/93)	2.7%	Total Assets	$121 million

IAI - Bond
Investment grade corps; governments; comm pap

Costs		Performance	
Sales Load	None	1-Year Return (1993)	+12%
Redemption Fee	None	3-Year Return (1991–93)	+41%
Tax Load (Estimated)	1%	5-Year Return (1989–93)	+75%
Annual 12b-1 Fee	0.25%	10-Year Return (1984–93)	NA
Annual Expense Ratio	1.10%	Worst-Ever Loss (1989–90)	6%
Annual Portfolio Turnover	374%	Bond Market Correlation	81%
5-Year Cost Estimate	7%	Up/Down Market Rank	A – E

Benefits		Investment Information	
Investment Objective	Income	Telephone	800-945-3863
5-Year Projected Return	+33%	Minimum Investment	$5,000
Safety Rating (0-100)	83%	Telephone Switching	Unlimited;free
Yield	5.9%	Total Assets	$129 million

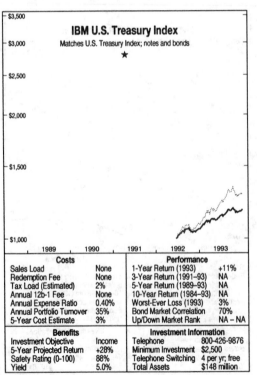

IBM U.S. Treasury Index
Matches U.S. Treasury Index; notes and bonds
★

Costs		Performance	
Sales Load	None	1-Year Return (1993)	+11%
Redemption Fee	None	3-Year Return (1991–93)	NA
Tax Load (Estimated)	2%	5-Year Return (1989–93)	NA
Annual 12b-1 Fee	None	10-Year Return (1984–93)	NA
Annual Expense Ratio	0.40%	Worst-Ever Loss (1993)	3%
Annual Portfolio Turnover	35%	Bond Market Correlation	70%
5-Year Cost Estimate	3%	Up/Down Market Rank	NA – NA

Benefits		Investment Information	
Investment Objective	Income	Telephone	800-426-9876
5-Year Projected Return	+28%	Minimum Investment	$2,500
Safety Rating (0-100)	88%	Telephone Switching	4 per yr; free
Yield	5.0%	Total Assets	$148 million

Idex II Flexible Income "A"
Low-medium grade bonds; all maturities

Costs		Performance	
Sales Load	5.0%	1-Year Return (1993)	+14%
Redemption Fee	None	3-Year Return (1991–93)	+57%
Tax Load (Estimated)	0%	5-Year Return (1989–93)	+54%
Annual 12b-1 Fee	0.35%	10-Year Return (1984–93)	NA
Annual Expense Ratio	1.85%	Worst-Ever Loss (1989–90)	13%
Annual Portfolio Turnover	139%	Bond Market Correlation	25%
5-Year Cost Estimate	16%	Up/Down Market Rank	B – D

Benefits		Investment Information	
Investment Objective	Income	Telephone	800-624-4339
5-Year Projected Return	+35%	Minimum Investment	$50
Safety Rating (0-100)	90%	Telephone Switching	See prospectus
Yield (5/93)	6.2%	Total Assets	$31 million

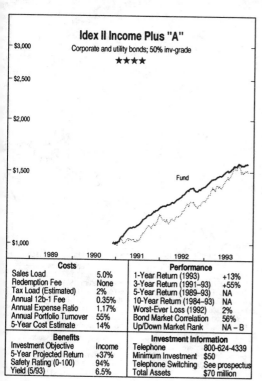

Idex II Income Plus "A"

Corporate and utility bonds; 50% inv-grade

★★★★

Fund

Costs		Performance	
Sales Load	5.0%	1-Year Return (1993)	+13%
Redemption Fee	None	3-Year Return (1991–93)	+55%
Tax Load (Estimated)	2%	5-Year Return (1989–93)	NA
Annual 12b-1 Fee	0.35%	10-Year Return (1984–93)	NA
Annual Expense Ratio	1.17%	Worst-Ever Loss (1992)	2%
Annual Portfolio Turnover	55%	Bond Market Correlation	56%
5-Year Cost Estimate	14%	Up/Down Market Rank	NA – B

Benefits		Investment Information	
Investment Objective	Income	Telephone	800-624-4339
5-Year Projected Return	+37%	Minimum Investment	$50
Safety Rating (0-100)	94%	Telephone Switching	See prospectus
Yield (5/93)	6.5%	Total Assets	$70 million

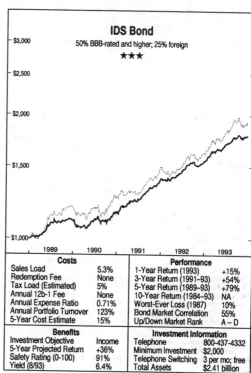

IDS Bond

50% BBB-rated and higher; 25% foreign

★★★

Costs		Performance	
Sales Load	5.3%	1-Year Return (1993)	+15%
Redemption Fee	None	3-Year Return (1991–93)	+54%
Tax Load (Estimated)	5%	5-Year Return (1989–93)	+79%
Annual 12b-1 Fee	None	10-Year Return (1984–93)	NA
Annual Expense Ratio	0.71%	Worst-Ever Loss (1987)	10%
Annual Portfolio Turnover	123%	Bond Market Correlation	55%
5-Year Cost Estimate	15%	Up/Down Market Rank	A – D

Benefits		Investment Information	
Investment Objective	Income	Telephone	800-437-4332
5-Year Projected Return	+36%	Minimum Investment	$2,000
Safety Rating (0-100)	91%	Telephone Switching	3 per mo; free
Yield (8/93)	6.4%	Total Assets	$2.41 billion

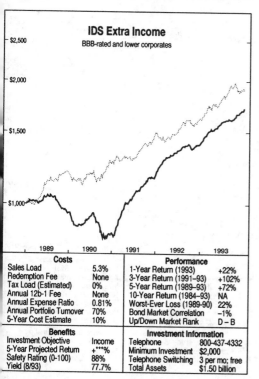

IDS Extra Income

BBB-rated and lower corporates

Costs		Performance	
Sales Load	5.3%	1-Year Return (1993)	+22%
Redemption Fee	None	3-Year Return (1991–93)	+102%
Tax Load (Estimated)	0%	5-Year Return (1989–93)	+72%
Annual 12b-1 Fee	None	10-Year Return (1984–93)	NA
Annual Expense Ratio	0.81%	Worst-Ever Loss (1989-90)	22%
Annual Portfolio Turnover	70%	Bond Market Correlation	–1%
5-Year Cost Estimate	10%	Up/Down Market Rank	D – B

Benefits		Investment Information	
Investment Objective	Income	Telephone	800-437-4332
5-Year Projected Return	+***%	Minimum Investment	$2,000
Safety Rating (0-100)	88%	Telephone Switching	3 per mo; free
Yield (8/93)	77.7%	Total Assets	$1.50 billion

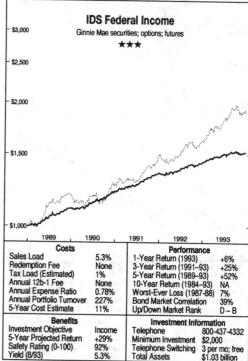

IDS Federal Income

Ginnie Mae securities; options; futures

★★★

Costs		Performance	
Sales Load	5.3%	1-Year Return (1993)	+6%
Redemption Fee	None	3-Year Return (1991–93)	+25%
Tax Load (Estimated)	1%	5-Year Return (1989–93)	+52%
Annual 12b-1 Fee	None	10-Year Return (1984–93)	NA
Annual Expense Ratio	0.78%	Worst-Ever Loss (1987-88)	7%
Annual Portfolio Turnover	227%	Bond Market Correlation	39%
5-Year Cost Estimate	11%	Up/Down Market Rank	D – B

Benefits		Investment Information	
Investment Objective	Income	Telephone	800-437-4332
5-Year Projected Return	+29%	Minimum Investment	$2,000
Safety Rating (0-100)	92%	Telephone Switching	3 per mo; free
Yield (8/93)	5.3%	Total Assets	$1.03 billion

BOND

IDS Global Bond
Foreign & U.S. - 80% BBB & higher corp bonds

Costs		Performance	
Sales Load	5.3%	1-Year Return (1993)	+17%
Redemption Fee	None	3-Year Return (1991–93)	+46%
Tax Load (Estimated)	3%	5-Year Return (1989–93)	NA
Annual 12b-1 Fee	None	10-Year Return (1984–93)	NA
Annual Expense Ratio	None	Worst-Ever Loss (1991)	6%
Annual Portfolio Turnover	160%	Bond Market Correlation	20%
5-Year Cost Estimate	8%	Up/Down Market Rank	A – C

Benefits		Investment Information	
Investment Objective	Income	Telephone	800-437-4332
5-Year Projected Return	+19%	Minimum Investment	$2,000
Safety Rating (0-100)	86%	Telephone Switching	3 per mo; free
Yield (5/93)	3.5%	Total Assets	$165 million

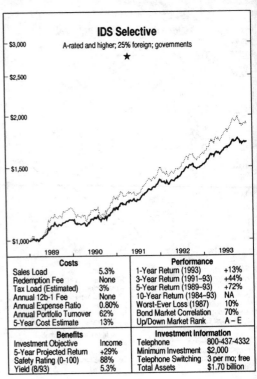

IDS Selective
A-rated and higher; 25% foreign; governments
★

Costs		Performance	
Sales Load	5.3%	1-Year Return (1993)	+13%
Redemption Fee	None	3-Year Return (1991–93)	+44%
Tax Load (Estimated)	3%	5-Year Return (1989–93)	+72%
Annual 12b-1 Fee	None	10-Year Return (1984–93)	NA
Annual Expense Ratio	0.80%	Worst-Ever Loss (1987)	10%
Annual Portfolio Turnover	62%	Bond Market Correlation	70%
5-Year Cost Estimate	13%	Up/Down Market Rank	A – E

Benefits		Investment Information	
Investment Objective	Income	Telephone	800-437-4332
5-Year Projected Return	+29%	Minimum Investment	$2,000
Safety Rating (0-100)	88%	Telephone Switching	3 per mo; free
Yield (8/93)	5.3%	Total Assets	$1.70 billion

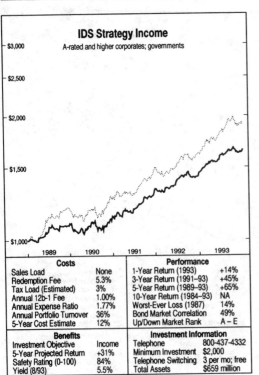

IDS Strategy Income
A-rated and higher corporates; governments

Costs		Performance	
Sales Load	None	1-Year Return (1993)	+14%
Redemption Fee	5.3%	3-Year Return (1991–93)	+45%
Tax Load (Estimated)	3%	5-Year Return (1989–93)	+65%
Annual 12b-1 Fee	1.00%	10-Year Return (1984–93)	NA
Annual Expense Ratio	1.77%	Worst-Ever Loss (1987)	14%
Annual Portfolio Turnover	36%	Bond Market Correlation	49%
5-Year Cost Estimate	12%	Up/Down Market Rank	A – E

Benefits		Investment Information	
Investment Objective	Income	Telephone	800-437-4332
5-Year Projected Return	+31%	Minimum Investment	$2,000
Safety Rating (0-100)	84%	Telephone Switching	3 per mo; free
Yield (8/93)	5.5%	Total Assets	$659 million

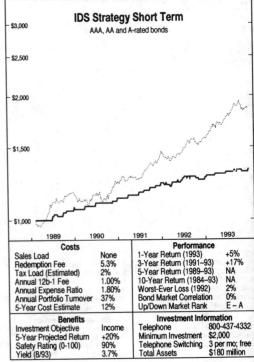

IDS Strategy Short Term
AAA, AA and A-rated bonds

Costs		Performance	
Sales Load	None	1-Year Return (1993)	+5%
Redemption Fee	5.3%	3-Year Return (1991–93)	+17%
Tax Load (Estimated)	2%	5-Year Return (1989–93)	NA
Annual 12b-1 Fee	1.00%	10-Year Return (1984–93)	NA
Annual Expense Ratio	1.80%	Worst-Ever Loss (1992)	2%
Annual Portfolio Turnover	37%	Bond Market Correlation	0%
5-Year Cost Estimate	12%	Up/Down Market Rank	E – A

Benefits		Investment Information	
Investment Objective	Income	Telephone	800-437-4332
5-Year Projected Return	+20%	Minimum Investment	$2,000
Safety Rating (0-100)	90%	Telephone Switching	3 per mo; free
Yield (8/93)	3.7%	Total Assets	$180 million

B
O
N
D

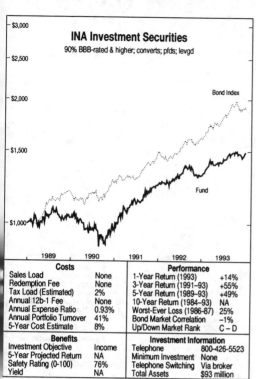

INA Investment Securities
90% BBB-rated & higher; converts; pfds; levgd

Bond Index

Fund

Costs		Performance	
Sales Load	None	1-Year Return (1993)	+14%
Redemption Fee	None	3-Year Return (1991–93)	+55%
Tax Load (Estimated)	2%	5-Year Return (1989–93)	+49%
Annual 12b-1 Fee	None	10-Year Return (1984–93)	NA
Annual Expense Ratio	0.93%	Worst-Ever Loss (1986-87)	25%
Annual Portfolio Turnover	41%	Bond Market Correlation	−1%
5-Year Cost Estimate	8%	Up/Down Market Rank	C – D

Benefits		Investment Information	
Investment Objective	Income	Telephone	800-426-5523
5-Year Projected Return	NA	Minimum Investment	None
Safety Rating (0-100)	76%	Telephone Switching	Via broker
Yield	NA	Total Assets	$93 million

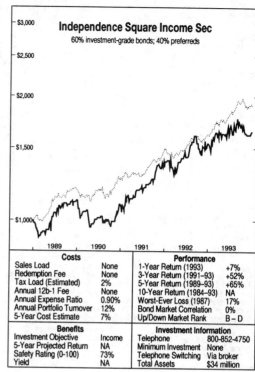

Independence Square Income Sec
60% investment-grade bonds; 40% preferreds

Costs		Performance	
Sales Load	None	1-Year Return (1993)	+7%
Redemption Fee	None	3-Year Return (1991–93)	+52%
Tax Load (Estimated)	2%	5-Year Return (1989–93)	+65%
Annual 12b-1 Fee	None	10-Year Return (1984–93)	NA
Annual Expense Ratio	0.90%	Worst-Ever Loss (1987)	17%
Annual Portfolio Turnover	12%	Bond Market Correlation	0%
5-Year Cost Estimate	7%	Up/Down Market Rank	B – D

Benefits		Investment Information	
Investment Objective	Income	Telephone	800-852-4750
5-Year Projected Return	NA	Minimum Investment	None
Safety Rating (0-100)	73%	Telephone Switching	Via broker
Yield	NA	Total Assets	$34 million

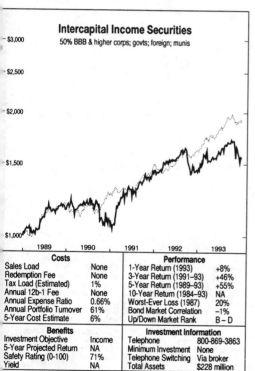

Intercapital Income Securities
50% BBB & higher corps; govts; foreign; munis

Costs		Performance	
Sales Load	None	1-Year Return (1993)	+8%
Redemption Fee	None	3-Year Return (1991–93)	+46%
Tax Load (Estimated)	1%	5-Year Return (1989–93)	+55%
Annual 12b-1 Fee	None	10-Year Return (1984–93)	NA
Annual Expense Ratio	0.66%	Worst-Ever Loss (1987)	20%
Annual Portfolio Turnover	61%	Bond Market Correlation	−1%
5-Year Cost Estimate	6%	Up/Down Market Rank	B – D

Benefits		Investment Information	
Investment Objective	Income	Telephone	800-869-3863
5-Year Projected Return	NA	Minimum Investment	None
Safety Rating (0-100)	71%	Telephone Switching	Via broker
Yield	NA	Total Assets	$228 million

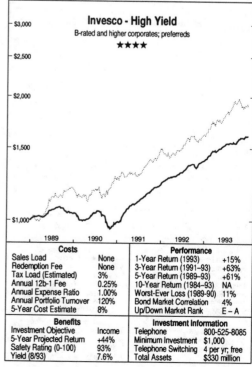

Invesco - High Yield
B-rated and higher corporates; preferreds
★★★★

Costs		Performance	
Sales Load	None	1-Year Return (1993)	+15%
Redemption Fee	None	3-Year Return (1991–93)	+63%
Tax Load (Estimated)	3%	5-Year Return (1989–93)	+61%
Annual 12b-1 Fee	0.25%	10-Year Return (1984–93)	NA
Annual Expense Ratio	1.00%	Worst-Ever Loss (1989-90)	11%
Annual Portfolio Turnover	120%	Bond Market Correlation	4%
5-Year Cost Estimate	8%	Up/Down Market Rank	E – A

Benefits		Investment Information	
Investment Objective	Income	Telephone	800-525-8085
5-Year Projected Return	+44%	Minimum Investment	$1,000
Safety Rating (0-100)	93%	Telephone Switching	4 per yr; free
Yield (8/93)	7.6%	Total Assets	$330 million

ISI Total Return U.S. Treasury
U.S. Treasury securities

(Chart: $1,000–$3,500 scale, 1989–1993, showing "Bond Index" and "Fund" lines)

Costs		Performance	
Sales Load	4.7%	1-Year Return (1993)	+13%
Redemption Fee	None	3-Year Return (1991–93)	+37%
Tax Load (Estimated)	1%	5-Year Return (1989–93)	NA
Annual 12b-1 Fee	0.25%	10-Year Return (1984–93)	NA
Annual Expense Ratio	0.77%	Worst-Ever Loss (1989-90)	6%
Annual Portfolio Turnover	191%	Bond Market Correlation	85%
5-Year Cost Estimate	10%	Up/Down Market Rank	A – E

Benefits		Investment Information	
Investment Objective	Income	Telephone	800-955-7175
5-Year Projected Return	+24%	Minimum Investment	$5,000
Safety Rating (0-100)	81%	Telephone Switching	Unlimited;free
Yield (8/93)	4.4%	Total Assets	$225 million

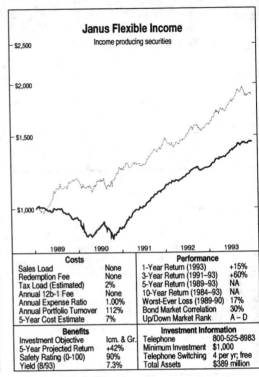

Janus Flexible Income
Income producing securities

(Chart: $1,000–$2,500 scale, 1989–1993)

Costs		Performance	
Sales Load	None	1-Year Return (1993)	+15%
Redemption Fee	None	3-Year Return (1991–93)	+60%
Tax Load (Estimated)	2%	5-Year Return (1989–93)	NA
Annual 12b-1 Fee	None	10-Year Return (1984–93)	NA
Annual Expense Ratio	1.00%	Worst-Ever Loss (1989-90)	17%
Annual Portfolio Turnover	112%	Bond Market Correlation	30%
5-Year Cost Estimate	7%	Up/Down Market Rank	A – D

Benefits		Investment Information	
Investment Objective	Icm. & Gr.	Telephone	800-525-8983
5-Year Projected Return	+42%	Minimum Investment	$1,000
Safety Rating (0-100)	90%	Telephone Switching	4 per yr; free
Yield (8/93)	7.3%	Total Assets	$389 million

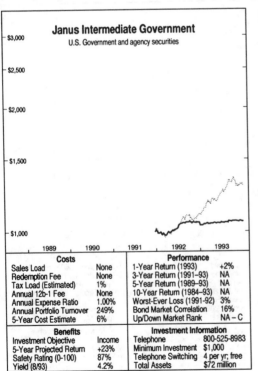

Janus Intermediate Government
U.S. Government and agency securities

(Chart: $1,000–$3,000 scale, 1989–1993)

Costs		Performance	
Sales Load	None	1-Year Return (1993)	+2%
Redemption Fee	None	3-Year Return (1991–93)	NA
Tax Load (Estimated)	1%	5-Year Return (1989–93)	NA
Annual 12b-1 Fee	None	10-Year Return (1984–93)	NA
Annual Expense Ratio	1.00%	Worst-Ever Loss (1991-92)	3%
Annual Portfolio Turnover	249%	Bond Market Correlation	16%
5-Year Cost Estimate	6%	Up/Down Market Rank	NA – C

Benefits		Investment Information	
Investment Objective	Income	Telephone	800-525-8983
5-Year Projected Return	+23%	Minimum Investment	$1,000
Safety Rating (0-100)	87%	Telephone Switching	4 per yr; free
Yield (8/93)	4.2%	Total Assets	$72 million

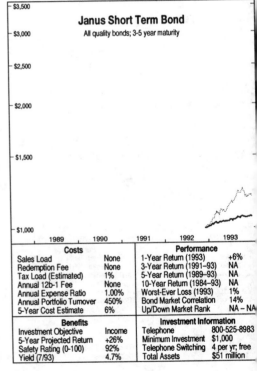

Janus Short Term Bond
All quality bonds; 3-5 year maturity

(Chart: $1,000–$3,500 scale, 1989–1993)

Costs		Performance	
Sales Load	None	1-Year Return (1993)	+6%
Redemption Fee	None	3-Year Return (1991–93)	NA
Tax Load (Estimated)	1%	5-Year Return (1989–93)	NA
Annual 12b-1 Fee	None	10-Year Return (1984–93)	NA
Annual Expense Ratio	1.00%	Worst-Ever Loss (1993)	1%
Annual Portfolio Turnover	450%	Bond Market Correlation	14%
5-Year Cost Estimate	6%	Up/Down Market Rank	NA – NA

Benefits		Investment Information	
Investment Objective	Income	Telephone	800-525-8983
5-Year Projected Return	+26%	Minimum Investment	$1,000
Safety Rating (0-100)	92%	Telephone Switching	4 per yr; free
Yield (7/93)	4.7%	Total Assets	$51 million

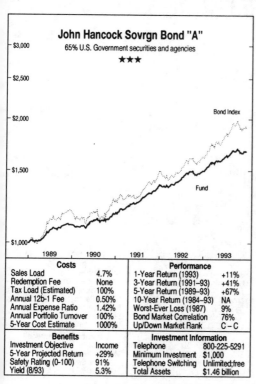

John Hancock Sovrgn Bond "A"
65% U.S. Government securities and agencies
★★★

Costs		Performance	
Sales Load	4.7%	1-Year Return (1993)	+11%
Redemption Fee	None	3-Year Return (1991–93)	+41%
Tax Load (Estimated)	100%	5-Year Return (1989–93)	+67%
Annual 12b-1 Fee	0.50%	10-Year Return (1984–93)	NA
Annual Expense Ratio	1.42%	Worst-Ever Loss (1987)	9%
Annual Portfolio Turnover	100%	Bond Market Correlation	76%
5-Year Cost Estimate	1000%	Up/Down Market Rank	C – C

Benefits		Investment Information	
Investment Objective	Income	Telephone	800-225-5291
5-Year Projected Return	+29%	Minimum Investment	$1,000
Safety Rating (0-100)	91%	Telephone Switching	Unlimited;free
Yield (8/93)	5.3%	Total Assets	$1.46 billion

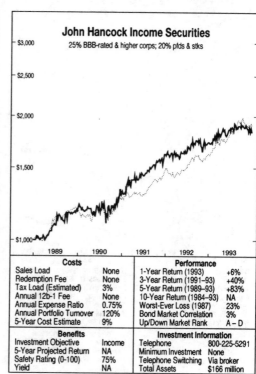

John Hancock Income Securities
25% BBB-rated & higher corps; 20% pfds & stks

Costs		Performance	
Sales Load	None	1-Year Return (1993)	+6%
Redemption Fee	None	3-Year Return (1991–93)	+40%
Tax Load (Estimated)	3%	5-Year Return (1989–93)	+83%
Annual 12b-1 Fee	None	10-Year Return (1984–93)	NA
Annual Expense Ratio	0.75%	Worst-Ever Loss (1987)	23%
Annual Portfolio Turnover	120%	Bond Market Correlation	3%
5-Year Cost Estimate	9%	Up/Down Market Rank	A – D

Benefits		Investment Information	
Investment Objective	Income	Telephone	800-225-5291
5-Year Projected Return	NA	Minimum Investment	None
Safety Rating (0-100)	75%	Telephone Switching	Via broker
Yield	NA	Total Assets	$166 million

John Hancock Investors
50% BBB & higher corps; 50% restructured secs

Costs		Performance	
Sales Load	None	1-Year Return (1993)	+3%
Redemption Fee	None	3-Year Return (1991–93)	+47%
Tax Load (Estimated)	4%	5-Year Return (1989–93)	+76%
Annual 12b-1 Fee	None	10-Year Return (1984–93)	NA
Annual Expense Ratio	0.74%	Worst-Ever Loss (1987)	27%
Annual Portfolio Turnover	120%	Bond Market Correlation	5%
5-Year Cost Estimate	11%	Up/Down Market Rank	A – E

Benefits		Investment Information	
Investment Objective	Income	Telephone	800-225-5291
5-Year Projected Return	NA	Minimum Investment	None
Safety Rating (0-100)	69%	Telephone Switching	Via broker
Yield	NA	Total Assets	$161 million

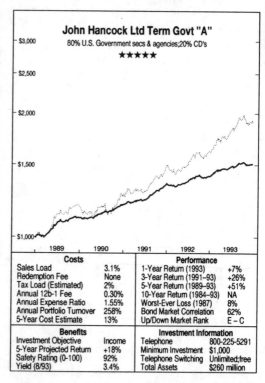

John Hancock Ltd Term Govt "A"
80% U.S. Government secs & agencies;20% CD's
★★★★★

Costs		Performance	
Sales Load	3.1%	1-Year Return (1993)	+7%
Redemption Fee	None	3-Year Return (1991–93)	+26%
Tax Load (Estimated)	2%	5-Year Return (1989–93)	+51%
Annual 12b-1 Fee	0.30%	10-Year Return (1984–93)	NA
Annual Expense Ratio	1.55%	Worst-Ever Loss (1987)	8%
Annual Portfolio Turnover	258%	Bond Market Correlation	62%
5-Year Cost Estimate	13%	Up/Down Market Rank	E – C

Benefits		Investment Information	
Investment Objective	Income	Telephone	800-225-5291
5-Year Projected Return	+18%	Minimum Investment	$1,000
Safety Rating (0-100)	92%	Telephone Switching	Unlimited;free
Yield (8/93)	3.4%	Total Assets	$260 million

BOND

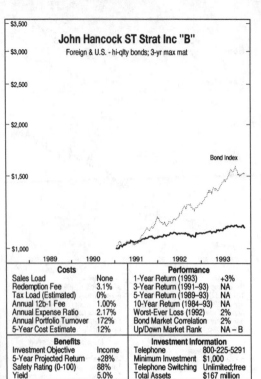

John Hancock ST Strat Inc "B"
Foreign & U.S. - hi-qlty bonds; 3-yr max mat

Bond Index

Costs		Performance	
Sales Load	None	1-Year Return (1993)	+3%
Redemption Fee	3.1%	3-Year Return (1991–93)	NA
Tax Load (Estimated)	0%	5-Year Return (1989–93)	NA
Annual 12b-1 Fee	1.00%	10-Year Return (1984–93)	NA
Annual Expense Ratio	2.17%	Worst-Ever Loss (1992)	2%
Annual Portfolio Turnover	172%	Bond Market Correlation	2%
5-Year Cost Estimate	12%	Up/Down Market Rank	NA – B

Benefits		Investment Information	
Investment Objective	Income	Telephone	800-225-5291
5-Year Projected Return	+28%	Minimum Investment	$1,000
Safety Rating (0-100)	88%	Telephone Switching	Unlimited;free
Yield	5.0%	Total Assets	$167 million

JP Income
90% A-rated and higher corporates; 5% stocks
★★

Costs		Performance	
Sales Load	5.8%	1-Year Return (1993)	+10%
Redemption Fee	None	3-Year Return (1991–93)	+34%
Tax Load (Estimated)	4%	5-Year Return (1989–93)	+60%
Annual 12b-1 Fee	None	10-Year Return (1984–93)	NA
Annual Expense Ratio	0.93%	Worst-Ever Loss (1987)	8%
Annual Portfolio Turnover	14%	Bond Market Correlation	80%
5-Year Cost Estimate	12%	Up/Down Market Rank	B – D

Benefits		Investment Information	
Investment Objective	Income	Telephone	800-458-4498
5-Year Projected Return	+29%	Minimum Investment	$300
Safety Rating (0-100)	89%	Telephone Switching	Unlimited;free
Yield (8/93)	5.2%	Total Assets	$22 million

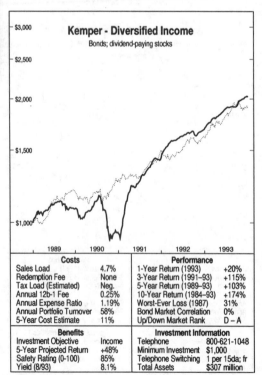

Kemper - Diversified Income
Bonds; dividend-paying stocks

Costs		Performance	
Sales Load	4.7%	1-Year Return (1993)	+20%
Redemption Fee	None	3-Year Return (1991–93)	+115%
Tax Load (Estimated)	Neg.	5-Year Return (1989–93)	+103%
Annual 12b-1 Fee	0.25%	10-Year Return (1984–93)	+174%
Annual Expense Ratio	1.19%	Worst-Ever Loss (1987)	31%
Annual Portfolio Turnover	58%	Bond Market Correlation	0%
5-Year Cost Estimate	11%	Up/Down Market Rank	D – A

Benefits		Investment Information	
Investment Objective	Income	Telephone	800-621-1048
5-Year Projected Return	+48%	Minimum Investment	$1,000
Safety Rating (0-100)	85%	Telephone Switching	1 per 15da; fr
Yield (8/93)	8.1%	Total Assets	$307 million

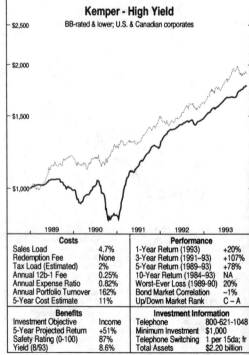

Kemper - High Yield
BB-rated & lower; U.S. & Canadian corporates

Costs		Performance	
Sales Load	4.7%	1-Year Return (1993)	+20%
Redemption Fee	None	3-Year Return (1991–93)	+107%
Tax Load (Estimated)	2%	5-Year Return (1989–93)	+78%
Annual 12b-1 Fee	0.25%	10-Year Return (1984–93)	NA
Annual Expense Ratio	0.82%	Worst-Ever Loss (1989-90)	20%
Annual Portfolio Turnover	162%	Bond Market Correlation	–1%
5-Year Cost Estimate	11%	Up/Down Market Rank	C – A

Benefits		Investment Information	
Investment Objective	Income	Telephone	800-621-1048
5-Year Projected Return	+51%	Minimum Investment	$1,000
Safety Rating (0-100)	87%	Telephone Switching	1 per 15da; fr
Yield (8/93)	8.6%	Total Assets	$2.20 billion

BOND

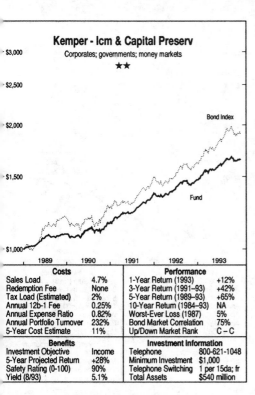

Kemper - Icm & Capital Preserv
Corporates; governments; money markets
★★

Bond Index

Fund

Costs		Performance	
Sales Load	4.7%	1-Year Return (1993)	+12%
Redemption Fee	None	3-Year Return (1991–93)	+42%
Tax Load (Estimated)	2%	5-Year Return (1989–93)	+65%
Annual 12b-1 Fee	0.25%	10-Year Return (1984–93)	NA
Annual Expense Ratio	0.82%	Worst-Ever Loss (1987)	5%
Annual Portfolio Turnover	232%	Bond Market Correlation	75%
5-Year Cost Estimate	11%	Up/Down Market Rank	C – C

Benefits		Investment Information	
Investment Objective	Income	Telephone	800-621-1048
5-Year Projected Return	+28%	Minimum Investment	$1,000
Safety Rating (0-100)	90%	Telephone Switching	1 per 15da; fr
Yield (8/93)	5.1%	Total Assets	$540 million

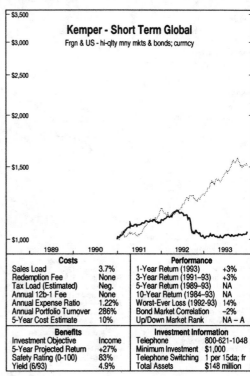

Kemper - Short Term Global
Frgn & US - hi-qlty mny mkts & bonds; currncy

Costs		Performance	
Sales Load	3.7%	1-Year Return (1993)	+3%
Redemption Fee	None	3-Year Return (1991–93)	+3%
Tax Load (Estimated)	Neg.	5-Year Return (1989–93)	NA
Annual 12b-1 Fee	None	10-Year Return (1984–93)	NA
Annual Expense Ratio	1.22%	Worst-Ever Loss (1992-93)	14%
Annual Portfolio Turnover	286%	Bond Market Correlation	–2%
5-Year Cost Estimate	10%	Up/Down Market Rank	NA – A

Benefits		Investment Information	
Investment Objective	Income	Telephone	800-621-1048
5-Year Projected Return	+27%	Minimum Investment	$1,000
Safety Rating (0-100)	83%	Telephone Switching	1 per 15da; fr
Yield (6/93)	4.9%	Total Assets	$148 million

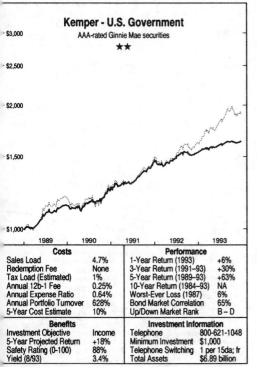

Kemper - U.S. Government
AAA-rated Ginnie Mae securities
★★

Costs		Performance	
Sales Load	4.7%	1-Year Return (1993)	+6%
Redemption Fee	None	3-Year Return (1991–93)	+30%
Tax Load (Estimated)	1%	5-Year Return (1989–93)	+63%
Annual 12b-1 Fee	0.25%	10-Year Return (1984–93)	NA
Annual Expense Ratio	0.64%	Worst-Ever Loss (1987)	6%
Annual Portfolio Turnover	628%	Bond Market Correlation	65%
5-Year Cost Estimate	10%	Up/Down Market Rank	B – D

Benefits		Investment Information	
Investment Objective	Income	Telephone	800-621-1048
5-Year Projected Return	+18%	Minimum Investment	$1,000
Safety Rating (0-100)	88%	Telephone Switching	1 per 15da; fr
Yield (8/93)	3.4%	Total Assets	$6.89 billion

Kemper Intermediate Government
Foreign & U.S. - At least 65% U.S. Govt secs

Costs		Performance	
Sales Load	None	1-Year Return (1993)	+3%
Redemption Fee	None	3-Year Return (1991–93)	+21%
Tax Load (Estimated)	0%	5-Year Return (1989–93)	+44%
Annual 12b-1 Fee	None	10-Year Return (1984–93)	NA
Annual Expense Ratio	0.93%	Worst-Ever Loss (1990)	19%
Annual Portfolio Turnover	334%	Bond Market Correlation	–1%
5-Year Cost Estimate	5%	Up/Down Market Rank	E – D

Benefits		Investment Information	
Investment Objective	Income	Telephone	800-537-6006
5-Year Projected Return	+50%	Minimum Investment	None
Safety Rating (0-100)	73%	Telephone Switching	Via broker
Yield	8.4%	Total Assets	$0 million

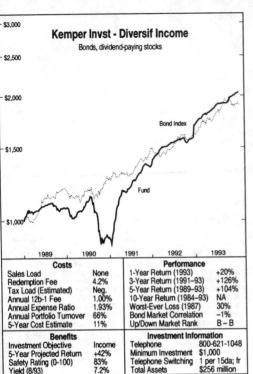

Kemper Invst - Diversif Income
Bonds, dividend-paying stocks

Bond Index

Fund

Costs		Performance	
Sales Load	None	1-Year Return (1993)	+20%
Redemption Fee	4.2%	3-Year Return (1991–93)	+126%
Tax Load (Estimated)	Neg.	5-Year Return (1989–93)	+104%
Annual 12b-1 Fee	1.00%	10-Year Return (1984–93)	NA
Annual Expense Ratio	1.93%	Worst-Ever Loss (1987)	30%
Annual Portfolio Turnover	66%	Bond Market Correlation	–1%
5-Year Cost Estimate	11%	Up/Down Market Rank	B – B

Benefits		Investment Information	
Investment Objective	Income	Telephone	800-621-1048
5-Year Projected Return	+42%	Minimum Investment	$1,000
Safety Rating (0-100)	83%	Telephone Switching	1 per 15da; fr
Yield (8/93)	7.2%	Total Assets	$256 million

Kemper Invst - Government
U.S. Government securities; AAA-rated repos

Costs		Performance	
Sales Load	None	1-Year Return (1993)	+5%
Redemption Fee	4.2%	3-Year Return (1991–93)	+28%
Tax Load (Estimated)	Neg.	5-Year Return (1989–93)	+53%
Annual 12b-1 Fee	1.00%	10-Year Return (1984–93)	NA
Annual Expense Ratio	1.75%	Worst-Ever Loss (1987)	7%
Annual Portfolio Turnover	551%	Bond Market Correlation	64%
5-Year Cost Estimate	10%	Up/Down Market Rank	C – E

Benefits		Investment Information	
Investment Objective	Income	Telephone	800-621-1048
5-Year Projected Return	+19%	Minimum Investment	$1,000
Safety Rating (0-100)	86%	Telephone Switching	1 per 15da; fr
Yield (8/93)	3.5%	Total Assets	$4.29 billion

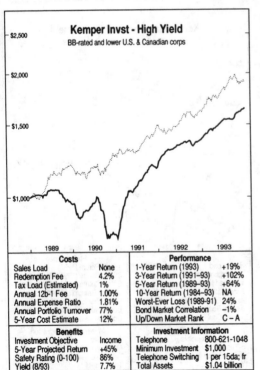

Kemper Invst - High Yield
BB-rated and lower U.S. & Canadian corps

Costs		Performance	
Sales Load	None	1-Year Return (1993)	+19%
Redemption Fee	4.2%	3-Year Return (1991–93)	+102%
Tax Load (Estimated)	1%	5-Year Return (1989–93)	+64%
Annual 12b-1 Fee	1.00%	10-Year Return (1984–93)	NA
Annual Expense Ratio	1.81%	Worst-Ever Loss (1989-91)	24%
Annual Portfolio Turnover	77%	Bond Market Correlation	–1%
5-Year Cost Estimate	12%	Up/Down Market Rank	C – A

Benefits		Investment Information	
Investment Objective	Income	Telephone	800-621-1048
5-Year Projected Return	+45%	Minimum Investment	$1,000
Safety Rating (0-100)	86%	Telephone Switching	1 per 15da; fr
Yield (8/93)	7.7%	Total Assets	$1.04 billion

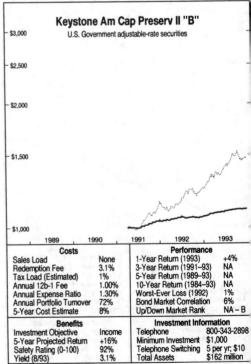

Keystone Am Cap Preserv II "B"
U.S. Government adjustable-rate securities

Costs		Performance	
Sales Load	None	1-Year Return (1993)	+4%
Redemption Fee	3.1%	3-Year Return (1991–93)	NA
Tax Load (Estimated)	1%	5-Year Return (1989–93)	NA
Annual 12b-1 Fee	1.00%	10-Year Return (1984–93)	NA
Annual Expense Ratio	1.30%	Worst-Ever Loss (1992)	1%
Annual Portfolio Turnover	72%	Bond Market Correlation	6%
5-Year Cost Estimate	8%	Up/Down Market Rank	NA – B

Benefits		Investment Information	
Investment Objective	Income	Telephone	800-343-2898
5-Year Projected Return	+16%	Minimum Investment	$1,000
Safety Rating (0-100)	92%	Telephone Switching	5 per yr; $10
Yield (8/93)	3.1%	Total Assets	$162 million

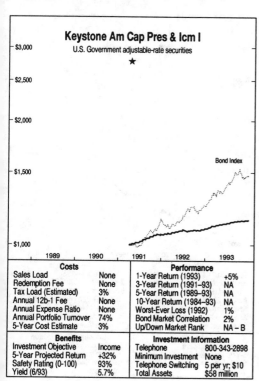

Keystone Am Cap Pres & Icm I
U.S. Government adjustable-rate securities
★

Bond Index

		1989	1990	1991	1992	1993

Costs		Performance	
Sales Load	None	1-Year Return (1993)	+5%
Redemption Fee	None	3-Year Return (1991–93)	NA
Tax Load (Estimated)	3%	5-Year Return (1989–93)	NA
Annual 12b-1 Fee	None	10-Year Return (1984–93)	NA
Annual Expense Ratio	None	Worst-Ever Loss (1992)	1%
Annual Portfolio Turnover	74%	Bond Market Correlation	2%
5-Year Cost Estimate	3%	Up/Down Market Rank	NA – B

Benefits		Investment Information	
Investment Objective	Income	Telephone	800-343-2898
5-Year Projected Return	+32%	Minimum Investment	None
Safety Rating (0-100)	93%	Telephone Switching	5 per yr; $10
Yield (6/93)	5.7%	Total Assets	$58 million

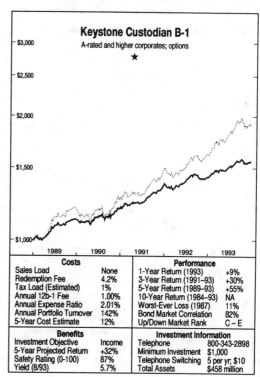

Keystone Custodian B-1
A-rated and higher corporates; options
★

Costs		Performance	
Sales Load	None	1-Year Return (1993)	+9%
Redemption Fee	4.2%	3-Year Return (1991–93)	+30%
Tax Load (Estimated)	1%	5-Year Return (1989–93)	+55%
Annual 12b-1 Fee	1.00%	10-Year Return (1984–93)	NA
Annual Expense Ratio	2.01%	Worst-Ever Loss (1987)	11%
Annual Portfolio Turnover	142%	Bond Market Correlation	82%
5-Year Cost Estimate	12%	Up/Down Market Rank	C – E

Benefits		Investment Information	
Investment Objective	Income	Telephone	800-343-2898
5-Year Projected Return	+32%	Minimum Investment	$1,000
Safety Rating (0-100)	87%	Telephone Switching	5 per yr; $10
Yield (8/93)	5.7%	Total Assets	$458 million

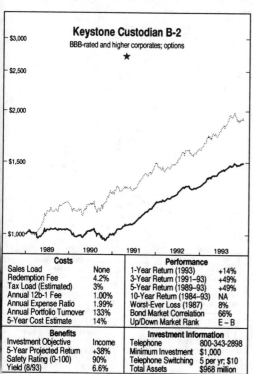

Keystone Custodian B-2
BBB-rated and higher corporates; options
★

Costs		Performance	
Sales Load	None	1-Year Return (1993)	+14%
Redemption Fee	4.2%	3-Year Return (1991–93)	+49%
Tax Load (Estimated)	3%	5-Year Return (1989–93)	+49%
Annual 12b-1 Fee	1.00%	10-Year Return (1984–93)	NA
Annual Expense Ratio	1.99%	Worst-Ever Loss (1987)	8%
Annual Portfolio Turnover	133%	Bond Market Correlation	66%
5-Year Cost Estimate	14%	Up/Down Market Rank	E – B

Benefits		Investment Information	
Investment Objective	Income	Telephone	800-343-2898
5-Year Projected Return	+38%	Minimum Investment	$1,000
Safety Rating (0-100)	90%	Telephone Switching	5 per yr; $10
Yield (8/93)	6.6%	Total Assets	$968 million

Keystone Custodian B-4
BBB-rated and lower corporates; options

Costs		Performance	
Sales Load	None	1-Year Return (1993)	+26%
Redemption Fee	4.2%	3-Year Return (1991–93)	+111%
Tax Load (Estimated)	Neg.	5-Year Return (1989–93)	+57%
Annual 12b-1 Fee	1.00%	10-Year Return (1984–93)	NA
Annual Expense Ratio	2.17%	Worst-Ever Loss (1989-91)	30%
Annual Portfolio Turnover	125%	Bond Market Correlation	–1%
5-Year Cost Estimate	12%	Up/Down Market Rank	E – A

Benefits		Investment Information	
Investment Objective	Income	Telephone	800-343-2898
5-Year Projected Return	+48%	Minimum Investment	$1,000
Safety Rating (0-100)	87%	Telephone Switching	5 per yr; $10
Yield (8/93)	8.1%	Total Assets	$962 million

BOND

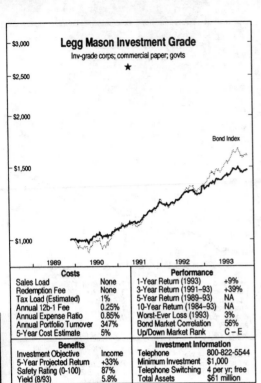

Legg Mason Investment Grade

Inv-grade corps; commercial paper; govts

★

Bond Index

Costs		Performance	
Sales Load	None	1-Year Return (1993)	+9%
Redemption Fee	None	3-Year Return (1991–93)	+39%
Tax Load (Estimated)	1%	5-Year Return (1989–93)	NA
Annual 12b-1 Fee	0.25%	10-Year Return (1984–93)	NA
Annual Expense Ratio	0.85%	Worst-Ever Loss (1993)	3%
Annual Portfolio Turnover	347%	Bond Market Correlation	56%
5-Year Cost Estimate	5%	Up/Down Market Rank	C – E

Benefits		Investment Information	
Investment Objective	Income	Telephone	800-822-5544
5-Year Projected Return	+33%	Minimum Investment	$1,000
Safety Rating (0-100)	87%	Telephone Switching	4 per yr; free
Yield (8/93)	5.8%	Total Assets	$61 million

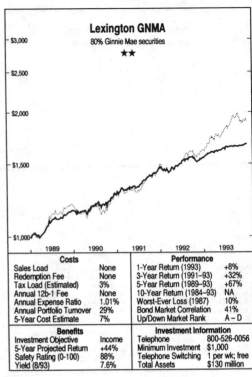

Lexington GNMA

80% Ginnie Mae securities

★★

Costs		Performance	
Sales Load	None	1-Year Return (1993)	+8%
Redemption Fee	None	3-Year Return (1991–93)	+32%
Tax Load (Estimated)	3%	5-Year Return (1989–93)	+67%
Annual 12b-1 Fee	None	10-Year Return (1984–93)	NA
Annual Expense Ratio	1.01%	Worst-Ever Loss (1987)	10%
Annual Portfolio Turnover	29%	Bond Market Correlation	41%
5-Year Cost Estimate	7%	Up/Down Market Rank	A – D

Benefits		Investment Information	
Investment Objective	Income	Telephone	800-526-0056
5-Year Projected Return	+44%	Minimum Investment	$1,000
Safety Rating (0-100)	88%	Telephone Switching	1 per wk; free
Yield (8/93)	7.6%	Total Assets	$130 million

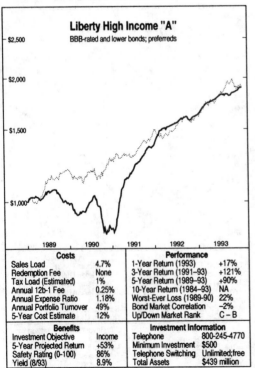

Liberty High Income "A"

BBB-rated and lower bonds; preferreds

Costs		Performance	
Sales Load	4.7%	1-Year Return (1993)	+17%
Redemption Fee	None	3-Year Return (1991–93)	+121%
Tax Load (Estimated)	1%	5-Year Return (1989–93)	+90%
Annual 12b-1 Fee	0.25%	10-Year Return (1984–93)	NA
Annual Expense Ratio	1.18%	Worst-Ever Loss (1989-90)	22%
Annual Portfolio Turnover	49%	Bond Market Correlation	–2%
5-Year Cost Estimate	12%	Up/Down Market Rank	C – B

Benefits		Investment Information	
Investment Objective	Income	Telephone	800-245-4770
5-Year Projected Return	+53%	Minimum Investment	$500
Safety Rating (0-100)	86%	Telephone Switching	Unlimited;free
Yield (8/93)	8.9%	Total Assets	$439 million

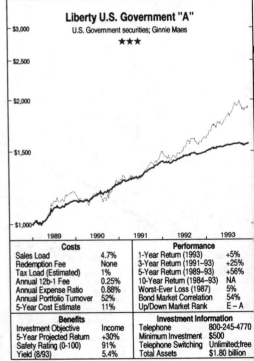

Liberty U.S. Government "A"

U.S. Government securities; Ginnie Maes

★★★

Costs		Performance	
Sales Load	4.7%	1-Year Return (1993)	+5%
Redemption Fee	None	3-Year Return (1991–93)	+25%
Tax Load (Estimated)	1%	5-Year Return (1989–93)	+56%
Annual 12b-1 Fee	0.25%	10-Year Return (1984–93)	NA
Annual Expense Ratio	0.88%	Worst-Ever Loss (1987)	5%
Annual Portfolio Turnover	52%	Bond Market Correlation	54%
5-Year Cost Estimate	11%	Up/Down Market Rank	E – A

Benefits		Investment Information	
Investment Objective	Income	Telephone	800-245-4770
5-Year Projected Return	+30%	Minimum Investment	$500
Safety Rating (0-100)	91%	Telephone Switching	Unlimited;free
Yield (8/93)	5.4%	Total Assets	$1.80 billion

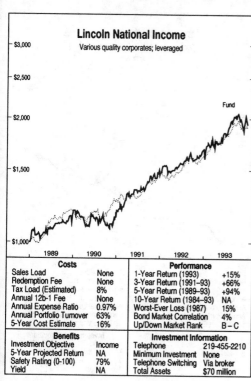

Lincoln National Income
Various quality corporates; leveraged

Fund

Costs		Performance	
Sales Load	None	1-Year Return (1993)	+15%
Redemption Fee	None	3-Year Return (1991–93)	+66%
Tax Load (Estimated)	8%	5-Year Return (1989–93)	+94%
Annual 12b-1 Fee	None	10-Year Return (1984–93)	NA
Annual Expense Ratio	0.97%	Worst-Ever Loss (1987)	15%
Annual Portfolio Turnover	63%	Bond Market Correlation	4%
5-Year Cost Estimate	16%	Up/Down Market Rank	B – C

Benefits		Investment Information	
Investment Objective	Income	Telephone	219-455-2210
5-Year Projected Return	NA	Minimum Investment	None
Safety Rating (0-100)	79%	Telephone Switching	Via broker
Yield	NA	Total Assets	$70 million

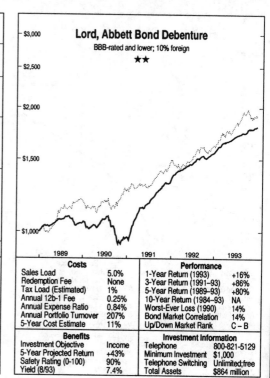

Lord, Abbett Bond Debenture
BBB-rated and lower; 10% foreign
★★

Costs		Performance	
Sales Load	5.0%	1-Year Return (1993)	+16%
Redemption Fee	None	3-Year Return (1991–93)	+86%
Tax Load (Estimated)	1%	5-Year Return (1989–93)	+80%
Annual 12b-1 Fee	0.25%	10-Year Return (1984–93)	NA
Annual Expense Ratio	0.84%	Worst-Ever Loss (1990)	14%
Annual Portfolio Turnover	207%	Bond Market Correlation	14%
5-Year Cost Estimate	11%	Up/Down Market Rank	C – B

Benefits		Investment Information	
Investment Objective	Income	Telephone	800-821-5129
5-Year Projected Return	+43%	Minimum Investment	$1,000
Safety Rating (0-100)	90%	Telephone Switching	Unlimited;free
Yield (8/93)	7.4%	Total Assets	$864 million

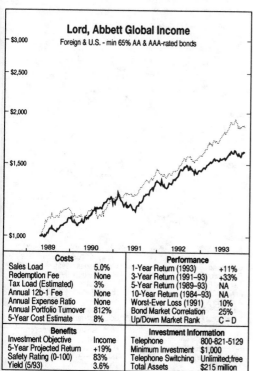

Lord, Abbett Global Income
Foreign & U.S. - min 65% AA & AAA-rated bonds

Costs		Performance	
Sales Load	5.0%	1-Year Return (1993)	+11%
Redemption Fee	None	3-Year Return (1991–93)	+33%
Tax Load (Estimated)	3%	5-Year Return (1989–93)	NA
Annual 12b-1 Fee	None	10-Year Return (1984–93)	NA
Annual Expense Ratio	None	Worst-Ever Loss (1991)	10%
Annual Portfolio Turnover	812%	Bond Market Correlation	25%
5-Year Cost Estimate	8%	Up/Down Market Rank	C – D

Benefits		Investment Information	
Investment Objective	Income	Telephone	800-821-5129
5-Year Projected Return	+19%	Minimum Investment	$1,000
Safety Rating (0-100)	83%	Telephone Switching	Unlimited;free
Yield (5/93)	3.6%	Total Assets	$215 million

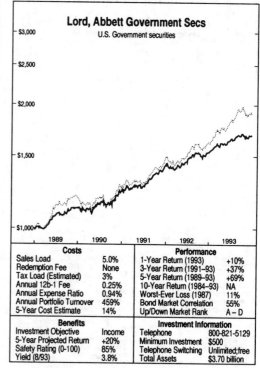

Lord, Abbett Government Secs
U.S. Government securities

Costs		Performance	
Sales Load	5.0%	1-Year Return (1993)	+10%
Redemption Fee	None	3-Year Return (1991–93)	+37%
Tax Load (Estimated)	3%	5-Year Return (1989–93)	+69%
Annual 12b-1 Fee	0.25%	10-Year Return (1984–93)	NA
Annual Expense Ratio	0.94%	Worst-Ever Loss (1987)	11%
Annual Portfolio Turnover	459%	Bond Market Correlation	55%
5-Year Cost Estimate	14%	Up/Down Market Rank	A – D

Benefits		Investment Information	
Investment Objective	Income	Telephone	800-821-5129
5-Year Projected Return	+20%	Minimum Investment	$500
Safety Rating (0-100)	85%	Telephone Switching	Unlimited;free
Yield (8/93)	3.8%	Total Assets	$3.70 billion

B O N D

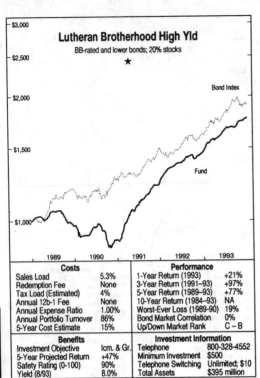

Lutheran Brotherhood High Yld
BB-rated and lower bonds; 20% stocks
★

Costs		Performance	
Sales Load	5.3%	1-Year Return (1993)	+21%
Redemption Fee	None	3-Year Return (1991–93)	+97%
Tax Load (Estimated)	4%	5-Year Return (1989–93)	+77%
Annual 12b-1 Fee	None	10-Year Return (1984–93)	NA
Annual Expense Ratio	1.00%	Worst-Ever Loss (1989-90)	19%
Annual Portfolio Turnover	86%	Bond Market Correlation	0%
5-Year Cost Estimate	15%	Up/Down Market Rank	C – B

Benefits		Investment Information	
Investment Objective	Icm. & Gr.	Telephone	800-328-4552
5-Year Projected Return	+47%	Minimum Investment	$500
Safety Rating (0-100)	90%	Telephone Switching	Unlimited; $10
Yield (8/93)	8.0%	Total Assets	$395 million

Lutheran Brotherhood Income
Corporate bonds; U.S. Government securities
★★★★

Costs		Performance	
Sales Load	5.3%	1-Year Return (1993)	+10%
Redemption Fee	None	3-Year Return (1991–93)	+39%
Tax Load (Estimated)	3%	5-Year Return (1989–93)	+66%
Annual 12b-1 Fee	None	10-Year Return (1984–93)	NA
Annual Expense Ratio	0.82%	Worst-Ever Loss (1987)	9%
Annual Portfolio Turnover	104%	Bond Market Correlation	62%
5-Year Cost Estimate	13%	Up/Down Market Rank	D – C

Benefits		Investment Information	
Investment Objective	Income	Telephone	800-328-4552
5-Year Projected Return	+26%	Minimum Investment	$500
Safety Rating (0-100)	90%	Telephone Switching	Unlimited; $10
Yield (8/93)	4.7%	Total Assets	$1.06 billion

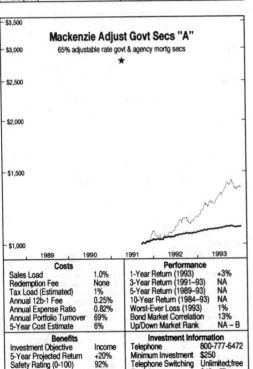

Mackenzie Adjust Govt Secs "A"
65% adjustable rate govt & agency mortg secs
★

Costs		Performance	
Sales Load	1.0%	1-Year Return (1993)	+3%
Redemption Fee	None	3-Year Return (1991–93)	NA
Tax Load (Estimated)	1%	5-Year Return (1989–93)	NA
Annual 12b-1 Fee	0.25%	10-Year Return (1984–93)	NA
Annual Expense Ratio	0.82%	Worst-Ever Loss (1993)	1%
Annual Portfolio Turnover	69%	Bond Market Correlation	13%
5-Year Cost Estimate	6%	Up/Down Market Rank	NA – B

Benefits		Investment Information	
Investment Objective	Income	Telephone	800-777-6472
5-Year Projected Return	+20%	Minimum Investment	$250
Safety Rating (0-100)	92%	Telephone Switching	Unlimited;free
Yield (7/93)	3.8%	Total Assets	$42 million

MacKenzie Fixed Income
Long-term investment-grade corps and govts

Costs		Performance	
Sales Load	5.0%	1-Year Return (1993)	+15%
Redemption Fee	None	3-Year Return (1991–93)	+43%
Tax Load (Estimated)	1%	5-Year Return (1989–93)	NA
Annual 12b-1 Fee	0.25%	10-Year Return (1984–93)	NA
Annual Expense Ratio	1.49%	Worst-Ever Loss (1989-90)	8%
Annual Portfolio Turnover	139%	Bond Market Correlation	76%
5-Year Cost Estimate	14%	Up/Down Market Rank	A – E

Benefits		Investment Information	
Investment Objective	Income	Telephone	800-777-6472
5-Year Projected Return	+34%	Minimum Investment	$1,000
Safety Rating (0-100)	82%	Telephone Switching	Unlimited;free
Yield (8/93)	6.0%	Total Assets	$130 million

BOND

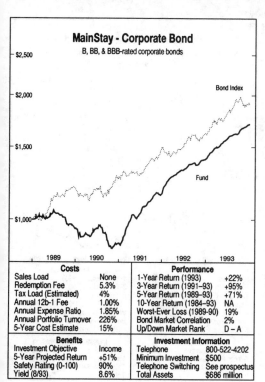

MainStay - Corporate Bond
B, BB, & BBB-rated corporate bonds

Bond Index

Fund

	Costs		Performance	
Sales Load	None	1-Year Return (1993)	+22%
Redemption Fee	5.3%	3-Year Return (1991–93)	+95%
Tax Load (Estimated)	4%	5-Year Return (1989–93)	+71%
Annual 12b-1 Fee	1.00%	10-Year Return (1984–93)	NA
Annual Expense Ratio	1.85%	Worst-Ever Loss (1989-90)	19%
Annual Portfolio Turnover	226%	Bond Market Correlation	2%
5-Year Cost Estimate	15%	Up/Down Market Rank	D – A
	Benefits		Investment Information	
Investment Objective	Income	Telephone	800-522-4202
5-Year Projected Return	+51%	Minimum Investment	$500
Safety Rating (0-100)	90%	Telephone Switching	See prospectus
Yield (8/93)	8.6%	Total Assets	$686 million

MainStay - Government
U.S. Government securities; futures; options

	Costs		Performance	
Sales Load	None	1-Year Return (1993)	+6%
Redemption Fee	5.3%	3-Year Return (1991–93)	+25%
Tax Load (Estimated)	3%	5-Year Return (1989–93)	+50%
Annual 12b-1 Fee	1.00%	10-Year Return (1984–93)	NA
Annual Expense Ratio	1.75%	Worst-Ever Loss (1989-90)	5%
Annual Portfolio Turnover	613%	Bond Market Correlation	78%
5-Year Cost Estimate	13%	Up/Down Market Rank	D – B
	Benefits		Investment Information	
Investment Objective	Income	Telephone	800-522-4202
5-Year Projected Return	+19%	Minimum Investment	$500
Safety Rating (0-100)	86%	Telephone Switching	See prospectus
Yield (8/93)	3.6%	Total Assets	$1.18 billion

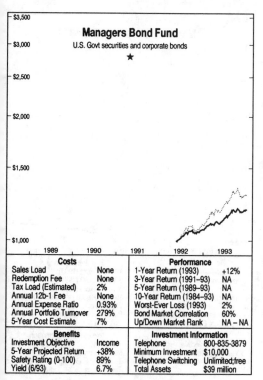

Managers Bond Fund
U.S. Govt securities and corporate bonds
★

	Costs		Performance	
Sales Load	None	1-Year Return (1993)	+12%
Redemption Fee	None	3-Year Return (1991–93)	NA
Tax Load (Estimated)	2%	5-Year Return (1989–93)	NA
Annual 12b-1 Fee	None	10-Year Return (1984–93)	NA
Annual Expense Ratio	0.93%	Worst-Ever Loss (1993)	2%
Annual Portfolio Turnover	279%	Bond Market Correlation	60%
5-Year Cost Estimate	7%	Up/Down Market Rank	NA – NA
	Benefits		Investment Information	
Investment Objective	Income	Telephone	800-835-3879
5-Year Projected Return	+38%	Minimum Investment	$10,000
Safety Rating (0-100)	89%	Telephone Switching	Unlimited;free
Yield (6/93)	6.7%	Total Assets	$39 million

Managers Intermed Mortgage Sec
65% mortgage securities
★★

	Costs		Performance	
Sales Load	None	1-Year Return (1993)	+11%
Redemption Fee	None	3-Year Return (1991–93)	NA
Tax Load (Estimated)	5%	5-Year Return (1989–93)	NA
Annual 12b-1 Fee	None	10-Year Return (1984–93)	NA
Annual Expense Ratio	0.79%	Worst-Ever Loss (1993)	3%
Annual Portfolio Turnover	290%	Bond Market Correlation	22%
5-Year Cost Estimate	10%	Up/Down Market Rank	NA – NA
	Benefits		Investment Information	
Investment Objective	Income	Telephone	800-835-3879
5-Year Projected Return	+47%	Minimum Investment	$10,000
Safety Rating (0-100)	92%	Telephone Switching	Unlimited;free
Yield (8/93)	8.0%	Total Assets	$185 million

BOND

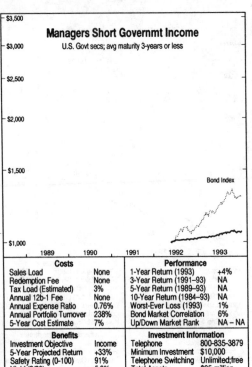

Managers Short Governmt Income

U.S. Govt secs; avg maturity 3-years or less

Costs		Performance	
Sales Load	None	1-Year Return (1993)	+4%
Redemption Fee	None	3-Year Return (1991–93)	NA
Tax Load (Estimated)	3%	5-Year Return (1989–93)	NA
Annual 12b-1 Fee	None	10-Year Return (1984–93)	NA
Annual Expense Ratio	0.76%	Worst-Ever Loss (1993)	1%
Annual Portfolio Turnover	238%	Bond Market Correlation	6%
5-Year Cost Estimate	7%	Up/Down Market Rank	NA – NA

Benefits		Investment Information	
Investment Objective	Income	Telephone	800-835-3879
5-Year Projected Return	+33%	Minimum Investment	$10,000
Safety Rating (0-100)	91%	Telephone Switching	Unlimited;free
Yield (8/93)	5.9%	Total Assets	$95 million

Managers Short-Intermed Bond

U.S. Govt secs & agencies; 1-5 years avg maty
★★★★

Costs		Performance	
Sales Load	None	1-Year Return (1993)	+8%
Redemption Fee	None	3-Year Return (1991–93)	NA
Tax Load (Estimated)	3%	5-Year Return (1989–93)	NA
Annual 12b-1 Fee	None	10-Year Return (1984–93)	NA
Annual Expense Ratio	0.86%	Worst-Ever Loss (1992)	1%
Annual Portfolio Turnover	144%	Bond Market Correlation	35%
5-Year Cost Estimate	7%	Up/Down Market Rank	NA – NA

Benefits		Investment Information	
Investment Objective	Income	Telephone	800-835-3879
5-Year Projected Return	+34%	Minimum Investment	$10,000
Safety Rating (0-100)	96%	Telephone Switching	Unlimited;free
Yield (8/93)	6.1%	Total Assets	$98 million

Mariner Fixed Income

Diversified investment-grade bonds

Costs		Performance	
Sales Load	5.0%	1-Year Return (1993)	NA
Redemption Fee	None	3-Year Return (1991–93)	NA
Tax Load (Estimated)	2%	5-Year Return (1989–93)	NA
Annual 12b-1 Fee	0.35%	10-Year Return (1984–93)	NA
Annual Expense Ratio	0.93%	Worst-Ever Loss (1993)	2%
Annual Portfolio Turnover	143%	Bond Market Correlation	NA
5-Year Cost Estimate	12%	Up/Down Market Rank	NA – NA

Benefits		Investment Information	
Investment Objective	Income	Telephone	800-753-4462
5-Year Projected Return	NA	Minimum Investment	$1,000
Safety Rating (0-100)	NA	Telephone Switching	1 per 7da;free
Yield (6/93)	6.2%	Total Assets	$82 million

Merrill Lynch Adjust Rate "B"

Adjustable-rate AA-rated corps and govts

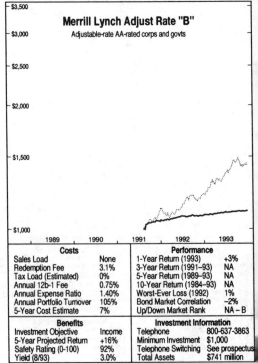

Costs		Performance	
Sales Load	None	1-Year Return (1993)	+3%
Redemption Fee	3.1%	3-Year Return (1991–93)	NA
Tax Load (Estimated)	0%	5-Year Return (1989–93)	NA
Annual 12b-1 Fee	0.75%	10-Year Return (1984–93)	NA
Annual Expense Ratio	1.40%	Worst-Ever Loss (1992)	1%
Annual Portfolio Turnover	105%	Bond Market Correlation	–2%
5-Year Cost Estimate	7%	Up/Down Market Rank	NA – B

Benefits		Investment Information	
Investment Objective	Income	Telephone	800-637-3863
5-Year Projected Return	+16%	Minimum Investment	$1,000
Safety Rating (0-100)	92%	Telephone Switching	See prospectus
Yield (8/93)	3.0%	Total Assets	$741 million

BOND

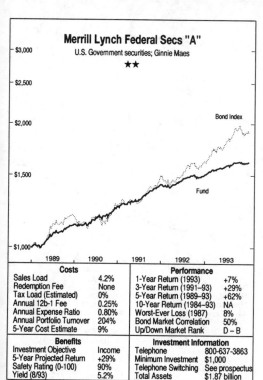

Merrill Lynch Federal Secs "A"
U.S. Government securities; Ginnie Maes
★★

Costs		Performance	
Sales Load	4.2%	1-Year Return (1993)	+7%
Redemption Fee	None	3-Year Return (1991–93)	+29%
Tax Load (Estimated)	0%	5-Year Return (1989–93)	+62%
Annual 12b-1 Fee	0.25%	10-Year Return (1984–93)	NA
Annual Expense Ratio	0.80%	Worst-Ever Loss (1987)	8%
Annual Portfolio Turnover	204%	Bond Market Correlation	50%
5-Year Cost Estimate	9%	Up/Down Market Rank	D – B

Benefits		Investment Information	
Investment Objective	Income	Telephone	800-637-3863
5-Year Projected Return	+29%	Minimum Investment	$1,000
Safety Rating (0-100)	90%	Telephone Switching	See prospectus
Yield (8/93)	5.2%	Total Assets	$1.87 billion

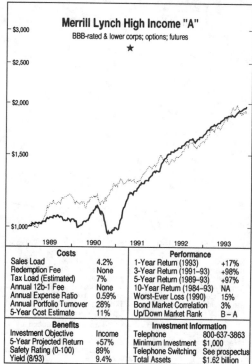

Merrill Lynch High Income "A"
BBB-rated & lower corps; options; futures
★

Costs		Performance	
Sales Load	4.2%	1-Year Return (1993)	+17%
Redemption Fee	None	3-Year Return (1991–93)	+98%
Tax Load (Estimated)	7%	5-Year Return (1989–93)	+97%
Annual 12b-1 Fee	None	10-Year Return (1984–93)	NA
Annual Expense Ratio	0.59%	Worst-Ever Loss (1990)	15%
Annual Portfolio Turnover	28%	Bond Market Correlation	3%
5-Year Cost Estimate	11%	Up/Down Market Rank	B – A

Benefits		Investment Information	
Investment Objective	Income	Telephone	800-637-3863
5-Year Projected Return	+57%	Minimum Investment	$1,000
Safety Rating (0-100)	89%	Telephone Switching	See prospectus
Yield (8/93)	9.4%	Total Assets	$1.62 billion

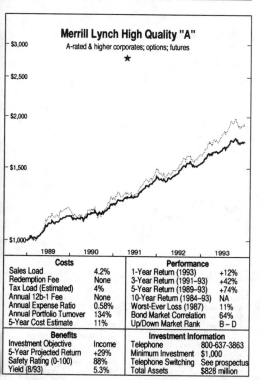

Merrill Lynch High Quality "A"
A-rated & higher corporates; options; futures
★

Costs		Performance	
Sales Load	4.2%	1-Year Return (1993)	+12%
Redemption Fee	None	3-Year Return (1991–93)	+42%
Tax Load (Estimated)	4%	5-Year Return (1989–93)	+74%
Annual 12b-1 Fee	None	10-Year Return (1984–93)	NA
Annual Expense Ratio	0.58%	Worst-Ever Loss (1987)	11%
Annual Portfolio Turnover	134%	Bond Market Correlation	64%
5-Year Cost Estimate	11%	Up/Down Market Rank	B – D

Benefits		Investment Information	
Investment Objective	Income	Telephone	800-637-3863
5-Year Projected Return	+29%	Minimum Investment	$1,000
Safety Rating (0-100)	88%	Telephone Switching	See prospectus
Yield (8/93)	5.3%	Total Assets	$828 million

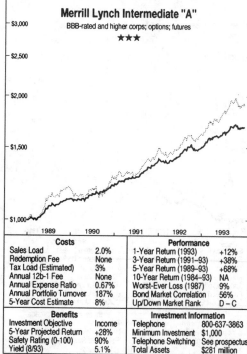

Merrill Lynch Intermediate "A"
BBB-rated and higher corps; options; futures
★★★

Costs		Performance	
Sales Load	2.0%	1-Year Return (1993)	+12%
Redemption Fee	None	3-Year Return (1991–93)	+38%
Tax Load (Estimated)	3%	5-Year Return (1989–93)	+68%
Annual 12b-1 Fee	None	10-Year Return (1984–93)	NA
Annual Expense Ratio	0.67%	Worst-Ever Loss (1987)	9%
Annual Portfolio Turnover	187%	Bond Market Correlation	56%
5-Year Cost Estimate	8%	Up/Down Market Rank	D – C

Benefits		Investment Information	
Investment Objective	Income	Telephone	800-637-3863
5-Year Projected Return	+28%	Minimum Investment	$1,000
Safety Rating (0-100)	90%	Telephone Switching	See prospectus
Yield (8/93)	5.1%	Total Assets	$281 million

BOND

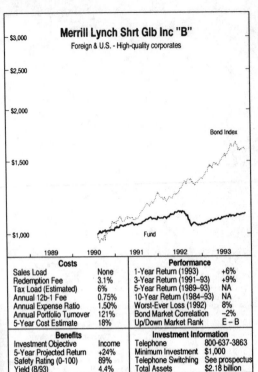

Merrill Lynch Shrt Glb Inc "B"
Foreign & U.S. - High-quality corporates

Costs		Performance	
Sales Load	None	1-Year Return (1993)	+6%
Redemption Fee	3.1%	3-Year Return (1991–93)	+9%
Tax Load (Estimated)	6%	5-Year Return (1989–93)	NA
Annual 12b-1 Fee	0.75%	10-Year Return (1984–93)	NA
Annual Expense Ratio	1.50%	Worst-Ever Loss (1992)	8%
Annual Portfolio Turnover	121%	Bond Market Correlation	−2%
5-Year Cost Estimate	18%	Up/Down Market Rank	E – B

Benefits		Investment Information	
Investment Objective	Income	Telephone	800-637-3863
5-Year Projected Return	+24%	Minimum Investment	$1,000
Safety Rating (0-100)	89%	Telephone Switching	See prospectus
Yield (8/93)	4.4%	Total Assets	$2.18 billion

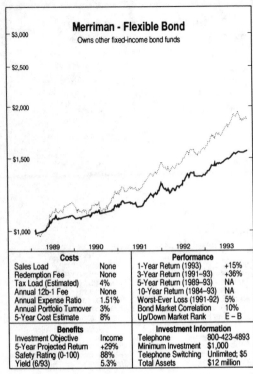

Merriman - Flexible Bond
Owns other fixed-income bond funds

Costs		Performance	
Sales Load	None	1-Year Return (1993)	+15%
Redemption Fee	None	3-Year Return (1991–93)	+36%
Tax Load (Estimated)	4%	5-Year Return (1989–93)	NA
Annual 12b-1 Fee	None	10-Year Return (1984–93)	NA
Annual Expense Ratio	1.51%	Worst-Ever Loss (1991-92)	5%
Annual Portfolio Turnover	3%	Bond Market Correlation	10%
5-Year Cost Estimate	8%	Up/Down Market Rank	E – B

Benefits		Investment Information	
Investment Objective	Income	Telephone	800-423-4893
5-Year Projected Return	+29%	Minimum Investment	$1,000
Safety Rating (0-100)	88%	Telephone Switching	Unlimited; $5
Yield (6/93)	5.3%	Total Assets	$12 million

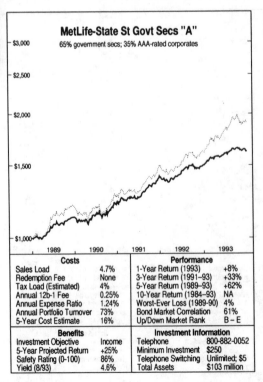

MetLife-State St Govt Secs "A"
65% government secs; 35% AAA-rated corporates

Costs		Performance	
Sales Load	4.7%	1-Year Return (1993)	+8%
Redemption Fee	None	3-Year Return (1991–93)	+33%
Tax Load (Estimated)	4%	5-Year Return (1989–93)	+62%
Annual 12b-1 Fee	0.25%	10-Year Return (1984–93)	NA
Annual Expense Ratio	1.24%	Worst-Ever Loss (1989-90)	4%
Annual Portfolio Turnover	73%	Bond Market Correlation	61%
5-Year Cost Estimate	16%	Up/Down Market Rank	B – E

Benefits		Investment Information	
Investment Objective	Income	Telephone	800-882-0052
5-Year Projected Return	+25%	Minimum Investment	$250
Safety Rating (0-100)	86%	Telephone Switching	Unlimited; $5
Yield (8/93)	4.6%	Total Assets	$103 million

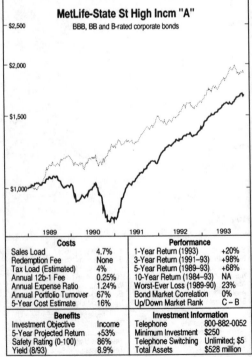

MetLife-State St High Incm "A"
BBB, BB and B-rated corporate bonds

Costs		Performance	
Sales Load	4.7%	1-Year Return (1993)	+20%
Redemption Fee	None	3-Year Return (1991–93)	+98%
Tax Load (Estimated)	4%	5-Year Return (1989–93)	+68%
Annual 12b-1 Fee	0.25%	10-Year Return (1984–93)	NA
Annual Expense Ratio	1.24%	Worst-Ever Loss (1989-90)	23%
Annual Portfolio Turnover	67%	Bond Market Correlation	0%
5-Year Cost Estimate	16%	Up/Down Market Rank	C – B

Benefits		Investment Information	
Investment Objective	Income	Telephone	800-882-0052
5-Year Projected Return	+53%	Minimum Investment	$250
Safety Rating (0-100)	86%	Telephone Switching	Unlimited; $5
Yield (8/93)	8.9%	Total Assets	$528 million

BOND

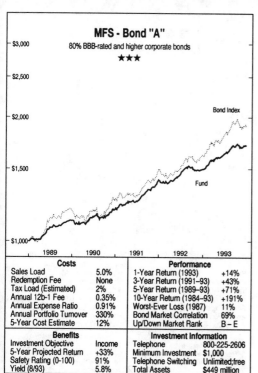

MFS - Bond "A"
80% BBB-rated and higher corporate bonds
★★★

Bond Index

Fund

Costs		Performance	
Sales Load	5.0%	1-Year Return (1993)	+14%
Redemption Fee	None	3-Year Return (1991–93)	+43%
Tax Load (Estimated)	2%	5-Year Return (1989–93)	+71%
Annual 12b-1 Fee	0.35%	10-Year Return (1984–93)	+191%
Annual Expense Ratio	0.91%	Worst-Ever Loss (1987)	11%
Annual Portfolio Turnover	330%	Bond Market Correlation	69%
5-Year Cost Estimate	12%	Up/Down Market Rank	B – E

Benefits		Investment Information	
Investment Objective	Income	Telephone	800-225-2606
5-Year Projected Return	+33%	Minimum Investment	$1,000
Safety Rating (0-100)	91%	Telephone Switching	Unlimited;free
Yield (8/93)	5.8%	Total Assets	$449 million

MFS - Govt Markets Income
BBB-rated and higher bonds

Costs		Performance	
Sales Load	None	1-Year Return (1993)	+9%
Redemption Fee	None	3-Year Return (1991–93)	+26%
Tax Load (Estimated)	2%	5-Year Return (1989–93)	+31%
Annual 12b-1 Fee	None	10-Year Return (1984–93)	NA
Annual Expense Ratio	1.04%	Worst-Ever Loss (1990)	19%
Annual Portfolio Turnover	482%	Bond Market Correlation	6%
5-Year Cost Estimate	10%	Up/Down Market Rank	E – C

Benefits		Investment Information	
Investment Objective	Income	Telephone	800-343-2829
5-Year Projected Return	NA	Minimum Investment	None
Safety Rating (0-100)	66%	Telephone Switching	Via broker
Yield	NA	Total Assets	$761 million

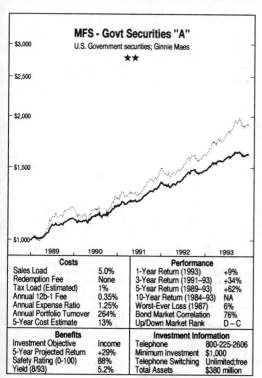

MFS - Govt Securities "A"
U.S. Government securities; Ginnie Maes
★★

Costs		Performance	
Sales Load	5.0%	1-Year Return (1993)	+9%
Redemption Fee	None	3-Year Return (1991–93)	+34%
Tax Load (Estimated)	1%	5-Year Return (1989–93)	+62%
Annual 12b-1 Fee	0.35%	10-Year Return (1984–93)	NA
Annual Expense Ratio	1.25%	Worst-Ever Loss (1987)	6%
Annual Portfolio Turnover	264%	Bond Market Correlation	76%
5-Year Cost Estimate	13%	Up/Down Market Rank	D – C

Benefits		Investment Information	
Investment Objective	Income	Telephone	800-225-2606
5-Year Projected Return	+29%	Minimum Investment	$1,000
Safety Rating (0-100)	88%	Telephone Switching	Unlimited;free
Yield (8/93)	5.2%	Total Assets	$380 million

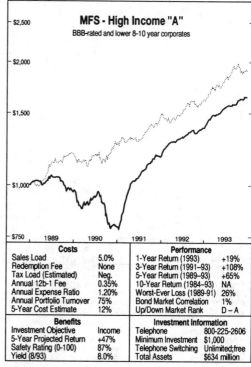

MFS - High Income "A"
BBB-rated and lower 8-10 year corporates

Costs		Performance	
Sales Load	5.0%	1-Year Return (1993)	+19%
Redemption Fee	None	3-Year Return (1991–93)	+108%
Tax Load (Estimated)	Neg.	5-Year Return (1989–93)	+65%
Annual 12b-1 Fee	0.35%	10-Year Return (1984–93)	NA
Annual Expense Ratio	1.20%	Worst-Ever Loss (1989-91)	26%
Annual Portfolio Turnover	75%	Bond Market Correlation	1%
5-Year Cost Estimate	12%	Up/Down Market Rank	D – A

Benefits		Investment Information	
Investment Objective	Income	Telephone	800-225-2606
5-Year Projected Return	+47%	Minimum Investment	$1,000
Safety Rating (0-100)	87%	Telephone Switching	Unlimited;free
Yield (8/93)	8.0%	Total Assets	$634 million

BOND

MFS - Multi-Mkt Income Trust
Frgn & U.S. - BBB-rated & higher corps; govts

Bond Index

Fund

Costs		Performance	
Sales Load	None	1-Year Return (1993)	+6%
Redemption Fee	None	3-Year Return (1991–93)	+42%
Tax Load (Estimated)	2%	5-Year Return (1989–93)	+31%
Annual 12b-1 Fee	None	10-Year Return (1984–93)	NA
Annual Expense Ratio	1.11%	Worst-Ever Loss (1989-90)	24%
Annual Portfolio Turnover	474%	Bond Market Correlation	7%
5-Year Cost Estimate	10%	Up/Down Market Rank	D – D

Benefits		Investment Information	
Investment Objective	Income	Telephone	800-343-2829
5-Year Projected Return	NA	Minimum Investment	None
Safety Rating (0-100)	67%	Telephone Switching	Via broker
Yield	NA	Total Assets	$947 million

MFS - World Governments "A"
Foreign & U.S. - fixed income and currencies

Costs		Performance	
Sales Load	5.0%	1-Year Return (1993)	+18%
Redemption Fee	None	3-Year Return (1991–93)	+36%
Tax Load (Estimated)	1%	5-Year Return (1989–93)	+72%
Annual 12b-1 Fee	0.35%	10-Year Return (1984–93)	+275%
Annual Expense Ratio	1.61%	Worst-Ever Loss (1984-85)	8%
Annual Portfolio Turnover	163%	Bond Market Correlation	18%
5-Year Cost Estimate	15%	Up/Down Market Rank	C – B

Benefits		Investment Information	
Investment Objective	Income	Telephone	800-225-2606
5-Year Projected Return	+23%	Minimum Investment	$1,000
Safety Rating (0-100)	88%	Telephone Switching	Unlimited;free
Yield (8/93)	4.3%	Total Assets	$386 million

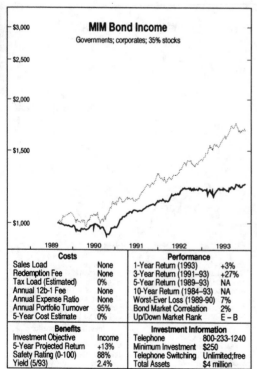

MIM Bond Income
Governments; corporates; 35% stocks

Costs		Performance	
Sales Load	None	1-Year Return (1993)	+3%
Redemption Fee	None	3-Year Return (1991–93)	+27%
Tax Load (Estimated)	0%	5-Year Return (1989–93)	NA
Annual 12b-1 Fee	None	10-Year Return (1984–93)	NA
Annual Expense Ratio	None	Worst-Ever Loss (1989-90)	7%
Annual Portfolio Turnover	95%	Bond Market Correlation	2%
5-Year Cost Estimate	0%	Up/Down Market Rank	E – B

Benefits		Investment Information	
Investment Objective	Income	Telephone	800-233-1240
5-Year Projected Return	+13%	Minimum Investment	$250
Safety Rating (0-100)	88%	Telephone Switching	Unlimited;free
Yield (5/93)	2.4%	Total Assets	$4 million

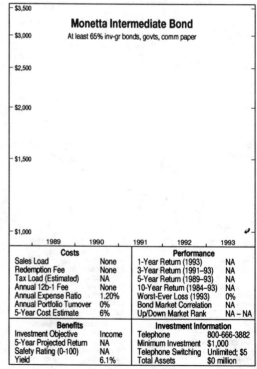

Monetta Intermediate Bond
At least 65% inv-gr bonds, govts, comm paper

Costs		Performance	
Sales Load	None	1-Year Return (1993)	NA
Redemption Fee	None	3-Year Return (1991–93)	NA
Tax Load (Estimated)	NA	5-Year Return (1989–93)	NA
Annual 12b-1 Fee	None	10-Year Return (1984–93)	NA
Annual Expense Ratio	1.20%	Worst-Ever Loss (1993)	0%
Annual Portfolio Turnover	0%	Bond Market Correlation	NA
5-Year Cost Estimate	6%	Up/Down Market Rank	NA – NA

Benefits		Investment Information	
Investment Objective	Income	Telephone	800-666-3882
5-Year Projected Return	NA	Minimum Investment	$1,000
Safety Rating (0-100)	NA	Telephone Switching	Unlimited; $5
Yield	6.1%	Total Assets	$0 million

BOND

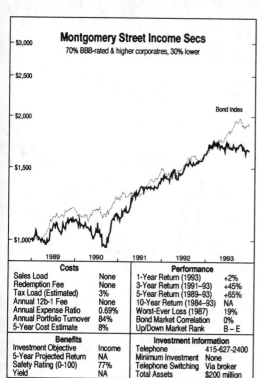

Montgomery Street Income Secs
70% BBB-rated & higher corporatres, 30% lower

Bond Index

Costs		Performance	
Sales Load	None	1-Year Return (1993)	+2%
Redemption Fee	None	3-Year Return (1991–93)	+45%
Tax Load (Estimated)	3%	5-Year Return (1989–93)	+65%
Annual 12b-1 Fee	None	10-Year Return (1984–93)	NA
Annual Expense Ratio	0.69%	Worst-Ever Loss (1987)	19%
Annual Portfolio Turnover	84%	Bond Market Correlation	0%
5-Year Cost Estimate	8%	Up/Down Market Rank	B – E

Benefits		Investment Information	
Investment Objective	Income	Telephone	415-627-2400
5-Year Projected Return	NA	Minimum Investment	None
Safety Rating (0-100)	77%	Telephone Switching	Via broker
Yield	NA	Total Assets	$200 million

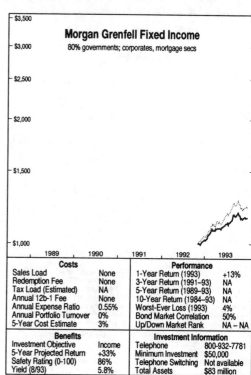

Morgan Grenfell Fixed Income
80% governments; corporates, mortgage secs

Costs		Performance	
Sales Load	None	1-Year Return (1993)	+13%
Redemption Fee	None	3-Year Return (1991–93)	NA
Tax Load (Estimated)	NA	5-Year Return (1989–93)	NA
Annual 12b-1 Fee	None	10-Year Return (1984–93)	NA
Annual Expense Ratio	0.55%	Worst-Ever Loss (1993)	4%
Annual Portfolio Turnover	0%	Bond Market Correlation	50%
5-Year Cost Estimate	3%	Up/Down Market Rank	NA – NA

Benefits		Investment Information	
Investment Objective	Income	Telephone	800-932-7781
5-Year Projected Return	+33%	Minimum Investment	$50,000
Safety Rating (0-100)	86%	Telephone Switching	Not available
Yield (8/93)	5.8%	Total Assets	$83 million

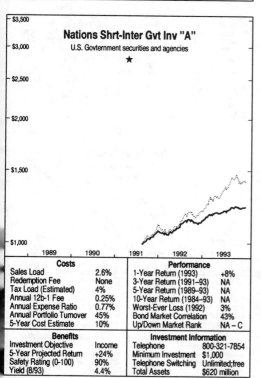

Nations Shrt-Inter Gvt Inv "A"
U.S. Govternment securities and agencies
★

Costs		Performance	
Sales Load	2.6%	1-Year Return (1993)	+8%
Redemption Fee	None	3-Year Return (1991–93)	NA
Tax Load (Estimated)	4%	5-Year Return (1989–93)	NA
Annual 12b-1 Fee	0.25%	10-Year Return (1984–93)	NA
Annual Expense Ratio	0.77%	Worst-Ever Loss (1992)	3%
Annual Portfolio Turnover	45%	Bond Market Correlation	43%
5-Year Cost Estimate	10%	Up/Down Market Rank	NA – C

Benefits		Investment Information	
Investment Objective	Income	Telephone	800-321-7854
5-Year Projected Return	+24%	Minimum Investment	$1,000
Safety Rating (0-100)	90%	Telephone Switching	Unlimited;free
Yield (8/93)	4.4%	Total Assets	$620 million

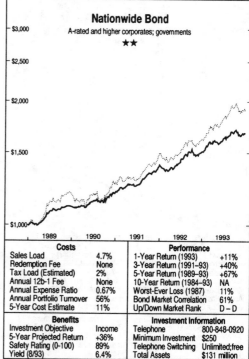

Nationwide Bond
A-rated and higher corporates; governments
★★

Costs		Performance	
Sales Load	4.7%	1-Year Return (1993)	+11%
Redemption Fee	None	3-Year Return (1991–93)	+40%
Tax Load (Estimated)	2%	5-Year Return (1989–93)	+67%
Annual 12b-1 Fee	None	10-Year Return (1984–93)	NA
Annual Expense Ratio	0.67%	Worst-Ever Loss (1987)	11%
Annual Portfolio Turnover	56%	Bond Market Correlation	61%
5-Year Cost Estimate	11%	Up/Down Market Rank	D – D

Benefits		Investment Information	
Investment Objective	Income	Telephone	800-848-0920
5-Year Projected Return	+36%	Minimum Investment	$250
Safety Rating (0-100)	89%	Telephone Switching	Unlimited;free
Yield (8/93)	6.4%	Total Assets	$131 million

BOND

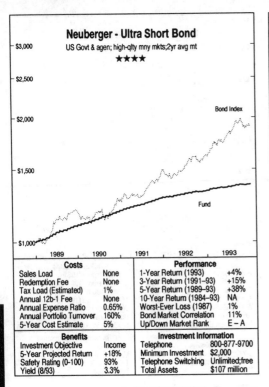

Neuberger - Ultra Short Bond
US Govt & agen; high-qlty mny mkts;2yr avg mt
★★★★

Bond Index

Fund

Costs		Performance	
Sales Load	None	1-Year Return (1993)	+4%
Redemption Fee	None	3-Year Return (1991–93)	+15%
Tax Load (Estimated)	1%	5-Year Return (1989–93)	+38%
Annual 12b-1 Fee	None	10-Year Return (1984–93)	NA
Annual Expense Ratio	0.65%	Worst-Ever Loss (1987)	1%
Annual Portfolio Turnover	160%	Bond Market Correlation	11%
5-Year Cost Estimate	5%	Up/Down Market Rank	E – A

Benefits		Investment Information	
Investment Objective	Income	Telephone	800-877-9700
5-Year Projected Return	+18%	Minimum Investment	$2,000
Safety Rating (0-100)	93%	Telephone Switching	Unlimited;free
Yield (8/93)	3.3%	Total Assets	$107 million

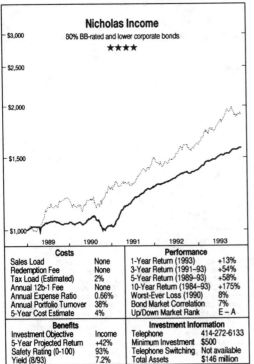

Nicholas Income
80% BB-rated and lower corporate bonds
★★★★

Costs		Performance	
Sales Load	None	1-Year Return (1993)	+13%
Redemption Fee	None	3-Year Return (1991–93)	+54%
Tax Load (Estimated)	2%	5-Year Return (1989–93)	+58%
Annual 12b-1 Fee	None	10-Year Return (1984–93)	+175%
Annual Expense Ratio	0.66%	Worst-Ever Loss (1990)	8%
Annual Portfolio Turnover	38%	Bond Market Correlation	7%
5-Year Cost Estimate	4%	Up/Down Market Rank	E – A

Benefits		Investment Information	
Investment Objective	Income	Telephone	414-272-6133
5-Year Projected Return	+42%	Minimum Investment	$500
Safety Rating (0-100)	93%	Telephone Switching	Not available
Yield (8/93)	7.2%	Total Assets	$146 million

New America High Income
BB-rated and lower corporate bonds

Costs		Performance	
Sales Load	None	1-Year Return (1993)	+40%
Redemption Fee	None	3-Year Return (1991–93)	+191%
Tax Load (Estimated)	Neg.	5-Year Return (1989–93)	+6%
Annual 12b-1 Fee	None	10-Year Return (1984–93)	NA
Annual Expense Ratio	1.87%	Worst-Ever Loss (1989-90)	72%
Annual Portfolio Turnover	130%	Bond Market Correlation	–1%
5-Year Cost Estimate	12%	Up/Down Market Rank	A – C

Benefits		Investment Information	
Investment Objective	Income	Telephone	800-426-5523
5-Year Projected Return	NA	Minimum Investment	None
Safety Rating (0-100)	37%	Telephone Switching	Via broker
Yield	NA	Total Assets	$187 million

Northeast Investors Trust
80% B-rated and lower bonds
★★★

Costs		Performance	
Sales Load	None	1-Year Return (1993)	+24%
Redemption Fee	None	3-Year Return (1991–93)	+84%
Tax Load (Estimated)	0%	5-Year Return (1989–93)	+67%
Annual 12b-1 Fee	None	10-Year Return (1984–93)	+214%
Annual Expense Ratio	0.79%	Worst-Ever Loss (1989-91)	14%
Annual Portfolio Turnover	59%	Bond Market Correlation	0%
5-Year Cost Estimate	4%	Up/Down Market Rank	D – A

Benefits		Investment Information	
Investment Objective	Income	Telephone	800-225-6704
5-Year Projected Return	+47%	Minimum Investment	$1,000
Safety Rating (0-100)	92%	Telephone Switching	Unlimited;free
Yield (8/93)	8.0%	Total Assets	$498 million

B O N D

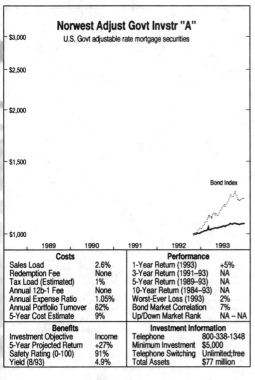

Norwest Adjust Govt Invstr "A"
U.S. Govt adjustable rate mortgage securities

Costs		Performance	
Sales Load	2.6%	1-Year Return (1993)	+5%
Redemption Fee	None	3-Year Return (1991–93)	NA
Tax Load (Estimated)	1%	5-Year Return (1989–93)	NA
Annual 12b-1 Fee	None	10-Year Return (1984–93)	NA
Annual Expense Ratio	1.05%	Worst-Ever Loss (1993)	2%
Annual Portfolio Turnover	62%	Bond Market Correlation	7%
5-Year Cost Estimate	9%	Up/Down Market Rank	NA – NA

Benefits		Investment Information	
Investment Objective	Income	Telephone	800-338-1348
5-Year Projected Return	+27%	Minimum Investment	$5,000
Safety Rating (0-100)	91%	Telephone Switching	Unlimited;free
Yield (8/93)	4.9%	Total Assets	$77 million

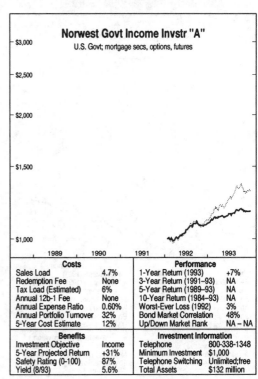

Norwest Govt Income Invstr "A"
U.S. Govt; mortgage secs, options, futures

Costs		Performance	
Sales Load	4.7%	1-Year Return (1993)	+7%
Redemption Fee	None	3-Year Return (1991–93)	NA
Tax Load (Estimated)	6%	5-Year Return (1989–93)	NA
Annual 12b-1 Fee	None	10-Year Return (1984–93)	NA
Annual Expense Ratio	0.60%	Worst-Ever Loss (1992)	3%
Annual Portfolio Turnover	32%	Bond Market Correlation	48%
5-Year Cost Estimate	12%	Up/Down Market Rank	NA – NA

Benefits		Investment Information	
Investment Objective	Income	Telephone	800-338-1348
5-Year Projected Return	+31%	Minimum Investment	$1,000
Safety Rating (0-100)	87%	Telephone Switching	Unlimited;free
Yield (8/93)	5.6%	Total Assets	$132 million

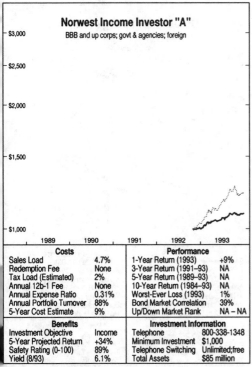

Norwest Income Investor "A"
BBB and up corps; govt & agencies; foreign

Costs		Performance	
Sales Load	4.7%	1-Year Return (1993)	+9%
Redemption Fee	None	3-Year Return (1991–93)	NA
Tax Load (Estimated)	2%	5-Year Return (1989–93)	NA
Annual 12b-1 Fee	None	10-Year Return (1984–93)	NA
Annual Expense Ratio	0.31%	Worst-Ever Loss (1993)	1%
Annual Portfolio Turnover	88%	Bond Market Correlation	39%
5-Year Cost Estimate	9%	Up/Down Market Rank	NA – NA

Benefits		Investment Information	
Investment Objective	Income	Telephone	800-338-1348
5-Year Projected Return	+34%	Minimum Investment	$1,000
Safety Rating (0-100)	89%	Telephone Switching	Unlimited;free
Yield (8/93)	6.1%	Total Assets	$85 million

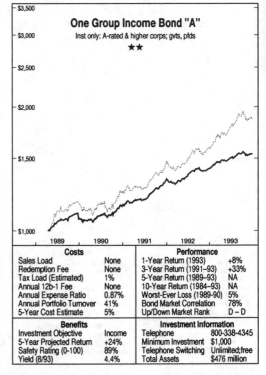

One Group Income Bond "A"
Inst only: A-rated & higher corps; gvts, pfds
★★

Costs		Performance	
Sales Load	None	1-Year Return (1993)	+8%
Redemption Fee	None	3-Year Return (1991–93)	+33%
Tax Load (Estimated)	1%	5-Year Return (1989–93)	NA
Annual 12b-1 Fee	None	10-Year Return (1984–93)	NA
Annual Expense Ratio	0.87%	Worst-Ever Loss (1989-90)	5%
Annual Portfolio Turnover	41%	Bond Market Correlation	78%
5-Year Cost Estimate	5%	Up/Down Market Rank	D – D

Benefits		Investment Information	
Investment Objective	Income	Telephone	800-338-4345
5-Year Projected Return	+24%	Minimum Investment	$1,000
Safety Rating (0-100)	89%	Telephone Switching	Unlimited;free
Yield (8/93)	4.4%	Total Assets	$476 million

BOND

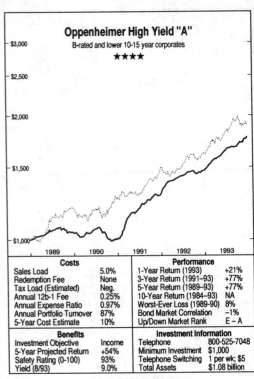

One Group Ltd Volat Bond "A"

Inst only: A-rated & higher corporate bonds

★★★

Bond Index

Fund

Costs		Performance	
Sales Load	None	1-Year Return (1993)	+7%
Redemption Fee	None	3-Year Return (1991–93)	+29%
Tax Load (Estimated)	2%	5-Year Return (1989–93)	NA
Annual 12b-1 Fee	None	10-Year Return (1984–93)	NA
Annual Expense Ratio	0.87%	Worst-Ever Loss (1992)	2%
Annual Portfolio Turnover	40%	Bond Market Correlation	48%
5-Year Cost Estimate	6%	Up/Down Market Rank	NA – B

Benefits		Investment Information	
Investment Objective	Income	Telephone	800-338-4345
5-Year Projected Return	+22%	Minimum Investment	$1,000
Safety Rating (0-100)	93%	Telephone Switching	Unlimited;free
Yield (8/93)	4.1%	Total Assets	$404 million

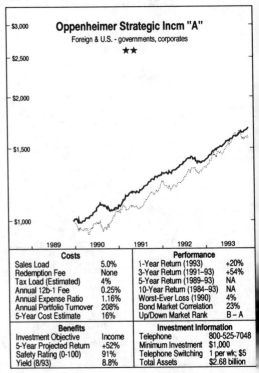

Oppenheimer High Yield "A"

B-rated and lower 10-15 year corporates

★★★★

Costs		Performance	
Sales Load	5.0%	1-Year Return (1993)	+21%
Redemption Fee	None	3-Year Return (1991–93)	+77%
Tax Load (Estimated)	Neg.	5-Year Return (1989–93)	+77%
Annual 12b-1 Fee	0.25%	10-Year Return (1984–93)	NA
Annual Expense Ratio	0.97%	Worst-Ever Loss (1989-90)	8%
Annual Portfolio Turnover	87%	Bond Market Correlation	−1%
5-Year Cost Estimate	10%	Up/Down Market Rank	E – A

Benefits		Investment Information	
Investment Objective	Income	Telephone	800-525-7048
5-Year Projected Return	+54%	Minimum Investment	$1,000
Safety Rating (0-100)	93%	Telephone Switching	1 per wk; $5
Yield (8/93)	9.0%	Total Assets	$1.08 billion

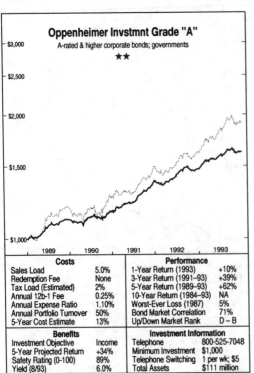

Oppenheimer Invstmnt Grade "A"

A-rated & higher corporate bonds; governments

★★

Costs		Performance	
Sales Load	5.0%	1-Year Return (1993)	+10%
Redemption Fee	None	3-Year Return (1991–93)	+39%
Tax Load (Estimated)	2%	5-Year Return (1989–93)	+62%
Annual 12b-1 Fee	0.25%	10-Year Return (1984–93)	NA
Annual Expense Ratio	1.10%	Worst-Ever Loss (1987)	5%
Annual Portfolio Turnover	50%	Bond Market Correlation	71%
5-Year Cost Estimate	13%	Up/Down Market Rank	D – B

Benefits		Investment Information	
Investment Objective	Income	Telephone	800-525-7048
5-Year Projected Return	+34%	Minimum Investment	$1,000
Safety Rating (0-100)	89%	Telephone Switching	1 per wk; $5
Yield (8/93)	6.0%	Total Assets	$111 million

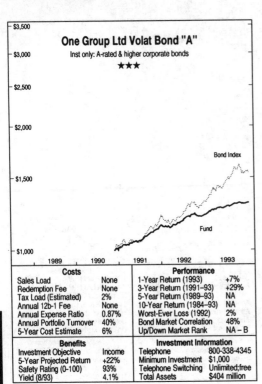

Oppenheimer Strategic Incm "A"

Foreign & U.S. - governments, corporates

★★

Costs		Performance	
Sales Load	5.0%	1-Year Return (1993)	+20%
Redemption Fee	None	3-Year Return (1991–93)	+54%
Tax Load (Estimated)	4%	5-Year Return (1989–93)	NA
Annual 12b-1 Fee	0.25%	10-Year Return (1984–93)	NA
Annual Expense Ratio	1.16%	Worst-Ever Loss (1990)	4%
Annual Portfolio Turnover	208%	Bond Market Correlation	23%
5-Year Cost Estimate	16%	Up/Down Market Rank	B – A

Benefits		Investment Information	
Investment Objective	Income	Telephone	800-525-7048
5-Year Projected Return	+52%	Minimum Investment	$1,000
Safety Rating (0-100)	91%	Telephone Switching	1 per wk; $5
Yield (8/93)	8.8%	Total Assets	$2.68 billion

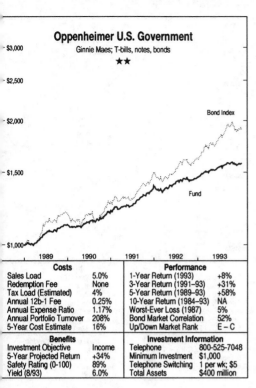

Oppenheimer U.S. Government
Ginnie Maes; T-bills, notes, bonds
★★

Bond Index

Fund

Costs		Performance	
Sales Load	5.0%	1-Year Return (1993)	+8%
Redemption Fee	None	3-Year Return (1991–93)	+31%
Tax Load (Estimated)	4%	5-Year Return (1989–93)	+58%
Annual 12b-1 Fee	0.25%	10-Year Return (1984–93)	NA
Annual Expense Ratio	1.17%	Worst-Ever Loss (1987)	5%
Annual Portfolio Turnover	208%	Bond Market Correlation	52%
5-Year Cost Estimate	16%	Up/Down Market Rank	E – C

Benefits		Investment Information	
Investment Objective	Income	Telephone	800-525-7048
5-Year Projected Return	+34%	Minimum Investment	$1,000
Safety Rating (0-100)	89%	Telephone Switching	1 per wk; $5
Yield (8/93)	6.0%	Total Assets	$400 million

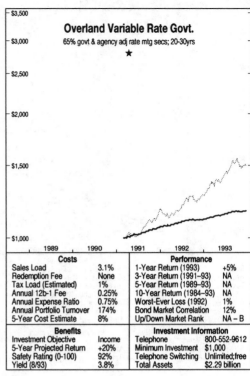

Overland Variable Rate Govt.
65% govt & agency adj rate mtg secs; 20-30yrs
★

Costs		Performance	
Sales Load	3.1%	1-Year Return (1993)	+5%
Redemption Fee	None	3-Year Return (1991–93)	NA
Tax Load (Estimated)	1%	5-Year Return (1989–93)	NA
Annual 12b-1 Fee	0.25%	10-Year Return (1984–93)	NA
Annual Expense Ratio	0.75%	Worst-Ever Loss (1992)	1%
Annual Portfolio Turnover	174%	Bond Market Correlation	12%
5-Year Cost Estimate	8%	Up/Down Market Rank	NA – B

Benefits		Investment Information	
Investment Objective	Income	Telephone	800-552-9612
5-Year Projected Return	+20%	Minimum Investment	$1,000
Safety Rating (0-100)	92%	Telephone Switching	Unlimited;free
Yield (8/93)	3.8%	Total Assets	$2.29 billion

Pacific American Income Shares
75% BBB-rated and higher; 25% convert & pfds

Costs		Performance	
Sales Load	None	1-Year Return (1993)	+17%
Redemption Fee	None	3-Year Return (1991–93)	+60%
Tax Load (Estimated)	3%	5-Year Return (1989–93)	+74%
Annual 12b-1 Fee	None	10-Year Return (1984–93)	NA
Annual Expense Ratio	0.90%	Worst-Ever Loss (1989-90)	16%
Annual Portfolio Turnover	74%	Bond Market Correlation	–2%
5-Year Cost Estimate	10%	Up/Down Market Rank	B – D

Benefits		Investment Information	
Investment Objective	Income	Telephone	800-368-2558
5-Year Projected Return	NA	Minimum Investment	None
Safety Rating (0-100)	73%	Telephone Switching	Via broker
Yield	NA	Total Assets	$146 million

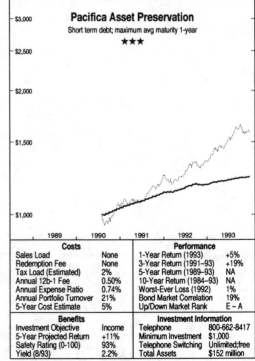

Pacifica Asset Preservation
Short term debt; maximum avg maturity 1-year
★★★

Costs		Performance	
Sales Load	None	1-Year Return (1993)	+5%
Redemption Fee	None	3-Year Return (1991–93)	+19%
Tax Load (Estimated)	2%	5-Year Return (1989–93)	NA
Annual 12b-1 Fee	0.50%	10-Year Return (1984–93)	NA
Annual Expense Ratio	0.74%	Worst-Ever Loss (1992)	1%
Annual Portfolio Turnover	21%	Bond Market Correlation	19%
5-Year Cost Estimate	5%	Up/Down Market Rank	E – A

Benefits		Investment Information	
Investment Objective	Income	Telephone	800-662-8417
5-Year Projected Return	+11%	Minimum Investment	$1,000
Safety Rating (0-100)	93%	Telephone Switching	Unlimited;free
Yield (8/93)	2.2%	Total Assets	$152 million

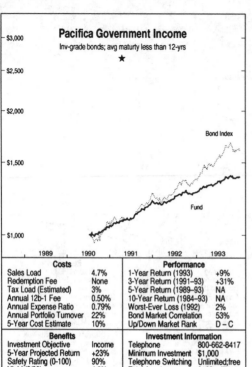

Pacifica Government Income
Inv-grade bonds; avg maturity less than 12-yrs
★

Costs		Performance	
Sales Load	4.7%	1-Year Return (1993)	+9%
Redemption Fee	None	3-Year Return (1991–93)	+31%
Tax Load (Estimated)	3%	5-Year Return (1989–93)	NA
Annual 12b-1 Fee	0.50%	10-Year Return (1984–93)	NA
Annual Expense Ratio	0.79%	Worst-Ever Loss (1992)	2%
Annual Portfolio Turnover	22%	Bond Market Correlation	53%
5-Year Cost Estimate	10%	Up/Down Market Rank	D – C

Benefits		Investment Information	
Investment Objective	Income	Telephone	800-662-8417
5-Year Projected Return	+23%	Minimum Investment	$1,000
Safety Rating (0-100)	90%	Telephone Switching	Unlimited;free
Yield (8/93)	4.2%	Total Assets	$163 million

Paine Webber Global Income "B"
Foreign & U.S. - government bonds

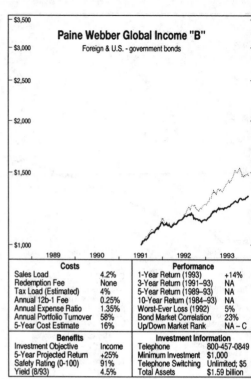

Costs		Performance	
Sales Load	4.2%	1-Year Return (1993)	+14%
Redemption Fee	None	3-Year Return (1991–93)	NA
Tax Load (Estimated)	4%	5-Year Return (1989–93)	NA
Annual 12b-1 Fee	0.25%	10-Year Return (1984–93)	NA
Annual Expense Ratio	1.35%	Worst-Ever Loss (1992)	5%
Annual Portfolio Turnover	58%	Bond Market Correlation	23%
5-Year Cost Estimate	16%	Up/Down Market Rank	NA – C

Benefits		Investment Information	
Investment Objective	Income	Telephone	800-457-0849
5-Year Projected Return	+25%	Minimum Investment	$1,000
Safety Rating (0-100)	91%	Telephone Switching	Unlimited; $5
Yield (8/93)	4.5%	Total Assets	$1.59 billion

Paine Webber High Income "A"
65% BBB-rated & lower corps; options; futures

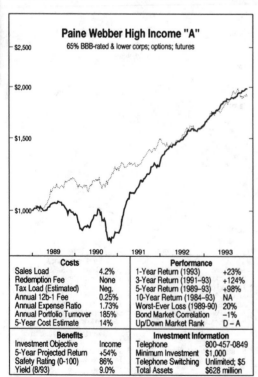

Costs		Performance	
Sales Load	4.2%	1-Year Return (1993)	+23%
Redemption Fee	None	3-Year Return (1991–93)	+124%
Tax Load (Estimated)	Neg.	5-Year Return (1989–93)	+98%
Annual 12b-1 Fee	0.25%	10-Year Return (1984–93)	NA
Annual Expense Ratio	1.73%	Worst-Ever Loss (1989-90)	20%
Annual Portfolio Turnover	185%	Bond Market Correlation	–1%
5-Year Cost Estimate	14%	Up/Down Market Rank	D – A

Benefits		Investment Information	
Investment Objective	Income	Telephone	800-457-0849
5-Year Projected Return	+54%	Minimum Investment	$1,000
Safety Rating (0-100)	86%	Telephone Switching	Unlimited; $5
Yield (8/93)	9.0%	Total Assets	$628 million

Paine Webber Income "B"
Foreign & U.S. - govt mtg secs, AA & up bonds

Costs		Performance	
Sales Load	None	1-Year Return (1993)	+12%
Redemption Fee	5.3%	3-Year Return (1991–93)	+53%
Tax Load (Estimated)	Neg.	5-Year Return (1989–93)	+69%
Annual 12b-1 Fee	1.00%	10-Year Return (1984–93)	NA
Annual Expense Ratio	1.95%	Worst-Ever Loss (1987)	13%
Annual Portfolio Turnover	24%	Bond Market Correlation	52%
5-Year Cost Estimate	11%	Up/Down Market Rank	A – E

Benefits		Investment Information	
Investment Objective	Income	Telephone	800-457-0849
5-Year Projected Return	+30%	Minimum Investment	$1,000
Safety Rating (0-100)	88%	Telephone Switching	Unlimited; $5
Yield (8/93)	5.4%	Total Assets	$33 million

BOND

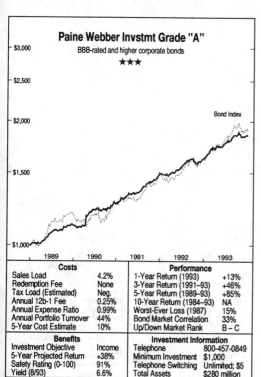

Paine Webber Invstmt Grade "A"
BBB-rated and higher corporate bonds
★★★

Bond Index

Costs		Performance	
Sales Load	4.2%	1-Year Return (1993)	+13%
Redemption Fee	None	3-Year Return (1991–93)	+46%
Tax Load (Estimated)	Neg.	5-Year Return (1989–93)	+85%
Annual 12b-1 Fee	0.25%	10-Year Return (1984–93)	NA
Annual Expense Ratio	0.99%	Worst-Ever Loss (1987)	15%
Annual Portfolio Turnover	44%	Bond Market Correlation	33%
5-Year Cost Estimate	10%	Up/Down Market Rank	B – C

Benefits		Investment Information	
Investment Objective	Income	Telephone	800-457-0849
5-Year Projected Return	+38%	Minimum Investment	$1,000
Safety Rating (0-100)	91%	Telephone Switching	Unlimited; $5
Yield (8/93)	6.6%	Total Assets	$280 million

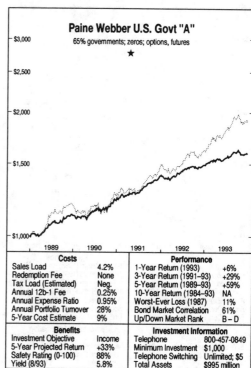

Paine Webber U.S. Govt "A"
65% governments; zeros; options, futures
★

Costs		Performance	
Sales Load	4.2%	1-Year Return (1993)	+6%
Redemption Fee	None	3-Year Return (1991–93)	+29%
Tax Load (Estimated)	Neg.	5-Year Return (1989–93)	+59%
Annual 12b-1 Fee	0.25%	10-Year Return (1984–93)	NA
Annual Expense Ratio	0.95%	Worst-Ever Loss (1987)	11%
Annual Portfolio Turnover	28%	Bond Market Correlation	61%
5-Year Cost Estimate	9%	Up/Down Market Rank	B – D

Benefits		Investment Information	
Investment Objective	Income	Telephone	800-457-0849
5-Year Projected Return	+33%	Minimum Investment	$1,000
Safety Rating (0-100)	88%	Telephone Switching	Unlimited; $5
Yield (8/93)	5.8%	Total Assets	$995 million

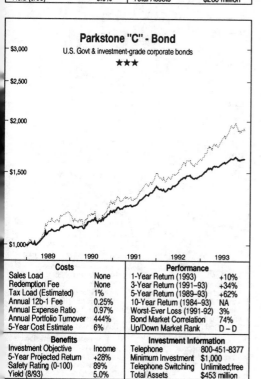

Parkstone "C" - Bond
U.S. Govt & investment-grade corporate bonds
★★★

Costs		Performance	
Sales Load	None	1-Year Return (1993)	+10%
Redemption Fee	None	3-Year Return (1991–93)	+34%
Tax Load (Estimated)	1%	5-Year Return (1989–93)	+62%
Annual 12b-1 Fee	0.25%	10-Year Return (1984–93)	NA
Annual Expense Ratio	0.97%	Worst-Ever Loss (1991-92)	3%
Annual Portfolio Turnover	444%	Bond Market Correlation	74%
5-Year Cost Estimate	6%	Up/Down Market Rank	D – D

Benefits		Investment Information	
Investment Objective	Income	Telephone	800-451-8377
5-Year Projected Return	+28%	Minimum Investment	$1,000
Safety Rating (0-100)	89%	Telephone Switching	Unlimited;free
Yield (8/93)	5.0%	Total Assets	$453 million

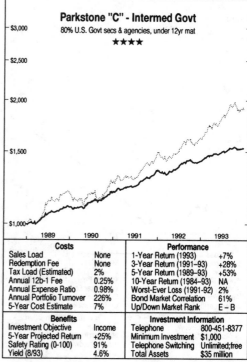

Parkstone "C" - Intermed Govt
80% U.S. Govt secs & agencies, under 12yr mat
★★★★

Costs		Performance	
Sales Load	None	1-Year Return (1993)	+7%
Redemption Fee	None	3-Year Return (1991–93)	+28%
Tax Load (Estimated)	2%	5-Year Return (1989–93)	+53%
Annual 12b-1 Fee	0.25%	10-Year Return (1984–93)	NA
Annual Expense Ratio	0.98%	Worst-Ever Loss (1991-92)	2%
Annual Portfolio Turnover	226%	Bond Market Correlation	61%
5-Year Cost Estimate	7%	Up/Down Market Rank	E – B

Benefits		Investment Information	
Investment Objective	Income	Telephone	800-451-8377
5-Year Projected Return	+25%	Minimum Investment	$1,000
Safety Rating (0-100)	91%	Telephone Switching	Unlimited;free
Yield (8/93)	4.6%	Total Assets	$35 million

BOND

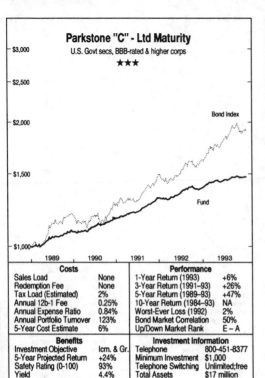

Parkstone "C" - Ltd Maturity

U.S. Govt secs, BBB-rated & higher corps

★★★

Bond Index

Fund

Costs		Performance	
Sales Load	None	1-Year Return (1993)	+6%
Redemption Fee	None	3-Year Return (1991–93)	+26%
Tax Load (Estimated)	2%	5-Year Return (1989–93)	+47%
Annual 12b-1 Fee	0.25%	10-Year Return (1984–93)	NA
Annual Expense Ratio	0.84%	Worst-Ever Loss (1992)	2%
Annual Portfolio Turnover	123%	Bond Market Correlation	50%
5-Year Cost Estimate	6%	Up/Down Market Rank	E – A

Benefits		Investment Information	
Investment Objective	Icm. & Gr.	Telephone	800-451-8377
5-Year Projected Return	+24%	Minimum Investment	$1,000
Safety Rating (0-100)	93%	Telephone Switching	Unlimited;free
Yield	4.4%	Total Assets	$17 million

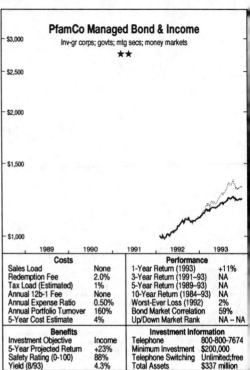

PfamCo Managed Bond & Income

Inv-gr corps; govts; mtg secs; money markets

★★

Costs		Performance	
Sales Load	None	1-Year Return (1993)	+11%
Redemption Fee	2.0%	3-Year Return (1991–93)	NA
Tax Load (Estimated)	1%	5-Year Return (1989–93)	NA
Annual 12b-1 Fee	None	10-Year Return (1984–93)	NA
Annual Expense Ratio	0.50%	Worst-Ever Loss (1992)	2%
Annual Portfolio Turnover	160%	Bond Market Correlation	59%
5-Year Cost Estimate	4%	Up/Down Market Rank	NA – NA

Benefits		Investment Information	
Investment Objective	Income	Telephone	800-800-7674
5-Year Projected Return	+23%	Minimum Investment	$200,000
Safety Rating (0-100)	88%	Telephone Switching	Unlimited;free
Yield (8/93)	4.3%	Total Assets	$337 million

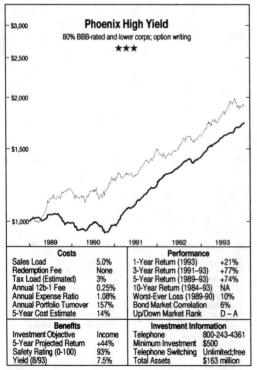

Phoenix High Yield

80% BBB-rated and lower corps; option writing

★★★

Costs		Performance	
Sales Load	5.0%	1-Year Return (1993)	+21%
Redemption Fee	None	3-Year Return (1991–93)	+77%
Tax Load (Estimated)	3%	5-Year Return (1989–93)	+74%
Annual 12b-1 Fee	0.25%	10-Year Return (1984–93)	NA
Annual Expense Ratio	1.08%	Worst-Ever Loss (1989-90)	10%
Annual Portfolio Turnover	157%	Bond Market Correlation	6%
5-Year Cost Estimate	14%	Up/Down Market Rank	D – A

Benefits		Investment Information	
Investment Objective	Income	Telephone	800-243-4361
5-Year Projected Return	+44%	Minimum Investment	$500
Safety Rating (0-100)	93%	Telephone Switching	Unlimited;free
Yield (8/93)	7.5%	Total Assets	$163 million

Pilgrim High Yield

65% B-rated and lower; option writing

Costs		Performance	
Sales Load	5.0%	1-Year Return (1993)	+19%
Redemption Fee	None	3-Year Return (1991–93)	+78%
Tax Load (Estimated)	Neg.	5-Year Return (1989–93)	+64%
Annual 12b-1 Fee	0.75%	10-Year Return (1984–93)	NA
Annual Expense Ratio	1.89%	Worst-Ever Loss (1989-90)	16%
Annual Portfolio Turnover	64%	Bond Market Correlation	–1%
5-Year Cost Estimate	16%	Up/Down Market Rank	E – A

Benefits		Investment Information	
Investment Objective	Income	Telephone	800-334-3444
5-Year Projected Return	+53%	Minimum Investment	$1,000
Safety Rating (0-100)	90%	Telephone Switching	1 per mo; free
Yield (8/93)	8.9%	Total Assets	$19 million

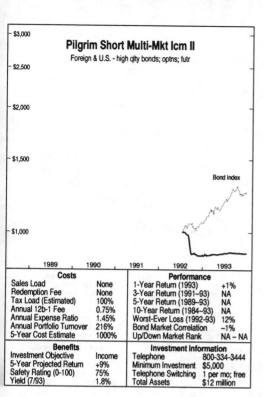

Pilgrim Short Multi-Mkt Icm II

Foreign & U.S. - high qlty bonds; optns; futr

Bond Index

Costs		Performance	
Sales Load	None	1-Year Return (1993)	+1%
Redemption Fee	None	3-Year Return (1991–93)	NA
Tax Load (Estimated)	100%	5-Year Return (1989–93)	NA
Annual 12b-1 Fee	0.75%	10-Year Return (1984–93)	NA
Annual Expense Ratio	1.45%	Worst-Ever Loss (1992-93)	12%
Annual Portfolio Turnover	216%	Bond Market Correlation	–1%
5-Year Cost Estimate	1000%	Up/Down Market Rank	NA – NA

Benefits		Investment Information	
Investment Objective	Income	Telephone	800-334-3444
5-Year Projected Return	+9%	Minimum Investment	$5,000
Safety Rating (0-100)	75%	Telephone Switching	1 per mo; free
Yield (7/93)	1.8%	Total Assets	$12 million

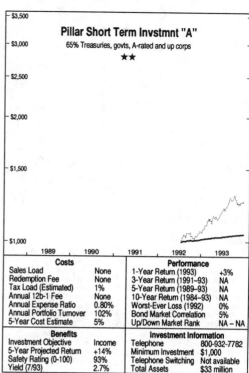

Pillar Short Term Invstmnt "A"

65% Treasuries, govts, A-rated and up corps
★★

Costs		Performance	
Sales Load	None	1-Year Return (1993)	+3%
Redemption Fee	None	3-Year Return (1991–93)	NA
Tax Load (Estimated)	1%	5-Year Return (1989–93)	NA
Annual 12b-1 Fee	None	10-Year Return (1984–93)	NA
Annual Expense Ratio	0.80%	Worst-Ever Loss (1992)	0%
Annual Portfolio Turnover	102%	Bond Market Correlation	5%
5-Year Cost Estimate	5%	Up/Down Market Rank	NA – NA

Benefits		Investment Information	
Investment Objective	Income	Telephone	800-932-7782
5-Year Projected Return	+14%	Minimum Investment	$1,000
Safety Rating (0-100)	93%	Telephone Switching	Not available
Yield (7/93)	2.7%	Total Assets	$33 million

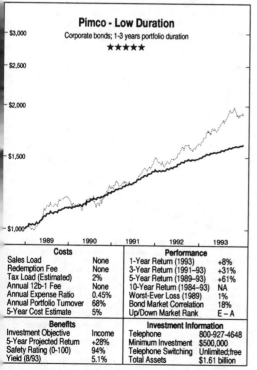

Pimco - Low Duration

Corporate bonds; 1-3 years portfolio duration
★★★★★

Costs		Performance	
Sales Load	None	1-Year Return (1993)	+8%
Redemption Fee	None	3-Year Return (1991–93)	+31%
Tax Load (Estimated)	2%	5-Year Return (1989–93)	+61%
Annual 12b-1 Fee	None	10-Year Return (1984–93)	NA
Annual Expense Ratio	0.45%	Worst-Ever Loss (1989)	1%
Annual Portfolio Turnover	68%	Bond Market Correlation	18%
5-Year Cost Estimate	5%	Up/Down Market Rank	E – A

Benefits		Investment Information	
Investment Objective	Income	Telephone	800-927-4648
5-Year Projected Return	+28%	Minimum Investment	$500,000
Safety Rating (0-100)	94%	Telephone Switching	Unlimited;free
Yield (8/93)	5.1%	Total Assets	$1.61 billion

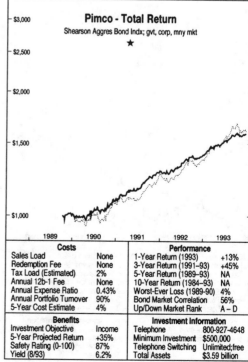

Pimco - Total Return

Shearson Aggres Bond Indx; gvt, corp, mny mkt
★

Costs		Performance	
Sales Load	None	1-Year Return (1993)	+13%
Redemption Fee	None	3-Year Return (1991–93)	+45%
Tax Load (Estimated)	2%	5-Year Return (1989–93)	NA
Annual 12b-1 Fee	None	10-Year Return (1984–93)	NA
Annual Expense Ratio	0.43%	Worst-Ever Loss (1989-90)	4%
Annual Portfolio Turnover	90%	Bond Market Correlation	56%
5-Year Cost Estimate	4%	Up/Down Market Rank	A – D

Benefits		Investment Information	
Investment Objective	Income	Telephone	800-927-4648
5-Year Projected Return	+35%	Minimum Investment	$500,000
Safety Rating (0-100)	87%	Telephone Switching	Unlimited;free
Yield (8/93)	6.2%	Total Assets	$3.59 billion

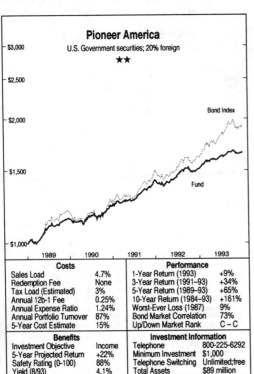

Pioneer America
U.S. Government securities; 20% foreign
★★

Bond Index

Fund

Costs		Performance	
Sales Load	4.7%	1-Year Return (1993)	+9%
Redemption Fee	None	3-Year Return (1991–93)	+34%
Tax Load (Estimated)	3%	5-Year Return (1989–93)	+65%
Annual 12b-1 Fee	0.25%	10-Year Return (1984–93)	+161%
Annual Expense Ratio	1.24%	Worst-Ever Loss (1987)	9%
Annual Portfolio Turnover	87%	Bond Market Correlation	73%
5-Year Cost Estimate	15%	Up/Down Market Rank	C – C

Benefits		Investment Information	
Investment Objective	Income	Telephone	800-225-6292
5-Year Projected Return	+22%	Minimum Investment	$1,000
Safety Rating (0-100)	88%	Telephone Switching	Unlimited;free
Yield (8/93)	4.1%	Total Assets	$89 million

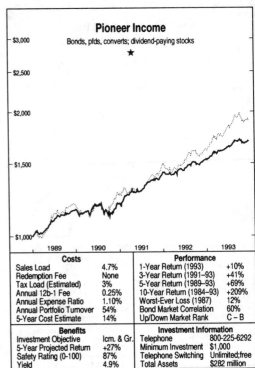

Pioneer Income
Bonds, pfds, converts; dividend-paying stocks
★

Costs		Performance	
Sales Load	4.7%	1-Year Return (1993)	+10%
Redemption Fee	None	3-Year Return (1991–93)	+41%
Tax Load (Estimated)	3%	5-Year Return (1989–93)	+69%
Annual 12b-1 Fee	0.25%	10-Year Return (1984–93)	+209%
Annual Expense Ratio	1.10%	Worst-Ever Loss (1987)	12%
Annual Portfolio Turnover	54%	Bond Market Correlation	60%
5-Year Cost Estimate	14%	Up/Down Market Rank	C – B

Benefits		Investment Information	
Investment Objective	Icm. & Gr.	Telephone	800-225-6292
5-Year Projected Return	+27%	Minimum Investment	$1,000
Safety Rating (0-100)	87%	Telephone Switching	Unlimited;free
Yield	4.9%	Total Assets	$282 million

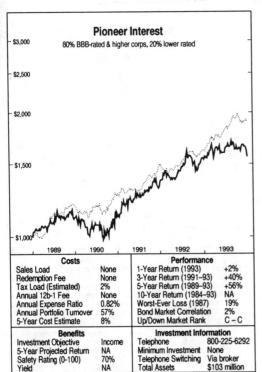

Pioneer Interest
80% BBB-rated & higher corps, 20% lower rated

Costs		Performance	
Sales Load	None	1-Year Return (1993)	+2%
Redemption Fee	None	3-Year Return (1991–93)	+40%
Tax Load (Estimated)	2%	5-Year Return (1989–93)	+56%
Annual 12b-1 Fee	None	10-Year Return (1984–93)	NA
Annual Expense Ratio	0.82%	Worst-Ever Loss (1987)	19%
Annual Portfolio Turnover	57%	Bond Market Correlation	2%
5-Year Cost Estimate	8%	Up/Down Market Rank	C – C

Benefits		Investment Information	
Investment Objective	Income	Telephone	800-225-6292
5-Year Projected Return	NA	Minimum Investment	None
Safety Rating (0-100)	70%	Telephone Switching	Via broker
Yield	NA	Total Assets	$103 million

Piper Jaffray Govt Income
65% U.S. Government secs & agencies; mortgage

Costs		Performance	
Sales Load	5.3%	1-Year Return (1993)	+10%
Redemption Fee	None	3-Year Return (1991–93)	+37%
Tax Load (Estimated)	2%	5-Year Return (1989–93)	+62%
Annual 12b-1 Fee	0.50%	10-Year Return (1984–93)	NA
Annual Expense Ratio	1.14%	Worst-Ever Loss (1987)	8%
Annual Portfolio Turnover	191%	Bond Market Correlation	47%
5-Year Cost Estimate	13%	Up/Down Market Rank	A – E

Benefits		Investment Information	
Investment Objective	Income	Telephone	800-866-7778
5-Year Projected Return	+46%	Minimum Investment	$250
Safety Rating (0-100)	84%	Telephone Switching	4 per yr.fr;$5
Yield	7.8%	Total Assets	$154 million

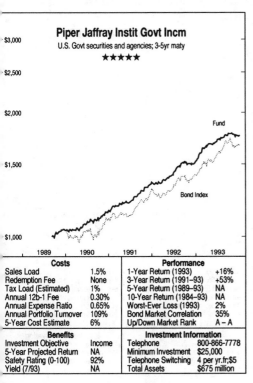

Piper Jaffray Instit Govt Incm

U.S. Govt securities and agencies; 3-5yr maty

★★★★★

Costs		Performance	
Sales Load	1.5%	1-Year Return (1993)	+16%
Redemption Fee	None	3-Year Return (1991–93)	+53%
Tax Load (Estimated)	1%	5-Year Return (1989–93)	NA
Annual 12b-1 Fee	0.30%	10-Year Return (1984–93)	NA
Annual Expense Ratio	0.65%	Worst-Ever Loss (1993)	2%
Annual Portfolio Turnover	109%	Bond Market Correlation	35%
5-Year Cost Estimate	6%	Up/Down Market Rank	A – A

Benefits		Investment Information	
Investment Objective	Income	Telephone	800-866-7778
5-Year Projected Return	NA	Minimum Investment	$25,000
Safety Rating (0-100)	92%	Telephone Switching	4 per yr.fr;$5
Yield (7/93)	NA	Total Assets	$675 million

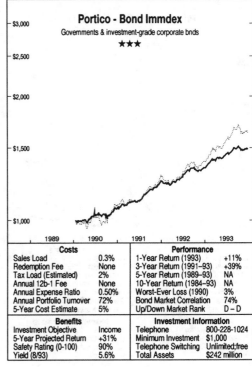

Portico - Bond Immdex

Governments & investment-grade corporate bnds

★★★

Costs		Performance	
Sales Load	0.3%	1-Year Return (1993)	+11%
Redemption Fee	None	3-Year Return (1991–93)	+39%
Tax Load (Estimated)	2%	5-Year Return (1989–93)	NA
Annual 12b-1 Fee	None	10-Year Return (1984–93)	NA
Annual Expense Ratio	0.50%	Worst-Ever Loss (1990)	3%
Annual Portfolio Turnover	72%	Bond Market Correlation	74%
5-Year Cost Estimate	5%	Up/Down Market Rank	D – D

Benefits		Investment Information	
Investment Objective	Income	Telephone	800-228-1024
5-Year Projected Return	+31%	Minimum Investment	$1,000
Safety Rating (0-100)	90%	Telephone Switching	Unlimited;free
Yield (8/93)	5.6%	Total Assets	$242 million

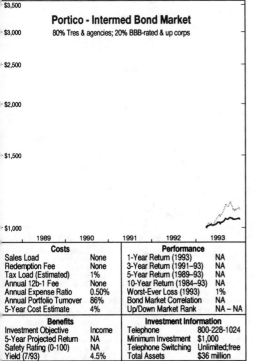

Portico - Intermed Bond Market

80% Tres & agencies; 20% BBB-rated & up corps

Costs		Performance	
Sales Load	None	1-Year Return (1993)	NA
Redemption Fee	None	3-Year Return (1991–93)	NA
Tax Load (Estimated)	1%	5-Year Return (1989–93)	NA
Annual 12b-1 Fee	None	10-Year Return (1984–93)	NA
Annual Expense Ratio	0.50%	Worst-Ever Loss (1993)	1%
Annual Portfolio Turnover	86%	Bond Market Correlation	NA
5-Year Cost Estimate	4%	Up/Down Market Rank	NA – NA

Benefits		Investment Information	
Investment Objective	Income	Telephone	800-228-1024
5-Year Projected Return	NA	Minimum Investment	$1,000
Safety Rating (0-100)	NA	Telephone Switching	Unlimited;free
Yield (7/93)	4.5%	Total Assets	$36 million

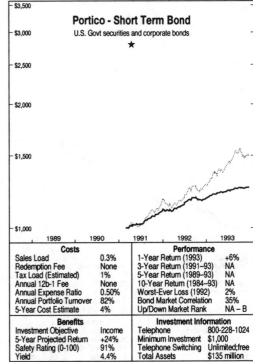

Portico - Short Term Bond

U.S. Govt securities and corporate bonds

★

Costs		Performance	
Sales Load	0.3%	1-Year Return (1993)	+6%
Redemption Fee	None	3-Year Return (1991–93)	NA
Tax Load (Estimated)	1%	5-Year Return (1989–93)	NA
Annual 12b-1 Fee	None	10-Year Return (1984–93)	NA
Annual Expense Ratio	0.50%	Worst-Ever Loss (1992)	2%
Annual Portfolio Turnover	82%	Bond Market Correlation	35%
5-Year Cost Estimate	4%	Up/Down Market Rank	NA – B

Benefits		Investment Information	
Investment Objective	Income	Telephone	800-228-1024
5-Year Projected Return	+24%	Minimum Investment	$1,000
Safety Rating (0-100)	91%	Telephone Switching	Unlimited;free
Yield	4.4%	Total Assets	$135 million

BOND

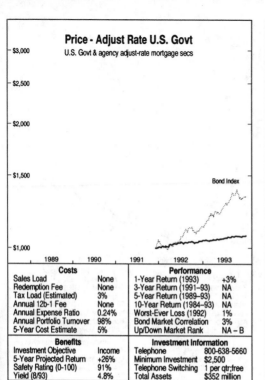

Price - Adjust Rate U.S. Govt
U.S. Govt & agency adjust-rate mortgage secs

$3,000
$2,500
$2,000
$1,500
$1,000

Bond Index

1989 1990 1991 1992 1993

Costs		Performance	
Sales Load	None	1-Year Return (1993)	+3%
Redemption Fee	None	3-Year Return (1991–93)	NA
Tax Load (Estimated)	3%	5-Year Return (1989–93)	NA
Annual 12b-1 Fee	None	10-Year Return (1984–93)	NA
Annual Expense Ratio	0.24%	Worst-Ever Loss (1992)	1%
Annual Portfolio Turnover	98%	Bond Market Correlation	3%
5-Year Cost Estimate	5%	Up/Down Market Rank	NA – B

Benefits		Investment Information	
Investment Objective	Income	Telephone	800-638-5660
5-Year Projected Return	+26%	Minimum Investment	$2,500
Safety Rating (0-100)	91%	Telephone Switching	1 per qtr;free
Yield (8/93)	4.8%	Total Assets	$352 million

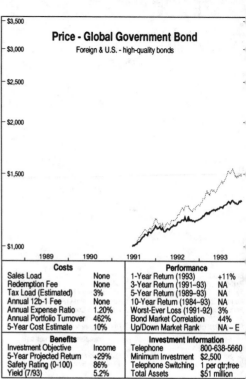

Price - Global Government Bond
Foreign & U.S. - high-quality bonds

$3,500
$3,000
$2,500
$2,000
$1,500
$1,000

1989 1990 1991 1992 1993

Costs		Performance	
Sales Load	None	1-Year Return (1993)	+11%
Redemption Fee	None	3-Year Return (1991–93)	NA
Tax Load (Estimated)	3%	5-Year Return (1989–93)	NA
Annual 12b-1 Fee	None	10-Year Return (1984–93)	NA
Annual Expense Ratio	1.20%	Worst-Ever Loss (1991-92)	3%
Annual Portfolio Turnover	462%	Bond Market Correlation	44%
5-Year Cost Estimate	10%	Up/Down Market Rank	NA – E

Benefits		Investment Information	
Investment Objective	Income	Telephone	800-638-5660
5-Year Projected Return	+29%	Minimum Investment	$2,500
Safety Rating (0-100)	86%	Telephone Switching	1 per qtr;free
Yield (7/93)	5.2%	Total Assets	$51 million

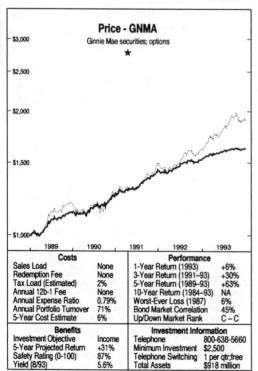

Price - GNMA
Ginnie Mae securities; options
★

$3,000
$2,500
$2,000
$1,500
$1,000

1989 1990 1991 1992 1993

Costs		Performance	
Sales Load	None	1-Year Return (1993)	+6%
Redemption Fee	None	3-Year Return (1991–93)	+30%
Tax Load (Estimated)	2%	5-Year Return (1989–93)	+63%
Annual 12b-1 Fee	None	10-Year Return (1984–93)	NA
Annual Expense Ratio	0.79%	Worst-Ever Loss (1987)	6%
Annual Portfolio Turnover	71%	Bond Market Correlation	45%
5-Year Cost Estimate	6%	Up/Down Market Rank	C – C

Benefits		Investment Information	
Investment Objective	Income	Telephone	800-638-5660
5-Year Projected Return	+31%	Minimum Investment	$2,500
Safety Rating (0-100)	87%	Telephone Switching	1 per qtr;free
Yield (8/93)	5.6%	Total Assets	$918 million

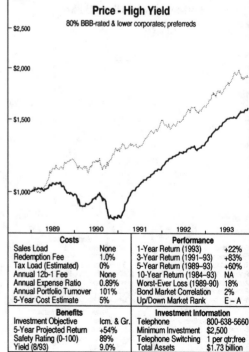

Price - High Yield
80% BBB-rated & lower corporates; preferreds

$3,000
$2,500
$2,000
$1,500
$1,000

1989 1990 1991 1992 1993

Costs		Performance	
Sales Load	None	1-Year Return (1993)	+22%
Redemption Fee	1.0%	3-Year Return (1991–93)	+83%
Tax Load (Estimated)	0%	5-Year Return (1989–93)	+60%
Annual 12b-1 Fee	None	10-Year Return (1984–93)	NA
Annual Expense Ratio	0.89%	Worst-Ever Loss (1989-90)	18%
Annual Portfolio Turnover	101%	Bond Market Correlation	2%
5-Year Cost Estimate	5%	Up/Down Market Rank	E – A

Benefits		Investment Information	
Investment Objective	Icm. & Gr.	Telephone	800-638-5660
5-Year Projected Return	+54%	Minimum Investment	$2,500
Safety Rating (0-100)	89%	Telephone Switching	1 per qtr;free
Yield (8/93)	9.0%	Total Assets	$1.73 billion

BOND

Price - International Bond
Foreign - high quality bonds

(chart: Bond Index, Fund; y-axis $1,000–$3,000; years 1989–1993)

Costs		Performance	
Sales Load	None	1-Year Return (1993)	+19%
Redemption Fee	None	3-Year Return (1991–93)	+45%
Tax Load (Estimated)	2%	5-Year Return (1989–93)	+62%
Annual 12b-1 Fee	None	10-Year Return (1984–93)	NA
Annual Expense Ratio	1.24%	Worst-Ever Loss (1988-89)	14%
Annual Portfolio Turnover	349%	Bond Market Correlation	15%
5-Year Cost Estimate	8%	Up/Down Market Rank	C – B

Benefits		Investment Information	
Investment Objective	Income	Telephone	800-638-5660
5-Year Projected Return	+35%	Minimum Investment	$2,500
Safety Rating (0-100)	82%	Telephone Switching	1 per qtr;free
Yield (8/93)	6.2%	Total Assets	$611 million

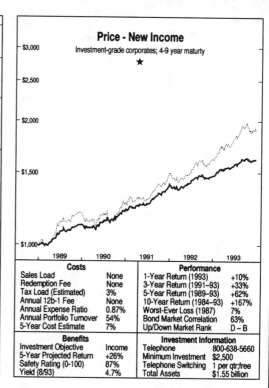

Price - New Income
Investment-grade corporates; 4-9 year maturity
★

(chart: y-axis $1,000–$3,000; years 1989–1993)

Costs		Performance	
Sales Load	None	1-Year Return (1993)	+10%
Redemption Fee	None	3-Year Return (1991–93)	+33%
Tax Load (Estimated)	3%	5-Year Return (1989–93)	+62%
Annual 12b-1 Fee	None	10-Year Return (1984–93)	+167%
Annual Expense Ratio	0.87%	Worst-Ever Loss (1987)	7%
Annual Portfolio Turnover	54%	Bond Market Correlation	63%
5-Year Cost Estimate	7%	Up/Down Market Rank	D – B

Benefits		Investment Information	
Investment Objective	Income	Telephone	800-638-5660
5-Year Projected Return	+26%	Minimum Investment	$2,500
Safety Rating (0-100)	87%	Telephone Switching	1 per qtr;free
Yield (8/93)	4.7%	Total Assets	$1.55 billion

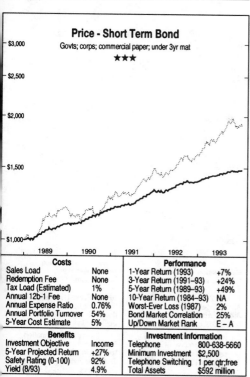

Price - Short Term Bond
Govts; corps; commercial paper; under 3yr mat
★★★

(chart: y-axis $1,000–$3,000; years 1989–1993)

Costs		Performance	
Sales Load	None	1-Year Return (1993)	+7%
Redemption Fee	None	3-Year Return (1991–93)	+24%
Tax Load (Estimated)	1%	5-Year Return (1989–93)	+49%
Annual 12b-1 Fee	None	10-Year Return (1984–93)	NA
Annual Expense Ratio	0.76%	Worst-Ever Loss (1987)	2%
Annual Portfolio Turnover	54%	Bond Market Correlation	25%
5-Year Cost Estimate	5%	Up/Down Market Rank	E – A

Benefits		Investment Information	
Investment Objective	Income	Telephone	800-638-5660
5-Year Projected Return	+27%	Minimum Investment	$2,500
Safety Rating (0-100)	92%	Telephone Switching	1 per qtr;free
Yield (8/93)	4.9%	Total Assets	$592 million

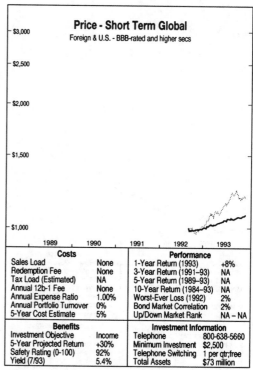

Price - Short Term Global
Foreign & U.S. - BBB-rated and higher secs

(chart: y-axis $1,000–$3,000; years 1989–1993)

Costs		Performance	
Sales Load	None	1-Year Return (1993)	+8%
Redemption Fee	None	3-Year Return (1991–93)	NA
Tax Load (Estimated)	NA	5-Year Return (1989–93)	NA
Annual 12b-1 Fee	None	10-Year Return (1984–93)	NA
Annual Expense Ratio	1.00%	Worst-Ever Loss (1992)	2%
Annual Portfolio Turnover	0%	Bond Market Correlation	2%
5-Year Cost Estimate	5%	Up/Down Market Rank	NA – NA

Benefits		Investment Information	
Investment Objective	Income	Telephone	800-638-5660
5-Year Projected Return	+30%	Minimum Investment	$2,500
Safety Rating (0-100)	92%	Telephone Switching	1 per qtr;free
Yield (7/93)	5.4%	Total Assets	$73 million

BOND

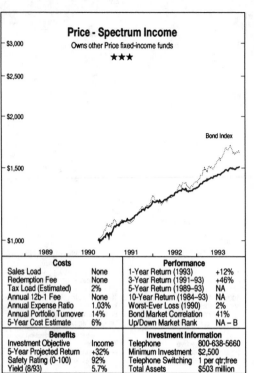

Price - Spectrum Income
Owns other Price fixed-income funds
★★★

Bond Index

Costs			Performance	
Sales Load	None		1-Year Return (1993)	+12%
Redemption Fee	None		3-Year Return (1991–93)	+46%
Tax Load (Estimated)	2%		5-Year Return (1989–93)	NA
Annual 12b-1 Fee	None		10-Year Return (1984–93)	NA
Annual Expense Ratio	1.03%		Worst-Ever Loss (1990)	2%
Annual Portfolio Turnover	14%		Bond Market Correlation	41%
5-Year Cost Estimate	6%		Up/Down Market Rank	NA – B

Benefits			Investment Information	
Investment Objective	Income		Telephone	800-638-5660
5-Year Projected Return	+32%		Minimum Investment	$2,500
Safety Rating (0-100)	92%		Telephone Switching	1 per qtr;free
Yield (8/93)	5.7%		Total Assets	$503 million

Primary U.S. Government
U.S. Government securities
★

Costs			Performance	
Sales Load	None		1-Year Return (1993)	+8%
Redemption Fee	None		3-Year Return (1991–93)	+28%
Tax Load (Estimated)	2%		5-Year Return (1989–93)	NA
Annual 12b-1 Fee	None		10-Year Return (1984–93)	NA
Annual Expense Ratio	0.75%		Worst-Ever Loss (1990)	4%
Annual Portfolio Turnover	109%		Bond Market Correlation	59%
5-Year Cost Estimate	5%		Up/Down Market Rank	C – E

Benefits			Investment Information	
Investment Objective	Income		Telephone	800-443-6544
5-Year Projected Return	+25%		Minimum Investment	$500
Safety Rating (0-100)	86%		Telephone Switching	5 per yr; $5
Yield (8/93)	4.5%		Total Assets	$1 million

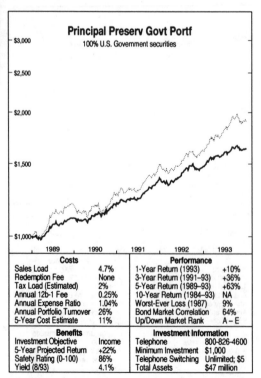

Principal Preserv Govt Portf
100% U.S. Government securities

Costs			Performance	
Sales Load	4.7%		1-Year Return (1993)	+10%
Redemption Fee	None		3-Year Return (1991–93)	+36%
Tax Load (Estimated)	2%		5-Year Return (1989–93)	+63%
Annual 12b-1 Fee	0.25%		10-Year Return (1984–93)	NA
Annual Expense Ratio	1.04%		Worst-Ever Loss (1987)	9%
Annual Portfolio Turnover	26%		Bond Market Correlation	64%
5-Year Cost Estimate	11%		Up/Down Market Rank	A – E

Benefits			Investment Information	
Investment Objective	Income		Telephone	800-826-4600
5-Year Projected Return	+22%		Minimum Investment	$1,000
Safety Rating (0-100)	86%		Telephone Switching	Unlimited; $5
Yield (8/93)	4.1%		Total Assets	$47 million

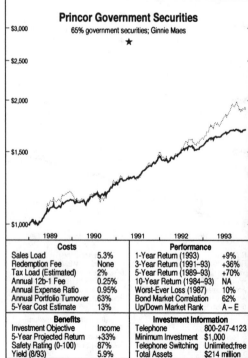

Princor Government Securities
65% government securities; Ginnie Maes
★

Costs			Performance	
Sales Load	5.3%		1-Year Return (1993)	+9%
Redemption Fee	None		3-Year Return (1991–93)	+36%
Tax Load (Estimated)	2%		5-Year Return (1989–93)	+70%
Annual 12b-1 Fee	0.25%		10-Year Return (1984–93)	NA
Annual Expense Ratio	0.95%		Worst-Ever Loss (1987)	10%
Annual Portfolio Turnover	63%		Bond Market Correlation	62%
5-Year Cost Estimate	13%		Up/Down Market Rank	A – E

Benefits			Investment Information	
Investment Objective	Income		Telephone	800-247-4123
5-Year Projected Return	+33%		Minimum Investment	$1,000
Safety Rating (0-100)	87%		Telephone Switching	Unlimited;free
Yield (8/93)	5.9%		Total Assets	$214 million

Prospect Street High Income
BB-rated and lower corporates; 20% zero coupn

Bond Index

Fund

Costs		Performance	
Sales Load	None	1-Year Return (1993)	+10%
Redemption Fee	None	3-Year Return (1991–93)	+119%
Tax Load (Estimated)	Neg.	5-Year Return (1989–93)	–20%
Annual 12b-1 Fee	None	10-Year Return (1984–93)	NA
Annual Expense Ratio	2.28%	Worst-Ever Loss (1989-90)	72%
Annual Portfolio Turnover	154%	Bond Market Correlation	1%
5-Year Cost Estimate	14%	Up/Down Market Rank	C – E

Benefits		Investment Information	
Investment Objective	Income	Telephone	800-524-4458
5-Year Projected Return	NA	Minimum Investment	None
Safety Rating (0-100)	31%	Telephone Switching	Via broker
Yield	NA	Total Assets	$94 million

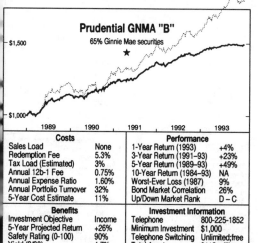

Prudential GNMA "B"
65% Ginnie Mae securities
★

Costs		Performance	
Sales Load	None	1-Year Return (1993)	+4%
Redemption Fee	5.3%	3-Year Return (1991–93)	+23%
Tax Load (Estimated)	3%	5-Year Return (1989–93)	+49%
Annual 12b-1 Fee	0.75%	10-Year Return (1984–93)	NA
Annual Expense Ratio	1.60%	Worst-Ever Loss (1987)	9%
Annual Portfolio Turnover	32%	Bond Market Correlation	26%
5-Year Cost Estimate	11%	Up/Down Market Rank	D – C

Benefits		Investment Information	
Investment Objective	Income	Telephone	800-225-1852
5-Year Projected Return	+26%	Minimum Investment	$1,000
Safety Rating (0-100)	90%	Telephone Switching	Unlimited;free
Yield (8/93)	4.7%	Total Assets	$118 million

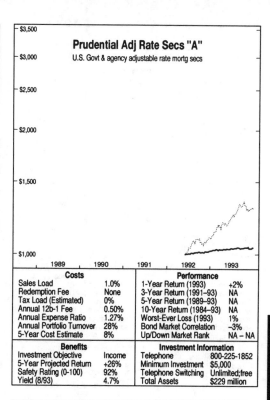

Prudential Adj Rate Secs "A"
U.S. Govt & agency adjustable rate mortg secs

Costs		Performance	
Sales Load	1.0%	1-Year Return (1993)	+2%
Redemption Fee	None	3-Year Return (1991–93)	NA
Tax Load (Estimated)	0%	5-Year Return (1989–93)	NA
Annual 12b-1 Fee	0.50%	10-Year Return (1984–93)	NA
Annual Expense Ratio	1.27%	Worst-Ever Loss (1993)	1%
Annual Portfolio Turnover	28%	Bond Market Correlation	–3%
5-Year Cost Estimate	8%	Up/Down Market Rank	NA – NA

Benefits		Investment Information	
Investment Objective	Income	Telephone	800-225-1852
5-Year Projected Return	+26%	Minimum Investment	$5,000
Safety Rating (0-100)	92%	Telephone Switching	Unlimited;free
Yield (8/93)	4.7%	Total Assets	$229 million

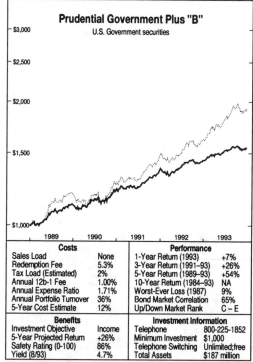

Prudential Government Plus "B"
U.S. Government securities

Costs		Performance	
Sales Load	None	1-Year Return (1993)	+7%
Redemption Fee	5.3%	3-Year Return (1991–93)	+26%
Tax Load (Estimated)	2%	5-Year Return (1989–93)	+54%
Annual 12b-1 Fee	1.00%	10-Year Return (1984–93)	NA
Annual Expense Ratio	1.71%	Worst-Ever Loss (1987)	9%
Annual Portfolio Turnover	36%	Bond Market Correlation	65%
5-Year Cost Estimate	12%	Up/Down Market Rank	C – E

Benefits		Investment Information	
Investment Objective	Income	Telephone	800-225-1852
5-Year Projected Return	+26%	Minimum Investment	$1,000
Safety Rating (0-100)	86%	Telephone Switching	Unlimited;free
Yield (8/93)	4.7%	Total Assets	$187 million

BOND

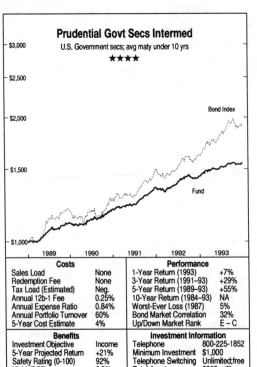

Prudential Govt Secs Intermed

U.S. Government secs; avg maty under 10 yrs

★★★★

Bond Index

Fund

Costs		Performance	
Sales Load	None	1-Year Return (1993)	+7%
Redemption Fee	None	3-Year Return (1991–93)	+29%
Tax Load (Estimated)	Neg.	5-Year Return (1989–93)	+55%
Annual 12b-1 Fee	0.25%	10-Year Return (1984–93)	NA
Annual Expense Ratio	0.84%	Worst-Ever Loss (1987)	5%
Annual Portfolio Turnover	60%	Bond Market Correlation	32%
5-Year Cost Estimate	4%	Up/Down Market Rank	E – C

Benefits		Investment Information	
Investment Objective	Income	Telephone	800-225-1852
5-Year Projected Return	+21%	Minimum Investment	$1,000
Safety Rating (0-100)	92%	Telephone Switching	Unlimited;free
Yield (8/93)	3.9%	Total Assets	$323 million

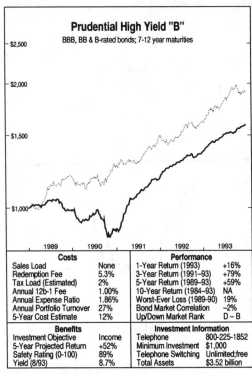

Prudential High Yield "B"

BBB, BB & B-rated bonds; 7-12 year maturities

Costs		Performance	
Sales Load	None	1-Year Return (1993)	+16%
Redemption Fee	5.3%	3-Year Return (1991–93)	+79%
Tax Load (Estimated)	2%	5-Year Return (1989–93)	+59%
Annual 12b-1 Fee	1.00%	10-Year Return (1984–93)	NA
Annual Expense Ratio	1.86%	Worst-Ever Loss (1989-90)	19%
Annual Portfolio Turnover	27%	Bond Market Correlation	–2%
5-Year Cost Estimate	12%	Up/Down Market Rank	D – B

Benefits		Investment Information	
Investment Objective	Income	Telephone	800-225-1852
5-Year Projected Return	+52%	Minimum Investment	$1,000
Safety Rating (0-100)	89%	Telephone Switching	Unlimited;free
Yield (8/93)	8.7%	Total Assets	$3.52 billion

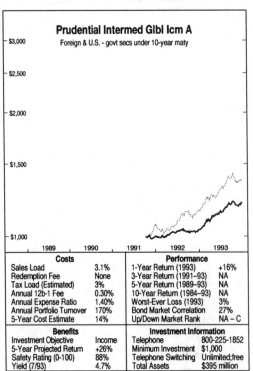

Prudential Intermed Glbl Icm A

Foreign & U.S. - govt secs under 10-year maty

Costs		Performance	
Sales Load	3.1%	1-Year Return (1993)	+16%
Redemption Fee	None	3-Year Return (1991–93)	NA
Tax Load (Estimated)	3%	5-Year Return (1989–93)	NA
Annual 12b-1 Fee	0.30%	10-Year Return (1984–93)	NA
Annual Expense Ratio	1.40%	Worst-Ever Loss (1993)	3%
Annual Portfolio Turnover	170%	Bond Market Correlation	27%
5-Year Cost Estimate	14%	Up/Down Market Rank	NA – C

Benefits		Investment Information	
Investment Objective	Income	Telephone	800-225-1852
5-Year Projected Return	+26%	Minimum Investment	$1,000
Safety Rating (0-100)	88%	Telephone Switching	Unlimited;free
Yield (7/93)	4.7%	Total Assets	$395 million

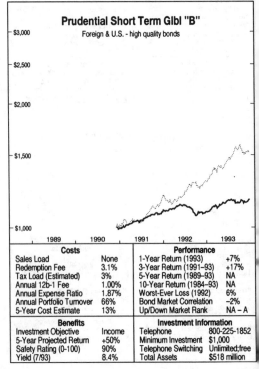

Prudential Short Term Glbl "B"

Foreign & U.S. - high quality bonds

Costs		Performance	
Sales Load	None	1-Year Return (1993)	+7%
Redemption Fee	3.1%	3-Year Return (1991–93)	+17%
Tax Load (Estimated)	3%	5-Year Return (1989–93)	NA
Annual 12b-1 Fee	1.00%	10-Year Return (1984–93)	NA
Annual Expense Ratio	1.87%	Worst-Ever Loss (1992)	6%
Annual Portfolio Turnover	66%	Bond Market Correlation	–2%
5-Year Cost Estimate	13%	Up/Down Market Rank	NA – A

Benefits		Investment Information	
Investment Objective	Income	Telephone	800-225-1852
5-Year Projected Return	+50%	Minimum Investment	$1,000
Safety Rating (0-100)	90%	Telephone Switching	Unlimited;free
Yield (7/93)	8.4%	Total Assets	$518 million

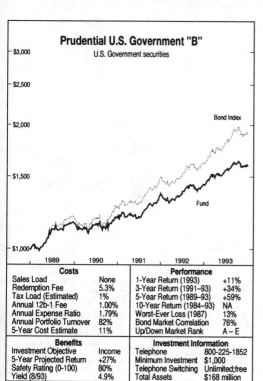

Prudential U.S. Government "B"
U.S. Government securities

Bond Index

Fund

Costs		Performance	
Sales Load	None	1-Year Return (1993)	+11%
Redemption Fee	5.3%	3-Year Return (1991–93)	+34%
Tax Load (Estimated)	1%	5-Year Return (1989–93)	+59%
Annual 12b-1 Fee	1.00%	10-Year Return (1984–93)	NA
Annual Expense Ratio	1.79%	Worst-Ever Loss (1987)	13%
Annual Portfolio Turnover	82%	Bond Market Correlation	76%
5-Year Cost Estimate	11%	Up/Down Market Rank	A – E

Benefits		Investment Information	
Investment Objective	Income	Telephone	800-225-1852
5-Year Projected Return	+27%	Minimum Investment	$1,000
Safety Rating (0-100)	80%	Telephone Switching	Unlimited;free
Yield (8/93)	4.9%	Total Assets	$168 million

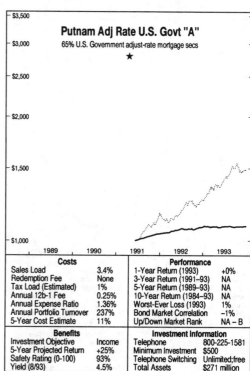

Putnam Adj Rate U.S. Govt "A"
65% U.S. Government adjust-rate mortgage secs
★

Costs		Performance	
Sales Load	3.4%	1-Year Return (1993)	+0%
Redemption Fee	None	3-Year Return (1991–93)	NA
Tax Load (Estimated)	1%	5-Year Return (1989–93)	NA
Annual 12b-1 Fee	0.25%	10-Year Return (1984–93)	NA
Annual Expense Ratio	1.36%	Worst-Ever Loss (1993)	1%
Annual Portfolio Turnover	237%	Bond Market Correlation	–1%
5-Year Cost Estimate	11%	Up/Down Market Rank	NA – B

Benefits		Investment Information	
Investment Objective	Income	Telephone	800-225-1581
5-Year Projected Return	+25%	Minimum Investment	$500
Safety Rating (0-100)	93%	Telephone Switching	Unlimited;free
Yield (8/93)	4.5%	Total Assets	$271 million

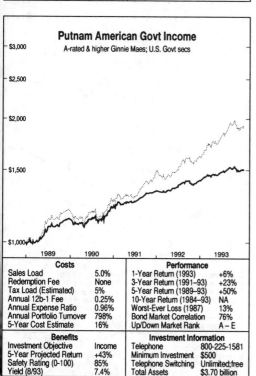

Putnam American Govt Income
A-rated & higher Ginnie Maes; U.S. Govt secs

Costs		Performance	
Sales Load	5.0%	1-Year Return (1993)	+6%
Redemption Fee	None	3-Year Return (1991–93)	+23%
Tax Load (Estimated)	5%	5-Year Return (1989–93)	+50%
Annual 12b-1 Fee	0.25%	10-Year Return (1984–93)	NA
Annual Expense Ratio	0.96%	Worst-Ever Loss (1987)	13%
Annual Portfolio Turnover	798%	Bond Market Correlation	76%
5-Year Cost Estimate	16%	Up/Down Market Rank	A – E

Benefits		Investment Information	
Investment Objective	Income	Telephone	800-225-1581
5-Year Projected Return	+43%	Minimum Investment	$500
Safety Rating (0-100)	85%	Telephone Switching	Unlimited;free
Yield (8/93)	7.4%	Total Assets	$3.70 billion

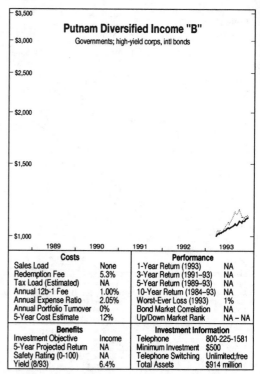

Putnam Diversified Income "B"
Governments; high-yield corps, intl bonds

Costs		Performance	
Sales Load	None	1-Year Return (1993)	NA
Redemption Fee	5.3%	3-Year Return (1991–93)	NA
Tax Load (Estimated)	NA	5-Year Return (1989–93)	NA
Annual 12b-1 Fee	1.00%	10-Year Return (1984–93)	NA
Annual Expense Ratio	2.05%	Worst-Ever Loss (1993)	1%
Annual Portfolio Turnover	0%	Bond Market Correlation	NA
5-Year Cost Estimate	12%	Up/Down Market Rank	NA – NA

Benefits		Investment Information	
Investment Objective	Income	Telephone	800-225-1581
5-Year Projected Return	NA	Minimum Investment	$500
Safety Rating (0-100)	NA	Telephone Switching	Unlimited;free
Yield (8/93)	6.4%	Total Assets	$914 million

BOND

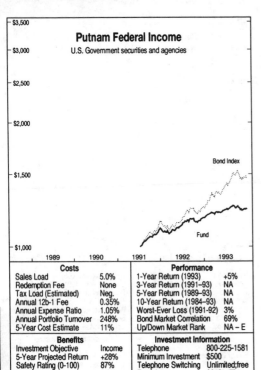

Putnam Federal Income
U.S. Government securities and agencies

Bond Index

Fund

Costs		Performance	
Sales Load	5.0%	1-Year Return (1993)	+5%
Redemption Fee	None	3-Year Return (1991–93)	NA
Tax Load (Estimated)	Neg.	5-Year Return (1989–93)	NA
Annual 12b-1 Fee	0.35%	10-Year Return (1984–93)	NA
Annual Expense Ratio	1.05%	Worst-Ever Loss (1991-92)	3%
Annual Portfolio Turnover	248%	Bond Market Correlation	69%
5-Year Cost Estimate	11%	Up/Down Market Rank	NA – E

Benefits		Investment Information	
Investment Objective	Income	Telephone	800-225-1581
5-Year Projected Return	+28%	Minimum Investment	$500
Safety Rating (0-100)	87%	Telephone Switching	Unlimited;free
Yield (8/93)	5.0%	Total Assets	$640 million

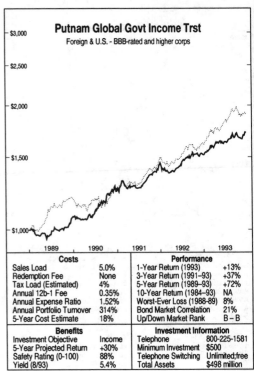

Putnam Global Govt Income Trst
Foreign & U.S. - BBB-rated and higher corps

Costs		Performance	
Sales Load	5.0%	1-Year Return (1993)	+13%
Redemption Fee	None	3-Year Return (1991–93)	+37%
Tax Load (Estimated)	4%	5-Year Return (1989–93)	+72%
Annual 12b-1 Fee	0.35%	10-Year Return (1984–93)	NA
Annual Expense Ratio	1.52%	Worst-Ever Loss (1988-89)	8%
Annual Portfolio Turnover	314%	Bond Market Correlation	21%
5-Year Cost Estimate	18%	Up/Down Market Rank	B – B

Benefits		Investment Information	
Investment Objective	Income	Telephone	800-225-1581
5-Year Projected Return	+30%	Minimum Investment	$500
Safety Rating (0-100)	88%	Telephone Switching	Unlimited;free
Yield (8/93)	5.4%	Total Assets	$498 million

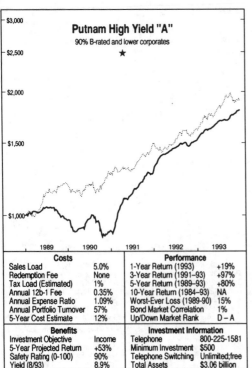

Putnam High Yield "A"
90% B-rated and lower corporates
★

Costs		Performance	
Sales Load	5.0%	1-Year Return (1993)	+19%
Redemption Fee	None	3-Year Return (1991–93)	+97%
Tax Load (Estimated)	1%	5-Year Return (1989–93)	+80%
Annual 12b-1 Fee	0.35%	10-Year Return (1984–93)	NA
Annual Expense Ratio	1.09%	Worst-Ever Loss (1989-90)	15%
Annual Portfolio Turnover	57%	Bond Market Correlation	1%
5-Year Cost Estimate	12%	Up/Down Market Rank	D – A

Benefits		Investment Information	
Investment Objective	Income	Telephone	800-225-1581
5-Year Projected Return	+53%	Minimum Investment	$500
Safety Rating (0-100)	90%	Telephone Switching	Unlimited;free
Yield (8/93)	8.9%	Total Assets	$3.06 billion

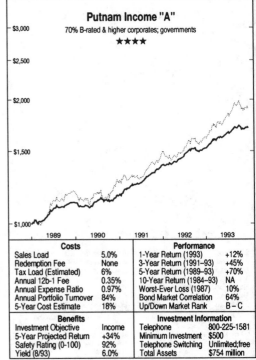

Putnam Income "A"
70% B-rated & higher corporates; governments
★★★★

Costs		Performance	
Sales Load	5.0%	1-Year Return (1993)	+12%
Redemption Fee	None	3-Year Return (1991–93)	+45%
Tax Load (Estimated)	6%	5-Year Return (1989–93)	+70%
Annual 12b-1 Fee	0.35%	10-Year Return (1984–93)	NA
Annual Expense Ratio	0.97%	Worst-Ever Loss (1987)	10%
Annual Portfolio Turnover	84%	Bond Market Correlation	64%
5-Year Cost Estimate	18%	Up/Down Market Rank	B – C

Benefits		Investment Information	
Investment Objective	Income	Telephone	800-225-1581
5-Year Projected Return	+34%	Minimum Investment	$500
Safety Rating (0-100)	92%	Telephone Switching	Unlimited;free
Yield (8/93)	6.0%	Total Assets	$754 million

BOND

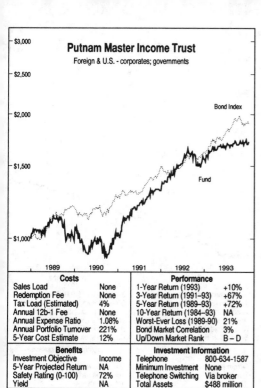

Putnam Master Income Trust
Foreign & U.S. - corporates; governments

Bond Index

Fund

Costs		Performance	
Sales Load	None	1-Year Return (1993)	+10%
Redemption Fee	None	3-Year Return (1991–93)	+67%
Tax Load (Estimated)	4%	5-Year Return (1989–93)	+72%
Annual 12b-1 Fee	None	10-Year Return (1984–93)	NA
Annual Expense Ratio	1.08%	Worst-Ever Loss (1989-90)	21%
Annual Portfolio Turnover	221%	Bond Market Correlation	3%
5-Year Cost Estimate	12%	Up/Down Market Rank	B – D

Benefits		Investment Information	
Investment Objective	Income	Telephone	800-634-1587
5-Year Projected Return	NA	Minimum Investment	None
Safety Rating (0-100)	72%	Telephone Switching	Via broker
Yield	NA	Total Assets	$488 million

Putnam Premier Income Trust
Foreign & U.S. - governments; high-yld corps

Costs		Performance	
Sales Load	None	1-Year Return (1993)	+13%
Redemption Fee	None	3-Year Return (1991–93)	+56%
Tax Load (Estimated)	5%	5-Year Return (1989–93)	+59%
Annual 12b-1 Fee	None	10-Year Return (1984–93)	NA
Annual Expense Ratio	1.06%	Worst-Ever Loss (1989-90)	23%
Annual Portfolio Turnover	203%	Bond Market Correlation	0%
5-Year Cost Estimate	13%	Up/Down Market Rank	C – C

Benefits		Investment Information	
Investment Objective	Income	Telephone	800-634-1587
5-Year Projected Return	NA	Minimum Investment	None
Safety Rating (0-100)	74%	Telephone Switching	Via broker
Yield	NA	Total Assets	$504 million

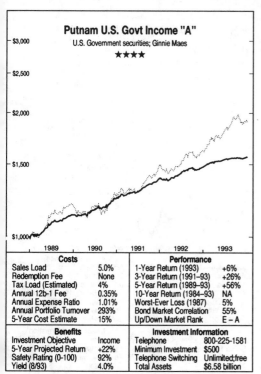

Putnam U.S. Govt Income "A"
U.S. Government securities; Ginnie Maes
★★★★

Costs		Performance	
Sales Load	5.0%	1-Year Return (1993)	+6%
Redemption Fee	None	3-Year Return (1991–93)	+26%
Tax Load (Estimated)	4%	5-Year Return (1989–93)	+56%
Annual 12b-1 Fee	0.35%	10-Year Return (1984–93)	NA
Annual Expense Ratio	1.01%	Worst-Ever Loss (1987)	5%
Annual Portfolio Turnover	293%	Bond Market Correlation	55%
5-Year Cost Estimate	15%	Up/Down Market Rank	E – A

Benefits		Investment Information	
Investment Objective	Income	Telephone	800-225-1581
5-Year Projected Return	+22%	Minimum Investment	$500
Safety Rating (0-100)	92%	Telephone Switching	Unlimited;free
Yield (8/93)	4.0%	Total Assets	$6.58 billion

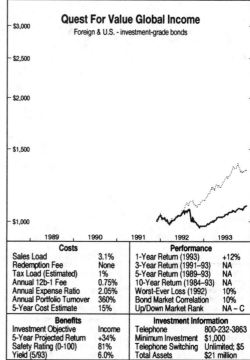

Quest For Value Global Income
Foreign & U.S. - investment-grade bonds

Costs		Performance	
Sales Load	3.1%	1-Year Return (1993)	+12%
Redemption Fee	None	3-Year Return (1991–93)	NA
Tax Load (Estimated)	1%	5-Year Return (1989–93)	NA
Annual 12b-1 Fee	0.75%	10-Year Return (1984–93)	NA
Annual Expense Ratio	2.05%	Worst-Ever Loss (1992)	10%
Annual Portfolio Turnover	360%	Bond Market Correlation	10%
5-Year Cost Estimate	15%	Up/Down Market Rank	NA – C

Benefits		Investment Information	
Investment Objective	Income	Telephone	800-232-3863
5-Year Projected Return	+34%	Minimum Investment	$1,000
Safety Rating (0-100)	81%	Telephone Switching	Unlimited; $5
Yield (5/93)	6.0%	Total Assets	$21 million

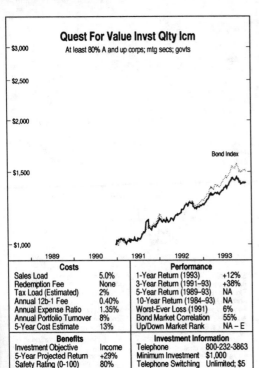

Quest For Value Invst Qlty Icm

At least 80% A and up corps; mtg secs; govts

Bond Index

Costs		Performance	
Sales Load	5.0%	1-Year Return (1993)	+12%
Redemption Fee	None	3-Year Return (1991–93)	+38%
Tax Load (Estimated)	2%	5-Year Return (1989–93)	NA
Annual 12b-1 Fee	0.40%	10-Year Return (1984–93)	NA
Annual Expense Ratio	1.35%	Worst-Ever Loss (1991)	6%
Annual Portfolio Turnover	8%	Bond Market Correlation	55%
5-Year Cost Estimate	13%	Up/Down Market Rank	NA – E

Benefits		Investment Information	
Investment Objective	Income	Telephone	800-232-3863
5-Year Projected Return	+29%	Minimum Investment	$1,000
Safety Rating (0-100)	80%	Telephone Switching	Unlimited; $5
Yield	5.2%	Total Assets	$0 million

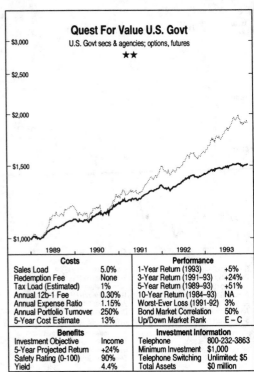

Quest For Value U.S. Govt

U.S. Govt secs & agencies; options, futures
★★

Costs		Performance	
Sales Load	5.0%	1-Year Return (1993)	+5%
Redemption Fee	None	3-Year Return (1991–93)	+24%
Tax Load (Estimated)	1%	5-Year Return (1989–93)	+51%
Annual 12b-1 Fee	0.30%	10-Year Return (1984–93)	NA
Annual Expense Ratio	1.15%	Worst-Ever Loss (1991-92)	3%
Annual Portfolio Turnover	250%	Bond Market Correlation	50%
5-Year Cost Estimate	13%	Up/Down Market Rank	E – C

Benefits		Investment Information	
Investment Objective	Income	Telephone	800-232-3863
5-Year Projected Return	+24%	Minimum Investment	$1,000
Safety Rating (0-100)	90%	Telephone Switching	Unlimited; $5
Yield	4.4%	Total Assets	$0 million

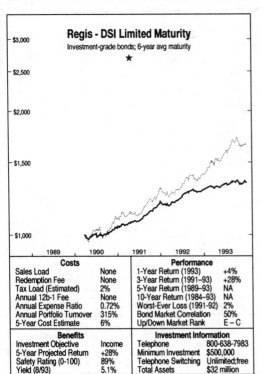

Regis - DSI Limited Maturity

Investment-grade bonds; 6-year avg maturity
★

Costs		Performance	
Sales Load	None	1-Year Return (1993)	+4%
Redemption Fee	None	3-Year Return (1991–93)	+28%
Tax Load (Estimated)	2%	5-Year Return (1989–93)	NA
Annual 12b-1 Fee	None	10-Year Return (1984–93)	NA
Annual Expense Ratio	0.72%	Worst-Ever Loss (1991-92)	2%
Annual Portfolio Turnover	315%	Bond Market Correlation	50%
5-Year Cost Estimate	6%	Up/Down Market Rank	E – C

Benefits		Investment Information	
Investment Objective	Income	Telephone	800-638-7983
5-Year Projected Return	+28%	Minimum Investment	$500,000
Safety Rating (0-100)	89%	Telephone Switching	Unlimited;free
Yield (8/93)	5.1%	Total Assets	$32 million

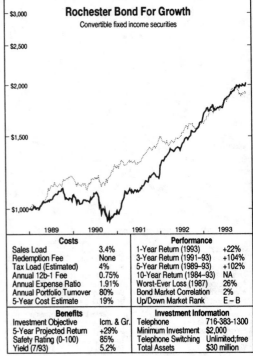

Rochester Bond For Growth

Convertible fixed income securities

Costs		Performance	
Sales Load	3.4%	1-Year Return (1993)	+22%
Redemption Fee	None	3-Year Return (1991–93)	+104%
Tax Load (Estimated)	4%	5-Year Return (1989–93)	+102%
Annual 12b-1 Fee	0.75%	10-Year Return (1984–93)	NA
Annual Expense Ratio	1.91%	Worst-Ever Loss (1987)	26%
Annual Portfolio Turnover	80%	Bond Market Correlation	2%
5-Year Cost Estimate	19%	Up/Down Market Rank	E – B

Benefits		Investment Information	
Investment Objective	Icm. & Gr.	Telephone	716-383-1300
5-Year Projected Return	+29%	Minimum Investment	$2,000
Safety Rating (0-100)	85%	Telephone Switching	Unlimited;free
Yield (7/93)	5.2%	Total Assets	$30 million

B O N D

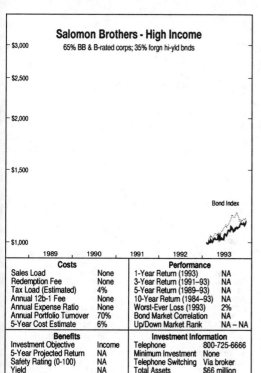

Salomon Brothers - High Income
65% BB & B-rated corps; 35% forgn hi-yld bnds

Bond Index

| 1989 | 1990 | 1991 | 1992 | 1993 |

Costs		Performance	
Sales Load	None	1-Year Return (1993)	NA
Redemption Fee	None	3-Year Return (1991–93)	NA
Tax Load (Estimated)	4%	5-Year Return (1989–93)	NA
Annual 12b-1 Fee	None	10-Year Return (1984–93)	NA
Annual Expense Ratio	None	Worst-Ever Loss (1993)	2%
Annual Portfolio Turnover	70%	Bond Market Correlation	NA
5-Year Cost Estimate	6%	Up/Down Market Rank	NA – NA

Benefits		Investment Information	
Investment Objective	Income	Telephone	800-725-6666
5-Year Projected Return	NA	Minimum Investment	None
Safety Rating (0-100)	NA	Telephone Switching	Via broker
Yield	NA	Total Assets	$66 million

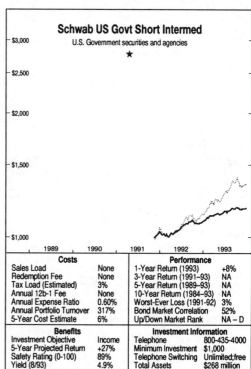

Schwab US Govt Short Intermed
U.S. Government securities and agencies
★

| 1989 | 1990 | 1991 | 1992 | 1993 |

Costs		Performance	
Sales Load	None	1-Year Return (1993)	+8%
Redemption Fee	None	3-Year Return (1991–93)	NA
Tax Load (Estimated)	3%	5-Year Return (1989–93)	NA
Annual 12b-1 Fee	None	10-Year Return (1984–93)	NA
Annual Expense Ratio	0.60%	Worst-Ever Loss (1991-92)	3%
Annual Portfolio Turnover	317%	Bond Market Correlation	52%
5-Year Cost Estimate	6%	Up/Down Market Rank	NA – D

Benefits		Investment Information	
Investment Objective	Income	Telephone	800-435-4000
5-Year Projected Return	+27%	Minimum Investment	$1,000
Safety Rating (0-100)	89%	Telephone Switching	Unlimited;free
Yield (8/93)	4.9%	Total Assets	$268 million

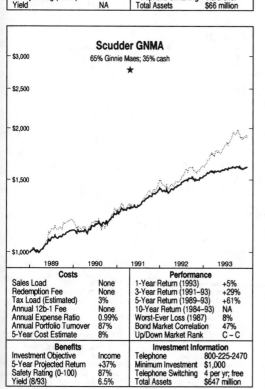

Scudder GNMA
65% Ginnie Maes; 35% cash
★

| 1989 | 1990 | 1991 | 1992 | 1993 |

Costs		Performance	
Sales Load	None	1-Year Return (1993)	+5%
Redemption Fee	None	3-Year Return (1991–93)	+29%
Tax Load (Estimated)	3%	5-Year Return (1989–93)	+61%
Annual 12b-1 Fee	None	10-Year Return (1984–93)	NA
Annual Expense Ratio	0.99%	Worst-Ever Loss (1987)	8%
Annual Portfolio Turnover	87%	Bond Market Correlation	47%
5-Year Cost Estimate	8%	Up/Down Market Rank	C – C

Benefits		Investment Information	
Investment Objective	Income	Telephone	800-225-2470
5-Year Projected Return	+37%	Minimum Investment	$1,000
Safety Rating (0-100)	87%	Telephone Switching	4 per yr; free
Yield (8/93)	6.5%	Total Assets	$647 million

Scudder Income
Bonds, preferreds; stocks; governments
★★

| 1989 | 1990 | 1991 | 1992 | 1993 |

Costs		Performance	
Sales Load	None	1-Year Return (1993)	+13%
Redemption Fee	None	3-Year Return (1991–93)	+41%
Tax Load (Estimated)	2%	5-Year Return (1989–93)	+70%
Annual 12b-1 Fee	None	10-Year Return (1984–93)	+193%
Annual Expense Ratio	0.97%	Worst-Ever Loss (1987)	10%
Annual Portfolio Turnover	137%	Bond Market Correlation	76%
5-Year Cost Estimate	8%	Up/Down Market Rank	A – E

Benefits		Investment Information	
Investment Objective	Income	Telephone	800-225-2470
5-Year Projected Return	+30%	Minimum Investment	$1,000
Safety Rating (0-100)	88%	Telephone Switching	4 per yr; free
Yield (8/93)	5.4%	Total Assets	$503 million

BOND

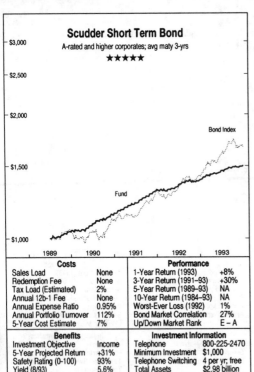

Scudder Short Term Bond
A-rated and higher corporates; avg maty 3-yrs
★★★★★

Bond Index
Fund

Costs		Performance	
Sales Load	None	1-Year Return (1993)	+8%
Redemption Fee	None	3-Year Return (1991–93)	+30%
Tax Load (Estimated)	2%	5-Year Return (1989–93)	NA
Annual 12b-1 Fee	None	10-Year Return (1984–93)	NA
Annual Expense Ratio	0.95%	Worst-Ever Loss (1992)	1%
Annual Portfolio Turnover	112%	Bond Market Correlation	27%
5-Year Cost Estimate	7%	Up/Down Market Rank	E – A

Benefits		Investment Information	
Investment Objective	Income	Telephone	800-225-2470
5-Year Projected Return	+31%	Minimum Investment	$1,000
Safety Rating (0-100)	93%	Telephone Switching	4 per yr; free
Yield (8/93)	5.6%	Total Assets	$2.98 billion

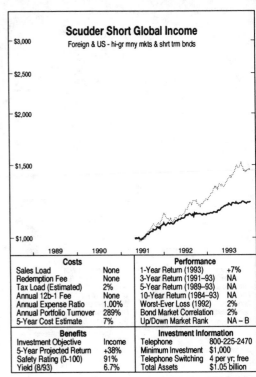

Scudder Short Global Income
Foreign & US - hi-gr mny mkts & shrt trm bnds

Costs		Performance	
Sales Load	None	1-Year Return (1993)	+7%
Redemption Fee	None	3-Year Return (1991–93)	NA
Tax Load (Estimated)	2%	5-Year Return (1989–93)	NA
Annual 12b-1 Fee	None	10-Year Return (1984–93)	NA
Annual Expense Ratio	1.00%	Worst-Ever Loss (1992)	2%
Annual Portfolio Turnover	289%	Bond Market Correlation	2%
5-Year Cost Estimate	7%	Up/Down Market Rank	NA – B

Benefits		Investment Information	
Investment Objective	Income	Telephone	800-225-2470
5-Year Projected Return	+38%	Minimum Investment	$1,000
Safety Rating (0-100)	91%	Telephone Switching	4 per yr; free
Yield (8/93)	6.7%	Total Assets	$1.05 billion

Scudder Zero Coupon 2000
Zero coupon; U.S. Government securities

Costs		Performance	
Sales Load	None	1-Year Return (1993)	+16%
Redemption Fee	None	3-Year Return (1991–93)	+51%
Tax Load (Estimated)	0%	5-Year Return (1989–93)	NA
Annual 12b-1 Fee	None	10-Year Return (1984–93)	NA
Annual Expense Ratio	1.00%	Worst-Ever Loss (1989-90)	11%
Annual Portfolio Turnover	119%	Bond Market Correlation	83%
5-Year Cost Estimate	5%	Up/Down Market Rank	A – E

Benefits		Investment Information	
Investment Objective	Income	Telephone	800-225-2470
5-Year Projected Return	+26%	Minimum Investment	$1,000
Safety Rating (0-100)	75%	Telephone Switching	4 per yr; free
Yield (8/93)	4.8%	Total Assets	$34 million

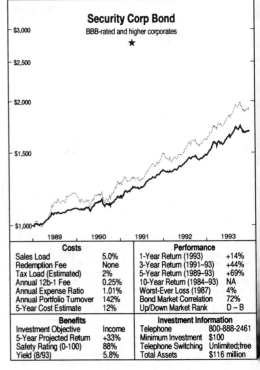

Security Corp Bond
BBB-rated and higher corporates
★

Costs		Performance	
Sales Load	5.0%	1-Year Return (1993)	+14%
Redemption Fee	None	3-Year Return (1991–93)	+44%
Tax Load (Estimated)	2%	5-Year Return (1989–93)	+69%
Annual 12b-1 Fee	0.25%	10-Year Return (1984–93)	NA
Annual Expense Ratio	1.01%	Worst-Ever Loss (1987)	4%
Annual Portfolio Turnover	142%	Bond Market Correlation	72%
5-Year Cost Estimate	12%	Up/Down Market Rank	D – B

Benefits		Investment Information	
Investment Objective	Income	Telephone	800-888-2461
5-Year Projected Return	+33%	Minimum Investment	$100
Safety Rating (0-100)	88%	Telephone Switching	Unlimited;free
Yield (8/93)	5.8%	Total Assets	$116 million

B O N D

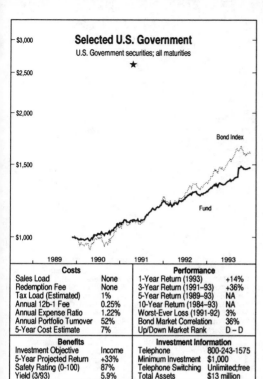

Selected U.S. Government
U.S. Government securities; all maturities
★

Bond Index

Fund

| | | 1989 | 1990 | 1991 | 1992 | 1993 |

Costs		Performance	
Sales Load	None	1-Year Return (1993)	+14%
Redemption Fee	None	3-Year Return (1991–93)	+36%
Tax Load (Estimated)	1%	5-Year Return (1989–93)	NA
Annual 12b-1 Fee	0.25%	10-Year Return (1984–93)	NA
Annual Expense Ratio	1.22%	Worst-Ever Loss (1991-92)	3%
Annual Portfolio Turnover	52%	Bond Market Correlation	36%
5-Year Cost Estimate	7%	Up/Down Market Rank	D – D

Benefits		Investment Information	
Investment Objective	Income	Telephone	800-243-1575
5-Year Projected Return	+33%	Minimum Investment	$1,000
Safety Rating (0-100)	87%	Telephone Switching	Unlimited;free
Yield (3/93)	5.9%	Total Assets	$13 million

Seligman High Yield Bond "A"
BBB-rated and lower corporatae bonds

| | | 1989 | 1990 | 1991 | 1992 | 1993 |

Costs		Performance	
Sales Load	5.0%	1-Year Return (1993)	+29%
Redemption Fee	None	3-Year Return (1991–93)	+101%
Tax Load (Estimated)	Neg.	5-Year Return (1989–93)	+92%
Annual 12b-1 Fee	0.25%	10-Year Return (1984–93)	NA
Annual Expense Ratio	1.29%	Worst-Ever Loss (1989-90)	14%
Annual Portfolio Turnover	200%	Bond Market Correlation	–2%
5-Year Cost Estimate	12%	Up/Down Market Rank	E – A

Benefits		Investment Information	
Investment Objective	Income	Telephone	800-221-2450
5-Year Projected Return	+52%	Minimum Investment	$1,000
Safety Rating (0-100)	87%	Telephone Switching	Unlimited;free
Yield (8/93)	8.8%	Total Assets	$51 million

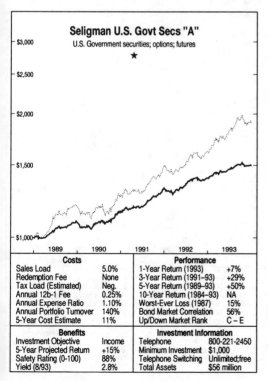

Seligman U.S. Govt Secs "A"
U.S. Government securities; options; futures
★

| | | 1989 | 1990 | 1991 | 1992 | 1993 |

Costs		Performance	
Sales Load	5.0%	1-Year Return (1993)	+7%
Redemption Fee	None	3-Year Return (1991–93)	+29%
Tax Load (Estimated)	Neg.	5-Year Return (1989–93)	+50%
Annual 12b-1 Fee	0.25%	10-Year Return (1984–93)	NA
Annual Expense Ratio	1.10%	Worst-Ever Loss (1987)	15%
Annual Portfolio Turnover	140%	Bond Market Correlation	56%
5-Year Cost Estimate	11%	Up/Down Market Rank	C – E

Benefits		Investment Information	
Investment Objective	Income	Telephone	800-221-2450
5-Year Projected Return	+15%	Minimum Investment	$1,000
Safety Rating (0-100)	88%	Telephone Switching	Unlimited;free
Yield (8/93)	2.8%	Total Assets	$56 million

Sentinel Bond
Investment-grade bonds
★★

| | | 1989 | 1990 | 1991 | 1992 | 1993 |

Costs		Performance	
Sales Load	5.3%	1-Year Return (1993)	+12%
Redemption Fee	None	3-Year Return (1991–93)	+43%
Tax Load (Estimated)	1%	5-Year Return (1989–93)	+71%
Annual 12b-1 Fee	0.20%	10-Year Return (1984–93)	NA
Annual Expense Ratio	0.94%	Worst-Ever Loss (1987)	10%
Annual Portfolio Turnover	153%	Bond Market Correlation	76%
5-Year Cost Estimate	11%	Up/Down Market Rank	B – D

Benefits		Investment Information	
Investment Objective	Income	Telephone	800-282-3863
5-Year Projected Return	+25%	Minimum Investment	$500
Safety Rating (0-100)	89%	Telephone Switching	1 per 15da; fr
Yield (8/93)	4.6%	Total Assets	$74 million

BOND

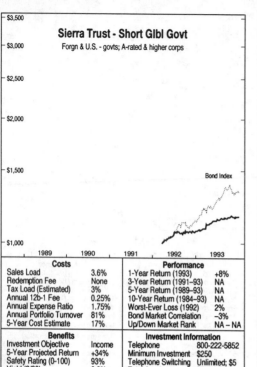

Sierra Trust - Short Glbl Govt

Forgn & U.S. - govts; A-rated & higher corps

Bond Index

Costs		Performance	
Sales Load	3.6%	1-Year Return (1993)	+8%
Redemption Fee	None	3-Year Return (1991–93)	NA
Tax Load (Estimated)	3%	5-Year Return (1989–93)	NA
Annual 12b-1 Fee	0.25%	10-Year Return (1984–93)	NA
Annual Expense Ratio	1.75%	Worst-Ever Loss (1992)	2%
Annual Portfolio Turnover	81%	Bond Market Correlation	–3%
5-Year Cost Estimate	17%	Up/Down Market Rank	NA – NA

Benefits		Investment Information	
Investment Objective	Income	Telephone	800-222-5852
5-Year Projected Return	+34%	Minimum Investment	$250
Safety Rating (0-100)	93%	Telephone Switching	Unlimited; $5
Yield (8/93)	6.0%	Total Assets	$214 million

Sierra Trust - U.S. Govt

Intermediate-long term U.S. Government secs

★★

Costs		Performance	
Sales Load	4.7%	1-Year Return (1993)	+7%
Redemption Fee	None	3-Year Return (1991–93)	+31%
Tax Load (Estimated)	4%	5-Year Return (1989–93)	NA
Annual 12b-1 Fee	0.50%	10-Year Return (1984–93)	NA
Annual Expense Ratio	0.72%	Worst-Ever Loss (1991-92)	3%
Annual Portfolio Turnover	35%	Bond Market Correlation	40%
5-Year Cost Estimate	11%	Up/Down Market Rank	E – B

Benefits		Investment Information	
Investment Objective	Income	Telephone	800-222-5852
5-Year Projected Return	+28%	Minimum Investment	$250
Safety Rating (0-100)	90%	Telephone Switching	Unlimited; $5
Yield (8/93)	5.1%	Total Assets	$839 million

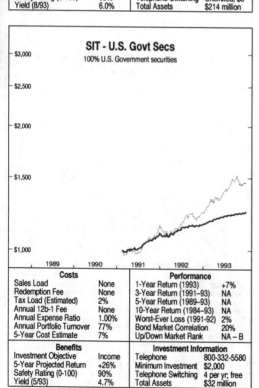

SIT - U.S. Govt Secs

100% U.S. Government securities

Costs		Performance	
Sales Load	None	1-Year Return (1993)	+7%
Redemption Fee	None	3-Year Return (1991–93)	NA
Tax Load (Estimated)	2%	5-Year Return (1989–93)	NA
Annual 12b-1 Fee	None	10-Year Return (1984–93)	NA
Annual Expense Ratio	1.00%	Worst-Ever Loss (1991-92)	2%
Annual Portfolio Turnover	77%	Bond Market Correlation	20%
5-Year Cost Estimate	7%	Up/Down Market Rank	NA – B

Benefits		Investment Information	
Investment Objective	Income	Telephone	800-332-5580
5-Year Projected Return	+26%	Minimum Investment	$2,000
Safety Rating (0-100)	90%	Telephone Switching	4 per yr; free
Yield (5/93)	4.7%	Total Assets	$32 million

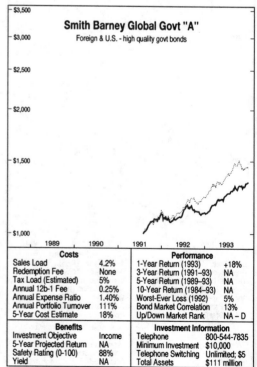

Smith Barney Global Govt "A"

Foreign & U.S. - high quality govt bonds

Costs		Performance	
Sales Load	4.2%	1-Year Return (1993)	+18%
Redemption Fee	None	3-Year Return (1991–93)	NA
Tax Load (Estimated)	5%	5-Year Return (1989–93)	NA
Annual 12b-1 Fee	0.25%	10-Year Return (1984–93)	NA
Annual Expense Ratio	1.40%	Worst-Ever Loss (1992)	5%
Annual Portfolio Turnover	111%	Bond Market Correlation	13%
5-Year Cost Estimate	18%	Up/Down Market Rank	NA – D

Benefits		Investment Information	
Investment Objective	Income	Telephone	800-544-7835
5-Year Projected Return	NA	Minimum Investment	$10,000
Safety Rating (0-100)	88%	Telephone Switching	Unlimited; $5
Yield	NA	Total Assets	$111 million

BOND

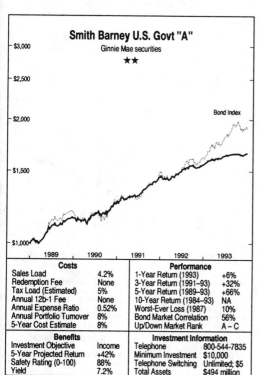

Smith Barney U.S. Govt "A"
Ginnie Mae securities
★★

Costs		Performance	
Sales Load	4.2%	1-Year Return (1993)	+6%
Redemption Fee	None	3-Year Return (1991–93)	+32%
Tax Load (Estimated)	5%	5-Year Return (1989–93)	+66%
Annual 12b-1 Fee	None	10-Year Return (1984–93)	NA
Annual Expense Ratio	0.52%	Worst-Ever Loss (1987)	10%
Annual Portfolio Turnover	8%	Bond Market Correlation	56%
5-Year Cost Estimate	8%	Up/Down Market Rank	A – C

Benefits		Investment Information	
Investment Objective	Income	Telephone	800-544-7835
5-Year Projected Return	+42%	Minimum Investment	$10,000
Safety Rating (0-100)	88%	Telephone Switching	Unlimited; $5
Yield	7.2%	Total Assets	$494 million

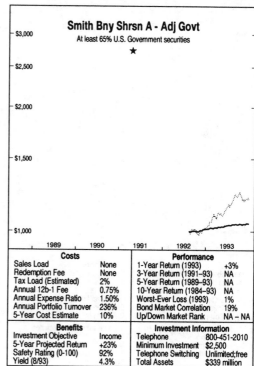

Smith Bny Shrsn A - Adj Govt
At least 65% U.S. Government securities
★

Costs		Performance	
Sales Load	None	1-Year Return (1993)	+3%
Redemption Fee	None	3-Year Return (1991–93)	NA
Tax Load (Estimated)	2%	5-Year Return (1989–93)	NA
Annual 12b-1 Fee	0.75%	10-Year Return (1984–93)	NA
Annual Expense Ratio	1.50%	Worst-Ever Loss (1993)	1%
Annual Portfolio Turnover	236%	Bond Market Correlation	19%
5-Year Cost Estimate	10%	Up/Down Market Rank	NA – NA

Benefits		Investment Information	
Investment Objective	Income	Telephone	800-451-2010
5-Year Projected Return	+23%	Minimum Investment	$2,500
Safety Rating (0-100)	92%	Telephone Switching	Unlimited; free
Yield (8/93)	4.3%	Total Assets	$339 million

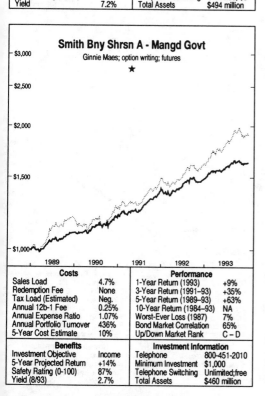

Smith Bny Shrsn A - Mangd Govt
Ginnie Maes; option writing; futures
★

Costs		Performance	
Sales Load	4.7%	1-Year Return (1993)	+9%
Redemption Fee	None	3-Year Return (1991–93)	+35%
Tax Load (Estimated)	Neg.	5-Year Return (1989–93)	+63%
Annual 12b-1 Fee	0.25%	10-Year Return (1984–93)	NA
Annual Expense Ratio	1.07%	Worst-Ever Loss (1987)	7%
Annual Portfolio Turnover	436%	Bond Market Correlation	65%
5-Year Cost Estimate	10%	Up/Down Market Rank	C – D

Benefits		Investment Information	
Investment Objective	Income	Telephone	800-451-2010
5-Year Projected Return	+14%	Minimum Investment	$1,000
Safety Rating (0-100)	87%	Telephone Switching	Unlimited; free
Yield (8/93)	2.7%	Total Assets	$460 million

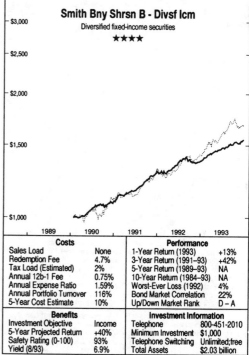

Smith Bny Shrsn B - Divsf Icm
Diversified fixed-income securities
★★★★

Costs		Performance	
Sales Load	None	1-Year Return (1993)	+13%
Redemption Fee	4.7%	3-Year Return (1991–93)	+42%
Tax Load (Estimated)	2%	5-Year Return (1989–93)	NA
Annual 12b-1 Fee	0.75%	10-Year Return (1984–93)	NA
Annual Expense Ratio	1.59%	Worst-Ever Loss (1992)	4%
Annual Portfolio Turnover	116%	Bond Market Correlation	22%
5-Year Cost Estimate	10%	Up/Down Market Rank	D – A

Benefits		Investment Information	
Investment Objective	Income	Telephone	800-451-2010
5-Year Projected Return	+40%	Minimum Investment	$1,000
Safety Rating (0-100)	93%	Telephone Switching	Unlimited; free
Yield (8/93)	6.9%	Total Assets	$2.03 billion

BOND

Smith Bny Shrsn B - Global Bnd
Foreign & U.S. - 85% AA-rated & higher bonds

Costs		Performance	
Sales Load	None	1-Year Return (1993)	+15%
Redemption Fee	4.7%	3-Year Return (1991–93)	+38%
Tax Load (Estimated)	3%	5-Year Return (1989–93)	+58%
Annual 12b-1 Fee	0.75%	10-Year Return (1984–93)	NA
Annual Expense Ratio	2.22%	Worst-Ever Loss (1987)	6%
Annual Portfolio Turnover	216%	Bond Market Correlation	21%
5-Year Cost Estimate	15%	Up/Down Market Rank	D – B

Benefits		Investment Information	
Investment Objective	Income	Telephone	800-451-2010
5-Year Projected Return	+22%	Minimum Investment	$1,000
Safety Rating (0-100)	88%	Telephone Switching	Unlimited;free
Yield (4/93)	4.1%	Total Assets	$65 million

Smith Bny Shrsn B - Govt Secs
Government securities; option writing

Costs		Performance	
Sales Load	None	1-Year Return (1993)	+10%
Redemption Fee	4.7%	3-Year Return (1991–93)	+35%
Tax Load (Estimated)	Neg.	5-Year Return (1989–93)	+66%
Annual 12b-1 Fee	0.75%	10-Year Return (1984–93)	NA
Annual Expense Ratio	1.46%	Worst-Ever Loss (1986-87)	14%
Annual Portfolio Turnover	200%	Bond Market Correlation	70%
5-Year Cost Estimate	8%	Up/Down Market Rank	B – E

Benefits		Investment Information	
Investment Objective	Income	Telephone	800-451-2010
5-Year Projected Return	+18%	Minimum Investment	$1,000
Safety Rating (0-100)	85%	Telephone Switching	Unlimited;free
Yield (8/93)	3.4%	Total Assets	$950 million

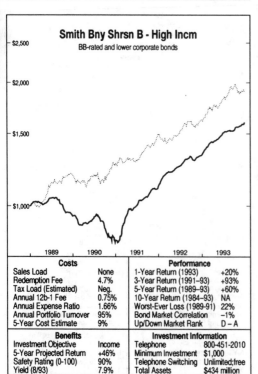

Smith Bny Shrsn B - High Incm
BB-rated and lower corporate bonds

Costs		Performance	
Sales Load	None	1-Year Return (1993)	+20%
Redemption Fee	4.7%	3-Year Return (1991–93)	+93%
Tax Load (Estimated)	Neg.	5-Year Return (1989–93)	+60%
Annual 12b-1 Fee	0.75%	10-Year Return (1984–93)	NA
Annual Expense Ratio	1.66%	Worst-Ever Loss (1989-91)	22%
Annual Portfolio Turnover	95%	Bond Market Correlation	–1%
5-Year Cost Estimate	9%	Up/Down Market Rank	D – A

Benefits		Investment Information	
Investment Objective	Income	Telephone	800-451-2010
5-Year Projected Return	+46%	Minimum Investment	$1,000
Safety Rating (0-100)	90%	Telephone Switching	Unlimited;free
Yield (8/93)	7.9%	Total Assets	$434 million

Smith Bny Shrsn B - Inv Grade
Investment-grade corporates; government secs

Costs		Performance	
Sales Load	None	1-Year Return (1993)	+18%
Redemption Fee	4.7%	3-Year Return (1991–93)	+57%
Tax Load (Estimated)	3%	5-Year Return (1989–93)	+83%
Annual 12b-1 Fee	0.75%	10-Year Return (1984–93)	NA
Annual Expense Ratio	1.54%	Worst-Ever Loss (1987)	18%
Annual Portfolio Turnover	50%	Bond Market Correlation	71%
5-Year Cost Estimate	11%	Up/Down Market Rank	A – E

Benefits		Investment Information	
Investment Objective	Income	Telephone	800-451-2010
5-Year Projected Return	+36%	Minimum Investment	$1,000
Safety Rating (0-100)	82%	Telephone Switching	Unlimited;free
Yield (8/93)	6.3%	Total Assets	$473 million

BOND

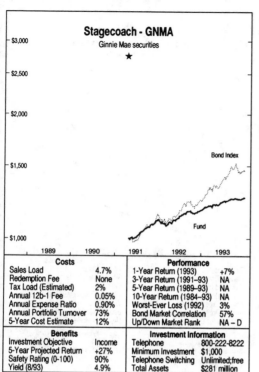

Stagecoach - GNMA
Ginnie Mae securities
★

Bond Index

Fund

Costs		Performance	
Sales Load	4.7%	1-Year Return (1993)	+7%
Redemption Fee	None	3-Year Return (1991–93)	NA
Tax Load (Estimated)	2%	5-Year Return (1989–93)	NA
Annual 12b-1 Fee	0.05%	10-Year Return (1984–93)	NA
Annual Expense Ratio	0.90%	Worst-Ever Loss (1992)	3%
Annual Portfolio Turnover	73%	Bond Market Correlation	57%
5-Year Cost Estimate	12%	Up/Down Market Rank	NA – D

Benefits		Investment Information	
Investment Objective	Income	Telephone	800-222-8222
5-Year Projected Return	+27%	Minimum Investment	$1,000
Safety Rating (0-100)	90%	Telephone Switching	Unlimited;free
Yield (8/93)	4.9%	Total Assets	$281 million

Stagecoach - U.S. Government
U.S. Government securities and agencies

Costs		Performance	
Sales Load	4.7%	1-Year Return (1993)	+19%
Redemption Fee	None	3-Year Return (1991–93)	+47%
Tax Load (Estimated)	2%	5-Year Return (1989–93)	NA
Annual 12b-1 Fee	0.05%	10-Year Return (1984–93)	NA
Annual Expense Ratio	1.03%	Worst-Ever Loss (1991-92)	5%
Annual Portfolio Turnover	33%	Bond Market Correlation	73%
5-Year Cost Estimate	12%	Up/Down Market Rank	B – D

Benefits		Investment Information	
Investment Objective	Income	Telephone	800-222-8222
5-Year Projected Return	+28%	Minimum Investment	$1,000
Safety Rating (0-100)	83%	Telephone Switching	Unlimited;free
Yield (8/93)	5.1%	Total Assets	$218 million

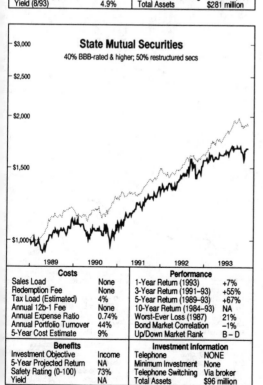

State Mutual Securities
40% BBB-rated & higher; 50% restructured secs

Costs		Performance	
Sales Load	None	1-Year Return (1993)	+7%
Redemption Fee	None	3-Year Return (1991–93)	+55%
Tax Load (Estimated)	4%	5-Year Return (1989–93)	+67%
Annual 12b-1 Fee	None	10-Year Return (1984–93)	NA
Annual Expense Ratio	0.74%	Worst-Ever Loss (1987)	21%
Annual Portfolio Turnover	44%	Bond Market Correlation	–1%
5-Year Cost Estimate	9%	Up/Down Market Rank	B – D

Benefits		Investment Information	
Investment Objective	Income	Telephone	NONE
5-Year Projected Return	NA	Minimum Investment	None
Safety Rating (0-100)	73%	Telephone Switching	Via broker
Yield	NA	Total Assets	$96 million

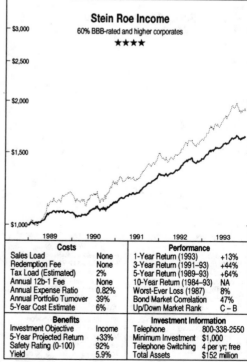

Stein Roe Income
60% BBB-rated and higher corporates
★★★★

Costs		Performance	
Sales Load	None	1-Year Return (1993)	+13%
Redemption Fee	None	3-Year Return (1991–93)	+44%
Tax Load (Estimated)	2%	5-Year Return (1989–93)	+64%
Annual 12b-1 Fee	None	10-Year Return (1984–93)	NA
Annual Expense Ratio	0.82%	Worst-Ever Loss (1987)	8%
Annual Portfolio Turnover	39%	Bond Market Correlation	47%
5-Year Cost Estimate	6%	Up/Down Market Rank	C – B

Benefits		Investment Information	
Investment Objective	Income	Telephone	800-338-2550
5-Year Projected Return	+33%	Minimum Investment	$1,000
Safety Rating (0-100)	92%	Telephone Switching	4 per yr; free
Yield	5.9%	Total Assets	$152 million

BOND

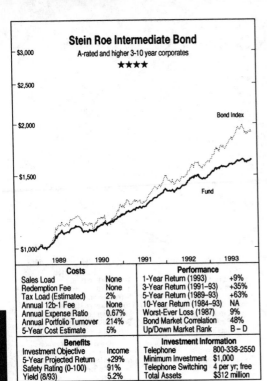

Stein Roe Intermediate Bond
A-rated and higher 3-10 year corporates
★★★★

Bond Index

Fund

Costs		Performance	
Sales Load	None	1-Year Return (1993)	+9%
Redemption Fee	None	3-Year Return (1991–93)	+35%
Tax Load (Estimated)	2%	5-Year Return (1989–93)	+63%
Annual 12b-1 Fee	None	10-Year Return (1984–93)	NA
Annual Expense Ratio	0.67%	Worst-Ever Loss (1987)	9%
Annual Portfolio Turnover	214%	Bond Market Correlation	48%
5-Year Cost Estimate	5%	Up/Down Market Rank	B – D

Benefits		Investment Information	
Investment Objective	Income	Telephone	800-338-2550
5-Year Projected Return	+29%	Minimum Investment	$1,000
Safety Rating (0-100)	91%	Telephone Switching	4 per yr; free
Yield (8/93)	5.2%	Total Assets	$312 million

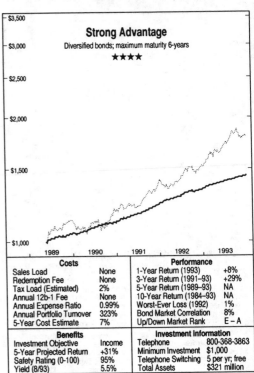

Strong Advantage
Diversified bonds; maximum maturity 6-years
★★★★

Costs		Performance	
Sales Load	None	1-Year Return (1993)	+8%
Redemption Fee	None	3-Year Return (1991–93)	+29%
Tax Load (Estimated)	2%	5-Year Return (1989–93)	NA
Annual 12b-1 Fee	None	10-Year Return (1984–93)	NA
Annual Expense Ratio	0.99%	Worst-Ever Loss (1992)	1%
Annual Portfolio Turnover	323%	Bond Market Correlation	8%
5-Year Cost Estimate	7%	Up/Down Market Rank	E – A

Benefits		Investment Information	
Investment Objective	Income	Telephone	800-368-3863
5-Year Projected Return	+31%	Minimum Investment	$1,000
Safety Rating (0-100)	95%	Telephone Switching	5 per yr; free
Yield (8/93)	5.5%	Total Assets	$321 million

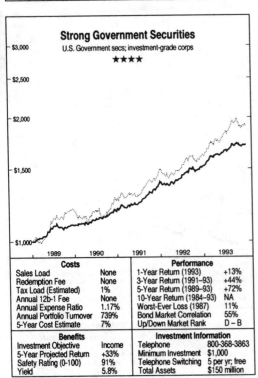

Strong Government Securities
U.S. Government secs; investment-grade corps
★★★★

Costs		Performance	
Sales Load	None	1-Year Return (1993)	+13%
Redemption Fee	None	3-Year Return (1991–93)	+44%
Tax Load (Estimated)	1%	5-Year Return (1989–93)	+72%
Annual 12b-1 Fee	None	10-Year Return (1984–93)	NA
Annual Expense Ratio	1.17%	Worst-Ever Loss (1987)	11%
Annual Portfolio Turnover	739%	Bond Market Correlation	55%
5-Year Cost Estimate	7%	Up/Down Market Rank	D – B

Benefits		Investment Information	
Investment Objective	Income	Telephone	800-368-3863
5-Year Projected Return	+33%	Minimum Investment	$1,000
Safety Rating (0-100)	91%	Telephone Switching	5 per yr; free
Yield	5.8%	Total Assets	$150 million

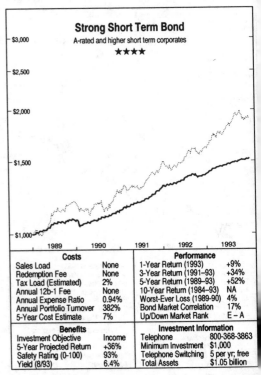

Strong Short Term Bond
A-rated and higher short term corporates
★★★★

Costs		Performance	
Sales Load	None	1-Year Return (1993)	+9%
Redemption Fee	None	3-Year Return (1991–93)	+34%
Tax Load (Estimated)	2%	5-Year Return (1989–93)	+52%
Annual 12b-1 Fee	None	10-Year Return (1984–93)	NA
Annual Expense Ratio	0.94%	Worst-Ever Loss (1989-90)	4%
Annual Portfolio Turnover	382%	Bond Market Correlation	17%
5-Year Cost Estimate	7%	Up/Down Market Rank	E – A

Benefits		Investment Information	
Investment Objective	Income	Telephone	800-368-3863
5-Year Projected Return	+36%	Minimum Investment	$1,000
Safety Rating (0-100)	93%	Telephone Switching	5 per yr; free
Yield (8/93)	6.4%	Total Assets	$1.05 billion

BOND

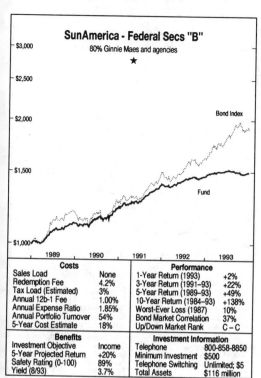

SunAmerica - Federal Secs "B"
80% Ginnie Maes and agencies
★

Bond Index

Fund

Costs		Performance	
Sales Load	None	1-Year Return (1993)	+2%
Redemption Fee	4.2%	3-Year Return (1991–93)	+22%
Tax Load (Estimated)	3%	5-Year Return (1989–93)	+49%
Annual 12b-1 Fee	1.00%	10-Year Return (1984–93)	+138%
Annual Expense Ratio	1.85%	Worst-Ever Loss (1987)	10%
Annual Portfolio Turnover	54%	Bond Market Correlation	37%
5-Year Cost Estimate	18%	Up/Down Market Rank	C – C

Benefits		Investment Information	
Investment Objective	Income	Telephone	800-858-8850
5-Year Projected Return	+20%	Minimum Investment	$500
Safety Rating (0-100)	89%	Telephone Switching	Unlimited; $5
Yield (8/93)	3.7%	Total Assets	$116 million

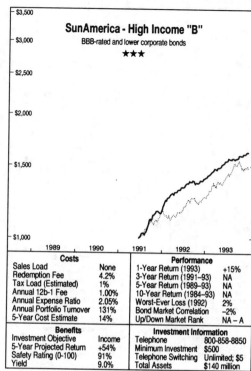

SunAmerica - High Income "B"
BBB-rated and lower corporate bonds
★★★

Costs		Performance	
Sales Load	None	1-Year Return (1993)	+15%
Redemption Fee	4.2%	3-Year Return (1991–93)	NA
Tax Load (Estimated)	1%	5-Year Return (1989–93)	NA
Annual 12b-1 Fee	1.00%	10-Year Return (1984–93)	NA
Annual Expense Ratio	2.05%	Worst-Ever Loss (1992)	2%
Annual Portfolio Turnover	131%	Bond Market Correlation	–2%
5-Year Cost Estimate	14%	Up/Down Market Rank	NA – A

Benefits		Investment Information	
Investment Objective	Income	Telephone	800-858-8850
5-Year Projected Return	+54%	Minimum Investment	$500
Safety Rating (0-100)	91%	Telephone Switching	Unlimited; $5
Yield	9.0%	Total Assets	$140 million

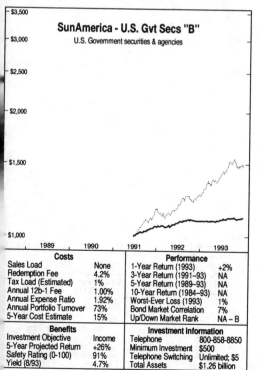

SunAmerica - U.S. Gvt Secs "B"
U.S. Government securities & agencies

Costs		Performance	
Sales Load	None	1-Year Return (1993)	+2%
Redemption Fee	4.2%	3-Year Return (1991–93)	NA
Tax Load (Estimated)	1%	5-Year Return (1989–93)	NA
Annual 12b-1 Fee	1.00%	10-Year Return (1984–93)	NA
Annual Expense Ratio	1.92%	Worst-Ever Loss (1993)	1%
Annual Portfolio Turnover	73%	Bond Market Correlation	7%
5-Year Cost Estimate	15%	Up/Down Market Rank	NA – B

Benefits		Investment Information	
Investment Objective	Income	Telephone	800-858-8850
5-Year Projected Return	+26%	Minimum Investment	$500
Safety Rating (0-100)	91%	Telephone Switching	Unlimited; $5
Yield (8/93)	4.7%	Total Assets	$1.26 billion

Templeteon Emerging Mkts Incme
Foreign - 65% high-yield bonds

Costs		Performance	
Sales Load	None	1-Year Return (1993)	NA
Redemption Fee	None	3-Year Return (1991–93)	NA
Tax Load (Estimated)	NA	5-Year Return (1989–93)	NA
Annual 12b-1 Fee	None	10-Year Return (1984–93)	NA
Annual Expense Ratio	1.00%	Worst-Ever Loss (1993)	3%
Annual Portfolio Turnover	0%	Bond Market Correlation	NA
5-Year Cost Estimate	5%	Up/Down Market Rank	NA – NA

Benefits		Investment Information	
Investment Objective	Growth	Telephone	800-292-9293
5-Year Projected Return	NA	Minimum Investment	None
Safety Rating (0-100)	NA	Telephone Switching	Via broker
Yield	NA	Total Assets	$0 million

Templeton Global Income

Foreign & U.S. - Government securities

Chart showing values from $1,000 to $3,000, years 1989–1993, with "Bond Index" and "Fund" lines

Costs		Performance	
Sales Load	None	1-Year Return (1993)	–8%
Redemption Fee	None	3-Year Return (1991–93)	+22%
Tax Load (Estimated)	3%	5-Year Return (1989–93)	+41%
Annual 12b-1 Fee	None	10-Year Return (1984–93)	NA
Annual Expense Ratio	0.81%	Worst-Ever Loss (1990)	18%
Annual Portfolio Turnover	198%	Bond Market Correlation	1%
5-Year Cost Estimate	10%	Up/Down Market Rank	E – C

Benefits		Investment Information	
Investment Objective	Income	Telephone	800-292-9293
5-Year Projected Return	NA	Minimum Investment	None
Safety Rating (0-100)	69%	Telephone Switching	Via broker
Yield	NA	Total Assets	$995 million

Templeton Income

Foreign & U.S. - bonds; dividend-paying stks

Chart showing values from $1,000 to $3,000, years 1989–1993

Costs		Performance	
Sales Load	4.7%	1-Year Return (1993)	+11%
Redemption Fee	None	3-Year Return (1991–93)	+32%
Tax Load (Estimated)	2%	5-Year Return (1989–93)	+58%
Annual 12b-1 Fee	0.25%	10-Year Return (1984–93)	NA
Annual Expense Ratio	1.24%	Worst-Ever Loss (1987-88)	8%
Annual Portfolio Turnover	267%	Bond Market Correlation	17%
5-Year Cost Estimate	13%	Up/Down Market Rank	E – B

Benefits		Investment Information	
Investment Objective	Income	Telephone	800-292-9293
5-Year Projected Return	+36%	Minimum Investment	$100
Safety Rating (0-100)	89%	Telephone Switching	Unlimited;free
Yield (4/93)	6.4%	Total Assets	$199 million

Thomson - U.S. Government "B"

U.S. Government securities; options

★

Chart showing values from $1,000 to $3,000, years 1989–1993

Costs		Performance	
Sales Load	None	1-Year Return (1993)	+7%
Redemption Fee	1.0%	3-Year Return (1991–93)	+27%
Tax Load (Estimated)	0%	5-Year Return (1989–93)	+52%
Annual 12b-1 Fee	1.00%	10-Year Return (1984–93)	NA
Annual Expense Ratio	1.80%	Worst-Ever Loss (1987)	8%
Annual Portfolio Turnover	156%	Bond Market Correlation	68%
5-Year Cost Estimate	10%	Up/Down Market Rank	D – D

Benefits		Investment Information	
Investment Objective	Income	Telephone	800-628-1237
5-Year Projected Return	+23%	Minimum Investment	$1,000
Safety Rating (0-100)	87%	Telephone Switching	Unlimited;free
Yield (8/93)	4.2%	Total Assets	$554 million

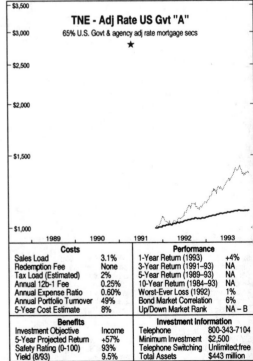

TNE - Adj Rate US Gvt "A"

65% U.S. Govt & agency adj rate mortgage secs

★

Chart showing values from $1,000 to $3,500, years 1989–1993

Costs		Performance	
Sales Load	3.1%	1-Year Return (1993)	+4%
Redemption Fee	None	3-Year Return (1991–93)	NA
Tax Load (Estimated)	2%	5-Year Return (1989–93)	NA
Annual 12b-1 Fee	0.25%	10-Year Return (1984–93)	NA
Annual Expense Ratio	0.60%	Worst-Ever Loss (1992)	1%
Annual Portfolio Turnover	49%	Bond Market Correlation	6%
5-Year Cost Estimate	8%	Up/Down Market Rank	NA – B

Benefits		Investment Information	
Investment Objective	Income	Telephone	800-343-7104
5-Year Projected Return	+57%	Minimum Investment	$2,500
Safety Rating (0-100)	93%	Telephone Switching	Unlimited;free
Yield (8/93)	9.5%	Total Assets	$443 million

BOND

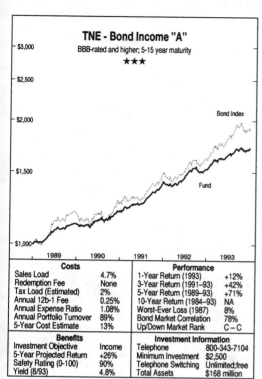

TNE - Bond Income "A"
BBB-rated and higher; 5-15 year maturity
★★★

$3,000
$2,500
$2,000 — Bond Index
$1,500 — Fund
$1,000

1989　1990　1991　1992　1993

Costs		Performance	
Sales Load	4.7%	1-Year Return (1993)	+12%
Redemption Fee	None	3-Year Return (1991–93)	+42%
Tax Load (Estimated)	2%	5-Year Return (1989–93)	+71%
Annual 12b-1 Fee	0.25%	10-Year Return (1984–93)	NA
Annual Expense Ratio	1.08%	Worst-Ever Loss (1987)	8%
Annual Portfolio Turnover	89%	Bond Market Correlation	78%
5-Year Cost Estimate	13%	Up/Down Market Rank	C – C

Benefits		Investment Information	
Investment Objective	Income	Telephone	800-343-7104
5-Year Projected Return	+26%	Minimum Investment	$2,500
Safety Rating (0-100)	90%	Telephone Switching	Unlimited;free
Yield (8/93)	4.8%	Total Assets	$168 million

TNE - Global Government "A"
Foreign & U.S. - government securities

$3,000
$2,500
$2,000
$1,500
$1,000

1989　1990　1991　1992　1993

Costs		Performance	
Sales Load	4.7%	1-Year Return (1993)	+13%
Redemption Fee	None	3-Year Return (1991–93)	+30%
Tax Load (Estimated)	1%	5-Year Return (1989–93)	+50%
Annual 12b-1 Fee	0.25%	10-Year Return (1984–93)	NA
Annual Expense Ratio	2.19%	Worst-Ever Loss (1991)	7%
Annual Portfolio Turnover	278%	Bond Market Correlation	30%
5-Year Cost Estimate	18%	Up/Down Market Rank	C – D

Benefits		Investment Information	
Investment Objective	Income	Telephone	800-343-7104
5-Year Projected Return	+14%	Minimum Investment	$2,500
Safety Rating (0-100)	86%	Telephone Switching	Unlimited;free
Yield (8/93)	2.6%	Total Assets	$18 million

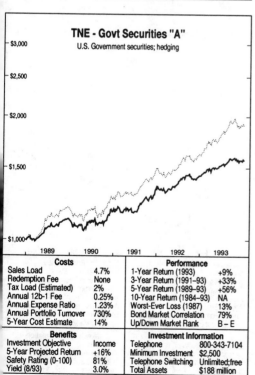

TNE - Govt Securities "A"
U.S. Government securities; hedging

$3,000
$2,500
$2,000
$1,500
$1,000

1989　1990　1991　1992　1993

Costs		Performance	
Sales Load	4.7%	1-Year Return (1993)	+9%
Redemption Fee	None	3-Year Return (1991–93)	+33%
Tax Load (Estimated)	2%	5-Year Return (1989–93)	+56%
Annual 12b-1 Fee	0.25%	10-Year Return (1984–93)	NA
Annual Expense Ratio	1.23%	Worst-Ever Loss (1987)	13%
Annual Portfolio Turnover	730%	Bond Market Correlation	79%
5-Year Cost Estimate	14%	Up/Down Market Rank	B – E

Benefits		Investment Information	
Investment Objective	Income	Telephone	800-343-7104
5-Year Projected Return	+16%	Minimum Investment	$2,500
Safety Rating (0-100)	81%	Telephone Switching	Unlimited;free
Yield (8/93)	3.0%	Total Assets	$188 million

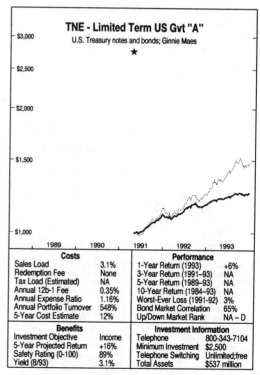

TNE - Limited Term US Gvt "A"
U.S. Treasury notes and bonds; Ginnie Maes
★

$3,000
$2,500
$2,000
$1,500
$1,000

1989　1990　1991　1992　1993

Costs		Performance	
Sales Load	3.1%	1-Year Return (1993)	+6%
Redemption Fee	None	3-Year Return (1991–93)	NA
Tax Load (Estimated)	NA	5-Year Return (1989–93)	NA
Annual 12b-1 Fee	0.35%	10-Year Return (1984–93)	NA
Annual Expense Ratio	1.16%	Worst-Ever Loss (1991-92)	3%
Annual Portfolio Turnover	548%	Bond Market Correlation	65%
5-Year Cost Estimate	12%	Up/Down Market Rank	NA – D

Benefits		Investment Information	
Investment Objective	Income	Telephone	800-343-7104
5-Year Projected Return	+16%	Minimum Investment	$2,500
Safety Rating (0-100)	89%	Telephone Switching	Unlimited;free
Yield (8/93)	3.1%	Total Assets	$537 million

BOND

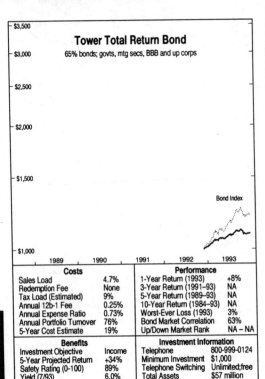

Tower Total Return Bond
65% bonds; govts, mtg secs, BBB and up corps

Bond Index

Costs		Performance	
Sales Load	4.7%	1-Year Return (1993)	+8%
Redemption Fee	None	3-Year Return (1991–93)	NA
Tax Load (Estimated)	9%	5-Year Return (1989–93)	NA
Annual 12b-1 Fee	0.25%	10-Year Return (1984–93)	NA
Annual Expense Ratio	0.73%	Worst-Ever Loss (1993)	3%
Annual Portfolio Turnover	76%	Bond Market Correlation	63%
5-Year Cost Estimate	19%	Up/Down Market Rank	NA – NA

Benefits		Investment Information	
Investment Objective	Income	Telephone	800-999-0124
5-Year Projected Return	+34%	Minimum Investment	$1,000
Safety Rating (0-100)	89%	Telephone Switching	Unlimited;free
Yield (7/93)	6.0%	Total Assets	$57 million

Transamerica - Government Secs
U.S. Government securities; Ginnie Maes

Costs		Performance	
Sales Load	5.0%	1-Year Return (1993)	+8%
Redemption Fee	None	3-Year Return (1991–93)	+34%
Tax Load (Estimated)	Neg.	5-Year Return (1989–93)	+61%
Annual 12b-1 Fee	0.25%	10-Year Return (1984–93)	NA
Annual Expense Ratio	1.20%	Worst-Ever Loss (1987)	5%
Annual Portfolio Turnover	199%	Bond Market Correlation	72%
5-Year Cost Estimate	12%	Up/Down Market Rank	C – E

Benefits		Investment Information	
Investment Objective	Income	Telephone	800-472-3863
5-Year Projected Return	+19%	Minimum Investment	$1,000
Safety Rating (0-100)	83%	Telephone Switching	Unlimited;free
Yield (8/93)	3.6%	Total Assets	$708 million

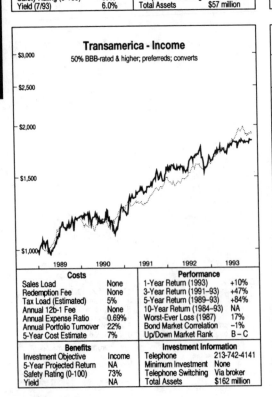

Transamerica - Income
50% BBB-rated & higher; preferreds; converts

Costs		Performance	
Sales Load	None	1-Year Return (1993)	+10%
Redemption Fee	None	3-Year Return (1991–93)	+47%
Tax Load (Estimated)	5%	5-Year Return (1989–93)	+84%
Annual 12b-1 Fee	None	10-Year Return (1984–93)	NA
Annual Expense Ratio	0.69%	Worst-Ever Loss (1987)	17%
Annual Portfolio Turnover	22%	Bond Market Correlation	–1%
5-Year Cost Estimate	7%	Up/Down Market Rank	B – C

Benefits		Investment Information	
Investment Objective	Income	Telephone	213-742-4141
5-Year Projected Return	NA	Minimum Investment	None
Safety Rating (0-100)	73%	Telephone Switching	Via broker
Yield	NA	Total Assets	$162 million

Transamerica - Investment Qlty
BBB-rated and higher corporates; options

Costs		Performance	
Sales Load	5.0%	1-Year Return (1993)	+9%
Redemption Fee	None	3-Year Return (1991–93)	+37%
Tax Load (Estimated)	3%	5-Year Return (1989–93)	+65%
Annual 12b-1 Fee	0.25%	10-Year Return (1984–93)	NA
Annual Expense Ratio	1.28%	Worst-Ever Loss (1987)	8%
Annual Portfolio Turnover	316%	Bond Market Correlation	69%
5-Year Cost Estimate	16%	Up/Down Market Rank	A – E

Benefits		Investment Information	
Investment Objective	Income	Telephone	800-472-3863
5-Year Projected Return	+20%	Minimum Investment	$1,000
Safety Rating (0-100)	85%	Telephone Switching	Unlimited;free
Yield (8/93)	3.8%	Total Assets	$109 million

BOND

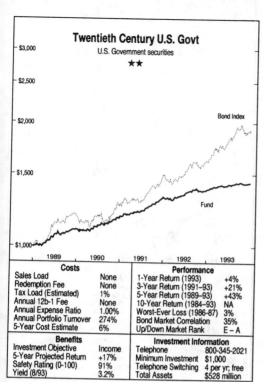

Twentieth Century U.S. Govt
U.S. Government securities
★★

Bond Index

Fund

Costs		Performance	
Sales Load	None	1-Year Return (1993)	+4%
Redemption Fee	None	3-Year Return (1991–93)	+21%
Tax Load (Estimated)	1%	5-Year Return (1989–93)	+43%
Annual 12b-1 Fee	None	10-Year Return (1984–93)	NA
Annual Expense Ratio	1.00%	Worst-Ever Loss (1986-87)	3%
Annual Portfolio Turnover	274%	Bond Market Correlation	35%
5-Year Cost Estimate	6%	Up/Down Market Rank	E – A

Benefits		Investment Information	
Investment Objective	Income	Telephone	800-345-2021
5-Year Projected Return	+17%	Minimum Investment	$1,000
Safety Rating (0-100)	91%	Telephone Switching	4 per yr; free
Yield (8/93)	3.2%	Total Assets	$528 million

United - Bond
Government securities; options; futures

Costs		Performance	
Sales Load	6.1%	1-Year Return (1993)	+13%
Redemption Fee	None	3-Year Return (1991–93)	+45%
Tax Load (Estimated)	2%	5-Year Return (1989–93)	+66%
Annual 12b-1 Fee	0.25%	10-Year Return (1984–93)	NA
Annual Expense Ratio	0.90%	Worst-Ever Loss (1987)	7%
Annual Portfolio Turnover	189%	Bond Market Correlation	75%
5-Year Cost Estimate	13%	Up/Down Market Rank	B – E

Benefits		Investment Information	
Investment Objective	Income	Telephone	800-366-5465
5-Year Projected Return	NA	Minimum Investment	$500
Safety Rating (0-100)	85%	Telephone Switching	Mail only
Yield	NA	Total Assets	$631 million

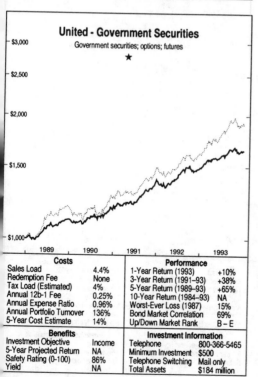

United - Government Securities
Government securities; options; futures
★

Costs		Performance	
Sales Load	4.4%	1-Year Return (1993)	+10%
Redemption Fee	None	3-Year Return (1991–93)	+38%
Tax Load (Estimated)	4%	5-Year Return (1989–93)	+65%
Annual 12b-1 Fee	0.25%	10-Year Return (1984–93)	NA
Annual Expense Ratio	0.96%	Worst-Ever Loss (1987)	15%
Annual Portfolio Turnover	136%	Bond Market Correlation	69%
5-Year Cost Estimate	14%	Up/Down Market Rank	B – E

Benefits		Investment Information	
Investment Objective	Income	Telephone	800-366-5465
5-Year Projected Return	NA	Minimum Investment	$500
Safety Rating (0-100)	86%	Telephone Switching	Mail only
Yield	NA	Total Assets	$184 million

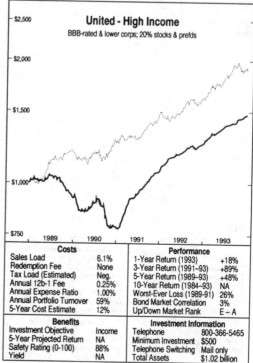

United - High Income
BBB-rated & lower corps; 20% stocks & prefds

Costs		Performance	
Sales Load	6.1%	1-Year Return (1993)	+18%
Redemption Fee	None	3-Year Return (1991–93)	+89%
Tax Load (Estimated)	Neg.	5-Year Return (1989–93)	+48%
Annual 12b-1 Fee	0.25%	10-Year Return (1984–93)	NA
Annual Expense Ratio	1.00%	Worst-Ever Loss (1989-91)	26%
Annual Portfolio Turnover	59%	Bond Market Correlation	3%
5-Year Cost Estimate	12%	Up/Down Market Rank	E – A

Benefits		Investment Information	
Investment Objective	Income	Telephone	800-366-5465
5-Year Projected Return	NA	Minimum Investment	$500
Safety Rating (0-100)	88%	Telephone Switching	Mail only
Yield	NA	Total Assets	$1.02 billion

BOND

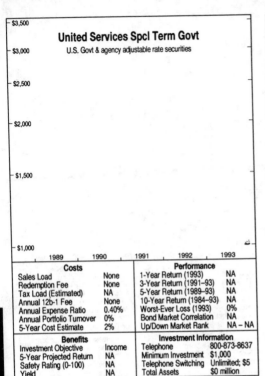

United Services Spcl Term Govt
U.S. Govt & agency adjustable rate securities

Costs		Performance	
Sales Load	None	1-Year Return (1993)	NA
Redemption Fee	None	3-Year Return (1991–93)	NA
Tax Load (Estimated)	NA	5-Year Return (1989–93)	NA
Annual 12b-1 Fee	None	10-Year Return (1984–93)	NA
Annual Expense Ratio	0.40%	Worst-Ever Loss (1993)	0%
Annual Portfolio Turnover	0%	Bond Market Correlation	NA
5-Year Cost Estimate	2%	Up/Down Market Rank	NA – NA

Benefits		Investment Information	
Investment Objective	Income	Telephone	800-873-8637
5-Year Projected Return	NA	Minimum Investment	$1,000
Safety Rating (0-100)	NA	Telephone Switching	Unlimited; $5
Yield	NA	Total Assets	$0 million

US Life Income
50% BBB & higher corps; converts; pfds; levgd

Costs		Performance	
Sales Load	None	1-Year Return (1993)	+6%
Redemption Fee	None	3-Year Return (1991–93)	+75%
Tax Load (Estimated)	Neg.	5-Year Return (1989–93)	+75%
Annual 12b-1 Fee	None	10-Year Return (1984–93)	NA
Annual Expense Ratio	1.38%	Worst-Ever Loss (1986-90)	36%
Annual Portfolio Turnover	37%	Bond Market Correlation	0%
5-Year Cost Estimate	9%	Up/Down Market Rank	D – E

Benefits		Investment Information	
Investment Objective	Income	Telephone	212-709-6000
5-Year Projected Return	NA	Minimum Investment	None
Safety Rating (0-100)	71%	Telephone Switching	Via broker
Yield	NA	Total Assets	$55 million

USAA Income
Bonds; preferreds; stocks; governments
★★★★

Costs		Performance	
Sales Load	None	1-Year Return (1993)	+10%
Redemption Fee	None	3-Year Return (1991–93)	+42%
Tax Load (Estimated)	3%	5-Year Return (1989–93)	+77%
Annual 12b-1 Fee	None	10-Year Return (1984–93)	+204%
Annual Expense Ratio	0.41%	Worst-Ever Loss (1987)	9%
Annual Portfolio Turnover	45%	Bond Market Correlation	68%
5-Year Cost Estimate	4%	Up/Down Market Rank	A – D

Benefits		Investment Information	
Investment Objective	Income	Telephone	800-531-8181
5-Year Projected Return	+38%	Minimum Investment	$1,000
Safety Rating (0-100)	89%	Telephone Switching	6 per yr; $5
Yield (8/93)	6.7%	Total Assets	$1.79 billion

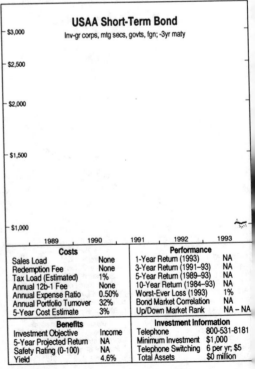

USAA Short-Term Bond
Inv-gr corps, mtg secs, govts, fgn; -3yr maty

Costs		Performance	
Sales Load	None	1-Year Return (1993)	NA
Redemption Fee	None	3-Year Return (1991–93)	NA
Tax Load (Estimated)	1%	5-Year Return (1989–93)	NA
Annual 12b-1 Fee	None	10-Year Return (1984–93)	NA
Annual Expense Ratio	0.50%	Worst-Ever Loss (1993)	1%
Annual Portfolio Turnover	32%	Bond Market Correlation	NA
5-Year Cost Estimate	3%	Up/Down Market Rank	NA – NA

Benefits		Investment Information	
Investment Objective	Income	Telephone	800-531-8181
5-Year Projected Return	NA	Minimum Investment	$1,000
Safety Rating (0-100)	NA	Telephone Switching	6 per yr; $5
Yield	4.6%	Total Assets	$0 million

BOND

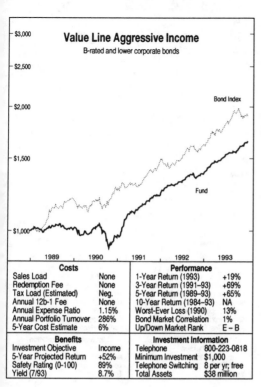

Value Line Aggressive Income
B-rated and lower corporate bonds

Costs		Performance	
Sales Load	None	1-Year Return (1993)	+19%
Redemption Fee	None	3-Year Return (1991–93)	+69%
Tax Load (Estimated)	Neg.	5-Year Return (1989–93)	+65%
Annual 12b-1 Fee	None	10-Year Return (1984–93)	NA
Annual Expense Ratio	1.15%	Worst-Ever Loss (1990)	13%
Annual Portfolio Turnover	286%	Bond Market Correlation	1%
5-Year Cost Estimate	6%	Up/Down Market Rank	E – B

Benefits		Investment Information	
Investment Objective	Income	Telephone	800-223-0818
5-Year Projected Return	+52%	Minimum Investment	$1,000
Safety Rating (0-100)	89%	Telephone Switching	8 per yr; free
Yield (7/93)	8.7%	Total Assets	$38 million

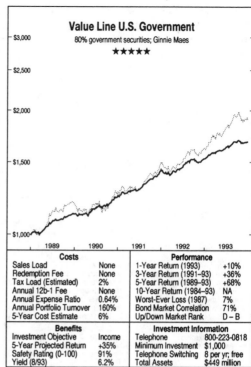

Value Line U.S. Government
80% government securities; Ginnie Maes
★★★★★

Costs		Performance	
Sales Load	None	1-Year Return (1993)	+10%
Redemption Fee	None	3-Year Return (1991–93)	+36%
Tax Load (Estimated)	2%	5-Year Return (1989–93)	+68%
Annual 12b-1 Fee	None	10-Year Return (1984–93)	NA
Annual Expense Ratio	0.64%	Worst-Ever Loss (1987)	7%
Annual Portfolio Turnover	160%	Bond Market Correlation	71%
5-Year Cost Estimate	6%	Up/Down Market Rank	D – B

Benefits		Investment Information	
Investment Objective	Income	Telephone	800-223-0818
5-Year Projected Return	+35%	Minimum Investment	$1,000
Safety Rating (0-100)	91%	Telephone Switching	8 per yr; free
Yield (8/93)	6.2%	Total Assets	$449 million

Van Eck - World Income
Global debt securities

Costs		Performance	
Sales Load	5.0%	1-Year Return (1993)	+5%
Redemption Fee	None	3-Year Return (1991–93)	+21%
Tax Load (Estimated)	Neg.	5-Year Return (1989–93)	+57%
Annual 12b-1 Fee	0.25%	10-Year Return (1984–93)	NA
Annual Expense Ratio	1.32%	Worst-Ever Loss (1992-93)	12%
Annual Portfolio Turnover	52%	Bond Market Correlation	4%
5-Year Cost Estimate	12%	Up/Down Market Rank	D – B

Benefits		Investment Information	
Investment Objective	Income	Telephone	800-221-2220
5-Year Projected Return	+40%	Minimum Investment	$1,000
Safety Rating (0-100)	84%	Telephone Switching	Unlimited;free
Yield (8/93)	7.0%	Total Assets	$297 million

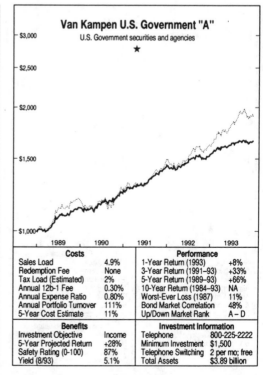

Van Kampen U.S. Government "A"
U.S. Government securities and agencies
★

Costs		Performance	
Sales Load	4.9%	1-Year Return (1993)	+8%
Redemption Fee	None	3-Year Return (1991–93)	+33%
Tax Load (Estimated)	2%	5-Year Return (1989–93)	+66%
Annual 12b-1 Fee	0.30%	10-Year Return (1984–93)	NA
Annual Expense Ratio	0.80%	Worst-Ever Loss (1987)	11%
Annual Portfolio Turnover	111%	Bond Market Correlation	48%
5-Year Cost Estimate	11%	Up/Down Market Rank	A – D

Benefits		Investment Information	
Investment Objective	Income	Telephone	800-225-2222
5-Year Projected Return	+28%	Minimum Investment	$1,500
Safety Rating (0-100)	87%	Telephone Switching	2 per mo; free
Yield (8/93)	5.1%	Total Assets	$3.89 billion

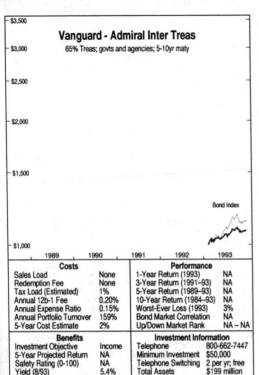

Vanguard - Admiral Inter Treas
65% Treas; govts and agencies; 5-10yr maty

Bond Index

Costs		Performance	
Sales Load	None	1-Year Return (1993)	NA
Redemption Fee	None	3-Year Return (1991–93)	NA
Tax Load (Estimated)	1%	5-Year Return (1989–93)	NA
Annual 12b-1 Fee	0.20%	10-Year Return (1984–93)	NA
Annual Expense Ratio	0.15%	Worst-Ever Loss (1993)	3%
Annual Portfolio Turnover	159%	Bond Market Correlation	NA
5-Year Cost Estimate	2%	Up/Down Market Rank	NA – NA

Benefits		Investment Information	
Investment Objective	Income	Telephone	800-662-7447
5-Year Projected Return	NA	Minimum Investment	$50,000
Safety Rating (0-100)	NA	Telephone Switching	2 per yr; free
Yield (8/93)	5.4%	Total Assets	$199 million

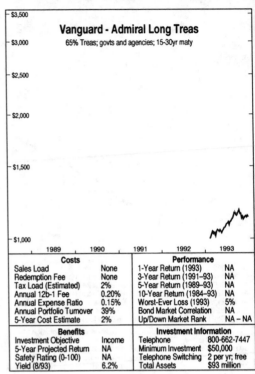

Vanguard - Admiral Long Treas
65% Treas; govts and agencies; 15-30yr maty

Costs		Performance	
Sales Load	None	1-Year Return (1993)	NA
Redemption Fee	None	3-Year Return (1991–93)	NA
Tax Load (Estimated)	2%	5-Year Return (1989–93)	NA
Annual 12b-1 Fee	0.20%	10-Year Return (1984–93)	NA
Annual Expense Ratio	0.15%	Worst-Ever Loss (1993)	5%
Annual Portfolio Turnover	39%	Bond Market Correlation	NA
5-Year Cost Estimate	2%	Up/Down Market Rank	NA – NA

Benefits		Investment Information	
Investment Objective	Income	Telephone	800-662-7447
5-Year Projected Return	NA	Minimum Investment	$50,000
Safety Rating (0-100)	NA	Telephone Switching	2 per yr; free
Yield (8/93)	6.2%	Total Assets	$93 million

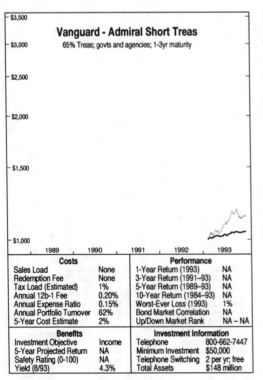

Vanguard - Admiral Short Treas
65% Treas; govts and agencies; 1-3yr maturity

Costs		Performance	
Sales Load	None	1-Year Return (1993)	NA
Redemption Fee	None	3-Year Return (1991–93)	NA
Tax Load (Estimated)	1%	5-Year Return (1989–93)	NA
Annual 12b-1 Fee	0.20%	10-Year Return (1984–93)	NA
Annual Expense Ratio	0.15%	Worst-Ever Loss (1993)	1%
Annual Portfolio Turnover	62%	Bond Market Correlation	NA
5-Year Cost Estimate	2%	Up/Down Market Rank	NA – NA

Benefits		Investment Information	
Investment Objective	Income	Telephone	800-662-7447
5-Year Projected Return	NA	Minimum Investment	$50,000
Safety Rating (0-100)	NA	Telephone Switching	2 per yr; free
Yield (8/93)	4.3%	Total Assets	$148 million

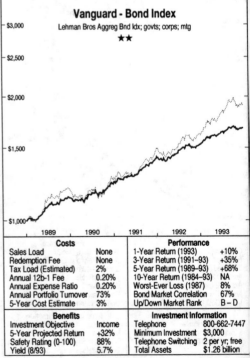

Vanguard - Bond Index
Lehman Bros Aggreg Bnd Idx; govts; corps; mtg
★★

Costs		Performance	
Sales Load	None	1-Year Return (1993)	+10%
Redemption Fee	None	3-Year Return (1991–93)	+35%
Tax Load (Estimated)	2%	5-Year Return (1989–93)	+68%
Annual 12b-1 Fee	0.20%	10-Year Return (1984–93)	NA
Annual Expense Ratio	0.20%	Worst-Ever Loss (1987)	8%
Annual Portfolio Turnover	73%	Bond Market Correlation	67%
5-Year Cost Estimate	3%	Up/Down Market Rank	B – D

Benefits		Investment Information	
Investment Objective	Income	Telephone	800-662-7447
5-Year Projected Return	+32%	Minimum Investment	$3,000
Safety Rating (0-100)	88%	Telephone Switching	2 per yr; free
Yield (8/93)	5.7%	Total Assets	$1.26 billion

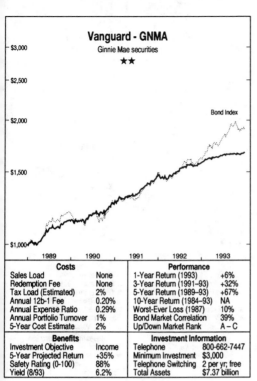

Vanguard - GNMA
Ginnie Mae securities
★★

Bond Index

Costs		Performance	
Sales Load	None	1-Year Return (1993)	+6%
Redemption Fee	None	3-Year Return (1991–93)	+32%
Tax Load (Estimated)	2%	5-Year Return (1989–93)	+67%
Annual 12b-1 Fee	0.20%	10-Year Return (1984–93)	NA
Annual Expense Ratio	0.29%	Worst-Ever Loss (1987)	10%
Annual Portfolio Turnover	1%	Bond Market Correlation	39%
5-Year Cost Estimate	2%	Up/Down Market Rank	A – C

Benefits		Investment Information	
Investment Objective	Income	Telephone	800-662-7447
5-Year Projected Return	+35%	Minimum Investment	$3,000
Safety Rating (0-100)	88%	Telephone Switching	2 per yr; free
Yield (8/93)	6.2%	Total Assets	$7.37 billion

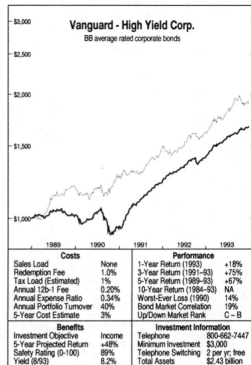

Vanguard - High Yield Corp.
BB average rated corporate bonds

Costs		Performance	
Sales Load	None	1-Year Return (1993)	+18%
Redemption Fee	1.0%	3-Year Return (1991–93)	+75%
Tax Load (Estimated)	1%	5-Year Return (1989–93)	+67%
Annual 12b-1 Fee	0.20%	10-Year Return (1984–93)	NA
Annual Expense Ratio	0.34%	Worst-Ever Loss (1990)	14%
Annual Portfolio Turnover	40%	Bond Market Correlation	19%
5-Year Cost Estimate	3%	Up/Down Market Rank	C – B

Benefits		Investment Information	
Investment Objective	Income	Telephone	800-662-7447
5-Year Projected Return	+48%	Minimum Investment	$3,000
Safety Rating (0-100)	89%	Telephone Switching	2 per yr; free
Yield (8/93)	8.2%	Total Assets	$2.43 billion

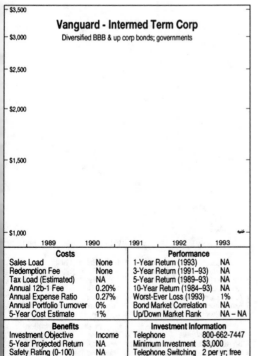

Vanguard - Intermed Term Corp
Diversified BBB & up corp bonds; governments

Costs		Performance	
Sales Load	None	1-Year Return (1993)	NA
Redemption Fee	None	3-Year Return (1991–93)	NA
Tax Load (Estimated)	NA	5-Year Return (1989–93)	NA
Annual 12b-1 Fee	0.20%	10-Year Return (1984–93)	NA
Annual Expense Ratio	0.27%	Worst-Ever Loss (1993)	1%
Annual Portfolio Turnover	0%	Bond Market Correlation	NA
5-Year Cost Estimate	1%	Up/Down Market Rank	NA – NA

Benefits		Investment Information	
Investment Objective	Income	Telephone	800-662-7447
5-Year Projected Return	NA	Minimum Investment	$3,000
Safety Rating (0-100)	NA	Telephone Switching	2 per yr; free
Yield (8/93)	5.1%	Total Assets	$0 million

Vanguard - Long Term Corporate
Investment-grade corporate bonds

Costs		Performance	
Sales Load	None	1-Year Return (1993)	+14%
Redemption Fee	None	3-Year Return (1991–93)	+52%
Tax Load (Estimated)	3%	5-Year Return (1989–93)	+86%
Annual 12b-1 Fee	0.20%	10-Year Return (1984–93)	NA
Annual Expense Ratio	0.31%	Worst-Ever Loss (1987)	13%
Annual Portfolio Turnover	80%	Bond Market Correlation	75%
5-Year Cost Estimate	5%	Up/Down Market Rank	A – E

Benefits		Investment Information	
Investment Objective	Income	Telephone	800-662-7447
5-Year Projected Return	+36%	Minimum Investment	$3,000
Safety Rating (0-100)	82%	Telephone Switching	2 per yr; free
Yield (8/93)	6.4%	Total Assets	$3.17 billion

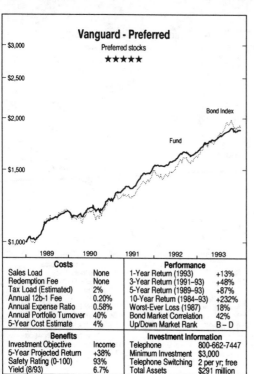

Vanguard - Preferred

Preferred stocks

★★★★★

Bond Index

Fund

$3,000					
$2,500					
$2,000					
$1,500					
$1,000					
	1989	1990	1991	1992	1993

Costs		Performance	
Sales Load	None	1-Year Return (1993)	+13%
Redemption Fee	None	3-Year Return (1991–93)	+48%
Tax Load (Estimated)	2%	5-Year Return (1989–93)	+87%
Annual 12b-1 Fee	0.20%	10-Year Return (1984–93)	+232%
Annual Expense Ratio	0.58%	Worst-Ever Loss (1987)	18%
Annual Portfolio Turnover	40%	Bond Market Correlation	42%
5-Year Cost Estimate	4%	Up/Down Market Rank	B – D

Benefits		Investment Information	
Investment Objective	Income	Telephone	800-662-7447
5-Year Projected Return	+38%	Minimum Investment	$3,000
Safety Rating (0-100)	93%	Telephone Switching	2 per yr; free
Yield (8/93)	6.7%	Total Assets	$291 million

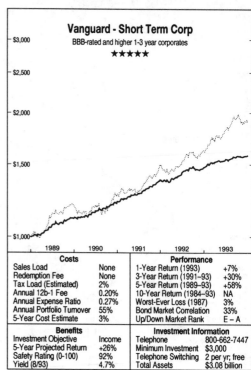

Vanguard - Short Term Corp

BBB-rated and higher 1-3 year corporates

★★★★★

$3,000					
$2,500					
$2,000					
$1,500					
$1,000					
	1989	1990	1991	1992	1993

Costs		Performance	
Sales Load	None	1-Year Return (1993)	+7%
Redemption Fee	None	3-Year Return (1991–93)	+30%
Tax Load (Estimated)	2%	5-Year Return (1989–93)	+58%
Annual 12b-1 Fee	0.20%	10-Year Return (1984–93)	NA
Annual Expense Ratio	0.27%	Worst-Ever Loss (1987)	3%
Annual Portfolio Turnover	55%	Bond Market Correlation	33%
5-Year Cost Estimate	3%	Up/Down Market Rank	E – A

Benefits		Investment Information	
Investment Objective	Income	Telephone	800-662-7447
5-Year Projected Return	+26%	Minimum Investment	$3,000
Safety Rating (0-100)	92%	Telephone Switching	2 per yr; free
Yield (8/93)	4.7%	Total Assets	$3.08 billion

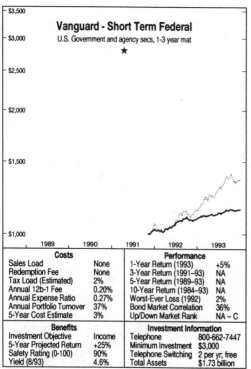

Vanguard - Short Term Federal

U.S. Government and agency secs, 1-3 year mat

★

$3,500					
$3,000					
$2,500					
$2,000					
$1,500					
$1,000					
	1989	1990	1991	1992	1993

Costs		Performance	
Sales Load	None	1-Year Return (1993)	+5%
Redemption Fee	None	3-Year Return (1991–93)	NA
Tax Load (Estimated)	2%	5-Year Return (1989–93)	NA
Annual 12b-1 Fee	0.20%	10-Year Return (1984–93)	NA
Annual Expense Ratio	0.27%	Worst-Ever Loss (1992)	2%
Annual Portfolio Turnover	37%	Bond Market Correlation	36%
5-Year Cost Estimate	3%	Up/Down Market Rank	NA – C

Benefits		Investment Information	
Investment Objective	Income	Telephone	800-662-7447
5-Year Projected Return	+25%	Minimum Investment	$3,000
Safety Rating (0-100)	90%	Telephone Switching	2 per yr; free
Yield (8/93)	4.6%	Total Assets	$1.73 billion

Vanguard - US Treas Long Term

U.S. Treasury bonds; 15-30 year maturity

$3,000					
$2,500					
$2,000					
$1,500					
$1,000					
	1989	1990	1991	1992	1993

Costs		Performance	
Sales Load	None	1-Year Return (1993)	+16%
Redemption Fee	None	3-Year Return (1991–93)	+47%
Tax Load (Estimated)	4%	5-Year Return (1989–93)	+84%
Annual 12b-1 Fee	0.20%	10-Year Return (1984–93)	NA
Annual Expense Ratio	0.27%	Worst-Ever Loss (1987)	16%
Annual Portfolio Turnover	6%	Bond Market Correlation	83%
5-Year Cost Estimate	2%	Up/Down Market Rank	A – E

Benefits		Investment Information	
Investment Objective	Income	Telephone	800-662-7447
5-Year Projected Return	+35%	Minimum Investment	$3,000
Safety Rating (0-100)	75%	Telephone Switching	2 per yr; free
Yield (8/93)	6.2%	Total Assets	$826 million

BOND

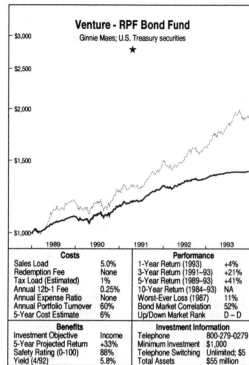

Venture - Income Plus
80% BBB-rated and lower corporates

Bond Index

Fund

Costs		Performance	
Sales Load	5.0%	1-Year Return (1993)	+17%
Redemption Fee	None	3-Year Return (1991–93)	+71%
Tax Load (Estimated)	Neg.	5-Year Return (1989–93)	+31%
Annual 12b-1 Fee	0.25%	10-Year Return (1984–93)	NA
Annual Expense Ratio	1.75%	Worst-Ever Loss (1989-91)	27%
Annual Portfolio Turnover	90%	Bond Market Correlation	–2%
5-Year Cost Estimate	15%	Up/Down Market Rank	E – A

Benefits		Investment Information	
Investment Objective	Income	Telephone	800-279-0279
5-Year Projected Return	+48%	Minimum Investment	$1,000
Safety Rating (0-100)	90%	Telephone Switching	Unlimited; $5
Yield (7/92)	8.2%	Total Assets	$47 million

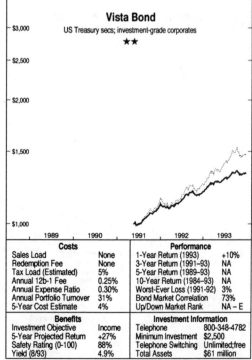

Venture - RPF Bond Fund
Ginnie Maes; U.S. Treasury securities
★

Costs		Performance	
Sales Load	5.0%	1-Year Return (1993)	+4%
Redemption Fee	None	3-Year Return (1991–93)	+21%
Tax Load (Estimated)	1%	5-Year Return (1989–93)	+41%
Annual 12b-1 Fee	0.25%	10-Year Return (1984–93)	NA
Annual Expense Ratio	None	Worst-Ever Loss (1987)	11%
Annual Portfolio Turnover	60%	Bond Market Correlation	52%
5-Year Cost Estimate	6%	Up/Down Market Rank	D – D

Benefits		Investment Information	
Investment Objective	Income	Telephone	800-279-0279
5-Year Projected Return	+33%	Minimum Investment	$1,000
Safety Rating (0-100)	88%	Telephone Switching	Unlimited; $5
Yield (4/92)	5.8%	Total Assets	$55 million

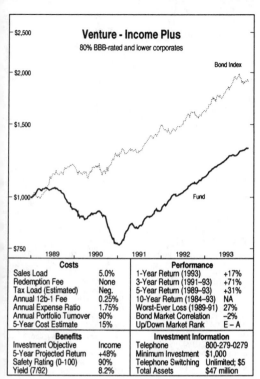

Vestaur Securities
75% BBB-rated & higher corps; pfds; conv; lvg

Costs		Performance	
Sales Load	None	1-Year Return (1993)	+7%
Redemption Fee	None	3-Year Return (1991–93)	+36%
Tax Load (Estimated)	0%	5-Year Return (1989–93)	+74%
Annual 12b-1 Fee	None	10-Year Return (1984–93)	NA
Annual Expense Ratio	0.90%	Worst-Ever Loss (1987)	18%
Annual Portfolio Turnover	42%	Bond Market Correlation	–1%
5-Year Cost Estimate	7%	Up/Down Market Rank	A – B

Benefits		Investment Information	
Investment Objective	Income	Telephone	215-567-3969
5-Year Projected Return	NA	Minimum Investment	None
Safety Rating (0-100)	79%	Telephone Switching	Via broker
Yield	NA	Total Assets	$100 million

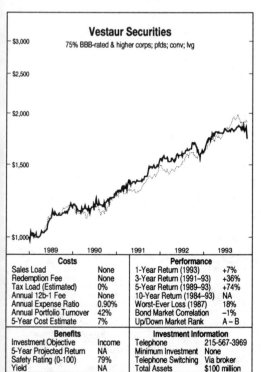

Vista Bond
US Treasury secs; investment-grade corporates
★★

Costs		Performance	
Sales Load	None	1-Year Return (1993)	+10%
Redemption Fee	None	3-Year Return (1991–93)	NA
Tax Load (Estimated)	5%	5-Year Return (1989–93)	NA
Annual 12b-1 Fee	0.25%	10-Year Return (1984–93)	NA
Annual Expense Ratio	0.30%	Worst-Ever Loss (1991-92)	3%
Annual Portfolio Turnover	31%	Bond Market Correlation	73%
5-Year Cost Estimate	4%	Up/Down Market Rank	NA – E

Benefits		Investment Information	
Investment Objective	Income	Telephone	800-348-4782
5-Year Projected Return	+27%	Minimum Investment	$2,500
Safety Rating (0-100)	88%	Telephone Switching	Unlimited;free
Yield (8/93)	4.9%	Total Assets	$61 million

BOND

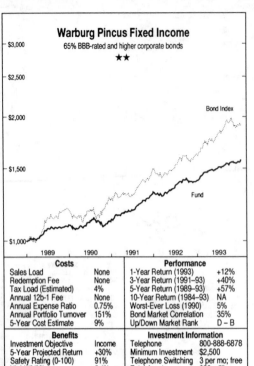

Warburg Pincus Fixed Income
65% BBB-rated and higher corporate bonds
★★

Bond Index

Fund

Costs		Performance	
Sales Load	None	1-Year Return (1993)	+12%
Redemption Fee	None	3-Year Return (1991–93)	+40%
Tax Load (Estimated)	4%	5-Year Return (1989–93)	+57%
Annual 12b-1 Fee	None	10-Year Return (1984–93)	NA
Annual Expense Ratio	0.75%	Worst-Ever Loss (1990)	5%
Annual Portfolio Turnover	151%	Bond Market Correlation	35%
5-Year Cost Estimate	9%	Up/Down Market Rank	D – B

Benefits		Investment Information	
Investment Objective	Income	Telephone	800-888-6878
5-Year Projected Return	+30%	Minimum Investment	$2,500
Safety Rating (0-100)	91%	Telephone Switching	3 per mo; free
Yield (8/93)	5.4%	Total Assets	$80 million

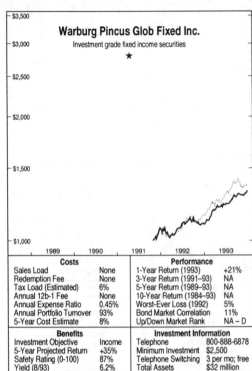

Warburg Pincus Glob Fixed Inc.
Investment grade fixed income securities
★

Costs		Performance	
Sales Load	None	1-Year Return (1993)	+21%
Redemption Fee	None	3-Year Return (1991–93)	NA
Tax Load (Estimated)	6%	5-Year Return (1989–93)	NA
Annual 12b-1 Fee	None	10-Year Return (1984–93)	NA
Annual Expense Ratio	0.45%	Worst-Ever Loss (1992)	5%
Annual Portfolio Turnover	93%	Bond Market Correlation	11%
5-Year Cost Estimate	8%	Up/Down Market Rank	NA – D

Benefits		Investment Information	
Investment Objective	Income	Telephone	800-888-6878
5-Year Projected Return	+35%	Minimum Investment	$2,500
Safety Rating (0-100)	87%	Telephone Switching	3 per mo; free
Yield (8/93)	6.2%	Total Assets	$32 million

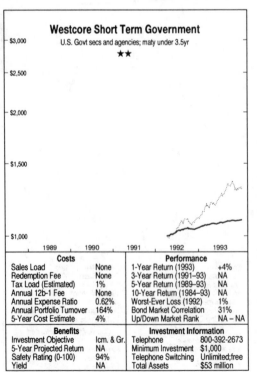

Westcore Short Term Government
U.S. Govt secs and agencies; maty under 3.5yr
★★

Costs		Performance	
Sales Load	None	1-Year Return (1993)	+4%
Redemption Fee	None	3-Year Return (1991–93)	NA
Tax Load (Estimated)	1%	5-Year Return (1989–93)	NA
Annual 12b-1 Fee	None	10-Year Return (1984–93)	NA
Annual Expense Ratio	0.62%	Worst-Ever Loss (1992)	1%
Annual Portfolio Turnover	164%	Bond Market Correlation	31%
5-Year Cost Estimate	4%	Up/Down Market Rank	NA – NA

Benefits		Investment Information	
Investment Objective	Icm. & Gr.	Telephone	800-392-2673
5-Year Projected Return	NA	Minimum Investment	$1,000
Safety Rating (0-100)	94%	Telephone Switching	Unlimited;free
Yield	NA	Total Assets	$53 million

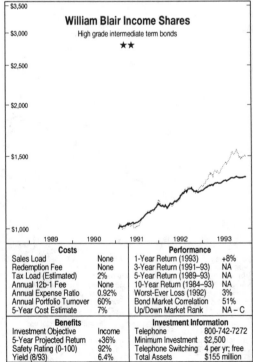

William Blair Income Shares
High grade intermediate term bonds
★★

Costs		Performance	
Sales Load	None	1-Year Return (1993)	+8%
Redemption Fee	None	3-Year Return (1991–93)	NA
Tax Load (Estimated)	2%	5-Year Return (1989–93)	NA
Annual 12b-1 Fee	None	10-Year Return (1984–93)	NA
Annual Expense Ratio	0.92%	Worst-Ever Loss (1992)	3%
Annual Portfolio Turnover	60%	Bond Market Correlation	51%
5-Year Cost Estimate	7%	Up/Down Market Rank	NA – C

Benefits		Investment Information	
Investment Objective	Income	Telephone	800-742-7272
5-Year Projected Return	+36%	Minimum Investment	$2,500
Safety Rating (0-100)	92%	Telephone Switching	4 per yr; free
Yield (8/93)	6.4%	Total Assets	$155 million

BOND

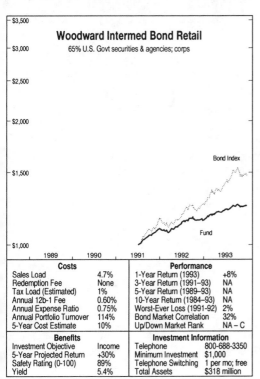

Woodward Intermed Bond Retail

65% U.S. Govt securities & agencies; corps

Bond Index

Fund

Costs		Performance	
Sales Load	4.7%	1-Year Return (1993)	+8%
Redemption Fee	None	3-Year Return (1991–93)	NA
Tax Load (Estimated)	1%	5-Year Return (1989–93)	NA
Annual 12b-1 Fee	0.60%	10-Year Return (1984–93)	NA
Annual Expense Ratio	0.75%	Worst-Ever Loss (1991-92)	2%
Annual Portfolio Turnover	114%	Bond Market Correlation	32%
5-Year Cost Estimate	10%	Up/Down Market Rank	NA – C

Benefits		Investment Information	
Investment Objective	Income	Telephone	800-688-3350
5-Year Projected Return	+30%	Minimum Investment	$1,000
Safety Rating (0-100)	89%	Telephone Switching	1 per mo; free
Yield	5.4%	Total Assets	$318 million

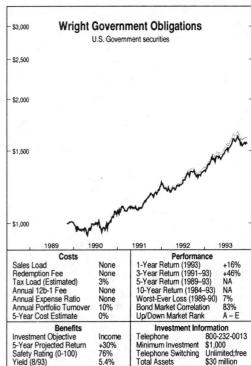

Wright Government Obligations

U.S. Government securities

Costs		Performance	
Sales Load	None	1-Year Return (1993)	+16%
Redemption Fee	None	3-Year Return (1991–93)	+46%
Tax Load (Estimated)	3%	5-Year Return (1989–93)	NA
Annual 12b-1 Fee	None	10-Year Return (1984–93)	NA
Annual Expense Ratio	None	Worst-Ever Loss (1989-90)	7%
Annual Portfolio Turnover	10%	Bond Market Correlation	83%
5-Year Cost Estimate	0%	Up/Down Market Rank	A – E

Benefits		Investment Information	
Investment Objective	Income	Telephone	800-232-0013
5-Year Projected Return	+30%	Minimum Investment	$1,000
Safety Rating (0-100)	76%	Telephone Switching	Unlimited;free
Yield (8/93)	5.4%	Total Assets	$30 million

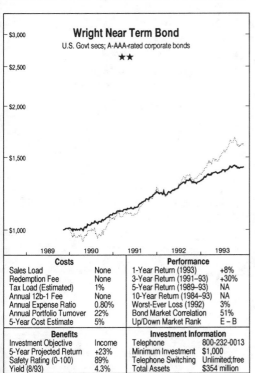

Wright Near Term Bond

U.S. Govt secs; A-AAA-rated corporate bonds

★★

Costs		Performance	
Sales Load	None	1-Year Return (1993)	+8%
Redemption Fee	None	3-Year Return (1991–93)	+30%
Tax Load (Estimated)	1%	5-Year Return (1989–93)	NA
Annual 12b-1 Fee	None	10-Year Return (1984–93)	NA
Annual Expense Ratio	0.80%	Worst-Ever Loss (1992)	3%
Annual Portfolio Turnover	22%	Bond Market Correlation	51%
5-Year Cost Estimate	5%	Up/Down Market Rank	E – B

Benefits		Investment Information	
Investment Objective	Income	Telephone	800-232-0013
5-Year Projected Return	+23%	Minimum Investment	$1,000
Safety Rating (0-100)	89%	Telephone Switching	Unlimited;free
Yield (8/93)	4.3%	Total Assets	$354 million

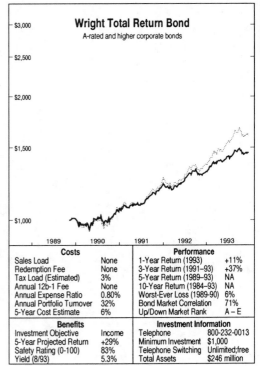

Wright Total Return Bond

A-rated and higher corporate bonds

Costs		Performance	
Sales Load	None	1-Year Return (1993)	+11%
Redemption Fee	None	3-Year Return (1991–93)	+37%
Tax Load (Estimated)	3%	5-Year Return (1989–93)	NA
Annual 12b-1 Fee	None	10-Year Return (1984–93)	NA
Annual Expense Ratio	0.80%	Worst-Ever Loss (1989-90)	6%
Annual Portfolio Turnover	32%	Bond Market Correlation	71%
5-Year Cost Estimate	6%	Up/Down Market Rank	A – E

Benefits		Investment Information	
Investment Objective	Income	Telephone	800-232-0013
5-Year Projected Return	+29%	Minimum Investment	$1,000
Safety Rating (0-100)	83%	Telephone Switching	Unlimited;free
Yield (8/93)	5.3%	Total Assets	$246 million

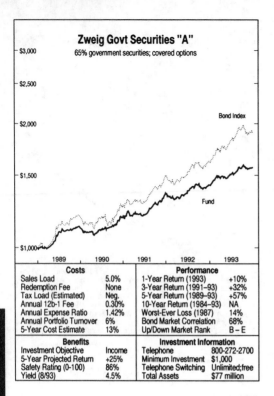

Zweig Govt Securities "A"
65% government securities; covered options

Costs		Performance	
Sales Load	5.0%	1-Year Return (1993)	+10%
Redemption Fee	None	3-Year Return (1991–93)	+32%
Tax Load (Estimated)	Neg.	5-Year Return (1989–93)	+57%
Annual 12b-1 Fee	0.30%	10-Year Return (1984–93)	NA
Annual Expense Ratio	1.42%	Worst-Ever Loss (1987)	14%
Annual Portfolio Turnover	6%	Bond Market Correlation	68%
5-Year Cost Estimate	13%	Up/Down Market Rank	B – E

Benefits		Investment Information	
Investment Objective	Income	Telephone	800-272-2700
5-Year Projected Return	+25%	Minimum Investment	$1,000
Safety Rating (0-100)	86%	Telephone Switching	Unlimited;free
Yield (8/93)	4.5%	Total Assets	$77 million

Chapter Ten

The Buyer's Guide to Tax-Free Funds

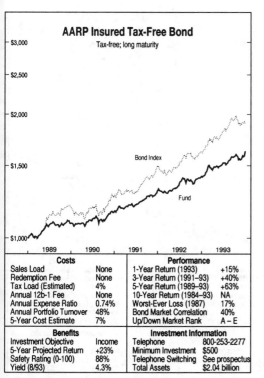

AARP Insured Tax-Free Bond
Tax-free; long maturity

Costs		Performance	
Sales Load	None	1-Year Return (1993)	+15%
Redemption Fee	None	3-Year Return (1991–93)	+40%
Tax Load (Estimated)	4%	5-Year Return (1989–93)	+63%
Annual 12b-1 Fee	None	10-Year Return (1984–93)	NA
Annual Expense Ratio	0.74%	Worst-Ever Loss (1987)	17%
Annual Portfolio Turnover	48%	Bond Market Correlation	40%
5-Year Cost Estimate	7%	Up/Down Market Rank	A – E

Benefits		Investment Information	
Investment Objective	Income	Telephone	800-253-2277
5-Year Projected Return	+23%	Minimum Investment	$500
Safety Rating (0-100)	88%	Telephone Switching	See prospectus
Yield (8/93)	4.3%	Total Assets	$2.04 billion

Aim - Municipal Bond "A"
80% BBB-rated and higher municipals
★

Costs		Performance	
Sales Load	5.0%	1-Year Return (1993)	+12%
Redemption Fee	None	3-Year Return (1991–93)	+38%
Tax Load (Estimated)	3%	5-Year Return (1989–93)	+60%
Annual 12b-1 Fee	0.25%	10-Year Return (1984–93)	NA
Annual Expense Ratio	0.90%	Worst-Ever Loss (1987)	17%
Annual Portfolio Turnover	30%	Bond Market Correlation	49%
5-Year Cost Estimate	12%	Up/Down Market Rank	A – E

Benefits		Investment Information	
Investment Objective	Income	Telephone	800-959-4246
5-Year Projected Return	+23%	Minimum Investment	$500
Safety Rating (0-100)	90%	Telephone Switching	Unlimited;free
Yield (8/93)	4.2%	Total Assets	$293 million

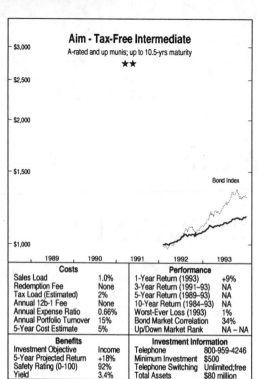

Aim - Tax-Free Intermediate
A-rated and up munis; up to 10.5-yrs maturity
★★

Bond Index

Costs		Performance	
Sales Load	1.0%	1-Year Return (1993)	+9%
Redemption Fee	None	3-Year Return (1991–93)	NA
Tax Load (Estimated)	2%	5-Year Return (1989–93)	NA
Annual 12b-1 Fee	None	10-Year Return (1984–93)	NA
Annual Expense Ratio	0.66%	Worst-Ever Loss (1993)	1%
Annual Portfolio Turnover	15%	Bond Market Correlation	34%
5-Year Cost Estimate	5%	Up/Down Market Rank	NA – NA

Benefits		Investment Information	
Investment Objective	Income	Telephone	800-959-4246
5-Year Projected Return	+18%	Minimum Investment	$500
Safety Rating (0-100)	92%	Telephone Switching	Unlimited;free
Yield	3.4%	Total Assets	$80 million

Alliance Insured Municipal "A"
Insured municipal bonds

Costs		Performance	
Sales Load	4.4%	1-Year Return (1993)	+9%
Redemption Fee	None	3-Year Return (1991–93)	+33%
Tax Load (Estimated)	3%	5-Year Return (1989–93)	+56%
Annual 12b-1 Fee	0.30%	10-Year Return (1984–93)	NA
Annual Expense Ratio	0.72%	Worst-Ever Loss (1987)	25%
Annual Portfolio Turnover	152%	Bond Market Correlation	40%
5-Year Cost Estimate	12%	Up/Down Market Rank	C – C

Benefits		Investment Information	
Investment Objective	Income	Telephone	800-221-5672
5-Year Projected Return	+27%	Minimum Investment	$250
Safety Rating (0-100)	88%	Telephone Switching	Unlimited;free
Yield (8/93)	4.9%	Total Assets	$171 million

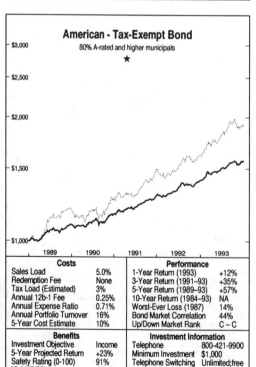

American - Tax-Exempt Bond
80% A-rated and higher municipals
★

Costs		Performance	
Sales Load	5.0%	1-Year Return (1993)	+12%
Redemption Fee	None	3-Year Return (1991–93)	+35%
Tax Load (Estimated)	3%	5-Year Return (1989–93)	+57%
Annual 12b-1 Fee	0.25%	10-Year Return (1984–93)	NA
Annual Expense Ratio	0.71%	Worst-Ever Loss (1987)	14%
Annual Portfolio Turnover	16%	Bond Market Correlation	44%
5-Year Cost Estimate	10%	Up/Down Market Rank	C – C

Benefits		Investment Information	
Investment Objective	Income	Telephone	800-421-9900
5-Year Projected Return	+23%	Minimum Investment	$1,000
Safety Rating (0-100)	91%	Telephone Switching	Unlimited;free
Yield (8/93)	4.3%	Total Assets	$1.06 billion

American Capital Muni Bond "A"
50% A-rated and higher municipals
★★★

Costs		Performance	
Sales Load	5.0%	1-Year Return (1993)	+11%
Redemption Fee	None	3-Year Return (1991–93)	+36%
Tax Load (Estimated)	3%	5-Year Return (1989–93)	+59%
Annual 12b-1 Fee	0.25%	10-Year Return (1984–93)	NA
Annual Expense Ratio	0.90%	Worst-Ever Loss (1987)	19%
Annual Portfolio Turnover	2%	Bond Market Correlation	43%
5-Year Cost Estimate	10%	Up/Down Market Rank	D – C

Benefits		Investment Information	
Investment Objective	Income	Telephone	800-421-5666
5-Year Projected Return	+23%	Minimum Investment	$500
Safety Rating (0-100)	92%	Telephone Switching	1 per mo; $5
Yield (8/93)	4.2%	Total Assets	$325 million

TAX FREE

Atlas National Municipal
AA-rated and higher municipals

Bond Index

	1989	1990	1991	1992	1993

Costs		Performance	
Sales Load	3.1%	1-Year Return (1993)	+13%
Redemption Fee	None	3-Year Return (1991–93)	NA
Tax Load (Estimated)	4%	5-Year Return (1989–93)	NA
Annual 12b-1 Fee	0.25%	10-Year Return (1984–93)	NA
Annual Expense Ratio	0.83%	Worst-Ever Loss (1992)	4%
Annual Portfolio Turnover	6%	Bond Market Correlation	40%
5-Year Cost Estimate	8%	Up/Down Market Rank	NA – D

Benefits		Investment Information	
Investment Objective	Income	Telephone	800-933-2852
5-Year Projected Return	+26%	Minimum Investment	$2,500
Safety Rating (0-100)	89%	Telephone Switching	Unlimited;free
Yield	4.8%	Total Assets	$0 million

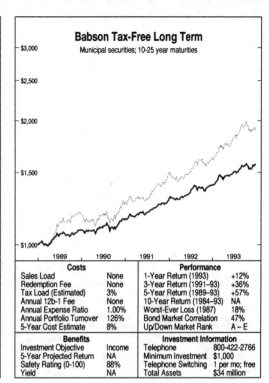

Babson Tax-Free Long Term
Municipal securities; 10-25 year maturities

	1989	1990	1991	1992	1993

Costs		Performance	
Sales Load	None	1-Year Return (1993)	+12%
Redemption Fee	None	3-Year Return (1991–93)	+36%
Tax Load (Estimated)	3%	5-Year Return (1989–93)	+57%
Annual 12b-1 Fee	None	10-Year Return (1984–93)	NA
Annual Expense Ratio	1.00%	Worst-Ever Loss (1987)	18%
Annual Portfolio Turnover	126%	Bond Market Correlation	47%
5-Year Cost Estimate	8%	Up/Down Market Rank	A – E

Benefits		Investment Information	
Investment Objective	Income	Telephone	800-422-2766
5-Year Projected Return	NA	Minimum Investment	$1,000
Safety Rating (0-100)	88%	Telephone Switching	1 per mo; free
Yield	NA	Total Assets	$34 million

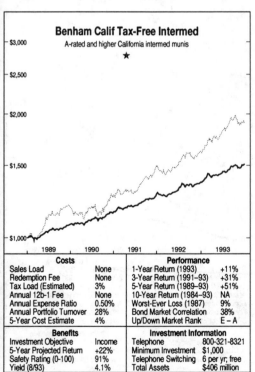

Benham Calif Tax-Free Intermed
A-rated and higher California intermed munis

★

	1989	1990	1991	1992	1993

Costs		Performance	
Sales Load	None	1-Year Return (1993)	+11%
Redemption Fee	None	3-Year Return (1991–93)	+31%
Tax Load (Estimated)	3%	5-Year Return (1989–93)	+51%
Annual 12b-1 Fee	None	10-Year Return (1984–93)	NA
Annual Expense Ratio	0.50%	Worst-Ever Loss (1987)	9%
Annual Portfolio Turnover	28%	Bond Market Correlation	38%
5-Year Cost Estimate	4%	Up/Down Market Rank	E – A

Benefits		Investment Information	
Investment Objective	Income	Telephone	800-321-8321
5-Year Projected Return	+22%	Minimum Investment	$1,000
Safety Rating (0-100)	91%	Telephone Switching	6 per yr; free
Yield (8/93)	4.1%	Total Assets	$406 million

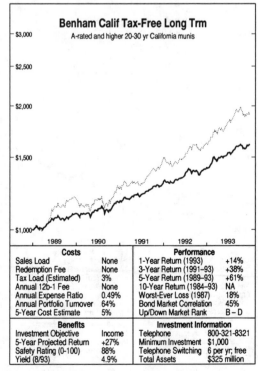

Benham Calif Tax-Free Long Trm
A-rated and higher 20-30 yr California munis

	1989	1990	1991	1992	1993

Costs		Performance	
Sales Load	None	1-Year Return (1993)	+14%
Redemption Fee	None	3-Year Return (1991–93)	+38%
Tax Load (Estimated)	3%	5-Year Return (1989–93)	+61%
Annual 12b-1 Fee	None	10-Year Return (1984–93)	NA
Annual Expense Ratio	0.49%	Worst-Ever Loss (1987)	18%
Annual Portfolio Turnover	64%	Bond Market Correlation	45%
5-Year Cost Estimate	5%	Up/Down Market Rank	B – D

Benefits		Investment Information	
Investment Objective	Income	Telephone	800-321-8321
5-Year Projected Return	+27%	Minimum Investment	$1,000
Safety Rating (0-100)	88%	Telephone Switching	6 per yr; free
Yield (8/93)	4.9%	Total Assets	$325 million

Benham Natl Tax-Free Long Term
A-rated and higher long-term municipals

Bond Index

Fund

Costs		Performance	
Sales Load	None	1-Year Return (1993)	+14%
Redemption Fee	None	3-Year Return (1991–93)	+41%
Tax Load (Estimated)	2%	5-Year Return (1989–93)	+65%
Annual 12b-1 Fee	None	10-Year Return (1984–93)	NA
Annual Expense Ratio	0.72%	Worst-Ever Loss (1987)	19%
Annual Portfolio Turnover	105%	Bond Market Correlation	51%
5-Year Cost Estimate	6%	Up/Down Market Rank	B – E

Benefits		Investment Information	
Investment Objective	Income	Telephone	800-321-8321
5-Year Projected Return	+25%	Minimum Investment	$1,000
Safety Rating (0-100)	87%	Telephone Switching	6 per yr; free
Yield (8/93)	4.6%	Total Assets	$69 million

BlackRock Investment Qlty Muni
80% BBB-rated and higher municipals

Costs		Performance	
Sales Load	None	1-Year Return (1993)	NA
Redemption Fee	None	3-Year Return (1991–93)	NA
Tax Load (Estimated)	1%	5-Year Return (1989–93)	NA
Annual 12b-1 Fee	None	10-Year Return (1984–93)	NA
Annual Expense Ratio	0.87%	Worst-Ever Loss (1993)	9%
Annual Portfolio Turnover	234%	Bond Market Correlation	NA
5-Year Cost Estimate	7%	Up/Down Market Rank	NA – NA

Benefits		Investment Information	
Investment Objective	Income	Telephone	800-688-0928
5-Year Projected Return	NA	Minimum Investment	None
Safety Rating (0-100)	NA	Telephone Switching	Via broker
Yield	6.5%	Total Assets	$236 million

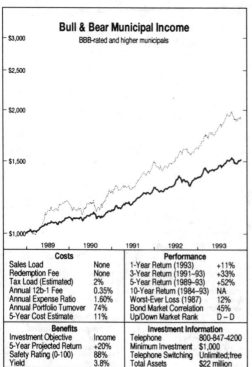

Bull & Bear Municipal Income
BBB-rated and higher municipals

Costs		Performance	
Sales Load	None	1-Year Return (1993)	+11%
Redemption Fee	None	3-Year Return (1991–93)	+33%
Tax Load (Estimated)	2%	5-Year Return (1989–93)	+52%
Annual 12b-1 Fee	0.35%	10-Year Return (1984–93)	NA
Annual Expense Ratio	1.60%	Worst-Ever Loss (1987)	12%
Annual Portfolio Turnover	74%	Bond Market Correlation	45%
5-Year Cost Estimate	11%	Up/Down Market Rank	D – D

Benefits		Investment Information	
Investment Objective	Income	Telephone	800-847-4200
5-Year Projected Return	+20%	Minimum Investment	$1,000
Safety Rating (0-100)	88%	Telephone Switching	Unlimited;free
Yield	3.8%	Total Assets	$22 million

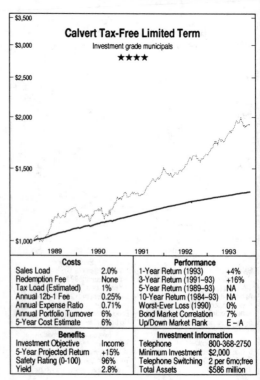

Calvert Tax-Free Limited Term
Investment grade municipals
★★★★

Costs		Performance	
Sales Load	2.0%	1-Year Return (1993)	+4%
Redemption Fee	None	3-Year Return (1991–93)	+16%
Tax Load (Estimated)	1%	5-Year Return (1989–93)	NA
Annual 12b-1 Fee	0.25%	10-Year Return (1984–93)	NA
Annual Expense Ratio	0.71%	Worst-Ever Loss (1990)	0%
Annual Portfolio Turnover	6%	Bond Market Correlation	7%
5-Year Cost Estimate	6%	Up/Down Market Rank	E – A

Benefits		Investment Information	
Investment Objective	Income	Telephone	800-368-2750
5-Year Projected Return	+15%	Minimum Investment	$2,000
Safety Rating (0-100)	96%	Telephone Switching	2 per 6mo;free
Yield	2.8%	Total Assets	$586 million

TAX FREE

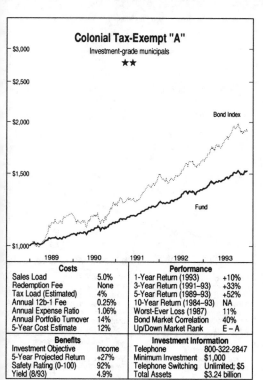

Colonial Tax-Exempt "A"

Investment-grade municipals
★★

Bond Index

Fund

| | | 1989 | 1990 | 1991 | 1992 | 1993 |

Costs		Performance	
Sales Load	5.0%	1-Year Return (1993)	+10%
Redemption Fee	None	3-Year Return (1991–93)	+33%
Tax Load (Estimated)	4%	5-Year Return (1989–93)	+52%
Annual 12b-1 Fee	0.25%	10-Year Return (1984–93)	NA
Annual Expense Ratio	1.06%	Worst-Ever Loss (1987)	11%
Annual Portfolio Turnover	14%	Bond Market Correlation	40%
5-Year Cost Estimate	12%	Up/Down Market Rank	E – A

Benefits		Investment Information	
Investment Objective	Income	Telephone	800-322-2847
5-Year Projected Return	+27%	Minimum Investment	$1,000
Safety Rating (0-100)	92%	Telephone Switching	Unlimited; $5
Yield (8/93)	4.9%	Total Assets	$3.24 billion

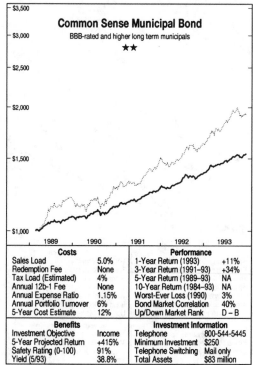

Colonial Tax-Exempt Insrd "A"

Investment-grade municipals; 20+ yr maturity
★

| | | 1989 | 1990 | 1991 | 1992 | 1993 |

Costs		Performance	
Sales Load	5.0%	1-Year Return (1993)	+10%
Redemption Fee	None	3-Year Return (1991–93)	+33%
Tax Load (Estimated)	4%	5-Year Return (1989–93)	+54%
Annual 12b-1 Fee	0.25%	10-Year Return (1984–93)	NA
Annual Expense Ratio	1.06%	Worst-Ever Loss (1987)	17%
Annual Portfolio Turnover	7%	Bond Market Correlation	46%
5-Year Cost Estimate	11%	Up/Down Market Rank	D – C

Benefits		Investment Information	
Investment Objective	Income	Telephone	800-322-2847
5-Year Projected Return	+20%	Minimum Investment	$1,000
Safety Rating (0-100)	90%	Telephone Switching	Unlimited; $5
Yield (8/93)	3.8%	Total Assets	$239 million

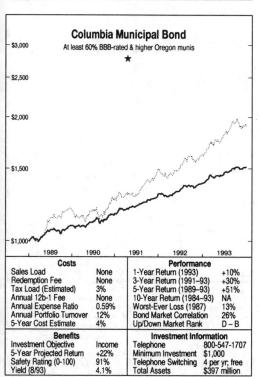

Columbia Municipal Bond

At least 60% BBB-rated & higher Oregon munis
★

| | | 1989 | 1990 | 1991 | 1992 | 1993 |

Costs		Performance	
Sales Load	None	1-Year Return (1993)	+10%
Redemption Fee	None	3-Year Return (1991–93)	+30%
Tax Load (Estimated)	3%	5-Year Return (1989–93)	+51%
Annual 12b-1 Fee	None	10-Year Return (1984–93)	NA
Annual Expense Ratio	0.59%	Worst-Ever Loss (1987)	13%
Annual Portfolio Turnover	12%	Bond Market Correlation	26%
5-Year Cost Estimate	4%	Up/Down Market Rank	D – B

Benefits		Investment Information	
Investment Objective	Income	Telephone	800-547-1707
5-Year Projected Return	+22%	Minimum Investment	$1,000
Safety Rating (0-100)	91%	Telephone Switching	4 per yr; free
Yield (8/93)	4.1%	Total Assets	$397 million

Common Sense Municipal Bond

BBB-rated and higher long term municipals
★★

| | | 1989 | 1990 | 1991 | 1992 | 1993 |

Costs		Performance	
Sales Load	5.0%	1-Year Return (1993)	+11%
Redemption Fee	None	3-Year Return (1991–93)	+34%
Tax Load (Estimated)	4%	5-Year Return (1989–93)	NA
Annual 12b-1 Fee	None	10-Year Return (1984–93)	NA
Annual Expense Ratio	1.15%	Worst-Ever Loss (1990)	3%
Annual Portfolio Turnover	6%	Bond Market Correlation	40%
5-Year Cost Estimate	12%	Up/Down Market Rank	D – B

Benefits		Investment Information	
Investment Objective	Income	Telephone	800-544-5445
5-Year Projected Return	+415%	Minimum Investment	$250
Safety Rating (0-100)	91%	Telephone Switching	Mail only
Yield (5/93)	38.8%	Total Assets	$83 million

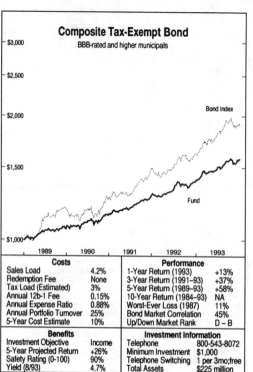

Composite Tax-Exempt Bond
BBB-rated and higher municipals

Costs		Performance	
Sales Load	4.2%	1-Year Return (1993)	+13%
Redemption Fee	None	3-Year Return (1991–93)	+37%
Tax Load (Estimated)	3%	5-Year Return (1989–93)	+58%
Annual 12b-1 Fee	0.15%	10-Year Return (1984–93)	NA
Annual Expense Ratio	0.88%	Worst-Ever Loss (1987)	11%
Annual Portfolio Turnover	25%	Bond Market Correlation	45%
5-Year Cost Estimate	10%	Up/Down Market Rank	D – B

Benefits		Investment Information	
Investment Objective	Income	Telephone	800-543-8072
5-Year Projected Return	+26%	Minimum Investment	$1,000
Safety Rating (0-100)	90%	Telephone Switching	1 per 3mo;free
Yield (8/93)	4.7%	Total Assets	$225 million

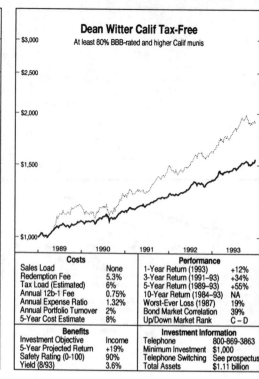

Dean Witter Calif Tax-Free
At least 80% BBB-rated and higher Calif munis

Costs		Performance	
Sales Load	None	1-Year Return (1993)	+12%
Redemption Fee	5.3%	3-Year Return (1991–93)	+34%
Tax Load (Estimated)	6%	5-Year Return (1989–93)	+55%
Annual 12b-1 Fee	0.75%	10-Year Return (1984–93)	NA
Annual Expense Ratio	1.32%	Worst-Ever Loss (1987)	19%
Annual Portfolio Turnover	2%	Bond Market Correlation	39%
5-Year Cost Estimate	8%	Up/Down Market Rank	C – D

Benefits		Investment Information	
Investment Objective	Income	Telephone	800-869-3863
5-Year Projected Return	+19%	Minimum Investment	$1,000
Safety Rating (0-100)	90%	Telephone Switching	See prospectus
Yield (8/93)	3.6%	Total Assets	$1.11 billion

Dean Witter New York Tax-Free
BBB-rated and higher New York municipals

Costs		Performance	
Sales Load	None	1-Year Return (1993)	+14%
Redemption Fee	5.3%	3-Year Return (1991–93)	+40%
Tax Load (Estimated)	6%	5-Year Return (1989–93)	+59%
Annual 12b-1 Fee	0.75%	10-Year Return (1984–93)	NA
Annual Expense Ratio	1.40%	Worst-Ever Loss (1987)	17%
Annual Portfolio Turnover	10%	Bond Market Correlation	38%
5-Year Cost Estimate	9%	Up/Down Market Rank	B – E

Benefits		Investment Information	
Investment Objective	Income	Telephone	800-869-3863
5-Year Projected Return	+57%	Minimum Investment	$1,000
Safety Rating (0-100)	90%	Telephone Switching	See prospectus
Yield (8/93)	9.5%	Total Assets	$232 million

Dean Witter Tax-Exempt Secs
BBB-rated and higher municipal bonds
★

Costs		Performance	
Sales Load	4.2%	1-Year Return (1993)	+11%
Redemption Fee	None	3-Year Return (1991–93)	+37%
Tax Load (Estimated)	5%	5-Year Return (1989–93)	+60%
Annual 12b-1 Fee	None	10-Year Return (1984–93)	NA
Annual Expense Ratio	0.49%	Worst-Ever Loss (1987)	18%
Annual Portfolio Turnover	8%	Bond Market Correlation	46%
5-Year Cost Estimate	7%	Up/Down Market Rank	C – C

Benefits		Investment Information	
Investment Objective	Income	Telephone	800-869-3863
5-Year Projected Return	+25%	Minimum Investment	$1,000
Safety Rating (0-100)	90%	Telephone Switching	See prospectus
Yield (8/93)	4.5%	Total Assets	$1.47 billion

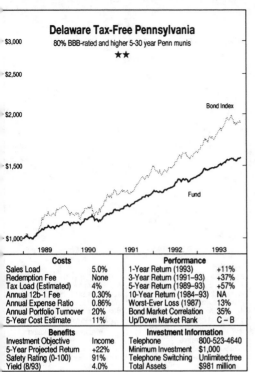

Delaware Tax-Free Pennsylvania

80% BBB-rated and higher 5-30 year Penn munis

★★

Bond Index

Fund

Costs		Performance	
Sales Load	5.0%	1-Year Return (1993)	+11%
Redemption Fee	None	3-Year Return (1991–93)	+37%
Tax Load (Estimated)	4%	5-Year Return (1989–93)	+57%
Annual 12b-1 Fee	0.30%	10-Year Return (1984–93)	NA
Annual Expense Ratio	0.86%	Worst-Ever Loss (1987)	13%
Annual Portfolio Turnover	20%	Bond Market Correlation	35%
5-Year Cost Estimate	11%	Up/Down Market Rank	C – B

Benefits		Investment Information	
Investment Objective	Income	Telephone	800-523-4640
5-Year Projected Return	+22%	Minimum Investment	$1,000
Safety Rating (0-100)	91%	Telephone Switching	Unlimited;free
Yield (8/93)	4.0%	Total Assets	$981 million

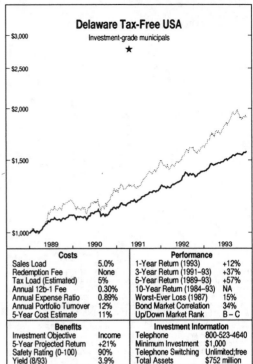

Delaware Tax-Free USA

Investment-grade municipals

★

Costs		Performance	
Sales Load	5.0%	1-Year Return (1993)	+12%
Redemption Fee	None	3-Year Return (1991–93)	+37%
Tax Load (Estimated)	5%	5-Year Return (1989–93)	+57%
Annual 12b-1 Fee	0.30%	10-Year Return (1984–93)	NA
Annual Expense Ratio	0.89%	Worst-Ever Loss (1987)	15%
Annual Portfolio Turnover	12%	Bond Market Correlation	34%
5-Year Cost Estimate	11%	Up/Down Market Rank	B – C

Benefits		Investment Information	
Investment Objective	Income	Telephone	800-523-4640
5-Year Projected Return	+21%	Minimum Investment	$1,000
Safety Rating (0-100)	90%	Telephone Switching	Unlimited;free
Yield (8/93)	3.9%	Total Assets	$752 million

Dreyfus California Tax-Exempt

At least 60% BBB-rated & higher Calif munis

Costs		Performance	
Sales Load	None	1-Year Return (1993)	+12%
Redemption Fee	None	3-Year Return (1991–93)	+31%
Tax Load (Estimated)	4%	5-Year Return (1989–93)	+52%
Annual 12b-1 Fee	0.25%	10-Year Return (1984–93)	NA
Annual Expense Ratio	0.69%	Worst-Ever Loss (1987)	15%
Annual Portfolio Turnover	46%	Bond Market Correlation	42%
5-Year Cost Estimate	6%	Up/Down Market Rank	D – C

Benefits		Investment Information	
Investment Objective	Income	Telephone	800-645-6561
5-Year Projected Return	+26%	Minimum Investment	$2,500
Safety Rating (0-100)	89%	Telephone Switching	Unlimited;free
Yield (8/93)	4.7%	Total Assets	$1.85 billion

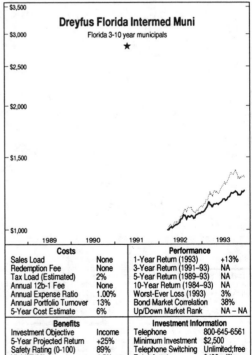

Dreyfus Florida Intermed Muni

Florida 3-10 year municipals

★

Costs		Performance	
Sales Load	None	1-Year Return (1993)	+13%
Redemption Fee	None	3-Year Return (1991–93)	NA
Tax Load (Estimated)	2%	5-Year Return (1989–93)	NA
Annual 12b-1 Fee	None	10-Year Return (1984–93)	NA
Annual Expense Ratio	1.00%	Worst-Ever Loss (1993)	3%
Annual Portfolio Turnover	13%	Bond Market Correlation	38%
5-Year Cost Estimate	6%	Up/Down Market Rank	NA – NA

Benefits		Investment Information	
Investment Objective	Income	Telephone	800-645-6561
5-Year Projected Return	+25%	Minimum Investment	$2,500
Safety Rating (0-100)	89%	Telephone Switching	Unlimited;free
Yield (7/93)	4.5%	Total Assets	$430 million

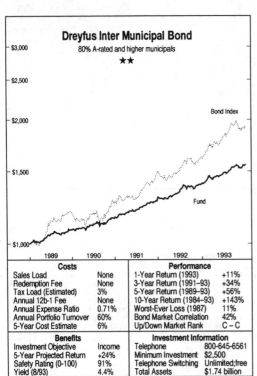

Dreyfus Inter Municipal Bond
80% A-rated and higher municipals
★★

Bond Index

Fund

Costs		Performance	
Sales Load	None	1-Year Return (1993)	+11%
Redemption Fee	None	3-Year Return (1991–93)	+34%
Tax Load (Estimated)	3%	5-Year Return (1989–93)	+56%
Annual 12b-1 Fee	None	10-Year Return (1984–93)	+143%
Annual Expense Ratio	0.71%	Worst-Ever Loss (1987)	11%
Annual Portfolio Turnover	60%	Bond Market Correlation	42%
5-Year Cost Estimate	6%	Up/Down Market Rank	C – C

Benefits		Investment Information	
Investment Objective	Income	Telephone	800-645-6561
5-Year Projected Return	+24%	Minimum Investment	$2,500
Safety Rating (0-100)	91%	Telephone Switching	Unlimited;free
Yield (8/93)	4.4%	Total Assets	$1.74 billion

Dreyfus Mass Tax-Exempt
At least 65% BBB-rated and higher Mass munis
★

Costs		Performance	
Sales Load	None	1-Year Return (1993)	+12%
Redemption Fee	None	3-Year Return (1991–93)	+36%
Tax Load (Estimated)	4%	5-Year Return (1989–93)	+56%
Annual 12b-1 Fee	0.25%	10-Year Return (1984–93)	NA
Annual Expense Ratio	0.81%	Worst-Ever Loss (1987)	17%
Annual Portfolio Turnover	68%	Bond Market Correlation	47%
5-Year Cost Estimate	9%	Up/Down Market Rank	D – D

Benefits		Investment Information	
Investment Objective	Income	Telephone	800-645-6561
5-Year Projected Return	+26%	Minimum Investment	$2,500
Safety Rating (0-100)	90%	Telephone Switching	Unlimited;free
Yield (8/93)	4.8%	Total Assets	$185 million

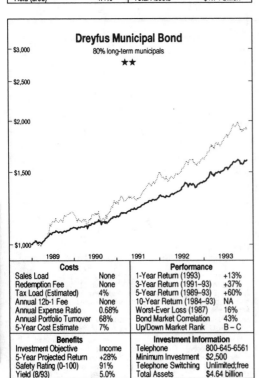

Dreyfus Municipal Bond
80% long-term municipals
★★

Costs		Performance	
Sales Load	None	1-Year Return (1993)	+13%
Redemption Fee	None	3-Year Return (1991–93)	+37%
Tax Load (Estimated)	4%	5-Year Return (1989–93)	+60%
Annual 12b-1 Fee	None	10-Year Return (1984–93)	NA
Annual Expense Ratio	0.68%	Worst-Ever Loss (1987)	16%
Annual Portfolio Turnover	68%	Bond Market Correlation	43%
5-Year Cost Estimate	7%	Up/Down Market Rank	B – C

Benefits		Investment Information	
Investment Objective	Income	Telephone	800-645-6561
5-Year Projected Return	+28%	Minimum Investment	$2,500
Safety Rating (0-100)	91%	Telephone Switching	Unlimited;free
Yield (8/93)	5.0%	Total Assets	$4.64 billion

Dreyfus New York Tax-Exempt
At least 65% BBB-rated and higher N.Y. munis
★

Costs		Performance	
Sales Load	None	1-Year Return (1993)	+13%
Redemption Fee	None	3-Year Return (1991–93)	+37%
Tax Load (Estimated)	4%	5-Year Return (1989–93)	+59%
Annual 12b-1 Fee	None	10-Year Return (1984–93)	NA
Annual Expense Ratio	0.70%	Worst-Ever Loss (1987)	16%
Annual Portfolio Turnover	40%	Bond Market Correlation	44%
5-Year Cost Estimate	6%	Up/Down Market Rank	B – D

Benefits		Investment Information	
Investment Objective	Income	Telephone	800-645-6561
5-Year Projected Return	+24%	Minimum Investment	$2,500
Safety Rating (0-100)	90%	Telephone Switching	Unlimited;free
Yield (8/93)	4.4%	Total Assets	$2.11 billion

TAX FREE

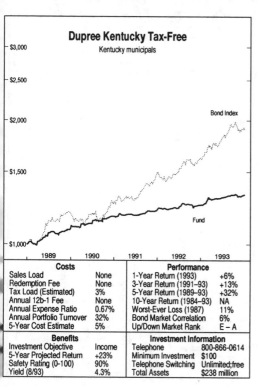

Dupree Kentucky Tax-Free
Kentucky municipals

(chart: Bond Index vs Fund, 1989–1993, $1,000–$3,000 scale)

Costs		Performance	
Sales Load	None	1-Year Return (1993)	+6%
Redemption Fee	None	3-Year Return (1991–93)	+13%
Tax Load (Estimated)	3%	5-Year Return (1989–93)	+32%
Annual 12b-1 Fee	None	10-Year Return (1984–93)	NA
Annual Expense Ratio	0.67%	Worst-Ever Loss (1987)	11%
Annual Portfolio Turnover	32%	Bond Market Correlation	6%
5-Year Cost Estimate	5%	Up/Down Market Rank	E – A

Benefits		Investment Information	
Investment Objective	Income	Telephone	800-866-0614
5-Year Projected Return	+23%	Minimum Investment	$100
Safety Rating (0-100)	90%	Telephone Switching	Unlimited;free
Yield (8/93)	4.3%	Total Assets	$238 million

Eaton Vance - Municipal Bond
80% A-rated & higher municipals; 20% unrated
★★

(chart: 1989–1993, $1,000–$3,000 scale)

Costs		Performance	
Sales Load	5.0%	1-Year Return (1993)	+14%
Redemption Fee	None	3-Year Return (1991–93)	+40%
Tax Load (Estimated)	5%	5-Year Return (1989–93)	+67%
Annual 12b-1 Fee	None	10-Year Return (1984–93)	NA
Annual Expense Ratio	0.74%	Worst-Ever Loss (1987)	15%
Annual Portfolio Turnover	60%	Bond Market Correlation	47%
5-Year Cost Estimate	14%	Up/Down Market Rank	A – D

Benefits		Investment Information	
Investment Objective	Income	Telephone	800-225-6265
5-Year Projected Return	+29%	Minimum Investment	$1,000
Safety Rating (0-100)	91%	Telephone Switching	Unlimited;free
Yield (8/93)	5.2%	Total Assets	$110 million

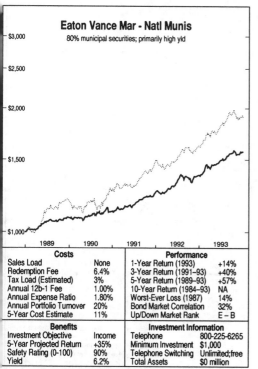

Eaton Vance Mar - Natl Munis
80% municipal securities; primarily high yld

(chart: 1989–1993, $1,000–$3,000 scale)

Costs		Performance	
Sales Load	None	1-Year Return (1993)	+14%
Redemption Fee	6.4%	3-Year Return (1991–93)	+40%
Tax Load (Estimated)	3%	5-Year Return (1989–93)	+57%
Annual 12b-1 Fee	1.00%	10-Year Return (1984–93)	NA
Annual Expense Ratio	1.80%	Worst-Ever Loss (1987)	14%
Annual Portfolio Turnover	20%	Bond Market Correlation	32%
5-Year Cost Estimate	11%	Up/Down Market Rank	E – B

Benefits		Investment Information	
Investment Objective	Income	Telephone	800-225-6265
5-Year Projected Return	+35%	Minimum Investment	$1,000
Safety Rating (0-100)	90%	Telephone Switching	Unlimited;free
Yield	6.2%	Total Assets	$0 million

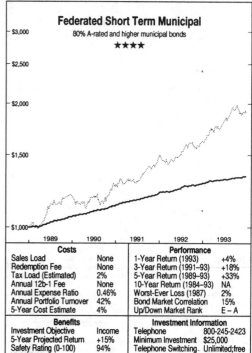

Federated Short Term Municipal
80% A-rated and higher municipal bonds
★★★★

(chart: 1989–1993, $1,000–$3,000 scale)

Costs		Performance	
Sales Load	None	1-Year Return (1993)	+4%
Redemption Fee	None	3-Year Return (1991–93)	+18%
Tax Load (Estimated)	2%	5-Year Return (1989–93)	+33%
Annual 12b-1 Fee	None	10-Year Return (1984–93)	NA
Annual Expense Ratio	0.46%	Worst-Ever Loss (1987)	2%
Annual Portfolio Turnover	42%	Bond Market Correlation	15%
5-Year Cost Estimate	4%	Up/Down Market Rank	E – A

Benefits		Investment Information	
Investment Objective	Income	Telephone	800-245-2423
5-Year Projected Return	+15%	Minimum Investment	$25,000
Safety Rating (0-100)	94%	Telephone Switching	Unlimited;free
Yield (8/93)	2.9%	Total Assets	$318 million

TAX FREE

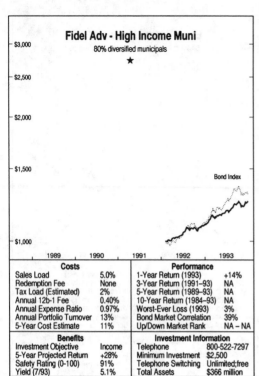

Fidel Adv - High Income Muni
80% diversified municipals
★

Bond Index

Costs		Performance	
Sales Load	5.0%	1-Year Return (1993)	+14%
Redemption Fee	None	3-Year Return (1991–93)	NA
Tax Load (Estimated)	2%	5-Year Return (1989–93)	NA
Annual 12b-1 Fee	0.40%	10-Year Return (1984–93)	NA
Annual Expense Ratio	0.97%	Worst-Ever Loss (1993)	3%
Annual Portfolio Turnover	13%	Bond Market Correlation	39%
5-Year Cost Estimate	11%	Up/Down Market Rank	NA – NA

Benefits		Investment Information	
Investment Objective	Income	Telephone	800-522-7297
5-Year Projected Return	+28%	Minimum Investment	$2,500
Safety Rating (0-100)	91%	Telephone Switching	Unlimited;free
Yield (7/93)	5.1%	Total Assets	$366 million

Fidelity Aggressive Tax-Free
High-yield municipals; 10% defaulted
★★★★

Costs		Performance	
Sales Load	None	1-Year Return (1993)	+14%
Redemption Fee	1.0%	3-Year Return (1991–93)	+39%
Tax Load (Estimated)	3%	5-Year Return (1989–93)	+64%
Annual 12b-1 Fee	None	10-Year Return (1984–93)	NA
Annual Expense Ratio	0.69%	Worst-Ever Loss (1987)	11%
Annual Portfolio Turnover	32%	Bond Market Correlation	35%
5-Year Cost Estimate	5%	Up/Down Market Rank	C – A

Benefits		Investment Information	
Investment Objective	Income	Telephone	800-544-8888
5-Year Projected Return	+32%	Minimum Investment	$2,500
Safety Rating (0-100)	92%	Telephone Switching	4 per yr; free
Yield (7/93)	5.7%	Total Assets	$903 million

Fidelity Calif Tax-Free Hi Yld
80% investment-grade California municipals

Costs		Performance	
Sales Load	None	1-Year Return (1993)	+13%
Redemption Fee	None	3-Year Return (1991–93)	+36%
Tax Load (Estimated)	4%	5-Year Return (1989–93)	+59%
Annual 12b-1 Fee	None	10-Year Return (1984–93)	NA
Annual Expense Ratio	0.58%	Worst-Ever Loss (1987)	20%
Annual Portfolio Turnover	32%	Bond Market Correlation	38%
5-Year Cost Estimate	5%	Up/Down Market Rank	B – D

Benefits		Investment Information	
Investment Objective	Income	Telephone	800-544-8888
5-Year Projected Return	+28%	Minimum Investment	$2,500
Safety Rating (0-100)	90%	Telephone Switching	4 per yr; free
Yield (8/93)	5.0%	Total Assets	$582 million

Fidelity High Yield Tax-Free
Long-term, medium-low quality municipals

Costs		Performance	
Sales Load	None	1-Year Return (1993)	+13%
Redemption Fee	None	3-Year Return (1991–93)	+35%
Tax Load (Estimated)	4%	5-Year Return (1989–93)	+58%
Annual 12b-1 Fee	None	10-Year Return (1984–93)	NA
Annual Expense Ratio	0.57%	Worst-Ever Loss (1987)	17%
Annual Portfolio Turnover	56%	Bond Market Correlation	33%
5-Year Cost Estimate	7%	Up/Down Market Rank	B – C

Benefits		Investment Information	
Investment Objective	Income	Telephone	800-544-8888
5-Year Projected Return	+29%	Minimum Investment	$2,500
Safety Rating (0-100)	90%	Telephone Switching	4 per yr; free
Yield (8/93)	5.3%	Total Assets	$2.21 billion

TAX FREE

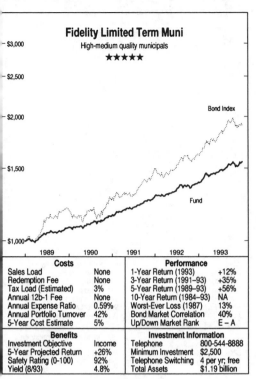

Fidelity Limited Term Muni
High-medium quality municipals
★★★★★

Bond Index

Fund

	1989	1990	1991	1992	1993

Costs		Performance	
Sales Load	None	1-Year Return (1993)	+12%
Redemption Fee	None	3-Year Return (1991–93)	+35%
Tax Load (Estimated)	3%	5-Year Return (1989–93)	+56%
Annual 12b-1 Fee	None	10-Year Return (1984–93)	NA
Annual Expense Ratio	0.59%	Worst-Ever Loss (1987)	13%
Annual Portfolio Turnover	42%	Bond Market Correlation	40%
5-Year Cost Estimate	5%	Up/Down Market Rank	E – A

Benefits		Investment Information	
Investment Objective	Income	Telephone	800-544-8888
5-Year Projected Return	+26%	Minimum Investment	$2,500
Safety Rating (0-100)	92%	Telephone Switching	4 per yr; free
Yield (8/93)	4.8%	Total Assets	$1.19 billion

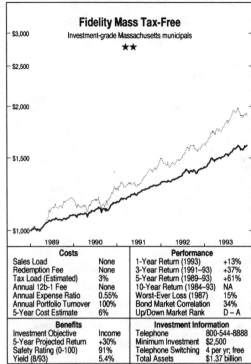

Fidelity Mass Tax-Free
Investment-grade Massachusetts municipals
★★

	1989	1990	1991	1992	1993

Costs		Performance	
Sales Load	None	1-Year Return (1993)	+13%
Redemption Fee	None	3-Year Return (1991–93)	+37%
Tax Load (Estimated)	3%	5-Year Return (1989–93)	+61%
Annual 12b-1 Fee	None	10-Year Return (1984–93)	NA
Annual Expense Ratio	0.55%	Worst-Ever Loss (1987)	15%
Annual Portfolio Turnover	100%	Bond Market Correlation	34%
5-Year Cost Estimate	6%	Up/Down Market Rank	D – A

Benefits		Investment Information	
Investment Objective	Income	Telephone	800-544-8888
5-Year Projected Return	+30%	Minimum Investment	$2,500
Safety Rating (0-100)	91%	Telephone Switching	4 per yr; free
Yield (8/93)	5.4%	Total Assets	$1.37 billion

Fidelity Michigan Tax-Free
Investment-grade Michigan municipals
★

	1989	1990	1991	1992	1993

Costs		Performance	
Sales Load	None	1-Year Return (1993)	+14%
Redemption Fee	None	3-Year Return (1991–93)	+40%
Tax Load (Estimated)	3%	5-Year Return (1989–93)	+62%
Annual 12b-1 Fee	None	10-Year Return (1984–93)	NA
Annual Expense Ratio	0.61%	Worst-Ever Loss (1987)	19%
Annual Portfolio Turnover	4%	Bond Market Correlation	41%
5-Year Cost Estimate	3%	Up/Down Market Rank	A – D

Benefits		Investment Information	
Investment Objective	Income	Telephone	800-544-8888
5-Year Projected Return	+29%	Minimum Investment	$2,500
Safety Rating (0-100)	89%	Telephone Switching	4 per yr; free
Yield (5/93)	5.2%	Total Assets	$537 million

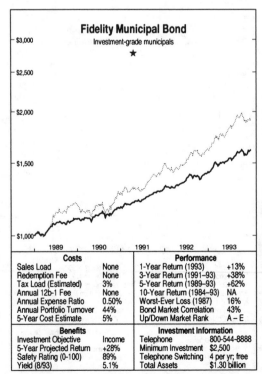

Fidelity Municipal Bond
Investment-grade municipals
★

	1989	1990	1991	1992	1993

Costs		Performance	
Sales Load	None	1-Year Return (1993)	+13%
Redemption Fee	None	3-Year Return (1991–93)	+38%
Tax Load (Estimated)	3%	5-Year Return (1989–93)	+62%
Annual 12b-1 Fee	None	10-Year Return (1984–93)	NA
Annual Expense Ratio	0.50%	Worst-Ever Loss (1987)	16%
Annual Portfolio Turnover	44%	Bond Market Correlation	43%
5-Year Cost Estimate	5%	Up/Down Market Rank	A – E

Benefits		Investment Information	
Investment Objective	Income	Telephone	800-544-8888
5-Year Projected Return	+28%	Minimum Investment	$2,500
Safety Rating (0-100)	89%	Telephone Switching	4 per yr; free
Yield (8/93)	5.1%	Total Assets	$1.30 billion

TAX FREE

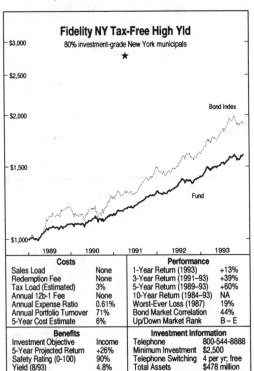

Fidelity NY Tax-Free High Yld
80% investment-grade New York municipals
★

(Chart showing Bond Index and Fund lines, $1,000–$3,000 scale, 1989–1993)

Costs		Performance	
Sales Load	None	1-Year Return (1993)	+13%
Redemption Fee	None	3-Year Return (1991–93)	+39%
Tax Load (Estimated)	3%	5-Year Return (1989–93)	+60%
Annual 12b-1 Fee	None	10-Year Return (1984–93)	NA
Annual Expense Ratio	0.61%	Worst-Ever Loss (1987)	19%
Annual Portfolio Turnover	71%	Bond Market Correlation	44%
5-Year Cost Estimate	6%	Up/Down Market Rank	B – E

Benefits		Investment Information	
Investment Objective	Income	Telephone	800-544-8888
5-Year Projected Return	+26%	Minimum Investment	$2,500
Safety Rating (0-100)	90%	Telephone Switching	4 per yr; free
Yield (8/93)	4.8%	Total Assets	$478 million

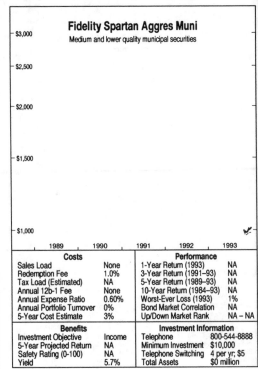

Fidelity Spartan Aggres Muni
Medium and lower quality municipal securities

(Chart, $1,000–$3,000 scale, 1989–1993)

Costs		Performance	
Sales Load	None	1-Year Return (1993)	NA
Redemption Fee	1.0%	3-Year Return (1991–93)	NA
Tax Load (Estimated)	NA	5-Year Return (1989–93)	NA
Annual 12b-1 Fee	None	10-Year Return (1984–93)	NA
Annual Expense Ratio	0.60%	Worst-Ever Loss (1993)	1%
Annual Portfolio Turnover	0%	Bond Market Correlation	NA
5-Year Cost Estimate	3%	Up/Down Market Rank	NA – NA

Benefits		Investment Information	
Investment Objective	Income	Telephone	800-544-8888
5-Year Projected Return	NA	Minimum Investment	$10,000
Safety Rating (0-100)	NA	Telephone Switching	4 per yr; $5
Yield	5.7%	Total Assets	$0 million

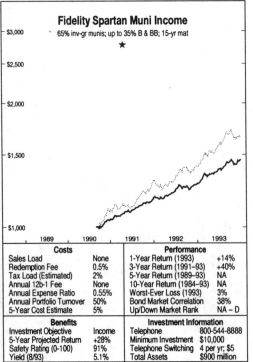

Fidelity Spartan Muni Income
65% inv-gr munis; up to 35% B & BB; 15-yr mat
★

(Chart, $1,000–$3,000 scale, 1989–1993)

Costs		Performance	
Sales Load	None	1-Year Return (1993)	+14%
Redemption Fee	0.5%	3-Year Return (1991–93)	+40%
Tax Load (Estimated)	2%	5-Year Return (1989–93)	NA
Annual 12b-1 Fee	None	10-Year Return (1984–93)	NA
Annual Expense Ratio	0.55%	Worst-Ever Loss (1993)	3%
Annual Portfolio Turnover	50%	Bond Market Correlation	38%
5-Year Cost Estimate	5%	Up/Down Market Rank	NA – D

Benefits		Investment Information	
Investment Objective	Income	Telephone	800-544-8888
5-Year Projected Return	+28%	Minimum Investment	$10,000
Safety Rating (0-100)	91%	Telephone Switching	4 per yr; $5
Yield (8/93)	5.1%	Total Assets	$900 million

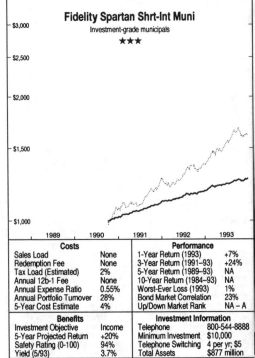

Fidelity Spartan Shrt-Int Muni
Investment-grade municipals
★★★

(Chart, $1,000–$3,000 scale, 1989–1993)

Costs		Performance	
Sales Load	None	1-Year Return (1993)	+7%
Redemption Fee	None	3-Year Return (1991–93)	+24%
Tax Load (Estimated)	2%	5-Year Return (1989–93)	NA
Annual 12b-1 Fee	None	10-Year Return (1984–93)	NA
Annual Expense Ratio	0.55%	Worst-Ever Loss (1993)	1%
Annual Portfolio Turnover	28%	Bond Market Correlation	23%
5-Year Cost Estimate	4%	Up/Down Market Rank	NA – A

Benefits		Investment Information	
Investment Objective	Income	Telephone	800-544-8888
5-Year Projected Return	+20%	Minimum Investment	$10,000
Safety Rating (0-100)	94%	Telephone Switching	4 per yr; $5
Yield (5/93)	3.7%	Total Assets	$877 million

TAX FREE

1994 Mutual Fund Buyer's Guide

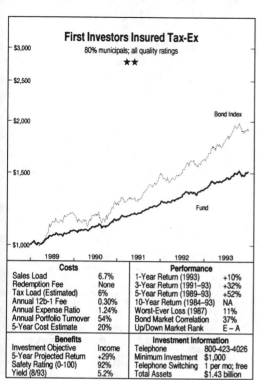

First Investors Insured Tax-Ex

80% municipals; all quality ratings

★★

Bond Index

Fund

| | | | 1989 | 1990 | 1991 | 1992 | 1993 | |

Costs		Performance	
Sales Load	6.7%	1-Year Return (1993)	+10%
Redemption Fee	None	3-Year Return (1991–93)	+32%
Tax Load (Estimated)	6%	5-Year Return (1989–93)	+52%
Annual 12b-1 Fee	0.30%	10-Year Return (1984–93)	NA
Annual Expense Ratio	1.24%	Worst-Ever Loss (1987)	11%
Annual Portfolio Turnover	54%	Bond Market Correlation	37%
5-Year Cost Estimate	20%	Up/Down Market Rank	E – A

Benefits		Investment Information	
Investment Objective	Income	Telephone	800-423-4026
5-Year Projected Return	+29%	Minimum Investment	$1,000
Safety Rating (0-100)	92%	Telephone Switching	1 per mo; free
Yield (8/93)	5.2%	Total Assets	$1.43 billion

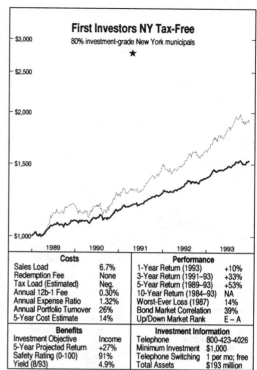

First Investors NY Tax-Free

80% investment-grade New York municipals

★

| | | | 1989 | 1990 | 1991 | 1992 | 1993 | |

Costs		Performance	
Sales Load	6.7%	1-Year Return (1993)	+10%
Redemption Fee	None	3-Year Return (1991–93)	+33%
Tax Load (Estimated)	Neg.	5-Year Return (1989–93)	+53%
Annual 12b-1 Fee	0.30%	10-Year Return (1984–93)	NA
Annual Expense Ratio	1.32%	Worst-Ever Loss (1987)	14%
Annual Portfolio Turnover	26%	Bond Market Correlation	39%
5-Year Cost Estimate	14%	Up/Down Market Rank	E – A

Benefits		Investment Information	
Investment Objective	Income	Telephone	800-423-4026
5-Year Projected Return	+27%	Minimum Investment	$1,000
Safety Rating (0-100)	91%	Telephone Switching	1 per mo; free
Yield (8/93)	4.9%	Total Assets	$193 million

Flagship MI Triple Tax-Ex "A"

BBB-rated & higher 15-25 year Michigan munis

| | | | 1989 | 1990 | 1991 | 1992 | 1993 | |

Costs		Performance	
Sales Load	4.4%	1-Year Return (1993)	+12%
Redemption Fee	None	3-Year Return (1991–93)	+37%
Tax Load (Estimated)	4%	5-Year Return (1989–93)	+59%
Annual 12b-1 Fee	0.40%	10-Year Return (1984–93)	NA
Annual Expense Ratio	0.95%	Worst-Ever Loss (1987)	17%
Annual Portfolio Turnover	10%	Bond Market Correlation	48%
5-Year Cost Estimate	10%	Up/Down Market Rank	A – C

Benefits		Investment Information	
Investment Objective	Income	Telephone	800-227-4648
5-Year Projected Return	+22%	Minimum Investment	$3,000
Safety Rating (0-100)	89%	Telephone Switching	Unlimited;free
Yield (8/93)	4.1%	Total Assets	$232 million

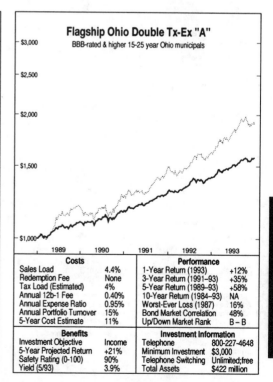

Flagship Ohio Double Tx-Ex "A"

BBB-rated & higher 15-25 year Ohio municipals

| | | | 1989 | 1990 | 1991 | 1992 | 1993 | |

Costs		Performance	
Sales Load	4.4%	1-Year Return (1993)	+12%
Redemption Fee	None	3-Year Return (1991–93)	+35%
Tax Load (Estimated)	4%	5-Year Return (1989–93)	+58%
Annual 12b-1 Fee	0.40%	10-Year Return (1984–93)	NA
Annual Expense Ratio	0.95%	Worst-Ever Loss (1987)	16%
Annual Portfolio Turnover	15%	Bond Market Correlation	48%
5-Year Cost Estimate	11%	Up/Down Market Rank	B – B

Benefits		Investment Information	
Investment Objective	Income	Telephone	800-227-4648
5-Year Projected Return	+21%	Minimum Investment	$3,000
Safety Rating (0-100)	90%	Telephone Switching	Unlimited;free
Yield (5/93)	3.9%	Total Assets	$422 million

TAX FREE

Franklin California Tax-Free

California 20-25 year municipals

★★★

Bond Index

Fund

$3,000
$2,500
$2,000
$1,500
$1,000

1989 1990 1991 1992 1993

Costs		Performance	
Sales Load	4.2%	1-Year Return (1993)	+9%
Redemption Fee	None	3-Year Return (1991–93)	+31%
Tax Load (Estimated)	4%	5-Year Return (1989–93)	+50%
Annual 12b-1 Fee	None	10-Year Return (1984–93)	NA
Annual Expense Ratio	0.49%	Worst-Ever Loss (1987)	13%
Annual Portfolio Turnover	19%	Bond Market Correlation	43%
5-Year Cost Estimate	8%	Up/Down Market Rank	E – A

Benefits		Investment Information	
Investment Objective	Income	Telephone	800-632-2180
5-Year Projected Return	+26%	Minimum Investment	$100
Safety Rating (0-100)	93%	Telephone Switching	Unlimited;free
Yield (8/93)	4.8%	Total Assets	$13.66 billion

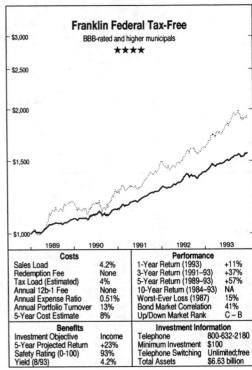

Franklin Federal Tax-Free

BBB-rated and higher municipals

★★★★

$3,000
$2,500
$2,000
$1,500
$1,000

1989 1990 1991 1992 1993

Costs		Performance	
Sales Load	4.2%	1-Year Return (1993)	+11%
Redemption Fee	None	3-Year Return (1991–93)	+37%
Tax Load (Estimated)	4%	5-Year Return (1989–93)	+57%
Annual 12b-1 Fee	None	10-Year Return (1984–93)	NA
Annual Expense Ratio	0.51%	Worst-Ever Loss (1987)	15%
Annual Portfolio Turnover	13%	Bond Market Correlation	41%
5-Year Cost Estimate	8%	Up/Down Market Rank	C – B

Benefits		Investment Information	
Investment Objective	Income	Telephone	800-632-2180
5-Year Projected Return	+23%	Minimum Investment	$100
Safety Rating (0-100)	93%	Telephone Switching	Unlimited;free
Yield (8/93)	4.2%	Total Assets	$6.63 billion

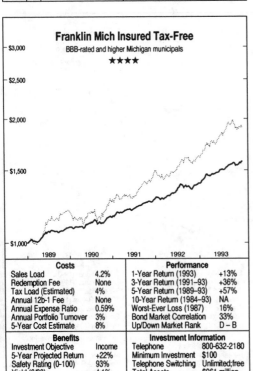

Franklin Mich Insured Tax-Free

BBB-rated and higher Michigan municipals

★★★★

$3,000
$2,500
$2,000
$1,500
$1,000

1989 1990 1991 1992 1993

Costs		Performance	
Sales Load	4.2%	1-Year Return (1993)	+13%
Redemption Fee	None	3-Year Return (1991–93)	+36%
Tax Load (Estimated)	4%	5-Year Return (1989–93)	+57%
Annual 12b-1 Fee	None	10-Year Return (1984–93)	NA
Annual Expense Ratio	0.59%	Worst-Ever Loss (1987)	16%
Annual Portfolio Turnover	3%	Bond Market Correlation	33%
5-Year Cost Estimate	8%	Up/Down Market Rank	D – B

Benefits		Investment Information	
Investment Objective	Income	Telephone	800-632-2180
5-Year Projected Return	+22%	Minimum Investment	$100
Safety Rating (0-100)	93%	Telephone Switching	Unlimited;free
Yield (6/93)	4.1%	Total Assets	$961 million

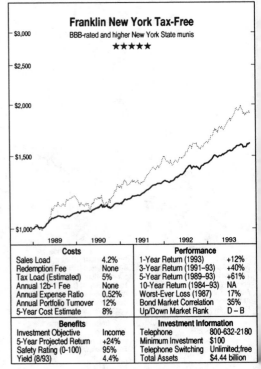

Franklin New York Tax-Free

BBB-rated and higher New York State munis

★★★★★

$3,000
$2,500
$2,000
$1,500
$1,000

1989 1990 1991 1992 1993

Costs		Performance	
Sales Load	4.2%	1-Year Return (1993)	+12%
Redemption Fee	None	3-Year Return (1991–93)	+40%
Tax Load (Estimated)	5%	5-Year Return (1989–93)	+61%
Annual 12b-1 Fee	None	10-Year Return (1984–93)	NA
Annual Expense Ratio	0.52%	Worst-Ever Loss (1987)	17%
Annual Portfolio Turnover	12%	Bond Market Correlation	35%
5-Year Cost Estimate	8%	Up/Down Market Rank	D – B

Benefits		Investment Information	
Investment Objective	Income	Telephone	800-632-2180
5-Year Projected Return	+24%	Minimum Investment	$100
Safety Rating (0-100)	95%	Telephone Switching	Unlimited;free
Yield (8/93)	4.4%	Total Assets	$4.44 billion

TAX FREE

1994 Mutual Fund Buyer's Guide

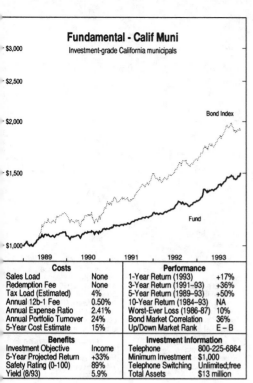

Fundamental - Calif Muni
Investment-grade California municipals

$3,000	
$2,500	
$2,000	Bond Index
$1,500	
	Fund
$1,000	

1989　1990　1991　1992　1993

Costs		Performance	
Sales Load	None	1-Year Return (1993)	+17%
Redemption Fee	None	3-Year Return (1991–93)	+36%
Tax Load (Estimated)	4%	5-Year Return (1989–93)	+50%
Annual 12b-1 Fee	0.50%	10-Year Return (1984–93)	NA
Annual Expense Ratio	2.41%	Worst-Ever Loss (1986-87)	10%
Annual Portfolio Turnover	24%	Bond Market Correlation	36%
5-Year Cost Estimate	15%	Up/Down Market Rank	E – B

Benefits		Investment Information	
Investment Objective	Income	Telephone	800-225-6864
5-Year Projected Return	+33%	Minimum Investment	$1,000
Safety Rating (0-100)	89%	Telephone Switching	Unlimited;free
Yield (8/93)	5.9%	Total Assets	$13 million

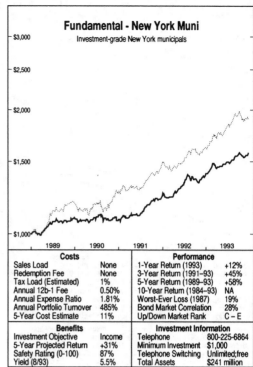

Fundamental - New York Muni
Investment-grade New York municipals

$3,000	
$2,500	
$2,000	
$1,500	
$1,000	

1989　1990　1991　1992　1993

Costs		Performance	
Sales Load	None	1-Year Return (1993)	+12%
Redemption Fee	None	3-Year Return (1991–93)	+45%
Tax Load (Estimated)	1%	5-Year Return (1989–93)	+58%
Annual 12b-1 Fee	0.50%	10-Year Return (1984–93)	NA
Annual Expense Ratio	1.81%	Worst-Ever Loss (1987)	19%
Annual Portfolio Turnover	485%	Bond Market Correlation	28%
5-Year Cost Estimate	11%	Up/Down Market Rank	C – E

Benefits		Investment Information	
Investment Objective	Income	Telephone	800-225-6864
5-Year Projected Return	+31%	Minimum Investment	$1,000
Safety Rating (0-100)	87%	Telephone Switching	Unlimited;free
Yield (8/93)	5.5%	Total Assets	$241 million

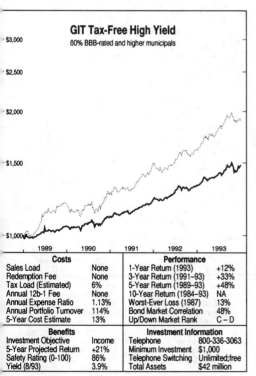

GIT Tax-Free High Yield
80% BBB-rated and higher municipals

$3,000	
$2,500	
$2,000	
$1,500	
$1,000	

1989　1990　1991　1992　1993

Costs		Performance	
Sales Load	None	1-Year Return (1993)	+12%
Redemption Fee	None	3-Year Return (1991–93)	+33%
Tax Load (Estimated)	6%	5-Year Return (1989–93)	+48%
Annual 12b-1 Fee	None	10-Year Return (1984–93)	NA
Annual Expense Ratio	1.13%	Worst-Ever Loss (1987)	13%
Annual Portfolio Turnover	114%	Bond Market Correlation	48%
5-Year Cost Estimate	13%	Up/Down Market Rank	C – D

Benefits		Investment Information	
Investment Objective	Income	Telephone	800-336-3063
5-Year Projected Return	+21%	Minimum Investment	$1,000
Safety Rating (0-100)	86%	Telephone Switching	Unlimited;free
Yield (8/93)	3.9%	Total Assets	$42 million

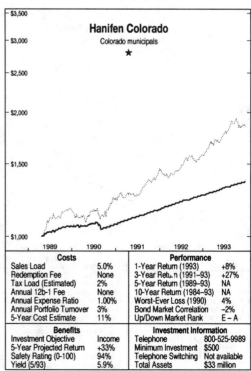

Hanifen Colorado
Colorado municipals
★

$3,500	
$3,000	
$2,500	
$2,000	
$1,500	
$1,000	

1989　1990　1991　1992　1993

Costs		Performance	
Sales Load	5.0%	1-Year Return (1993)	+8%
Redemption Fee	None	3-Year Return (1991–93)	+27%
Tax Load (Estimated)	2%	5-Year Return (1989–93)	NA
Annual 12b-1 Fee	None	10-Year Return (1984–93)	NA
Annual Expense Ratio	1.00%	Worst-Ever Loss (1990)	4%
Annual Portfolio Turnover	3%	Bond Market Correlation	-2%
5-Year Cost Estimate	11%	Up/Down Market Rank	E – A

Benefits		Investment Information	
Investment Objective	Income	Telephone	800-525-9989
5-Year Projected Return	+33%	Minimum Investment	$500
Safety Rating (0-100)	94%	Telephone Switching	Not available
Yield (5/93)	5.9%	Total Assets	$33 million

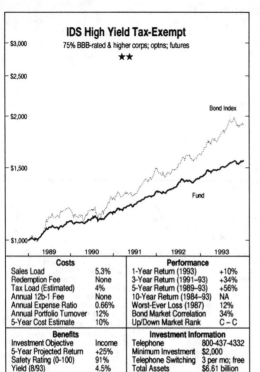

IDS High Yield Tax-Exempt

75% BBB-rated & higher corps; optns; futures

★★

Bond Index

Fund

$3,000
$2,500
$2,000
$1,500
$1,000

1989 1990 1991 1992 1993

Costs		Performance	
Sales Load	5.3%	1-Year Return (1993)	+10%
Redemption Fee	None	3-Year Return (1991–93)	+34%
Tax Load (Estimated)	4%	5-Year Return (1989–93)	+56%
Annual 12b-1 Fee	None	10-Year Return (1984–93)	NA
Annual Expense Ratio	0.66%	Worst-Ever Loss (1987)	12%
Annual Portfolio Turnover	12%	Bond Market Correlation	34%
5-Year Cost Estimate	10%	Up/Down Market Rank	C – C

Benefits		Investment Information	
Investment Objective	Income	Telephone	800-437-4332
5-Year Projected Return	+25%	Minimum Investment	$2,000
Safety Rating (0-100)	91%	Telephone Switching	3 per mo; free
Yield (8/93)	4.5%	Total Assets	$6.61 billion

IDS Tax-Exempt Bond

75% BBB-rated & higher munis; optns; futures

$3,000
$2,500
$2,000
$1,500
$1,000

1989 1990 1991 1992 1993

Costs		Performance	
Sales Load	5.3%	1-Year Return (1993)	+13%
Redemption Fee	None	3-Year Return (1991–93)	+33%
Tax Load (Estimated)	3%	5-Year Return (1989–93)	+65%
Annual 12b-1 Fee	None	10-Year Return (1984–93)	NA
Annual Expense Ratio	0.65%	Worst-Ever Loss (1987)	13%
Annual Portfolio Turnover	75%	Bond Market Correlation	35%
5-Year Cost Estimate	13%	Up/Down Market Rank	B – D

Benefits		Investment Information	
Investment Objective	Income	Telephone	800-437-4332
5-Year Projected Return	+25%	Minimum Investment	$2,000
Safety Rating (0-100)	88%	Telephone Switching	3 per mo; free
Yield (8/93)	4.6%	Total Assets	$1.29 billion

Invesco - Tax-Free Long Term

BBB-rated and higher municipals

$3,000
$2,500
$2,000
$1,500
$1,000

1989 1990 1991 1992 1993

Costs		Performance	
Sales Load	None	1-Year Return (1993)	+11%
Redemption Fee	None	3-Year Return (1991–93)	+36%
Tax Load (Estimated)	3%	5-Year Return (1989–93)	+63%
Annual 12b-1 Fee	0.25%	10-Year Return (1984–93)	NA
Annual Expense Ratio	1.03%	Worst-Ever Loss (1987)	19%
Annual Portfolio Turnover	28%	Bond Market Correlation	47%
5-Year Cost Estimate	7%	Up/Down Market Rank	A – E

Benefits		Investment Information	
Investment Objective	Income	Telephone	800-525-8085
5-Year Projected Return	+28%	Minimum Investment	$1,000
Safety Rating (0-100)	87%	Telephone Switching	4 per yr; free
Yield (8/93)	5.1%	Total Assets	$332 million

John Hancock Tax-Exempt

80% A-rated and higher; 15% BBB & lower munis

★★

$3,000
$2,500
$2,000
$1,500
$1,000

1989 1990 1991 1992 1993

Costs		Performance	
Sales Load	4.7%	1-Year Return (1993)	+11%
Redemption Fee	None	3-Year Return (1991–93)	+35%
Tax Load (Estimated)	3%	5-Year Return (1989–93)	+56%
Annual 12b-1 Fee	0.30%	10-Year Return (1984–93)	NA
Annual Expense Ratio	1.28%	Worst-Ever Loss (1987)	14%
Annual Portfolio Turnover	104%	Bond Market Correlation	52%
5-Year Cost Estimate	15%	Up/Down Market Rank	B – C

Benefits		Investment Information	
Investment Objective	Income	Telephone	800-225-5291
5-Year Projected Return	+21%	Minimum Investment	$1,000
Safety Rating (0-100)	91%	Telephone Switching	Unlimited;free
Yield (8/93)	3.9%	Total Assets	$513 million

TAX FREE

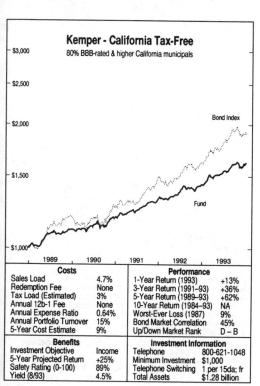

Kemper - California Tax-Free
80% BBB-rated & higher California municipals

Costs		Performance	
Sales Load	4.7%	1-Year Return (1993)	+13%
Redemption Fee	None	3-Year Return (1991–93)	+36%
Tax Load (Estimated)	3%	5-Year Return (1989–93)	+62%
Annual 12b-1 Fee	None	10-Year Return (1984–93)	NA
Annual Expense Ratio	0.64%	Worst-Ever Loss (1987)	9%
Annual Portfolio Turnover	15%	Bond Market Correlation	45%
5-Year Cost Estimate	9%	Up/Down Market Rank	D – B

Benefits		Investment Information	
Investment Objective	Income	Telephone	800-621-1048
5-Year Projected Return	+25%	Minimum Investment	$1,000
Safety Rating (0-100)	89%	Telephone Switching	1 per 15da; fr
Yield (8/93)	4.5%	Total Assets	$1.28 billion

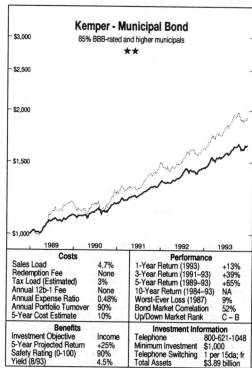

Kemper - Municipal Bond
85% BBB-rated and higher municipals
★★

Costs		Performance	
Sales Load	4.7%	1-Year Return (1993)	+13%
Redemption Fee	None	3-Year Return (1991–93)	+39%
Tax Load (Estimated)	3%	5-Year Return (1989–93)	+65%
Annual 12b-1 Fee	None	10-Year Return (1984–93)	NA
Annual Expense Ratio	0.48%	Worst-Ever Loss (1987)	9%
Annual Portfolio Turnover	90%	Bond Market Correlation	52%
5-Year Cost Estimate	10%	Up/Down Market Rank	C – B

Benefits		Investment Information	
Investment Objective	Income	Telephone	800-621-1048
5-Year Projected Return	+25%	Minimum Investment	$1,000
Safety Rating (0-100)	90%	Telephone Switching	1 per 15da; fr
Yield (8/93)	4.5%	Total Assets	$3.89 billion

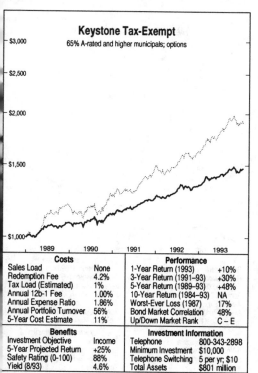

Keystone Tax-Exempt
65% A-rated and higher municipals; options

Costs		Performance	
Sales Load	None	1-Year Return (1993)	+10%
Redemption Fee	4.2%	3-Year Return (1991–93)	+30%
Tax Load (Estimated)	1%	5-Year Return (1989–93)	+48%
Annual 12b-1 Fee	1.00%	10-Year Return (1984–93)	NA
Annual Expense Ratio	1.86%	Worst-Ever Loss (1987)	17%
Annual Portfolio Turnover	56%	Bond Market Correlation	48%
5-Year Cost Estimate	11%	Up/Down Market Rank	C – E

Benefits		Investment Information	
Investment Objective	Income	Telephone	800-343-2898
5-Year Projected Return	+25%	Minimum Investment	$10,000
Safety Rating (0-100)	88%	Telephone Switching	5 per yr; $10
Yield (8/93)	4.6%	Total Assets	$801 million

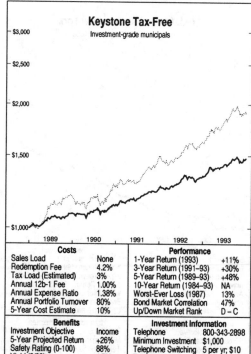

Keystone Tax-Free
Investment-grade municipals

Costs		Performance	
Sales Load	None	1-Year Return (1993)	+11%
Redemption Fee	4.2%	3-Year Return (1991–93)	+30%
Tax Load (Estimated)	3%	5-Year Return (1989–93)	+48%
Annual 12b-1 Fee	1.00%	10-Year Return (1984–93)	NA
Annual Expense Ratio	1.38%	Worst-Ever Loss (1987)	13%
Annual Portfolio Turnover	80%	Bond Market Correlation	47%
5-Year Cost Estimate	10%	Up/Down Market Rank	D – C

Benefits		Investment Information	
Investment Objective	Income	Telephone	800-343-2898
5-Year Projected Return	+26%	Minimum Investment	$1,000
Safety Rating (0-100)	88%	Telephone Switching	5 per yr; $10
Yield (8/93)	4.7%	Total Assets	$1.54 billion

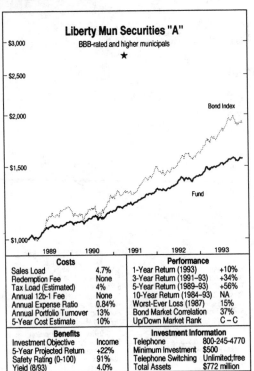

Liberty Mun Securities "A"
BBB-rated and higher municipals
★

Bond Index

Fund

Costs		Performance	
Sales Load	4.7%	1-Year Return (1993)	+10%
Redemption Fee	None	3-Year Return (1991–93)	+34%
Tax Load (Estimated)	4%	5-Year Return (1989–93)	+56%
Annual 12b-1 Fee	None	10-Year Return (1984–93)	NA
Annual Expense Ratio	0.84%	Worst-Ever Loss (1987)	15%
Annual Portfolio Turnover	13%	Bond Market Correlation	37%
5-Year Cost Estimate	10%	Up/Down Market Rank	C – C

Benefits		Investment Information	
Investment Objective	Income	Telephone	800-245-4770
5-Year Projected Return	+22%	Minimum Investment	$500
Safety Rating (0-100)	91%	Telephone Switching	Unlimited;free
Yield (8/93)	4.0%	Total Assets	$772 million

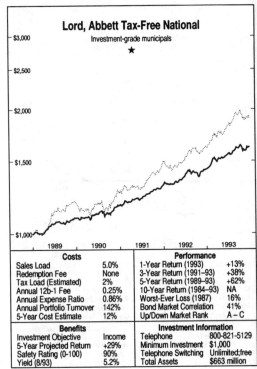

Lord, Abbett Tax-Free National
Investment-grade municipals
★

Costs		Performance	
Sales Load	5.0%	1-Year Return (1993)	+13%
Redemption Fee	None	3-Year Return (1991–93)	+38%
Tax Load (Estimated)	2%	5-Year Return (1989–93)	+62%
Annual 12b-1 Fee	0.25%	10-Year Return (1984–93)	NA
Annual Expense Ratio	0.86%	Worst-Ever Loss (1987)	16%
Annual Portfolio Turnover	142%	Bond Market Correlation	41%
5-Year Cost Estimate	12%	Up/Down Market Rank	A – C

Benefits		Investment Information	
Investment Objective	Income	Telephone	800-821-5129
5-Year Projected Return	+29%	Minimum Investment	$1,000
Safety Rating (0-100)	90%	Telephone Switching	Unlimited;free
Yield (8/93)	5.2%	Total Assets	$663 million

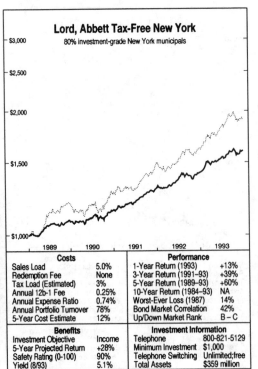

Lord, Abbett Tax-Free New York
80% investment-grade New York municipals

Costs		Performance	
Sales Load	5.0%	1-Year Return (1993)	+13%
Redemption Fee	None	3-Year Return (1991–93)	+39%
Tax Load (Estimated)	3%	5-Year Return (1989–93)	+60%
Annual 12b-1 Fee	0.25%	10-Year Return (1984–93)	NA
Annual Expense Ratio	0.74%	Worst-Ever Loss (1987)	14%
Annual Portfolio Turnover	78%	Bond Market Correlation	42%
5-Year Cost Estimate	12%	Up/Down Market Rank	B – C

Benefits		Investment Information	
Investment Objective	Income	Telephone	800-821-5129
5-Year Projected Return	+28%	Minimum Investment	$1,000
Safety Rating (0-100)	90%	Telephone Switching	Unlimited;free
Yield (8/93)	5.1%	Total Assets	$359 million

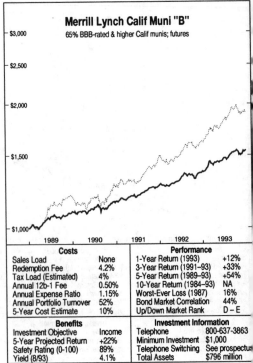

Merrill Lynch Calif Muni "B"
65% BBB-rated & higher Calif munis; futures

Costs		Performance	
Sales Load	None	1-Year Return (1993)	+12%
Redemption Fee	4.2%	3-Year Return (1991–93)	+33%
Tax Load (Estimated)	4%	5-Year Return (1989–93)	+54%
Annual 12b-1 Fee	0.50%	10-Year Return (1984–93)	NA
Annual Expense Ratio	1.15%	Worst-Ever Loss (1987)	16%
Annual Portfolio Turnover	52%	Bond Market Correlation	44%
5-Year Cost Estimate	10%	Up/Down Market Rank	D – E

Benefits		Investment Information	
Investment Objective	Income	Telephone	800-637-3863
5-Year Projected Return	+22%	Minimum Investment	$1,000
Safety Rating (0-100)	89%	Telephone Switching	See prospectus
Yield (8/93)	4.1%	Total Assets	$796 million

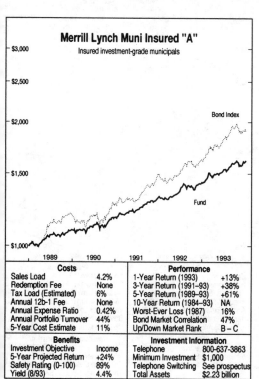

Merrill Lynch Muni Insured "A"
Insured investment-grade municipals

(chart showing Bond Index and Fund, years 1989–1993, $1,000–$3,000 scale)

Costs		Performance	
Sales Load	4.2%	1-Year Return (1993)	+13%
Redemption Fee	None	3-Year Return (1991–93)	+38%
Tax Load (Estimated)	6%	5-Year Return (1989–93)	+61%
Annual 12b-1 Fee	None	10-Year Return (1984–93)	NA
Annual Expense Ratio	0.42%	Worst-Ever Loss (1987)	16%
Annual Portfolio Turnover	44%	Bond Market Correlation	47%
5-Year Cost Estimate	11%	Up/Down Market Rank	B – C

Benefits		Investment Information	
Investment Objective	Income	Telephone	800-637-3863
5-Year Projected Return	+24%	Minimum Investment	$1,000
Safety Rating (0-100)	89%	Telephone Switching	See prospectus
Yield (8/93)	4.4%	Total Assets	$2.23 billion

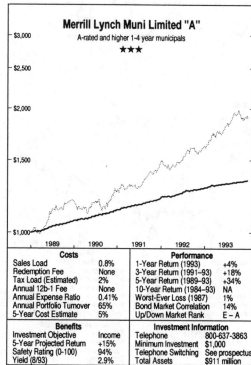

Merrill Lynch Muni Limited "A"
A-rated and higher 1-4 year municipals
★★★

(chart, years 1989–1993, $1,000–$3,000 scale)

Costs		Performance	
Sales Load	0.8%	1-Year Return (1993)	+4%
Redemption Fee	None	3-Year Return (1991–93)	+18%
Tax Load (Estimated)	2%	5-Year Return (1989–93)	+34%
Annual 12b-1 Fee	None	10-Year Return (1984–93)	NA
Annual Expense Ratio	0.41%	Worst-Ever Loss (1987)	1%
Annual Portfolio Turnover	65%	Bond Market Correlation	14%
5-Year Cost Estimate	5%	Up/Down Market Rank	E – A

Benefits		Investment Information	
Investment Objective	Income	Telephone	800-637-3863
5-Year Projected Return	+15%	Minimum Investment	$1,000
Safety Rating (0-100)	94%	Telephone Switching	See prospectus
Yield (8/93)	2.9%	Total Assets	$911 million

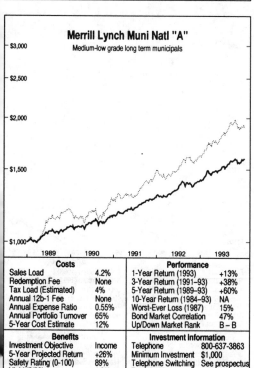

Merrill Lynch Muni Natl "A"
Medium-low grade long term municipals

(chart, years 1989–1993, $1,000–$3,000 scale)

Costs		Performance	
Sales Load	4.2%	1-Year Return (1993)	+13%
Redemption Fee	None	3-Year Return (1991–93)	+38%
Tax Load (Estimated)	4%	5-Year Return (1989–93)	+60%
Annual 12b-1 Fee	None	10-Year Return (1984–93)	NA
Annual Expense Ratio	0.55%	Worst-Ever Loss (1987)	15%
Annual Portfolio Turnover	65%	Bond Market Correlation	47%
5-Year Cost Estimate	12%	Up/Down Market Rank	B – B

Benefits		Investment Information	
Investment Objective	Income	Telephone	800-637-3863
5-Year Projected Return	+26%	Minimum Investment	$1,000
Safety Rating (0-100)	89%	Telephone Switching	See prospectus
Yield (8/93)	4.8%	Total Assets	$1.35 billion

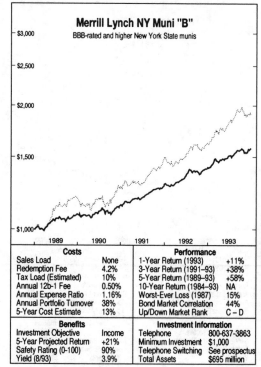

Merrill Lynch NY Muni "B"
BBB-rated and higher New York State munis

(chart, years 1989–1993, $1,000–$3,000 scale)

Costs		Performance	
Sales Load	None	1-Year Return (1993)	+11%
Redemption Fee	4.2%	3-Year Return (1991–93)	+38%
Tax Load (Estimated)	10%	5-Year Return (1989–93)	+58%
Annual 12b-1 Fee	0.50%	10-Year Return (1984–93)	NA
Annual Expense Ratio	1.16%	Worst-Ever Loss (1987)	15%
Annual Portfolio Turnover	38%	Bond Market Correlation	44%
5-Year Cost Estimate	13%	Up/Down Market Rank	C – D

Benefits		Investment Information	
Investment Objective	Income	Telephone	800-637-3863
5-Year Projected Return	+21%	Minimum Investment	$1,000
Safety Rating (0-100)	90%	Telephone Switching	See prospectus
Yield (8/93)	3.9%	Total Assets	$695 million

TAX FREE

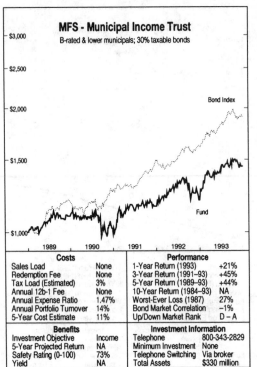

MFS - Municipal Income Trust
B-rated & lower municipals; 30% taxable bonds

(Chart showing Bond Index and Fund lines, 1989–1993, y-axis $1,000 to $3,000)

Costs		Performance	
Sales Load	None	1-Year Return (1993)	+21%
Redemption Fee	None	3-Year Return (1991–93)	+45%
Tax Load (Estimated)	3%	5-Year Return (1989–93)	+44%
Annual 12b-1 Fee	None	10-Year Return (1984–93)	NA
Annual Expense Ratio	1.47%	Worst-Ever Loss (1987)	27%
Annual Portfolio Turnover	14%	Bond Market Correlation	–1%
5-Year Cost Estimate	11%	Up/Down Market Rank	D – A

Benefits		Investment Information	
Investment Objective	Income	Telephone	800-343-2829
5-Year Projected Return	NA	Minimum Investment	None
Safety Rating (0-100)	73%	Telephone Switching	Via broker
Yield	NA	Total Assets	$330 million

MFS - Muni Ltd Maturity "A"
80% BBB-rated & higher municipals; govts

(Chart, 1989–1993, y-axis $1,000 to $3,500)

Costs		Performance	
Sales Load	2.6%	1-Year Return (1993)	+8%
Redemption Fee	None	3-Year Return (1991–93)	NA
Tax Load (Estimated)	NA	5-Year Return (1989–93)	NA
Annual 12b-1 Fee	0.35%	10-Year Return (1984–93)	NA
Annual Expense Ratio	0.85%	Worst-Ever Loss (1993)	1%
Annual Portfolio Turnover	0%	Bond Market Correlation	43%
5-Year Cost Estimate	7%	Up/Down Market Rank	NA – NA

Benefits		Investment Information	
Investment Objective	Income	Telephone	800-225-2606
5-Year Projected Return	+18%	Minimum Investment	$1,000
Safety Rating (0-100)	91%	Telephone Switching	Unlimited;free
Yield (7/93)	3.4%	Total Assets	$71 million

National - Calif Tax-Exempt
BBB-rated and higher California municipals
★

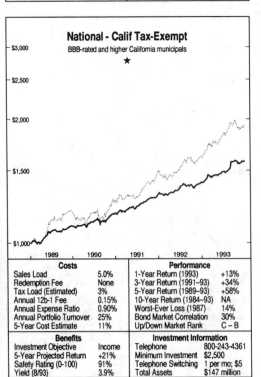

(Chart, 1989–1993, y-axis $1,000 to $3,000)

Costs		Performance	
Sales Load	5.0%	1-Year Return (1993)	+13%
Redemption Fee	None	3-Year Return (1991–93)	+34%
Tax Load (Estimated)	3%	5-Year Return (1989–93)	+58%
Annual 12b-1 Fee	0.15%	10-Year Return (1984–93)	NA
Annual Expense Ratio	0.90%	Worst-Ever Loss (1987)	14%
Annual Portfolio Turnover	25%	Bond Market Correlation	30%
5-Year Cost Estimate	11%	Up/Down Market Rank	C – B

Benefits		Investment Information	
Investment Objective	Income	Telephone	800-243-4361
5-Year Projected Return	+21%	Minimum Investment	$2,500
Safety Rating (0-100)	91%	Telephone Switching	1 per mo; $5
Yield (8/93)	3.9%	Total Assets	$147 million

Norwest Tax-Free Icm Invstr"A"
High and medium grade municipals

(Chart, 1989–1993, y-axis $1,000 to $3,000)

Costs		Performance	
Sales Load	4.7%	1-Year Return (1993)	+10%
Redemption Fee	None	3-Year Return (1991–93)	NA
Tax Load (Estimated)	2%	5-Year Return (1989–93)	NA
Annual 12b-1 Fee	None	10-Year Return (1984–93)	NA
Annual Expense Ratio	0.34%	Worst-Ever Loss (1993)	2%
Annual Portfolio Turnover	43%	Bond Market Correlation	35%
5-Year Cost Estimate	8%	Up/Down Market Rank	NA – NA

Benefits		Investment Information	
Investment Objective	Income	Telephone	800-338-1348
5-Year Projected Return	+25%	Minimum Investment	$1,000
Safety Rating (0-100)	91%	Telephone Switching	Unlimited;free
Yield (7/93)	4.6%	Total Assets	$110 million

TAX FREE

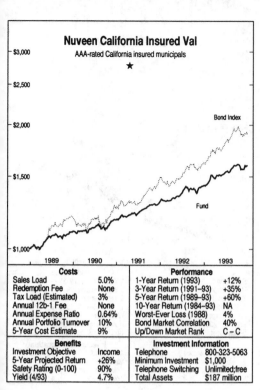

Nuveen California Insured Val
AAA-rated California insured municipals
★

Costs		Performance	
Sales Load	5.0%	1-Year Return (1993)	+12%
Redemption Fee	None	3-Year Return (1991–93)	+35%
Tax Load (Estimated)	3%	5-Year Return (1989–93)	+60%
Annual 12b-1 Fee	None	10-Year Return (1984–93)	NA
Annual Expense Ratio	0.64%	Worst-Ever Loss (1988)	4%
Annual Portfolio Turnover	10%	Bond Market Correlation	40%
5-Year Cost Estimate	9%	Up/Down Market Rank	C – C

Benefits		Investment Information	
Investment Objective	Income	Telephone	800-323-5063
5-Year Projected Return	+26%	Minimum Investment	$1,000
Safety Rating (0-100)	90%	Telephone Switching	Unlimited;free
Yield (4/93)	4.7%	Total Assets	$187 million

Nuveel Calif Tax-Free Value
BBB-rated & higher 20-30-yr California munis
★★

Costs		Performance	
Sales Load	5.0%	1-Year Return (1993)	+11%
Redemption Fee	None	3-Year Return (1991–93)	+35%
Tax Load (Estimated)	4%	5-Year Return (1989–93)	+60%
Annual 12b-1 Fee	None	10-Year Return (1984–93)	NA
Annual Expense Ratio	0.67%	Worst-Ever Loss (1987)	12%
Annual Portfolio Turnover	11%	Bond Market Correlation	43%
5-Year Cost Estimate	9%	Up/Down Market Rank	C – B

Benefits		Investment Information	
Investment Objective	Income	Telephone	800-323-5063
5-Year Projected Return	+27%	Minimum Investment	$1,000
Safety Rating (0-100)	91%	Telephone Switching	Unlimited;free
Yield (4/93)	4.9%	Total Assets	$198 million

Nuveen Florida Quality Income
80% BBB & higher 20-30yr Florida munis; levgd

Costs		Performance	
Sales Load	None	1-Year Return (1993)	+12%
Redemption Fee	None	3-Year Return (1991–93)	NA
Tax Load (Estimated)	3%	5-Year Return (1989–93)	NA
Annual 12b-1 Fee	None	10-Year Return (1984–93)	NA
Annual Expense Ratio	0.65%	Worst-Ever Loss (1993)	9%
Annual Portfolio Turnover	14%	Bond Market Correlation	–1%
5-Year Cost Estimate	6%	Up/Down Market Rank	NA – C

Benefits		Investment Information	
Investment Objective	Income	Telephone	800-323-5063
5-Year Projected Return	NA	Minimum Investment	None
Safety Rating (0-100)	74%	Telephone Switching	Via broker
Yield	NA	Total Assets	$272 million

Nuveen Michigan Quality Income
80% BBB & higher 20-30yr Michigan munis; levg

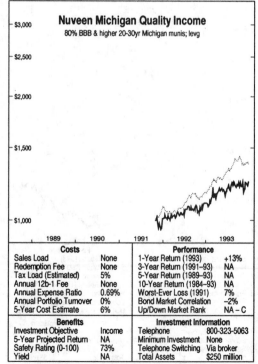

Costs		Performance	
Sales Load	None	1-Year Return (1993)	+13%
Redemption Fee	None	3-Year Return (1991–93)	NA
Tax Load (Estimated)	5%	5-Year Return (1989–93)	NA
Annual 12b-1 Fee	None	10-Year Return (1984–93)	NA
Annual Expense Ratio	0.69%	Worst-Ever Loss (1991)	7%
Annual Portfolio Turnover	0%	Bond Market Correlation	–2%
5-Year Cost Estimate	6%	Up/Down Market Rank	NA – C

Benefits		Investment Information	
Investment Objective	Income	Telephone	800-323-5063
5-Year Projected Return	NA	Minimum Investment	None
Safety Rating (0-100)	73%	Telephone Switching	Via broker
Yield	NA	Total Assets	$250 million

TAX FREE

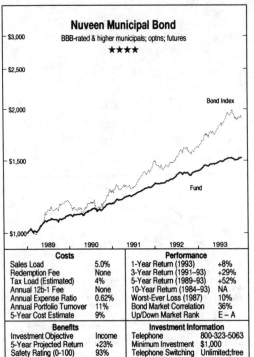

Nuveen Municipal Bond
BBB-rated & higher municipals; optns; futures
★★★★

Bond Index

Fund

Costs		Performance	
Sales Load	5.0%	1-Year Return (1993)	+8%
Redemption Fee	None	3-Year Return (1991–93)	+29%
Tax Load (Estimated)	4%	5-Year Return (1989–93)	+52%
Annual 12b-1 Fee	None	10-Year Return (1984–93)	NA
Annual Expense Ratio	0.62%	Worst-Ever Loss (1987)	10%
Annual Portfolio Turnover	11%	Bond Market Correlation	36%
5-Year Cost Estimate	9%	Up/Down Market Rank	E – A

Benefits		Investment Information	
Investment Objective	Income	Telephone	800-323-5063
5-Year Projected Return	+23%	Minimum Investment	$1,000
Safety Rating (0-100)	93%	Telephone Switching	Unlimited;free
Yield (9/93)	4.3%	Total Assets	$2.49 billion

Nuveen Municipal Value
80% BBB-rated and higher municipals

Costs		Performance	
Sales Load	None	1-Year Return (1993)	–2%
Redemption Fee	None	3-Year Return (1991–93)	+25%
Tax Load (Estimated)	6%	5-Year Return (1989–93)	+51%
Annual 12b-1 Fee	None	10-Year Return (1984–93)	NA
Annual Expense Ratio	0.75%	Worst-Ever Loss (1987)	20%
Annual Portfolio Turnover	4%	Bond Market Correlation	8%
5-Year Cost Estimate	6%	Up/Down Market Rank	C – B

Benefits		Investment Information	
Investment Objective	Income	Telephone	800-323-5063
5-Year Projected Return	NA	Minimum Investment	None
Safety Rating (0-100)	80%	Telephone Switching	Via broker
Yield	NA	Total Assets	$1.80 billion

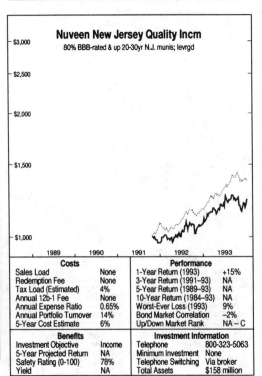

Nuveen New Jersey Quality Incm
80% BBB-rated & up 20-30yr N.J. munis; levrgd

Costs		Performance	
Sales Load	None	1-Year Return (1993)	+15%
Redemption Fee	None	3-Year Return (1991–93)	NA
Tax Load (Estimated)	4%	5-Year Return (1989–93)	NA
Annual 12b-1 Fee	None	10-Year Return (1984–93)	NA
Annual Expense Ratio	0.65%	Worst-Ever Loss (1993)	9%
Annual Portfolio Turnover	14%	Bond Market Correlation	–2%
5-Year Cost Estimate	6%	Up/Down Market Rank	NA – C

Benefits		Investment Information	
Investment Objective	Income	Telephone	800-323-5063
5-Year Projected Return	NA	Minimum Investment	None
Safety Rating (0-100)	78%	Telephone Switching	Via broker
Yield	NA	Total Assets	$158 million

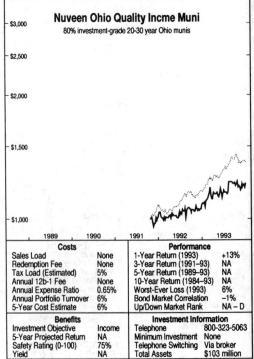

Nuveen Ohio Quality Incme Muni
80% investment-grade 20-30 year Ohio munis

Costs		Performance	
Sales Load	None	1-Year Return (1993)	+13%
Redemption Fee	None	3-Year Return (1991–93)	NA
Tax Load (Estimated)	5%	5-Year Return (1989–93)	NA
Annual 12b-1 Fee	None	10-Year Return (1984–93)	NA
Annual Expense Ratio	0.65%	Worst-Ever Loss (1993)	6%
Annual Portfolio Turnover	6%	Bond Market Correlation	–1%
5-Year Cost Estimate	6%	Up/Down Market Rank	NA – D

Benefits		Investment Information	
Investment Objective	Income	Telephone	800-323-5063
5-Year Projected Return	NA	Minimum Investment	None
Safety Rating (0-100)	75%	Telephone Switching	Via broker
Yield	NA	Total Assets	$103 million

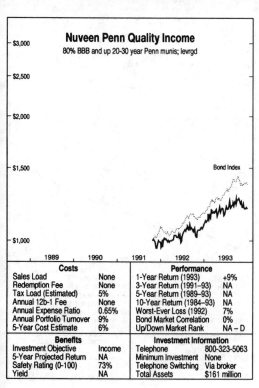

Nuveen Penn Quality Income
80% BBB and up 20-30 year Penn munis; levrgd

Costs		Performance	
Sales Load	None	1-Year Return (1993)	+9%
Redemption Fee	None	3-Year Return (1991–93)	NA
Tax Load (Estimated)	5%	5-Year Return (1989–93)	NA
Annual 12b-1 Fee	None	10-Year Return (1984–93)	NA
Annual Expense Ratio	0.65%	Worst-Ever Loss (1992)	7%
Annual Portfolio Turnover	9%	Bond Market Correlation	0%
5-Year Cost Estimate	6%	Up/Down Market Rank	NA – D

Benefits		Investment Information	
Investment Objective	Income	Telephone	800-323-5063
5-Year Projected Return	NA	Minimum Investment	None
Safety Rating (0-100)	73%	Telephone Switching	Via broker
Yield	NA	Total Assets	$161 million

Nuveen Tax-Free NY Value
BBB-rated & higher N.Y. munis; futures; optns
★★

Costs		Performance	
Sales Load	5.0%	1-Year Return (1993)	+13%
Redemption Fee	None	3-Year Return (1991–93)	+41%
Tax Load (Estimated)	4%	5-Year Return (1989–93)	+62%
Annual 12b-1 Fee	None	10-Year Return (1984–93)	NA
Annual Expense Ratio	None	Worst-Ever Loss (1992)	3%
Annual Portfolio Turnover	12%	Bond Market Correlation	39%
5-Year Cost Estimate	6%	Up/Down Market Rank	B – B

Benefits		Investment Information	
Investment Objective	Income	Telephone	800-323-5063
5-Year Projected Return	+26%	Minimum Investment	None
Safety Rating (0-100)	91%	Telephone Switching	Unlimited;free
Yield (4/93)	4.7%	Total Assets	$120 million

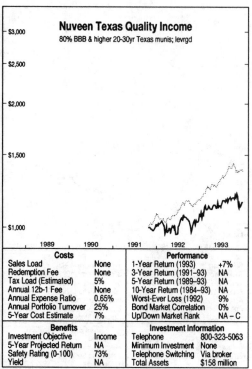

Nuveen Texas Quality Income
80% BBB & higher 20-30yr Texas munis; levrgd

Costs		Performance	
Sales Load	None	1-Year Return (1993)	+7%
Redemption Fee	None	3-Year Return (1991–93)	NA
Tax Load (Estimated)	5%	5-Year Return (1989–93)	NA
Annual 12b-1 Fee	None	10-Year Return (1984–93)	NA
Annual Expense Ratio	0.65%	Worst-Ever Loss (1992)	9%
Annual Portfolio Turnover	25%	Bond Market Correlation	0%
5-Year Cost Estimate	7%	Up/Down Market Rank	NA – C

Benefits		Investment Information	
Investment Objective	Income	Telephone	800-323-5063
5-Year Projected Return	NA	Minimum Investment	None
Safety Rating (0-100)	73%	Telephone Switching	Via broker
Yield	NA	Total Assets	$158 million

One Group Intermed Tax-Fr "A"
Inst only: 80% A-rated and up 5-15 year munis
★★

Costs		Performance	
Sales Load	None	1-Year Return (1993)	+10%
Redemption Fee	None	3-Year Return (1991–93)	NA
Tax Load (Estimated)	NA	5-Year Return (1989–93)	NA
Annual 12b-1 Fee	None	10-Year Return (1984–93)	NA
Annual Expense Ratio	0.85%	Worst-Ever Loss (1993)	2%
Annual Portfolio Turnover	0%	Bond Market Correlation	37%
5-Year Cost Estimate	4%	Up/Down Market Rank	NA – A

Benefits		Investment Information	
Investment Objective	Income	Telephone	800-338-4345
5-Year Projected Return	+20%	Minimum Investment	$1,000
Safety Rating (0-100)	92%	Telephone Switching	Unlimited;free
Yield (8/93)	3.7%	Total Assets	$167 million

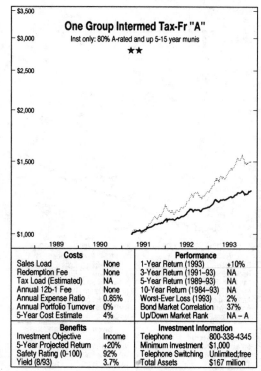

TAX FREE

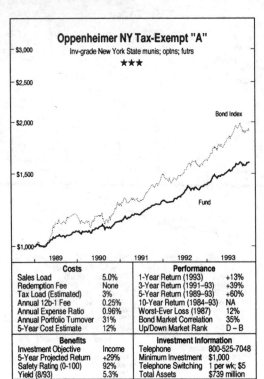

Oppenheimer NY Tax-Exempt "A"
Inv-grade New York State munis; optns; futrs
★★★

Bond Index

Fund

Costs		Performance	
Sales Load	5.0%	1-Year Return (1993)	+13%
Redemption Fee	None	3-Year Return (1991–93)	+39%
Tax Load (Estimated)	3%	5-Year Return (1989–93)	+60%
Annual 12b-1 Fee	0.25%	10-Year Return (1984–93)	NA
Annual Expense Ratio	0.96%	Worst-Ever Loss (1987)	12%
Annual Portfolio Turnover	31%	Bond Market Correlation	35%
5-Year Cost Estimate	12%	Up/Down Market Rank	D – B

Benefits		Investment Information	
Investment Objective	Income	Telephone	800-525-7048
5-Year Projected Return	+29%	Minimum Investment	$1,000
Safety Rating (0-100)	92%	Telephone Switching	1 per wk; $5
Yield (8/93)	5.3%	Total Assets	$739 million

Oppenheimer Tax-Free "A"
Investment-grade 20-30 year municipals
★★

Costs		Performance	
Sales Load	5.0%	1-Year Return (1993)	+13%
Redemption Fee	None	3-Year Return (1991–93)	+39%
Tax Load (Estimated)	3%	5-Year Return (1989–93)	+61%
Annual 12b-1 Fee	0.25%	10-Year Return (1984–93)	NA
Annual Expense Ratio	0.89%	Worst-Ever Loss (1987)	13%
Annual Portfolio Turnover	27%	Bond Market Correlation	38%
5-Year Cost Estimate	11%	Up/Down Market Rank	C – C

Benefits		Investment Information	
Investment Objective	Income	Telephone	800-525-7048
5-Year Projected Return	+12%	Minimum Investment	$1,000
Safety Rating (0-100)	92%	Telephone Switching	1 per wk; $5
Yield (8/93)	2.3%	Total Assets	$593 million

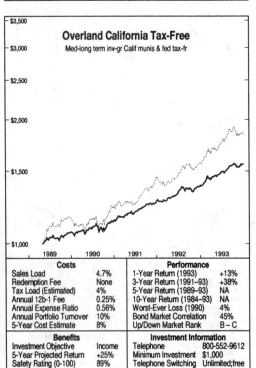

Overland California Tax-Free
Med-long term inv-gr Calif munis & fed tax-fr

Costs		Performance	
Sales Load	4.7%	1-Year Return (1993)	+13%
Redemption Fee	None	3-Year Return (1991–93)	+38%
Tax Load (Estimated)	4%	5-Year Return (1989–93)	NA
Annual 12b-1 Fee	0.25%	10-Year Return (1984–93)	NA
Annual Expense Ratio	0.56%	Worst-Ever Loss (1990)	4%
Annual Portfolio Turnover	10%	Bond Market Correlation	45%
5-Year Cost Estimate	8%	Up/Down Market Rank	B – C

Benefits		Investment Information	
Investment Objective	Income	Telephone	800-552-9612
5-Year Projected Return	+25%	Minimum Investment	$1,000
Safety Rating (0-100)	89%	Telephone Switching	Unlimited;free
Yield (5/93)	4.5%	Total Assets	$380 million

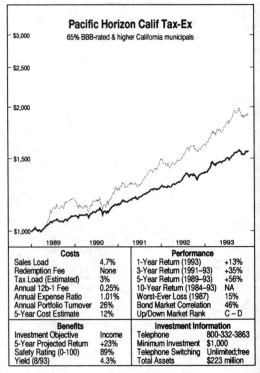

Pacific Horizon Calif Tax-Ex
65% BBB-rated & higher California municipals

Costs		Performance	
Sales Load	4.7%	1-Year Return (1993)	+13%
Redemption Fee	None	3-Year Return (1991–93)	+35%
Tax Load (Estimated)	3%	5-Year Return (1989–93)	+56%
Annual 12b-1 Fee	0.25%	10-Year Return (1984–93)	NA
Annual Expense Ratio	1.01%	Worst-Ever Loss (1987)	15%
Annual Portfolio Turnover	26%	Bond Market Correlation	46%
5-Year Cost Estimate	12%	Up/Down Market Rank	C – D

Benefits		Investment Information	
Investment Objective	Income	Telephone	800-332-3863
5-Year Projected Return	+23%	Minimum Investment	$1,000
Safety Rating (0-100)	89%	Telephone Switching	Unlimited;free
Yield (8/93)	4.3%	Total Assets	$223 million

Paine Webber Calif Tax-Fr "A"

80% BBB-rated & higher California municipals

Bond Index

Fund

Costs		Performance	
Sales Load	4.2%	1-Year Return (1993)	+12%
Redemption Fee	None	3-Year Return (1991–93)	+34%
Tax Load (Estimated)	3%	5-Year Return (1989–93)	+56%
Annual 12b-1 Fee	0.25%	10-Year Return (1984–93)	NA
Annual Expense Ratio	0.91%	Worst-Ever Loss (1987)	14%
Annual Portfolio Turnover	19%	Bond Market Correlation	36%
5-Year Cost Estimate	10%	Up/Down Market Rank	D – B

Benefits		Investment Information	
Investment Objective	Income	Telephone	800-457-0849
5-Year Projected Return	+27%	Minimum Investment	$1,000
Safety Rating (0-100)	89%	Telephone Switching	Unlimited; $5
Yield (8/93)	4.9%	Total Assets	$236 million

Paine Webber Natl Tax-Free "A"

BBB-rated and higher municipals; all maturtys

Costs		Performance	
Sales Load	4.2%	1-Year Return (1993)	+12%
Redemption Fee	None	3-Year Return (1991–93)	+34%
Tax Load (Estimated)	3%	5-Year Return (1989–93)	+56%
Annual 12b-1 Fee	0.25%	10-Year Return (1984–93)	NA
Annual Expense Ratio	0.91%	Worst-Ever Loss (1987)	13%
Annual Portfolio Turnover	15%	Bond Market Correlation	40%
5-Year Cost Estimate	10%	Up/Down Market Rank	C – B

Benefits		Investment Information	
Investment Objective	Income	Telephone	800-457-0849
5-Year Projected Return	+28%	Minimum Investment	$1,000
Safety Rating (0-100)	90%	Telephone Switching	Unlimited; $5
Yield (8/93)	5.0%	Total Assets	$427 million

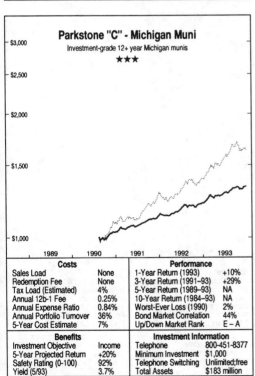

Parkstone "C" - Michigan Muni

Investment-grade 12+ year Michigan munis

★★★

Costs		Performance	
Sales Load	None	1-Year Return (1993)	+10%
Redemption Fee	None	3-Year Return (1991–93)	+29%
Tax Load (Estimated)	4%	5-Year Return (1989–93)	NA
Annual 12b-1 Fee	0.25%	10-Year Return (1984–93)	NA
Annual Expense Ratio	0.84%	Worst-Ever Loss (1990)	2%
Annual Portfolio Turnover	36%	Bond Market Correlation	44%
5-Year Cost Estimate	7%	Up/Down Market Rank	E – A

Benefits		Investment Information	
Investment Objective	Income	Telephone	800-451-8377
5-Year Projected Return	+20%	Minimum Investment	$1,000
Safety Rating (0-100)	92%	Telephone Switching	Unlimited;free
Yield (5/93)	3.7%	Total Assets	$183 million

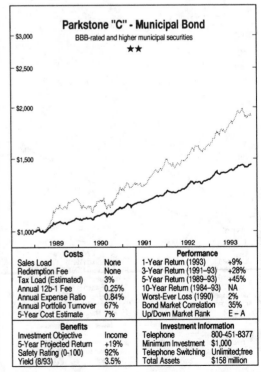

Parkstone "C" - Municipal Bond

BBB-rated and higher municipal securities

★★

Costs		Performance	
Sales Load	None	1-Year Return (1993)	+9%
Redemption Fee	None	3-Year Return (1991–93)	+28%
Tax Load (Estimated)	3%	5-Year Return (1989–93)	+45%
Annual 12b-1 Fee	0.25%	10-Year Return (1984–93)	NA
Annual Expense Ratio	0.84%	Worst-Ever Loss (1990)	2%
Annual Portfolio Turnover	67%	Bond Market Correlation	35%
5-Year Cost Estimate	7%	Up/Down Market Rank	E – A

Benefits		Investment Information	
Investment Objective	Income	Telephone	800-451-8377
5-Year Projected Return	+19%	Minimum Investment	$1,000
Safety Rating (0-100)	92%	Telephone Switching	Unlimited;free
Yield (8/93)	3.5%	Total Assets	$158 million

Pioneer Tax-Free Income

A-rated and higher municipals

★

Bond Index

Fund

$3,000					
$2,500					
$2,000					
$1,500					
$1,000					
	1989	1990	1991	1992	1993

Costs		Performance	
Sales Load	4.7%	1-Year Return (1993)	+13%
Redemption Fee	None	3-Year Return (1991–93)	+38%
Tax Load (Estimated)	3%	5-Year Return (1989–93)	+64%
Annual 12b-1 Fee	0.25%	10-Year Return (1984–93)	NA
Annual Expense Ratio	0.87%	Worst-Ever Loss (1987)	17%
Annual Portfolio Turnover	60%	Bond Market Correlation	42%
5-Year Cost Estimate	13%	Up/Down Market Rank	A – E

Benefits		Investment Information	
Investment Objective	Income	Telephone	800-225-6292
5-Year Projected Return	+21%	Minimum Investment	$1,000
Safety Rating (0-100)	91%	Telephone Switching	Unlimited;free
Yield (8/93)	3.9%	Total Assets	$513 million

Price - Tax-Free High Yield

Medium quality municipals

★★★★

$3,000					
$2,500					
$2,000					
$1,500					
$1,000					
	1989	1990	1991	1992	1993

Costs		Performance	
Sales Load	None	1-Year Return (1993)	+13%
Redemption Fee	None	3-Year Return (1991–93)	+38%
Tax Load (Estimated)	3%	5-Year Return (1989–93)	+62%
Annual 12b-1 Fee	None	10-Year Return (1984–93)	NA
Annual Expense Ratio	0.83%	Worst-Ever Loss (1987)	11%
Annual Portfolio Turnover	34%	Bond Market Correlation	45%
5-Year Cost Estimate	6%	Up/Down Market Rank	C – A

Benefits		Investment Information	
Investment Objective	Income	Telephone	800-638-5660
5-Year Projected Return	+29%	Minimum Investment	$2,500
Safety Rating (0-100)	92%	Telephone Switching	1 per qtr;free
Yield (8/93)	5.3%	Total Assets	$900 million

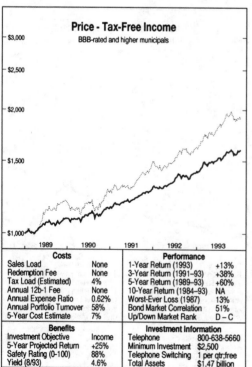

Price - Tax-Free Income

BBB-rated and higher municipals

$3,000					
$2,500					
$2,000					
$1,500					
$1,000					
	1989	1990	1991	1992	1993

Costs		Performance	
Sales Load	None	1-Year Return (1993)	+13%
Redemption Fee	None	3-Year Return (1991–93)	+38%
Tax Load (Estimated)	4%	5-Year Return (1989–93)	+60%
Annual 12b-1 Fee	None	10-Year Return (1984–93)	NA
Annual Expense Ratio	0.62%	Worst-Ever Loss (1987)	13%
Annual Portfolio Turnover	58%	Bond Market Correlation	51%
5-Year Cost Estimate	7%	Up/Down Market Rank	D – C

Benefits		Investment Information	
Investment Objective	Income	Telephone	800-638-5660
5-Year Projected Return	+25%	Minimum Investment	$2,500
Safety Rating (0-100)	88%	Telephone Switching	1 per qtr;free
Yield (8/93)	4.6%	Total Assets	$1.47 billion

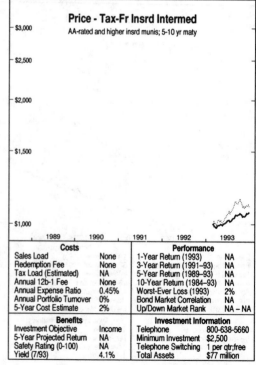

Price - Tax-Fr Insrd Intermed

AA-rated and higher insrd munis; 5-10 yr maty

$3,000					
$2,500					
$2,000					
$1,500					
$1,000					
	1989	1990	1991	1992	1993

Costs		Performance	
Sales Load	None	1-Year Return (1993)	NA
Redemption Fee	None	3-Year Return (1991–93)	NA
Tax Load (Estimated)	NA	5-Year Return (1989–93)	NA
Annual 12b-1 Fee	None	10-Year Return (1984–93)	NA
Annual Expense Ratio	0.45%	Worst-Ever Loss (1993)	2%
Annual Portfolio Turnover	0%	Bond Market Correlation	NA
5-Year Cost Estimate	2%	Up/Down Market Rank	NA – NA

Benefits		Investment Information	
Investment Objective	Income	Telephone	800-638-5660
5-Year Projected Return	NA	Minimum Investment	$2,500
Safety Rating (0-100)	NA	Telephone Switching	1 per qtr;free
Yield (7/93)	4.1%	Total Assets	$77 million

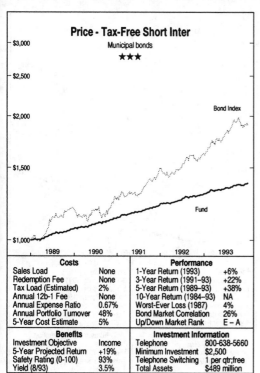

Price - Tax-Free Short Inter
Municipal bonds
★★★

Bond Index

Fund

Costs		Performance	
Sales Load	None	1-Year Return (1993)	+6%
Redemption Fee	None	3-Year Return (1991–93)	+22%
Tax Load (Estimated)	2%	5-Year Return (1989–93)	+38%
Annual 12b-1 Fee	None	10-Year Return (1984–93)	NA
Annual Expense Ratio	0.67%	Worst-Ever Loss (1987)	4%
Annual Portfolio Turnover	48%	Bond Market Correlation	26%
5-Year Cost Estimate	5%	Up/Down Market Rank	E – A

Benefits		Investment Information	
Investment Objective	Income	Telephone	800-638-5660
5-Year Projected Return	+19%	Minimum Investment	$2,500
Safety Rating (0-100)	93%	Telephone Switching	1 per qtr;free
Yield (8/93)	3.5%	Total Assets	$489 million

Prudential California Muni "B"
Investment-grade California long term munis

Costs		Performance	
Sales Load	None	1-Year Return (1993)	+12%
Redemption Fee	5.3%	3-Year Return (1991–93)	+34%
Tax Load (Estimated)	4%	5-Year Return (1989–93)	+53%
Annual 12b-1 Fee	0.50%	10-Year Return (1984–93)	NA
Annual Expense Ratio	1.28%	Worst-Ever Loss (1987)	15%
Annual Portfolio Turnover	53%	Bond Market Correlation	44%
5-Year Cost Estimate	12%	Up/Down Market Rank	E – C

Benefits		Investment Information	
Investment Objective	Income	Telephone	800-225-1852
5-Year Projected Return	+23%	Minimum Investment	$1,000
Safety Rating (0-100)	89%	Telephone Switching	Unlimited;free
Yield (8/93)	4.3%	Total Assets	$203 million

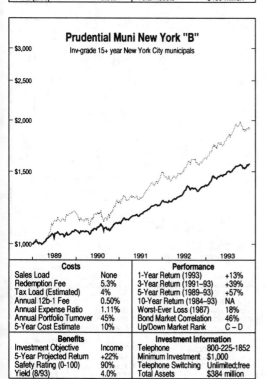

Prudential Muni New York "B"
Inv-grade 15+ year New York City municipals

Costs		Performance	
Sales Load	None	1-Year Return (1993)	+13%
Redemption Fee	5.3%	3-Year Return (1991–93)	+39%
Tax Load (Estimated)	4%	5-Year Return (1989–93)	+57%
Annual 12b-1 Fee	0.50%	10-Year Return (1984–93)	NA
Annual Expense Ratio	1.11%	Worst-Ever Loss (1987)	18%
Annual Portfolio Turnover	45%	Bond Market Correlation	46%
5-Year Cost Estimate	10%	Up/Down Market Rank	C – D

Benefits		Investment Information	
Investment Objective	Income	Telephone	800-225-1852
5-Year Projected Return	+22%	Minimum Investment	$1,000
Safety Rating (0-100)	90%	Telephone Switching	Unlimited;free
Yield (8/93)	4.0%	Total Assets	$384 million

Prudential National Muni "B"
A and BBB-rated long term municipals

Costs		Performance	
Sales Load	None	1-Year Return (1993)	+12%
Redemption Fee	5.3%	3-Year Return (1991–93)	+37%
Tax Load (Estimated)	3%	5-Year Return (1989–93)	+56%
Annual 12b-1 Fee	0.50%	10-Year Return (1984–93)	NA
Annual Expense Ratio	1.15%	Worst-Ever Loss (1987)	16%
Annual Portfolio Turnover	124%	Bond Market Correlation	48%
5-Year Cost Estimate	10%	Up/Down Market Rank	B – E

Benefits		Investment Information	
Investment Objective	Income	Telephone	800-225-1852
5-Year Projected Return	+25%	Minimum Investment	$1,000
Safety Rating (0-100)	90%	Telephone Switching	Unlimited;free
Yield (8/93)	4.5%	Total Assets	$866 million

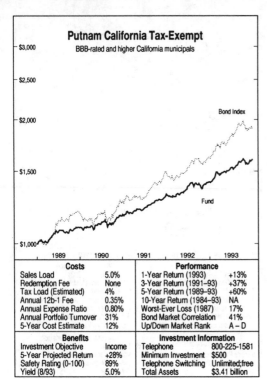

Putnam California Tax-Exempt
BBB-rated and higher California municipals

Costs		Performance	
Sales Load	5.0%	1-Year Return (1993)	+13%
Redemption Fee	None	3-Year Return (1991–93)	+37%
Tax Load (Estimated)	4%	5-Year Return (1989–93)	+60%
Annual 12b-1 Fee	0.35%	10-Year Return (1984–93)	NA
Annual Expense Ratio	0.80%	Worst-Ever Loss (1987)	17%
Annual Portfolio Turnover	31%	Bond Market Correlation	41%
5-Year Cost Estimate	12%	Up/Down Market Rank	A – D

Benefits		Investment Information	
Investment Objective	Income	Telephone	800-225-1581
5-Year Projected Return	+28%	Minimum Investment	$500
Safety Rating (0-100)	89%	Telephone Switching	Unlimited;free
Yield (8/93)	5.0%	Total Assets	$3.41 billion

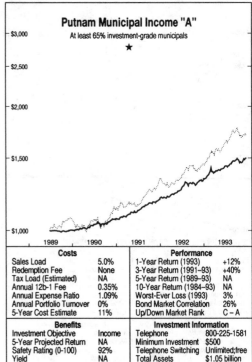

Putnam Municipal Income "A"
At least 65% investment-grade municipals
★

Costs		Performance	
Sales Load	5.0%	1-Year Return (1993)	+12%
Redemption Fee	None	3-Year Return (1991–93)	+40%
Tax Load (Estimated)	NA	5-Year Return (1989–93)	NA
Annual 12b-1 Fee	0.35%	10-Year Return (1984–93)	NA
Annual Expense Ratio	1.09%	Worst-Ever Loss (1993)	3%
Annual Portfolio Turnover	0%	Bond Market Correlation	26%
5-Year Cost Estimate	11%	Up/Down Market Rank	C – A

Benefits		Investment Information	
Investment Objective	Income	Telephone	800-225-1581
5-Year Projected Return	NA	Minimum Investment	$500
Safety Rating (0-100)	92%	Telephone Switching	Unlimited;free
Yield	NA	Total Assets	$1.05 billion

Putnam New York Tax-Exempt
BBB-rated and higher long-term New York munis

Costs		Performance	
Sales Load	5.0%	1-Year Return (1993)	+14%
Redemption Fee	None	3-Year Return (1991–93)	+44%
Tax Load (Estimated)	5%	5-Year Return (1989–93)	+63%
Annual 12b-1 Fee	0.35%	10-Year Return (1984–93)	NA
Annual Expense Ratio	0.90%	Worst-Ever Loss (1987)	16%
Annual Portfolio Turnover	40%	Bond Market Correlation	38%
5-Year Cost Estimate	14%	Up/Down Market Rank	A – E

Benefits		Investment Information	
Investment Objective	Income	Telephone	800-225-1581
5-Year Projected Return	+27%	Minimum Investment	$500
Safety Rating (0-100)	89%	Telephone Switching	Unlimited;free
Yield (8/93)	4.9%	Total Assets	$2.22 billion

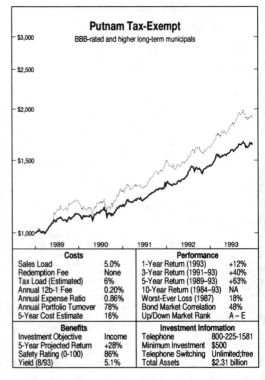

Putnam Tax-Exempt
BBB-rated and higher long-term municipals

Costs		Performance	
Sales Load	5.0%	1-Year Return (1993)	+12%
Redemption Fee	None	3-Year Return (1991–93)	+40%
Tax Load (Estimated)	6%	5-Year Return (1989–93)	+63%
Annual 12b-1 Fee	0.20%	10-Year Return (1984–93)	NA
Annual Expense Ratio	0.86%	Worst-Ever Loss (1987)	18%
Annual Portfolio Turnover	78%	Bond Market Correlation	48%
5-Year Cost Estimate	16%	Up/Down Market Rank	A – E

Benefits		Investment Information	
Investment Objective	Income	Telephone	800-225-1581
5-Year Projected Return	+28%	Minimum Investment	$500
Safety Rating (0-100)	86%	Telephone Switching	Unlimited;free
Yield (8/93)	5.1%	Total Assets	$2.31 billion

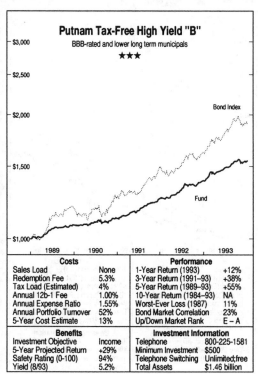

Putnam Tax-Free High Yield "B"

BBB-rated and lower long term municipals

★★★

Chart: $1,000 to $3,000 scale, years 1989–1993, showing Bond Index and Fund lines

Costs		Performance	
Sales Load	None	1-Year Return (1993)	+12%
Redemption Fee	5.3%	3-Year Return (1991–93)	+38%
Tax Load (Estimated)	4%	5-Year Return (1989–93)	+55%
Annual 12b-1 Fee	1.00%	10-Year Return (1984–93)	NA
Annual Expense Ratio	1.55%	Worst-Ever Loss (1987)	11%
Annual Portfolio Turnover	52%	Bond Market Correlation	23%
5-Year Cost Estimate	13%	Up/Down Market Rank	E – A

Benefits		Investment Information	
Investment Objective	Income	Telephone	800-225-1581
5-Year Projected Return	+29%	Minimum Investment	$500
Safety Rating (0-100)	94%	Telephone Switching	Unlimited;free
Yield (8/93)	5.2%	Total Assets	$1.46 billion

Putnam Tax-Free Insured

AAA-rated government guaranteed municipals

Chart: $1,000 to $3,000 scale, years 1989–1993

Costs		Performance	
Sales Load	None	1-Year Return (1993)	+11%
Redemption Fee	5.3%	3-Year Return (1991–93)	+32%
Tax Load (Estimated)	4%	5-Year Return (1989–93)	+49%
Annual 12b-1 Fee	1.00%	10-Year Return (1984–93)	NA
Annual Expense Ratio	1.79%	Worst-Ever Loss (1987)	15%
Annual Portfolio Turnover	57%	Bond Market Correlation	36%
5-Year Cost Estimate	15%	Up/Down Market Rank	D – D

Benefits		Investment Information	
Investment Objective	Income	Telephone	800-225-1581
5-Year Projected Return	+23%	Minimum Investment	$500
Safety Rating (0-100)	89%	Telephone Switching	Unlimited;free
Yield (8/93)	4.2%	Total Assets	$569 million

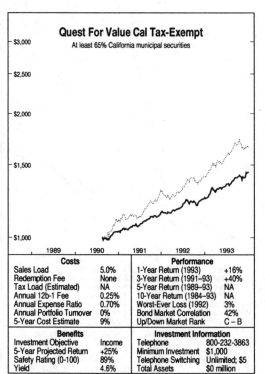

Quest For Value Cal Tax-Exempt

At least 65% California municipal securities

Chart: $1,000 to $3,000 scale, years 1989–1993

Costs		Performance	
Sales Load	5.0%	1-Year Return (1993)	+16%
Redemption Fee	None	3-Year Return (1991–93)	+40%
Tax Load (Estimated)	NA	5-Year Return (1989–93)	NA
Annual 12b-1 Fee	0.25%	10-Year Return (1984–93)	NA
Annual Expense Ratio	0.70%	Worst-Ever Loss (1992)	3%
Annual Portfolio Turnover	0%	Bond Market Correlation	42%
5-Year Cost Estimate	9%	Up/Down Market Rank	C – B

Benefits		Investment Information	
Investment Objective	Income	Telephone	800-232-3863
5-Year Projected Return	+25%	Minimum Investment	$1,000
Safety Rating (0-100)	89%	Telephone Switching	Unlimited; $5
Yield	4.6%	Total Assets	$0 million

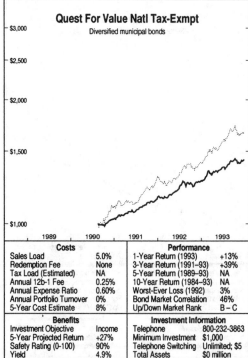

Quest For Value Natl Tax-Exmpt

Diversified municipal bonds

Chart: $1,000 to $3,000 scale, years 1989–1993

Costs		Performance	
Sales Load	5.0%	1-Year Return (1993)	+13%
Redemption Fee	None	3-Year Return (1991–93)	+39%
Tax Load (Estimated)	NA	5-Year Return (1989–93)	NA
Annual 12b-1 Fee	0.25%	10-Year Return (1984–93)	NA
Annual Expense Ratio	0.60%	Worst-Ever Loss (1992)	3%
Annual Portfolio Turnover	0%	Bond Market Correlation	46%
5-Year Cost Estimate	8%	Up/Down Market Rank	B – C

Benefits		Investment Information	
Investment Objective	Income	Telephone	800-232-3863
5-Year Projected Return	+27%	Minimum Investment	$1,000
Safety Rating (0-100)	90%	Telephone Switching	Unlimited; $5
Yield	4.9%	Total Assets	$0 million

TAX FREE

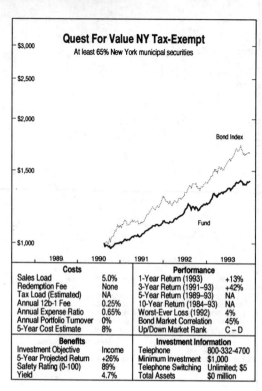

Quest For Value NY Tax-Exempt
At least 65% New York municipal securities

(chart: Bond Index and Fund lines, 1989–1993, $1,000–$3,000 scale)

Costs		Performance	
Sales Load	5.0%	1-Year Return (1993)	+13%
Redemption Fee	None	3-Year Return (1991–93)	+42%
Tax Load (Estimated)	NA	5-Year Return (1989–93)	NA
Annual 12b-1 Fee	0.25%	10-Year Return (1984–93)	NA
Annual Expense Ratio	0.65%	Worst-Ever Loss (1992)	4%
Annual Portfolio Turnover	0%	Bond Market Correlation	45%
5-Year Cost Estimate	8%	Up/Down Market Rank	C – D

Benefits		Investment Information	
Investment Objective	Income	Telephone	800-332-4700
5-Year Projected Return	+26%	Minimum Investment	$1,000
Safety Rating (0-100)	89%	Telephone Switching	Unlimited; $5
Yield	4.7%	Total Assets	$0 million

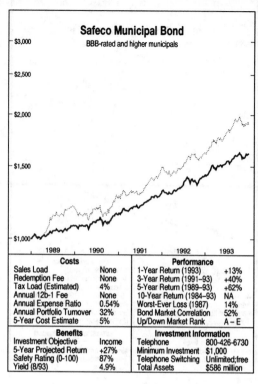

Safeco Municipal Bond
BBB-rated and higher municipals

(chart: 1989–1993, $1,000–$3,000 scale)

Costs		Performance	
Sales Load	None	1-Year Return (1993)	+13%
Redemption Fee	None	3-Year Return (1991–93)	+40%
Tax Load (Estimated)	4%	5-Year Return (1989–93)	+62%
Annual 12b-1 Fee	None	10-Year Return (1984–93)	NA
Annual Expense Ratio	0.54%	Worst-Ever Loss (1987)	14%
Annual Portfolio Turnover	32%	Bond Market Correlation	52%
5-Year Cost Estimate	5%	Up/Down Market Rank	A – E

Benefits		Investment Information	
Investment Objective	Income	Telephone	800-426-6730
5-Year Projected Return	+27%	Minimum Investment	$1,000
Safety Rating (0-100)	87%	Telephone Switching	Unlimited;free
Yield (8/93)	4.9%	Total Assets	$586 million

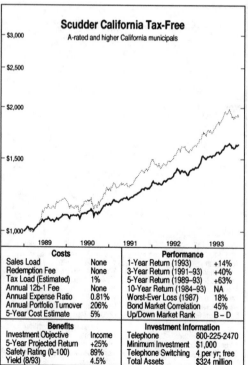

Scudder California Tax-Free
A-rated and higher California municipals

(chart: 1989–1993, $1,000–$3,000 scale)

Costs		Performance	
Sales Load	None	1-Year Return (1993)	+14%
Redemption Fee	None	3-Year Return (1991–93)	+40%
Tax Load (Estimated)	1%	5-Year Return (1989–93)	+63%
Annual 12b-1 Fee	None	10-Year Return (1984–93)	NA
Annual Expense Ratio	0.81%	Worst-Ever Loss (1987)	18%
Annual Portfolio Turnover	206%	Bond Market Correlation	45%
5-Year Cost Estimate	5%	Up/Down Market Rank	B – D

Benefits		Investment Information	
Investment Objective	Income	Telephone	800-225-2470
5-Year Projected Return	+25%	Minimum Investment	$1,000
Safety Rating (0-100)	89%	Telephone Switching	4 per yr; free
Yield (8/93)	4.5%	Total Assets	$324 million

Scudder Managed Municipal Bond
A-rated & higher municipals; 20% taxable bnds

(chart: 1989–1993, $1,000–$3,000 scale)

Costs		Performance	
Sales Load	None	1-Year Return (1993)	+13%
Redemption Fee	None	3-Year Return (1991–93)	+38%
Tax Load (Estimated)	3%	5-Year Return (1989–93)	+61%
Annual 12b-1 Fee	None	10-Year Return (1984–93)	NA
Annual Expense Ratio	0.64%	Worst-Ever Loss (1987)	14%
Annual Portfolio Turnover	63%	Bond Market Correlation	45%
5-Year Cost Estimate	7%	Up/Down Market Rank	B – C

Benefits		Investment Information	
Investment Objective	Income	Telephone	800-225-2470
5-Year Projected Return	+26%	Minimum Investment	$1,000
Safety Rating (0-100)	89%	Telephone Switching	4 per yr; free
Yield (8/93)	4.8%	Total Assets	$900 million

Scudder New York Tax-Free
Investment-grade New York State municipals

Bond Index
Fund

Costs		Performance	
Sales Load	None	1-Year Return (1993)	+13%
Redemption Fee	None	3-Year Return (1991–93)	+42%
Tax Load (Estimated)	1%	5-Year Return (1989–93)	+62%
Annual 12b-1 Fee	None	10-Year Return (1984–93)	NA
Annual Expense Ratio	0.87%	Worst-Ever Loss (1987)	15%
Annual Portfolio Turnover	201%	Bond Market Correlation	47%
5-Year Cost Estimate	5%	Up/Down Market Rank	C – D

Benefits		Investment Information	
Investment Objective	Income	Telephone	800-225-2470
5-Year Projected Return	+22%	Minimum Investment	$1,000
Safety Rating (0-100)	89%	Telephone Switching	4 per yr; free
Yield (8/93)	4.1%	Total Assets	$214 million

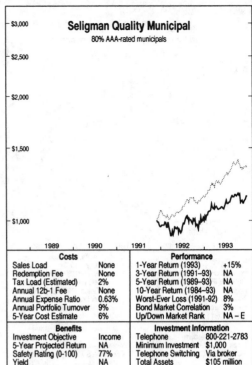

Seligman Quality Municipal
80% AAA-rated municipals

Costs		Performance	
Sales Load	None	1-Year Return (1993)	+15%
Redemption Fee	None	3-Year Return (1991–93)	NA
Tax Load (Estimated)	2%	5-Year Return (1989–93)	NA
Annual 12b-1 Fee	None	10-Year Return (1984–93)	NA
Annual Expense Ratio	0.63%	Worst-Ever Loss (1991-92)	8%
Annual Portfolio Turnover	9%	Bond Market Correlation	3%
5-Year Cost Estimate	6%	Up/Down Market Rank	NA – E

Benefits		Investment Information	
Investment Objective	Income	Telephone	800-221-2783
5-Year Projected Return	NA	Minimum Investment	$1,000
Safety Rating (0-100)	77%	Telephone Switching	Via broker
Yield	NA	Total Assets	$105 million

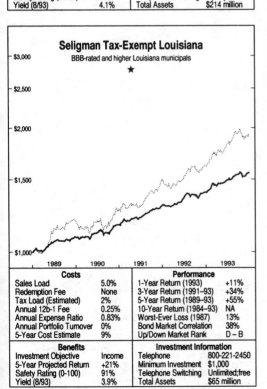

Seligman Tax-Exempt Louisiana
BBB-rated and higher Louisiana municipals
★

Costs		Performance	
Sales Load	5.0%	1-Year Return (1993)	+11%
Redemption Fee	None	3-Year Return (1991–93)	+34%
Tax Load (Estimated)	2%	5-Year Return (1989–93)	+55%
Annual 12b-1 Fee	0.25%	10-Year Return (1984–93)	NA
Annual Expense Ratio	0.83%	Worst-Ever Loss (1987)	13%
Annual Portfolio Turnover	0%	Bond Market Correlation	38%
5-Year Cost Estimate	9%	Up/Down Market Rank	D – B

Benefits		Investment Information	
Investment Objective	Income	Telephone	800-221-2450
5-Year Projected Return	+21%	Minimum Investment	$1,000
Safety Rating (0-100)	91%	Telephone Switching	Unlimited;free
Yield (8/93)	3.9%	Total Assets	$65 million

Seligman Tax-Exempt Maryland
BBB-rated and higher Maryland municipals
★★

Costs		Performance	
Sales Load	5.0%	1-Year Return (1993)	+12%
Redemption Fee	None	3-Year Return (1991–93)	+34%
Tax Load (Estimated)	3%	5-Year Return (1989–93)	+56%
Annual 12b-1 Fee	0.25%	10-Year Return (1984–93)	NA
Annual Expense Ratio	0.88%	Worst-Ever Loss (1987)	17%
Annual Portfolio Turnover	0%	Bond Market Correlation	38%
5-Year Cost Estimate	10%	Up/Down Market Rank	D – C

Benefits		Investment Information	
Investment Objective	Income	Telephone	800-221-2450
5-Year Projected Return	+23%	Minimum Investment	$1,000
Safety Rating (0-100)	91%	Telephone Switching	Unlimited;free
Yield (8/93)	4.2%	Total Assets	$62 million

TAX FREE

Seligman Tax-Exempt Mass
BBB-rated and higher Massachusetts municipals

Costs		Performance	
Sales Load	5.0%	1-Year Return (1993)	+12%
Redemption Fee	None	3-Year Return (1991–93)	+37%
Tax Load (Estimated)	3%	5-Year Return (1989–93)	+55%
Annual 12b-1 Fee	0.25%	10-Year Return (1984–93)	NA
Annual Expense Ratio	0.83%	Worst-Ever Loss (1987)	16%
Annual Portfolio Turnover	42%	Bond Market Correlation	40%
5-Year Cost Estimate	12%	Up/Down Market Rank	C – B

Benefits		Investment Information	
Investment Objective	Income	Telephone	800-221-2450
5-Year Projected Return	+23%	Minimum Investment	$1,000
Safety Rating (0-100)	91%	Telephone Switching	Unlimited;free
Yield (8/93)	4.2%	Total Assets	$137 million

Seligman Tax-Exempt Michigan
BBB-rated and higher Michigan municipals
★

Costs		Performance	
Sales Load	5.0%	1-Year Return (1993)	+11%
Redemption Fee	None	3-Year Return (1991–93)	+36%
Tax Load (Estimated)	3%	5-Year Return (1989–93)	+57%
Annual 12b-1 Fee	0.25%	10-Year Return (1984–93)	NA
Annual Expense Ratio	0.80%	Worst-Ever Loss (1987)	17%
Annual Portfolio Turnover	6%	Bond Market Correlation	39%
5-Year Cost Estimate	10%	Up/Down Market Rank	B – C

Benefits		Investment Information	
Investment Objective	Income	Telephone	800-221-2450
5-Year Projected Return	+22%	Minimum Investment	$1,000
Safety Rating (0-100)	91%	Telephone Switching	Unlimited;free
Yield (8/93)	4.1%	Total Assets	$160 million

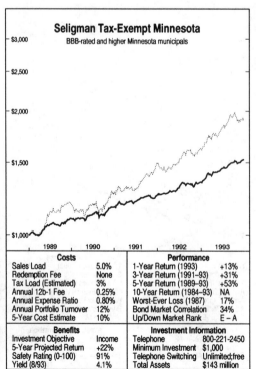

Seligman Tax-Exempt Minnesota
BBB-rated and higher Minnesota municipals

Costs		Performance	
Sales Load	5.0%	1-Year Return (1993)	+13%
Redemption Fee	None	3-Year Return (1991–93)	+31%
Tax Load (Estimated)	3%	5-Year Return (1989–93)	+53%
Annual 12b-1 Fee	0.25%	10-Year Return (1984–93)	NA
Annual Expense Ratio	0.80%	Worst-Ever Loss (1987)	17%
Annual Portfolio Turnover	12%	Bond Market Correlation	34%
5-Year Cost Estimate	10%	Up/Down Market Rank	E – A

Benefits		Investment Information	
Investment Objective	Income	Telephone	800-221-2450
5-Year Projected Return	+22%	Minimum Investment	$1,000
Safety Rating (0-100)	91%	Telephone Switching	Unlimited;free
Yield (8/93)	4.1%	Total Assets	$143 million

Seligman Tax-Exempt National
BBB-rated and higher municipals

Costs		Performance	
Sales Load	5.0%	1-Year Return (1993)	+14%
Redemption Fee	None	3-Year Return (1991–93)	+37%
Tax Load (Estimated)	1%	5-Year Return (1989–93)	+56%
Annual 12b-1 Fee	0.25%	10-Year Return (1984–93)	NA
Annual Expense Ratio	0.80%	Worst-Ever Loss (1987)	21%
Annual Portfolio Turnover	68%	Bond Market Correlation	45%
5-Year Cost Estimate	10%	Up/Down Market Rank	A – E

Benefits		Investment Information	
Investment Objective	Income	Telephone	800-221-2450
5-Year Projected Return	+28%	Minimum Investment	$1,000
Safety Rating (0-100)	88%	Telephone Switching	Unlimited;free
Yield (8/93)	5.1%	Total Assets	$134 million

TAX FREE

Seligman Tax-Exempt New York

BBB-rated and higher New York municipals

(Chart showing Bond Index and Fund from 1989 to 1993, $1,000 to $3,000 scale)

Costs		Performance	
Sales Load	5.0%	1-Year Return (1993)	+13%
Redemption Fee	None	3-Year Return (1991–93)	+40%
Tax Load (Estimated)	3%	5-Year Return (1989–93)	+58%
Annual 12b-1 Fee	0.25%	10-Year Return (1984–93)	NA
Annual Expense Ratio	0.80%	Worst-Ever Loss (1987)	19%
Annual Portfolio Turnover	20%	Bond Market Correlation	42%
5-Year Cost Estimate	10%	Up/Down Market Rank	B – E

Benefits		Investment Information	
Investment Objective	Income	Telephone	800-221-2450
5-Year Projected Return	+25%	Minimum Investment	$1,000
Safety Rating (0-100)	89%	Telephone Switching	Unlimited;free
Yield (8/93)	4.5%	Total Assets	$101 million

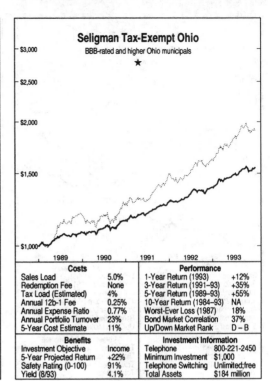

Seligman Tax-Exempt Ohio

BBB-rated and higher Ohio municipals

★

(Chart showing Bond Index and Fund from 1989 to 1993, $1,000 to $3,000 scale)

Costs		Performance	
Sales Load	5.0%	1-Year Return (1993)	+12%
Redemption Fee	None	3-Year Return (1991–93)	+35%
Tax Load (Estimated)	4%	5-Year Return (1989–93)	+55%
Annual 12b-1 Fee	0.25%	10-Year Return (1984–93)	NA
Annual Expense Ratio	0.77%	Worst-Ever Loss (1987)	18%
Annual Portfolio Turnover	23%	Bond Market Correlation	37%
5-Year Cost Estimate	11%	Up/Down Market Rank	D – B

Benefits		Investment Information	
Investment Objective	Income	Telephone	800-221-2450
5-Year Projected Return	+22%	Minimum Investment	$1,000
Safety Rating (0-100)	91%	Telephone Switching	Unlimited;free
Yield (8/93)	4.1%	Total Assets	$184 million

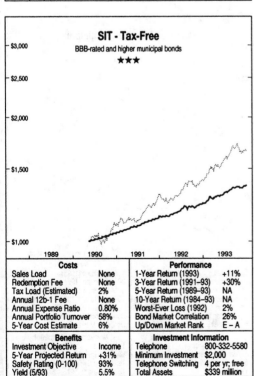

SIT - Tax-Free

BBB-rated and higher municipal bonds

★★★

(Chart showing fund from 1990 to 1993, $1,000 to $3,000 scale)

Costs		Performance	
Sales Load	None	1-Year Return (1993)	+11%
Redemption Fee	None	3-Year Return (1991–93)	+30%
Tax Load (Estimated)	2%	5-Year Return (1989–93)	NA
Annual 12b-1 Fee	None	10-Year Return (1984–93)	NA
Annual Expense Ratio	0.80%	Worst-Ever Loss (1992)	2%
Annual Portfolio Turnover	58%	Bond Market Correlation	26%
5-Year Cost Estimate	6%	Up/Down Market Rank	E – A

Benefits		Investment Information	
Investment Objective	Income	Telephone	800-332-5580
5-Year Projected Return	+31%	Minimum Investment	$2,000
Safety Rating (0-100)	93%	Telephone Switching	4 per yr; free
Yield (5/93)	5.5%	Total Assets	$339 million

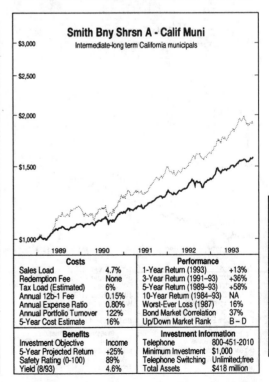

Smith Bny Shrsn A - Calif Muni

Intermediate-long term California municipals

(Chart showing fund from 1989 to 1993, $1,000 to $3,000 scale)

Costs		Performance	
Sales Load	4.7%	1-Year Return (1993)	+13%
Redemption Fee	None	3-Year Return (1991–93)	+36%
Tax Load (Estimated)	6%	5-Year Return (1989–93)	+58%
Annual 12b-1 Fee	0.15%	10-Year Return (1984–93)	NA
Annual Expense Ratio	0.80%	Worst-Ever Loss (1987)	16%
Annual Portfolio Turnover	122%	Bond Market Correlation	37%
5-Year Cost Estimate	16%	Up/Down Market Rank	B – D

Benefits		Investment Information	
Investment Objective	Income	Telephone	800-451-2010
5-Year Projected Return	+25%	Minimum Investment	$1,000
Safety Rating (0-100)	89%	Telephone Switching	Unlimited;free
Yield (8/93)	4.6%	Total Assets	$418 million

TAX FREE

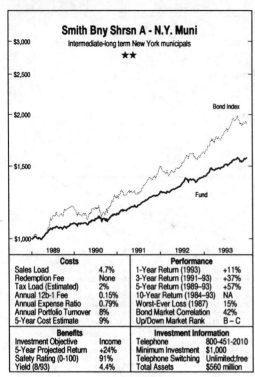

Smith Bny Shrsn A - N.Y. Muni
Intermediate-long term New York municipals
★★

Bond Index

Fund

Costs		Performance	
Sales Load	4.7%	1-Year Return (1993)	+11%
Redemption Fee	None	3-Year Return (1991–93)	+37%
Tax Load (Estimated)	2%	5-Year Return (1989–93)	+57%
Annual 12b-1 Fee	0.15%	10-Year Return (1984–93)	NA
Annual Expense Ratio	0.79%	Worst-Ever Loss (1987)	15%
Annual Portfolio Turnover	8%	Bond Market Correlation	42%
5-Year Cost Estimate	9%	Up/Down Market Rank	B – C

Benefits		Investment Information	
Investment Objective	Income	Telephone	800-451-2010
5-Year Projected Return	+24%	Minimum Investment	$1,000
Safety Rating (0-100)	91%	Telephone Switching	Unlimited;free
Yield (8/93)	4.4%	Total Assets	$560 million

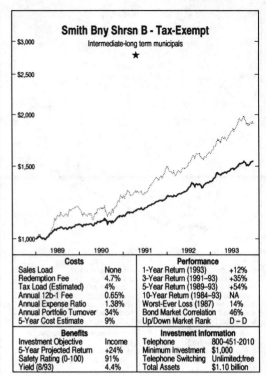

Smith Bny Shrsn B - Tax-Exempt
Intermediate-long term municipals
★

Costs		Performance	
Sales Load	None	1-Year Return (1993)	+12%
Redemption Fee	4.7%	3-Year Return (1991–93)	+35%
Tax Load (Estimated)	4%	5-Year Return (1989–93)	+54%
Annual 12b-1 Fee	0.65%	10-Year Return (1984–93)	NA
Annual Expense Ratio	1.38%	Worst-Ever Loss (1987)	14%
Annual Portfolio Turnover	34%	Bond Market Correlation	46%
5-Year Cost Estimate	9%	Up/Down Market Rank	D – D

Benefits		Investment Information	
Investment Objective	Income	Telephone	800-451-2010
5-Year Projected Return	+24%	Minimum Investment	$1,000
Safety Rating (0-100)	91%	Telephone Switching	Unlimited;free
Yield (8/93)	4.4%	Total Assets	$1.10 billion

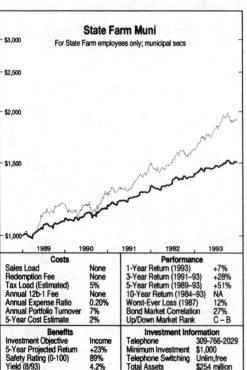

State Farm Muni
For State Farm employees only; municipal secs

Costs		Performance	
Sales Load	None	1-Year Return (1993)	+7%
Redemption Fee	None	3-Year Return (1991–93)	+28%
Tax Load (Estimated)	5%	5-Year Return (1989–93)	+51%
Annual 12b-1 Fee	None	10-Year Return (1984–93)	NA
Annual Expense Ratio	0.20%	Worst-Ever Loss (1987)	12%
Annual Portfolio Turnover	7%	Bond Market Correlation	27%
5-Year Cost Estimate	2%	Up/Down Market Rank	C – B

Benefits		Investment Information	
Investment Objective	Income	Telephone	309-766-2029
5-Year Projected Return	+23%	Minimum Investment	$1,000
Safety Rating (0-100)	89%	Telephone Switching	Unlim,free
Yield (8/93)	4.2%	Total Assets	$254 million

Stein Roe Managed Municipals
75% A-rated and higher municipals
★★★★★

Costs		Performance	
Sales Load	None	1-Year Return (1993)	+11%
Redemption Fee	None	3-Year Return (1991–93)	+35%
Tax Load (Estimated)	3%	5-Year Return (1989–93)	+60%
Annual 12b-1 Fee	None	10-Year Return (1984–93)	NA
Annual Expense Ratio	0.64%	Worst-Ever Loss (1987)	15%
Annual Portfolio Turnover	63%	Bond Market Correlation	36%
5-Year Cost Estimate	6%	Up/Down Market Rank	A – D

Benefits		Investment Information	
Investment Objective	Income	Telephone	800-338-2550
5-Year Projected Return	+25%	Minimum Investment	$1,000
Safety Rating (0-100)	92%	Telephone Switching	4 per yr; free
Yield (8/93)	4.6%	Total Assets	$776 million

TAX FREE

Strong High Yield Muni Bond
Medium and low quality municipals

Costs		Performance	
Sales Load	None	1-Year Return (1993)	NA
Redemption Fee	None	3-Year Return (1991–93)	NA
Tax Load (Estimated)	NA	5-Year Return (1989–93)	NA
Annual 12b-1 Fee	None	10-Year Return (1984–93)	NA
Annual Expense Ratio	1.10%	Worst-Ever Loss (1993)	0%
Annual Portfolio Turnover	0%	Bond Market Correlation	NA
5-Year Cost Estimate	6%	Up/Down Market Rank	NA – NA

Benefits		Investment Information	
Investment Objective	Income	Telephone	800-368-3863
5-Year Projected Return	NA	Minimum Investment	$1,000
Safety Rating (0-100)	NA	Telephone Switching	5 per yr; free
Yield	7.1%	Total Assets	$0 million

Strong Insured Municipal Bond
65% diversified insurd muni secs; 35% AAA-rtd

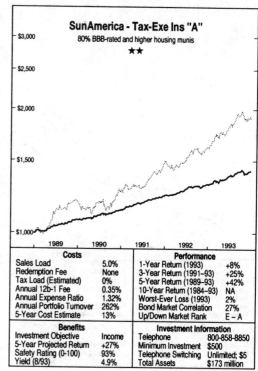

Costs		Performance	
Sales Load	None	1-Year Return (1993)	NA
Redemption Fee	None	3-Year Return (1991–93)	NA
Tax Load (Estimated)	2%	5-Year Return (1989–93)	NA
Annual 12b-1 Fee	None	10-Year Return (1984–93)	NA
Annual Expense Ratio	1.15%	Worst-Ever Loss (1993)	2%
Annual Portfolio Turnover	136%	Bond Market Correlation	NA
5-Year Cost Estimate	8%	Up/Down Market Rank	NA – NA

Benefits		Investment Information	
Investment Objective	Income	Telephone	800-368-3863
5-Year Projected Return	NA	Minimum Investment	$2,500
Safety Rating (0-100)	NA	Telephone Switching	5 per yr; free
Yield (8/93)	4.4%	Total Assets	$52 million

Strong Municipal Bond
BBB-rated and higher municipals
★

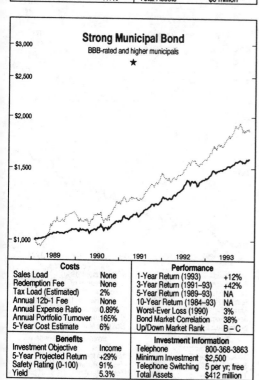

Costs		Performance	
Sales Load	None	1-Year Return (1993)	+12%
Redemption Fee	None	3-Year Return (1991–93)	+42%
Tax Load (Estimated)	2%	5-Year Return (1989–93)	NA
Annual 12b-1 Fee	None	10-Year Return (1984–93)	NA
Annual Expense Ratio	0.89%	Worst-Ever Loss (1990)	3%
Annual Portfolio Turnover	165%	Bond Market Correlation	38%
5-Year Cost Estimate	6%	Up/Down Market Rank	B – C

Benefits		Investment Information	
Investment Objective	Income	Telephone	800-368-3863
5-Year Projected Return	+29%	Minimum Investment	$2,500
Safety Rating (0-100)	91%	Telephone Switching	5 per yr; free
Yield	5.3%	Total Assets	$412 million

SunAmerica - Tax-Exe Ins "A"
80% BBB-rated and higher housing munis
★★

Costs		Performance	
Sales Load	5.0%	1-Year Return (1993)	+8%
Redemption Fee	None	3-Year Return (1991–93)	+25%
Tax Load (Estimated)	0%	5-Year Return (1989–93)	+42%
Annual 12b-1 Fee	0.35%	10-Year Return (1984–93)	NA
Annual Expense Ratio	1.32%	Worst-Ever Loss (1993)	2%
Annual Portfolio Turnover	262%	Bond Market Correlation	27%
5-Year Cost Estimate	13%	Up/Down Market Rank	E – A

Benefits		Investment Information	
Investment Objective	Income	Telephone	800-858-8850
5-Year Projected Return	+27%	Minimum Investment	$500
Safety Rating (0-100)	93%	Telephone Switching	Unlimited; $5
Yield (8/93)	4.9%	Total Assets	$173 million

TAX FREE

Thomson - Tax-Exempt "B"
80% BBB-rated and higher municipals; options

Bond Index

Fund

Costs		Performance	
Sales Load	None	1-Year Return (1993)	+11%
Redemption Fee	1.0%	3-Year Return (1991–93)	+30%
Tax Load (Estimated)	3%	5-Year Return (1989–93)	+50%
Annual 12b-1 Fee	1.00%	10-Year Return (1984–93)	NA
Annual Expense Ratio	1.80%	Worst-Ever Loss (1987)	16%
Annual Portfolio Turnover	107%	Bond Market Correlation	41%
5-Year Cost Estimate	13%	Up/Down Market Rank	C – E

Benefits		Investment Information	
Investment Objective	Income	Telephone	800-628-1237
5-Year Projected Return	+18%	Minimum Investment	$1,000
Safety Rating (0-100)	89%	Telephone Switching	Unlimited;free
Yield (8/93)	3.3%	Total Assets	$73 million

TNE - Tax-Exempt Income "A"
80% BBB-rated and higher; options; futures
★

Costs		Performance	
Sales Load	4.7%	1-Year Return (1993)	+13%
Redemption Fee	None	3-Year Return (1991–93)	+39%
Tax Load (Estimated)	3%	5-Year Return (1989–93)	+61%
Annual 12b-1 Fee	0.25%	10-Year Return (1984–93)	NA
Annual Expense Ratio	0.95%	Worst-Ever Loss (1987)	18%
Annual Portfolio Turnover	85%	Bond Market Correlation	47%
5-Year Cost Estimate	13%	Up/Down Market Rank	A – E

Benefits		Investment Information	
Investment Objective	Income	Telephone	800-343-7104
5-Year Projected Return	+25%	Minimum Investment	$2,500
Safety Rating (0-100)	90%	Telephone Switching	Unlimited;free
Yield (8/93)	4.6%	Total Assets	$214 million

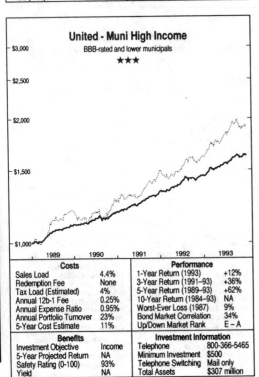

United - Muni High Income
BBB-rated and lower municipals
★★★

Costs		Performance	
Sales Load	4.4%	1-Year Return (1993)	+12%
Redemption Fee	None	3-Year Return (1991–93)	+36%
Tax Load (Estimated)	4%	5-Year Return (1989–93)	+62%
Annual 12b-1 Fee	0.25%	10-Year Return (1984–93)	NA
Annual Expense Ratio	0.95%	Worst-Ever Loss (1987)	9%
Annual Portfolio Turnover	23%	Bond Market Correlation	34%
5-Year Cost Estimate	11%	Up/Down Market Rank	E – A

Benefits		Investment Information	
Investment Objective	Income	Telephone	800-366-5465
5-Year Projected Return	NA	Minimum Investment	$500
Safety Rating (0-100)	93%	Telephone Switching	Mail only
Yield	NA	Total Assets	$307 million

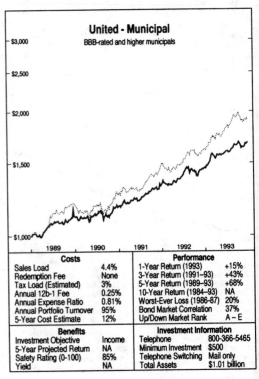

United - Municipal
BBB-rated and higher municipals

Costs		Performance	
Sales Load	4.4%	1-Year Return (1993)	+15%
Redemption Fee	None	3-Year Return (1991–93)	+43%
Tax Load (Estimated)	3%	5-Year Return (1989–93)	+68%
Annual 12b-1 Fee	0.25%	10-Year Return (1984–93)	NA
Annual Expense Ratio	0.81%	Worst-Ever Loss (1986-87)	20%
Annual Portfolio Turnover	95%	Bond Market Correlation	37%
5-Year Cost Estimate	12%	Up/Down Market Rank	A – E

Benefits		Investment Information	
Investment Objective	Income	Telephone	800-366-5465
5-Year Projected Return	NA	Minimum Investment	$500
Safety Rating (0-100)	85%	Telephone Switching	Mail only
Yield	NA	Total Assets	$1.01 billion

TAX FREE

1994 Mutual Fund Buyer's Guide

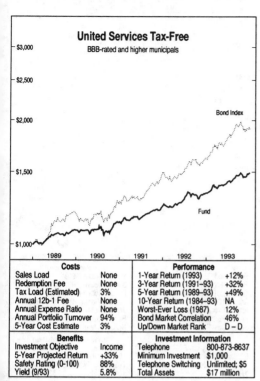

United Services Tax-Free
BBB-rated and higher municipals

Costs		Performance	
Sales Load	None	1-Year Return (1993)	+12%
Redemption Fee	None	3-Year Return (1991–93)	+32%
Tax Load (Estimated)	3%	5-Year Return (1989–93)	+49%
Annual 12b-1 Fee	None	10-Year Return (1984–93)	NA
Annual Expense Ratio	None	Worst-Ever Loss (1987)	12%
Annual Portfolio Turnover	94%	Bond Market Correlation	46%
5-Year Cost Estimate	3%	Up/Down Market Rank	D – D

Benefits		Investment Information	
Investment Objective	Income	Telephone	800-873-8637
5-Year Projected Return	+33%	Minimum Investment	$1,000
Safety Rating (0-100)	88%	Telephone Switching	Unlimited; $5
Yield (9/93)	5.8%	Total Assets	$17 million

USAA Tax-Exempt Intermediate
A-rated and higher municipals; 10-yr avg maty
★★

Costs		Performance	
Sales Load	None	1-Year Return (1993)	+11%
Redemption Fee	None	3-Year Return (1991–93)	+34%
Tax Load (Estimated)	3%	5-Year Return (1989–93)	+57%
Annual 12b-1 Fee	None	10-Year Return (1984–93)	NA
Annual Expense Ratio	0.42%	Worst-Ever Loss (1987)	9%
Annual Portfolio Turnover	35%	Bond Market Correlation	41%
5-Year Cost Estimate	4%	Up/Down Market Rank	E – A

Benefits		Investment Information	
Investment Objective	Income	Telephone	800-531-8181
5-Year Projected Return	+26%	Minimum Investment	$3,000
Safety Rating (0-100)	91%	Telephone Switching	6 per yr; $5
Yield (8/93)	4.7%	Total Assets	$1.49 billion

USAA Tax-Exempt Long Term
Investment grade municipals
★

Costs		Performance	
Sales Load	None	1-Year Return (1993)	+13%
Redemption Fee	None	3-Year Return (1991–93)	+37%
Tax Load (Estimated)	3%	5-Year Return (1989–93)	+62%
Annual 12b-1 Fee	None	10-Year Return (1984–93)	NA
Annual Expense Ratio	0.39%	Worst-Ever Loss (1987)	17%
Annual Portfolio Turnover	53%	Bond Market Correlation	45%
5-Year Cost Estimate	5%	Up/Down Market Rank	A – D

Benefits		Investment Information	
Investment Objective	Income	Telephone	800-531-8181
5-Year Projected Return	+28%	Minimum Investment	$3,000
Safety Rating (0-100)	90%	Telephone Switching	6 per yr; $5
Yield (8/93)	5.1%	Total Assets	$2.00 billion

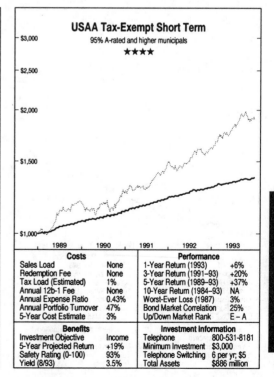

USAA Tax-Exempt Short Term
95% A-rated and higher municipals
★★★★

Costs		Performance	
Sales Load	None	1-Year Return (1993)	+6%
Redemption Fee	None	3-Year Return (1991–93)	+20%
Tax Load (Estimated)	1%	5-Year Return (1989–93)	+37%
Annual 12b-1 Fee	None	10-Year Return (1984–93)	NA
Annual Expense Ratio	0.43%	Worst-Ever Loss (1987)	3%
Annual Portfolio Turnover	47%	Bond Market Correlation	25%
5-Year Cost Estimate	3%	Up/Down Market Rank	E – A

Benefits		Investment Information	
Investment Objective	Income	Telephone	800-531-8181
5-Year Projected Return	+19%	Minimum Investment	$3,000
Safety Rating (0-100)	93%	Telephone Switching	6 per yr; $5
Yield (8/93)	3.5%	Total Assets	$886 million

T A X

F R E E

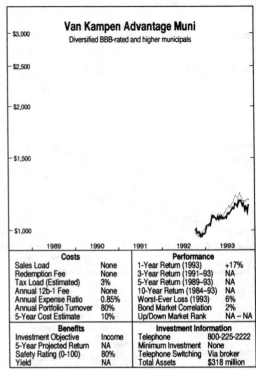

Value Line Tax-Exempt Hi Yield
Investment grade 10-40 year municipals

Bond Index

Fund

Costs		Performance	
Sales Load	None	1-Year Return (1993)	+13%
Redemption Fee	None	3-Year Return (1991–93)	+37%
Tax Load (Estimated)	2%	5-Year Return (1989–93)	+57%
Annual 12b-1 Fee	None	10-Year Return (1984–93)	NA
Annual Expense Ratio	0.74%	Worst-Ever Loss (1987)	11%
Annual Portfolio Turnover	30%	Bond Market Correlation	41%
5-Year Cost Estimate	5%	Up/Down Market Rank	E – B

Benefits		Investment Information	
Investment Objective	Income	Telephone	800-223-0818
5-Year Projected Return	+28%	Minimum Investment	$1,000
Safety Rating (0-100)	89%	Telephone Switching	8 per yr; free
Yield (8/93)	5.0%	Total Assets	$297 million

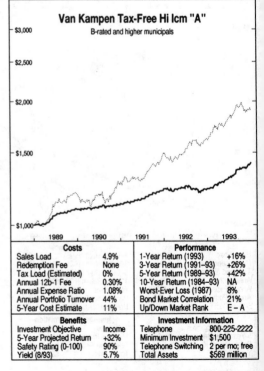

Van Kampen Advantage Muni
Diversified BBB-rated and higher municipals

Costs		Performance	
Sales Load	None	1-Year Return (1993)	+17%
Redemption Fee	None	3-Year Return (1991–93)	NA
Tax Load (Estimated)	3%	5-Year Return (1989–93)	NA
Annual 12b-1 Fee	None	10-Year Return (1984–93)	NA
Annual Expense Ratio	0.85%	Worst-Ever Loss (1993)	6%
Annual Portfolio Turnover	80%	Bond Market Correlation	2%
5-Year Cost Estimate	10%	Up/Down Market Rank	NA – NA

Benefits		Investment Information	
Investment Objective	Income	Telephone	800-225-2222
5-Year Projected Return	NA	Minimum Investment	None
Safety Rating (0-100)	80%	Telephone Switching	Via broker
Yield	NA	Total Assets	$318 million

Van Kampen Insured Tax-Fr "A"
Diversified insured municipals

Costs		Performance	
Sales Load	4.9%	1-Year Return (1993)	+12%
Redemption Fee	None	3-Year Return (1991–93)	+36%
Tax Load (Estimated)	3%	5-Year Return (1989–93)	+59%
Annual 12b-1 Fee	0.30%	10-Year Return (1984–93)	NA
Annual Expense Ratio	0.83%	Worst-Ever Loss (1987)	13%
Annual Portfolio Turnover	112%	Bond Market Correlation	40%
5-Year Cost Estimate	13%	Up/Down Market Rank	D – B

Benefits		Investment Information	
Investment Objective	Income	Telephone	800-225-2222
5-Year Projected Return	+23%	Minimum Investment	$1,500
Safety Rating (0-100)	90%	Telephone Switching	2 per mo; free
Yield (8/33)	4.2%	Total Assets	$1.14 billion

Van Kampen Tax-Free Hi Icm "A"
B-rated and higher municipals

Costs		Performance	
Sales Load	4.9%	1-Year Return (1993)	+16%
Redemption Fee	None	3-Year Return (1991–93)	+26%
Tax Load (Estimated)	0%	5-Year Return (1989–93)	+42%
Annual 12b-1 Fee	0.30%	10-Year Return (1984–93)	NA
Annual Expense Ratio	1.08%	Worst-Ever Loss (1987)	8%
Annual Portfolio Turnover	44%	Bond Market Correlation	21%
5-Year Cost Estimate	11%	Up/Down Market Rank	E – A

Benefits		Investment Information	
Investment Objective	Income	Telephone	800-225-2222
5-Year Projected Return	+32%	Minimum Investment	$1,500
Safety Rating (0-100)	90%	Telephone Switching	2 per mo; free
Yield (8/93)	5.7%	Total Assets	$569 million

TAX FREE